Wagner Handbook

Wagner Handbook

EDITED BY
ULRICH MÜLLER
PETER WAPNEWSKI

TRANSLATION EDITED BY
JOHN DEATHRIDGE

HARVARD UNIVERSITY PRESS
CAMBRIDGE, MASSACHUSETTS
LONDON, ENGLAND   1992

Originally published as *Richard-Wagner-Handbuch,* © 1986
by Alfred Kröner Verlag, Stuttgart.

This book has been supported by a grant from the
National Endowment for the Humanities,
an independent federal agency.

Publication of this book has also been supported through
the generous provisions of the Maurice and Lula Bradley Smith
Memorial Fund.

This book is printed on acid-free paper, and its binding
materials have been chosen for strength and durability.

Library of Congress Cataloging-in-Publication Data

Richard-Wagner-Handbuch. English
   Wagner handbook / edited by Ulrich Müller and Peter Wapnewski;
translation edited by John Deathridge.
      p.   cm.
Translation of: Richard-Wagner-Handbuch.
Includes bibliographical references and index.
ISBN 0-674-94530-1 (alk. paper)
   1. Wagner, Richard, 1813–1883.   I. Wagner, Richard, 1813–1883.
II. Müller, Ulrich, 1940–   .   III. Wapnewski, Peter.   IV. Title.
ML410.W131R41613   1992
782.1'092—dc20
   [B]   91-42202
                                                     CIP

Contents

Works: Sources, Influences, Aesthetics

Biography and Reception: Decadence and the Dawn of "Wagnerism"

Works: The Composer

Biography and Reception: Bayreuth, Performance, Musical Influence

Works: The Writer

Foreword to the German Edition

That Richard Wagner is one of the figures in world history about whom the greatest number of books and articles has been written is both a true and, by now, a trivial statement. It is also a simple fact that in the German-speaking world Wagner is one of the most quoted and most controversial authors and artists of the nineteenth and twentieth centuries, in this respect comparable only to Karl Marx and Sigmund Freud. A book that focuses on the key topics and issues that have arisen in discussions about Wagner to date therefore hardly needs elaborate justification.

We conceived this book for all those interested in the personality and works of Richard Wagner who are looking for information about him that is comprehensive yet relatively concisely presented and in tune with the current state of individual disciplines that have some claim on him. The aim was to keep the text free of jargon without undermining scholarly standards and to attain a degree of clarity that will enrich the much-vaunted "interested layman" as well as the Wagner scholar, and indeed to suggest important ideas that may give even the experts food for thought.

The *Wagner Handbook* is the combined effort of scholars from several academic disciplines. It almost goes without saying that the complexity of the Wagner phenomenon can be treated in anything remotely like a thorough and proper manner only if it is approached from several different angles. Nonetheless, we were only occasionally tempted to succumb to the illusion that we would be able to cover every aspect of the topic in appropriate depth. The reality of producing this book has been a constant reminder of the limitations on what is humanly possible and the discrepancy between our original intention and the final result.

As the structure of the book shows, it was important for us not only to place Wagner in historical context but also to focus on the diversity of his influence. In presenting this variety of essays we hoped to highlight the fact that, to the present day, discussion about Wagner and his works has never ceased to stimulate fresh controversy, some of which—albeit now for rather different reasons—can still be surprisingly vehement.

The wide range of subjects and issues that the single name of Wagner attracts is reflected by the diversity of the contributors to this book. As all the chapters are meant to be self-contained and read as independent pieces, we have deliberately not adjusted them to avoid repetition and overlap. Equally, we have refrained from smoothing out the contributors' varied and even sometimes contradictory opinions on certain issues, preferring to accept them without resistance as a natural consequence of any discussion of this extraordinary figure. Indeed, the controversies are so much an integral part of the many-faceted and vexing peculiarity of the subject of Wagner that they cannot be suppressed.

Having planned this project together and carried it out with the help of many of our colleagues, we hope that most readers of these pages will find in them what they are looking for. We shall also be pleased if, besides all the information they will find here, this book can help to provide a solid basis for further debates about the Wagner phenomenon.

Ulrich Müller   Peter Wapnewski
Salzburg 1985   *Berlin 1985*

Introduction

JOHN DEATHRIDGE

Brahms once said of Richard Wagner that he was "a man with a gigantic capacity for work, colossal industry and horrendous energy." Few would seriously disagree. Wagner wrote the text and music for thirteen operas and music dramas, at least half of which still count as towering masterpieces. He planned at least ten more works for the operatic stage, some in considerable detail, only to set them aside for one reason or another. He wrote dozens of minor works: string quartets, sonatas, overtures, symphonies, lieder, a near oratorio, and numerous choral pieces. An outstanding performer, Wagner profoundly influenced a whole generation in the art of conducting. He produced his own operas and music dramas whenever he could, and spent a great deal of energy conducting and arranging operas by others as well, including Gluck and Mozart. He took part in a revolution and had the ear of kings and highly placed diplomats. Wagner's collected writings on a huge variety of subjects fill sixteen substantial volumes. He organized the building of the Bayreuth festival theater and established it as one of the focal points of European culture in the late nineteenth century. His private life was eventful (to say the least), and on top of everything else he penned thousands of letters (about ten thousand have so far been traced), many of them running to several densely written pages.

The bald facts are still startling. For Brahms—himself no idle worker—the sheer copiousness of Wagner's output was remarkable and at the same time almost dreadful to contemplate. Today the prospect of coming to terms with it is still daunting, if not more so in view of the notorious literature about it that has proliferated in the meantime, and relentlessly continues to accumulate. Critics often argue, sometimes rather irritably, that the Wagnerian terrain is littered with too many library corpses for most of it ever to have even a semblance of life. Why exhume the maudlin reminiscences, the psychiatric studies, the countless hagiographies or resurrect the (supposedly) turgid and obscure writings when we have *Tristan* and the *Ring*? Why bother with Wagner's life and mind at all when the sheer greatness of his art makes his love affairs, his pompous theories about the end of opera, even his anti-Semitism seem almost an irrelevance? "What Wagner's triumphant *oeuvre* validates is not his theory," Thomas Mann wrote a trifle indignantly in 1933, "but simply itself."

When seen in context Mann's overemphatic (not to say circular) dictum is understandable. In 1933 Wagner was already being misused as a prestigious and neatly ordered cultural shop window by the Nazis. Mann's essay, "The Sorrows and Grandeur of Richard Wagner," from which the quoted sentence is taken, was a valiant attempt to protect Wagner from this obnoxious brand of ideological hygiene by probing into the strange and deeply problematic amalgam of the premodern and the modern in Wagner's works which still haunts even his staunchest admirers. The predilection for the mythic and legendary, for the medieval world of miracles and burning religious faith, for Protestant nationalism and Catholic ritual—all these elements of backward looking, of obscurantist worship of the past, Mann thought, are embedded in the "triumphant oeuvre," but not in a real sense. Wagner's creative mind was "charged with life and vehemently progressive" despite its melancholia and attachment to death. His is "an artistic idiom of a highly figurative kind," whose real purport is "entirely revolutionary." Even his Germanness was refracted and fragmented in the modern mode, "decorative, analytical and intellectual—hence its powerful fascination, its innate capacity for cosmopolitan, not to say planetary influence."

Mann's carefully nuanced phrases were almost certain to be grievously misinterpreted. The signatories of the notorious *Protest from Richard Wagner's Own City of Munich* (who, besides Hans Pfitzner and Richard Strauss, included, appropriately enough, Dr. Ludwig Hoeflmayer, Munich's senior public health officer) launched a vitriolic attack on Mann's essay, taking him to task for his unpatriotic views. What was at issue, however, was not so much Mann's faith in German culture (which, as he rightly protested in turn, was unshakable) as his up-to-date interpretation of it. At a stroke Mann had managed to turn Wagner's Germanness into a model of progress and internationalism, "a powerful and complex phenomenon of German and European life." Indeed, to his critics in 1933 the essay must have had the familiar and unwelcome ring of that highbrow Weimar liberalism (since the rise of Hitler now rapidly dwindling) which only relatively recently, in the 1920s, had succumbed to the "decadent" fever of modernity. Not surprisingly, the violent reaction to the Wagner essay was the immediate reason (though by no means the only one) for Mann's decision to leave Germany.

In the long run Mann's defense of Wagner in the name of modernity has been enormously successful. Not that later influential interpreters, who acknowledged both the stature of the works and the fact that they had been severely compromised politically, had much option but to rescue them from the debris of the past with similar strategies. The most radical was Theodor Adorno, who claimed to have dug away the historical rubbish heap piled on top of Wagner to reveal a few black, jagged measures of *Tristan* that pointed unmistakably in the direction of Schoenberg. After two hundred pages of polemics about, among other things, the relation between Wagnerian mythology and the fading world of the German Empire, Adorno used these few measures to build a brief and unlikely "redemptive" happy ending during which he established Wagner's credentials as a bona fide humanist after all, though a disconcertingly pessimistic one whose bleak view of humanity (like Adorno's own) was supposedly uncompromising in the extreme. Wieland Wagner, with his famous sparsely lit stages and monolithic, smoothly surfaced scenery, was no less eager to create the impression that the painfully embarrassing moments in the history of Wagner's fame (the aesthetic as well as the political ones) were a thing of the past. Boulez's bracing and deliberately antirhetorical readings of *Parsifal* and the *Ring* in the 1960s and 1970s consolidated the modernist vision of Wagner as the key link between Beethoven and Schoenberg, and the first serious composer to bring tonality to the brink of destruction.

Mann and Adorno have both had a significant impact on the way we see Wagner, and critical evaluations of equal penetration have arguably been in dismayingly short supply ever since. Yet perhaps the modernist spirit has done Wagner less than justice. The "strange pathos of purity" (Peter Bürger) at the center of the project of modernity has had the odd effect of pricking our moral conscience about the painful moments in the history of Wagner's fame, thereby allowing us to reject as reactionary everything we associate with them, while at the same time leaving us with the comfortable feeling that it is possible nonetheless to sit back and enjoy those things about him that we can safely call progressive. That there are no such shortcuts to an appreciation of Wagner and his works, and the enormous resonance they have found, should be clear to anyone after consulting this book.

A lasting faith in aesthetics, as opposed to a critical view of history, has never looked more problematic than it does with Wagner. This is my own, doubtless unhealthily overskeptical view of the Bayreuth Master, and, as this volume shows, there are many who disagree with it. Indeed, from the start the lack of consensus about Wagner has been such a consistent feature in the history of his fame that any wide-ranging book trying desperately to present him and his aura in a systematic and presumably objective fashion runs the risk of distorting this key fact. The present volume is therefore a "handbook" only in the widest sense of the word: a thoroughly diverse collection of twenty-three essays by eighteen authors which considers Wagner and his influence in a variety of historical, cultural, literary, and musical contexts. One assumption behind the book, as the German editors Ulrich Müller and Peter Wapnewski originally conceived it, is that it is simply not possible, especially in Wagner's case, to make a clean division between fact and value, or to reduce his collected works to a neat and unified image, modernist or otherwise. Müller and Wapnewski, whose cooperation in the preparation of this English-language edition has been immensely valuable, have therefore tried to make the book as comprehensive as possible, although they would be the last to claim that it is exhaustive.

In editing the English edition I have overhauled the bibliographical apparatus and rearranged the order of chapters: the three longest—the in-depth surveys of Wagner's activities as dramatist, composer, and writer—now appear at the beginning, in the middle, and at the end of the book, respectively. Interleaved with them are shorter chapters which, in serving as a counterpoint to the longer essays, give the reader information about specific aspects of Wagner's works and their influence. For a number of reasons some chapters in the original German edition have been excluded (the puns and numerous plays on words in local dialects in Manfred Eger's excellent piece on Wagner parodies and caricatures, for instance, proved impossible to translate), and two have been added: Jens Malte Fischer's chapter on singing (the longer German version of which first appeared in *Opernwelt* in 1986) and Isolde Vetter's specially commissioned survey "Wagner in the History of Psychology." Other additions are my discussion of Wagner, the Jews, and Jakob Katz (the substance of which I first published in the *Times Literary Supplement* in November 1986) appended to the chapter on Wagner research; Ulrich Müller's postscript to his survey "Wagner in Literature and Film"; and the checklist of writings at the end of Jürgen Kühnel's chapter on Wagner's prose works. Although the checklist is now one of the most detailed currently available, the absence of a proper catalogue and critical edition of Wagner's writings means that it is still to be regarded as no more than tentative. (A strictly chronological list can be found in Nattiez 1990.)

I have not included still another inventory of Wagner's musical works, as a full-scale catalogue (WWV) and offshoots from it are now easily available, including the list in Deathridge-Dahlhaus 1984, where the reader will also find an extensive select bibliography. Other Wagner bibliographies which the reader may consult with profit are in Newman 1976, WWV, Gregor-Dellin 1980 and 1983, Field 1981 (an especially useful annotated bibliography on Wagner and Bayreuth), Millington 1984, Nattiez 1990, Bartlett 1990, Kropfinger 1991, and the original German edition of this book. I am even more convinced now than I was when I compiled the bibliography for the German edition that the Wagner literature is simply too copious to be conveniently catalogued at all, especially in a relatively short list. For the sake of greater clarity and economy, therefore, I have limited the bibliography in the present edition (see the Bibliographical Abbreviations at the end of the book) to items actually referred to in the main text. Given the range of subjects touched on by the contributors, it is inevitably no longer a bibliography devoted solely to Wagner, although in a book trying to build bridges between disciplines in order to understand him better, I hope a more suitable one.

Note on Citations

Citations appear in the text in abbreviated form; full publishing information is provided in the list of Bibliographical Abbreviations.

Wherever possible, quotations are from English-language editions. The only major exception is Wagner's prose works, which in view of the rather dated standard translation by Ellis have been retranslated and cited directly from the most extensive German edition (SSD). This edition in any case contains items which are not to be found in Ellis. For those who want to consult the translations in the Ellis edition, I have given page references to them in the checklist of writings appended to the final chapter.

Andrew Gray's translation of Wagner's autobiography, *Mein Leben* (ML), and Geoffrey Skelton's prodigious rendering into English of Cosima Wagner's diaries (CT) are cited throughout, though occasional modifications have been made to suit the context of the narrative. Cosima's diaries are usually cited by date, as are Wagner's letters—in the latter case to avoid, with a few exceptions, cumbersome references to many different German and English editions long out of print. Stewart Spencer's concise modern translation of selected letters (SL) has been used wherever possible.

As the German titles of Wagner's operas and music dramas are so familiar, they have not been translated. Many of the titles of Wagner's prose works, on the other hand, are much less well known and have therefore been given in English. The original German titles can be found in the checklist of writings.

The occasional comment by me is marked "[Ed.]."

J. D.

Works: The Dramatist

CHAPTER I

The Operas as Literary Works

PETER WAPNEWSKI

First Attempts: *Die Hochzeit* and *Die Feen*

The premiere of Wagner's earliest opera did not take place until five years after his death, on 29 June 1888 in Munich, adding one final unexpected twist to a musical career that teems with oddities and marvels. *Die Feen* was a great success, though mainly because of Wagner's fame, and above all owing to the enchanting stage designs by the "Imperial chief stage technician Karl Lautenschläger," as he was listed in the program (Bauer 1983, p. 12).

Did I say Wagner's earliest opera? Actually, an even earlier one had preceded it: *Die Hochzeit*. It was never more than a fragment, however, and the young Wagner wrote off even the bit he had finished. In so doing he was swayed by the disapproval of his "motherly sister" Rosalie, whom he loved and respected, and who had no stomach for an "out-and-out night piece in the blackest of colours." Ossian and Werther were its spiritual fathers. Its source was Büsching's *Ritterzeit und Ritterwesen,* which Wagner adapted as an opera text in Prague in November 1832 (ML 66–69).

The composition of *Die Hochzeit* was limited to a couple of scenes (Westernhagen 1978, I, 36); but it is notable precisely for its theme of *Ritterwesen,* or chivalry. Wagner began his output just as he was to conclude it half a century later, with the topic of chivalry. As a dramatist he concentrated on medieval Europe, from the myths of Celtic and Nordic legend to the Nuremberg of *Die Meistersinger* and the dawn of the modern age. One can say that medieval history was the crucible of Wagner's operas without unfairly overlooking the timeless myth of *Holländer* or the Renaissance hero of *Rienzi.* Wagner's penchant for adapting history shows that he was a true Romantic, although he was as boldly and willfully unorthodox here as he was in other respects. Romantic historians and philologists had rediscovered a historical epoch. Wagner vindicated it and turned it into a universal age sui generis—a Wagnerian eon.

In 1833 Wagner's brother Albert found him a position as chorus master in

Würzburg. There he learned his craft and made himself useful, not only as a musician but behind the scenes and onstage as well. More than anything else, though, he was composing music. He had brought with him the text of his new opera, *Die Feen,* and the orchestral sketch for act 3 was finished on 7 December. Four days later his sister Rosalie heard the proud news: "It was just midday—12 o'clock, and bells were ringing in all the church towers as I wrote *finis* at the foot of the very last page;—what pleasure it gave me!" (11 December 1833). Here the budding theatrical genius makes sure that every meaningful second in his creative life receives a suitably dramatic staging: the church bells of Würzburg join in a joyful chorus to the finale he has just finished writing.

The whole opera was ready to be performed when Wagner completed the overture on 6 January 1834. "Deus laudetur," he wrote at the end; but his real troubles were only just beginning. The subsequent history of *Die Feen* is a story of rejection—to Wagner's distress a story that was to be repeated throughout his career.

On 15 January Wagner traveled to Leipzig with the three bulky volumes of *Die Feen.* Again we see his highly developed sense of theater. Wagner's debut was to be reserved for his birthplace: the big city and her ambitious native son were to enhance each other's fame. Nor did the son lack practical support. His sister Rosalie was a celebrated actress at the Leipzig theater, and Friedrich Brockhaus duly delivered his brother-in-law's opera to the theater's director. Indications looked favorable; but seldom in artistic organizations does the man at the top have the final say. Kapellmeister Stegmayer and Franz Hauser, a producer who was also a singer, succeeded in thwarting the project with endless queries, requests for changes, and suggested emendations. The rehearsals fizzled out.

All the same, the overture was played on 10 January 1835—not in Leipzig but in Magdeburg, where Wagner had become musical director of a theater company. After this performance before an audience of local Freemasons, there were to be no further airings of *Die Feen.* Wagner would never see a stage production of his first opera, and this seems to have had harmful consequences for both the composer and the work. *Die Feen* was shelved.

Wagner owed the actual subject matter of the opera to Carlo Gozzi (whose writings later inspired operas by Busoni, Puccini, Prokofiev, and Hans Werner Henze). It must have been E. T. A. Hoffmann, one of Wagner's favorite authors, who drew his attention to *La donna serpente.* With his sure sense of style and atmosphere, Hoffmann had recognized in Gozzi's dramatic fairy tales a "rich treasure trove of excellent subjects for operas" (Soden-Loesch 1983, p. 60). Here—in contrast to Goldoni's realism, for example—the whole panoply of the vanishing commedia dell'arte was revealed once more, with its fairy-tale atmosphere and stock comic characters. In the programmatic *A Communication to My Friends* (1851), Wagner included an outline of *Die Feen,* in which he discovered "the seeds of an important element" in all his later opera writing. Presumably he meant its anticipation of many of the basic themes that govern the later works. Redemption through love, the forbidden question, the erotic component in the brother-sister relationship, the magic charms of a demonic lover, feudal service and allegiance, immortality through love—these and other elements run through all Wagner's dramas from *Die Feen* on. This early work derived the names of its leading characters from the Gaelic bard Ossian as well as from the lore of the Middle Ages. It also owed something to Schikaneder's and Mozart's *Die Zauberflöte*. It was to influence the libretto and, to an even greater extent, Hofmannsthal's narrative version of *Die Frau ohne Schatten* of 1919 (this applies to the details as much as to the general outline).

The story concerns the love of a mortal for a fairy, a magic condition, and the breaking of that condition. Like Arthurian romance, it tells of a guilty lapse on the part of the hero and of his long and arduous road to redemption. He has to face severe trials. Finally, since the fairy can never turn into a mortal, the human hero becomes immortal instead and is crowned king of the fairies: "A lofty fate has he achieved, / He is removed from earthly dross! / So now forever let us sing, / The blessings thus bestowed through love!"[1]

Wagner soon learned how to manipulate spectacular stage effects: choruses of spirits and warriors, manifestations of magic and oaths, and the portrayal of madness, which never fails in the theater. More important still is the way he mastered the great Romantic theme of a clash between the spirit world and the world of humans, which had fascinated such classical Romantics as the writers Hoffmann, Fouqué, and Novalis and the composers Marschner and Weber.

All these elements were to influence Wagner's future stage works: they reappear in *Holländer*, in *Tannhäuser*, and in *Lohengrin*. Moreover, love as a means of overcoming and removing human limitations is the core of the *opus metaphysicum* (to use Nietzsche's phrase) of *Tristan*, and a Christian variant of it constitutes the essence of *Parsifal*. Such an elixir also gives life to *Die Feen*, and anybody deploring its more than obvious textual, dramaturgic, and musical shortcomings might stop to consider Wagner's letter of 11 December 1833 to Rosalie. In a manner both touching and self-aware, and with that pathos which never deserted him, Wagner begged his whole family to pardon him, exclaiming: "All I can do is to ask you most fervently to be kind and forbearing throughout! God, I'm only twenty years of age!"

Grand Comic Opera: *Das Liebesverbot oder Die Novize von Palermo*

To gain some respite from the troubles surrounding the production of *Die Feen*, Wagner traveled in June 1834 with his friend Theodor Apel to Bohemia, a country he had always loved. In addition to Teplitz he visited Carlsbad and Prague (where he offered the theaters *Die Feen*—in vain, of course). This trip

---

1. Extracts from Wagner's libretti have been quoted, with occasional revisions, from the following translations: *Holländer* David Pountney (1982); *Tannhäuser*, Rodney Blumer (1988); *Ring* cycle, Andrew Porter (1976); *Tristan*, Andrew Porter (1980); *Meistersinger*, Frederick Jameson, rev. Norman Feasey and Gordon Kember (1983); *Parsifal*, Stewart Robb (1962). Extracts from other works have been translated afresh. [Ed.]

saw a fresh spate of artistic activity in a life constantly marked by creative spurts and upheavals. A new opera was conceived, initially as a prose draft; by autumn Wagner had reworked *Das Liebesverbot* in verse. This was a work very different from *Die Feen*—so different, in fact, that even their composer would one day express astonishment at their proximity in time. Despite its Italian literary source, *Die Feen* belonged entirely to the German Romantic tradition dominated by Beethoven's *Fidelio* and by the operas of Weber and Marschner. But the new work was tied to the opposite aesthetic and artistic principle, that of French and Italian light opera, with its modish posturings, its transparent frivolities.

This new trend can be summed up in names of authors and composers whose work offers clues to Wagner's reasons for changing direction. They include Heinse, Heine, and Laube; Bellini and Auber; Boieldieu, Adam, and Halévy. Existing information about the role that these artists and their works played in Wagner's output derives less from the biographical data than from his theoretical writings. Wagner now embarked on an inexhaustible stream of reflections and proposals, rodomontades and arguments. In 1834 his (anonymously published) manifesto *German Opera* appeared in his friend Heinrich Laube's *Zeitung für die elegante Welt*. This was the first of a vast number of programmatic essays the writing of which would have taken the average person a lifetime. Wagner, of course, was no average person.

In his manifesto Wagner dismissed the "eternally allegorizing orchestral tumult" of German composers (and yet, later on, he was repeatedly charged with being its primary practitioner). He expressed a decided preference for French opéra comique and Italian lyrical opera. In short, he was against Weber and for Bellini, to whom he devoted an essay in 1837. In broad terms, this statement marked his reorientation toward sensuality and lightness, freedom and lucidity. Wagner's new personal and political outlook stemmed from his association with his Leipzig friend and colleague Laube, and also from the Young Germans, a literary movement that had taken up arms against the reactionary forces of the Biedermeier restoration. Its manifesto was Laube's epistolary novel *Das junge Europa,* part one of which appeared in 1833. A follow-up to Heinse's *Ardinghello* (1787), this work expounded a utopian design for freedom, extending from the rejection of property to demands for free love. It supported the Greek and Polish independence movements, just as it supported the aims of the July revolution in Paris. And that meant, in the words of Dieter Borchmeyer, opposing "Romantic mysticism, the reactionary orthodoxy of the Church, a moral code implacably hostile to the life of the senses, backward particularistic politics" (DS X, 215).

Understandably, then, the main topics of conversation during Wagner's Bohemian journey with Apel were Beethoven and Heinse, Hoffmann, and Shakespeare. Wagner now conceived a new dramatic subject drawn from Shakespeare's *Measure for Measure,* "but with the difference that I took out the predominant seriousness and reshaped the material in the spirit of Young Europe: by virtue of its very nature, openly expressed sensuality defeated puritan hypocrisy," as he put it in the *Autobiographical Sketch* (1842–43).

In Shakespeare the scene is Vienna. Wagner set his drama in the passionate world of Palermo in the sixteenth century. His cast list follows the conventions of his time: there are two noble couples and a contrasting pair of buffo characters. The locations include a piazza, the courtyard of a convent, a courtroom, a dungeon, and a street. The action involves imprisonment and liberation, self-sacrifice, and intense suffering. And of course there is also the element of disguise and mistaken identity: only deception can lead to the truth. Wagner presents all these themes in a mixture of rhyming and un-rhymed verse, colored by pathos and sentimentality and laced with many exclamations of "Ha!"

Underlying the run-of-the-mill stage activity is a pointed fable. The king of Sicily has designated a deputy to rule in his absence. The deputy is a German named Friedrich who lives up to the Teutonic stereotype. He is a pedantic sobersides, devoid of humor, opposed to sensuality, and crafty to boot. He closes the taverns and prohibits the delights of carnivals and free love. It would not take a Freud to perceive what underlies such crude puritanism: the compulsive need to compensate. Indeed, Friedrich is a lecher as well as a scoundrel. To further his career he has banished his wife, Mariana, whom he has only just married; now she is a novice in a convent, cut off from the world. But Friedrich is himself dangerously susceptible to that power whose exercise he so ruthlessly forbids—the power of eros and sex. He falls head over heels in love with another novice, Isabella, whose brother Claudio he has imprisoned and condemned to death for the "crime" of love. This is the start of a highly moral intrigue. To rescue her brother, Isabella pretends to agree to the regent's shameless offer: her love in return for Claudio's liberty. But at the appointed rendezvous it is not the desired Isabella whom the hot-blooded schemer finds behind the carnival mask but his wife (this is reminiscent of the finale of *Figaro*). Friedrich is now seen to be doubly guilty—as an erring husband and as the transgressor of his own decree.

Das Liebesverbot forms a Young German protest against hypocrisy and the suppression of natural urges by the state and monarchy. Its finale leads to a dizzying carnival, which amounts to more than merely a dramatic stage effect. A carnival is a licensed eruption of primitive forces, of anarchic energy within a circumscribed area; it is, as it were, a prearranged and officially approved demonstration. It is not a popular celebration, although it is a celebration of the people, a "latent political uprising," to use Borchmeyer's phrase (DS X, 217). So strong and secure is Wagner's triumphant, jubilant populace that it can waive punishment and retribution and magnanimously allow the corrupt deputy to lose himself in its midst. Unlike Shakespeare, as Wagner wrote in his *Communication,* he had used a revolution rather than the monarch to reach a denouement. It was certainly a very humane revolution. "The carnival that Goethe, when in Italy, had perceived as a covert political phenomenon turns into a celebration of a democracy ruled by eros" (Borchmeyer, in DS X, 218).

In the *Communication,* Wagner stressed the antithetical aspect of the work's place in his musical development. In *Das Liebesverbot* he had countered the "deadly seriousness" dominating *Die Feen* with a "tendency that seems sharply at odds with it and is nurtured by vital impressions; a cheeky tendency towards wild and impetuous sensuality and a joyful defiance. This is quite obvious to me when I compare the musical treatment of the two operas . . . Anyone studying *Liebesverbot* side by side with *Die Feen* could scarcely imagine how such a striking change of direction could have occurred in such a short space of time. To harmonize the two was to be the object of my further artistic development."

On the one hand, we have the "pathos-laden mysticism" of German opera, with its profoundly intimate feelings and sentiments. On the other, we have the "beauty of the material, the wit and the spirit" that characterize the playfulness and the frivolous splendor of French opera and Italian bel canto. Avowedly Wagner did not make the slightest effort to avoid suggesting either type of opera.

What is the dramaturgic significance of this phase in Wagner's output? Three basic themes emerge. The first is the theme of democratic revolution, whose impulses lay deep within Wagner. He may have expressed this drive in different forms and shapes, but he was always a political and artistic radical. He stood for a victory of the people and its natural energies over the abstract laws of tyrants.

The second theme is the peculiar one of laws against love. Notably it appears in various forms throughout Wagner's works. Thus any woman who loves the Dutchman is doomed. Tannhäuser is not allowed to love Venus. Alberich, thwarted in his desires, pronounces a curse on love (in the name of that other primal force, domination). Siegmund and Sieglinde come to grief because they have broken the law against incest. Hans Sachs, who renounces love in noble, sonorous tones, is made to suffer for observing his self-imposed ban. And finally, both Amfortas and Parsifal are forbidden to give in to Kundry's amorous charms.

Despite these examples, one hesitates to infer a sexual neurosis on Wagner's part, mainly because the story of Tristan and Isolde is about the triumphant breaking of a law against love. The power of love is correlated to these ordinances that forbid it, tending to confirm them dialectically rather than contradicting them, since love is a right and proper means of redemption. To some extent an element of happiness may be involved. Love to the rescue: in various forms (although the rescue never serves worldly interests) this ideal holds true in all of Wagner's dramas. *Holländer* reflects it, as do *Tannhäuser* and *Lohengrin*. It is also seen in Siegfried and Brünnhilde, in Tristan and Isolde, and in Hans Sachs. Even the unhappily loving Kundry is saved by love—a spiritual love, that is. But only Stolzing and Eva can look forward with some confidence to that cozy happiness which is the bourgeois version of love triumphant.

The third theme is that of comic opera; and, in light of the foregoing, it may have wider implications than the other two for Wagner's output. It involves the idea of a master who becomes the slave of his own plan for domination, the victim of his own regime. "What, O pitiful man, has become

/ Of the system so neatly built up?" In this apothegm, which could easily come from Wotan (assuming he were to speak in such terms), the infamous Friedrich anticipates the plight of a creator overcome and threatened by his own creation. By the same token, the doctrine of chastity imposed by the emotionally and spiritually crippled deputy foreshadows a cult of purity which, transfigured and sanctified, will govern the kingdom of the Grail as well as Parsifal himself, its eventual ruler. Purity is achieved by suppressing sensuality in the one case and by conquering it in the other. At the very least, Wagner seems on the verge of proclaiming the dramatic truth of the one realm as much as the alternative.

"Can be performed": so wrote the Magdeburg censor on the title page of the libretto of *Das Liebesverbot*. Because it was Holy Week, however, the magistrate insisted on deleting the frivolous title in favor of the subtitle, *Die Novize von Palermo*. Wagner's assurance that it was based on a very serious play by Shakespeare did the rest.

Magdeburg was now Wagner's base. After returning from Bohemia he had been appointed musical director of the theater company run by Heinrich Bethmann. "The die was cast," he wrote in his autobiography, a remark that refers primarily to the troupe's young female lead, Fräulein Minna Planer. After mentioning the first night he spent with the pretty actress, Wagner proceeds to the heavy-hearted observation (made, of course, with the benefit of hindsight): "Care had entered my life, as I had sensed it would" (ML 88, 95).

It is with self-deprecating irony that Wagner, looking back in some amusement thirty years later, describes the hapless state of this touring company and its "chronically bankrupt" manager. But, less amusingly, the young genius's second opera was to have only one performance during his lifetime. The premiere took place on 29 March 1836, and as a result of the singers' and players' shortcomings, the audience was left completely in the dark as to the nature of the piece. Not altogether unexpectedly, the second night degenerated into farce. Only three people were in the audience; the real drama, however, went on behind the closed curtain. The participants were the leading lady, the second tenor, and a husband seething with jealousy. Blows were exchanged, blood flowed, and the leading lady threw a tantrum. "The stage director was sent before the curtain to advise . . . that 'owing to unforeseen difficulties' the performance of the opera could not take place" (ML 119).

Grand Tragic Opera: *Rienzi, der Letzte der Tribunen*

It was during the summer of 1837 in, of all places, Blasewitz near Dresden that Wagner first discovered the tragic pathos of the tale of Rienzi. Indeed, Wagner's situation had its own pathos, although the drama did not transcend the boundaries of his private life. Minna, whom Wagner had married in Königsberg on 24 November 1836, had run off with a businessman named Dietrich. Wagner, despairing yet courageous, pursued the absconding couple, catching up with Minna at Blasewitz, but he lost her once more when she again vanished with Dietrich without even saying good-bye. "During the miserable days of my last stay with Minna in Blasewitz I had read Bulwer's novel about Cola Rienzi," Wagner reports in his autobiography (ML 142), and in typical fashion he immediately worked out "a plan for a grand opera."

The libretto and composition of *Rienzi* took up all of 1838, when Wagner was conducting in Riga. Minna, by now forgiven, had returned to live with him. By April 1839 he had prepared the full score of the first act and the first complete draft of the second. Work was then interrupted by their hazardous escape from creditors in Riga (then part of Russia) to Pillau, and thence via Norway to England in a small sailing boat. On 20 August the couple stepped ashore in France, a country that was to have a momentous effect on the composer's career. The sea passage involved three dreadful storms; one, which forced them to anchor at Sandvike, near Arendal on the Norwegian coast, helped to inspire the text and music of *Holländer*. Subsequently Wagner spent two and a half years in Paris—probably the most humiliating and grinding years of his life. He was to suffer physical and emotional deprivation, hunger, and loss. Minna saw the hard times bravely through, but her husband was reduced almost to a shadow, his hopes repeatedly crushed by agonizing realities. During this period his grateful admiration for Meyerbeer, whose patronage he had sought, eventually turned into hostility, indeed hatred. The misery of his Paris years explains a great deal of Wagner's subsequent anti-Semitism, his need to be pampered, and his Francophobia. "No one can imagine a more terrible time," Wagner wrote to his friend Laube on 3 December 1840. He was referring to two wearying days of going around cap in hand, but the remark applies to the whole period. The suffering and pathos, for once, were quite real.

Wagner completed the full score of *Rienzi* on 19 December 1840. The work was accepted at Dresden, which had just witnessed the opening of Gottfried Semper's new opera house. The first performance took place on 20 October 1842. Although its enormous success was possibly matched by that of *Die Meistersinger,* it was never to be surpassed in Wagner's career.

The libretto is based on a novel by Edward Bulwer, the first Baron Lytton (1803–1873), a politician of note and a successful author. He called his novel *Rienzi: The Last of the Roman Tribunes* (Bulwer Lytton was a great fan of finales and loved to include phrases such as "the last" in his titles, as in *The Last Days of Pompeii*). Published in 1834, the book appeared in German translation in 1836, and Wagner was not slow to acquire it. After the "German" *Die Feen* and the "Italian" *Das Liebesverbot*, Bulwer Lytton's subject matter was just what Wagner needed to give, or indeed to impose on, the world *le grand opéra* in all its monumentality. With excusable arrogance he planned it on such a vast scale that only opera houses with a very large stage would be able to mount it, thus safeguarding himself from artistic ruin at the hands of impecunious strolling players. His only thought when writing the libretto was its suitability for and effect on the music (which, for its own part, was equally bent on effect).

The historical Rienzi was not overshadowed by tragedy to quite the extent the radical tragic dramatist would have it. (Wagner reshaped the character accordingly.) Born in 1313 the son of a Roman tavern keeper, Cola di Rienzo was elected tribune by the people, fell victim to hubris, and died in a rebellion in 1354. In his "grand tragic-heroic opera," Wagner used this subject to create a cosmos governed by a combination of historical, religious, social, and personal forces. In act 1 Rome has been torn apart by the rivalry and feuding of the corrupt nobles. Rienzi restores order with the promise of freedom and happiness. The people greet him with joy and elect him tribune.

In act 2 the subdued nobles swear allegiance to Rienzi. The new ruler arranges a grand celebration (in a ballet interlude with dumb show), but the cunning nobles revolt and attempt to assassinate him. Their plot fails when Adriano Colonna, son of the nobles' leader, betrays the conspirators out of love for Rienzi's sister, Irene. Together they plead for mercy for the noblemen. Rienzi agrees, for he is a man of moods, easily swayed, dazzled, and deceived (which makes him something of an artist by temperament). The nobles again swear allegiance. Nonetheless, they remain as ambitious and cunning as ever. In act 3 they raise an army outside the gates of Rome and join battle. After much bloodshed and loss of life, Rienzi emerges victorious. But when Adriano finds his own father among the fallen, his love and admiration for the tribune turn to hatred, and he makes plans to destroy him.

In act 4 the tables are turned. Deserting their leader, the Roman people exchange tales and rumors about him. They suspect Rienzi of conspiring with the nobles, and they criticize him for his laxity, claiming that by making a firmer stand he could have avoided the slaughter. Even the papal envoy (the Holy See is in Avignon rather than Rome) hurls anathema on Rienzi. The man of the people is now a man without a people, a man alone; only his sister, Irene, stands by him.

Finally, in act 5 Rienzi beseeches God in a mighty aria not to abandon him before he has accomplished his mission. From the balcony of the Capitol he tries one last time to exert his old effect on the people. But in vain; the crowd throws stones at him and sets the Capitol on fire. The building collapses. Rienzi and his utopia are buried under its ruins, together with his loving sister and Adriano Colonna, who has sought at the last moment to save her.

Rienzi has been described by jocular admirers as Meyerbeer's greatest opera. Its stage apparatus is indeed enormous, and so are the demands on the singers and orchestra. In that sense Wagner had calculated rightly. Only opera houses that could afford both the scenery and the singers, including a ringing Heldentenor and a virtuosic mezzo-soprano in the trouser role of Adriano, could venture a production.

For his own part, Wagner quickly dissociated himself from his "bawling infant," his unloved "monstrosity." This sin of his youth, as he put it, became an embarrassment to him. A composer is probably bound to adopt this attitude after he has gone on to explore new avenues. And yet Wagner's clattering, flattering showpiece is not without merit. It is no accident that the overture and Rienzi's prayer figure in many concert performances. Understandably enough, *Rienzi* enjoyed a swift success, first in Dresden, next in Hamburg (where the composer conducted it), then in Berlin; eventually all the great opera houses of Europe were staging it. In Germany in particular, however, *Rienzi* was soon to be overshadowed by Wagner's "authentic" operas, as sanctioned by the guardians and priests of the true faith at Bayreuth. And that series of works only began with *Holländer*.

Let us now consider the place of *Rienzi* in Wagner's output. Themes that *Das Liebesverbot* had presented through colorful masquerades assume sharper political forms in *Rienzi*. Again Wagner adopts some of the ideas of Young Germany, but with a greater degree of militant pathos and fervor. Civil liberty (meaning, primarily, freedom for the hitherto oppressed classes); revolt against the despotism of an obsolescent aristocracy; equality before the law: these battle cries were being raised by freedom fighters across Europe, and they resound again in *Rienzi*. And yet, as is so often true with Wagner, we find a vexing contradiction if we look at the opera closely. For what kind of a role do the people play? In *Das Liebesverbot*, with its final apotheosis, the people are, or rather become, a sovereign power. But in *Rienzi* they represent a multitude, which means they are pitifully indecisive and shabbily corruptible. The hero is not the populace but that central character who, appearing in various guises, would henceforth determine and dominate Wagner's operas. From now on the hero would be a great individual to whom there attaches both charisma and a stigma, and who—Parsifal excepted—eventually comes to grief. Rienzi, the Roman tribune made and subsequently undone by the people, is the first of a line that includes the Dutchman, Tannhäuser, Lohengrin, Siegfried, and Tristan. The melancholy god Wotan can also be viewed in this light. Hans Sachs, who achieves a substitute form of happiness, is a contrastingly popular character. But even he has scarcely any illusions about the people's fickleness, if we understand his "Wahn" monologue rightly.

In *Rienzi* the great individual—the savior, the tragic hero—makes his debut in Wagner's oeuvre. This grand opera and its hero are thus clearly distinguishable from the amiable characters of *Die Feen* and *Das Liebesverbot*, who are ultimately only types. Here the people are a disappointment, although none of Wagner's dramas portray them as actively saving the day. Rather, they themselves are saved by a powerful individual facing personal ruin. Thus Lohengrin saves Brabant; and the survival, the new beginning of the men and women in the finale of *Götterdämmerung*, can be seen ultimately as Siegfried's act of redemption, an act that negates the power of the gods. Moreover, we know from innumerable comments by Wagner, particularly those recorded in Cosima Wagner's diaries, that although he was genuinely full of revolutionary ardor and was also a political activist at one crucial point, the artist in him despised the people—that is, the common people—and time and again was deeply repelled by their behavior.

As a work of art, *Rienzi* derives a considerable portion of its troubling charm from this contrast. On the one hand, it characterizes the people and solo figures with the utmost splendor: "finales, ensembles, huge choral scenes, the clash of arms, chorales, duets and trios and the whole gamut of passions, all of which were larger than life" (Bauer 1983, p. 27). Yet, on the other hand, it takes the lonely individual as its real central subject.

It is characteristic of Wagner that he graciously spares lazy-minded listeners from having to think by indulging them with orchestral sounds that reach to the farthest limits of sensuous power and touch "our earthly horizon," as Busoni aptly put it (Busoni 1911, p. 80). This creates a barrier to a considered response to his work; and it explains why the history of his operas is "also a history of their reinterpretation" (Bauer 1983, p. 37). Admittedly this applies in principle to all responses to art, especially drama. But the effect has proved to be infinitely more drastic in Wagner's case than in the case of, say, Shakespeare or Schiller.

To illustrate the point, let us imagine ourselves in Linz, on the Danube, in the year 1906. A seventeen-year-old youth goes to the theater, experiences *Rienzi*, and—this is a typical reaction to Wagner—feels personally affected, stirred to the depths of his being. More than that, it gives him a sense of mission. "The words tumbled from him like a flood breaking through a bursting dam. In thrilling and grandiose imagery, he unfolded to me his future and that of his people." Thus August Kubizek recalled a walk with his old friend Adolf Hitler after a performance of *Rienzi*. And in 1939, according to the same witness, Hitler himself recollected that memorable evening with the words: "In that hour it began" (Kubizek 1954, p. 66). Another source, Albert Speer, quotes Hitler as saying: "Hearing that divine music as a young man in Linz, I was inspired to think that I too would succeed in uniting the German Reich and making it great."

Here we have a shocking case of blindness and self-delusion. It is a symptomatic response to a work of art that this petty-bourgeois fanatic should extract his own message from it, a message corresponding to extravagant private ambitions and fantasies but not to the artistic reality. In this instance the message did not even conform to historical reality. Hitler, the product of an obscure lower-middle-class background, contrived to view the grandeur of the Roman innkeeper's son in a way that respected neither history nor Wagner. He patently overlooked the fact that Wagner's Rienzi is a vacillating, mercurial character. Enthralled by power, and intoxicated by a frenzy of mass rejoicing, Rienzi is irrationally tied to the people in a kind of erotic relationship, with "Roma" as his bride. He is only briefly successful in the brittle and chimerical task of unification. The young Hitler could not possibly have seen this, or he would not have felt Rienzi's career to be a challenge, and one worth emulating. This lends an even eerier quality to the sequence of events which, it now seems, sprang from that night at the opera. For it was precisely on this model that Hitler's destiny, the Hitlerian persona, developed historically. A gruesome parallel can also be drawn between their similar deaths: the one perishes, surrounded by his nearest and dearest, in the blazing ruins of the Capitol, the other in his bunker beneath the blazing ruins of the Chancellery. But for all his faults, Rienzi was a hero, whereas Hitler was a barbaric paranoiac. Both had the fatal gift of charisma. Another eerie note is Hitler's saying "In that hour it began" in 1939, thus marking that year as already the beginning of the end. Although Hitler himself may not have been conscious of it, Rienzi is recalled in the lachrymose and self-lacerating pathos of the Führer's last recorded words. The nobles, and even the pope, were only Rienzi's immediate enemies; the real adversary—in the sense of a defaulting partner—was the populace. One can translate these factors into the psychological world of a Hitler who, in the end, querulously complained that his people had not been worthy of him. Adorno is right in detecting a parallel between Rienzi, the "first servant of the greater social totality," and the fascist Adolf Hitler (Adorno 1981, p. 13).

Here were two deluded men, beset by utopian visions from phantasmagoric regions of the soul, and led astray by their own delirious sense of power at a historically propitious moment. And each met with or brought about an end very different from the one foreseen in his utopian dreams. Over and above this, however, Wagner's summing up of Rienzi in a letter of 25 January 1859 to the singer Albert Niemann is accurate, but definitely not applicable to the insane ambition of the young operagoer in Linz. Rienzi's tragedy, Wagner wrote, was "that only his idea was true, and the people were not."[2]

Romantic Opera: *Der fliegende Holländer*

Wagner's circle of friends in Paris was what would be popularly described as a merry band of artists. They included the painters Ernst Benedikt Kietz and Friedrich Pecht, the librarian Gottfried Englebert Anders, and the philosopher Samuel Lehrs. Although they may well have made merry together, their life was hard. Wagner's story *An End in Paris* catches something of its real flavor. The story ends with a credo ("I believe in God, Mozart and Beethoven . . ."). This patently rings true, but the names that dominated the Paris salons were of more immediate significance: such names as Meyerbeer or the famous and successful Heinrich Heine, whose character was similar to Wagner's in certain respects.

Nonetheless, it was probably in Riga, rather than Paris, where Wagner found the inspiration for the libretto of his first "authentic" opera, as Riga was the place where he read Heine's *Memoirs of Herr von Schnabelewopski*.

2. Reproduced as "probably Wagner's most important statement" on his *Rienzi* in SW 23, document 256.

Moreover, as an avid reader he may also have known Wilhelm Hauff's fairy tale *Geschichte vom Gespensterschiff* (1825).

These threads, however, became woven together only because of a personal experience: the Wagners' sea journey of 1839, when their boat had to anchor in Sandvike Bay, off the Norwegian island of Boröya. Here the steeply shelving coast formed a wall which bounced back the shouts and singing of the sailors, creating an echo. This was an impressive experience for a past master of theatrical effects, and by his own account it inspired the Norwegian Sailors' Chorus in the opera.

The libretto of *Holländer* was written between 18 and 28 May 1841. Wagner finished composing the whole work a few months later, on 19 November, but another year went by before it had its first performance. This took place not in Paris but in Dresden on 2 January 1843. Wagner himself conducted the performance, but it was a mere succès d'estime and could not compare with the triumph of *Rienzi,* even though the part of Senta was sung by Wilhelmine Schröder-Devrient, who had been widely admired in the role of Adriano. The run ended with the fourth performance. On 2 February 1843, one month after the premiere, Wagner was appointed to the post of Kapellmeister by the Saxon royal court. Despite his aversion to permanent engagements, he accepted, mainly at Minna's (understandable) insistence. In so doing he wrought a momentous change in his life. But I am anticipating events.

Art was assiduously cultivated at the Dresden Opera, but it was no match for the Paris Opéra. Wagner would naturally have preferred to stage the premiere of *Holländer* in Paris, the capital city of European culture, the musical metropolis that had seen the triumphs of Spontini and Auber, of Rossini, Cherubini, Donizetti, Bellini, and Meyerbeer. But whatever its importance, musically and otherwise, it was simply not a lucky place for Wagner. Extreme penury induced him to sell his *Holländer* libretto, the synopsis of which he had submitted (in French) to the Paris Opéra management in the summer of 1840. Wagner was hoping to be commissioned to write a one-act piece of the kind then in fashion as curtain raisers (see Bauer 1983, p. 42). The management liked his text—and asked a house composer, Pierre Louis Philippe Dietsch, to write the music. For Wagner this was an acute humiliation, but it was standard practice. Plagued by debts, Wagner had to be content with five hundred francs, and Dietsch composed his *Vaisseau phantôme,* which had a total of eleven performances before disappearing into the oblivion it merited.

The text by Heine gives a clear idea of the original subject matter, and of what Wagner, abandoning the tastes of the Parisian salons for the misty atmosphere of a Nordic world, chose to make of it. The fact that it contains its share of banalities and absurdities should enhance one's understanding of Wagner's version of it. Heine's narrator tells of a stage play which he professes to have seen in Amsterdam (the text can be found in Dahlhaus 1979, pp. 7–9). Although the Heine text reads like a simplified version of the opera plot, Wagner endowed it nonetheless with dignity, profundity, and drama. He did so by compressing the story and increasing the tension. The original config-

uration of three characters—the father, the daughter, and the Dutchman—becomes an interplay of four main characters, the stranger being contrasted with a sexual rival, Erik the huntsman (this character is Wagner's invention), whose touching but hopeless love makes Senta's superiority and her isolation that much clearer because of his pronounced insignificance. Senta has long since outgrown the narrow world dominated by the shrewd business deals of her father, Daland, and Erik's good-natured platitudes; she has been visualizing her destiny for a long time. The figure of Erik takes on a useful dramatic function in the finale. The Dutchman overhears the last conversation between the pair. In the time-honored tradition of opera plots he interprets it wrongly, but in a most significant way, for it motivates his departure and thus Senta's sacrificial death.

The finale reveals the real significance of Wagner's changes to the story. The ironic Heine regarded the faithful woman's suicide as the only means of achieving eternal fidelity; with Wagner, irony is turned into tragic pathos (see Dahlhaus 1979, pp. 10ff.). Certainly Heine had opened up the possibility with his emotional climax to the traditional tale of a Jew condemned to wander until Judgment Day. This climax, however, amounted to little more than the odd touch of sentimentality. But Wagner's heroine dies because this is the only way she can show the Dutchman that he is mistaken in thinking he has been duped by a woman again. What justifies her act of redemption is that the beneficiary has at last earned it. In a significant twist on the original story, the Dutchman invokes a formal point: Senta has sworn to be faithful to him. When he rejects punishment and vengeance, he achieves a kind of renunciation, as well as expressing a desire to redeem his betrothed ("Countless victims have already paid / the price: but Senta, I am saving your soul!"). This change in him shows the effect of love, an emotion he has never felt before. The principal characters in the "dramatic ballad," as Wagner once called the opera, are acted upon rather than active. From the very beginning both are driven by a fervent longing for death—a death that will redeem them, a sacrificial death in a logically constructed martyr play (Dahlhaus 1979, p. 12).

It has rightly been said that in this opera "one can observe for the first time those tragically interwoven themes of escape, allegiance, deception and redemption that run through Wagner's whole output in ever-new variations" (Gregor-Dellin/Soden 1983, pp. 63ff.). Let us single out some of those themes and their variants. One is the Wandering Jew who has made a devil's pact and is condemned to roam the world forever. This theme applies to Kundry as well as the Flying Dutchman (Telramund and Wotan also touch on the thematic note of a devil's pact). Second, there is the theme of a disastrous greed for gold: we see this in Alberich as well as Daland. Third, we have the theme of supposed deception, or a simple lack of faith. Elsa is one of its victims; another is the tragically perplexed Brünnhilde, who only perceives her mistake when she is dying. Wagner also returns to curses and sorcery as dramatic devices: Ortrud, Kundry, and Alberich belong to this

magic domain, as does Isolde's mother. (The machinations of the gods constitute a separate theme.)

Above all there is the theme of death—death as sacrifice, death as redemption, the woman-redeemer as a goddess of death. This applies to Elisabeth, and also to a limited extent to the Brünnhilde whom Siegmund sees and to the essentially magical Isolde. Male characters, too, can represent a god of death who brings redemption. Lohengrin assumes this role for Elsa, and Parsifal for Kundry (and in this sense Senta and Parsifal are very closely linked).

As was his wont when called upon to interpret his own works, Wagner placed *Holländer* in a wider, more universal context. In *A Communication to My Friends* (1851) he described the figure of the Dutchman as "the poetic myth of the people." The Dutchman, he said, expressed "an age-old feature of man's character . . . with a power that grips the heart"; the characteristic in question was a "longing for respite from the storms of life." This sounds suspiciously like autobiography, and it smacks too of Biedermeier values. Senta, however, opposes any such longing. She yearns, in Hans Mayer's words, "for the new and unknown, and longs to escape from her present surroundings. Senta is not a foolish hysteric, as many have described and portrayed her. She is a passionate and very lonely young woman in cramped and uninspiring surroundings" (Mayer 1966, p. 36).

Let us return to Wagner's commentary. At the close of the Middle Ages, he states, mankind was agitated by a new thirst for action (previously embodied by the figures of Odysseus and the Wandering Jew). On the "plane of world-history" the impulse found its strongest outlet during the age of exploration. The view of the seas as the "bedrock of life" and the longing for a homeland turn into their opposite: a yearning for the new and unknown, for things instinctively sensed. This impulse is encapsulated in the myth of the Flying Dutchman—a designation, it may be remarked, that identifies the Dutch as great seafaring explorers. To a certain extent the Dutchman is a combination of Odysseus, the Wandering Jew, and Columbus. "Swirling seas and storms" are obvious physical signs of his damnation by the devil. Mortally sick, the condemned man pines for redemption "through the agency of—a woman." Penelope at her loom can no longer fulfill this role. Instead, "it is womankind in general, but the longed-for, half-sensed, infinitely feminine woman who does not yet exist—in short, the woman of the future."

Whenever he was stuck for a definition, Wagner was fond of invoking the future. It is not easy to grasp what he meant by the woman of the future. But this much is evident: the man is damned by his own (masculine) element, condemned to turmoil, danger, curiosity, conquest, activity, ambition, the joy of success, and the desire for gain. The opposed feminine element provides shelter, tranquillity, a homeland, a romantic return to the mother's lap, as well as darkness, oblivion, a dissolution into nature. The redemption of the masculine element comes through that peace which a woman's (self-denying) love bestows. The collision point of these two worlds is where a great man, and especially a great artist, proves himself. And it is not just in this sense that all Wagner's dramas are also dramatizations of an artist's life (as noted in Mayer 1966, pp. 36ff.).

In *Holländer* these opposed spheres are also depicted as the world of concrete reality (Daland's world) on the one hand and the reality of dreams and visions (Senta's world) on the other. The two are irreconcilable. Senta resolves and redeems matters by passing into the nocturnal world of the Dutchman (see Dahlhaus 1979, p. 12).

Senta as a character is unfathomable. Wagner describes her ballad as the core of the opera: "I remember sketching Senta's ballad in the second act, writing both the text and the melody, before going on . . . to the composition proper. I unconsciously incorporated in this piece the thematic seeds of the music for the whole opera: it was the compressed image of the whole drama as I saw it in my mind's eye. When I had to find a title for the finished work, I was strongly tempted to call it a 'dramatic ballad.'"

There is certainly no disputing the central position of the ballad, in which Senta conjures up the Dutchman in person, just as Elsa will conjure up Lohengrin (and Hagen Siegfried). But Wagner's statement needs to be qualified (Dahlhaus 1979, pp. 14ff.). The ballad actually contains only two of the opera's musical motifs. Wagner happily indulged in tall tales about how he was inspired to write his works—such as the story of the primary chord of the *Rheingold* prelude and the alleged Good Friday inspiration of *Parsifal,* or the prelude to *Die Meistersinger* (see Deathridge/Dahlhaus 1984, pp. 39ff.). In this particular instance, however, the salient point is the reduction of the whole opera to the character of a ballad. In 1901 the first work by Wagner that was worthy of Bayreuth became the last to be staged there. Cosima and Siegfried Wagner introduced a production detail that harked back to the original autograph score, and because of the point just mentioned it was highly convincing: they allowed the opera to proceed continuously, uninterrupted by breaks between acts.[3]

From a poetic standpoint, certainly, Senta's Ballad is indeed a microcosm reflecting the whole (see Borchmeyer 1982, p. 178). In writing it, the poet of *Holländer* forsook the career of a "manufacturer of opera libretti," as he says in *A Communication to My Friends*.

Wagner's own interpretation of his work sketches a mythology that boldly revokes time and space. "Antiquity (the longing for a homeland), medieval times (the longing for death) and the modern age (the longing for the new)" are combined "in an utopian myth" (Borchmeyer 1982, p. 184). This myth encompasses—albeit in shadowy outline—the image of the "woman of the future." Like the hero of a medieval romance, Wagner perceives a utopian homeland "in the image of the *femme introuvable*." Such a preordained state

---

3. A practice observed by Harry Kupfer in his fascinating 1978 Bayreuth production. See Werner Breig's remarks on the matter in Chapter 18 of this volume.

of homelessness is the stigma that attaches to the modern artist. "Two symbols are therefore contained in the figure of the Flying Dutchman. He is the mythical image of modern man, whose urge to explore has become a homeless journeying into an infinite void, and who is now seeking a *terra utopica* he can adopt as a homeland. At the same time he is . . . an existential symbol of the modern, absolute artist in his alienation from life" (Borchmeyer 1982, p. 185).

Death and transfiguration: the Dutchman's end is a classic Wagnerian finale. Wagner's stage direction reads: "Both of them, transfigured, are seen rising from the sea." This poses a problem in any production, for how can the scene be staged without lapsing into kitsch? The really crucial point, however, is the possibility of happiness, of a concrete utopia: "He holds her in a close embrace."

Grand Romantic Opera: *Tannhäuser und der Sängerkrieg auf Wartburg*

In April 1842 Richard and Minna Wagner returned from Paris to Germany and breathed a great sigh of relief. It was a moving moment for them when they crossed the Rhine, turning their backs on the salons, *les paradis artificiels,* and a world of frivolous hedonism—not that Wagner had been allowed to sample the delights of that world. On their way to Dresden they traveled past the Wartburg. This journey from Parisian grand opera to a Thuringian stronghold symbolized for Wagner the path toward an ideal he was doggedly, desperately seeking: a sublimation of importunate sensual urges and the raising of the commonplace to a nobler level. To resolve the conflict between sensual pleasure and peace of mind in favor of the latter was a goal that seemed truly "German" to Wagner at this stage in his life. He expressed his yearning for such a Germany in *Tannhäuser,* which he called a "Grand Romantic Opera." It was a yearning for which he found a name and a concept then and there. It bears little relation to his real attitude toward the German character, which he was to criticize most bitterly, especially in his later years.

The Genesis of Tannhäuser

Between 6 and 10 September 1842 Wagner wrote a long letter from Dresden to his friend Ernst Benedikt Kietz in Paris: "The only thing I have achieved for myself this summer is the detailed stage draft of the 'Venusberg' [the original title of *Tannhäuser*]. I consider it a complete success and am convinced that this opera will be my most original creation . . . I began working out the details of the draft in the course of a short journey which I made on foot from Teplitz to Aussig and beyond in the mountains; I spent the night on the Schreckenstein . . . and started work on it there." Wagner also relates how he came across a reproduction of Carlo Dolci's Madonna in the Aussig parish church during his outing. (We shall return to this episode in connection with *Die Meistersinger.*)

Wagner completed the libretto of *Tannhäuser* in April 1843, and in July he began work on the music. This took another year, the full score eventually being completed in April 1845. In his letter of 5 June to the writer and music critic Karl Gaillard, Wagner again places a notable emphasis on the "German" element: "I am enclosing with this letter a copy of my 'Tannhäuser' as he lives and breathes, a German from head to toe . . . May he be capable of winning me the hearts of my fellow Germans in far greater numbers than my earlier works have thus far succeeded in doing!"

The opera had its first performance in Dresden on 19 October 1845. Audience reception was muted, in spite of a brilliant cast. (The composer himself conducted, and the title role was sung by Joseph Tichatschek, the foremost Heldentenor of the day. Wilhelmine Schröder-Devrient sang Venus, and Wagner's niece Johanna appeared in the part of Elisabeth.) Press reaction ranged from cautious to dismissive. People also objected, ironically enough, to what they felt was a lascivious subject. Moreover, the tolling of a bell from the Wartburg was the only indication of Elisabeth's sacrificial death, and the audience did not find this ending sufficiently clear.

Wagner immediately began to revise the opera. The corrections, changes, and efforts to intensify and clarify it are now part of its history. When *Tannhäuser* returned to the repertory on 1 August 1847, it had acquired a more concrete finale. The dramatic effect was appreciably enhanced by the reemergence of Venus from her subterranean world. Elisabeth, her antagonist, also reappears, although she is now a lifeless figure in a coffin, at whose side Tannhäuser collapses. This was the second stage of the composition and revision of the opera and part of the so-called Dresden version. (For details of the four stages in the writing of *Tannhäuser,* see WWV 70.)

Although the opera did not enjoy instant success, interest in it grew steadily and inexorably. After Liszt had taken the initiative in Weimar (1849), nearly all the German opera houses staged *Tannhäuser* during the 1850s, and foreign companies followed suit. This spate of productions gave rise to an ever-growing stream of interpretations of the work from Wagner's pen, starting in 1853 with a "communication to conductors and performers of this opera," *On Performing "Tannhäuser."* It was Paris, however, that marked a decisive point in the reception history of the piece.

Much, to be sure, had happened in the meantime. Several noteworthy, indeed epoch-making, events had occurred. In 1848 Wagner completed *Lohengrin.* That year he became involved with the revolution in Dresden, and had to flee via Weimar to Zurich to escape arrest (an episode discussed in detail in Chapter 4). His Zurich exile lasted nearly ten years. There he completed his libretto for the *Ring* and worked on the music to *Das Rheingold, Die Walküre,* and *Siegfried* (to the end of act 2). While living in Zurich, Wagner also fell in love with Otto Wesendonck's wife, Mathilde. The experience inspired him to write the libretto of *Tristan* and to compose the first act. The year 1858 found him once more on the run, this time to Venice, where he composed the second act of *Tristan* in the Palazzo Giustiniani. After the Austrian authorities had caused him to flee yet again, Wagner finished *Tristan* in Lucerne on 6 August 1859. Then came the move to Paris.

In Paris Wagner enjoyed the protection of the Austrian ambassador, or rather the ambassador's wife, Princess Pauline Metternich. She induced Emperor Napoleon III to decree a new production of *Tannhäuser* (the French court was happy to oblige Austria if it meant annoying the Prussians).

For the first and only time in the history of Wagner's operas, a stubborn battle arose between the work's author and its public, or that public's normal expectations. The Parisians were not exactly noted for the seriousness and profundity of their tastes, and in line with their need for amusement they demanded some changes and additions. On 10 April 1860 Wagner wrote to Mathilde Wesendonck: "Not one note, not one word of *Tannhäuser* will be altered." (This was overconfidence speaking. In fact Wagner did have to make changes, and make them with a good grace. For details of the changes, see Abbate 1985 and WWV, pp. 290–293.) He went on: "But a 'ballet' was said to be imperative, and this ballet was supposed to occur in the second act, since the subscribers to the Opera always arrive at the theatre somewhat later, after a heavy dinner, never at the beginning. Well, I declared that I would not take my orders from the Jockey Club, but that I would withdraw my work. But now I intend to help them out of their difficulty: the opera does not need to begin until 8 o'clock, and then I shall have another go at the unholy Venusberg, and this time I'll do it properly."

This may look like a concession to the tastes of high society, but actually it reflects Wagner's sure dramatic instincts. The original version had depicted Venus' world, the world of the senses, in colors that were too drab and pallid: Venus never developed into a powerful and dangerous rival to the spiritual Elisabeth. Wagner needed to inject more energy into this world—and he had discovered a way of doing it. His letter of 10 April continues: "But I now also recognize that at the time that I wrote *Tannhäuser* I was not yet able to do the sort of thing that is necessary here: for this I should have required a far greater mastery such as I have only now acquired: only now that I have written Isolde's final transfiguration have I been able to find the right ending for the *Flying Dutchman* Overture, as well as—the horrors of the Venusberg. One becomes all-powerful only by playing with the world."

This last statement is a flirtatious yet bitter allusion to the personally shattering effect of the Wesendonck affair, which led to a productive act of renunciation on Wagner's part. It opened up reserves of energy, an electrical charge of spiritual and sensual impressions. And these were creatively transformed into the inspiration for *Tristan,* as well as the new bacchanal in *Tannhäuser.*

On 30 March 1860 Wagner drew up an account of the envisaged changes in the form of a "complete poetic sketch of the Venusberg." Rehearsals began in September, and they benefited from the exceptional stagecraft and technical facilities available in Paris. On 28 January 1861 Wagner finished the score of the new first act. The first performance of the so-called Paris version took place on 13 March—after no fewer than 164 rehearsals—under Pierre Louis Philippe Dietsch. This was the same man who had turned Wagner's draft for

Holländer into the opera *Le vaisseau phantôme*. Bülow, in his typically forthright way, described him as "the meanest of blockheads," aurally deficient and with no capacity for study. In fact he was a competent musician and conductor, but nothing more.

The performance unleashed a mighty storm. As was to be the pattern with Wagner's music, the public was split into two camps. Albert Niemann, who sang the part of Tannhäuser, had the temerity to fling his pilgrim's hat into the rowdy audience; he subsequently had to apologize to the emperor, who was present. Wagner withdrew his opera after three performances. The sets were used for other productions in the repertory. The hostility of the Jockey Club eventually abated. On 4 April 1861 Wagner wrote to Bülow: "Thanks to the fury of the Jockeys, this much-hampered performance has acquired a real halo. Already groups are being specially formed in my honour, and that includes some of the common people." The most illustrious and sensitive spokesman for these partisans, the "Wagnerites," was Charles Baudelaire (Baudelaire 1861). Once again Wagner displayed his insatiable need to be the chronicler of his own history; he published his own account of the affair in Leipzig in the *Deutsche Allgemeine Zeitung* on 7 April 1861 (see appendix to Chapter 23, item 90).

Sources and Models

Wagner states in *My Life* that the subject of *Tannhäuser* came to him "quite by chance through a folk book about the Venusberg. All I regarded as inherently German had attracted me with ever-increasing force and impelled me to look for its deepest meaning with enthusiastic longing, and here I suddenly found it in the simple re-telling of the legend, based on the ancient, well-known ballad of Tannhäuser" (ML 212).

With regard to this "simple re-telling," Wagner owed his acquaintance with the ancient ballad to Heinrich Heine; but with what Borchmeyer calls shameless ingratitude (Borchmeyer 1982, p. 198), he kept quiet about the debt. Once more it was from the work of this elegant cynic that Wagner drew the material which fired him. In the third volume of his *Salon* (1836), Heine deliberately prefaced his strophic Tannhäuser legend with the "well-known ballad"—well-known from the *Wunderhorn* collection—to point up the contrast between them. Wagner's other sources included Ludwig Tieck's story *Der getreue Eckart und der Tannenhäuser* (from the *Phantasus* collection of 1812–1817) and Novalis' *Heinrich von Ofterdingen* (1802). He also drew on several of the *Deutsche Sagen* published in 1816 by the Brothers Grimm—notably number 173, the *Hö[r]selberg* (synonymous with Venusberg). And *Der Kampf der Sänger* (from *Die Serapionsbrüder* of 1819) by Wagner's favorite author, E. T. A. Hoffmann, was more than familiar to him; indeed, he had it very much in mind.

A decisive factor in Wagner's dramatization of the material was, however, an unexpected encounter with two books of a very different type. In his repeated references to the Tannhäuser "folk book" as a source, Wagner is, perhaps unwittingly, misleading us, since no such book exists. But this may really be a reference to a work whose title he neglects to mention: Ludwig Bechstein's *Sagenschatz des Thüringerlandes* (a "treasury of tales from Thuringia") of 1835. This book unexpectedly associates the Wartburg song contest with the name of Tannhäuser. At roughly the same time, in 1838, a learned treatise that Wagner obtained through his Paris friend the philologist Samuel Lehrs similarly suggested a link between these two heterogeneous and previously unconnected subjects. Written by a Königsberg philologist, C. T. L. Lucas, and published by the Royal German Society of Königsberg, it was called *Der Krieg von Wartburg*. For chronological reasons alone, its quirky thesis would be hard to defend. (Lucas speculated that the legendary Heinrich von Ofterdingen, the problematic hero of the ballad of the Wartburg contest, was related to Tannhäuser, even though tales and legends were already attaching the Venusberg exploit to Tannhäuser soon after his death in the thirteenth century.) At any rate, given the link established by each of these publications, Wagner's pent-up dramatic instincts caused the dam to break. All at once he found himself able to combine the two subjects, the world of Tannhäuser and Venus and the Marian world of the Wartburg contest, within the framework of a single tragic drama.

For the sake of clarity let us reconstruct the sequence in which Wagner assembled his source material. First came Tannhäuser himself, a Middle High German lyric poet from the first part of the thirteenth century (circa 1200–1270). Colorful and (pseudo)learned, imaginative and formally skillful, he was a writer of songs and lays who exists for us only through his poetry and not as a historically tangible figure. Very soon he underwent a transformation through an association in various legends with Wagner's second source: the tale of the Venusberg and the knight who succumbs to the goddess of love in her grotto. This conjunction gave rise to the ancient poem transmitted— in a version dating from 1521—in the first volume of *Des Knaben Wunderhorn* (1806). But until Bechstein published his version of the tale in 1835, and until Lucas' wrongheaded thesis (which the tale may have inspired), neither of the two sources had had any connection with Wagner's third source: a collection of Middle High German poems about the Wartburg contest.

The *Wartburgkrieg* collection, which probably came into existence in Thuringia around 1260–1270, was an amalgam of a number of independent pieces. One of the key elements is the *Sängerkrieg,* or tournament of song, which belongs to the genre of the *Fürstenpreis,* in which the poet addresses his sovereign. The piece tells how, under Landgrave Hermann I, the court poets vie with one another in song. In the course of the contest the unorthodox minstrel Heinrich von Ofterdingen is ostracized as an outcast, defeated, and threatened with death.

In the other outstanding piece in the collection a singer is again defeated in a contest. Ofterdingen has summoned the magician Klingsor to his aid, but in a game of riddles Klingsor is vanquished by Wolfram von Eschenbach. The piece is a late flowering of the courtly poetic art. Summarizing and transfiguring past achievements, it is a model of how to portray profane magic and religious piety, and proves that those minstrels who directly or indirectly contributed to the tradition were descended from noble antecedents.

In any event, all three sources are made up of descriptive material that tends toward epic narrative. None of them revolves around a dramatic or tragic conflict, for disputes between professional artistic rivals are not the stuff of such conflicts. But a conflict was what Wagner was looking for: his genius lay not just in the linking of the Tannhäuser legend with the singing contest, but in his perception and use of its implicit drama. (The link had been merely adumbrated in the two sources.)

The linkage accounts for the opera's double title: *Tannhäuser und Der Sängerkrieg auf Wartburg*. Combining two alternative titles (like *Das Liebesverbot oder Die Novize von Palermo*) was a literary fashion in the eighteenth and nineteenth centuries, "summarizing the argument or the gist of the plot" (Dahlhaus 1979, p. 21). But here we have something else. The traditional "or" in the title has been replaced by "and." The idea is not to explain the title by paraphrasing it but rather to augment it: without the second part it would not be complete. In other words, a dramatic relationship is being established between two different subjects; the theme of Tannhäuser and Venus becomes interwoven with that of Ofterdingen's defeat in the song contest. Wagner had conceived a drama that takes place on two levels, and the nub of the drama is their interrelation. Since the first strand is motivated by the Tannhäuser-Venus link, his concept necessarily entails the creation of a fresh antagonist for the second strand of the plot. But naturally neither the landgrave nor the competing singers would make an acceptable counterpart to Venus. Hence the appearance of Elisabeth, a contrasting character to the pagan goddess of love, and a woman whose love reflects a Marian form of Christian worship. Also, since the Virgin-like Elisabeth could not possibly be married to the landgrave, Wagner had to turn the ruler's daughter-in-law of the original tale into his niece (the historical Elisabeth, later a saint, had been the Hungarian king's daughter).[4]

The ancient Tannhäuser ballad[5] tells how the hero extricates himself from the enticement of voluptuous carnal delights (just as Odysseus managed to wriggle out of the embraces of Calypso and Circe):

> No longer goes it well with me,
> I must away already.
> Free me, gentle lady, from
> your proud and noble body.

4. Elisabeth (1207–1231) was married to Hermann's son, Landgrave Ludwig IV (1200–1227).

5. The German text quoted herein is from *Des Knaben Wunderhorn: Alte deutsche Lieder*, vol. 1, compiled by Achim von Arnim and Clemens Brentano, collected edition (Munich: DTV, 1963), pp. 56–59. The version of the Tannhäuser ballad included in Bechstein's *Sagenschatz* has (among other things) a different ending. It can be found (with minor variations) in ENO Tannhäuser 1988, pp. 58–59, together with an English translation by J. W. Thomas. Wagner knew both versions. [Ed.]

Driven by pangs of conscience and a pious desire to do penance, Tannhäuser goes on a pilgrimage to Rome to see the pope, Urban IV. He begs for his sins to be forgiven, but the pope refuses absolution. The old *Wunderhorn* ballad relates:

> The Pope he has a staff of white,
> Made of a withered tree-bough:
> "When this my staff begins to flower,
> Then shall all your sins be forgiven."

This condition is an apparent impossibility. There is nothing Tannhäuser can do but return to the Venusberg and his pagan queen.

> And then upon the third day after
> The staff it started to flower,
> And messengers were sent abroad
> To seek the knightly Tannhäuser.

> Within the Venusberg was he,
> And there henceforth would he tarry
> Until the very end of time,
> Awaiting God's own judgement.

This, far from amounting to a tragic denouement, is almost a happy ending. Johann Nestroy adopted the same tone in his Wagner parody.[6]

The other piece, the *Sängerkrieg,* is similar in poetic structure. In a contest a minstrel is defeated by another competitor. His defeat comes as a devastating blow, but it does not have the makings of a moving and exciting drama.

At this point Wagner the instinctive dramatist stepped in with an inspired idea. He sternly confronts Venus' intoxicating artificial paradise with its opposite, namely a German paradise, the ascetic domain of the Wartburg. The hero who struggles out of the Venusberg is acting for the sake of the Wartburg and in order to win the latter's acknowledgment. The Venus apostate becomes a singer of praises. But what does he praise? He praises love. And this is the tragic element that Wagner injected into his drama, for Tannhäuser celebrates the very love from which he has just escaped. He does so before a courtly gathering that is absolutely opposed to the love of Venus. What they uphold and practice is a cult of renunciation and a high-minded courtly love—the secularized form of Mariolatry and *Gottesminne,* the noble love of God.

This situation is bound to lead to catastrophe; it is itself catastrophic. The singer must offend both others and himself. The pope is not going to absolve him, despite his repentance and unquestionably sincere remorse. This forces him ineluctably back into the Venusberg. Tannhäuser is confronted by the Christian principle in accordance not with a pious medieval reading of the narrative, but rather with a worldly, modern way of thinking: he stands in

6. Nestroy, a popular Viennese dramatist, wrote a *Tannhäuser* parody in 1857. This moderately witty "farce of the future" (*Zukunftsposse*) ends happily for all concerned: Venus restores the two lovers to life and blesses their union.

need of redemption, just like everyone else. But this cannot be achieved through the kind of hedonism expounded by Heinse and Feuerbach. The only way to gain it is through sacrifice—through renunciation and a readiness for martyrdom. As his advocate before God, Elisabeth atones for Tannhäuser just as Gretchen atones for Goethe's Faust. By dying for Tannhäuser, Elisabeth enables Tannhäuser to die a pure death.

The Duality Principle

On 23 January 1883, three weeks before Wagner's death, Cosima noted in her diary: "Chat in the evening, brought to an end by R. with the 'Shepherd's Song' and 'Pilgrims' Chorus' from *Tannhäuser*. He says he still owes the world *Tannhäuser*." An enigmatic remark—but what is certain is that Wagner never stopped thinking about *Tannhäuser* (two more diary entries that illustrate this will follow shortly). It is fair to speculate that his preoccupation or anxiety had to do with the theme of a personal dichotomy, which he fully explored for the first time in *Tannhäuser*. In that sense it is his testament, part of an attempt to master the meaning of his own life.

The dichotomy is the contradiction or antagonism between the artist and society. It is also the contrast between the world of the senses and the world of the spirit. By devoting a great deal of energy and effort to its resolution, Wagner succeeded in accommodating the first contradiction within his personal life. But the other conflict gnawed at him to the end of his days.

Commentators (Hans Mayer and Dieter Borchmeyer are recent examples) have frequently observed that Wagner's operas can be interpreted as dramas about an artist's life, among other things. This is particularly true of the Romantic, prerevolutionary works; *Holländer, Tannhäuser,* and *Lohengrin* have been described as "symbols of the artist's existence" (Borchmeyer 1982, p. 185). Wagner's own exegesis in his *Communication* of 1851 supports this view, and it was through this that the 1972 Bayreuth production of *Tannhäuser* by Götz Friedrich, for instance, acquired its dramatic intensity. But the conflict must not be exaggerated. Granted, Wagner deals with it in all his dramas, and it becomes crucial to *Die Meistersinger,* although the personalities of those Wagner heroes who are not artists can also be summed up as artistic. It would, however, be stretching a point to identify Tannhäuser's situation with that of Goethe's Tasso. Torquato Tasso was an artist of modest social standing who depended on a noble protector. Tannhäuser, by contrast, is a gentleman and knightly minstrel surrounded by his peers. And unlike Tasso, who is obliged to stay away from the princess in Goethe's play, he is brought straight to the lady of the court. Thus the conflict in *Tannhäuser* is not so much between the artist and society as between libertinism and convention within the social framework. The drama contrasts the passionate advocate of a new sensuality in art and life with the proponents of an ossified Christian morality. In that respect it anticipates the antagonism between Old Art and New Art in *Die Meistersinger*.

In 1861 Baudelaire wrote his striking essay "Richard Wagner and *Tannhäuser* in Paris." In a way this was an apology to the composer on behalf of the French intelligentsia. In it Baudelaire states firmly and succinctly: "*Tannhäuser* presents the struggle of the two principles which have selected the human heart as their chief arena, i.e. the struggle of the flesh with the spirit, of hell with heaven and of Satan with God" (Baudelaire 1861, p. 794).

It is, however, the Paris version of the opera rather than the earlier ones that develops the theme of dualism. Although Wagner refused to make concessions to the habitués who would arrive at the opera during the intermission and came to applaud their favorite ballet dancers, he did extend the first act. Not for extraneous reasons, however, but for reasons that lay within the opera itself. In his letter to Mathilde of 10 April 1860 he wrote: "This court of Frau Venus was clearly the weak point in my work: lacking a good ballet, I resorted at the time to a few coarse brush-strokes, and in that way spoiled a great deal: in particular, the Venusberg left a very dull and indecisive impression, and, as a result, I lost an important foundation upon which the whole of the subsequent tragedy should have been built to shattering effect."

Wagner enlarged the bacchanal appreciably, in both words and music, and depicted the fascination and seductive charm of Venus' realm in glowing colors. But he could achieve this musically only after he had composed Isolde's transfiguration, only after having expressed extreme dread and rapture in the glittering chromaticism of *Tristan,* a style that could be adapted quite easily to the 1845–1847 version of *Tannhäuser.* As he repeatedly said in so many words, Wagner owed *Tristan* to his love affair with Mathilde. Hence it was also to her that he owed the fresh riches of *Tannhäuser,* as he knew when he described them to her in elaborate detail.[7]

In this sense *Tannhäuser* can be regarded as a first draft for *Parsifal,* a preliminary study. It can be seen as a monument to the enormous effort that Wagner made to settle the destructive conflict between two opposed worlds. In *Tannhäuser* as in *Parsifal* he achieved only the "Christian solution." In both cases this solution is patently inadequate, and possibly absurd. *Tannhäuser* shows us the world of Venus, the underworld of Romantic myth, Baudelaire's *paradis artificiel.*[8] To quote Borchmeyer: "This underworld is in artificial contrast to the prosaic upper world, symbolizing the hermetic and demonic realm of art, and involving its denizens in a profoundly ambiguous relationship to reality: the rejection of reality is typical, but so is the longing for it (Borchmeyer 1982, p. 206). Tannhäuser escapes from this realm, by the skin of his teeth. But what, having just evaded Venus' golden chains of erotic desire,

7. In the 1859–61 revision of *Tannhäuser,* Wagner replaced his description of it in the score as a "grand romantic opera" with the more abstract "Handlung in drei Aufzügen"—literally, "action in three acts." The new description is identical to the one used for *Tristan.* [Ed.]

8. This underworld theme brings to mind Wagner's scenario for a projected opera, *The Mines of Falun* (*Die Bergwerke zu Falun,* 1842), a subject treated successively by Arnim, Hoffmann, J. P. Hebel, Rückert, and Hugo von Hofmannsthal (*Das Bergwerk von Falun,* 1899). Heine deals with a similar theme in his "Gods in Exile." See Borchmeyer 1982, pp. 189ff., 197; see also Weiner 1982.

does he proclaim to the contrasting world he has striven so hard to reach, the courtly world with its sublimated, high-minded concept of love (*Minne*)? He fervently proclaims an erotic doctrine unworthy of a minnesinger. To combat Wolfram's noble and knightly renunciation and Biterolf's dogma of illumination, Tannhäuser—after several frenzied trial runs—finally offers a song that takes up the jubilant melody of the hymn to Venus:

> Goddess of love, to you my life is given,
> in praise of love I'll sing for evermore.
> By lust for love man's heart and soul are driven,
> his hopes made flesh by you whom all adore.
> And blest the man who on your beauty has feasted,
> for he alone knows all that love can be.
> Poor mortals, who true love have never tasted,
> make haste, haste to the Venusberg with me!

This is strong stuff—too strong, inevitably, for the high-sounding, stiffly intolerant advocates of *Minne,* the would-be guardians of morality. The song causes a terrible scandal. Elisabeth rescues the transgressor from the swords of the moralizers, who are far from averse to violence, whereupon the offender sinks to his knees and acknowledges himself to be a sinner. Pleading for mercy, he condemns his "depraved tongue," despite the fact that he was also singing in Elisabeth's honor. And now,

> To Rome I take the journey,
> and there repent afresh,
> to kneel in dust and ashes,
> and mortify my flesh.

The singer of this confession has not been enlightened in any way; he has made not the slightest progress on the road to knowledge. Violently but naively he has lurched from one form of enchantment into another. Robbed of his independence, Tannhäuser is not accountable for his actions.

This is a gaping flaw in the drama, and Wagner managed it no better than he dealt with the purity cult in *Parsifal.* Tannhäuser (but not *Tannhäuser*) triumphantly proclaims the joys of free and openly sensual love. Such were the joys that Heinse, Laube, and Young Germany preached; and Feuerbach provided the philosophical rationale. But Wagner did not dare to stand by Tannhäuser, any more than he stood by his love for Mathilde Wesendonck or his later love for Judith Gautier. Instead he composed *Tristan* and *Parsifal,* thereby replacing an affirmation of the physical world with the *opus metaphysicum,* the *opera metaphysica.* Wagner's solutions were, successively, escape from the world and transfiguration (in *Tristan*), jovial renunciation *(Die Meistersinger),* and angelic infallibility *(Parsifal).* These are towering monuments to a personal conflict translated into art. Through art, Wagner achieved things he could not achieve in life. These solutions would be more aptly described as declarations: documents, that is to say, of a human personality with its stigmas and its burden of suffering.

A few further observations may serve to reinforce and enlarge on this thesis (which will be expanded and rounded out with my thoughts on *Parsifal*). First, Wagner does find a thoroughly organic means of bringing Tannhäuser out of the sultry world of the classical pagan goddess of love and into the spiritual world of the minnesingers' devotions in German Thuringia. He achieves this through the agency of a Germanic spring goddess, and hence love goddess. The shepherd sings in praise of Frau Holda, and it is his song that first introduces Tannhäuser to the German world after the scene changes.[9] Because of the spare, unaccompanied setting this engaging song is not erotic in character. And yet it invokes that female incarnation of the spirit of love— "Freia die holde [noble], Holda die freie [free]," to cite the 1852 libretto— who remains Tannhäuser's escort, making him a knight who serves love and not the servant of *Minne,* the courtly ideal.

The next point is a detail, but it has wide implications (see Pahlen 1981, p. 223). Wolfram represents the mannerly principle of kindly wisdom and, to a still greater degree, of noble renunciation. In act 3 he launches the second scene with the famous song that popular artists turned into a drawing-room ballad: he addresses the "loveliest of stars," praising it as a polestar. When his adored Elisabeth passes from "the earthly vale" to the heights of a "blessed angel," she will be greeted by this "friendly" guiding light: "O thou, my noble star of eve." But the evening star—again we find the adjective *noble*— is Venus, and while Wolfram hardly realizes the fact, Wagner certainly did. For Wagner, Elisabeth belonged in the same constellation as Venus. Here again we can clearly sense that the opera's real governing deity is, if not Venus, then at any rate love. And this is love in all its complexity—not entirely sensual, but not in its purely spiritual form either. As Wagner himself said in his *Tannhäuser* article of 1853, Wolfram is chiefly a poet and artist, whereas Tannhäuser is first and foremost a human being.[10]

There is, moreover, a notable affinity not only between Tannhäuser and Parsifal but also between these two and Tristan. By their actions Tannhäuser and Parsifal accept the impossibility of reconciling the two different worlds of love.[11] Tristan, by contrast, gives himself up completely and utterly to a fusion of the two—at the cost of his earthly life, for such a destiny goes beyond human bounds. It can be sustained only through the death of the body; immortality is achieved through death and beyond it. In a diary entry for 20 July 1880, Cosima recorded this statement by Wagner: "Everything cries! . . . It is the same in the Venusberg as in *Tristan,* in the one it is resolved

9. In the opening scene of *Tristan,* the young sailor's song has a similar function.

10. Hence Wolfram anticipates the relationship between artistic power and renunciation to be demonstrated by the melancholy victory of Hans Sachs.

11. But whereas Tannhäuser is "beaten," one would hesitate to say the same of Parsifal. Yet it remains to elucidate the final promise or requirement: "Redemption to the Redeemer." See the section on *Parsifal* in this chapter.

in grace, in the other in death. Everywhere this cry, this lament." And in an entry for 6 October 1882: "*Tannhäuser, Tristan* and *Parsifal,* he thinks, belong together." This remark was made during the planning of a Bayreuth Festival repertory, but it indicates an internal correspondence among the three works as well. In the same context Wagner let slip that he regarded the drama of *Tannhäuser* as "finished, and yet unfinished, because it seems to him that some of the music is underdeveloped." These and other statements that the composer made in his old age are not entirely explicit.[12] They prove, nonetheless, that he never stopped thinking about this opera, its themes, and its problems.

Tannhäuser is a love tragedy. The music of *Tristan,* composed in 1856–59, is of a piece with the Paris bacchanal of 1861. On 15 March 1881 Cosima noted: "R. tells me that during the rehearsals in Paris Wesendonck said to him, 'What utterly voluptuous sounds these are!' 'I suppose he was afraid I had been dancing something like that in front of his wife,' R. says! And then he calls the passage with the Three Graces 'the bit Wesendonck likes.'" Wagner's detachment is as unconvincing as his belated sarcasm is feeble. Of course the distant friend had heard rightly. Wagner had indeed "been dancing something like that" in front of Wesendonck's wife.

Romantic Opera: *Lohengrin*

The date is 28 August 1850 and the scene is the terrace of the Swan, a restaurant in Lucerne. Among the patrons are a curious couple: a lady in the company of a man who is holding a watch and is lost in rapt concentration. Richard Wagner, accompanied by Minna, is mentally following the first performance of *Lohengrin,* produced and conducted by Liszt. Staged in honor of Goethe's birthday, it is being performed at this very moment in the theater of the ducal court at Weimar.

It was, of course, inevitable that Wagner, with his unerring flair for theatrical effect, would find a restaurant called the Swan to mark the occasion. As for keeping track of the performance, however, he was blissfully unaware of one thing. Despite detailed discussions by mail, the tempi adopted by Liszt were slower than Wagner's. Once again, the composer's imagination was running ahead of him.

One must admit that there is something very touching about this episode. Wagner had never actually heard his opera performed. It was not until thirteen years after the completion of the score that he first had an opportunity to hear (and check) it. This was on 11 May 1861, a few weeks after the *Tannhäuser* scandal in Paris. Wagner—the one German who had not yet heard *Lohengrin,* as he wryly put it—attended a rehearsal in Vienna, where he saw a public

---

12. See the statement "still owes the world *Tannhäuser,*" quoted at the beginning of this section. To supplement my account I would draw attention to my remarks on the production of *Tannhäuser* in Wapnewski 1985.

performance on 15 May. The opera was applauded vociferously, and Wagner himself was deeply moved.

At around the same time, a handsome young Bavarian prince attended a performance of *Lohengrin* in Munich. The experience was to color his whole life and take on a historic significance for Wagner's career.

The Genesis of Lohengrin

With *Lohengrin,* Wagner's sources are more easily established than with his other operas. In July 1845 the Dresden court conductor set off on his summer holidays. His doctor having advised treatment at a spa, he traveled (together with his wife, Minna, Peps the dog, and Papo the parrot) to Marienbad in his beloved Bohemia. But the stay had effects other than those calculated to improve his health. His reading matter profoundly shaped his dramatic plans for the whole of his remaining output. To quote Wagner himself:

> Once again I found myself on the volcanic soil of this singular and, for me, always stimulating country of Bohemia; a marvelous, almost overly hot summer served to heighten my spirits still further. I intended to abandon myself to a life of the utmost leisure, as is in any case essential when undergoing the exhausting regime of a cure. I had therefore chosen my summer reading with care: the poems of Wolfram von Eschenbach in the versions of Simrock and San Marte, together with the anonymous epic of Lohengrin with the great introduction by Görres. With a book under my arm I betook myself to the seclusion of the neighboring woods, where I would lie beside a brook communing with Titurel and Parzifal in this strange and yet so intimately appealing poem of Wolfram. But soon the longing to create something of my own from what I found here became so strong that, although I had been warned against any stimulus of this kind while taking the waters of Marienbad, I had difficulty fighting off the impulse. This soon put me into a highly overwrought state of mind: *Lohengrin,* the first conception of which dates from the latter part of my time in Paris, stood suddenly revealed before me in full armor at the center of a comprehensive dramatic adaptation of the whole material. Among all the many strands in the complex of myths that I was studying at this time, it was the legend of the Knight of the Swan, occupying such a significant position in their midst, which now stimulated my fantasy inordinately. Mindful of the doctors' warnings, I struggled manfully against the temptation to put the plan down on paper and resorted to a most curious and strenuous means to that end.   (ML 302–303)

Wagner's remedy was to turn to *Die Meistersinger.* For this he promptly devised "a comic scene" which he thought a "less exciting subject." He drafted it in defiance of his doctors' orders, not least in the hope of forgetting—or suppressing—the more stimulating *Lohengrin.* "But," he tells us, "I was fooling myself: no sooner had I stepped into my noonday bath than I was seized by such desire to write *Lohengrin* that, incapable of lingering in the bath for the prescribed hour, I leapt out again after only a few minutes, scarcely took the time to clothe myself again properly, and ran like a madman to my quarters to put what was obsessing me on paper. This went on for several days, until the entire dramatic plan for *Lohengrin* had been set down in full detail."

The "first conception" from the latter part of Wagner's time in Paris was inspired by the selfsame philological monograph that had crucially affected the structure of *Tannhäuser*. This was Lucas' 1838 study of the *Krieg von Wartburg,* a poem that also deals with the subject of *Lohengrin*. In addition, Wagner's preparatory reading included the stimulating *Deutsche Sagen* of the Brothers Grimm.

Wagner finished the original draft of his text in November 1845. On 17 December he recited it for the first time in Dresden's so-called Engelklub, a group of artists who met regularly to discuss one another's work. Robert Schumann for one was evidently impressed, although he doubted the feasibility of setting it to music. This was good thinking as far as it went, because Wagner's libretto reflects a development that was already clearly impending in *Tannhäuser*. He was now moving on from the aria-studded numbers style of opera to through-composed music drama—that sung, so to speak, according to the rhythm of naturally declaimed speech.

In May 1846 Wagner started to compose the music—a process that entailed continually making changes in the text (for details, see WWV 75 and Deathridge 1989). He completed a fair copy of the score on 28 April 1848, the year of the revolution. The director of the Dresden Opera, Baron von Lüttichau, authorized the first performance, only to retract his promise shortly afterwards. The climate of opinion at court lashed out against the rebellious propagandist in Wagner—the debating companion of Bakunin and Röckel, the tireless author of programs for political reform, the ardent speech maker. His private response to this setback was equally radical. Understandably disappointed and irked by the petty restrictions placed on his art, he "henceforth spurned the theater altogether and on principle, rejected any attempt" to involve him with it. He was referring, of course, not to the art of theater but to the prevailing administrative situation; Bayreuth would prove the point once and for all.

The setback released energies that he channeled into the original version of the text of *Siegfrieds Tod* (later to be *Götterdämmerung*) and a draft of a social revolutionary drama, *Jesus of Nazareth*. By this time Wagner had put Romantic opera behind him.

On 30 April 1849 revolution spread to Dresden. Wagner's pragmatic activism would not allow him to remain a mere bystander. He therefore joined the struggle against the Prussian troops that the government of Saxony had summoned to its aid. After removing Minna and their pets to the safety of his sister Clara Wolfram's home in Chemnitz, Wagner then fled by a hazardous roundabout route, carrying a false passport, and eventually reached Zurich. At the time anyone overtly opposed to authoritarian monarchy was welcome in liberal Switzerland. Wagner was to remain in Zurich for nearly ten years, until 1858.

Lohengrin *as Tragic Romance*

Lohengrin is strongly animated by themes of the miraculous, magic and dreams, remoteness in time—and also the longing for redemption through love. (Incidentally, and somewhat surprisingly, the opera bears no traces of those political energies unleashed in Wagner during its creation, significant as they were in other respects.) Wagner, as we have seen, had deliberately departed from the conventional structure of the numbers style of opera, with its exquisite bel canto and its blissful duets. Nonetheless, audiences came to regard *Lohengrin* as his most beautiful work; up until the Second World War it was performed more often in Germany than any other Wagner opera. Our present age, in contrast, appears to be drawn more strongly to the post-*Lohengrin* works, which it sees as "authentic" Wagner. Yet time and again, descriptions of the musical impression left by *Lohengrin* have pointed to the personal authenticity of the prelude and its magical use of divided violins (four tutti parts, four solo). Wagner's tentative description of these sounds was "ethereal blue," while Thomas Mann was one day to speak of them as "silvery-blue." Eduard Hanslick, however, remarked scornfully that *Lohengrin* was the favorite opera of sentimental ladies. All the same, it has also been a favorite of discerning Italians, and not simply because it is the only Wagner opera in which an Italian tenor (meaning a certain type of voice) has a chance to shine.

The story blends will and idea, illusion and reality, airy magic and down-to-earth power politics. Such themes are quite legitimate and indeed natural in the operatic genre. Wagner himself prefigured them in *Holländer* and *Tannhäuser* as well as *Die Feen*: supernatural and subterranean powers are called into play in all these operas. Since stage directors are skilled in the art of illusion, creating two contrasting worlds and making the transition between them presents no special aesthetic problems; what does make a director's task difficult in *Lohengrin* is the swan. In myth this proud and handsome creature was ennobled through the story of Leda, if not earlier, and touching legends have earned it a niche in ballet. Later in his career Wagner would turn the swan into a symbol of peace—a peace cruelly shattered by an (as yet) guileless fool. Experts in bird lore praise the swan's monogamous habits and revere it as the epitome of fidelity. It became only too obvious a focus for King Ludwig's vivid imagination to fix on. But it is increasingly difficult for a modern production to show the swan pulling Lohengrin's boat on stage, especially since it was clearly the composer's intention that any theatrical depiction of this scene should match the naiveté of the story.

Owing once again to Wagner's sound instincts, indeed his genius for dramaturgy, he provided this narrative with a taut, contrapuntal structure. His sources were *Parzifal* (ll. 824.1ff.) by Wolfram von Eschenbach and the strophic epic *Lohengrin,* an anonymous work from the end of the thirteenth century. The events are recounted one after another, in the epic manner, and there is a complete absence of suspense (though not of tension). We read the old story of a wrongfully accused princess (the Genoveva theme), her miraculous rescue at the hands of a wonder-working savior, a love that flares up like a *coup de foudre,* a magical condition imposed on Elsa's relationship with Lohengrin (the forbidden question), and the heroine's final victory over her accusers. Yet the ending is a sad one: the condition is broken when Elsa asks the forbidden question, and the lovers are obliged to part. To be sure, once the tale's subject matter became associated with the Grail theme, the magical question found a rationale of its own within that topos. From then on the forbidden question ceased to evoke the Sphinx's riddles or the (pseudo)triumph of Rumpelstiltskin; instead it related to a group of Grail motifs. A *forbidden* question had supplanted an *obligatory* question (whereby a failure to answer meant immediate calamity and prolonged suffering).

Because it was so straightforward, the original tale could never have yielded a Wagner opera. So out of the traditional components Wagner constructed his own dramatic framework. As in *Tannhäuser,* he needed to supply his main characters not only with opponents but also with counterparts. Hence he conceived of the black figure of Ortrud in contrast to the lily-white Elsa and made her his Christian miracle worker's antagonist. Ortrud, the rabid embodiment of an ancient heathen religion, is as potent a magician as the hero. And although Wagner was prepared to put the swan on stage, it would not have been a strong enough figure for his purposes had it been merely a fabulous creature. He therefore took the logical step of giving it a role to play; it became, if not an active character, at any rate an object of intrigue and mystery. The culprits are the accusers themselves; the murderers are the plaintiffs. And the swan is the heir to the throne, a prince bewitched by the heathen enchantress who is slanderously claiming that the prince has been killed by his sister. It is through these devices that the interplay of dramatic forces acquires its tension and its balance.

Redemption

Since Nietzsche it has been repeatedly stated, and rightly so, that Wagner's dramatic tragedies are always concerned with the possibility of, and need for, redemption. Such is the case with *Lohengrin.* But it would be false to assume that Elsa is the relevant character here. This duchess, this shining, vulnerable, and imperiled figure, needs no redeeming but only rescuing. Wagner arranged matters so subtly that the character who is actually in need of redemption is Lohengrin. He needs to be redeemed from his contrived and narrow world of art, from a masculine sphere that is sterile and isolated, from the confines imposed by his statutory role. The key text is found, once again, in *A Communication to My Friends,* where Wagner says of him:

> Lohengrin was in search of a woman who would believe in him . . . , to whom he did not need to explain or justify himself. For this reason he had to conceal

his higher nature, for it was precisely the non-discovery, the non-revelation of this higher—or rather, heightened—nature that was his sole guarantee that he was not being admired and marvelled at purely because of that quality . . . What he desired was not admiration or adoration but the one thing that could release him from his isolation . . . namely love, the sense of being loved, of being understood through love. In his highest aspirations . . . he wanted to become and to remain nothing other than a full and complete human being who would feel warm emotion and inspire it in another—not God, which is to say the absolute artist . . . Doubt and jealousy prove to him that he was not understood but only adored, and tear from him the admission of his divinity, with which, his hopes shattered, he reverts to his isolation.

A great thought, this: the humanization of what is divine. A god is impelled to leave the isolation that his position dictates. He wants to share in the chance of happiness that is available to those he has created; he wants to love and to be loved, to suffer and to experience fear and rapture. Take Zeus, who appears in the human guise of Amphitryon and yet wishes to remain himself. Or the mermaids who, like Melusine, want to leave their own native element and embrace a mortal in order to experience love, but must kill that mortal in the event of betrayal. There is still something of the river Elbe sprite in Isolde, that figure out of Celtic mythology. And Wotan, who tends to be on friendlier terms with human beings than with gods and demons, humanizes himself through an association with a mortal woman, through the procreation of Siegfried by Siegmund and Sieglinde.

"You have the greatest faith to thank me for," sings Lohengrin. But Elsa does not thank him for it; she is unable to respond. Marveling unquestioningly at the miracle of his existence, she nonetheless feels a desire and a need to fathom this man who shares her bridal chamber now that a shadow of doubt has been cast on him. Elsa is unaware that Lohengrin is seeking redemption through her, the woman he has rescued. He seeks to be redeemed not in love, which of itself is a law of nature, a mere urge, but in understanding, that is, through a profoundly human, cultured quality. But that is denied him; and the denial is what shatters him by forcing him back into a distant and lonely divinity.

As always with Wagner, this situation probably involves an element of autobiography. We are presented with a *deus artifex,* a divine creator who is also an artist. And we see the artist as a god in his creative activities; but he does not wish to be loved for his creativity. What he wants is to be understood for his humanity: therein lies his chance of happiness. That may explain Wagner's phrase "God, which is to say the absolute artist." Man, the "relative" artist, is a "relative" god.

The silvery blue *Lohengrin,* on the face of it the most delightful and endearing of Wagner's works, is really his darkest tragedy. Everywhere else the great rift, the insuperable paradox which is part of one's existence, is radiantly bridged by the musical promise of a reconciliation in the hereafter. It happens in *Holländer* and *Tannhäuser,* in *Tristan,* and even amid the global conflagration of *Götterdämmerung*—to say nothing of the finales of *Die Meistersinger* and *Parsifal,* which express a blissful release. *Lohengrin,* by contrast, admits of no further hope. Contrary to the medieval sources, Elsa is punished with death for her narrowness, her foolish naiveté, her incomprehension. Lohengrin, unredeemed, returns to his gilded cage, the near-divine realm of the Holy Grail. This dread-inspiring, unresolved finale conceals what was soon to emerge at Nietzsche's instigation: Western nihilism.

This component of *Lohengrin* is anti-Romantic and modern. In a contemporary production it would need developing, overriding such features as the conspirators' oath, the charms of the bridal chamber, and the pseudonational tones of Heinrich der Vogler with his militant pathos. Such pathos has now become hard to accept (although it makes sense in the context of a prerevolutionary feeling of solidarity). Nowadays, the elevated figure of divine light that Lohengrin presents is no longer credible; from the very outset the hero was all too angelic and otherworldly to be an example and model at all, and there is nothing genuinely German about him either. That rapt and fanciful dreamer King Ludwig of Bavaria had to come forward to offer the Knight of the Swan a temporary refuge in a world that understands neither kings nor swans.

Stage Festival Play: *Der Ring des Nibelungen*

Wagner completed the score of *Lohengrin* on 28 April 1848. That was the year of volcanic upheaval inside Germany; and, as always, the easily excitable Wagner, constantly in a state of extreme unrest, busied himself with projects. The director of the Dresden Opera had approved the first performance of *Lohengrin* but then postponed it because Wagner had displeased the Saxon court with his conspicuous political activity. Very understandably he responded with ambitious plans for the reorganization of the authoritarian but sluggish management of German theaters. He made speeches about "the republic and kingship," and engaged in eloquent debate with his musical and political intimate August Röckel, as well as with Liszt and Bakunin. With his proposed theater reforms still in mind, he traveled to Vienna, where he began working on the draft of a drama about Barbarossa. Amid all the turmoil and chaos he hit on the subject of a lifetime, the work he was born to create. From now on—although there would be major interruptions—it was to occupy, burden, torment, and inspire Wagner persistently. The subject was the saga of the Nibelungs.

It began with a curious mix-up. In the course of his Barbarossa studies Wagner thought he had detected a line leading back from the Stauffers (that is, the Ghibellines) to the Nibelungs. The latter, however, would have had to be spelled with an initial *W,* since the Italian language replaced the German *W* with *Gh* (*Ghibelline* for *Waibling*). If the Ghibelline dynasty of the Stauffers was in fact genealogically linked to the Nibelungs, Wagner thought, the

Nibelungs must formerly have been called Wibelungs (and thus similarly linked to the Welfs, or Guelphs). Late in the summer of 1848 these early studies yielded an essay called *The Wibelungs: World History from the Saga.*[13] In October this led to the sketch *The Nibelung Legend (Myth),* which was subsequently printed under the title *The Nibelung Myth, as Sketch for a Drama.* The same month Wagner duly turned it into the prose version of a Siegfried drama entitled *Siegfrieds Tod.* A verse adaptation followed in November, and in December Wagner gave it the usual recital in the presence of some friends.

Revolution, however, was boiling up everywhere. It was on Wagner's mind as well as on that of the imaginary Siegfried. In 1849, the year of the Dresden riots, he drafted (along with his Nibelung plans) a drama called *Jesus of Nazareth.* Here Christ, the Son of God, is depicted as a social revolutionary who proclaims the political message of love.

The uprising in Dresden broke out on 30 April (see Chapter 4). Wagner supported it to the hilt and may have been personally involved in the fighting before escaping to his friend Liszt in Weimar. Liszt supplied him with money and a false passport, and Wagner crossed Lake Constance, arriving in Zurich on 28 May. Ahead of him lay nine years of exile broken by frequent travels. At no time, of course, could he venture onto German soil, where there were warrants out for his arrest.

Between December 1849 and March 1850 Wagner wrote a sketch for another drama. Once again the subject was drawn from German antiquity. *Wieland der Schmied* appealed to Wagner because it contained what were already classic Wagnerian themes: enchantment, redemption, fire, and of course the wings that carry the crippled hero to freedom. During this period Wagner also felt an ever more pressing need to define and justify his artistic activity in theoretical writings. They poured forth from him in a rushing and constantly widening stream. Abruptly dislodged from what had been the center of his existence, he now justified himself and his work in the first of his great speculative treatises, *Opera and Drama* (1851).

Siegfrieds Tod, however, had to be elaborated. As early as October 1848 Eduard Devrient, an experienced man of the theater, was already warning Wagner that the story included rather too much background material; this exposition needed to be acted out, not just referred to. Wagner reacted promptly and sensitively. Prior to the original entry into the hall of the Gibichungs, he introduced the fond leave-taking of Siegfried and Brünnhilde.

---

13. The chronology of *The Wibelungs* and the first drafts of *Siegfrieds Tod* is more complex than has hitherto been realized. The first surviving draft for *The Wibelungs* was written in late December 1848 or early in 1849 (see WWV, p. 329). Wagner recited it to friends on 22 February 1849, when, according to Eduard Devrient's diaries, he expressed an interest in turning it into a drama. Wagner may well have written a first draft in the summer of 1848; but the existing document and Devrient's diaries prove that he was still interested in Barbarossa and the Wibelungs after he had written *Siegfrieds Tod,* contrary to the impression given in his collected writings and in his autobiography. The first layer of the document uses the name *Gibelinen.* The name *Wibelungen* was introduced at a later stage (see WWV, p. 404). [Ed.]

This private yet heroic idyll found a place in the overall scheme with the aid of another scene that preceded it: that of the Norns, with their "solemn cosmic tittle-tattle" (Thomas Mann). But even this addition, it now appeared, was not sufficient. Siegfried's death presupposes his life. In May and June 1851 Wagner drafted *Der junge Siegfried,* and in consequence was drawn forcibly into the undertow of his myth-building exercise. He was obliged to go farther and farther backwards. First the prose draft and then the verse libretto of *Die Walküre* (June–July 1852) and *Das Rheingold* (autumn 1852) were produced in rapid succession. Finally, and again from inner necessity, Wagner made extensive revisions to the libretti for *Der junge Siegfried* and *Siegfrieds Tod,* whose content had to be squared with the story now leading up to them. (Parts of *Der junge Siegfried* were to be recast once again in 1856). By 15 December 1852 the libretto of the whole *Ring* cycle was basically finished. In the new year its author published it in a limited edition of fifty copies, and on four evenings in February 1853 he recited it to an interested gathering of friends in the Baur au Lac hotel in Zurich. He began to set the huge libretto to music that same year.

The poet-composer himself commented on his conception of the *Ring* on innumerable occasions. Let us consider two such statements that will help to define it more precisely. On 12 November 1851, while taking the waters in Albisbrunn, Wagner wrote a letter to his faithful Dresden friend Theodor Uhlig, the violinist and writer on music. In it he set out the necessity of expanding the twofold drama of Siegfried into a tetralogy. He went on to say (in what almost sounds like an anticipation, more than a century in advance, of the iconoclastic Pierre Boulez):

> With this new conception of mine, I am departing *completely* from anything related to our present-day theatres and audiences: I am making a clean break with present forms of theatre . . . The only *performance* I can contemplate will be *after the revolution:* only the revolution can provide the appropriate artists and listeners. The next revolution must of necessity put an end to the whole *way we run our theatres:* it must and will knock them all down, inevitably so. I shall gather up what I need from the ruins: I shall *then* obtain what is required. Then I shall set up a theatre on the Rhine and launch a great festival of drama: following a year of preparation I shall perform my whole work over a period of *four days:* and *with* this work, I shall enable the people who have experienced the revolution to perceive its *meaning,* in the noblest sense. *This audience* will understand me; the present ones cannot.

Wagner reckoned that the execution of the *Ring* would take him at least another "*three whole years.*" In fact it was to take up more than a quarter of a century. But the intensity of the vision remained constant throughout. It foresaw a drama of mankind in which the hero would realize the highest possibilities in life, free of all compulsion and constraints, free of the curse of inheritance and the curse of capital. A life dominated by debt-laden gods and base demons would give way to one lived in the purest state of humanity, that is to say, in freedom. Siegfried, the hero of the drama, would incorporate

Rienzi and Barbarossa and Christ the social revolutionary—and also, of course, Richard Wagner. Yet Siegfried's downfall was already certain, despite all the straining for success. The story would end with his death, which was immanent from the beginning, as the ancient Nordic and medieval sources acknowledge; there is no alternative. The great undertaking was designed as a tragedy from the outset. But we must bear in mind that tragedy as a dramatic genre inculcates not absolute hopelessness but the relative possibility of hope.

While designing and animating his great world theater, however, Wagner was always determining his own position in it as well. The revolution formed part of his artistic creation, just as it formed part of the revolution. We come now to the second personal statement on the *Ring*. In his autobiography Wagner looks back to a Dresden on the verge of violent upheaval and writes:

> During my walks, which I now took utterly alone, I relieved my spirits by working out in my head, in ever more elaborate detail, my conception of a state of human society, for which the boldest wishes and goals of the socialists and communists, then so actively constructing their systems, offered me a mere foundation. Their efforts would assume significance and value for me only when they had completed their political upheavals and reforms, for it was only at that point that I could begin to realize my new ideal of art.   (ML 376)

This reveals the nucleus of Wagner's conception of the *Ring*. If one substitutes a more sober tone, what Wagner is actually saying in the passage is this: During my solitary walks I visualized human society as it would be as a result of the enthusiastic efforts of the socialists and communists, and how it could then afford the precondition and platform whereby my artistic revolution might be carried out (Wapnewski 1978b, pp. 120ff.). At this stage Wagner had not yet heard of the works of Schopenhauer. Not until 1854, when he was engaged in composing the music of *Die Walküre,* did Herwegh acquaint him with that book which was to endorse and influence his ideas at the deepest level (ML 508–510).

The Composition and Its Sources

In 1853 Wagner traveled to Italy and, on 5 September, found himself in La Spezia. Racked with fever, insomnia, and the aftereffects of seasickness, he took an afternoon nap, and it was then that he had his initial musical vision of the *Ring*. His autobiography gives a graphic account (ML 499). As he was dozing, the basic germ cell of the *Rheingold* prelude—its E-flat major chord, the "cradle song of the world"—came to him, murmurs of nature and water music in figured triads stretching over 136 bars, and thus emerging as a structural law of cosmic harmony based on the oceanic primary note E flat.

Wagner was fond of telling such tales about his inspiration; probably he sincerely believed them.[14] In this instance it would be a long time—by his standards—before the vision was translated into actual notes. But the account

---

14. For more detailed critical appraisals of Wagner's La Spezia vision, see WWV 408–409, Deathridge-Dahlhaus 1984, pp. 39–40, and Darcy 1989. [Ed.]

in his autobiography does offer us a starting date. Wagner completed the music of *Das Rheingold* in September 1854. Henceforth the composition of the *Ring* proceeded in the correct order. The music of *Die Walküre* was written between June 1854 and March 1856, and in the summer of 1856 Wagner set to work on the music for *Siegfried*.

At that point, however, another claim presented itself with imperious insistence. Once again it confirms the indissoluble link, in Wagner's career, between the life and the creative power, between personal and artistic experience. It was now that he met Mathilde Wesendonck and became infatuated with her; he also became enthralled by Schopenhauer's philosophy, with its disdain for the real world and impulse to transcend it. In short, *Tristan* was beginning to register its claims. And of course *Tristan* would be—had to be—followed by *Die Meistersinger*. After the ecstasy that transcends life came the radiant work of renunciation to subdue that ecstasy, calmly and lightly touching it with its own vein of melancholy. In *Die Meistersinger* the heightening and justification of life itself through art became the central idea.

On 28 June 1857 Wagner wrote to Liszt the oft-quoted words: "I have finally decided to give up my obstinate attempt to complete my *Nibelungen*. I have got as far as leading my young Siegfried into the forest's lovely solitude, where I left him under a linden tree and bade him farewell with tears of heartfelt sorrow: he is better off there than anywhere else. —Should I ever resume the work, either it would have to be made very easy for me to do so, or I myself would need in the meantime to have put myself in a position to make the world a *present* of it, in the fullest meaning of the word." For the time being, however, Wagner had something else in mind. He was planning to give the world "an eminently practicable opus," absurd as it was of him to think of *Tristan,* of all operas, in those terms, and to cherish the illusion that it might "quickly provide me with a good income and keep me afloat for a while." His letter then returned to the subject of the *Nibelungen*. "This time," Wagner wrote, "I have been severe on myself; just when it was all going so well, I tore Siegfried out of my heart and put him under lock and key, as though I were burying him alive. There I intend him to stay, and nobody is to get a glimpse of him, since I must banish him from my own mind. Well, maybe the sleep will do him good." (Wagner did in fact go on to finish composing the second act of *Siegfried* before starting in earnest on the music of *Tristan*.)

In any event, it was not made "very easy" for Wagner to resume the work. But there is no denying that the sleep did do Siegfried some good, inasmuch as the third act is clear evidence that its composer had in the meantime passed the tests of *Tristan* and *Die Meistersinger* with flying colors. The interruption lasted a total of twelve years, but by 1869 Wagner had found a patron for his work. On 23–24 February he wrote to King Ludwig of the "dark, sublime and awesome sensations with which I enter the realm of my third act." "An interruption to a work lasting *twelve* years is surely unprecedented in the history of the arts" was Wagner's own comment on the situation, and in principle he was right. It is nothing short of a miracle that, against all odds, the abandoned threads were tied together again and the extensive network of mighty parts was joined up and combined in a prodigious whole. (There was one break in the period: between December 1864 and December 1865 Wagner orchestrated his sketch of the music for the second act of *Siegfried*.) The score of the third act of *Siegfried* was completed in February 1871. By then Wagner had already started work on the music of *Götterdämmerung* as well. At the bottom of the final page of the entire *Ring* score he wrote: "Completed in Wahnfried on 21 November 1874. I shall say no more!! R.W."

Wagner designed his "everlasting work" for a particular place and a particular time. Beyond any lofty display of an artist's individual will, this concept was well founded from a dramaturgic, aesthetic, and sociological standpoint (and it has held good right up to the present). Hence the impatient royal patron—who was not qualified to make artistic pronouncements—was committing no minor error when he commanded the premiere of *Das Rheingold* to be given in Munich on 22 September 1869, and that of *Die Walküre* to follow on 26 June 1870. Wagner never forgave the dreamy royal dilettante for issuing such orders, and his resentment is understandable.

The premiere of the whole *Ring* cycle inaugurated the first Bayreuth Festival. Hopes were high, and an enormous amount of effort went into the project. But the artistic success was moderate and the financial outcome disastrous.

The *Ring* is a great parable of life, which Wagner presents as innocent by nature and as encumbered with guilt by its history. It comprehends its own finite character, and yet it is not prepared to give up hoping against hope for the infinite. Wagner gives us a utopian history of the universe which takes the form of a vast drama about the world's beginning and end. Two precepts motivate this drama. One holds that all of life is essentially linked with guilt and the other that all of life wants to be redeemed from its guilt.

From what basic elements did Wagner assemble the material of this cosmic social utopia? If one proceeds to list them, one immediately realizes how little they matter, because Wagner regarded them as no more than a pretext for a new mythology. In other words, it is not Odin-Wotan who matters; what does matter is the supreme skepticism of Arthur Schopenhauer that issues from his mouth (irrespective of whether Wagner was consciously borrowing Schopenhauer's ideas). It is not Brünnhilde who matters but the spirit of Ludwig Feuerbach as it blazes up on her funeral pyre (Wagner wrote several different versions of this ending). Sigurd-Siegfried is far less important than Mikhail Bakunin's rhetorical visions of a hard-won freedom, as realized through the act of revolt. Alberich and the giants matter less than the curse of capital which they represent and which destroys them, a curse that Wagner had come to understand through "the socialist theories of Proudhon and others" (ML 373). And the *Ring* owes its underlying tragic mood as much to a passionate and continual study of Greek and Shakespearean drama as to the somber heaven of the Germanic gods.

Nonetheless, Wagner himself has left us an interesting record of the sources of which he made substantial use. On 9 January 1856 he listed the following titles for Franz Müller, a Weimar privy councillor who was preparing a book on the poem of the *Ring* (published in 1862):

1. *Der Nibelungen Noth und Klage,* edited by Lachmann. 2. *Zu den Nibelungen etc.* by Lachmann. 3. Grimm's *Mythologie.* 4. *Edda.* 5. *Volsunga-Saga* (translated by Hagen-Breslau). 6. *Wilkina and Niflungasaga* (ditto). 7. *Das deutsche Heldenbuch—* old edition, reissued by Hagen. —Adapted by Simrock, six volumes. 8. *Die deutsche Heldensage,* by Wilhelm Grimm. 9. *Untersuchungen zur deutschen Heldensage* by Mone (very important). 10. *Heimskringla*—translated by Mohnike (I think!) (not the Wachter translation—bad). (See Wapnewski 1978b, pp. 24ff.; Spencer 1985)

As detailed monographs have shown, Wagner knew and made use of a great many additional sources.[15] He did so with a view to mastering for himself that subject which the Romantics had seized on so ardently, whether as scholars or as poets. The crucial point is that Wagner's role was not primarily an interpretive one. He had no desire either to carry on and preserve an old tradition or to revive and renew it. Wagner was using traditional forms and themes in order to establish new ones of his own. "The myth is not so much restored by Wagner as destroyed, or, rather, it is restored in order to be destroyed" (Dahlhaus 1979, p. 114).

"The *Nibelungenlied* still makes a powerful impression on us (particularly the second part). Whoever wrote it was greater than Wolfram," Cosima remarked on 2 July 1873. Here her diary records Richard's thoughts during the final stage of the composition of *Götterdämmerung*. But despite his admiration for the Middle High German epic, Wagner had a more ambitious concept in mind. The epic was produced (in its final version) anonymously around the year 1200, in the region of the Danube. It gave a contemporary quality to legendary material which it regarded as historical, and the purpose of this was to confront the age with its own story, the human experience of inhumanity. The era was to be presented with a monumental likeness of itself and its destructive potential. The epic was based on a magnificent but limited concept, one that was conservative in its desire to preserve established values. Wagner wanted to do more than that. He did not wish to save an old world but to found a new one, the world of the free man who revokes the obsolescent power of the old gods. This man is divorced from any historical past, that is, from the fetters of all debts and obligations incurred throughout history. His sole obligation is to himself and his own law. The *Nibelungenlied* no longer recognized any gods (at the most it shows an unconscious inkling of them in fragments from ancient times); it acknowledged the God of Christianity. Wagner, by contrast, did not recognize the Christian God (nor did he wish to). Rather, he was familiar with the ancient gods as projections of

15. The difficulties of establishing a reliable bibliography for the sources of the *Ring,* and precisely what Wagner gleaned from those sources, are discussed in detail in Magee 1990. [Ed.]

everything that had brought misery and impending doom to the world and its inhabitants. Human inadequacy formed part of the splendor of those gods, and in them it was blown up to majestic proportions. Dictators responsible for the workings of fate, they "are called gods without being gods" (Ernst Bloch).

Thus Wagner could borrow only some individual though significant features of the *Nibelungenlied* for his cosmic drama. These he exploited in all their fascinating detail.[16] But he went farther back in his delvings; and in any event the traditional Old Norse versions of the subject were bound to strike him as earlier deposits, archaic and original to a greater degree. I refer to the heroic lays of the *Edda* and the *Volsunga Saga*. Granted these texts were written down roughly one generation later than the Middle High German *Nibelungenlied,* and they included some thoroughly modern ingredients. But Wagner was not mistaken in perceiving some extremely ancient and original features in their outlook, style, and material. Above all, he discovered in them those gods whose challenged and damaged status was the reflection of a challenged and damaged world.

Here Wagner at last came across the language that he felt to be the only suitable form of expression for his dramatic purposes: *Stabreim* poetry. Much mockery has been made of it over the years; Wagner's parodists have thought the stringing together of words beginning with the same consonant a tremendous joke. But this attitude shows a lack of historical understanding. *Stabreim* is a genuine connecting device in a language (that is, the Germanic language group) based on stressing the first syllable. Thus in principle every word has an initial accent. The inevitable result of this emphasis and verbal melody is a connection between the respective word beginnings as the stressed particles, in terms of both sound and sense, rather than between the unaccentuated, weak-sounding final syllables. This is what Nietzsche meant by his lordly aphorism that *Stabreim* was "language raised to the strongest degree of expression." The German language still bears the imprint of this rhyming technique in colloquial phrases such as "Mann und Maus" ("mice and men"; or compare the English "part and parcel," "signed and sealed"). But what, because of its familiarity, we can accept as natural in common usage will always be an annoyance in the language of artistic expression. The fact remains that this technique enabled Wagner to give his subject matter the only diction that was suited to it; moreover, he adapted and exploited it as part of his musical syntax. Wagner was moving away from the traditional language of opera, with its clearly distinguishable, self-contained set pieces and numbers, its arias and ensembles. And just as *Stabriem* seems closer to prose than ordinary end rhyme does, so Wagner's music was approaching a new syntax of his own devising. Like prose, this syntax was constantly advancing in "unending melody," prompted and guided by the "art of transition."

16. On this and my next remarks, see Wapnewski 1978b, pp. 123ff.

Prologue: Das Rheingold

Once upon a time the whole of creation was innocent, the image of perfection, born of the primal element of water. Caught by the sun's fire, the golden treasure of the Rhine shone with a brilliance that was pure and value free (that is, it was not debased as a medium of exchange, mere capital). All this is expressed in the music of *Das Rheingold* as it rises, murmuring, out of the primordial depths to the bright beacons of light from above.

But then evil enters this world. A lustful dwarf, a black goblin, Alberich, attempts to seize hold of the bobbing and bantering Rhine Maidens, daughters of the great river. The maidens are quite willing to play tag with him, provided he does not capture them. So he seizes the Rhine Gold instead and reduces it to a commodity. The latent power of the precious metal can be released only through the enforced renunciation of the power of love. Having uttered a curse on love, Alberich is able to snatch the gold for himself. This represents the Fall of Man. The complementary relationship between worldly power and the power of love, between the renunciation of love and the accumulation of power, will shape the tetralogy to its very finish.

Wotan, the creator-god, seeks to purge a nature that has now been damaged and jeopardized. He intends at least to forestall its ruin, and hence his own—the ruin of the world of the gods. Not even his own past and prehistory, however, are untouched by ugly and violent events; evil has cast its shadow here. In order to achieve wisdom, Wotan has had to sacrifice an eye, and the World Ash Tree from which he once broke off a bough is now withering and wasting away. It was from this bough that the god carved his emblem of power, his spear. These myths are deeply symbolic. The first takes up the theme of an exchange, of compensation. He who wants wisdom must suffer for it; he who desires inner vision must forfeit an eye as a sacrifice. And he who wants to exercise universal dominion must mutilate nature by his actions. Any human encroachment in the interests of civilization—and hence the exercise of power—is an attack on the natural order of creation.

"Wotan made / holy laws and treaties; / then Wotan / cut their words in the spear: / he held it to rule all the world," comments the Second Norn in the prelude to *Götterdämmerung*. Wotan is even harsher on himself when addressing Brünnhilde in *Die Walküre*. Impelled by both love and the lust for power, "and driven / by impetuous desires, / I won myself the world; / yet all unwitting, / I acted wrongly; / trusted in treaties / where evil lay" (*Die Walküre,* act 2, scene 2). Thus Wotan has achieved knowledge and wisdom. He has endeavored to reconcile the two elementary, mutually opposed forces: the will to love and the will to power. He has tried not to give up the one for the sake of the other. He has sacrificed something, and the opposing energies of an imperiled world of nature have been forcibly contained within an orderly system. This has been done through the binding power of contracts, and his sacred spear is the guarantor of their continuous validity. Even

Wotan himself is bound by the contracts: "Since by my treaties I rule, / by those treaties I am enslaved" (*Die Walküre,* act 2, scene 2).

The evil Alberich uses the Rhine Gold to produce a ring, whose magic the Rhine Maiden Wellgunde reveals to him. "The world's wealth can / be won by a man who, / seizing the Rhinegold, / fashions a ring: / that ring makes him lord of the world." To counter the threat of this ever-increasing power Wotan, looking to his own defense, builds a castle for protection. Here, to prevent "the shameful defeat of the immortals," the wild Valkyries, his daughters, will commandeer glorious warriors "till valiant hosts of heroes / are gathered in Walhall's hall." (These lines are again addressed to Brünnhilde in *Die Walküre,* act 2, scene 2. Brünnhilde, of course, is supposed to have been long aware of all this. But in the first place Wotan is reviewing events for his own benefit, and second he is speaking to listeners not yet familiar with the story.) These warriors are to form a praetorian guard, armed for the final battle. Posted at Wotan's fortress, they will join forces with the noble gods to resist and stave off the end.

Inevitably, however, building the castle has sunk its architect in debt. Wotan has overreached himself and is unable to pay his laborers, the giants Fafner and Fasolt. Trusting too much in the ingenuity of a dubious adviser ("craftily counselled by Loge"), Wotan has already been frivolous enough to mortgage the goddess Freia, his sister-in-law, who represents eternal youth. This leads to a fresh source of guilt. Hard-pressed by his lumbering creditors who want to take possession of their prize, Wotan resorts to the one expedient that is barred to him, since he has declared that contracts are binding. He proceeds to turn the tables on the thieving Alberich. Together with Loge, his oily accomplice, he descends into Nibelheim, the netherworld where the nouveau riche dwarf is churning out money. Alberich is seduced into making a boastful show of his wealth; drunk with power, he pays for his misstep (again the process is a complementary one) with a temporary loss of reason and intelligence, allowing the gods to trick the black elf. The nearly omnipotent Alberich, who is capable of turning himself into any shape he pleases, appears first as a giant serpent and then as a little toad. But his second transformation is an error. The intruders can now easily seize him and tie him up before dragging him aloft.

Once more a fateful bargain is struck: Freia for the Nibelung gold, Alberich's magic helmet (Tarnhelm), and finally his magic ring. (Here Wagner, the master magician, allows his plot to defy common sense, for how is it possible for the two brutal, scheming gods to seize Alberich and spirit him away when he possesses the ring that confers all worldly power? We must be content with the thought that myths are immune from ordinary logic.) Alberich lays a deadly curse on the treasure that has been snatched from his grasp.

How does Wotan justify his appropriation of the ring? After all, its possession does not seem any more lawful because it was stolen from an illegitimate owner—on the principle, perhaps, that universal power must not be allowed to remain in evil hands. What is evil? What is good? Parsifal, too, will be faced with these questions.

The ring does not stay in "good" hands—that is, Wotan's—much as he clings to the treasure and denies it to the giants, who have claimed it against Wotan's debt. The last word goes to the ancestral mother Erda, the goddess Wala. When Wotan demurs, she warns him of the end of the gods and implores him to avoid the ring's curse. In the face of her omniscience, Wotan gives in: "You giants, there is your ring!"

This triggers the series of events inspired by the terrible curse that the swindler Alberich, himself defrauded, has laid on his artifact. The dwarf exchanges one curse for another. With the first he had gained the gold and forfeited love. Now he has forfeited the ring, which has been extorted from him by brute force, but he endows it now with the power of death: "Let it now bring / but death, death to its lord! / Its wealth shall yield / pleasure to none; / let no fortunate owner / enjoy its gleam! / Care shall consume / the man who commands it, / and mortal envy / consume those who don't!"

The curse takes effect immediately, for rather than share the gold, the giant Fafner (Cain) murders his more ingenuous brother Fasolt (Abel) for it. "Fearful power / lies hid in that fatal curse!" exclaims Wotan, whereupon Loge cynically comments: "Your luck, Wotan, / what could surpass it? / . . . For your enemies, see, / murder each other / for the gold that you let go." Fafner now literally sits on his treasure. Under the cloak of invisibility he has turned himself into that most vigilant of creatures, a dragon, avariciously brooding over his unproductive capital. In a sense he freezes his assets and becomes a slave to them, forgoing any production of surplus value. This extremely noncapitalistic attitude on the part of the stupid and unimaginative guardian of the hoard is in stark contrast to the artfulness of Alberich, the shrewd capitalist, who had added to his wealth by producing goods with the aid of (truly alienated) labor.

The gods now create for themselves the illusion of a perfect, reunited world. Donner clears the stifling atmosphere with a purifying clap of thunder, while Froh makes a rainbow bridge into the castle. But this shimmering vision is countered by the somber orchestral music, which contains themes of warning and reminiscence. There is a long-range significance in the fact that at this very point, despite the castle's deceptive splendor, the Sword motif resounds for the first time, and "with great energy," in the brass. What is it telling us? Wotan sees the castle as a stronghold: "The night is near: / from its envy / we have our refuge now." As if to bolster his courage the motif blares out, according to the stage direction, "very resolutely, as though seized by a grand thought." The father of the gods can now safely utter his salutation: "So greet I the hall, / safe from all fear and dread—."

What has given Wotan courage? What grand thought has emboldened him? He knows that the events in which he is culpably involved have upset the balance of universal government. He must try to put matters right, but this can be achieved only if power does not rest in evil hands. The grand thought, then, is the idea of the sword that will one day be wielded by the "free man," an individual not beholden to mortgages and contracts. This man will be able, indeed fated, to break the calamitous chain of trickery and rapine, lies and murder. As for the ring, what will he do with it? There may be some comfort in the thought that when the gold has been returned to its source, the cycle will be complete. The old innocence, now raised to a new and conscious level, will be reinstated, and the world will be granted a fresh start.

But can that be accomplished with the sword? Wotan thinks so. The relevant passage seems to have meant so much to Wagner that in his capacity as stage director he was loath to leave its elucidation entirely to the "allusive magic" (Thomas Mann) of the leitmotif. According to Felix Mottl, Wagner's rehearsal pianist in 1876, the inaugural year of the Bayreuth Festival, Wagner had Wotan pick up a sword at this point. Since it was just one item in Alberich's hoard, Fafner has ignored it. But now Wotan raises it in the direction of the castle to salute and to symbolize his grand thought.[17]

The gods are on dangerous ground, but they fail to recognize the fact, dazzled as they are by their own splendor, their foolish arrogance, and their delight in illusions. They are participating in a glorious, richly costumed dance of death. Looking to his own safety, Loge remains behind as the others proceed toward the castle. He perceives the gods' blindness and contemplates finishing them off in his role of Fire: "I must consider: / who knows what I'll do?"

The lament of the wronged Rhine Maidens mingles with the pomp and majesty of the procession into the castle. Angrily Wotan dismisses their pleas, as though he were unaware of his impotence and were refusing them by choice: "Stop their tiresome lament!" he commands his steward. Loge obeys him, but in his own way, cynically advising the maidens to "let the gods' new golden splendour / shine upon you instead!"

The events of this prologue conclude with a fatal judgment delivered by the Rhine Maidens: there can be no other ending to the story but the end of the gods. "Goodness and truth / dwell but in the waters: / false and base / all those who dwell up above!"

First Day: Die Walküre

"On this unknown hearth, / here I must shelter." The first words of *Die Walküre* are sung by an unaccompanied human voice, quite alone and seemingly deserted by men and gods. A fearful storm has forced the singer to take shelter. In a state of nervous suspense, and in the violent grip of the Thunder motif, the orchestral prelude depicts the flight of the outcast, the lone wolf. Then silence reigns, and the music adopts a new tempo. It signals a paradise regained, but also a paradise lost.

Siegmund, who does not know who he is, has been blown off course to

17. This idea is discussed at greater length in Wapnewski 1978b, pp. 271–273.

this place, and to Sieglinde, who does not know who she is either. The wounded, defenseless man is protected by the laws of hospitality. Yet we can tell from the words and, still more, the music that he is not in for a pleasant encounter with the master of the house, the Germanic tribal chieftain Hunding. The name comes from the Old Norse, and it is an indication of Hunding's houndlike character, which will be too strong even for the *Sieg* or victorious element in the names of the other two characters. At the outset, to be sure, the stranger is still nameless; he lacks a discernible identity. Quickly revived by warmth and refreshment, he gives his name: Wehwalt—"woe lord."

Hunding's return home is signaled by his orchestral motif, an ominous-sounding staccato call. The two men size each other up at once: they sense that they are inveterate enemies. Then the visitor introduces himself. He gives an account of his youth and tells the story of a father and son, Wolfe and Wölfing. He recalls their hunting expeditions together, the slaying of the mother "by ruffians who sought revenge," a twin sister's disappearance, and the fugitive life of the outlawed father and son. Eventually the father too disappears. A wolf skin is the sole relic left by this werewolf. Consumed by unhappiness, the son knows neither peace nor a home. This tale only reinforces Hunding's distrust of the baneful visitor, who claims to bring calamity wherever he goes: "So the Norn who dealt you this fate, / she felt no love for you: / No-one greets you with joy / when you arrive as guest."

At this point Wagner brings the story up to the present by incorporating a lengthy ballad recounting a bloody and dramatic story. This ballad, although essentially irrelevant to the logic and progress of the action, is intended to establish right from the start the antagonism between Siegmund and Hunding. This lone wolf has been summoned to the aid of a bride about to be married off by her brothers against her will. He fights and kills the brothers with ferocity before finally being driven off by their kinsmen, and also by a peculiar change of heart in the "ill-fated bride." It is here that the paths of Siegmund and Hunding first crossed, so to speak, as Hunding says he was himself involved in that bloody dispute, called by his kinsmen to their aid, only to arrive too late and to discover that they had been slain by a stranger. "I heard a summons to vengeance: / . . . Too late came I, / but now that I'm home, / I find that stranger here." For the night "Wölfing" will be his guest, but they are obliged to do battle the next day. They are already foes before the stranger has proceeded to abuse Hunding's hospitality.

The story of the love affair between the stranger and Sieglinde is an analytical drama revealing the true origins of the pair. What precipitates events is the sword. The father had spoken of the weapon to his son long ago. During the celebration of Hunding's and Sieglinde's unhappy wedding, it was plunged into the trunk of an ash tree by a stranger, "an old man dressed all in grey; / his hat hung so low / that one of his eyes was hidden." Here the music proclaims what the central characters do not as yet know. Underlying Sieglinde's narrative is the Valhalla motif, indicating Wotan's unseen presence as author, conductor, and producer of the fateful drama.

The world now changes in a flash, and a new era begins. As the buds of

May succeed winter's storms, the two lovers are increasingly, compulsively drawn to each other. "The bride and sister / is freed by her brother." This is a metaphor for love and spring, but it also refers to Siegmund and Sieglinde. Hazy memories and shadowy presentiments take on sharper outlines. Sieglinde's shimmering image, as she saw it reflected in a stream, merges with the image of the stranger, who is no longer unfamiliar to her. The voice she hears is the echo of a sound that rang out long ago. Now comes the revelation of the true name of Siegmund's father, Wälse (the name under which the multifaceted god played this divine role). Wälse has thus brought two people face to face with their destiny. Now Sieglinde speaks her guest's own, original name, hence giving him an identity and character. But while the first part of his response—"Siegmund is my name"—is correct, he is dreadfully mistaken in adding, "Siegmund am I!" (literally "victory's guardian"). He is not fated to be a victor, even though he unsheathes the sword from the ash tree's trunk, violently and yet effortlessly. This sword he proffers as a "bridal gift," a fateful love token. The lovers recognize each other as brother and sister, and brother and sister succumb to each other as lovers: "Bride and sister," sings Siegmund, "be to your brother; / the blood of these Wälsungs is blessed!" As the curtain falls, the music evokes the pounding of the blood in their veins, coursing in passionate fervor.

Wotan's plans have gone awry, at least for the time being; the god has miscalculated. The task he has set himself arises from the political situation: he must have that ring. At the very least he must prevent the powers of evil, embodied by Alberich, from getting it back. Both these adversaries—the forces of light and the forces of darkness—are unable to accomplish anything by their own efforts. Alberich's power has been curbed: it is flawed and damaged as a result of his curse on love, which was partly a curse on himself. And Wotan's power has been weakened by the dialectics of lawgiving, whereby the lawmaker must bow to his own law. For this reason the two opposed demigods create, almost simultaneously, instruments or agents to proceed on their behalf. Although incapable of love, Alberich produces a son, that pale hero Hagen, by committing a form of rape on the Gibichung queen he has paid for, Kriemhild (the mother of Gunther and Gutrune). Wotan, too, has sought out a mortal woman, and as Wälse he has fathered by her the twins Siegmund and Sieglinde. Wotan's hope is that the "free man," not being bound by a self-imposed law as Wotan himself is, will win back the magic ring—by force, naturally. From his viewpoint this would have the effect of restoring the balance of the universe.

But Wotan will not be able to achieve his goal if the chosen agent commits an offense. Siegmund seizes upon the sword as the emblem and instrument of his destiny, but by recapturing his sister in order to become her lover, he is implicating both of them in adultery and incest. This was not what the ruler of the gods intended. He did not reckon with the possibility that spring, as a force of nature, would confound his cleverly devised plans. Again we find the theme of a choice between observing the law and breaking it.

Now Fricka throws herself in the path of Wotan's calculations. She is acting by virtue of her authority as the scourge of anarchy. She is the goddess responsible for the preservation of hearth and home and the integrity of marriage. In the ensuing dispute, which is overlaid with the clash of invisible arms, she completely demolishes Wotan with her arguments. It is more than the act of incest that enrages Fricka (although she asks in horror: "When came it to pass / that brother and sister were lovers?"—to which Wotan calmly and rather jovially replies: "Now it's come to pass!"). Fricka stands for conservatism and the status quo ("Your concern / is for things that have been," comments Wotan). She takes umbrage because she is "wedlock's guardian." With inflexible arguments she mercilessly uncovers Wotan's self-deception point by point. These two young people, she asserts, have not been free to act as they choose; they have been mechanically playing predetermined roles. Both Siegmund and Sieglinde have been merely the instruments of Wotan's political will, of his general tactics and strategy, and he must therefore take responsibility for his creatures' infringement of the law, which he sanctioned. That is to say, he must retract his instruction to the Valkyrie Brünnhilde, his beloved child, that Siegmund is to kill Hunding in battle. "Abandon the Wälsung!" demands Fricka. Wotan believes that this fate can still be avoided. "Let him go his way," he says, and later adds: "The Valkyrie is free to choose." But Fricka sees through this subterfuge as well. Pitilessly she orders: "Command her that Siegmund dies!" Wotan, bowed and indeed broken, gives the goddess his oath.

Fricka's standpoint is unassailable, for it is not a human one. The gods would be ruined if they revoked their own law, the universal order the gods represent. "For men in their scorn / would laugh at our might, / jeer at the glorious gods."

From the philosophical point of view the second scene of act 2 constitutes the core of the great tetralogy. Wotan gives his summing-up, his self-analysis. The colloquy with his favorite daughter, Brünnhilde, is really a soliloquy ("I think aloud, then, / speaking to you"). He is ruthless with himself and no longer has any illusions when he confesses his failure: "I forged the fetters; / now I'm bound, / I, least free of all living!" This leads to the outburst: "The saddest of beings is Wotan!" Then he describes a vast panorama in which ancient times, the present, and the future are combined. He outlines to Brünnhilde—who is supposedly aware of all this but who must assume ignorance for our benefit—the tangled web of violence and lies and liabilities that the accursed ring presents. It is the ring that is the key if there is to remain any hope for the world, and thus for the gods. But there is a contradiction: Wotan is bound to Fafner by their contract, and "the bond that I made / forbids me to harm him; / if I should try / my power would fail. / These are the fetters / which have bound me; / since by my treaties I rule, / by those treaties I am enslaved." The god is in need of a man, a free man, "foe to the gods, / free of soul, / fearless and bold, / who acts alone." For "that man can do / what the god must shun." With absolute clarity Wotan perceives the dreadful paradox that is involved here. Whoever he creates to save the gods will remain his puppet: "I have no power to make the free man; / my hand can only make slaves!"

There is no way out of the dilemma. "I leave all my work; / but one thing I desire: / the ending, / the ending!" Wotan sets this in motion by ordering Brünnhilde: "Let Siegmund fall!" Subsequently he is to delay this ending through the rough benevolence with which, almost against his better judgment, he will cautiously direct his unintended grandson, Siegfried.

Siegfried is the child Brünnhilde helps to bring into the world after rebelling against Wotan's order and vainly attempting to save Siegmund. She succeeds in rescuing the pregnant Sieglinde. Having done so, she gives her as Siegmund's sole legacy the fragments of the sword that Wotan, in a terrible rage, has shattered with his spear. This sword is destined to exact revenge; wielded by the dragon slayer, it will one day shatter the spear of the Law. Siegfried will then be on his way to fortune and his end, which will also mark the end of his era.

Siegfried, Wotan's grandson, is scarcely any closer to him than his father, Siegmund, was. Perhaps, however, he stands closer to Wagner. A child born out of incest implies an intermingling of powers that are very intimately related. It implies a pure distillation of the noblest blood, for the purest breeding is achieved through inbreeding. For all his reams of theoretical statements, Wagner never expressed an opinion on the subject. Yet it must have exerted a strong, indeed a compelling influence on him. But this is just vague speculation based on his own close relationship with his elder sisters Luise Brockhaus, Clara Wolfram, and Ottilie Brockhaus, and above all his warm and intense affection for his eldest sister, Rosalie (born in 1803).[18] All the heroes of Wagner's dramas are motherless. Often they are in search of a mother, and not a few of them have a close and tenderly loving relationship with their sisters. This is first seen in Arindal and Lora in *Die Feen*. It continues with Claudio and Isabella *(Das Liebesverbot),* and becomes more pronounced in the case of Rienzi and Irene. Sachs's relation to Eva in *Die Meistersinger* is even like a highly erotic father-daughter relationship. The incestuous Wälsung blood Siegfried inherits from Siegmund and Sieglinde makes him Brünnhilde's nephew.

As the *Ring* drama progresses, Brünnhilde is punished for her disobedience by being shorn of her identity. She is forcibly removed from the company of her sisters, the "barbarous maidens" (to quote Fricka in act 2, scene 1), and from the activity sparked by her bloodthirsty battle cry. Wotan strips her of

18. Also worthy of note is Wagner's relationship with his mother, Johanna, which was both heartfelt and problematic. It may have been the cause of the fact that he was attracted "only to women 'with ties.'" Martin Gregor-Dellin has tackled the subject in his biography by way of the Freudian concept of the injured third party (Gregor-Dellin 1983, p. 23). This is clearly important, although equally clearly there are limits to what can be read into it without losing oneself in a maze of conjecture and obsession. On the incest theme, see also Gutman 1968, p. 83. [The source of Gregor-Dellin's approach, which he does not acknowledge, is discussed briefly in Family Letters, p. xxxii.—Ed.]

her divine status. Undine-like, she leaves her proper fairy element for the sake of that earthly love which alone can redeem her from banishment. We leave her fast asleep, reserved for the bravest of heroes and protected from the world's mediocrity by a fiery rampart. Now, encircled though she may be, Brünnhilde is free to experience the purely human element, love. It is love that will snatch her up to the peaks of rapture. It is also love that will destroy Brünnhilde, and her lover with her, along with all the gods and their ruler, Wotan.

Second Day: Siegfried

The son of Siegmund and Sieglinde grows up in a cave in the forest, where Mime the smith has brought him up grudgingly rather than in any spirit of kindness. When the dying Sieglinde gave birth to her child, it was to this dwarf that she entrusted him, together with the fragments of the shattered sword, Nothung.

Siegfried has now to discover his own identity. This is a gradual process. Dourly and slowly, his presumed father begins by enlightening him as to the facts of his birth and his name. The news makes sense to Siegfried, with his primitive theory of evolution, because it was only with loathing that he could ever endure his foster father's care. Having seen his own face in a stream, he remarks: "It wasn't like yours, / . ˙. no more than a toad / resembles a fish. / No fish had a toad for a father!" (see Wapnewski 1978b, pp. 164ff.). Nothing weak earns any respect from this sturdy child of nature. His next step is to be united with the sword, for each is meant for the other. But the sword Mime produces in his forge lacks durability in the hands of this superhuman swordsman. So Siegfried masters the hammer and bellows, and skillfully welds together the fragments, loudly singing his blacksmith's songs.

Mime watches his progress with mixed feelings. On the one hand, he wants to make use of the young hero. Only the strength of Siegfried can slay the dragon Fafner, who is brooding over his hoard, and thus put Mime in possession of the ring, the instrument of power. On the other hand, Mime has every reason to fear the youngster's weapon himself. Through Wotan he has been allowed a glimpse of the future. In the anonymous role of the Wanderer, the god has paid him an unexpected visit while Siegfried is out in the forest. He cruelly confronts the weakling and outcast, taunting him with his helplessness (just as the boy did in his own fashion). Wotan forces Mime to take part in a game of riddles, another idea that Wagner derived from Old Norse sources.[19] The price of the wager is the loser's head. Here Mime makes a mistake. His questions are on abstruse general subjects, and he asks them in order to confirm rather than add to his personal fund of knowledge. A wiser man would have asked the stranger—whose identity is beginning to dawn on Mime—for information of some practical use. The uncanny visitor then poses his own questions; and in this way Mime discovers that his death

---

19. On this point, see Wapnewski 1978b, pp. 158ff.; see also Brinkmann 1972.

is to come at the hand of a man who has not yet learned the meaning of fear—none other than Siegfried. It is Siegfried who will mend the sword—and who will thus cost Mime his life. This is the meaning of Wotan's riddles. Having been trapped into proposing to forfeit his head, Mime must now pay the price. Wotan, however, departs, whimsically delegating the prize to him "who has never learnt to fear." This leaves Mime in a dilemma. In order to realize his designs on the ring, he has need of the very person who will prevent him from enjoying the spoils. The agent of his stratagem is also going to be the agent of his death. In desperation the hapless Mime resorts to a coward's weapon. Brewing a potion, he induces in himself (and here he strongly resembles Alberich, another dwarf deluded by his own arrogance) the euphoria of a man who rules the world: "And the dwarf they despised / they will treat as a king!" While Siegfried is hammering out his song of feudalistic morality at the top of his voice, Mime is envisaging handsome compensation for his lowly, subhuman life of drudgery: "The world will cower / when I command." He affirms his new status with boundless glee: "Hi, Mime! You fortunate smith!" But the dwarf is not the least bit fortunate. His end will be every bit as wretched as his life.

Meanwhile, the lad that Mime has reared in the forest has started off on his worldly career. His encounter with the dragon and his victory over it should be seen as a kind of initiation ceremony. Once this rite has been undergone, Siegfried will understand nature. He will also be ripe for the supreme human experience—the experience of love.

As the Wanderer, Wotan has met Alberich lurking eagerly in front of Fafner's cavern, the Neidhöhle. He enlightens the dwarf about the future with a lofty calm. The god's consciousness of the coming apocalypse, his terrible sadness and black melancholy have made him free, and he is capable of distancing himself from events. The passionate creature of action has turned into an almost dispassionate spectator. With seeming indifference he allows events to take their course, knowing, to be sure, that initially all will go well. Even though he has consciously experienced what Schopenhauer's philosophy teaches in principle (see *Die Walküre*, act 2, scene 2), there is in Wotan's attitude just a glimmer of hope that peaceful negotiations with the ring's owner may yet be possible.

The "giant worm," however, will take neither advice nor warnings to heart. Fafner is not prepared to engage in friendly bargaining with Siegfried. "I'll keep what I hold," he retorts with a yawn, and goes back to sleep. Meanwhile, Mime has tried but failed to teach Siegfried the meaning of fear on their long journey to the Neidhöhle. Being still in a prehuman state, Siegfried lacks this emotion; his first experience of it will be afforded by a woman, and by love. The present exploit, the trial of strength, is a preparation for it. As Siegfried rests underneath a linden tree, he is happily reminded once more that he is not Mime's son. He describes the wretched dwarf and born loser in terms as cynical as they are wicked. We may not concur with Adorno, who sees a caricature of the Jews in this description. All the same, Wagner never minces either words or music when he has a specific target in mind.[20] The grotesque and unfeeling portrait that Mime's foster son paints of the dwarf strikes one as being in fairly poor taste.

The simple drama of the scene under the linden tree (act 2, scene 2), stems from the youth's innocent attempt to whittle a reed. One might be tempted to view this as merely a burlesque episode in the midst of tragedy, or even to find some deep psychological explanation for it, the flute being an obvious Freudian symbol. In fact the scene has a dramatic logic which is rooted in the actual situation. Siegfried is delighted by the sound of the Woodbird's song, and already suspecting that it has something important to tell him, he tries to understand it by an entirely logical method: that of imitating it. But this will not work. As yet, only his pipe offers a suitable expression of his state of awareness (see Wapnewski 1978b, pp. 171ff.).

Thanks to Mime's training, the lad is fully prepared for his clash with the dragon. He has learned about tactics and knows where a dragon's heart is; his hero's strength does the rest. What the dying Fafner fails to tell him ("The dead can tell no tidings") Siegfried learns from its fiery blood. As he raises his scorched hand to his mouth and moistens it with his tongue, the taste of the dragon's blood makes him part of all-seeing nature. Now he can understand what the birds are saying. The experience gives him what his rude strength needs if he is to progress to a higher stage, namely, knowledge (if not wisdom). With magic inevitability it leads him first to the dragon's hoard. He leaves the pile of gold but takes the Tarnhelm and the ring. The magic then protects Siegfried from Mime's attempt to drug him (although one should point out that this attempt does not in itself absolutely justify Mime's murder).

The scheming villain blunders and thus goes to his death. He dies because, amazingly enough, he reveals his intentions to Siegfried, describing them in detail and with great forcefulness in the course of his babblings. This is not an episode that should be taken literally. Wagner put a great deal of thought into it. Siegfried has acquired "an ear for the universe": by conquering the dragon he has gained access to the world of nature and man. Having assumed this crucial extra dimension, he finally understands what his foolish state prevented him from grasping before. That is, he can now hear what other characters are thinking—in this case the murderous thoughts of the dwarf (Wapnewski 1978b, pp. 158ff.). Thus Siegfried now has to get rid of him. In theory he needs only to dismiss him with a sharp kick, but instead he actually takes Mime's life. This gives Siegfried his first sight of a corpse other than an animal's, an experience that leaves him unmoved. After throwing the corpse into the dragon's cave, he drags Fafner's lifeless body to the entrance: "And so you both have found your rest!"

But Siegfried himself remains restless. Under the linden tree once more,

---

20. Adorno 1981, pp. 20–25. Adorno goes so far as to maintain that Wagner was caricaturing himself as well.

he again entrusts himself to the guidance of the Woodbird. As it sings of Brünnhilde and of love, his chest swells with ardor at the thought that *he* is the man who can save her: "Only he wakes Brünnhilde who is unacquainted with fear!" In obeying the bird, he will be obeying his personal demon.

Compared to the music for the first two acts, the terse orchestral prelude to the third act, with its strong dynamic contrasts, is clear evidence of a new phase in Wagner's development. This passage serves as a bridge to the dramatic prelude. With his opening song the Wanderer awakens Erda, the ancient mother-goddess, from her "slumbering wisdom." It was she who had prophesied (*Das Rheingold,* scene 4): "All things that are, perish! / An evil day / dawns for the immortals." It was also Erda who later bore Wotan his favorite daughter. At this stage in the world's course he expects her to advise him afresh on the question of how "a god can master his care." She begins by scolding Wotan for his extreme and petulant behavior toward Brünnhilde, who was, after all, merely carrying out his own wishes. At this point, however, Wotan affirms in pithy phrases his ideas of willing and yielding: "That the gods may die soon / gives me no anguish; / I have willed that end! / What in an hour of fiercest anguish / despairing once I resolved, / freely and gladly / I shall now bring to pass." His legacy can be safely handed down to the morally spotless Siegfried ("today to the Wälsung / I have bequeathed my realm"). Alberich's curse will be ineffective once the ring is with Siegfried, through whom Brünnhilde will achieve that deed "that will free our world." Erda, says Wotan, must go back to sleep and dream of his end, which he confirms of his own free will: "Whatever may happen / the god will gladly / yield his rule to the young!"

Wotan's plans have been determined by that spirit of optimism for which Schopenhauer's favorite epithet was "infamous." Surprisingly, he still believes that all will end well. But although he has the last word in sending Erda back to sleep, there is menace in her line: "You are not what you declare!"[21] It goes on reverberating long after she has delivered it.

There is also much truth in Erda's line: Wotan's grandson is going to overthrow him, and thereafter he will no longer be a god. Coming after the images of himself and the future that Wotan has projected, the ensuing scene between the Wanderer and Siegfried is a painful contrast. Siegfried behaves like a thoughtless lout, just as he always has, and after his experience with Mime, he has a particular mistrust of the old. Through Wotan, Wagner gives us the usual thorough recapitulation of past events. Siegfried is eager to get back to the present and to embark on his future. He insults the old Wanderer, denigrating him as a rowdy who has lost an eye in a brawl. Wotan's cryptic reply and rebuke have not the slightest effect on him. But his impetuosity is countered—not quite logically, in view of what Wotan envisaged in his last argument with Erda—with stolid resistance on the god's part. Although

21. "Wagner never created anything more noble and moving than this scene of farewell to an ideal" (Gutman 1968, p. 300).

avowedly ready to retire, he now obstructs the very path that he has prepared for his grandson and heir. He indulges in a fit of rage and lapses into his former—younger, emotionally ruled—self, although what causes this outburst is an old man's anger at a young rebel. The ruler exerts his authority one last time: "I am the rock's defender! / And mine the spell / that enfolds the slumbering maid." But how can he ask Siegfried to fear his authority without abolishing the young man's sole distinction, which is his ignorance of fear? When talking with Erda, Wotan had portrayed the voluntary abdication of power as a desirable and comforting response to the problem of evil. Now, however, he is clinging to his throne and seems to dread losing it. He who can wake Brünnhilde, "he who can win her, / makes me powerless for ever!"

Wotan stretches out his spear against Siegfried's sword in a symbolic unmasking of himself: "The sword that you bear / was broken by this shaft; / and once again / I'll break it on this my spear!" Siegfried grasps the connection. Recognizing his father's enemy, he strikes out with the sword, and this time it is the spear—the "eternal" spear—that breaks. Wotan is stripped of his power, but not in the way he meant it to happen. This act of annexation spells doom for the gods, and for the superhuman Siegfried as well. His deed will prevent him from altering the world's fate and deny him the freedom to administer the god's legacy.

For now, what draws the young hero on is love. He rushes off toward the rampart of fire and passes through it triumphantly. Having awakened the sleeping figure, he listens to her fervent hymn to the sun. Carried away by her supreme femininity, he at last learns the meaning of fear and joins in an ecstatic song of joy with her. Siegfried becomes united with love, with the all-embracing, terrible, unconscious cry of an unending *Liebestod:* "Light of our loving, / laughter in death!"[22]

Third Day: Götterdämmerung

On 23–24 February 1869 Wagner wrote to King Ludwig II: "*Siegfried* is divine. It is my greatest work!" Both the superlative and the artistic judgment are subjective; to question them is not only legitimate but necessary. Even from the genealogical angle, Wagner's comment is only half true. Since Siegfried's father and mother were of partly human parentage, he himself is no less human than he is divine. What makes him most human is his thirst for the world, and hence his blindness to it. Though seemingly free, he is so dazzled that he stumbles into traps and snares.

At the start of *Götterdämmerung* we hear from the Norns, who are weaving (but not determining) the rope of the world's fate. Sublimely at their ease, they are discussing past, present, and future events. Of Wotan they have

---

22. Gutman comments on this scene rather more coolly, from a musical standpoint. Siegfried and Brünnhilde, he suggests, bid a lyrical farewell to music drama and push on with the composer "toward that rediscovered goal of the ultimate grand opera" *Götterdämmerung* (Gutman 1968, p. 299).

nothing good to say. His spear broken from the wood of the World Ash Tree pulled the whole tree out with it. The god had it chopped down and the branches piled around Valhalla in anticipation of the ultimate fire for which he once yearned.

Wotan is now a broken god. In his dialogue with Erda at the beginning of act 3 of *Siegfried,* he voiced a resignation that was almost cheerful. Why has this mood now turned into one of dull and gloomy despair? Is it because he has suddenly perceived that his successor is unworthy, that the man chosen to save the world cannot be someone so fanatically ruthless as to have no sense of duty to anybody but himself? That he is someone who hacks down all real or imagined obstacles and has no respect or reverence for anything? Or has Wotan realized the flaw in his scheme for maintaining the universe? Has he seen that even Siegfried's freedom is specious, since his criminal deeds merely amount to a carrying out of his grandfather's wishes? Fricka's arguments concerning the supposed freedom of Siegmund are equally true of his son; all that separates them is the different generations. As a savior Siegfried has been, as it were, set up for his task. Wotan, formerly that lordly figure who renounced all power, is now a shamefully deposed ruler. What is vaguely implied by the Norns will be spelled out by Waltraute's dramatic account in act 1, scene 3 of *Götterdämmerung*.

First, however, Siegfried bids farewell to Brünnhilde, the woman he loves. As Wotan has taken away her divinity, Siegfried has awakened her humanity. Brünnhilde parts from her love, who was invested with divinity by Wotan and whose humanity has been aroused by her waking. As her wedding gift she gives him her runes, representing her divine power to bless and protect. In return Siegfried gives her the ring, whose potent magic he no more suspects than she does—and whose curse cannot take effect if the ring is worn by an innocent. This gift is a symbol of their unending bond. But then, to our irritation, Siegfried has to go off—"to fresh deeds," sings Brünnhilde, who can actually see some point in his going. To us his reason is questionable. After all, he has won the finest woman on earth, and has held in his hands the source of all power. So why this need to prove himself afresh as a conquering hero? Why this complaisant assertion of his military glory? The couple's farewells mark their separation. When they meet again, they will see only a dreadful travesty of their former selves, Siegfried having been seriously corrupted.

The rushing sounds of his *Rhine Journey* carry Siegfried to the court of the Gibichungs. Hagen initiates his intrigues, and at first they succeed beautifully. Like Siegmund (and hence Siegfried as well), Alberich's son owes his own life entirely to the battle between the two great powers for possession of the ring. With that prize in view, he binds Siegfried in an alliance with the Gibichungs. This is achieved with the aid of that familiar theatrical device, a magic potion. "He'll forget all women but you; / the past will fade from his mind; / all memory he will have lost," sings Hagen to his sister, Gutrune. There is more to this scene than meets the eye. What it involves is not simply a drug-induced personality change; rather, the potion brings Siegfried's true character to light. He wants to be free in his own way—that is, to revoke the past and to shed both the burden of memory and a duty imposed by a too-constraining bond. If a man goes wrong because he has been poisoned, this is sad but not tragic. Siegfried, however, is the author of his own misfortune: while not desiring it consciously, he still actively brings it upon himself. His seduction takes place because he wants to be seduced. He desires Gutrune almost as soon as he sees her; the potion is merely the catalyst of his wishes and lusts. Moreover, it has only a limited effect. It effaces Siegfried's memory not of his whole past life but only of those things he needs to forget if he is to achieve worldly glory and if Hagen is to have the ring: that is, he must forget Brünnhilde and her love.[23]

Hagen's guest only too gladly allows himself to be reduced to an agent of the other's cynical plans for achieving power. Siegfried is now joined to Gunther by a vow of blood brotherhood. With an atypical display of moral scruples, Hagen finds an excuse for not joining with them. The ill-starred alliance is intended to gain Brünnhilde as Gunther's bride, Gutrune as a bride for Siegfried, and the ring for Hagen. A deal has been made, and the one partner's hand has been sullied by the other's. Siegfried, alienated from Brünnhilde and thus from himself, sets off on his journey, taking Gunther with him: "There lies my boat; / swiftly sail to the mountain!" One thing he has not forgotten is the route.

The same route has been taken by Waltraute, one of the other eight Valkyries. With a desperate urgency she tries to save Wotan and the world from ruin by begging her half-sister Brünnhilde for the ring. To return it to the Rhine, she says, will be to restore the original truth of the universe. Wotan himself has said that "if once the Rhine's fair daughters / win back their ring from Brünnhilde again, / then the curse will pass; / she will save both god and the world." At first this means nothing to Brünnhilde. Only gradually does she begin to grasp the truth. But she rejects her sister's plea in a furious outburst. Brünnhilde is completely obsessed by her love for Siegfried—even at the very moment when he is betraying her. Totally possessed by the idea of fidelity, she hurls at Waltraute and the gods a forthright "No," Herostratus-like in its frenzy.

> More than Walhall's pleasures,
> more than the fame of the gods,
> more is this ring . . .
> The shine of this gold
> tells me that Siegfried loves me! . . .
> Go home to the sacred
> clan of the gods!
> And of my ring

23. On this and the discussion that follows, see Wapnewski 1978b, pp. 174–184.

you may give them this reply:
My love shall last while I live,
my ring in life shall not leave me!
Fall first in ruins
Walhall's glorious pride!

So Brünnhilde drives away her agitated sister: "Back to your horse!" Waltraute's last word is "woe."

Waltraute's account of Wotan's condition is like a report on a sick patient, telling of the pathological case of a great man racked by depression. He is being torn apart by rational fears and irrational anxieties; or rather, his rational worries have turned into irrational specters and imagined threats, throwing him into a state of panic. He has suffered an inner disfigurement, a depersonalization triggered by the loss of his spear. Since falling prey to such anxieties, the patient has lost his sense of identity. Restlessly he roams the world as a Wanderer, or else he falls into melancholy brooding, locked in a state of apathy and aphasia. His readiness to give up his power voluntarily has turned into a fear of another's power, a fear of retaliation.

From now on everything Siegfried does will justify Wotan's anxieties and engineer the world's destruction. The scene in which he returns to Brünnhilde and overpowers her, brutally and pitilessly, is a horrifying one. Initially the horror derives from the violence, but even more horrific is the picture thus presented of Wotan's grandson. The Tarnhelm, hitherto unused and hence value free or neutral, now, thanks to Hagen's tutelage, has become an instrument of evil. "Ein Freier kam" is how Siegfried, disguised as Gunther, announces his arrival. This punning phrase contains a dreadful irony, for neither is he a *Freier* (suitor), nor is he *frei* (free). Brünnhilde's warning gesture with her ring finger is wasted; the ring is no protection. She does not know its power, and its true master is no longer himself. The potion may offer some excuse for the foolish hero's behavior. But we cannot simply dismiss the fact that he is lending himself to an absolutely shameless deception. Nor can Siegfried fail to realize that he is making the finest of women another man's helpless captive—even if he does fail to recognize her. By means of lies, deceit, and physical violence, a character part goddess and part human is being deprived of her predestined role. Who would call this Siegfried "divine"?

After nightfall we see the broken Brünnhilde lying beside her conqueror, with the sword placed between them. Ties of blood brotherhood are still observed where love has been trampled.

Meanwhile, the scheming Hagen has been keeping watch over the Gibichung hall. Although seemingly asleep, he gives soothing answers when his father addresses him. Their eerie dialogue lets us know that the opposing factions in the war have regrouped; Alberich's adversary is no longer Wotan but Siegfried. Alberich fears that the unsuspecting hero, being immune to the ring's curse, could return the gold to the Rhine Maidens, which would spell final defeat for Alberich and Hagen. Hagen must stand on his own from now on. Like Wotan in the opposing camp, Alberich has long been reduced to a mere shadow of himself. The scene ends with Alberich's call: "Be true! True!" Again this contains a dreadful irony, for who would count on Hagen for loyalty?

Events are now subject to the ineluctable workings of evil, which can only create further evil. The ring is an instrument not of power but of bloody confusion and gruesome disclosures. After Gunther's vassals have sung loud wedding greetings, he presents his bride Brünnhilde, the downcast captive. Then a second illustrious couple enters, Siegfried and Gutrune. Brünnhilde notices the ring worn by Siegfried. This, she realizes, is the ring that was snatched from her by the supposed Gunther the evening before. Siegfried denies it—which is an odd thing to do, for how can he have forgotten a deed that was so recent and deliberate? It was, he claims, from a "giant worm" (Fafner) that he won the ring. At this point Hagen sees his chance to destroy Siegfried. He tells a deliberate lie and suggests that Siegfried has obtained the ring by treachery. The quarrel becomes heated, and in terrible anguish the cruelly deceived Brünnhilde astounds everyone by declaring that she is married to "that man there"—Siegfried. If we are to follow the flurry of arguments about the wedding night, we must bear three points in mind. First, the official court view is that Brünnhilde has been won by King Gunther. Second, what the conspirators are privately thinking is based on the unconsummated "chaste nuptials" of Brünnhilde and the disguised Siegfried. The frenzied Brünnhilde, however, is referring to her night of love with Siegfried when he first awakened her. This memory, still fresh in her mind, has assumed for her a mythical and timeless quality.

Unnerved by Brünnhilde's towering fury, Siegfried loses his composure and defends his actions. In so doing, he reveals the shabby plot at which the men have connived. He invokes his blood brotherhood with Gunther, which he has fully respected: "Nothung, my faithful sword, / guarded that holy vow; / this shining blade divided me / from this unhappy wife." This is quite true, and by admitting it Siegfried reveals the monstrous deception to the vassals and the entire court. But a king ceases to be a king when his honor has been impugned and his weakness thus proved. For the time being, however, Gunther is saved by the urgent issue of resolving the previous night's events. A solemn oath is called for. On the point of Hagen's spear, Siegfried and Brünnhilde swear the truth as each sees it. But their versions of the truth differ: Brünnhilde is thinking back to Siegfried's actual, initial conquest of her, whereas Siegfried himself is thinking of his second, vicarious one. The vassals react with rage and bewilderment; their immediate response is to appeal to Donner, the god of thunder. But Siegfried makes himself heard, posturing in a typically shallow and banal way. Here, as elsewhere, he behaves like what we would nowadays call a male chauvinist: "You vassals, leave her alone! / Leave this woman to scold! / Like cowards, men quit the field / when it's a battle of words." Note the dismissal of Brünnhilde as a mere scold. This reflects an unpardonable lack of understanding. Siegfried has clearly been abandoned by his god, his inner demon.

Siegfried leads his bride Gutrune into the palace. He is in high spirits: "Follow, you vassals! / On to the feast! / Come, fair women, / help at our wedding! / Share my delight / laugh at my joy!" But the scene outside the hall presents a terrifying contrast. While the cheerful hero is praising love with a "happy heart," his death is being decided.

Brünnhilde, Gunther, and Hagen remain behind. In agonized thought the desperate goddess tries to see through the web of confusion. Hagen exploits the situation by offering to avenge her. He learns from Brünnhilde how even a weak man might topple the mightiest. Knowing that Siegfried would never turn his back to an enemy, she did not guard it with her magic runes. Gunther now speaks up, grieving over his disgrace. In the wake of Siegfried's explanation Brünnhilde has grasped the deception, but without detecting any mitigating circumstances in Siegfried's blood brotherhood with Gunther. She attacks Gunther with the words: "O cowardly man! / falsest of friends! / Sheltering behind him, / scared by the flames, / and then when he'd won me, / daring to claim me!" This provocative statement is left dangling, a loose end amid the tangle of motives. In a formidable revenge trio, the three resolve to kill Siegfried. By combining their voices, Wagner went against his own aesthetic precepts, but to powerful effect. Within its harmonic fabric the trio expresses several separate and indeed clashing ideas. Brünnhilde is bent on avenging the betrayal of her love, her very existence. Gunther swears revenge for the shame brought on him by Siegfried's disclosure of the trickery involved in Brünnhilde's conquest. For Hagen the sole object of Siegfried's death is to acquire the ring. This is a trio of dissonances, a dreadful summons to gods and demons to abet the most evil of human deeds. Hagen invokes Alberich, the "night guardian," while Gunther and Brünnhilde call upon Wotan. Thus the two ruling powers are invisibly present on the bloody stage—the powers at whose behest these blind and deluded characters, half superhuman and half human, are about to take their last desperate steps. With Siegfried and Gutrune leading them, the dazzled courtiers file past in a joyful wedding procession.

Once more, however, fate seems about to smile on the hard-pressed evildoers and give them another chance. In their frivolous way the Rhine Maidens gaily flirt with Siegfried, who, having got lost during a bear hunt, has been cut off from Hagen's craftily planned expedition. Further bartering now takes place: the maidens offer him the bear in return for the ring. Typically Siegfried almost gives in to their seductive cooing, but the bargain is such a bad one that he fears, of all things, his wife's scolding! The Rhine Maidens scoff at this picture of a henpecked husband and dive into the river's depths. But no sooner have they vanished than Siegfried changes his mind. To prove he is no miser, he is now willing to make them a present of the ring. This illustrates his unstable and impulsive character: he can never be faithful to anyone for long. Suddenly the bobbing nymphs reappear, now wearing very different expressions. Gravely and solemnly they tell the unsuspecting hero about the ring and the curse, predicting his death that very day "unless you obey and give the ring to our care." This tactic is a mistake; but as we have known from the outset, psychology is not the Rhine Maidens' forte. Siegfried might have responded to flattery, but threats not only leave him unmoved but actually provoke his stubborn resistance. Life and limb are of no account to him, as he proves by lifting a clod of earth in a statuesque pose and then tossing it contemptuously behind him. The sisters resign themselves to his folly. "He thinks he is wise, / he thinks he is strong, / but he's as stupid and blind as a child!" Deciding to turn to his next of kin, they swim off in search of Brünnhilde. Siegfried merely behaves like a fool once more, taking refuge in barracks-room bluster. He knows, he says, what women are like. Furthermore, were it not for his duty to Gutrune, "I'd try to capture / one of those pretty maids."[24]

Siegfried's death, ironically, is to be his salvation. At last he ceases to be an unwitting puppet, a rash daredevil, artless and happy-go-lucky. He dies as his true self: that man to whom love brought an awakening, if only temporary, and who himself awakened a woman through love and for one fateful second had the chance to become the savior of the world. He dies conscious of all this, aware once again of what was, and what he was, and what Brünnhilde was to him.

It is Hagen who is the force behind Siegfried's death and transfiguration. In act 3, scene 2, the hunting party stops for refreshment. Siegfried, who has been reunited with his comrades, unwittingly makes a sacrificial gesture. Having poured an offering, he lets the drink overflow from his horn, moistening the earth. Then he decides to enliven the company, the gloomy and anxious Gunther included. He sings of exploits in his past life, particularly the Woodbird and its advice. The fact that he had forgotten the birds—"For a long while I've paid no heed to their song"—is highly significant, for it means that Siegfried has lost that contact with omniscient nature that he was granted when he slew the dragon. By giving himself up to worldly pleasures, he has alienated himself from nature again.

Siegfried's story is interrupted at the point where, having killed Mime, he starts following the Woodbird—to Brünnhilde's rock. This comes too close to the truth for Hagen; yet, strangely enough, he also seems to want that truth to be told, although it will exonerate Siegfried and deeply incriminate himself, especially in the eyes of Gunther. He slips an antidote into Siegfried's drink, reviving that area of his memory that was previously lost to him. Siegfried now recalls the moment when he woke "the splendid maid." The moment of truth has arrived. Two ravens fly up, and using them to divert Siegfried's attention, Hagen thrusts a spear into his back. Helpless as ever,

24. On the Rhine Maidens in general, and this scene in particular, see Wapnewski 1978b, pp. 147–153.

and stunned by what he has just learned, Gunther tries too late to seize the murderer's arm.

The melody of the dying man's final words takes up the melody of Brünnhilde's awakening. It is as though in dying Siegfried were at last being awakened himself. Brünnhilde had not been forced "back to sleep," as he has supposed; rather, he has been a prisoner of his own blindness. His end is a rapturous and visionary *Liebestod:* "Joyful surrender! / Sweet are these terrors!"

To the grieving Gutrune, Hagen subsequently owns up to the murder "with terrible defiance." Even though Siegfried is still wearing the ring, its curse strikes again. Hagen kills Gunther but shrinks back in alarm when Siegfried's dead hand raises itself threateningly.

Brünnhilde enters and sees the tragic scene before her. She now perceives that Siegfried betrayed her because he himself was the only too willing victim of a deception. What really betrayed Siegfried, to be sure, was that the god who conceived and created him as a free man then took away that freedom by reducing him to a mere agent of his own will. When love brought out the human being in Siegfried and made him independent, he quickly fell from grace, became a different person—an individual in his own right and no longer a commission personified—and as such he ceased to recognize Brünnhilde, in whom his mission was embodied.

Throughout the rest of the scene Brünnhilde announces the end of the tragedy in powerful and fearsome tones. "For vengeance," she declares, "here I have come." In reality she is wholly incapable of revenge; she can only pass judgment, particularly on the doomed gods. Wagner's emotions were strongly stirred by the final apotheosis. He sketched three different versions of it, expanding and pruning and altering. In the final version Brünnhilde's farewell is partly an indictment of the gods. Her targets are those who condoned—indeed initiated—the plot that ensnared Siegfried, who had no power over himself because he was being used as a pawn.

> Never was man
> more loyal to friendship;
> never was man
> more true to his promise;
> never was known
> love more faithful.
> And yet he was faithless,
> broke every promise;
> the truest of lovers—
> none falser than he!

Then, gazing upward, she sings:

> Look down, you guardians,
> look down and hear me!
> Turn your regard
> on my shame and my grief;

> and learn your eternal disgrace!
> And Wotan, hear
> you mighty god!

With this lament she unmasks the god just as Fricka once did. She exposes his ulterior motive, a motive he preferred to conceal from himself.

> By his most valiant deed
> he fulfilled your desire,
> but he was forced
> to share in your curse—
> that curse which has doomed your downfall.
> He, truest of all men,
> betrayed me,
> that I in grief might grow wise!
> Know I now what must be?

Yes, Brünnhilde knows that Wotan's end has come. "Rest now, rest now, O god!"

Brünnhilde's song is also partly her testament. She leaves the ring to the Rhine Maidens "who dwell in the waters." The funeral fire that will consume her body will purge the ring of its curse; and once restored to its element, the gold will regain its pristine purity. The same fire will set Valhalla ablaze and destroy its "glorious fortress." Brünnhilde's last words, however, are devoted to Siegfried. Hence her farewell is ultimately an avowal of her love, a finale in the manner of *Tristan*. It desires to immortalize love beyond life and even beyond death: "Siegfried! Siegfried! See! / Brünnhilde greets you as wife!"[25]

The funeral pyre blazes up, burning Siegfried's body together with Brünnhilde and her horse, Grane. The Rhine Maidens have won back the ring. Hagen tries to snatch it from them, just as his father snatched the gold; but whereas the maidens had avoided embracing Alberich, they enfold Hagen in their arms. True to their demonic nature, this embrace is a lethal one. As he drowns, Hagen utters the last words of the entire tragedy: "Give back the ring!"

The blaze has its counterpart in a second fire. On the far horizon Valhalla goes up in flames from the heaped-up branches of the toppled World Ash Tree. This was how Wotan had prepared for the end. The god will rest now.

But what is meant by "the end"? There are still men and women. How Wagner viewed their particular role is not wholly clear. In his early "sketch for a drama," *The Nibelung Myth*, he proposed one interpretation: "The gods

---

25. This *Liebestod* conclusion is stressed even more strongly in thirty lines Wagner deleted from the final version but then set to music separately at King Ludwig's insistence. They end with the vigorous statement: "selig in Lust und Leid/läßt—die Liebe nur sein!" (blessed in joy and grief/let there be only—love). [A facsimile of Wagner's musical setting of the deleted text can be found in SW 29, I, 177.—Ed.]

now raise men for the lofty purpose of purging their own guilt, and if they destroyed themselves in this creation of men, their aim would be achieved."

How do these humans stand, and what becomes of them in the end? If we listen to the music closely, it offers as much comfort and hope as the Old Norse sources on which Wagner depended. According to the poem *Der Seherin Gesicht* (The vision of the prophetess), land will rise out of the waters and put forth new shoots, and fields will bear crops (see Wapnewski 1978b, pp. 194ff.). Within the finale's great fabric of musical motifs the dominant one is the theme commonly known as the Reconciliation motif, although Dieter Schnebel aptly calls it the "motif of unconditional love." It is a melodic sequence that has been heard only once before in the cycle, in the second act of *Die Walküre*, where Brünnhilde resolves "unconditionally" to sacrifice herself for Sieglinde and hence for Siegfried.[26] Miraculously, this motif stayed secretly lodged in Wagner's mind for some twenty years (years that were taxing from a personal as well as a professional standpoint). Then, at precisely the right moment, it reappeared. On 23 July 1872 Cosima recorded Wagner as saying: "Music has no ending . . . I am glad that I kept back Sieglinde's theme of praise to Brünnhilde, to become as it were a hymn to the heroine."[27]

Leaving the music aside, however, there are several other points to consider. Power has neutralized itself, of its own volition. And in so doing it has drawn into the resulting vacuum those who are loath to renounce their power, like Wotan and Alberich. The element of water, the source of all life, has been purified with the aid of primordial fire. It receives the gold within its depths, making it the plaything of the Rhine Maidens and once again devoid of commercial value. *Das Rheingold* ended with the line: "Goodness and truth / dwell but in the waters: / false and base / all those who dwell up above!" The phrase was a reference to the deluded gods as they crossed their bridge of light into the castle, blissfully basking in their new splendor and deaf to Loge's scorn for their arrogance. There were already undertones of doom in the music at that stage. Now that the gods' splendor has faded away, what do we find "up above"? The final stage direction is transparently clear: "From the ruins of the fallen hall, the men and women, in great agitation, watch the growing firelight in the heavens."

The watchers belong to a human race which plays only a supporting part in the tetralogy. Where it does come briefly to the forefront, it is passive rather than active. Think of Hunding, Gunther, and Gutrune, as well as the anonymous walk-ons. (Like Hagen, both Siegmund and Sieglinde are only half human in origin, as is Siegfried. And although Wotan revokes the divinity

---

26. The whole subject of Brünnhilde's special position in the cycle—and by extension Wagner's general attitude toward his female characters—is aired in a most enlightening discussion in Schickling 1983, which I was unable to appraise and make express use of in the present survey but would strongly recommend.

27. In the original German edition of CT the word for "heroine" has been incorrectly transcribed as *Helden* and rendered accordingly as "heroes" in Skelton's English translation. Cosima actually wrote "Heldin" (heroine), which makes much more sense in the context. [Ed.]

of Brünnhilde, whose parents were both gods, that does not make her a human being.) Hence the moving spirits of this world are, or were, "white" and "black" goblins, the gods and demons and giants, all of them craving happiness but actually creating sorrow. All are projections of constraints and laws, of hardship and sacrifice, and they inflict bondage even when they represent love. Therefore man must get rid of them. The world must be cleansed through their death by fire, clearing the way for the truly "free" individuals to come.

There are human survivors. The world is theirs from now on. It has been entrusted to their care. The rest is up to them.

Tristan und Isolde

Wagner first met Otto and Mathilde Wesendonck in Zurich in February 1852. The couple had been married for five years. Otto was a well-to-do business-man from the Rhineland, a partner in a New York silk firm. The lovely Mathilde, with her artistic gifts and enthusiasms, was the daughter of a leading Elberfeld financier named Luckemeyer. Husband and wife were thirty-seven and twenty-three, respectively, which made Wagner two years older than Otto. The three of them became good friends; Otto also began to play the part of a benevolent patron. But this was not all the relationship amounted to. Wesendonck was building an imposing neo-Renaissance villa in the Zurich suburb of Enge, and when he learned that a Dr. Binswanger was planning to put up a mental hospital next door, he swiftly bought the adjoining land. This plot was the site of a half-timbered dwelling which Wesendonck offered the Wagners for a nominal rent. On 28 April 1857 the happy pair moved into their "refuge on the green hill." Four months later the Wesendoncks took up residence in the neighboring villa.

Wagner's orchestral sketch for the second act of *Siegfried* contains this revealing note, written on 18 June 1857: "*Tristan* already decided." Having put *Siegfried* aside, he produced the prose and then the verse libretto of *Tristan* in August. He handed Mathilde the original manuscript of the complete text on 18 September, a date they would treat as an anniversary in years to come. In October Wagner began work on the music for the first act, creating sounds that no one had imagined before. This has been described as the moment when modern music began.

While working on *Tristan* the composer was also setting Mathilde's poetry to music. His original title reads: *Five Poems by an Amateur Set to Music for a Woman's Voice by Richard Wagner.* Later known as the Wesendonck lieder, these settings were to become famous examples of the late-Romantic art song. They constitute one of the rare instances of Wagner's using lyrics that were not his own (the other exceptions to the rule were dictated by his poverty in Paris). This fact too, of course, says something about his relationship with Mathilde. He himself described the second song to be written (*Träume*, 4–5 December 1857) and the last (*Im Treibhaus*, 1 May 1858) as "studies for

Tristan." Indeed they do match or anticipate the opera's harmonic and melodic style; and another of the songs (*Stehe still*) is also clearly evocative of act 1. Since the idea was that Mathilde would accompany herself at the piano, Wagner orchestrated only one setting, *Träume*, for her birthday in December 1857. The orchestral versions of the other four songs most frequently heard nowadays are the work of Felix Mottl (although Hans Werner Henze rescored them in 1977).

Wagner completed the score of act 1 of *Tristan* on 3 April 1858. Four days later Minna intercepted a letter from her husband to Mathilde. It had been written in a state of high emotion, exhibiting a mixture of jealousy, love, and wounded feelings, and as usual with Wagner it included some far-ranging speculations of a cultural nature, having to do with Goethe's *Faust*. (Wagner called it a *Morgenbeichte,* or "morning confession," and with good reason.) The discovery led to a stormy scene. The association with Mathilde had to cease. The happy days at the "refuge" were over, and the composer and Minna were now married in name only. Minna gave up running a home for him, and their furniture was put up for sale. Wagner left for Venice on 17 August. He lived there until March 1859, in the Palazzo Giustiniani, and composed act 2 of *Tristan,* while also recounting the details of his daily life in letters to Mathilde. Then, as a political refugee, he was ordered to leave Venice. Returning to Switzerland, he finished *Tristan* on 6 August 1859 in the Schweizerhof Hotel at Lucerne. Despite his stormy personal life at the time, and several changes of residence, the whole opera had taken him no more than two years to complete.

The ensuing years were spent in restless wandering, or rather flight. Wagner met with setbacks and disappointments of both an artistic and a private nature, and creditors were at his heels wherever he went. In Vienna the first performance of *Tristan* was called off after seventy-seven rehearsals. The official reason—that it was unperformable—seems not unlikely in view of the work as well as the times. Then Wagner was rescued by the "Munich miracle." On 3 May 1864 King Ludwig II summoned to his presence the composer he had admired since boyhood. This marked the start of a new phase in Wagner's life and career. At last it would be possible to stage a production of *Tristan*. Again there was a fateful link between the composer's work and the life he was leading. The conductor of *Tristan* was to be his pupil and friend Hans von Bülow, and, on 10 April 1865, exactly two months before the premiere, von Bülow's wife, Cosima, gave birth to a child by Wagner. The parents named their daughter Isolde; less appropriately, but in deference to the demands of convention and the law, she bore the surname von Bülow.[28]

28. A second daughter, Eva, was born to Richard and Cosima in 1867, and a son, Siegfried (Fidi), in 1869. Their names are reflected in Wagner's compositions. On 25 August 1870 Wagner married Cosima, née Liszt (now divorced from Hans von Bülow). In April 1872 the family made its home in Bayreuth, the location of Wagner's future theater. The foundation stone of the Festspielhaus was laid on 22 May 1872 (Wagner's fifty-ninth birthday). On 28 April 1874 the family moved into Wahnfried. Over the front entrance to the house was inscribed: "Hier wo

The performer who sang the role of Tristan, Ludwig Schnorr von Carols-feld, seems to have surpassed himself; at any rate, that was Wagner's verdict. Six weeks after the premiere he died suddenly, after having appeared in only four performances. His death added to the uncanny, mystical, even demonic atmosphere that surrounded this opera from the very start.

Sources and Inspiration

Wagner was fond of apocryphal tales about inspiration and enjoyed contrib-uting to them, not without a certain ironic detachment. But no such tale attaches to his most personal work, for which he wrote a text that in terms of expression outstripped all his others, and in which he extended the bound-aries of his music to an extreme point. Indeed, his source and inspiration were never more obvious.

The literary source for *Tristan* was the lucid, virtuosic Middle High German epic by Gottfried von Strassburg. It dates from around 1200. In 1843, feeling secure in his position as Saxon court conductor, Wagner started to acquire a comprehensive personal library. After his flight from Dresden in 1849, this library passed into the hands of a creditor, his brother-in-law Heinrich Brock-haus, and Wagner never saw it again. (It now forms part of the Richard Wagner Foundation in Bayreuth; see Westernhagen 1966.) Old German lit-erature, Wagner tells us in *My Life,* made up the bulk of the collection. It included two editions of Gottfried's epic, by Friedrich Heinrich von der Hagen (1823) and Hans Ferdinand Massmann (1843), along with Heinrich Kurtz's translation (1844).[29] Nonetheless, Gottfried von Strassburg seems not to have been one of the Old German authors whose works Wagner took with him to Marienbad in July 1845. He had momentous encounters with Wolfram von Eschenbach, *Lohengrin,* and Hans Sachs during his holiday, but not with *Tristan.* Even if the last-named simply slipped Wagner's mind when he was writing *My Life,* the omission is a striking one.

From 1854 on, Wagner was thinking about the subject; and by 1857, the year he moved into his Zurich refuge, it had taken a firm hold on his imagination. He had three very dissimilar sources of inspiration for writing *Tristan,* evidence of which has been cited time and again.

First there was the philosophy of Schopenhauer. In *My Life* Wagner relates that in October 1854 his friend Georg Herwegh drew his attention to Scho-penhauer's *Die Welt als Wille und Vorstellung* (The world as will and idea), a magnum opus which only then was becoming well known in Germany. To Wagner the work was a revelation. He saw it as fulfilling—in advance—his personal concept of life and death. Looking at his "Nibelung poems," he recognized to his amazement "that the very things I now found so unpalatable

mein Wähnen Frieden fand—WAHNFRIED—Sei dieses Haus von mir genannt" (Here where my illusions found peace, let me call this house Peace from Illusion).

29. For a discussion of Hanslick's involuntary mediation with regard to Wagner's discovery of the Tristan tales, see Wapnewski 1978b, pp. 83–85.

in the theory were already long familiar to me in my own poetic conception. Only now did I understand my own Wotan myself and, greatly shaken, I went on to a closer study of Schopenhauer's book" (ML 510).

Schopenhauer then led Wagner on from Wotan to Tristan. For, to quote again from *My Life:* "It was no doubt in part the earnest frame of mind produced by Schopenhauer, now demanding some rapturous expression of its fundamental traits, which gave me the idea for a Tristan and Isolde . . . Returning from a walk one day, I jotted down the contents of the three acts . . . I wove into the last act an episode I later did not use: this was a visit by Parzival, wandering in search of the Grail, to Tristan's sickbed. I identified Tristan, wasting away but unable to die of his wound, with the Amfortas of the Grail romance."

The connection sounds very straightforward. Wagner had already come to share Schopenhauer's ideas, and after registering this fact he consistently built them into the remainder of his *Ring* cycle. Yet this scarcely explains why he suspended work on the cycle in order to draft *Tristan,* leaving Siegfried under his linden tree. To account for that momentous break in the *Ring,* we must look to another reason. Wagner was involved in a love affair that was fated to follow a Schopenhauerian course. Inasmuch as it offended against convention and tradition and all norms of social behavior, it stamped out the infamous will to life and sought a true consummation in a vision of the Beyond. We can see from a letter Wagner sent to Liszt how close the two groups of themes were to each other. As biographical documents Wagner's letters are generally more reliable than his memoirs, which he touched up both because of Cosima and with an eye to his later reputation. For obvious reasons, this applies especially to passages in *My Life* concerning *Tristan* and Mathilde Wesendonck. Wagner wrote to Liszt about Schopenhauer on 16 December 1854. He berated the German professors who had loftily ignored their great colleague ever since his masterpiece had first appeared (in 1819). Then he went on to the subject of *Siegfried,* which he hoped to complete by 1856. Here he makes an interesting mental leap: "Then I can perform it in 1858, the tenth year of my hegira—if it's to be. But as I have never in my life tasted the true joy of love, I will set up a memorial to this fairest of all dreams, where from first to last this love shall, for once, be properly sated. For I have planned in my head a *Tristan and Isolde,* the simplest but most full-blooded musical conception."

Wagner could justifiably have pointed to Schopenhauer as his guide if he were now proposing to complete the *Ring.* But this letter even holds Schopenhauer responsible for the suspension of his work on it, which jeopardized the whole project. No such hiatus would have occurred without a burning desire on Wagner's part to "set up a memorial to this fairest of all dreams." Somebody else was also behind his need: Mathilde Wesendonck.

Wagner's love for Mathilde was his second—and main—inspiration for writing *Tristan.* His feelings for her were seeking an outlet; they persistently demanded to be translated into art, and the claim grew violent. To stress this point does not necessarily make one guilty of crudely ascribing all works of art to specific events in the artist's life. During the period in question Wagner's favorite reading material consisted of Goethe's *Werther* and *Elective Affinities,* as well as dramas by Calderón depicting the conflict between honor and courtly codes of behavior. (All these books were shared with Mathilde.) There is no accounting for the way that imagination and everyday reality, abstract vision and intuitive experience, interact within the creative soul. But it was Wagner's passion for Mathilde that inspired *Tristan,* an opera intoxicated by passion almost to the point of depravity. That much will be evident to anyone who has ever felt this music's unprecedented depths and its power to illuminate fervent human emotion from every conceivable angle. To suppress evidence of Wagner's cardinal source of inspiration may be the clever thing to do, but there are countless signs of its vitality, above all from Wagner's own pen. His letters to Mathilde offer moving and often disturbing proof of the great passion that released so much creative energy within him. They provide a perfect example of the inseparable link between private experience and a public—that is, artistic—confession.[30]

No witness could have been closer to events than Minna Wagner. She can certainly be accused of failing to appreciate the immense genius of her unruly and often insufferable spouse. Yet it would hardly be fair to say that she was merely imagining a connection between Mathilde and *Tristan.* Minna left Zurich in September 1858, "noisily, with dire consequences," according to Wagner. On 15 December she wrote to Johann Jakob Sulzer, a family friend, from Dresden: "The performance of *Tristan und Isolde* is due to take place under W[agner]'s personal supervision in Karlsruhe next Easter. He wants me to go there and join him on his travels, but I shan't—I want nothing to do with the success of this opera which I can't stand anyway, as I know what caused it. The text is appalling: the passion in it is almost indecent. Later on I can perhaps send you a copy, and then you can say I'm an evil-minded woman" (Fehr II, 149). In reality Minna was not evil-minded but pitiable— and besides, she had good reason to feel embarrassed. It should also be added that the passion of the music far outstrips the libretto in "indecency."

Finally we come to Wagner's third incentive for writing *Tristan,* one that shows a comic side: his perennial eagerness for cash. He wanted not only to express his emotional upheavals in art but also to make a living from doing so, and a comfortable one at that. In his letter to Liszt he had written of the "sincere and heartfelt longing for death: complete unconsciousness, total non-being, the vanishing of all dreams—the purest final release." But this philosophy prevented neither Schopenhauer nor Wagner from welcoming what the world had to offer with open arms and doing his best to enjoy it. Thus

30. See Wapnewski 1978b, pp. 32–36, and also Wapnewski 1981, pp. 124–149. For my attempt to show the links between Wagner's personal experience, his understanding of Goethe's *Faust,* and his debt to Schopenhauer, see Wapnewski 1984.

Wagner seriously pursued what now seems the weird idea of exploiting *Tristan*—a quite "practicable work," he thought—as a money-maker. He planned to dedicate an Italian version to Dom Pedro, the emperor of Brazil, fondly imagining that he could thus earn enough to keep the wolf from the door for a time.[31] Before he had actually written a single note of *Tristan,* he was already discussing ideas for staging it with his old Dresden friend Eduard Devrient, now the director of the Karlsruhe theater.

The story of Tristan and Isolde as Wagner saw it depicted a victory over the material things of this world so as to achieve a complete independence from personal wants and enter a state of insensible nothingness (nirvana). The aim was to fuse subject (ego) and object (world) to the point where "I, myself, am the world"—the sublimation expressed in Isolde's final "unbewusst—höchste Lust" (unconscious—supreme bliss). Wagner was recreating Schopenhauer's somber ideal of transcendence for the sake of the purest personal happiness in a transfigured Beyond. This makes *Tristan* the most intimate and personal of all Wagner's tragedies, an ecstatic act of total internalization. But given the eloquence with which the opera rejects the world and society (and in this respect it is radically outward-looking), *Tristan* is also a fierce critique of a society so constituted as to exclude the possibility of personal happiness. This was a rebellious and indeed revolutionary idea. Far from being a modern one, however, it is inherent in the *Tristan* epic. Gottfried von Strassburg was already beating down the walls of medieval stability and a closed, dogmatic society.

Action and Characters

Of all Wagner's dramas *Tristan* is the most rigorous—one could also say the boldest—in structure. The way in which Wagner lopped off the ramifications of the medieval epic shows his mastery of dramatic design. Leading up to Tristan's story is that of his parents, Rivalin and Blanchefleur, whose "tristful" fate determines their son's. Wagner presents this aspect of the tale entirely in flashbacks. He also leaves out the colorful events of the second part, concerning Tristan's separation from Isolde, his marriage to a second Isolde, and his mortal wound, which is incurred by accident. The drama is pared down to the core, to the story of two lovers and their impossible love—impossible because political and social circumstances forbid it. What society requires is a settlement between the warring kingdoms of Ireland and Cornwall by means of an alliance between the two ruling houses. Adultery in this context is a shocking crime in the sight of both God and man.

Love is the subject and moving spirit of Wagner's *Tristan.* The flame is lit aboard ship, where Tristan is escorting Isolde to his king, on whose behalf he has wooed her. The rest of the opera is static; all the action is internalized.

---

31. See Wagner's letter to Liszt of 28 June 1857. The same plan is described in more detail in ML 548.

This is what Wagner meant by the term "Eine Handlung" (literally a plot or an action) on the title page of the printed orchestral and vocal score. His aim, as Carl Dahlhaus defines it, was to surprise us with his use of words: one is brought up short and reminded of the original meaning of the hackneyed term *drama*. Thus he gives us to understand that in *Tristan* the all-important inner drama has been stripped of any encrustation produced by outward drama, by the bustle of events (Dahlhaus 1979, p. 65).

The cast and the settings of *Tristan* are as simple as the form. With regard to the cast, two principals are responsible for—indeed *are*—the action. Tristan and Isolde entirely dominate the stage. Brangäne and Kurwenal are supporting figures in the dramatic tradition of the confidante and nurse, on the one hand, and the friend and vassal, on the other. King Marke is remote from the rest and stands alone as the drama's victim. Wagner thus presents us with a triangle, a prototype of that stock device of domestic comedy. The remaining characters are walk-ons. Even Melot is used merely to engineer the crisis through his act of betrayal in the crucial scene depicting the discovery of the lovers and Tristan's deliberate (and delayed) suicide.

The structure and the settings have an archaic simplicity to match. Act 1: The Ship. Act 2: Garden of Marke's Castle. Act 3: Tristan's Courtyard. Each of these settings is related to the internal situation: (1) the couple fall in love; (2) their love becomes a reality; (3) *Liebestod* (which does not mean the death of love or death through love but death for the sake of love, in the sense that it is carried into infinity).

Wagner's most inspired touch as a dramatist, however, is his handling of the love potion. In the oldest versions of the story the potion serves to excuse the lovers' strange and infamous behavior. Because of the drug they have no will of their own and are therefore blameless.

The way that Gottfried von Strassburg dealt with this device is of some significance. Like others before him, he treats the episode as an accident. Isolde has been given the potion by her anxious mother so that bride and groom may be magically united after their nuptials. When Tristan and Isolde ask for something to drink, a maid carelessly pours them the magic potion instead of wine. Gottfried's forerunners, like Hans Sachs after him, regarded the story as a simple case of poisoning (see Wapnewski 1978a, pp. 39ff.). The subtle and sophisticated Gottfried, by contrast, seized on the theme as a dramatic symbol. He makes it clear that the pair are already in love before they become aware of the fact; they are, as the saying goes, meant for each other from the start. With Gottfried the purpose of the love potion is to advance visibly what is already happening secretly in the lovers' hearts.

Delving much deeper still, Wagner gives a strong moral and philosophical twist to the story. Isolde's thoughts are dominated by her unhappy perception that matters have reached an impasse. Accordingly she displays the attitude of a classical heroine. Tristan adopts her monumental composure. They "drink atonement." Isolde has ordered Brangäne to fetch a lethal poison from the medicine chest, and Tristan understands at once:

Well known to me
Is Ireland's queen
And all her mighty
Wond'rous art.
The balm she gave me
Eased my pain:
The cup that now I take
Will cure my hurt completely . . .
Oblivion's healing draught,
I drink it all to you!

Here, already, is the idea of a *Liebestod*. Tristan drinks, and Isolde wrests the cup from his hands: "Betrayed once more? / Half to me now!" Since they cannot live together, they want to die together.

Brangäne, however, has substituted the love potion for the deadly poison. She appears to be playing the role of fate, yet in reality she is only fate's puppet. By giving the couple the love potion, she is leading them toward their destiny and absolving them of blame once and for all. Both were intent on dying. Now they go on "living" in a great fervor of love with its attendant guilt and intrigue, deceptions and crimes. But they are not really living out this love so much as living through it, being far away in spirit. Finally, in dramatic slow motion, they are overtaken by the death they have long since chosen, and it carries them off to their proper sphere: the world of night, the mothers, the safety of nothingness, unconscious eternity, the Beyond.

Die Meistersinger von Nürnberg

"Whoever can feel perplexed at the proximity of *Tristan* and the *Meistersinger* has failed to understand the life and nature of all truly great Germans on an important point: he does not know upon what basis alone that uniquely *German cheerfulness* exhibited by Luther, Beethoven and Wagner can grow, a kind of cheerfulness which other nations completely fail to understand and which contemporary Germans themselves appear to have lost" (Nietzsche 1983, pp. 232–233).

By contrast with Nietzsche in the fourth of his *Untimely Meditations,* Carl Dahlhaus has called *Die Meistersinger* "the brainchild of an untrustworthy sense of humour" (Dahlhaus 1979, p. 65). The two views are not incompatible. Dahlhaus is warning us not to misjudge what first appears to be popular merrymaking, and not to regard the brawling and trickery as a humorous element. The good-natured soul of the German nation conceals a predilection for force and violence; and, as Dahlhaus perceives, Wagner incorporated it in this opera. What Nietzsche had in mind was something different. He was delving right to the foundations of *Die Meistersinger.* (Wagner had termed it a "comic" opera in his first prose draft of 1845, and a "grand comic" opera in the second of 1861; these adjectives were deleted when the opera had its premiere in 1868; see WWV, p. 483.) Nietzsche was not primarily concerned with the cheerful side at all: it was the *grounds* for cheerfulness that mattered. His crucial insight was that the only people able to recognize these grounds would be those "who have suffered profoundly from life and return to it with, as it were, the smile of convalescents."

Die Meistersinger had its foundations in *Tristan*. Derived from the suffering that life brings, the cheerfulness signals a recovery. Besides coming one after the other, the two operas share certain features. Of Wagner's major works only *Tristan* and *Meistersinger* are devoid of gods and demons, "white" and "black" goblins, giants and gnomes, flower maidens and magicians. In other words, they contain no mythical characters. True, there is still an element of myth in both of them, but this element is represented by human beings, and extremely human ones at that. In *Die Meistersinger* they have biblical names: Eva, Hans (from Johannes, or John), David, and Magdalena. The names in *Tristan* derive from the distant twilight of primitive Celtic myth: Drostan and Essylt and Mark. Moreover, both operas are based on the theme of forbidden love. They vibrate with the underlying tensions that an overt or suppressed eroticism produces. *Die Meistersinger* provides the answer—the humanly possible answer—to the open question with which the world-negating tragedy of *Tristan* concludes.

The two operas also have another feature in common: several of the main characters have suffered early bereavement. Tristan's father died before he was born, and his mother died in childbirth. Marke took him into his affectionate care and was willing to forgo marriage and progeny for his nephew's sake. Walther von Stolzing, too, though still a young man, has evidently lost his parents (a fate he shares with most of the heroes of Wagner's operas). Evchen is motherless, and she takes refuge from her father's patriarchal authority ("A child obeys and is not heard," act 2, scene 2) in an erotically tinged relationship with a substitute father, the childless widower Hans Sachs. In his own way Stolzing also becomes attached to Sachs.

The vital difference between the two operas can be summed up from the perspective of a heightened potential for intimate personal experience: whereas Tristan and Isolde renounce the world for their love's sake, Hans Sachs renounces love for the world's sake—that is, for the sake of his own particular world, the world of art.

Realism in Die Meistersinger

It can truthfully be said that *Meistersinger* is Wagner's most down-to-earth work, for it gets by without any divine or superhuman characters. It is the only one of Wagner's operas to have a traditional happy ending (we may have our doubts with regard to *Parsifal*). Only in *Die Meistersinger* do two lovers attain a happiness that is more than fleeting. Senta, Elisabeth, Elsa, Sieglinde, Brünnhilde, Isolde, and Kundry are all doomed to die.[32] But Evchen survives:

---

32. The same applies to Irene in *Rienzi*. *Das Liebesverbot* and *Die Feen* do not affect the validity of this point.

surrounded by the crowd, she finally joins with Stolzing in looking forward to being happily married.

It is also true to say that the sturdy realism of *Meistersinger* owes something to its realistic historical setting and relative closeness to the modern age (the historical Hans Sachs lived from 1494 to 1576). In that sense it is Wagner's most modern drama. But there can still be demons even if none are listed in the cast of characters, getting up to their tricks inside the doublets, jerkins, and bodices of the human dramatis personae. *Die Meistersinger* amounts to more than the expressions of jovial delight that are conventionally assigned to its characters.

Models and Genesis

During his Marienbad holiday in July 1845 Wagner became creatively occupied not only with Wolfram von Eschenbach and Lohengrin but also with the mastersingers (though not with *Tristan,* as we have seen). At the time he was also studying the *History of German Literature* by Georg Gottfried Gervinus, published in five volumes between 1835 and 1840. Although he had started it out of intellectual curiosity, he was inspired "by a few remarks" in the work to dash off a prose sketch for a drama (ML 303). Chances are, however, that Wagner was not previously unfamiliar with the subject of Hans Sachs and the mastersingers. He already knew the historical novella *Meister Martin der Küfner und seine Gesellen* by his favorite writer, E. T. A. Hoffmann (who in 1820 had included it in the cycle *Die Serapionsbrüder*). He also knew Lortzing's opera *Hans Sachs* (1840) and its literary model, a dramatic poem of the same title by the Viennese court dramatist Johann Ludwig Deinhardstein. This feeble but successful play was first performed in 1827 (see Wapnewski 1978a, pp. 51ff.).

Wagner later gave the first prose sketch for *Meistersinger* to Mathilde Wesendonck. It already included some of the elements of the final version, but not—and this has a major bearing on the opera's foundation—the theme of the love between Sachs and Evchen.

For sixteen years the project lay dormant. Then, after reaching act 2 of *Siegfried* in his *Ring* cycle and writing *Tristan,* Wagner was impelled to carry it out. The year 1861 marked the start of his series of agonized demands for money from the publisher Schott; this correspondence was to drag on for years. In November 1861 a Titian Madonna, the *Assunta dei Frari,* which Wagner saw in Venice, had a surprising effect on him: "I decided to write *Die Meistersinger,*" he states in his autobiography. Precisely because of the apparent incongruity between the painting and the opera, the link between them merits close attention. It will shed some crucial light on the essence of the opera, which was to be anything but comic in the end.

The event in Venice gave rise to the second prose draft, and also to Wagner's first sketches for the music. *My Life* mentions his return journey by train to Vienna: "During this journey I first thought of the musical treatment of *Die Meistersinger,* the poem for which I had retained in my mind only in its earliest form; I conceived the main part of the overture in C major with the greatest clarity" (ML 668).

In Vienna he set to work at once, loyally assisted by Peter Cornelius (Wagner always found people to help him and exploited them to the point of ruthlessness). Above all, he needed information on the doctrine, system, and practices of the historical mastersingers. His main source was *Von der Meister-Singer Holdseligen Kunst,* a famous book by the Altdorf professor Johann Christoph Wagenseil. Published in 1697, it was a kind of scholarly summing up of this urban, middle-class art, which endured for a long time but soon grew set in its ways. Here again, one marvels at Wagner's skill in digesting a subject so complex that even experts can master it only after long and laborious study. His genius extended to the learning of new subjects—a gift, of course, whose real merit lies in the artistic process of assimilation, translation, and re-creation. Sitting in dingy taverns, Wagner jotted down the names, techniques, and terminology and the original words and melodies of the mastersingers. Subsequently he wrote the whole libretto for *Meistersinger* in the Hôtel Voltaire in Paris, between December 1861 and 25 January 1862. Because the contents steered clear of historical accretions and mythological models, the language acquired a new freedom.

Until King Ludwig came to his rescue, the years 1862 to 1864 were a period of terrible uneasiness for Wagner. Money was scarce; he had worries about his health; and his travels were merely attempts to escape from his troubles. He set up house in Penzing near Vienna, again on a lavish scale, and recklessly ran up debts. From Penzing he wrote to Mathilde on 28 June 1863: "Were I now to say that a master needs his rest, I'd have to declare right away that *I* get no peace, and what's worse, probably never will. That's the ugly situation, and I now realize it: I'm getting no peace. I'm shunning other people, conditions, any kind of contact—utterly so, because basically everything's a torture—that's simply the way I'm made!"

Despite his rescue by Ludwig, Wagner soon had to leave Munich again. Public opinion was to blame—or, rather, the way Wagner was riding roughshod over that public with his extravagant demands and behavior. He finished the first act of *Die Meistersinger* in Geneva on 23 March 1866. The second act was completed in Tribschen on Lake Lucerne 6 September 1866; and on 24 October 1867 Wagner finished the whole opera "at eight in the evening," as he wrote on the score. A telegram he sent to Bülow is graphic proof of how far he identified himself with his creation: "The last C written this evening on the stroke of 8. Please join in quiet celebration. Sachs."

The premiere was given in Munich on 21 June 1868, two evenings before Midsummer's Eve. It was a huge success for Wagner and certainly ranks with the early triumph he had with *Rienzi.* Contrary to all tradition and etiquette, King Ludwig invited his protégé into the royal box and allowed him to acknowledge the public ovation from the balcony, a sensational event in itself. From that moment on *Die Meistersinger* began to establish itself in the minds of Wagner's compatriots as *the* German festival opera. Not even the disastrous Berlin premiere on 1 April 1870 was to alter that fact.

External Drama

The characters in this German festival opera, and the situations they find themselves in, are traditional in type. The principal pair of lovers, Stolzing and Eva, are paralleled by a buffo couple, David and Magdalena. There is also a jealous rival, and a wise mediator and peacemaker. Finally, since the opera calls for a chorus, there are "the people," as they are usually called.

The dramatic action seems equally straightforward. It shows the coming together of two lovers—a process which, as we all know, is often uncertain in life, and always in opera. The young hero is at loggerheads with prevailing customs; this is reflected in his failure to observe the rules for the master song. The father of Evchen, the girl whom the hero loves, appears to have placed her beyond his reach by offering her—most reprehensibly—to the winner of the mastersingers' contest. Beckmesser, the rival suitor, is a virtuoso in the officially approved style and thus seems assured of success. Events are impelled toward a climax. What cannot be won on the prescribed terms must be taken by subterfuge. Stolzing and Evchen, being game for anything, plan to elope by night in the accepted traditions of opera and knight-errantry. The plan is thwarted by the unexpected tumult arising out of the private actions of the three central characters and the person who is guiding them. Accompanied by the cobbler-poet's merciless hammering, Beckmesser's serenade under Eva's window stirs up all the aggressive feelings simmering in "dear old Nuremberg" and whips the crowd into a frenzy. The scent of the *Flieder* (which could mean "lilac" but here clearly means "elder") combines with the sound of Beckmesser's lute to lay bare the secret unrest. A wild, barbaric uproar ensues, setting every man against his fellows. Here—and this too is peculiarly German—we see an embarrassing affinity between the idyll and the atrocity, between order and anarchy. The situation alters more suddenly than the observer can take in. The momentary raging of all these unleashed passions is reproduced musically in the strict form of a fugue.

The hubbub quickly dies down. As though from a different world the contrasting note of the Night Watchman's horn rings out, and we hear his "Praise ye God the Lord!" The only characters left on the stage are a battered Beckmesser and a pair of lovers who have been saved from their own folly.

Things subsequently go well for the lovers, but at someone else's expense, and with the aid of intrigue. The jovial poet Hans Sachs lures Beckmesser into a trap by leaving a copy of a song lying around for him to find and letting him take it as an authentic composition by Sachs. The besotted Beckmesser—his thrashing by the crowd seems to have affected his brain as much as his limbs—thinks that with this unexpected gift he will be sure to win the forthcoming contest. In fact he will make a pitiable fool of himself with it, for the song is really a sample of Stolzing's art, whose newness has been a source of surprise and fascination to Sachs. Since the intellectual Beckmesser is the servant—indeed the slave—of a tradition, this song will be beyond his grasp, and hence his powers as an interpreter.

Sachs has done his work well. Beckmesser proceeds to make complete nonsense of the puzzling lyrics with his ridiculous paraphrases, and his performance is a fiasco. This gives Stolzing (whose name, incidentally, implies pride) his opportunity. His is an art that draws on ancient sources: Walther von der Vogelweide was "the Master who taught me." But at the same time he is striking out in a new direction, breaking the rigid pattern of the bar form (AAB) with superlative skill. Stolzing can now freely display this art, and he is also free to woo Evchen. But the finale is devoted not to an agreeable apotheosis of love but to the "spirit of the people" as embodied by Sachs. In his closing address he eloquently extols the people and the realm, decrying foreign flimflam and alien influences. For him, however, even the Holy Roman Empire in all its splendor is second to "holy German art," with its claim to immortality. This final scene belongs to Sachs. It climaxes in a radiant C major: "Hail, Sachs . . . Nuremberg's poet Sachs!" *Die Meistersinger* began with a chorale to John the Baptist; it ends with a hymn to John, or Hans, the Poet.

And what of Beckmesser? He too used to be cherished by the people of Nuremberg, and he does after all hold the important office of town clerk (which puts him in a unique position among all these master craftsmen). In his stage direction Wagner dismisses him: "He rushes away in fury and is lost in the crowd." Beckmesser disappears from the picture, unless the stage director rescues him, and significantly, modern directors have repeatedly ventured to do this. There is a complementary relationship between the traditionalist and the innovator, the intellectual and the artist, the loner and the popular favorite. But we can also look at him another way. Beckmesser cuts an altogether tragic figure—the only one in this supposedly comic opera. He has paid for the others' final rejoicing with his personal misfortune. Yet he neither meant nor did any harm. It was Evchen's wealthy and influential father, Pogner, who encouraged Beckmesser to regard himself as his future son-in-law and to compete for the prize: "Be well assured of my good favour" (act 1, scene 3). As is well known, Wagner originally conceived the Beckmesser character as a satire of the Viennese scholar Eduard Hanslick, who was his leading critic. For his part, Hanslick was wise enough to give this particular opera a moderately good review. Again one is reminded of Dahlhaus' phrase "the brainchild of an untrustworthy sense of humour."

Wagner may have been amusing himself at somebody else's expense, but it is for other qualities that this great opera is chiefly renowned. On German soil, at least, its fame was enhanced by the deep, rich note of national feeling in Sachs's lengthy address—a sentiment that is not so easy to stomach in an age that has grown chary of patriotic declarations. One should not, of course, overlook the fact that the main emphasis is on German art rather than on

nationalistic power and glory. "Then may depart / the holy Roman state, / We have at home / our sacred German art!"

Die Meistersinger is indeed a German work. But before we start to fret about such expressions of ceremonious self-esteem, let us be clear about the eminently democratic slant that Wagner gave his drama. Deinhardstein's play ends, embarrassingly, with a great scene in praise of the monarch, thereby dubiously deferring to a servile tradition of court theater. Wagner turned this ending firmly on its head: the people are now cheering a hero who is a personification of themselves. And Sachs in turn redirects the plaudits to the masters of art—German masters, to be sure, and German art (see Wapnewski 1978a, p. 53).

Wagner, though the king's protégé, was never a courtier or servant. He voiced his staunchly democratic outlook with astonishing assurance in a letter to King Ludwig of 11 December 1866: "Oh, who could say what it means to be a German king! Look around you, dear friend, look at your footling royal household, that welfare organization for a ramshackle, useless and unmanly nobility; take a good look at this callous display they strive to keep up, this once-fashionable copy of the court of Louis XIV."

Because the king was so susceptible to his music, Wagner boldly attempted time and again to influence him in political matters as well—which did neither of them any good. From the angle of Wagner's own political perceptions, the official sentiments expressed by Hans Sachs were well founded. Sachs was clearly speaking for a powerful contemporary movement that was tired of petty states and longed for national unity. And it must be remembered that music (especially the music of Verdi and the Slavonic composers) played an important role in the course of the nineteenth-century nationalist movements. Yet *Meistersinger* came within an inch of avoiding this cheerful nationalistic bias. The finale is another example of Cosima's influence, and again it was not wholly harmless. For in the end, Wagner had been of the opinion that the opera should close with Stolzing's Prize Song, and he had been tempted to cut the speech he had written for Sachs. As Cosima wrote to King Ludwig:

> He thought the drama would be complete with Walther's poem and that Sachs' great speech, being more of an author's speech to the audience, were best left out as an irrelevance. At this I pulled such a doleful face, adding that Walther's refusal of official honours was very much a part of his character, that he thought again, although naturally he still had his own viewpoint. The matter gave him no rest in the night: he rewrote the stanza, cutting what I'd suggested, and also pencilled in a draft of the music.[33]

This episode occurred on the night before 28 January 1867. It shows that originally Wagner was more concerned with the inner drama than with the outward expression of an ideological stance.

33. Original text in Eckart 1929, pp. 333–334. According to Otto Strobel (König-Briefe II, p. 110) the date of the letter is 31 January 1867. [Ed.]

Apart from the first and last pieces in the *Ring* cycle, *Meistersinger* is the only one of Wagner's major operas not to be named after its hero (or, in *Die Walküre,* after the central figure). One would have expected it to be called *Hans Sachs,* or, to avoid duplicating Lortzing's title, *The Mastersinger of Nuremberg,* for the leading lights of the guilds are too limited to serve as heroes of the drama, either subliminally or overtly. Whatever Wagner's reason for the camouflage, *Die Meistersinger* is the drama of Hans Sachs. It tells of his self-denial and inner victory. Overestimations of the opera's popular, humorous, and burlesque features stem mainly from a failure to perceive its true core; for this Wagner's listeners have been more to blame than he himself was.

Internal Drama

The action of *Die Meistersinger* is motivated by three basic forces. First, Wagner was dramatizing the confrontation between two eras (in which respect he came very close to the contemporary tragedies of Hebbel, although Hebbel was not a writer he admired). We are witnessing a clash between medievalism and the modern age. We have, on the one hand, the feudal world of a knightly class that has had its day but is still ruled by the pride of rank, and on the other the world of a self-aware, increasingly settled bourgeoisie. This latter class was especially assiduous in adapting the art that the nobility used to engage in, mastersinging being a sequel to the aristocratic *Minnesang.* The clash is reflected and harmoniously resolved in Stolzing's love for Eva: the marriage between the impoverished knight and the wealthy goldsmith's daughter marks the wedding of two epochs. In fact we may view the opera in an even wider historical context. It can be said to chart the transformation of the medieval world's unity and religious order—the Holy Roman Empire—into the secular, bourgeois nation-state of the modern era.

The opera's second underlying impulse is linked with the first, one that, although a universal problem, had acquired specific meaning for Wagner. This was the conflict between old and new art, tradition and modernity, discipline and freedom. Hence the opera embraces the perennial battle between the artist and society (which had been one of the themes of Wagner's Romantic operas—notably *Tannhäuser* but the others as well). The figure of Hans Sachs towers over this conflict, bestriding the two camps as the "spirit of the people in its latest artistically productive form," to quote from Wagner's *Communication to My Friends* of 1851. But what was meant by the "spirit of the people"? This rather hazy vision derived from Romantic aesthetics and its doctrine of the creative artist, a doctrine strongly influenced by the Brothers Grimm. Here Wagner outdoes himself in dialectical dramaturgy. While representing a vanquished *social* reality, Stolzing stands at the same time for a triumphant *artistic* reality, the rise of the new art. On the social plane the bourgeoisie is taking over from the nobility. Bourgeois art, however, is being supplanted by a nobility, part old and part new, of the artist stationed outside society.

(But, in another dialectical twist, this artist harks back to Walther von der Vogelweide.)

Third and last, *Die Meistersinger* can be properly understood only if—as Nietzsche exhorts—we view it as complementing *Tristan*. The opera is about renunciation. All that keeps it from plunging into the murky abyss of tragedy is its hero's rational switch from the personal to the universal—that is, the act of self-denial whereby a private need is converted into artistic achievement. Only the self-denying Hans Sachs can, in the role of the representative artist, become the people's hero.

But is it Sachs we are talking about? No, we are actually talking about Wagner. In *Tristan* he depicted the absolute claims of love and the lover's absolute destiny, things that necessarily transcend this world. Through Hans Sachs he shows how the personal renunciation of love can lead one to redirect one's efforts outward, into the world. *Die Meistersinger* is the artistic product and expression of a lover's resignation. It marks Wagner's victory over his love for Mathilde Wesendonck. This reading of the opera is confirmed by any number of striking proofs, especially the composer's own statements. Some six weeks after meeting and again parting from Mathilde in Venice, he wrote to her from Paris on 21 December 1861: "The return trip from Venice to Vienna was a pretty long one: for two whole nights and a day I was stuck helplessly between Once and Now, and so it got pretty dismal. I had to have some fresh work, or else—I was done for!" This work "was a life-saver, just as the beginning of madness can be one's salvation!" A few days later Wagner wrote: "Only now am I completely resigned." For only a "victory over all wishing and desiring" can conclude the "immense struggles we went through," as he had already confided to his beloved during the Zurich period.[34]

In the summer of the first Bayreuth Festival, Wagner was to conceive a burning passion for Judith Mendès-Gautier (this love would again be reflected dialectically in his work on *Parsifal,* with its purity cult). In 1868 he wrote to Judith from Lucerne, explaining the meaning of the "little orchestral piece," namely, the prelude to act 3 of *Die Meistersinger:* "To be sure, the first motif in the strings has already been heard in the second act, during the third stanza of the Cobbling Song. There it expressed the sorrow of a resigned man who's showing the world a cheerful, vigorous countenance. Eva had grasped this hidden lament and, deeply saddened, she wanted to flee so as to avoid hearing any more of this seemingly happy song. This motif is now sounded on its own and develops in intensity before finally fading away with a resigned melancholy." And then—for "I can make music do this"—the orchestra depicts the switch from the intimate and personal sphere to the external world of public life and the poet's mission. "But at the same time, as if from far

34. For a detailed discussion and further evidence, see Wapnewski 1978b, pp. 103ff.

away, the horns give out the solemn air with which Hans Sachs once hailed Luther and the Reformation, and which earned the poet a unique popularity."

A couple of sentences further on we read: "The first motif for the full strings returns once more and expresses the vehement and beneficial emotion of a soul deeply stirred. The motif grows calm, ebbs away, and then rises to the supreme ecstasy of a mild and blessed resignation."[35]

Sachs is not afraid of sharing the fate (the *Glück,* or fortune) of King Marke. He does not renounce love in order to avoid that fate, although one could easily assume so from the famous passage quoting *Tristan* in the fourth scene of act 3. Here Evchen, captivated by her new fortune, confesses to Sachs: "And if my soul gave voice, / And were my heart my own; / Then thou would'st be my choice, / The prize thine alone!" To which Sachs replies: "My child, / Of Tristan and Isolde, / A grievous tale I know: / Hans Sachs was wise and would not / Endure King Marke's woe." And the orchestra quotes the Tristan motif of infinite yearning.

Sachs is still a young man (Franz Betz was thirty-three when he sang the role in the first performance of *Die Meistersinger*). Nonetheless, he has become firmly convinced that this *Glück,* this fortune or misfortune, is not for him. His own "grievous tale" concerns the pain of renunciation and the agonized self-conquest that are part of the artist's mission; at all events that was how Wagner saw it. In that sense the figures of Hans Sachs and Beckmesser correspond to each other. Both have to find their true selves by dismissing love, and both must transform this imposed or self-imposed denial into an effort to live. Amid the jostling crowd in the finale nobody is more alone than these men, though the one has been raised up and the other cast down.

Heavenly Love

For Wagner the Virgin Mary symbolized a love that abjures earthly bliss. As I have noted, Wagner decided—without stopping to explain himself—"to write *Die Meistersinger*" the moment he saw Titian's Madonna in Venice. What accounts for this curious decision is the meaning this image had long held for him in the context of renunciation. On 10 September 1842 he had written about his *Tannhäuser* plans to Ernst Benedikt Kietz, a painter friend in Paris. He had been with Minna to Bohemia, and "in the parish church of Aussig I asked to see the Madonna by Carlo Dolci: the picture gave me enormous pleasure, & if Tannhäuser had seen it, I'd have fully understood how he came to turn from Venus to Mary, without being gripped by any great piety."[36]

It is beside the point that the painting was not an original Dolci, as everyone up till then (including Goethe) had supposed, but a copy of Ismael Mengs. The crucial point is that this comment contains the key to Wagner's response to the Titian *Assunta* in Venice. He saw the Madonna's portrait as an image

35. Schuh 1936, pp. 102–106. Original French text in Guichard 1964.
36. On this statement and the remarks that follow, see Wapnewski 1978b, pp. 103ff.

of heavenly love. It represented the transcending of earthly love, a transfiguration achieved through painful self-denial. Hans Sachs presents a self-denying variation on Tristan, a variant released to go on living on the earth. Just as the sacrifice of the purest of women (Elisabeth) leads Tannhäuser to heavenly love, so Wagner—not without sacrificing Mathilde—leads the Tristan within himself to renunciation in the form of Hans Sachs's existence. In his own life Wagner could not go the way of Tristan; this was his only alternative.

In the letter of 10 April 1860 to Mathilde from Paris, Wagner started to explain the devilish, visually outlandish and antique yet nonclassical goings-on in his new version of the Venusberg (*Tannhäuser,* act 1). But how did he address Mathilde? "Don't be surprised," Wagner wrote, "at finding this in a letter to Elisabeth." Mathilde was now his Elisabeth, virginal, Madonna-like, his companion on the road to resignation.

It is thus no longer surprising that the first sketch for *Die Meistersinger,* written in July 1845, contains no hint of love between Eva and Sachs. Only after Wagner's affair with Mathilde could the theme come into the drama. And Wagner bade it farewell in the seraphic quintet in which Sachs, all on his own and no longer a part of the group, sings: "To this lovely child I long / Now to sing of gladness, / But must hide my heart's sweet pain / Hide my tender sadness. / Such a wondrous evening dream; / Dare I think what it may mean?"

Now that it has been dreamed, one is allowed to flirt with that dream. Although the hero is renouncing love, he is still entitled to love, albeit of a different kind. "Keep your heart firmly barred against Sachs: you're going to fall in love with him!" Thus Wagner to Mathilde in a message from Paris at the end of December 1861.[37]

Sacred Festival Drama: *Parsifal*

In a passage from *My Life,* referring to April 1857, Wagner wrote:

> Beautiful spring weather now set in; on Good Friday I awoke to find the sun shining brightly into this house for the first time: the garden was blooming, and the birds singing, and at last I could sit out on the parapeted terrace of the little dwelling and enjoy the longed-for tranquillity that seemed so fraught with promise. Filled with this sentiment, I suddenly said to myself that this was Good Friday and recalled how meaningful this had seemed to me in Wolfram's *Parzival.* Ever since that stay in Marienbad, where I had conceived *Die Meistersinger* and

---

37. Wapnewski 1978b, p. 109. Incidentally, there could be some substance in the notion that *Der Rosenkavalier* was modeled on *Die Meistersinger,* if we bear in mind how well Strauss and Hofmannsthal knew Wagner's operas. At the center of each work is a mature figure who carefully and selflessly guides the course of events. Both the Marschallin and Sachs lead the young person they love to his or her "real" partner—Rofrano to Sophie and Eva to Stolzing. In each case a rival suitor opposes the union with the encouragement of the prospective father-in-law. And although acting in good faith, Ochs and Beckmesser are both reduced to figures of fun as a result of some dubious machinations.

Lohengrin, I had not taken another look at that poem; now its ideality came to me in overwhelming form, and from the idea of Good Friday I quickly sketched out an entire drama in three acts. (ML 547)

Here again Wagner was dramatizing his own feelings, with an unerring flair for atmosphere. If we check the dates, we find that in 1857 Good Friday fell on 10 April, whereas the Wagners did not move into their "refuge" until 28 April. So Wagner's account of his inspiration is a fictitious one, but one which has added to the spiritual aura of sublime ritual that has always surrounded *Parsifal.* The composer himself knew the facts of the matter, and he must have been aware of them long before Cosima noted in a diary entry for 22 April 1879: "R. today recalled the impression which inspired his 'Good Friday Music'; he laughs, saying that he had thought to himself, 'In fact it is all as far-fetched as my love affairs, for it was not Good Friday at all—just a pleasant mood in Nature which made me think, "This is how a Good Friday ought to be."'"

How farfetched the love affairs were is an open question. But at all events, Wagner had surrounded his conception of *Parsifal* with this imagined legendary aura so that the time and the subject could neatly coincide.

Once again the material underwent a long period of incubation before coming to fruition. The image of Parzival had already become vivid to him during the unhappy Paris year of 1842, the time of his encounter with Tannhäuser and the Grail themes associated with *Lohengrin.*[38] This impression was greatly enhanced by his reading during the Marienbad summer holiday in 1845—Gervinus' *History of Literature,* Görres' *Lohengrin* edition, and the works of Wolfram von Eschenbach. There matters rested until that April day in Zurich in 1857. Having finished *Die Walküre,* Wagner was at work on *Siegfried,* and *Tristan* was already bidding for attention. Under Schopenhauer's influence he was planning a Buddhist drama of renunciation, *Die Sieger* (The Victors). It was now that he drafted a "hastily sketched" outline of *Parsifal.* This draft is missing (it may not be altogether perverse to wonder if it ever actually existed).

A further incubation period ensued. On 29–30 May 1859, in the middle of composing act 3 of *Tristan,* Wagner wrote a long letter to Mathilde Wesendonck. In it he launched into a penetrating critique of Wolfram von Eschenbach and his *Parzival,* examined from both a poetic and a dramatic standpoint. His criticism of the medieval epic was as unjust as it was acute; had it been Wolfram's aim to write poetry like Wagner's, the critique might have had a

---

38. As far as the spelling is concerned, Wagner always uses Parzifal (or Parcival) up to 14 March 1877. On that date Cosima noted in her diary: "And his name will be Parsifal." The blame for this incorrect spelling rests with Görres, who had discovered the Arabic formulation *fal parsi* (meaning "pure fool") and confused it with a German name. In differentiating between the two versions, I use Parzival for Wolfram's hero and Parsifal for Wagner's.

certain validity.[39] After this the subject again lay dormant, although it continued to crop up at intervals. Cosima's *Brown Book* includes this entry for 3
September 1865: "What a wonderful thing—the king is passionately keen to
hear about Parzival." In fact it was no great wonder, since Wagner had written
a detailed prose draft between 27 and 30 August 1865 (reproduced in SW 30,
pp. 68–77). King Ludwig would have known of it, and on 5 September he
thanked Wagner effusively for the draft he had received. Subsequently they
exchanged letters on the subject. By its very nature it was one that offered
plenty of scope for fantasizing—either in mythical and romantic terms or in
a sentimental and homoerotic vein.

Still the incubation period went on. Meanwhile, Wagner's life was one of
turmoil. He had to seek refuge in Switzerland again, in Geneva and Tribschen.
Major events included the first performance of *Die Meistersinger* (21 June 1868),
his marriage to Cosima (25 August 1870), the laying of the foundation stone
of the Bayreuth Festival Theater (22 May 1872), and the completion of the
Ring (21 November 1874). The first Bayreuth Festival took place in August
1876, and shortly afterward, in September, Wagner set off for Italy, where he
found his model for the temple of the Grail: Siena Cathedral. Then in Sorrento
on 26 November he parted for good from his dear friend Nietzsche; in the
future Nietzsche was to feel a mixture of love and hatred for him. They could
no longer be close.

In her diary Cosima records Wagner's saying to her on 25 January 1877: "I
am going to begin *Parzival* and shan't let it out of my sight until it is finished."
As usual he wrote the text in a very short space of time, in March and April
1877. Then he started work on the music. Cosima heard "a few of the first
notes" on 2 August, according to her diary. Wagner's labors filled the years
1878 to 1880. He "discovered" Klingsor's magic garden in Ravello above the
Bay of Naples on 26 May 1880 while visiting the Palazzo Rufulo. On 13
January 1882 he orchestrated the cryptic, celestial final words, "Redemption
to the Redeemer," thus completing the opera.

The publisher Schott acquired *Parsifal* for the vast sum of 100,000 gold
marks. The sacred festival drama had its premiere in Bayreuth on 26 July
1882 and took up the second festival, receiving sixteen performances. It was
a great success, although a controversy arose over the applause, which has
had tiresome consequences right up to the present. There is a myth that
Wagner considered silence to be the only suitable reaction to act 1. This myth
clearly stems from a clumsy moment at the premiere when he seemed to be
gesturing for the applause to stop but was in fact trying to prevent the singers
from taking a curtain call.

The final performance ended in a way that was deeply moving for everyone
involved. During the Transformation music in the third act, Wagner took

39. For a discussion of this and the next several points, see Wapnewski 1978b, pp. 201–268.

over the baton from his conductor, Hermann Levi, and conducted the remainder of the opera himself. Six months later he was dead.

The thirty-year embargo on productions outside Bayreuth expired in 1913. Since then, opera houses all over the world have been able to include *Parsifal* in their repertory. Wagner was firmly against this, but the work itself has certainly benefited.

Wolfram's Poem and Wagner's Drama

The dramaturgic thinking behind *Parsifal* evolved from Wagner's long letter of 29–30 May 1859 to Mathilde Wesendonck. Just as he had done when recasting his literary model for *Tristan,* Wagner adopted a thoroughly radical approach. He simplified and compressed the 25,000 lines of Wolfram's poem, converting its linear, epic technique into a tightly knit structure in which the settings and dramatic situations were made either to correspond to or to contrast with one another. In this way the confusing ramifications of the story of the Grail became, if not transparently clear, at any rate comprehensible. The traditional versions included those by Wolfram and his own model, Chrestien de Troyes; the legend of the platter from the Last Supper in which Joseph of Arimathea caught the blood of the crucified Christ; and the story of Longinus' spear, with which the Savior's side was pierced by the Roman soldier. Wagner's crucial dramatic invention, however, is the figure of Kundry. Showing all his old ingenuity, he presents Kundry as a woman torn in two and condemned to live on two different levels. On the one hand, she is reluctantly serving the Grail to expiate her sin; on the other, she is subservient to the wizard Klingsor. Terrorized by his sorcery, she must practice her deadly arts of seduction on the knights of the Grail, playing the part of a decoy and a whore.

Wagner left out the preliminary events in Wolfram's account: the story of Parzival's parents, Gahmuret and Herzeloyde, which is one of love, adventure, and premature death. He also omitted Wolfram's elaborate treatment of Gawan (Gawain), the heroic soldier and lover who is both a reflection of Parzival and his antithesis. The opera's action begins with Parsifal's first visit to the Grail kingdom. The necessary background details are supplied by the loyal Gurnemanz, a typically talkative old man. Wagner took this character from Wolfram, but he gave him a completely new function. And, as he so often did, he posits a rather improbable ignorance on the part of certain characters in order to impart information to his audience. It is in this way that we learn of the two opposing kingdoms. One, the Grail kingdom, is called Monsalvat, and its location appears to be a mountainous area of northern Spain. The other kingdom centers on the magic castle of Klingsor (whose ambition it was to be a knight of the Grail, and who castrated himself to conquer sensual desire). We are to imagine this castle as facing Moorish Spain. The Grail kingdom is in serious danger because Amfortas, the king and chief priest who guards the holy spear and platter, has been mortally injured. While doing battle with Klingsor, he succumbed to the lure of Kundry, and his opponent wounded him with his own spear. The Grail vessel is now unguarded, Klingsor has the holy spear, and Amfortas feels infinitely weary. But according to a prophecy he may expect the arrival of a healer, savior, and successor made "knowing through pity, the holy fool."

Parsifal duly enters the sacred realm, whereupon he proves his foolishness. In his boyish fondness for sport, he kills a swan, the symbol of fidelity. When questioned, he is unable to say who he is or where he comes from. Being a child of nature, he does not acknowledge any moral code. Thus, when Kundry tells him that his mother is dead, his first response is alarm, and he instinctively makes to attack his informant, the "restlessly nervous maid." But Gurnemanz begins to suspect that this fool is a holy one, possibly even the promised savior. So, accompanied by the powerful tone painting of the Transformation music, he escorts Parsifal to the Gralsburg, the Grail castle. "I hardly walk," sings Parsifal, "yet seem to have gone quite far." Gurnemanz replies with a profound aphorism: "You see, my son, that here time turns to space." Despite his Saxon rationalism, Wagner did not bother to give a cogent explanation for fusing these basic concepts. Cosima records him as commenting on 21 December 1877: "Today I composed a philosophical maxim: 'here space becomes time.'"

The tormented king is forced by his old father, Titurel, and his knights into an agonized celebration of the Grail's bloody ritual. The pallid company is succored by the transubstantiation of Christ's blood and body, and this moves Parsifal deeply. Understandably, however, the youth is left speechless. He cannot take the sacrament, and so he is driven out. The old man offers some parting advice: "Yet hark to Gurnemanz: / Hereafter do not go after our swans. / Just seek, foolish gander, a goose!"

But that is not what Parsifal has in mind. In Wolfram's poem there follows a series of exploits along the lines of Arthurian romance. These are meant to illustrate the boy's knightly prowess, and Wolfram recounts them one after another. The point is that Parzival is made to realize his unwitting sinfulness: when out on his horse, he brought about his mother's death, and then he sought to win Arthur's favor by recklessly slaying a distinguished knight, who was moreover a relative (the theme of Cain and Abel). Although he did these things by accident, he was guilty of acting blindly and has thus removed himself from God's sight (*haz gein gote,* in Middle High German). Eventually Trevrizent, a grandson of Titurel, leads him to God and to his own true self. Wagner's approach is fundamentally different. For him, the young man's heroic deeds as a knight can be taken as read. It was, he thought, more important to provide the dramatic interplay which Wolfram's epic inherently lacks. Wolfram's Parzival has no serious adversary or antagonist: all he has to contend with are jousting knights—and, of course, himself. Wagner provides his Parsifal with an opponent.

His logical starting point was the story's nucleus: the infirm king of the Grail. Amfortas has been wounded by the opposing ruler, Klingsor (who plays only a fleeting part in Wolfram's poem). Klingsor's power has increased to a dangerous extent since he seized the holy spear, and with the connivance of Kundry, who wickedly seduced the lords of the Grail. With Wolfram this episode is merely incidental; nobody blames the king for having been injured in a *Minnekampf,* or love contest, by a heathen with a poisoned spear. At the time he was seeking to win the gorgeous Orgeluse, whose alluring features Wagner transfers to his Kundry. (The Kundrîe of Wolfram's poem represents the bizarre, exotic Grail messenger.)

The effective dynamism behind Wagner's drama derives from the opposition of Amfortas with Klingsor and Amfortas with Kundry. This antagonism has had dreadful results, and it logically follows from the situation that they can be remedied only by someone who faces the same danger as the stricken king. Nor is that impossible, for the danger still exists.

Parsifal gains entry to the evil sorcerer's realm. With a mighty oath Klingsor resorts to his strongest weapon: Kundry. She is obliged to obey, for Klingsor can no longer be seduced in his maimed state, and hence she has no hold over him. Moreover he knows her secret—the fact that, like the legendary Wandering Jew, she once mocked the Savior bearing his cross and is now condemned to wander forever. In an initial test Parsifal resists the blandishments of the sparkling Flower Maidens. By calling his name, Kundry leads him to his innermost self ("only music can do it," said the composer of this moment in the drama). Running the whole gamut of erotic emotion, the scene reaches the peak of audacity with Kundry's gift of his mother's "final blessing and farewell" to Parsifal: "She gives you love's first kiss."

As a temptress Kundry uses the most subtly refined of psychological tools in masterly fashion. She deliberately evokes Parsifal's mother to exploit her chance of his falling in love with her. Here, quite rightly, Wagner's commentators have marveled once again at his ability to reveal the soul's hidden depths, and at his anticipation of concepts that Freud was the first to bring to our attention.

Kundry's kiss marks the turning point in the drama. The fervor of it gives Parsifal a glimpse of the "love that torments," but also of Amfortas' wound. The knowledge hits him like a thunderclap. He now comprehends not love but sorrow: "The spear-wound! the spear-wound! / A burning pain in my heart. / Oh, sorrow! sorrow! / Terrible torture! / A cry of anguish wells from this heart." Hitherto no more than a "pure fool," Parsifal becomes wise through pity at this point. He realizes that he has failed the anguished king, whose lament he did not grasp. "And I, the fool, the coward, / to wild and childish actions hurried on!" Kundry does not understand the words: "O valiant knight! cast off your spell! / Look up! and love the one who loves!" But her wiles are in vain. Parsifal has grasped the terrible lesson of Amfortas: "She kissed away the salvation of his soul!" Wildly he thrusts the gleaming temptress away from him: "You sorceress! out of my sight! / Leave me, ever be gone!" At this, "very passionately," she abruptly shrinks back within herself, repeating her damnable story and basing her hope of salvation on being united with Parsifal in love. Indeed, Kundry wants this union even at the cost of being rejected forever by "God and the world." Suspecting that, contrary to her intentions, her kiss has made Parsifal "all-seeing," she renews her efforts to seduce him, but his one thought is to reach Amfortas. "Have pity on me!" she begs ("Were you just one hour mine! / Were I just one hour yours!") and curses him furiously when he again forcibly thrusts her away. This is the cue for Klingsor to enter. He hurls the spear at the spiritually awakened hero, and it remains in the air over his head. Seizing hold of it, Parsifal exorcises the spell, and Klingsor's illusory splendor crumbles to dust. Parsifal leaves.

"You know where you can find me once again" are his parting words in act 2. Kundry does indeed know. She wakes from a deep sleep in a meadow bedecked with early spring flowers "in the Grail kingdom." Gurnemanz enters and immediately notices that she is now a different person. Gurnemanz has grown truly old, for in his longing for death Amfortas has refused to administer the Grail sacrament, denying his subjects its life-giving power. By so doing he has killed his father: Titurel has died, "human like everyone."

A knight enters in full armor, disturbing the sanctity of Good Friday. Both Gurnemanz and Kundry recognize him as the young man who killed the swan. When Gurnemanz recognizes as well the holy spear the knight carries, the old man, deeply moved, grasps the divine miracle: the savior has come. While Kundry—reminiscent of Mary Magdalene—washes Parsifal's feet, Gurnemanz sprinkles water from the sacred stream over his head. "Thus was it all predicted," he sings. "My blessing on your head: / I greet you as our sovereign."

Not yet crowned in public but already conscious of his new title, Parsifal bends toward Kundry. In the role of priest he grants her that deliverance which, misguidedly, she was ardently seeking by other means. "I thus perform my first of tasks: / be now baptized, / believe in the Redeemer!" Acting as his servant, Gurnemanz now escorts Parsifal to the Grail, again to the accompaniment of the tersely condensed Transformation music. There they meet Titurel's funeral procession. In a suicidal frenzy Amfortas calls upon his knights to plunge their swords into his body "to the hilt." Parsifal intervenes: "One weapon only serves: / thus the spear which / gave the wound heals the wound." Amfortas is now "whole, forgiven and absolved," and the holy spear is reunited with the vessel. Assuming his royal office, Parsifal waves the Grail in blessing over his new kingdom, whereupon Kundry sinks lifeless to the ground. Die she must, for her immortal existence was derived from a curse. Her baptism has removed that curse, but it must also take her life, since now she too is "human like everyone."

"Everyone" sings the final words of the drama, in a chorus mystically echoing far into the distance, beyond the domed hall and the Grail kingdom: "Highest healing's wonder! / Redemption to the Redeemer!"

A Troubling Purity

In a very specific and also dubious way, Wagner's *Parsifal* is an altogether personal work. This applies in the first place to the powerful reshaping of the traditional material—although that feature is of course typical of Wagner's whole output. But his Kundry, for instance, can only be described as a highly original and fascinating creation. She commutes between the two kingdoms without realizing it, involuntarily helping to destroy the powers of darkness. She leads a double life as both a demonic temptress and a humble penitent, as "archetype of the sinner who is condemned to wander restlessly and stands in need of salvation" (Floros 1982, p. 31). There is no doubt that her characterization was a stroke of genius. By her own account Kundry is a Jewess. That point is particularly fascinating in view of Wagner's militant anti-Semitism, for Thomas Mann was surely right in describing her as one of the strongest figures, and poetically one of the boldest, ever conceived by Wagner (Mann 1985, p. 98). She is also among the most sexually attractive. Significantly, Wagner confessed to Cosima that what he really wanted in the stage production was for Kundry to be "lying there naked, like a Venus by Titian" (CT, 4 January 1881). This tells us, among other things, that as a spiritual mentor, Titian led Wagner into very disparate worlds. The composer also succeeded admirably in constructing this divided and yet consistent character from three different figures in Wolfram's poem, Orgelûse, Sigûne, and Kundrîe. To these, moreover, he added the biblical component of Mary Magdalene.[40]

The attribute of knowledge through pity whereby Parsifal achieves his messianic calling is another original idea on Wagner's part. Though a Christian one, this feature is not as marked in the Parzival of medieval Christianity (who was more concerned with "knowingly" coming to terms with himself and his sinful condition, and hence with making his peace with God). The Christian element is also seen in the resemblance of the suffering Amfortas to the suffering Christ, and again in Parsifal's resemblance to Christ as a savior.[41]

It is this Christian element that makes *Parsifal* a troubling work, and one that has attracted much censure and controversy. Nietzsche launched the first attack ("Wagner as the Apostle of Chastity," in Nietzsche 1910, p. 70):

> Is this the German way?
> Comes this low bleating forth from German hearts?
> Should Teutons, sin repenting, lash themselves,
> Or spread their palms with priestly unctuousness,
> Exalt their feelings with the censer's fumes,
> And cower and quake and bend the trembling knee,
> And with a sickly sweetness plead a prayer?
> Then ogle nuns, and ring the Ave-bell,
> And thus with morbid fervour outdo heaven?

40. Floros 1982, pp. 53–57, makes the highly interesting discovery that Frank Wedekind devised his Lulu as a female counterpart to Wagner's Parsifal and conceived the plays *Erdgeist* (1895) and *Büchse der Pandora* (1904) "as a kind of anti-*Parsifal*."

41. See Wapnewski 1978b, pp. 230ff., 246ff., 250ff. On Wagner's own special philosophy of compassion, and its role in a Schopenhauer-based philosophy, see Wapnewski 1984.

> Is this the German way?
> Beware, yet are you free, yet your own Lords.
> What yonder lures is Rome, Rome's faith sung without words!

To answer Nietzsche's question more briefly than it warrants, no, this is not the German way. But that is no real criticism of the opera. And it is doubtful that Wagner was speaking for Rome. What he gives us in *Parsifal* is rather his own private religion, a religion which is provocative by dint of its very singularity. The troubling core of it is the equation of human purity with sexual asceticism. The messianic state is associated with an immunity to carnal temptation, and sexual desire is associated with sin. One proves one's nobility by resisting sensual urges.

Nietzsche's diatribe was right inasmuch as a Pauline Christianity, with all its ruinous consequences, dominates the morality of *Parsifal*. It is ascetic in outlook, opposed to the senses, and misogynistic. Exploring the typical case of a character involved in sensual indulgence and sexual debauchery, and the possibility of extricating him from it, is well worth a dramatist's time and effort. But *Parsifal* does not deal with that theme; it does not present a Doctor Faustus' progress from sinfulness to transfiguration. Parsifal is not even a fallible character. Rather he is a young man without qualities acting solely as a catalyst for the qualities of others. In this way he enables Amfortas and Kundry to be restored to their former state of innocence.

In its hostility to the senses and to women, *Parsifal* is a profoundly inhuman spectacle, glorifying a barren masculine world whose ideals are a combination of militarism and monasticism. But its dramaturgic structure is admirable, and the music amazing. Even the fiercest critics of Wagner as a person have paid tribute to the music of *Parsifal*—from Hanslick (who liked the Flower Maidens) and Nietzsche to Debussy and Adorno.

A Passion and a Passion Play

The drama's ceremony and its fanaticism derive from aspects of the composer's own soul and nature. This point is easily established; what is harder to explain is just why this is so.

As I argued in my discussion of *Tannhäuser* under the heading "The Duality Principle," *Tannhäuser* and *Parsifal* are complementary. Each turns on the unresolved—and perhaps insoluble—problem of the conflict between the claims of sensual love on the one hand and moral requirements, religious laws, and social codes on the other. For Wagner this was a very personal problem. One cannot emphasize too strongly the remarkable fact that underlying and stimulating all his work on *Parsifal* was his love for a woman. Though certainly not the deepest love of his life, it was possibly the most ardent. It was an elderly man's passion, and it had all the touching, poignant, perhaps even ridiculous features usually associated with such an obsession.

Born in 1846, Judith Gautier was the daughter of the writer Théophile Gautier; she herself had literary ambitions. The wife of the author Catulle

Mendès, she had been engaged in friendly social intercourse with Wagner and Cosima since 1869. Her contemporaries agree in describing her as a classic beauty. That she must have possessed a refined erotic appeal is confirmed by her nickname, "the Whirlwind." In 1876, aged just thirty and already divorced for two years, she went to the first Bayreuth Festival. The "Whirlwind" took hold of Wagner, disturbing and tantalizing him. Some of his letters to her which have been preserved are written in a touchingly labored French. His intermediary was a close friend, the surgeon Schnappauf (the name, reminiscent of *Meistersinger,* adds to the operatic flavor of the affair). In the fervor of their language these letters leave us in no doubt as to the incandescence of the passion that gripped Wagner. Later on, when writing to Judith in Paris, he repeatedly asked to be sent luxurious fabrics, cosmetics, and perfumes: these articles were meant to remind him of her physical presence. This correspondence went on for a year and a half, and then, very suddenly, it stopped. Evidently Cosima had found out about it, for Wagner broke it off with a request that any future letters be sent in care of his wife. The request, dated 10 February 1878, thus concluded a series of letters full of references to kisses and embraces, passion and longing. Wagner was prepared to give in. But does such a passion just stop? Two days later Cosima noted in her diary: "The sorrow I was dreading didn't pass me by; it burst in from outside. God help me!"

The amorous pair had parted company in September 1876. Wagner wrote the text for *Parsifal* in March and April 1877, and simultaneously his passionate letters to Judith. In December 1877 he sent her the libretto. During November he confessed to her: "Je me sens aimé, et j'aime. Enfin, je fais la musique du Parsifal." A stage play about the suppression of the senses was rescuing him from a personal drama of sensual desire. Wagner had already sent Judith a musical excerpt; one wonders whether this reflects an ingenuity of the most frivolous sort, or an astonishing naiveté regarding his own frame of mind and what lay behind the gesture. What he sent was the text and music of the passage "Take my body and eat," thereby suggesting a parallel between the mystery of the Eucharist—the transformation of matter into the most sacred substance—and the ardent physical surrender of sensual love.

The last love letter bears the date 6 February. "My dear beloved," it reads, "I have finished the first act." Wagner goes on to say: "Why in heaven's name didn't I find you after *Tannhäuser* flopped in Paris? Were you too young at the time? Let's keep silent, silent! But let's be loving, loving! Your Richard" (again the association of *Tannhäuser* with *Parsifal*). Four days later he wrote his farewell letter.

One suspects that Wagner always suffered in a sense from Amfortas' wound. That is, he was never able to tame the sexual urge in accordance with socially approved norms or integrate it into his love affairs, marriages, and life generally. Minna, Jessie Laussot(-Taylor), Mathilde Wesendonck, Mathilde Maier, Friederike Meyer: all these relationships, and others as well, suggest a tormenting sense of incompleteness, with significant consequences.

Finally there was Judith, the femme fatale. It was clearly she who inspired the iridescent colors and glittering charms of Wagner's Kundry, the character possessing the sensuality of a naked Venus by Titian. To ask whether her own motivation for the affair was love or simply a careless vanity would be beside the point.

"Learn the meaning of love": the author and composer of those words knew what love meant and worked it into his sacred drama. In order to tame and chastise the strongest of all urges, and to guard against its destructive potential, Wagner conjured up a purification exercise. Through an emotional celebration of Christian ritual, with its repressive laws, he was staging a masochistic ceremony of self-punishment. *Parsifal* was an attempt to overcome the Klingsor, the Kundry inside all of us. One can extend the idea to Wagner's entire oeuvre: all his operas portray an attempt to come to terms with personal guilt. If personal failings cannot be eradicated, at least we can try to live with them on a higher, artistic level and to proceed from darkness toward enlightenment.[42]

Egon Voss quotes an Indian epigram which Cosima noted in her diary on 28 January 1876: "He who produces beautiful works throughout his life has conquered sensuality." In this connection Voss sees *Parsifal* "as the composer's attempt to transfigure his own deeply internalized guilt feelings." He describes the music of the opera as basically expressing the "torment of love"—an expression above all of pain and sorrow caused by the guilty conviction that sensual desires are ignoble. "To that extent *Parsifal*—whose music is assuredly of more general interest nowadays than the libretto—is not so much a statement or glorification of bourgeois Christian sexual morality as a disturbing testimony to its consequences. *Parsifal* is a tragedy" (Voss 1984, p. 18).

Wagner's artistic farewell to the world ends with the equivocal and much-debated phrase "Redemption to the Redeemer!" This could be taken as a factual reference to Parsifal, who henceforth will be demonstrating his redeemed state by bestowing redemption. Or it could be supposed to mean that he must now seek his own salvation, and that of his fellow knights, in a reconstituted Grail community that will abandon a barren masculine self-sufficiency. But the phrase can also be related to Christ.

In 1878 Wagner published an essay, *Public and Popularity*, in the first volume of the *Bayreuther Blätter*. This is less a statement of aesthetic principles than a voluble invective against his disloyal friend Nietzsche, whose aphoristic essays *Human, All Too Human* appeared the same year. In the third part of his invective Wagner turns to theological matters and takes issue with the Jewish origin of the Christian God. "To regard the God of our Saviour as deriving from the Israelites' tribal god is one of the most terrible mistakes in history; every period has paid for that mistake, and the price we are paying today is the increasingly overt atheism of both our crudest thinkers and our finest."

---

42. This account is closely based on the final chapter of Wapnewski 1981, pp. 173–191. For the original French text of Wagner's letters to Judith, see Guichard 1964.

Further on we read: "Critics will go on regarding the God whom Jesus revealed to us with suspicion, because they always feel obliged to take Him for the Jehovah who created the world of the Jews!" And: "Is it utterly beyond the theologians to take a big step forward by granting theology its indisputable truth, through delivering up Jehovah, while also granting the Christian world its purely revealed God in the form of Jesus, the one and only?" (SSD X, 86–88).

This is irrational, emotionally charged rhetoric. It aspires to a Christianity which is not all too human but "purely" human—that is, non-Semitic—and which interested Wagner for ideological reasons, for he was not a religious man. It was in that spirit that he quoted Schopenhauer, as we read in this extract from Cosima's diary (26 July 1878): "Yes, Schop[enhauer] and others have already spoken about the misfortune that Christianity was propped up on Judaism, but nobody has yet said, 'That is God!'"

This statement is as hazy as Wagner's other theorizings frequently are. But it is clear what Cosima saw as the basic hypothesis of his essay, which, she noted on 25 July 1878, "is no more an article than the *Kaisermarsch* is a march!" How, then, did she interpret these propositions? "'Redemption to the Redeemer,' I say to R., 'that is the motto for this concluding article.'"

If Cosima was right in her reading of the opera's cryptic final message, its meaning would be plain at last. Jesus, the Christian God and Savior, himself needs to be saved from the legacy of his Jewish descent. This is a reading with which Hartmut Zelinsky agrees.[43] But Wagner's own reaction to it is crucial to our inquiry. If that was his meaning, one would expect him to have confirmed it promptly. Wagner's actual response, though, was to say that his wife's idea was a "bold" one. However one paraphrases the sentence, it does not confirm Cosima's reading, but it does say roughly: there are many conceivable interpretations of the final gesture, and yours is a bright and unusual one.

The message's possible ultimate meaning has, however, been summed up by Mazzino Montinari:

> What was going on in Wagner's mind at the time was a final artistic shaping of the redemption myth, part *à la* Schopenhauer, part Buddhist and part Christian. But such redemption is only possible if one consciously clings to the metaphysical illusion. Consequently it lacks the spontaneity that comes of faith and amounts to an ideology, rather than myth. While resorting to every artistic device of mystification in order to create it, Wagner treats the so-called myth as a mere pretext and incentive for his "artefact." With *Parsifal* he was superseding all previous antithetical tendencies in his ideology and his false consciousness, including their "human, all too human" and *inhuman* elements (like antisemitism); for as an artist, Wagner could not be ultimately serious about those. All that remains is the existential core of the whole thing: the basic metaphysical propo-

43. See the chapter "Auseinandersetzungen um die Ideologie des 'Parsifal'" (Coming to terms with the ideology of "Parsifal"), in Csampai-Holland 1984, pp. 214–269. See particularly the cogent summary by Dahlhaus, pp. 262ff.

sition about the negation of the will and the denial of life—of something that is inherently sinful. Despite the music of *Parsifal,* which is immensely fascinating and of beguiling loveliness, one cannot get away from the fact that in this opera the whole German Romantic movement is seen in its most advanced, exhausted and decadent form. It is submitting totally to the yearning for death and for nothingness. (Montinari 1985, p. 16)

To some ears, however, the opera's enigmatic conclusion may also sound like the personal hope of Richard Wagner—the salvation of a miraculous artist who wanted to redeem himself and the world with his art.

Translated by Peter Palmer

Biography and Reception:
History, Ideology, Research

CHAPTER 2

Wagner's Place in the History of Music
CARL DAHLHAUS

A Historiographical Schema

A composer's place in the history of music is usually determined by noting the influences to which he was subjected until he reached the point of achieving what can be called a style of his own, and then by describing the influence he had on others. Thus, although there is hardly a historian who fails at least to mention interrelationships, music history takes three different forms. First, it provides a system of reference within which a composer finds his bearings (in the case of Wagner these references were, first, Weber and Marschner, then Auber, Bellini, and Donizetti, and Spontini and Meyerbeer). Second, it defines the process of internal development which a composer undergoes at the dictates of a personal inner law. Third, it acts as reception history, the context in which the composer's contemporaries and successors become acquainted with and absorb his work or various aspects of it. (The transition from Romantic opera to music drama, the "qualitative leap" between *Lohengrin* and *Das Rheingold,* and the origin of musical modernism in *Tristan,* a modernism that came into being at the same time as Baudelaire's *Fleurs du mal,* are aspects of Wagner's internal development that require special explanation.)

Although, generally speaking, this schema may appear to be problematic, it seems fairly unobjectionable in the case of Wagner. For it was precisely his career that formed the model from which the schema was first abstracted around 1900, at a time when music history was gradually becoming a discipline. Wagner's influence had then reached its peak, and historians were beginning to devise a pattern for studying the inner artistic biography of a composer by dividing it into the three phases: dependence on models, attainment of independence, and influence on others. (In his book on Mozart, Hermann Abert acknowledges the general influence of Italian opera, yet ignores Italian operas written in the 1780s. Virtually the only explanation for this fact is that he believed that from a certain point on, the work of a composer develops on its own, independently of what others are doing—an idea that takes its direction from Wagner but is not valid for Mozart.)

That the schema needs to be modified here and there even in the case of Wagner is irrefutable, though not of crucial importance. It is not difficult to hear in *Die Feen* foreshadowings of the style of the Romantic operas from *Holländer* to *Lohengrin,* foreshadowings which cannot be attributed solely to the influence of Weber and Marschner, and which became blurred in *Das Liebesverbot* and *Rienzi.* Nonetheless, it seems probable that in the 1850s Wagner was influenced by Liszt's *Symphonic Poems,* although by this time his originality as a composer was no longer in doubt, even if his contemporaries found it disconcerting.

The decisive factor, however, is the extent to which the history of composition is perceived in terms of the influence exerted on and emanating from a composer. If one decides to define Wagner's place in the development of music drama and the symphonic style in terms of the rival positions taken up in vastly different ways by Meyerbeer, Berlioz, Verdi, Gounod, Bizet, and Mussorgsky, the historiographical schema, with its bias toward biography, proves to be inadequate. The history of music in general, and the history of nineteenth-century music in particular, turns out to consist of events that are and yet are not simultaneous. (In view of the fact that music drama can be defined as symphonic opera, even its relation to the distinctive forms that the symphonic style assumed in other genres, from the symphonic poem to the symphonic cantata, is certainly not irrelevant to a historical portrayal of Wagner's oeuvre, or at any rate to one that goes beyond the factional strife between Wagnerians and Brahmsians.)

Opera and Instrumental Music

The most important musical influences of Wagner's youth were the symphonies of Beethoven. Later on, in the 1850s, he conceived of music drama as symphonic opera, and finally, after completing *Parsifal,* he expressed a wish to write only symphonies. In fact, when Wagner was born, music history had reached a stage that, in the minds of contemporaries, was characterized by the mutually exclusive contrast between German instrumental music and Italian and French opera. In the nineteenth century Italy had no instrumental music to speak of, and in Paris music existed merely in the form of the virtuoso piece. Conversely, German Romantic opera, in spite of the Paris success of Weber's *Freischütz* in 1824 in the guise of *Robin des Bois,* was not a European phenomenon but one confined by national boundaries. German music was largely synonymous with Beethoven's symphonies, which were championed with the same fervor in London by George Smart as in Paris by François-Antoine Habeneck, whose Conservatoire concerts excited Wagner's enthusiasm.

Wagner's music dramas were the first German operas—that is, operas rooted in the German language—which were destined to achieve European renown during the lifetime of the composer. (Handel was essentially an Italian composer; Gluck in his late works a Parisian, meaning a cosmopolitan, one; and Mozart's German operas were slow to gain acceptance in Italy and France.) Wagner's attempt to overcome the provincialism of German opera was halting at first, but eventually he achieved complete success. The hypothesis that this success occurred not in spite of but because of the symphonic style—a style that marked a profound difference between music drama and the traditions of French and Italian opera—is less paradoxical than it might at first seem. The symphonic element was after all the essence of what had been expected of German music since the time of Haydn and Beethoven.

As long as Wagner tried to conform to the main traditions of opera—the Italian in *Das Liebesverbot,* the French in *Rienzi*—he was stuck in the rut of provincialism. *Rienzi,* originally destined for Paris, was a triumph in Dresden in 1842, but this success had hardly any effect elsewhere (Hamburg in 1844, Königsberg in 1845, Berlin in 1847). Yet the aesthetic and historical significance of Wagner's music dramas was quickly recognized. (Wagner did not relish the term *music drama,* incidentally, although his objection to it was ignored.) In fact the importance of these works was acknowledged even when they were not performed, or where they were performed without apparent success as with *Tannhäuser* in Paris in 1861. This phenomenon is documented by the large number of both polemics and apologias his work excited. Despite Wagner's complaints about the hostility toward him, the apologias were very much in the majority.

The decisive factor, it seems, was the rigorous artistic claim that Wagner made for opera. (The fact that this was a striking venture in the history of ideas and institutions was the reason why so many French poets, who knew only a few short fragments of Wagner's music, became enthusiastic Wagnerians.) A Wagnerian music drama, like a Beethoven symphony, is a work of art, an inviolable text to be taken at its word and conveyed to the understanding of an audience capable of aesthetic contemplation by means of a staged interpretation that serves the work. By contrast, an Italian opera, for example by Rossini or even the early and middle Verdi, was nothing more than a blueprint for an evening in the theater, and the production succeeded or failed on those grounds alone. This attitude provided the rationale for the ruthless and, from a Wagnerian point of view, inartistic adaptation of operas to changing local tastes. The concept of a *work* in the strictest sense of the word—which Wagner inherited from the tradition of German instrumental music—did not exist in Italy until Verdi's late period. Then, after lengthy struggles, the composer, supported by his unassailable reputation, finally assumed control over the libretto and the staging of his operas.

In order to determine Wagner's place in the history of music, therefore, we must recognize that in technical and aesthetic terms music drama subsumed the symphonic style—the style that gave opera the character of a distinct work in its own right. Wagner's concept of art came from the poetic theory of the Weimar classical period, whose terms of reference were transferred to the aesthetics of music of the Viennese classical period, which in turn had developed in northern Germany. But the symphonic style that Wagner carried over into his music dramas had been characterized since Beethoven by a number of features, four of which stand out.

First, the theory of the symphony was based on the idea of the sublime, which, since the last third of the eighteenth century—the time of Edmund Burke and Immanuel Kant—had laid claim to a place next to the idea of the beautiful in the philosophy of art. (This theory was already present toward the end of the eighteenth century in Johann Georg Sulzer's influential *Allgemeine Theorie der schönen Künste* and appears in even more pronounced form in E. T. A. Hoffmann's Beethoven reviews of 1810, which document the origins of the Romantic aesthetic of music.)

Second, a symphony conceived in the spirit of Beethoven had to solve the problem of reconciling a monumentalism whose utopian audience was "humanity" (both as a mass and as the actual or at least ideally anticipated humanity of the individual) and a kind of thematic-motival complexity taken to extremes. This complexity tended to become esoteric, and as a result the work threatened to deteriorate into a text for initiates that was difficult to decipher on the one hand and became a façade for naive enthusiasts on the other.

Third, the cyclic cohesion of a symphony was guaranteed by thematic-motival links and associations enveloping the work like an overt or latent network, and no longer by the principle of balance that in the classical period had made movements that contrasted in tempo seem parts of a self-contained whole.

Fourth, in the aesthetic theory of the Romantic epoch, which took its direction from Beethoven (though not without a certain degree of misunderstanding), a symphony was of importance as an artwork of ideas precisely because it was an integral whole rather than mere program music. By detaching itself from clearly defined, mundane content and emotion it conveyed, as Wackenroder, Tieck, Hoffmann, and Schopenhauer believed, an idea of the absolute. As a form of language that was lifted above the language of words by its lack of concepts (rather than lagging behind because of a lack of clarity, as was thought in the eighteenth century), the symphony was an expression of the inexpressible, an "organon of philosophy" (Friedrich Schelling).

That Wagner's aesthetics proceeded not from the idea of the beautiful but from the idea of the sublime need not be demonstrated in painstaking detail. The mythological subject matter that he chose, like the symphonic style through which he sought to elicit an empathic (or, as Hanslick thought, pathological) emotional understanding of the scenic action, was characterized by the representation of the sublime, though sometimes in precarious relation to the Romantic principle of the characteristic and the interesting (Friedrich Schlegel). Furthermore, no one who can read a score would deny that the monumentalism that Wagner pushed to the limit in passages such as the

Vassals' Chorus in *Götterdämmerung* and the choruses of the Knights of the Grail in *Parsifal* is offset by an intricate tissue of motifs, a technique that prompted Nietzsche to make the seemingly paradoxical remark that Wagner was really a musical m niaturist. Yet the fatal habit of affixing labels to leitmotifs conceals this technique to an extent that has prevented due recognition of Wagner's art of "developing variation" (Arnold Schoenberg). By hearing how the Ring motif is transformed into the Valhalla motif in the orchestral interlude between the first and second scenes of *Das Rheingold* (and it is hardly possible *not* to hear the transition), we cannot fail to see that the assertion that the motifs are stuck together rather than evolving out of each other is a prejudice and a crude mistake. Wagner, however, did not merely adopt the Romantic method of linking motifs into a network as a way of bringing together the diverging movements of a symphony; he took the method to extremes. As his contemporaries put it, it became a system.

From 1854 on, Wagner began to absorb the Romantic metaphysics of instrumental music, or more precisely the version he found in the writings of Schopenhauer. At first sight, Schopenhauer's philosophy of music seems impossible to reconcile with music drama. Wagner circumvented the difficulty by declaring that drama, the stage action, was nothing less than "a musical deed made visible" (*On the Term "Musikdrama,"* 1872). What he meant was that, in the musical-scenic work of art, music represents the essence, whereas the text and the scenic action are merely "phenomenal." It is not that absolute music, the real object of Schopenhauer's aesthetics, keeps programmatic and scenic connotations at a distance, but that the "extramusical" forms the "exterior" while the music forms the "interior." It was this aspect of Schopenhauer's metaphysics that Wagner was able to adapt. Thus, the music does not illustrate the text and the stage action so much as the text and the stage action illustrate the music. For a listener who is completely immersed in the flow of the music, the sense of sight diminishes. As Wagner put it in his essay *Beethoven* (1870), the listener's visual faculties are eventually "deprived of their potency" *(depotenziert)*.

Operatic Traditions

Music history, if it is not to be narrowly nationalistic, must proceed from the fact that the dominant genres of opera in the early nineteenth century were *grand opéra, opéra comique,* and *opera seria* or *semiseria.* (The history of the *opera buffa* genre came to an end in 1816 with Rossini's *Barbiere di Siviglia.* Donizetti's *Don Pasquale* and Verdi's *Falstaff* were exceptional works.)

Wagner would have been the last to deny that he took his lead in *Das Liebesverbot* from opéra comique and opera semiseria, and in *Rienzi* from the grand opera of Spontini and Meyerbeer. Italian and French influences are unmistakable even in *Die Feen,* which is usually classified as a German Romantic opera. This categorization is not really remarkable, for the carefree mixture of styles that Robert Schumann bemoaned as musical "juste milieu" in the case of Heinrich Marschner had always been a feature of German Romantic opera, which was not in fact as German as it was made out to be by a nation that firmly asserted its cultural identity because it lacked a political one.

Thus it is not disputed that Wagner's early operas (to call them youthful works is an exaggeration that smacks of apology) are the typical products of a composing kapellmeister who made ready use of ideas from various quarters (and who, in this case, had a genuine talent for the theater), taking them to crass extremes by piling up all the available means. Yet it is questionable to what extent operatic convention continued to influence his works after *Holländer*, in which Wagner believed he had found himself as a composer and as a musical dramatist.

As we see in the case of *Tannhäuser*, music history can emphasize and highlight either the traditions from which a composer took his bearings or the innovations upon which he was embarked. Elisabeth's aria at the beginning of the second act can in fact be called an aria without doing it an injustice. The scene between Tannhäuser and Elisabeth is undoubtedly more of a duet than a musical dialogue. And in the finale of the second act Wagner, as later in *Lohengrin*, did not wish to forgo the *pezzo concertato* that had long since become a topos in Italian opera. Here, after a dramatic revelation, the surprise and tension provide a desired opportunity for a long, sustained cantabile that groups the characters into a living picture, a tableau vivant: the real time of the action seems expanded many times over.

It cannot be denied, however, that the difference between the division of an opera into musical numbers, to which form Wagner still adhered in *Holländer*, and the division into scenes, to which he progressed in *Tannhäuser*, signifies a qualitative leap in the formal history of the genre. It is not merely a superficial matter of nomenclature. That scenes were prefigured in the numbers of the earlier operas, and, conversely, that the outlines of numbers still shine through in the scenes of the later works, is difficult to deny. Nonetheless, it is not a good enough reason to challenge the historical fact that *Tannhäuser* marked a stage of development in which the dominance of the one principle yielded to that of the other.

It was hardly possible (except for adherents of the old Bayreuth orthodox view) to overlook the fact that Wagner had continued the dominant tradition of grand opera in *Lohengrin*. Even the musical form of *Götterdämmerung* bore clear traces that the text had been written decades earlier (*Siegfrieds Tod*, 1848). Still, the *Gesamtkunstwerk* that Wagner proclaimed in his writings around 1850 was less the result of a real operatic tradition than of a utopian one whose arena was not the stage but all of aesthetic theory. It would be shortsighted, however, to deny that the literary debate about opera in the form of "interpretive anticipation" of the stage works themselves is part of theatrical culture. Besides, an idea that after a long prior development finally makes music history is a piece of that history and not merely the dead past, even in its early manifestations, which may initially have seemed mere peripheral speculation. To a certain extent the *Ring* can indeed be seen as the result of an ideal operatic tradition of the late eighteenth and early nineteenth centuries.

The idea of the Gesamtkunstwerk assumed changing guises derived from the context of the history of ideas in the case of Herder, the early Romantics, and Hoffmann. It is endangered in two ways: either by being reduced to the trivial insight that in an opera music, language, staging, and scenic-mimetic action work together; or by being turned into an abstruse utopian vision through the claim that the individual arts are actually parts of what was originally a whole—in other words, that, separated from one another, they are nothing but fragments of their true selves. Wagner's historical myth—the reckless notion that Shakespeare's dramas and Beethoven's symphonies were incomplete artistic genres that needed to be supplemented and demanded salvation from their isolated existence in the wholeness of the music drama (*Opera and Drama*, 1851)—should be consigned to Hegel's "fury of disappearing" in the wake of controversies that were both persistent and superfluous. In the first place, the idea is empirically without substance. Second, it was not even representative of the spirit of the nineteenth century, except perhaps with regard to a certain megalomaniac streak. And third, it remained without discernible influence on the actual form of the music drama. The appropriate object of a worthwhile, empirically based debate—a debate that examines the palpable difficulties and their successful or unsuccessful solutions instead of clinging to speculations—would not be the fictitious "historical necessity" of subsuming the symphonies of Beethoven within the music drama. Rather, it would be something Wagner only hinted at: the aesthetic and technical possibility of utilizing fundamental categories of absolute instrumental music such as theme, elaboration, and development in music drama without loss of substance.

There is another feature complementing the historical construct which shows that Wagner's conception of the Gesamtkunstwerk differs quite fundamentally from the Romantic or pre-Romantic manifestations of the idea. This is the assertion, inspired by the philosophy of Ludwig Feuerbach, that the living human being forms (or should form) the center around which, in the music drama, the various interlocking arts group themselves. In terms of musical dramaturgy the claim is a problematic one. After 1854 Feuerbach's anthropology was subject to competition from Schopenhauer's metaphysics in Wagner's aesthetic thinking. He was never able to decide conclusively (the baldest example of this ambivalence being the Beethoven essay of 1870) whether it was the music metaphysically interpreted in the spirit of Schopenhauer or the singer-actor placed in the foreground on the lines of Feuerbach's anthropological destruction of metaphysics that constituted the substance of what was to be understood as drama. Wagner certainly felt that he was the legitimate and sole heir of Beethoven in channeling the history of the symphony into that of the symphonic opera. But he was also an "actor" and obsessed with the theater, a quality for which Nietzsche upbraided him. In aesthetic terms this meant that, although he appropriated Romantic metaphysics, originally a philosophy of absolute music, he was in tune with a realistic epoch that demanded immediacy. It was precisely this discord manifest in him that showed he was typical of the century against which he believed he was rebelling.

The Romantic and pre-Romantic idea of the Gesamtkunstwerk belongs to the development of theatrical culture, if not of opera, for it was an aesthetic theory that was historically influential. In the works of Wagner it was given a specific shape that owed its substance to a historical myth on the one hand and to an anthropology on the other. Yet it cannot be taken at face value and has to be decoded, so to speak, as a metaphor for unresolved problems. These are the difficulties that arise from Wagner's attempts to transfer the symphonic style to music drama, or symphonic opera, and at the same time to find an aesthetic compromise between the orchestral melody, in which, contrary to all operatic traditions, the musical substance was concentrated, and the performer, who inevitably attracts the primary attention of the audience. Here the philosophical hyperbole in Wagner's writings is of less importance than theatrical practice, from which the debate should take its bearings instead of drifting off into the realm of weltanschauung.

Romantic Opera as Idea and Genre

Holländer, Tannhäuser, and *Lohengrin,* and, in an anticipatory form, *Die Feen,* belong to a type of musical drama whose name, Romantic opera, suggests a clearly defined genre with a history of its own: a history that in Germany extends from Hoffmann's *Undine* (1816) and Louis Spohr's *Faust* (1816) to *Lohengrin* or even beyond, and whose outstanding representatives before Wagner are considered primarily to be Carl Maria von Weber and, at a slightly lower level, Heinrich Marschner.

The distinction between the genre of Romantic opera and Wagner's music dramas from *Das Rheingold* on can be demonstrated compellingly in terms of the history of composition, although Bayreuth tradition denied this. The leitmotif technique is the binding together of a music drama through a dense web of motivic connections from within. It differs so tremendously from the older method of citing reminiscence motifs at dramatically decisive moments (their aesthetic effect was doubtless significant, but their structural function was negligible) as to mark a caesura in the history of music itself. (The leitmotif technique was conceived originally in the 1850s with the particular preconditions of the *Ring* in mind. On the one hand, the motival web formed the necessary inner support for a composition in which the traditional melodic phrase and periodic structure had been destroyed by a language whose alliterative verse was merely prose, in terms of purely musical criteria. Wagner believed this language was made imperative by the Germanic myths on which the subject matter was based. On the other hand, leitmotifs that to all intents and purposes perform the dramaturgical function of reminiscence motifs are appropriate to an action in which an overwhelming past throws a continually waxing shadow on the scenic present. The fact that the leitmotif technique was then transferred to dramatic actions that, as in *Tristan* and *Parsifal,* are closer to those of *Lohengrin* than of the *Ring* should not lead us to minimize the difference between music drama and Romantic opera. In the late works the dramaturgy that corresponded to the leitmotif technique, whose basic trait is the continual presence of an oppressive past, was foisted on the literary subject matter or inferred to be an interpretive possibility.)

Despite the doubts of historians and theorists about the terms *Romantic opera* and *music drama,* it is justifiable to speak of both a prior and a subsequent history of Romantic opera: a prior history in the eighteenth century and a subsequent history around 1900 in the neo-Romantic style espoused by Hans Pfitzner. In the eighteenth century the Romantic element in opera was understood as being merely a feature of the libretto with no tangible effect on the music. But fin-de-siècle neo-Romanticism was indebted to Wagner to an extent that clearly suggests the concept of the epigone. (Pfitzner's opera *Der arme Heinrich* is a kind of variation on *Tannhäuser.*)

In the previous history of the genre, as represented, for example, by Paul Wranitzky's *Oberon* (1789), Romanticism—the miraculous, exotic, fairy-tale elements—remained restricted to the subject matter, never assuming musical shape. The problem for Romantic opera in the nineteenth century lay in the difficulty of defining the Romantic element in musical terms. In order to explain the rise of true Romantic opera, a genre that *Undine* and *Faust* represent only to a certain degree, we may proceed from the hypothesis that the musical realization of the Romantic aesthetic was based on features such as the characteristic, the striking, and the interesting, which Schlegel had used around 1800 to define the concept in literary theory. (In opera the musical rather than the literary manifestation of what Schlegel had postulated was crucial. From a literary point of view Friedrich Kind's libretto for *Der Freischütz* is trivial Romanticism. To quote Chateaubriand, it should not be reckoned to belong to the Romantic, which arises from a "sublime imagination," but rather to the mere Romanesque, which in the tradition of certain low eighteenth-century genres speculates with the attraction of miraculous, exotic, fairy-tale subject matter.)

Yet the musical realization of the aesthetic categories with which Schlegel defined what was modern in the early nineteenth century was not unproblematic, even in the Romantic operas whose stature no one denies. Weber sought the characteristic and interesting detail, the striking momentary effect, instead of the kind of unbroken melodic continuity that was considered the embodiment of the beautiful in music. Weber's method was felt to be a disunity of the musical structure and was criticized as such by Grillparzer, Hegel, and even the Weber enthusiast Wagner (*Opera and Drama,* 1851). The musical representation of the features that were miraculous or derived from gruesome legends—for example, the use of the Samiel motif in *Der Freischütz* to depict the supernatural element—presupposed nothing less than the emancipation of tone color. (It is not the harmony but the instrumentation that defines the Samiel motif.) This autonomy was persistently denied by nine-teenth-century music theory and aesthetics, despite Berlioz. Its mental repres-sion can indeed be construed as a sign of the profound significance of the step in the history of composition. (Even Gustav Mahler and Arnold Schoenberg still clung to the idea that color was merely incidental to the drawing of melodic and contrapuntal or melodic and harmonic part writing. In theory they were still paying tribute to a classicism which in compositional practice they had already left far behind.)

Thus the aesthetic idea of the Romantic was to all intents and purposes rendered in musical terms by characteristic, "disunited" melody and an eman-cipated use of tone color which defined and were independent of the structure of the part writing. This meant that they could determine neither the form nor the genre. Romantic opera as a genre does not exist, contrary to the historical prejudice mentioned earlier. From a formal and dramaturgical point of view *Der Freischütz* is a Singspiel (one might even say an opéra comique, at the risk of offending the nationalistic emotions that helped bring the work its triumph in 1821); *Euryanthe* is the failed attempt to develop by force a grand Romantic opera using the forms of the Singspiel and the elements of the Romantic tradition ("grand" meaning nothing more than through-com-posed, without spoken dialogue); and *Lohengrin* is a grand opera. *Lohengrin* can in fact be construed as the perfected manifestation of a pattern developed by Scribe and Meyerbeer in which affairs of state grow out of private actions and, in an exact dramaturgical analogy, large-scale choral and ensemble scenes evolve from arias and duets. Nonetheless, once it has been established that Romanticism in opera is not a clearly defined genre—not the embodiment of forms and how they are arranged, but an aesthetic idea and a set of features that can be rendered in different and even sharply diverging genres—then it can no longer be denied that Meyerbeer's *Robert le diable* is also a Romantic opera, although it is undoubtedly a grand opera. Features such as the Romantic or medieval and demonic character of the subject matter, the disunity of the melody which characterizes details, and the emancipatory tendency of tone color do not deny the work its place in the genre of grand opera. (The fact that Weber and Meyerbeer were both pupils of Abbé Vogler is more signifi-cant in terms of the history of composition than a historical account dictated by nationalistic feelings might admit, especially when such an account de-nounces the cosmopolitan element in Meyerbeer's music and denies its pres-ence in Weber's.)

Wagner, Beethoven, and the Tradition of the Symphonic Style

In 1851 Wagner proclaimed the end of the symphony in *Opera and Drama*, and in the same breath claimed that the tradition of the symphonic style as established by Beethoven had been subsumed within the music drama. His-torians who do not share the orthodox Bayreuth view have interpreted this as the arrogant presumption of an unscrupulous egocentric who unashamedly presented his own work to his astonished contemporaries as the culmination of the history of drama and of music, as the synthesis of Shakespeare and Beethoven. Yet Wagner's provocative claim must be taken more seriously in historical terms than it has been, except by the older Bayreuth circle, which has long been discredited as a sect. The claim expresses something, albeit in the distorted form of a historical myth, that seems as significant as it is paradoxical: the fact that no symphonies of note were written between 1850 and 1870, that is, between Schumann's Third Symphony and Bruckner's Second. Concurrently the symphonic style began to permeate other genres whose traditions had previously considered it a foreign element. Liszt transformed the concert overture into the symphonic poem, Henry Litolff the solo concerto into the *concert symphonique,* and Wagner opera into symphonic opera or music drama.

Wagner's transition from Romantic opera *(Lohengrin)* to music drama *(Das Rheingold)* was thus part of the historical process in music, occurring around 1850, in which the decline in importance of the symphony as a genre represented the obverse of an inexorable expansion of the symphonic style in other genres. The symphonic ambition was in turn the compositional and technical manifestation of an aesthetic claim: the claim that a work was "art" in the emphatic sense. The libretto and the score of the music drama were, as we have seen, supposed to be an inviolable text, the significance of which was conveyed to the public by an interpretation, rather than a flexible outline for a theatrical performance. Bayreuth was founded to ensure a fidelity to the work, which took its cue from this concept of the text as a "classic." Together with innovations such as the appropriation of the symphonic style, which was the outstanding historical manifestation of the classical period in music, this idea of the text was part and parcel of the claim that the theatrical work aspired to the status of art.

Throughout the nineteenth century Beethoven's symphonies constituted the paradigmatic realization of the symphonic idea. The history of the genre thus proceeded in a circumpolar (to use Theodor Kroyer's term) instead of a linear fashion. Brahms did not start where Schumann left off, and Bruckner did not begin where Schubert ended. Rather, Brahms and Bruckner bypassed Schumann and Schubert and referred directly to Beethoven. The symphonic idea was determined in both an exoteric and an esoteric way. In exoteric terms it was the sublime power of imagination. As early as the end of the eighteenth century Johann Abraham Peter Schulz, writing in Johann Georg Sulzer's *Allgemeine Theorie der schönen Künste,* had extolled this sublime power in the case of an Allegro movement of a symphony, which reminded him of a Pindaric ode. In esoteric terms it was a dense web of thematic-motivic relationships that, as Hoffmann put it in 1810 in his review of Beethoven's Fifth Symphony, provided a firm inner structure and thus held together a work from within (which, when heard casually, had the effect of an "inspired rhapsody") and constituted its aesthetic and technical unity.

Wagner enlarged the motivic network that encompassed single movements in the case of Beethoven, and whole groups of movements in certain Romantic symphonies by Berlioz, Mendelssohn, and Schumann. It became a system of leitmotifs that formed the inner structure of four music dramas and grew to assume proportions that were to all intents and purposes immeasurable. The sheer quantity of the approximately 120 motifs that Wagner needed to fill fifteen hours of orchestral melody signified, to put it in the language of Hegel, a qualitative leap in the evolution of the symphonic style. It is unclear, however, what the concept of musical or musical-dramatic coherence can mean in the face of the continual and often abrupt scenically or linguistically motivated alternation of motifs.

In an essay describing the composition of the *Ring* (*Report to the German Wagner Society*, 1871), Wagner remarked that the whole stock of motifs of the cycle had evolved from a few "malleable nature motifs" *(plastische Naturmotive)*. The remark is initially mystifying and is understandable only if we admit that not only variation but also contrast can be a form of musical relationship (as opposed to nonrelational dissimilarity), and also if we understand the derivation of the motifs from one another not merely as an abstract musical process but also as a musical-dramatic one resulting from the interaction of and correspondence between musical and dramatic events. The musical techniques of transformation and contrast and the scenic-poetic links and association of ideas cannot be separated if the "allusive magic" (Thomas Mann) that ensures the systematic character of the ensembles of leitmotifs linked by threads running hither and thither is to become effective.

The network technique that derived from the Romantic symphony was taken to its limits by Wagner, who, however, acknowledged only the influence of Beethoven. In symphonic opera, that is, the music dramas after 1853, he also restored the outwardly directed, exoteric feature of a Beethoven symphony, the sublime or monumental style that had been retracted and toned down in the Romantic symphonies of Schumann and Mendelssohn. In the 1850s the motivic web technique that had been developed in the Romantic era and the symphonic pathos that had been repressed between 1830 and 1850 (except in the case of Berlioz) formed a new historical configuration in the case of Wagner and Liszt.

Thus, the monumentalism to which the symphonic style was unable to rise in the intermediate period, with the contradictory and not wholly successful exception of Schumann's Second Symphony, was perhaps restored by Wagner and Liszt after the middle of the century (in a political context overshadowed by resignation after the failure of the 1848–49 Revolution) and even intensified. Yet this took place under changed aesthetic conditions. Unlike Beethoven's symphonies, which are, so to speak, artworks of ideas, the music dramas and the symphonic poems are based on myths in which a Romantic spirit directed against the Enlightenment is at work. This is apparent in the music dramas, whereas in the symphonic poems it becomes noticeable only if we are aware that Liszt considered not just Orpheus and Prometheus but also Hamlet and Faust to be mythical figures. He did not set Shakespeare's and

Goethe's dramas to music, but rather invented musical equivalents of Hamlet and Faust as the archetypes which, half released from the poetic works themselves, they had in the meantime become in the general European consciousness.

Liszt's method of motivic and thematic transformation—the procedure of developing from an identical diastematic substance distinct themes and motifs distinguished from one another by sharp differences in character and tempo—also represents an intensification of the Romantic network technique. Thus it is evident that in the case of both Wagner and Liszt, the historically representative composer of the postrevolutionary epoch, the "allusive magic" formed a contraposition and counterbalance to the character contrasts that both composers needed in order to do justice to the scenic or programmatic subject matter, which they wished to convey to the listener's emotional understanding, as Wagner put it, with musical means. According to Hoffmann (1810), Beethoven was able to counter the danger of rhapsodic disunity only by the "great circumspection" with which he elaborated the inner structure of a symphony as a tissue of motifs. This danger had in the meantime grown to such an extent that an increase in the systemization of the thematic-motival interrelationships, in the form of Wagner's leitmotif technique and Liszt's transformation method, seemed necessary as an aesthetic and technical counterbalance. Yet the semblance of rhapsody, which Schulz thought the symphony shared with the Pindaric ode, was a sign or expression of the sublime power of the imagination. In the history of the symphonic style, at the beginning of the century in the case of Beethoven and after the middle of the century in the case of Wagner and Liszt, this was the reason for the monumental tendency that was felt to be the aesthetic counterpart to the technical or material existence of the large orchestral forces. In the large form expressed in exemplary fashion by the beginning of Beethoven's Ninth Symphony, a work that molded Wagner's feeling for style, the exposition of the themes and motifs is at one and the same time an exposition of the instruments: the orchestral voices whose differences in tone color Adolf Bernhard Marx described as being aesthetic character differences.

If we translate Wagner's historical myth into sober history, the historical position of music drama can thus be described using the categories he proffers in *Opera and Drama*. The crisis of the symphony around 1850 coincided with a transfer of the symphonic style to other genres, and the "symphonic ambition" (Egon Voss) meant nothing less than that both the exoteric and the esoteric aspects of a Beethoven symphony were restored under changed aesthetic premises—to be precise, under the influence of the Romantic myth instead of the classical and Enlightenment idea of an "education to humanity" (Herder). The exoteric element was restored by reestablishing the sublime, monumental style, which, after the post-1830 retrenchment, again seemed possible and replete with substance. The esoteric element, by contrast, was restored by an intensification of the classic motivic network technique, which in the Romantic era progressed from a single movement to a whole cycle, thereby becoming systematic. The density of the motivic web ensured inner coherence in the face of the swift and often abrupt changes in melodic character which were necessary for the musical presentation of the events onstage and the literary programs, staged events, and the like to which in turn the restoration of what was now a mythically based symphonic pathos was attached.

Contrary Views of Opera

An opera that is dependent on Wagner is not necessarily identical to what Bayreuth approved of as the kind of opera that could be tolerated in the same company as Wagner, or be seen as worthy of following in his footsteps. According to the Bayreuth doctrine, the only path still open to a composer who did not wish to produce superfluities was not imitation pure and simple, but in fact the avoidance of the genre of heroic and mythical music drama that Wagner had perfected. This path led to fairy-tale opera (Engelbert Humperdinck was Siegfried Wagner's teacher) or comic opera, which had already been propagated in the 1850s by Liszt as an alternative to music drama (for example, Peter Cornelius' *Barbier von Bagdad* of 1858) and in which Hugo Wolf, enthusiastic Wagnerian that he was, later sought a kind of refuge from Wagner (as with *Der Corregidor*).

Wagner's German successors were thus divided into epigones who were not even recognized in Bayreuth and admirers who took pains to express their reverence by avoiding the area in which there was nothing new to say. By contrast, Wagner's relationship to the developing operatic traditions in Italy, France, and Russia in the late nineteenth century is characterized by a curious lack of interaction that can only be explained by sharply diverging conceptions of the fundamental tenets of music drama. (There was no such thing as "Wagnerismo," of which Verdi was accused by incomprehending critics. Rather, when, after the triumphs of the early 1850s, Verdi attempted to become an international—that is, a Parisian—composer in addition to being an Italian one, he had to come to terms with the grand opera of Giacomo Meyerbeer.)

It was impossible to bridge the gap between Wagner's music dramas and the various kinds of opera that were produced in a never-ending stream in the late nineteenth century. One should mention the *drame lyrique* of Gounod, Massenet, and Tchaikovsky; tragico-realistic opera such as Verdi's *Traviata* (1853) and Bizet's *Carmen* (1875); the character tragedy or comedy in the spirit of Shakespeare, such as Verdi's *Otello* (1887) and *Falstaff* (1893); and the historical drama or chronicle play that also derived from Shakespeare (Mussorgsky's *Boris Godunov* of 1874; Borodin's *Prince Igor* of 1889). The reason for the gap between Wagner's music dramas and other kinds of opera was the sharp divergence not only between ways of solving problems, but also between the problems one started with. (That both Mussorgsky and Massenet, to name two very different composers, adopted rudiments of the leitmotif technique as their own is nothing but a superficial technical detail of minor musical and dramaturgical importance.)

In order to define in conceptual terms the chasm that separated Wagner from his contemporaries and, paradoxically, made him an outstanding figure outside the mainstream, we can proceed from the contrast between mythical and realistic subject matter, overwhelming memory and stage presence, or orchestral melody and vocal cantabile. A plot set in the past is as realistic in the broadest sense of the word as one set in the present, provided history is not merely used as the source of names for intrigues centered on the unchanging conflicts between love and honor. A historical plot is realistic as long as epoch-making events form the main theme of the opera, which, through musical and scenic color, tries to paint a (naturally fictitious) portrait of the past. But from the time of *Das Rheingold* on, Wagner kept his distance both from history and from the present (except in *Die Meistersinger,* that paradoxical phenomenon of a music drama that is a historically localized comedy). He sought the common human element in myth rather than in history or the present, where he believed it was distorted and restrained by convention.

Thus, the problem faced by every other opera composer of the late nineteenth century—making it seem plausible that characters realistically depicted on the stage should sing instead of speaking—did not exist for Wagner.

Yet we would be doing an injustice to the history of opera after 1850 if we believed that creating musical dialogue that was both realistic and impassioned was the highest achievement a composer could attain. The technique of employing a dense network of orchestral motifs—whether repeated situational motifs (as in Verdi) or leitmotifs that change from one moment to the next—to carry a dialogue that veers between different stylistic levels was generally available in the late nineteenth century. The real problem of operatic composition, for Verdi as for Bizet, Tchaikovsky, or Mussorgsky, was not "melody as dialogue" (Wagner). Rather, it was the challenge of not surrendering the cantabile melody, of preserving it dramaturgically in spite of the continuity of the musical dialogue. However different the paths pursued by operatic composers after the middle of the century, from the inserted song and scenically motivated music to the monologue of solitude (even solitude in the presence of others) and the duet in situations of estrangement, the problem for which they were seeking a solution was always the same: how to reconcile, uninterruptedly if possible, realism and cantabile melody. This was not a problem for Richard Wagner.

If, in the case of other composers, leitmotifs or reminiscence motifs served as an orchestral support for the musical-dramatic dialogue, in Wagner the reverse seems true: the dialogue is a function of and initiating factor in an orchestral melody in which the true inner action takes place. The essential subject of the music (of which the orchestral melody speaks) is not the palpable action onstage, in which the emotions of the characters collide, but a past that throws an imaginary though overwhelming shadow over the visible action. Strictly speaking, the past, according to the criterion that the genuine reality in opera is the one constituted by musical means, is in Wagner's case "more real" than the present. In his case, and only his case, the object of the musical presentation is always something that happened in the past and weighs oppressively on the present. (In other operas memory can also become a musical-dramatic theme from which moving effects emanate, for example, in *Boris Godunov, Eugen Onegin,* or *Werther*. But this fact has virtually no bearing on the fundamental difference between opera and music drama. In the former the music is aimed at the direct presence of emotions and not at contemplative immersion in the distant past.)

There is a connection, however, between myth and the oppressive weight of memory, the factors that determine the subject matter and the musical structure in Wagnerian dramaturgy. For only through memory, a musical reminiscence conjured up through leitmotifs, does the world of the gods in whom the nineteenth century no longer believed assume a theatrically convincing form. In *Götterdämmerung,* Wotan is present exclusively in the music. But he seems more powerful and impressive than the indecisive and sometimes wretched god who appears onstage in *Das Rheingold* (a fact rooted not only in the action but also in the relationship between myth and music, a relationship to which Wagner, with sure musical-dramaturgical instinct, adapted the plot). The same holds true for the dazzling hero, who proves to be rather childish in *Siegfried* and actually deluded—the deceiver deceived—in *Götterdämmerung*. Only in musically evoked memory, above all in the funeral music, a musically inspired glance *behind* the action, is he the mythical hero that Wagner intended him to be, and whom Nietzsche praised. (Actually, the visible action of *Götterdämmerung* must have seemed repugnant to Nietzsche, who praised severity for reasons of self-denial but never crudity.)

The complex of problems with which Wagner grappled, the connection between myth, overwhelming memory, and leitmotivic orchestral melody, was thus totally different from the difficulty that confronted other late-nineteenth-century opera composers: the difficulty of reconciling realistic dialogue, the action on the stage, and cantabile melody.

Wagner, Brahms, and the New German School

The name New German School was suggested in 1859 by Franz Brendel, Schumann's successor as editor of the *Neue Zeitschrift für Musik,* for the Wagner-Liszt-Berlioz triumvirate. But the term is simply absurd in reference to Berlioz and, strictly speaking, Liszt, who must be counted as a French composer despite his German origins and the fact that he considered himself to be a Hungarian. Although the term is a misnomer and seems nonsensical in retrospect, it had a far-reaching effect in that it burdened music history and reflection about it with the taint of party strife, an issue that, in politics, obtruded on the public consciousness as a result of the French Revolution and the backlash of conservatism that it provoked. (Conservatism differs from simple traditionalism, in which one's own position is regarded as self-evident and not in need of justification, in that it is often characterized by polemical reflection, a characteristic that has been taken over by its opponent, liberalism.)

Brendel considered the New German School a progressive party. In 1860, however, an opposing conservative party was established in the mind of the musical public through the provocative manifesto against the New Germans issued by certain "serious-minded musicians," to which Brahms, to his detriment, put his signature (less of his own accord than because his friends pressed him to do so). Schoenberg discerned in Brahms a progressive composer who anticipated part of the future through his use of musical prose and a sophisticated kind of developing variation. And Ernst Kurth considered Bruckner to be a latter-day baroque composer transported into the nineteenth century, despite the fact that Bruckner's contemporaries saw him as a member of the progressive faction. These differences do not alter the fact that after the middle of the nineteenth century the division into factions became part of the thinking about music, intervening in the process of musical development and directing or diverting its course. It was a theory that had a practical effect.

Yet the controversy, contrary to nineteenth-century practice, should not be personalized. Brahms studied the score of *Tristan* very carefully, and undoubtedly realized Wagner's stature as the outstanding figure of half a century of music history. (That he erred mightily in the case of Bruckner, whom he viewed with the arrogance of the sophisticated toward the unsophisticated, is of secondary importance.) It seems less likely that Wagner felt the same in return, though we should not take his malicious comments about Brahms too seriously; they were occasioned primarily by his anger toward his musical antagonist's journalistic partisans. Wagner read, or rather read aloud, insatiably, but after his time as a kapellmeister he seems to have taken hardly any notice of the music of his contemporaries.

Such party strife remains incomprehensible as long as we cling to individual figures. We are almost inevitably led to the conclusion, as we look back historically, that the debates were superfluous and detrimental, and that the vehemence with which they were conducted must be put down to the prejudices and biases of the epoch. The personalization that emerges from a formula such as Wagnerians versus Brahmsians distracts our attention from the problems at the root of the controversy. To conjecture in terms of the current ruling intellectual fashion that political and social dissent inspired the factional strife, albeit in a concealed manner, would also be pointless, merely a move to the opposite methodological extreme. True, anti-Wagnerian sentiments were in certain respects similar to those that in politics underlay the distrust of Louis Napoleon and suspicion of the prevailing confused mixture of populism, Caesarism, technical and industrial progress, and a penchant for speculation.

An attempt at an explanation in terms of the history of ideas, and with sociohistorical implications, is probably more to the point, although for the present it must remain fragmentary and sketchy.

First, in thinking *about* music, from which thinking *in* music is never quite independent, the modern belief in progress as proclaimed by Brendel radicalized the older one that derived from the eighteenth century in a manner that marked a significant qualitative shift in the debate about history. Not only the discovery and realization of what was musically reasonable but the reasonable itself was drawn into the inexorable movement of historical change. Beethoven, who termed the rules of thoroughbass irrefutable, was still convinced that music was based on timeless structural principles that were not affected by history. And musical revolutions from Monteverdi to Gluck were interpreted by Beethoven as restorations. Yet with Berlioz, Liszt, and Wagner (and to this extent Brendel, although he expressed himself in an unfortunate way, understood something that was crucial), a process began which in a manner of speaking dynamized the concept of music, and even freed the fundamental assumptions of the technique of composing to accept possible or necessary changes.

Second, closely connected with the "dynamizing" process was the tendency, which began to be generally accepted in scholarship at this time, to admit the validity of nothing in composition except technical empiricism. It was no longer a rule that decided what was and was not musically permissible but solely the "inner experience" of the composer. He could, for example, perceive unusual chords and progressions as meaningful even if, at least for the time being, they eluded the terminology of music theory. (The empiricism characteristic of the age and the aesthetics of genius that emerged in the latter part of the eighteenth century blended to form an unusual notion in the fundamental concept of musical experience. Among the theorists Gottfried Weber was the first to emphasize it. The concept gave primary importance to the subjective experience of the composer and weighed as secondary the intrasubjective one of the audience.) That the *Tristan* chord seems meaningful and not absurd can be substantiated only in an empirical way and not in theoretical terms. For the category to which it belongs, a suspension resolving onto an altered seventh chord on the dominant of the dominant, which in turn resolves onto the dominant seventh chord (in more general terms, a dissonance of the third degree), also admits the construction of countless nonsensical forms.

Third, the basic premise of the progressive party was that music, like all forms of "objectified spirit," is historical through and through. This thought was simply unbearable for the good musicians of the nineteenth century, who clung, albeit with increasing unease, to timeless norms, structural rules, and principles of genre. (Brahms thought he knew once and for all what was a lied and what was not.) Thus, in music as in other walks of life, the substance of conservatism was not the simple affection for what was old but the conviction of being firmly rooted in what is timeless (and that which is timeless seems to have been handed down from the past only insofar as it has always been true). Musical conservatism was less an undifferentiated enmity toward Wagner than a point of view that discerned in his indisputable greatness an aspect of historical doom. This conservatism resisted for understandable reasons the idea of progress as reaching into an undefined future (instead of merely, as people thought in the eighteenth century, into the present). It also resisted the surrender of inalienable musical principles, without the general acceptance of which, it was thought, progress would be at the mercy of sheer caprice. And, finally, it rejected the idea that the inner experience of the composer, which could be comprehended by an empathetic audience without being dependent on their consent, should be regarded as the final court of appeals for determining what was musically permissible and what was not. In contrast to the progressive party, the conservatives clung to the conviction that there was such a thing as musical truth or reason (Moritz Hauptmann), partly discovered and in part still to be discovered, but at least existing unto itself, and which should not be sacrificed to a total, inexorable historicization.

Translated by Alfred Clayton

CHAPTER 3

Wagner in the History of Psychology

ISOLDE VETTER

The Historical Framework

During Wagner's lifetime there was little scientific involvement in psychology and certainly no academic discipline that could be said to cover, even approximately, what we traditionally understand by the term today. Although it is customary to date the birth of psychology to 1879, with the foundation of the first "psychological laboratory" in Leipzig by Wilhelm Wundt (1832–1920), the main emphasis in psychological research until well into the twentieth century was to remain in the fields of sensory physiology, perceptual psychology, and the psychology of thinking, areas defined by the beginnings of the discipline but relatively remote from any concern with art and with the personality of the artist.

Nonetheless, the place of psychology was not altogether untenanted in Wagner's day. It was occupied, for the most part, by another discipline—psychiatry—which, in the course of the nineteenth century, had developed into a special branch of medicine. It was not until the early twentieth century that the emergent doctrine of psychoanalysis and other derivative schools of depth psychology (all of them offshoots of psychiatric and neurological medicine) came to dispute the position held by psychiatry in the psychological approach to art and artists. The years following the end of the Second World War finally witnessed the academic triumph of empirical psychology, a discipline which, influenced by American behaviorism, has yet to achieve the popularity enjoyed by depth psychology in the area of interest to us here.

The "Problem" of Genius

The so-called problem of genius is one which had exercised the minds of classical Greek and Roman writers, Plato and Aristotle having been among the first to discuss the idea of a relationship between genius and supposedly divine madness. The ancient Greeks had already divined a solution to the problem of genius in their belief that the genius had to pay for his gift, or to "provide compensation" *(Ersatz)* for it. The obvious example was the seer who paid for the gift of prophecy with the loss of his eyesight. Even as late as the twentieth century, attempts to explain the abilities of the genius, or creative personality, have been bedeviled by more and more diluted variants of this *Ersatz* hypothesis (to quote the term used in Groeben/Vorderer 1986, p. 106).

With the establishment in the nineteenth century of psychiatry as a scientific and academic discipline, the theme of the "mad genius" again came in for detailed attention. It is to the French psychiatrist Jacques-Joseph Moreau de Tours (1804–1884) that we owe a variant of the *Ersatz* hypothesis according to which *génie* was synonymous with *névrose* (neurosis in the sense of an organic change). Now accorded scientific respectability, this view was advanced in his *Morbid Psychology in Its Relations with the Philosophy of History or of the Influence of Neuropathies on Intellectual Dynamism* (Moreau 1859). But the real apostle of this idea was the Italian psychiatrist Cesare Lombroso (1836–1909) with his book *Genius and Insanity* (Lombroso 1897; see also Mora 1964). For Lombroso genius represented a kind of degenerative and epileptic psychosis, without, however, necessarily implying any disparagement of genius in general.

Alongside the claim that genius was close to madness there now emerged another doctrine, that of degeneration (or, in German, *Entartung*), a doctrine whose leading representative is generally held to have been Bénédict Auguste Morel (1809–1873). In his *Treatise on the Physical, Intellectual, and Moral Degeneration of the Human Race and of Its Causes Which Produce These Unhealthy Varieties* (Morel 1857), he advanced the view that degeneration was a morbid deviation from the normal type, a deviation which could be passed on by hereditary means and which would lead to the progressive extinction of later generations.

The joint doctrines of degeneration on the one hand and genius as madness on the other were bound to produce an explosive mixture. They enjoyed a meteoric rise in popularity and exercised a baleful influence not only on medicine but on large areas of aesthetics and cultural theory, as well as on political ideology, contributing to the persecution of numerous artists as proponents of "degenerate art" *(entartete Kunst)* and to the murder of several million members of "degenerate races" in National Socialist concentration camps. Even during the twentieth century few writers have taken exception to the fact that both theses were mere assertions for which no rational evidence existed and which therefore appear to today's observer as no more than examples of nineteenth-century bourgeois morality dressed up as science. In the first place, scientific writers of the time did not even have a theory to explain the normal process of heredity, still less to show how symptoms of acquired degeneracy could be passed on by hereditary means. What is more, writers on the theory of degeneracy not infrequently admitted that their doctrine involved an act of faith, but a faith to which they nonetheless remained unwaveringly loyal (see Weingart/Kroll/Bayertz 1988, pp. 73–74).

In the second place, there was of course no statistically corroborated evidence that geniuses were in fact more disposed to mental illness than the average man in the street. Only in the course of the twentieth century has the growth of modern genetics gradually put paid to the doctrine of degeneration; the thesis that genius was equivalent to madness disappeared, too, once it was possible to prove statistically that men and women of genius do not exhibit a higher rate of mental illness than the rest of a given population. (For further reading, see Becker 1978, Gold 1960, Walter 1956, and Weingart/Kroll/Bayertz 1988.)

The Age of Psychiatric Pathobiography

The first "pathobiography" is generally held to have been *Le démon de Socrate* (1836) by the French psychiatrist L. F. Lélut (see Lange-Eichbaum 1967, pp. 221 and 711, source 3411), who, according to Mora (1964, p. 568, n. 7), "considered Socrates as afflicted by sensorial hallucinations without, however, arriving at a delusional or manic psychosis." After 1860 pathobiography inevitably became caught up in the wake of the two doctrines discussed in the preceding section of this chapter. It was to be more than a century before the discipline was able to shake itself free once again. The ne plus ultra of pathobiographical inquiry, at least in quantitative terms, was *Genius, Madness, and Fame* by the psychiatrist Wilhelm Lange-Eichbaum, first published in 1928. Its latest complete edition—the sixth—contains case histories of about six hundred figures from world history, together with no fewer than 3,655 references to secondary sources (Lange-Eichbaum 1967).

The normal procedure adopted by psychiatric pathobiography was to derive an unfavorable psychiatric diagnosis of some man or woman of genius from (ostensibly) biographically ascertainable characteristics while leaving open (at least in principle) the question of what merit lay in the works of the individual concerned, despite his or her having been placed in an unflattering category psychiatrically. Still, it was extraordinarily tempting to infer on the basis of such a diagnosis that the works themselves were of inferior quality. What might be described as a pathobiographical shortcut consisted in deriving the unfavorable diagnosis of the person directly from the (ostensible) qualities of his or her works, so that it then became unnecessary to engage in a separate discussion about the merits of those works. Psychiatrists who indulged in pathobiography finally went so far as to claim that they were "educating the people," arrogating to themselves and to their profession the right to decide what was art and what was not (Glatzel 1986, p. 19).

According to another line of thinking, writers and painters—whether wittingly or unwittingly—supposedly describe in their works certain psychiatric syndromes that have to be identified. (Even today, attempts are still being made to unearth examples of psychic illness in literary texts; see Stone 1966.) This assumption was unconnected with the claim that an artist must necessarily have suffered from any illness he or she describes.

From Pathobiography to Psychobiography

Freud's first analysis of a literary work, "Delusions and Dreams in Jensen's *Gradiva*" (Freud 1907), heralded the start of a psychoanalytic interest in art and literature. At about the same time he also gave programmatical expression to his ideas on the psychology of poets and artists in general in "Creative Writers and Day-Dreaming" (Freud 1908). These two essays were followed by other pieces on individual words and particular poets or artists but not, however, on music or musicians. Freud described his personal reasons for this choice as follows:

> Works of art do exercise a powerful effect on me, especially those of literature and sculpture, less often of painting . . . [I] spend a long time before them trying to apprehend them in my own way, i.e. to explain to myself what their effect is due to. Wherever I cannot do this, as for instance with music, I am almost incapable of obtaining any pleasure. Some rationalistic, or perhaps analytic, turn of mind in me rebels against being moved by a thing without knowing why I am thus affected and what it is that affects me.   (Freud 1914, p. 211)

Both areas of psychoanalysis inaugurated by Freud—those dealing with the lives of artists on the one hand and with the interpretation of their works on the other—continue to occupy considerable space in psychoanalytic literature. By 1960 there were more than three hundred international psychoanalytic biographies emanating from the Freudian school (Cremerius 1971, p. 10), although of these only two are on the subject of Richard Wagner (Racker 1948 and Marcuse 1963), in addition to an untold number of interpretive studies (see Eck 1979).

Freud had declared that artistic creativity belonged in the realm of the unconscious and that it was analogous to dreaming (Freud 1908), its predominant concern being wish fulfillment—in other words, the symbolic realization of repressed desires. In this way not only the unconscious wishes of the artist himself but, vicariously, those of his audience are fulfilled: "There is no longer any need for one to murder, since *he* [the criminal as Redeemer in Dostoyevski's *Crime and Punishment*] has already murdered; and one must be grateful to him, for, except for him, one would have been obliged oneself to murder" (Freud 1928, p. 190). According to this interpretation the work of art owes its existence to an act of regression, parallel to neurosis, on the part of the artist toward those oral, anal, and phallic desires which accompany the different stages of development of infantile psychosexuality and which can be revealed behind the aesthetic facade by means of psychoanalysis.

"What psycho-analysis was able to do," according to Freud, was to "construct" that part of the artist "which he shared with all men"; it "can do nothing towards elucidating the nature of the artistic gift, nor can it explain the means by which the artist works—artistic technique" (Freud 1925, p. 65); "investigations of this kind are not intended to explain an author's genius"

(Freud 1933, p. 254). In this way psychoanalysis fell short of the claims of pathobiography with its hypothesis which had sought in particular to explain the exceptional nature of genius by reference to madness. If psychoanalysis attempted to distance itself from this view by constantly stressing the fact that neurosis (which had replaced *madness* as the preferred term) was a "ubiquitous phenomenon" (Cremerius 1971, p. 16)—in other words, "that part of the artist which he shared with all men"—it nonetheless took over the legacy of psychiatric pathobiography to the extent that it still attempted to locate the driving force of creativity in neurosis. According to Wilhelm Stekel, it is neurosis that "presses the pen into the hand" of the poet (Stekel 1909, p. 12). And ultimately, by concentrating on universally human neurosis, psychoanalytic interpretations of artists' lives and works had to contend with a certain sense of predictability since, notwithstanding the great variety of authors and their works, the findings were inevitably the same—namely, those basic structures of the psychoanalytic theory of neurosis which Freud himself had developed: "The Oedipus complex, for example, has long since become a cliché; what was rightly regarded as a discovery during the early days of psychoanalysis has in the meantime been pressed into the service of a reductionism which . . . believes it can see everywhere the same material for the father/son conflict, not least in respect of artistic creativity" (Kudszus 1980, p. 1122).

The Analytical Psychology of Jung

In contrast to Freudian psychoanalysis, Jung's analytical psychology denies any connection between artistry and neurosis. It distinguishes the psychological structure of the work of art from that of the artist who created it: neither can be wholly traced back to the other any more than they can help to explain each other. For Jung there are two kinds of creativity, the psychological and the visionary. The former depicts actual experiences and passions and remains within the realm of human consciousness. Here the psychologist can add nothing to what has already been said in the work of art. The latter, by contrast, requires interpretation. This, however, will not be achieved by recourse to the author or to his individual unconscious but rather to that "collective unconscious" which is common to all and which preserves the experiences of the whole of humanity in symbolic form—in other words, in the form of archetypes. By sharing these mental and spiritual elemental forces, the artist becomes a human being in the highest sense of the word: it is not the art which must be explained in terms of the artist, but the artist who must be explained through his art. The artist might have his own personal problems, but these are of no significance to the "essential nature of the work of art" (see Jung 1930, 1932; for Jungian studies of individual works of literature, see Eck 1979, pp. 863–864).[1]

---

1. A whole series of other schools of psychology and psychotherapy—individual psychology, existential analysis, humanistic psychology, phenomenological psychology, and so on—has also

Empirical Psychology

In its attempts to explain creativity, modern psychology has undergone a "democratization of the creativity construct" (Groeben/Vorderer 1986, p. 106). Creativity is no longer regarded as the unattainable gift of individual geniuses but as a quality which, in principle, is within the reach of every individual. Its actual extent is presumably learned, while it can, within certain limits, be increased by appropriate training. (To date this aspect has been exploited to an appreciable degree only in industry and commerce.) Accordingly, there is no longer a scientific problem concerning genius inasmuch as geniuses, like everyone else, are now investigated with the methods of empirical personality research. Since these methods are largely dependent on the cooperation of the analysand, they appear to be of only limited application in the case of historical figures.

As to the psychoanalytic interpretation of literature, many literary psychologists had earlier come to the conclusion that the collaboration of a "living consciousness" was necessary if free association was to be used in interpreting the text. But since the authors of the works being interpreted were not or are not, as a rule, available, many interpreters would tacitly use their own associative ideas as an instrument of interpretation. It was perhaps out of dissatisfaction with a state of affairs which, if tolerated, was methodologically unsound that Norman Holland developed a psychoanalytic approach to textual analysis using the free associations of several readers (Holland 1975; for reasons of time and expense Holland was obliged to limit himself initially to five such persons). In this unexpected way "the psychoanalytic method of interpretation" saw itself "transformed into a variant of empirical audience research" (Groeben/Vorderer 1986, p. 117). This is a method which can be applied unrestrictedly to all historical works of art that are read, or listened to, by an audience alive today (and, in a restricted way, perhaps also to the reception of works in the past).

The Contribution of Music Psychology

Although Wagner was unquestionably a composer of music, the foregoing discussion has been confined, perhaps to the surprise of a number of readers, to the field of literary psychology. This focus, however, is neither an accident nor an oversight: to date, music psychology has been concerned almost exclusively with the physiology of hearing and the psychology of perception, along with musicality tests, research into the conditions that influence musical taste and musical behavior, and other related subjects (see, for example, Hodges 1980). Within the framework of music psychology there has been no attempt to conduct psychological analyses of the personality of individual

---

taken up literary interpretation. Since their number appears to include only one study on Wagner, however (Sehulster 1979/80), it will be sufficient here merely to list the relevant bibliographical references: Eck 1979, Natoli 1984, Natoli/Rusch 1984, and Halász 1987.

composers on the basis of their work, or on the basis of any individual work, and the (marginal) contributions that psychoanalysis has made to the subject are generally ignored by music psychology. (There are no relevant source references in Motte-Haber 1979 or Hodges 1980, the only exception being Haesler 1985.) Music psychologists claim that the reason for their self-denial lies in the fact that "music resists content analysis" (Motte-Haber 1979, p. 186). This claim is of course true only if, in attempting to analyze the work, we aim to establish a single, unambiguous, and quasi-objective meaning. By applying the methods of audience psychology, by contrast, we might very well find ourselves in a position to comment on how disparate are the meanings attributed to music (in other words, to the different styles of music, different works of music, and even individual musical moments), whether certain personality types are more inclined than others to produce certain types of content, and whether similar socialization experiences suggest similar meanings. It then becomes possible to speak of particular subcultures in terms of musical meaning, and much else besides. This kind of research, especially as it relates to "highbrow" music, seems, however, to be still in its earliest infancy, not least because the traditional aesthetic postulate of an autonomous art with objective significance still appears to be in the ascendant. (On the psychoanalysis of music, see Haesler 1985, Haisch 1953, Michel 1948 and 1965, and Musique en jeu 1972.)

Psychological Literature on Wagner

In turning now to the existing psychological literature on Wagner and examining individual instances of its principal manifestations, we must not forget that there is no clear-cut distinction between psychological and nonpsychological literature. Unless it confines itself exclusively to facts, almost every statement concerning the composer will contain an element of psychology if it seeks to interpret those facts with any degree of sensitivity. This is especially true, of course, of large-scale biographies such as those of Robert Gutman and Martin Gregor-Dellin (Gutman 1968 and Gregor-Dellin 1980), which set themselves the task of providing a detailed interpretation of Wagner's life as well as his works.

It was necessary, therefore, to keep the present survey within reasonable bounds. To that end, only those writings have been included which adopt an exclusively psychological approach and whose authors either are professional psychologists, psychiatrists, or psychoanalysts, or have based their work on some acknowledged psychological, psychiatric, or psychoanalytic theory. A third group of writers consists of those who, although themselves not specialists, and although in some cases only borrowing from psychological theories, could not be ignored in the present context. One thinks here, for example, of the numerous editions of Wagner's *Letters to a Seamstress* (Spitzer 1877), which may well have had a considerable influence on the picture that subsequent specialists have had of Wagner. Nor, in this regard, is it possible to overlook Friedrich Nietzsche, for all that he made only atmospheric use of the twin theories of degeneracy and of genius as madness that were current in his day. Mention should also be made of the musicologist Robert Donington, whose 1963 book on the *Ring* is generally regarded as a Jungian interpretation of the work.

Wagner in Psychiatric Pathobiography

As far ,as it has been possible to ascertain, the psychological literature on Wagner begins, spectacularly, in 1872 with the publication of *Richard Wagner: A Psychiatric Study,* a pamphlet by the aspiring psychiatrist Theodor Puschmann, who, out of hand, declared the composer to be mentally ill (Puschmann 1873). According to Puschmann's diagnosis, Wagner was suffering from what in his day were regarded as three of the principal categories of psychiatric pathology, namely, megalomania, persecution mania, and moral insanity (the last-named an invention of the English physician and ethnologist James Cowles Prichard, dating from 1835). By seeking to derive his diagnoses from both the personality and the works of his subject, Puschmann combined the two different kinds of psychiatric pathobiography outlined earlier to produce a virtually unassailable argument. As the motive behind his essay the author cites scientific interest, well-meaning sympathy, and the hope of saving Wagner's supporters. (Wagner himself was evidently held to be beyond redemption.) But in spite of these assurances, the essay's function as a political slap in the face to Wagner and the so-called Wagner movement is plain to see.

The agenda of later psychiatric diatribes against the composer was thus defined. With Puschmann's piece they may all be seen as evidence of the political and philosophical corruptibility of science. At the same time, the doctrine of degeneration which held sway during this period must, for many people, have had the force of a sword of Damocles permanently suspended above their heads (one thinks here of Strindberg, for instance). Diagnosing the symptoms of degeneration in others may well have helped them overcome their own anxieties (see Vetter 1988a).

Only a few years after Puschmann's pamphlet, another sensation rocked the Wagnerian world when the well-known Viennese journalist Daniel Spitzer published sixteen letters from Wagner to a Viennese seamstress in the well-respected Vienna daily *Neue Freie Presse* (Spitzer 1877). Dating from the years 1864–1868, these letters contained orders for countless satin dressing gowns and satin bedspreads, together with untold quantities of satin fabrics, silk ribbons, rose garlands, and so on. (A single one of the surviving invoices includes an order for, in addition to countless other items, no fewer than 491 ells of satin, or between 275 and 435 yards.) Spitzer headed the letters with Hunding's line from act 1 of *Die Walküre,* "How like the woman he looks!" which in its original context has a totally different meaning from the one Spitzer gave it. Paul Tausig, the editor of the 1906 edition, assured his readers that these letters "should not and cannot impugn the *artist* and creator of so many immortal masterpieces," while in almost the same breath he spoke ominously of the "teachings" of figures such as Lombroso and Krafft-Ebing, a professor of psychiatry in Vienna and a famous sexual pathologist.

In fact the *Letters to a Seamstress* helped fuel a whole series of quasi-scientific reflections on Wagner's sexual "perversions." The other stumbling block was the composer's friendship with King Ludwig II of Bavaria. Whereas the orders for "women's dressing-gowns at fabulous prices" had persuaded Lombroso to classify Wagner as a "sexual psychopath" (Lombroso 1897), the publication of several effusively worded letters from Ludwig II to Wagner in the *Jahrbuch für sexuelle Zwischenstufen* of Magnus Hirschfeld (in his day one of the leading campaigners for homosexual emancipation) suggested that the relationship between king and composer was at the very least homoerotically tinged (Anonymous 1901). And there is no doubt that the study *Richard Wagner and Homosexuality* (H. Fuchs 1903) was indebted to the self-same movement: its author, Hanns Fuchs, left no stone unturned in his attempts to prove Wagner's predisposition toward "mental" homosexuality at the very least. One of the leading sexologists of the time, albeit a scholar more associated with the opponents of homosexual emancipation, was Albert Moll. Unimpressed by satin fabrics, he rejected Fuchs's tentative line of argument and inveighed against that "obsession," which he claimed existed "in certain homosexual circles," which persuaded writers "to describe as homosexual anyone who has achieved anything of greatness" (Moll 1910, p. 80). Another writer on Wagner who managed to avoid all mention of dressing gowns and the like was the playwright, novelist, and former psychiatrist Oskar Panizza, whose essay "Bayreuth and Homosexuality" was first published in 1895. Picking up Schopenhauer's postulate of a link between homosexuality and old age, Panizza ascribed to *Parsifal,* and hence to its creator, a homosexuality which, like Fuchs's, was more or less "sublimated" (Panizza 1895). In his 1907 essay "Richard Wagner's Bisexuality" (Pudor 1907), Heinrich Pudor, former director of the Dresden Conservatory and, by his own later admission, "champion of *Deutschtum* and anti-Semitism" (Pudor 1934), cited the composer as an example of the "dual bisexual nature" of the genius in general and of the musician in particular, concluding from Wagner's predilection for satin that the composer was by nature *feminin-urnindenhaft* (*Urninde* is a feminine form of the word *Urning,* which in turn means a male homosexual; Pudor 1907, pp. 141, 144).

The evidence mentioned so far seems to be only the tip of the iceberg, or so it would appear from Alfred Kind's *Gynaeocracy in the History of Humankind,* a monumental work published shortly before the outbreak of the First World War, in which the author, a sexologist, looks back, from an ironic distance, at the veritable flood of condemnations dressed up in psychiatric guise which the *Letters to a Seamstress* apparently produced:

A considerable stir has also been caused by another case in which an artist singled out by genius surrounded himself with signs of gender [Kind's rather coy way of saying the female sex] in order to enhance his mood and increase his artistic productivity. It is for this reason that homosexual circles have claimed him as their own and that he has, at the very least, been dubbed a fetishist . . . It is *Richard Wagner*. I have spoken my mind far too often to find it necessary now to explain once again, in detail, to what extent the male artist requires a womanly atmosphere in order to create his work. [There follows the text of one of Wagner's letters to the seamstress, together with one of the latter's invoices.] In its day the *Neue freie Presse* in Vienna blurted out these secrets from an artist's boudoir. Since then many value judgements have been passed: sybaritic, homosexual, dermatitic [!], fetishistic, transvestite, feminine streak. Much to the dismay of the diagnosticians, none of these assessments is wholly true. The way is therefore still open for new sideheads of pathological morality. A competition should be set up in time for the next psychiatric congress: Wagner's illness.   (Fuchs-Kind 1913, II, 528–530)

In 1923 Kind's coauthor, Eduard Fuchs (a man famous even today as a collector and student of erotic art), published the second volume of his *History of Erotic Art*. Entitled *The Individual Problem*, it contains this piquantly exaggerated passage, which, it may be added, could be read as an indictment and equally well as a defense:

Since, in the process of artistic creation, the creative artist engages, first and foremost, in an act of self-gratification—and this irrespective of whether he writes poetry or composes music, whether he works in clay or gives structure to space— it is entirely logical if, during the creative process, the individual artist adopts the role that most closely corresponds to his sex life and if he feels most creatively aroused while playing this role. Or, to cite an entirely concrete example: it is not in the least surprising if, while composing, Richard Wagner ran around in bisexually suggestive lace drawers. For this is wholly appropriate apparel for his markedly masochistic character, a character wholly consonant with the fervently androgynous nature of an art which lacks all true masculinity.   (E. Fuchs 1923, p. 128)

It was finally inevitable that the judiciary itself, in the person of the Dresden public prosecutor Erich Wulffen, should enter the fray. In 1928, in his *Sexual Mirror: On Art and Criminality,* Wulffen claimed to have discovered something "criminal" beneath the silk covers, posthumously stringing up poor Richard by his dearly bought "rose garlands":

Only a brief sketch on Richard Wagner. A pathological and criminal element is unmistakable in his nature. Relentless egoism in his real life and constant self-admiration to the point of narcissism in his works . . . Additionally, the noticeably feminine streak in his nature, evident even in his facial features, the effeminate elements in all his characters; the Meister has not been able to create a single genuine man, to say nothing of a Germanic man . . . And then there is the idea of redemption through womankind, an idea to which feminine natures are covertly responsive. The feminine element in his character corresponds to the

decorative element in his stage designs, the sonorousness of his music . . .
Feminine, too, the straining after effect in a theatrical context . . . In life too he
loved ostentation, he dressed like a woman—even the everyday clothes that he
wore were of velvet and silk—and he ordered vast quantities of fabrics from
milliners; the bills he received for what they supplied are well known . . . His
friendships with men such as Nietzsche and Ludwig II were effeminate and
mawkish . . . And his logic was marked by feminine sophistry.   (Wulffen 1928,
pp. 366–367)

According to Cosima Wagner's diaries, Wagner himself had his own say
on the subject on 20 July 1881, when he adapted the final lines of Goethe's
Faust—"Das Unbeschreibliche, / Hier ist's getan, / Das Ewig-Weibliche /
Zieht uns hinan" ("All that's mysterious / here finds the day. / Woman in all
of us / shows us the way," to quote Robert David Macdonald's translation)—
and told Cosima, "Das sanft Bestreichliche hat's uns getan, das angenehm
Weichliche zieht man gern an" (an untranslatable pun that means approximately "What's gently strokable's done for us all, what's pleasantly soft is
nice to put on"). (See also Karpath 1906 and Kusche 1967.)

Whereas the publication of Puschmann's pamphlet in 1872 had initially
persuaded Nietzsche to see in it an example of "insidious and deeply malicious
innuendo" calculated to "undermine" the "confidence of the coming generation" (Nietzsche 1978, pp. 85–86), he himself was quite prepared, sixteen
years later, to continue the task of undermining the composer in his
essay "The Case of Wagner" (Nietzsche 1967), even going so far as to use the
degeneration theory as the instrument with which to administer his assault:
"*Wagner est une névrose*. Perhaps nothing is better known today, at least nothing
has been better studied, than the Protean character of degeneration that here
conceals itself in the chrysalis of art and artist. Our physicians and physiolo-
gists confront their most interesting case in Wagner, at least a very complete
case" (Nietzsche 1967, p. 166). The "real" reasons for Nietzsche's apostasy
continue to be hotly debated even today (see Dieter Borchmeyer's essay on
Wagner and Nietzsche, Chapter 14 of this volume). The only certainty is that
Nietzsche's attitude toward the composer was characterized by increasing
ambivalence, not to say inconsistency, as he himself was the first to admit.
He summarized his feelings in the preface to "The Case of Wagner": "I am,
no less than Wagner, a child of this time; that is, a decadent: but I comprehended this, I resisted it" (Nietzsche 1967, p. 155; see also Koppen 1973,
pp. 315–324; and the afterword in Borchmeyer 1983, pp. 632–637).

Nietzsche's verdict on Wagner clearly found immediate support among the
ranks of those petit-bourgeois critics who sought to exploit it for their own
aims, whether hyper-German or any other. Heinrich Pudor, for example,
paraphrased Nietzsche in a lecture delivered in 1891 under the title *Morality
and Wholesomeness in Music*: "But [Wagner's] Teutons are sick; they are hysterical. Or is Isolde not hysterical? Love makes her hysterical . . . Wagner
was sick . . . The healthiest kind of Wagnerian music is *Die Meistersinger*.
This is music which can be recommended even to a young German lady and

a German youth; members of either sex who are not yet mature ought not to be admitted to any other music by Wagner" (Pudor 1891, pp. 16–17).

A writer who had even more impact than Nietzsche, at least in the short term, was Max Nordau. Born in Budapest, Nordau was a doctor and writer, and later, with Theodor Herzl, a leading Zionist. His two-volume study *Degeneration* (Nordau 1895) was immediately translated into several languages and was frequently reprinted. Wholly imbued with the doctrine of degeneration, Nordau was able to appeal to Lombroso in his castigation of a whole series of fin-de-siècle cultural phenomena, including the "Richard Wagner cult." Not pausing to examine biographical detail, he derived his damning account of the composer directly from the latter's literary works. Wagner's writings led him to diagnose "persecution mania, megalomania and mysticism," "vague philanthropy, anarchism, a craving for revolt and contradiction," and finally "graphomania, namely incoherence, fugitive ideation, and a tendency to idiotic punning" (p. 171), and he discovered in the texts of the music dramas an "erotic madness" which he regarded as "a form of Sadism" (pp. 181–182) expressed, for example, in the "amorous whinings, whimperings and ravings of *Tristan und Isolde*" (p. 181; see also Sutor 1893; Jachino 1894; Ziehen 1895; Koppen 1973, pp. 308–313, 325–328; and Fischer 1977).

Not infrequently—and somewhat cheaply—Nordau's critics simply tried to turn the tables on him, declaring him to be mentally disturbed (Hirsch 1894, Seidl 1895, Shaw 1895). Not so Cesare Lombroso, Nordau's (unwilling) spiritual mentor; he distanced himself expressly from Nordau's theory and, while happy to classify Wagner as "mentally disturbed," acknowledged—in line with his own theory—that the composer was "perhaps an epileptic" genius (Lombroso 1897).

As I noted earlier, Lombroso had already dismissed Wagner as a "sexual psychopath" on the evidence of his dressing gowns; the letters additionally served to convince the Italian that Wagner was "feeble-minded." Even though Lombroso may not have intended to engage in open defamation of the various celebrities whom he favored with his diagnoses, the ridiculous list of characteristics attributed not only to Wagner but to other great minds as well, cobbled together on the basis of little more than hearsay, certainly demonstrates the shortcomings of his scientific "method" (Lombroso 1891, 1897; cf. Mora 1964; and for further examples set in motion by Lombroso, see Roncoroni 1899a, b).

In a work dated 1907–08 a certain P. H. (believed to have been attached in some way to the University of Brussels) analyzed the character of Tannhäuser in an attempt to demonstrate that the figure, whether wittingly or unwittingly on Wagner's part, shows all the symptoms of general paralysis (P. H. 1907–08): act 1, agitated melancholy: act 2, periods of lucidity alternating with amnesia, a decline in the hero's mental powers, and depression; in act 3 the syndrome is less well depicted, since, according to the anonymous author, paralysis in real life becomes inexorably worse. His interpretation appears to have met with little response.

As early as 1910 Oswald Feis had expressed the view that nothing further could be gained by giving detailed consideration to writings such as those by Puschmann and Nordau in which Wagner was held "by common consent" to be "mentally ill" (Feis 1910, p. 79). But this did not discourage a number of latecomers from entering the field, all of them fired by an enthusiastic desire to engage in psychiatric diagnosis. In addition to Lange-Eichbaum's compilatory classic (Lange-Eichbaum 1967) and the velvet-and-silk brigade discussed earlier, the French neurologist Augustin Cabanès must also be mentioned. Although he was careful to distance himself, at least in part, from the vogue for equating genius with madness, Cabanès was nonetheless reluctant to abandon completely the concept of the *grand névropathe* or *malade immortel:* thus in one of his innumerable and cheaply sensationalist books he found himself in a position to brand the composer a "hysteric" suffering from "erotomania" (Cabanès 1920[?], p. 374). Another work published at around the same time was *Psychopathological Documents: Confessions and Eye-Witness Accounts from the Border Areas of the Mind* by the psychiatrist Karl Birnbaum (Birnbaum 1920). Drawing on passages from Wagner's autobiography, *My Life,* Birnbaum cites examples to prove his claims about "border areas," including the composer's "childhood fears and nightmares," an episode in Wagner's youth when he indulged his craze for gambling, and the composer's part in the student riots of 1830. Rather astonishingly, by contrast, there is no mention of Wagner under the heading "Psychosexual Aberrations," although the composer's dressing gowns could have been effortlessly included here, not only in the form of "confessions" but as "eye-witness accounts" as well.

The treatment of Wagner during the period of National Socialist rule represents a chapter in and of itself, inasmuch as psychology was suddenly required to perform a complete about-face. Wagner was now accounted among the party saints, so there could no longer be any question of seeking out psychic abnormalities The result was that for a period of some twelve years the composer was virtually ignored as an object of psychiatric inquiry. Such psychological accounts as there were had to give exclusive emphasis to Wagner's greatness and to a talent that could be deduced from race. To the extent that they were mentioned at all, qualities which had earlier been the subject of psychiatric diagnosis were now reinterpreted in a positive light and seen from the standpoint of the prevailing Nazi ideology.

In the fourth edition of the standard reference work on eugenics, *Human Heredity and Eugenics* by Erwin Baur, Eugen Fischer, and Fritz Lenz (all of them leading racial theorists at the Kaiser Wilhelm Institute for Anthropology, Human Heredity, and Eugenics in Berlin), Wagner (together with a number of other famous figures) is accused of having a "hysterical disposition"; but the charge is immediately qualified with the claim that such a predisposition "is no doubt of greater significance for intellectual creativity than any other anomaly . . . Particularly in the religious, artistic and political sphere, an abnormally great wish-conditionability [that is, the way in which the individual is conditioned by his or her wishes] appears capable of contributing to great achievements, more especially when the soul is governed by a great desire for admiration, as is the rule with persons of an hysterical disposition" (Lenz, in Baur-Fischer-Lenz 1936, p. 677). It may be added that Adolf Hitler read the second (1923) edition of this work while in prison in Landsberg (in other words, before or during his work on *Mein Kampf*) and that in the view of one of its authors, Fritz Lenz, he "assimilated the essential ideas of eugenics and their significance with great intellectual sensitivity and energy" (quoted in Weingart/Kroll/Bayertz 1988, p. 373).

Whereas in *Human Heredity and Eugenics* there is still a glimmer of the categories of traditional psychiatric pathology, one searches in vain for such terminology in Walther Rauschenberger's reflections on racial psychology, *Richard Wagner's Origins and Racial Characteristics* (Rauschenberger 1937). According to his findings Wagner was to be regarded, in racial terms, as Nordic-Dinaric. The composer's exceptional creative powers, his boldness, and his tenacity were all Nordic, as was his poetical and dramatic gift (in addition, of course, to his musical talent). Alongside these qualities, however, were other non-Nordic features, which were predominantly Dinaric. The most striking of these was his extraordinarily passionate nature, together with a sensuality which regularly came to the fore and which explained Wagner's predilection for strong perfumes, for the effect of color and light, for full-bodied sound, and for velvet, silk, and satin garments. The goal to which Wagner's art aspired was *"intoxicated exuberance, an extreme intensification of ego feeling, and a Dionysian revelling in emotion"* (Rauschenberger 1937, p. 167; italics in original). Even more pronounced Dinaric characteristics were supposedly found in Wagner's urge to preach his own private gospel: "Wagner wants to *redeem* humanity through his art" (Rauschenberger 1937, p. 167). The composer's "Dinaric bent," then, was clearly multifaceted if it could be made to explain not only his hankering after silken dressing gowns but also, for example, "the (Baroque) notion of the total work of art," "verbal accretions," and an "inflated way of speaking." Rauschenberger's tract was reprinted in 1942, three years after the outbreak of war, when the author was evidently struck, just in time, by the opportune idea that in Wagner's art "even dying becomes a fervent frenzy" (p. 147).

There was not, however, total agreement among those scholars who had placed their services at the disposal of national socialism. The leading authority on such matters, Fritz Lenz, considered, for example, that it was "not expedient" to "posit a special 'Dinaric race'" (Lenz in Baur-Fischer-Lenz 1936, p. 731). But there was no need to feel apprehensive about Wagner's satin excesses or, indeed, about any of his other exuberances: another (racist) solution would no doubt have been found to escape from the impasse.

After the evils of racist thinking had been brought to an end, at least officially, it seems to have taken a little time for the psychiatric advocates of bourgeois morality to recover themselves sufficiently to pick up from where they had left off in the years leading up to 1933. (See, in this context, Chessick

1983, cited later in this chapter in the section titled "Wagner in Psychoanalytic Psychobiography.") At all events, it is not until 1963 that we find James A. Brussel, M.D., offering a highly moralistic—and monstrously distorted—description of Wagner's life in his article "The Brobdingnag of Bayreuth," a description which might equally well have been written in 1863. Brussel ends with a surprise attack, his "diagnosis" wielded with all the elegance of the executioner's ax: "It is simple to diagnose Wagner as an aggressive type of the emotionally unstable personality. A more venturesome but nonetheless quite probably nosological label is petit mal epilepsy. Possibly Richard Wagner *merits both*" (Brussel 1963, p. 229; emphasis added). A similar spirit of perversity invests a factually inaccurate article by Robert Greenblatt, professor emeritus of endocrinology at an American medical school, published to mark the centenary of Wagner's death and titled "Richard Wagner (1813–1883): The Voluptuary Genius." In it Greenblatt takes evident pleasure in quoting a remark by a certain William B. Ober: Wagner "suffered from haemorrhoids, and there will be some who say that he *deserved them*" (Greenblatt 1983, p. 18; emphasis added).

In the autumn of 1989 the Technics company ran an advertising campaign in England for a new stereo system (with full-page advertisements in, inter alia, the *Sunday Times* of 17 September 1989, p. A18). The advertisement showed part of a human face with deep-set, widely staring eyes beneath demonically arching brows. Beneath it, in bold letters, were the words: "To hear what he intended, a hi-fi system has to be perfectly composed." The text of the advertisement went on: "The insane glint in Wagner's eyes may have something to do with the events that unfolded before them. Between spells in debtors prison [sic], he founded a revolutionary movement, married Liszt's daughter and had an affair with King Ludwig II." Ought we ultimately to welcome the fact that psychiatric diagnoses which have been hawked around for over a century have finally finished up as advertising copy?

Wagner in Psychoanalytic Psychobiography

Freud himself left no writings on music or on Wagner. He did, however, make this (negative) remark in a letter to an unknown correspondent: "I am . . . completely unmusical. I am, as it were, stunted in this area of feeling; barely capable of enjoying a few pretty tunes by Mozart, I find even Wagner foreign to my nature, while everything approaching 'modern' music is simply inaccessible. I know it isn't easy for you to conceive of such a pitiful response" (Vienna, 18 January 1928; facsimile in Caïn 1982, pp. 105–106). As it turned out, Freud's "unmusical" nature need not have prevented him from writing about a kind of music which, like Wagner's operas, was textually based. Indeed, those psychoanalysts who were to write about Wagner generally did not mention the fact that he also set his texts to music.

Psychoanalytic literature on Wagner began in 1911 with the publication of *Richard Wagner in "The Flying Dutchman": A Contribution to the Psychology of Artistic Creativity* by Max Graf, a writer on music closely associated with

Freud. Writing wholly in the spirit of the theory of art propounded by Freud, Graf sets out from the belief that the "typical motifs found in an artist's work" "always" represent the artist's attempt to find the "solution to some emotional problem" (Graf 1911, p. 23). The typical motif with Wagner is said to be that of the woman caught between two men, a relationship embodied not only by his heroines Senta, Elisabeth, Sieglinde, Isolde, and Eva but also, in his own life, by Mathilde Wesendonck and Cosima von Bülow. This central motif allows Graf, in keeping with Freud's theory of the Oedipus complex, to posit "childhood fantasies" on Wagner's part concerning his mother's infidelity: as a "little Oedipus" (p. 34), Wagner had imagined himself to be the son of his stepfather, Ludwig Geyer (who, at least in Wagner's imagination, must therefore have stolen his mother away from his father), and identified with Geyer. This motif, Graf argues, is as true of Wagner's life as it is with his operatic characters. In consequence the picture of the heroine in Wagner's later works always derives from a transformation and idealization of the image of the mother. Hence, for example, Siegfried's and Parsifal's longing for their respective mothers.

Freud's pupil Otto Rank comes to similar conclusions. In the Wagner chapter of his substantial book *The Lohengrin Legend: A Contribution to Its Motivic Structure and Meaning* (Rank 1911), Rank essentially reduces the Oedipal events of the legend to those "necessary conditions for loving" which Freud had identified in 1910 and which describe the conditions to which neurotics frequently regress in order to be able to love at all, namely, the fantasy of "rescuing" the beloved, and the requirement of the "injured third party" (see Freud 1910). Through both one aims to obtain the mother as wife (hence Elsa's rescue by Lohengrin and Siegfried's rescue of Brünnhilde from the flickering flames), and indeed the "redemption fantasy" that can also be observed in Wagner reflects the intention to rescue the individual from (adolescent) love sickness through a sexual relationship with the mother. Thus even the hero's refusal to divulge his name in *Lohengrin,* where it is linked with the famous "forbidden question," can mean only one thing: that is, he is covering up the act of incest with the mother.

Rank followed up these ideas a year later with his book *The Incest Motif in Poetry and Legend: Elements of a Psychology of Poetic Creativity* (Rank 1912). Here he notes a whole series of examples of love between siblings in Wagner's works. Their unconscious model is said to have been furnished by the composer's "overaffectionate" relations with his sisters, especially with Rosalie. The "lovers' union in death"—in other words, the so-called *Liebestod*—is seen by Rank as a defense against the motif of "bride-taking": as such it is an "ambiguous symbolic substitute for proscribed sexual union" (proscribed, that is, because it forms part of an incest fantasy; Rank 1912, p. 641).

Sabina Spielrein, an early psychoanalyst whose writings have only recently been rediscovered, ascribed a "destructive component" to the "sexual instinct" in her 1912 essay "Destruction as a Cause of Becoming," arguing that the "reproductive instinct demands the destruction of the individual" (Spielrein

1912, p. 101; 1987, p. 134), and thereby anticipating, in the view of many, Freud's later postulate of a death instinct. In a section titled "Life and Death in Mythology," Spielrein goes on to suggest that in Wagner "death is often no more and no less than the destructive component of the instinct for becoming." This, she claims, is particularly well illustrated by the figure of Senta in *Holländer,* inasmuch as the heroine "agrees to being completely destroyed in her love for the Dutchman" (pp. 132–133). After returning to the mother (the sea), the lovers rise up from the water as though reborn. Senta's love is said to be the "rescue type" of love mentioned by Freud (Freud 1910); and the same, Spielrein argues, is true of the love felt by Siegfried and Brünnhilde, who sacrifice themselves to their love and die.

Leo Kaplan's observations on *Tannhäuser* and "erotic dualism" (Kaplan 1912) are on the same lines as an essay of Freud's published at the same time, in which the latter attributed the "universal tendency to debasement in the sphere of love" to the gap between sensuality and tenderness (Freud 1912).

Whereas the Oedipus complex (culminating in the phallic phase of libidinal development) had hitherto dominated all attempts at interpretive exegesis, Walter Samuel Swisher now turned his attention to the anal phase in "The Symbolism of Wagner's 'Rheingold'" (Swisher 1923). Swisher discovered elements of an anal libido fixation in Wagner (love of ostentation and grandiosely ambitious dreams of a total work of art) and found them mirrored in Alberich's repudiation of love and his regression to ownership of the Rhine Gold (whereby gold equals feces).

Its title notwithstanding, the somewhat disorganized study by Louise Brink, *Women Characters in Richard Wagner* (Brink 1924), deals not only with women characters but with male ones too, namely Wotan, Siegfried, and Alberich. According to Katherine Jones (Jones 1925) the central topic is Brünnhilde's development, which must be seen as prototypical of the development of womankind to a more mature kind of love. Like any typical growing daughter, Brünnhilde is not prepared to accept a woman's passive role; on the one hand she subordinates herself to her father in loving obedience, while on the other hand she rebels against him. Her later failing is the result of her father fixation. In contrast to Brünnhilde, Siegfried grows up without knowing his parents and is therefore free of all such fixations.

Another psychiatrist who concerned himself with Wagner was Georg Groddeck, variously known as the "wild analyst" and as the "father of psychosomatics." Groddeck, who ran a sanatorium at Baden-Baden, regarded his public lectures as largely therapeutic in aim. In one such lecture on the *Ring* he had no hesitation in describing not only the tetralogy but other poems too as "textbooks in psychoanalysis." Yet, far from advancing theories of his own or applying preexisting ones, he promised only "to communicate fairly randomly whatever happens to spring to mind" (Groddeck 1927, p. 136). These random thoughts extend from the claim that there is in fact no love but mother love and that no one who recognizes this fact needs to study psychoanalysis, to his conservative views on appropriate roles for the different sexes to play and the interpretation of various symbols (such as Wotan's spear as the god's male member).

In spite of its title, J. F. Flugel's work "The Tannhäuser Motif" (Flugel 1936) is concerned less with Wagner's opera than with the fact that, although much had been written about the triangular relationship between "two men and a woman" in light of the discovery of the Oedipus complex (Rank's *Incest Motif* being a prime example), little had been written, in the author's view, on the triangular relationship of "two women and a man" (in this case Venus, Elisabeth, and Tannhäuser). This, Flugel went on, should henceforth be known as the "Tannhäuser motif." The author traces the motif through various literary works but has little new to offer on Wagner's opera itself.

The best commentary on Enrique Racker's "Psychoanalytical Essay on the Personality and Dramatic Works of Richard Wagner" (Racker 1948) is the brief summary in English which he himself appends to the end of his piece, cited here verbatim:

> In the first place the author sets forth Wagner's fixation to the Oedipus complex and the conflicts related to this, on the basis of an examination of his work and life. After this there is a description of his pregenital conflicts and their manifestation in the form of manic-depressive and paranoic processes. It is attempted in particular to understand, with the help of these mechanisms, Wagner's complex temper and his fluctuations between depression and aggressiveness, self-destruction and destruction of the world, contrition and megalomania, rebellion and submissiveness, etc. It is also attempted to clarify the mythical obscurity of several of his works and to bring to consciousness the universal conflicts and problems contained in these. (p. 79)

One thing at least is clear from this description, namely, that in advancing his interpretation, Racker no longer draws exclusively on what had hitherto been regarded as the three phases of libidinal infantile development (the oral, anal, and phallic), but that he also includes the "pregenital" phase, which had been introduced into psychoanalysis during the intervening period.

"An Insight into Richard Wagner and His Works," by James Clark Moloney and Laurence A. Rockelein (Moloney/Rockelein 1948), offers the case history of a patient obsessed with *Tannhäuser* (90 percent of which is taken up with a verbatim account of the analysand's remarks). The authors' theoretical starting point (in keeping with Freud's assumption that the unconscious is both the creator and the recipient of art) is that the reactions of patients to works of art contain pointers not only to the problems of the patient but also to the conflicts felt by the artist. Their method, however, fails to shed any further light on Wagner's *Tannhäuser* beyond pointing out the fact that it deals with the "basic triangle between the man, the mother, and the wife."

The author of "Les guerres péniques chez Wagner," André Michel, considers the Oedipal motif the "most consistent leitmotif" in Wagner (Michel 1948, p. 75). The Dutchman's crime, Michel claims, is clear: he has overstepped a forbidden barrier, coition with the mother (*mère* / mother = *mer* / sea);

Tannhäuser's Oedipal guilt renders him incapable of mature love, so he remains split between carnal and spiritual love; Lohengrin cannot consummate his love in the earthly world; the love between Tristan and Isolde is symbolically incestuous and punished by death. Turning to Parsifal, Michel draws on the writings of Marie Bonaparte (Bonaparte 1933), citing sentences which similarly harp on the Oepidal theme (bound homoerotically to his father, Parsifal revolts against him, only to unite with him in the end). In the *Ring,* finally, all the libidinal phases are said to be present, with the Oedipal phase in particular evidence: the soul (Wotan) joins forces with childlike powers (Siegmund, Sieglinde, Siegfried) in order to contend with guilt (Alberich, Hagen). These are the *guerres péniques* (penile battles) of Michel's title. In the Wagner chapter of his book *L'école freudienne devant la musique* (Michel, 1965), Michel provides a comprehensive survey of psychoanalytic writings on Wagner, beginning with Max Graf's 1911 study and ending with Anton Ehrenzweig's 1949 essay. (He also includes a number of other works not classified here under the headings of either psychology or psychoanalysis.)

In "Some Psychoanalytic Concepts in Richard Wagner's 'The Ring of the Nibelung'" Irving Levin attempts an analytical interpretation of the symbols contained in Wagner's libretti (Levin 1959). But, having expended his talents on elaborate synopses, the author offers only a mechanical presentation of his symbolic interpretations, which give the impression of having been copied straight out of a textbook, without making any connections among them. Thus the waters of the Rhine at the beginning of *Das Rheingold* stand for the birth fantasy; the gold itself naturally represents feces and points in the direction of an anal-erotic fixation; Wotan's loss of an eye indicates symbolic castration (as it had for Groddeck); and so on.

"A Freudian View of *The Ring,*" by the English writer on music Robert L. Jacobs, is another analysis in the light of the Oedipus complex (Jacobs 1965). Whereas the early drafts of the *Ring* centered on the conflict between relatively abstract forces (gods and heroes), the final version shows Wagner transferring the battle between power and love to the field of sexuality, where it is distorted by the Oedipus complex. The root of all evil in the *Ring* is not Alberich's rejection by the Rhine Maidens but Wotan's loveless marriage with Fricka. Wotan's Oedipus complex forces him to conclude that love and power are antithetical forces. Siegfried, growing up without ever knowing his parents, can approach Brünnhilde with feelings of quasi-incestuous love, but Wotan is capable only of acting out his incestuous desires in unconscious fantasies projected onto Siegmund. These fantasies are associated in his mind with a plan for redeeming the world, which is of course foredoomed to failure.

In the preface to his book *Poetry and Psychoanalysis* (Dettmering 1969) the psychoanalyst Peter Dettmering announces that it is his intention neither to follow a pathobiographical, psychoanalytic line of inquiry nor to translate "cogent poetic symbols into sexual symbols at any price." By extending the psychoanalytic approach from what was predominantly a psychology of the contents of the id to include ego and object psychology, he hoped to benefit literature and art, where the aim was no longer exposure but a deepening of our understanding. Dettmering's analyses of Wagner are published under the title "The Redemption Motif in Richard Wagner's Music Dramas" (Dettmering 1969, pp. 155–211) and, as I have suggested, are conducted in the vocabulary of object psychology, with its changing role attributions such as the "Good Mother" and the "Bad Mother," while at the same time harking back to the "love requirements" postulated by Freud (see Freud 1910). The "requirement of the injured third party" (chap. 1) appears to Dettmering to go back almost as far as *Rienzi,* before emerging in fully recognizable form in *Holländer, Tannhäuser, Lohengrin,* and (chap. 5) in *Tristan. Das Rheingold* is analyzed (chap. 2) under the heading "The Struggle for Power," a struggle said to take place in the "anal-sadistic sphere of instinctual drives." The *Ring* as a whole, in Dettmering's view, is dominated by the "activities of the Oedipus fantasy" (chap. 3). In *Götterdämmerung* we witness the "failure of the hero" (chap. 4): "frustrated parent *imagines*" (imago = an idealized mental picture of oneself or another person) have turned against the son and brought about his downfall. In *Tristan* (chap. 5) we have an example of regression on the part of the hero, the love potion having the function of overcoming the incest taboo. The final chapter, "Redemption to the Redeemer," concerns itself with ultimate liberation from the role of "injured third party," an act prepared for in *Die Meistersinger* and then achieved in *Parsifal.* By freeing himself from his parent *imagines* (Amfortas and Kundry), Parsifal also redeems himself, just as Wagner frees himself from the "requirement of the injured third party" and resolves the Oedipus complex (although Dettmering does not use this term, preferring, as he states in his preface, to avoid psychoanalytic nomenclature).

In "Richard Wagner and the Ur Maternal Sea" (Cody 1975), John Cody, a professor of psychiatry, considers the role ostensibly played by Wagner's identification of the maternal element with the sea, especially during his six-year absence from composition between 1847 and 1853. Cody attempts to reduce the events to the language of object psychology: the "Good Mother/Good Self Merger" is said to correspond to Wagner's account of the "oceanic" embrace of poet and musician in *Opera and Drama.* This period of barren unproductiveness in Wagner's compositional output began, Cody argues, with the death of Wagner's mother on 9 January 1848, but the wellspring of his creative powers began to flow again with the Water music of *Das Rheingold* in 1853, when Wagner's relationship with Mathilde Wesendonck began to deepen. (There is, it has to be said, no conclusive evidence that Wagner's relationship with Mathilde had indeed begun to "deepen" by 1853.) The "Bad Self" that developed during Wagner's childhood had led to a "borderline" adolescence (that is, a personality type lying between neurosis and psychosis). At a later date, too, Wagner had been governed by two separate "self-images," the "bad" one of which he projected onto the French, the Jews, and the Italians. It was this "Bad Self" which was activated during his period of compositional sterility (witness his involvement in the 1848 revolution); only in his relationship with Mathilde Wesendonck did Wagner rediscover his "Good Self."

In "Wagner and *Lohengrin:* A Psychoanalytic Study" (Graham 1978) another professor of psychiatry, Lindsay A. Graham, sets out to show how Wagner sought to resolve his Oedipal problems through the creative process. Over and above the usual (Oedipal) interpretation of Wagner's uncertainty as to his father's true identity and his nighttime fears as a child, Graham examines a further episode in Wagner's life: his fear of cholera following his participation in an orgy with a friend when the composer was nineteen or twenty. Wagner's fear, the author maintains, was bound up with homosexual fantasies and the fear of castration. Graham then turns his attention to *Lohengrin* and to the composer's attempt to resolve these Oedipal problems through the opera. If, in Marienbad in 1844–45, Wagner had leaped out of his bath prematurely in order to dash off a sketch of *Lohengrin,* it was presumably because guilt over masturbatory fantasies during the bath had driven him to sublimate those fantasies in the form of the opera. Of the changes which Wagner had made to the legend, Gottfried's return at the end of the opera was dramatically unnecessary in Graham's view; thus Wagner must have had a particular, unconscious reason for introducing it. The truth of the matter, Graham believes, is that the relationships depicted in the opera mirrored those in Wagner's own family: the dead duke of Brabant is a reflection of Wagner's dead father, while Friedrich mirrors his stepfather, Ludwig Geyer, and he himself and his sister Cäcilie, Gottfried and Elsa. Graham concludes from all this that Gottfried represents Wagner's tabooed, incestuous self and Lohengrin his pure, asexual self. Wagner is said to have made ample use—not only here but with his other characters, too—of the defense mechanism of "object splitting" and also of the rescue fantasy. Finally, Graham ends up discussing the "manifestly homosexual relationship" between Parsifal and Lohengrin.

In my own essay "Senta and the Dutchman: A Narcissistic Collusion with a Fatal Outcome" (Vetter 1982), I have been guided by pair-related aspects of narcissism theory, itself a relatively recent development in psychoanalysis. Here I argue that both Senta and the Dutchman possess only a partial self, and that each strives to become a complete self by fusing with the longed-for Other. They engage in a complementary "narcissistic collusion" with each other, but it is a collusion which is highly unstable and, being liable to implode at the least disruption from outside (in this case through the figure of Erik), ends in both their deaths. This interpretation does not make any assumptions about Wagner's own personality but rather suggests a possible reason for the opera's continuing popularity today.

Another writer to draw on narcissism theory, this time in an approach to the *Ring,* is the professor of psychiatry Richard D. Chessick, whose article "'The Ring': Richard Wagner's Dream of Pre-Oedipal Destruction" (Chessick 1983) interprets the action of the tetralogy as a reflection of Wagner's catastrophic personality. The composer—according to Chessick one of the most repulsive human beings ever known—allegedly failed to progress beyond the pre-Oedipal stage and hence never achieved maturity. The curse on the ring represents self-destructive narcissism and narcissistic rage. The characters in the *Ring* are divided, nonintegrated object *imagines* from Wagner's pre-Oedipal phase: Alberich, for example, is the incestuous, narcissistic side of the father *imago,* which, following the Rhine Maidens' rejection of the love that is offered them, falls prey to classic narcissistic rage. Fricka, who represents Wagner's wife, Minna, is typical of the uncreative, rigid "German Hausfrau," a woman incapable of giving. And so on. The "redemption" at the end of the work offers the confused and confusing message that even in death, love is superior to hate. But, according to Chessick, no previous interpreter has explained why everything has to end in wholesale death and destruction. Oedipal explanations were not sufficient to account for this; rather, unresolved archaic pre-Oedipal conflicts were sexualized in the *Ring.*

In his book *Farewell to Valhalla: Richard Wagner's Erotic Society* (Schickling 1983), the author and journalist Dieter Schickling has attempted, by his own account, to provide a guide to a better understanding not only of Wagner's literary and musical works but also of Wagner the man. His aim, however, is not to offer "a precisely worded thesis" (p. 7). The result is a lively and often briskly written psychology of common sense, which, in an age when psychoanalytic ideas have already been debased as cultural assets, can apparently no longer get by without appealing to "the sacred name of Freud" (p. 14). It is, for example, now a foregone conclusion, even for the general public, that the "incest complex" must be accorded "the greatest significance in Wagner's poetic oeuvre" (p. 238, where Schickling cites Rank). That Wagner (as the dust jacket informs us) "granted women the utopian role of redemption" is no doubt a valid observation. But whether this also means that "the feminine element" becomes "the dream of a social alternative" and that Wagner is therefore an "emancipated composer in the midst of a male-dominated nineteenth century" remains open to serious question. Given his restorative ideas about redemption, the reception of Wagner and his works, not only in the nineteenth century but also in the twentieth, speaks a somewhat different language, a language which cannot simply be dismissed as the result of "many misunderstandings."

In a long essay titled "Richard Wagner as Cult Hero: The Tannhäuser Who Would Be Siegfried" Melvin Kalfus, president of the International Psychohistorical Society, lists all the psychologically revealing facts known, or believed to be known, about Wagner's childhood, life, and influences, from the unresolved question of his parentage to his marriages and his resurrection under national socialism (Kalfus 1984). Interspersed with all these facts and pseudofacts are random observations on the content of the operas, together with quotations from the writings of psychoanalysts, describing early childhood relationships apparently echoed in Wagner's own life and the resultant character traits. But the reader runs the repeated risk of losing sight of the theme that seems to be alluded to in Kalfus' title.

In his article "Parsifal and the Compassionate Psychoanalyst" (Canzler 1987), the psychoanalyst Peter Canzler sets out to trace the development that Parsifal has to undergo if he is to become capable not only of feeling pity but of redeeming Amfortas and "entering upon the dynastic succession." (The second half of Canzler's account is given over to the role of various kinds of compassion in psychoanalytic therapy.) According to Canzler, this development consists in resolving the Oedipus complex. Parsifal is reluctant to ask the question which will release Amfortas from his suffering since it would reveal his own Oedipal guilt at Amfortas' torment. During the five or so years of his quest (the approximate time taken to undergo psychoanalysis) Parsifal falls into Klingsor's anal trap, a trap representing Parsifal's divided self, an anal-sadistic part of him which he denies. As the kiss of the mother, Kundry's kiss arouses incestuous desires in Parsifal, who now has to suffer the Oedipal drama. He suddenly has the physical sensation of having injured his father (Amfortas) by desiring his mother (Kundry). By repudiating Kundry, he renounces incest and a primary relationship with the mother, in consequence of which Klingsor's anal magic becomes superfluous and disintegrates. There is now no longer anything to prevent Parsifal from realizing his wish to make up with Amfortas and to cure him, nothing to prevent him from returning as King of the Grail.[2]

In his essay "Parsifal: A Betrayed Childhood: Variations on a Leitmotif by Alice Miller" the musicologist Martin Geck attempts a radical reinterpretation of *Parsifal* using the unconventional views of the psychoanalyst Alice Miller (Geck 1988). Whereas the drama, in keeping with Freud's Oedipus theory (or Jung's idea of self-becoming, which I discuss in the next section), has invariably been seen hitherto as the symbolic enactment of a necessary process of development by which the individual learns to conform, Geck seeks to turn this positive interpretation right side up. The process of development depicted here is not in the least necessary for Parsifal either as boy or as adolescent. Rather it is necessary for the patriarchal society of the Grail brotherhood, which seizes the opportunity offered by the "pure fool," mistreating him as a sacrificial lamb and expecting him to solve the problems which their society

---

2. If Canzler, like others before him (see, for example, Rank 1912, p. 640), claims that Wagner, having lost his father at an early age, thus enjoyed undivided possession of his mother, psychoanalytic theory has once again done violence, albeit on a limited scale, to historical truth. Wagner, who was born on 22 May 1813, was only six months old when his father died (23 November 1813). Barely six months after that, in mid-May 1814 (by which time Wagner himself was just twelve months old), his mother conceived another child, Wagner's half-sister Cäcilie, who was born on 16 February 1815. The father on this occasion was the family friend Ludwig Geyer, whom Wagner's mother married on 28 August 1814, three months after the child was conceived. In other words, the infant Richard can have enjoyed "undivided possession" of his mother from at best the age of six months (when his father died) to the age of twelve months (when his half-sister was conceived). But even during these six months undivided possession is extremely unlikely. Geyer had been a close friend of the family for some time, and Wagner's mother could well have been having sexual intercourse with him before she conceived Cäcilie, or at least may have become more friendly with him immediately after her husband's death.

has brought on itself. Just as Alice Miller sees Freud's drive theory, and the kind of psychoanalysis practiced on the basis of that theory, as a means by which to implement paternalistic interests at the cost of children's rights in life, so Geck shows how the Grail fathers unload their own sense of guilt onto the shoulders of the next generation in the person of Parsifal, thereby breaking that generation on the wheel of their demands and rendering its members sufficiently submissive as to rid them of their guilt, while in actual fact forcing them to accept the same obligation to atone for that guilt, an obligation which passes ineluctably from one generation to the next in a never-ending spiral. (See also Lorenz 1914, Stekel 1917, Angelucci 1928, Bugard 1932, Caftale 1933, Ehrenzweig 1949, Jones 1959, Burke 1963, Lehmann 1986, and Miller 1988.)

Wagner in Jungian Psychology

The first significant reference to Wagner in the writings of Carl Gustav Jung, the Swiss psychiatrist who later founded his own school of psychotherapy, is in his *Transformations and Symbols of the Libido,* later revised and translated into English as *Symbols of Transformation* (Jung 1911/12). According to Jung's pupil Jolande Jacobi, it was here that he first drew attention to a number of archetypal motifs in the *Ring,* "investigating their symbolic content while drawing upon them in order to shed light on the phantasies of a mentally ill patient, and thus not only providing a better understanding of those phantasies by comparing them with certain historico-mythological evidence but also comprehending them psychologically by examining their place in the history of ideas" (Jacobi 1958, p. 140). Among examples of the kind of archetypal motif to which Jung was referring are two of the important "basic motifs" of the dramatic action which Jacobi herself mentions, namely, the "threefold anima-role of Brünnhilde as daughter, lover, and mother" (by *anima* Jung means those feminine characteristics present in the male psyche), and Wotan's role as an old man who has to give way to his successor, Siegfried, in order to be rejuvenated in him. But there are also interpretations of individual objects and events: the sword, for example, is seen as a symbol of the sun's power, while incest is the universal longing to return to a paradisal state of unconsciousness (Jacobi 1958, pp. 142–143).

Jung's interpretations—in other words, his assumptions concerning the psychological import of the various motifs—begin by comparing different mythological sources. According to Ralph Langner (1986b, p. 47), however, Jungian psychology lacks a large part of the theoretical basis that supports psychoanalysis. In consequence the theory and technique of literary interpretation have yet to find "explicit expression." This, it may be added, is hardly surprising, given that "intuition" is "the preferred instrument of interpretation" (p. 70). This means that a Jungian interpretation undoubtedly leaves a great deal of scope to the interpreter's subjective feelings—an attractive feature of Jung's ideas, perhaps, in comparison to psychoanalysis. Nonetheless, there have been relatively few Jungian interpretations of Wagner. An interpretation based on Jungian psychology, however, scarcely differs in its aims from one that is undertaken with the help of mythologically inspired words of wisdom. Thus it is difficult to draw a clear distinction between this kind of interpretation and the untold numbers of nonpsychological interpretations of Wagner.

Among Wagnerian writers of a Jungian orientation, pride of place must go to the philosophy professor Hans Grunsky and his numerous contributions to the Bayreuth program booklets. For the reasons just given, however, an account of them may be limited to his first such essay, "'Parsifal' in the Light of Depth Psychology" (Grunsky 1951), which at least makes its reference to depth psychology plain in its title.[3] In Grunsky's eyes Parsifal undergoes a process of self-discovery. Even a fatherless child, according to Jung, contains within him the "archetype of the father," and it is this that Parsifal sets out to find. His immoderate, and hence suppressed, relationship with his mother, together with his unfulfilled longing for his father, characterize him as a "fool" who does not know his name and who therefore has no identity of his own. Although he passes the "test of suffering" in the Temple of the Grail, where he shows fellow feeling for the wounded king of the Grail, he fails to find "what is most important," in other words, his name. Only when Kundry tells him his name, which she "of course" imagines "as an initiation into the secrets of physical love" (p. 8), does Parsifal put aside his foolish ways and really become aware of his great mission, which is to guide "humankind in general" back to the Grail, from which they had turned away. Parsifal achieves this by "reuniting spear and Grail," an act which produces a "creative synthesis of his male and female forces" (p. 11) and hence brings about the "enthronement of that androgynous human being" who acquires "his highest kingdom with his self" (p. 27).

Robert Donington's study *Wagner's "Ring" and Its Symbols: The Music and the Myth* is widely recognized as the definitive Jungian interpretation of the tetralogy (Donington 1963). A musicologist by training, Donington follows the four dramas, act by act, through the sixteen chapters of his book, offering an interpretation which, according to the dust jacket of the German edition, embraces "several levels: musical, dramatic, poetical, and psychological in the widest sense of the word." In spite of numerous references to the writings of Jung and others, long stretches of Donington's work in fact offer no more than a kind of homespun psychology and philosophy, a state of affairs for

---

3. For Grunsky's other interpretations of Wagner, see Vogt 1986. Grunsky's predilection for Jung goes back, of course, to a much earlier date than emerges from his essay on *Parsifal*, written for the reopening of "New Bayreuth" in 1951. As long since as 1935 he had found that it was "certainly no accident that those two Bolshevising psychologists Freud and Adler were Jews" (Grunsky 1935, p. 106), whereas Jung had "not gone along with Freud in Bolshevising the human mind. But no more has he found the right National Socialist solution, however close he appears to have come to it—so close, indeed, that we might, at first sight, attribute to him a certain sympathy with what we call the unity of mind and blood" (p. 99). It is no wonder that on 3 October 1935, the official party Board of Inspectors for the protection of National Socialist writings decreed that "the NSDAP [National Socialist Workers' party] has no objections to the publication of this essay" (verso of title page).

which the lack of any interpretive methodology on the part of Jungian psychology must largely be held responsible. Lengthy passages consist of detailed paraphrases of the operas' action enlivened by psychological explanations of a commonsensical kind. Elsewhere the author engages in anthropological speculations on a variety of themes drawn from here, there, and everywhere: in his discussion of act 1 of *Die Walküre,* for example, he speculates about the incest taboo and its "purpose," about the allegedly rare occurrence of physical incest, and much else besides. The musical interpretation is confined to an accompanying description of what goes on in the score. (See also Teillard 1948 and Kester 1984.)

Wagner in Transpersonal Psychology
In Jerome R. Sehulster's article "The Role of Altered States of Consciousness in the Life, Theater, and Theories of Richard Wagner" (Sehulster 1979/80) an attempt is made to analyze Wagner's works from a perspective largely ignored hitherto: that of the listener. (The term *altered states of consciousness* was devised by a particular school of humanistic psychology, namely, transpersonal psychology, and refers to those experiences that transcend what we see and feel during our normal waking consciousness.) In Sehulster's view the "secret" of the impact which Wagner's works have on the listener is in their ability to induce a trancelike state. Wagner himself, Sehulster argues, was familiar with such states, as is clear from his own accounts of (for example) the somnambulist state in which he claims to have conceived the prelude to *Das Rheingold* in La Spezia. His operatic characters, too, often experience similar states. But Wagner was particularly adept at designing his works and the conditions under which they were (and are) performed in such a way as to produce altered states of consciousness in members of his audience. The chief factors here are their extraordinary length and the density of the information they contain, together with the darkening of the auditorium, the complete invisibility of the orchestral apparatus that produces the music, and much else besides. Wagner's music, too, is said to possess trance-inducing characteristics in the form of a constant, regular pulse, gradual transitions, and the omnipresence of the past in the shape of leitmotifs, as well as a sequential technique that gradually heightens the listener's feelings, a style of harmonic writing that never comes to rest, and so on. All of this, Sehulster maintains, was recognized by Hanslick, and especially by Nietzsche, who called Wagner a "master of hypnotic tricks" (Nietzsche 1967, p. 166). Bertolt Brecht was reacting against Wagner's "theatre of intoxication" when he described it as a mass drug which dulled all social criticism and thereby maintained the status quo. According to Sehulster, Wagner associated changing political aims with the inducement of altered states of consciousness in the listener: during his pre-Schopenhauerian period Wagner had located the basis of capitalism in the individual "egoistical" consciousness, whereas he found the basis of communism to lie in a collective consciousness. At a later date he saw a unifying link in the German national spirit. But Sehulster concludes that it is ultimately

left to the listener whether or not he chooses to hear Wagner's work as a form of intoxication, as a link with this German national spirit, or as an outstanding work of art.

Wagner's Dreams: The Artist's "Darker Side"?

When Cosima Wagner's long-awaited diaries (CT) were finally published in Germany in 1976–77 (the English translation followed in 1978–80), it emerged that several hundred of Wagner's dreams were recorded there, a number probably greater than for any other historical personality. It must of course be remembered that Wagner did not write down his dreams himself, and a greater-than-average degree of conscious or unconscious censorship, not only on his own part but on Cosima's as well, almost certainly must be reckoned with.

One of the first to attempt to take account of the existence of this exceptional corpus of dreams was Martin Gregor-Dellin, whose chapter "What a Man Dreams" in his 1980 biography of the composer lists Wagner's "hundred most remarkable dreams." (This chapter is not included in the English translation.) "Even without interpretative obscurantism," Gregor-Dellin claims, these dreams convey "something of the darker side" of Wagner the artist (Gregor-Dellin 1980, p. 694). For the purposes of his survey he arranges them into different groups, as indicated by the running heads in the German edition: "Phantasms" (also referred to in the text as "empty dreams"), "A Guilty Conscience," "Burden of Guilt," "Loss Anxiety," "Women," "An Artist's Predicament," and "Death." (Since Gregor-Dellin, like Hall 1983, does not give the date of the dreams in question, the reader is prevented from checking their original wording in either the German edition or, in the case of Hall, in the English translation.) Although at least some of these dreams inspired Gregor-Dellin to exclaim, "What a goldmine for Sigmund Freud and the psychiatrists of his school! What a piling up of symbols of the Oedipus complex" (Gregor-Dellin 1980, p. 703), they do not appear to have been systematically investigated in any great detail by Freudians in the years since the diaries' first publication, although it could of course be said in the Freudians' favor that they had already discovered Wagner's Oedipus complex in his works a good three-quarters of a century previously, so that an analysis of his dreams could not be expected to reveal anything significantly new.

As I have mentioned, empirical personality research is dependent, for almost all its procedures, on data obtained from *living* persons. In the strict sense of the word, empirical research cannot, therefore, be carried out on historical persons, since, as a rule, such systematic data simply do not exist. In this case, however, dreams represent a certain exception; because they cannot be obtained directly from the analysand (by means of an electroencephalogram, for example), today's researcher must rely on the subject's oral or written report, much as the interpreter of dreams has always had to do during however many millennia the art of oneiromancy has been practiced.

In *Wagner par ses rêves* (Wagner through his dreams) Philippe Muller, a professor of psychology, examines Wagner's dreams in the course of conducting empirical research into dreams and personality in general (Muller 1981). At the same time he offers what appears to be a complete list (together with his own translation) of all the dreams contained in Cosima's diaries—421 in number. Muller argues that, for the dreams of a historical figure, a psychoanalytic method (which, strictly speaking, would require the dreamer's free associations) is less appropriate than a descriptive approach. He uses his own method of classifying the dreams into forty-one categories according to their content (listed on p. 43), a system he had originally designed for the projective personality test known as TAT (Thematic Apperception Test). In Appendix III (pp. 212–228) Muller examines the dreams in the light of a second system of categories. Developed by Calvin S. Hall (Hall/Van de Castle 1966), this system draws on an analysis of the content of the dreams of five hundred male and five hundred female subjects, thereby providing an additional instrument with which to measure the comparative frequency of different dream contents. When applied to Wagner, however, neither Muller's own approach to dream analysis nor the method borrowed from Hall leads to any clearly recognizable goal or result.

Hall's own contribution to the subject is his popular-scientific article "Wagnerian Dreams: One Hundred Years after Richard Wagner's Death, a Study of the Composer's Dreams Offers Clues to His Odious Behavior," in which the number of dreams is given as only 293 (Hall 1983, p. 36). Even if the principal subject of the dreams is "Wagner as victim," it would be wrong, Hall argues, to suggest that Wagner suffered from a persecution mania, since in his case, in contrast to that of paranoid personalities, almost every other character who figures in his dreams appears similarly in the role of victim. And one must not forget that Wagner believed in his own musical genius, and everything else was subordinate to that belief. Moreover, much of Wagner's reprehensible behavior was grounded in a basic insecurity, which found expression in his dreams.

Another article published to coincide with the anniversary of Wagner's death in 1983 is Justus Noll's witty piece, inspired as much by Karl Marx as by Sigmund Freud (Noll 1983). The title of the essay, "'Es wollte ihn wecken'—oder: Bach auf gehacktem Fleisch spielen" ("It[d] threatened to wake him"—or, performing Bach on chopped meat), refers to two entries in Cosima's diaries (24 November 1878 and 14 March 1878).

For his psychoanalytically colored account "Richard Wagner's Dream of Redemption" (Strunz 1986), the psychologist Franz Strunz has drawn on the descriptive findings established by Hall and Muller. But, independently of them, Strunz is convinced that it is "almost certain that Wagner was irredeemably marked by a childhood trauma." It was "difficult to ascertain in precisely what way he was marked," but not only Wagner's own remarks but also certain clear-cut sections of his biography provide a clue (p. 560). According to Strunz, Wagner's works "stand revealed as a highly varied wish phantasy concerning an imaginary relationship between a man and a woman and intended to overcome some early misfortune" (p. 562). Like Hall, however, Strunz is of the view that this insight does not affect the actual genesis of Wagner's music dramas, since many such psychic patterns exist without giving rise to creative works.

For studies of Wagner in other schools of psychology, see Vauzanges 1913 and also Caftale 1933 (graphology); Müller-Freienfels 1919 (German philosophical psychology, or *geisteswissenschaftliche Psychologie*); and Cox 1926 (test psychology).

Themes for Future Research

Essentially there are two possible points of departure in the psychology of art: it can take as its starting point either the personality of the author or, alternatively, that of the listener or reader, in other words, the author's audience. (The psychology of literary characters is included here as an example of the way in which the psychology of an individual can be applied to fictional characters; it is not, therefore, treated as an independent category.) As we have seen, traditional art psychology has in effect been concerned with only the first of these alternative approaches, that is, with the psychology of creative artists (and of their fictional characters). I shall start, therefore, with this approach.

Author Psychology

There are few who would give credence any longer to the claim, formerly advanced by psychiatry, that Wagner was a genius in spite of or even precisely because of the fact that he suffered from this or that form of mental illness (or, alternatively, that he was *not* a genius for the same reasons). The mad-ergo-a-genius theory has long since been scientifically laid to rest, and the mad-ergo-*not*-a-genius theory ought to have been exposed for what it always was, even at the time of its first appearance more than a century ago, namely, an ideological maneuver on the part of conservative cultural politicians carried out under the guise of science. (One thinks here, for example, of the criticisms leveled at Puschmann's pamphlet at the time of its publication in 1872; see Vetter 1988a.)

In much the same way the claim, formerly advanced by psychoanalysis, that those basic human structures (principally the Oedipus complex) which it assumed were universally present were shared by the artist Richard Wagner and that they revealed themselves in his works is basically of little interest any longer: the Oedipus complex has outlived its usefulness as the bogey of the middle classes. But what has emerged in the process are two highly remarkable and interconnected contradictions. The first is that, according to the theory of psychoanalysis, the Oedipus complex is present in each of us. But if this is so, why is it necessary to prove that it is also present in artists such as Wagner? After all, it has never been considered necessary to adduce special proof that artists also have, say, an appendix.

Whether or not psychoanalysts have recognized this first contradiction, even on a subliminal level, what is even more remarkable is the second, related contradiction: Freud himself had declared in no uncertain terms that psychoanalysis could say "nothing" that would "throw light on artistic talent"; it could not "explain the poet's genius" but only "construct" that part of the artist which he "shared with all men" (Freud 1925 and 1933; and see my discussion earlier in this chapter). What this means, however, is that, according to Freud, there can be no such thing as a specific psychoanalytic psychology of art and artists. (Of the writers on psychoanalysis discussed here, only Strunz appears to have recognized this with any clarity, when he says that Wagner's psychic makeup is insufficient reason to explain the existence of his works, since many such patterns may be found in other persons without enabling them to produce creative works of art; see the section on Wagner's dreams earlier in this chapter). If writers have nonetheless continued to "demonstrate" the existence of the Oedipus complex in artists (when what they really ought to have explained is why *all* creative artists do not write works *exclusively* about adultery and incest), this analysis was bound to give the impression—as, indeed, it clearly has done—that they had thereby said all, or virtually all, that needed to be said about the artist and the artistic process. Unless we are to assume that psychoanalysts are less than entirely clear as to the logic and effectiveness of their undertaking, it is difficult to avoid the suspicion that psychoanalytic interest in art and artists has been less concerned, in the main, with insight (apart from the banalities about human "universals") than with harnessing the public prestige that attaches to the person of the artist and pressing it into the service of presenting an apparently cogent demonstration of the truth of psychoanalytic theories. The school associated with the name of Jung, by contrast, did not initially claim that it wished to explain the artist's art by reference to his psyche; quite the opposite, it was the artist's psyche which was to be explained by his art—whatever that may mean.

In short, whole armies of experts from a variety of psychological disciplines have fallen on Wagner without ultimately being able to discover anything sufficiently specific in his artistic persona that would "explain" his artistry or his art. Not even empirical psychology appears to be anywhere near to developing theories potent enough either to enable it to predict an individual's creative abilities on the basis of conditions of socialization (or even of "creative genes," assuming such things to exist) or, conversely, to take a genius already recognized as such (Wagner, for example), and then to ask itself how the conditions known to have existed in that individual's life contributed toward the shaping of that genius in order to be able to obtain a test case with which to verify the original theory. The main obstacle here would seem to be the scant interest that empirical psychologists have hitherto shown in historical figures.

It would seem, in any case, that present-day psychology is still teetering on the brink of being able to explain the existence of a work of art in terms of the psychology of the artist who created it. Whereas the representatives of the different branches of psychology have already tried to operate on a *theoretical* level, the more basic *descriptive* level (which ought in fact to precede any attempt at theoretical exegesis) is still far from exhausted in the case of Wagner: the surviving historical material relating to the composer's life remains largely untapped, at least as far as his personality traits are concerned. Certain characteristics of his personality can be identified, for example, through comparison, wherever possible, of his own account of events as it appears in his autobiographical writings with the actual events in his life as recorded elsewhere.

Two examples will suffice. In his autobiography Wagner claims that the original title of *Tannhäuser—Der Venusberg* (literally, "The Mount of Venus")—was changed only when the publisher of the vocal score pointed out that obscene jokes were being made about it (ML 301). In fact, Wagner had altered the title as early as 1843, shortly after completing the text—in other words, years before the publication of a vocal score was even being discussed (WWV, p. 287). Wagner's reason for offering this distorted account may perhaps lie in his wish to present himself as a naively innocent artist who suddenly and unwittingly finds himself the victim of an uncomprehending (in this case obscenely so) audience. The second example concerns a letter to Wagner from the composer Gaspare Spontini ostensibly reproduced verbatim in *My Life* and showing its writer to have been a senile idiot. But when Spontini's original letter turned up little over a decade ago, it was seen to have a very different wording, moreover one that reflects the workings of a rational and responsible mind (see Deathridge 1979). Here, in a case of willful misquotation, we can exclude any possibility of an *unconscious* error on Wagner's part. The reason for his *conscious* distortion may once again have been his attempt to elevate his own reputation at the expense of someone else's.

In general, Wagnerian biography has hitherto followed a single source, namely, the composer's own account of his life in his autobiography. Far too little attention has been paid to the fact that, as Nietzsche (one of the few selected readers of the original, privately printed edition of *My Life*) recognized over a century ago: "What has hitherto circulated as "Wagner's Life" is *fable convenue*, if not worse. I confess my mistrust of every point attested to only by Wagner himself. He did not have pride enough for any truth about himself; . . . he remained faithful to himself in biographical questions, too—he remained an actor" (Nietzsche 1967, p. 182).

A somewhat more authentic account of Wagner's life than the one to be found in his autobiographical writings, penned as they were with an eye to public consumption, may well be reflected in his letters. But, although the letters have been less distorted for the benefit of posterity, they can as yet be of only limited use since, out of an estimated total of some ten thousand, only about a third have ever appeared in print (and then often in obscure publications). What from this point of view promises to be a more convenient edition, the *Collected Letters* (SB), inaugurated over twenty years ago, is still only fractionally complete. Not only has the publication of Wagner's letters suffered serious shortcomings and delays, but the genre of Wagner "literature" (which can normally be relied on to bring forth lengthy articles on even the most minor aspects of Wagner's works) has—unbelievable as it may sound—hitherto paid only scant attention to a dramatic work by the master, a tragedy entitled *Leubald* (WWV 1), which runs to over one hundred pages of printed text. Now that the disagreeable task of deciphering the manuscript has been completed (Vetter-Voss 1988), it emerges that this tale of Gothic horror by the fifteen-year-old Wagner is a psychologically remarkable piece of writing, pandemonically presaging his later oeuvre. It also appears to reflect certain aspects of Wagner's childhood and adolescence—and does so, moreover, with a vividness and coarseness that had not been recognized before (Vetter 1988a).

In addition to all this primary source material, which still remains to be made available, there presumably exists a virtually incalculable number of unknown documents by Wagner's contemporaries containing essential information on his life and psychological makeup. A single example must suffice. Not until relatively recently (Sigismund 1984/85 and Gregor-Dellin 1985) did it emerge that Wagner's mother (who seems to have veiled her past in a certain secrecy) had, in her youth, been the lover of Prince Constantin of Saxe-Weimar, the younger brother of Goethe's patron, Carl August, a revelation which must surely produce shock waves in every Oedipal theorist.

Audience Psychology

The second possible perspective for a psychology of art—research into the reception of works of art—is a relative latecomer to the field of art psychology and seems not yet to have found a sure footing for itself. One wonders whether there are any conceivable explanations that can be attributed to the nature of the historical origins of author psychology.

From the point of view of the two different kinds of pathobiography designed to account for genius, it seems unnecessary to posit a separate audience psychology, although the reasons for this differ slightly, depending on the kind of pathobiography under review: in the case of the milder variety (the artist is mad but capable of producing works of genius) the audience could scarcely have a role to play, for even if the genius *is* mad, his works themselves nonetheless remain precisely what they have always been on the strength of traditional aesthetic postulates; in other words, they are still works of genius. What could an audience add that would in any way be relevant? In the case of the stricter interpretation (the works are mad, and therefore the genius himself is either equally mad or else not a "true" genius) the psychology of the audience has more or less been accounted for in advance, since it goes without saying that only an audience of madmen could enjoy mad works written by mad artists.

Psychoanalysis, too, has answered both questions in one and the same breath by assigning art to the realm of the unconscious. If the artist created his works out of the suppressed wishes of his unconscious, those works, of course, would be nothing more nor less than a reflection of those wishes, and it is this in turn that casts a spell on an audience already possessed of the same forbidden wishes.

Jungian psychology adopted a different approach, but it too tended, of course, to exclude the audience: although its concern was the preexistent archetypal symbols undoubtedly present in the collective unconscious of artists and audiences alike, it was equally indubitable that only trained Jungian psychologists could be called on to identify and interpret them.

Audience psychology (or reader psychology; see Groeben/Vorderer 1986), which has begun to emerge as a separate discipline, more especially in the field of literature, has replaced the earlier concept that a work of art must have an objective psychological meaning. Indeed, even traditional schools of aesthetics had not, as a rule, reached any agreement as to what this ostensibly objective content might be, although they had all, independently and unwaveringly, clung to the *idea* that such a content existed. Audience psychology, by contrast, has moved away from an elitist definition of that content, in which only experts had a say, and turned instead to a democratic definition in which the man in the street is sounded for his opinion. The work of art can now have many meanings: in an extreme case it may have as many meanings as it has readers or listeners. It is therefore as a genuinely empirical science that audience psychology has responded to the long-established fact that works of art have always tended to be subjected to the most varied meanings and interpretations. Such an assessment of the empirically existent state of affairs is of course completely at odds with traditional notions of autonomous aesthetics, which seek to establish the "true" meaning of a work of art by recourse to the age-old art of hermeneutics.

In spite of the many hopes and fears that it has aroused, this move toward greater democratization (perhaps indicative of a paradigmatic change that is beginning to take place in research into art psychology) is still far from having solved all the problems with which traditional hermeneutics has hitherto had to wrestle. The question which must be at the top of the agenda as far as audience psychology is concerned should be less that of solving old problems than that of declaring new ones amenable to scientific inquiry. It may of course be of interest to us to know what the man or woman in the street thinks of *Parsifal,* however many "misconceptions" students of hermeneutics may wish to point out in his or her reaction to the piece. (Until recently, this right to express a private opinion has been conceded to only a select few at best—people such as Nietzsche and Adorno—with the result that their opinion has not infrequently been treated as if it expressed the "one true" meaning of the work in question.) It would be wrong to wish to see a populist egalitarianism in this democratic trend in audience psychology: questions that only experts can answer remain precisely that, even here. In other words, anyone wanting to know what Wagner, for example, thought of as the meaning of one or another of his works will not consult the aforementioned man or woman in the street but will instead turn to the relevant Wagnerian expert.

The only difference now is that the question as to the content, interpretation, or meaning of the piece will have to be couched in much more specific terms. Meaning is no longer meaning *in itself* but meaning *for someone:* in other words, the meaning of *Parsifal,* say, for Wagner himself, for this or that member of the first-night audience, for the average operagoer under the Second Reich, for the dictator Adolf Hitler, for the young Karl Popper in the Vienna of the interwar years, and so on. (That it may turn out that not all of these questions can be answered conclusively is, of course, another story.)

An early, isolated example of empirical audience research is *Music and Its Lovers: An Empirical Study of Emotion and Imaginative Responses to Music* by Violet Paget, an essayist and writer on aesthetics who wrote under the name of Vernon Lee. The dust jacket states the book's purpose as follows: "It seeks to understand why the same piece of music will seem good, i.e. worth hearing, to some people and bad to others. It describes the various responses of listeners and hearers to music and attempts to account for these being so various" (Lee 1932). Paget devised a questionnaire soon after the turn of the century (pp. 563–567), which, in the course of the ensuing years, she submitted in slightly altered form to some 150 experimental subjects. (This would not, of course, meet the standards required of modern surveys.) Two of her questions made particular reference to Wagner, and her study reproduces the brief descriptions supplied by about seventy of her subjects concerning the way in which Wagner's music affected them (pp. 533–542; see also index).

The present day has produced nothing more than isolated attempts at empirical research into responses to Wagner's music, the majority of which have been in the field of psychophysiology (Vehrs 1987 [in a research project which is still in progress, the so-called Vehrs lever is used to measure the degree of excitement felt during the *Meistersinger* prelude]; Sternagel 1989).

Ecstasy and Eroticization Aroused by Wagner's Music

In the case of Wagner, research in the field of audience psychology has hitherto been hindered by a certain taboo, inasmuch as his music—or rather his music drama—has repeatedly been associated with trancelike states and feelings of ecstasy. Susanna Großmann-Vendrey, one of the most knowledgeable experts on reactions to Bayreuth in the German press, speaks, for example, of "numerous accounts of trance-like states of near-ecstasy in the Bayreuth audience" (see Großmann-Vendrey 1977/83, III, 16, where, unfortunately, no detailed source references are given). Such experiences, however, were subject to powerful social constraints: "In the west, states of music-induced trance and ecstasy were frowned upon from the nineteenth century onwards, at least outside the realm of national customs, so that descriptions of them (such as the Viennese waltz) are, for the most part, correspondingly pejorative" (Brandl 1985, p. 424). However explicitly belletristic writers have seized on the theme of Wagnerian intoxication (see Koppen 1973), it has been stubbornly ignored by science, perhaps in keeping with the idea that the left (or "rational") half of the brain is not supposed to know what the right (or "emotional") half can feel. That this prejudice is by no means a thing of the past is clear, for example, from the way in which Funkkolleg Musik—a public broadcasting body in Germany set up in 1978 to promote a musical education among the population at large—was able to sum up, without further comment, the alleged views of the Marxist writer on musical aesthetics, Georg Lukács: "Allowing the feelings free rein would lead to non-conformism and inefficiency, even if they did not lead straight to the madhouse" (Zimmermann 1978, p. 74). This is a statement one might expect to find in some nineteenth-century treatise on the perils of masturbation.

In the case of Wagner's works, the aesthetic taboo bound up with musical ecstasy must have combined with the moral taboo associated with the ecstasy of sexual love to produce a particularly unassailable barrier, so that only in the subculture of nonprofessional musical audiences has justice been done to the eroticizing effect of Wagner's music in the form of a more or less self-evident open secret. Only a handful of brave souls from the "educated" classes have occasionally dared to confide their feelings to a secret diary or to refer to them in hushed voices as the "vices" of "others," let alone to speak of them in public. But even then what were presumably their own reactions were regularly passed off as the observations of some third party or as "general statements." The maverick writer Oskar Panizza, for example, devoted not only a poem but also an essay to the secret priapic pleasures of *Tristan*'s bourgeois audience—and perhaps also to his own orgasmic ecstasies (Panizza 1899 and 1900). Bernard Shaw, already an acknowledged music critic, openly admitted in *The Perfect Wagnerite,* first published in 1898, that Wagner had followed back "poetic love" to its "alleged origin in sexual passion, the emotional phenomena of which he has expressed in music with a frankness and forcible naturalism which would possibly have scandalized Shelley. The love duet in the first act of The Valkyries [sic] is brought to a point at which the conventions of our society demand the precipitate fall of the curtain; whilst the prelude to Tristan and Isolde is . . . an astonishingly intense and faithful translation into music of the emotions which accompany the union of a pair of lovers" (Shaw 1898, p. 74). Christian von Ehrenfels, respected in his day as a professor of philosophy in Prague but remembered now only for having coined the term "Gestalt quality" (a term taken over by Gestalt psychology), was himself an advocate of sexual reform who saw in Wagner "the most powerful eroticist yet produced by Mother Earth"; even now, Ehrenfels wrote, Wagner's eroticism was still regarded by the majority of people as a "partie honteuse" (Ehrenfels 1931, p. 9). In Ehrenfels's view, Wagner's "revelatory work" entitled him to be ranked alongside figures such as Heinrich Heine and Sigmund Freud, of all people (p. 11). Surpassing even Shaw in his physiological exactitude (although still not exact enough in terms of the precise number of bars involved), Ehrenfels reveals that it is possible to "point to the bars" in the second act of *Tristan* "in which the orgiastic ejaculations of that night twice burst forth and detumesce" (p. 10). Elsewhere in Wagner's works, by contrast, or at least in *Parsifal,* the opposite message has been uncovered, a message which may perhaps act on a more subliminal level: sexual pleasure is held out as mankind's greatest sin and source of guilt (Voss 1984).

In general, however, this sensitive issue has been treated only indirectly in the form of discussions of the "morality" or "immorality" of Wagner's music: his supporters pleaded for the former (M. 1870), while his opponents demanded the vice squad be brought in (Dorn 1879). Private censorship, principally (if not exclusively) to protect women's sensibilities (and here one thinks of the subtitle of Heinrich Dorn's 1879 tract, *Legislation and Opera Libretti (An Essay for Men),* was of course common from the outset and made no exceptions, not even in the case of female members of dynastic houses: Duchess Sophie of Bavaria (1845–1867) was excluded from the first performance of *Tristan* in Munich in June 1865 "out of moral considerations" (Sexau 1963, p. 141), and this in spite of the fact that she was no longer an innocent young girl but the wife (since February of that year) of Duke Carl Theodor of Bavaria (1839–1909). While working on the score of *Tristan,* Wagner himself had written these half-joking but also perhaps half-serious lines to Mathilde Wesendonck in mid-April 1859: "Child! This Tristan is turning into something *terrible!* This final act!!! . . . I fear the opera will be banned—unless the whole thing is parodied in a bad performance—: only mediocre performances can save me! Perfectly *good* ones will be bound to drive people mad,—I cannot imagine it otherwise. This is how far I have gone!! Oh dear!"

Nonetheless, the moral dangers posed by Wagner's works were occasionally judged in virtually the opposite way, as emerges, for example, from the reminiscences of the psychoanalyst Georg Groddeck, who, looking back on his youth from the vantage point of 1927, was to write: "When I was still young [Groddeck was born in 1866] and the world was a more moral place than it is today, young seventeen-year-old girls were still not allowed to attend a performance of *Faust* or to read [Gottfried] Keller's *A Village Romeo and Juliet,* but Wagner's *Die Walküre* could be admired and idolatrised without reservation, although its central concern is adultery and incest. If things are dressed up in heroic guise, they cease to be immoral, as we have learnt from Wagner's analytical textbook" (Groddeck 1927, p. 150). One can only hope that a careful and imaginative search for even more private accounts such as letters and diaries will throw further light on this aspect of historical responses to Wagner. In *The Bourgeois Experience: Victoria to Freud,* the cultural historian Peter Gay has shown that even in the field of nineteenth-century sexuality, where far stronger taboos might be thought to exist, it is possible to unearth an unexpectedly large number of private confessions, even if that number is still small in absolute terms. A number of splendid examples of the type of reaction provoked by Wagner are included in his chapter "The Food of Love" in volume two, *The Tender Passion* (Gay 1986/87). For the present, it goes without saying that the whole range of methods available to empirical psychology must, in turn, be enlisted in order to establish whether Wagner's music has any erotic effect on present-day audiences.

A number of pieces of nineteenth-century evidence suggest, however, that Wagner's effect was not due exclusively to the magical power of his music (or to that of the music drama as a whole). Nietzsche (even if we allow for a degree of irony) described certain sectors of Wagner's audience in this way: "Just look at these youths—rigid, pale, breathless! These are the Wagnerians: they understand nothing about music—and yet Wagner becomes master over them" (Nietzsche 1967, p. 172). And, even more clearly: "It was not with his music that Wagner conquered [these youths], it was with the 'idea'" (p. 178). In much the same way Max Nordau found every reason for believing that "all the mystics of the Jewish sacrifice of blood, of woollen shirts, of the vegetable *menu,* and sympathy cures, were compelled to raise their paeans in [Wagner's] honour, for he was the embodiment of all their obsessions." But "as for his music, they simply threw that into the bargain . . . The vast majority of Wagner fanatics understood nothing of it. The emotional excitement which the works of their idol made them experience did not proceed from the singers and the orchestra, but in part from the pictorial beauty of the scenic tableaux, and in a greater measure from the specific craze each brought with him to the theatre, and of which each worshipped Wagner as the spokesman and champion" (Nordau 1895, I, 210). And in her article "From Wagner to Nietzsche: A Youthful Experience" the Viennese writer and feminist theorist Rosa Mayreder (born 1858) recalls how, in her youth, what had impressed her more than anything else was Wagner's early writings, with their polemical onslaught on Christianity (Mayreder 1936, p. 8). She gave the eighteen-year-old brother of her future husband "*Art and Revolution* to read; and from that moment onwards he was a believer in, and a disciple of, Wagner" (p. 10).

Nor, in this context, can we forget Wagner's influence on the National Socialists. Pride of place must go here, of course, to Adolf Hitler, for whom (according to the much later account of August Kubizek, a friend of his youth) a performance of *Rienzi* in Linz in 1906 or 1907 was of immense political significance: even as late as 1939 Hitler is still said to have recalled the performance with the enthusiastic words, "In that hour it began" (Kubizek 1954, p. 66). The extent to which Wagner continues, even today, to exert an ideological influence on others is something which would be well worth investigating from an empirical standpoint.

Faced with all these potentially eroticizing and politicizing views, with left- and right-wing Wagnerism, and with the whole confusing spectrum of different meanings and interpretations, we are bound to ask ourselves (and this is a question which may even assume the nature of a hypothesis) whether the impact of music—and not only Wagner's music—should rather be construed according to the attributive theory of emotion advanced by Schachter and Singer. These two psychologists have shown that test subjects administered the hormone epinephrine without their knowledge, and thereby "neutrally" stimulated, experienced this stimulation as a source of enjoyment or annoyance depending on whether they had been placed in contact with pleasant or unpleasant people (Schachter/Singer 1962). By analogy we might regard the role of music as that of an equally nonspecific agent which raises the general *level* of stimulation while not prejudging the particular *content* of that sensation. Music—whether by Wagner or any other composer—would therefore increase the intensity of the stimulation felt by the listener, but the cognitive interpretation of that stimulation—whether it be the right-wing politicization associated, say, with the National Socialists or the left-wing politicization associated with Adorno, or whether it be the right-wing eroticization associated with Schopenhauer (among others) or the left-wing alternative associated with Ehrenfels—would be dependent, first, on the immediate environment (a Nuremberg party rally, for instance) in which the musical offering that provided the stimulation took place and second, on the interpretational pattern (Nordau's "specific craze") which each listener brings with himself or herself. According to this hypothesis, music itself has (initially) no fixed meaning for the listener; rather it intensifies the emotional charge of interpretational patterns which are offered at that particular moment and/or which already exist for the listener, even though each particular interpretation will strike him (or her) as a genuine property of the music itself.

Translated by Stewart Spencer

CHAPTER 4

The Revolutionary of 1848–49

RÜDIGER KROHN

"The Dresden revolution and all its consequences have now taught me that I am by no means made out to be a real revolutionary: I realized from the unhappy outcome of the uprising that a true victorious revolutionary must act in total disregard for others . . . But it is not people like us who are destined to carry out this fearful task: we are only revolutionaries in order to be able to *build* on new ground; what attracts us is not to *destroy* things but to *refashion* them, and that is why we are not the people that fate needs . . . *I herewith sever my links with the Revolution*" (emphasis in original). The Dresden uprising had ended only five days earlier when Wagner wrote these words in a letter to his wife, Minna (14 May 1849)—a brief span indeed between active involvement in the uprising and this "parting" from its ideals and principles.

Like all the autobiographical statements to which Wagner is so prone both in his private correspondence and in his writings, these remarks must be treated with considerable caution. Immediately after the crushing of the revolution, Wagner went to great lengths to play down his part in the unrest and the events leading up to it, to present himself as a harmless witness. These efforts are most apparent in *My Life,* the autobiography that Wagner dictated to Cosima—a work intended for his royal patron, Ludwig II of Bavaria. Wagner's account of his part in the Dresden uprising was produced almost twenty years after the actual events, yet for many years *My Life* was the decisive source for determining Wagner's role in the events of May 1849. His own account fitted in neatly with the intentions of his biographers, because for decades Wagnerian scholars were anxious to avoid too great a politicization of Wagner's life and work. His art was their sole concern.

There is, however, no longer any real doubt that Wagner was involved in this unsuccessful revolution. His biased testimony has been disproved by documentary and archival material, contemporary accounts, and historical studies. Although there is no evidence to support the occasional claims that Wagner was one of the leaders of the uprising, the fact of his participation is no longer in dispute. Discussion now centers on the motives for his involvement—an involvement that emphatically did not end with the failure of the uprising but continued to make itself felt in his writings on art, and not only in his Zurich essays.

The revolutionary energies of the man who had been royal kapellmeister at the Dresden Opera since 1843 derived not so much from a realization of the political necessity of violent revolution as from those sources that always decisively influenced his actions and his creative work: his self-obsession and conception of a new art on the one hand, and his financial difficulties and dogged self-assertiveness on the other. To stress these motives, however, is not to minimize once again Wagner's involvement, but to show how the social revolutionary and even anarchistic impulses that determined his behavior during and after the May uprising are explainable in terms of his personality and of fundamental modes of thought and action which manifested themselves on other occasions.

Wagner's remarks, as well as his activities in the Dresden uprising and the events connected with it, display the wild enthusiasm, the spontaneous emotionalism, and the dubious tendency toward speculative exaggeration so typical of the composer. They reveal that once again the sublime and the trivial combined in Wagner to form a dangerous mixture whose explosive force was further magnified by the circumstances of the time, although it is impossible to define causal and temporal sequence in the interaction between these subjective and objective factors.

Wagner's conceptual apparatus for analyzing the revolutionary movements of the time was chiefly provided by August Röckel, whose political views had been powerfully shaped by his experience of the July revolution in Paris in 1830 and by close study of social reform movements, particularly in England. Wagner had been instrumental in finding Röckel a post as assistant conductor (Musikdirektor) in Dresden in 1843, since which time Röckel had been extremely active politically. He was well versed in the relevant political and socialist writings of these turbulent years, and he clearly exerted a lasting, indeed a "demonic"[1] influence on the composer. (It is significant that Wagner's library in Dresden did not contain a single political work until he met Röckel.)

According to Wagner, Röckel's "oratorical gift . . . evolved in private conversation to a stupefying intensity" (ML 364), and no doubt in their private conversations Röckel expatiated on the "social-utopian and revolutionary intellectual impulses" (Gregor-Dellin 1973, p. 26) provided by works such as Proudhon's Qu'est-ce que la propriété? (What is property?, 1840); Weitling's Evangelium des armen Sünders (The poor sinner's gospel, 1843); Feuerbach's Grundsätze der Philosophie der Zukunft (Principles of the philosophy of the future, 1843) and Wesen der Religion (The essence of religion, 1845); or Stirner's Der Einzige und Sein Eigentum (The individual and his property, 1845). It is

1. Dinger 1892, p. 96. This source gives a detailed account of the relationship between Wagner and Röckel. For a more recent version, see Gregor-Dellin 1983, pp. 128ff.

unlikely that Wagner, always a master of the rapid, purposive acquisition of ideas, had read these works himself. His knowledge was probably based on his lengthy discussions with Röckel in particular but also with other members of the group of intellectuals who met regularly for discussions in the Engel restaurant in Dresden. (The group included, among others, the architect Gottfried Semper and the painter Friedrich Pecht; see ML 318ff.)

The knowledge of Marx which is occasionally evident in Wagner's writings and remarks is probably also secondhand, the result of conversations with Röckel about his reading of Proudhon or (in later years) of his discussions with Georg Herwegh. There is no evidence that Wagner studied Karl Marx's writings, either before or after 1848. (The *Communist Manifesto,* written by Marx and Engels, appeared in February 1848.) Wagner does not refer to Marx at all. In 1876, however, Marx contemptuously described Wagner as a "state composer."

The passage in *My Life* in which Wagner lists the reasons for Röckel's passionate political commitment is revealing. Wagner writes that Röckel "had long since abandoned all hope of earning a decent living from his musical career," and that his job as assistant conductor "had become pure drudgery." He says that Röckel, "who had to plug along miserably, getting increasingly into debt," hoped to improve his position through the reading of "books on political economy" (ML 363). Röckel believed that this improvement could be achieved only by the "reshaping of the bourgeois order . . . after a complete transformation of its social basis" (ML 373; translation modified). Wagner thus implies that the motives for Röckel's political commitment are at least in part egotistical and apolitical.

Another significant feature is that in retrospect Wagner stresses the contrast between his motives and those of his friend: "On the basis of the socialist theories of Proudhon and others pertaining to the annihilation of the power of capital by direct productive labor, he constructed a whole new order of things to which . . . he little by little converted me, to the point where I began to rebuild upon it my hopes for the realisation of my artistic ideals" (ML 373). But before this, in the letter to Minna (14 May 1849) quoted earlier, he had described his position in entirely different terms: "Deeply dissatisfied with my position and finding little pleasure in my art . . . so deeply in debt that my regular income would have satisfied my creditors only after many years and the most shameful constraints,—I was at odds with the world, I ceased to be an artist, frittered away my creative abilities and became—in thought, if not in deed—a revolutionary plain and simple. In other words I sought fresh ground for my mind's latest artistic creations in a radically transformed world."

As early as the mid-1840s, Wagner had plunged into political discussion with characteristic gusto and total commitment to his convictions, and his fervent advocacy of these convictions drove him—beyond the liberal positions of the Young Germans—to increasingly radical statements. The socialist writer Alfred Meissner gives this account of a conversation with Wagner in

September 1846: "Richard Wagner considered the political situation ripe for fundamental change and thought it inevitable that there would be an upheaval in the near future . . . I still recall his precise words: that revolution had already been accomplished in the minds of all; that the new Germany was as complete as a casting and required but a single hammerblow on the clay mold to emerge" (quoted in Gregor-Dellin 1983, p. 134). But the true meaning of the longed-for revolution becomes clear in a letter Wagner wrote to the critic Ernst Kossak on 23 November 1847, following his disappointing stay in Berlin in the autumn of that year: "My Berlin ambitions are also a thing of the past . . . There is a dam to be broken through here, and the means is: revolution! The positive foundations must be built." But this foundation was to be no more than that of Wagner's art. The letter culminates in the surprising but symptomatic statement: "Just one sensible decision by the King of Prussia for his opera-theatre and everything will be in order again!"

In view of this blithe equation of his private interests with political objectives—however much Wagner may have felt and argued that the former were the expression of higher needs—it is hardly surprising that he was mocked by some contemporaries, who described him as a revolutionary on behalf of the theater, an accusation Wagner vehemently rejects in his essay *A Communication to My Friends*. Nonetheless, this autobiographical sketch, written in 1851, only two years after the Dresden uprising, confirms yet again the close and indissoluble link between the artistic and social driving forces that shaped his thoughts and actions. "Reflections on the possibility of a fundamental transformation of our theatrical system," he writes, "have driven me to a realisation of the *unworthiness of political and social conditions that are capable of bringing about only the artistic situation which I have just been attacking*" (emphasis in original). Therefore, he continues, he was "capable of completely recognising the necessity of the revolution dawning in 1848" (SSD IV, 308ff.).

In the *Communication,* where Wagner is obviously trying to correct his own image, he stresses that he had never "really" been involved in politics, or rather that his "participation in the political world of appearances had always been artistic in nature" (SSD IV, 309ff.). A work that certainly belongs in this category is the pamphlet *Concerning the Royal Orchestra,* which Wagner presented to the management of the Hoftheater in 1846. It outlines a scheme for substantially improving the income and the social security of the musicians and for raising the artistic quality of their work. Wagner's petition met with no success, and his relationship with the theater director, August von Lüttichau, deteriorated rapidly. Wagner had every reason to be dissatisfied with his work and its moderate success. He reduced his conducting activities to the bare minimum. In August 1847 he even offered to resign, and when this offer was rejected, he applied for a drastic increase in salary.

Wagner's financial situation was desperate. He was already heavily in debt, and unsuccessful speculations on the sale of his opera scores plunged him even deeper into the red. His application for a raise—in reality a promotion to parity with the court kapellmeister Reissiger, whom he envied—was granted, but on such humiliating terms as to fuel his resentment of the theater management. Thus in this respect, too, Wagner had little to lose in Dresden, and in his bitterness over the obstruction of his artistic and personal advancement he "inclined—naturally, one is tempted to say—towards republican tendencies" (Mayer 1978, p. 75).

The news of the uprising and proclamation of a republic in Paris in February 1848 therefore found Wagner in a most receptive frame of mind for revolutionary developments. When the uprising spread to Germany, reaching Saxony by the end of February, King Frederick August II, pressed by petitions from several towns, at first rejected all demands for reform. But under the pressure of events, in March he declared that he was prepared to make compromises, including a partial restructuring of the cabinet, the appointment of liberal ministers, and certain changes in the law. This limited success was greeted enthusiastically by the people, and Wagner, now seeing hope for his own plans, was among the most vociferous in the general acclaim for the king (cf. ML 36off.).

At this time Wagner was in the midst of finishing the score of *Lohengrin,* and his role in the events of the following weeks was marginal, that of a distant observer. After the fall of Metternich, fierce street fighting broke out in Berlin and Frankfurt on 18 March, and on 31 March a provisional parliament was set up to work out the constitution for a national assembly, developments that Wagner described as "oddly pleasant" (ML 361). On 28 April, having completed *Lohengrin,* he found "the leisure necessary to look about and study the course of events" (ML 362).

Wagner soon saw cause for concern that the results of the radical political changes could jeopardize his artistic plans. In response to proposals to cut subsidies for the Hoftheater, he wrote a lengthy paper titled *Plan for the Organization of a German National Theater for the Kingdom of Saxony,* which he presented on 11 May. Wagner's *Plan* included measures designed to democratize the running of the theater and the orchestra, the founding of an association of playwrights and composers, salary increases, and the establishment of a drama school and choral institute. But the telltale point was one he was careful to suppress from his *Collected Writings:* the demand that managing the theater be the responsibility of a single kapellmeister. There is no doubt that this director was to be none other than himself, and the proposal was therefore doomed to failure. It is possible that this new defeat made the composer even more sensitive and more receptive to the revolutionary events of his time. At any rate his "previous plans, such as those for a reform of the theatre," as he tells us in the *Communication,* now seemed "childish"; he shunned "any concern with artistic proposals," for they suddenly appeared "ridiculous." He "no longer had any choice" but "emphatically turned [his] back . . . on a world to which in [his] true nature [he] no longer belonged." Instead, he began "to speak out against this entire system of art in its connection with the political-social conditions of the modern world" (SSD IV, 333ff.).

Wagner now devoted his time to "politics, socialism, communism" (BB

95). He wrote "a popular appeal in verse" to the German princes and their peoples (ML 362), and on 19 May 1848 sent a letter to Franz Wigard, the Saxon deputy in the Frankfurt National Assembly, containing proposals for a new political order, including demands for "immediate issue of arms to the whole country" and a solution to the "territorial question": *Parliament must first revolutionize the individual states . . . If you seek less rigorous means, you will not achieve your goal"* (emphasis in original).

Wagner now gave himself up completely to the revolutionary impetus of subsequent events. He joined the Dresden Vaterlandsverein (Association of the Fatherland), a left-wing republican counterweight to the Deutscher Verein (German Association) with its program for a constitutional monarchy. He later declared that he had taken part in this organization's activities simply, "as in all these things, as a friend of the arts" (ML 364). But he made his debut in Dresden's political life with a much-discussed speech, *How Do Republican Aspirations Stand in Relation to the Monarchy?* Given on 14 June 1848 to the Vaterlandsverein, the speech had previously been published anonymously in the *Dresdener Anzeiger*.

In this address Wagner showed that he was at best a "synthesizer of other people's philosophies, an imitative thinker, not an original philosophical genius" (Gregor-Dellin 1973, p. 21). His proposal, which was chiefly influenced by the ideas of Proudhon and Weitling, included demands for the abolition of the First Chamber and of the aristocracy, but emphatically rejected "the most fatuous and futile doctrine" of communism, and advocated that "the king should be the first and most genuine republican" (SSD XII, 223, 225). This somewhat muddled attempt to reconcile the ideas of the monarchists with those of the republicans caused widespread indignation, particularly at the Hoftheater, whose management immediately removed *Rienzi* from the repertoire.

Wagner responded to the attacks from all sides by writing several self-justificatory letters, the most important being to Lüttichau and the king. Then, after several attempts to consolidate his financial position had failed, he set off for Vienna, in the hope of realizing his schemes for theatrical reform and possibly even finding a new position there. Eduard Hanslick gives this account of a meeting with the composer: "Wagner was full of politics; he expected that the victory of the revolution would bring a complete rebirth of art, society and religion, a new theater, a new music" (quoted in Gregor-Dellin 1973, p. 21). Yet again it became apparent that this victory of the revolution was "conceived of as the victory of the theory and practice of Richard Wagner" (Mayer 1978, p. 75).

These plans also came to nothing, and Wagner returned to Dresden, where he became absorbed in a study of the Nibelungen saga: literary speculations on a revolution inspired from above in which heterogeneous social utopias and mythical dreams of redemption combine to form a confused and confusing doctrine of salvation.

Further humiliations at the Hoftheater followed, among them the cancellation of scheduled performances of *Lohengrin* because of Wagner's article *Germany and Its Rulers,* a sharp attack on the dominant aristocracy which appeared anonymously in Röckel's new, extreme left-wing newspaper *Volksblätter*. The upshot of all this was that Wagner, now increasingly under the influence of Röckel, burned all his bridges behind him, later writing in his *Annals* of the autumn of 1848: "Break now decided.—Solitude: communist ideas on fashioning of mankind of the future in a way conducive to art" (BB 95; translation modified).

From this point on Wagner, apart from his work on the prose draft and the first version of the libretto for *Siegfrieds Tod,* devoted more and more of his attention to the revolution then brewing in Saxony—and not merely as an apolitical spectator, concerned only with his own vision of art, who is suddenly sucked into events (these are the terms in which he later attempted to trivialize his involvement); on the contrary, an undoubted purposefulness of behavior was evident both in his revolutionary writings of 1849 and in his actions during the May uprising. Nor can this behavior be explained away by reference to the frustrated royal kapellmeister's volatility or by his obvious expectation that a radical political transformation could only prove favorable to his artistic vision. The main motivation behind Wagner's social revolutionary disposition in the thirteen months of the German uprising was clearly personal, focusing chiefly on the realization of his private goals, a fact that is proven by numerous documents and writings: "The revolution is *his* revolution" (Mayer 1978, p. 75).

In January 1849 the newly constituted representatives of the people of Saxony demanded recognition of the basic rights proclaimed by the Frankfurt National Assembly—but these demands were rejected. During the period of smoldering political conflict Wagner produced a draft of a "tragedy," *Jesus von Nazareth* (Jesus of Nazareth), which portrays Christ as a social revolutionary, links the idea of redemption to the abolition of property, and culminates in Jesus' self-sacrifice—an interpretation typical of Wagner's thinking in 1848–49. His tone became even more radical in an article published anonymously in Röckel's *Volksblätter* on 10 February. The article, titled *Man and Existing Society,* claimed that society's task is to educate mankind, to "perfect [men's] spiritual, moral and physical capabilities," and thus to "lead them to an ever-higher, purer happiness" (SSD XII, 241), a mission in which art, of course, could—or rather had to—play a decisive part.

On 25 February 1849 the Reform Ministry in Saxony, founded in March 1848, was abolished, and the reactionary forces in the government, led by the conservative Freiherr von Beust, gained control. Wagner, the "political rhymester" (Gregor-Dellin 1983, p. 163), responded with *Die Not* (SSD XII, 361ff.), a passionate poem which betrays a conspicuous delight in the radical destruction of the existing order. It is possible that this work was inspired by the anarchist Mikhail Bakunin, whom Wagner had met through Röckel and who made a lasting impression on the composer, although his grasp of Wagner's artistic ambitions was tenuous. Bakunin even suggested to the admiring composer that he create a work in which the tenor sings, "Off with his head!"; the soprano, "To the gallows!"; and the basso continuo, "Fire, fire!" (ML 387).

The hopes of the reformers were dashed on 3 April 1849, when King Friedrich Wilhelm IV of Prussia refused the Imperial Crown, which the Frankfurt National Assembly had offered him on 28 March. Wagner immediately wrote a furious hymn in prose, *The Revolution,* which was published in the *Volksblätter* on 8 April (SSD XII, 245ff.). "From now on the socialist revolution took the form of a rhapsody" (Mayer 1978, p. 81), whose author chanted a powerful dithyramb on the all-destroying, chain-breaking, victorious power of radical change, the only force capable of creating the "free human being." At the same time, Wagner was taking part in discussions and plans for an armed insurrection. It has even been claimed, though of course never proved or disproved, that Wagner, together with Röckel, ordered a large supply of hand grenades. There is nonetheless no doubt that Wagner was a remarkably active conspirator in the period leading up to the May riots in Dresden.

On 30 April Friedrich August II, following the example of Prussia, blatantly violated the constitution by dissolving both chambers of the Saxon parliament and dismissing most of his ministers. The king, strongly supported by his foreign minister, von Beust, was demonstratively steering a collision course and seeking confrontation even before the opposition could finalize its plans to counter these measures. On 2 May Dresden was full of rumors of imminent invasion by Prussian troops, and the Communal Guards and Saxon militia confronted each other, awaiting developments. On 3 May the Town Council, summoned as a precautionary measure, set up a Defense Committee against foreign troops, and on the same day hostilities broke out between troops loyal to the king and the Communal Guards. The Dresden May uprising had begun.

Faced with this new situation, Wagner was overcome by a sense of "great, almost extravagant well-being" (ML 391) and was reminded of Goethe's sensations at the battle of Valmy—a further example of his persistent tendency to strip concrete events of all reality and to transform them into aesthetic impressions. Despite this inclination, Wagner set about making himself useful in the struggles that were under way—for example, by buying rifles for the Patriotic Club—since the Defense Committee had ordered the arming of citizens and the building of barricades. In the small hours of 4 May the king and his ministers fled the city; the bewildered troops agreed to a five-hour truce; and the rebellious townspeople formed a provisional government—with O. L. Heubner, K. Todt, and S. E. Tzschirner among its members—who swore an oath of loyalty to the German constitution.

Wagner, although also affected by the general bewilderment and excitement, took advantage of the truce for a daring stroke. He drafted and had printed an appeal with the heading: "Are you with us against foreign troops?" This he distributed to the Saxon soldiers in an effort to persuade them to make common cause with the Communal Guards, both to avoid further bloodshed and—as had already happened in Württemberg—by this demonstration of unity to force the politicians to accept the Paulskirche constitution. Wagner's actions came to nothing, although, amazingly, he was not harmed. That evening he returned home, and on the way, at least according to his account in *My Life,* he found sufficient artistic leisure to muse on his plans for an opera about Achilles.

In the days that followed, Wagner worked indefatigably for the provisional government as an envoy, intermediary, and scout. From the tower of the Kreuzkirche he observed the street fighting that had broken out again, as well as troop movements and the arrival of reinforcements for both his own and the enemy's side. He spent the nights at this far-from-safe post, holding philosophical, theological, and aesthetic discussions with his comrades Berthold and Thum. The arrival of Prussian troops early in the morning of 6 May brought matters to a head. The fighting at the barricades—some of them erected under the expert guidance of the architect Semper—became fiercer, and many of the Communal Guards' positions were captured. Suddenly the Old Opera House burst into flames, set ablaze for strategic reasons and not, as some later claimed, by Wagner.

As the situation deteriorated, Wagner escorted his wife to safety away from the city. Then he returned to Dresden. The rebels, now at the end of their rope, were preparing to retreat to the Erzgebirge, where they proposed to fight an "all-German popular war." At this point Wagner "quite consciously abandoned all personal considerations" (ML 402), and in this final phase of the unequal struggle he demonstrated considerable revolutionary energy. He remained in constant touch with the provisional government (especially with its leader Heubner) and with Bakunin, who throughout the chaos displayed astonishing circumspection. Wagner's euphoric enthusiasm, his "acquiescence born of despair" (ML 402), which formed a stark contrast to the grimness of the situation around him, manifested itself in passionate speeches and appeals, in spontaneous embraces and undaunted confidence.

All this enthusiasm could not prevent the crushing of the Dresden uprising on 8 May 1849. Its leaders (Heubner, Bakunin, Röckel, and others) were imprisoned, and most remained in prison for many years. Wagner himself escaped arrest by sheer luck and a series of grotesque misunderstandings. He left for Weimar on 10 May, arriving on the thirteenth. There he was welcomed by his friend and patron Franz Liszt. The next morning he attended an orchestral rehearsal of *Tannhäuser,* which "again stimulated me artistically in manifold ways" (ML 413). He also visited Princess Caroline von Sayn-Wittgenstein, went to the Wartburg (for the first time), and was received in Eisenach by the Grand Duchess Maria Pavlovna. The world of the arts now reclaimed its prodigal son.

In letters to his wife (14 and 16 May 1849) and to Eduard Devrient (17 May 1849), Wagner attempted at some length to justify his involvement in the uprising and at the same time to minimize his role. On 16 May "Wanted" posters bearing his name were printed; they were published in the *Dresdener Zeitung* on 19 May, and later in other local newspapers. Wagner was forced to flee to neutral Switzerland. Escaping with the help of Liszt, and using a forged passport, he arrived in Zurich on 28 May.

Wagner was now finished with the revolution, which according to official figures had claimed over two hundred lives, although the real toll was probably considerably higher. It is impossible to establish the extent of Wagner's actual involvement in the uprising, or the degree to which his motives were artistic as opposed to political—the extent to which he saw the rebellion as a means of furthering art or art as a means of furthering revolution. Even the official documents provide only approximate, relative indications: the police file compiled in 1856, when Wagner put in his first appeal for a pardon, lists all the charges against him (Lippert 1927, pp. 17ff.), accusing him of giving considerable support to the insurgents, whereas Wagner himself always claimed that he had been nothing but a harmless spectator, interested primarily in the artistic and philosophical aspects of the events. In his exile in Switzerland he avoided any contact with his comrades from Dresden.

In 1862 Wagner was finally granted a full amnesty. His revolutionary spark, although no longer fanned into theatrical ecstasy and emotional fever, still continued to glimmer, flaring up occasionally. Nor would it be extinguished in the years to come.

There is no doubt that Wagner's convictions during his turbulent Dresden years continued to make their mark on his creative work long after the events of 1848–49, albeit in fragmented and indirect form. There are clear traces of stock socialist ideas in the libretto of the *Ring,* for instance, the very first drafts of which go back to the autumn of 1848. The early studies and sketches (*The Wibelungs, The Nibelung Legend [Myth],* and the first drafts of the libretto for *Siegfrieds Tod*) were all produced in 1848–49 and influenced by the brew of revolutionary ideas found in Wagner's other writings of this time. The path that leads from here to the rather different world of ideas that the *Ring* came to inhabit by the time it was finished in 1874 was often interrupted, but nonetheless direct.

It is precisely in these delayed effects that the crucial impact on Wagner's development of the May uprising and its intellectual ramifications emerges, and in view of its obvious significance the discussion of how deeply Wagner was involved in the actual historic events may seem somewhat superfluous. For with Wagner, more than with other artists, all thought and action is directed toward the furtherance of his artistic creativity and the realization of his artistic concepts. Those who seek Wagner the revolutionary must therefore look for him chiefly in his works. Wagner's biography can at best sketch in the background; it cannot make a more substantial contribution to an understanding of his work.

Translated by Paul Knight

CHAPTER 5

The Question of Anti-Semitism

DIETER BORCHMEYER

It was not until 1879 that the concept of anti-Semitism gained currency, with the publication of Wilhelm Marr's pamphlet *Der Sieg des Judenthums über das Germanenthum* (The victory of Judaism over Germanism). The term spread rapidly across Europe, giving outward expression to a distinction which, in spite of many areas of overlap, defined the essential dissimilarity between traditional anti-Jewish feeling, stretching back to the Jewish Diaspora of the Hellenic age, and modern anti-Jewish hostility, which can be adequately explained only in terms of political, social, and economic developments of the 1870s. Wagner's infamous essay *Judaism in Music,* published in the Leipzig *Neue Zeitschrift für Musik* in September 1850 (and reissued in revised form in Leipzig in 1869 in the form of a separate brochure with an introductory essay *Elucidation of "Judaism in Music"*), stands, as it were, on the dividing line between traditional and modern anti-Semitism.

Although Wagner always enclosed the term *anti-Semitism* within quotation marks, and although in his letter of 23 February 1881 to one of his many Jewish friends, the Berlin theater manager Angelo Neumann, he insisted that he had "absolutely nothing in common" with the "modern 'anti-Semitic' movement," it is difficult to deny that his 1850 article belongs to the forefront of that movement. Cosima Wagner's diaries reveal, moreover, that Wagner followed with considerable interest the growth of the modern anti-Semitic movement in and around 1880, and he appears to have identified to an appreciable extent, if not with all of its aims, then at least with its ideological premises. He read the pamphlet by Wilhelm Marr, among other works, as soon as it appeared in print. Cosima's entry in her diary for 27 February 1879 notes that the brochure contained "views which are very close to R.'s." It must be said, however, that Marr's later anti-Semitic tracts, which Wagner received on a regular basis, struck the composer as "rather superficial" (CT, 14 July 1879).

Be that as it may, Wagner read almost all the leading anti-Semitic writings published around 1880, including works by Constantin Frantz, Paul de Lagarde,[1] Wilhelm Marr, and Eugen Dühring. He was largely dismissive of Dühring's book *Die Judenfrage als Racen-, Sitten- und Culturfrage* (The Jewish question as a racial, moral, and cultural question), which appeared in 1881, rejecting it on both stylistic and conceptual grounds, not least because of Dühring's negative remarks about Wagner himself (see CT, 12 January and 1 February 1881). But to judge from his private remarks, Wagner appears in principle to have accorded anti-Jewish publications his wholehearted, if occasionally skeptical, approval.

Certainly he was openly sympathetic toward the views of the Prussian court chaplain Adolf Stöcker, the movement's most influential political representative. Stöcker had founded the Christian Social Movement in 1880, a body which two years later spawned the Berlin Movement, the cell from which grew all the anti-Semitic parties that sprang up in Germany over the course of the following decades, culminating in the National-Socialist German Workers' party, founded in 1919. Stöcker fanned the flames of a fanatical opposition to "Jewish domination" of economics, politics, and the press, a zealotry whose goal was the abolition of the Jews' political rights. In the course of his conversations with Cosima, Wagner repeatedly expressed support of Stöcker's ideas. "I read a very good speech by the preacher Stöcker about the Jews," she wrote in her diary on 11 October 1879. "R. is in favour of expelling them entirely. We laugh to think that it really seems as if his article on the Jews marked the beginning of this struggle." Wagner himself was clearly pleased to regard his essay on Judaism in music as the spark, so to speak, which had set off anti-Semitism.

It must be said that only in private conversation did Wagner assert himself so unequivocally with regard to the new anti-Semitic movement. He consistently avoided undertaking any official defense of the movement's aims; indeed, in the letter to Angelo Neumann of 23 February 1881, he went out of his way to distance himself from such aims. In 1880, when Bernhard Förster, one of the most outspoken representatives of political anti-Semitism at that time, initiated a mass petition against the "rampancy of Judaism" *(Überhandnehmen des Judentums)*, Wagner declined to add his signature to it. According to an entry in Cosima's diary for 16 June 1880, he considered that such a petition ("demanding emergency laws against the Jews") was inappropriate for three reasons: "(1) he has already done what he can [evidently through his essay on the Jews]; (2) he dislikes appealing to Bismarck [the addressee of the petition], whom he now sees as irresponsible, just following his own caprices; (3) nothing more can be done in the matter." Resignation, dislike of Bismarck, a disinclination to bring down on himself once more the

---

1. It is not clear, however, which works by Frantz and Lagarde Wagner actually read. He was presumably acquainted with Frantz's book *Der Nationalliberalismus und die Judenherrschaft* (National liberalism and the hegemony of the Jews), published in Munich in 1874. And on 22 January 1881, according to Cosima, Wagner received a "brochure" by Lagarde. The editors of CT conjecture that this was *Semitica* (1879). [Ed.]

wrath of the liberal world (as he had earlier done with his essay on Judaism in music), and, undoubtedly not least, the diplomatic consideration that a renewed admission of his own anti-Semitism would certainly impede the dissemination of his works: these are the essential reasons why Wagner preferred to distance himself from the movement.

This is true not only of his refusal to sign Förster's petition but also of his attitude toward Angelo Neumann, who realized that his elaborate plans for staging Wagner's works in Berlin would be jeopardized by rumors of Wahnfried's active anti-Semitism. Nevertheless, Wagner's official reserve toward anti-Jewish propaganda cannot be dismissed simply as opportunism on his part, since he had certainly not balked at the idea of republishing his essay in 1869, a move which clearly ran counter to his own best interests. We may, rather, suppose that the violent escalation of political and racial attacks on the Jews had left Wagner with a feeling of apprehension and encouraged him to adopt an air of public caution, the more so since—as we shall see shortly—in the final years of his life he came to embrace a profoundly mystical racist ideology which, in spite of his unabated anti-Jewish feelings, could no longer be reconciled with militant anti-Semitism as we understand it today. The reason why such a reconciliation was no longer possible was that the aim of his new ideology was the suppression of racial differences in the spirit of the "blood of Christ."

Seen from the standpoint of social psychology, anti-Semitism and its various historical manifestations have been conditioned not only by the role which the Jews have played in the history of religion and society, but also by the Jews' highly developed sense of racial solidarity. Whereas traditional antagonism towards the Jews was directed against the policy of integrating the religious and social practices of a minority into the rest of society, modern anti-Semitism takes as its starting point the fact that the basic solution to the Jewish "question," the granting of equal political and social rights to the Jews, is already a part of history. The end of the process of emancipation was marked in Germany by the constitution of the North German Federation of 3 July 1869, which became law in all of Germany two years later with the founding of the Reich. Not until 1871 was the last of the ghettoes closed. The anti-Semitic movement which dates from the 1870s, and which, in the newly united German Empire, was of course an outgrowth of the nascent sense of national identity and the resultant rejection of "undesirable aliens," attempted to reverse the historical process of Jewish integration, and to force the Jews back into the very situation which had been the initial justification for traditional anti-Jewish feeling, namely, a state of racial isolation. This is what, in spite of all the underlying similarities of prejudice and the same cliché-ridden arguments, separates modern anti-Semitism from its forerunner in the days before emancipation. Modern anti-Semitism is the dialectical opposite of traditional anti-Jewish sentiment, coming after (and as a direct result of) the political and legal solution to the Jewish "question."

Judaism in Music

The Jewish "Question" and Liberalism

As I have remarked, Wagner's essay of 1850 stands at the crossroads of traditional and modern anti-Semitism. In it Wagner himself admits that he is not concerned with challenging the principle of religious, political, and social equality for the Jews, although he is certainly not averse to making sarcastic comments on the historical developments which had led to their equality of status. If he identifies with the liberal movement—a movement he had embraced as an active revolutionary and whose ideas had left their mark on his writings up until 1852—and if he adopts the persona of the democratic "we," he does so with an ironic awareness of the role he is playing. He seeks to criticize the liberal movement and its attitude toward the Jewish question not as an outsider but apparently from within, as a participant who has contributed toward the emancipation of the Jews; and he does so in order to give his arguments more rhetorical weight—that is, to render the failure of Jewish integration all the more plausible. The "special status of the Jews has been regarded as an invitation to practise humane justice from the moment that we ourselves became fully conscious of the urge for social liberation. Yet when we fought for the emancipation of the Jews, we were in fact fighting far more for an abstract principle than for a concrete cause." Just as "all of our liberal thinkers" became committed to the abstract idea of "freedom for the people," irrespective of the concrete reality of the people, "so our eagerness to accord the Jews equal rights sprang from the stimulus of a general idea rather than from any genuine sympathy" (SSD V, 67).

Here we find Wagner repeating an argument which had earlier been adduced by opponents of the French Revolution, most notably Edmund Burke, who argued that the Revolution had set out from the abstract idea of Man, and not from the empirical reality of human beings in general. This same objection to bourgeois liberalism was later repeated by Jean-Paul Sartre, who uses terms similar to those employed by Wagner in his discussion of the Jewish question (Sartre 1948). Sartre is primarily concerned with a critique of French anti-Semitism, which had a profound influence on Wagner's own thinking. The liberal democrat, according to Sartre, is a poor advocate of the Jews, since he is committed to the spirit of analysis and therefore blind to "the synthetic patterns of history. He knows neither the Jew nor the Arab nor the black nor the bourgeois, or the worker. He knows only man, who is always and everywhere the same . . . Thus the democrat . . . fails to see the individual since for him the individual is merely the sum total of general characteristics. It follows, therefore, that his defence of the Jew rescues the Jew as an individual, but destroys him as a Jew." Whereas the anti-Semite "desires the annihilation of the Jew as a man, so as to leave behind only the Jew, the pariah and the untouchable," the democrat wishes to "annihilate him as a Jew in order to preserve him as a man, as a general, abstract object worthy of human and civil rights." Sartre concludes, "There is one point on which we agree with the anti-Semite," namely the view that humanitarian and social problems must be examined in the spirit of philosophical synthesism. In his essay of 1850 we find Wagner demanding much the same kind of thing, at least from the point of view of logical method; his ethical and practical aims are not, of course, the same. According to Wagner, the starting point for any discussion should not be the abstract idea of the Jew as an object of persecution, since that object has been transformed into an equally abstract subject for democratic rights; rather it should be the concrete reality of Jews in general. But that reality, "in terms of actual, physical contact," remains for the non-Jew something "instinctively repugnant" (SSD V, 67).

On the purportedly enlightened pretext of exposing this "repugnant" element in order to rid us of our "self-deception," Wagner describes the characteristics of "the physical appearance of the Jews" which produce such "instinctive revulsion" in the non-Jew. He gives the game away by claiming in one and the same breath that his intention is to "explain" anti-Jewish sentiment, while at the same time confessing that the purpose of his exposé is indeed to "justify the instinctive revulsion which we clearly recognise to be stronger and greater than our conscious desire to overcome those feelings of revulsion" (SSD V, 67). In other words, Wagner's purportedly enlightened method serves a decidedly unenlightened aim, which is to legitimize rather than to overcome his readers' presumed aversion to all things Jewish, an aversion which has now been brought out into the open and which Wagner invests with an air of moral creditworthiness. By lifting "the darkness into which we good-natured humanists have cast [the Jew], in order to render him less repugnant in our eyes" (SSD V, 69), Wagner hopes to throw light on what it is about the Jews that is so repellent.

This idea is repeated in *Elucidation of "Judaism in Music,"* where we find a significant shift of emphasis by means of which Wagner endeavors to clear himself of the suspicion that he still subscribes to "the medieval notion of anti-Jewish sentiment, a feeling which puts to shame our own more enlightened times" (SSD VIII, 241): if the Jewish element "is to be assimilated in such a way that it develops in common with us, in the direction of a more mature cultivation of our nobler human qualities, then it is obvious that what is needed here is not the concealment of the difficulties which beset that process of integration, but rather their most candid exposure" (SSD VIII, 260). This line of reasoning is intended to gloss over the underlying inhumanity of the original essay, which at least suggests that by 1869 Wagner was no longer a part of that trend. In his 1850 article Wagner had drawn a stereotyped and negative picture of the Jewish character, a picture which had encouraged him to generalize about "the Jew" and thus to commit the same mistake which he reproached the liberals for having made. Thus, the "repulsive" (to quote Wagner) outward appearance of the Jew, the ugliness of his language in matters of both articulation and syntax, his dispassionate rationality, his inability to produce works of creative genius (his only genuine talent

being for financial transactions), and, last but not least, the "grotesque caricature" of his form of religious worship, and especially of his chanting in the
synagogue, a remarkable criticism in view of Wagner's later encomium to
Jacques-François Halévy's opera *La juive,* in which he singled out for particular
praise the composer's presentation of the Passover feast, which, he said,
"contains the best expression of the Jewish character" (CT, 27 June 1882).
Wagner exhausts the whole xenophobic arsenal of traditional anti-Jewish
feeling, not in order to define, in rational terms, the catalogue of prejudices,
stereotyped images, and antipathetic emotions and thus to overcome them in
a spirit of enlightened humanism, but rather to invest them with a greater
legitimacy.

Although Wagner's concern, in his essays on aesthetic reform of 1849–1852,
with a "social" explanation for cultural phenomena suggests that he was fully
alive to the sociohistorical reasons for the supposedly "repugnant" aspects of
Jewish character and Jewish life, he declines to examine those reasons in detail,
and hence fails to question whether his instinctive antipathy toward the Jews
is justified. That is, he fails to expose prejudices for what they are, still less
to explain and tolerate the ethnological and cultural peculiarities of Judaism
by questioning those assumptions. "The fact that the historical penury of the
Jews and the rapacious savagery of their Christian-German oppressors have
between them led to the transfer of this power [in the modern financial sense]
to the sons of Israel does not need to detain us here" (SSD V, 68). Wagner
has no intention of embarking on such a discussion since he is instead concerned with depicting the aspects of Judaism which are the butt of his attack
not as a function of social history but as an expression of the Judaic character.
Wagner's refusal to adopt a historical perspective (something he does as a
matter of course in his other, theoretical writings) prevents him from seeing
that the Jews' self-evident lack of intellectual and artistic independence in the
cultural life of Germany was directly attributable to the unconscionable delay
in their emancipation.

The purpose of Wagner's argument is to shed light on the failure, and
indeed the impossibility, of genuine integration. He transgresses the boundaries of traditional anti-Jewish sentiment and points irrefutably in the direction
of modern anti-Semitism, a movement from which he nevertheless stands
apart by virtue of his lack of any clearly defined statement of racial ideology
and by the fact that he expressly limits himself to a consideration of the role
of Judaism in contemporary artistic life. Nor does he make any political or
legal demands aimed at depriving the Jews of their recently acquired equality.
Yet it cannot be denied that the basic thesis of modern anti-Semitism is already
implicit in *Judaism in Music* in embryonic form: from the standpoint of political
anti-Semitism, emancipation had not led to the Jews' loss of their special
status; rather, oppression had turned into domination. Being racially different,
so the argument continues, the Jews had not been properly assimilated but
had continued to exist as a self-contained group, seeking in that way to
monopolize every aspect of culture, economics, and politics. In the view of

confirmed political anti-Semites, this process could be counteracted only by abolishing the equal rights which the Jews now enjoyed. Unlike traditional anti-Jewish feeling, which was as widespread in the nineteenth century in radical democratic and socialist circles as it was elsewhere in society, modern anti-Semitism was reactionary in its racial ideology, and could find acceptance among the middle classes only when they turned their collective back on the liberalism of the revolutionary years, a change of attitude manifest in their identification with the Second Reich, which owed its existence to authoritarian intervention rather than to democratic means.

Wagner's critique of liberalism in *Judaism in Music* prepared the way for this reactionary turn of events, even though, as we have seen, he still shrank from openly disavowing the ideals and achievements of the revolution and from demanding that political and legal change be achieved through the breakdown of Jewish integration. He nonetheless states that, "while we were lost in the clouds, fighting our liberal battle" for Jewish emancipation, the Jews themselves had their feet firmly planted on the ground of actual reality, with the result that "we" now find ourselves in the position of having to fight for "emancipation *from* the Jews." "In the present state of things, the Jew is already more than emancipated: he holds sway, and will continue to hold sway as long as money remains the force before which all our actions are rendered ineffectual" (SSD V, 68).

Wagner, of course, assumes that he is perfectly aware of the historical process by which the Jews have acquired their power: "From the moment when humankind first began to develop in the direction of society and when, with increasingly frank acceptance, money effectively conferred on its owner the status of a plutocrat, it was no longer possible to deny the Jews—who had been left with no professional alternative to that of earning their money without doing any actual work, i.e. usury—the patent of nobility which modern money-grubbing society arrogated to itself; more than that, the Jews themselves brought about this state of affairs without any help from outside" (SSD V, 73). The Jews' enforced and exclusive involvement in financial dealings was a direct result of the medieval ban on collecting interest and of their exclusion from public office and agrarian pursuits. This is a fact of social history of which Wagner was fully aware, for all his insistence that the Jews had a natural affinity for money. In consequence, Wagner argued, the Jews had come to see every aspect of life in monetary terms, commercializing everything and reinterpreting the mediation of art as an "exchange of artistic produce" (SSD V, 68).

The Jews in Music

Wagner's attack is aimed principally at the role played by Jews in music. He demonstrates the power of their influence by reference to the figures of Meyerbeer—whom he contemptuously dismisses, not even deigning to mention him by name—and of Mendelssohn, more discriminatingly assessed as a "tragic" figure who, for all his musical talent, never progressed beyond a merely imitative formalism, since he lacked the "popular or nationalist spirit" *(Volksgeist)* which alone would have enabled him to write a creative work of art capable of "gripping both heart and soul."

Wagner refuses to accept that there may have been a connection between the rapid advance in Jewish emancipation and the fact that only after the death of Beethoven were Jewish composers able to exert such a powerful influence on the musical life of the nation. Instead he ascribes that influence to the paralysis and "lack of inner viability" of contemporary music in general, which had allowed foreign elements to lodge in it like maggots in a corpse— a simile regularly applied to the Jews. In other words, the increasing importance of the Jews is proof of *"the artistic incompetence of our musical epoch"* (SSD V, 83; emphasis in original), and of the inartistic nature of modern civilization in general, its "bad conscience" being represented by the Jews (SSD V, 85). For Wagner, the phrase "Judaism in music" simply summed up the paradigm of corrupt civilization alienated from art and governed only by the laws of a market economy. This civilization is the dark background against which the "artwork of the future" is destined to emerge. Wagner purposefully declines to speak of this here, but the idea of such a work of art is all the more implicit for its methodical exclusion from his essay on Judaism.

Right up to the penultimate paragraph of the essay, Wagner appears to hold out little hope of the Jews' entering into a positive relationship with contemporary society; but then, in the final paragraph, he opens up a hitherto unannounced perspective which makes sense only if we interpret the passage as an implicit allusion to this artwork of the future. This perspective provides a clear contrast with the anti-Semitism of the succeeding decades, and yet these very same sentences have inadmissibly allowed a link to be forged between Wagner and genocidal anti-Semitism. Wagner reminds his readers of Ludwig Börne: "He relinquished his special status as a Jew and came among us in search of redemption: he failed to find it and was forced to realise that he would only do so *when we ourselves were redeemed as true human beings.* But for the Jew to become human together with us is tantamount to his ceasing to be a Jew" (SSD V, 85; emphasis in original). In Wagner's view it is not possible for the Jew to achieve this goal simply by means of some straightforward and superficial process of assimilation with the rest of existing society, but only by means of his active participation in the revolutionary process of self-annihilation and redemption, a process to which the whole of humankind must submit in consequence of our alienation from our true humanity.

Redemption through Self-Annihilation: Ahasuerus

In the original version of the text there follows an appeal to the Jews: "Join unreservedly in this self-destructive and bloody battle, and we shall all be united and indivisible!" When republishing the article in 1869, Wagner altered this sentence in a significant way to read: "Join unreservedly in this work of redemption that you may be reborn through the process of self-annihilation, and we shall all be united and indistinguishable." He goes on: "But remember that one thing alone can redeem you from the curse which weighs upon you: the redemption of Ahasuerus—*destruction!*" (SSD V, 85; emphasis in original). To quote this final sentence out of context and to read into it the idea of genocide, as Hartmut Zelinsky has done, is completely misleading (Zelinsky 1978, pp. 94ff.). The question is not simply one of self-annihilation and self-destruction—the voluntary nature of which excludes any thought of physical liquidation—but one of rebirth and redemption through this act of (self-) destruction, an act, it goes without saying, of a symbolic nature, intended to bring about a mystic transformation of the whole of humankind. Only as a result of this process of transformation will the Jew become a true human being—something the integrated Jew can never be, since the rest of mankind with whom he is assimilated is just as remote from the true human being as he is himself. There can be no doubt but that this quasi-mystic transubstantiation of the Jew, enacted in a realm remote from concrete sociohistorical experience, is none other than the effect which will be produced by the unnamed artwork of the future.

This passage explains the curious attraction Wagner exerted on Jews both within his immediate orbit and in his wider sphere of influence. The strange ritual of his dealings with his Jewish friends fluctuated between humiliation and offers of salvation. Joseph Rubinstein, for example, interpreted the revised ending in precisely the sense I have just outlined, when, in his letter to Wagner of February 1872, he sought admission to Wagner's household, defending his willingness to devote himself wholeheartedly to the Bayreuth enterprise with the argument "that the Jews must perish." He did not, of course, mean physical death, any more than Wagner himself did when he reinterpreted the peroration at the end of the 1850 version as an appeal to "higher Judaism" (SSD VIII, 241) for an "acceptance which offers hope" to the Jews themselves (SSD VIII, 258). For all his passionate chauvinism, it was Wagner's aim that "we" should be "united with and indistinguishable from" the Jews. In this way he appears to return by a mysterious route to the liberal position which he had earlier abandoned. Political liberalism has been transformed into an aesthetic doctrine of salvation. Only the artwork of the future can "redeem" the Jew in Wagner's eyes, provided the Jew is prepared to submit unconditionally to the process of self-annihilation, a process intended to lead us all away from the depravity of contemporary civilization toward the utopian ideal incarnate in that work of art.

It is worth emphasizing once more, in view of recent academically suspect speculation, that the metaphorical imagery of annihilation and destruction has nothing in common with the theoretical possibility of genocide. Instead it harks back to the imaginative world and the symbolism of a type of poetry, which flourished in Europe in the early decades of the nineteenth century, whose theme was weltschmerz, or world-weariness. A leading exponent of the theme, who turns up in a variety of poetical disguises, is the figure of Ahasuerus, the Wandering Jew, evoked by Wagner at the end of the essay. According to medieval legend, Ahasuerus prevented Christ from resting with his cross on the way to Calvary and was therefore condemned to eternal wandering.

One of the disguises assumed by Ahasuerus, according to Wagner's own exegesis, was the Flying Dutchman, in what he described as his romantic opera of that name, a work which might more appropriately be termed an opera of world-weariness. In Karl Immermann's novel *Epigonen* (1825) it is said: "Men of all ages have had their fill of misfortune, but the curse of modern man is to feel unhappy in the absence of all suffering." Life as such is a misfortune from which the individual longs to escape into death and to sink into the peace of oblivion. There can be no more terrible thought than that of being condemned, like Ahasuerus, to everlasting life. In his ballad of 1833, *Ahasver, der ewige Jude* (Ahasuerus the Wandering Jew), the German poet Nikolaus Lenau, who was his period's leading advocate of the theme of weltschmerz, has his eternally wandering hero report his countless attempts at suicide and his ardent longing for annihilation, very much as Wagner does with his own Flying Dutchman. Indeed, Wagner's metaphoric imagery of death, annihilation, and redemption may, to a large extent, be explained by reference to this affinity with death, which is typical of the age. This was not something he learned from Schopenhauer, although Schopenhauer was certainly the philosopher of world-weariness par excellence; well before reading his chief work, *The World as Will and Representation,* Wagner had already become familiar with such imagery, thanks to the general mood of the time, and was thus spiritually related to Schopenhauer by virtue of their shared sense of world-weary melancholy.

From the middle of the nineteenth century on, the myth of Ahasuerus became increasingly associated with the fate of the Jewish people, not least in the works of Jewish writers themselves. But anti-Semitic literature also seized hold of the subject, especially in the rabid world of National Socialist racism, where the meaning of the old legend was radically altered by Fritz Hippler, for example, in his notorious film *Der ewige Jude* (The Wandering Jew) of 1940. Wagner, by contrast, did not interpret the myth of Ahasuerus in this anti-Semitic sense, since for him the myth embodied the inconstancy of his own life as an artist. It was, moreover, a myth of salvation and redemption which specifically included the Jews, as we have seen. The figure of the Wandering Jew, wrote Wagner with reference to *Holländer* in *A Communication to My Friends,* was a creation of "displaced Christianity": "There was no hope of earthly redemption to comfort this traveller, condemned for ever and all time to a life devoid of purpose and joy, a life which long ago had run its course; the only desire left to him was his longing for death, his only hope an end to existence" (SSD IV, 265). But unlike the Wandering Jew of the legend, both the Flying Dutchman and Kundry, the female counterpart of Ahasuerus, are finally granted redemption in death.

It is in this sense that the myth of Ahasuerus is reworked at the end of the essay. If Wagner appears to offer the Jews redemption in death as the only means of expunging the mark of Cain which stigmatizes their race, making them unassimilable aliens among the nations of the world, and if, in addition, he says of Hermann Levi that he "—as a Jew—has merely to learn to die, but Levi shows understanding" (CT, 12 November 1880), it must be remembered that, under the influence of the melancholy philosophy of weltschmerz, Wagner had come to view life in general as a rehearsal for dying, whereby the force of the will (in the Schopenhauerian sense) is finally broken. Schopenhauer's "leading idea, the final denial of the will to live," the "sincere and heartfelt yearning for death," is uniquely redeeming, Wagner wrote to Franz Liszt in mid-December 1854. Judaism, which seemed to be striving for power in every area of modern civilization, was therefore the quintessential embodiment of the will to live, whose *Wahn,* or illusion, Wagner believed, conditioned the state of the modern world. If the Jew had to learn how to die, what that meant was that he had to break the power of his will by means of renunciation, an idea which both Levi and Rubinstein "understood"—a remark of Cosima's which would be absurd if the notion of physical liquidation was implied, as some writers have assumed on the basis of this entry in her diary.

Judaism in Music has repeatedly been compared with Karl Marx's essay "On the Jewish Question," written seven years earlier. (It has so far proved impossible to answer the question as to whether Marx's influence on Wagner was direct or not.) Marx, too, was concerned with the problem of how the Jews might cease to be Jews. His hypostatizations are every bit as ahistorical and defamatory as Wagner's and show the extent to which even the Jews themselves had adopted the clichés of traditional anti-Jewish feeling. Marx asks: "What is the worldly religion of the Jews? *Huckstering.* What is its worldly god? *Money.* Very well then! . . . An organisation of society which would abolish the preconditions for huckstering, and therefore the possibility of huckstering, would make the Jew impossible." The Jewish spirit *(Judengeist),* according to Marx, has become the spirit of modern society. In this sense the Jew, for Marx as for Wagner, has long since been "emancipated." The emancipation of the Jews can therefore be effected only through "the emancipation of mankind from *Judaism,*" Marx argues, agreeing almost word for word with Wagner. If "the Jew recognises that this *practical* nature of his is futile and works to abolish it, he . . . works for *human emancipation* as such" (Marx 1975, p. 170; emphasis in original). What Marx terms "abolishment" *(Aufhebung)* and "emancipation" become, in Wagner's partly revolutionary, partly world-weary vocabulary, "annihilation" and "redemption." In spite of the ideological gulf that separates Wagner's confused philosophy of redemption from Marx's stringent and dialectical line of reasoning, there is nonetheless one point which the two writers have in common, namely, the belief that the Jewish question cannot be solved by integrating the Jews into existing society. It can be addressed only by abolishing Judaism as part of a more general process involving the struggle to overcome man's alienation from self, which is itself the result of the domination of capital.

Wagner's Hostility toward the Jews

Psychological Causes

In his letter to Liszt of 18 April 1851 Wagner admitted that his "long-suppressed resentment against this Jewish business" was as necessary to his nature "as gall is to the blood." The psychological causes of this resentment have not yet been adequately investigated. The findings of sociopsychological investigations into the type of person who tends to be anti-Semitic can be applied to Wagner only with considerable reservation, since they generally relate to the average petty bourgeois. The description of the typical anti-Semite, which is propounded, for example, by Alphons Silbermann, in part reads almost like the polar opposite of Wagner's own character study. This typical individual, we read in Silbermann's account, is an "unquestioning conformist, who shows signs of anxiety at any sign of social deviation" (Silbermann 1981, pp. 40–41); he is lacking in imagination, his way of thinking is stereotyped and his behavior conventional; he feels a constant need to subject himself to some higher authority and to external controls; and so on. All of these are features which clearly contradict the accepted portrait of Wagner's character, although the fact that extreme anti-Semites are always highly neurotic personalities—an observation unanimously stressed by students of social psychology—will not, of course, be denied in the case of Wagner.

Nietzsche was the first of the composer's critics to ascribe his anti-Semitism to self-hatred. This line of argument generally presupposes that Wagner believed that his stepfather, Ludwig Geyer, was his real father, and that he believed Geyer to be Jewish because of his name. The result was a psychoanalytical package of anti-Semitic and Oedipal complexes. But here we find ourselves on the unstable ground of unsupportable speculation. And we are no more likely to be convinced by references to contemporary caricatures and polemical writings (which frequently drew attention to Wagner's allegedly Semitic nose and depicted the composer as a Jew, surrounded by his Jewish acolytes) than by the conclusion that such personal attacks produced in Wagner the effect of a trauma that expressed itself in hostility toward the Jews. For what we are dealing with in the majority of such cases are replies to Wagner's brochure of 1869. The caricaturists and polemicists were simply attempting to beat Wagner at his own game. It was in this sense that Gustav Freytag first took the side of the Jews against Wagner, affirming that "to judge from his brochure he himself appears as the greatest Jew of all." The argument that Wagner was traumatized by the belief that he himself was a Jew is one which confuses cause and effect.

The Influence of French Anti-Semitism

Leaving aside psychological speculations, we can state that Wagner's anti-Jewish sentiments seem to have been in part an outcome of his experiences in Paris between 1839 and 1842 (see Katz 1986). This becomes obvious when we compare, for example, Wagner's passionate defense of Heinrich Heine in an article for the Dresden *Abendzeitung* of 6 July 1841 (Jacobs-Skelton 1973, pp. 161–162) and the embarrassed way in which he later attempted to disassociate himself from the exiled German poet, an attempt which simply serves to highlight Wagner's desire to minimize the extent of Heine's influence on his own works. The markedly Jewish presence in the artistic life of Paris (where Wagner himself failed to make any impression); the humiliation of repeated defeat; the sense of rivalry with Meyerbeer, who Wagner believed had failed to offer the appropriate patronage; his own material poverty in the face of luxury, which—under the influence of fiercely anti-Semitic early socialist thinkers—Wagner regarded as the product of exploitive Jewish capitalists; the amalgamation of a deep-seated envy with an ideology newly acquired from books: all these factors explain only too clearly Wagner's increasingly idiosyncratic attitude toward all things Jewish. It was an outlook encouraged by virulent anti-Jewish trends in French intellectual circles, for which there was scarcely a parallel in Germany at that time.

Whereas hardly any of the major German writers of the nineteenth century were anti-Semitic, many of the leading French writers (including Chateaubriand, Victor Hugo, Alfred de Vigny, and Balzac) reveal signs of an often open hostility toward the Jews. Above all, however, it was the early representatives of the socialist movement—Charles Fourier, Toussenel, and above all Proudhon, whose chief work *Qu'est-ce que la propriété?* Wagner is known to have read—who established a new concept of the Jew as the common enemy and the basic evil of society, a view whose effects on Wagner cannot be underestimated. In Proudhon he had already found the beginnings of an ideological racial devaluation of the Jews. This mixture of religious and racial anti-Semitism against a background of socialism, such as may be found in Proudhon's thinking, constitutes the specific content of Wagner's remarks on the Jewish question from the 1860s on.

Nietzsche repeatedly emphasized that, as an artist Wagner really belonged in Paris, in the company of Delacroix, Berlioz, and Baudelaire, France's late Romantics and decadents; Wagner was a German, Nietzsche argued, only by virtue of his crude ideology, an ideology which Nietzsche, whose views in this regard were quite the opposite, saw as including anti-Semitism as its major component. In this light it must be said that Wagner's anti-Jewish sentiments were considerably more French than German in origin. In his later years, too, Wagner's increasingly racially oriented attitude toward the Jews remained indebted to French sources, his chief informant in these matters being his wife, Cosima, who, like Wagner himself, had brought her extremist views back with her from Paris. Among these sources one thinks of Ernest Renan, whose epoch-making *Vie de Jésus* (1863) Wagner studied in depth in 1878. In Renan's work "Semites" are clearly depicted as an inferior type of humanity, albeit for reasons of religion and cultural sociology rather than on the biological grounds of race. But this was one of the aspects of Renan's system which Wagner quite openly criticized. Renan had referred "solely to the Jews who have remained Jewish," Wagner explained to Cosima on 25 May 1878, and in that way had overlooked that "Jews can never really become anything else." Whereas Renan's opposition to the Jews was religious and cultural in its motivation (and the same was true of the majority of anti-Semites in France before 1870), Wagner's argument was now being conducted in terms of racial ideology: because of their innate and therefore immutable biological characteristics, the Jews can never be fully integrated into society.

Although Gobineau's *Essai sur l'inégalité des races humaines* (1853–1855), which Wagner discovered in 1881, accorded the Jews sub-Aryan status in a racial hierarchy of white (Aryan) nobility, yellow petty bourgeoisie, and a black proletariat or slave class, there was no question of Gobineau's dismissing or condemning the Jews as an inferior race. On the contrary, he praised the consistency of Judaism to such an extent that even Zionist ideologists have subsequently had recourse to his principal work in support of their arguments. Modern racial theories were initially far from being anti-Semitically oriented. "Not until the final decades of the nineteenth century did racial theories combine with what had earlier been religious or socio-cultural forms of anti-Jewish feeling, to produce a true racial anti-Semitism" (Mühlen 1977, p. 126). Only when these two types combined did anti-Jewish feeling necessarily become politically reactionary, now that the Jews were seen as an alien group which, because of biologically determined characteristics, could never be integrated with the rest of humanity. Prior to that date, making scornful remarks about the Jews was almost, in Sartre's words, a parlor game in politically progressive circles. This explains why *Judaism in Music* was not necessarily interpreted as a betrayal of the ideals of the 1848 revolution.

There is clear evidence that Wagner had justified his hostility toward the Jews on the grounds of racial biology long before he read Gobineau, who, as we shall see, actually provoked him into contradicting the French writer's fatalistic approach to racial thinking. When, in a conversation on the Jewish problem, someone advanced the view that the solution lay in intermarriage, Wagner objected that "the Germans would then cease to exist, since the fair German blood is not strong enough to withstand this 'alkali'" (CT, 7 April 1873). Ludwig II, who was a staunch advocate of Jewish emancipation, wrote to Wagner in a letter dated 11 October 1881 dealing with Hermann Levi's appointment as the conductor of *Parsifal* that there was "nothing more repugnant and more unedifying" than intolerance toward the Jews since, "after all, we are all basically brothers." Wagner gave vent to his displeasure (CT, 14 October 1881) and wrote back to the king on 22 November, saying that he considered "the Jewish race the born enemy of pure humanity and all that is noble in man." He even announced: "We Germans especially will be destroyed by them." (There are, of course, other, more conciliatory statements about the Jews in Wagner's correspondence with the king.)

The Evidence of Cosima Wagner's Diaries

The most extreme expression of Wagner's anti-Semitism is unquestionably to be found in the pages of his wife's diary, although it must be remembered that what we are dealing with here are unauthenticated quotations at second hand. On 18 December 1881, in the course of a conversation concerning Lessing's *Nathan der Weise* (a play of which Wagner predictably thought very little) he made "a fierce joke" to the effect that "all Jews should be burned at a performance of *Nathan.*" However intolerable such a joke must seem to us today in the light of the National Socialists' "final solution," historical objectivity nevertheless forbids us to read into the remark an anticipation of genocide. Wagner indulged in extreme outbursts of emotion such as this in private conversation, and they were by no means always directed against the Jews. Witness his remarks about other groups whom he detested, such as the Jesuits, who, he said, should all be "wiped out" (CT, 27 April 1870).

Of course Cosima's diaries also repeat somewhat more benevolent remarks by Wagner about the Jews, revealing a gamut of acceptance ranging from ironical recognition to unconcealed admiration. It was, after all, through the power of capital that the Jews had prevented themselves from becoming enslaved by the state, and were hence "the only truly free people among us" (CT, 22 December 1880). This remark shows that Wagner conformed to the prevailing prejudices about a handful of leading Jewish financiers while ignoring the fact (as Karl Marx did too, incidentally) that the majority of Jews, especially in Germany, belonged professionally to the lower-middle class. The Jews alone "have preserved a feeling for genuineness which the Germans have entirely lost, and that is why many of them cling" to Wagner (CT, 22 November 1881; and see a similar remark in Wagner's letter to King Ludwig of the same date). As representatives of the oldest religion, the Jews were "the most superior of all" (CT, 2 July 1878), an idea we find echoed in a conversation concerning Joseph Rubinstein: "Jews like him behave quite differently from us Germans; they know the world belongs to them, we are *déshérités* [outcasts of fortune]!" (CT, 15 May 1878). This and other remarks demonstrate how Wagner judged the Jews not as outsiders but as a superior cultural power. Indeed, the last of these quotations reveals a very real metaphysical jealousy toward Judaism, a feeling of envy which had its roots in the conviction that Jewishness is the "only possible counterpart" to Germanness in world history. In his letter to Nietzsche of 23 October 1872, Wagner describes Germanness, like Jewishness, as "a purely metaphysical concept"—in other words, not simply a national identity.

A belief which returns repeatedly in his conversations with Cosima is the view that the Jews "have been amalgamated with us at least fifty years too soon: 'We must first be something ourselves.'" In other words, the Germans should first have become culturally emancipated, following their long dependence on the Romantic model (CT, 1 December 1878). As a result, the Jews "have intervened too early in our cultural condition," and as a result "the human qualities the German character might have developed from within itself and passed on to the Jewish character have been stunted by their premature interference in our affairs, before we have become fully aware of ourselves" (CT, 13 January 1879). "If ever I were to write again about the Jews, I should say I have nothing against them, it is just that they descended on us Germans too soon, we were not yet steady enough to absorb them" (CT, 22 November 1878).

Persecution Complex

Wagner's attitude toward the Jews is marked by his neurotic obsession with the idea that he and his works were being persecuted. In *Elucidation of "Judaism in Music"* this obsession comes undisguisedly to the surface. Virtually all opposition to his work is interpreted as an unacknowledged vendetta waged by the Jews against the essay of 1850. He attempts to demonstrate "Jewish opposition to me, which curiously seeks to conceal its motives" (SSD VIII, 254) by means of the example of his archenemy Eduard Hanslick, a critic who until 1850 had been thoroughly sympathetic to Wagner's cause. During the final decades of Wagner's life, his persecution mania became so intense that on one occasion he even told Cosima that the Jews were "just waiting for his death, for then, as they well know, all will be ended" (CT, 15 May 1879).

Wagner was constantly irritated by the power of attraction which he and his works exercised on Jewish audiences. His comments on this attraction reveal a mixture of affection and irony. On one occasion he said that he would have to build a synagogue in Bayreuth for his Jewish friends, and on another that "we ought to give Fidi [his son, Siegfried] a crooked nose" (CT, 7 August 1879); the Jews, he said, were "like flies—the more one drives them away, the more they come" (CT, 12 September 1880); and so on. Basically, however, the very real longing for redemption which drew so many Jews into his orbit corresponded to his own metaphysical and aesthetic "plan for the world's salvation." Wagner's apologists like to gloss over his anti-Semitism by drawing attention to his intimate circle of Jewish friends, from Samuel Lehrs and Karl Tausig to Heinrich Porges, Joseph Rubinstein, Hermann Levi, and Angelo Neumann. But this is just as unsatisfactory a solution to the problem as the contrasting attempt to justify his friendship with these men on the grounds of pure opportunism. In Wagner's personal dealings with Jews, he always gave the impression of performing an act of charity, almost a ritual of exquisite torment, according to Cosima's diary, even if Wagner himself may not always have been conscious of that fact.

Religion and Art and the "Regeneration" Essays

In his treatise *Religion and Art* and its elaboration in the so-called regeneration essays of 1880–81, Wagner once more broached the Jewish question, this time arguing from new and theologically oriented premises based on the works he had read while writing *Parsifal*. His experience of the aftermath of the Franco-Prussian War and of the European arms race had led him to adopt a radically pacifist stance in these essays. He contrasted modern civilization, bent increasingly on war, with the idea of a true religion, which, for Wagner, meant the Christian religion—the religion of the Cross—combined with the ethics of Buddhism. Like the early Christian heretic Marcion, whom he got to know chiefly through Renan (CT, 23 January 1880), he saw the religion of the New Testament as one of love and compassion, in marked contrast with the Old Testament Judaic religion of terror and law, which had eclipsed the Christian message of peace and become the spirit of modern militarism—or so Wagner argued, idiosyncratically reversing the traditional prejudice about the Jews' antimilitarist tendencies. This reawakening of a true religion therefore aimed at rooting out all the genuinely Jewish elements in the Christian religion. At the same time Wagner was fascinated by Jewish mysticism and the Cabala, which he had discovered through reading the first volume of August Friedrich Gfrörer's *Geschichte des Urchristenthums* (History of Early Christianity), first published in 1838. According to Cosima's diaries, Wagner studied this work intensively during 1874–75 (see the entry for 25 January 1875).

Armed with the standard of his new Christian-Buddhist creed (of which Nietzsche was so violently critical), Wagner now set about attacking the racial theory of his new friend, the Comte Joseph-Arthur de Gobineau, whose relevant work he had read for the first time following the completion of *Religion and Art*. Although he accepted Gobineau's central thesis of the inequality of the races, he rejected its fatalistic consequences. On this point he concurs with the criticism of Alexis de Tocqueville, who, in his correspondence with Gobineau, had rejected on humanitarian and liberal grounds the idea of man's total abandonment to his racial constitution. Wagner advances a similar criticism against Gobineau, but in this case argues from a religious standpoint. "If one remembers the Gospels," he remarked to Cosima on 14 February 1881, soon after beginning Gobineau's *Nouvelles asiatiques,* "one knows that what really matters is something different from racial strength." Under the date 23 April 1882 we find this observation by Cosima: "He reproaches Gobineau for leaving out of account one thing which was given to mankind—a Saviour, who suffered for them and allowed himself to be crucified." On 17 December 1881 he remarked: "But one thing is certain: races are done for, and all that can now make an impact is—as I have ventured to express it—the blood of Christ." (He had attempted—in vain—to persuade Levi to join him in receiving the blood of Christ in the form of Communion.)

This final remark of Wagner's contains an allusion to his essay *Remarks on "Religion and Art": Heroism and Christianity,* written in 1881. Here he emphasizes that the blood of Christ flowed not for any "one privileged race" but for "the whole of humankind" (SSD X, 283). The natural inequality of the races—which he never denied but which, he argued, had led to "a fundamentally immoral world-order" as a result of the "domination and exploitation of the inferior races"—was to be compensated by a moral equality, "such as true Christianity must seem to us to be called upon to encourage" (SSD X, 284–285). Wagner regarded this essay as his final contribution to a solution of the Jewish question, as is clear from his letter to Angelo Neumann of 23 February 1881, cited at the beginning of this chapter: "I have absolutely nothing in common with the modern 'anti-Semitic' movement: an essay of mine which is shortly to appear in the *Bayreuther Blätter* will clarify this, to the extent that it should henceforth be impossible for *anyone of intelligence* to associate me with that movement." Indeed, Wagner draws a clear line in *Heroism and Christianity* between his own individual philosophy and a movement whose racist principle, emblazoned on its banners, was the strengthening of the Aryan race.

Do the Music Dramas Contain Traces of Anti-Semitism?

Ever since 1952 and the publication of Theodor W. Adorno's *In Search of Wagner*,[2] it has been repeatedly claimed that Wagner's music dramas contain unequivocal traces of anti-Semitism. Against this it must be said that, in all of Wagner's innumerable commentaries on his own works, there is not a single statement which would entitle us to interpret any of the characters in the music dramas or any of the details of their plots in anti-Semitic terms, or even to interpret them as allusions to the Jews. The attempt to interpret the Nibelungs, and especially the figure of Mime, as mythic projections of the Jews—an interpretation based on Wagner's description of the physical appearance and speech patterns of Jews in his 1850 essay—is no more than an unverifiable hypothesis. And it is an implausible hypothesis, if for no other reason than that Wagner admitted to Cosima on 2 March 1878 that "he had once felt every sympathy for Alberich." In fact, in its original conception the prose scenario (*The Nibelung Legend [Myth]* of 1848) had ended with the liberation of all the Nibelungs, including Alberich, by Brünnhilde.

We may also discount the view that Beckmesser is a caricature of the Jewish intellectual, an interpretation based on the fact that in the 1861 prose drafts of *Die Meistersinger* the Marker was given the name of Hanslich. Quite apart from the fact that, in their professional status and social roles, town clerks and Jews were never one and the same, it can only have been *after* Wagner's altercation with the Viennese critic that he identified Beckmesser in *Die Meistersinger* with Hanslick. When he first sketched the opera in 1845, Wagner was on the best of terms with Hanslick, as is clear from the critic's favorable review of *Tannhäuser,* which had received its world premiere that same year. In this sketch the character is already firmly established in each of the basic comic situations. Beckmesser is the embodiment of the academic and purist critic in the tradition of humanist satire, in which the pedant is regularly

---

2. The first chapter of Adorno's book, containing his ideas about Wagner's anti-Semitism, had been published thirteen years earlier as "Fragmente über Wagner," in *Zeitschrift für Sozialforschung,* vol. 8, ed. Max Horkheimer (Paris, 1939–40), pp. 1–14. [Ed.]

exposed to popular ridicule (for instance the Dottore of commedia dell'arte); as such a pedant—but not necessarily as a Jew—Hanslick is one of the butts of Wagner's satire.

The only one of Wagner's characters to be associated with a Jewish figure in the work itself is Kundry in *Parsifal,* whom Wagner himself interprets as a female counterpart to the Wandering Jew (SS XI, 404). But Kundry's racial identity is certainly not one of the themes of the opera, and her capacity for evoking our sympathy—a capacity with which Wagner has richly endowed her both poetically and musically—excludes from the outset any possibility of our interpreting her as an anti-Semitic statement. Like the Flying Dutchman, who is no more a Jew than Kundry herself, she simply enacts the mythical role of the Wandering Jew. Admittedly she was descended from the biblical Herodias, an earlier figure who, from the Middle Ages right up to the nineteenth century, recurs repeatedly as a female version of Ahasuerus. She is often confused with her daughter Salome, as in Heinrich Heine's *Atta Troll.* Since that time, however, the type has undergone countless rebirths in a sort of literary metempsychosis. She is portrayed not as Jewish but as a heathen. Awakened each spring to a new life, she embodies the eternal cycle of unredeemed nature. Her yearning for redemption in death in *Parsifal* echoes the theme of world-weariness which had first been heard in *Höllander.* Some writers have attempted to interpret *Parsifal* in the light of the later regeneration essays and to see the work as an ideological parable whose final phrase, "Redemption to the Redeemer," looks forward to the aryanization of Christianity. But such an interpretation is impossible to substantiate either textually or musically, and belongs to the realm of unverifiable speculation of a kind which inadmissibly turns the text of *Parsifal* into an allegorical poem. In any case, the words "Redemption to the Redeemer" refer quite unmistakably to the redemption of Christ, immanent within the Grail, from the hands of its sinful guardian Amfortas.

We are bound to ask ourselves why, in spite of his violently anti-Semitic polemical writings, there is not a single trace in Wagner's music dramas of any similar tendencies (a claim which is philologically unassailable, notwithstanding speculative suggestions to the contrary). The basic reason is clearly that Wagner would have given the lie to the promise of redemption held out by the artwork of the future if he had used his music dramas—which promised to free the Jews from the "curse" of their race—as an instrument of anti-Jewish propaganda. Within the utopian framework of the mythopoeic music drama, the Jewish problem is solved by means of Wagner's mystical doctrine of redemption.

Wagner's anti-Semitism is a mixture of elements borrowed from traditional and modern anti-Jewish sentiment. His ideas cannot be reduced to an unambiguous common denominator, not least because, in the final years of his life, Wagner drew a clear distinction between his private views on the one hand and his public statements on the other. The result was an ever-increasing sense of contradiction in his attitude toward the Jews. Such contradictions demonstrate that he was basically undecided as to which of the sociopolitical solutions was best suited to deal with the Jewish question. He transformed the whole problem into an aesthetic doctrine of redemption whose aim was the abolition of racial differences. In this respect Wagner's opposition to the Jews differs fundamentally from the racial fanaticism which emerged at the turn of the century, generating various programs for racial breeding. In contrast to such trends Wagner gave unequivocal expression in the final years of his life to the hope that the principle of racial strength, and the races in general, would soon have acted out their respective roles in the history of world events.

Translated by Stewart Spencer

CHAPTER 6

The Political Influence and Appropriation of Wagner

ERNST HANISCH

The German "Special Path"

The central question for German history since 1945 has been the vexing one of why it was Germany, alone among the developed industrial nations, in which a radical fascist regime came to power. When did this German *Sonderweg,* or historical "special path," begin, and what course did it take? This *Sonderweg* shows that in Germany the industrialization of society was successful but the democratization of it was not. The search for continuities in German history has stressed the unity of the period from 1871 to 1945, dissociating it from the "normal" development of Western European history. The debate soon came to concentrate on the special development of the German mind and of German culture. The attempt to discover the causes of the German catastrophe led to the reconstruction of a specifically German ideology; this ideology, rooted in Romanticism, cast the taint of irrationalism over German culture as a whole. Thus, it was assumed that there was a path leading straight from Richard Wagner to Adolf Hitler.

To write about Richard Wagner, then, is to write about a central problem in German and European history. No other composer or writer of the nineteenth century was as ideologically charged as Wagner, but then no other composer or writer attained comparable European standing. Postwar research has abandoned the task of simple classification. In this it has been powerfully inspired by the writings of Thomas Mann (1985), which stressed the contradictions and complexities of Wagner's nature, its ambivalence and multivalence. This is also true of Wagner's ideology, or rather his ideologies.

To state the position clearly from the outset, Wagner cannot be reduced to Hitler's idiosyncratic view of him. Where has the hubris of power been more convincingly denounced than in Wagner? Where else does everything lead so inevitably to its downfall? Yet Hitler and his followers were not merely laboring under a misunderstanding. There is material in Wagner's works—

and still more in his theoretical writings—that lends credence to their interpretations.

Founding of the Empire and of the Bayreuth Festival

Again it was Thomas Mann (following a long German tradition) who ranked
Wagner and Bismarck together as twin culminations of the hegemony of the
German mind. "Revolution from above" (Nietzsche mocked the German
propensity for "always wanting to reform, not to make revolution") was
reflected in the founding of the empire on the one hand and of the Bayreuth
Festival as the expression of German cultural dominance on the other. Wagner
himself sometimes saw the parallel, only to be bitterly disappointed. In the
end he claimed that the empire had been created merely to provide an appropriate backdrop for his music dramas.

The outbreak of the Franco-Prussian War of 1870 sent Wagner into a
"chauvinistic frenzy" (Gregor-Dellin 1983, p. 397). He hoped that Paris would
be burned to the ground, as a "symbol of the world's liberation at last from
the pressure of all that is bad" (CT, 18 August 1870). His poem *An das deutsche
Heer von Paris* (To the German army at Paris) marks a low point in his poetry
and is marred by appeals to aggressive imperialism—forming a link with the
"ideas of 1914"—to quiet force and pious discipline. A copy of the poem was
sent to Bismarck, who reacted with polite indifference; nor was he to show
great interest in Wagner later, despite the composer's attempts to curry favor.
The *Kaisermarsch* (WWV 104), and that "piece of fatuous buffoonery," as
Catulle Mendès put it, titled *Eine Kapitulation* (WWV 102), both follow the
same ideological line: that of asserting the fundamental existential differences
between Germany and the West. On 9 December 1870 Wagner summarized
this idea for Cosima. Basically, the two sides adopt opposing principles: the
West, with its great revolutions, believes in the possibility of (political) bliss
on earth, whereas Germany, which instinctively rejects such utopianism, finds
security in the Prussian officer's principle of authority. Wagner concludes with
a note of resignation: "I have lived through all these illusions myself and have
now got to the point of understanding the meaning of a limited sense of
duty."

In 1872, by the time of the laying of the foundation stone for the Festival
Theater, Wagner had abandoned hopes that Bayreuth could be a cultural
equivalent to the founding of the empire. In defiant resignation, Wagner
appealed to the German mind *(Geist)*, whose natural inclination, he said, was
to build from within. Such pithy, forceful sayings were soon taken up in
schoolrooms, quoted approvingly in bourgeois drawing rooms, and later
greedily appropriated by nationalist circles.

The economy in 1872 was booming, and had indeed reached its peak.
Wagner and his disciples changed their plans for the theater, reorganizing the
project as the most modern form of enterprise: the joint-stock company. This

was also an excellent publicity stunt that served to keep the German press in the dark about their intentions. The esoteric and mysterious, combined with a hint of scandal, exerted a powerful appeal. Meanwhile, the Viennese press, who had been let in on the secret, beat the publicity drum all the more eagerly. From a distance Wagner and the "German cause" were all the more closely identified. The Battle of Sedan was followed by the founding of the Bayreuth Festival, the manifestation of the united German mind (as shown in the essays by Ludwig Speidel and Oscar Berggrün in Großmann-Vendrey 1977/83, I, 20–24). It was also thoroughly modern to exploit the network of voluntary associations *(Vereine)* in Germany as vehicles for communication and to use the Wagner associations *(Wagner-Vereine)* for formal and informal publicity.

A year after the laying of the foundation stone, the overheated economy, fueled partly by speculation, fizzled out, and a long period of economic instability ensued. At the same time, economic and political liberalism plunged into their most serious crisis. A shift occurred in the political constellation of the German Empire. The policy of the new coalition was intended to guarantee the privileged position of the old elites. The ideological thrust of this group was directed against liberalism, political Catholicism, the Jews, and, above all, social democracy. The ideological adversaries of this coalition thus included at least some of the customary objects of Wagner's hostility: Jews, Jesuits, and journalists, the three J's.

At the end of the 1870s, German nationalism underwent a change of direction. It lost its left-wing, emancipatory impetus and developed into a right-wing, chauvinist ideology of integration, which soon incorporated imperialist elements. The conditions for the reception of Wagner's works also changed as a result. The constant *Heil*s and other nationalistic touches, in *Lohengrin* for instance, contained clearly progressive features in the political context of the 1840s: they were directed against the Holy Alliance, and in particular against tsarist Russia. Karl Marx saw matters in a similar light. By the 1880s, however, the idea of the East had been partly reconfigured into the internal "enemies" of the empire (Jews and Slavs) and partly infused with imperialist ambitions and thereby revealed as the object of Germany's traditional imperialist desires. By 1876 it was already too late for Wagner's dream of Bayreuth as a democratic festival. Instead, the first festivals were a glittering party for the ruling classes. If reports of the social composition of the audience are to be believed, Bayreuth in 1876 was a preview of the coalition to come: the kaiser and the German princes, the aristocracy, the bankers, the educated classes, and the artistic elites were all present. But the architect of the new policies, Bismarck, did not attend; nor did his opponents—the classical liberals, the Catholic center, and, most notably, the social democrats. In nearby Karlsbad, Karl Marx, a man of private means, railed in a letter to his daughter, Jenny Longuet, at the "new German-Prussian Empire-musician" (a crude distortion) and, from a thoroughly bourgeois perspective, mocked Wagner's complicated family circumstances (Marx–Letters, p. 312). Later, too, Marx referred to Wagner's "lecherous gods" (Engels 1985, p. 67).

The reaction of the public was mixed. Considerations of musical taste apart, political dividing lines can be drawn. Disapproval of Wagner came primarily from the liberal camp. Bourgeois liberalism was able to cope with the *Nibelungenlied* but balked at the somber Old Norse *Edda*. Eduard Hanslick, the music critic of the *Neue freie Presse* and professor of aesthetics in Vienna, can be taken as a typical representative of this political camp. His criticism of the first festivals clearly formulates liberal reservations. He was the city man condemning the narrow-minded provincial atmosphere of the small town, the Viennese aesthete complaining at length about uncomfortable accommodations and poor food. He was the bourgeois moralist who had internalized the Victorian ideal of the family and who was confronted in the *Ring* with deception, lies, violence, brutish sensuality, and disgusting incestuous relationships. He was the moderate nationalist bemused by the slavering chauvinism of some of the Wagnerians. He was the bourgeois dignitary, long accustomed to the limited politics of deals made in smoke-filled rooms, who now saw signs of an excessive cult of master and Führer. Moderate-liberal disapproval of the festivals, which was at least based on a knowledge of music, was taken to strident extremes by another liberal Viennese journalist, Ludwig Speidel: "No, no, and no again, the German people has nothing in common with what has now been revealed as a laughable flop, and if it were ever to derive true pleasure from the false gold of the Nibelung Ring, this fact alone would be enough to strike it from the list of the artistic nations of the West" (Großmann-Vendrey 1977/83, I, 229).

Cultural Crisis

The economic crisis of the 1870s triggered and intensified the crisis of liberal bourgeois political culture. Discontent with and within the modern capitalist industrial society, with its many forms of alienation, motivated a vehement critique of culture from the perspective of the educated classes. One manifestation of this crisis was the new anti-Semitism, which emerged at the end of the decade. It saw the Jews as epitomizing all the negative features of modernity. Richard and Cosima Wagner participated wholeheartedly in this trend. A further sign of the crisis was the spirit of bourgeois anticapitalism, which adopted elements of the preindustrial, Romantic critique of capitalism and regarded money as a destructive force. The attempt to escape from industrial society then superimposed itself on the national myth. Myth has always played an important part in the formation of nations as a resource for establishing social meaning and purpose and as a vehicle for defining national identity. In the case of Germany, myth soon became part of the so-called aberration in the nation's historical development. The image of Siegfried, the young golden-blond hero, caused "the breasts of German youth to swell with the elation of male glory," as Thomas Mann observed. This was a trivialized image, ideally suited for distinguishing tough, aggressive German youth from its stereotypically cowardly, spoiled Latin counterpart. It was an image that could easily be filled with racist content and used to justify imperialism both at home and abroad, if initially only in the form of extreme cultural Darwinism. By 1936 the German ancestral portrait gallery (described in Ritter 1936) included Siegfried, Parsifal, and Horst Wessel.

Of course this use of the pretentious kitsch image of the German Siegfried to stabilize the insecure egos of German schoolboys and depraved young traveling salesmen had become dissociated from the image of Siegfried the free man in Wagner's *Ring*. But no one contributed more than Wagner to the popularization of Germanic myth. Theodor Adorno was not the only critic to interpret the structure of the Siegfried-Mime relationship in terms of the superman–subhuman model.

The spreading cultural crisis soon began to affect Bismarck's celebrated empire, too. The German Reich of Richard Wagner and the German Reich of Otto von Bismarck had been identical for only a brief moment; they soon began to diverge. Wagner's criticism of Bismarck was undoubtedly based, at least in part, on a personal grievance: he could not forgive the chancellor for his failure to become a Wagnerite. But Wagner also quickly understood the prussification, militarization, and centralization behind the unsuccessful attempt to unify the empire. On 16 December 1878 Cosima quotes Wagner as saying: "What does a Junker of that sort know about Germany?" And on 12 November 1880 she reports that when the painter Lenbach mentioned Bismarck, Wagner flew into a rage, calling Bismarck "bulldog-face." This hatred made Wagner perceptive and productive; on several occasions he referred to Bismarck's strategy of creating enemies within the empire as a method of distracting attention from internal problems. Wagner's rejection of the empire as a "dead body" even took the extreme form of the ironic yet emotional declaration that he wished to resign his membership in the German Empire (CT, 5 January, 13 September 1879, 10 November 1881). On 9 November 1892, in a letter to Bodo von dem Knesebeck, Cosima even went so far as to ascribe Bismarck's political failure to his attitude toward Bayreuth (Cosima 1980, p. 310).

Wagner's criticism of the existing German Empire became increasingly fierce: "Really, the Germans are imbeciles" (CT, 23 July 1879). But the true, genuine, apolitical Germany only shone all the more radiantly; or, as Wagner put it in *Meistersinger*: "Zerging in Dunst das Heil'ge Römische Reich, uns bliebe gleich die heil'ge deutsche Kunst" ("If the Holy German Empire disappeared in smoke, holy German art would still remain"). Wagner's dream of a different, eternal Germany was characterized by a number of dichotomies typical of his age, which formed the ideological basis of the German *Sonderweg* and were admirably suited for exploitation in 1914 and again in 1933. Such antinomies, which are to be found in Wagner's writings, can be listed in tabular form:

German	Not German
province	city
culture	civilization
inwardness	superficiality
nonpolitical orientation	political orientation
conservatism	revolution
authority	democracy
idealism	materialism
depth of feeling	superficial distractedness
creativity and originality	imitation and exploitation
morality	intellect

All these negative, non-German qualities came together in one figure of hate: the Jew.

The Bayreuth Circle

Wagner's message—whatever he had said, revoked, and then restated in a new form—was raised to the status of gospel by the Bayreuth circle, who dwelt on his every word and at the same time narrowed his ideas down into a Germanic-Christian doctrine of salvation. Friedrich Nietzsche was one of the first to diagnose this as ideology: "The Germans have constructed a Wagner for themselves whom they can revere" (Nietzsche 1967, p. 165). In *Ecce Homo* Nietzsche sees Wagner as epitomizing foreignness, opposition, protest against all German virtues: "Wagner had been translated into German!—*German* art! The *German* master! *German* beer!" Nietzsche then directs his incomparably cutting derision against the Bayreuth "idealists": "Truly, a hair-raising crowd! Nohl, Pohl, *Kohl*, charmingly *in infinitum*! Not an abortion was missing, not even the anti-Semite" (Nietzsche 1979, p. 90).

Such an ideology could gain influence only if certain prerequisites were in place. And the most important of these was Wagner himself. Nietzsche drew the dividing line as sharply as possible: "What I have never forgiven Wagner for? That he *condescended* to the Germans—that he became *reichsdeutsch*" (Nietzsche 1979, pp. 60–61). The process of secularization had to be well advanced—the established churches had to have lost much of their integrative power—before art could be experienced as bourgeois religion. This religion of aesthetics was still intermingled with Christianity, but it sought redemption in this world through great art. Another prerequisite was that the crisis of meaning in modern industrial society had to have broken out, and partial democratization and mass phenomena such as the labor movement had to be present as a visible threat to the educated bourgeoisie. And indeed these phenomena were observable in all other industrial societies at the time. But mental adjustment to industrial society proved particularly difficult in Germany. The reins of power were firmly in the hands of the preindustrial classes, and preindustrial structures and attitudes were deeply rooted in society. It was only in Germany that such a collective refuge was sought in culture: in a culture decked out, among other things, in Germanic Wagnerian heroes, a culture which at its most extreme could create for itself a delusional world. In Bayreuth world history, so to speak, culminated—as the fulfillment of the Aryan mystery, as the India scholar Leopold von Schroeder described it. It was only in Germany that such a powerful bourgeois anticapitalist movement developed, in conjunction with the so-called Conservative Revolution. The cultural pessimism then gaining ground had hardly any connection with economic facts; the sphere of production was ignored. On this subject the master, loquacious though he was on other occasions, remained silent.

In his analysis of charismatic rule, Max Weber stressed the element of emotional identification and community. In the Bayreuth circle, for the first time in modern cultural history, the model of the master and his disciples, the leader and his retinue, was presented, in an extreme and secularized form; this went deeper, had a more radical effect, than the mere educated-bourgeois cult of genius. It was precisely in this connection that the real contribution to fascism made by the Bayreuth idealists lay: not so much in their nationalist ideology nor in their racist ideas, both of which were also found elsewhere, as in their exclusiveness, their Knights of the Holy Grail mentality, their total and uncritical devotion to the master, their complete submissiveness. Here were prepared and rehearsed sociopsychological mechanisms which became politically exploitable in the twentieth century.

It was the liberals who first identified and criticized the threat which these tendencies posed to a democratic political culture. Daniel Spitzer ridiculed the "Council Hall in which representatives of the various Wagnerian dioceses met to proclaim the infallibility of the master"; he was referring to Bayreuth in 1876 (Spitzer 1881, III, 351). Eduard Hanslick referred dismissively to "Wagner's dancing dervishes" (Hanslick 1894, p. 222), and Eduard Kulke accused Wagner of "artistic megalomania" (Zelinsky 1976, p. 65).

After Wagner's death the Bayreuth circle became increasingly sectlike, with a core of devotees (Cosima, Wolzogen, Stein, Glasenapp, and others) surrounded by satellites, with a fully formulated orthodoxy and a group of dissidents to go with it. A journey to Bayreuth was no ordinary journey; it was more like a pilgrimage. In extreme cases, such as that of Friedrich Eckstein, a Wagnerian and a friend of Bruckner's, it was a literal pilgrimage: he arrived on foot, with pilgrim's staff and knapsack, because he felt the railway journey would have been a profanation of his sacred mood (Eckstein 1936, p. 213). At the same time, the group's political allegiances became more sharply defined, and more strongly sympathetic toward national *völkisch* ideology.

The two leading ideologues of the Bayreuth circle were Ludwig Schemann and Houston Stewart Chamberlain. Both were physically weak and sickly, which perhaps explains their particularly intense longing for Aryan heroism, for "a breed of eagles among men." Schemann, the translator and biographer of Gobineau, had close contacts among the pan-German movement. In time he came to reject the orthodox affectation of the inner circle, but he still maintained that "whoever goes on the pilgrimage to Bayreuth should do so in the consciousness of strengthening his Germanness," and "Only those who take upon themselves the corresponding duties to the Fatherland have a right to Bayreuth" (Schemann 1925, p. 224).

Chamberlain, the fashionable German philosopher of English descent, was a widely read dilettante whose major work, *Foundations of the Nineteenth Century,* went through twenty-seven editions by 1941. Like Schemann, he was not a member of the academic fraternity. Chamberlain was Wagner's son-in-law and so had family ties in Bayreuth. He was highly thought of by Kaiser Wilhelm II and formed the personal link in the chain from Wagner to Adolf Hitler. Indeed, national socialism began to make Chamberlain "its own special prophet and herald" (Field 1981, p. 445) well before its attainment of power. Chamberlain's popular book on Wagner described him as "the most German of all artists" (Chamberlain 1900, p. 28), retouched his revolutionary past, and made him acceptable to the educated bourgeoisie.

The *Bayreuther Blätter,* the journal published by the circle, accurately reflected the superficiality and the expansion of the Bayreuth ideology. The journal's subtitle, originally *Monatsschrift des Bayreuther Patronatsvereins* (Monthly journal of the Bayreuth Patronage Association), was later changed to the characteristically ponderous *Zur Verständigung über die Möglichkeit einer deutschen Kultur* (On communication about the possibility of a German culture). The journal later resurfaced with the simple but ambitious subtitle *Deutsche Zeitschrift im Geiste Richard Wagners* (German journal in the spirit of Richard Wagner). The journal propagated the racist myth in all its forms, wallowed in exclusive Germanness, and tried to drum up support for Wilhelminian imperialism. With its bombastic, imprecise, and ideologically distorted language, it makes thoroughly unbearable reading. But its contribution to German ideology is indisputable.

The journal's editor was Hans von Wolzogen, whose specialty was the proselytization of Germanic Christianity. The *Ring* had inspired him to become a Christian, and he now preached his version of the reconciliation between Christianity and Teutonism. His attacks were directed at the emerging cult of the Teutons, which worshiped Wotan instead of the God of Abraham, Isaac, and Jacob, celebrated its own festivals, and wanted to introduce a Germanic calendar. But the attacks were also directed at a Christianity bound to church and dogma and—with intense vehemence—at materialistic, un-German social democracy. What Wolzogen was aiming to achieve during his editorship of the *Bayreuther Blätter* was nothing less than the moral rebirth or regeneration of the whole of mankind. Parsifal, the misunderstood individual seeking his God, was the appropriate symbol of this endeavor. Parsifal decisively shaped the guiding image of the great, untimely individual, the heroic man, the pure-hearted fool who struggles against the civilization of the West, who condemns industry, and who summons up German depth to oppose the Anglo-Saxon worship of Mammon. The primary schoolteacher with his many frustrations (including financial problems) was now able to feel like a Knight of the Holy Grail, a member of a spiritual elite who "privately ascends his petit-bourgeois mountain of the Grail and surveys with satisfaction the heights of spiritual education" (Hermand 1962, pp. 528–529). The vague notion of the Aryan Christ, already hinted at in Wagner and expounded in more detail by Chamberlain, merged with the myth of Parsifal: the content of the Grail changed from the blood of Christ into Aryan blood. Only when the race is pure will the Grail shine.

It is against this complex ideological and political background that the dispute about the copyright of *Parsifal* raged.[1] There was more at stake here than the wishes of the master: a wide range of religious and national emotions had been aroused. The performances of *Parsifal* in New York (24 December 1903) and Amsterdam (20 June 1905) seemed like the theft of the Grail. Not only was the West refusing to allow Germany to play its part in world domination, but it was also stealing its most sacred and most characteristic treasure, the symbol of German culture. The reaction of the Bayreuth circle was ambivalent. On the one hand, attempts were made to use all the instruments of democracy, with signatures being collected and representations made to members of the Reichstag; on the other hand, the circle played its antidemocratic, elitist arrogance to the hilt. The most blatant example of this approach was that of Richard Strauss, who, in the context of the debate about the copyright of *Parsifal,* fulminated against "imbecilic universal suffrage" and argued that the vote of Richard Wagner was worth the votes of a hundred thousand others, and also said that ten thousand servants should have only one vote among them (Zelinsky 1976, p. 122). There was nothing at all new about this argument; it was part of the standard repertoire of the German antidemocratic tradition.

The Wagner associations also adopted this dual strategy. According to democratic theory, voluntary associations are organizations that concentrate on particular interests and present these interests to the ruling elites. But in fact the Wagner associations were pursuing larger goals than just supporting the festivals and propagating the work of Richard Wagner. They were one pebble in a mosaic of national action associations, from the Naval Association to the Colonial Association—groups which, in partial opposition to the Wilhelminian system, cultivated a highly emotional form of populist nationalism and paved the way for the annexation plans of 1914–15.

The Richard Wagner associations had about five thousand members in 1884 (*Bayreuther Blätter* 8, 1885, supplement). They came for the most part from

---

1. *Parsifal,* which Wagner decreed could be performed only in Bayreuth, was protected by copyright until 1913. The Wagner family tried unsuccessfully to persuade the German parliament to create a special "lex *Parsifal*" that would extend the copyright beyond this date. [Ed.]

the wealthy and educated bourgeoisie, interspersed with aristocrats, some members of the lesser landed gentry, and more than a few military officers. The people as such were conspicuously absent: neither farmers nor workers were represented. The day-to-day business of the association was also thoroughly bourgeois in character. Houston Stewart Chamberlain gave a mocking account to Cosima: "Basically it is the usual monstrous clubbableness. All that happens is drinking, eating and smoking, and now and then someone gets up and hammers something out on the piano" (letter to Cosima, 20 February 1891). But the speeches given on these occasions were not so harmless, and the reading of Wagner's regenerative writings, which was later made compulsory, nurtured anti-Semitism and more besides.

The Beginnings of a Left-Wing Interpretation

Although the right-wing national movement was dominant among Wagner's followers, some attempts were made even in the nineteenth century to interpret his work in left-wing and even in socialist terms. Toward the end of the 1870s in Vienna, a circle of young Wagnerians and vegetarians formed around Engelbert Pernerstorfer. Some of the circle were Jewish, and one of the members was Victor Adler, later the leader of the Austrian Social Democratic party. This group, confused by the crisis of liberalism, sought refuge in Wagner's music and in the world of culture. Although the group's sympathies were German nationalist, they took the revolutionary impetus in Wagner more seriously than did his right-wing admirers. In the founding phase of Austrian social democracy at the end of the 1880s and the early 1890s, Pernerstorfer tried to rescue Wagner for socialism and to acclaim him as a socialist artist (see McGrath 1974; Zelinsky 1976, p. 72). Richard von Kralik was also a member of the Pernerstorfer circle; after his conversion to Catholicism he interpreted Wagner's music and writings in Catholic terms. Von Kralik's disciple Anton Orel later produced a series of obscure interpretations in which he claimed Wagner for Catholicism.

The most significant impetus toward a left-wing interpretation of Wagner was provided by the work of Friedrich Nietzsche and George Bernard Shaw. Nietzsche was constantly trying to rescue Wagner from the Germans and to place him above Wagnerism, by portraying him as a Frenchman—that is, as a revolutionary and a decadent. He, like Wagner, saw in Siegfried not the typically German hero but the typical revolutionary, who spurns all contracts, all custom, law, and morality. Nietzsche wrongly argued that Wagner failed because of the influence of Schopenhauer, which caused his revolutionary optimism to lose its utopian content and drift into pessimism. A start had been made, nonetheless. Thenceforth socialist intellectuals approached Wagner's work in the footsteps of Nietzsche, except for those who, like Marx and Engels, rejected Wagner completely. The unorthodox socialist George Bernard Shaw, for example, interpreted the *Ring* quite logically as a drama of contemporary capitalism. In this interpretation Siegfried is a completely immoral character, a born anarchist à la Bakunin; Alberich is seen as a nasty Manchester factory owner who, by 1876, is well on the way to becoming a Krupp of Essen; the realm of the Nibelungs becomes an exploitive coal mine or a stinking, murderous match factory; and Wotan appears as a deceitful ruler who uses every means at his disposal to maintain his antiquated throne; he seemingly reaches a triumphant peak by means of a revolution from above (in the manner of Bismarck in 1871), but he leads his realm to destruction.

Such interpretations remained merely an undercurrent during the nineteenth century. The great tide of German Wagnerism flowed into the nationalist camp to form an element of the ideas of 1914.

The Ideas of 1914

The long drawn-out cultural crisis culminated in a burst of frenetic enthusiasm in the summer of 1914. The war seemed to open a path toward the longed-for regeneration. The German intelligentsia, reveling in self-destruction, joined wholeheartedly in the war propaganda. It is said that about fifty thousand war poems a day were being written in August 1914. Constant appeals were made to the German "mission" and the German *Sonderweg*. The ideological trends that had been building up for years were incorporated in concentrated form in agitation for war. And of course Wagner had to be included. Countless newspaper articles acclaimed him as the guarantor of essential Germanness, a figure from whom the Germans could take their bearings. Fragments of Wagnerian mythology even penetrated to the army High Command, as the names of his characters were misappropriated to describe military formations: Wotan, Siegfried, Brünnhilde, and Hunding all lent their names to the war effort.

The Bayreuth circle played an active part in this propaganda. Cosima Wagner wrote to Ernst zu Hohenlohe-Langenburg (1 January 1915): "War seems to suit us Germans far more than peace, when everything un-German flourished" (Cosima 1980, p. 730). Chamberlain's war essays were extremely popular. Hans von Wolzogen hoped that the war would bring about a more noble, purely German culture; Germans would return from this war as "Wagner-ripe souls" (*Bayreuther Blätter* 38, 1915, p. 100). Naturally, *Siegfried* came to be identified with the essence of Germanness, the world war was seen as the *Götterdämmerung* of the West, and the West was associated with the curse of gold and the treachery of Hagen. The exploitation of Wagner occurred in the ponderous, quotation-ridden style of German academics, but also in the highly subtle, ironically dialectical, and playful manner of Thomas Mann.

Richard Sternfeld's pamphlet *Richard Wagner und der heilige deutsche Krieg* (Richard Wagner and the Holy German War), published in 1916, serves as a typical example of the academic style. As one would expect, he takes *Lohengrin* as his key text. Wagner's utopian-revolutionary hope that the rays of German liberty and "mildness," of all things, would warm the Bushmen and the Chinese is turned into an imperialist-annexationist slogan, and this in turn is used to justify Germany's claim to world domination. Inevitably, the famous sentence from Wagner's *German Art and German Politics* is invoked, to the effect that to be German means to do something for its own sake, a sentiment that had acquired an almost sacrosanct status in nationalist circles. Siegfried, symbol of victory *(Sieg)* and peace *(Frieden),* appears as the poetic exemplification of this thought, whereas Mime, the symbol of all that is un-German, of the enemy powers, is motivated only by considerations of egoistic utility and self-interest. More artistically, but to no less devastating ideological effect, Thomas Mann adopted all the clichés attached to the idea of a special historical development in Germany in his First World War essay of "Reflections of a Nonpolitical Man"; in it he used Wagnerian categories to attack the West and civilized literati. The Wagnerian antinomies are distorted into existential categories and interpreted historically as part of the age-old German struggle against the West. In opposition to the Western categories of politics, civilization, revolution, democracy, and the masses, Mann set the German categories of rank, authority, duty, the military, and the people. Of course Mann distanced himself from the approved literature on Wagner; he saw Wagner's Germanness as fragmented and subverted in a modern sense, "calculated to make Germanness interesting even to an ass of a foreigner"; but in the final analysis the essay amounts to an artistic apotheosis of the German *Sonderweg,* with Richard Wagner giving his blessing. The adversary, the hated civilized literatus, was none other than Thomas Mann's brother Heinrich Mann, whose recent novel *Man of Straw* contained a magnificent parody of the way *Lohengrin* was used to inflame national emotions.

Revolution and the Weimar Republic

The unacknowledged defeat of the German Empire activated other symbolic uses of Wagner's opus. Contrary to expectation, the German *Sieg-Fried* did not kill the gold-seeking Mime (that is, the West) but was defeated by the treacherous Hagen. The German sword was broken. It was now necessary to wait for the hero, the Führer, who would forge Nothung anew and lead it to victory. Until that time Bayreuth had to guard the holy flame, the Grail of true Germanness, as the secret armorer of the nation. The enemies were the same: the West with its democracy and its "anal art," which were now spreading through Germany; and the East, whose "hordes" had taken on a far more threatening dimension after the Bolshevik Revolution of 1917. Cosima commented maliciously on the murder of Kurt Eisner, the "Galician Semite." In her opinion the murderer was a "martyr" (Cosima 1980, p. 744).

In 1924 the Bayreuth Festival reopened with *Die Meistersinger.* The performance ended with a provocative political demonstration: the singing of all the verses of the German national anthem. The indefatigable Hans von Wolzogen gave a commemorative speech on the festival of 1924 (reproduced in Zelinsky 1976, p. 184). Although its poetic quality is abysmal, it perfectly summarizes the Bayreuth ideology: the power of the German Empire has been broken;

then comes the revealing line, "The loud word of the master is suppressed." In other words, the German people are being treated like slaves by the victorious powers. Now Wolzogen strikes a defiant note: Bayreuth has spoken; the initiates have seen the Grail! As long as Bayreuth exists, Germany is not lost. As long as Bayreuth exists, the sacred relic will be preserved (as he puts it in another poem) from "the plague of the West" (Wessling 1983, pp. 83, 119). August Püringer drew a political conclusion from this thinking: Wagner and Bismarck foundered on each other. This is why the empire collapsed. Only if Wagner and a new political leader joined forces could they create "salvation for us Germans!" (Wessling 1983, p. 161).

One must bear in mind that while this sour, antimodern, and antirepublican ideology was being purveyed in Bayreuth, the Roaring Twenties were in full swing in Berlin, and Germany was experiencing a broad cultural breakthrough into modernity. The Bayreuth circle regarded this influence as mere "foreign trash," the pollution of the German soul by Western civilization. In this respect Bayreuth was the antithesis of Berlin. Those who attempted to rescue Wagner from the morass of national ideology were rare and isolated. Bernhard Diebold made an impressive attempt, stressing the liberal intentions in Wagner's work and accusing the European left of failing to appreciate his significance (Zelinsky 1976, p. 191).

The labor movement, however, was not completely hostile to Wagner. The Workers' Symphony Concerts, established in Vienna in 1905, regularly played works by Wagner. But it was Wagner the revolutionary of 1848 who was appreciated by the labor movement. In 1933 Anatoli Lunacharsky, People's Commissar for Education, advocated the subtle socialist appropriation of Wagner, whom he described as a "deep thinker" and a "significant poet," who nonetheless went over to the reactionaries after the failure of the 1848 revolution, became a renegade, and "kissed the slippers of the Pope of Rome." But *Lohengrin* contains a progressive dimension, and *Siegfried* celebrates the anarchically free personality. "Woe to him who impoverishes the world by crossing out Wagner's name with a censor's pencil. Woe to him who would let this cunning magician, this talent tainted by an evil disease, into our camp . . . Beware! Quarantine! All baggage must be checked! We must see what is what!" (Lunacharsky 1965, p. 352).

Thomas Mann's masterly essay "The Sorrows and Grandeur of Richard Wagner" (1933) remains the most effective liberal defense of the composer, the best attempt to rescue him from the clutches of nationalist circles, including, of course, Bayreuth. Mann brought on himself the hatred of the Bayreuth clientele. The protest against him by Wagner's city of Munich in the form of a petition signed by Richard Strauss, Hans Pfitzner, and many others (reproduced in Zelinsky 1976, p. 195) is a shameful document in the history of German intellectual life. It was not an attempt to bring political pressure to bear; it was rather an eruption of the pure intellectual will to destroy, a blatant effort by the German intelligentsia to curry favor with the Nazi rulers. In a diary entry for 19 April 1933, Thomas Mann described the petition, quite accurately, as a craven document, and resolved not to return to Germany.

Hitler as Wagnerian

In his autobiography, *Mein Kampf,* Adolf Hitler proclaimed that Wagner was one of the key influences on his life. At the age of twelve he saw *Lohengrin* at the Linz Opera, and his political awakening came a few years later when he saw *Rienzi* at the same theater. The Linz Realschule, which he left without receiving his diploma, was regarded as a center of radical German nationalism. By about 1900 Wagner had become completely integrated into the German nationalist ideology of the provincial bourgeoisie.

Some elements of the fascination which Wagner exerted on Hitler can be isolated and identified. For instance, the tendency toward dilettantism, which both Friedrich Nietzsche and Thomas Mann discovered in Wagner, was also a striking feature of Hitler's character; so too, was the lack of formal training, compensated for by extraordinary talent. Another powerful influence was the image of the genius who prevails against a world of enemies and achieves his goal. In a speech to a party gathering in Munich, Hitler described three men as his models: Luther, Friedrich II, and Richard Wagner. All three were men who "against the will of all enacted real heroism" and won. Hitler added: "We consider the artist Richard Wagner to be so great because he depicts heroic nationality, Germanness. The Heroic is the Great. This is what our people longs for" (HSA 1032). On the one hand, Hitler's understanding of art was conventionally middle class. He expected a "dedicated" stage work *(Weihespiel)* to provide: "ultimate exaltation, the freeing of the individual from all the wretchedness and misery, but also from the rottenness, which unfortunately we encounter in the rest of our lives" (HSA 197). On the other hand, this conception of Wagner's art contained another, dangerously iridescent dimension. In 1912 Hitler designed a costume for Wagner's Siegfried. Under the design he wrote: "Young Siegfried, well known from the days of the Linz Opera. Wagner's work was the first to show me what blood-myth is" (HSA 53). He is said to have expanded on this subject in his conversations with Hermann Rauschning (although their value as a source is disputed); he argued that *Parsifal* was a glorification not of the Christian-Schopenhauerian religion of compassion but of pure aristocratic blood. By an act of providence, he had come across the work of Wagner at an early age; and he found that "everything he read by this great mind corresponded to his innermost, unconscious, dormant views" (Rauschning 1940, pp. 228ff.). But this means that Hitler's interpretation of Wagner was influenced by the ideology of the Bayreuth circle. He adopted their omissions and added a few of his own. He took no notice of the downfall of Wagnerian heroes, from Rienzi to Siegfried.

Hitler entered Haus Wahnfried for the first time in October 1923 to visit the ailing Houston Stewart Chamberlain and the Wagner family. The letter

Chamberlain wrote to Hitler on 7 October is one of the "classic texts" (Paul Bülow) of national socialism. In it Chamberlain defines the basic pattern of the charismatic Führer myth. Hitler, who awakens "people from sleep and humdrum routines," had so inspired him that for the first time since 1914 he had enjoyed a long, "refreshing sleep" (Field 1981, p. 436). Chamberlain is consciously evoking the image of the healer-king here.

Here was the hero the Bayreuth circle had longed for, who would forge Nothung anew. Hitler was truly moved as he stood at the grave of Richard Wagner, the hero of his youth. And the ripples of this emotion were perceptible even in his speech at his trial following the unsuccessful putsch of November 1923.

Bayreuth deployed its tried-and-true double strategy with regard to national socialism. Given the international aura of the festival, Siegfried Wagner kept his distance. He defended the Jews in a conversation with August Püringer and kept the festival open to them as performers and visitors. This brought criticism from Goebbels and Hitler. Hitler, in one of his endless monologues in his headquarters, said that in the 1920s Siegfried Wagner had been "in the hands of the Jews a little" (HSC, 28 February 1942). And on 8 May 1926, after a visit to Bayreuth, Goebbels noted angrily in his diary: "Siegfried is so feeble. Ugh! He ought to be ashamed in the master's eyes! . . . Feminine. Good-natured. Slightly decadent." Siegfried's wife, Winifred Wagner, by contrast, he described as "a superb woman . . . And fanatically on our side."

Winifred Wagner had brought Bayreuth and national socialism together, as Hitler appreciatively noted. She was one of his "show" women, one of the select few to be honored with the familiar *Du* form of address. The fact that Bayreuth functioned as a means of boosting Hitler into power was due in large part to Winifred. She met Hitler at Haus Bechstein in 1922 and was deeply impressed. She fought "like a lioness" for him and remained loyal even after the failed putsch.

In the Third Reich

The dreams of many of the Bayreuth circle came true in 1933. Just as industry had supported Hitler financially, Bayreuth helped him ideologically by making him respectable in the eyes of the bourgeoisie. The sight of Hitler in tails, listening to Wagner's music, humbly effacing himself before the master's work made Bayreuth hearts beat faster. The union of art and power, which had not been achieved in 1871, became a reality for many in 1933.

National socialists and emigrants agreed on one point at least: that Wagner had forged the sword which national socialism wielded. Wagner and national socialism were inseparable. Hitler himself used precisely this formulation. Ernst Bloch was one of the few who protested. Without denying the "real Nazi germ-cells in Wagner," Bloch refused to be cheated of a German cultural possession: "The music of the Nazis is not the prelude to *Die Meistersinger,* it is the *Horst-Wessel-Lied*" (Zelinsky 1976, p. 237).

Despite its eminence the Bayreuth Festival was in the midst of a financial crisis in 1933. The war horses of the Nazi storm troopers were certainly not Wagnerians. "It is deeply tragic that Bayreuth has never been attacked so heavily on all fronts as in the Third Reich," wrote Liselotte Schmidt to her parents on 26 May 1933 (Karbaum 1976, p. 77). But Wolf (as Hitler was called in the Wagner family circle) proved his worth: he ensured that Bayreuth was given the financial support of the Reich. Winifred Wagner tried to pursue her old strategy of supporting Hitler publicly and out of conviction while keeping the internal control of the festival as free as possible from Nazi influence—an approach which was bound to fail in the face of the totalitarian reality of the Third Reich. Thanks to her personal friendship with Hitler, Winifred enjoyed a relatively large degree of independence; she could therefore afford to make personal representations on behalf of the victims of political persecution (see Karbaum 1976, pp. 113ff.).

The Bayreuth Festival of 1933 was a Hitler festival, with swastika flags in all the windows, and *Mein Kampf* instead of *My Life* taking pride of place in the bookshops. There were black SS uniforms everywhere. Hitler's ceremonious Austrian-style kissing of Winifred Wagner's hand paralleled the handshake and stiff bow to Hindenburg in Potsdam. The former represented the symbolic union between national socialism and German art, the latter the union with the old power elites.

Richard Wagner's music was completely integrated into the national socialist political liturgy. The radio marked the chancellor's forty-fourth birthday with the strains of Wagner, as *Lohengrin* or *Die Meistersinger* was being performed throughout the country. The Nuremberg party conference opened to the music of *Rienzi* and *Die Meistersinger* was performed at the City Opera. On Hitler's fiftieth birthday the representatives of German industry and the Labor Front presented him with some of Wagner's manuscript scores and sketches. Ignorance of Wagner could even be politically dangerous. Hitler dismissed Walther Dönicke, the mayor of Leipzig, for this reason. The general view at home and abroad was that Wagner and the Third Reich were one and the same.

The National Socialists also attempted to make one of Wagner's dreams come true by opening the Bayreuth Festival to a wider public. The organization of the wartime festivals was in the hands of the Labor Front *(Arbeitsfront)*. Masses of ill-prepared soldiers and "members of the folk community" were brought to the Festival Theater. But as military defeat loomed, the fascination with Wagner declined. The *Götterdämmerung* could no longer be staved off. In the end, it was the inspiration of the Prussian King Friedrich II to which Hitler adhered, not to Wagner.

Translated by Paul Knight

CHAPTER 7

A Brief History of Wagner Research

JOHN DEATHRIDGE

Sermon on the History of Wagner Research

It may seem foolhardy to begin an outline of Wagner research by announcing that such a thing is virtually impossible to write. Yet the fact must be faced at the outset that the bewildering variety of interests and standards in Wagner scholarship (or what passes for it) is congenitally resistant to systematic study. It is tempting to see the Bayreuth ideology that is part and parcel of Wagner and so-called Wagnerism as the root of the problem. (Houston Stewart Chamberlain's "Bayreuthians" and their dreadful mouthpiece the periodical *Bayreuther Blätter* alone wreaked havoc with Wagner research by surrounding it with an impenetrable ideological web.) Yet the question of ideology is not enough to explain the many paradoxes in Wagner studies. Nor is it the only reason for the tension between partisan special pleading (usually disguised as "objective" study) and the truly critical scholarship that runs beneath the surface of most writings on Wagner. Many scholars have felt compelled to distinguish between Wagner literature and Wagner research (WlWf), as if the apparent antithesis were a way out, as well as an accurate definition, of an acute dilemma. The distinction has something utopian about it: while Shakespeare and Beethoven scholarship can boast some vigorous interaction (not all of it friendly) between well-defined schools of analysis and historical study,[1] Wagner research presents a more diffuse picture which, although brightened by some of the most brilliant interpretive writing ever lavished on a major composer, is clouded by hagiography, dilettantish scholarship (much of it influential), and intellectual pretentiousness. Only comparatively recently have there been signs of a fruitful confrontation between dispassionate historical investigation on the one hand and a strong tradition of criticism and analysis on the other.

---

1. See *Shakespeare-Handbuch* (Stuttgart: Kröner Verlag, 1978), pp. 917ff., and D. Johnson, "Beethoven Scholars and Beethoven Sketches," *Nineteenth-Century Music* 2 (1978), 3ff.

Many shortcomings of Wagner research in the strictest sense can be traced to Wagner himself, whose lukewarm interest in and skepticism about factual historical investigation undoubtedly left their mark on his followers. On receiving the first volume of Nikolaus Oesterlein's *Katalog einer Richard Wagner-Bibliothek* he remarked, "Now I can relish all the fuss and bother that'll be made about me fifteen years after my death" (CT, 11 July 1882), a light-hearted comment revealing more than a hint of mistrust of scholarly method. Cosima Wagner, after remarking on Oesterlein's Wagner Museum in Vienna in a letter to Chamberlain (23 November 1891), reiterated a not dissimilar view with the telling sentence: "Whatever I feel, it is impossible for me to feel historically." Chamberlain himself carried this attitude farther when, in a letter to Cosima dated 13 January 1905, he denied the value of archival research altogether. "I am of the opinion," he wrote, "that all of us today suffer from a mania for documents, and that a great man has to be judged on the strength of his works and very little factual evidence—the less the better."

Wagner almost certainly bears partial responsibility for the influential anti-historical stance of his wife and son-in-law. Yet his sensitivity to history and the world of scholarship (academic traits not always recognized by his followers) was doubtless one factor that prompted him to use his considerable skill as a writer to furbish his public image with plentiful historical "facts." Egon Voss has rightly spoken of an "authenticity bonus" (Voss 1982, p. 77) in Wagner research that has prevented many scholars from challenging what we claim to know about Wagner simply because much of it comes from the master's pen. (It is less Wagner's flights of fantasy per se than his theatrical talent for weaving fiction with sometimes astonishingly accurate accounts of his life that has caused most of the trouble.) Furthermore, Wagner continually amplified his view of himself with new information and ideas, often changing important details in the process, so that not even his own writings can be said to present a coherent and consistent whole. The situation is complicated, too, by an unusually large number of primary sources that form a dense counterpoint to the conflicting evidence of Wagner's writings. Finally, given the difficulties of presenting dry and unglamorous contradictions to a world fascinated by Wagner's theatrical genius (and sated with books about it), it is no exaggeration to say that accurate documentation has become one of the thorniest problems facing the Wagner scholar.

Any history of Wagner research must broach the question of interdisciplinary study while concentrating on specialized source analysis and the overwhelming influence of Wagner biography. It would be a narrow historian who ignored Wagner's reaction to the artistic and moral realities of the nineteenth century and the literature it produced. Yet, despite the intellectual challenge Wagner's many-sided personality poses, scholars who can bridge interdisciplinary boundaries to do justice to the phenomenon have been surprisingly rare. On the one hand, "musicology's remoteness from the mundane" (Meyer 1978, p. 350) has never been more apparent than in musicological studies of the suggestive subject of Wagner. On the other hand, musically untrained historians confronted with the elusiveness of musical material are understandably reluctant to deal with the subject from the inside, on its own terms. Except, therefore, for scarce and widely scattered shorter studies, Wagner has not received his due from intellectual historians. Nor have musicologists (except in the rarest instances) given his music the kind of detailed treatment its extramusical ambitions demand. Even Wagner's political role in the nineteenth century and in the rise of Nazi ideology in the twentieth is an important subject that is seldom examined without polemics, largely because the common denominators of music and ideology are usually denied vigorous scholarly treatment.

Nevertheless, the attractive image of the versatile scholar who can do everything *(Gesamtforscher),* as well as the question of competence, needs careful handling by the historian of Wagner scholarship. It is easier to lament the lack of well-grounded books embracing several disciplines than it is to explain the gap, or to evaluate isolated studies that point tentatively in this direction. (The unwritten history of what is loosely known as Wagnerism— a field of study that would include many cultural and political as well as specifically musical dimensions—is readily yearned for regardless of scattered attempts to grapple with the problems it poses.) A purist overemphasis on scholarly competence can easily distort the interplay of ideology and scholarship in the history of Wagner research. My own description of the *Bayreuther Blätter* as "dreadful" in the opening paragraph of this essay is a good example of how tempting it is, especially in the heated vicinity of Wagner's reputation, to take sides on ideological issues while projecting partisan feeling onto the kind of scholarship associated with them. To say that the Bayreuthians "wreaked havoc with Wagner research" is in any case to imply that a scholarly tradition can be measured against another, more contemporary one in a way that surrounds the latter with the aura of an absolute ideal. The implicit judgments are unreal in the context since they tend to belittle the historical role of the Bayreuthians and to create a false picture of Wagner scholarship as inevitably groping toward, or being "rescued" by, modern research techniques.

Wagner research is so closely bound up with the paradoxes of the phenomenon it tries to dissect that any systematic study claiming to see it in terms of tidy periods of development and scholarly achievement invariably runs the risk of gross distortion. No one would seriously claim today that Carl Friedrich Glasenapp's biography of Wagner—to take just one prominent example— is a scholarly masterpiece. Yet in the fifth edition of *Grove's Dictionary of Music and Musicians* Eric Blom not only succeeded in turning a real virtue into a vice by calling the biography "worthless . . . so far as the facts are concerned" (many of the facts are surprisingly accurate), but also ignored the ideological landscape of Wagner research by seriously underestimating Glasenapp's leading, and by no means entirely negative, role as the guardian of a powerful biographical myth. If we are to understand, too, how Wagner's public image as a musical progressive and an intellectual enfant terrible complicated his reputation by (in part) diverting attention from the complex reality of his music and the content of his theories, the influence of the multifarious liter-ature that contributed to the peculiar dynamic of the Wagner "question" in the nineteenth century is clearly more important than its scholarly worth might suggest.

I am aware that any attempt to define the unwieldy and atomized corpus of writing that amounts to Wagner research in the broadest sense is bound to seem simplistic. I am also aware that concentrating on the dynamic rather than the content of Wagner scholarship will make my allegiances seem suspect to anyone unwilling to suspend belief—momentarily at least—in favored scholarly methods for the sake of insight into the field. This essay is not an apologia for the Bayreuthians; nor is its prime purpose to belittle modern research by placing it on the same pedestal as more old-fashioned philosophies of scholarship. Rather its aim is to highlight the main contours of Wagner research, past and present, without pressing value judgments too much into the foreground. No one, least of all myself, can remain entirely neutral on the subject of what has been written about Wagner in the name of scholarship. Yet a dispassionate distinction between ideology and scholarship is essential if their interaction—and, at the same time, their independence from each other—is to be shown clearly. There is little point in condemning the prob-lematic strategies of Wagner and many of his biographers with the "facts" of his life when the important thing is to show his influence on the kind of scholarship he attracted. Above all, the idea of a kind of research that is totally emancipated from its subject and seen as a preordained goal in the history of Wagner scholarship is a chimera I have tried to resist. Like the ever-recurring specter of the "truth" about Wagner, a viable view of Wagner research has more to do with the dynamics of history than with an absolute vision of how it should be.

Source Studies

There are few subjects that have generated more heat in the history of Wagner research than the publication and interpretation of primary sources. "It stands to reason," Ernest Newman wrote on 22 August 1930 to Elbert Lenrow, the editor of the English translation of Wagner's letters to Anton Pusinelli, "that the nearer the publication stood to the date of Wagner's death, and the more people who were still alive at the time, the more scruples Wahnfried would have about publication in full. Perhaps what Cosima and the others did was no more than any widow and any friends would do in similar circumstances." Newman's charitable view is nonetheless a kind way of saying that the sensitivity of Wahnfried toward information that could throw a negative light on the paradoxical and inconsistent character of Wagner was a not inconsid-erable obstacle to serious research at the outset. The negative effects of

Bayreuth censorship were probably more psychological than practical. Righteous indignation at publications approved by Wahnfried quickly became de rigueur among Wagner experts, many of whom wasted valuable time complaining about what was missing instead of concentrating on what was not. Even scholars unwilling to attract attention with pointless sensationalism, however, were nagged by the frustration (in the early years of Bayreuth at least) of being unable to check printed texts against original documents contained in what the English scholar William Ashton Ellis aptly called the "Wahnfried strong-box."

Cosima's reputation as the ruthless expurgator of all undesirable knowledge about Wagner has unquestionably been exaggerated. (After much hue and cry about Wagner's "repressed" autobiography, the editions of *My Life* published in 1911 and 1914 contained, apart from editorial errors, a mere seventeen passages modified "out of consideration for those yet living and their relatives," as Wagner's step-daughter Daniela Thode put it. See ML 755.) Yet the notion that "the Wahnfried strong-box . . . must have been an incinerator as well" (Burrell 1929, p. xi) had more than a grain of truth. Cosima, who—perhaps rightly—did not share the rest of the world's almost voyeuristic interest in intimate correspondence, is known to have destroyed the originals of Wagner's letters to Mathilde Wesendonck (except for the musical examples), Nietzsche's letters to herself, and Peter Cornelius' letters to Wagner, as well as several important communications from Hans von Bülow to Wagner between the middle of May 1861 and the end of November 1867. The fate of Wagner's missing letters to Cosima is inextricably linked with the eccentric behavior of Cosima's daughter Eva Chamberlain. And according to Houston Stewart Chamberlain, Cosima carried out "an *auto-da-fé* with old letters in Wahnfried" (Eger 1979, p. 26) with Eva in 1909, a report that scarcely diminishes the impression of brutal Realpolitik concerning sensitive documents, even if the motives behind it were not always entirely reprehensible.

Yet not all the sensitive gaps among the Wahnfried manuscripts and other collections are attributable to "Cosima and the others." The fact that nearly half of Wagner's early works up to 1832 have disappeared is probably due to a variety of reasons ranging from sheer carelessness to Wagner's habit of settling debts by making presents of his own manuscripts. More important later sources, including the scores of *Die Feen, Das Liebesverbot, Rienzi, Das Rheingold,* and *Die Walküre,* have been lost only since 1945. Wagner presented them on various occasions in the 1860s to King Ludwig II of Bavaria, and it was from Ludwig's estate that they passed into the possession of the Wittelsbacher Ausgleichsfonds. They were given to Adolf Hitler in 1939 on his fiftieth birthday as a gift from the German Chamber of Industry and Commerce. Wagner's peripatetic existence as the conductor and manager of concerts, usually of his own works, is certainly the reason for the lamentably small number of concert versions of excerpts from works such as *Lohengrin* and the *Ring* that have survived. The missing links in Wagner's sketches and drafts are more difficult to explain. In one case, however—the first complete draft of *Lohengrin*—it is easy to prove that some of the gaps have something to do with the misguided generosity of the Wagner family in making gifts of manuscripts to prominent personalities and institutions without retaining copies (Deathridge 1989, p. 57).

Nevertheless, the sheer number of primary sources that have survived is a far greater stumbling block than lost manuscripts or editorial garbling. The problem of emendations by Cosima and the others to, say, the first editions of Wagner's correspondence with Liszt or his letters to his Dresden friends, inexplicable and clumsy as they often are, pales before the virtually insuperable difficulties of editing Wagner's letters as a whole. The quantity of material is immense, and not even the most clairvoyant scholar can envisage how much remains to be discovered. There is no modern equivalent of Wilhelm Altmann's *Richard Wagner's Letters: Chronology and Content* (Altmann 1905), which registered the existence of no fewer than 3,143 autograph letters. (The number has more than trebled in the meantime.) And progress on the first and so far only complete critical edition of the letters (SB) has been hindered by limited resources and uncertain editorial principles (Voss 1978).

The vast quantity of surviving sources for Wagner's musical works is the main reason why no scholarly catalogue has been devoted to either the works or the sources until recently. Wagner's skepticism about such publications and the people who make them (both Wagner and Cosima referred disparagingly to *rubrizierende Menschen,* or "people who like to put things in pigeonholes") doubtless did little to encourage such projects. In the hundred years after Wagner's death, at any rate, scant progress was made beyond simply compiling work lists that are neither complete nor reliable. Emerich Kastner's *Wagner-Katalog* admittedly aspired to greater heights, only to be promptly—and rightly—dismissed by Wagner himself as "exacting work carelessly done" (CT, 5 April 1878). An unpublished inventory of sources compiled by Otto Strobel intended for internal use in the Bayreuth archives never progressed beyond its initial stages. And publications such as Cecil Hopkinson's book on the printed sources of *Tannhäuser* (Hopkinson 1973) or the bibliographies of first editions by Horst Klein (Klein 1979 and 1983) have dealt exclusively with specialized areas. The first attempt at a larger systematic catalogue of Wagner's musical works and their sources, the *Wagner Werk-Verzeichnis* (WWV), is among other things a necessary step toward an objective Wagner biography since, for the first time on this scale, its commentaries confront many "facts" in Wagner's autobiographical writings with analyses of primary sources (Deathridge 1983, Deathridge-Voss 1985).

The work of the former Bayreuth archivist Otto Strobel on Wagner sources is still a mainstay of research in the field. Strobel is a classic example of a Wagner scholar whose influence was seriously impaired by his association with the Nazis. No one today can regard a scholarly credo with equanimity that saw Wagner research as a "service to the people" (*Dienst am Volke*) which must negate the "conscious transformation of Wagner's personality and influence into kitsch" by a press "largely in Jewish hands" (Strobel 1943, pp. 16, 32). Yet Strobel's role as the leading light of the Richard-Wagner-Forschungsstätte—a short-lived research institution brought into being on Wagner's 125th birthday (22 May 1938) at the decree of Hitler—cannot be dismissed lightly. He not only planned and made preparations for "a new large-scale biography of Wagner taking into consideration all relevant source material" and "a historico-critical collected edition of Wagner's writings, verse texts and letters" (NWF 9), but he also began research for a projected complete edition of Wagner's musical works that greatly profited later generations of scholars. His work on Wagner's methods of composition in particular became an important stepping-stone for future studies (Deathridge 1974/5).

Political developments and Strobel's entrenched position outside the mainstream of traditional musicology were two reasons why a revival of interest in Wagner's sketches had to wait for over two decades. In 1963 Curt von Westernhagen published a study of an incomplete composition draft of *Siegfrieds Tod* (1850), the first version of *Götterdämmerung,* and five years later Robert Bailey followed suit with a more detailed study of all the fragmentary sketches and drafts of the same work (Westernhagen 1963, Bailey 1968). Yet, contrary to expectations, the interest aroused by these publications did not precipitate a scholarly industry on the scale of Beethoven sketch studies. Research undertaken so far has attempted to illuminate two key stylistic thresholds in Wagner's evolution with an analysis of relevant sketch materials (Breig 1973, Deathridge 1977). Many sketches have been examined that shed light on the genesis of, and on alterations to, *Holländer* (Vetter 1982), *Tannhäuser* (Abbate 1985), and *Lohengrin* (Schmid 1988, Deathridge 1989). A few sketches have assisted music analysis (Bailey 1968, Brinkmann 1972, Abbate 1989), while Westernhagen's pioneer work on the composition sketches of the *Ring* (1976; for a detailed critique, see Deathridge 1977a) has at least drawn public attention to the documents, even if it falls below the high standard of Strobel's study of manuscripts for the libretto of the same work (1930). Despite this flurry of activity, however, Wagner's sketches have arguably still not been given the critical attention they deserve. (For a full inventory of the sketches, see WWV.)

Collected editions of Wagner's musical and literary works inevitably raise the question of interpretation as a conscious or unconscious by-product of the editorial process. Wagner's own edition of his collected writings neatly dovetails method and interpretation. At first, Wagner wanted to arrange his writings roughly according to subject matter (see BB 131–133). He eventually decided, however, to publish them chronologically since this best suited his view of the edition—stated in the preface to the first volume—as a "record of an artist's activity throughout his life." Wagner's editorial intentions were biographical rather than scholarly; but they had a unity of purpose that was ignored when Richard Sternfeld expanded the edition from ten to sixteen volumes without much thought as to either the arrangement or the sources of the additional texts. Sternfeld's edition has still not been superseded. The difficulties facing a modern edition are admittedly enormous: Wagner wrote a great deal that was published in obscure newspapers and periodicals that are not easily available today. He also published many essays, reviews, and speeches either anonymously or under a pseudonym. Even the fundamental editorial problem of whether to present the writings systematically, according to subject, or chronologically as Wagner eventually did is fraught with questions that are far from easy to answer. Selections and inventories of the writings by scholars acquainted with primary sources (Voss 1978, Borchmeyer 1983, Kropfinger 1984, Nattiez 1990), and a thorough discussion of editorial method (Dahlhaus 1985), are nonetheless important signposts toward the emergence of a reliable critical edition.

Plans for collected editions of Wagner's musical works, too, were inevitably influenced from the beginning by the question of interpretation. On 26 August 1871 Wagner wrote to the publisher Hermann Müller that he was considering a "complete edition of the scores" of his operas, clearly intimating that revisions were in order that would raise the scores to the status of definitive versions. (The edition never materialized.) The conductor Michael Balling, who began publishing a collected edition in 1912, thought nothing of "improving" dynamics and phrasing in keeping with the kapellmeister tradition of the nineteenth century. Strobel's projected complete edition for the Richard-Wagner-Forschungsstätte was to be a continuation of Balling's, and its failure to materialize is a significant loss, if only because Strobel had access to the manuscripts in Hitler's possession that are now missing. We shall never know exactly how Strobel's scholarly credo would have influenced his edition. Despite the radical change in the political climate of Germany after the war, Strobel's attack on "pseudo-scholarship" (Strobel 1943, p. 16), by which he meant a lax interpretation of primary sources endemic to most Wagner studies, is echoed by the understandably stringent stance toward documentary evidence taken by the complete edition of Wagner's works initiated by Carl Dahlhaus in 1968 (SW). One of the declared aims of the edition is the *Entmythologisierung,* or demystification, of Wagner (Voss 1976/7), an approach based on the premise that documents can be used as effective critical tools to penetrate the thicket of myth and half-truth that has rapidly grown around Wagner and his works since the nineteenth century.

Biography

In a letter to Anton Pusinelli (12 January 1870) Wagner described his autobiography as "a document by means of which all the misrepresentations and calumnies that circulate about me, as they do about no one else, may be refuted." Soon after the appearance of the first public edition of *My Life* (1911) it was itself described as a misrepresentation and a perfect example of Wagner's myth-making prowess. Despite the doubts of scholars, however, the book never received the systematic critique it deserved. After coming into possession of the first private edition not long after Wagner's death, Mary Burrell, the most conscientious of Wagner's early biographers, declared outright that "Richard Wagner is not responsible for the book" (Burrell 1898). Others, no less critical, nevertheless succumbed to Wagner's powerful autobiographical images, as if relentless detail were enough to banish doubts about the "unadorned truthfulness" which, in a short preface, Wagner claimed *My Life* represented. George Ainslie Hight, for example, believed that Wagner "or someone else" had transformed the affair with Jessie Laussot "into a romance in the doubtful taste of a third-rate French novel, with all the regular apparatus of neglected wife, union of souls, proposed elopement, challenge to a duel, etc." (Hight 1925, I, 230–231). Yet Hight's justifiable skepticism was not enough to prevent him from basing a full-scale biography on an uncritical acceptance of information drawn largely from the book.

In addition to exposing *My Life* to a rigorous analysis of other documents, one must place it in context with the traditions of nineteenth-century autobiography. Wagner's stylization of his life and work on a grand historical scale and his transformation of empirical data into highly suggestive images have their roots in Goethe. Yet *My Life* is not only an Olympian view of *Dichtung und Wahrheit;* it is also a polemical vindication that abandons poetry and philosophy for a more journalistic discourse in order to defend an idealistic image of the artist. In a sense, it is the reverse of Tolstoy's *Confessions* and its negative critique of art. Wagner was not simply justifying a life of moral turpitude (at least in the eyes of the public) with the argument that art must take precedence over sordid reality; he was also defending the cause of art itself, the very existence of which was threatened by the decline of Western civilization.

Houston Stewart Chamberlain and Carl Friedrich Glasenapp, who tried to stress Wagner's artistic mission by fusing his life and art into a quasi-mystical unity, were major scholars in the eyes of the Bayreuthians, a term invented by Chamberlain to distinguish the idealists from mere Wagnerites, who were allegedly oblivious to Wagner's cultural message. In a sense, Chamberlain and Glasenapp continued in the spirit of Wagner's own autobiographical narratives. Glasenapp's monumental biography, for instance, which is concerned with the "facts" of Wagner's life rather than with a critique of his life and work, is—on one level at least—an elaboration of the direct but nonetheless tendentious dramaturgy of *My Life* (Glasenapp I–VI). Wagner told Cosima three days before he died that he still intended "to finish the biography" (*My Life* ends with the call to Munich by Ludwig II on 3 May 1864). Not only does the remark cast at least one shadow of doubt on the optimal authenticity that Cosima's diaries are generally thought to represent; it also expresses Wagner's need to interpret the final and most decisive part of his life, a task he bequeathed to his Bayreuthian disciples, and Glasenapp in particular. (The sixth volume of Glasenapp's biography, which covers only the last six years of Wagner's life, is noticeably larger and more copious than any of the other five.)

The mixture of pedantry and devout prose in Glasenapp's biography found many imitators. The assiduous Wagner scholar William Ashton Ellis, founder of the English periodical *The Meister,* began translating Glasenapp freely into English (1900–1908) and elaborated the researches of the famous Bayreuth "house biographer" to such an extent that the translation gradually changed, almost unnoticeably, into an independent and by no means entirely insignificant study of Ellis' own.. Westernhagen, who liked to describe himself as a pupil of Glasenapp, achieved success with a biography (Westernhagen 1978) which, despite adopting Glasenapp's Old Bayreuthian approach in muted form, fitted comfortably into the ideological landscape of Wieland Wagner's New Bayreuth. (Westernhagen's use of his mentor's methods, which consisted mainly of hagiography carefully disguised as apparently solid scholarship, is discussed in detail in Deathridge 1981 and Rose 1982.) Chamberlain's idiosyncratic dovetailing of facts and uninhibited subjective interpretation to create "not a biography in the narrower sense of the word, but so to speak a *picture*" (Chamberlain 1900, p. v; emphasis in original) set an influential example. (The distance between Chamberlain's use of luxurious facsimiles to enhance his aesthetic view of Wagner's life and the modern documentary biography, despite all differences in scholarly method, is not as great as it appears to be at first sight.) Scholars who were critical of Chamberlain profited nevertheless from his consciously antihistorical methods. In an important study of Wagner's exile from Germany after the Dresden revolution and the amnesty that eventually allowed him to return, Woldemar Lippert quotes Chamberlain's golden rule that for the Wagner scholar, "Wagner's writings, letters and works will always be the most important, and actually the only, source" (Lippert 1927, p. 8). Nevertheless, Lippert rightly refused to turn Chamberlain's rule into an absolute and attempted to see Wagner's sometimes contradictory statements in a historical context that could be presented more precisely by recourse to archival material.

If specialized studies of Wagner's life concentrating on specific issues in depth (for example, Kropfinger 1991) or shorter periods (Arro 1965) are surprisingly scarce, the opposite is true of the popular, all-embracing Wagner biography. Dahlhaus' comment that "the story of Wagner's life has been told so often that it can be told no longer" (Dahlhaus 1979, p. 2) is an exasperated, and for the serious scholar a sympathetic, reaction to countless books that are either pale repetitions of *My Life* or glorified historical gossip columns. Even the highly respected biographies by Robert Gutman (1968) and Martin Gregor-Dellin (1983), both of which easily transcend the feebleminded spirit of most accounts, have more than a trace of the *biographie romanesque.* Richly embroidered narratives animate great figures of the nineteenth century to the point where merciless criticism of Wagner's behavior, too, becomes part of the dramatic effect. Theodor Adorno claimed that Ernest Newman's four-volume biography (Newman 1976) "shares nothing with novel writing and is guided by a thoroughly English aversion against 'dramatization'" (Adorno 1947, p. 155). Yet for all Newman's critical sense and sobriety, his zealous detective work in combating established *convenus* (created mainly by Wagner and the Glasenapp-Chamberlain school) did not escape theatrical distortion.

Newman's biography is nonetheless a landmark in Wagner research. Whereas its detractors decried Newman's lack of scholarly method, Adorno, one of Newman's most sharp-witted defenders, praised the latter's exaggerated use of empirical analysis, which, in Adorno's view, was taken to such extremes that it began to throw doubt on the value of empirical research itself. "His search for truth," Adorno wrote, "is not that of a detached scholar. He may be compared to a gambler whose stake is the work of his life, whose price the absolute reconstruction of reality as it was, and whose risk the ultimate doubt about the existence of such an objective reality itself" (Adorno 1947, pp. 155–156). Newman's gamble was to desecrate for the first time certain sacred symbols of the Wagnerian gospel: the idea of Liszt as unstinting benefactor and unselfish servant of Wagnerism, of the "mad" King Ludwig, of Cosima as the liberal protector of the Holy Grail, and many others. For Newman, the effort of archival labor and scholarly precision paled before the more onerous critical task of undermining an entrenched myth of formidable power. (The task was made more urgent by the falsification and exploitation of Wagner's life and work by the Nazis, which gained ground while Newman was at work on his biography.) Forgivably in the circumstances, Newman's zest was often misplaced. Ironically, too, he undoubtedly succeeded in creating legends of his own, including a mythical piece of music, the so-called *Starnberg Quartet* (for details, see WWV, pp. 508–509), and a wrongheaded analysis of the case Nietzsche built against Wagner. Yet if the monumental scale and intellectual bluster of Newman's biography is unsympathetic to the modern scholar, it is still a work of unshakable distinction and critical flair which, combined with greater accessibility to, and a more sophisticated handling of, original documents, could point the way to future studies.

Analysis and Criticism

It has often been said that Wagner laid down a law of obligatory silence about musical technique. Yet the claim that he was uninterested in analyses of his music is difficult to reconcile with several remarks in his writings and correspondence. In a letter to Theodor Uhlig (December 1851) he actively encouraged Uhlig to write a musical analysis of *Lohengrin* (an invitation Uhlig did not accept). And in a late essay, *On the Application of Music to the Drama* (1879), Wagner claimed to have shown the way toward what he called a "useful critique" of the musical forms in his dramas. The dramatic significance and effect of the so-called leitmotifs had already been examined by his "young friend" (Hans von Wolzogen), he wrote, but their place in the musical structure of the dramas remained to be examined in detail (SSD X, 185). Such remarks are not without tinges of self-glorification and hardly envisaged the kind of music analysis we are accustomed to today. The idea of musical autonomy within a musical-dramatic work, too, is clearly part of the philosophy of the composer of *Parsifal,* who had become disappointed with the theater and whose ambition to write symphonies increasingly came to dominate his ideas on music and aesthetics in his last years. Indeed, the importance Wagner attached late in life to musical structure allowed the question of the role of the extramusical in opera to be forgotten—a debate that had received considerable impetus from *Opera and Drama* (1851), written by a younger Wagner who had not yet read Schopenhauer and still believed in operatic reform. Because of a scholarly tradition that regarded Wagner's final words on the subject of music and drama as definitive, the earlier author of *Opera and Drama* was either misunderstood or simply ignored for a hundred years after his death.

On 12 May 1921 Hans von Wolzogen wrote to Alfred Lorenz: "I am very glad that you want to study and present the musical form in Wagner's works in a serious manner. That is what Wagner himself always wanted; but he could never get the musicians among his admirers to write anything about it" (Grunsky 1943, p. 42). Wolzogen's words contain three unmistakable ingredients of Bayreuthian dogma: a bid for "authenticity"; the presentation as an absolute of a view peculiar to Wagner's last years; and an undisguised contempt for the Wagnerites. Not surprisingly, all these ingredients are faithfully incorporated into Alfred Lorenz's monumental four-volume study of the "secret" of form in Wagner's music dramas, published between 1924 and 1933 (Lorenz I–IV). Lorenz was the Glasenapp of Wagnerian music analysis: his work was less a dispassionate study than a scholarly offensive not averse to the corruption of empirical observation for the sake of ideological argument. Yet his attempt to prove that Wagner was the exact opposite of the "actor" Nietzsche accused him of being was a landmark not only in Wagner research but also in the history of music analysis. Never had a musicologist sustained a piece of analytical writing on this scale before; and no one, not even Glasenapp, had taken up the cudgel on Wagner's behalf with such devastating diligence.

The crux of Lorenz's argument was the claim that Wagner's dramas are coherent musical structures that have to do neither with operatic devices nor with the mechanical application to a text of leitmotifs that creates something anarchic and entirely arbitrary. Using an array of graphs and tables that presented Wagner's music principally in terms of spatial analogies, Lorenz set out to dislodge the criticism implicit in Nietzsche's shrewd epithets. According to Lorenz, Wagner was neither a superficial *histrio* masquerading as Beethoven's successor nor a failed opera composer whose music was shallow and formless. Rather he was a master of minutely organized musical edifices of astounding formal complexity "relentlessly saturated with the flow of symphonic argument" (Grunsky 1943, p. 42).

Lorenz's work has been described as a "*reductio ad absurdum* of certain valid insights" (Kerman 1989, p. 170) and as having "little in common with the realities of Wagner's music" (Voss 1983a, p. 73). Yet criticism of Lorenz has been carried to such extremes that one feels compelled to leap to his defense, even if one has to start with the modest, and decidedly subjective, point that a scholar whose work was still causing such controversy so many years after its publication must have said something significant. Lorenz's position in the history of Wagner research is seldom noted in judgments of his methods. Lorenz believed that he had successfully refuted the reproach of formlessness which Hanslick had leveled at Wagner by constructing immaculate tables demonstrating the huge, formal expanses of the music dramas (Dahlhaus 1969, Stephan 1970). He is seldom appreciated, however, as part of the movement inspired by Wagner's advocacy of Schopenhauer. Lorenz's predecessors—Hostinsky (1877), Ehrenfels (1896, 1913), Grunsky (1906, 1907), Halm (1916), and Kurth (1920)—were all sympathetic to the interpretation Wagner gave to Schopenhauer's metaphysics; and, like Lorenz, they tended to a mystical interpretation of Wagner's music that ignored its roots in operatic tradition. (Lorenz said of August Halm, who coined the suggestive, Schopenhauerian term *Formwille,* that Halm had "stood close to the threshold of finding the solutions" that he himself had found.) Lorenz's tightrope walk between metaphysics and systematic presentations of musical data is another aspect of his analyses that is hardly ever mentioned. The central question concerning Lorenz is not so much one of his diligent obsessions or the fact that he often ignored the reality of Wagner's music. Nor is it enough to say, with Patrick McCreless (1982), that "Lorenz erred seriously" in relating the discussion of tonality and form in Wagner's treatise *Opera and Drama* to all Wagner's works, beginning with *Das Rheingold,* particularly as the argument assumes the validity of Lorenz's interpretation of *Opera and Drama* (or at least a tiny portion of it) in the first place.[2] Rather the fragility of Lorenz's analyses—at least in a narrow sense—could be seen as a mirror of the daring chasms between detail and monumental form in Wagner's music which Lorenz's scholarly apparatus unwittingly traces. An objective attempt at interpreting Lorenz's system has to start at the point where his analyses of small forms turn into elaborate metaphors masquerading as quasi-scientific grand designs. In other words, a profitable study of Lorenz must begin with the details of his analyses while treating more skeptically the "giant" forms in Wagner's dramas that Lorenz claimed to have discovered, but which, nevertheless, can

2. Lorenz concentrated on the concept of the "poetic-musical period," a didactic paradigm Wagner invented to illustrate a possible way of combining musical structure with the content and form of *Stabreim* verse. According to *Opera and Drama,* the period is defined by a "main key" (*Haupttonart*). Lorenz took this to mean that every passage in Wagner's dramas defined by a "main key" (anything from a few bars to hundreds) is therefore a "poetic-musical period." The reversal is "logically tenuous" (Dahlhaus 1965) and is one symptom of Lorenz's support for the later Wagner's view of his works, which, unlike *Opera and Drama,* uses the authority of Schopenhauer to give greater weight to the role of music in his dramas than to their other components.

be seen as allegories for the symphonic ambition in Wagner's works that Lorenz rightly felt they contained.

Even in Wagner's lifetime serious studies of the mythological background to the *Ring* were being published by Franz Müller (1862) and Ernst Koch (1875), a line of inquiry subsequently developed by Ernst Meinck (1892), Wolfgang Golther (1902), and more recently by Deryck Cooke (1979) and Elizabeth Magee (1990). Scholars have not been slow, either, to sift the sources of Wagner's other mature works (see Weston 1896, Bowen 1897, Golther 1907, Zademack 1921, and Newman 1949). Nor has there been a lack of richly embroidered interpretations of Wagner's sources, of which Peter Wapnewski's studies (1978b, 1981) are a particularly good example. Wagner, whom Lévi-Strauss called "le père irrécusable de l'analyse structurelle des mythes" (*Mythologiques: le cru et le cruit,* Paris, 1964, p. 23), has also prompted psychoanalytical and structural analyses of his works (notably Donington 1963, Ingenschay-Goch 1982, Kester 1984; for a detailed survey, see Chapter 3 of this volume).

Yet despite this activity, Wagner's invitation in *Opera and Drama* to see his works in an extramusical context or to analyze them from (an albeit tendentious) historical point of view has not been critically scrutinized until relatively recently. Apart from Guido Adler (1904), scholars have subscribed too often to the banal idea that *Opera and Drama* was merely a confused theoretical blueprint for the *Ring* and have tended instead—like Lorenz, although often rejecting him—toward a purely musical analysis that reduces Wagner's music to precisely organized tables and diagrams. It is certainly true that in the century since Wagner's death, there have been only scattered attempts at more differentiated interpretations of *Opera and Drama*. Even an excellent essay by Klaus Just (1978) that focuses Wagner's position in the history of the libretto omits mention of the treatise. Although *Opera and Drama* is "today part and parcel of the Wagner Monument, parts of it, and certain ways it has been interpreted, are still controversial" (Kropfinger 1984, p. 532). With rare exceptions (Rather 1979, Borchmeyer 1982), Wagner's own interpretation of myth in the treatise has been virtually ignored. Nor have Wagner's ideas in *Opera and Drama* about the role of words and music in his dramas received the critical attention they deserve, even though studies by Jack Stein (1960), Alan Laing (1973), Frank W. Glass (1982), Thomas Grey (1987), and Carolyn Abbate (1989) point tentatively in this direction.

If Wagner's major theoretical work (Richard Strauss called it "the book of books about music") has never been interpreted in toto, the rarity of comprehensive analyses of the dramas is hardly surprising. The postwar reaction to Lorenz's ideologically colored analyses is partly responsible; but so is a more complex view of the works which compels the analyst to study them in the small rather than in the large. Alternatives to Lorenz's approach such as intensive analysis of single scenes or sections (Brinkmann 1972, Breig 1980, McCreless 1989, Brown 1989); reappraisals of leitmotif technique (Dahlhaus

1971, Steinbeck 1984); Schenkerian analysis (Mitchell 1967); and semiology (Renk 1978, Nattiez 1990) are all part of the colorful palette of postwar analysis of Wagner's works. Reflections on the structuralist approach to myth in Wagner's dramas (Prox 1974, Brinkmann 1978) have opened perspectives that need further exploration. Even Lorenz's obsession with tonal structure has been sensibly realigned (in Bailey 1969 and 1977/8, Josephson 1979, Newcomb 1981/2, McCreless 1982, Kinderman 1983, and Lewin 1984). An alternative analytical model that could replace Lorenz's fragile explanation of large-scale form in Wagner's dramas, however, has yet to be developed.

In a speculative study of Patrice Chéreau's Bayreuth centenary production of the *Ring*, Jean-Jacques Nattiez asks: "Le Ring de Wagner a-t-il un sens?" (Nattiez 1983, p. 57). The question is not meant to imply that the *Ring* is merely a critical vacuum, a kind of prestigious tabula rasa on which all and sundry can simply spell out their latest obsessions. Rather it raises the issue of how many narrative levels there are in the *Ring*, of its discontinuities as well as its undeniable unity and nobility. Nattiez's ideas also extend to the staging, the extent to which it can "orchestrate" the different narrative elements in the work and, through stylistic variation, preserve, in the words of Pierre Boulez, the unity of each "multiple level of signification" (Nattiez 1980, p. 88). In a further study, *Wagner Androgyne*, arguably the most elaborate interpretation of the *Ring* to date, Nattiez extends these ideas in parallel with his semiotic approach to include a variety of other themes such as psychoanalysis and the history of music itself (Nattiez 1990).

"Few puzzle anymore," Susan Sontag has written, "in the way generations of Wagner lovers and Wagner fearers did, about what Wagner's operas *mean*. Now Wagner is just enjoyed as a drug" (Sontag 1987, p. 9). The puzzlers of earlier generations used to be so numerous, however, that serious critics often reacted sharply against them. The doctrinal views of Houston Stewart Chamberlain, for instance, were not shared by independent minds that had difficulty in accepting the narrowly defined Bayreuthian interpretation of Wagner's works. Indeed, many critics and admirers felt compelled to raise the question of meaning as an issue in itself, or to invent strategies that skirted it altogether. Nietzsche, who sensed "the apologetic desire" in the religion of redemption and "the truly systematic totality of the Wagnerian music drama" (Adorno 1947, p. 160), tried to expose the ideological character of Wagner's work by elevating the Wagner "case" to the level of a historical and artistic catastrophe. Lorenz, a Bayreuthian, certainly, but no leitmotif-hunting Wagnerite, was able to trace what he claimed to be vast and intricate formal patterns in the dramas only by rigorously separating form from content. Paul Bekker (1924) even managed to write an entire book based on a single aesthetic concept, "the art of expression" *(Ausdruckskunst)*, without seriously asking what it was that Wagner was supposed to have been expressing. Cleansing Wagner from contamination with the ideology of the Third Reich also required some spectacular critical somersaults, especially in postwar Bayreuth. Wieland Wagner spoke of "the clearing away of old lumber" *(Entrümpelung)*, producing stage pictures bereft of their "reactionary" ethos—and, as skeptics were prone to add, most of their content as well.

First published in 1952, Adorno's *Versuch über Wagner* (Essay on Wagner) follows Nietzsche by treating Wagner's art critically as "ideology."[3] Yet it also tries more positively to "rescue" Wagner (as Adorno himself put it), or in other words to wrest what is left of Wagner's humanity from the forces of history that threaten to engulf him. Adorno sees Wagner as a heavily damaged bourgeois individual whose weaknesses are so great that his very decadence becomes a critical weapon against the powers he allegedly serves. The book distances itself from Wagner with a method that is deliberately antimonumental or "micrological" *(mikrologisch)*. "[In my book] there is nothing that is generally fundamental, there are no complete analyses of the works, no summaries and no conclusions" (Adorno 1952, p. 505). Eight bars of *Tannhäuser* are analogous to Wagner's futile rebellion against the powers that be— a rebellion that "is more clearly inscribed in the formal principles underlying his music than it ever was in his philosophical opinions" (Adorno 1981, p. 40). And contradictory musical strategies in the opening bars of *Tristan* "resist . . . the aesthetic claims of 'symbolism,' in short, the entire tradition of German idealism" (1981, p. 48). With a tightly-knit chain of similar analogies (here simplified) Adorno claims that "Wagner's giant forms stand confronted . . . within two hundred pages" (1952, p. 505).

Adorno's "sociological decoding" *(soziologische Dechiffrierung)* of Wagner's music has been sharply criticized by Dahlhaus (1970b). Yet, although Dahlhaus rejects Adorno's sociological analogies, he accepts the latter's fundamental assertion "that progress and reaction in Wagner's music cannot be separated out like sheep and goats. The two are indissolubly intertwined" (Adorno 1981, pp. 47–48). The dialectical sting in Adorno's premise is nonetheless undermined when Dahlhaus, in an almost positivistic way, resolves Adorno's image of indissoluble contradiction into one of straightforward paradox. Indeed, it is less Adorno than the spirit of Ernst Bloch's "Paradoxes and the Pastorale in Wagner's Music" (Bloch 1985) that stands in the wings of Dahlhaus' seminal study *Richard Wagner's Music Dramas.* "The categories of 'progressive' and 'conservative'," Dahlhaus writes, "become rather confused when applied to Wagner, with musical factors contradicting dramatic situations . . . It is the 'villains,' the 'antis,' Venus in *Tannhäuser,* Ortrud in *Lohengrin* and Beckmesser in *Meistersinger,* who are presented in exploratory and adventurous musical language" (Dahlhaus 1979, p. 47).

The postwar habit of reducing Wagner to a manageable size (one could almost speak of domestication) is a striking contrast to other, less stringent interpretations. With a critical method strongly influenced by F. R. Leavis, Michael Tanner (1979) probes Wagner's major works with the concept of

---

3. The title of the English translation, *In Search of Wagner* (London: Adorno, 1981), is based on a misunderstanding. See my review in *Nineteenth-Century Music* 7 (1983), 81ff.

"moral vitalism," an idea reminiscent of parts of Shaw's *Perfect Wagnerite* (Shaw 1898). Wagner's surprisingly rich and varied approach to the theater, too, is scrutinized by Dieter Borchmeyer (1982), who, instead of containing Wagner in yet another intellectual straitjacket, almost chases too many hares in his efforts to show how wide-ranging Wagner's interest in the theater really was. One of the strongest reactions to the reductive abstractions of New Bayreuth, however, is the work of Hans Jürgen Syberberg. Susan Sontag has described him as a "great Wagnerian, the greatest since Thomas Mann." But she also adds that Syberberg's "attitude to Wagner and the treasures of German romanticism is not only pious. It contains more than a bit of malice, the touch of the cultural vandal." On the one hand, Syberberg's film of *Parsifal* is consciously overloaded with symbols on different levels of meaning, almost as if he were agreeing with the idea that the work is little more than an empty space to be filled with cultural detritus. On the other hand, without resorting to the rigid absolutes of the Old Bayreuthians or the neutral abstractions of New Bayreuth, he sets as his goal nothing less than obtaining our undivided attention to, and passionate involvement with, the work of art itself—a quintessentially Wagnerian claim, as Sontag notes, that "manages to perpetuate in a melancholy, attenuated form something of Wagner's notions of art as therapy, as redemption and catharsis" (Sontag 1980).

Reception

Apart from endless performance statistics published by Eichberg, Kastner, Wolzogen, and others for the benefit of admirers seeking confirmation of the growth of Wagner's reputation at the end of the nineteenth century, investigations into the reception of Wagner's works are a comparatively recent development. Wagner himself was uninterested in studying the history of his fame (although he kept a sharp eye on its progress) and would doubtless have agreed with Chamberlain that to preserve and examine, say, the judgment of an obscure music critic as a "historical document" is absurd (Chamberlain 1900, p. 5). Yet, happily free from Wagner's influence as this branch of Wagner research is, it is faced with another, far more crushing problem: a virtually unconquerable mass of archival material. In an introductory chapter to two books evaluating the immense number of sources that document press reactions to the Bayreuth festivals of 1876 and 1882, Susanna Großmann–Vendrey speaks frankly of the initial "impotence of the scholar when faced with historical reality" (1977/83, I, 7). In another, no less ambitious undertaking, Ute Jung (1974) examines the reception of Wagner's art in Italy and, after finding herself confronted with so much material, relinquishes systematic method altogether in favor of a blanket claim on all information (*Totalitätsanspruch*) that can help to reconstruct history "as it really was."

The "ultimate doubt" about the existence of objective reality that Adorno read into Newman's zealous positivism would have been even more appropriate had Adorno mentioned it in the present context. Certainly this branch of Wagner research is not without acrimonious debate that raises doubts in the mind of the dispassionate observer about the feasibility of the undertaking. Jung's *Totalitätsanspruch* has been sharply criticized by Großmann-Vendrey for its "irresponsible neglect of the dimension of time that is the only way of illuminating historical contexts" (Großmann-Vendrey 1976). Großmann-Vendrey herself has been taken to task by Isolde Vetter for an overselective publication of sources—a decision prompted not only by stringent methods of "research into reception history that has been strategically and methodologically thought out" from a bland and unsystematic "anthology," but also by limited funds and space for publication. Indeed, the institutional structure of organized research in the field tends to encourage scholars to keep documents jealously hidden from the public eye—a mentality described by Vetter as being more akin to "treasure hunting" *(Schatzgräbermentalität)* than to serious research, and one that tends to turn empirical historical scholarship into its own worst enemy (Vetter 1980).

Scholars interested in what Großmann-Vendrey calls "creative statements" [*schöpferische Aussagen*] about Wagner have rarely bothered with questions of method, as though the search for Wagnerism, one of the most famous phantoms of Western culture, were in itself enough to exempt them from critically scrutinizing the haphazard ways of reconstructing history in which they usually indulge. Most studies of this kind end up in a sort of intellectual no-man's-land. Yet there are notable exceptions where self-imposed limitations to, say, a single concept, one person, or a group of persons are at least fruitful attempts to focus the unwieldy amount of available material. Erwin Koppen places the idea of decadence at the center of his study of Wagner and the literature of the fin de siècle (Koppen 1973). Responses to Wagner in nineteenth-century English literature are examined by Anna Dzamba Sessa as part of a concern with "the inadequacies of the reigning scientism as a metaphysic" (Sessa 1979, p. 11). The proceedings of the 1983 Salzburg Symposium, too, contain some telling contributions precisely because of strict limits imposed on the participants. Private and public attitudes to composers, works, and institutions—a category Großmann-Vendrey defines as "communicative statements" *(kommunikative Aussagen)*—as well as the views of individual artists or groups of artists are discussed in a series of sharp vignettes that create the effect of a scholarly kaleidoscope (see Salzburg Symposium). A similar though more broadly defined approach can be found in *Wagnerism in European Culture and Politics,* edited by David Large and William Weber, the most substantial book on the reception of Wagner's works yet to appear in English (Large-Weber 1985).

Winfried Schüler's study of the Bayreuth circle from its inception up to the First World War is still the standard work on this aspect of Wagner reception (Schüler 1971). Yet the world of scholarship has still to produce a comprehensive, and at the same time a convincing, investigation of the extremely delicate topic of Bayreuth and the Third Reich. It would be wrong, of course, to interpret this lack as a definitive sign of impotence in this branch of Wagner studies; yet it is worth noting that discussions of the subject, despite all the claims made for them on the basis of the documents that have been brought to light, constantly seem to miss their target. Hartmut Zelinsky's writings on Wagner and Bayreuth, provided with informative footnotes and numerous facsimiles of relevant material, have prompted reactions in the German-speaking media that are unwittingly more revealing than the source of the provocation. (Zelinsky's thesis of Wagner's alleged "'new religion' of 'redemption' through 'destruction'," which he has repeated with variations in three bravely polemical publications, is a juicy conspiracy theory that has been almost universally condemned in a way that at least gives the lie to the notion that serious controversy about Wagner has long since been defused and enshrined by history. See Zelinsky 1976, 1978, and 1982. Part of the controversy is documented in Csampai-Holland 1984; see also Mork 1990.)

The centenary of Bayreuth in 1976 saw not only Chéreau's controversial production of the *Ring,* but also the appearance of two books about the Bayreuth festivals by Michael Karbaum and Hans Mayer that appeared amidst a swirl of invective about the supposedly unacknowledged use of documents in Mayer's book that Karbaum had already collected and evaluated in his own study (Karbaum 1976 and Mayer 1976), an affair described by Reinhold Brinkmann in *Melos/Neue Zeitschrift für Musik* (1, 1977) as a "scandal." Yet, apart from the squabble about the knowing or unknowing use of another scholar's material, few noticed the more interesting, though no less disturbing, fact that both Karbaum and Mayer had arrived at widely divergent interpretations of the history of the Bayreuth Festival by apparently using the same documentary material. If the reception of Wagner's works is so diffuse that systematic study of it, particularly when undertaken by a single scholar, seems impossible from the outset, it is clear that the relation between empirical research into the history of Bayreuth on the one hand and a narrative approach to that history on the other has to be thought through again, the valuable achievements of Karbaum and Mayer notwithstanding. Joseph Kerman has described Bayreuth as "the most formidable move in the history of Wagnerism" (Kerman 1961). It almost goes without saying that formidable research skills (and formidable tact) are still needed to study the history of the Bayreuth Festival and the web of aesthetics and ideology at its core.

Translated by the author

Postscript: Wagner, the Jews, and Jakob Katz

By far the most sensitive subject in the history of Wagner research is Wagner's anti-Semitism. Apart from Leon Stein's *The Racial Thinking of Richard Wagner* (1950), full-length studies of the subject are surprisingly hard to come by, although there has been no shortage of brief articles and heated exchanges. The most incisive study is Jakob Katz's work *The Darker Side of Genius* (1985). By way of a conclusion to this chapter, I append here a review of his book in which I outline some of the issues arising from this central and (for many) highly problematic aspect of Wagner. These issues are also raised in more detail by Dieter Borchmeyer in Chapter 5 of this volume. My purpose here is not to repeat or elaborate them, but—with Katz's book as a basis—to present them in a somewhat different light.

To the critical historian concerned with Wagner's anti-Semitism, Katz argues, the "evidence" of Wagner's music dramas and the outcry that in some, by no means only Jewish, circles has enveloped the issue since the Second World War offer no rewards. The scruples of the conscientious scholar compel one to concentrate only on the "facts" taken from Wagner's writings and other contemporary testimony while leaving to the "historians of literature and music" the question of whether Wagner's anti-Semitic views can deepen our understanding of his art (Katz 1986, p. 123). If this looks like an evasion of some tricky issues in the name of professional ethics, it is certainly not intended in Wagner's defense. Even putting aside the Nazi horrors and questions of aesthetics, Katz comes to the remarkable conclusion that "the historical condemnation of Wagner by no means rests on the belated insight of the historian, but results from the correct understanding of his own statements and actions. Wagner himself sits in judgement on Wagner and is unable to grant himself a historical acquittal" (p. 132).

Coming at the end of a levelheaded account of Wagner's anti-Semitic passions, this is a surprising, not to say contorted, deus ex machina. This is a pity, since the book is in many respects a welcome antidote to the sanitized image of Wagner's anti-Semitism in the popular biographies by Westernhagen (1978) and Gregor-Dellin (1983) that has played a minor role in Germany's so-called coming to terms with the past, and an informed rebuttal of some senseless Wagner battering which—in the German-speaking media at least—has passed for an adequate answer to a feeble cover-up. At the last minute Katz seems to have sensed that by steering a severely factual course between these two implacably opposed camps he had knocked the stuffing out of his own position. He saves the situation by turning the tables on his method with an interpretation of Wagner's well-known dislike of the anti-Semitic movement of the 1870s and early 1880s that is quickly turned into the "fact" that Wagner shrank "from the practical consequences of his way of thinking" (p. 131). Wagner had his own, and not exactly liberal-minded, reasons for publicly distancing himself from the movement, including the view that it was vulgar and not very intelligent. But the idea that he could foresee "the potential for disaster embedded in his life-work" is both too kind and too cruel, since Katz assumes too readily that Wagner had consistent and serious moral qualms about his anti-Semitic philosophy, a thesis that is difficult to prove, while also implying that he was already imagining the possibility of a wholesale massacre of the Jews, a leap of faith influenced by the kind of historical insight that Katz explicitly rejects.

Although everyone has heard about Wagner and the Jews, few have actually read what he said about them or bothered to grasp his dialectical, quasi-

Hegelian train of thought and its significant changes of emphasis in the later stages of his life. Katz treads warily through the complicated reasoning of *Judaism in Music* (1850) and is careful to distinguish between Wagner's arguments and those of Bruno Bauer and Karl Marx, whose overparadoxical young Hegelian idiom and stereotype of the Jew as a symbol of market relations are only a prelude in Wagner's polemic to a jungle of biological metaphor and jingoistic palaver quite alien to the spirit of his predecessors. Liberal guilt about Wagner's anti-Semitism is often assuaged by some healthy finger wagging at Marx in particular; but there is a world of difference between Marx's equation of the social emancipation of the Jews with the emancipation of society from Judaism and Wagner's more visceral, demonic version that vilifies Jews on a personal level and burdens them collectively with the "curse" of Ahasuerus and the prospect of "redemption" through self-willed "destruction" *(Untergang)*.

Katz rightly warns against reading into Wagner's notion of "destruction" anything more than a drastic expression for the de-Judaization of the Jews. Still, Wagner clearly wanted to hit below the belt with *Judaism,* and hit even harder when he republished it in 1869, this time with a preface and an afterword denouncing the alleged Jewish conspiracy against his works supposedly brought about by the first edition. The reaction to the original had been strong, as Katz shows; but by 1869 it was virtually forgotten—so much so that critics of the new version had little trouble in parrying Wagner's contention about Jewish revenge for the piece with the almost unanimous declaration that they had never heard of it.

By 1869 Wagner was very famous indeed, and *Judaism,* first published in a music periodical *(Neue Zeitschrift für Musik)* with limited circulation, had been transformed into a full-fledged brochure that could be reissued according to demand—two factors ensuring that it got more attention than it deserved. Wagner's victims had proliferated, too. To Mendelssohn and Meyerbeer, the central targets of the early version, he added Hanslick and Joachim, among others, and also the "truly sympathetic friends" delivered to Wagner by "fate from their tribal kinship [with the Jews]" (SSD VIII, 239). How Wagner rationalized the well-known fact that by 1869 some of his most active collaborators, such as Karl Tausig and Heinrich Porges, were Jews simply defies logical analysis. Katz battles with the arguments nevertheless and clearly shows how Wagner used what he presented as his friends' attempts to exorcise their Jewishness to reinforce the impression that his libelous brochure was really a praiseworthy way of guiding all Jews along the thorny road to assimilation, as opposed to a "violent ejection" of them, which was plainly impractical.

What happened next has opened a Pandora's box of innuendo and bizarre interpretation in the Wagner literature which Katz obviously finds difficult to close. Nietzsche for one knew that Wagner's phobias about the Jews got worse in his last years, despite a theoretical readiness to accept them with Gobineau's theory of "race," corrected, so to speak, through the doctrine of

Christian salvation. Nietzsche's fleeting allusion in "The Case of Wagner" to the possibility that Wagner was himself a Jew, or thought he was in part (Nietzsche 1967, p. 182), has spawned a great deal of speculation which Katz tries to do away with "once and for all" with the simple observation that Geyer, the name of Wagner's stepfather, on which the issue rests, "scarcely ever appears among Jews" (Katz 1986, p. 121). Geyer may not seem to us a distinctively Jewish name now; but it did to Nietzsche and his friend Peter Gast, who, after hearing a false rumor that the maiden name of Wagner's mother was "Beer," spent a malicious evening referring to Wagner as "Geyerbeer." The obscure way Nietzsche phrased his remark was not "completely" arbitrary, as Katz thinks, but was—as Roger Hollinrake (1970) has shown— a cutting reference to the family crest at the head of the privately published first edition of *My Life,* which only Bayreuth's innermost circle could fully understand. It was a willful distortion of "facts," yet it started a powerful legend that struck at the heart of Bayreuth hypocrisy about the Jews—a legend unfortunately so insidious that the historian can only delude himself if he thinks that merely by putting the facts right again he can dispose of it for good.

Katz avoids the question of why, in spite of Wagner's polemics against the Jews, it seems impossible to prove that his music dramas have anti-Semitic characteristics. In Chapter 5 of this volume Dieter Borchmeyer suggests that "Wagner would have given the lie to the promise of redemption held out by the artwork of the future if he had used his music dramas—which promised to free the Jews from the 'curse' of their race—as an instrument of anti-Jewish propaganda" (see also the appendix to the English translation of Borchmeyer 1982). The defense is shaky, to say the least, since it implicates Wagner's aesthetics in a world view conditioned by anti-Semitism while at the same time seeming to exonerate them from it. Once the ideological purpose of Wagner's music dramas is seen to include the redemption of the Jews, it is only a small step to the argument that he defined the boundaries of the lost paradise he wanted to conjure up in his works by including in them anti-Semitic stereotypes in the form of social outcasts such as Mime and Kundry. With Borchmeyer, Katz would dismiss this line of reasoning as speculative and in any case, since it is supposedly influenced by the Nazi appropriation of Wagner, of only relatively recent origin. Yet its history is much older (it begins tentatively with Paul Lindau's critique of *Parsifal* in 1882; see Großmann-Vendrey 1977/83, II, 32). In choosing not to confront the issue with anything more than a blind faith in empirical "fact," Katz and Borchmeyer dismiss too hastily as inadmissible "evidence" the deeper, more subjective motives at the root of Wagner's anti-Semitism and the controversy it has caused. This may come as a relief for admirers of Wagner's music. For the dispassionate reader and listener, however, it leaves the unsettling impression that in trying to put out the fire with a detailed and sensible account of this— by far the most unpalatable—subject in the history of Wagner research, Katz and Borchmeyer have simply left it to smolder.

Works: Sources, Influences, Aesthetics

CHAPTER 8

Wagner and Antiquity

ULRICH MÜLLER

"I do not believe there can ever have been a boy or young man who was more enthusiastic about classical antiquity than I was during the time I attended the Kreuzschule in Dresden; and yet, fascinated though I was by Greek mythology and history, it was above all the study of Greek as a language to which I felt most drawn, to such an extent, indeed, as to be guilty of a total and almost rebellious avoidance of Latin." These remarks of Wagner's, it must be admitted, occur in a polemical context, namely his *Open Letter to Friedrich Nietzsche* (SSD IX, 295–302), first published in the *Norddeutsche Allgemeine Zeitung* of 23 June 1872. Nonetheless, the sentence provides a wholly pertinent summary of the importance which classical antiquity had for Wagner, in addition to offering a clear demonstration of the way in which Wagner's enthusiasm for the Greeks, and his lack of interest in Latin, were entirely typical of nineteenth-century educational trends. In fact, if Wagner was well versed in the literature, mythology, and history of ancient Greece, he owed his knowledge less to the lessons he had received at school than to his own intensive private study; and the results of this study are clearly discernible in his works. To this point, too, he made frequent and explicit reference.

Earlier writings on the subject of Wagner and the Greeks include various works by Robert Petsch (1907), Otto Strobel (1930), Arthur Drews (1931), Paul Maas (1932), Walther Vetter (1953), and Curt von Westernhagen (1956). These, however, are little more than preliminary studies to three longer essays by Wolfgang Schadewaldt (1970) which originated as three lectures given in Bayreuth between 1962 and 1964 at the invitation of Wieland Wagner. Schadewaldt examines the theme of Wagner and the Greeks in all its complexity, listing all of Wagner's relevant remarks on the subject (and listing them, moreover, in far more manageable form than Gerhard Frommel had done in 1933).[1] In discussing influences and parallels, and revealing much that was

---

1. Many of Schadewaldt's observations were subsequently confirmed by Westernhagen (1966) and CT.

previously unknown, Schadewaldt influenced the production style of New
Bayreuth during the years in question, an influence that was most clearly
discernible in the pseudoclassical costumes worn by the gods in the *Ring*.[2]
The survey by Hugh Lloyd-Jones (1982) is based in part on Schadewaldt, as
are three complementary studies published in 1982 by Dieter Borchmeyer,
Karl Bertau, and Michael Ewans, each of which deals for the most part only
with individual points. The present survey is based on all of these earlier
investigations, but most especially on those of Schadewaldt.[3] It attempts,
however, to complement them and, in certain cases, to shift the emphases
somewhat. It must be stated at the outset that Wagner offers "neither an
imitation, nor a classicistic idealization of the Greeks, no immediate and naïve
reversion to the Greeks such as one finds with Goethe or Hölderlin . . . but,
conditioned by the new age of science and historicism, it offers a conscious
return to the Greeks that is characterized by a certain erudition and a constant
awareness of their historical remoteness; it is a return in which this sense of
historical distance exercises a quite remarkable creative influence" (Schadewaldt 1970, p. 386).

Wagner's Interest in the Greeks

Wagner's earliest interest in the Greeks dates from his youthful years in
Dresden and Leipzig (ca. 1822–1827), when the chief influence was that of his
"favourite teacher at the Kreuzschule," Julius Sillig (SSD IX, 295), together
with that of his uncle Adolf Wagner. A more intensive interest followed
during his years in Paris from 1839 to 1842, when he was guided in his studies
by his friend Samuel Lehrs, a student of classical and Germanic philology
from Königsberg, who eked out a living in the French metropolis as a reader
for a publisher. What could be called the decisive breakthrough for Wagner
finally came in the summer of 1847, when he was in Dresden working on
the composition of *Lohengrin*. It was then that he first read Aeschylus (in the
1832 translation and reconstruction of Johann Gustav Droysen),[4] Aristophanes, and Plato (in translations by Hieronymus Müller, 1843–1846, and Friedrich Schleiermacher, 1817–1828), together with Droysen's *History of Hellenism*
(1836–1843) and the major accounts of Roman history by Edward Gibbon
(German translation of 1840) and Barthold Georg Niebuhr (1833–1845). All
these works were in Wagner's library in Dresden, which he began to assemble

2. Schadewalt had many conversations with Wieland Wagner during the years leading up to
the publication of the three lectures; see also Jürgen Kühnel's 1984 article in *Salzburg Symposium*.

3. I should like to take this opportunity to record my gratitude to Wolfgang Schadewaldt,
from whom I learned a great deal, in both seminars and private conversations, on a subject that
was of intense interest to him during my years as a student in Tübingen in the early 1960s.

4. Here and in subsequent references the dates represent the date of publication of the relevant
volume in Wagner's Dresden library; no indication is given as to the particular edition that he
used.

in 1842, and which he had to leave behind when he fled the city in 1849.[5] Also present were translations of Euripides by J. J. C. Donner (1841–1845), Herodotus by Friedrich Lange (1842), Homer by Johann Heinrich Voss (1840 and 1843), Pindar by Johannes Tycho Mommsen (1846), Sophocles by Donner (1842), and Thucydides by Maximilian Jacobi (1804–1808), as well as translations of Horace, Livy, Tacitus, and Virgil.

At the same time—and with no less intense an interest—Wagner continued to devote his attention, just as he had in Paris, to "German antiquity" (ML 343), especially to Jacob Grimm's *German Mythology* (2nd ed., 1844). Indeed, by far the majority of the books that made up his Dresden library dealt with medieval subjects. It was, however, his reading of Aeschylus, and above all the *Oresteia,* that left the liveliest impression on Wagner: "My ideas about the significance of drama, and especially of the theatre itself, were decisively moulded by these impressions" (ML 342–343). From now on the Greeks were to be of undiminished importance for Wagner.[6] Among other works that later made an impression, those that deserve to be mentioned here are the *Odyssey* (which Wagner read in Zurich in 1850), the *Iliad,* works by Sophocles and Aristophanes, and, above all, the *Oresteia,* which Wagner reread at the Villa Angri outside Naples, reciting the work to his family and friends on three consecutive evenings (CT, 23–25 June 1880) and engaging in a critique of the drama.

Evidence of Wagner's interest in the Greeks is clearly discernible in a number of aspects of his work, including his theoretical writings, his conception of the Bayreuth Festival, his attempts at a comedy "in the antique manner," *Eine Kapitulation* (WWV 102), and, finally, in the music dramas themselves.

The Greeks and Wagner's Theoretical Writings

It is certainly no exaggeration to claim that the three essays on the theory of art which Wagner wrote in Zurich between 1849 and 1851 (*Art and Revolution, The Art-Work of the Future,* and *Opera and Drama*) were influenced by his critical confrontation with Greek antiquity. To quote Wolfgang Schadewaldt: "Confirmation of his own ideas by relating them to, and deriving them from, the Greeks almost becomes a way of thinking for him" (1970, p. 353; for more details, see Chapter 23). As Wagner himself insists at the beginning of *Art and Revolution* (SSD III, 9): "If we reflect even for a moment on present-day art, we are bound to be struck at each step we take by its links with *Greek art.* Indeed, our modern art is but a link in the chain that binds the whole of Europe together in a single artistic development, a development

---

5. The library was donated to the Richard Wagner Archive in Bayreuth in 1979, and is now on permanent display in the museum at Wahnfried.

6. See Wagner's remark, as noted by Cosima on 6 March 1870, "If I were locked up in prison, I should ask only for Greek literature and things about Greece."

which begins with the Greeks." In the Greek word *mūsikē* Wagner sees "the three purely human artistic genres in their original unity," that is, "*dance, music* and *poetry*" (SSD III, 67). It is a sense of unity that was later lost and which Wagner sought to reestablish with his new *Gesamtkunstwerk,* or total work of art. The idea propounded by Nietzsche in his *Birth of Tragedy out of the Spirit of Music* of 1872 (an idea explicit in the title of that work) had already been developed by Wagner with reference to Greek drama both in the basic outline of his argument and in the metaphorical language which he had used to expound it (for a more detailed discussion, see Chapter 14). With the full score of *Lohengrin* behind him (it was completed on 28 April 1848) Wagner now rejected the use of a chorus in opera,[7] appealing in support of his argument to what, in this case, was a misunderstood classical model; in the "drama of the future" the function of the classical chorus was to pass to the orchestra. "The *orchestra* thus plays an uninterrupted and, from every point of view, a leading and elucidatory role in the overall impression that the performer conveys both to the ear and to the eye; it is the teeming womb of music from which the unifying bond of expression grows.—*The chorus of Greek tragedy* has bequeathed to the *modern orchestra* the significance that is felt as being necessary to the drama, for only in the orchestra can it be developed, free from all constraint, and achieve so immeasurably varied an expression" (SSD IV, 190–191). The Greek *orchestra*—the onstage space in classical drama where the chorus danced and sang—is replaced by the modern orchestra, which "carries" the staged events and "elucidates" them. Unlike Nietzsche, however, Wagner always drew a functional distinction between the classical *orchestra* and the modern orchestra.

Wagner's Ideas for a Festival

As early as 1849, in *Art and Revolution,* Wagner had complained that "in the case of the Greeks" art "existed in the public consciousness, whereas today it exists only in the individual consciousness, in contrast to public unconsciousness of it" (SSD III, 28). Throughout his life the composer strove to reestablish a "public art," and he believed that he had finally achieved that aim in building the Festival Theater in Bayreuth and in establishing a festival there (see Chapter 19). The audience was not to be divided up according to social class, as in the old "system of tiered boxes," but would sit together in democratic equality, as in a classical *theatron,* confronted by the events onstage and controlled by them. The invisible orchestra and the removal of the proscenium boxes were intended to create a "mystic abyss" which, on the one hand, would convey to the spectator "the mysterious illusion whereby the actual stage appears to be more remote" but, on the other, would enable him to experience "the clarity of real proximity," a clarity "leading to another illu-

---

7. But not forever, as is evident from act 2 of *Götterdämmerung,* and, above all, *Die Meistersinger* and *Parsifal.*

sion, ensuring that the characters onstage appear to be magnified and super-human in size," as in the classical theater (all quotations from *The Stage Festival Theater in Bayreuth* of 1873, SSD IX, 336–338). Of course, Wagner was fully conscious of the differences that existed between his Bayreuth audiences and the ideal classical populace, and he was aware of the dissimilarity between a genuinely classical theater (he speaks somewhat confusingly of the seating arrangement of the classical *amphitheater*, whereas what he really meant was a normal Greek theater such as the Theater of Dionysius in Athens or that in Epidaurus) and his own theater, with its roof and proscenium stage. And, finally, his festival at Bayreuth had as little in common with an ideal Greek performance (which, being a religious event, lasted the whole day) as the modern Olympic Games, founded at a somewhat later date by Baron Pierre de Coubertin, had with their classical counterpart.

Attempts to Write in the Antique Manner

Wagner made a number of attempts at a direct adaptation of classical subjects, or, rather, he attempted to write plays "in the antique manner." In 1849, stimulated by his reading of Droysen, he planned an *Alexander* in three acts; in 1849–50 an *Achilles* (WWV 81); and, two decades later, a "comedy in the antique manner," *Eine Kapitulation* (WWV 102), indebted to Aristophanes' *Frogs* and the Romantic literary comedy, this last work a somewhat macabre joke about the Franco-Prussian War (autumn 1870), for which he envisaged music "in the style of Offenbach as being truly necessary" (SSD IX, 4). Mention should also be made here of a "curiously silly sketch for a comedy" (Borchmeyer 1982, p. 359), noted down in the *Brown Book* (BB) in 1868 in emulation, once again, of Aristophanes, whom he admired so much. Our only information concerning the projected *Alexander* comes from Cosima's diaries, which contain brief references to the content of the individual acts.[8] At least a few preliminary notes have survived on the subject of Achilles, although it is far from certain that they have anything to do with the project of 1849–50 (see WWV, p. 340). Both works bear distant resemblances in outline to *Siegfried*. But it is to the completed music dramas that we must turn for the best reflection of Wagner's preoccupation with the Greeks, a reflection which, if less direct, is all the more impressive and effective.

Wagner's Music Dramas and the Greeks

Considered superficially, all of Wagner's operas and music dramas are medieval in the sense that, without exception, they take place in a medieval setting or adapt medieval themes. This element played an extremely important part in later attitudes toward Wagner's works. Yet the medieval aspect was to a

8. See CT 1 April 1878: "The first act was the murder of Clitos, the second the decision to return from Asia, the third his death."

large extent present only in the characters, their costumes, and the plot structures; it was less a part of the content and message. Indeed, up to and including *Parsifal,* the content gradually assumed the opposite meaning to that contained within the medieval source material (see Müller 1986). As Wagner himself was frequently to observe, and later commentators have argued at length, the stage works contain a great deal of classical material buried within their "deep structure," or, to use another current expression, their "mythic construction."

Myth was of fundamental significance for Wagner. "What is so incomparable about myth is that it is true for all time, and that its content, with its extreme concision, is inexhaustible for every age" (SSD IV, 64). It is myth which has made Greek tragedy so incomparable: "The subject-matter of this drama, however, was myth, from whose essential nature alone we can grasp the supreme work of Greek art and the form which so enthralls us" (SSD IV, 31). And it was specifically Greek myth which Wagner used as an ever-present interpretive model both in drawing comparisons and in interpreting even the most everyday things (Borchmeyer 1982, pp. 79–80). From this point of view it would have been natural for Wagner to have used Greek myths as the material for his music dramas rather than the legends of the Germanic tribes and of the Middle Ages. But for Wagner there was an essential difference between "the autochthonous legend of the more modern European and, above all, *German* nations" and the myths of the Greeks, and this difference lay in the fact that in Greek myth "natural phenomena such as day and night, or the rising and setting of the sun, are transformed by an act of imagination into characters who act and who are worshiped or feared because of their actions, so that gods who are thought of as human finally become truly anthropomorphized heroes." In other words, religious myth, with its pantheon of gods, is turned into anthropocentric heroic legend, which remains, however, deeply rooted "in the same religious perception of nature as that which had once produced the primeval myth" (*Opera and Drama,* SSD IV, 38–39).

Wagner himself observed—albeit at a later date, in *A Communication to My Friends* of 1851—that Greek myths were a "fundamental feature," part of the "deep structure," of *Holländer, Tannhäuser,* and *Lohengrin.* The fundamental feature of the Flying Dutchman myth is to be found in the earlier figure of the Hellenic Odysseus, in a form that is still intelligible to us today. Odysseus, in tearing himself away from Calypso's embrace, in his flight from Circe's allurements, and in his yearning for the wife from his homeland who is familiar to him in mortal form, expresses the fundamental features of yearning that were recognizable to the Hellenic mind and that we ourselves rediscover in *Tannhäuser,* where the sense of longing is infinitely more intense and more enriched in its content. Similarly, we also encounter the fundamental features of the Lohengrin myth in Greek mythology, although even this is by no means the oldest form in which we know it. "Who has not heard of Zeus and Semele?" (SSD IV, 289)—that same Semele who ignored express warnings and insisted on seeing her lover, Zeus, in his actual form, thereby destroying both her love and herself. It is a motif which is also found in the classical tale of Cupid and Psyche, as well as in Wagner's early opera *Die Feen*. It would be wrong to assume in these and later cases that Wagner was from the outset aware of the mythic parallels and worked on them consciously. Psychoanalytical and structural analyses of myth have shown that deep archetypal relationships exist between the myths, narratives, and characters of the various cultural and linguistic regions of the world, however remote they may be geographically. As a result, it is unjustifiable to interpret every parallel of plot, character, or myth in terms of influence and imitation, and the same degree of caution is also necessary in the case of a nineteenth-century author such as Wagner.

Doubts must therefore be raised as to the validity of Schadewaldt's assumption that the figure of Socrates, so memorably portrayed by Plato in his *Symposium,* is "the prototype of Wagner's Hans Sachs" (Schadewaldt 1970, p. 397). Such doubts become even stronger when, citing Hugo von Hofmannsthal, Schadewaldt discovers an (admittedly vague) "Homeric" character to *Die Meistersinger.* The same is no doubt also true in the case of the alleged relationship between Wagner's *Tristan* and the myths of Narcissus, Daphne, and Phaedra and Hippolytus which Schadewaldt and Bertau, among others, claim to have found. An indisputably classical symbol (albeit more familiar from Lessing's essay of 1769, *How the Ancients Depicted Death*) is the torch that, as an emblem of death, is extinguished in act 2 of *Tristan* (Wapnewski 1978b, p. 53). Wagner himself pointed out links between Aeschylus and the second act of *Tristan* (CT, 25 June 1880); and we also know that Hans Sachs's closing address in *Die Meistersinger* was, surprisingly enough, inspired by the ending of Aeschylus' *Eumenides* (see Schadewaldt 1970, p. 393, and Cosima Wagner's letter to Hermann Levi of late summer 1880 in Eckart 1929, pp. 913–914). Nor is it possible to dismiss out of hand the importance of Aristophanes' *Frogs* for *Die Meistersinger,* an influence pointed out by both Schadewaldt and Lloyd-Jones (1982), for Wagner keenly admired it.

Wagner's greatest debt to the Greeks, however, and especially to Aeschylus, is to be found in the *Ring.* Schadewaldt gives a detailed account, whereas Michael Ewans (1982) displays an obsessive preoccupation with the *Oresteia,* which seems tangential in comparison. The *Ring,* conceived and expanded "retrogressively" (according to Peter Wapnewski 1978b), corresponds in its large-scale dramatic format to the (Athenian) Greek tetralogy of four dramas (generally related in content and comprising either three tragedies and a satyr play or four tragedies), written by a single poet for the tragedy competition held in Athens on the occasion of the Greater Dionysia and performed, in succession, in the course of a single day. Wagner admittedly specified that the *Ring* should be performed on four successive days, or, more precisely, on a "preliminary evening" (*Vorabend*) and the three following days.

The classical models that Wagner knew were the *Oresteia,* the only dramatic trilogy to have survived complete and one of the most frequently read works in the composer's library, and Droysen's reconstruction of a Prometheus trilogy, also by Aeschylus. According to this reconstruction (which modern scholars do not accept), the first part of the trilogy (no longer extant) dealt with the theft of fire, the second part with the binding of Prometheus (extant as *Prometheus Bound*), and the third (also missing) with the freeing of Prometheus. The parallelism with *Das Rheingold,* originally titled *Der Raub* (The theft), *Die Walküre* (The binding of Brünnhilde), and *Siegfried* is clear at a glance, even if it is not consistently carried through. More general parallels between Aeschylus and the *Ring* may be seen in three of the later work's basic qualities: first, its "epic form developed over long periods" (Schadewaldt 1970, p. 388), including its large-scale dialogues and long epic narrations; second, the interaction of the divine and human planes, which is not as pronounced in Wagner's Scandinavian sources as "the association of heroic tragedy and divine destiny which makes the poem of the *Ring* what it is and which represents a poetic reflex of the [reconstructed] *Prometheus* of Aeschylus"; and finally, the resultant expansion of a drama dealing with individual characters, *Siegfrieds Tod* (as *Götterdämmerung* was originally called), to become "a universal poem in the sense understood by Aeschylus" (Schadewaldt 1970, p. 362). Hugh Lloyd-Jones (1982) even argues, with some plausibility, that Aeschylus' choral style may have been the model that helped Wagner develop his leitmotif technique.

A number of convincing correspondences have been found between the two plots: the Oceanides in the extant *Prometheus Bound* are reminiscent of the Rhine Maidens; and the tetralogy's central scene in act 3 of *Die Walküre,* where Brünnhilde prophetically reveals to the fleeing Sieglinde the birth of her deliverer Siegfried, "proves at a glance to reflect an equally central scene" in Aeschylus (Schadewaldt 1970, p. 361), in which the bound Prometheus helps Io to escape the pursuing Hera and announces the birth of Epaphos, the forefather of the hero (Heracles) who will eventually release him. Moreover, there are echoes of Droysen's introduction and reconstruction in the prelude to *Das Rheingold* (Droysen speaks of "the twilight of becoming"), in the building of the citadel of the gods, and in the giants. The figure of Wagner's Brünnhilde bears basic similarities not only with the daughter of Zeus, Pallas Athena, as depicted by Homer, but also to the Prometheus of Aeschylus (for more details, see Schadewaldt 1970, pp. 371–372).[9] More generally, the Valhalla of the *Ring* is palpably inspired by the Greek Olympus. Wotan's various love affairs clearly recall those of Zeus, the father of the Greek gods. The arguments between Wotan and Fricka in *Das Rheingold* and act 2 of *Die Walküre* resemble corresponding scenes between Zeus and Hera in Homer's *Iliad* (books 4 and 14–15): marital feuds in Homer, Ibsen, and Wagner are clearly interlinked. There are also links between the figures of Siegfried and Homer's radiant hero Achilles, who is similarly vulnerable in only a single spot and who is characterized by hubris. And Erda, an invention of Wagner's, is

9. Parallels between Prometheus and Loge were noted by Theodor Schaefer as early as 1899.

unmistakably based on the Greek figure of Gaea, the mother of Prometheus. In contrast, Wagner's borrowings from the *Oresteia* are far less direct: Michael Ewans (1982) has certainly got the emphasis wrong here. At the time of writing, the most recently noted—and most surprising—traces of classical antiquity to be found in the *Ring* are those pointed out by Dieter Borchmeyer (1982). He has cited not only allusions to the Narcissus myth in act 1 of *Die Walküre* but also repeated correspondences with the myths centered on Oedipus and Antigone, of which Wagner himself offers a substantial interpretation in *Opera and Drama* (SSD IV, 55–67). Once again, Wagner's models were classical dramas, namely the *Oedipus* and *Antigone* of Sophocles, and Aeschylus' *Seven Against Thebes*.

Finally, *Parsifal* attests to a resurgence of interest in Aeschylus in the early 1870s. There is no doubt that it was this that Cosima had in mind when she subtitled it "The Redeemer Unbound" (CT, 28 February 1877). The influence of Aeschylus is apparent here not only (as with the *Ring*) in the epic-dramatic structure but also in the extreme ritualization of the action, in its conception as a *sacred* stage festival play ("Bühnen*weih*festspiel": the term recalls both the religious grounding of Greek drama and the tradition of the Christian liturgy), in the new importance given to the chorus, and, finally, in individual characters and motifs. Amfortas is related to Prometheus, who similarly suffers from a wound that keeps on reopening, is unable to die, and—in the version of Aeschylus—laments his fate in lengthy monologues. Parsifal resembles Heracles, who finally releases Prometheus as Parsifal releases Amfortas. And the manner in which Amfortas is healed by the very spear that dealt him his wound calls to mind not only the way in which Achilles heals Telephus but also a similar episode in Sophocles' *Philoctetes* that tells of Philoctetes and Neoptolemus.

Wagner must certainly have been thinking first and foremost of himself when he penned these words in his essay *What Is German?* (1865; first published in 1878): "Through the most intimate understanding of antiquity the German spirit has acquired the ability to imitate the purely human in all its original freedom, which it does, not by using classical forms to depict a particular subject, but by using the classical view of the world to produce the new and necessary form" (SSD X, 41). It is in this sense—that is, not as a model to be copied directly but as an invitation to question and to recreate anew, and to do so, moreover, in full consciousness of the historical distance involved—that the importance for Wagner of Greek antiquity, and especially Greek myth and Greek drama, cannot be underestimated.

Translated by Stewart Spencer

CHAPTER 9

Wagner's Middle Ages

VOLKER MERTENS

In *Lohengrin,* Wagner told Cosima on 6 June 1879, he felt he had "provided a complete picture of the Middle Ages"; to which Cosima replied that *Lohengrin* was "the only monument that shows the *beauty* of the Middle Ages."

It sounds from this as though it was less the medieval works themselves that provided a complete and beautiful picture of the Middle Ages than their nineteenth-century adaptations. Implicit in such a view is the belief that the epics of Wolfram von Eschenbach and Gottfried von Strassburg, together with the anonymous *Nibelungenlied* and *Lohengrin,* are in some way inadequate reworkings of the narrative material that they contain, and that they even distort or misrepresent the treasury of old legends in folk poetry, a view that was typical of the early nineteenth century. Wagner believed that he himself was the first person to have extracted the essential mythical meaning of these medieval narratives, and to have portrayed that meaning onstage, whereas what he actually staged, with the help of characters and episodes from these older accounts, were the problems of his own age, even of his own life. That is why a glance at these literary sources and a comparison between them and his own adaptation of the material reveals essential aspects of his oeuvre, and of the conditions that gave rise to his works, together with the aims that he hoped to achieve in writing them.

In terms of the history of ideas in general and of the history of art in particular, Wagner's change of course in the direction of German antiquity came relatively late. It can be explained in part by his experiences as a German musician in Paris and his striving for originality, and in part by a biographical coincidence.

Tannhäuser is, of course, the first of Wagner's operas to deal with a specifically medieval subject, but *Holländer* had already marked the decisive change of direction. It was neither (Italian) history (as in *Rienzi*) nor a remodeling of vaguely historical dramas (as in *Die Feen* and *Das Liebesverbot*), but rather a folk poem which Wagner sought to interpret and adapt, in contrast to the salon literature of contemporary Paris. But the historically German aspect of

Tannhäuser is further contrasted with the French and Italian influence that prevailed at the Paris Opéra. Having failed to find recognition in Paris, Wagner looked for an explanation for his lack of success in the domination of French and Italian taste in opera, setting himself apart from such taste by recalling his own "Germanness."

It had become traditional by this time to look back on the Middle Ages as a utopian era that offered the possibility of national identity. Admittedly, the rediscovery of medieval literature in the mid-eighteenth century had been little influenced by such an outlook, and it was really only at the beginning of the nineteenth century, with the growth of Germanic philology, that national enthusiasm was revived and intensified, especially in the wake of the Wars of Liberation (1813–1815). Owing to the efforts of the philologists, Wagner was able to draw on a rich fund of editorial experience and a preexisting, and by no means rudimentary, interpretive understanding of medieval texts. Indeed, about half the books in his Dresden library (which has survived almost intact) are medieval texts or accounts of medieval literature and history. Classical literature, even if represented by important works, occupies, by contrast, a secondary position. Wagner could therefore be said to have pursued a thorough course of medieval studies: he read Middle High German, although he always used translations to help him, and was familiar (albeit in a somewhat unsystematic way) with Old Icelandic.

The classical myths were incapable of satisfying Wagner's desire for originality. He still regarded them as relevant, but only insofar as they had been assimilated into Germanic myth, which they influenced and modified. If medieval themes had formed the basis for earlier works such as Carl Maria von Weber's opera *Euryanthe,* it was less because of their mythic potential than because of their Romantic coloring. What Wagner sought in medieval works, by contrast, was a universal humanity (which is how he interpreted myth), something which he could equally well have found, of course, in tales about Zeus and Semele, or Theseus and Oedipus.

As I have said, Wagner's interest in the German Middle Ages was sparked by a biographical coincidence. One of his friends in Paris was the philologist Samuel Lehrs, who had taken a lively interest in *Holländer.* When Wagner announced his intention to dig deeper into mythology and study the Greek classics in the original language (see ML 209–210), Lehrs dissuaded him from doing so; indeed, it appears to have been he who steered Wagner in the direction of German history. It was Wagner's first intensive encounter with this subject since his schooldays. He studied Friedrich von Raumer's *History of the Hohenstaufens,* and was fascinated above all by the figure of the Emperor Friedrich II and his son, King Manfred. On the strength of this interest he sketched a five-act drama suitable for setting to music, later elaborating the sketch in Dresden in the winter of 1842–43 as the text for an opera, *Die Sarazenin* (WWV 66). It allows us to identify important aspects of Wagner's incipient interest in the German Middle Ages. It is clear that the actual historical subject matter created difficulties for him since he was artistically unable to depict Friedrich (ML 210). Instead, he turned his attention to the emperor's son, Manfred, whose fate left him more scope for invention, most notably in the case of the Saracen Woman herself, "a female principal of highly Romantic significance," as he described her. Historical specificity can be a hindrance to dramatic characterization. In addition, the nationalistic element tended to overlap, he said, with the "purely human," thus revealing the extent to which the German spirit was "related to the Greek spirit." What both had in common was a mythic aspect which the Romantics interpreted as a poetic and symbolic realization of the ontological conditions of man and his world (in contrast to a conceptual and abstract portrayal).

In other words, Wagner sought the suprahistorical in the historical and the human in the national. He followed Schiller's maxim of "taking only the general situation, the time and the characters from history, and of inventing everything else" (letter to Goethe, 20 August 1799), and in doing so came close to the Romantic historical tragedy of, say, Schiller's *Die Jungfrau von Orleans*. But *Die Sarazenin* was incapable of satisfying Wagner, or of inspiring him to set it to music. It has a historical framework, to be sure, but is several stages removed from myth. The progress that had been marked by *Holländer* would have been forfeited had Wagner merely returned to Romantic historical drama in the manner of Schiller. Both elements, however, were successfully combined in his very next piece, *Tannhäuser*.

Tannhäuser: A Medieval Tale of Penance

As with *Holländer,* Wagner owed his knowledge of the Tannhäuser legend to Heinrich Heine, whose poem *Tannhäuser: A Legend* had appeared in 1837, in the third volume of *Der Salon,* together with a late medieval version of the poem. In addition Wagner knew Ludwig Tieck's short story *Der getreue Eckart und der Tannenhäuser* from his collection *Phantasus,* and the Tannhäuser Ballad from *Des Knaben Wunderhorn* of 1806, itself based on a late medieval version. Although Wagner claimed in *A Communication to My Friends* that he had acted "entirely without reflection in choosing the subject of Tannhäuser," and that he had reached his decision "in a wholly arbitrary manner, without critical awareness" (SSD IV, 272), there is no doubt that he studied the relevant source material in a thoroughly systematic way. In *My Life* (ML 212) and *A Communication to My Friends* he mentions "a folk book about the Venusberg" as his primary source, a version said to go back to "the well-known old Ballad" (presumably the version contained in *Des Knaben Wunderhorn*). What particularly attracted him was "the connection, if only fleetingly set forth, of Tannhäuser with the contest of song at the Wartburg" (ML 212).

Scholarly attempts to identify this folk book have so far proved unsuccessful, although of course that does not mean that such a book never existed. It is possible to imagine a Tannhäuser folk book, no longer extant, based on the late medieval poems about Tannhäuser. What is curious about Wagner's statement, however, is his remark that Tannhäuser was loosely connected with the song contest on the Wartburg, for Ludwig Bechstein's 1835 collection of *Legends of Eisenach and the Wartburg, Hörselberg, and Reinhardsbrunn* contains just such a link. Bechstein notes that Tannhäuser lived at the time when Hermann of Thuringia "had gathered around him at his Court on the Wartburg so many singers who vied to win great prizes in proud song contests." And since Wagner appears to have been influenced by this account in formulating the Landgrave's address in act 2 of his opera, it is tempting to suggest that the composer used Bechstein and, consciously or unconsciously, concealed his debt.

Wagner was familiar with the song contest from E. T. A. Hoffmann's *Battle of the Bards* (part of the *Serapionsbrüder* cycle), but he felt that Hoffmann "had a distorted view of this old material," and he conceived the desire "to form a more authentic picture of this attractive legend" (ML 212). The picture he was looking for was provided by Samuel Lehrs, who brought him a copy of Christoph Theodor Leopold Lucas' *Über den Krieg von Wartburg* (On the Wartburg contest; Annual Proceedings of the Royal German Society in Königsberg, 1838). Here he found not only an annotated edition of the story of the song contest but an even more detailed link with the Tannhäuser legend: Lucas assumed that the minnesinger Tannhäuser had later become identified in the popular imagination with Heinrich von Ofterdingen, one of the participants in the Wartburg song contest, an identification attributable to "their being originally related, or to some later connection" (p. 270). Although Wagner, by his own account, "could use virtually none of the material from this authentic version," he nonetheless felt that Lucas' edition had shown him "the German Middle Ages in a significant colouring" of which he had previously been completely unaware (ML 213). He felt drawn toward all that was "German," which attracted him "with ever-increasing force" (ML 212); and he appears to have discovered that "Germanness" first and foremost in the Middle High German language. Certainly the old poem has little actual color, if one ignores its mixture of linguistic ineptitude and formal complexity (the latter the result of the poem's strophic form). Far more important were E. T. A. Hoffmann, Tieck, and Heine's *Tannhäuser* ballad, all of them Romantic adaptations of medieval source material. In addition there was the late medieval Tannhäuser Ballad, as transmitted by Bechstein, Heine, and Achim von Arnim and Clemens von Brentano's *Des Knaben Wunderhorn* of 1806.

The late medieval Tannhäuser legend, which forms the basis of the Tannhäuser Ballad, is believed to date from around 1400. It provided Wagner with the outline of his plot: Tannhäuser has entered the Venusberg, but has grown weary of sensual pleasure and is ready to atone for his sins. He goes on a pilgrimage to Rome and confesses his failing to the pope, who makes his forgiveness dependent on a miracle: as soon as his staff bursts into leaf, Tannhäuser's sins will be remitted. In his despair Tannhäuser returns to Lady Venus. Too late the staff puts forth green shoots; Tannhäuser remains in the Venusberg until the Day of Judgment. In addition to his earlier sin of turning away from God and abandoning himself to sensuality, he is also guilty of *desperatio,* the sin of despair in the possibility of divine forgiveness. This is the only sin that can never be forgiven, since it is a sin against the Holy Ghost. That is why Tannhäuser is damned, not because he worships Venus.

Wagner inserted the Wartburg song contest before Tannhäuser's decision to atone. It is a contest in which, originally, Wolfram von Eschenbach triumphed over Heinrich von Ofterdingen (the latter replaced in Wagner's opera by Tannhäuser). The change is linked with another alteration which Wagner made to his source, and which concerns the theme of the contest itself. In the Middle High German poem the minnesingers sing the praises of various princes, but in Wagner's case it is "love's supreme essence" of which they sing. Wagner's inspiration here was probably the love lyrics of the historical Tannhäuser, with which he may have been familiar from Friedrich Heinrich von der Hagen's collection *Minnesinger.* The Tannhäuser of the ballad, it should be added, is nowhere described as a love poet, but only as a "doughty knight"; nonetheless, it might well be expected that, as a result of his stay in the Venusberg, he would be more than competent to discourse on matters of love.

Of crucial dramaturgical importance here is the introduction of a female figure who not only presides over the song contest and, like the Landgravine in the medieval poem, crowns the victor, but who is wooed by the contest's two most prominent participants. The character in question, Elisabeth, owes no more than her name to the historical Saint Elisabeth of Hungary (1207–1231), who was the wife of Landgrave Ludwig IV.

The theme of a woman as the object of more than one man's attentions had already been introduced into the story by E. T. A. Hoffmann in his *Battle of the Bards,* where Countess Mathilde receives the singers' praise. She is at first attracted to Wolfframb von Eschimbach, but then finds herself drawn under the spell of Heinrich von Ofterdingen, whose songs she attempts to imitate, before being released from Heinrich's demonic enchantment by a song sung by Wolfframb.

Wagner omitted the idea of having the woman feel any renewed regard for Wolfram: instead, the sinner is redeemed by the sacrifice of her love and her life. Having reworked the song contest in this way (an adaptation which owes more to Hoffmann than to the Middle High German poem), Wagner then picked up the thread of the Tannhäuser Ballad once more, but in so doing altered its meaning entirely. What Tannhäuser regrets here is not his earlier involvement with Venus but his inability to respond in kind to Elisabeth's physical *and* spiritual love. Confronted by the desensualized love of the other singers, Tannhäuser had praised the physical love of Venus, and thus struck at the very existence of Elisabeth as a loving woman, for the latter can give herself only to a man for whom sex is merely a single part of an overall ethical conception of love. Tannhäuser hopes that, by means of "penance and repentance," and by going to Rome and confessing his sins to the pope, God will save him from eternal damnation: he sees in Elisabeth God's divine representative. As in the ballad his hopes are misplaced; the Pope proclaims his eternal perdition. In his despair he seeks to return to the Venusberg. At this point Wagner picks up the motif of friendship which he had found in Hoffmann (and Tieck): Wolfram attempts to hold Tannhäuser back, but what saves the latter is not Wolfram's friendship but Elisabeth's love. Through her vicarious penance and intercession she ensures that the man she loves is saved, in token of which the papal staff puts forth green shoots.

In one respect Wagner goes back to the original meaning of the ballad: for him the miracle of the burgeoning staff is a symbol of God's grace for all mankind, including the most wicked of sinners, rather than a sign of the pope's sinful arrogance, as it is in the ballad. The sinner's act of penance, however, does not lead to his salvation, since—as in the ballads—he falls victim to the deadly sin of *desperatio,* or doubt in the possibility of salvation. The idea that another person's intercession and death can redeem the individual sinner is a profoundly Christian concept, exemplified in Christ's sacrificial death and imitated by countless saints. Wagner's motivation for the sacrifice, however, is anything but medieval in its appeal to Elisabeth's (purified) sexual love. But this, after all, is a recurrent theme of Wagner's works, and a theme prefigured by Gretchen's redemption of Faust in the second part of Goethe's drama. Tannhäuser, for his part, shows a last-minute change of heart, as required by medieval belief, when he calls on Saint Elisabeth to intercede for him, so that her vicarious plea may profit him and lead to his salvation.

Although Wagner's knowledge and understanding of the Middle Ages was still secondhand at the time, *Tannhäuser* remains his most medieval work, inasmuch as the spirit of German Romanticism encouraged him to go beyond the ballads that were familiar to him and rediscover the legend's original meaning. If the role of sexual love in the relationship between Tannhäuser and Elisabeth came to seem problematic, it was not because of anything Wagner found in his medieval sources. In Heine's own reworking of the Tannhäuser Ballad, the hero does not ask the pope to remit his sins, as he does in the oldest version of 1515 (reproduced by Bechstein); instead he asks for help in resisting the powerful constraints of his love for Venus. The same is true of Wagner's Tannhäuser. As a result of his stay in the Venusberg, he had fallen prey to that "yearning which no penance has yet cooled." That the love between him and Elisabeth must remain unfulfilled is the result of *his* past, a past which can be corrected only by her renunciation, and by her mortifying the longing within her own heart.

Wagner's later Schopenhauerian interpretation of *Tannhäuser* in his letter to August Röckel of 23 August 1856 ("If there is a single poetic feature underlying [it], it is the high tragedy of renunciation, the well-motivated, ultimately inevitable and uniquely redeeming denial of the will") does less than full justice to the work. Its underlying theme is not the tragedy of renunciation but redemption through love. That this redemption is not effective in terms of man's earthly existence but only in an afterlife that is deemed to be real is entirely within the spirit of the medieval tale of penance.

Lohengrin: A Fairy Tale with Medieval Color

In his choice of *Lohengrin* as the subject for an opera, Wagner went back for the first time to exclusively medieval sources, for, unlike *Tannhäuser,* this was a theme to which the German Romantics had paid no attention. The contents of the medieval epic were already familiar to Wagner from his Paris days, when he had read Lucas' detailed synopsis of the poem while studying the *Song Contest on the Wartburg.* The medieval *Lohengrin,* an anonymous poem written between 1283 and 1288, is a political work in praise of the German king. It is clearly Rudolf of Habsburg to whom the poet pays homage in his portrayal of the first king of Saxony, Henry the Fowler, whose campaigns and battles take up most of the poem. Lohengrin's own story merely provides the poem with a framework, in which the character plays a specific, and exemplary, heroic role in battle. The epic ends with a chronology of Ottonian rulers. In addition, Wagner must have been familiar with *The Swan-Knight* of Konrad von Würzburg, although probably only in the modern version published by Johann Wilhelm Wolf in his *Legends of the Netherlands* (1843). Konrad's poem has survived only in fragmentary form, and neither its hero nor its heroine is named.

Whereas the medieval *Lohengrin* turns the hero into a stylized knight who rides out in search of adventures and in defense of women, and contains elaborate descriptions of courtly ritual and religious ceremonies and detailed accounts of battles, Konrad von Würzburg's short romance is remarkably concentrated in its form, confining itself to the decisive elements that make up its plot: the arrival of the Swan Knight, the duchess' plaint to the emperor, the duel, the question, and the knight's departure. According to *A Communication to My Friends,* Wagner's first reaction on reading *Lohengrin* was "distrust and a sense of repugnance." Only later did he get to know the "Lohengrin myth in its simpler outline, and, at the same time, in its deeper significance as an actual poem of the people, a myth which has come to light thanks to the expurgations of more recent research into the history of legends" (SSD IV, 288). Among these simpler versions were presumably Konrad's poem and, above all, the account contained in the *German Legends* of the Brothers Grimm, together, finally, with the tale of the Swan Children available to Wagner in the Grimms' anthology, in Wolf's *Legends of the Netherlands,* and in Ludwig Bechstein's collection of fairy tales.

According to the version given by the Brothers Grimm, a young nobleman is out hunting when he comes upon a young girl bathing, with a golden chain in her hand. He takes the chain and brings her back home as his wife. She duly gives birth to seven children, six boys and a girl, all of whom wear golden chains around their necks. Her wicked mother-in-law abducts the children, replacing them with young dogs. She instructs a servant to kill them, but the servant spares their lives and leaves them in the forest at the mercy of the elements. They are discovered while the six brothers, transformed into swans, are bathing in a river, and while their sister guards the chains which will restore them to human shape. Their grandmother has the six chains taken away, but she is unsuccessful in her attempts to gain possession of the girl's chain. The girl feeds and looks after the swans, until she comes to her father's attention because of her golden chain. By dint of his questioning he learns all about her, and the grandmother confesses her guilt. The chains are produced, and the swans change back into men—all but one. Of him it is said merely that he later drew a knight's boat by means of a golden chain.

Unlike *Tannhäuser,* in which two originally independent traditions have been brought together, *Lohengrin* represents Wagner's own version of various medieval recensions of a single theme (including later reworkings in books of legends). Perhaps this is the reason why *Lohengrin* seemed to Wagner an ideal picture of the Middle Ages, precisely because it was purged of all extraneous material.

Wagner's Middle High German source provided him with the elements of his plot and its leading figures: these include Elsa of Brabant, whom Friedrich von Telramund accuses of breaking her promise to marry him; Henry the Fowler, who decrees an ordeal as a means of deciding the issue (and later musters his troops for war with Hungary); the victory of the Swan Knight Lohengrin; the forbidden question which Lohengrin poses to Elsa before their marriage; the duchess' question, asked at the prompting of a countess whose husband had been defeated by Lohengrin; the official announcement of Lohengrin's name, background, and family in the presence of the monarch and his princes and people; and, finally, the Swan Knight's departure after he has bestowed his horn, sword, and ring on those he leaves behind. Certain details derive from Konrad's version, namely the chain by which the swan draws Lohengrin's vessel, the Swan Knight's farewell to the swan, the duchess' accusation before the emperor denouncing her accuser's false claim, Gottfried's name (used here of the dead man, and therefore dynastically fixed), and the opponent's suspicion that the Swan Knight may have magical powers. *The Younger Titurel* by Albrecht (von Scharfenberg?), which Wagner knew from the detailed summary in San-Marte's edition of Wolfram's *Willehalm; Titurel* and lyric verse (Magdeburg 1841); and, for the Lohengrin section, Wolf's *Legends of the Netherlands* (no. 61) and Joseph Görres' 1813 introduction to his edition of *Lohengrin:* all these provided Wagner with the motif whereby Lohengrin's alleged magic powers would fail him were he to lose the smallest piece of his flesh. The idea that the Grail is "a *vessel* of wondrous benediction" also comes from *The Younger Titurel:* in both the Middle High German *Lohengrin* and Wolfram's *Parzival* the Grail is a stone.

Important details were also provided by the story of the Swan Children, which contains the figure of the jealous intriguer or wicked woman responsible for turning another character into a swan, proof of her guilt being the golden chain. Ortrud, an amalgamation of the wicked mother-in-law of this version and the Countess of Cleves in the *Lohengrin* epic, has cast a spell on Elsa's brother, Gottfried: "For by that sign significant, / the chain I fastened round his throat, / I know the true heir of Brabant!" This is the reason why Elsa can be accused of fratricide, and additionally reproached for having a secret paramour (a motif invented by Wagner). Ortrud thus becomes a demonic and evil counterpart to the divinely appointed Swan Knight; Telramund is her innocent agent. Lohengrin's connection with the Christian Grail myth is counterbalanced by Ortrud's appeal to the pagan gods of pre-Christian Friesland. Elsa succumbs to the baleful influence not of an accidental and insignificant peripheral character but of a genuine rival. This emerges with particular clarity in the women's confrontation outside the minster, a motif which Wagner borrowed from the *Nibelungenlied*. The role of Brünhild— who, in the *Nibelungenlied,* has magic powers at her command—is transferred to the similarly powerful Ortrud; like her, she insists on entering the minster before her rival, Elsa, who is married to a man of unknown background and hence of indeterminate social status (as Brünhild believes Siegfried to be), a man, moreover, whom the Frisian princess suspects of magic. By availing himself of one of the most dramatic and vivid scenes in the *Nibelungenlied,* Wagner has found a way of making his antagonist (whom he himself has introduced into the piece) dramaturgically effective. He builds up a successful contrast by means of two unequal pairs: the savior Lohengrin and the passive and impressionable Elsa, contrasted with the baneful figure of Ortrud and her equally dependent consort Telramund. Wagner must have realized that the tension between good and evil, between light and dark (or something comparable), was lacking in the medieval versions. That is why the ending of his opera, with the hero's departure, loses some of its incomprehensible harshness: the principle of goodness prevails, the spell cast on the brother is broken by Lohengrin's prayer (a feature paralleled in the Old French *Chevalier au Cygne*), and proper order is restored to Brabant through the reinstatement of the country's rightful heir. Although Lohengrin's departure is a personal catastrophe for Elsa—and for him—it does not affect the universal order: on a superficial level it is good that triumphs. In the medieval epic the hero's departure is subsumed into imperial history and (by extension) into the history of the world's salvation, whereas Konrad's *Swan-Knight* ends on a note of unease.

For a time Wagner was persuaded by the criticism of one of his friends to think of giving the work a less tragic ending and of having Elsa go off with Lohengrin. But he soon realized that such an ending ran counter to the actual substance of the tale: "The symbolic meaning of the tale I can best sum up as follows: contact between a metaphysical phenomenon and human nature, and the impossibility that such contact will last" (letter to Hermann Franck of 30 May 1846). Scholars who have conducted research into fairy tales speak of the motif of the disturbed Mahrte marriage (a reference to the girl whose spirit leaves her body at night and plagues sleeping men), and this indeed forms the basic tale, which Wagner has left unaltered. The medieval poems had turned the fairy-tale motif into a genealogical legend; this is true, certainly, of both the *Chevalier au Cygne* and Konrad's *Swan-Knight*. And it is this that gives Wagner his final note of conciliation, with Gottfried's being named leader of Brabant. But the composer was obliged (and only too pleased) to dispense with the genealogical implications of the story. Since Elsa asks the forbidden question on her wedding night (as a result of Wagner's compression of the time scale of the work), Lohengrin has no children to found a royal house, as he does in the Middle High German epic and in Konrad's version of the story. Dynastic considerations were in any case "medieval" (conditioned as they were by the situation), and therefore just as unusable as the original theme of the *Song Contest on the Wartburg,* where dynastic princes had been praised in song.

Wagner shows how Lohengrin's tragedy arises from his being bound by the Grail's decree that no questions be asked of him. A comparable injunction is by no means uncommon in other variants of this same motif, which tells of the disturbed relationship between a supernatural being and a human (one thinks, for example, of the Undine tradition). In other words, *Lohengrin* is a fairy-tale opera in medieval guise, a guise which is evident above all, as in the Middle High German epic, in the ceremonial action and therefore, first and foremost, in the stage directions, where the impression is of a kind of dramatized historical painting. Wagner himself regarded the theme of the "old German kinship" in *Lohengrin* as local color, as he told Ferdinand Heine in a letter of 31 October 1853. It is clear, however, from this same letter that Wagner's portrayal of kingship has an element of social criticism to it. In *A Communication to My Friends* he interpreted the work as an expression of the problematic nature of the artist's life, and it can indeed be understood as such. But it equally clearly contains other themes, such as the clash between the powers of light and darkness and the tension between the sexes; and it is open to additional interpretations besides.

Wagner was right to regard "the Christian Romantic category" as an "accidental and external characteristic" of the hero rather than as the "essence of his nature" (SSD IV, 298). The Lohengrin myth is said to be "an age-old poem about human nature" (SSD IV, 289; the motif of the disturbed Mahrte marriage can be found in almost every culture). Wagner himself draws attention to Zeus and Semele as a classical variant on the theme. It is certainly not a Christian myth, for in Christianity the bond or covenant between God and man does not break: even after his ascension Christ remains present in the Eucharist for all who believe in him—not just for the chosen fellowship of the Grail, as in Wagner. The Christian Middle Ages were predisposed to interpret the Lohengrin myth as a genealogical rather than a theological or anthropological one. Wagner freed it from this genealogical overlay, but in so doing removed what was specifically medieval about it, so that only the local color remained. The conflict between the powers of light and darkness which Wagner introduced into his material through his invention of the figure of Ortrud was not originally part of the legend. And it is this conflict that gives the ending of the opera its ambivalence: although good triumphs over evil, the union between an earthly figure and one from the other world proves

impossible. The contrast between light and darkness is not specifically medieval, although the early Middle Ages provided the appropriate historical
situation, for the old pagan beliefs had not yet been wholly supplanted by
Christianity. The Christian element is the manifestation of the power of light
in a form appropriate to the Middle Ages, and this is another reason why the
Middle Ages are largely present in the work as local color.

Der Ring des Nibelungen: From Legend to World Myth

In *Lohengrin*, as in *Tannhäuser*, Wagner had placed an individual figure at the
center of his work: the Swan Knight fails not because of outward circumstances but because of his own determinedness. Wagner's concern in the case
of the *Ring,* by contrast, was not the hero alone but the circumstances as well
and the future he dreamed of in the politically bleak present he sought to
"create out of images of the past in order to make them recognizable to the
senses" (SSD IV, 311). Wagner's change of direction from Lohengrin to
Siegfried is that from an apolitical artist to a political human being. What he
now looked for in myth was "the social circumstances in equally simple,
specific and graphic outline" as he had "previously recognized it to contain
the human form itself" (SSD IV, 312).

The contemporary, historical element of the *Nibelungenlied* was bound to
be as unacceptable to him as it had been in *Lohengrin,* which is why he adopted
a similar method in both cases, drawing on a number of different versions of
the same subject matter, including the Old Norse Eddic poems, the account
of the Nordic myths contained in the *Prose Edda* of Snorri Sturluson, and the
prose compilation of the *Volsunga Saga,* all in addition to the Middle High
German *Nibelungenlied.* He considered the Norse versions to be more archaic
and closer to the original than the *Nibelungenlied,* a belief which is in fact only
partially true. But he needed them first and foremost in order to be able to
find the mythically simplified social conditions which he had sought in vain
in the *Nibelungenlied* as he had in the history of Frederick Barbarossa. What
he was looking for was not the advanced feudal society of the late twelfth
century, but those very conditions which, in combination with the Germanic
gods and heroes, seemed to him to have archetypal significance and hence
provided a key to interpret the present.

Wagner's first adaptation of the various medieval sources was the prose
scenario *The Nibelung Legend (Myth),* in the course of which it dawned on
Wagner that the myths could be fashioned into a musical drama. His library
in Dresden contained two editions of the *Nibelungenlied* in the original Middle
High German, and two modern translations, and it was this text which
provided the starting point for Wagner's studies. This emerges with particular
clarity from his earliest poetic reworking of the Siegfried myth in *Siegfrieds
Tod,* written between 12 and 28 November 1848. This poem, the heart of the
later *Götterdämmerung,* takes as its framework the events of the first part of
the *Nibelungenlied* but also incorporates elements from other accounts of the

myth. The Middle High German *Nibelungenlied,* which may have assumed written form in Passau sometime around the year 1200, consists of two originally unconnected halves, recounting the life of Siegfried and the downfall of the Burgundians. In all probability the two parts were not linked together until the twelfth century, and it may indeed have been the *Nibelungenlied* which first made that connection. The link between the two parts is provided by the figure of Kriemhild: in the first part her husband, Siegfried, is murdered, and in the second part she avenges his death by slaying her brothers. (In the older version it was a quarrel over the treasure which led to the downfall of the Burgundians.) Wagner used only the first part (*âventiuren* 1–19) for the action of his drama, borrowing only individual motifs from the second part.

Ever since its rediscovery by Johann Jakob Bodmer in the middle of the eighteenth century, the *Nibelungenlied* has been seen as the German national epic, a German *Iliad* and popular epic poem in contrast to the allegedly superficial courtly romance that was based on French models. Even before Wagner's day the poem had tempted writers to adapt it as a drama. The most significant of these generally ineffective adaptations is *The Hero of the North* by Friedrich de la Motte-Fouqué, who, like Wagner, drew upon the Old Norse tradition, and who may have influenced the composer in certain details.

The large-scale epic form of the *Nibelungenlied* is not found in Old Icelandic, where the legend of the Nibelungs (or Niflungs) gained poetic expression in the shorter individual songs of the so-called *Poetic Edda.* These poems take as their theme specific episodes in the legend and rely for their effect on a preexisting knowledge of the material as a whole. For Wagner, and for today's reader, this knowledge could be obtained only from the explanatory details which Snorri Sturluson gives in his *Prose Edda,* and in the narrative prose rendition of the *Volsunga Saga,* an account set down in the second half of the thirteenth century as an attempt to incorporate elements of the various related legends into a vast narrative complex.

The Eddic poems, written down around 1270, go back to an older oral tradition and must have undergone numerous transformations and alterations in the course of time. In the context of Wagner's *Ring,* the most important poems are the *Brot af Sigurdharkvidhu* (Fragment of a lay of Sigurd) and the *Sigrdrífumál* (also known as *The Valkyrie's Awakening*), the first of which dates from the eighth to eleventh centuries, and the later *Sigurdharkvidha in scamma* (Short lay of Sigurd), *Helreidh Brynhildar* (Brynhild's ride to hell), *Reginsmál* (Sayings of Regin), and *Fáfnismál* (Sayings of Fafnir), together with the *Grípisspá* (Gripir's prophecy), a compilation of all the Sigurd lays. The poetic form of the Eddic lays is that of *fornyrdhislag,* in which pairs of lines are linked together by alliteration or *Stabreim,* generally in groups of eight. Each half-line contains two main stresses and a variable number of unstressed syllables. A second verse form is also found, namely the *ljódhaháttr,* in which two half-lines are followed by an independent full line with (usually) three lifts or main stresses. In his *Eddic Songs of the Nibelungs,* Ludwig Ettmüller attempted to reproduce the verse form of the original Eddic strophe when translating these poems into German, and it was from Ettmüller that Wagner borrowed the meter and *Stabreim* that characterize his poem for the *Ring*. Presumably the discussions which Wagner held with "Eddamüller" following their meeting in Zurich in 1849 left their mark on the linguistic form of the definitive texts when these came to be set down in writing in 1851–52. This is particularly clear when one compares *Siegfrieds Tod* and *Götterdämmerung,* which, textually, are almost identical.

There was also the *Volsunga Saga*. At some date during the second half of the thirteenth century, a storyteller at the royal court in Norway rewrote the Eddic lays about Sigurd in the form of a saga or prose romance, linking together previously independent sections of the narrative and incorporating some of the myths relating to the Norse gods in order to forge a link between Odin (Wotan) and the race of the Volsungs. The saga represents a late synthesis of legend and myth, and makes connections which did not exist in the oldest layer of myth.

An important influence on Wagner's handling of the myths and on the way he restructured, expanded, and linked the material together was Karl Simrock's attempt in his *Lay of the Amelungs* (1843–1849) to depict "the whole of German heroic legend in a single large-scale poem, at least to the extent that this has not survived in the Nibelungs and in Gudrun." The "old account," he argued, had been "lost, or else preserved only in late and in part very crude reworkings." His aim was to breathe new life into the old legend by going back to a multiplicity of sources. Wagner was an enthusiastic admirer of Simrock's edition. (In 1849–50 he sketched a drama entitled *Wieland der Schmied,* which, in its essential outline, derives from Simrock.) On the basis of his reading of Simrock he adopted and extended the practice of linking together the myths and legends, taking one stage further the integration of the divine and heroic cycles of myths which the *Volsunga Saga* had already initiated and which Simrock himself had developed. His technique of "mythic reportage" on the part of his dramatic characters is an additional feature which Wagner owed to the *Lay of the Amelungs.*

Wagner, it must be said, was a much more fundamentally consistent and comprehensive creator of myths than Simrock, since the Bonn professor, for all his poetic ambitions, was not concerned with creating a world myth. Of decisive importance for Wagner was Jacob Grimm's *German Mythology,* in which the mythic material was reproduced not in a narrative context but in fragmentary and thematic form. Wagner realized that the myth had to provide him with the building blocks rather than the ground plan before he himself could create his own myth. His first act of mythic conflation was to provide his protagonist Siegfried with a mythically distinguished ancestry, something that the hero lacks in both the Old Norse tradition and in the *Nibelungenlied.* Wagner makes him a grandson of Wotan and the offspring of an incestuous union. The motif of incestuous ancestry comes from the *Volsunga Saga,* where Sinfjötli is the son of the twins Signy and Sigmund. Wagner not only conflates the figure of Sinfjötli with that of Siegfried, but he makes Wotan the twins' natural father. The composer's change is intended above all to elevate the hero, Siegfried, but it serves first and foremost to create a "free human being" who can change the existing world order, an order which is based on injustice, and which Wotan himself is incapable of altering since he is bound by treaties, unlike Siegfried, who was conceived outside the bonds of wedlock.

In dealing with the details of Siegfried's life, Wagner stayed mainly with the *Nibelungenlied* and the compilation of the various tales concerning Sigurd contained in the *Volsunga Saga.* Siegfried is the son of Siegmund and Sieglinde (their names are taken from the *Nibelungenlied* and their fates from the *Volsunga Saga* through the identification of Sinfjötli and Sigurd, while Sieglinde's death may be influenced by the fate of Tristan's mother in Gottfried von Strassburg's *Tristan*). He grows up with a wise smith who forges a sword for him and incites him to slay the dragon Fafner. Following the dragon's death, Siegfried also kills the villainous dwarf Mime; in contrast to the traditional version, Wagner gives a detailed account of the way in which Mime has long had designs on Siegfried's life, and he further excuses the murder by having the dwarf forfeit his life in the Riddle scene with Wotan. This is a motif which Wagner took over from the *Vafdhrúdhnismál* (Sayings of Vafdhrudhnir), an Eddic poem from the mythological cycle of songs surrounding the figure of Odin. The identification of the Sigrdrifa of the *Sigrdrífumál* and the Brynhild of the *Brot af Sigurdharkvidhu,* which had already been begun in the thirteenth century, is completed by Wagner through the device of the wall of flame (originally one of the conditions imposed on Brynhild's would-be suitors), the woman's awakening (including verbal reminiscences of the poem), and the oaths and information concerning runic charms. Wagner's Siegfried owes his invulnerability and unprotected back to the Valkyrie. The composer evidently found it too banal that the hero's vulnerable spot should be the result of chance, as it is in the *Nibelungenlied,* where a leaf falls between his shoulder blades as he is bathing in the dragon's blood. As a result he invented Brünnhilde's "blessing," the limitations of which she herself betrays to Hagen, fully conscious of what she is doing, unlike Kriemhild in the *Nibelungenlied,* who is tricked by Hagen into revealing Siegfried's vulnerable spot. Siegfried's arrival at Gunther's court is taken from the *Nibelungenlied,* but Hagen's status as Alberich's son and Gunther's half-brother is an invention of Wagner's intended to link Siegfried's murderer with Wotan's adversary. Siegfried's wooing of Gutrune also comes from the *Nibelungenlied* (her name derives from the Norse tradition), as does her brother's consent to the match on condition that Siegfried help him woo Brünnhilde. The potion which makes Siegfried lose his memory is taken from the *Volsunga Saga* (or *Grípisspá*); it reveals Siegfried's erotic susceptibility, a quality which also emerges in his conversation with the Rhine Maidens. As a result, his betrayal of his love for Brünnhilde (which leads ultimately to his downfall) shows him to be both guilty and innocent: his desire for action, which in the prose draft is said to be a "primeval law" which he must obey and which draws him away from

Brünnhilde, is part of his heroic nature, for, as conceived by Wagner, the "free" human being, guided as he is by fate, cannot be bound even in love. The potion both absolves him and, at the same time, makes his *lack* of freedom all the more obvious.

The wooing of Brünnhilde follows the pattern set by the later Norse sources, with Siegfried and Gunther changing shapes, and Siegfried riding through the rampart of flame and placing his sword between himself and Brünnhilde as a sign of his loyalty to Gunther. His forceful appropriation of the ring is a motif which Wagner found in the *Volsunga Saga* and *Nibelungenlied,* and he uses it in an entirely similar manner: the ring that once bestowed power has now become a token of love, and the fact that Siegfried, rather than Gunther, possesses it signifies deception and, at the same time, a higher truth. In the *Nibelungenlied* the ring has no past, whereas in the *Volsunga Saga,* at the point where the ring is stolen, the prose redactor recalls how it was once owned by the dwarf Andvari; but this plays no part in the quarrel between Brynhild and Gudrun. Wagner gives Brünnhild's ring from the *Nibelungenlied* the past history of Andvari's ring from the *Volsunga Saga,* a history which invests it with its tragic potential: for Brünnhilde it signifies only Siegfried's love, but for Siegfried himself, once he has wrested it back from Brünnhilde, it is no longer a symbol of loyalty but merely booty gained in his fight with the dragon. (In the prose draft he still knows that it confers power on its wearer.) As a symbol of love's betrayal it later causes his death, for this, after all, is what power entails, according to Alberich's curse. Brünnhilde, too, will wear it in death, but she decrees that the Rhine Maidens shall repossess it: her voluntary death cleanses the gold so that it may return to what the prose draft describes as the "harmless" state of nature.

Siegfried clears himself of Brünnhilde's accusation that he has broken faith with her—in the prose draft she accuses him "intentionally, being bent only on destroying him"—and he does so by means of the very oath which Gunther dispenses with in the *Nibelungenlied.* Since the accusation and the vow relate to two different situations (as Brünnhilde must know, even if she cannot understand how), the oath is both true and false.

As Alberich's ambivalent son, Hagen becomes Siegfried's murderer in Wagner. In the *Nibelungenlied* he is motivated not only by the pursuit of power but also by feudal loyalty toward his queen and by his overlord's loss of honor, which affects him, too, as Gunther's vassal. In the Old Norse tradition the murderer's name is Guthorm, but, on the strength of the *Nibelungenlied*'s version of events, the name of Hagen had entered the general consciousness as that of Siegfried's murderer, and so this was the name Wagner used. He was unable to rid himself of the fascination which this character exercised over him and which the *Nibelungenlied* poet develops, especially in the second half of his poem, where Hagen is characterized by his bold defiance of fate. This is clear from Wagner's transference of the Watch scene from Etzel's court (where Hagen watches over the sleeping Burgundians) to Gunther's court in the definitive version of *Götterdämmerung*. (There is no corresponding scene in *Siegfrieds Tod*.)

From the *Nibelungenlied* comes the idea of having Siegfried murdered in the course of a hunt, as do the scene in which the murdered man's corpse is left outside his wife's room and Hagen's exposure as the murderer when he approaches Siegfried's bier. Wagner's characterization of Siegfried also includes features of the Norse god Baldr, whose supposed invulnerability is pierced by Loki, using the only weapon that can harm him. Baldr's body is cremated on a funeral pyre together with that of his wife, while Odin places his ring beside the two bodies. According to Snorri's account in the *Prose Edda*, Baldr's death was the most terrible loss the gods could have suffered.

Even in the 1848 prose draft the myth of the gods already motivates the story of Siegfried: by stealing Alberich's ring, the gods have made themselves guilty. The man who will absolve them of their guilt, or redeem them, is the free human being, who, in the prose draft, is not yet mentioned by name. It is left to the definitive version to tackle this problem head on: as Wotan's offspring, Siegmund cannot be free; only someone fathered and conceived against the will of the gods can fulfill that function, and that hero is Siegfried. His role, it must be said, changes: in the prose draft his atonement for the gods' guilt consolidates Wotan's supremacy following his death: "One alone shall rule, / Almighty father, thou glorious god!" The idea that power involves renouncing love, and that the rule of the gods is thereby tainted by guilt but that they may nonetheless be redeemed, is one which Wagner would have sought in vain in the Old Norse myths. Instead he arranged mythic elements to form a new myth that told of the beginning and end of the world, and of the "Twilight of the Gods." (The title rests on a misunderstanding that goes back to Snorri Sturluson, who had written of *ragnarökkr*, or dusk of the gods, in preference to *ragnarök*, fate of the gods.)

Odin, or Wotan (the Old High German form *Wuotan* ought to be *Wuten* in modern German), plays a role in the *Reginsmál* (and hence in the *Volsunga Saga*), which Wagner elaborates in *Das Rheingold*, and which had already been hinted at in *The Nibelung Legend (Myth)*: he is forced to hand over, in the form of a ransom, the gold which had previously been stolen from the dwarf Andvari (the name Alberich comes from the *Nibelungenlied*), and to relinquish, moreover, a magic ring in order to meet the demands of the ransom in full. The curse which the dwarf lays on the ring triggers all that takes place later in the legend, but it required Wagner to turn this into a universal symbol of the entanglements inherent in power: its name was then used as the title of the completed poem. Wagner combined the theft of the ring and the curse with the fairy-tale motif of the giant builder which he found in the *Gylfaginning* (The beguiling of Gylfi), the first part of Snorri's *Edda*: Asgard, the citadel of the gods (which includes the hall of Walhall), is built by a giant who is promised Freyja as his wife. Owing to a trick played by Loki, however, the giant fails to meet the agreed deadline and is struck down by the hammer of Thor (Donner). Wagner transfers to this tale the motif whereby the sons of Hreidmar murder their father and steal the ransom that is rightfully his. One of the sons is called Fafnir (it is he who transforms himself into a dragon), while the name and fate of his brother, Reigin, are transferred to Alberich's brother Mime, who is still called Reigin in the prose draft. The name of Wagner's second giant, Fasolt, comes from one of the Middle High German heroic poems: he is the brother of the giant Ecke in the *Lay of Ecke*.

Die Walküre follows the *Volsunga Saga* closely, although it transfers to the figure of Siegmund the story of Sinfjötli's adolescence. And, once again, Simrock's *Lay of the Amelungs* was a determining influence, for it was here that Wagner found a key reference to "the blood of the Wälsungs." The Annunciation of Death *(Todverkündigung)* is based on a tenth-century Norwegian skaldic poem. The Valkyries come from Norse mythology: Wagner could have found details concerning them in Jacob Grimm's *German Mythology,* which contains frequent references to the Eddic poems. Most sources list nine Valkyries, and Wagner, too, has nine, including Brünnhilde. The quarrel between Wotan and Fricka may well derive from a remark of Grimm's to the effect that Frigg had once acted to the detriment of a hero favored by Odin. Entirely of Wagner's own creation is the preeminent role which Wotan plays in this part of the tetralogy, together with his relationship with Brünnhilde: these characteristics of the chief god have no precedent in Norse mythology. Wagner has invested the action with archetypally human situations, with Brünnhilde as Wotan's alter ego and, ultimately, as his "wish-maid," someone who will accomplish his wish for the end.

Wagner's synthetic world myth, as set forth in *Das Rheingold,* brings together a number of originally heterogeneous motifs. In the case of the "black elves," he was able to refer to Snorri's *svartalfar,* whom the Icelandic writer had equated with the dwarfs; their home in Niflheim also comes from Snorri, for whom, however, the "world of darkness" was the abode of departed spirits. The giants can be found in both Norse mythology and in German medieval literature: they are strong, violent, and stupid, but originally they present a threat to the gods (at least in the Old Norse sources). For the old Germanic gods Wagner went back to the Eddic songs that retell the divine myths, as well as to Snorri and to Grimm's *German Mythology.* Here Wotan is presented as the chief of the gods and as warlord, as "All-Father" *(alfödhr)* and "Father of Victory" *(Sigfödhr),* his attributes being a spear, a ring (Draupnir, the circlet of authority), and two ravens; his role as Wanderer is also mentioned here (see my discussion earlier of the Riddle scene). Fricka (Frigg in Old Norse) is Odin's wife and the guardian of wedlock. With his hammer Donner (Thor) is known, among other things, for his encounters with giants. Freia (Freyja) is the goddess of love and fertility; her golden apples, with their power to rejuvenate, belong to the goddess Idun, who, according to Snorri, was abducted by the giant Thrazi and brought back by Loki. Froh (Freyr), who plays an insignificant part in *Das Rheingold,* was one of the most important gods. Since Snorri reports that rain and sunshine are dependent on him,

Wagner has him summon up the rainbow which acts as a bridge to Valhalla. Loge, the cunning god of fire, did not become fully developed as a character until the final version of the text, where he appears as an amalgamation of Loki, the gods' assistant and opponent (as in the Old Norse *Reginsmál*), and Logi, the enemy of the gods, a giant who is the personification of fire. Erda goes back to the Old Norse goddess, or giantess, Jörd (Earth): she was regarded as Odin's lover, but it is Wagner's invention that Wotan fathered Brünnhilde by her. Her talents as a seer derive from the Old Norse *völva* (Wagner's Wala), who is the subject of the *Völuspá* (The seeress's vision). The role of the Valkyries as Wotan's "wish-maids" (Old Norse *óskmeyjar*) comes from Nordic mythology, although their names are Wagner's invention. The Rhine Maidens come from the *Nibelungenlied*: in the course of the Burgundians' journey to Hungary at the invitation of King Etzel, Hagen meets two water sprites who prophesy disaster. Their opening role as custodians of the Rhine Gold is, again, Wagner's own invention, introduced into the poem at a fairly late stage when he was working out the *Ring*'s past history. Whether Alberich's theft of the Rhine Gold—the "original sin" of Wagner's world myth—goes back to the *Völuspá* is highly questionable. Rather it appears to be Wagner's own interpretation of world events.

Das Rheingold is a particularly clear example of Wagner's technique of mythic synthesis: he combines a number of disparate myths, some of which derive from existing traditions, others of which are his own invention, and from them he develops his own myth telling how the gods acquired power through ownership and repression and how they thus became ensnared by guilt. In the prose draft the new myth is still relatively unambiguous, whereas in the tetralogy proper it is overlaid with problems concerning the freedom of the individual, the redemption of the gods through the supersession of the old order, and the latter's replacement by the establishment of a new rule. As we know, Wagner had difficulties staging the end of the gods' domination, and he wrestled with the ending of *Götterdämmerung*: at least three different endings are traditionally distinguished, associated with the names and influence of Mikhail Bakunin, Ludwig Feuerbach, and Arthur Schopenhauer.

The final version is not unambiguous: does it represent a return to nature, with the possibility of a cyclical development, or do the men and women who look on "in deepest emotion" embody the new liberated society? Or is the ending entirely open, suggesting hope beyond death and the expectation of a (generative) wonder such as is perhaps implied by the musical theme which brings the work to its conclusion, a theme first heard at Sieglinde's words "O radiant wonder" in act 3, scene 1 of *Die Walküre,* when Brünnhilde tells her that she bears Siegfried within her womb? Germanic mythology may have been familiar with the idea of a cyclical development in world history; certainly the fire which destroys the world in the *Völuspá* (strophes 59–66) is followed by the emergence of a new world. But Wagner consciously refrained from adopting this aspect of the Nordic myth of the gods. It is this very ambiguity which is the hallmark of Wagner's new myth: if his original scenario still had the character of a social parable, Wagner's work on the material and his increasing inclusion of additional heterogeneous mythic elements led to the development of a narrative tale that can no longer be interpreted unambiguously. Through a synthesis of heterogeneous myths, he created a new myth for mankind and the world.

Tristan und Isolde: From Immanent Eros to Transcendent Love

In Gottfried von Strassburg's *Tristan* Wagner found a text which may be numbered among the finest poetic achievements of the Middle Ages: the lucidity and musicality of the language, the art of representation, and the (problematic) subject matter place the poem in a class of its own in medieval German literature. Scholarly research has identified various stages in the development of the tale, and traced it back to Celtic origins which contained the work's basic conflict between a hero's erotic attachment to the wife of his king and the loyalty which the hero owes to his king.

In the course of time the basic story was elaborated: the love between the two protagonists was explained and justified by their drinking a magic potion together, and a preliminary history was added that told of the hero's fight with a dragon and his wooing expedition. Further adventures were incorporated, some of them burlesque in tone, and the hero's fidelity was put to the test by a second Isolde—Isolde of the White Hands. The first French Tristan romance, known as the *estoire,* appears to date from the mid-twelfth century, but we know it only from the German reworking of Eilhart von Oberge (ca. 1190). The Old French version of the Anglo-Norman poet Thomas d'Angleterre has survived in only fragmentary form and, like Eilhart's version, dates from the years just before the end of the twelfth century. It was followed around 1215 by the *Tristan* of Gottfried von Strassburg. Gottfried's romance breaks off before Tristan's marriage to the second Isolde, but two later poets, Ulrich von Türheim and Heinrich von Freiberg, completed the poem, and it was their versions that Wagner also knew through von der Hagen's edition of Gottfried.

Within the framework of the courtly tradition that existed around 1200, Gottfried's *Tristan* occupies a somewhat extreme position. The kind of fated and enchanted love that he depicts, in contrast to courtly love, with its concept of service or servitude, is found, at least as a theoretical possibility, in discussions about love in the lyric and epic traditions, but nowhere else is it developed at such epic length or in such absolute terms. *Tristan* explores the tensions that exist between unquestioning, existential love and the claims of society, but finds no harmonious solution to the problem; rather it leads the lovers to physical destruction as the only possible means of making their love public. But society's victory is merely apparent, for love remains the greatest good. In Gottfried's romance love is no longer excused by the effects of the potion; rather, it is treated as a potent instrument of fate, embodying a power which is consciously accepted by both the lovers as the supreme and deciding force in their lives (and deaths). The question as to whether Tristan and Isolde were unconsciously in love *before* they drank the potion, or whether it is the potion that brings about their love, is one on which scholars disagree; but it is clear that the lovers belong to each other by virtue of their exemplary courtly attributes and education. Within the context of courtly society, existential love can be depicted only as adulterous passion, marriage being a purely social institution entered into for political reasons; at best it could be said that marriage did not necessarily exclude love. In terms of the theory of courtly love, however, marriage and passionate love were irreconcilable opposites. In order to portray love's absolutist claims, Gottfried used a means of expression offered him by the one thing that, in the medieval world, could lay claim to absolute status—namely religion. The poem's extensive religious overlay culminates in the temple of the Cave of Lovers, with its Bed of Love in place of the usual altar and with the lovers sustained not by food but by a love construed in terms of the sacrament. By treating love as something absolute, Gottfried justifies his own ethical conception of it: the lovers' actions bespeak a type of honor which is at odds with society's view of honor, a view which involves social standing and which both the lovers nonetheless feel committed to uphold. It is an irreconcilable conflict. The idea of the *Liebestod* or love-death is already hinted at by Gottfried in Tristan's reference to "êweclîchez sterben," or "eternal death," in contrast to eternal life and as a consequence of the love potion. It almost certainly does not have a transcendental dimension, however, but merely points to the biblical equation of existential love and the experience of death: "fortis ut mors dilectio" (may death be as strong as love).

Wagner's personal situation in the 1850s—his affair with Mathilde Wesendonck and the chance occurrence that his friend Karl Ritter was planning a drama on the subject of *Tristan* that would have centered on the work's superficial adventures and intrigues—ensured that he would be attracted by Gottfried's work, especially by its "profound tragedy." In consequence he determined "to cut away all the inessentials from this central theme" (ML 511) and sketched out a three-act drama, concentrating on three basic episodes and introducing all preliminary details in a merely allusive or referential way.

The first act deals with the initial stirrings of love between Tristan and Isolde, and their awareness of their feelings for each other. The action takes place on board the ship that is bringing Isolde from Ireland to Cornwall. Wagner makes it clear that there is already a predestined attachment between the lovers. Isolde reminds Brangäne of Tristan's first voyage to Ireland, when she cured him of a poisoned wound, and how, in spite of his calling himself Tantris (as in the medieval romance), she had recognized him as the murderer of her betrothed, Morold. Wagner makes Morold her fiancé rather than her uncle, since the clan relationship and medieval motif of vengeance seemed less compelling to him than the emotional tie that binds Isolde to her betrothed. But Tristan's glance prevents her from killing him as she stands over him, her sword unsheathed. In Gottfried it is both her outward status and her internal state of mind that make her incapable of avenging herself on Tristan, for not only would killing him dishonor her in the eyes of society, but also she herself is incapable of such cruelty and hardness. In addition, Isolde's mother had promised to protect Tantris in return for his agreement to contest the claims of a deceitful steward. In Wagner's interpretation, however, it is not Isolde's general situation that prevents her from striking Tristan but something much more specific: her incipient (or already existent) love for Tristan.

In Wagner, unlike in Gottfried, this scene of discovery and Isolde's failure to exact vengeance have already taken place when Tristan sets out for the second time to woo Isolde on King Marke's behalf, an expedition which he undertakes because he is still committed to the values of courtly society and still unconscious of his love for Isolde: "Unknown and unexpressed, / A vision scarcely guessed; / A vision whose enchantment / I scarcely dared to gaze on," he says in act 2. He obeys social constraints in taking on the apparently hopeless task of wooing Isolde on behalf of Marke. Isolde's notion that Tristan has praised her as a bride for his uncle, an idea with which she repeatedly torments herself, arises from her misinterpretation of the glance that gave rise to their love, seeing in it the gaze of a procurer sizing her up.

Gottfried's Isolde, like Wagner's, is not sufficiently impressed by the official reconciliation between Ireland and Cornwall (a reconciliation to be sealed by Marke's marriage) to accept Tristan's service as a vassal on board ship. But in Wagner's version, as his Tristan immediately realizes, this is merely a pretext: Isolde intends them to die together, since life together seems to her impossible. In the medieval romance Isolde the Wise, the Queen Mother, has entrusted a love potion to Brangäne which is to be given to the newlywed couple so that not merely political calculation but also love should bind them together. This too is the primary purpose of Wagner's love potion. When Isolde considers her fate in Cornwall ("Unbeloved / Beside that man / Every day to see him! / Ah how could I bear such anguish?"), it is Tristan whom she is thinking of. Brangäne fails to understand her and, believing she is referring to Marke, recalls her "mother's magic arts," and specifically the love potion. But the mother has given her daughter more than this to take with her on her journey to Cornwall: she also has a wondrous balsam, an antidote, and a death potion. It is the death potion that she intends to drink with Tristan. But Brangäne, acting out of "foolish loyalty," intentionally exchanges it for the love potion. In Gottfried the substitution is the result of a banal mix-up, when a lady-in-waiting mistakes the potion for wine. In Wagner, by contrast, the lovers' plan to leave this world behind them is wholly intentional, a willing abandonment of their earthly existence. In consequence, Brangäne's exchange of the one potion for the other is only logical, for it is this that will betoken love between Tristan and Isolde.

In Gottfried the lovers consummate their union on board the ship, whereas

Wagner separates their consummation from the drinking of the potion and gives it a dramatic space of its own in the second act. In addition to deciding, on dramaturgical grounds, to make the emergence of love, its consummation, and its transcendency the main emphases of his action, Wagner no doubt had an additional reason for delaying the moment of consummation until after the bride has been handed over to her intended husband. In the medieval romance the loss of Isolde's virginity leads to Brangäne's replacing her mistress on the wedding night and to a subsequent attempt on Brangäne's life. But the hint of farce that is evident in the first of these episodes was an example of what Wagner considered the "inessentials" of the story. The idea that, following her wedding, Isolde sleeps with two men does not seem to have been a serious problem for any of the medieval poets, all of whom drew a distinction between marital duty and love. Wagner's version differs from theirs inasmuch as his King Marke has not consummated his marriage: "I have never / Dared to lie beside her, / My desire / Only could revere her," he says of Isolde in his great lament. In Gottfried, Marke is himself to blame for the deception that is practiced on him since he desires Isolde only with instinctive lust, quite apart from the fact that—as Gottfried comments when Brangäne stands in for Isolde on the wedding night—one woman is no different from another as far as he is concerned. Wagner's resigned and sensitive king, who seeks spiritual but not physical sustenance in his love for Isolde, is the exact opposite of Gottfried's King Marke.

The second act is a compilation of all the lovers' secret meetings, including the Cave of Lovers episode and their discovery in the orchard. According to Peter Wapnewski's interpretation, Wagner's model here was the medieval dawn song, or *aubade,* a lyric poem that describes a lovers' farewell after a night spent together, as the encroaching dawn instills in them the fear of discovery. At the moment of parting they become conscious once more of the intensity of their love, before the watchman's warning call finally forces them apart. It is to Gottfried that Wagner owes the idea of transferring the watchman's role to Brangäne; but whereas the servant remains silent in the medieval romance, Wagner's Brangäne has two strophes to sing. The corresponding figure in the medieval dawn song is frequently given strophes to sing. The lyrical intensification of the ideal moment of love which we find in the dawn song is the inspiration behind Wagner's idea of compressing the lovers' various encounters into a single ideal assignation. As a result this one meeting can fulfill the same function in the drama as that performed in the epic by the allegory of the Cave of Lovers, namely transcendence and transfiguration.

Wagner's version differs from the medieval *aubade* in that his lovers are taken unawares by "desolate day," with the discovery compromising the ideal moment. In Gottfried, Marke comes upon the lovers in each other's arms but then goes off to find witnesses, an unnecessary step in terms of medieval law but one which gives the lovers an opportunity to bid each other a long farewell. In the course of her extended monologue, Isolde caps Tristan's traditional metaphor of lovers exchanging hearts by claiming that they have exchanged identities. She calls Tristan "ir lîp," in other words her life, but also herself as a person. By the same token she refers to herself as "iuwer lîp," his body and person, so that she can then summarize this in the words "Tristan and Isolde, you and I, we are both one forever more, undivided" (Tristan und Isôt, ir und ich, / wir zwei sîn iemer beide / ein dinc âne underscheide). Wagner takes up this idea: "You Isolde, / Tristan I, / no more Isolde!"—"You Tristan, / Isolde I, / no more Tristan!"

As Wapnewski has made clear, the action would have had to end with act 2 if Wagner had wished to distill from the romance only its mythic kernel, the old Celtic tale, in which the discovery of the lovers leads straightaway to their deaths. But Wagner refused to make things easy for his lovers by having their deaths follow immediately upon the ecstasies of their love; and in making this decision he has the support of the medieval tradition, in which Tristan flees Cornwall following his discovery and marries Isolde of the White Hands. Struck down in battle by a poisoned spear, he sends for the Irish Isolde. A white sail will herald her impending arrival; but Isolde of the White Hands falsely reports that the sail is black, whereupon Tristan dies in despair. Isolde the Fair lands, lies down beside her lover's body, and dies in turn. The wound from which Wagner's Tristan suffers and dies is a self-inflicted one, dealt by Melot's sword, unlike in the medieval versions, where the wound is the result of a chance encounter. The composer's aim in presenting the torments of desire and the love-death on stage was to show the impossibility of living a life of love which is greater than human strength. The issues raised by Isolde of the White Hands were also inessentials as far as Wagner was concerned (although he retained a reminiscence of the sail motif in Tristan's question, "What flag is she flying?"). But, by portraying Isolde as the longed-for healer, the composer invested her with the same features of woman as redeemer that he had given his earlier female characters from Senta to Brünnhilde. In so doing he introduced into the work some of the religious transcendence which Gottfried had used in his desire to clarify love's claims to be seen as something absolute: in the "final refreshment" which Isolde brings Tristan, there is more than a chance allusion to the sacrament of the Eucharist. But on the whole the fact that religion could no longer claim to be binding by nature meant that religion was no longer suited, as it had been with Gottfried, to represent absolute values.

The tension between honor and love which besets Gottfried's lovers in spite of love's superior value (thus ensuring that love remains immanent) is resolved in Wagner in favor of a transcendental view of love: Marke still speaks of shame, but Tristan gazes upon him "compassionately"; love belongs to the "other" world. In Gottfried, Tristan and Isolde leave the Cave of Lovers in order to return to society, since it is precisely through their love that they can grant absolute status to the highest of all courtly values and remain members of courtly society. In Wagner, by contrast, the lovers' end is one of mystic transfiguration. For the Middle Ages only what is divine is transcendent, so that love is transcendent only by analogy. But for Wagner, love is the *only* transcendental entity in a world that has become trivial.

Die Meistersinger: The Middle Ages as Social Milieu

Unlike all of Wagner's other operas from *Tannhäuser* to *Parsifal, Die Meistersinger* was not based on any narrative source material from which he could have distilled or (as in the *Ring*) synthesized his own private myth. His stimulus in this instance was merely poetic adaptations dating from the eighteenth and nineteenth centuries which dealt with a single historical figure and the literary and social background associated with him. They include Goethe's poem *An Account of an Old Woodcut Showing Hans Sachs's Poetic Calling* and Albert Lortzing's 1840 opera *Hans Sachs,* whose libretto, by Philipp Reger, was based on Johann Ludwig Ferdinand Deinhardstein's 1827 play. In consequence Wagner had to invent the entire story himself. Whereas in his other operas the medieval social background was reduced to local color or else (as in the *Ring*) abandoned completely, it has been incorporated into *Die Meistersinger* with a great wealth of detail. In order to achieve this aim, Wagner went back to at least one older source, Johann Christoph Wagenseil's *Book of the Master-Singers' Gracious Art,* of 1697. As a result Wagner's conception of *Die Meistersinger* arose in a way precisely opposite to that of his other works, inasmuch as on this occasion he took a plot which was no longer mythical in origin but was clearly indebted to contemporary operatic tradition and placed it within an older framework. It was a procedure far removed from that of rediscovering the mythic substratum of medieval poems that had become obscured by contemporary detail.

At the time of his work on the first draft of the libretto in Marienbad in July 1845, Wagner was still largely ignorant of the art of the mastersingers. A "young man, the son of an impoverished knight," arrives in Nuremberg; he is self-taught and owes his knowledge not to the lyric poetry of Walther von der Vogelweide, for example, but to epic verse. Wagner's poetic imagination had been fired by the idea of a tournament of song, by a comparison between artistic competence and the consequences of such competence in terms of an artist's life, and, finally, by the function of the Marker. The first prose draft already contains hints of a contrast between cheerful middle-class conventionality and the oppressive constrictions of municipal life. The second draft, written in Vienna sixteen years later, in November 1861, shows signs of a more detailed interest in the art of the mastersingers: the knight has heard of the "gracious cultivation of art" (a turn of phrase reminiscent of Wagenseil's title), the "rules of the *Tabulatur*" are read to him, and "all kind of melodies presented by name: the Rainbow, Nightingale Melody, etc." Before elaborating the definitive libretto Wagner studied Wagenseil in detail, copying out four pages of extracts, some of which were incorporated word for word into the text of the opera. But Wagner's basic concept was already fixed, and could no longer be affected by his more recent acquisition of a detailed knowledge of the mastersingers and their art.

The mastersingers were craftsmen (at least as a general rule) who united to form guilds in various south German towns in order to perform and compose songs. They practiced their art according to strict and complicated rules that were laid down in the "school regulations," or *Tabulatur*. Songs were performed in public or within the circle of the singers, and had the character of a competition. The oldest such guild is generally held to be the one in Mainz, believed to have been founded in the fourteenth century. The fifteenth and early sixteenth centuries saw guilds established in Nuremberg, Augsburg, and Strasbourg, although only the Nuremberg guild is recorded in much detail. Among the fifteenth-century mastersingers who appear in Wagner's opera are Fritz Kettner, Konrad Nachtigall, Fritz Zorn, Sixt Beckmesser, and Hans Folz. A generation later the art of the mastersingers culminated in the works of the shoemaker-poet Hans Sachs (1494–1576). In addition to creating thirteen original melodies, Sachs wrote some 4,400 songs, 70 comedies, and 58 tragedies (including one on the subject of Tristan and Isolde), together with some 85 Shrovetide plays, prose dialogues, gnomic verse, and sacred and secular songs.

By far the majority of the mastersingers' poems deal with religious subjects: from the Reformation on it was one of their chief aims to versify Luther's translation of the Bible and thus make it available to laymen. A public concert, or *Singschule,* was normally held once a month on Sunday in church at which only songs based on religious themes could be performed; other sessions held in taverns *(Zechsingen)* would include fabliaux and farces, narrative works of the most disparate origins, and songs in praise of the singers' art. Aspiring mastersingers would practice their understanding of the rules by performing set pieces before creating their own text to a preexisting *Ton* (tone) or melody, and finally writing their own song to their own melody. The performance of the song was assessed by four Markers, who judged it according to its theological accuracy, its conformity with the rules of the genre, and the correctness of its rhyme scheme and melody. The victor received the "school trinket," a chain with a King David medallion, while the runner-up was awarded a garland. At the *Zechsingen* only garlands were awarded, although money prizes were also sometimes given. The guild set great store by its exclusiveness and had a strict admission procedure. The songs could be performed only within the framework of the *Singschule* or *Zechsingen* and were not allowed to appear in print. In terms of numbers the mastersingers were an insignificant group: a mere half of one percent of all Nuremberg's master craftsmen belonged to this particular guild.

The tones were described by reference to the name of their creator and to their melody, for example, "Hans Sachs, Rose Tone" or "Heinrich Frauenlob,

Forgotten Tone." They have survived from every century of *Meistergesang*, and were used again and again. They generally consist of twelve to twenty-four verses, divided into three sections according to their strophic structure and melody, having two metrically and musically identical *Stollen* and an *Abgesang* which differed from them, although the *Stollen* was sometimes repeated, metrically and musically, at the end. The *Meisterlied* (not the individual strophe) was described as a *Bar,* and always consisted of an uneven number of strophes. The songs were performed only vocally, and never had any instrumental accompaniment.

When Johann Christoph Wagenseil, professor of public law and history, Oriental languages, and canon law at the University of Altdorf, wrote his treatise on *Meistergesang,* he relied not only on older source material but also on his own observations. The picture he drew was a uniform one without any real sense of historical differentiation.

What is "medieval" about *Die Meistersinger* is the Romantics' Janus-faced myth of Nuremberg as a free city in which the arts flourish, but petit-bourgeois narrowness and small-mindedness also abound. The music of the mastersingers stands for both of these attributes: it is "German and true," in that it preserves the old and authentic art through lean years, but at the same time its narrowness is manifest in the quaint laws and customs which Wagner evokes in such graphic terms. The contrast between an ossified dependence on rules on the one hand and artistic originality on the other required that the rules be made more precise, and for this Wagner turned to Wagenseil. In the noisy festivities on the banks of the Pegnitz the problematic and threatening aspects of the mastersingers and their art are lost in the utopian vision of an artist who, rejected by the pedantic guild, is acknowledged instead by the "folk." This typically Romantic utopia required a multidimensional social milieu such as was to be found in the late medieval town with its guilds and town council, its craftsmen and apprentices, and its knights and burghers. The fact that Wagner has neglected social reality in favor of a transfiguration of the (lower) middle classes (for it is from here that he has recruited his "folk") is another story. The most important sector of Nuremberg's populace in terms of political and cultural power occupies only a modest place in *Die Meistersinger* in the figure of the "much-traveled" Pogner, and there is no sign at all of the patrician merchants or the learned humanists. What emerges in triumph is a narrow middle-class world, in spite of the presence of the young aristocrat Walther von Stolzing. After all, *his* desire is to be assimilated into the middle classes, a desire which he finally realizes. It is ultimately a utopia tinged with resignation, not least for "holy German art." The medievalism of the work is not merely a matter of local color, as it had been in *Lohengrin:* rather it is the form in which the social element appears as an integrative factor, an element which, according to Wagner's understanding, was "German and true" in the Romantic tradition. The work confirms this tradition, albeit not in a completely benign manner.

Parsifal: From Universal Chivalric Romance to Mystery Play

Among the works which Wagner read during his medieval summer of 1845 were the *Parzival* and *Titurel* of Wolfram von Eschenbach, and Albrecht's *Younger Titurel* in a version by San-Marte. In this way he was introduced to the main branches of the German Grail tradition. But, as in the case of *Tristan,* his knowledge lay fallow for a number of years, before being briefly revived at the time of his initial conception of *Tristan.* In 1859, however, he became reacquainted with Wolfram's major work, and he was both attracted by "the genuine features of the legend" and "brusquely repelled by the poet's incompetence," as he told Mathilde Wesendonck on 29–30 May 1859. What repelled him was what he saw as the lack of any overall plan, the ambiguity of important motifs and situations, the narrative digressions which Wolfram consciously introduces, and the lack of concentration on "key situations of graphic purport"—precisely those qualities which constitute the complexity and universality of *Parzival* and guarantee its fascination for today's reader.

Wolfram von Eschenbach's romance was written around the years 1205–1210, and consists of some 25,000 lines. It opens with an account of the lives of the hero's parents—his father, Gahmuret, and his mother, Herzeloyde. Gahmuret falls in battle before his son is born, and Herzeloyde retires to the wilderness in order to raise her son in ignorance of chivalry. But when Parzival comes upon three knights in the forest and hears about King Arthur, he flouts his mother's wishes and sets off for Arthur's court, oblivious to the fact, as he takes his leave of her, that his mother has collapsed in a dead faint. On his way to Arthur's court he meets his cousin Sigune, who reveals to him his name; he now knows himself to be related both to Arthur and to the Grail family. He arrives at Arthur's court, where he murders his kinsman Ither in a provoked attack and thus obtains his horse and armor. From Gurnemanz he receives instruction in knighthood and courtly behavior but still remains inexperienced—*tump,* as Wolfram describes him. He raises the siege of Pelrapeire and marries Condwiramurs, the country's queen. He leaves her with the intention of seeking out his mother, but comes upon a mysterious castle where he sees a magnificent procession, a bleeding lance, and a mysterious object, which is the Grail. The king, Anfortas, is suffering from a wound he has sustained, but Parzival does not ask about it, having learned not to ask inopportune questions. A second meeting with Sigune reveals the extent of his failing. Gawan takes him to Arthur's court, where he is given a festive welcome and treated with great honor, but the hideous Grail messenger Cundrie curses him in the presence of all the other knights and reviles him for having omitted to ask the question of Anfortas: had he done so, the king would have been healed.

The narrative then switches to the model Arthurian knight Gawan, whose adventures take up a third of the romance. The world of Arthurian society guarantees immanent knightly perfection. Gawan's chief act is to liberate Schastel Marveile, the Castle of Wonders, and to win Orgeluse. The magician

Klinschor, who was castrated as a punishment for his adultery, has imprisoned four hundred noblewomen in the castle, including Gawan's mother and sister. Gawan breaks the spell on the castle and frees his kinfolk. Wolfram characterizes this adventure as an act of redemption, paralleled by Parzival's act of redemption at the Castle of the Grail at Munsalvaesche, an act which is similarly performed to redeem a kinsman. Orgeluse, the Duchess of Logroys, is an embittered woman who is quick to give and take offense. Since her lover was killed in single combat, she is bound to attract all knights to her, only to reject them all in scornful contempt. Parzival is the only knight to have resisted her. Gawan serves her with patience and equanimity, and succeeds in freeing her from the condition in which she is trapped, before leading her back to Arthurian society.

Meanwhile Parzival, having been cursed by Cundrie, has turned his back on God and gone out into the world in search of adventure. One Good Friday he meets a penitent knight and realizes how far he has strayed from God. He comes upon his uncle Trevrizent, who leads the life of a hermit, and is enlightened as to the story of his family, his mother's death, the Grail, and the Grail family. The Grail is said to be a stone, brought to earth by angels. The first Grail King was Titurel, followed by Frimutel and now Anfortas, who is attended by the Knights Templar who guard the Grail's domain. The Grail feeds them and keeps them alive: anyone who sets eyes on the Grail will not die during the whole of the ensuing week. Every Good Friday a dove brings a wafer which gives the stone its power. An inscription on the Grail summons young boys and girls: the latter are subsequently given in marriage, and the men become Grail Knights, who on occasion are sent out to bring stability to rulerless lands (a prefiguration here of the Loherangrin episode at the end of the poem). The knights are not allowed to marry, the only exception being the Grail King, whose wife is allocated by the Grail. Anfortas, however, chose his own lover, Orgeluse, and in serving her was wounded in the genitals by a spear wielded by a heathen intent on capturing the Grail. The blade, which had remained embedded in the wound, was drawn out by a doctor. Anfortas is now kept alive by the sight of the Grail; no medicine can help him. The Grail announces that a knight will ask the reason for Anfortas' wound, and that the king will then be cured; but no one must explain to the stranger what he must do. The heathen's spear which wounded Anfortas is replaced in the wound in an attempt to reduce the pain. The king can neither ride nor walk, lie, or stand, but occasionally he seeks to alleviate his suffering by bathing in Lake Brumbane, which is why he is falsely believed to be a fisherman. (It is at the lake that Parzival first meets him.)

Trevrizent, too, had initially devoted his life to secular knighthood, but the wound suffered by his brother Anfortas has led to his conversion. He takes Parzival's sins upon himself and absolves him. Parzival then has to undergo further adventures. But the Grail cannot be obtained by force. Finally the inscription calls him to Munsalvaesche, a summons that is communicated by

Cundrie. As his companion he takes with him his half-brother Feirefiz (the son of Gahmuret's marriage to the Mooress Belakane). He asks Anfortas the question, "Uncle, what ails thee?" ("Oeheim, waz wirret dier?"). The question has nothing to do with miracles or the lance and the Grail; it is prompted only by compassion for a kinsman's suffering. Parzival now becomes Grail King, the precondition for which is his acquiescence in God's will and his insight into the limitations of knighthood (although knighthood nonetheless remains a prerequisite); but no less important are Parzival's acceptance of his fellow men and his legitimization by virtue of being a member of the Grail family. The question concerning redemption can be asked only by one who is called; but here it is the legitimate heir who is called.

In his letter to Mathilde Wesendonck (29–30 May 1859) Wagner took exception to several specific aspects of Wolfram's narrative: (1) the interpretation of the Grail as a stone, for from San-Marte's edition he knew of the identification of the Grail with the chalice used at the Last Supper, in which Joseph of Arimathea caught Christ's blood, and he quotes the etymology, mentioned by San-Marte, whereby *San gréal* derives from *Sang real,* "royal blood" or "blood of Our Lord"; (2) Parzival's rejection of God and his subsequent conversion, both of which Wagner felt to be lacking all motivation; (3) the question, which seemed to Wagner to be "altogether fatuous and entirely meaningless"; and (4) the fact that Anfortas and Parzival vie for the reader's attention. Wagner felt a particular affinity for Anfortas, whom he described in the same letter to Mathilde Wesendonck as "my third-act Tristan inconceivably intensified"; but at the same time he could see that Parzival's "development and the profound sublimity of his purification" would have to be the focus of the action if the hero were not to appear "as a deus ex machina who leaves us completely cold." (In Wolfram's poem Anfortas is important only as a touchstone for Parzival's behavior.) Ultimately, Wagner said, he would have to "compress everything into *three* climactic situations," just as he had done with *Tristan* and as he proposed to do with Hartmann von Aue's *Erec,* according to a letter to Mathilde Wesendonck in which he expounded the contents of Hartmann's romance in dramatically finished form (see Müller 1985). In 1859 he "took leave of this senseless project," preferring at that stage not to turn Wolfram's romance into a music drama; but in August 1865 he sketched out the plot in the form of an extended prose draft. He retained Wolfram's orthography of the hero's name, not altering it to Parsifal until 1877, when his authority was the (incorrect) Arabian etymology of Joseph Görres.

Among Wagner's most significant additions is the figure of Kundry, who is a conflation of various characters in his source, but to whom he has given a very distinctive profile. She is the messenger of the Grail, and the characterization of her outward appearance as "wild and terrible" reflects the peculiar hideousness of Wolfram's Cundrie. But her appearance serves a totally different purpose in Wagner, for whom Kundry is a heathen, someone "accursed," whereas Wolfram's character is a learned woman who transcends courtly norms. The figure also includes characteristics of Orgeluse, inasmuch as she is Klingsor's agent and Amfortas' lover, and only Parsifal has resisted her. Her contradictory nature, and even her need to be redeemed, are qualities she shares with Orgeluse. To Sigune she owes her knowledge of Parsifal, including her knowledge of his name, which, as in Wolfram, she is the first to reveal to him. There are also elements of the biblical figure of the sinner Mary Magdalene, who had played an important role in Wagner's 1849 poetic draft *Jesus of Nazareth,* where she appears as paramour, lover, and servant. Above all, the scene in which Kundry anoints Parsifal's feet and dries them with her hair—a scene incorporated into the opera—is based on the corresponding episode in the Bible (John 12:3). Kundry is a reincarnation of all the figures who "cause men to suffer the anguish of love's seduction" (1865 prose draft). The idea of rebirth came to Wagner from Buddhism, and it plays a part in his 1856 sketch for *Die Sieger.* Here, as there, rebirth involves a search for redemption and for a man who will resist the woman's attempts to seduce him. Woman as temptress—and here one thinks of Eve—is a thoroughly medieval idea, but Kundry's feeling of despair at being exposed to that fate derives from a modern reflection and from her sense of distance from her own nature.

Wagner's community of the Grail is an all-male society of ascetics, the antithesis of Klingsor's castle of she-devils (as they are called in the prose draft) and their lovers. Wolfram's Grail community consists of men *and* women, although they, too, lead ascetic lives and abjure sexuality. His Parzival, by contrast, is married and remains so: for him the issue of the correct kind of sexual relationship is not a problem. In Wolfram's Castle of Wonders, by contrast, there are only women and no men; after being freed they are integrated into courtly society and restored to a secular existence, an existence in which sexual relationships are the "correct" way of life.

In many religions the renunciation of sexuality is considered a means of attaining godliness, of breaking free from the world in order to meet with God. In Christianity religiously motivated chastity has been institutionalized in monasticism, an evangelical recommendation that was turned into a regulation and taken over by the religious orders of chivalry, which further linked it with their unconditional and active support of the Church Militant. It was on this that Wolfram based the law governing his Grail Knights, and Wagner followed him in turn. To that extent the latter's Grail Knights are not unmedieval: only the extremely problematic treatment of chastity as the supreme virtue, with compulsive desire and total (but equally compulsive) abstinence being held out as mutually exclusive alternatives, is typical of Wagner's own nineteenth century. The interpretation of sex as a manifestation of original sin emerges equally clearly from the figure of Klingsor: in Wolfram he is castrated as punishment for an adulterous affair, but in Wagner his castration is a compulsive form of self-chastisement intended to help him attain the Grail. Wagner reduces the "varieties of love," which are a part of the universality of Wolfram's romance (where fourteen relationships are recounted), to one that is either compulsive and destructive or negative, an alternative scarcely suggested by even the most antisexual of medieval theologians. The courtly world of chivalry and its values (including sexual love) Wagner eliminates as inessential, and the romance's wealth of content is reduced to three situations depicting first Parsifal as a fool incapable of redemption, second his experience of suffering, and third his act of redemption. He is predestined to accomplish this act, but not by his knightly strength in battle, a necessary prerequisite for Wolfram's hero even if it is not the most decisive factor by which he is judged; Parsifal defeats Klingsor not in battle but by scoring a moral and spiritual victory over him. In this way the romance is turned into a modern mystery play. The mystery, however, is not asceticism itself, which is merely a precondition for the initiated, but the fact that man suffers as a result of his animal existence, a form of suffering which he can transcend if he learns to recognize this limitation in his nature. The cryptic words "Redemption to the Redeemer" refer first and foremost to God's redemption "from hands defiled and guilty," an act of redemption which Parsifal himself accomplishes; but it also symbolizes man's existential suffering and the possibility of redemption from such suffering. A figure of redemption, Parsifal is at the same time redeemed from suffering, for only as such can he be a redeemer. It is at this point that Buddhist ideas and Schopenhauer's philosophy become merged. In addition to the concept of a real transcendence to which man can aspire through (a nonspecifically Christian) asceticism, the Middle Ages also provided elements of the narrative and the symbols of lance and Grail. But the message of the work has changed, issuing as it does from the "sufferings and greatness" of the nineteenth century and of Wagner himself.

The Middle Ages Transformed

Wagner's works aroused and stimulated interest in the Middle Ages not only in the late nineteenth century but also in the twentieth. One example of their far-reaching influence may be found in the "Grail Castle" of Neuschwanstein, which owes its origins to Ludwig II's enthusiasm for the composer: Tannhäuser, Lohengrin, Tristan, Sachs's beloved Nuremberg, the Nibelung legend, and finally Parsifal/Parzival are all represented in murals in the palace, where they were painted between the years 1880 and 1884. Many of the nearly 1 million tourists who visit Neuschwanstein each year make their first acquaintance here not only of Wagner's works but also his medieval sources, since the frescoes relate both to scenes from his music dramas and to events from the older versions which Wagner did not adapt, blending them together to form an ideal picture of the Middle Ages. Here Wagner has clearly helped transmit the Middle Ages to the present day, inasmuch as the scenes depicted in the frescoes are based on the original legends rather than on his adaptation of them. For, like *Lohengrin* in the remark quoted at the beginning of this chapter, the original legend is located in an ideal realm of beauty.

The Middle Ages had been seen as an escapist goal by other writers before Wagner, but it was he who really opened up the period to a broad and educated public and in that way aroused interest in the original texts. There is no doubt that an acquaintance with Wagner's works created an audience for Gottfried's *Tristan* and Wolfram's *Parzival,* and the same is still true today. But this later audience read the old romances through Wagner's eyes: Wolfram's *Parzival* was reduced to the hero's quest for the Grail and the "pure fool's" capacity for compassion, with the result that readers overlooked Gawan and his love affairs, the whole of the Arthurian world and its genealogical program, and the entire feudal world that the work portrays, seeing only the "mystery" or Grail. In the case of *Tristan* they concentrated on the theme of love and the tension between the self and the world (or, at best, between the individual and society), and ignored the problems of redefining the chivalric ideal, of dynastic succession, and of feudal loyalty. It has always been difficult, especially with Gottfried, for scholars to think beyond Wagner and to adopt a less one-sided interpretation of the work than one which concentrates exclusively on the mysteries of love. An assessment of the problems associated with Isolde of the White Hands, including the belief that Gottfried did not care to lead his hero into a state of alienation, is prejudiced by Wagner's concentration on the basic plot of the romance. Because of the tradition within which he was working, Gottfried could not simply pass from the lovers' farewell to their deaths, as Wagner could; hence, according to one school of thought, he broke off his work before he had completed it. Wagner's *Tannhäuser* has given rise not only to a one-sided picture of Wolfram as a representative of nonsexual courtly love (a picture which ignores the poet's delight in sexual jokes and overlooks all forms of love which do not conform to this ideal image), but also to a dualistic view of women which admits only of coarse sensuality or renunciation, a view which even today continues to color many readers' perceptions of *Minnesang.* Wagner's *Meistersinger* conditioned the belief that the art of the mastersingers was a continuation of "German art," that the singers themselves cultivated and safeguarded that art, and that Hans Sachs was a respectable, if cunning, burgher. The opera was deemed an accurate reflection of the practice of this art, which was in fact one of the most arid branches on the tree of poetry. And the *Ring,* finally, has not only conditioned later reaction to the *Nibelungenlied* but, even more profoundly, has influenced our view of the Germanic gods, humanizing them like the Greek gods and fostering a false image of Norse mythology as tragic and obsessed with death (with the result that the Funeral March from *Götterdämmerung* could provide a musical commentary on the fall of Stalingrad).

What is missing from Wagner's picture of the Middle Ages is its social aspect. If it appears at all, as in *Die Meistersinger,* it is a backward projection of nineteenth-century society. Wagner's medieval heroes are reduced to a single heroic dimension and traced back to their archetypal origins; in the process they lose all sense of triviality, but also their actual humanity. His myth is a nineteenth-century myth rather than a prehistorical one: if it appears as such, this is merely a quasi-rhetorical means of presenting a contemporary myth to his own generation as though it were archetypal—as Wagner himself liked to believe that it was.

Nevertheless, this realization should not mislead us into declaring Wagner's adaptation of the Middle Ages to be a mere distortion. Admittedly, his response to the Middle Ages says more about his own age than it does about the medieval period, but it also releases possibilities inherent in the older texts. Wagner's "false" perception of the Middle Ages is repeatedly capable of increasing our own sensitivity and understanding: after all, does not Gottfried's *Tristan* contain a greater degree of subjectivity than we generally concede to be typical of the Middle Ages? Is the dimension that is added by a rationally inexplicable "mythical" component not something which was equally fascinating for a medieval reader or audience of *Lohengrin,* and especially of *Parzival?* And is not Wolfram's work invested with a problematic claim to totalitarianism which Wagner's *Parsifal* makes manifest? In this way Wagner's works not only reveal significant aspects of his own time but, if we follow him at a certain critical distance, act as a mediator in our understanding of the Middle Ages.

Translated by Stewart Spencer

CHAPTER 10

The Dramatic Texts

PETER BRANSCOMBE

Writing from Dresden on 30 January 1844, Wagner offered his Berlin corre-spondent Karl Gaillard a forceful summary of his current views on the rela-tionship between drama and the subject matter of opera, and on the difference between setting his own texts to music and setting the words of another librettist: "And so anyone who knows only my *Flying Dutchman* generally holds it against me that I write my own texts for my operas: because of the difficulties which—as I freely admit—I make for myself in this area, people think themselves justified in concluding that I am not equal to the task. Those who know my *Rienzi* judge differently . . . I really have no illusions about my reputation as a poet, & I confess that it was only as a last resort that I adopted the expedient of writing my own libretti, since no decent texts were offered me. But it would now be totally impossible for me to set another's text to music." These lines bespeak a combination of modesty and clear-cut judgment that shows Wagner standing at a fork in the road, as is amply confirmed by the subsequent course of his compositional development. The new path on which he embarked with *Holländer* was to leave its mythological mark on the whole of his future, discouraging him from ever again returning to the world of history, which he had left behind him with *Rienzi*.

The letter to Gaillard, however, gives further insights into the uniqueness of Wagner's inspiration: "Even before I set about writing a single line of the text or drafting a scene, I am already thoroughly immersed in the musical aura of my new creation, I have the whole sound & all the characteristic motifs in my head so that when the poem is finished & the scenes are arranged in their proper order the actual opera is already completed." It is a sentence that could just as well have been written ten or twenty years later, so admir-ably does it encapsulate the composer's working method at the time of the *Ring*. Of course, Wagner is exaggerating when in speaking of elaborating the score he claims that "its detailed musical treatment is more a question of calm & reflective revision, the moment of actual creativity having already passed."

No composer before Wagner, nor any since, was as skilled in forging so compelling and indissoluble a synthesis of words, music, stage picture, and gesture to produce a dramatic whole. His confidence in his own talent, so unmistakably expressed in his letter to Gaillard, even allowed him to conclude that the future course of opera lay not in staging "trivialities, intrigues & so on" by "modern writers of comedies & plays," but in conjuring up "the unique & characteristic aura of sanctity associated with poetry as it wafts across the centuries in the form of legends & tales from the dawn of history."

Earliest Attempts at Drama

Wagner's first attempt to write a drama was the tragedy *Leubald* (WWV 1), completed in 1828 when he was only fifteen. It is of significance that, according to *My Life* (ML 34), he intended to set it to music a few years later. But the text itself is not without interest. A member of the British House of Lords, whose name it has unfortunately not been possible to establish, mentions the play and quotes from it in his copy of the Notices and Orders of the Day for Tuesday, 25 July 1893. But what is of most interest to the modern reader of this blank-verse drama (see Vetter-Voss 1988 for the first complete transcription of it) is the occasional appearance of alliterative verse, or *Stabreim,* the form of rhyme that is so characteristic of the later Wagner: "So lag der Vater vor mir auf der Bahre, / Als unsrer Liebe fluchend er verschied" (Thus lay my father on his bier before me, / And with his final breath our love did curse), and "Woher um mich dies wonnigliche Wehen" (Whence wafts the wind that thrills my senses; SSD XVI, 182 and Vetter-Voss 1988, pp. 182, 164). As for the language of *Leubald,* Wagner had this to say: "One of the main ingredients of my poetic fancy I owed to Shakespeare's mighty diction, emotional and humorous" (ML 27). And he consoled himself in the face of his family's indignant reaction by recalling that the work "could only be judged rightly when provided with the *music* I now had decided to write for it and which I intended to start composing immediately"; it was to be "incidental music . . . like Beethoven's for *Egmont*" (ML 27, 31). But the music never materialized.

Four years later motifs from *Leubald* were taken up again and used in Wagner's first operatic venture, *Die Hochzeit* (Prague, 1832), a work which he subsequently destroyed almost in its entirety. Here one can already sense the mature composer's stark originality. He subsequently wrote of the piece: "This blackest nocturnal epic, through which echoed *Leubald und Adelaïde* from my distant youth in a somewhat more refined strain, was executed in black on black, with disdain for any ray of light and in particular for all operatic embellishments" (ML 68). Almost forty years later Wagner recalled his youthful drama when his sketch for *Götterdämmerung* was not progressing as he would have wished: "'I am no composer,' he says, 'I wanted only to learn enough to compose *Leubald und Adelaïde;* and that is how things have remained—it is only the subjects which are different'" (CT, 31 January 1870).

The libretto of Wagner's first music drama, *Die Feen,* is a reworking of

Carlo Gozzi's *La donna serpente,* mixed in with reminiscences of Marschner's *Hans Heiling,* Kleist's *Käthchen von Heilbronn,* Schiller's *Die Jungfrau von Orleans,* Kotzebue's *Spiegelritter,* and Schikaneder's *Die Zauberflöte* (the source of "the dark gate of terror" and the Two Armed Men). Of interest here are the early pointers to *Tannhäuser* and other later works, but more especially to Richard Strauss's *Die Frau ohne Schatten,* with a libretto by Hugo von Hofmannsthal. The text of *Die Feen* is highly conventional, though well suited to the musical design. Even this first completed stage work of Wagner's shows his typical handling of dramatic contrasts between chorus, ensemble, and solo singing, and also between various verse forms. Dactylic, iambic, and trochaic feet alternate frequently, rhyme is used only rarely, and the length of the lines is extremely varied. It is a language which is felt by the reader—and even more by the listener—to be prose rather than verse. Even so, one finds the odd series of iambic pentameters, as well as many examples of the sort of grammatical inversion that Wagner so favored:

> Denn unvergänglicher Schöne
> nie verblühender Hauch
> durchweh't die herrlichen Welten,
> athmet froh dieser Kreis.

> For sempiternal beauty's
> never fading breeze
> wafts through these glorious worlds,
> gladly breathes this realm.

Examples such as this one, from the opening chorus of the work, stand side by side with passages of a more simple and direct diction. A further contrast, no doubt indispensable in drama, is that between long speeches and an ensuing short-breathed dialogue known as stichomythia; and yet another contrast, more frequently found in opera, is that between long and short lines. The music of *Die Feen* occasionally recalls the later Wagner; but an unbiased reader of the poem would discover nothing of any significance if he did not already know the librettist's name. Wagner himself was aware of his own achievement when he wrote of *Die Feen:* "While I had written *Die Hochzeit* without operatic embellishments and treated the material in the darkest vein, this time I festooned the subject with the most manifold variety . . . As to the poetic diction and the verses themselves, I was almost intentionally careless about them. I was not nourishing my former hopes of making a name as a poet; I had really become a 'musician' and a 'composer' and wanted simply to write a decent libretto, for I now realized nobody else could do this for me, inasmuch as an opera book is something unique unto itself and cannot be easily brought off by poets and literati" (ML 72).

In his autobiography Wagner tells how, in writing *Das Liebesverbot,* he turned away from the symphony, "whereas the opera, on the contrary, in which I increasingly felt myself to have no real predecessor, presented itself in varied and alluring shapes as a fascinating art form" (ML 91). On this occasion he was "much more careful as regards diction and versification than with the preparation of my book for *Die Feen*" (ibid.). Shakespeare's *Measure for Measure* was "very freely" adapted: "*Das junge Europa* and *Ardinghello* now set the tone for my basic conception" (ML 83).

In the 1879 essay *The Work and Mission of My Life* (written by Hans von Wolzogen and signed by Wagner; see CT, 1 May 1879), *Das Liebesverbot* is held out as an attempt to reconcile the demands of the composer's art with those of his life. The work's chaotic premiere in Magdeburg in 1836 was the first and last occasion on which he heard the piece. When, in 1871, the contents of the first volume of his collected writings seemed to him somewhat thin, he wondered "whether to include his youthful works in it. However, he finds them too childish" (CT, 16 July 1871). By 1879 he was even astonished to discover "how bad it is: 'What phases one goes through! It is hard to believe it is the same person'" (CT, 1 February 1879). In his old age Wagner undervalued the work, perhaps in compensation for his earlier overvaluation: "These spirited and in many respects boldly devised scenes I had clothed with commensurate diction and meticulous verses" (ML 118) was the comment he had added to his long synopsis of the plot in *My Life*.

During his years of apprenticeship, Wagner the musical-dramatic poet fell, so to speak, between two stools. On the one hand we find him ready to write libretti for other composers, and on the other maintaining contact with poets whom he saw as potential librettists. In 1833 Heinrich Laube declared his readiness "to consign to me [Wagner] an opera text [*Kocziusko*] he had intended for Meyerbeer"; Wagner declined the offer since he already had his own "definite and instinctive idea as to how such a text had to be written" (ML 79). And in 1836 he wrote to Eugène Scribe, offering him his sketch of *Die hohe Braut* (The high-born bride, WWV 40) to be worked up into a libretto, but on condition that Scribe obtain a commission for him to compose the work for Paris. The plan came to nothing, although Wagner himself later versified *Die hohe Braut* for his Dresden colleague Karl Reissiger, who was then preparing the first performance of *Rienzi*. In the end it was Wagner's Czech friend Johann Friedrich Kittl who successfully set the text to music under the title *Bianca und Giuseppe, oder Die Franzosen vor Nizza* (Bianca and Giuseppe, or the French outside Nice). In 1842 Wagner planned a libretto for Josef Dessauer, based on E. T. A. Hoffmann's *Die Bergwerke zu Falun*, but technical difficulties prevented the plan from coming to fruition (see WWV 67). A final example of Wagner as potential librettist for another composer is provided by *Holländer*. In the summer of 1841, Wagner, in need of money, reluctantly sold the rights to *Holländer* to the Paris Opéra for five hundred francs, although Paul Foucher and Bénédict-Henry Révoil made little or no use of it in their libretto *Le vaisseau fantôme*, which they wrote for Pierre Louis Philippe Dietsch.

Wagner himself was not unaware of his ambivalent position as poet-composer in the eyes of his contemporaries. In *My Life* he mentions that, according to a critic in Prague, his text for Kittl's opera "was proof of my true calling as a librettist, and that I was only going astray in attempting also to compose; whereas Laube asserted on the basis of my *Tannhäuser* that it was my bad luck not to have found a practised dramatist to produce a decent text for my music" (ML 229). As late as 1849 Wagner was still preoccupied with the same concern: on 5 December 1849 he wrote to tell Liszt that he "found it utterly impossible merely to set to music another writer's poem,—not because I regard it as too slight, but because I know—and know from experience—that I would write only poor and indifferent music."

Rienzi and *Holländer*

That Wagner worked on *Rienzi* and *Holländer* simultaneously only serves to highlight the considerable differences between them—differences which consist not only in the fact that *Rienzi* is Wagner's longest work and *Holländer* almost his shortest, and that *Holländer,* with a cast of six, is extremely concentrated, whereas *Rienzi,* written in the five-act tradition of Meyerbeer's grand operas, contains a full-scale plot on a personal and political level. More decisive is the fact that in writing *Holländer,* Wagner was entering the world of myth, a world he was later to leave only once, in *Die Meistersinger,* whereas the approach he adopted in writing *Rienzi* was somewhat derivative, with its more or less conscious borrowing of elements from the French operas of Auber, Meyerbeer, and Spontini and from the Italian operas of Bellini.

As far as the poetic language of *Rienzi* is concerned, Wagner was relatively modest, particularly in light of his spectacular aim of "outdoing 'grand opera'" (SSD IV, 258): "And so I devoted no greater care to the language and prosody than seemed to me necessary to produce a decent *opera text* that was not too trivial" (SSD IV, 259; cf. I, 2). He availed himself chiefly of an iambic meter, with lines of five feet often replacing the predominantly octosyllabic lines; rhyme appears irregularly, occurring, for example, in Rienzi's Prayer, and often in choruses and ensemble passages, but rarely in monologues. Of interest here are the changes that Wagner made in the course of composition, especially in the number of syllables per line and in the way they are accented. One example among many is the Prayer, lines 5–6. The printed text (SSD I, 82) reads: "Du stärktest mich, du gabst mir Kraft, / Verlieh'st mir hohe Eigenschaft" (Thou strengthend'st me and gav'st me power / With lofty virtue didst me shower). In the full score these lines have been expanded to: "Du stärktest mich, du gabst mir hohe Kraft, / Du liehest mir erhab'ne Eigenschaft" (Thou strengthend'st me and gav'st me lofty power, / Sublimity on me thou didst shower). If we compare the prose draft of the fourth-act finale, "Irene, you—there is still a Roman man & woman!" with the definitive text, "Irene, you? *There's still a Rome!*" (SSD I, 82), we can see at once that even at this date Wagner was already a master of contraction and of intensification (Deathridge 1977, p. 184). Nonetheless, he was still not wholly consistent in his handling of stressed and unstressed syllables: in the final scene between

Irene and Adriano, the former is made to place a false stress on the fourth syllable of "Ihr seid Treulose" (You are faithless men):

In 1871, in his introduction to the first volume of his collected writings, Wagner came back to the text of *Rienzi:* he saw himself exposed to the risk of being misunderstood for apparently "trying to gain attention as a *poet,*" and felt that he might perhaps have done better not to have republished the text of the opera, since, in writing it, he had consciously avoided giving himself "the airs and graces of a poet." In judging the type of versification and diction used, one had to draw a distinction, he went on, between correctness and success, especially in the context of *Das Liebesverbot* and the libretto for *Rienzi,* with its "striking neglect of diction and versification" (SSD I, 2). He had learned from experience that literary qualities tended to get in the way of an opera's effectiveness. "Since I myself longed for a theatrical success, I was seized, the moment I set about looking for opera texts, by a very real loathing for all the so-called 'fine verses and elegant rhymes' that now and again had been offered me" (SSD I, 2–3). He was concerned only with writing "a decent stage play to go with music which, in turn, would have nothing whatever to do with flowery musical language . . . An effective 'stage play' lies behind *The Flying Dutchman* no less, indeed, than it does behind *The Last of the Tribunes*" (SSD I, 3).

What Wagner could not know at the time he was writing *Rienzi* was that it was precisely the historical aspect of this work which would prove to be a dead end as far as his subsequent development was concerned. This is also the reason why he did not complete his later plans for a *Friedrich I* (WWV 76) and *Jesus von Nazareth* (WWV 80). After *Rienzi* he wrote only three-act works (with the single exception of *Das Rheingold*), a development which is particularly striking in view of his earlier vacillation between operas of two or three acts at the one extreme and five at the other.

During his months in Paris, as he later explained in *A Communication to My Friends,* Wagner embarked on a new course: "*that of a revolution against the public life of present-day art* . . . The feeling that my indignation was a necessary emotion made a writer of me first and foremost" (SSD IV, 262). And, especially, a German writer: "A sensitive, yearning patriotism made itself felt, a feeling of which I had earlier had no inkling" (SSD IV, 268).

In the figure of the Flying Dutchman, of course, Wagner had hardly stumbled on a German character but rather on one with whom he himself could identify. "The figure of the 'Flying Dutchman' is the mythical poem of the people: a primeval trait of man's essential nature expresses itself here with heart-enthralling power. This trait, in its most general significance, is a yearning for rest from life's storms" (SSD IV, 265). Wagner was aware of how closely related the Dutchman or "Wandering Jew" was to the hero of the *Odyssey,* and in adapting his material, he was able to draw on his own experiences as a traveler. More important still, "it was the first *folk-poem* to penetrate my heart, encouraging me as an artist to interpret and adapt it in a work of art. It is here that my career as a *poet* begins, a career with which I abandoned the mere manufacture of opera texts" (SSD IV, 266).

As for the quality of his dramatic poem, Wagner's claims were relatively modest: so much about the poem was "still so undecided, the situations still so vaguely structured on the whole, the poetic language and the verses often still so lacking in individual character" (SSD IV, 267) that contemporary playwrights must certainly have criticized him for describing the text as a poem. What are its chief characteristics? Wagner describes it as being popular above all else. Some fifty pages later in the same essay he returns to the subject of the "folk legend": "From now on I was first and foremost a *poet* with regard to all my dramatic works, and only in elaborating and completing the poem did I become a musician once more" (SSD IV, 316).

Wagner's handling of the poetic language is uneven, alternating between traditional elements and much else that is new. Textual repetitions are rare, except in the choruses which the work contains: they are particularly striking in the rather more old-fashioned Romantic passages such as the act 1 duet for the Dutchman and Daland, and the act 2 duet between Senta and Erik. End rhyme is used to underline the work's key moments, such as the final dialogue between Senta and the Dutchman; it also occurs toward the end of long solo scenes, such as the Dutchman's opening scena, as well as in the lyrical, more leisurely paced, and often more traditional passages in the work, whereas the score's most musically inspired and original pages coincide for the most part with lines of blank verse. As for the meter, iambic pentameter predominates, but alexandrines are also found—"Erfahre das Geschick, vor dem ich dich bewahre!" (Now learn the dreadful fate from which you have been saved!; SSD I, 290)—in addition to lines of two or three feet. The rhythmic structure is flexible: the Steersman's Song begins anapestically, whereas the Sailors' Chorus, "Steuermann, lass' die Wacht!" (Steersman leave the watch!) is cretic by contrast; Senta's Ballad, described by Wagner as "the condensed image of the whole drama" (SSD IV, 323), alternates between iambic and trochaic tetrameter, interspersed with dactyls and other additional stressed and unstressed syllables. That Wagner was concerned with emphasizing the popular folkloric element is clear not only from the first part of *Opera and Drama* (especially SSD III, 266–267) but also from a remark in his letter to Ferdinand Heine of early August 1843: "From the outset I had to abandon the modern arrangement of dividing the work into arias, duets, finales etc., and instead relate the legend in a single breath, just as a good poem should be."

Tannhäuser

With his next opera Wagner immersed himself in the world of Middle High German literature. "It is a well-known fact that this poem [*Tannhäuser*] is directly linked with a longer epic poem *Lohengrin:* this, too, I studied and in doing so found a new world of poetic possibilities had opened up to me at a *single* stroke, a world of which I had previously had no inkling, since until that time I had generally taken as my starting-point subjects that were already fully fashioned and suited to the genre of opera" (SSD IV, 269–270). In *A Communication to My Friends* Wagner gives compelling reasons for preferring *Tannhäuser* to *Friedrich I*: "Here it was the *folk*-poem that always captures the *essence* of the phenomenon and reveals it, in turn, in simple, graphic outline; whereas there, in an historical context—i.e. not as it was in essence but as it exists in the only form that is recognizable to *us*—this phenomenon reveals itself in an endlessly colourful superficial diffuseness, and achieves graphic form only when the popular eye perceives it in its *essential nature,* endowing it with the form of an artistic myth" (SSD IV, 272). What Wagner rediscovered first and foremost in the Tannhäuser legend was "the simple, genuine folk-poem" (SSD IV, 269). As he was later to write in *My Life,* "I had not yet arrived at any close study of medieval poetry: the classical side of the poetry of the Middle Ages had so far only faintly dawned on me, partly from youthful recollections" (ML 259).

The text and the score of *Tannhäuser* evolved in two stages: first between 1842 and 1845 for the Dresden premiere of the work, and second in 1860–61 for the so-called Paris version. The textual changes for the Paris production are less interesting than the musical revisions which Wagner undertook immediately after he had put the finishing touches to *Tristan*. The text can basically be ascribed to the older type, with its longer, regular strophes interrupted by the stichomythia of shorter, more dramatic exchanges (for example, the dialogue between Wolfram and Tannhäuser in act 3, scene 3). The lines are predominantly iambic tetrameter and pentameter, although lines of three feet are also found, as in the duet "Gepriesen sei die Stunde" (O joyful hour of meeting) in act 2, scene 2. A typical monologue contains a group of pentameters followed by one of tetrameters ("Dir töne Lob!" [Thee will I praise] in act 1, scene 2; and "Als du in kühnem Sange uns bestrittest" [When in the hall of song we strove together] in act 1, scene 4); but short lines are also found, as in the Sirens' Song in act 1, scene 1, where trochee follows dactyl. Unrhymed passages often alternate fairly abruptly with ones in which a varied rhyme scheme is used. Nor is Wagner always successful in avoiding the ridiculous, as at the end of the Younger Pilgrims' final chorus: "Hoch über aller Welt ist Gott, / und sein Erbarmen ist kein Spott!" (High o'er the world God rules His folk, / and His compassion is no joke!).

Anyone reading the text is bound to form the impression that the verse is far too conventional and monotonous in its effect; but a comparison between the printed libretto and the two versions of the score shows Wagner's increasing mastery in expanding or compressing the regular meter in keeping with the demands of his musical imagination. Among noteworthy examples here are the textual and musical concentration with which the individual phrases of Wolfram, Tannhäuser, and the distant male chorus are woven together at the cry "Elisabeth!" in act 3, scene 3, or the dialogue between Venus and Tannhäuser at the beginning of the opera. Here there are only insignificant discrepancies between the printed text and the Dresden score ("Was ficht dich an?" [What possesses thee?] becomes "Was fasst dich an?" [What preys on thee?]), whereas for the French score Wagner was obliged to adapt both the music and the new German text to meet the requirements of the French language: "Sag', was kümmert dich?" (Say, what worries thee?) is expanded to become "Sag' mir, was dich mühet?" (Tell me what thee troubles), or "Dis-moi ce qui t'attriste?"; and "Was fasst dich an?" becomes "Was fasst dich an? wohin verlierst du dich?" (What preys on thee? and whither fly thy thoughts?), or "Combien sont folles tes peines! quel vain souci!" For all its occasional subtleties, *Tannhäuser* remains a fairly conventional opera from a formal point of view, with more or less self-contained arias, duets, ensembles, choruses, recitatives, marches, and so on, even if the individual numbers generally run into one another and are built up into finely structured acts.

Lohengrin

With *Lohengrin* Wagner entered "a new world of poetical possibilities" (SSD IV, 269–270) which he was scarcely ever again to leave. In the summer of 1845 he took with him to Marienbad "the poems of Wolfram von Eschenbach in the versions of Simrock and San Marte, together with the anonymous epic of Lohengrin with the great introduction by Görres," and "communed with Titurel and Parzival in this strange and yet so intimately appealing poem of Wolfram" (ML 302). Characteristic of almost all of Wagner's works during his middle and later years is the clear and graphic way in which each new subject suddenly revealed itself to his inner eye: "*Lohengrin,* the first conception of which dates from the latter part of my time in Paris, stood suddenly revealed before me in full armor at the center of a comprehensive dramatic adaptation of the whole material" (ML 302–303). The poem was quickly drafted, but when, in December 1845, Wagner read the text aloud to a circle of friends, he found that even experts had difficulty in understanding its form: "It was praised and deemed 'effective.' Schumann also liked it, yet couldn't figure out the musical form I had in mind for it, as he couldn't find any passages suitable for traditional musical numbers. I then had some fun reading different parts of my poem just as if they were in aria and cavatina form, so that in the end he smilingly conceded the point" (ML 326).

Like *Tannhäuser, Lohengrin* contains set pieces: one thinks of Elisabeth's Greeting to the Hall of Song and Wolfram's Ode to the Evening Star in the earlier work, and Elsa's "Einsam in trüben Tagen" (Oft when the hours were lonely) and Lohengrin's Grail narration in the later one. But individual speeches no longer simply follow one another, as in the earlier works, and the overlapping of phrases points to the later dramas. The language is uneven—it is not difficult to find rhymes that might have been lifted from second- or third-rate Romantic operas. There is something almost inept about the frequency of particles serving an exclusively metrical function, as in Friedrich's "Gar bald will ich wohl weiter noch mich wagen! / Vor euren

Augen soll es leuchtend tagen!" (literally, "Right soon shall I no doubt risk one more additional step! / Before your eyes the light shall brightly dawn!") in act 2, scene 3. The regular pentameters and tetrameters, normally rhyming in pairs, produce a sense of monotony, in spite of the sophistication with which Wagner the composer displaces the accents, alters the rhyme scheme, and weaves in verbal repetitions or contracted forms. The meter is predominantly iambic, although shorter lines and rhythmic variants are also found from time to time, as in Elsa's "Einsam in trüben Tagen." Occasionally the listener may feel himself approaching the world of the *Ring,* less in Ortrud's conjuration of her profaned gods Wodan and Freia than in the use of alliteration in Friedrich's plaint against Elsa: "Du hörst die Klage! König, richte recht!" (O King, thou'st heard my case, now justly judge it!). On the whole the libretto is fairly conventional, although Wagner could properly boast of a certain stylistic innovation when he wrote to Liszt on 8 September 1850, following the premiere of the work the previous month, noting that he had been at pains "to take account of the spoken emphasis of the words." The singers were instructed to show "animation rather than reserve" and to "produce the impression of an impassioned and poetical mode of delivery." Wagner was eager for the most part to abandon the distinction between the lyrical and narrative sections of his works, a desire which can be deduced from his correspondence with Liszt on the subject of the *Ring.*

Der Ring des Nibelungen

Both in his letter to Liszt of 20 November 1851 and in *A Communication to My Friends* of the preceding summer, Wagner emphasizes the need to depict the *Ring*'s dramatic relationships "in *moments of actual visual action on stage,*" such moments being "uniquely intelligible *in drama* alone" (SSD IV, 343). It was for this reason that he resolved to preface his original plan for *Siegfrieds Tod* with another work, *Der junge Siegfried,* and then to add another drama and a prelude. As he wrote to Liszt, his final plan was aimed at a "detailed depiction of all that occurs in *Der junge Siegfried* in narrative form," an aim he would achieve "by discarding, at the same time, all the narration-like passages which are now so extensive, or else by compressing them into a number of much more concise moments." Of course, it was not possible to eliminate the narrative passages quite so ruthlessly, although there is no doubting Wagner's success in achieving an incomparable "clarity of presentation."

The text of the *Ring* underwent relatively few alterations after Wagner had had it privately printed in 1853 for the benefit of his immediate circle of friends. Although he renamed the last two parts of the cycle and reworked the first act of *Siegfried,* and although he wrote a new ending for the work, prepared after he had read Schopenhauer's *World as Will and Representation,* Wagner did not consider it necessary to publish the revised version of the text as it appears in the completed score. An observant reader, familiar with the full score of the work, will notice, for example, that Donner's words "Schuldig blieb ich / Schächern nie" (I never remained indebted to robbers; SSD V, 222) or Erda's "Friedloser, / lass' mich frei! / Lose des Zaubers Zwang!" (Restless man, / let me go! / Loosen the spell's constraint!; *Siegfried*; SSD VI, 155) were not set to music. Far more striking, of course, are such major changes as the one that involves the scene between Wotan and Fricka (*Die Walküre,* act 2, scene 1, where there are four speeches in the full score and ten in the printed text), or the extensive revision of act 1 of *Siegfried*. In comparing the original version of *Siegfrieds Tod* (SSD II, 167–228) with the text of *Götterdämmerung,* one is struck by Wagner's initial preference for Old High German long lines:

> Zu neuen Thaten, theurer Helde,
> wie liebt' ich dich,—liess' ich dich nicht?

> To deeds of glory, brave beloved!
> My love for you bids you be gone.

Later he decided in favor of short lines, dividing each long line into two half-lines.

What are the characteristic qualities of the text of the *Ring* that strike the unprejudiced reader? First and foremost there are the significant differences in the length of the lines and the layout, between Brünnhilde's question to Hagen, "An wem?" (On whom?), or the Vassals' cry "Heil! Heil!" (Hail! Hail!) and the eleven syllables of Brünnhilde's lament in act 3 of *Die Walküre,* "dass mein Verbrechen so schmählich du bestrafst" (that you must punish my deed with endless shame). A comparison between text and score shows the most subtle handling of stressed and unstressed syllables, and the considerable degree of flexibility which Wagner achieved by dint of minor changes in the word order. In the course of elaborating the text and setting it to music, he made the language much more vivid and poetic, as a single example may serve to show. Hagen's original lines in *Siegfrieds Tod,* "Verstehst du auch dieser Raben Spruch? / Sie eilen, Wotan dich zu melden!" (Can you also tell what these ravens said? / They hasten to announce you to Wotan!; SSD II, 221) have become a more succinct and more dramatic alliterative question that no longer preempts Hagen's action: "Erräth'st du auch / dieser Raben Geraun'?" (Canst read the speech of those ravens aright?).

Of course, the most typical and most widely debated characteristic of the poem is its alliteration. Toward the end of the second part of *Opera and Drama* Wagner considers the device from a relatively theoretical point of view (SSD IV, 94–96), whereas in *A Communication to My Friends* he explains why this verse form in particular is appropriate to his purpose. It was clear to him that he could not have written *Siegfried* in a traditional meter: "I had thus to think of another speech melody; and yet, in truth, I had no need to think at all, but merely to make up my mind, for at the archetypally mythic source where I found the youthful and handsome human being, Siegfried, I also found, quite involuntarily, the sentiently consummate linguistic expression in which this man could alone manifest himself. This was *alliterative verse* which, in keeping with genuine speech inflections, can be adapted to suit the most natural and lively of rhythms; which is at all times readily capable of the most infinitely varied expression; and in which the folk themselves once wrote poetry at a time when they were still poets and creators of myths" (SSD IV, 329). It is in this sense that we must interpret Nietzsche's enthusiastic remark in part nine of *Richard Wagner in Bayreuth,* where he speaks of the way in which Wagner "forced language back to a primordial state in which it hardly yet thinks in concepts and in which it is itself still poetry, image and feeling."

In the third part of *Opera and Drama* Wagner stresses one of the main advantages of alliterative verse—its conceptual concentration—when he speaks of the possibility of combining "linguistic roots that express contrasting emotions (e.g. 'pleasure and pain' or 'weal and woe')." With the help of musical modulation the composer is able to illustrate such a combination. By way of an example Wagner contrasts "an alliterative line of verse with a perfectly uniform emotional content . . . such as 'love gives joy to life,'" where it is unnecessary "to step outside the chosen key," with a line "of mixed emotion, such as 'love brings pleasure and pain,'" where the composer would feel obliged to modulate to a different key at the word *pain,* where a second emotion is introduced (SSD IV, 152). Herein lay an essential advantage of *Stabreim* for Wagner the music dramatist. The fact that he flogged this linguistic horse to death was condemned by his own contemporaries, and it remains an object of censure today. "Woe is me, what a wearisome walk through Wagner's Vienna *Valkyrie,*" Daniel Spitzer complained at the beginning of his review of the Vienna premiere of *Die Walküre* in *Die Neue Freie Presse* of 18 March 1877.

Wagner's skill with words, especially in the *Ring,* is based on the linguistic sensitivity of a born philologist. Chamberlain reports that Wagner's teachers at the Kreuzschule in Dresden recognized him as such (Chamberlain 1900, p. 37). Proper names are treated etymologically and figuratively by turns ("Freia, die holde, / Holda, die freie" [literally, "Freia, the fair one, / Holda, the free one"] and—in reference to Gutrune—"Sind's gute Runen, / die ihrem Aug' ich entrathe?" [Are good the runes / that now in her eyes I am reading?]). Wagner also uses elements from the most disparate regions and dialects: Low German ("glau," or "bright," in *Das Rheingold;* SSD V, 205); Middle German ("grieseln," "to shudder," in *Siegfried;* SSD VI, 112, and "lackern," "to lick," in *Siegfried;* SSD VI, 108); and Upper German ("zu best," "for the best," in *Siegfried;* SSD VI, 89).

He also uses archaic forms, as in the complex "waten / wüten / Wotan" (to wade / to rage / Wotan) or, in *Siegfrieds Tod,* "Hier giebt es Wal zu küren!" (Here is the pick of the battlefield!); individual archaisms include "wonnig" (winsome) and "Schächer" (robber). His neologisms include both contracted and expanded forms, exclamations and invectives, and compound nouns ("Wehwalt," or "Prince of Woe," and "Des Angstversehrten," or "fear-consumed," in *Das Rheingold;* SSD V, 253) and newly coined verbs such as "umbangen" (to shroud in terror) in *Siegfried* (SSD VI, 171). Even traditional end rhyme is found on occasion, and in the opening scene of act 2 of *Götter-dämmerung* we have a kind of textual rondo with variations on the phrase "Schläfst du, Hagen, mein Sohn?" (Sleeping, Hagen, my son?). All of these devices are aimed at achieving the greatest concision and vividness of expression (Wolzogen 1878).

Tristan und Isolde

When Wagner completed the prose draft of *Tristan* in the summer of 1857, not only did he have the first musical impulses for the work already behind him (see his letter to Liszt of 16[?] December 1854), but he had already sketched *Die Sieger* (WWV 89), a Buddhist tragedy that he regarded as "the continuation and conclusion of *Lohengrin*" (letter to Mathilde Wesendonck of early August 1860) and which he hoped, even more than with *Tristan,* would provide "that most sacred of objects, total redemption" (letter to Liszt of 12 July 1856). The shared features with *Tristan,* the plans for a drama based on *Die Sieger,* and *Parsifal* (the hero, wandering in search of salvation and the Grail, was to have encountered the dying Tristan in Kareol) resolved themselves into two music dramas and one fragmentary prose sketch.

A similar phenomenon can be seen in the case of *Die Meistersinger:* the first prose draft of July 1845 contains a kind of preview of Wagner's later music dramas: "The young man [later named Konrad, and finally, in 1862, Walther] plucks up courage: 'in what tone shall I sing: of Siegfried and Grimmhilde?'—The Masters are shocked and shake their heads.—*The young man:* 'Well then, shall I sing of Parzival in Wolfram's tone?'—Renewed sense of shock" (SSD XI, 346).

The *Tristan* prose draft anticipates many of the linguistic details contained in the final libretto, although it remains no more than a sketch in several places. A comparison, for example, between the end of act 2 in the draft and the same passage in the full score shows how much richer and more refined the definitive version is, not only from a rhythmic point of view but also in that it is more elaborate now, more direct—in a word, more poetic. The linguistic structure of Isolde's Transfiguration is left completely open in the draft. By contrast, Marke's closing speech is already sketched out in quite precise detail, although still somewhat prosaic in its effect: "Why do this to me, Isolde? It was revealed to me what I could not grasp: to make you happy I hurried here after you: but who has attained misfortune's fury?" (SSD XI, 343). This passage has been turned into fifteen lines of verse in the printed libretto; and even between the published text and the full score, additional minor discrepancies—inversions and metrical refinements—may be noted. Here, as elsewhere with Wagner, the look of the text cannot be reconstructed from a sung performance, chiefly because the lines are generally very short: lines of two feet (with dactyls and iambs alternating) predominate, although there is also frequent use of trimeters. Wagner is very free in his handling of the rhythm (as may be seen superficially from the varying numbers of unstressed syllables). And the poetic devices he uses are extraordinarily numerous. Marke's final speech, for example, contains all these stylistic features: alliteration in "hell" (clear) and "enthüllt" (disclosed)—weakly stressed prefixes are ignored for the purposes of alliteration—and "Freund / frei . . . fand" (friend / free . . . found); assonance (the recurrent *o* sounds); end rhyme as a final affirmation ("Tod . . . Noth!"—literally, "death . . . distress!"); metrical variation between the prevailing iambs of the dimetric half-lines and the mixture of iambs and trochees in the trimeters, with a group of trimeters following one of dimeters but avoiding the impression of a fixed verse scheme (what the eye reads as dactyls is resolved in the score by a different emphasis or by the absence of emphasis); inclusion or exclusion of unstressed final syllables and examples of double anacrusis ("was zuvor" [what before]); dactyl ("dass ich den" ["that I the . . .," altered in the full score to "dass den Freund ich"]); cretic ("frei von Schuld" [free from blame]); and—a whole line in the printed text—"Ungestüm" (fury), together with amphibrach ("Die Ärnte" [the harvest]) and anapest ("wie erreicht" [how attains]). Like all of Wagner's music dramas, *Tristan* has its own poetic language, its own verse structure and tone.

Die Meistersinger

Throughout its various stages of drafting and composition, *Die Meistersinger* retained a constant factor expressed in the lines that were added to the end of the 1845 prose sketch (SSD XI, 355; translation from Newman 1949, p. 413):

> Zerging' das heil'ge römische Reich in Dunst,
> uns bliebe doch die heil'ge deutsche Kunst.

> Though should depart the might of holy Rome,
> no harm will come to holy German art.

These lines not only encapsulate the opera's theme of patriotic art, but they also provide an outline of its characteristic verse form.

What is unique about the libretto of *Die Meistersinger* is its wholly conscious, archaic poetic language, a blend of Luther's language and that of the historical Hans Sachs on the one hand with that of the imaginary speech of the medieval middle classes as invented by the German Romantics and the *Knittelvers* of Goethe's *Hans Sachsens poetische Sendung* on the other.

Rhyming couplets predominate, but there are also numerous variants. Pogner's monologue, "Das schöne Fest, Johannis-Tag" (The feast of John, Midsummer Day), begins with the rhyme scheme *a b a a b b a,* which is then repeated, before rhyming couplets take over for almost all the remaining thirty-six lines. Walther's Prize Song similarly starts with a complex rhyme scheme (*a b b c c a d e d e f g f,* repeated in the second *Stollen* with repetitions of the rhyme), while the *Abgesang,* or concluding stanza, is even more daring, repeating rhymes from both the earlier *Stollen.* "Spring and love" fire Walther to trust to spontaneous inspiration and to improvise a second, substantially different version of his song on the Festival Meadow. Another side of Walther's character emerges in his outburst of anger against the Masters in act 2, scene 2, where the short, sharp, hurried lines, rhyming in pairs, are reminiscent rather of the sort of rhyme that Beckmesser uses. In the exchange between Sachs and the Marker before the third strophe of Sachs's Cobbling Song we even find prose. The flexibility of Wagner's handling of the language can be seen with particular clarity here, in the small variations produced by the insertion of catalectic and hypercatalectic unstressed syllables. The lines vary in length from a simple iamb ("Mein Kind" [My child; SSD VII, 254]) and cretic (in the Quintet "hell und laut" [bright and loud; SSD VII, 256]) to David's extended, almost alexandrinelike line, "Kann mir gar nicht mehr denken, wie der Knieriemen thut" (Now the feel of his leather strap has gone from my mind!; SSD VII, 233). Most of the lines are iambic trimeters or tetrameters, occasionally interrupted by groups of dimeters; but trochees, dactyls, and so on are also found here and there. *Knittelvers,* after all, is typified by the fact that the number of unstressed syllables in any given line is not fixed. A glance at Sachs's monologues will demonstrate the truth of these observations.

Interestingly, the 1845 draft contains scarcely any reference to the "Flieder" and "Wahn" monologues of the definitive text. Only in the final peroration does the passage "Ho, ho! Scheltet mir die Meistersinger nicht!" (Ho ho! Do not speak ill of the mastersingers!) recall the version that is found in the full score of the work. The second prose draft of 1861 is already much closer to the final version.

A further intermediate stage is also available here for the purposes of comparison in Dieter Borchmeyer's ten-volume edition of Wagner's *Poems and Writings* (1983; see especially IV, 214 and 222–223). Borchmeyer quotes excerpts from the original 1862 version, together with the early recension of Walther's Morning Dream (not contained in the drafts) and excerpts from Sachs's monologues. Nineteen lines of the "Wahn" monologue show how the themes have remained familiar but how the order in which they appear has been altered: "The elder it was: Midsummer Eve . . . a glowworm . . . caused the damage . . . the world is aflame in [men's brains] . . . and if folly gives its blessing . . . the conflagration may yet be quenched! / A goblin's folly!—Midsummer Eve!" Wagner evidently found himself in difficulties over the repeated "Midsummer Eve." The closing monologue was longer in the original version of the poem, containing allusions to Walther's arrival and its repercussions, together with unimpressive observations on the dangers that threaten all that is traditional. As is so often true of familiar works of art, one learns to admire the final version even more when one knows something of its earlier stages.

Parsifal

Wagner himself regarded *Parsifal* as the culmination of his life's work: "'And Parzival?' I [Cosima] asked. 'That will be done in my 80th year, I shall perhaps do *Die Sieger* as a play . . . But no more music. With my ten scores I should think I have done enough'" (CT, 27 June 1869). *Parsifal* occupies a central position in Wagner's oeuvre. He first planned to write it as early as 1845, at a time when he was working on *Tannhäuser*. But *Tannhäuser* is not the only work with which it is closely related; it also has links with *Lohengrin, Tristan,* and the *Ring* (in *The Wibelungs* Wagner wrote, "Striving for the Grail now represents the struggle to gain the Nibelung hoard"; SSD II, 151). More generally, the three-act format was clear to Wagner from an early stage, as with all the dramas of his middle and later years. In a letter to Mathilde Wesendonck of 30 May 1859, he complained that he "could not choose to work on such a broad scale as Wolfram was able to do: I have to compress everything into *three* climactic situations of violent intensity, so that the work's profound and ramified content emerges clearly and distinctly." By the summer of 1860 Wagner's ideas on how to elaborate the plan had already taken on a clearer outline: "One day, when everything has matured within me, it will be an unprecedented pleasure to complete this poem. . . . And I should like to be satisfied for once with the poem alone" (letter to Mathilde Wesendonck of early August 1860).

After thirty-two years of contemplating, planning, and sketching the work, Wagner finally set down the verse draft in the space of five weeks in March and April 1877, and scarcely a word of it was altered when he came to set the poem to music. More instructive are the differences between the prose drafts of August 1865 and February 1877. Some of them relate to purely visual aspects of the work, such as the gesture of benediction made by the dead Titurel, a gesture which was not incorporated into the full score. Many familiar phrases are already contained in the 1865 draft: "Mein Sohn Amfortas! Bist du am Amt?" (My son Amfortas! Are you prepared?), and "Das ist Charfreitagszauber, Herr" (It is Good Friday's magic, lord!); others came later. Cosima tells how Wagner welcomed her back from an outing one day with "the revelation of *'Nehmt hin mein Blut'* [Take ye my blood]—R. tells me he wrote it down shortly before my return . . . He has had to alter the words to fit it, he says; this scene of Holy Communion will be the main scene, the core of the whole work; with the 'Prize Song' in *Die Meistersinger,* too, the melody came first, and he had adapted the words to it. He had already told me yesterday that one must beware of having to extend a melody for the sake of the words—now today the chief passage (*'Nehmet hin mein Blut um unsrer Liebe willen, nehmet hin meinen Leib und gedenket mein' ewiglich'*) is there complete, in all its mildness, suffering, simplicity and exaltation" (CT, 11 August 1877). The minor changes that were made to these phrases can be seen at a glance if one turns to the published text and vocal score. A similar exercise is well worth the effort in the case of Gurnemanz's monologue "Du sieh'st, das ist nicht so" (You see, it is not so): only three images remain constant throughout: the Redeemer on the Cross and God's sacrifice, the untrampled flowers in the meadow that day, and the gratitude felt by nature on this day of innocence. The image of the tears of repentance and dew does not appear until the 1877 prose draft, and that of the prayer only in the completed poem, which is of course richer and more poetic than its antecedents. It is interesting, finally, to observe the way in which Wagner developed the idea of "all irrational creatures" and changed its position in the monologue from the beginning to shortly before the end.

On the third day after he had begun working on the final text, Cosima noted in her diary: "R. talks about his verses, he has not yet used a rhyme; the more natural the music, he says, the less appropriate an end rhyme" (CT, 16 March 1877). Indeed, rhyme does not appear until well into the libretto, after which it is used only at specific points such as Gurnemanz's speeches (for example, "Titurel, der fromme Held" [Titurel, our noble lord]) and in the first of the temple scenes. But Klingsor and his Flower Maidens also sing in rhyme, as does Kundry in her seduction scene (note the structure of "Ich sah das Kind" [I saw the child], a particularly striking example of Wagner's handling of rhyme). Parsifal himself uses rhyme only sparingly until "Auch dir bin ich zum Heil gesandt" (For your salvation I was sent) toward the end of the second act. In the third act rhyme really is found to any extent only in the Good Friday Magic scene and in the final speeches of Amfortas and Parsifal. The lines vary considerably in length; some have four or five lifts, but the majority are shorter, some very short indeed: "Nicht doch!" (Not so!) or "Mittag" (Midday). The meter is flexible, and it is often only the position of the words that shows the language to be poetry rather than prose. As in all the works of Wagner's middle and later years, it is the interaction of textual phrase and vocal melody, and the absolute indivisibility of these two elements, which leaves the most marked impression.

However admirably Wagner's texts may serve his musical-dramatic purposes, he showed little real talent as a lyric poet. From time to time he wrote worthy verses in ottava rima, his favorite form, including two eight-line strophes placed at the head of the *Siegfried Idyll* ("Es war dein opfermutig hehrer Wille" [It was thy noble will for sacrifice]). Other examples, including several in *The Brown Book,* are stiff and awkward, and final couplets tend to suffer from false pathos (see, for example, "Am Abgrund steh' ich" [Above the abyss I stand]). A number of Wagner's poems reveal a late-Romantic mixture of irony and artificiality of feeling, while he also experimented with the sonnet and (most depressing of all) with the patriotic hymn. Even in the case of those poems that are connected in some way with his music dramas there is a lack of originality and an absence of the qualities that make the sung texts unique.

"Individuality of expression, bold compression, forcefulness and rhythmic versatility, a remarkable richness in strong and significant words, simplification of sentence construction, an almost unique inventiveness in the language of surging feeling and presentiment, occasionally a quite pure bubbling up of popular colloquialisms and proverbiality": thus Nietzsche summarized Wagner's linguistic achievements in part nine of *Richard Wagner in Bayreuth,* adding, however, that Wagner's "mightiest and most remarkable" gift as a poet was "the ability to mint for every work a language of its own and to bestow upon a new subjectivity also a new body and a new sound." Thomas Mann required fewer words to come to the same conclusion (Mann 1985, p. 190): "It has always seemed to me absurd to question Wagner's poetic gifts."

Translated by Stewart Spencer

CHAPTER 11

Wagner and Schopenhauer

HARTMUT REINHARDT

When, on 28 June 1869, Cosima asked Wagner "whether he thought that much still remained to be discovered in the philosophical field after Schopenhauer," Wagner answered bluntly: "To be described, much; to be discovered, I think not" (CT, 28 June 1869). Philosophy, it would seem, had exhausted its possibilities, had discharged its obligation to decipher the world. It was now the task of art to "represent" philosophical insight as perfected by Schopenhauer, that is, to transform that insight into an aesthetic experience. It goes without saying that here Wagner had music in mind—his own music drama.

Biographical Background

The biographical circumstances surrounding Wagner's encounter with the philosophy of Arthur Schopenhauer can be quickly summarized. In the fall of 1854 the writer Georg Herwegh, who, like Wagner, was living in Zurich as a political refugee, presented him with Schopenhauer's chief work, *The World as Will and Representation*. When it had first appeared, in 1818, it was more or less ignored, but the second, enlarged edition of 1844 gradually reached a wider public. This is not the place to analyze the extent to which the long-delayed but increasingly urgent relevance of Schopenhauer's philosophy was due to the mood of skeptical resignation typical of the later nineteenth century, a mood which derived from the lack of political or historical progress. In any event, this "uncompromising and inhospitable, gloomy philosophy" (Sch I, 25) struck a deep chord in Wagner. In his autobiography, which may be taken as an essentially reliable source on this issue, Wagner mentions that, within a very short time, he repeatedly (four times in fact) studied Schopenhauer's work; and he describes its effect on him as fundamentally decisive. Wagner praises Schopenhauer's stylistic brilliance, "the clearness and manly precision with which the most difficult metaphysical problems were treated from the very beginning." And it is not surprising that he duly emphasizes Schopenhauer's aesthetics, in particular "his noble conception of music." Wagner forges a link between his study of Schopenhauer and his own creative work: the doctrine of the negation of the Will is linked with Wotan's great eruption of resignation in the second act of *Die Walküre;* the "serious mood" is linked with the conception of *Tristan* and also with the original plan to have Parsifal, in his search for the Holy Grail, visit Tristan's deathbed. In the end this plot did not materialize, but the idea was to have weighty ramifications (ML 509–511).

Wagner immediately attempted to convert his circle of friends and followers in Zurich, including Otto and Mathilde Wesendonck, to Schopenhauer's philosophy. But his hopes of persuading the philosopher, who was living in Frankfurt am Main, to come to Zurich bore no fruit: the "coterie of refined sensibilities" in distant Switzerland could not tempt the misanthropic begetter of all that enthusiasm to shake off his reserve. Thus, Wagner had to content himself with sending Schopenhauer the text for the *Ring,* which had appeared in 1853 in a private edition. There was no accompanying letter, but the text did have an inscribed dedication which spoke of Wagner's "reverence and gratitude." Schopenhauer did not reply—a fact which Wagner noted later, not without a measure of resentment (see CT, 29 March 1878, 15 February 1881, 6 December 1882). Schopenhauer perceived the text as a poetic prelude to *The Art-Work of the Future,* which Wagner had propagated in 1849. He wrote critical comments in the margin, such as those which refer to the incestuous love of the Wälsungen and its "affront to morality." Schopenhauer apparently did not question the literary merit of the *Ring;* he made no objection, for example, to the stylizing effect of alliteration. Furthermore, Wagner enthusiasts report that in various conversations the philosopher, who was so well versed in aesthetics, described the language of the tetralogy as totally commensurate with its mythological subject; he even suggested that Wagner "should give up music" as he clearly showed "a greater talent for poetry." Adopting a rather un-Wagnerian position, Schopenhauer held that opera should be confined to two hours at the most (see Sch V, 513), and the Frankfurt performances of *Holländer* and *Tannhäuser* which he attended did nothing to convert him to an admirer of Wagner's music. Throughout his life Schopenhauer remained faithful to his love of Mozart and above all Rossini: it was a favorite pastime of his to play Rossini operas to himself on the flute from arrangements specifically acquired for the purpose. Wagner was later to comment ironically on these tastes of his musical and aesthetic mentor (see CT, 16 January 1869, 8 March 1872).

On the whole, however, Wagner's comments on Schopenhauer bespeak agreement, even enthusiasm. He uses such expressions as "a gift from heaven" (to Franz Liszt, 16[?] December 1854), and between 1858 and 1860, in the letters and diary entries for Mathilde Wesendonck, Wagner refers four times to Schopenhauer as his friend. Within the framework of this brief sketch it is not possible to trace in any systematic way the various Schopenhauer references in the Cosima diaries covering the years 1869–1883: they abound with countless expressions of everlasting gratitude, allusions, and borrowings, with recurrent eulogies and defenses whenever Wagner felt the need to enlighten the ignorant or the critic. He commends and recommends Schopenhauer to one and all. Ignorance of his philosophy—Darwin being an example (see CT, 1 July 1872)—is lamented, and, as in the case of the renegade Nietzsche of *The Gay Science* (1882), its aftereffects and influences are asserted (see CT, 3 February 1883). Schopenhauer is the center of all things, even in dreams (see CT, 8 July 1880, 4 February 1883). The most peripheral areas are not exempt; one thinks of the nonsense about beards (see CT, 21 May 1880) or the business letters which Wagner found "quite splendid" (CT, 23 March 1878). As Cosima's detailed accounts illustrate exhaustively, not to say exhaustingly, Schopenhauer's philosophy was read again and again, endlessly rehearsed. Increasingly Wagner appropriated the categories and modes which marked the thinking of the philosopher. He experimented with Schopenhauer's compulsive tracing of the mechanisms of the Will, which are at work in all living matter, whether it be in nature or in the infant, in Frederick the Great (CT, 23 October 1871) or in Wagner's own figure of Siegfried (CT, 12 March 1872). Schopenhauer stands as the supreme legislator, whom Wagner would wish to be the mentor not only for his own son (CT, 20 March 1878) but for the totality of German culture. Above all it is in the sphere of the aesthetics of music that the "guiding hand of the philosopher" (SSD IX, 87) is utterly decisive.

Musical Aesthetics

As is generally known, Schopenhauer ascribes to music a unique role. Music differs from "all other forms of art in that it does not depict phenomena . . . , but is the direct expression of the Will itself and thus pits the metaphysical against the physical things of this world, the thing-in-itself against all phenomena" (Sch I, 366). In respect of the ultimate reality of the metaphysical Will, Schopenhauer ranked the "wonderful art of notes" (Sch I, 359) on a par with the World itself. Schopenhauer celebrates music in a subjectively colored language of evocative power unparalleled in previous aesthetic philosophy. It is admittedly a power bought at the price of an overt trait of irrational speculation (see Sch I, 358f.) whose general validity must remain open to question. It is certainly understandable that Wagner the musician should have been so profoundly moved by this panegyric, so rich in striking examples, detailed observations, and some rather strained analogies between the elements of music and the various levels of the phenomenal world (see Sch I, 360ff.; II, 573ff.). Wagner's enthusiasm helped to smooth over some points of disagreement, such as the fact that Schopenhauer, in defining music as the voice of the innermost being of the World, necessarily had to deny music's "common ground with poetry" (Sch I, 366f.; II, 575f.). Wagner, the theoretician of music drama (even if he did not accept this term), the pedagogue of *Die Meistersinger,* differed from his aesthetic mentor in that he conceived of a genuine fusion of "note and word" (SSD VII, 220). Yet he could invoke Schopenhauer's deliberations in order to justify his own method: one thinks, for example, of the point where Schopenhauer states that music can complement "any scene, action, event, or setting" as "the most accurate and distinct commentary on it" (Sch I, 366). Such a statement could be applied to the *Ring*.

By comparison with the Zurich program notes, Wagner's later treatises show a number of corrections, or at any rate changes of emphasis, which can all be traced back to Schopenhauer's musical aesthetics. This is most overtly the case in the Beethoven essay of 1870, which—in an entirely Schopenhauerian fashion—distinguishes between the world of phenomena and the metaphysical realm of the Will. The essay posits a "world of sound" alongside a "world of light" (SSD IX, 69) in analogy to the dream, again along the lines of Schopenhauer, and constantly concerns itself with the "prophetic articulation of the innermost tonal world" (SSD IX, 83). These deliberations are shot through with detailed analyses of Beethoven and eventually—and unfortunately—lapse into nationalistic drumbeating for the "German weapons" that were so victorious in those days. As regards musical aesthetics, the central thesis of this essay, with its many other ambitions, emerges in the conclusion that music as the "comprehensive idea of the world" by definition contains the drama within itself (SSD IX, 105). Here Wagner argues in terms of Schopenhauer: the philosopher rejected any subordination of music to the word as "misconception" and "perversity" (Sch I, 365). In this respect the essay is an attempt to modify such conceptions as are inherently present in *Opera and Drama* (SSD III, 231). Even if one agrees with Carl Dahlhaus that Wagner's programmatic main work does not primarily aim to modify the function of music for the sake of poetry, but rather to modify the functions of both in the service of the drama (qua music drama), there can be no doubt that in the wake of his Schopenhauer studies, Wagner expressly distanced himself from his earlier position and committed himself unambiguously to the notion that drama derives from music (see CT, 11 February 1872).

The Influence of Schopenhauer on Wagner's Music Dramas

Tristan und Isolde

If one wishes to trace Schopenhauer's influences in Wagner's musical-dramatic work, one thinks above all of *Tristan,* and not only for chronological reasons. The work was conceived in outline as early as 1854, the text was written by 1857, and the music was composed by 1859. The primary Schopenhauer source for this work is the treatise titled *Metaphysics of Sexual Love* (see Sch II, 678ff.). For Schopenhauer, the Will inherent in all being is metaphysical. It does not manifest itself as a phenomenon, does not enter the world of "representation." Wagner's *Tristan* is, in the words of Nietzsche, an "opus metaphysicum": it is metaphysical precisely insofar as it grants the Will an overwhelming musical-dramatic presence. The preconscious promptings of the Will express themselves above all in the sexual drive, whose power and intimation of bliss Schopenhauer never tires of delineating in inspired phrases. In *Tristan* Wagner takes Schopenhauer at his word: the lovers are driven to the brink; here the most loyal of men becomes a traitor through love (Sch II, 682); here all social obligations of honor and duty are canceled (Sch II, 707). It must be noted, however, that *Tristan* is not unadulterated Schopenhauer: in his preoccupations with *Tristan,* Wagner conceives of a redemptive path to salvation which the philosopher had not considered. In his Venetian diary for Mathilde Wesendonck, Wagner speaks of the salvation granted by the fullest consummation of the aroused sexual desire (1 December 1858). That same year Wagner wrote a letter along similar lines to Schopenhauer but prudently refrained from posting it. One can all too easily imagine how the philosopher would have responded to this theory whereby the Will is assuaged "through love." For the philosopher there is only one path leading to the redemption of the world, and that is the moral-ascetic negation of the Will (Sch I, 494). But there can be no doubt that Wagner's "night piece" in praise of love, conceived in the spirit of Schopenhauer's philosophy, has attained the status of a supreme work of art precisely because it reinterprets Schopenhauer in a dilettante yet bold fashion. The epoch-making power of *Tristan* is not even disputed by those who are most critical of Wagner.

Since Thomas Mann's Wagner essay of 1933 it has become customary to trace the worship of night in *Tristan* back to Romantic sources, particularly to Novalis, and thus to separate this strand from the influence of Schopenhauer. But even so, one should not overlook one particular link in the chain. In his Beethoven essay, Wagner follows the lead of Schopenhauer in that he perceives the worlds of "representation" and "Will," of the "phenomenon" and the "thing-in-itself," in terms of the opposition between day and night (SSD IX, 68). And this is exactly the case in *Tristan*. Love leads into the uncharted and in this sense night-bound realm of the Will. Those who have experienced that realm bear the marks as stigmata and perceive the world of day as illusion, the demands of friendship and marital loyalty as "the chimeras of day" (SSD VII, 52). Night becomes the primal, motherly realm prior to all individuation and its inherent delusions. The lovers know themselves to be "worshippers of night" (SSD VII, 43); through them flows the "deity of the world's eternal becoming" (SSD VII, 34). They are alienated from the realm of day; they have seen through its "deceiving folly" (SSD VII, 45), and they are impervious to its norms and struggles. Tristan does not defend himself against the accusing, questioning King Marke, but simply looks "pityingly" up at him, and then shows Isolde the only remaining path into the "wondrous realm of night"—the path of death (SSD VII, 55f.). All this suggests the assertion of the undifferentiated realm of the Will in Schopenhauer's sense; yet, in contradistinction to Schopenhauer, the "sweetest folly of the world" remains immune to all disillusioning questions. In the relevant chapter in Schopenhauer, "folly" *(Wahn)* is a key term; it signifies that the individual is permanently deceived by the Will of the species, which in its urge to exist exploits the love instinct toward its own ends (Sch II, 688ff.). For the philosopher, all the loving of men and women is in the service of a "crude realism" which has only scorn for the emotional aspirations of "enamoured souls" (Sch II, 684). By sharpest contrast, Wagner's *Tristan* never departs from its glorification of love. The bitter curses hurled at the love potion are not directed at love itself, as has been assumed. Rather, the curse, in its colossal musical climax, is directed at the torment of living in the absence of the beloved. Above all, Isolde's love-death is the very opposite of the negation of the Will: it affirms, indeed transfigures, the Will-driven creature entering into the ultimate unity with the other, the beloved, in death. On the basis of Schopenhauer's metaphysics Wagner builds a work of art which, in its tumultuous and ecstatic affirmation of love unto death, is at one and the same time Romantic and decadent.

Die Meistersinger von Nürnberg
The influence of Schopenhauer can also be easily detected in *Die Meistersinger* (text 1862, music 1862–1867). Hans Sachs's "*Wahn*" monologue captures, after all, the very essence of a world driven by blind urge, that vision which the philosopher rehearses time and again in pessimistically somber phrases. In the first prose draft of 1845, Wagner planned to have Hans Sachs reflect on the theme of the "death . . . of the beautiful art of poetry" (SSD XI, 351), such as we find in Gervinus. In the second prose sketch, however, Hans Sachs, in the wake of the brawl at night, searches "in the chronicle of the world for similar wild outbursts" which "are to tell him of the nature of folly" (SSD XI, 366). This is the concept which the final text develops. In Schopenhauer's view there is no end to "the examples of indescribable misery . . . which we find in common human experience and history, wherever we turn, whatever aspect we study" (Sch I, 443). Wagner's Hans Sachs sees "wherever I look" the same "folly" beneath the self-torment of man (SSD VII, 233f.). For Schopenhauer "the Will to life unceasingly consumes itself, feeds in various guises on itself" (Sch I, 218); everywhere there must inevitably arise "struggle, . . . jostling crowds, shortages, misery and fear, crying and howling" (Sch II, 458). All this and much like it is taken up by Hans Sachs, albeit it in meditatively muted form: a good deal is literally borrowed or only slightly modified. The "town and world chronicle" which Hans Sachs consults in his researches is to all intents and purposes Schopenhauer's *World as Will and Representation,* and the conclusion which Hans Sachs reaches is again entirely Schopenhauerian: whether a "goblin," a "glow worm," or even the "lilac" with its wonderful scent "has done the damage" (SSD VII, 234f.), in the final analysis it is all a matter of that same blind Will and that causality to which Schopenhauer is firmly committed (Sch I, 205f.).

Hans Sachs's monologue, so steeped in Schopenhauerian thought, lends Wagner's brightly festive comedy a fundamentally somber mood which differs very much from that of the first sketch. The melancholy reverberates even in the jubilance of the festival ground. The brawl at night—not exactly an example of bourgeois peacefulness—is pondered on; the subsequent conversation about art with Stolzing, that ardent enthusiast of song and love, concerns itself with "the truest folly of men," which, again along the lines of Schopenhauer, is sought "in the dream" (SSD VII, 235). Hans Sachs attempts to channel Stolzing's youthful "fire of poetry and love" into the guiding structure of the "master rules," which are explicated by reference to bourgeois family images. Following Egon Voss, we may perceive this doctrine as a kind of domestication of the Will (Voss 1981, p. 15), which, according to those recurrent formulations in Schopenhauer's work, is especially inclined to flare up in the sexual drive. In other words, Hans Sachs does not content himself with the resigned insight into the foolish essence of the Will-driven world (the original text of the Folly monologue spoke of the "world's conflagration"), but the solid craftsman-poet takes it upon himself scrupulously to channel the folly in order not necessarily to create a "work of benediction" (King Ludwig to Wagner, 30 November 1866), but at least to achieve "a more noble work" (SSD VII, 235). Hans Sachs, who, despite all disillusion, commits himself to the principle of hope, succeeds here—albeit at the price of renunciation—in ordering things for the best, in art as well as in life.

Der Ring des Nibelungen

Wagner's main work, the *Ring,* was conceived and poetically executed independent of Schopenhauer, in contrast to the two great works which "interrupted" its genesis. Nietzsche's account of the *Ring* may be suggestive and fruitful, but it is quite incorrect insofar as it envisages Wagner sailing happily with Siegfried and Brünnhilde from the old to the new world, until the ship founders on a reef—the reef of Schopenhauer's philosophy, which caused the change from a revolutionary argument into a pessimistic one (see Nietzsche 1967, p. 164). Siegfried's death was in fact the initial concept for the *Ring;* the link with *Götterdämmerung* had long been determined. Furthermore, the text of the tetralogy was already finished and printed before Wagner became acquainted with Schopenhauer's philosophy. Only one subsequently written strophe of Brünnhilde's final monologue ("I lead no longer to Valhalla's citadel") is clearly influenced by Schopenhauer's thought, specifically the negation of the Will. But, according to Wagner's notes, he did not set this strophe to music "because its meaning was already articulated in the musical language of the drama" (SSD VI, 256). The decision not to write a Schopenhauerian ending is linked with a typical Schopenhauerian reference to the expressive potential, the ability of music itself to comment on the action. Could one then argue in terms of semantic correspondences and suggest that Wagner's compositional insistence on certain motifs which from the second act of *Die Walküre* onward become more prominent—motifs such as those of anger, a curse, renunciation, or the farewell greeting—was stimulated by Schopenhauer? Could this also possibly apply to the motif of redemption through love as sung by Sieglinde in the third act of *Walküre,* a motif which Wagner called more modestly a "theme of praise for Brünnhilde" (CT, 23

July 1872) and which in the concluding music of *Götterdämmerung* is sounded once more so triumphantly and significantly? To ask this question is to admit its unanswerability. Whatever parallels between Wagner's main work and his philosophical source may seem to offer, it must remain a matter of retrospective discovery. Thus, to a certain extent, Wotan may be understood as representative of the Will, omnipresent in all its emanations from Brünnhilde to Hagen and then indelibly marked by the contradictions in his own design of the world, ready to renounce ("I renounce my work"), and finally (the Valhalla theme in the concluding music) ready to will his own destruction. Wagner himself explicitly linked his Wotan figure with the metaphysical agency of the Will in Schopenhauer (see CT, 29 March 1878). In this sense we may conjecture on the basis of the *Ring* that the former revolutionary in the footsteps of Proudhon, Bakunin, and Feuerbach was predisposed to become a follower of Schopenhauer. But it is unacceptable to trace the gigantic work or any of its so-called contradictions back to Schopenhauer. It would appear, however, that some legends are not so easily disposed of.

Parsifal

By contrast, *Parsifal,* Wagner's sacramentally stylized "farewell to the world," stands clearly under the aegis of Schopenhauer. The ecstasy of love may no longer be experienced tumultuously, but must serve instead as a transitional stage on the road to that fundamentally decisive insight which brings about the transcendence of the Will. The "pure fool" learns through Kundry's kiss to "see through the world." No sooner has the enticement of sex filled his heart with "terrible longing" than he awakens to the memory of Amfortas and that compassionate question which he has failed to ask (SSD X, 358ff.). In the fate of the Grail King we can perceive a concentrated summary of the Will's history, which, according to Schopenhauer, is marked by self-mutilation. Sex creates the life wound "which will never heal" (SSD X, 332) and which causes the sufferer to cry out in despair: "No—no more!" (SSD X, 374). Parsifal's compassion expresses itself in the recurrence of Amfortas' temptation, as an act of suffering with the king; and he is able to free himself from the threat and thereby comes to see himself as the chosen agent who (although one has to be cautious here) completes the task of redemption. The essay *Religion and Art* of 1880 views all this in the context of religious or quasi-religious aspirations: the "sacred drama" does not by any means intend to offer the theatrical exploitation of Christian-Catholic liturgy; rather, within the historical constellation of a religious crisis (which has assumed secular proportions), the "sacred drama" aims to "save" (SSD X, 211) the "essence" of Christian religion through and for art. That this "essence" of *Parsifal* is not to be identified as a racist–cum–anti-Semitic blood myth, as some interpretations critical of Wagner claim, must surely emerge from any dispassionate examination of the facts—that is, of the text. Wagner's work is organized through and through around the concept of compassion, and this concept derives directly from Schopenhauer.

Already at the time of *Tristan*, Wagner had sketched the outlines of the *Parsifal* project; as early as 1858 (diary for Mathilde Wesendonck, 1 October) he had developed on his own initiative such Schopenhauerian concepts as resignation and compassion and discovered in man "the disposition to redeem the world through pity." Born under these auspices, *Parsifal*, with its protracted inception, becomes an anti-*Tristan*. In a totally Schopenhauerian vein (see, for example, Sch I, 517), it pleads for chastity and asceticism as moral responses to the turmoil of the world, which is now seen as inherently burdened with guilt. Thus, the work consistently denounces Eros as "sin" which binds man to the sufferings of the Will itself. Amfortas is invested with the—now negatively conceived—role of Tristan, and Parsifal has to renounce love's longing, to put aside the "night of world's folly" (SSD X, 361) in order to attain redemption. In this sense, Wagner's last work follows Schopenhauer's moral tenets, which postulate the overcoming of the Will and the capacity of compassion: Eros no longer reigns; instead it is *agape* which opens up the path to salvation. It is nothing less than remarkable that Wagner should thank Schopenhauer, the atheistic critic of religion, for having "revealed Christianity to me" (CT, 19 February 1879). For this reason there is an almost theatrical symbolism to an event which occurred on 24 February 1880: Wagner speaks of "sainthood and withdrawal from life," in Schopenhauer's sense, and then, "in connection with that," he plays the prelude to *Parsifal* on the piano (CT, 24 February 1880). In June 1875, before the inception of the work was even under way, Wagner had made the decisive declaration: "Schopenhauerian philosophy and *Parcival* as the crowning achievement" (CT, 10 June 1875).

Even a short summary of Richard Wagner's reception of Schopenhauer shows that, although the topic may have worn thin—Wieland Wagner typically spoke of "the old Schopenhauer story"—Wagner scholarship cannot dispense with it. Of course, Wagner's work cannot be exhausted in terms of Schopenhauer's philosophical tenets; but without this link a number of crucial intentions and connections are simply incomprehensible. Wagner claimed that it was not without a struggle that he surrendered to "that difficult admission" which Schopenhauer forced on him (CT, 1 November 1870). But Cosima's diaries testify beyond any doubt to the reality of this "surrender," to the fact that the composer after 1854 increasingly understood both himself and his creative work in Schopenhauerian terms. Although Wagner's participation in the Hegelian left of 1849 has been judged by Hans Mayer as little more than a case of following the crowd, Wagner's relationship to Schopenhauer is considerably more substantial. It was surely a key experience, coming late in his life, which Thomas Mann has described so eloquently. In his *Genealogy of Morals,* Nietzsche, with his sharp eye for psychological issues, interprets this relationship in terms of a consciously cultivated myth of the artist whereby the metaphysical dignity of music as posited by Schopenhauer was grist for Wagner's mill. It is not possible to discuss here the extent to which Nietzsche's critical view was justified or not. But his argument may serve to suggest that Schopenhauer became such a mentor for Wagner precisely because his philosophy revealed ways in which political and personal disappointments could be not only endured but transformed, with overwhelming musical power, into "redemptions." The last word should go to Cosima Wagner. On 29 February 1872 she writes: "Reading the chapter yesterday in which Schopenhauer describes the nature of genius, I felt he had written it about R[ichard]."

Translated by Erika and Martin Swales

CHAPTER 12

The Music

CARL DAHLHAUS

Composition and Musical Dramaturgy

Although the term *dramaturgy* has many meanings, a digression on the history of the concept would be superfluous and pedantic. It will probably prove neither unusual nor disconcerting if musical dramaturgy is merely taken to signify the poetics of an operatic composer, whereby the word *poetics,* in the sober, Aristotelian sense of *poiesis,* without the speculative Romantic connotations, means nothing but the theory of how works are made.

The fact that Wagner described music *(Opera and Drama)* as a means to an end in drama, and drama *(On the Term "Musikdrama")* as a "musical deed made visible," causes the connection between music and drama, the central problem of musical dramaturgy, to become strangely opaque. The idea that, in musical drama, the music is supposed to be a function of the drama and the drama a function of the music at one and the same time is not immediately apparent. The attempt to resolve the paradox by means of the hypothesis that Wagner changed his aesthetic and dramaturgical convictions after 1854 under the influence of Schopenhauer's philosophy of music (see Chapter 11) fails, at least initially, on account of the fact that the writings of the 1870s veer between placing the emphasis on the metaphysical essence of music and placing it on the primacy of the singer-actor in the theater—the real human being playing his part on the stage.

As always, the most intractable difficulties are embedded in the fundamental concepts: the terms *music* and *drama.* Their frequent and casual use conceals the fact that we rarely know exactly what they mean. At first glance it seems that Wagner's concept of drama cannot be misunderstood. Again and again, in *Opera and Drama* before he was influenced by Schopenhauer, and subsequently in his later writings on the theater, he emphasizes that music and language are nothing more than the means to the end of imparting the action, the scenic-mimetic events, to the emotional understanding of the audience.

The emphasis is placed on the palpable, and thus on what the emotions can grasp.

Yet, at the same time, Wagner tended increasingly, albeit not without some vacillation, to view as decisive the inner, musically expressed action instead of the outer, scenically visible one. Music, according to Schopenhauer, is essential form, and stage action, which thus no longer coincides with the essence of the drama, merely phenomenal form. (The fact that it was *Tristan*, which has the least action of all Wagner's works for the stage, that he simply termed "action," meaning "drama," can only signify that the music has as it were usurped the concept of drama in place of the stage events.) Yet a certain kind of dramaturgy is always a way of expressing an anthropological attitude. (It is enough to compare the dramaturgy of Wagner and of Bertolt Brecht in order to realize that the sharp divergence has its roots in the contrast between Wagner's idea of the common human element and Brecht's ideas about social character.) The fact that Wagner exchanged the anthropology of Ludwig Feuerbach for that of Arthur Schopenhauer after 1854 (albeit never totally) could not fail to influence his musical dramaturgy. His philosophical change of heart was also not without influence on the poetics of musical drama. The real, physically present human being as the ultimately decisive authority gave way to the idea of redemption from blind instincts and urges through aesthetic contemplation. The love of Siegfried and Brünnhilde was no longer liberating but, as Wagner stated in a letter of 23 August 1856 to August Röckel, "completely devastating." The emphasis of the artwork of the future began to change from the notion of a "direct appeal to the senses" to that of an "elevation" above the distress of the present moment which can be brought about by aesthetic means. The result was that in the musical drama the role of Wagner's music, which Nietzsche praised as "opus metaphysicum" and in the *Fragment on Music and Language* (1871) appropriately called "absolute tonal art," became more and more prominent.

Strictly speaking, aesthetic theory does not have the final word in Wagner. Rather, he left open the central problem (it is impossible to put it any other way) of the relationship of music and drama. In other words, he left it open for changing solutions in the various music dramas, which do not constitute a fixed type. Without doubt Wagner remained throughout his life an "inspired ham actor," and Nietzsche maliciously denounced him on these grounds (wrongly, for it is absurd to denounce the theater for being the theater). Yet it is undeniable that the path he took in theory and in practice gradually led to the vicinity of the invisible theater, which he once postulated in a conversation with Cosima in a mood of extreme disgust with the realities of the stage (CT, 23 September 1878).

But Wagner's historical influence cannot be separated from the musical dramaturgy on which he based his works, and the contradiction returns once more in the history of their reception. The statement from the essay *On the Application of Music to the Drama* to the effect that extreme compositional risks can be justified only by the dramatic function they perform was, as it were, given the lie by the development of music after Wagner, which, at least in Germany, and to some extent in France, evolved in Wagner's shadow. In the late nineteenth and early twentieth centuries the chromaticism of *Tristan,* the technique of motivic combination in *Götterdämmerung,* and the variation technique of *Parsifal* became the basic assumptions not only of dramatic music and program music but also of absolute music.

If, however, we admit that in the case of Wagner himself—and not only in the works he influenced—the music to a certain extent, though never totally, emancipated itself from the motivation through an external action and, as inner action, as a likeness of the essence of the world, became the real substance of the drama, then we are confronted by a paradox. That is, in the same process of development in which Wagner took increasingly extreme compositional risks, the justification from without, which he still expressly demanded as late as 1879 in the essay *On the Application of Music to the Drama,* became weaker and weaker. To put it another way, the further forward the music ventured, the more it had to attain artistic consistency using only its own means, without relying on outside support.

When we try to make sense of the fact that in the late nineteenth century it was possible to transfer Wagner's compositional discoveries from musical drama to absolute music, then, in addition to the advanced details, the shocking chord, or the striking combination of motifs, we must also take note of the decisive role played by formal integration, which gives such details their aesthetic right to exist in the first place. The problem can be demonstrated with reference to the "art of transition," which Wagner, in a letter to Mathilde Wesendonck (29 October 1859), praised as being his "most subtle art." When, in the first orchestral interlude in *Das Rheingold,* the Ring motif, by means of an extremely subtle combination of melodic, harmonic, and instrumentational features, merges into the Valhalla motif, the listener is naturally supposed to read from the musical event its dramatic significance: the idea that one and the same fateful striving for power binds the opposing spheres of the light elves *(Lichtalben)* and the black elves *(Schwarzalben).* But if we take our bearings from Schopenhauer's philosophy of music, then the dramatic meaning does not form the substance of the music. The reverse is the case: the music forms the substance of the dramatic meaning. As an image of the will, of the blind urge, it lifts the listener, through perception, far above an entanglement in the affairs of the world by being an image—in other words, by keeping its distance.

If, in order to mediate between the dramaturgical and the metaphysical interpretation, we conceive of musical listening as a process not only in a temporal but also in an aesthetic sense, then the dramatic significance of the motivic transformation in the first interlude in *Das Rheingold* does indeed mark the inception of the emotional understanding at which Wagner was aiming, if not the goal. To put it metaphorically: the action on the stage has the first but not the final word. According to Schopenhauer, what the music says transcends what can be expressed by words or actions. Thus, an appropriate aesthetic perception does not consist in dwelling exclusively on either the dramaturgical or the musical factor, but rather in understanding the path from one to the other as the intrinsic truth to be comprehended. But if the aesthetic substance of the Wagnerian music drama—and that means the substance constituted in the awareness of the listener and spectator—is in itself "processive," then the historical fact that absolute musical conclusions (which finally led to the end of the nineteenth century in the history of music) were drawn from Wagner's compositional techniques, contrary to his declared intentions, is less surprising than it at first seems. History proves to be the image and reflection of what was prefigured in Wagner's work. In the final analysis the most important thing from the historical point of view was not the barrier that Wagner erected in the essay *On the Application of Music to the Drama* but what he attempted, in vain, to hold back.

Romantic Harmony?

The concept of Romantic harmony, which was originated by Ernst Kurth in his book *Romantic Harmony and Its Crisis in Wagner's "Tristan"* (Kurth 1920), is the expression of a view of music theory and music history that takes its bearings from Wagner. But it does insufficient justice to Wagner himself and to the overall development of music in the nineteenth century, something that cannot be reduced to a single formula.

The phenomenon that Kurth took as his starting point, and whose profound significance no one denies, was what is termed alteration: the chromatic inflection of a part of a chord by raising or lowering it a semitone. (Through augmentation the fifth c-e-g becomes c-e-g♯; through diminution, c-e-g♭.) Altered notes belong to the category of leading notes that strive toward a goal (the augmented g sharp to a; the diminished g flat, conversely, to f). Thus it was possible for Kurth to relate effortlessly and compellingly the technique of altered chords, in which he thought he perceived the most striking feature of Wagnerian harmony, to the fundamental idea of his theory of harmony: the premise that "leading-note energy" is the prime moving force of tonal harmony. The same leading-note energy that in the simple cadence conveys and clarifies the motion from the tonic to the subdominant and, by analogy, from the dominant back to the tonic (e-f in C major = tonic-subdominant; b-c in C major = dominant-tonic) proves to be the impulse spurring on relentless progress in nineteenth-century Romantic harmony, which reached a crisis in Wagner's *Tristan*. Finally, after 1900, the growing complexity of harmony caused by a plethora of alterations led to the decline of tonality and the transition to atonality. (The atonal whole-tone scale [g-a-b-c♯'-e♭'-f'-g'] is a result of the markedly tonal dominant-ninth chord which emphasizes the dominant tendency with double—that is, upward and downward—altered fifths [in C major: g-b-d♭'-d♯'-f'-a'] as soon as, contrary to a prohibition of traditional voice-leading theory, the ninth is transposed to the lower octave.) According to Kurth, the origin of tonal harmony, the cadence, prefigures its end, atonality, because one and the same principle, leading-note energy, proves to be both its foundation and its destructive force.

Kurth's idea was ingenious inasmuch as it provided a continuous mediation between theory and history, between a unified explanatory principle and a compelling process of development. Its merits—and to scorn these would be sheer arrogance on the part of a younger man who is nothing but a dwarf on a giant's shoulders—must be measured against its drawbacks, the fact that the self-contained theoretical and historical concept severely distorts nineteenth-century musical reality.

In the first place, it is doubtful whether a modern historian ought to share the nineteenth-century prejudice that musical progress manifests itself primarily in the degree of harmonic complexity, and use this as the basis for the writing of history. The complexity of thematic and motivic working in Brahms, which in the composer's lifetime was disparaged by the supporters of the so-called progressive party as being conservative pedantry, seems in retrospect to be an essential premise of twentieth-century New Music. It was a development that ran parallel to Wagnerian harmony, not in opposition to it, and thus in 1933 Arnold Schoenberg could even write an essay titled *Brahms the Progressive*.

Second, the increased use of altered chords was not the only tendency in nineteenth-century harmony which might be said to have prepared for or anticipated aspects of the New Music. Parallel chromatic sixth chords (Chopin) no longer fit into the system of functional harmony; nor does the symmetrical division of the octave (Liszt) into two tritones, three major thirds, or four minor thirds, a technique that at times aspires to the play of pure sound. But above all there were the modal progressions (Mussorgsky), passages that alluded to sixteenth-century harmony, even if this was at times misunderstood or consciously redefined. These constituted a phenomenon in which an archaizing tendency appeared interwoven with a rudimentary anticipation of twentieth-century characteristics (Stravinsky, Bartók).

Third, Wagner's injunction that his harmony should not be analyzed without reference to the instrumentation ought to be taken more seriously than it normally is under the assumptions of a harmonic theory that tends toward schematic abstraction rather than toward the concrete example. The enigmatic harmony of the Tarnhelm motif in the *Ring,* which resists attempts to explain it in functional terms (two remotely related chords, G-sharp minor and E minor, are placed together; in *Götterdämmerung* with an f underpinning G-sharp minor), can hardly be imagined without the orchestral color imparted to it by the muted brass.

Fourth, we can complement descriptions of Wagnerian harmony which proceed from its historical foundations with analyses that try to do justice to developments in the music of the late nineteenth and twentieth centuries. In musical modernism the principle of linking semitones without tonal implications resulted from a leading-note chromaticism with a dominant or subdominant character. "Complementary" harmony—the technique of complementing the notes of one chord with those of another—was a subsidiary result of the chromaticism in *Tristan*. In Schoenberg it became an independent principle in its own right. The virtually unending extension of the *Tristan* chord (f-b-d♯'-g♯'), delaying the dissonance resolution, that is, to the point where it becomes irrelevant, prefigures the possibility of construing single striking (dissonant) chords as harmonic motifs. It was a possibility which, by a process of generalization, became a basic principle of twelve-tone technique in the twentieth century. That it would be unhistorical to project the later significance of a phenomenon onto Wagnerian harmony is self-evident. Yet we should not ignore the fact that tracing something to a historically earlier event, the usual historical method, threatens to distort a set of facts in the other direction. Only the attempt to strike a balance between prior and subsequent history offers a chance to reconstruct, for modern consciousness, the past as the present which it once was.

Fifth, the concept of Romantic harmony as devised by Kurth is problematic, for the hypothesis that the increased complexity of chord structures in Wagner forms the obverse of an ever-closer integration in tonal cohesion brought about by the dominant or subdominant function of the altered chords—that is, that growing diversity leads to an intensified unity held in a classical balance—is at odds in terms of the history of ideas with the fact that it was the categories of the characteristic, the interesting, the striking, and the shocking that Friedrich Schlegel declared around 1800 to be Romantic. "Characteristic" harmonies (the Samiel motif in Weber's *Freischütz* or the Tarnhelm motif in the *Ring*) cannot be analyzed meaningfully unless we take into account the instrumentation, as we have seen (in the case of the Samiel motif it is indeed the primary factor). The shocking and unpredictable (such as the harmony in the development section of the first movement of Berlioz's *Symphonie fantastique*) abandons tonal coherence altogether. In other words, the idea of a stable, unendangered balance between harmonic complexity and integration is more classical than Romantic in origin (if we adopt Schlegel's definition). In addition, the degree to which the characteristic, interesting, and striking harmonic details in Wagner are truly integrated tonally has almost always been exaggerated. That in theory we can relate almost every chord to every tonal center says little or nothing about musical reality, that is, compositional practice and reception that retraces compositional intentions. (From an epistemological viewpoint the universality of a theory, which no phenomenon is capable of evading, is more of a drawback than an advantage, for as soon as a principle embraces everything, it no longer explains anything. The possibility of interpreting the twelve-tone chord as a "quadrisonance," as the sum of four triads, does not signify a triumph of von Oettingen's dual harmonic system but rather its downfall.)

Music Drama and Musical Form

It is hardly an exaggeration to claim that the problem of musical form in Wagner remains essentially unsolved, although there has been no lack of attempts to clarify the aesthetic assumptions of a meaningful formal analysis. It has become self-evident that the objection, raised by some of Wagner's contemporaries, that his music was amorphous was just as absurd and trivial as the apologetic reply that the musical form did not pose a problem because the law of the linking and contrasting of leitmotifs lay in the scenic events and the meaning conveyed by the words. The charge of formlessness presupposes a constricted concept of form stemming from the didactically based formal theory of the nineteenth century, whose narrow-mindedness transpires from the scheme of letters that forms its substance. The idea that evades the formal problem—namely, that it is enough to explain the connection and the alternation of the leitmotifs in scenic and linguistic terms, from without, as it were—ignores the aesthetic fact that music which sustains the metaphysical claim to express the innermost essence of the world must be consistent in itself. Obviously the essential form, the music, cannot be structurally dependent on the phenomenal form, the staged events and the language. That Wagner adopted Schopenhauer's metaphysics, which was originally a philosophy of absolute music, forced him, not altogether against his will, to engage in more rigorous musical formal thinking.

From 1924 on, Alfred Lorenz, in a number of books devoted to the "secret of form" in Wagner's works (Lorenz I–IV), attempted to counter the charge that Wagner's music was amorphous by dividing the music dramas into sections whose delimiting criterion was tonal unity, and second, by discovering or construing within the sections an arrangement of motifs according to a scheme such as ABA or AAB, which came up to the standards of the textbook idea of musical form. With regard to methodology the procedure seems plausible, for to a certain extent the tonal assumption represents a control of the formal one, and vice versa. That the tonal delimitation makes sense and is not irrelevant must become apparent in the internal formal consistency of the passages thus delimited. But objectively, Lorenz's analyses suffer from faults that are as fundamental as they are impossible to eradicate. First, the sections, whose length varies from the extremes of 14 to 840 bars, are not formal units from which the listener can take his bearings. The perception of musical form presupposes a prior idea of the sizes to be expected, and this is not infinitely variable. Second, the premise that tonal coherence can be ensured only by a reprise of the beginning at the end no longer applies to the stage of compositional development represented by Wagner. Mere concatenation (B is directly related to A, and C to B, but C to A exclusively through B) also produces tonal cohesion; and "wandering tonality," as Schoenberg called it, was rightly subsumed by him under the concept of tonal coherence. Third, the schemes of formal theory such as ABA, AAB, and

ABABA, which Lorenz took for granted as if they were beyond doubt, are fundamentally inappropriate to Wagner's formal thinking, which was based not on the principle of change but on that of development (*On Franz Liszt's Symphonic Poems,* 1857). And fourth, in formal aesthetics the relationship between A and B or B and C does not express the crucial difference between contrast and unrelated dissimilarity.

In the essay *On the Application of Music to the Drama* (1879) Wagner referred to the model of the unity of the symphonic movement in order to explain and justify the musical form of his dramas. "However, to be an artwork as music, the new form of dramatic music must have the unity of the symphonic movement; and this it attains by spreading itself over the whole drama, in the most intimate cohesion therewith, not merely over single smaller, arbitrarily selected parts. This unity consists in a web of basic themes pervading all the drama, themes which contrast, complete, re-shape, divorce and intertwine with one another as in a symphonic movement; only that here the needs of the dramatic action dictate the laws of parting and combining, which were there originally borrowed from the motions of the dance" (SSD X, 185). That Wagner characterized the structure of the orchestral melody in the music drama as a web and not, as Lorenz does, as tonal architecture should be taken seriously. One of the aesthetic implications of the traditional theory of form is the architectural metaphor that arose around 1800 and quickly advanced to become a topos. It proves inadequate in the case of the music dramas. The real difficulty, however, lies in the seeming contradiction that on the one hand Wagner speaks of a form that is to constitute an artwork as music—in other words, which lays claim to aesthetic autonomy in the sense of Schopenhauer's philosophy—and on the other hand postulates that "the needs of the dramatic action dictate the laws of parting and combining."

The idea that Wagner "composed along" the key words contained in the texts and the associations that were suggested by the scenic actions is nonsensical and unspeakably banal. The result would be a concatenation of leitmotifs lacking musical and formal consistency. Yet Wagner's reference to the unity of a symphonic movement (he meant the development section of sonata form) is problematic, for in the musical drama the parting and combining of the motifs does not refer to an exposition and its thematic and tonal contrast. Apart from this the interaction between modulatory progress (wandering tonality) and thematic-motivic working (basic themes which "contrast, complete, re-shape, divorce") borrowed from Beethoven does not prove to be formally meaningful and teleologically justified in striving toward a recapitulation, the restoration of tonal and thematic unity. The musical form of the Wagnerian drama is, to put it bluntly, like a symphonic development section without the support of an exposition as a fundamental precondition and the recapitulation as a determining goal.

But if we do not wish to fall back on the one-sided and inadequate idea, which denies the metaphysical claim of music to be essential form, that the musical structure is primarily determined from without by the dramatic action, then, in order to gain ground for the analysis, we can proceed from a theory of form that Wagner sketched out in his *Report to the German Wagner Society* (1871) on the circumstances which accompanied the first stages of the composition of the *Ring*. The problem that must have faced Wagner when he began to compose the cycle was the virtually hopeless task of holding together musically the roughly 120 leitmotifs that he needed to fill fifteen hours of music; that is, of how to link them to create a web and not merely to add one to another. The solution that Wagner had in mind is reminiscent of Goethe's morphology, the "idea" of the primeval plant that Goethe claimed was an "experience." "With *Rheingold* I at once began to pursue the new path. Here I had first of all to find the malleable nature motifs which, whilst becoming ever more individual and distinct, were to convey the various kinds of passion of the extensive plot and the characters who expressed themselves within it" (SSD VI, 266).

If we take this quotation literally, it means nothing less than that the leitmotifs represent an almost infinite branching out of variants and contrasts. In a process that Wagner thought of as metamorphosis in the Goethean sense, they emanate from one another or are contrasted, whereby the musical relationship gains in comprehensibility by forming an analogy to the dramatic one. The Valhalla motif, which gradually grows out of the Ring motif (by means of extremely complex melodic, harmonic, and instrumentational techniques) in the orchestral interlude between the first and second scenes of *Das Rheingold,* is a transformation conveyed in musical and dramatic terms through the principle of the blind greed for power expressed by both motifs. The musical connection ensures the metaphysical significance of the dramatic one and, vice versa, the dramatic connection the empirical immediacy of the musical one. (Only a listener who is not insensible to the poetic intention can also perceive undiminished the musical and structural process.)

That the dramatic action provides "the laws of parting and combining" of the leitmotifs, as Wagner wrote in 1879, thus refers not only to the grouping of the motifs in a single scene or section but also, and above all, to the motivic relationships in the whole of the musical drama, whereby it should not be forgotten that contrast and variant both represent a form of musical continuity, as opposed to an empty sense of variety for its own sake. The musical development, which in music drama lacks the buttresses of the exposition and recapitulation that are prerequisites for the development section of the symphonic movement, manifests itself as a systematic connection of variants and contrasts through direct or indirect reference to an original musical substance, which Wagner termed "malleable nature motifs." In aesthetic terms this means that a listener, whenever leitmotifs are juxtaposed that he initially feels to be musically unrelated, has to try to reconstruct the prior musical history, which is at the same time a dramatic one, in order to find the point where the motifs or their prototypes emanated from one another or were contrasted. The development of the orchestral melody, which Wagner modeled on the development section of a symphonic movement (though vastly expanded in the musical drama), is thus, other than in the case of Beethoven, not determined primarily by the goal to which it strives but by the origins from which it takes its being. Beethoven's sense of time was teleological, pushing eagerly into the future. In Wagner it is a continually waxing past that lies oppressively on each moment of the present. (In contrast to Siegfried's funeral music, which conjures up an oppressive excess of earlier and distant ideas, the *Eroica,* although it celebrates the memory of a hero, is, in terms of the temporal feeling that underlies the musical process, never structurally retrospective.)

Melody as Dialogue

The popular preconception that nineteenth-century Italian opera seria is a set of arias rests in part on the incorrect application of eighteenth-century operatic criteria to the nineteenth century, and partly on the audience's habit, or venial sin, of construing a few outstanding arias or parts of arias (a cantabile or a cabaletta) as the real substance around which the rest of the work is grouped (with little regard to the musical-dramatic structure of the whole). Yet, contrary to this view, an impartial analysis shows that it is not so much the arias as the duets and the large ensembles emphasizing the endings of acts that form the backbone of the Italian style of opera, with which Wagnerian music drama must be compared if its unique form is to become apparent.

The fundamental principle of European drama in modern times, which was inspired by humanistic ideas, underlay the opera seria of the nineteenth century just as much as it did Wagnerian music drama. It is the principle that all the essential conflicts that determine the course of a drama can be presented in the form of dialogues, in the form of interpersonal altercation—that is, by means of speech and counterspeech. But the musical means at the composers' disposal were extremely varied. The aim of turning the dialogue into melody and the melody into dialogue was achieved in opera seria by dividing the dialogue, as it were, into a surface structure narrating or commenting on events and an emotional deep structure. The former was consigned to the *recitativo accompagnato,* or the scena, so that in the cantabile, melodic sections it was possible to concentrate on emotions and emotional conflicts. Thus in opera seria the dialogue part (in the narrower sense) that sketched in the outer and inner situation (*recitativo accompagnato,* or scena) was separated from the actual melodic part, in which the characters' emotions collided. Also, the pattern of a slow cantabile in *primo tempo* followed by a fast cabaletta in *secondo tempo* formed a basic structure, even in the sometimes extremely complex variants that adapted themselves to the dramatic peculiarities of a scene. From this Italian composers involuntarily took their formal bearings because other ways of achieving musical coherence did not seem available. In addition, the popular nineteenth-century idea of melody, which was principally coined by Bellini, focused on the model of the symmetrical, "four-square" period, the regularity of which was based primarily on harmonic and metrical norms, on chordal patterns and harmonic rhythm. In contrast, the musical-dramatic dialogue as realized by Wagner in the music dramas from *Das Rheingold* on is characterized by the abolition of the difference between recitative and arioso sections that divided the interpersonal conflict into outer and inner layers; by the abandonment of the formal cantabile-cabaletta scaffolding, the persistent use of which was understandable inasmuch as it conjoined complementarity and intensification; and, finally, by the dissolution of the four-square period structure into "musical prose" that can consist of particles of differing lengths (1 + 3 + 2 bars). To stop short, however, at the negative characteristics that initially force themselves on our attention, as is always the case with something that is historically new, would be an admission of an analytical and historiographic dilemma. This is still a methodological weakness even if the abolition of the old is declared to be emancipation, or progress.

If we compare the melody as dialogue, which Wagner sought to realize in the music drama, with the most advanced form which, in the 1850s, Verdi had ventured upon at the same time in the duet between Rigoletto and Sparafucile, the difference in the motivic structure of the orchestral melody turns out to be the decisive feature. The "situation motifs" of opera seria can either change frequently and abruptly *(recitativo accompagnato)*, or they can achieve musical coherence by incessant repetition (which forms a firm basis for stylistically flexible dialogue) without there having to be a self-contained number with a fixed form (as defined by formal theory). Yet the problem that Wagner solved, of which Italian composers were not even aware, consisted of nothing less than the preservation of formal continuity in the orchestral melody, despite the continual change of motifs (that is, the transformation of the disunity of *recitativo accompagnato* into coherent melody). Furthermore, it involved retaining in the voice parts the possibility of swift changes in stylistic levels and syntactic structures—the possibility, that is, of dialogue in the strict sense of the word.

In accordance with Wagner's aesthetic theory, however, the connection between the leitmotifs that the unending melody of the music dramas suggests is constituted not purely musically, but is rather partially conveyed by the dramaturgy (the concept of the purely musical did not exist for Wagner). The memory of the prior history of the motifs and the consciousness of the meanings that they had acquired in earlier situations belong essentially to what Thomas Mann praised as the "allusive magic" that causes the orchestral melody to appear as an aesthetic whole, although it not infrequently consists of particles that the so-called good musicians of the nineteenth century (a group of Wagner opponents who can in fact be taken quite seriously) felt to be disparate. The "art of transition" to which Wagner, in a letter to Mathilde Wesendonck, referred as his "most subtle art," the technique of conjoining diverging motifs without a discernible break and of making it seem that they emanate from one another with compelling logic, should not blind us to the fact that the constituent elements of unending melody, according to abstract musical criteria (inappropriate ones, that is, but useful as something on which to base the analysis), often stand unrelated side by side. Moreover, the term *unending melody*—coined in 1860 in the essay *Music of the Future*—says nothing more than that in an unbroken (unending) continuity each note, indeed each rhythmic rest, is expressive and significant (melodic). The Wagnerian concept of melody, which is totally different from the popular Italian one, does not cling to the (harmonically and metrically based) period structure, but adheres instead to the substantiality and eloquence of the motifs and successions of notes (which are never exclusively musical but are always dramatically based as well).

The memory of the prior history of the leitmotifs is thus one of the basic assumptions underlying the creation of the aesthetic impression of self-contained musical coherence, of unbroken continuity. The fact that Wagner continually directs the listener back to the past, whereas the only thing that counts aesthetically in Italian opera seria is the present, the striking immediacy of a musically expressed emotional conflict, proves to be the fundamental difference between the types of opera, which in the final analysis is based on the feeling for time. It is an aesthetic and metaphysical difference with far-reaching consequences for the composer. Only the memory of the past that weighs heavily on the leitmotifs—and, contrary to the theory postulated in *Opera and Drama*, the leitmotifs are almost always an expression of memory and only seldom of presentiment—brings about the "allusive magic" that holds everything together from within (and not only through technical links imposed from without). The art of joining and presenting together diverging orchestral motifs without a disintegration of musical coherence makes possible a musical-dramatic dialogue in which the traditional contrast between passages with motivic repetition as the fundamental scaffold and recitatives with frequent changes of motif (but without a self-contained musical structure) is abolished, as is the difference between dialogue sections (in the narrower sense) and actual melodic ones. The "melody as dialogue," which Wagner believed he had discerned in Mozart, is both dialogue (supported by the use of orchestral motifs, whose cohesion makes possible the change of stylistic levels and syntactic structures that a musical dialogue needs if it is to retain a proximity to the spoken play) and melody (in the sense that every note seems significant and eloquent and the continuity of meaning guarantees musical continuity).

Musical Analysis

Leitmotif, orchestral melody, art of transition, unending melody, *Sprechgesang* (speech-song), musical prose—these are the technical terms on which analyses of Wagner's music rely. Some come from Wagner himself (art of transition); others were tolerated (leitmotif) or rejected by him (music drama); still others grew from a passing formulation never again used publicly into a slogan of inestimable historical importance (unending melody); and some, through re-definition of what Wagner originally intended, even to the extent of turning a polemical utterance into an affirmative one, were made serviceable for the interpretation of his works (musical prose). Yet it is not the philological authenticity of the nomenclature that primarily decides its usefulness. It is, in the first place, the ineradicable history of its influence; whoever, by appealing to Wagner, tried to attempt to stamp out the concept of music drama would be a fool. Second, it is the technically appropriate nature of the categories. Third, it is the extent to which we succeed in interpreting them as parts of a self-contained aesthetic and compositional functional context—that is, in making manifest the context that imparts legitimacy to them as attempts to grasp the conceptually determining factors of the *Gesamtkunstwerk.*

That a musical and structural significance is linked or intermingles with an aesthetic or dramaturgical one in all the terms mentioned is impossible to overlook. Analytical technique, which in the twentieth century tends to emphasize the abstract musical element even in the case of vocal music, is thus burdened with unusual difficulties. These are rooted, however, in the phenomenon itself and are not the product of or suggested by the language with which we talk about them.

As we have seen, Wagner understood endless melody to be an unbroken, coherent, and uninterrupted orchestral melody in which every note seems expressive and significant (melodic). The technical fact that musical continuity can be achieved by avoiding or bridging cadences is indissolubly linked with an aesthetic implication: the fact that cadences are well-worn formulas that in themselves seem meaningless. In Wagner's language that means unmelodic, so if at all possible they have to be eradicated. Yet the significance of a succession of notes, or lack of it, the melodic or unmelodic essence, is decided not exclusively on the basis of an abstract musical criterion or set of criteria, but on the relationship to a motif that performs a dramaturgical function. For Wagner something that is purely musical, because it seems unfounded, lacking any kind of raison d'être, is, as it were, an insubstantial sonorous shape that has little to justify it.

Whereas in the case of endless melody there is a danger of a one-sided and narrowly technical interpretation, the concept of the leitmotif (the expression was either coined or popularized by Hans von Wolzogen, although it appears in the catalogue of the works of Carl Maria von Weber that Friedrich Wilhelm Jähns published in 1871)[1] is burdened with another kind of difficulty. This is the fact that the viability and necessity of more complex music analysis either pales to insignificance or hardly comes into its own next to a kind of dramaturgical and philosophical exegesis (based on a certain weltanschauung) that not infrequently tends to lose all sense of proportion. It has to be drawn painstakingly to the attention of a Wagnerian public accustomed to superficial labels. (The rigid naming of the motifs, even though it distorts the facts, is unavoidable, at least as a starting point for comprehension. It represents,

---

1. Thomas Grey has pointed out that A. W. Ambros used the term *Leitmotiv* in 1860, when, in an article on the controversy surrounding the so-called music of the future, he applied "the term to both Wagner and Liszt without qualitative distinction" (see Grey 1987, p. 406). [Ed.]

strictly speaking, the fundamental error at the root of all interpretations of Wagner.)

If we take Wagner's appropriation of Schopenhauer's metaphysics after 1854 as seriously as it no doubt must be taken, the fundamental assertion that music is an image of the innermost essence of the world, whereas language and stage action merely attach to the superficial layer, or that, to put it in scholastic terms, music is essential form and language and stage merely phenomenal forms, actually signifies that the real meaning of the leitmotifs never becomes apparent in the linguistically or scenically determined labels applied to them. The conclusion drawn by Schopenhauer with philosophical rigor (although it is a rigor that seems to be the counterpart of insufficient musical experience) is that the music does not illustrate a text or an action. Rather, it is a text or an action that illustrates the music, and is thus in principle exchangeable.

This is in fact so exaggerated that one hesitates to admit its validity as a fundamental premise of the interpretation of a music drama. Yet at least it hints at the direction that the perception of the listener and spectator has to take in order to arrive at the level of aesthetic and metaphysical contemplation on which Schopenhauer thought he discerned a means of evading the enmeshment in the Will, the blind force and urge that destroyed oneself and others. Where words fail and cease to communicate, there enters music, which, because it is what Wagner called sounding silence (*Music of the Future*, 1860), speaks of that to which language and stage action cannot attain. The extremely complex system of variants and derivations, substitutions, contrasts, and interaction that comes to light as the result of a precise analysis that avoids the pitfalls of the unspeakable leitmotif guides is not an abstract musical tissue. Nor can the meaning that it implies be linguistically retraced by adding to, transforming, and contaminating the names of leitmotifs until they have become the verbal monstrosities that have always been the laughingstock of non-Wagnerians, and nowadays not infrequently of Wagnerians as well. The only appropriate kind of reception, as in the poetry of Stéphane Mallarmé, lies in a process which, to be sure, begins with the simple, linguistically expressible meanings of the motifs (in poetry it is the everyday meanings of the words), but which gradually, the more numerous and entangled the musical and musical-dramatic relationships between the motifs become, move further and further away from the original tangible meaning, without, however, crossing the boundary where the linguistically and scenically conveyed meaning dissolves totally in the absolute musical one. The aesthetic goal, paradoxically expressed, consists in the path from illustrative to absolute music, whereby the starting point, being a crude simplification, is immediately crossed, and the goal is never supposed to be reached. It is a final goal to which Wagner, who was, to be sure, a Schopenhauerian, but at the same time a "ham actor" (Nietzsche), did not seriously strive, although he once spoke of music as "depriving the visual senses of their potency" (*Beethoven*, 1870). The aesthetic process, in order to remain what it is, must be held in the balance.

Only the fact that the leitmotifs intertwine in the listener's consciousness to form an ever-denser network in which finally everything is directly or indirectly related to everything else makes the orchestral melody appear to be the never-ending musical continuum that Wagner, in the essay *Music of the Future,* compared with a forest melody in which countless voices intermingle. But as orchestral melody, which is melodic in the Wagnerian sense of the word, the instrumental writing can support or carry a speech melody, which, taken on its own, would be musically inconsistent, and which nevertheless, on the basis of the criteria from which Wagner proceeded, is wholly melodic and not, for example, a recitative that approximates an arioso. First, in the consciousness of the listener the speech melody participates involuntarily in what is happening in the orchestral melody. The motivic substance of the instrumental part is transferred to the vocal line as if it were its aesthetic property, so to speak, because the singing protagonist appears to be the bearer of all the music. Second, Wagner's concept of melody, whose criterion is the significance and expressivity of tonal configurations and not their syntactic and harmonic and metrical structure, also encompasses speech melody inasmuch as, in mutual interaction with the orchestral melody, it is substantial enough to induce the perceptual process just described, through which the linguistically and scenically determined conception of music turns to aesthetic and metaphysical contemplation. Third, in Wagner's aesthetic theory speech melody is melodic on account of a feature that, according to the usual concepts of his contemporaries, would make it the exact opposite: its irregular syntax, which is termed musical prose. The asymmetrical phrases are based on the structure of the alliterative verse which leaves open the number of strong and weak syllables (these can consist of two or four but also of two and a half, three, or five bars: it is impossible to explain the "irregular" forms, which they no longer are under the assumptions of musical prose, as deviations from the norm of the "regular" four-square ones). These asymmetrical phrases are distinguished aesthetically, as Schoenberg realized (*Brahms the Progressive,* 1933), by a strict avoidance of melodic padding, without which hardly any symmetrical phrase or period manages to get along. Thus they do justice to the essential criterion of what Wagner termed melodic, the criterion that no note should be devoid of meaning. Wagner's musical prose, which suggested the concept to Schoenberg, is at root the same thing as unending melody: music in which every note, "yes, indeed every rhythmic rest," as Wagner enthusiastically commented in discussing Beethoven's *Eroica,* is significant and seems to speak.

The Charge of Dilettantism: Wagner and Modernism

In contrast to his view of himself as a theatrical genius, Wagner was never altogether sure of himself as a composer, although his cry of despair—that the stagnation to which he was on occasion subject would have been unthinkable in the case of Mendelssohn—contained an element of irony that should not be overlooked. What the "good musicians" (a synonym for musical conservatives) objected to in Wagner was that the idea of the *Gesamtkunstwerk* smacked of amateurishness; that a leitmotif technique which replaced musical coherence with the suggestive effect of repetitions was a kind of music for the unmusical; or that the intoxication brought about by the music drama was based on a profoundly destructive penchant for the amorphous and the anarchical. In the final analysis this comes to one and the same thing: that in the case of Wagner the music as such, independent of the theatrical effect (which in the nineteenth century, despite Schiller, was still mistrusted on moral grounds), was questionable in some admittedly elusive way. (That Schumann, in order to express his aesthetic irritation, did not shrink from pointing out the consecutive fifths in *Tannhäuser* is only a sign of how baffled he was; one might also say it was a blunder caused by embarrassment.)

To ward off the aesthetic mistrust with the simple argument that it is inappropriate to judge music dramas in abstract musical terms would of course not be wrong, albeit one-sided and orthodox in a questionable sense. In the first place, a kind of music whose style and technique proved to be profoundly influential at the end of the nineteenth century in the symphony, the symphonic poem, and musical drama must be able to stand up to an analysis that does not always veer away from the music to the dramaturgy whenever interpretive difficulties arise. Wagner's oeuvre was not immune to the influence that it exerted, an influence that was primarily musical and only secondarily musical-dramatic. The historical consequences, as it were, are projected back onto, and become part and parcel of, the image of Wagner's works. Second, a musical drama that in Wagner's aesthetic theory was burdened with the claim of subsuming and perfecting Beethoven's symphonic style can hardly evade a judgment that also encompasses abstract musical criteria, or at least does not ignore them. And third, music which, in the spirit of Schopenhauer, is to be viewed as an essential and not a phenomenal form—which, that is, asserts its aesthetic and metaphysical primacy vis-à-vis language and stage action—is driven to formal consistency. This consistency, contrary to Wagner's own view of the matter, makes a sudden change from musical-dramatic to abstract musical structures seem possible and meaningful at all times.

The charge of amateurishness, which was leveled not only at Wagner but also at Berlioz, Liszt, and even Schumann, to say nothing of composers such as Charles Alkan, must be taken seriously in the context of nineteenth-century music history, however shabby it may appear. It represents the obverse of a fact whose historical significance and importance can hardly be overestimated: that from about 1830 on, compositional technique, which had provided earlier composers with a solid foundation, ran into the dilemma of being subject either to the danger of the erosion of criteria in the name of progress or, for the sake of aesthetic security, to the irrelevance of the academic style. An investigation willing to face the compositional facts of the post-Beethoven age, where they are difficult to pin down, could thus start from the seemingly naive yet actually vexing question of why in fact the work of Berlioz is not amateurish and that of Mendelssohn not academic. Wagner's basic insecurity is at any rate a key compositional phenomenon. For this reason it seems apposite to declare it to be the distinguishing feature of musical modernism, which had its origins in the score of *Tristan*. This would be insufficient, however, because reformulating the aesthetic and technical fact as a historical one does not solve the problem; it merely gives it a different slant.

The strange perseverance with which Wagner, in conflict with Schopenhauer's metaphysics of music which he had adopted in 1854, still insisted decades later on a dramaturgical justification of compositional risks (*On the Application of Music to the Drama,* 1879), is similar to the equally surprising obstinacy with which, throughout his life, Schoenberg clung to the notion of continuously developing variation, a technique that was supposed to ensure that the thread of musical coherence never broke. In the face of music whose real substance is uncompromising expressivity, an embodiment of what Schopenhauer termed the Will and Sigmund Freud translated into the id of psychoanalysis, the composers conjure up an outside support that is inherent partly in the thing itself and partly in the (intermingled) reflection about it. This is supposed to lend to something that is secretly moving toward anarchy an aesthetic appearance of complete consistency. Both Wagner and Schoenberg, to put it another way, were great precisely because, in a manner of speaking, they took upon themselves dangers they did not seek, but which they recognized as unavoidable, and which they were able to master because, unlike the reckless gamblers of the avant-garde, who have squandered modernity mindlessly, they never for one moment lost the feeling for the slender path along which they were traveling. They possessed a sure sense of the "feeling for form" (Schoenberg), the latent logic of which they believed in unerringly, although in fact there was nothing tangible to guarantee it.

If, in order to exemplify this in musical terms, we proceed from certain basic categories of the classical-Romantic tradition, including the four-measure period as the fundamental premise of the popular concept of melody, the functional coherence of chords grouped around a tonal center accentuated at the start and at the end, harmonic-motivic counterpoint, tonally based form, and the "developing variation of musical ideas" (Schoenberg) based on the correlation and interaction of themes and harmony, we can claim without exaggeration that virtually all of these categories were sooner or later suspended by Wagner, either firmly or hesitantly (and in doing so he indirectly, or negatively, confirmed the systematic character of tradition). Musical prose, wandering tonality, dramaturgically conveyed counterpoint as the stratification of musically heterogeneous motifs, form as tissue instead of architecture, and motivic combinations distantly established and made wholly comprehensible only through the memory of early relationships and not through the simple presence of variation and contrast: the characteristic features of Wagner's music dramas after *Das Rheingold* are, from the point of view of tradition, nothing more than negations whose historical significance cannot become visible unless it is possible to state them in the affirmative as determining aspects of the modernist movement, or of a prior history of the modernist movement.

Whereas it is still relatively natural to declare the chain structure of wandering tonality to be a harmonic principle in its own aesthetic and technical right (not, that is, as a deficient mode of tonality rooted in the identity of beginning and end that the development section of the classical-Romantic sonata form still permitted as a passing state striving toward the recapitulation), it is difficult to arrive at an appropriate evaluation of counterpoint as a stratification of heterogeneous motifs. The far-reaching significance of the phenomenon becomes visible only if we admit the validity of an unusual and initially striking premise that causes much conceptual confusion—the premise that the kind of harmonic distortion that progresses to the brink of atonality (in *On the Application of Music to the Drama,* see the example from *Die Walküre*) and the projection of extremely divergent melodic forms on immobile chords (*Siegfried* and *Die Meistersinger*) are at root different manifestations of the same tendency: the growing neutrality of functional harmony. Seeing this in slightly exaggerated form and exclusively from our perspective in the future, we could in fact speak of the emancipation of counterpoint. The voices were no longer related to one another harmonically but rather exclusively in terms of their motivic characteristics (albeit a relationship that has to be plausible as a complementary contrast instead of a nonexistent relation creating an empty sense of variety for its own sake). This determines whether the stratification is in fact true counterpoint (something Heinrich Schenker denied with regard to *Meistersinger*) or a simultaneity forcibly brought about from without, which may be well founded in terms of dramaturgy but which is musically of no consequence (or which proves to be musically of substance merely on account of the transmission and admixture of dramaturgical features just mentioned, which in the music drama complement the concept of the musical that is no longer to be grasped in abstract terms but rather as a component in the *Gesamtkunstwerk*).

The theory of music has still not done justice to Wagner; nor has music history, which, when engaged in analysis and interpretation, continually and in an almost obsessive manner tends to evade the musical element (on account of which the other aspects acquired such significance in the first place). It is as if the issue that is in fact central were an embarrassment that those thinking about it seek to avoid.

Translated by Alfred Clayton

Biography and Reception:
Decadence and the Dawn of
"Wagnerism"

CHAPTER 13

The Patronage of King Ludwig II

MANFRED EGER

The friendship between King Ludwig II of Bavaria and Richard Wagner owed as much to fate as it did to misfortune. Its significance was commensurate with its consequences: if the two men had never met, *Meistersinger* and the *Ring* might never have been finished, *Parsifal* probably never been written, and the Bayreuth Festival not have been founded; nor would Neuschwanstein have been designed as it was.

The events which preceded their friendship, its course, and its outcome evoke an impression of astonishing inevitability and logic. Ludwig was pre-programmed for Wagner. The young Crown Prince's favorite haunt was Hohenschwangau, named for the swan on the coat of arms of the castle's previous owners. The swan was also favored by Ludwig's father, Maximilian II, who had had one of the rooms in the castle decorated with frescoes from the legend of the swan-knight. The young Ludwig grew up in the shadow of this legendary figure: he used to draw swans, and when writing letters would sometimes append to his signature a motif made up of a swan and a cross. He was thirteen years old when he first read the poem *Lohengrin*. Of a dreamy and wistful disposition, yet conscious of his sovereign position, the youth was bound to identify with the figure of the knight. When, at the age of fifteen, he heard and saw the opera for the first time, he was moved to the very depths of his being. It was *Lohengrin* that sparked his fascination with Wagner's poems and writings. Above all, Wagner's music had an almost demonic effect on him. At an early date the young Prince Ludwig also read Wagner's other libretti and *The Art-Work of the Future*, an essay which discusses, among other things, the "redemption of the utilitarianist thinker" by "the artistic man of the future." He was familiar, too, with the essays *Music of the Future* and *Opera and Drama*. The first public edition of the *Ring* poem appeared in 1863. In the preface Wagner wondered where he might find the patron who would enable him to set the poem to music and to stage the completed work: "Will this prince be found?—In the beginning was the deed." The Crown Prince felt that the question was addressed to him personally.

Wagner was in Vienna at this time, on course for total disaster. To escape the threat of imprisonment for debt, he was finally forced to flee the city. Thus, on Good Friday, 25 March 1864, he found himself in Munich, his first intermediate port of call, where his eye was caught by a portrait of the newly crowned eighteen-year-old king in a shop window. Ludwig's beauty and youth moved him to tears. From Mariafeld near Zurich, where he was offered shelter for a time by friends, he wrote to Peter Cornelius on 8 April: "*Some light* must show itself: *someone* must come forward and *help* me *now* with his energetic support . . . As I say: *some good* and truly helpful miracle must now befall me, otherwise it will all be over! Your terrible silence seems to indicate that this delightful miracle is already on its way!"

Six days later, obsessed by the desire to make Wagner's acquaintance, the young king sent his cabinet secretary Franz Seraph von Pfistermeister in search of the composer, who was finally discovered, after tedious detours to Vienna and Mariafeld, in a Stuttgart hotel. On 3 May Pfistermeister brought him a portrait of the king, together with a ring and a message inviting him to Munich. With "tears of the most heavenly emotion" in his eyes, the fifty-one-year-old Wagner wrote to thank his eighteen-year-old monarch. The following day he stood in the royal presence for the first time, in Ludwig's Munich residence. "He is, alas, so fair of form, so spirited, soulful and sublime that I fear his life must slip away like some celestial dream in this base world of ours," he wrote prophetically to Eliza Wille immediately afterward. The king promised, "I shall do everything . . . to requite you for past sufferings. The meanest cares of everyday life I shall banish for ever from your brow . . . Unwittingly you were the only well-spring of my joy from the days of my tenderest youth, my friend who, as none other, spoke to my heart, my most worthy mentor and teacher" (5 May 1864). The tone of the letters that subsequently passed between them is marked by an almost unheard-of effusiveness: "Oh most blessed of men! How I worship you!" (1 January 1865). "Uniquely beloved!" (1 February 1865). "Everything, you are everything to me! . . . Ah, that I might die for you!" (21 June 1865). "For you alone, whom I love so ardently, have I come into the world" (9 July 1865). "All praise and adoration to you, who are more than human!" (12 July 1865). "Saviour that blesses me!" (1 January 1866). Thus the king to Wagner, whom he described as "God-sent" and "a child of Heaven" (22 May 1866). Wagner, believing himself caught up in some fairy-tale world of his imagination, wrote to Eliza Wille that he was so "moved by astonishment at the miracle of this heavenly youth" that he had been "close to sinking down at his feet and worshipping him" (8 October 1864). His own letters echoed the tone of Ludwig's: "I am nothing without you . . . Oh, my King, you are godlike!" (11 December 1864). These mutually ecstatic expressions—in which homoeroticism certainly played a part, albeit unwittingly, in the case of the king—were no doubt sincerely intended, at least at the outset.

The situation was unprecedented. Both men were carried away by feelings of ideal harmony, as yet blind to each other's failings. Haus Pellet in Kempfenhausen on Lake Starnberg was placed at Wagner's disposal, and, during the period when he stayed there, Wagner would visit Ludwig almost daily. It was while he was here that he wrote the *Huldigungsmarsch* (WWV 97) as an act of homage to Ludwig, and the essay *On State and Religion,* in which the author, once decried by his enemies as a street fighter, took the opportunity to modify his views on kingship. In September 1864 he moved into the house which the king had provided for him in Munich's Briennerstrasse, and resumed work on the *Ring* once Ludwig had signed a formal contract for its completion, while at the same time planning a monumental Festival Theater for its first performances. The triumphal climax of the following year, 1865, was the premiere of *Tristan* under the baton of Hans von Bülow. At the king's request Wagner began dictating his autobiography, and wrote out the prose draft of *Parsifal.*

In the meantime, however, trouble was brewing. Wagner's immodesty, his profligacy, and the expensive plans for a Festival Theater; his interference in political issues; rumors surrounding his relations with the wife of his friend Bülow; the king's obsessive interest in Wagner's person, works, and plans, and his resultant neglect of his official duties and affairs of state: all this gave rise to concern mixed with ignorance and personal animosity. This was particularly true in the case of Ludwig von der Pfordten, whom the king had appointed his minister of foreign affairs and head of his cabinet at the end of 1864, scarcely suspecting that, as Saxon minister of education, Pfordten was already the sworn enemy of the insurgent Dresden kapellmeister, and that as recently as 1858 he had been heard to remark that if Germany's princes stuck together as closely as democrats, no more of Wagner's operas would ever be performed. A united front was soon formed against the foreign "revolutionary and Lutheran supporter," comprising friends of Pfordten's among ministry officials, the clergy, and court aristocracy. Its effects were felt in the form of open harassment by subordinate officials.

Wagner was not the man to leave it to Ludwig to determine the amount and frequency of the financial aid he was to receive. Coming from an artist who had been rescued from the depths of utter despair, the composer's repeated requests for help were not exactly modest, marked as they sometimes were by a striking and not unjustified note of pride: "Be right royally generous, and leave it to my conscience as to how I repay this royal trust in days to come!" (16 October 1865). The defensive attitude on the part of ministry officials went beyond the bounds of honest concern. When Pfistermeister's position was threatened, for example, and he attempted to win over Wagner as an ally, he was able to promise, among other things, unlimited credit from the cabinet exchequer.

Ludwig himself had been the first to suggest the Festival Theater, an idea which Wagner's enemies in Munich found alarming. For his part, Wagner was unimpressed by the plan: "How I hate this projected theatre, indeed, how childish the King seems for insisting on this project so passionately" (BB, 9 September 1865). Secretly opposed to the idea, he had nonetheless recommended Gottfried Semper as architect. The theater was to have been built in stone on the opposite bank of the river Isar, and joined by means of a bridge to a magnificent new boulevard leading to the city center. Its cost was estimated at 5 million gulden, and it would have taken six years to build. By way of a diversion, Wagner suggested that an interim theater be erected instead. Semper was again to be the architect. This theater would be built in a wing of the Crystal Palace and would cost only 200,000 gulden. The plan came to nothing, partly because of practical objections by the senior planning authorities. All the more energetically, then, did Ludwig press ahead with his plans for a Festival Theater. Building work, which had been due to begin in 1867, was delayed not only by ministry officials and by the expense of planning the ill-fated royal wedding (the annulment of Ludwig's engagement to his cousin Sophie Charlotte was announced officially on 11 October 1867), but also by Wagner himself, for whom Munich was now an object of loathing. The project, which would have tied the king forever to his capital city, was finally abandoned altogether. Shortly afterwards the plans for Neuschwanstein were drawn up.

Neuschwanstein was intended as "a worthy temple for my godlike friend," as Ludwig wrote to inform Wagner on 13 May 1868, only a few months after the idea for the Festival Theater had come to grief. So close in time were the two events that it is virtually impossible not to see a causal connection between them. Two theatrical set designers, Christian Jank and Angelo Quaglio, were commissioned to draw up the plans. The castle courtyard and bedchamber were based on the sets that had been used for the first production of *Lohengrin* in Munich, while the Singers' Hall and Venus Grotto were inspired by *Tannhäuser*. At a later date Neuschwanstein became Ludwig's "Grail Castle." Wagner never set foot in the castle, which was still incomplete at the time of his death. Countless details of the furnishings both there and in Ludwig's Munich residence, and the name *Tristan,* which he gave to his steamer on Lake Starnberg, attest to the king's boundless fixation with Wagner's operas. The same is true of his castle at Linderhof, which included a vast Venus Grotto, a Hunding Hut, a Gurnemanz Hermitage, and a Good Friday Meadow.

Even as early as the spring of 1865 Ludwig's officials were at pains to restrict Wagner's influence on the king and to reduce his growing demands. The composer himself contributed to a temporary cooling off in their friendship by striking a table with his fist in Ludwig's presence: the king, after all, was used to expecting the most obsequious gestures from his servants, and even his ministers and his own mother were required to show respectful submission. The accusation of political interference that Wagner's enemies leveled at him was only too just. Certainly Wagner was fatally involved in politics from the time his friendship with Ludwig first began. A political gloss was put on the fact that, through his operas and writings, the composer had encouraged the young Crown Prince in his dangerous bent toward make-believe and daydreaming. In addition, Pfordten's aversion to the erstwhile revolutionary ensured that the situation would remain politically explosive. Such was the young king's enthusiasm for artistic projects that Wagner unwittingly aroused in him a disinclination for affairs of state and official duties. Wagner was genuinely concerned about Ludwig's inexperience and guilelessness, all the more so when he realized that the king's weakness was being exploited by Pfordten's minions for their own ultramontanist ends.

Not least in an attempt to divert attention from their policies, the papist faction embarked on a witch-hunt against the composer, thereby forcing him to adopt a formal position in political matters. Wagner's views and advice occasionally proved to be more far-sighted than those of many cabinet members. The situation became grotesque when the rival factions both endeavored to bribe the composer. The ultramontanists promised him theaters, conservatories, villas, private pensions, and stock certificates if he would agree to speak to the king on their behalf. Wagner refused. He wrote to Mathilde Maier in February 1865, telling her that it would be an act of betrayal to abandon the king to intrigue. When his enemies prepared to strike the first blow later that same month, accusing him of profligacy in the pages of the *Allgemeine Zeitung,* he replied with disarming restraint. In September 1865 he advised the king to abolish his standing army and form a national militia: Ludwig, he concluded, should place himself at the head of the German movement and have himself elected emperor. This was seen as an attack on the constitution of the military. Once again, Wagner had played into his enemies' hands, allowing them to incite the population and court aristocracy and to revive memories of Ludwig I's unfortunate affair with the Irish dancer Lola Montez.

During a week-long visit by Wagner to Hohenschwangau, accompanied by music from *Lohengrin* performed on the castle battlements and by the arrival of a swan-knight on the Alpsee, Ludwig wrote enthusiastically to Cosima von Bülow: "Oh, he is godlike, godlike!—It is my calling to live for him, to fight and to suffer." At exactly the same time Peter Cornelius was writing to his fiancée, Bertha Jung, to express his fears that Wagner's political involvement was "the beginning of the end" (15 November 1865). On 26 November, the *Münchner Volksbote* accused Wagner of, among other things, trying to displace Pfistermeister in order to be able to deplete the cabinet exchequer all the more easily. Having been attacked in this manner, Wagner in turn charged the cabinet secretary with intrigue and treacherous indiscretions, and demanded that the king form a new cabinet. When Ludwig tried to console him with the words, "Sublime God, your hero shall not cause you shame!" (27 November 1865), Wagner responded with an open letter in the *Neueste Nachrichten* (29 November). Although the article appeared anonymously, it was clearly the work of Wagner. In it the writer demanded that "two or three persons be removed who do not enjoy the least respect among the Bavarian people" so that the king and his people might be rid once and for all of "these vexatious alarms." Wagner thus placed the weapon of his own destruction in his enemies' hands. The cabinet threatened to resign if

Wagner was not removed from Munich. When the royal family and clergy added their voices to this demand and warned of the threat of popular insurrection, the king relented and begged his friend to leave Bavaria "for a few months."

The composer was thunderstruck. He left the city on 10 December 1865. Ludwig suffered even more than Wagner from their enforced separation, especially when he discovered that fears of a popular revolt had been a mere pretext. The realization that he had been forced to make an unnecessary sacrifice had disastrous repercussions. Suddenly everything around him, from his city to affairs of state, was deeply repugnant. "I am suffering fearfully," Ludwig complained in a letter to Cosima on 2 January 1866. "I want to be with him . . . or—to die!" He wrote to his friend on 28 January: "I kneel before your bust . . . and shed tears, bitter tears." More than once he expressed the intention of abdicating and of settling in Switzerland, close to his friend. On each occasion Wagner advised him to be patient and remember his duties; but the composer also took the opportunity to repeat his suggestion that the king should get rid of Pfordten and Pfistermeister. When word leaked out that Ludwig had paid a secret visit to Wagner at Tribschen in May 1866, the country was deeply dismayed—all the more so since the political situation at the time was extremely tense on account of the threat of war with Prussia. The extent to which Wagner was still believed to wield political influence is clear from an attempt on Bismarck's part to sway the king with help from the composer.

Wagner responded by drawing up yet another political program of reform, indebted to the ideas of Constantin Frantz and promising salvation for Germany if Bavaria were to place itself at the head of the German Confederation, thereby filling the void that had been left by Prussia and Austria. He entreated Ludwig to maintain a position of neutrality, but his advice was frustrated by parliament's decision to enter the war against Prussia on the side of Austria. The Bavarian position was weakened by the ensuing defeat, and the king once again began to toy with the idea of abdicating. Yet again Wagner begged him to persevere, while at the same time advising him to transfer his seat of government to Nuremberg (24 July 1866), a suggestion to which Ludwig appears to have given serious thought (letter to Cosima of 27 November 1866). Wagner showed far-sightedness in advising the king to take account of the new political situation, to adopt a conciliatory attitude toward Prussia, and, to that end, to replace the ultramontanist Pfordten with Prince Hohenlohe-Schillingsfürst. When Ludwig acceded to this final request in December 1866 (Pfistermeister having already been removed from office), it seemed as though the major obstacles had been removed that stood in the way of Wagner's return to Munich. But in spite of the king's passionate desire to see him back there, Wagner had long since given up the idea. In the autumn of 1867 he prevailed upon the king to finance a semiofficial *Süddeutsche Presse*, in which he published a series of articles titled *German Art and German Politics* critical of the middle class's philistine attitudes. He also warned against sacrificing great cultural values for the sake of a society greedy for profit. When the king ordered this "suicidal" series of essays to be discontinued, a long period of ill-feeling ensued between the two men. By 1870 the affair surrounding the performances of *Das Rheingold* and *Die Walküre* had persuaded Wagner to pin his artistic hopes on the German nation now that it had been united under Prussian rule.

A further target for hostile attack was provided by Wagner's relations with the wife of his pupil, friend, and colleague Hans von Bülow, whom the king had invited to Munich at Wagner's recommendation. It was Cosima herself who took the initiative in this relationship, and the decisive step may well have been encouraged, if not precipitated, by Wagner's new position. In response to his invitation, she arrived in Kempfenhausen, accompanied by her daughters, and proceeded to consummate her liaison with an initially surprised and hesitant Wagner. Nine months later, on the day of the first orchestral rehearsal for *Tristan* (conducted by Bülow), she brought Wagner's first daughter, Isolde, into the world. By this time Cosima was Wagner's secretary, diplomatic representative, and lover. The guileless Ludwig continued to see in her Wagner's soul mate, self-sacrificial collaborator, and trustworthy confidante, a view he maintained even after she had begun to pay frequent and lengthy visits to Tribschen. When the Munich press launched a smear campaign against Bülow, Cosima, and Wagner in July 1866, the composer drew up a formal statement in defense of their honor, which Cosima asked the king to sign and publish. Ludwig agreed to the request, without suspecting that Cosima was already expecting Wagner's second child. When rumors again reached his ears, he told his cabinet secretary Lorenz von Düfflipp, "If adultery were really involved after all, then woe betide them!" (13 December 1867). Not until the autumn of 1868 did Wagner admit the truth to Ludwig. The king was shocked, but his disfavor did not last for long. In fact, he appears never to have learned the whole truth—that Isolde was Wagner's daughter, and that his royal favor had been abused. It was no doubt out of shame that Cosima lived this lie to the end, refusing to admit to her duplicity even in a court of law.

The first performance of *Die Meistersinger* had already taken place in Munich on 21 June 1868. At Ludwig's request Wagner sat beside him in the royal box, from which he leaned forward to acknowledge applause. It was an unprecedented breach of etiquette but a triumphant rehabilitation for Wagner in the very city from which he had been hounded less than two years earlier.

The first performance of *Das Rheingold* in September 1869, ordered by Ludwig "against my wishes," as Wagner complained retrospectively in a letter to the king of 1 March 1871, had serious repercussions for the relations between the two men. Wagner had refused to sacrifice the *Ring* to what he regarded as the loathsome routine of ordinary opera houses, preferring instead to present it in model performances under "exceptional conditions." Only with reluctance did he agree to the king's entreaty. As a precautionary measure he proposed Hans Richter as his conductor, and sent instructions by way of intermediaries. These, however, were ignored by the Munich intendant, Karl von Perfall, and preparatory work on the staging proceeded in such a desultory and inadequate fashion that fears were expressed at the dress rehearsal that the work would be exposed to public ridicule. As a result Richter resigned as conductor, and telegraphed Wagner asking him to do what he could to prevent the performance from taking place. Wagner begged the king to agree to a delay, and drew his attention to the suggestions he had made for improving the production. Ludwig, sensing insubordination, gave vent to his indignation in a series of letters and telegrams to Düfflipp; "The behaviour of 'Wagner' and the theatre rabble is nothing less than a crime and a disgrace; it is open insurrection against my orders." He spoke of "abominable intrigues" on Wagner's part. "Never before have I encountered such impudence . . . : may the lot of them perish!" (30 August 1869). "If W. dares to oppose me again, his salary is to be permanently stopped, and no more of his works are to be performed on the Munich stage" (31 August 1869). When Wagner announced that he was arriving in person to superintend the rehearsals, the king ordered Düfflipp "to foil his coming here. He does not need to know that this is what I want, otherwise all hell will be loose" (31 August 1869). To Franz Wüllner, who had been appointed conductor, Wagner threatened: "Hands off my score! Take my advice, Sir, or may the devil take you!" (11 September 1869).

The first performance took place on 22 September 1869. The events which led up to it produced a deep division between the king and Wagner. As usual, it was Ludwig who was the first to break the silence after several weeks had gone by: "The desire to hear your divine work was so overwhelming . . . ; forgive your friend who is conscious of his guilt" (mid-November 1869). Immediately after the *Rheingold* performances, however, he had given Perfall secret instructions to "proceed with the production of *Die Walküre* without any further reference to Wagner." Wagner learned of what was going on from newspaper reports in the early months of 1870, after Ludwig had already assured him: "You remain . . . my King and God. It is for your sake that I wear my crown . . . ; but do not deprive me of the air I need to breathe by prohibiting a performance of your works" (6 January 1870). Once again Wagner was forced to relent, but among the conditions he set was the demand that he himself receive an official commission to mount model performances of his works, and that, while the rehearsals were in progress, Perfall should be sent away on leave of absence. Since Wagner's liaison with Cosima had still not been legalized, the king did not dare risk an official invitation. As with *Das Rheingold,* the performance of *Die Walküre* in June 1870 went ahead in Wagner's absence and without his cooperation. These experiences persuaded him to set in motion his plans for a festival in Bayreuth independent of the king, and to delay, and then conceal, his completion of the full score of *Siegfried,* which Ludwig was eager to get his hands on. For a long time the king maintained an attitude of disapproval toward the Bayreuth project, but he finally came around to supporting it.

The reproach has persistently been leveled against Wagner that he preyed on the treasury and shamelessly exploited the king, who is alleged to have spent a royal fortune on him. The truth is that all the help that Wagner received was paid for out of the king's civil list. During the nineteen years of their friendship Wagner received a total of 562,914 marks, including salary, rents, the value of gifts in kind, and also the 75,000 marks that were given to Wagner to finance the building of Wahnfried. The total sum is less than one-seventh of the annual budget provided for by the civil list (4.2 million marks), although it must be admitted that only a third of this figure was available for the king to spend as he pleased. His private performances cost him 987,609 marks over a space of thirteen years. And his castles cost him— and him alone—32.4 million marks. (The Bavarian state, by way of comparison, had to pay 51 million marks in reparations when it lost the war with Prussia.) The bedchamber alone at Herrenchiemsee cost the king an outlay of some 652,000 marks—90,000 marks more than the total sum that Wagner received—and the bridal coach for the royal wedding that never took place cost 1.7 million marks. (Meyerbeer, it may be added, received 750,000 marks in royalties for one hundred performances of his opera *Le prophète* in Berlin.) Wagner's gifts in return included the original scores of *Die Feen, Das Liebes-verbot, Die Meistersinger, Das Rheingold,* and *Die Walküre,* together with nu-merous other musical and literary manuscripts. When Ludwig made it possible to proceed with construction on the Bayreuth Festival Theater in 1874, and when, four years later, he paid off the remaining deficit on the first festival (a deficit which was Wagner's personal responsibility), it was only after repeatedly refusing his help, and in the form of interest-bearing loans amount-ing to 316,000 marks. Both these loans were fully paid off by Wagner's family. Nonetheless, one must be wary of underestimating Ludwig's help, since at the time in question the king was becoming increasingly mired in financial difficulties as a result of his own building projects. These difficulties later encouraged him to think of bizarre ways of obtaining money (raiding the banks was one possibility he is said to have ordered), and finally led to financial ruin.

By the date of the completion of the Festival Theater, the friendship between the two men had long since burned itself out. The utopian dream of the early years had inevitably been destroyed by contact with sordid reality, just as the elevated sense of ideal companionship was undermined by the two men's egocentricity. Their epistolary style, once fired by spontaneous enthusiasm, was now reduced to empty formulas and posturing platitudes, the hypocrisy of which was a source of shame to Wagner. Their ways had diverged, and all that was left was the fascination which Wagner's art had always exerted over the king. Although Ludwig attended the dress rehearsals and the final cycle at the first Bayreuth Festival in 1876, he stayed away from the opening of the *Ring,* no doubt because of the presence of the kaiser. And to Wagner's great disappointment, he also missed the performances of *Parsifal* in 1882. He had wanted the work to be staged instead in Munich. In the last letter Wagner ever wrote to the king, he did his best to dissuade him. According to the court secretary Ludwig Bürkel, the king received news of Wagner's death with the words, "Oh! I'm sorry, but then again not really. Only recently he caused me problems over Parsifal" (Karbaum 1976, document III/11). After the funeral ceremonies were over, he told Bürkel: "The artist for whom all the world now mourns . . . it was I who saved him for the world" (Newman IV, 713). On 4 August 1865 he had written to Wagner: "And when the two of us have long since ceased to be, our work will continue to serve as a shining example for those that come after us, an example that shall delight the coming centuries, so that men's hearts will glow with enthusiasm for art, for an art that is sprung from God, an art that will never die."

Translated by Stewart Spencer

CHAPTER 14

Wagner and Nietzsche

DIETER BORCHMEYER

The encounter between Richard Wagner and Friedrich Nietzsche (1844–1900) ranks with the most striking and momentous relationships in German cultural history. In its intellectual and cultural range it is perhaps comparable to the friendship between Goethe and Schiller. Furthermore, the purely personal aspects of the two epoch-making encounters share features. Goethe's preeminent place in the literary culture of his time was just as indisputable as Richard Wagner's in the musical and theatrical world of the nineteenth century at the point when each of the younger authors, both far from having reached the high point of their oeuvre, entered the elder man's circle. Schiller and Nietzsche were the propagandists in these friendships; through their fruitful support and theoretical-critical penetration of the lifework of Goethe and Wagner, respectively, they significantly advanced their understanding of themselves and freed in their mentor (this is of course not the case for Wagner to the same extent as for Goethe) new artistic energies.

Conversely, the lifework of Schiller, like that of Nietzsche, is not separable from the relationship to what was for them, in both affirmation and critique, the paradigmatic art of Goethe and Wagner, respectively. In spite of or even through this fundamental, exemplary significance of the other's art for their own, Schiller and Nietzsche both stood in a permanent tension of rivalry with their overpowering models, a tension that discharged itself over and over again in a more or less concealed hatred. Whereas Goethe's alliance with Schiller was able to avert this hatred, the friendship of Nietzsche and Wagner was destroyed forever by it. The chief reason for the rupture in their personal relations was undoubtedly Nietzsche's dependence on Wagner, who either shut out other strong personalities or consumed them until they were part of his own. Nietzsche found this dependence intolerable and inhibiting of his own personal and philosophical development. As Cosima Wagner remarked presciently in her diary for 3 August 1871: "It is as if he [Nietzsche] were trying to resist the overwhelming effect of Wagner's personality." Even a few months before that (11 May 1871) she had scented "a dubious streak" in

Nietzsche: "an addiction to treachery, as it were—as if he were seeking to avenge himself for some great impression," that is, the impression Wagner had made on him.

The workings of legend which have clung for more than a century to the demise of this friendship, and whose basic features stem from Nietzsche himself, can today no longer hide the fact that a full-fledged break with Wagner in aesthetic matters did not take place. Even before the alleged break, which Nietzsche located in 1876 (the year of the first Bayreuth Festival) and 1878 (the year in which Wagner sent Nietzsche the published libretto of *Parsifal*), he had taken a very close critical look at Wagner and had formulated a set of arguments which, polemically exaggerated, would reappear in his later anti-Wagnerian writings. Still, he never denied in these and in his post-humously published aphorisms his passion for Wagner's work, which indeed reached a peculiar level of intensity once again in the final period before his paralytic collapse on 3 January 1889.

Wagner had found in Nietzsche, as Goethe had in Schiller, the most astute analyst of the kind of artistic personality he embodied. Nietzsche's critical analysis of Wagner has still not been surpassed; it presents an enduring challenge. The exemplary importance which Nietzsche attached to Wagner's art throughout his life has been made discernible in its full extent only through the critical edition of his literary remains in the complete Nietzsche edition by Giorgio Colli and Mazzino Montinari *(Nietzsche Werke)*. The posthumous fragments which have in large part been published for the first time in this edition represent the most important and intellectually reliable part of the critical confrontation between Nietzsche and Wagner. The fragments lack on the one hand those tactical traits which repeatedly mark the writings and aphorisms published during Wagner's lifetime (thus Nietzsche had avoided all critical emphases in his Wagner appreciations before 1878 and until 1883 qualified his polemics in many ways out of personal considerations); but on the other hand they provide, with their richly pro and contra analyses, a counterweight to the exaggerations of the last anti-Wagnerian writings. On the basis of these fragments Nietzsche's published thoughts on Wagner can at any rate be read in a new light and placed in their proper perspective.

The inception of Nietzsche's concern with Wagner dates from 1861, when the seventeen-year-old studied, with his friend Gustav Krug, Bülow's vocal score of *Tristan,* which had come out in the same year. Seven years later Nietzsche met Wagner for the first time at the home of the orientalist Hermann Brockhaus in Leipzig (8 November 1868). Even at this early stage Nietzsche stood at a decided distance from the sectarian Wagnerians, whose ideological-dogmatic partisanship the later Nietzsche cited as one of the chief grounds for his estrangement from Wagner. In his letter to Erwin Rohde of 22–28 February 1869 he declined to write partisan literature on behalf of the Wagnerian school. He reproached the "Brothers in Wagnero" in particular for taking the accidents of Wagner's artistic personality for the substance, and for seeing the "progress of music" in the things "which Wagner's extraordinary, unique nature blew up here and there like bubbles."

Tribschen and *The Birth of Tragedy*

From Whitsun 1869 Nietzsche visited Wagner and his wife-to-be Cosima regularly in their house at Tribschen near Lucerne. They developed that close, familiar friendship on whose happiness Nietzsche, after his personal break with Wagner, looked back ever afterwards as on a golden age. What bound them most closely together, after music, was their admiration for Schopenhauer's philosophy. The company of Wagner, wrote Nietzsche to his friend Erwin Rohde on 16 June 1869, was "a practical course in Schopenhauerian philosophy." Wagner took a lively interest in Nietzsche's studies and lectures in classical philology. Until the end of their friendship he followed the writings of his young friend with critical sympathy, even when they appeared to have little point of contact with his own work. Indeed, Nietzsche later acknowledged the lively interest Wagner had taken in his early world of thought. Thus he wrote to Franz Overbeck at the end of June 1886: "For, considered all in all, Richard Wagner was the only one up to now, or at least the first, who had any feeling for what I was up to . . . Considering that I am someone who *diu noctuque incubando* from earliest youth on has lived among problems and has his need and his happiness alone there, who would sympathize with that? Richard Wagner did, as I said: and for that reason Tribschen was such a refreshment. Now I have nowhere to go and no one to talk to any more for my refreshment."

Ancient Tragedy and Modern Music Drama

The central intellectual event of the friendship between Wagner and Nietzsche is the coming into being of Nietzsche's book *The Birth of Tragedy out of the Spirit of Music* (1872) and its preliminary versions (for instance *The Greek Music Drama, Socrates and Tragedy,* and *The Birth of Tragic Thought*). Nietzsche's interest in Greek tragedy was directly tied up with his passion for Wagnerian music drama. Each was continually mirrored in the other. The final sentences of *The Greek Music Drama* are symptomatic of this: "Many arts in the highest state of activity and thus an art-work—that is ancient music drama. But anyone who remembers to take a glance at the ideal of contemporary art-reformers must immediately say to himself that the art-work of the future is quite certainly not some radiant but deceptive castle in the air: what we hope for from the future has already once been a reality—in a more than two thousand-year-old past." Thus Nietzsche canceled every historical difference between ancient and modern "music drama." His first book and its preparatory lectures reveal a system of reprojection of modern problems and conditions onto Greek tragedy and equally a projection of that onto the music drama of Richard Wagner. The artwork of the future was believed in and legitimized through the proof that it had already once existed.

The Birth of Tragedy is influenced down to its details by Wagner's theoretical works, above all by *Opera and Drama* (1851) and *Beethoven* (1870). Nietzsche owed his decisive insights not least to the conversations at Tribschen, especially where Greek tragedy was concerned. Wagner was familiar with the basic issues; indeed he had acquired considerable knowledge of classical times during his Dresden period, which he passed on to Nietzsche. It is in no respect true, as people used to assume, that Wagner owed his classical knowledge first and foremost to Nietzsche.

Also, the influence of Wagner's own theoretical explorations into Greek tragedy on *The Birth of Tragedy* is not to be underestimated. The basic idea of the growth of Attic tragedy "from the spirit of music" is already fully developed in Wagner's writings on reform. "Birth from music: Aeschylus. Décadence—Euripides" (SSD XII, 280), proclaims a note from Wagner's fragment *The Artists of the Future* (1849). The line of thought of *The Birth of Tragedy* is already prefigured here: the emergence of tragedy from a musical basis, which came to full fruition in Aeschylus, and its collapse through the withdrawal of the musical element in Euripidean tragedy. Nietzsche's sharp critique of Euripides is inspired not least by Wagner, who had previously reversed the conventional classical evaluation of the order of Attic tragedians: Sophocles and Euripides stand wholly in the shadow of Aeschylus.

Music is the "womb" of Greek drama. Nietzsche adopted the metaphor directly from Wagner. It is definitely the chorus which forms the musical womb of the tragic drama. The chorus, singing and dancing in the Greek orchestra and musically sustaining the dialogue, is replaced in contemporary drama by the modern orchestra. This is Wagner's tirelessly repeated thesis. Through the system of leitmotifs the modern orchestra plays a part "in the complete expression of all the performer's utterances" which is "uninterrupted, clarifying and all-embracing: it is the dynamic womb of music, out of which the unifying bond of expression grows" (*Opera and Drama*; SSD IV, 190f.). The chorus in ancient tragedy cannot play this "uninterrupted" part, according to Wagner, because its singing is separate from the dialogue. Wagner combined his analogy between the Greek chorus and the modern orchestra with a sober description of their functional differences. And he did not allow himself to be tempted by *The Birth of Tragedy* into equating the two elements.

It cannot be doubted that Nietzsche's writings on tragedy were decisively influenced by Wagner's theory of the orchestra as the modern chorus. Just as decisively, however, he chose to ignore Wagner's differentiation between the modern and the ancient elements. Not Wagner's description of the ancient chorus but that of its modern equivalent, the symphony orchestra, is the basis of *The Birth of Tragedy,* whose author now completely equated the chorus with the orchestra, a highly consequential anachronism which Wagner, in spite of his overwhelming enthusiasm for Nietzsche's book, never made his own.

In his "Attempt at a Self-Criticism," which prefaced a new edition of *The Birth of Tragedy*, published in 1886, Nietzsche considered that in his treatise he had "*spoiled* the grandiose *Greek problem*" as it had arisen before his eyes "by introducing the most modern problems" (Nietzsche 1967, p. 24; emphasis in the original). Naturally he was thinking in the first place of Richard Wagner. This self-critical outpouring does not do justice to the way that the tragedy book evolved. With greater correctness one could say that the "Greek problem" was mixed with "modern issues" only later. The problem of the polarity of the Apollonian and the Dionysian, the truly innovative concept of the treatise, surfaces at a relatively late stage in Nietzsche's preliminary studies for *The Birth of Tragedy*, namely in the lecture which he wrote in the summer of 1870, *The Dionysian World-View*.

Thus Nietzsche ascribed to the chorus of Aeschylean tragedy without qualification the function of the modern orchestra: "the chorus as orchestra" is indeed what he wrote in the spring of 1871 in a note among his literary remains. The relationship of the chorus to the action equals the relationship of modern music to the drama, as Wagner described it in his *Beethoven* festschrift of 1870, approvingly cited by Nietzsche in *The Birth of Tragedy*. Wagner was here proceeding from the principle of the Schopenhauerian metaphysics of music. In contradiction to the actual views of the philosopher, who was an unconditional supporter of absolute music, Wagner defined music as the a priori condition which made drama possible, and drama itself as "the counterpart of music made visible" (SSD IX, 112), or, in other words, as an analogous dream image in the sense of Schopenhauer's theory of dreams and somnambulism. Nietzsche developed this theory further with the idea of Attic drama as a visual "release" and as a visionary "radiance" of the Dionysian chorus, by means of which it is precisely the chorus which becomes "the womb of the whole so-called dialogue." Nietzsche likened the process (as did Wagner) to the way "a Beethoven symphony compels individual listeners to describe their experience of it in images," just as "allegorical ideas and symbols stimulated by music arise in the imagination of the composer" (Beethoven's Pastoral Symphony, for instance). That is the reason for the existence of musical drama. According to Nietzsche, the translation of these visions into scenic shapes is a consequence of the compulsive need of symphonic music to release its inner tension in the (Apollonian) form of pictorial images. "Music sounds," Wagner wrote in his essay *On the Term "Musikdrama,"* "and what it sounds you can see there on the stage; to this end it gathers you together." In other words, the essence of music is made palpable by means of "a scenic allegory," just as "a mother demonstrates the mysteries of religion to her children by telling them stories from the legends" (SSD IX, 305). The influence of *The Birth of Tragedy* on this statement of Wagner's written in 1872 is not beyond the bounds of possibility, though Wagner is only developing an idea here which is fundamentally already contained in his 1870 *Beethoven* festschrift.

Nietzsche also used Schopenhauer's metaphysics of music to define the relationship between chorus and drama. Certainly, he followed Schopenhauer's ideas less than Wagner's reinterpretation of them, who in *Beethoven* managed to turn the great philosophical apologist of absolute music into a guarantor of the musical drama that Schopenhauer had expressly rejected. Nietzsche made this reinterpretation completely his own, citing the same passages from Schopenhauer's writing on musical aesthetics that Wagner does. According to Schopenhauer, music presents "the heart of things," in other words, "the metaphysical in relation to all physical things of the world, the thing in itself [*das Ding an sich*] in relation to the world of appearances." Or, to express it in scholastic terminology: "Concepts are the *universalia post rem,* but music gives the *universalia ante rem* and the real world the *universalia in re*" (Nietzsche 1967, p. 103). Nietzsche applied this philosophical idea to the relationship between chorus and dialogue in Attic tragedy; the orchestra (in the Greek sense) is, so to speak, the region of *universalia ante rem,* and the scene the reflection of the *universalia in re.* Chorus and orchestra are thus assigned to two different levels of being. The metaphysical "ante" of music is symbolically embodied in the spatial layout of the orchestra in front of the scene.

Nietzsche believes that he has solved the "riddle" of the "orchestra in front of the scene" by interpreting the latter as a mere vision "generated" by the chorus and the chorus as the only true "reality" of tragedy (Nietzsche 1967, p. 65). This separation of orchestra and scene is of course historically untenable; Nietzsche is projecting the modern separation of stage and auditorium back onto the Attic amphitheater where the scene then becomes the peep show of the chorus, so to speak. The solution of the "riddle" of the orchestra before the scene consists in nothing but its identification with the orchestra pit, the "mystical abyss" in front of the modern stage. By sleight of hand the theater of Dionysus is turned into the precursor of the Bayreuth Festspielhaus.

Although the modern tendencies of *The Birth of Tragedy* owe a great deal to Wagner's aesthetics, they deviate just as much from the latter when it comes to evaluating Greek tragedy historically. Wagner did not go along with the eradication of the historical differences between Attic tragedy and musical drama, as those of his writings show which appeared after the publication of Nietzsche's treatise. In Wagner's view, the chorus in Aeschylean tragedy could not fulfill the same function as the modern orchestra in underpinning the action (as Nietzsche thought it could) because music as an emancipated art form was still unknown to the Greeks. Wagner repeatedly pointed out that the "inseparable and lively ensemble effect of dance gestures and the language of words with music"—what the Greeks called music *(mūsikē)*—did not allow music to unfold autonomously. "Greek music, by which poetry was nearly always meant as well," could "only be seen as the dance which was articulated through music and words" (SSD VII, 106).

In the *Beethoven* festschrift Wagner had concluded from the fact of the primal unity of the arts in Greek "music" that here the art of sound in Schopenhauer's sense of the voice of the In-itself *(An-sich)* had still not emancipated itself from its role as a reflection of the world of appearance. For Wagner the proof of this was the view the Pythagoreans held of the regular ordering of the cosmos and the "musical" harmony of the spheres which resulted from it. It was not true of Greek music that its kingdom "was not of this world," precisely because this world as yet could scarcely be regarded as a deprived civilization alienated from man. Thus music could still embrace the world of appearance and blend with its laws. Human beings needed only the redeeming powers of autonomous music when "to their despair the modern world of appearance began to engulf them everywhere with no possibility of escape." Wagner illustrated this power "vis-à-vis our whole modern civilisation" with this image: "Music sublates [civilisation] as daylight does the light of a lamp" (SSD IX, p. 120).

Nietzsche cites this comparison in *The Birth of Tragedy* to indicate the effect of Dionysian music: "Similarly, I believe, the Greek man of culture felt himself sublated [that is, nullified and then preserved at a higher level in the Hegelian sense of *aufgehoben*] in the presence of the satyric chorus" (Nietzsche 1967, p. 59; translation modified). This identification of the spirit of modern with ancient music has the consequence that Greek culture, which is supposed to be sublated by music, takes on the characteristics of modern civilization. What "in the face of the satyr chorus is sublated"—that is, "the Greek man of culture," "the state and society, in general the gulf between man and man"— they are the human being, the state, the society, and the social alienation of the late nineteenth century. The pessimistic features in Nietzsche's writings on tragedy are to a large extent the result of his projection of Wagner's critique of civilization onto the Greek world.

Absolute Music

If Nietzsche appears in this respect almost more Wagnerian than Wagner himself, he had already distanced himself from Wagner during the period of the gestation of *The Birth of Tragedy* on a point that would gain ever-greater significance for him in later years. Admittedly he did not publish his critique on the subject. It is to be found only in his posthumously published fragments. In a note of early 1871 Nietzsche speaks of the "monstrous aesthetic super-stition" which insists that "with the fourth movement of the Ninth Symphony Beethoven admitted to a solemn recognition of the limits of absolute music, indeed with that movement had so to speak unbolted the doors of a new art." This is precisely Wagner's central thesis, at least before his acceptance of Schopenhauer. The concept of absolute music was introduced by Wagner, and decidedly with a negative connotation. Musical drama signified for him the overcoming of absolute music; the symbolic step beyond it is taken in the final movement of the Ninth.

Nietzsche certainly knows that the reading of Schopenhauer led to a sig-nificant change of emphasis in Wagner's musical aesthetic. In a fragment from 1874 Nietzsche expressly distinguishes Wagner's "older teaching," according to which music was only the "means" to the end of "drama" *(Opera and*

Drama), from the "newer teaching" that "the drama should be understood in relation to the music as a schema, as an exemplar to a general concept." Nietzsche continues: "Music can generate pictures from itself, which will then always be only schemata, as it were images of its own general content." That is for Nietzsche perfectly legitimate. "But how should the image, the representation be able to generate music from itself!" This last thought—the determination of music through extramusical representation—appeared as absurd to Nietzsche as the thought that a son could beget his own father.

The metaphysical revolution of the relationship between music and drama, as Wagner had worked it out under the influence of Schopenhauer, no longer permitted the disqualification of absolute music in the sense of *Opera and Drama,* according to Nietzsche. He clarified the consequences of the arguments of the later Wagner, as Wagner himself had failed to do, in order not to have to disavow the principles of his chief theoretical work. If the "new teaching" is true, wrote Nietzsche in 1874, "the general should not be at all dependent on the specific, that is to say absolute music is in the right, so the music of drama must also be absolute music." That was already Nietzsche's conviction at the time he was composing *The Birth of Tragedy.* In the posthumous notes from 1870–71 he considers that the values of an opera "will be higher, freer, more unconditioned, more Dionysiac as the music unfolds itself and the more so as it despises all so-called dramatic necessities." Until his later notes Nietzsche always sets the concept of "dramatic" music in quotation marks in order to highlight its illusory character, the gap between it and what music ("pure music") is in and for itself.

The positive idea of absolute music also forms the philosophical turning point of *The Birth of Tragedy,* even though Nietzsche avoided that term out of consideration for Wagner's negative valuation, while he unhesitatingly used it in his unpublished notes. For him the death of tragedy coincided with the death of absolute music for the Greeks. He rebuked Euripidean tragedy and the new Attic dithyramb for having degraded music "to imitate as the slave of appearance the essential form of appearance," and he compared them in this respect with the false teaching of the Florentine Camerata, who considered "music as the servant, the libretto as the master." Wagner's musical drama meant for Nietzsche the rebirth of tragedy, because through the symphonic grounding of his works the drama would again be transformed into absolute music (a contradiction of Wagner's own theory in *Opera and Drama*).

After his break with Wagner, Nietzsche asked himself the skeptical question whether the "older teaching" of Wagner was not more constitutive of his work than the "newer." That is, he reproached him for having, in spite of his conversion to Schopenhauer, always wanted to compose music around the drama in practice. According to Nietzsche, Wagner was unable to write any absolute music, but always relied on the scenic element for stimulation. "Wagner begins from a hallucination—not of sounds but of gestures," he says in *The Case of Wagner.* "Then he seeks the sign language of sounds for them" (Nietzsche 1967, p. 170). "As a matter of fact, he repeated a single proposition all his life long: that his music did not mean mere music . . . 'motifs,' gestures, formulas, doing things double and even a hundredfold—he remained an orator even as a musician—he therefore had to move his 'it means' into the foreground as a matter of principle. 'Music is always a mere means': that was his theory, that above all the only *practice* open to him" (Nietzsche 1967, p. 177). As Wagnerian and as anti-Wagnerian, it appears here, Nietzsche is the out-and-out ideologue of absolute music.

The year 1872 was the high point of the relationship between Wagner and Nietzsche. At the beginning of the year *The Birth of Tragedy* appeared, and was received with rapture in Tribschen. "That is the book I have longed for" (Wagner to Cosima on 6 January). After a visit by Wagner to Basel, Nietzsche wrote on 28 January to Erwin Rohde: "I have formed an alliance with Wagner. You can't imagine how close we are now and how our plans coincide." Nietzsche even considered giving up his Basel professorship in the interests of preparing for the Bayreuth Festival, a plan which was disapproved of quite decisively by Wagner and Cosima. In general they tried, especially after the catastrophic failure of *The Birth of Tragedy* in the academic world, to get him back into the area of classical philology and to prevent him from placing the public relations work for Bayreuth before his own academic tasks. Cosima wrote in her letter of 22 August: "Philology is the secure ground, which you must always plant yourself on, to renew your power which is easily lost in the heavenly air of music and the watery depths of philosophy."

At the end of April Cosima disbanded the Tribschen household in Nietzsche's presence. He wrote about it to Karl von Gersdorff: "These three years which I have spent in the proximity of Tribschen, to which I have made twenty-three visits—what they mean for me! If I hadn't had them, what would I be! I am happy to have petrified for myself the world of Tribschen in my book *The Birth of Tragedy*" (1 May 1872).

Bayreuth

On the occasion of the laying of the foundation stone of the Festspielhaus in May, Nietzsche remained in Bayreuth. At the end of May, Ulrich von Wilamowitz-Moellendorff's pamphlet attacking *The Birth of Tragedy* appeared, titled *Philology of the Future,* which of course parodied Nietzsche's commitment to the "music of the future." Wagner wrote an open letter in defense of Nietzsche, which appeared in the *Norddeutscher Allgemeine Zeitung* for 23 June. It is one of the most significant autobiographical documents of Wagner's enthusiastic relationship with classical antiquity. The ostracism of Nietzsche by the guild of philologists brought him still closer to Wagner personally, who confessed in a letter of 25 June that he felt a kind of paternal love for Nietzsche: "Truly you are, after my wife, the one prize that life has brought me."

Nevertheless, in the period that followed, frictions accumulated in Nietzsche's relations with the Wagners, which were triggered by his bizarre judgments, especially on musical matters, his dilettantish ambitions as a composer, and the increasing personal reserve which he displayed toward Wagner. In spite of these more or less subterranean differences, Nietzsche remained unflaggingly true to Wagner and the Bayreuth undertaking. His loyalty was expressed especially in his *Exhortation to the German People,* a cry on behalf of Bayreuth which he laid before the delegates of the Patronatsverein in October 1873. But the "bold language" of the appeal (CT, 31 October), which dramatically called into question the tendencies of the existing world of culture, demanding their overthrow in the interests of supporting "with all possible energy a great artistic deed of German genius," disturbed the committee. On grounds of diplomatic tact the assembly declined to sign the exhortation.

Richard Wagner in Bayreuth

Nietzsche's notebooks of 1874 (one finds in them his most significant contribution to Wagnerian criticism) document an increasing distance from the personality and work of Wagner. They contain, with the possible exception of the analysis of decadence, nearly all the arguments of the later polemical writings. Of course they lack the harsh shrillness, paradoxical exaggerations, and ironic breaks of the late anti-Wagneriana. They still stand in the framework of a fundamentally favorable evaluation. Most of these critical reflections are preliminary studies for the fourth of the *Untimely Meditations: Richard Wagner in Bayreuth,* which was completed in 1876. In the final version the critical accents which Nietzsche had intended to include from the original conception on are almost completely missing. The fourth *Meditation* has the character of a purely apodictic piece of writing, a true "festival address," as Nietzsche himself said. He often speaks here in strange tongues, and one senses—especially with the critical aphorisms of 1874–75 in one's ears—the façade-like character of this official Wagner analysis.

In part the sketches of 1874 center on the problem of "absolute music"; and in part they are an attempt at a wide-ranging description of the artistic character of Wagner in terms of light and shadow. He is characterized as a musical rhetorician and a "displaced actor"; the first outline of the critique of theatrical art is adumbrated so that—and this is the stigma of modern art in general—the various spiritual worlds (*Tristan, Die Meistersinger,* the *Ring*) are put on and removed one after the other like masks; we hear about Wagner the "dilettante" and then we read the assessment: "None of the other great musicians was still in his twenty-eighth year such a bad artist." On this point he takes up Wagner's own statement in *My Life* and other autobiographical writings that he had come to music late through literature—a self-portrayal which is refuted by Wagner's first two operas (*Die Feen* and *Das Liebesverbot*). This remark of Nietzsche's (which testifies to his skepticism about Wagner's genuine musical gift) is an example of that revisionary appropriation of Wagner's self-portrayal, which the latter bitterly recognized in conversation with Cosima: "That bad person [Nietzsche] has taken everything from me, even the weapons with which he now attacks me" (2 August 1878). And nearly all the weaknesses in Wagner's character, which Nietzsche later emphasized, were already mentioned in the notes of 1874, although in a conciliatory light: his refusal to grant artistic individuality to anyone other than himself (for example, to Brahms), his desire for luxury, the "tyrannical urge to the colossal," the lack of restraint in his everyday relationships, and not least his anti-Semitism.

There is little to be noted of these critical insights in *Richard Wagner in Bayreuth*. Nietzsche here tries to equate his own perspectives with Wagner's in many respects, as it were to think his thoughts further. But in spite of the integration of the Wagnerian formulations, the metalevel from which he argues and evaluates cannot be overlooked. When he analyzes in the second chapter Wagner's artistic starting point, which he saw as representative of the modern artist, it is in terms of Wagner's "dilettantism," of "the dangerous desire for spiritual sampling," the "impotent many-sidedness of modern life" from which Wagner craves simplification, and Wagner's insistence on loyalty in the sense of a strong commitment to his artistic existence, which is mirrored in the theme of loyalty in his music dramas.

To the central thoughts of the extensive reflections belongs the recognition of Wagner as "anti-Alexander," retying the Gordian knots of culture, its tendency to disintegrate counteracted through the "astringent power" of his art—corresponding to the unifying, "simplifying" tendency of myth, as Wagner himself describes it in *Opera and Drama*. Again Nietzsche insists that Wagner is a sort of Aeschylus *redivivus;* again he denies the historical split between Greek tragedy and modern music drama. Time is "only a cloud"; the pendulum of history always swings back to its original position. The most philosophically significant parts of the piece are sections 5 and 9, in which Nietzsche predicates the return of mythic-musical drama on the sickness of language. (The relevant expositions of chapter 5 anticipate amazingly, and at times almost word for word, the skepticism about language of Hugo von Hofmannsthal's *Chandos Letter*.) In the "feeling-language" of musically authenticated myth, alienated speech experiences its *restitutio in integrum*. In general one of the basic purposes of the fourth *Meditation* is to make a just valuation of Wagner's much-mocked relationship to language, and his performance as a poet and prose writer.

Ten years later, in a posthumously published note, Nietzsche described his "Festival Oration" of 1876 as an "act of separation and alienation," despite its eulogistic gestures. He cited the following words from it: "Anyone who examines himself accurately knows that a secret enmity belongs to the act of observation, that of looking in the opposite direction." The fourth *Meditation* was supposed to have contributed to the glorification of the Bayreuth Festival of 1876—indeed, the Bayreuth undertaking is described there as the "first circumnavigation of the world of art"—yet Nietzsche now interpreted the event as the peripeteia of his relationship with Wagner. It was, he said, as if the scales had suddenly fallen from his eyes and everything became clear: that Wagner had fallen far away from himself, had become a "Wagnerian." "*What *had happened?* Wagner had been translated into German! The Wagnerian had become master of Wagner!—*German* Art! The *German* Master! *German* Beer!" (Nietzsche 1979, p. 90; emphasis in the original). It is necessary to look upon this later characterization with a certain skepticism. In reality it was not least Nietzsche's poor state of health which led to his flight from Bayreuth during the festival rehearsals; he was no longer physically capable of being present at the long performances. No conclusion can be drawn about a serious estrangement from Wagner at this point. At the end of October 1876, in the company of Malwida von Meysenbug, the last meeting between Nietzsche and Wagner took place in Sorrent.

The Break: Parsifal

According to Nietzsche, the real impetus for his break with Wagner was the publication of the libretto of *Parsifal* which Wagner sent him on 3 January 1878: "Richard Wagner, apparently most triumphant, but in truth a rotten despairing decadent, suddenly sank down, helpless and broken, before the Christian cross" (Nietzsche 1976, p. 676). Here one is definitely dealing with a dramatic invention of Nietzsche's. In fact he had known Wagner's detailed prose draft for *Parsifal* (1865) for a long time. He and Cosima had read it together on 25 December 1869; and on 10 October 1877 he could still write to Cosima: "The glorious promise of Parcival [sic] may comfort us in all things where we need consolation."

In a letter to Malwida von Meysenbug (published by Montinari for the first time in 1980) on the occasion of Richard Wagner's death on 13 February 1883, Nietzsche writes: "Wagner offended me in a fatal way—I'll say it to you!—his slow return and creeping back to Christianity and the church [which he could have known about from his first visits to Tribschen] I have experienced as a personal insult to me; my whole youth and direction seemed to me mocked, insofar as I had dedicated it to a spirit who was capable of this step." The next sentence betrays clearly that Nietzsche was stylizing retrospectively the case of *Parsifal* in the light of his present philosophical endeavor—his battle against Christianity: "To feel this so strongly—that I have penetrated through to unspoken goals and tasks" (cited in Montinari 1985, p. 21).

In this letter also appear the words "fatal offence," which Nietzsche employed in the long-known letter of the same time to Overbeck (22 February 1883), without further explanation. The "offence" is none other than Wagner's return to Christianity. The speculation about that term, at least as it figures in Martin Gregor-Dellin's biography of Wagner, has had the rug pulled out from under it by the publication of this important letter. Gregor-Dellin saw the basis of the "fatal offence" in the exchange of letters which the worried Wagner had had in October 1877 with Nietzsche's physician, Dr. Eiser, and in which Wagner traced the ill health of his young friend to frequent masturbation, in accordance with a widely held medical misconception of the nineteenth century (Gregor-Dellin 1983, pp. 451–456). Whether Nietzsche learned of this exchange through an indiscretion is not finally established, but it has in any case nothing to do with the "offence" of which he speaks in the two letters (cf. Montinari 1985, pp. 20–21).

Nietzsche's sending of *Human, All too Human* to Wagner at the end of April 1878 caused Wagner the same displeasure that Nietzsche had suffered from the receipt of the *Parsifal* poem a few months earlier. Nietzsche speaks in *Ecce Homo* of an ominous "crossing of two books," which had been "simultaneously" delivered to their respective addresses—likewise a distortion of the facts with stylizing intent, since the *Parsifal* libretto had been lying for more than three months on Nietzsche's desk. Wagner took Nietzsche's new book as a breaking off of their friendship, and in the August 1877 number of *Bayreuther Blätter* published an article, *Public and Popularity,* which contains a covert but for that reason all the more unpleasant polemic against the author of *Human, All too Human.* Thus was the personal break sealed.

Nietzsche followed the *Parsifal* festival of 1882 from a distance with strained attention, and studied the score carefully with his sister, who attended the festival. The comparison of *Parsifal* with his own youthful compositions seduced Nietzsche into writing to Peter Gast: "I confess: I have become aware with real horror of how close I really stand to Wagner" (25 July 1882).

After Wagner's Death

The death of Wagner on 13 February 1883 affected Nietzsche "terribly," as he wrote to Malwida von Meysenbug in the letter cited earlier. "In spite of which I believe that the experience, seen in the long view, is a relief for me. It was hard, very hard, to have to be for six years the enemy of someone one had so honoured and loved, as I have loved Wagner; yes, and to have to condemn oneself as an enemy to silence—for the sake of the respect which the man as a whole deserved." In all Nietzsche's letters after Wagner's death there emerges the same conflict of feeling: deep shock over the death of his one-time friend together with the sense of the "essential lightening" of his life (letter to Peter Gast, 19 February 1883). Again it shows that Nietzsche had suffered a terrible conflict of pressures from Wagner—the chief reason for the break. "In the last summer"—the *Parsifal* summer—"I felt that he had taken away from me all the people in Germany worth influencing," he writes in the letter to Gast. Here, as in other letters and conversations, he declares himself the "heir" of Richard Wagner, and indeed of the good, the "real Wagner," whom he played off against the Wagner of *Parsifal* "who had become old." When at the beginning of 1887 he heard for the first time the prelude to Wagner's last work, he turned his previous judgment about it, at least in musical respects, on its head. "Has Wagner ever done anything better?" he asks in his letter to Gast of 21 January, and there follows—as also in the posthumously published sketches—a eulogistic description of Wagner's late style.

Nietzsche's expressions about Wagner from the last years before his breakdown are characterized by extreme fluctuations of judgment. Effusive praise stands cheek by jowl with brusque dismissal. The latter results not least from the bitter insight that he had not got rid of the rival Wagner even after his death. "Even after his death the old seducer Wagner is still taking the few remaining people from me on whom I might have an effect," he wrote to Malwida von Meysenbug at the end of July 1888. Early in 1888 in Turin he began the attack, *The Case of Wagner,* whose shrill polemics, which are constantly turning into emphatic praise of Wagner's work, lost him many of his friends. It came almost to the point of breaking up his friendship with Malwida von Meysenbug, which Nietzsche, like Wagner, sought to preserve.

The second attack, *Nietzsche contra Wagner,* begun at the end of the year, is a collection and revision of the most important aphorisms on Wagner from Nietzsche's writings since *Human, All too Human.* On the day before his breakdown, 2 January 1889, he ordered that *Nietzsche contra Wagner* not be published. Thus the second attack belongs to Nietzsche's unauthorized literary remains. The nonpublication was no doubt connected with his new passionate turning toward *Tristan,* testified to by the last letters to Peter Gast and Carl Fuchs: "[*Tristan*] is the chief work and one which is without equal not only in music, but in all the arts" (to Carl Fuchs, 27 December 1888). The new passion for Wagner of the last period before the breakdown is also documented in the relevant passages in *Ecce Homo:* "Wagner is altogether the foremost name in *Ecce Homo*" (to Gast, 31 December 1888).

Wagner as Representative of Decadence

Nietzsche's debate with Wagner in the decade from 1878 to 1888 is too complex, and by virtue of its aphoristic and unsystematic form too diffuse, to be presented here in any more than its basic features. It will be considered only in what is certainly its central aspect: Wagner as representative of decadence. This concept surfaces for the first time in connection with Wagner in Nietzsche's letter to Peter Gast of 25 July 1882, with reference to *Parsifal:* "What sudden décadence! And what Cagliostism!" Nietzsche attached a new force to this concept after reading Paul Bourget's *Théorie de la décadence* in the first part of *Essais de psychologie contemporaine* (1883). Before that decadence was for him only a synonym for decline (as also for Wagner). Through Bourget he now became attentive to the modern revaluation, in France, of the originally pejorative concept, as it is found for the first time in Baudelaire: that is, decadence as biological weakening and nervous overrefinement; weary skepticism sick through knowledge, in contrast to the *vita activa;* a heightened responsiveness to perversity; the weakening of the naive, unmediated Will to Live and sympathy with death, in opposition to banal, everyday reality. This aesthetic revaluation of the concept of decadence was not capable in Nietzsche of wholly superseding its old meaning, and for him both senses often cross over dialectically. From this results the ever-renewed changing of Nietzsche's judgment on Wagner the decadent, the constant shifts of light in which his dispute with Wagner takes place. Thomas Mann, in his essay *The Sorrows and*

Grandeur of Richard Wagner, quite rightly characterizes Nietzsche's critique of Wagner as "a panegyric with reversed signs, as another form of glorification." The possibility that the signs of value can almost always be reversed in the case of Wagner goes along with Nietzsche's relation to decadence, which can only be grasped in contraries.

In the foreword to *The Case of Wagner,* Nietzsche justifies his opposition to Wagner: "I am, no less than Wagner, a child of this time; that is, a decadent: but I comprehended this, I resisted it." Wagner is a decadent without being aware that he is; Nietzsche, by contrast, moves after his self-testimony through reflection, through self-description as a decadent, to distance himself from the label. The fact that Wagner lacked the consciousness of decadence resulted in his always denying its positive worth and virtue; that is, he came to terms with that against which decadence defended itself: the established political and ideological powers, the Reich. Wagner, by nature an enemy of these, condescended to them, according to Nietzsche, through the "lie of the grand style," through the "alfresco" and monumentality of his art. One of the chief theses of the later Nietzsche is the double vision of the Wagnerian music drama: that he who "had created the most lonely music that there is" was indeed a theater lover who strove for the effects of representative mass art. Indeed, it is not in these traits that one finds the real Wagner but in artistic "délicatesse," in "psychological degeneracy," and from a perspective opposite to that of the theater lover and mass eloquence: Wagner is someone who "prefers to sit quietly in the nooks of collapsed houses: there, hidden, hidden from himself, he paints his real masterpieces." Nietzsche calls him "the master of the very minute," the "Orpheus of all secret misery," "our greatest miniaturist in music," and so on (Nietzsche 1976, p. 663ff.).

All the positive elements of Wagnerian art which Nietzsche describes here belong on the side of decadence; only when Wagner is a decadent is he credible. His heavy Teutonic tendencies, which bring him an obscure following, his keeping his eye on the established powers are for Nietzsche nothing but Wagner's attempts to escape from his true self. It is not life in the "ascendant" but life in "decline" that finds its legitimate expression in Wagner's art. With this judgment Nietzsche opposed the prevailing view of Wagner in Germany. Among Germans Wagner is "merely a misunderstanding," as he puts it in *Ecce Homo* and is always repeating in the posthumously published fragments. Wagner really belongs to Paris, in the circle of French late Romantics and decadents. The huge influence of Wagner on European, and particularly French, decadence proves that Nietzsche was right on this point.

Decadence can be overcome only by someone who faces up to it and sees through it. According to Nietzsche, this is precisely what Wagner avoided doing. At the same time, Wagner's ideal of the Dionysian as an art of life in the ascendant has its roots in his own experience as a decadent, and is hence dialectically related to it. Decadence is a necessary transitional stage in the developing process of life. In the epilogue to *The Case of Wagner,* Nietzsche emphasizes that master morality as well as Christian morality, classical as well as modern aesthetics (that is, the aesthetics of decadence), are necessarily related to one another. Dionysian art, the art propagated by Nietzsche that should emerge from life in the ascendant, must not forget the experience of life in decline: nervous susceptibility, psychological sensitivity, and all other virtues of decadence. This art must know whence the resurgence will begin; that is, it must really have taken the measure of Wagner's decadent modernity. "Wagner sums up modernity. There is no way out, one must first become a Wagnerian" (Nietzsche 1967, p. 156).

In spite of his many harsh judgments about Wagner, Nietzsche holds to the conviction, even in *The Case of Wagner,* that there is no musical alternative. The homage to Bizet at the beginning of *The Case of Wagner* was included only as a rhetorical device, as an "ironical antithesis," he confesses to Carl Fuchs in his letter of 27 December 1888. This homage was engendered by the desire for a music which obeys the "flute of Dionysus," a music which still "transfigures the world, says yes," from whose lack Nietzsche suffers as "from an open wound," as he puts it in *The Case of Wagner.* But Bizet appears no more after the opening pages of the pamphlet, and Brahms, who had been made the antipode of Wagner by the classical party of Hanslick, is scornfully dismissed by Nietzsche, in opposition to his earlier judgment, which he had used to snub Wagner. "Other musicians do not enter into consideration against Wagner" is his lapidary perception, for Wagner's music is the necessary revelation of "corruption," the paradigmatic expression of the modern as life in decline. Panegyric and critique here go once more inseparably together.

In the aphorism "Star-Friendship" of *The Gay Science,* which was originally to have appeared also in *Nietzsche contra Wagner,* Nietzsche moved his friendship with Wagner into a mythical sphere. "We were friends and have become estranged. But that is right," he says there. "That we have become estranged is the law *above* us: we should thereby become more honourable to one another! . . . There is probably a tremendous invisible stellar orbit in which our very different ways and goals may be *included* as small parts of the path,— let us rise up to this thought! But our life is too short and our power of vision too small for us to be more than friends in the sense of that sublime possibility." Nietzsche's belief in such a "star-friendship" between himself and Wagner exposes all attempts to take a partisan view of their epoch-making encounter as all too "earthly," as fanatical bias, which contrasts miserably with the intellectual dimensions of their friendship and enmity.

Translated by Michael Tanner

CHAPTER 15

Wagnerism as Concept and Phenomenon

ERWIN KOPPEN

Wagnerismus, or *Wagnerianismus* in German, *Wagnerisme* in French, Wagnerism or Wagnerianism in English—these are all imprecise labels which emerged in the last decade of the nineteenth century. Even then they defied all attempts at exact definition, and to this day, in spite of intense scholarly efforts (Woolley 1931; Jäckel 1931; Guichard 1963; Coeuroy 1965; Koppen 1973; Furness 1982), no greater clarity has resulted. But the scholarly use of these terms does reveal certain characteristic areas of overlap and consensus which can be summarized as follows:

First, Wagnerism is a predominantly, if not exclusively, *extramusical* form of Wagner reception. Wagner exerted a more extensive extramusical influence than any other composer before or after him. His impact was greater on contemporary literature, on aesthetic theory, on facets of philosophical and political thought, and—albeit to a lesser extent—on the plastic arts than it was, in fact, on contemporary music. This is especially true of France, less so of Germany, England, and Italy. Aspects of this far-reaching impact are subsumed in the term *Wagnerism.*

Second, Wagnerism differs from pure Wagner worship not so much in the sense that it is a more thoughtful and informed response to Wagner's art (Wagnerism does not exclude ignorance of whole areas of his work), but rather in the sense that his art becomes linked, frequently in a rather idiosyncratic fashion, to particular spiritual, literary, and other currents and conceptions, and is held to constitute their very basis and justification. Quite regularly, certain programs and ideologies are projected onto Wagner. (A similar tendency informs to a considerable degree those attempts, which can be observed in Germany, to make Wagner the symbol of nationalist, indeed fascist ideologies; in fact, however, neither at the time nor nowadays do such ideologies form part of the concept of Wagnerism, but rather constitute a different and quite separate chapter.)

Third, the notion of Wagnerism refers to a phenomenon that has acquired unmistakable historical contours. Its beginnings go back to the 1860s; it reached its heyday in the last three decades of the nineteenth century, and gradually subsided in the years leading up to the First World War. By the end of the war it was already felt to be part of history—and herein resides the contrast with Wagner worship, which operates without any sense of historical delimitation.

The Basis and Beginnings of Wagnerism

Even though Wagnerism is to be distinguished from Wagner worship, it undoubtedly arose because of the subterranean currents of enthusiasm. Moreover, it emerged as a countervailing voice to the widespread and virulent hatred of Wagner which was so much a feature of the late nineteenth century. These processes can best be illustrated with reference to France, which is the actual birthplace of Wagnerism. The term *Wagnerism* only established itself in the 1880s, but its origins go back well before that—to be precise, to 1861. Its birth certificate might well be said to be Baudelaire's article *Richard Wagner et "Tannhäuser" à Paris,* which initially appeared in the *Revue européenne* on 1 April 1861, and was later enlarged by the addition of a postscript (see Baudelaire 1861). The article came into being under characteristic circumstances. In 1860 three concerts of Wagner's music in Paris had produced both intense enthusiasm for and a repudiation of Wagner. The Paris premiere of *Tannhäuser* in March 1861 resulted in a famous scandal: political and musical opponents of Wagner joined forces with the aristocratic members of the Jockey Club, who deplored the absence of the customary ballet in the second act. They managed, by means of mass disturbances, to put an end to the run of *Tannhäuser* after its third performance—against the wishes of the enthusiastic majority of Wagner supporters, of whom Baudelaire was one. At one level his articles are the polemical broadside of an impassioned Wagnerian who portrays his opponents as ignorant philistines. But at another level Baudelaire attempts to offer a penetrating analysis of Wagner's music. He bases his arguments on the program for the 1860 concerts, on Wagner's *Music of the Future* (a summary, compiled for the French public, of key passages from *Art and Revolution, The Art-Work of the Future,* and *Opera and Drama*), and on an essay by Liszt, *Lohengrin and Tannhäuser.* Baudelaire's article is no mere polemic against Wagner's enemies; nor is it simply a straightforward attempt to convey information. Rather, it displays that feature which becomes so typical of later Wagnerism—a readiness to transfer one's own thinking, one's own aesthetic principles onto Wagner's art. Of particular interest in this context are those passages where Baudelaire describes his impressions on first hearing the *Lohengrin* prelude. He claims not only that he had sensations of weightlessness and strange visions of light, but also that he experienced forms of synesthesia. He summarizes these by quoting two stanzas from his famous poem *Correspondances,* in which synesthesia emerges as one of the cornerstones of his aesthetics. His interpretation of the Venus figure in *Tannhäuser* is also characteristic: her demonic power clearly reminds him of certain female figures in his own lyric poetry, and in his analysis of the overture to *Tannhäuser* we detect elements of his own satanism.

Baudelaire's Wagner essays are the earliest manifestations of French Wagnerism, the most substantial and significant expression of which is the *Revue wagnérienne,* which appeared in Paris between 1885 and 1887. A quarter of a century after Baudelaire's essay, and after the death of Wagner himself, this journal was born in a climate of Wagner enthusiasm which was in many ways distinct from that of the early 1860s. Wagner had by now managed to establish himself across a broad front and, as we shall see, had become an inseparable part of cultural life in general and of the literary scene in particular. He had even made inroads into the cultural awareness of the aristocracy and upper bourgeoisie, and, as Carassus showed in 1966, was very much part of the cultural snobbery of those circles. The Bayreuth Festival played no small part in this process: attendance was de rigeur not only on grounds of musical interest but, even at that time, because of the snob value which appealed so powerfully to aristocrats and upper-bourgeois circles alike.

The *Revue wagnérienne* was conceived by Houston Stewart Chamberlain, founded by Edouard Dujardin, and its presiding genius was Théodore de Wyzewa. As its name implies, the *Revue wagnérienne* was a journal devoted to Wagner. It published articles on Wagner and related themes, excerpts in French translation from Wagner's theoretical writings, and introductions to his theory; and, in addition, it gave factual information about performances and concerts and about the Bayreuth Festival, notes on Wagner literature, references to the *Bayreuther Blätter,* and so on. But the journal was shaped and dominated by a very different sort of contribution. The key authors were not expert musicologists: as a rule they were not even Wagner specialists. They were, rather, important figures in the intellectual and above all the literary circles of the time. Swinburne, Mallarmé, Verlaine, Ghil, Huysmans, Gérard de Nerval, and Villiers de L'Isle-Adam, and in addition Catulle Mendès, who was well known both as a lyric poet of the Parnassian school and as the author of successful decadent novels. Mendès was one of the most important and earliest Wagner enthusiasts in France, and he was for a time married to a celebrated Wagnerite, Judith Gautier. Another representative of Wagner circles in France was the esoteric dramatist and essayist Edouard Schuré. The editor of the *Revue* was the twenty-four-year-old Edouard Dujardin; in his case, too, the *Revue wagnérienne* marked the beginnings of a literary (and not, it should be noted, musical) career. Théodore de Wyzewa was a philosopher manqué.

It was because the interests of these men lay outside music that French Wagner enthusiasts who were musically knowledgeable refused to take the *Revue* seriously. And indeed, the *Revue*'s writers were not concerned with Wagner the musician. They sought to approach the Wagner phenomenon in literary and, to a certain extent, philosophical terms. For example, the *Revue wagnérienne* contains a cycle of eight sonnets in praise of Wagner which were for the most part contributed by leading representatives of contemporary French poetry: there is, for example, Mallarmé's famous Wagner poem and the equally well known *Parsifal* poem by Verlaine. The presence of other contributors such as Stuart Merrill and Charles Morice suggests that Wagner was the pretext for a symbolist anthology. Other pieces—such as Huysmans' prose paraphrase of the *Tannhäuser* overture (by no means a musical analysis, but rather the recording of a layman's subjective impressions)—take up motifs from decadent art. Mallarmé's *Richard Wagner: Rêveries d'un poète français* is at one and the same time a concentrated and hermetic prose text and a theoretical disquisition on the nature of drama. The contribution of Théodore de Wyzewa (whose name was actually Wyzewski) on Wagner's pessimism is a philosophical treatise which is indebted less to Wagner than to Schopenhauer and which essentially offers the personal responses of its young author (as Wyzewa's granddaughter, Isabelle Wyzewska, made clear in her dissertation on the *Revue wagnérienne;* see Wyzewska 1934). The journal gives a faithful, although not necessarily complete, picture of contemporary Wagnerism in which symbolism, decadence, esoteric philosophy, and reflections on innovative impulses in drama are brought very much to the fore. In the first number of the journal, Fourcaud's leading article defines the term *Wagnerism* exclusively in terms of music and the stage; but the contents tell another story. For the journal was concerned with interpreting Wagner not as a composer and dramatist, but as the decisive spiritual force of the second half of the century, as the leader and catalyst in all areas, and this transformed Wagner into a kind of magic focus on which all the lines of their own intuitions, poetic moods, and aesthetic programs converged. If Baudelaire's *Tannhäuser* article marked the birth of Wagnerism, the *Revue wagnérienne* may be seen as its veritable compendium.

The remarkable fact that a foreign composer should be accorded a journal of his own was not confined to France. In England there appeared in the years 1888–1895 the journal *The Meister,* which may conceivably have been inspired by the *Revue wagnérienne;* and in Italy, from 1893 to 1895 a *Cronaca wagneriana* was published. Such journals consisted largely of notes and information for the followers of Wagner who wished to know about the master and his work: there was no attempt to establish any particular connection with the cultural and literary situation of the time. In Germany the *Bayreuther Blätter* developed along quite different lines and unashamedly ignored the *Revue wagnérienne.* The fact that in the French journal Wagner was associated with such suspect movements as decadence and symbolism triggered nothing but perplexity and even disgust in Bayreuth. Indeed, Wagnerism developed entirely apart from the Bayreuth circle: Bayreuth and Wagnerism went their separate ways. It was the decadent moods and symbolist currents of the European fin de siècle which were most closely linked with Wagnerism, and they continued to determine its image.

Symbolism

It would not be entirely accurate to speak of Wagner's influence on the symbolist movement in Europe. The symbolists' view of Wagner was, in a particularly striking way, an exercise in self-projection, even identification. Wagner was first and foremost "the living banner of the Symbolist school" (Woolley 1931). Or, to put the matter in a different way, he was the prototype of the antibourgeois, innovative artist who defied any and every convention. He also personified the antirealist tendencies of the symbolist writers. Even Tolstoy's polemically intended assertion that the deliberate opacity and incomprehensibility of the symbolist poets derived from Wagner contains more than a grain of truth. But, contrary to the frequently held view, it must be noted that the ideal of musicality, worshiped by the symbolist poets, cannot possibly have derived from Wagner, for purely chronological reasons. Wagnerism did not create a symbolist climate. It simply surfaced at a particular time and raised the temperature of a musical climate which was already warm. But it did no more than to help the symbolists find a more precise conception of "musicality" (Coeuroy 1965). Verlaine's famous poem *Art poétique* was conceived at a time when its author had not yet concerned himself with Wagner. Only after the event was this worship of musicality linked with Wagner, particularly by Edouard Dujardin, Stuart Merrill, Gustave Kahn, Albert Mockel, and in England by Arthur Symons. In all such cases we are concerned not with influence but with a retrospective projection. When René Ghil in his theoretical treatise *Traité du verbe* developed his notion of "verbal instrumentation," according to which modern lyric poetry was supposed to represent a musical score couched in words, he did specifically add one chapter titled "Wagnérisme." The putative link with Wagner, however, is not a matter of "influence, of a shaping presence, but simply an analogy between Wagner's and Ghil's work" (Guichard 1964). Here, too, Wagner is associated with symbolism, but he did not exert a precise, demonstrable influence.

What is precise and demonstrable, however, is that phenomenon which Guichard calls "Wagnerian imagery," that is to say, a predilection for Wagnerian themes, images, and motifs, including allusions—in varying degrees of subtlety—to Wagner's work. Alongside the already mentioned poems in the *Revue wagnérienne* there are individual items by Jules Laforgue, Francis Viélé-Griffin, Stuart Merrill, and Charles Morice, who had already made names for themselves as contributors to the *Revue wagnérienne*. Such imagery is of course also to be found in the works of those poets who were not particularly close to symbolism: Pierre Louÿs, Robert de Montesquiou, and Catulle Mendès. It is not excessive to suggest that Wagner had furnished contemporary French lyric poetry with a whole system of images and symbols which facilitated the process of poetic communication.

A similar phenomenon, albeit in milder form, can be observed in English lyric poetry, in particular among the writers of the so-called Yellow Nineties.

Motifs from and allusions to Wagner can be found especially in the work of Richard Le Galienne, who also made a name for himself as translator of *Tristan*. One should further mention Eugene Lee-Hamilton, Winston O'Sullivan, John Payne, and in particular Theodore Wratislaw. There are, in addition, references to Wagner in the theoretical writings of William Butler Yeats. The Wagnerism of Aubrey Beardsley will be considered in the next section of this chapter. Suffice it to say that his Wagner drawings which appeared in *The Yellow Book,* which was utterly symptomatic of the English fin de siècle, and his *Tannhäuser* novel became inseparable from the Wagnerian climate of the time. One must also mention Arthur Symons, who not only included Wagner motifs in his poetry but also published analytical discussions of Wagner (Symons 1909). His drama *Tristan and Iseult* (1917) displays unmistakable traces of Wagner's *Tristan*. In Italy and Germany, symbolist and related poetry shows scarcely any echoes of Wagner. Even a Wagnerian such as Gabriele d'Annunzio did not work with Wagnerian themes in his lyric poetry, but tended to confine them to his narrative production. The same applies to contemporary German poetry, which was untouched by Wagnerism in the French manner—that is, by the attempt to place one's own poetic practice under Wagnerian "patronage" or to employ Wagnerian imagery.

Wagner and Decadence

From the very start, Wagner and the world of his music dramas took possession of decadent literature of the fin de siècle. In innumerable literary documents (most particularly in poetry and the novel) decadent writers countermanded those notions of inevitable historical progress which were so much a feature of the second half of the nineteenth century with assertions of an equally inescapable decline and decay. The universe of decadence was essentially a topsy-turvy world in which, by definition, all values of contemporary society were transformed into their polar opposite. Just as decay was claimed as a positive value and was made to defy progress, so too sickness challenged health, death challenged life, artificiality was pitted against naturalness, uselessness against practicality. This is compounded by that notion, which in the wake of Baudelaire runs through all decadent literature, that physical degeneration and sickliness are the most fertile basis for genuine sensibility and creativity. In this literature of "femmes fatales" and "femmes fragiles," of androgynous figures, of fragile aesthetes, of degenerate geniuses, of the sickly and sensitive, of declining families and dynasties, of decaying towns and kingdoms, of a weary disparagement of any and every belief in progress—in all this Wagner is an omnipresent force.

It is significant that the writer who first attributed a positive value to the word *decadence* and who first endowed the concept with its morbid appeal, Baudelaire, is one of the standard-bearers of Wagnerism. In his *Tannhäuser* essay he invokes the characteristic decadent motifs of drugs and aestheticism. It is equally significant that the author of the supreme decadent work *À rebours,* Joris K. Huysmans, published a paraphrase of the *Tannhäuser* overture in the *Revue wagnérienne* which is also shot through with decadent motifs. Here too, as with Baudelaire, the music of the overture suggests satanic sexuality, and furthermore, in typical decadent fashion, the cultural mode of late antiquity is invoked. Other decadent authors view *Tannhäuser* as the paradigm for the often-proclaimed sensuality of Wagnerian music. It is a point on which, for once, they agree with Wagner's detractors, Hanslick and Nordau, who accuse this music of lustfulness and salaciousness. *Tannhäuser* becomes the very emblem of decadent sexuality. This can be seen most clearly and explicitly in Beardsley's novel *Venus and Tannhäuser,* a work whose "unexpurgated" edition until a few decades ago existed only in private printings. Beardsley shows here what in Wagner's opera figures as prehistory: Tannhäuser's experiences with Venus on the Hörselberg, which are portrayed in a frivolous and fantastic review of decadent sexuality. In this context one should also mention Beardsley's Wagner drawings, which apply the decadent ideals of morbidity, hyperrefinement, and physical fragility to Wagnerian figures. *Die Walküre* is another work of Wagner's in which the writers of the decadent generation discovered a sexual motif which was close to their hearts: the incest between Siegmund and Sieglinde. Thomas Mann, who in his early works (up to *Death in Venice*) handled Wagner motifs in ways which can only be described as decadent, writes in his story *Wälsungenblut* the paradigmatic decadent tale of incest, and he explicitly sets it against the background of a performance of *Die Walküre.* Twenty years earlier, the motif of the brother and sister who are impelled to copy the model of Siegmund and Sieglinde had already appeared in a French decadent novel, Elémir Bourges's *Le crépuscule des dieux,* whose Wagnerian title alludes to the decline of a princely family.

Tristan was the work which the decadent writers most esteemed. The motif of the *Liebestod* was particularly cherished—more for its text than for its music: not only did it express the shared Romantic origins of both Wagner's work and decadent writing, but the notion that sexual love must lead to death rather than to the begetting of new life accorded with the cast of mind of the decadent generation. From Baudelaire on, the *Liebestod* is a favorite motif of decadent poetry, novels, and stories, and for the most part the link with Wagner's *Tristan* is made explicit. One thinks, for example, of the very title of Thomas Mann's *Tristan,* or d'Annunzio's novel *Trionfo della morte* (Triumph of death), where whole passages, verbally paraphrasing the *Tristan* prelude, serve to create a *Liebestod* atmosphere. Similarly, in works by Catulle Mendès and above all in Joséphin Péladan's esoteric Wagner novel *La victoire du mari,* as in many lesser works and poems, Wagner's *Tristan* is invoked. In this context Villiers' drama *Axël* deserves mention, although it is not characteristic of decadence: it ends with a love-death, and Wagner's *Tristan* is invoked both thematically and stylistically, not least in the stage directions.

The decadents found their favorite motif of the decline of whole families and races in the *Ring,* and especially in *Götterdämmerung,* where it was combined with an apocalyptic mood to which they were hardly strangers. In

Bourges's novel *Le crépuscule des dieux* the decline of a German princely house is expressed in terms of physical degeneration and gradual demoralization, and the process is constantly marked by Wagnerian allusions. At the beginning Wagner himself conducts a concert; at the end there is a performance of *Götterdämmerung* in Bayreuth. A work such as Thomas Mann's *Buddenbrooks* is a German parallel. It, too, concerns the decline of a family: as the dynastic line weakens, so there is a gain in artistic sensibility and refinement. Here the process also unfolds under Wagnerian auspices, for his music is invoked at key points in the novel.

Wagner himself appears in person or more or less in literary disguise and refraction in a number of decadent works and tales—as in Catulle Mendès' novel *Le roi vierge,* whose eponymous hero is clearly identifiable as Ludwig II of Bavaria, and in which a composer appears, trembling with nervousness, whose name is Hans Hammer. Wagner-Hammer is a type familiar in decadent literature; his nervous condition marks him out as a "higher degenerate." Wagner appears (under his own name) as a frail but still charismatic old man in d'Annunzio's novel *Il fuoco,* whose central theme is the relationship of the poet Stelio Effrena (a disguise for the writer himself) with the actress Foscarina (Eleonora Duse). This work stands as a document of decadent Wagnerianism not so much by the fact that the composer himself appears as by the combination of his appearance with the setting: Venice. The fact that Wagner died in Venice, the classic city of decay and death in European literature in general and decadent literature in particular, has left its mark on French literature (Maurice Barrès, *La mort de Venise*) and on English literature (Vernon Lee, *A Wicked Voice*). The figure of the hero in Thomas Mann's *Death in Venice* is indebted not only to Gustav Mahler but also to Richard Wagner.

Finally, it should be noted that Wagner was described as decadent in polemical attacks—by the Budapest cultural critic Max Nordau in his (at the time) greatly respected study *Degeneration* (Nordau 1895), and above all by Nietzsche. *The Case of Wagner,* in which the disappointed Wagnerian vents his hatred, can surely also be seen to partake of decadent Wagnerism: numerous formulations and allusions in the essay reveal that it was a phenomenon with which Nietzsche was completely familiar.

Other Facets of Wagnerism

Wagnerism is by no means confined to the writings of the symbolists and the decadents, although admittedly outside these two particular areas the picture becomes much more blurred. While it cannot be doubted that Wagnerism has implications for both philosophy and the theory of drama, the connections are anything but clear-cut. This has particularly to do with the fact that, for purely linguistic reasons, many people at the time had no direct access to Wagner's theoretical writings but frequently knew them only at second or even third hand, usually on the strength of salon or café conversations. It is also true that Wagnerism represents not an authentic reception of Wagner, but rather the attempt to claim one of the supreme geniuses of the century as patron saint of one's own concerns.

Wagner's notion of the total work of art found no true disciples, although in France there was certainly the tendency to call every theatrical form that was unrealistic, antinaturalist—and therefore symbolist, Romantic, or idealistic—Wagnerian. This applies not only to Villiers' work but also to the early Claudel, who expressly spoke of his allegiance to Wagner, and to Maurice Maeterlinck, in whose work there are no traces of direct Wagnerian influences. It applies also to Edouard Schuré, who is usually cited as proof positive of the impact of Wagnerism on drama theory: the second volume of his work *Le drame musical,* which is titled *Richard Wagner: Son oeuvre et son idée* (Schuré 1875), does indeed portray Wagner as the great—in principle exemplary— modern music dramatist. "The rebirth from the spirit of music, not only of tragedy, but of art itself and, supremely among the arts, of poetry—this is what he postulates" (Jäckel 1931). This was certainly a "Wagnerian ambition," as Guichard (1964) put it, but he also noted that, for Schuré, Wagner was less an exemplary than an initiating force. (As a footnote one could mention that Schuré, in his Celtic drama *Vercingétorix*—without music—failed in his attempt to bring Wagnerian drama onto the stage.) In this context, we should also recall Mallarmé, who in his article *Richard Wagner: Rêveries d'un poète français,* which appeared in the *Revue wagnérienne,* maps out an ideal theater; in the course of his argument Wagner is frequently invoked and praised. But even so, Mallarmé ultimately offers "another conception of art, theatre, and the use of music" (Guichard 1964)—namely his own. The article exudes an almost religious veneration for the master; in this sense it is a typical document of Wagnerism, although (and this, too, is characteristic of Wagnerism) Mallarmé had at the time, as he himself admitted, scarcely seen a work of Wagner's on the stage.

This religious, cultlike enthusiasm can be found in other authors. One thinks in the first place of Joséphin Péladan, one of the principal representatives of contemporary French occultism, who saw *Parsifal* in Bayreuth in 1888 and, by his own account, was inspired to found three esoteric orders (Rosicrucian, Temple, and Grail). Péladan not only wrote a work, *Théâtre complet de Wagner,* in which he offered detailed analyses of eleven of Wagner's music dramas, but he also used Wagner's music to underpin occult events in the many novels of his cycle *La décadence latine;* one thinks, for example, of *La victoire du mari.* Schuré should also be mentioned again in this context. He saw in Wagner not only the genius who had initiated the idea of modern drama but also "the magus and leader of souls, the greatest instructive occultist who ever lived." In comparison with this, the various attempts to take possession of Wagner in philosophical or ideological terms, which also belong to the phenomenon of Wagnerism, are relatively harmless. They frequently invoke Schopenhauer and Nietzsche; as is well known, the former exerted a lasting influence on Wagner, and the latter was bound to Wagner's work initially in admiration, then in repudiation. Hence, it came about that the philosophers' influence on contemporary literature went hand in hand with Wagner's, so that when the name Wagner was mentioned, it often meant in fact Schopenhauer or Nietzsche. The French-Swiss novelist Edouard Rod advocated Schopenhauerian Wagnerism in his novel *La course à la mort*, and similar views were expressed in England by John Payne. Wyzewa should again be mentioned here. D'Annunzio, in his study, which is significantly titled *Il caso Wagner*, views Wagner in the light of Nietzsche's ideas and defends him against Nietzsche (d'Annunzio 1893). The Italian writer Angelo Conti, in his essay *L'arte delle Muse*, offers an even more striking example of Nietzschean Wagnerism in Italy.

Finally in this context, one should refer to the brilliant study by George Bernard Shaw, *The Perfect Wagnerite* (Shaw 1898). With splendidly assured simplification of complex issues, he sees the *Ring* as an allegory of contemporary capitalist society—or, more accurately, of capitalism at the time of the composition of the *Ring*. Capitalism is represented in the figure of Alberich; Wotan embodies the power of religion and the state; Siegfried the unbroken anarchic force of protest. The whole drama revolves around money and the wielding of power resulting from money. This, as Shaw is able to show with much plausibility, corresponds at least in part to Wagner's essential ideas and conceptions. Shaw uses his reading of the *Ring*, however, to put forward his own analysis of contemporary society. By contrast with the argument of the *Ring*, Shaw holds that it is Alberich who prevails in reality; he gets hold of the ring again and, in return for decent payment, persuades Wotan and Loge "to organize society for him," while Fafner, deprived of any entrepreneurial activity, goes to seed both physically and morally. Such an intellectual game, which combines Wagnerian figures and motifs into a new, original system, is part of Wagnerism, not least because it is related to contemporary enthusiasm for Wagner and Wagner snobbery. The author communicates with his public by means of a system of signs, symbols, and motifs deriving from Wagner.

The phenomenon of Wagnerism must on no account be seen as merely a more or less esoteric enthusiasm of a limited coterie of writers, philosophers, and critics. In terms of the aesthetics of cultural reception, it derives from the interaction of this circle with a broad public for Wagner which was sufficiently well informed to understand the most important allusions, to follow the ramifications of Wagnerian symbolism, and to recognize musical and textual quotations.

Among the less significant, but still noteworthy aspects of Wagnerism there are a number of facets which deserve mention. One should refer to the attempts to link certain innovations in narrative literature with Wagner. It has been claimed that interior monologue is, in the final analysis, the literary correlative of the unending melody. One of the inventors of the inner monologue is none other than Edouard Dujardin, the editor of the *Revue wagnérienne* (see Dujardin 1931). Thomas Mann, by associating certain figures in his fiction with recurring epithets and phrases, sought to inform his work with leitmotif patterns after the model of Wagner. Admittedly, the literary leitmotif existed long before Wagner. Tolstoy certainly did not derive the interior monologue in *Anna Karenina* from Wagner, whom he despised. But here again, more often than not, it is not demonstrable evidence that counts, but rather the merely subjective belief that such innovations derive from the example of Wagner's genius. The same applies to painting, to the attempt to link his genius with the visual arts, for example in Fantin-Latour's *Peinture wagnérienne* or Beardsley's Wagner drawings (see Chapter 16).

One should perhaps conclude this necessarily brief discussion with a key witness for Wagnerism—one who is not always recognized in this role because he changed from advocate to prosecutor—the Friedrich Nietzsche of the *Fourth Untimely Meditation* and *The Birth of Tragedy*. Even in *The Case of Wagner* and *Nietzsche contra Wagner,* where he emerges as Wagner's embittered opponent, he draws on that reservoir of Wagner images which we know from Wagnerism. Although Nietzsche's debate with Wagner is unremittingly critical in spirit, it still represents a high point in European Wagnerism.

Translated by Erika and Martin Swales

CHAPTER 16

Wagner and the Visual Arts

GÜNTER METKEN

Richard Wagner was interested in his own concept of how a work of art should be rather than in historical accuracy. He rejected historicism. For his opera *Tannhäuser,* which has as its theme the song contest that took place on the Wartburg, he had no desire to reconstruct the historical Hall of Song. In 1862 he visited the restored castle with paintings by Moritz von Schwind depicting the song contest as a princely tribute, with Elisabeth as the Madonna of Mercy defending the weaker Tannhäuser against the attacks of the minnesingers. For Wagner, Tannhäuser represented the artist as an outsider, a breaker of taboos. His verdict was appropriately reserved: "I inspected the partial restorations undertaken at the behest of the Grand Duke, including the hall with its pictures by Schwind. But it all left me rather cold" (ML 696–697).

He also had serious reservations about the literal accuracy with which Ludwig II had had scenes from his operas drawn or painted by Wilhelm von Kaulbach, Ferdinand Piloty, Bonaventura Genelli, and Michael Echter. These works, he wrote in a letter to the king (21–22 July 1865), were created in the manner of Peter von Cornelius and recreated the perceptions, as it were, "of the classical Middle Ages in the way one might assume poetic objects would have been depicted in art if painting had developed to the same pitch as medieval poetry. That is why this style will never be free from the reproach of a certain affectation and artistic pretense." Wagner believed that, with his own poems and stage directions, he had demonstrated "that the objects of the Middle Ages can be depicted in a more ideal, more purely human and more generally valid manner than this school of painting sets out to achieve." He nevertheless saw opportunities in the linear late classicism of Genelli to transfer the essential features of mythology into the modern age. He also admired Anselm Feuerbach. But the painter who could match his own conception was "no doubt still to be found."

Wagner had no real aesthetic preferences and constantly saw the visual arts in terms of how they could be applied to his own works: hence his attempts to persuade Arnold Böcklin to undertake the scenic designs in Bayreuth.

(Nothing came of the plan.) Still, Böcklin's Italian spring scene, *Look! The Meadows, How They Laugh* ("Sieh! es lacht die Aue"), painted in 1887, took not only its mood from *Parsifal,* but also its title from Parsifal's words to Kundry after the Good Friday music in act 3.

In Dresden, musicians and literati as well as painters such as Julius Schnorr von Carolsfeld, Eduard Bendemann, Friedrich Pecht, Robert Reinick, and Julius Hübner, and also the sculptors Ernst Rietschel and Ernst Julius Hähnel, had belonged to the circle of friends to whom Wagner had recited the libretto of *Lohengrin* in the Engelklub on 17 December 1845. The artists Pecht and Ernst Bendikt Kietz were among his faithful companions in the 1850s, although their work did not attract much attention. Gustave Doré frequently attended Wagner's lectures in Paris, a fact that is perhaps reflected in the designs of his wood engravings. Later, after Wagner became successful, he visited the leading artistic lights of the Gründerzeit: the house in Munich of Franz von Lenbach, who painted him and his family (as he did all the celebrities of the period); the studio in Vienna of Hans Makart, whose services he was pleased to acquire as a set designer; and in Berlin, Adolf Menzel, who also drew the composer as he rehearsed in Bayreuth. Auguste Renoir painted Wagner's portrait almost by chance in Palermo in 1882, where he was working on the orchestration of *Parsifal.* There is no discernible aesthetic continuity in these friendships or in prestigious contacts he subsequently made. Wagner had no more of a relationship with the artistic avant-garde of his time than with contemporary literature. The appeal for him in old art was its sweetness of tone, its mellifluousness, rather than its characterization. He found Leonardo's *Last Supper* unsurpassed. After seeing an oleograph Mater Dolorosa by Carlo Dolci in Aussig, he wrote to Kietz on 6 September 1842: "The picture delighted me no end and if Tannhäuser had seen it I would have no difficulty in imagining how he came to turn from Venus to Mary, and not driven particularly by reasons of piety."

The Bayreuth atmosphere suited the Russian painter Paul von Joukovsky, who moved there in 1880 and designed the sets for *Parsifal.* At Christmas that year he gave the master a special surprise when he arranged his children in a tableau of the Holy Family. Wagner was deeply moved and asked the painter to preserve the scene with his brush. The painting, in the old German–late Nazarene style, hung in the great hall in the villa of Wahnfried.

Ultimately, perhaps, we are left with the idea of Wagner's dilettantism, to which Adorno (who turned it into an absolute), Nietzsche, and Thomas Mann all referred. Wagner had no appreciation for individual arts. Everything had to serve the "analogy to language" (Adorno) and the mimetic character in his music, to underline its "meaning."

Toward a Synthesis of the Arts

It is clear that the painting of the late nineteenth and early twentieth centuries, with its striving for freedom of expression and theoretical maturity, helped to make possible the synthesis of the arts which Wagner called for both implicitly and explicitly. Nostalgia for the *Gesamtkunstwerk* runs through the nineteenth century and into the modern age. The artist had been "free" since the beginning of the nineteenth century. Architecture let loose its children, who then developed as individual arts but soon began to long again for a restraining coherence. The search for the supposedly lost unity quickly took on speculative, even ideological features. Wagner felt that in music, which was close to language but also appealed to the emotions and which satisfied myth and logic at a historical distance, they had found the element that would bring the separate areas together again. The painters Philipp Otto Runge and Caspar David Friedrich composed picture cycles "like symphonies," which were hung in secular shrines and were to be accompanied by music.

Inspired by Wagner's music and the painting of Delacroix, the poet Charles Baudelaire made a system out of these correspondences. He wrote in his essay *Richard Wagner and "Tannhäuser" in Paris* (Baudelaire 1861): "It would be really surprising if notes were not able to suggest colors, if colors gave no idea of notes, and notes and colors could not convey thoughts. For things have always expressed themselves through mutual analogy since God created the world as a complex, indivisible whole."

After the Paris premiere of *Tannhäuser,* Wagner stood in the center of efforts toward achieving the synthesis of the arts. Its mouthpiece was the *Revue wagnérienne,* which was founded in 1885 and which publicized music dramas and discussed the theory of the *Gesamtkunstwerk.* Poets such as Mallarmé and Verlaine, and also Claudel and Paul Valéry early on, were attracted by such ideas. But painters referred above all to Wagner. After Whistler's *Harmony in White* (1862) and Monet's *Harmonie verte* (1872), they were searching for color tones and musical patterns, which let pictures become instruments of spiritual vibrations, intellectual meaning, and ultimately of ideas and symbols of a general kind. "We must rid painting of the old habit of copying for it to become supreme. Instead of reproducing things, it should compel excitement," the poet Rimbaud claimed bluntly. Artists such as Gustave Moreau and Odilon Redon took up these ideas, and their works in the Salon in 1885 were reviewed as "peinture symphonique" and "peinture wagnérienne." Paul Gauguin and the Nabis also took the composer as a model. A Wagnerian tenet was painted in color on the wall of the Pension Marie Henry in Le Pouldu (Brittany), where this group lived in 1889–90. A later, idealistic portrait of Wagner by Emile Bernard (1925) again goes back to this idea.

Redon produced a lithograph, *Brünnhilde,* for the *Revue wagnérienne* in 1886, followed six years later by *Parsifal.* The latter print shows, in fact, that it was a spiritual affinity rather than direct musical inspiration that was at work. Redon's *Parsifal* is a dream symbol of crystalline purity, an almost childlike knight rather than a character in an opera. Redon strived for picturesque, brilliant, vivid symbolic figures rather than a thematic overlay.

Henri Fantin-Latour, a close friend of Manet's, was certainly familiar with the rising Impressionists, but was himself drawn to the themes of dreams and the imagination. This proclivity was strengthened by his preference for Romantic music. He sought to translate musical moods into black and white shaded lithographs as the basis for pictures. The central experience for him, which came to him through the German painter Otto Scholderer, whom he had befriended, was Richard Wagner. In 1862 he produced the first Wagner lithograph, *Tannhäuser in the Venusberg,* and a painting the following year. The impression was of an Arcadia drawn by Titian, colored by Rubens, and adapted by Delacroix, in which there was music and dancing, atmospheric but muted. One thing alone disturbs the sensual harmony—Tannhäuser himself. Wan and dressed in black, he stares somberly at a glowing Venus. Like Fantin-Latour himself, like Hamlet, this skeptic experiences the drama of the artist, that of having to decide between duty and inclination, between the painter's existence with all its privations and the temptations of the world. The years that followed produced the group portraits that were to make Fantin-Latour's name. *Autour du piano* (1885) is pure Wagner. The painter had himself become a Wagnerian after attending the Bayreuth *Ring* in 1876 and seen the brilliant confirmation of his contention that art was "féerique," escapism into the fantastic. He immediately started the first of over twenty lithographs in which his visual and musical effects intensified. In the search for the fantastic, Fantin-Latour was particularly carried away in Bayreuth by the first scene in *Das Rheingold,* in which the Rhine Maidens circle Alberich and taunt him. "Unique," he reported on 28 August 1876. "There is nothing to compare with it. A feeling never experienced before. The movements of the singing maidens as they swim are perfect. Alberich when he steals the gold, the lighting, the gleaming gold—magical."

Something of this enthusiasm carries over into the lithograph and the pastel, which were produced immediately after his visit to Bayreuth. It is surprising to what extent the painter saw these Nordic scenes in the Mediterranean light of Venice, thereby altering the myth in an instructive way: we see a faun from ancient legend being teased by water nymphs.

Among his contemporaries, Wagner also inspired Hans Makart, the leading painter of Viennese costume historicism. In fact the example of the *Gesamtkunstwerk* showed him the way to freer expression and creativity, while he otherwise remained for all his vigor stuck in illustrative design. Makart was an admirer of Wagner. In 1875 he gave one of his famous costume balls in Vienna for Richard and Cosima Wagner. A year later he took part in the opening festivals in Bayreuth.

His admiration for the poet-composer can be seen in eight large-scale scenes from the *Ring,* which must date from immediately after Wagner's death in 1883, obviously painted as a spontaneous homage. The gray-on-gray canvases of varying sizes, most of which are today in museums in Riga and Kiev, form the basis of an idea for decoration of a room. The same is true of the design— also produced spontaneously—for a ceiling fresco with motifs from the *Ring* (1870–1872). In the center we see the globe with the ring of the Nibelung over it. The dome segments show four separate scenes: the battle of the giants, Brünnhilde and the Rhine Maidens, Hunding's hut, and the Norns.

The themes of the Norns and the Rhine Maidens overlap the segments. The grisailles, which were painted at least ten years later, are related to this design and take up some of the motifs. They have opened up in terms of both spirit and size, revealing a looseness in the painting (in spite of the art-historical references and considerable qualitative strides) which would not have been conceivable without Wagner's music.

It was above all symbolist painting which involved Wagner. Searching for color tones, a renewed iconography, and emotional expression, the symbolists found in Wagner the model of such autonomy. So it was that the *Revue wagnérienne* became the organ of French symbolism. In Barcelona the textile manufacturer Eusebi Güell was, as a dominant fin-de-siècle figure, very receptive to Richard Wagner's music. Between 1885 and 1889 Antonio Gaudí built his home in Carrer Nou around the three-story-high music room with its built-in organ, a domed building which let in light from above: a temple of the Grail and a shrine consciously copied from *Parsifal*. The plans include elements of the Alhambra in Grenada; the Arabic connection had also been important for Klingsor's world in *Parsifal*, as the Montserrat mountain monastery near Barcelona was for the Grail castle. In the Güell palace the ascent from darkness into light gives shape to Wagner's idea of redemption.

It was in Barcelona, too, that one of the few monumental Wagnerian sculptures was created. It was the work of Pablo Gargallo (1881–1934), who was associated with Picasso and cubism and who grew up amid Barcelona's prevailing symbolism and worked with the Art Nouveau architect Domènechi Montaner on his Catalan concert hall (1905–1908). For the proscenium of the stage he devised on the spandrel the furious *Ride of the Valkyries,* after Wagner, giving the appearance of galloping movement toward the audience. This white grouping presents an extraordinary contrast to the auditorium's colored glass and ceramic decor. The Valkyries ride out in file under the fan tracery of the ceiling; the first figure is sculpted in the round, the second in high relief, and a third is presented flat. Their shields are stone, but the lances and reins are made of authentic materials. The trompe-l'oeil effect makes the horses' legs seem to stride out into the space below. The baroque ceiling frescoes showing the ascent of Elias and the sun chariot of Helios appear to stand in the foreground of the subject. But Gargallo has also been inspired by the nineteenth century. There are clear similarities to the *Marseillaise* and the dance by François Rude, to the groups on the Arc de Triomphe and the Opéra, as the figures break dynamically free from the wall, and the influence of the naturalism of the Gründerzeit is also notable. But Gargallo is unmistakably striving, less inspired here perhaps by Wagner than by the much-admired Rodin, to achieve a synthesis of the arts by fusing architecture, sculpture, sound, and color in a baroque cycle, which can be traced in the splendor of the clouds behind the fiery, swooping steeds.

Belgium—at that time the crossroads of Europe—was also feeling the effects of Wagner by the end of the century. The seventh annual exhibition of the artists' group Les XX in Brussels in 1890 contained a satirical picture by James

Ensor, which bore the misleadingly harmless title *At the Conservatoire in Brussels* and depicted Richard Wagner's *Die Walküre* being performed by the institute's musicians so wretchedly that in a picture within the picture the composer is seen with his hands over his ears. Ensor, who identified himself in drawings with a crucified figure, here denounces, in the context of Wagner, the treatment, or maltreatment, of genius in the bourgeois world generally. The painter always supported Wagner, as his gouache *The Ride of the Valkyries* (ca. 1888) shows. He was not the only Belgian with such a penchant. Symbolic painters in particular have used Wagnerian heroes to express mystic-erotic reverie and the death wish, for example Jean Delville (*Tristan and Parsifal*, 1890), Henri de Groux (*Lohengrin*, 1908), and Fernand Khnopff (*Isolde*, 1905). Khnopff also designed costumes for *Parsifal* at the Théâtre Royal de la Monnaie in 1911.

Wagner caused a sensation in the English-speaking world, too. The drawings by Aubrey Beardsley for *Das Rheingold* and *Siegfried* and his portrayal of Wagnerians provide a morbid commentary on English decadence and the motivating structure of the aesthetic movement. In complete contrast is the American Albert Pinkham Ryder (1874–1917), whose small, visionary paintings are only now achieving proper recognition. Ryder preferred literary themes, which enabled him to conjure up in balladlike chiaroscuro the forces which prevail in nature and to which man is subject as a result of his dependence on myth. Two pictures on Wagnerian themes represent the best of his work. One, *The Flying Dutchman* (1887), shows an eerily empty ship drifting in the stormy elements. The painter said of the origin of the other work, *Siegfried and the Rhine Maidens* (1888 or 1889): "I had seen the opera and came home around midnight and started the picture straight away. I worked on it for 48 hours without eating or sleeping." His painting *Götterdämmerung* was produced in New York in 1888 and 1889. The canvas shows Siegfried hunting on horseback, as the Rhine Maidens in the glistening water ask him for the ring; utterly in the sway of the threatening natural mysticism of this stormy moonlit night, the individual is powerless against fate, even if he is an almost invincible hero. This painting owes more to Wagner's music than to the text.

While in 1894 August Strindberg was experimenting with a free, almost informal style of landscape painting, in which his wife spontaneously recognized Tannhäuser's cave, a student of law and economics named Wassily Kandinsky attended a performance of *Lohengrin* at the Court Theater in Moscow at which, as he recalled in Munich in 1913, he experienced his awakening: "The violins, the deep tones of the double bass and most particularly the wind instruments carried for me then all the power of the promise of destiny. I saw all my colours in my mind, standing before my eyes. Wild, almost crazy lines appeared before me. I did not dare to use the expression that Wagner had painted 'my destiny' in music. It became quite clear to me, nonetheless, that art in general was much more powerful than I had thought, and that on the other hand painting can develop the same power that music possesses" (Kandinsky 1982, I, 364; translation modified).

Vienna at the Turn of the Century

The idea of the total work of art was the impetus behind Austrian cultural reform at the turn of the century, and Richard Wagner, together with Nietzsche, must be considered its driving force. It was just that for Camillo Sitte, director of the State Trade School in Vienna, whose chief work, *Städtebau* (urban building, 1889), contains a fundamental rejection of the architecture of the Ringstrasse. Sitte defined the role of the city planner as Wagner had defined that of the composer: as the regenerator of culture. He criticized the cold modern city drenched in traffic and slums and—taking *Die Meistersinger* as his model—advocated instead a model of rehumanized urban space and community wholeness (Schorske 1980, pp. 71–72). With different premises, the model came into being after the First World War in the communal buildings of "red" Vienna (although they were mainly preempted by Otto Wagner's more modern concept of urban planning). In an address on Wagner and German art delivered in 1875 to the Vienna Wagner Verein, Sitte set out his ideas on artisan values and their role in a modern capitalist world and pointed to Wagner as an important influence. He had the living room ceiling of his official residence painted with scenes from the *Ring* (Hans Thoma produced wall paintings on the same subject in 1877–1880 for a Frankfurt physician, Dr. Eisen). The experience of a Wagner performance, one which united an audience from all backgrounds, was for Sitte an example of structured, modern coexistence.

This example had some effect on artists, too. Figures from the *Ring* can be seen in Gustav Klimt's ceiling frescoes for the atrium of Vienna University, which were withdrawn after objections from the academic staff. In an allegorical picture of Philosophy (1900), also at the university, which caused a scandal because of its Schoperhauerian drift of bodies lacking will (suggesting the Rhine Maidens), Peter Vergo has compared the figure of Knowledge, emerging from below, with the appearance of Erda in *Rheingold*. Yet Wagner's influence went beyond the absorption of his motifs. At the peak of its influence in 1902, the Vienna Secession organized its fourteenth exhibition around the Beethoven statue by Max Klinger. The whole of Josef Olbrich's building, the House of the Secession, was given over to the Beethoven exhibition, which was in itself an ephemeral *Gesamtkunstwerk*. Klimt contributed a Beethoven frieze on plaster. The theme is the rise of mankind and its apotheosis in a joyfully embracing couple. Klimt conceived the last panel around a phrase from Schiller's *Ode to Joy* in the final chorus of the Ninth Symphony: "This kiss to the whole world" (Schorske 1980, pp. 254–263). The way Klimt developed his theme owed a good deal to Wagner's programmatic interpretation of the Ninth, which was published as a form of explanatory introduction in 1846 when Wagner conducted a performance of the work in Dresden. The symphony was particularly dear to Wagner because of its liberating influence: for Wagner art alone was able to save suffering, yearning humanity and to overcome hostile forces. By turning this scenario into an image of a revelation of a new age, Klimt (whose own scenario was published in the catalogue of the exhibition) in effect made Wagner's interpretation of Beethoven, rather than Beethoven himself, the focal point of an event which attracted over fifty thousand paying visitors and became renowned throughout Europe as a manifesto (Vergo 1981, pp. 68–77).

Wagner can therefore be counted among Vienna's moving spirits at the turn of the century, a force for internationalism, dynamism, and emancipation. It should not come as any surprise, then, that Theodore Herzl drew up his broadsheet *Der Judenstaat* (The Jewish state) in 1896 following the rousing experience of a performance of *Tannhäuser*. As the Paris correspondent of the Vienna *Neue Freie Presse,* he had been a witness to the Dreyfus affair and the growth of anti–Semitism in France, the land of enlightenment and revolution, and thus lost his last illusions of a possible assimilation of the Jews in Europe; they would be able to survive only as Zionists and in their own country. For him, Tannhäuser, as an emancipator and ostracized outsider, fit into the same categories. This was an opera which particularly inspired artists at the beginning of their careers. So it was with the young Klee, as we can see from letters which he wrote to his mother on his first stay in Munich. He later produced an ironic print showing the Tannhäuser of the opera.

The more general initiatives inspired by Wagner's works can also be seen as individual metaphors. The Museum of Art in Basel contains Oskar Kokoschka's major work, *Die Windsbraut* (The bride of the wind), which took its title from a line of a poem by Georg Trakl. We know from Kokoschka's letters that it should in fact have been called *Tristan und Isolde*. It was painted in 1913, at the time of his passionate relationship with Alma Mahler, the widow of the composer, whose performance of *Tristan* in the Court Opera House in the production by Alfred Roller in 1903 had made theatrical history. The couple are drifting in a boat, exposed to the unfettered elements and, as it were, tossed by love's storm, already aware of their end. The painter wrote to Albert Ehrenstein shortly after the outbreak of war in 1914: "And the boat, in which we are both being tossed around on the sea of the world, is a house, large enough for all the pain in the world, which we have undergone together, and no house in the world stands firmer. And I am going to war secretly. I ought to bite the dust. I am curious and reconciled with God."

Experienced by a great mind, this is one man's passion projected onto the Wagnerian lover of death. The theme of the frustrated sexuality of the bourgeois age also crystallizes around Wagner's work, however, particularly *Tannhäuser* and the Venusberg. One man who broke away was the Karlsruhe artist Rudolf Schlichter, who described this so brilliantly in his autobiography, *Tönerne Füsse* (Feet of clay): "For me he was and remained during this time a fascinating, exotic wonder, the great magician, the high priest of all the dark gods. Never before, it seemed to me, had a mortal ever conjured up with such power the sensuous joys of the abyss, the sweet pain of alienation, the last secrets of a happiness pregnant with corruption, the intoxication of nothingness, the deathly breath of ecstatic lust." An etching by Schlichter from 1913, contemporary therefore with *Die Windsbraut,* which shows Venus dressed in only a collar, boots, and black stockings and with a rose in her hand, completes these adolescent confessions. It is easier, then, to understand why in his novel *Der Mann ohne Eigenschaften* (The man without qualities; also set in 1913) Robert Musil sneered so openly at the would-be composer Walter, who conceals his own lack of talent—and his inhibited relationship with his wife, Clarisse—thundering out Wagner at the piano "like a schoolboy's vice"; he succumbs to this music "as to a stiff-brewed, hot, overpowering drink."

Music Rooms and Individual Mythology

Musil's objective irony of the 1920s reduced Wagner to a private context. The painter Max Slevogt could surround himself at the time with Wagnerian figures, while Salvador Dalí usurped Wagner for his own individual mythology.

The best known of the wall decorations on Wagnerian themes are in Schloss Neuschwanstein, where Ludwig II had his protégé's operatic dreams depicted in his refuge. The attitude of Slevogt was quite different when, in 1924, after visiting the Bayreuth Festival, he set about painting the music room in his summer residence in Neukastel near Leinsweiler in the southern Rhineland. The shorter side walls show scenes from Mozart operas, whereas the long wall is reserved for the *Ring.* Siegfried's youth and his death stand opposite each other contrapuntally. The boy is to the left, blond and half dressed like a faun. His manner is relaxed and unconcerned; he is a child of nature. The colors are summery, effervescing up from the palette. Painted like a monkey in the corner is his mortal enemy Alberich, who wants to take the ring from him. This figure leads the eye to the large panel. To the left are the Rhine Maidens amidst bucolic nature, more akin to ancient bacchanalians in spite of the pine trees and the northern vegetation. And then Siegfried's death—what a contrast! Unconsolable barrenness, cold colors. The hero lies diagonally, stretched out in gray-white pallor in the light green meadow, his hands clasped around his shield, the deadly spear in his back. The empty slope seems all the more eerie now because the spear thrower Hagen and the Norns have almost faded away on the wall, which has become damp.

Wagner's special cult status in Catalonia without doubt reached its zenith in Dalí. Dalí's autobiography reveals the importance of the German composer, whom he wove into the hallucinations in his pictures. He was fascinated not only by the revelation of hidden impulses through the use of leitmotifs, but especially by the depiction of frustrated love, insatiable desire as a prerequisite for creativity. Dalí demonstrated this himself when he worked on theater projects in America. The 1939–40 season saw the production of the ballet *Bacchanal,* after the Venusberg scenes in *Tannhäuser,* at the Metropolitan Opera in New York. The idea, libretto, set design, and production were Dalí's, with choreography by Léonide Massine. Dalí wrote of his idea in the program:

"The stage shows the Venusberg near Eisenach; in the background Salvador Dalí's birthplace, in the middle a temple rises up like in Raffael's *Betrothal of the Virgin*. The Italian paved street leading to the temple is thus laid on Catalan soil." Because Dalí is attempting a psychoanalysis of the Tannhäuser phenomenon, the bacchanal is here "seen through the madly confused mind of Ludwig II who, with his nervous visual over-sensitivity, 'lived' all the Wagner myths profoundly and to the edge of madness. As the actual hero of the ballet he identifies with this legendary hero; the plot depicts the hallucinations and emotions to which he was prey." Dalí's set design, one of his most convincing creations, conveys this semantic density. The skeleton of a boat also suggests *Tristan,* the opera to which he turned in 1944, once again in New York and with Massine responsible for the choreography. *Mad Tristan* is the name not only of the ballet but also of a painting. The hero, caught in the black sails of the ship of fate, which also recalls *Holländer,* stumbles around blindly on the Costa Brava shore, a victim of his delusion.

Echoes in Present-Day Art

Since the jubilee of the *Ring* in 1976 and publication of Cosima's diaries, Wagner has fascinated more than ever as a problematic and quintessential figure of the nineteenth century. Artists have shown renewed interest in him in ways that are trivial and satirical (J. Grützke, Paul Flora) but also shimmering and ambivalent, as in the series of works by Alfred Hredlicka: *Adalbert Stifter–Richard Wagner, Richard Stifter–Adalbert Wagner, Revolutionary and Reactionary* (Vienna 1985). Nor should one forget the decadent, Pre-Raphaelite-style pictures based on *Lohengrin* and *Parsifal* by Ernst Fuchs, who also designed the sets for these works.

Wagner's music also plays a part in a group of works by Edward Kienholz: his *Volksempfänger* (the "people's wireless" introduced by Hitler) of 1977. The Californian artist, who lives part of the time in Berlin, builds tableaux from odd items and moldings with the intention of provoking moral outrage. He was attracted by the angular form of the mass-produced wireless, which he felt was "German." Hitler, subverter of a people; music, with which he claimed to identify; subverted youth: here the American artist has intuitively found a model which he then universalizes as a symbol of mass manipulation. The "people's wireless" as the masculine principle—the voice that gives orders—is matched by a ribbed washboard representing woman, for Kienholz usually the victim of history. The National Socialist medal for childbearing, the *Mutterkreuz,* often hangs around her neck. Symbolic groupings arise from both cooperation and antagonism, from combination with other objects, which also give the impression of wear and tear. They speak of the drudgery of work, the struggle of the sexes, and of a false Utopia, and evoke almost unavoidably musical quotations from Nibelheim, the Valkyries' cliffs, or the entry of the gods into Valhalla. Kienholz arranges his assemblages as Norns and Notung, as Siegfried and Brünnhilde, eloquent runes of German history for hundreds of years.

Anselm Kiefer, a pupil of Horst Antes and Joseph Beuys, is known as a historical painter in the sense that he reflects on history rather than reproducing what has happened in the past: allegory, as we would once have called it. And for Kiefer, born in the year of collapse, 1945, that history is German. Of course he does not go about depicting it from a blatantly polemical or critical angle. He too wants to sharpen memory, but the memory is drawn out further. The great areas which he creates with brown paint, charcoal, chalk, and pencil on canvas or burlap suggest the theater. *Deutschlands Geisteshelden* (Germany's spiritual heroes) is the largest of his works, with no less than six meters devoted to this backdrop, a huge hall, a wooden Valhalla with flames in front of the side windows. On the sides are written the names of writers, philosophers, and politicians, increasing in size as they approach the observer. The largest, at the front left, is the name of Richard Wagner, the epitome of German mythology, whose works have made history, been seized on by factions of all kinds, and still retain their shimmering, unfathomable aura. It is probably for this reason that Kiefer, in addition to his books and works on paper, has devoted some of his best-known pictures to Wagner: *Parsifal* and *Notung* (1973); *Brünnhilde's Death* (1976), with burning pieces of wood; and *Nuremberg and the Mastersingers* (1981–82). The last calls to mind Wagner's Festival Theater meadow, Reich party rallies, and the Nuremberg laws and trials in a desolate, retreating room of associations which evoke the scorched-earth policy. With some complexity Kiefer calls up the recent past with a sort of system of leitmotifs and brings them to mind in his theater of memory.

Memorials

There are relatively few monuments to Richard Wagner in existence. Essentially, his omnipresence made such reminders almost superfluous. After his death he was almost more vitally present than when he was alive. Perhaps no other composer has ever had such an afterlife: not for him the usual brief posterity. The figure of the master cast a shadow over a whole generation, and was both acclaimed and attacked.

People might imagine that they have seen monuments to Wagner in musical citadels, but this does not stand the test of a topographical survey. His bust in the Giardini park in Venice, where it stands opposite Giuseppe Verdi's, is an exception rather than the rule. Richard Wagner died in Venice, and people boating on the canals are familiar with the great marble tablet on the quay wall of Palazzo Vendramin, the house where he died. Chiseled in 1910, it shows the famous guest in profile wreathed by laurels, an honor which by virtue of its generous style counts as a monument. There is all the more reason to expect statues of Wagner in Switzerland, his refuge for many years. Yet there are no sculptural tributes to him in the Wesendonck's house in

Zurich, today the Rietberg Museum, or in the adjacent park. And although the Tribschen villa near Lucerne does house a Wagner museum, apart from the bust by Fritz Schaper there is no memorial for the man who spent six productive years there.

The memory of Wagner seems posthumously serene in the memorial edition of the *Bayreuther Blätter,* which was published as an international effort a year after his death. Henri Fantin-Latour contributed the lithograph *En mort de Richard Wagner,* which might be described as the first potential memorial. It shows the gravestone plaque engraved with his name and on which an angel of fate strews roses. Had there not been thoughts of reprisals as a consequence of the lost war of 1870, Fantin-Latour's idea would certainly have produced sculptures in France, where Wagner dominated intellectual thinking at the end of the century. By 1896, however, the turbulence had calmed sufficiently for a poll to be taken in Paris as to whether a memorial to Wagner should be put up. As Tappert's Wagner lexicon describes, this suggestion infuriated the chauvinist Déroulède to such an extent that he replied: "A memorial to this brigand? Never, in the name of patriotism!" Wagner did finally get his bust in 1903, an extremely conventional work by J. Bozzi which was placed discreetly in the lobby of the Paris Opéra. No memorial commensurate with Wagner's influence in France ever materialized, however.

In the summer of 1982 it seemed briefly that this omission might be rectified by the facial "landscape" in which Hans Jürgen Syberberg's film *Parsifal* is set. Paris clearly wanted to accept as a gift the recumbent head, which had been reconstructed in fourteen parts from Wagner's death mask, and to install it opposite the Eiffel Tower between the wings of the Palais de Chaillot—a brief and unfortunately unrealizable dream.

In Germany, too, Wagner memorials have been erected in only a few select places since the beginning of the century. It is true that every so often he was included among the patron saints deemed worthy of one of the busts which surround opera houses, concert halls, and academies of music. In the Valhalla which Ludwig I of Bavaria established for "notably distinguished Germans," a bust of him by Bernhard Bleeker was finally exhibited in 1913 on the one hundredth anniversary of his birth. And above all the good bourgeois brought him into the parlor. A drawing produced in the 1920s by Karl Habbuch captures exactly the petit-bourgeois nightmare of these crammed living rooms. Next to the monstrous Black Forest clock stands a head of Wagner on the piano as an item of cultural pride: "A troubled Wagner in a bronze beard and cap balanced on a pile of classical piano arrangements" (W. Koeppen, *Tauben im Gras,* 1951).

Two Versions: Berlin and Munich

The composer was not raised onto his pedestal until after the consolidation of the German Reich around 1900—and then emphatically. The most eloquent example, endowed by a cosmetics manufacturer, is the Wagner memorial by Gustav Eberlein in the Berlin Zoo, which was unveiled on 1 October 1903. Kaiser Wilhelm II made it a personal and national priority by himself drawing the figure of Wolfram von Eschenbach in the design and arranging for the dedication to be recorded by his painter of battle scenes, Anton von Werner.

The Wilhelminian concept of memorials was perfectly captured in a contemporary description in Berlin: "The writer-composer is enthroned on [the memorial] in a sumptuous, romantic chair with arm-rests which end in heraldically styled lions. The composer is shown in a creative pose. His head is turned slightly to the left and seems to be listening for inspiration from his muse. His left hand appears to be feeling its way for the notes and in doing so almost unconsciously disturbing the lion's head on the chair. His right hand is clasped almost into a fist and is resting on sheets of music, seeming with its energetic movement to lend particular emphasis to the chord he has found" (Zelinsky 1976, p. 97). On his tall pedestal Richard Wagner looks removed from all tribulations. Bareheaded and devoid of old German finery, he looks up and into the distance like the bearer of a new doctrine. But the great man in his Olympian pose is sold short. On the base Tannhäuser, Alberich, Kriemhilde, and Siegfried serve as Pietà figures to his work, but they convey nothing of the spirit of his music dramas. That lay outside the scope of Eberlein's monument, which was intended to be imposing and was torn between representation and an attempt at conveying significance.

It did, perhaps, lie within the scope of the competition design which Franz Metzner (1870–1919) submitted for the Berlin Wagner memorial. Metzner later turned to an archaic colossal style when producing the Battle of the Nations Memorial in Leipzig. This early work, however, which is a notable example of the Jugendstil and is in some respects reminiscent of early Wilhelm Lehmbruck (around 1902–1905 he also modeled Siegfried testing the sword), came under the salutary influence of Rodin and above all of the sensitive Belgian Georges Minne. Accordingly the figures, which seem to be emerging hesitantly from the relief, lack individuality and express a universal sense of doom. Fatalistically stooped, propped up, or cowering on the floor, when not looking up in dumb lamentation, these are suffering figures full of Schopenhauerian pessimism and Wagnerian illusion, states of living anxiety with no relationship to figures in the music dramas. Only Wagner himself is recognizable, and even he appears stylized and lacking in substance. Holding a score on his knees, his right hand dangling, he seems too lost in inner contemplation to act, the master in harmony with his creations, which hardly escape from their dreamy meditations. It is an inner world, a world where revolt is in vain, in complete contrast to Eberlein's spirit of voluntarism. Whereas the latter, garrulously vying with historical painting, piles up an agglomeration of detail, Metzner proposes a total composition (with a center that stands out vaguely between two side sections) which has one prevailing tone and contents itself with decorative traces.

The fact that Berlin, at most a performance venue and never a milestone in Wagner's biography, now had this monument led to a heated flareup over a national or popular memorial, which Germany believed it ought to erect to its recently elected herald. But where should it go? Not in Leipzig, which had treated its greatest son like a poor cousin; nor in Dresden, which had made its own arrangements; nor in ungrateful Munich, as Kurt Mey asserted in 1903. It should be in Eisenach, where the Wartburg stood, site of the historical song contest, the place where Luther experienced his awakening, and, above all, where Johann Sebastian Bach was born. "Let the German national memorial to Richard Wagner be placed here, in the sacred German forest," cried out the Wartburg's supporters, clearly unheeded. Instead, it was Munich that got the memorial. It is a notorious fact that the Saxon composer, with his special relationship with Ludwig II, was not exactly popular in the Bavarian capital. The king had moreover installed in his castles marble copies of the great busts produced by Caspar von Zumbusch in 1864 of the *Musikarrangeur,* and Wagner himself distributed plaster casts to his friends. Yet the glory of Wagner's work, which first developed and became institutionalized largely through the king's patronage, reflects credit on Munich, which Wagner had after all selected as the first Festival Theater city. In fact the Prince Regent Theater opened in 1901 with Wagner festival productions. Next to the building, whose amphitheater calls to mind Bayreuth and Gottfried Semper, the great man's memorial was unveiled in 1913 on the centennial of his birth.

It was the work of Heinrich Waderé (1865–1950) from Colmar, a sought-after architectural and tombstone sculptor, and professor at the Munich School of Arts and Crafts. The sculpture is in appearance considerably more placid than the rather sulky version in Berlin. This is not only because Waderé returns to a Biedermeier style: on a late-classical plinth the composer lies draped on a couch like a princely genius—like Goethe in the Campagna. It is also because this serene sage—again only a mature, indeed an old Wagner is imaginable on a memorial—suggests nothing at all of the hugely self-confident impression given by this genius and friend of kings, which is how the inhabitants of Munich hold him in eternal memory. All aggression has been bled from this man as he rests on his work and looks back at us, yet this attitude was known to be alien to the model to the last stroke of his pen. It would, however, appear to say much about his position as an acknowledged composer deemed worthy of festival performances at the Court Theater.

Leipzig and Unfinished Business

The city which would have had the best reason to celebrate the centenary, namely Leipzig, where Wagner was born on 22 May 1813, did not manage either on this occasion or later to produce a worthy memorial, although there was no shortage of initiatives. The story of these soaring schemes, foundation stones which were never laid, arrangements which were never finalized, and works which were no longer wanted on completion, reflects the city's difficult relationship with a man who was, after all, politically extreme.

With the anniversary of Wagner's birth drawing near, Leipzig's most eminent artist, Max Klinger, was approached in 1904. As the forty-seven-year-old sculptor had already been responsible for the Brahms memorial in the Musikhalle in Hamburg, the famous Beethoven made of multicolored stone, and a head of Franz Liszt, he seemed preordained for the job. He had even produced a head of Wagner for the Leipzig music room at the World's Fair in St. Louis that same year. But this larger-than-life marble head betrayed the uncertainty which was to characterize the memorial project. Ill-disposed to the ornateness and the borrowed Romanticism of the Gründerzeit, Klinger returned to a clear, classically ordered face. It radiates the energy and capacity for achievement of a statesman or businessman, but, with its deceptive polish, it conveys none of Wagner's turbulent genius.

Klinger's marble model for the memorial shows Wagner shrouded in a togalike cloak and standing on a podium, more like a Romantic field marshal or orator than a musician. In 1905 he produced sketches and modeled the head, for which he was provided with an album of photographs from the Wagner family's Wahnfried home. The sculpture, which was cast in bronze in 1921, is more lifelike than the head from 1904 but retains the stereometric, angular structure and indication of strength of mind. The memorial attempts to create clear proportions and to sweep Wagner clean of the dust of Wagnerism. This is achieved to such an extent that the result is almost a vacuum devoid of ideas. The artist may have felt this too, since he presented new designs to the committee in 1911. Instead of the podium there was now a high pedestal which was to be decorated with reliefs on three sides: on the front three female figures—representing Music, Poetry, and Drama—to symbolize Wagner's synthesis of the arts; on the left, Siegfried, Mime, and the slain dragon; and on the right Parsifal and Kundry. Klinger started on the work immediately, but only the laying of the stepped section took place on 23 May 1913. The reliefs were then sent to Laas in the Tyrol to be worked on. The thirty-ton block was rough-hewn from the marble quarry there but could not be transported because of the outbreak of war. The work was dropped in 1920 as a result of Klinger's death. In 1924 the block with the reliefs finally reached Leipzig and was installed in the palm garden there. Together with the statue it perhaps shows that Klinger's art was in decline, that the magic of the blending of the barbaric with the refined was gone. The allegorical sisterly arts suggest three Reformation graces, thin and with fashionable hairstyles. It is as though Siegfried is stepping down from the altar of Pergamon, jarring with the outlines of Fafner and Mime, who emerge eerily from the surface. Nevertheless, Klinger's torso remains the only sculptural reference to Wagner in his home town.

The next commemorative year fell, ominously enough, in 1933, a half-century after the master's death. And it was Adolf Hitler himself who laid the foundation stone on Frankfurt Common on the outskirts of Leipzig on 6 March 1934 to mark the National Richard Wagner Memorial, after the Stuttgart sculptor Emil Hipp had won a competition initiated by Leipzig's Mayor Goerdeler. Hipp's project aimed to rally "thousands" of devotees on a paved courtyard (120 by 80 meters) around a mighty block resembling an altar, the four sides of which were to measure ten meters and bear figures depicting Mythology, Fate, Redemption, and Bacchanalia, supposedly representing levels of Wagner's work. The courtyard, in which a *Rheingold* fountain and a statue of Siegfried were also planned, was enclosed by a wall with nineteen scenes from Wagner's operas in bas-relief. These scenes are of Attic-classical inspiration, whereas the allegories, which range from half-relief to free-standing sculpture, shift between Pergamene Hellenism and national socialism in their pathos and dislocated style (Zelinsky 1976, pp. 223–226). Originally fixed for 1940, the erection of the memorial was delayed by the outbreak of war. Then in 1945, when it was finally ready and almost paid for, the city of Leipzig, for political reasons, no longer showed any interest. The artist could not continue to bear the storage costs, so the memorial became the property of the Kiefersfelden marble works, which then sold it to interested parties piece by piece. So it was that what had begun arrogantly as a national memorial with Hitler's Leipzig "pledge to Wagner" ended up in private hands.

The fatal year of 1933 did nevertheless produce a memorial—in the Liebethal southeast of Dresden, where in 1846 in Grossgerau near Pillnitz the music for *Lohengrin* first came into being. "Under the protection of the community of Pirna here at the birthplace of *Lohengrin*," the inscription reads, "the first memorial in Saxony was erected to THE MASTER by grateful admirers with the voluntary assistance of working youths from surrounding districts . . . February 1933": Wagner as Keeper of the Grail. The historicism of Richard Guhr is seen in the bronze folds of Wagner's garments, suggesting a priest or Martin Luther rather than a composer; the figures crouching at his feet, which would be at home in a stylized fountain, are intended to evoke characters and sounds from his operas. As a sculptor Guhr embraced eclecticism, as a painter Germanic mysticism. Something of both went into this work.

From Stage Design to Bronze: Wotruba

Memorials to Wagner in Germany are thus also documents to their age. This is particularly true for the period of the Third Reich. Wagner did not escape the pan-German cult of heroes: witness the head by Arno Breker which has stood in front of the Festival Theater in Bayreuth since it was unveiled by the Führer in 1938. We have here a thoroughly heroic interpretation. The head is oversized and presented with signs of great energy which neutralize one another in their concentration—dramatic hairstyle and beard, furrowed and arched brows over deep-set eyes, pronounced cheekbones, prominent nose and chin emphasizing a strong will. Breker probably based his work on photographs by Hanfstaengl taken in 1871, but he created a synthetic physiognomy not helped by a brutal expression. This is a leader and member of the master race in contemporary terms, which—if we accept Thomas Mann's phrase "the sorrows and grandeur of Richard Wagner"—misses the first of these two elements. The second element, which is conditional upon the first, is therefore invalidated irrespective of the attitude struck.

The distancing from Wagner which followed is also conveyed by the only memorial to be erected to him after the war. The sculpture, bearing the inscription "Dedicated to the genius Richard Wagner by his publisher B. Schott & Sons of Mainz, 1970," was put up outside the Rheingoldhalle in Mainz on the occasion of the publisher's two hundredth anniversary celebration. The work is an abstract bronze made of layered plates and segments like ice floes. The sculptor is the Austrian Fritz Wotruba, who in 1967 designed for the Deutsche Oper in Berlin from his "box of giant bricks" (as the producer Gustav Rudolf Sellner called it) a production of the *Ring* which "deals with the decline of our own age using mythical figures."

That a leading sculptor of the modern movement should tackle Wagner and the tetralogy so intensively as, in his words, the "exposure of a nation" prompted the idea of a memorial by his publishers, which was willingly taken up by the artist. It is indeed possible to see in the prismatic memorial, which is positively turbulent compared with Wotruba's other structures, its origin in a scenic context—the world of the smith, Mime, and the Nibelungen—which is given universal meaning in this sculptural culmination, perhaps a Valhalla: an "architecture into the Unknown," according to Adorno. Its title is undecided: either *Wagner Memorial* or *"Rheingold" Sculpture*. Only Hans Jürgen Syberberg's use of a blown-up death mask as scenery in his film of *Parsifal* indicates a conscious return to Wagner as a person.

How Wagner Saw Himself

The series of memorials paraded before us can make us curious as to how Wagner saw himself and wanted to be seen. It is generally acknowledged that he projected himself brilliantly, even before artists, whom he brought to despair with his mercurial nature when posing; he would chatter away incessantly, interrupt himself with exclamations, sing with his head thrown back, grimace, jump up suddenly, and parody himself and others. There is a famous description in a letter (15 January 1882) by Auguste Renoir of his meeting with the master, who had just finished the orchestration of *Parsifal*. The scene in the Hôtel des Palmes in Palermo brings to mind commedia dell'arte and shows at the same time, when one considers Renoir's startling portrait sketches of the exhausted old man, the nervous tensions which Wagner carried within him throughout his life.

Being an instant medium, photography was well suited to capture his restlessness—all the more so since Wagner, as Martin Geck has shown in his fine book (Geck 1970), used his own image skillfully to promote himself and his work, even in the years in exile in Switzerland when it was important to be remembered in Germany. He used new methods of reproduction ranging from lithography to steel and wood engraving to photography in order to promote himself as an artist, and he had portraits engraved for reproduction and distributed plaster casts of marble busts. This was also the case with the very Olympian bust by Gustav Adolph Kietz, which found a place not only in the hall in Wahnfried but also as plaster replicas in railroad station restaurants throughout Franconia. On 16 December 1874 Wagner wrote to the artist:

> I think you should earn something from plaster casts. I am in a particularly awkward position here. In the station refreshment rooms in 1. Bayreuth, 2. Neuenmarkt and 3. Lichtenfels I keep seeing despicable little busts of me; I have told the landlords that they make me cross, at which they explain that they would gladly have something better if they knew how, whereupon I then—instinctively—said to them that I would take care of it.
>
> Now my wife has drawn my attention—quite rightly—to the scandal that our magnificent press could bring upon me if it were to become known (from bragging), that I had installed my own busts there. On the other hand I would like to clear up the difficulty there. So how would it be if you were to write to these 3 landlords that you had been irritated by these poor busts, offering them for that reason your bust of me, for which you could perhaps charge as little as possible, since I just want the busts replaced; I, however, will pay you the full price that you charge for casts. Simply so that the people imagine, and can boast accordingly, that they have acquired the busts themselves.   (Geck 1970, p. 47)

This humorous example shows how much attention Wagner paid to the image of him that came before the public. Beyond personal vanity, what mattered was recognition of his work. Its creator should appear calm, serene, braving life's tribulations, rather than depleted as in Renoir's work or harried by the demon of creativity as in the famous photograph taken by Pierre Petit in Paris in 1860, which Wagner criticized, although it seems to convey accurately the artist's state of extreme tension. The curt rejection can be explained in all probability in that Wagner felt he had been betrayed or exposed because he could have no influence over the result. He clearly became aware of this with the series of photographs which he had taken at major concert venues such as Brussels, London, Paris, St. Petersburg, and Moscow and distributed among his patrons—particularly in the case of the famous shots taken in the studios of Joseph Albert and Franz Hanfstaengl in Munich. Hanfstaengl's series shows the genius in semiprofile, marked by life's struggle and, having come through determinedly in the face of all adversity, going on in 1871 to turn the total work of art into a reality. At the same time this expensively dressed man in the velvet beret is also the very dean and prince of artists whom Franz von Lenbach left to posterity, painting from this and other photographs the "Reformer," as Cosima decided he was. It seems clear that this view, and the later photographs by Elliot and Fry (1877), have contributed to the stately element in the monuments to Wagner. As his own producer and strategist of his fame after death, Wagner was striving, in his own words, for "a calm and natural facial expression," but in so doing he has deprived the memorials of creative spontaneity. His devotees were not to capture what he wrote about himself to a friend in Dresden in 1858 over some apparently unsuccessful photographs: "I am too changeable in my expression."

Translated by Simon Nye

CHAPTER 17

Wagner in Literature and Film

ULRICH MÜLLER

The continuing influence of Wagner and his works on the various media—in other words, the use that has been made of the composer and the creative reception of his works—is not only a vast area, but it is also by its very nature one which, in theory at least, will never cease to expand. This survey was written from the perspective of the mid-1980s. A complete picture is neither intended nor feasible. I have chosen rather to list and discuss a selection of those authors and works which, in my opinion and in the opinion of previous writers on the subject, are of particular and characteristic importance (always allowing, of course, for gaps in knowledge of the subject). Whereas the only work to date to deal with Wagner and the cinema is the anthology of essays edited by Ermano Comuzio and Giuseppe Ghigi to coincide with the 1983 Wagner Film Festival in Venice, the composer's influence on literature (in the narrower sense of the word) has inspired numerous individual studies and longer surveys, of which the most outstanding are those by Curt Jäckel (1931), Anna Jacobson (1932), Rosemary Park (1935), Max Moser (1938), Werner Vordtriede (1958), William J. McGrath (1965), and Erwin Koppen (1973; and see Chapter 15 in this volume), Ute Jung (1974), John DiGaetani (1978), Dieter Borchmeyer (1982), and Danielle Buschinger (1984), together with the anthologies *Wagner in Italia* edited by Manera and Pugliese (1982) and *Wagner et la France* edited by Kahane and Wild (1983); Hans-Martin Plesske's "Bibliography of Publications in German" in his *Wagner in der Dichtung* (1971); the collection of essays *Wagnerism in European Culture and Politics* (Large-Weber 1985); the anthology of papers from the 1983 Salzburg Symposium, *Richard Wagner: 1883–1983* (1984); and finally, and most important of all, Raymond Furness' book *Wagner and Literature* (1982), which provides a comprehensive survey of all that has been written on the subject to date (together with plentiful references to secondary literature), as well as offering a great deal of new material besides. This chapter is based in part on the work of my predecessors, but also on my own findings when, in the course of a seminar held during the summer term of 1983 at the University of Salzburg, a team of researchers reexamined the greater part of the existing material, and at the same time were able to make a number of additional contributions to the subject.

First Principles: The Types, Levels, and Main Emphases of Wagner's Influence

In discussing Wagner's influence on literature, certain basic types may be distinguished: (1) descriptions of Wagner as a historical personage in literary works dealing with his life either in whole or in part (in other words, chiefly embroidered biographical narratives, in which the line of demarcation between fiction and actual biographies in the narrower sense is often difficult to define), and also films about Wagner; (2) the borrowing and adaptation of episodes, characters, and themes from Wagner's works, a form of creative reception that is oriented primarily toward content and substance; and (3) the borrowing and adaptation of specifically Wagnerian devices. Here one thinks chiefly of the transfer of the leitmotif[1] from a musical environment to a poetic one (although it is also found in the cinema), a use which many authors, including Dujardin, Joyce, and Thomas Mann, have expressly ascribed to Wagner's example. It should, however, be borne in mind that a musical leitmotif—which, after all, has its own existence alongside the text and the action of the (music) drama—is completely different from a literary leitmotif, which must necessarily be formulated in words and which to that extent is part of the textual structure itself. In many cases later authors explicitly claim dependence on Wagner, either by direct reference or by mentioning his name, his works, and his characters or by means of other unequivocal indicators. In other instances their dependence may be inferred with more or less sufficient certainty, although equally often it must remain a matter for conjecture: not every tale of sibling love, for example, nor every instance of alliteration and every typical verbal repetition can necessarily be traced back to Wagnerian influence. The danger of overinterpretation, resulting from an excessive investigative delight in searching for (and finding) traces of Wagner where none may exist, is not to be underestimated.

It goes without saying that Wagner's influence is to be found on the most disparate levels as far as quality is concerned, from so-called highbrow, serious, or good literature on the one hand to "inferior" poems on the other. Work that is inferior in terms of quality is widely known for only a short period, if at all; it has less influence and remains to be comprehensively assessed. Nonetheless, like all forms of "trivial" literature, the message that

---

1. The term *Leitmotif* is one which Wagner himself used only rarely and reluctantly. The concept has always played so firm and central a role in later interpretations of Wagner, however, that it will have to be retained here, if for no other reason. The same is true of the terms *total work of art, music drama,* and *unending melody* (see Deathridge-Dahlhaus 1984, p. 111).

it conveys is extremely important in terms of the period which produced it and the level of reception which it represents.

The creative reception of Wagner in literature can be summarized by categorizing it under various main emphases, although such an approach must inevitably involve considerable simplification. In this survey various aspects have been singled out for consideration: (a) Wagner as an aesthetic problem in terms of his music (beginning with Eduard Hanslick) and text (this latter point is of importance chiefly in the context of the countless parodies that have been written on the subject); (b) Wagner as an example of what Nietzsche called his frenzied, narcotic, and morbid aspect, but most of all as material for the decadents and fin-de-siècle writers, for whom the starting point was generally *Tannhäuser* and *Tristan;* (c) Wagner as an expression of philosophical and political significance, generally in the context of the "typically" Germanic or German, an abstract notion which could be either positive, in the sense of national identity, or else negative in its more or less critical formulation; and finally (d) Wagner as the preeminent creator of myth and archetype. Any survey of Wagner's literary influence can of course be structured in different ways; it may be arranged according to the composer's individual works, according to the aspects and emphases just outlined, or according to the various countries whose national literature Wagner has influenced. The third of these possible strategies is the one that has been adopted herein since it best takes account of the linguistically constituted cultural and literary entities involved, even if, in adopting this approach, one runs the occasional risk of having to ignore developments that transcend linguistic barriers.

Wagner in Literature

The term *literature* is taken here to mean poetic and/or fictional texts of every description (novels, plays, and poems); nonfictional texts such as essays are mentioned only if they are the work of writers who are principally known for the other kind of text, or if such writings are of particular importance for their oeuvre.

France

The first Wagnerians were French, and the composer's influence on French literature is to be found at a correspondingly early date in a correspondingly intensive form. Indeed, there was scarcely a French writer of the day who did not respond to Wagner in one way or another and who was not influenced by him. (See Buschinger 1984, Salzburg Symposium.) At the beginnings of French *wagnérisme* (for a more detailed treatment of this subject, see Chapter 15) stands the figure of Charles Baudelaire. He is important in this context for his letter to Wagner of 17 February 1860 and for his article *Richard Wagner et "Tannhäuser" à Paris* of 1861, written in response to the so-called *Tannhäuser* scandal. He and other writers refer to Wagner as someone on whom they modeled their own view of art, a view characterized by its lofty symbolism and rejection of naturalism, by the musicality and extreme poeticality of its language, and by a sense of ecstasy and eroticism. The Symbolist movement found its short-lived but successful vehicle of expression in the *Revue wagnérienne* (1885–1887), founded and edited by Edouard Dujardin. The poems that were published here, and the essays that were often mystically rhapsodical in tone, influenced avant-garde attitudes toward Wagner and colored the view of all French intellectuals. Among the works that deserve to be mentioned here are Verlaine's sonnet *Parsifal* (but see also his *Art poétique,* published as early as 1882, a programmatic poem on the dominant significance of music for poetry), Mallarmé's sonnet *Hommage* and his essay *Richard Wagner: Rêverie d'un poète français,* and Huysmans' *L'Ouverture de "Tannhauser"* (see his 1884 novel *À rebours,* translated into English in 1926 as *Against the Grain*). Other names include Catulle Mendès, whose first wife was Judith Gautier and whose writings include *Le roi vierge* of 1881, a roman à clef dealing with the lives of Ludwig II and Wagner that caused a sensation in its day; and the proponents of an *esthétique wagnérienne,* Edouard Schuré, Théodore de Wyzewa, and Dujardin himself, the last-named notable for his introductions and translations, his prose paraphrase *Amfortas,* and his poem in homage to Wagner.

In this context the most influential of Wagner's works were *Tannhäuser* and *Tristan,* works which even today remain the nucleus of *wagnérisme*. What Max Nordau condemned as the "sick, degenerate and neurotic" side of Wagner in his famous two-volume work *Degeneration* (1895) became a fascinating model for the decadents[2] to imitate, not only in France, where one thinks of Huysmans, Maurice Barrès, Elémir Bourges, and Joséphin Péladan, but in the whole of Europe, where the movement's leading representatives were Gabriele d'Annunzio, George Moore, and Thomas Mann. It is astonishing that the French view of Wagner was scarcely affected by the increasingly passionate political and military differences between France and Germany (including two world wars), and that it showed no appreciable reaction to the national and nationalistic exploitation of Wagner that was rife in Germany from the 1870s on. If criticism was leveled at Wagner in France, it was first and foremost at the French view of Wagner, at a composer whom Georges Duhamel was to call a "sorcerer" and "brewer of poison" (*La musique consolatrice,* 1944, esp. pp. 50, 54, 61, 62; see also François Mauriac, Julien Gracq, and Charles du Bos, all of whom were thoroughly ambivalent in their criticism of Wagner). A more radical position was adopted by Paul Claudel, especially in his *Richard Wagner: Rêverie d'un poète français* of 1926 and his *Poison wagnérien* of 1938 (the very titles speak volumes), where he takes the composer to task for his immorality and un-Christian outlook, condemning his new myths and a use of leitmotif characterized by excessive repetition which, because of this excess, reminded Claudel of Hitler.

Time and again Wagner's importance as a creator of myths was emphatically stressed; indeed, Claude Lévi-Strauss describes him, scarcely surprisingly, as

2. On this concept, see Koppen 1973, pp. 63–68.

"the indisputable father of the structural analysis of myth" (*Le cru et le cuit,* 1964, p. 23). Wagner also exercised a demonstrable influence, generally acknowledged as such by the authors themselves, on the novels of Marguerite Yourcenar (*Souvenirs pieux,* 1974) and Georges Duhamel (*Le jardin des bêtes sauvages,* 1934, and *Le désert de Bièvres,* 1937; in the former, as I have said, the author's attitude is highly ambivalent). But above all one thinks here of Romain Rolland (*Jean-Christophe,* published in fifteen parts between 1904 and 1912, the fictional biography of a brilliant German musician which, in its structure, has sometimes been likened to a symphony); Julien Gracq (especially *Au Château d'Argol,* 1939; *Un balcon en forêt,* 1958; and also the stage play *Le roi pêcheur* of 1948, each of which reveals its author's intense struggle to come to terms with Wagner's *Parsifal*); and finally Marcel Proust. Proust's cyclical novel *À la recherche du temps perdu* (completed in 1913 and published in three parts between 1913 and 1927) not only mentions Wagner's name on frequent occasions, generally in connection with his music, which is either referred to directly by the characters themselves or else used in countless comparisons, but the very structure of the work has been compared to that of a Wagnerian music drama. Proust made no explicit reference to this effect (although in a letter of 1911 he claimed to know all of Wagner's works by heart), but his motifs of reminiscence have been repeatedly associated with Wagner's leitmotivic technique (a claim which, it must be said, has also occasionally been called into question). As for the structure of his vast novel, Proust himself mentions Wagner in this context, and André Maurois gave expression to a widely held view in 1944 when he explained that *À la recherche du temps perdu* was constructed "like an opera by Wagner" (quoted in Buschinger 1984, pp. 393–394). As a curiosity it may be mentioned in conclusion that the young Jean-Paul Sartre wrote an unpublished novel, *La défaite,* on the subject of Wagner and Nietzsche, in which the characterization of the latter was based in part on a self-portrait of Sartre himself (see Buschinger 1984, p. 380). Buschinger is right to observe that French *wagnérisme* culminated in the Bayreuth *Ring* productions of 1976–1981, directed by Patrice Chéreau and conducted by Pierre Boulez.

Italy

As in France, so there was also a special Wagnerian journal in Italy, the *Cronaca wagneriana,* published in Bologna (Italy's second most important "Wagnerian" city after Venice) from 1893 to 1895. In both scope and significance, however, it was far inferior to the *Revue wagnérienne;* but to that extent it was symptomatic of the weaker influence of Wagner in the Italian peninsula. Although there are occasional traces of Wagner's influence on various other authors, it is principally Gabriele d'Annunzio who shows the most intense preoccupation with Wagner (and Nietzsche). His novel *Il trionfo della morte* of 1894, which is shot through with autobiographical reminiscences, tells, in a glowingly expressive language and with explicit and identifying references to *Tristan,* the story of an overblown love affair which finally ends when the

Roman decadent Giorgio Aurispa forces his lover to join him in a Wagnerian *Liebestod*. In his later novel *Il fuoco* of 1900, the only completed part of a planned trilogy, d'Annunzio describes in often intimate detail his passionate and problematic affair with Eleonora Duse, once again with reference to Wagner. This tale, interspersed with conversations on artistic problems, ends with the couple's decision to separate. It takes place against the background of Wagner's last days in Venice and ends with his death. It is thus one of a series of works which deal with what, for the decadents, was the important association of Venice,[3] Wagner, and death: among the names that spring to mind here are Nietzsche, Maurice Barrès' *Mort de Venise* of 1902, Vernon Lee's novel *A Wicked Voice* of 1890, and Thomas Mann's *Death in Venice* of 1912.

English-Speaking Countries

The nearly incomprehensible enthusiasm for Wagner which marked the end of the nineteenth century also found expression in England, where it led to the foundation of yet a third periodical devoted to Wagner, *The Meister,* a somewhat more durable enterprise than its continental counterparts (it appeared quarterly from 1888 to 1895), but comparable to the *Cronaca wagneriana* in terms of the relatively poor quality of its contents. In its intensity, however, if not in its outline and consequences, Wagnerism in England was entirely similar to its contemporary manifestation in France (see Chapter 15). It was influenced by a decadent view of art and style of life, and, as in France, it was a reaction first and foremost to the erotic and ecstatic elements in Wagner, most notably represented by *Tannhäuser* and *Tristan*. As a prime example of intoxicatingly ecstatic music, *Tannhäuser* was to leave its mark—as it had on Nietzsche, Baudelaire, and Huysmans—on Oscar Wilde's *Picture of Dorian Gray* of 1891, Edward Frederic Benson's *Rubicon* of 1894 (see also Arthur Holitscher's *Poisoned Well* of 1900), and especially on the text and illustrations to Aubrey Beardsley's *Venus and Tannhäuser,* a work which was published during its author's lifetime only in an expurgated and incomplete version titled *Under the Hill,* although Beardsley himself prepared this edition as a means of attracting subscribers to his short-lived periodical *The Savoy* (1896). The complete text was privately printed in 1907 (Sessa 1979, p. 101). In its mixture of Wagnerian and rococo motifs, of studied artificiality and the most ribald obscenity, the work is "one of the most remarkable and graphic demonstrations of decadent sexuality" (Koppen 1973, p. 134).

Wagner was also of considerable significance for those Irish-born authors writing in English, at least some of whose works were produced in Ireland. One thinks of William Butler Yeats, one of the leading figures of the Celtic Renaissance, who collaborated with his friend George Moore on a Wagner-

---

3. The significance of Venice in Wagner's life has often been stressed, notably in 1983, the centenary of his death in Venice. See the "collage" *Richard Wagner in Venice,* published by the East German writer Friedrich Dieckmann in 1983.

inspired national Irish drama *Diarmuid and Grania*. The work, however, met with no success at its first performance in the newly founded National Theatre in Dublin in 1901. Moore himself, in his novel *Evelyn Innes* of 1898, used the figure of a Wagnerian soprano to demonstrate the fatal entanglement of eroticism and music,[4] a favorite theme of the decadents and one which may have been suggested to Moore by his Parisian friend Edouard Dujardin. In Moore's case, however, the work ends with a Christian conversion, a development continued in Moore's next novel, *Sister Teresa,* of 1901. A third name to be mentioned in this context is that of George Bernard Shaw, who had no use for Wagnerian myth and irrationality but who applied his caustic wit to debunking the contemporary view of Wagner, proposing the first consistent socialist interpretation of the *Ring* in his *Perfect Wagnerite* of 1898, an interpretation which, after long years of neglect, was later to prove influential.[5] But the most important of these writers to be discussed here is James Joyce. First, there are cryptic references in *Ulysses* and *Finnegans Wake* to Wagnerian myths, as well as direct quotations from Wagner's works (the most famous example being the Sirens episode, with its reference to the opening of *Das Rheingold*), all of which have an important role to play. Second, it is often said, as it was of Proust, that Wagner's leitmotif technique was adopted by Joyce: his "stream of consciousness" is said to be based on Edouard Dujardin's "monologue intérieur," which Dujardin himself claimed to have invented. Indeed, at a later date, in 1931, Dujardin expressly stated that he had been inspired to do so by Wagner. Certainly Joyce, who knew Wagner's works very well, structured his "unending text" using a technique very similar to that of the leitmotif (DiGaetani 1978). Another key work of twentieth-century English literature, T. S. Eliot's poem *The Waste Land* (1922), also contains references to Wagnerian myths in a number of central passages, and it is significant, as William Blissett has remarked,[6] that the anti-Wagnerian Ezra Pound, who collaborated with Eliot on the final version of the poem and made suggestions for shortening it, had no proposals for cutting these particular lines.

4. Particularly unforgettable for today's reader is the scene in which the heroine is seduced to the strains of *Tristan* played on a harpsichord.

5. Productions of the *Ring* which deserve a mention here include Ulrich Melchinger's Cassel production (1970–1974), Joachim Herz's Leipzig production (1973–1976), Luca Ronconi's La Scala production (1974–75; only *Die Walküre* and *Siegfried* were staged), and Patrice Chéreau's Bayreuth presentation (1976). See Bauer 1983 and Mack 1978. The latter includes a detailed account of the background against which Chéreau's production was staged and which makes clear how many of his ideas Chéreau owed to the Leipzig production. Wieland Wagner's staging, in which Valhalla was seen to have parallels with Wall Street, had already provided pointers in this direction. What all these productions have in common is that they include some visual critique of capitalism, an element which is indisputably present as *one* aspect of the work. Furness (1982, p. 123) draws attention in this context to Upton Sinclair's novel *Prince Hagen* of 1901 and its later revisions. In a lecture delivered in Bayreuth in 1983 Joachim Herz mentioned a spiritual precursor of Shaw's, namely Moritz Wirth, whose work on the subject dates from 1888.

6. William Blissett, "Wagner in *The Waste Land*," in J. Campbell and J. Doyle, eds., *The Practical Vision: Essays in English Literature in Honour of Flora Roy* (Waterloo, Ont., 1978).

As DiGaetani has argued in his detailed study of 1978, Wagner's influence appears to extend to the works of four other major novelists of modern English literature. (I cannot, however, agree with DiGaetani on every point.) *Tristan* and the *Ring,* but also *Parsifal* and *Holländer,* are said to have provided mythic plot structures for many of Joseph Conrad's novels, including *Almayer's Folly* (1895), *The Lagoon* (1898), *Falk* (1903), *Nostromo* (1904), *Chance* (1914), and *Victory* (1915); and *Tristan* and *Die Walküre* on the one hand and the *Ring* on the other are claimed to be the influences behind D. H. Lawrence's novels *The Trespasser* (1912) and *Women in Love* (1920), where there is once again said to be "a pronounced use of Wagnerian patterns" inspired by Lawrence's reading of George Moore, Friedrich Nietzsche, and above all Houston Stewart Chamberlain. Similar claims are made for E. M. Forster's novels *Where Angels Fear to Tread* (1905), *The Longest Journey* (1907), *A Room with a View* (1908), and especially *Howards End* (1910), but also *A Passage to India* (1924) and the posthumously published *Maurice* (1971): although Forster alludes to Wagner and his works, what is more interesting in this context is his intensive handling of a leitmotivic technique used for the purpose of "rhythmic structuring."

Mention must be made finally of Virginia Woolf and her novels *The Voyage Out* (1915), *Jacob's Room* (1922), *The Waves* (1931), and *The Years* (1937). Woolf had already shown a sound knowledge of Wagner and a particular interest in *Parsifal* in her *Impressions at Bayreuth,* published in *The Times* in 1909. She, too, uses references to Wagner, and above all to the *Ring* and *Parsifal,* as a means of establishing a mythic background and, more especially, as a means of characterization. *Parsifal* also provides a "deep mythic structure" for Bernard Malamud's novel *The Natural* of 1952, in which the story of an American hero—a baseball star—is placed in a mythic framework. And the Indian novelist Raja Rao offers a highly impressive reworking of themes surrounding the Grail and Tristan in *The Serpent and the Rope,* written in English and first published in 1960: the themes derive in part from medieval works but also show clear signs of Wagnerian influence and reinterpretation. Many novels of a more trivial nature that have appeared in England and the United States use references to Wagner and his works simply as a means of characterizing what their authors see as typically German or Germanic elements, an association permanently fixed at the level of the purest cliché. An evident misunderstanding on the part of the thriller writer Robert Ludlum resulted in his 1982 million-copy best-seller's being given the title *The Parsifal Mosaic,* with explicit reference, moreover, to Wagner. As an example of a highly ambivalent attitude toward Wagner on the part of an American Jewish writer one may also mention Mark Neikrug's 1981 music drama *Through Roses,* a work written for a single performer and characterized by its author's fascination with and, at the same time, horror at music which is a product of genius and yet capable of being used in concentration camps. The topicality of its theme ensured that the piece was shown not only on British and German television but also on Israeli television in the centenary year of 1983.

Scandinavian Countries

Wagnerian influence can also be observed in Scandinavian literature. It was no less a writer than George Bernard Shaw, and somewhat later Thomas Mann, who drew attention to the demonstrable parallels between Wagner and Henrik Ibsen in the way that both dramatists associate myth and psychology. The Swedish dramatist August Strindberg, who was clearly inspired by Bayreuth in formulating his demand for a "hidden orchestra" in the foreword to *Miss Julie* (1888), and whose profound musicality encouraged an intense preoccupation with Wagner, uses thematic parallels with *Tristan* and the composer's swan myth in his *Svanehvit* of 1902, the same year in which he wrote a sketch for a Flying Dutchman drama directly inspired by Wagner.

Slavic Countries

The extent to which Wagner has left his mark on Slavic literature has received little critical attention to date. Exceptions are Bartlett 1990 and the brief studies (all in Salzburg Symposium) on Wagner in Russia and among the Slavs by Bernice Glatzer Rosenthal and Ewa Burzawa. (See also the examination by Peter Bayerdörfer.) Wagner's concepts of the total work of art and stage dedication festival play were not only important for the Russian symbolists (specifically Aleksandr Blok) and the Ballets Russes of Sergei Diaghilev but also—surprising only at first glance perhaps—for the Soviet understanding of culture in general, and for festival plans, especially in the aftermath of the October Revolution. Important names here are those of Vladimir Mayakovski, Anatoly Lunacharsky, and above all Vsevolod Meyerhold,[7] who had previously staged *Tristan* in St. Petersburg in 1909. Leo Tolstoy, by contrast, had already given thematic expression to the potentially harmful influence of music in his *Kreutzer Sonata* of 1890 (exemplified here, admittedly, in the figure of Beethoven), and used the occasion of a performance of *Siegfried* in Moscow to launch one of the most violent personal attacks on Wagner, whom he castigated in his 1898 essay *What Is Art?* for a unique ability to conjure up hollow but hypnotic images.

---

7. Meyerhold's later plan to stage *Rienzi* is not surprising when one considers that in the early days of the Soviet Union the work was regarded as that of a social revolutionary. The overture (a favorite piece of Hitler's and regularly used at the Nuremberg party rallies) was part of the official celebrations marking the tenth anniversary of the founding of the new state; see the articles by Hans-Peter Bayerdörfer, Ewa Burzawa, and Ernst Hanisch in Salzburg Symposium, and Chapters 1 and 6 in the present volume. A surprising response to Wagner in the Soviet Union was revealed when the Moscow Art Theater (the famous company founded by Stanislavsky, which enjoys quasi-official status) gave a number of guest performances in Austria in the summer of 1984. In Mikhail Shatrov's play about Lenin, *Thus We Shall Conquer* (1981), which takes place on the day of Lenin's death and documents his life in a series of flashbacks, Wagner's music is played onstage at particularly portentous moments in history. The critic Helmut Schneider, writing in the *Salzburger Nachrichten* of 3 September 1984, was wrong to be surprised at "seeing Lenin portrayed by a Soviet ensemble on a par with Lohengrin, Siegfried and even, allusively, with Tristan."

German-Speaking Countries

The first German man of letters to introduce Wagner into a work of literature was the writer and literary historian Johannes Scherr, who presents transparent caricatures of Liszt and Wagner in the figures of the "world-famous virtuoso" Dr. Gaukel and the "musical saviour and tyrant of the future" Schwarbel in an episode in his novel *Michel: History of a German in Our Time,* first published in 1858. Indeed, many German writers—most notably Johann Nestroy—felt drawn toward Wagner's works and person first and foremost in order to parody them, or to make other negative remarks about them. One thinks here, for example, of Paul Heyse, who in *Children of the World* (1873) wrote of "a kind of pathetic cancan, a musical narcosis induced by hashish." Equally outspoken were Karl Gutzkow, Friedrich Theodor Vischer (see his *Rheingold* parody of 1879, *Yet Another*), and especially the Viennese journalist Daniel Spitzer, whose short story *Wagnerians in Love* of 1878 hits out squarely at a composer who writes in the Wagnerian style, and also at Wagner fanatics. His critique of the composer is principally of an aesthetic and musical nature, and it was certainly not mere chance that Spitzer's close colleague on the *Wiener Presse* and later on the *Neue freie Presse* was the music critic Eduard Hanslick, the spokesman of an early form of Wagner criticism. Wagner's *Tristan,* together with discussions of the composer's music in general, later assume a functional significance in Theodor Fontane's *L'adultera* of 1880 (see Eilert 1978). Although Fontane was by no means a Wagnerian, his work contains certain foreshadowings of Thomas Mann's later adaptation of Wagner. Brief mention may also be made of a considerable number of short stories and stage works which use Wagner in one form or another, but which are all of an inferior quality. As Erwin Koppen has noted, "fourth- and fifth-rate authors dominate the field" of early attitudes toward Wagner in Germany (1973, p. 82). Or, to quote Dieter Borchmeyer on the same subject, "purely literary reaction to Wagner was limited almost exclusively to a level of greater or lesser triviality" (1982, p. 316). There were, of course, notable exceptions, and these will be considered later.

Critical reaction to Wagner in Germany differs from that in France and England not only in terms of its artistic quality but also in its outline and, above all, in the aspects it chooses to emphasize. And unlike the reaction of the French *symbolistes* and *décadents,* it remains remarkably diffuse, even if it largely neglects Wagner's literary and dramatic significance and that decadent aspect of his works which was to be so influential elsewhere. What Borchmeyer (1982, p. 316) has to say in this context cannot be stressed sufficiently often: "The fact that Wagner was also a literary phenomenon, indeed—as is clear from the unabating poetical impact of his works, which no other German writer can equal in terms of European influence—that Wagner was *the* literary phenomenon of the nineteenth century, a writer whose most appreciable contribution was to world literature and world theatre—this is something which even today educated Germans are generally reluctant to admit."

For the Germans Wagner was first and foremost a musical phenomenon and, in part, a musical problem. Later—from the time of Bismarck's Reich onward, and above all under the influence of Cosima's Bayreuth and the *Bayreuther Blätter*—he came to be seen as evidence of Germany's cultural greatness, as a figure with whom the nation could identify, and as the alleged founder of a nationalist, if not racist, philosophy. To that extent literary attitudes toward Wagner are an accurate reflection of Germany's political and ideological development from the time of Wilhelm I to the advent of national socialism and beyond, and it remains an open question, and the subject of correspondingly violent debate, whether German Wagnerism influenced and affected this development not only directly but perhaps even crucially. While Oskar Panizza was scoring a direct hit with his attack on "erotic" reactions to Wagner in his *Tristan and Isolde in Paris* of 1900, the typically German national variant was being exposed and denounced by Heinrich Mann with unsurpassed skill and caustic accuracy. His novel *Man of Straw,* written in 1911 in the heyday of the Kaiserreich but not published until 1918, cites the example of a performance of *Lohengrin* in order to demonstrate the sort of attitudes toward Wagner that were typical of large sections of the German middle classes, namely narrow-minded ignorance and above all a patriotic (if not culturally imperialistic) nationalism. Following the First World War, in 1919, Mann singled out Wagner in his essay *Kaiserreich and Republic,* criticizing the composer as one of the great corrupting influences on Germany. Carl Sternheim was another writer who used the image of the German Wagnerian for the purposes of social criticism (see also M. Linke in Salzburg Symposium).

The two outstanding figures among German writers on Wagner are Friedrich Nietzsche (1844–1900) and Thomas Mann (1875–1955). Almost all the arguments that were later adduced for and against Wagner and his works, and almost all the reactions that were subsequently to be of importance not merely in Germany but throughout Europe, are already found in Nietzsche's ambivalent but (whether he was writing pro or contra the composer) extraordinarily perceptive essays on Wagner, the first of which may, with some justification, be held to be *The Birth of Tragedy from the Spirit of Music* of 1872, but the most piercing of which were not published until after Wagner's death or else remained unpublished fragments. For a long time a proper understanding of the relationship between Nietzsche and Wagner was compromised by the willful distortions of his sister Elisabeth Förster-Nietzsche and her interference in his unpublished papers. Only with the appearance of the new critical edition of Giorgio Colli and Mazzimo Montinari has any really reliable and complete source material become available (see Chapter 14 in this volume).

It would be possible to fill a small library with all the books that have been written on the subject of Thomas Mann and Wagner over the years. Only a few essential details can be sketched in here. Mann's essay *The Sorrows and Grandeur of Richard Wagner,* written as a public lecture in 1933 on the occasion of the fiftieth anniversary of Wagner's death, unleashed such a campaign against its author in the still new Reich that Mann decided not to return to

Germany. Reviled as un-German, the essay characterizes Wagner as *the* out-standing representative of the nineteenth century, and sees the secret of his unbroken influence in the successful combination of apparently contradictory and incompatible elements, namely myth and psychology. In its succinctness and balance the essay remains, for all its subjectivity, among the best things that have ever been said and written on the phenomenon of Wagner (for Mann's collected writings on Wagner, see Mann 1985). Mann's preoccupation with the composer and his attempt to come to terms with him can be traced across the whole of his literary oeuvre: the short stories *Tristan* (1903) and *Blood of the Wälsungs* (published in 1906 but later withdrawn by the author) are bourgeois reworkings of *Tristan* and act 1 of *Die Walküre*. In accord with decadent attitudes, Wagner's music is depicted as an aphrodisiac which leads to incest and death. Even in so early a work as the short story *Little Herr Friedemann* of 1897, but more especially in *Buddenbrooks* of 1901, the novel which brought Mann worldwide fame as a writer, the composer's music is described as having an erotic effect or else as inspiring a death wish in its listeners. And although it would be wrong to claim that the multilayered novella *Death in Venice* of 1912 is a direct account of Richard Wagner's death in Venice (Vordtriede 1958), there is no doubt that this tale of the death of Gustav von Aschenbach incorporates references to Wagner in a cryptic and allusive manner. As Mann himself indicated, he had already been inspired by Wagner's leitmotivic technique in writing *Buddenbrooks* (albeit in a purely mechanical sense), and the same technique is deployed in his later works with virtuosic symbolism. The function of the Wagnerian orchestra, ever present in its role as commentator, he compares to that of the omniscient narrator in a novel.

For no other author writing in German was Wagner as important as he was for Thomas Mann, which is not to say that traces of Wagner's influence cannot be found in the works of other leading writers. Wagner's concept of music drama left its mark—long overlooked—on Hofmannsthal and Richard Strauss. Bertolt Brecht's "epic theater" certainly came into being, at least in part, as a reaction against Wagner. And Wagner's music, often portrayed in a critical light, plays a greater or lesser role in Annette Kolb's novella *Torso* (1905), Friedrich Huch's "musical novel" *Enzio* (1911),[8] Arthur Schnitzler's *Road to the Open* (1908), and Robert Musil's *Man without Qualities* (published in three volumes between 1930 and 1943), a work that is largely influenced by Nietzsche. In his short story *Klein and Wagner* of 1919, Hermann Hesse tells how the personality of the middle-class "small man" Friedrich Klein, a man who breaks away from existing ties, is fatally and subconsciously dominated by two Wagners, one the composer and the other a murderer with the same name. In his 1924 novel *Verdi* Franz Werfel, who like Hesse, albeit for different reasons, was a lifelong anti-Wagnerian, proposes the counterimage of a truly human composer who constantly observes the primacy of music

8. For more on this author, see Borchmeyer 1982, pp. 357–362.

but who is all but stifled by Wagner's rivalry. Hermann Bahr (1863–1934) is a remarkable case: he was the speaker at the infamous meeting held in Vienna in 1883, when the city's student population gathered to mourn the composer's death, as a result of which he was expelled from the university. Although he remained a staunch and ardent propagandist on Wagner's behalf,[9] the composer surprisingly plays no part in his works. Karl Kraus, himself a nonpolemical expert on Wagner, said somewhat maliciously of Bahr, "His name will go down in literary history as the husband of a first-class Wagnerian soprano." (He was referring to Anna Bahr-Mildenburg.) In a category of his own, finally, is Egon Wayrer-Fauland. His *Erda*, first sketched in 1938 but not published until 1977–78, is a drama written in the exact style and spirit of the *Ring,* and for long sections could be described very much as a Wagnerian pastiche. It is intended to fill the gap between *Das Rheingold* and *Die Walküre,* and thus to turn the tetralogy into a pentalogy. The author even sought a composer to set the text to music. Wayrer-Fauland has also turned Wagner's sketch *Wieland der Schmied* (for which none other than Adolf Hitler had earlier planned to write the music) into a full-length drama, and has additionally supplied us with Kundry's early history in his 1985 drama *The Rose of Hell.*

German-language reactions to *Parsifal* are a special case, marked as they are by a pronounced tendency to surround both the quest for the Grail and the Grail itself with an aura of mysticism. Such interpretations veer toward the *völkisch* element on the one hand and the mythically archetypal on the other. (See also in this context Denis de Rougemont's interpretation of *Tristan* in his *L'amour et l'occident* of 1939, where Wagner is discussed, albeit with a completely different aim, in terms of global ideology.) This approach is reflected in the writings of Carl Vollmoeller (1902), Will Vesper (1911), Gerhart Hauptmann (1911–12), Friedrich Lienhard (1912), and Albrecht Schaeffer (1922), and, more recently, in Tankred Dorst's anti-Wagner drama *Merlin, or the Waste Land* (1981) and Botho Strauss's novel *The Young Man* (1984), described by Fritz J. Raddatz as "a fairy-tale paraphrase of *Parsifal.*" Mention must also be made here of the ideas associated with Rudolf Steiner and Carl Gustav Jung. In addition to Jung's influential interpretation of *Parsifal* (an interpretation which has left its mark on Wieland Wagner among others), one thinks principally of *The Grail Legend: A Psychological Interpretation* (1960) by Emma Jung and Marie Louise von Franz, a work which left its mark in turn on the literary field, including, for example, the writings of Nathalie Harder, and even Tankred Dorst (see Müller 1982).

---

9. Bahr, incidentally, was among the spiritual fathers of the Salzburg Festival. Among the circle of Viennese writers of around 1900 who refer to Wagner, two names which ought also to be mentioned here—even if they have now fallen into almost total oblivion—are those of the nationalist Catholic writers Richard von Kralik and Siegfried Lipiner (see McGrath 1965, ch. 6). With the exception of the Austrian German Nationalists, responses to Wagner in Austria have tended to emphasize the musical and aesthetic aspects of the composer, beginning with Hanslick and ending, provisionally at least, with Herbert von Karajan's Wagner productions presented within the framework of the Salzburg Easter Festival from 1967 on.

Among contemporary works by German-speaking writers several remain to be mentioned here: Dieter Kühn's narrative *Ludwig's Delight* (1977) and his one-act drama *Private Performance* (1976), both of which center on the figure of King Ludwig II; the 1983 "collage" *Richard Wagner in Venice* by Friedrich Dieckmann, a work which in spite of its generic mixture of collage and essay really belongs in this list (see also note 3); and two radio plays dealing with Wagner's married life, Alexander Widner's highly experimental and ideologically critical *The Beautiful Gardens of Osaka, or Herr Richard Wagner's Marital Bliss* (1981–82), with music by Dieter Kaufmann (including use of Wagner's own music), and Peter Hacks's deeply ironical *Muses* (part 3, 1984–85); Reinhard Baumgart's 1985 television play *Wahnfried,* which depicts fictional scenes from a German marriage in the winter of 1870–71; *Columbus the Balloonist: A Play about Lou Salomé, Friedrich Nietzsche, and Other Well-Known Faces* (Hamburg, 1984), a Nietzsche revue by Yves Andlau (Ilo von Janko); Frido Mann's autobiographical novel *Professor Parsifal* (1985), a work which marks the literary debut of this grandson of Thomas Mann and which wavers irresolutely between novel and autobiography; and *The Union of Body and Spirit* (1980), a comic-romantic novel by Chlodwig Poth, one of the best-known satirists currently writing in Germany. Poth's novel is important less for its literary quality than for the way it lays bare and discusses problems which many left-wing intellectuals and members of the generation of 1968 experienced in dealing with Wagner. Mention may finally be made of those German-language writers of light fiction whose novels on the life of Wagner are apparently still widely read today and who include, for example, Zdenko von Kraft, the author of several biographical novels on the composer, of which three were published together in 1954 under the title *World and Folly,* and Joachim Kupsch, remembered for *An End in Dresden* of 1963.[10]

Transformations
One cannot conclude this survey without listing some particularly interesting literary transformations which Wagner's works have undergone in the recent past. They include the as yet unrealized project *Wagner Space Opera* by the two Frenchmen Humbert Camerlo and Philippe Druillet (see *Wagner et la France,* nos. 337–344); the comic strip version of the *Ring* by Numa Sadoul and France Renoncé (1982–1984; also available in German translation), a version which affords new and surprising insights into the work; the *Parsifal* comic strips by the two Americans P. Craig Russell and Patrick C. Mason, first published in 1978 (a German version by Robert Lug appeared in 1980); and two dramatic dance adaptations from 1983, *The Sacred Marriage: Reminiscences of a Utopian Symphony Freely Based on Wagner's "Ring,"* a "fermenta-

10. A more recent contribution to the genre is the Hungarian novel *A végtelen dallam: Wagner életregénye* by the Hungarian musicologist and writer Imre Keszi (1984; a German translation, *Unendliche Melodie: Lebensroman Richard Wagners,* appeared the same year). The narrator is one Dr. Franz Glasius, a fictional confidant of the composer.

tion" commissioned by the Frankfurt Alte Oper and performed by the Viennese Serapionstheater, a group already well known for its convincing experiments with mime; and the biographical ballet *Riccardo W.,* choreographed by Valery Panov and performed at the Deutsche Oper Berlin to mixed critical reception.

Wagner in Film

The cinematic treatment of Wagner can be subdivided into three groups: biographical and historical films; films using Wagner's music; and film versions of Wagner's music dramas. Many, but not all, films relating to Wagner were assembled and shown in February 1983 within the framework of Venice's Celebrazioni Wagneriane. They are documented in a slender but extremely informative anthology edited by Ermano Comuzio and Giuseppe Ghigi. With few exceptions the survey that follows considers only full-length films, that is, an hour or more. Documentaries and/or academic or educational films (at least those made for television) have not been included.

Biographical and Historical Films

As in so many things, Wagner is at the top of the list when it comes to counting up his appearances in biographical and historical films. (His nearest musical rivals are Verdi and Mozart.) The first historical film about Wagner was made as long ago as 1912 in Berlin and was directed by Carl Froelich, the director and producer of a number of successful later films. Froelich's Wagner film—which was shown on Swiss television in 1983 with an added soundtrack in keeping with the style of the original silent version—sought to portray the official Bayreuth line and grotesquely manipulated the picture of Cosima. But even today the film remains impressive for its atmospheric density and for the performance of its leading actor, the Italian composer Giuseppe Becce;[11] it also provides documentary evidence, even if only in the form of studio recordings, of the contemporary style of Wagnerian performance. The next example of note is *Magic Fire,* a 1955 Hollywood production by William Dieterle, who in 1929 had made a film about Ludwig II and who left Germany for America the following year. *Magic Fire* is memorable for its minutely observed detail and for having been made almost entirely on location, using authentic settings. It tells the story of Wagner's life (impressively acted by Alan Badel), but suffers, at least from a modern perspective, from a certain stiffness and two-dimensionality. The longest and most expensive (and to that extent the most appropriate to the subject) film biography of any composer to date is the one made by the British director Tony Palmer, with Richard Burton in the title role. First seen in London in 1983, the film was

---

11. Not only did Becce bear an astonishing physical resemblance to Wagner in the film, but he also wrote the music for it, Bayreuth having declined to release the original scores, which were still covered by copyright at that time. Unfortunately, Becce's music has not survived.

subsequently shown on television all over the world as a ten-part serial. As with *Magic Fire,* Palmer's film was largely made on location, at enormous expense and with an extravagant array of acting talent. The advance publicity was correspondingly overblown, but the film itself proved disappointingly long-winded, quite apart from the historical inaccuracies which it contained.

A particularly popular choice of theme in this context was, and remains, Wagner and Venice, a subject that has been treated in, among other films Vittorio Carpignano's *Wagner e Venezia,* made in Italy in 1943, largely a documentary account of the composer's association with the city; Josée Dayan's *La mort du titan,* made for French television in 1975 with Michel Vitold as Wagner, and repeated in 1983 under the title *Crépuscule à Venise ou la mort de Wagner;* Petr Ruttner's *Wagner e Venezia,* made in Italy in 1982 and lasting forty-three minutes; and, finally, Werner Friedel's prize-winning coproduction for German and Austrian television (ZDF/ORF) *I am like Othello, my day's work is done* (1983), a film which again involved considerable expense and which takes as its theme the music dramas *Tristan* and *Parsifal,* and above all Wagner's death, although the composer "appears" only as a Harlequin mask.

Wagner also plays an important supporting role in films based on the lives of contemporaries such as King Ludwig II (William Dieterle, 1929; Helmut Käutner, 1955; Hans Jürgen Syberberg, 1972; and Luchino Visconti, 1973) and Franz Liszt (Charles Vidor and George Cukor's *Song without End,* 1959). Wagner's most scurrilous film appearance to date is doubtless in Ken Russell's rock film *Lisztomania* (1976; music by Rick Wakeman), where the composer is portrayed as a vampire, Antichrist, and Hitlerian dictator, before finally being killed by Liszt in the guise of an astronaut. As in many of Hans Jürgen Syberberg's later films, Russell employs cinematic means to underline the indisputable importance which Wagner had for Hitler's ideology.

Film Music

There is no way of telling exactly when and how often Wagner's music has been used in films, but it has certainly not been infrequently (see Roberto Pugliese's article in Comuzio-Ghigi 1983). Among the most popular pieces are *Lohengrin, Tristan,* and the *Ring,* with *The Ride of the Valkyries,* predictably perhaps, at the head of the list. Once again, as in the more popular forms of light fiction, Wagner's music has been used up to the most recent times to represent national socialism. One thinks of Fritz Lang's *Testament of Dr. Mabuse* (Germany, 1933), Claude Chabrol's *Les Cousins* (France, 1958), Luchino Visconti's *The Damned* (Italy, 1969), and Hans Jürgen Syberberg's seven-hour epic *Hitler: A Film from Germany* (Federal Republic of Germany, 1977). But original excerpts from Wagner's music dramas have also been used for other expressive purposes such as indicating passion, secrets, battle and struggle, and so on. Examples include Jean Cocteau's *Le testament d'Orphée* (France, 1960; see the same director's screenplay for Jean Delannoy's 1943 film *L'éternel retour*), Federico Fellini's *Otto e mezzo* (Italy, 1963), Roger Vadim's *Le vice et la vertu* (France, 1963), Tony Richardson's *The Loved One*

(USA, 1964), Louis Malle's *Lacombe Lucien* (France, 1975), and Werner Herzog's *Nosferatu* (Federal Republic of Germany, 1978).[12] It may also be mentioned in this context that Sergei Eisenstein was a great admirer of Wagner: he not only produced *Die Walküre* in Moscow in 1940 (at the time of the pact between Hitler and Stalin), but in 1932 he had planned to make a Wagner-inspired film "as a kind of modern *Götterdämmerung*" (Large-Weber, 1985, p. 243). His sentimentally nationalistic films *Alexander Nevsky* (1938) and *Ivan the Terrible* (1944) reveal Wagner's influence in the staging of their action just as clearly as did the contemporary party rallies of Hitler and Goebbels, at which music from *Rienzi* was regularly performed.

Three particularly outstanding and characteristic examples of the use of Wagner's music in films are, first, in Charlie Chaplin's *Great Dictator* (USA, 1940), in which Chaplin, caricaturing Hitler, performs a grotesque balancing act with a globe-shaped balloon to the strains of *Lohengrin;* second, a sequence that must be counted among the most famous in the history of the cinema, the air raid on a Vietnamese village in Francis Ford Coppola's *Apocalypse Now* (USA, 1979), with *The Ride of the Valkyries* used functionally as an aphrodisiac designed to release aggressive and destructive tendencies;[13] and third, John Boorman's eerily beautiful film about King Arthur, *Excalibur* (Great Britain, 1981), whose soundtrack consists almost exclusively of music by Wagner, with the addition of some by Carl Orff.

Music *reminiscent* of Wagner also plays a major role in the cinema, especially in big-budget science fiction and fantasy films. This trend has been particularly apparent since the 1970s in the work of Hollywood composers such as John Williams (who also composes as Towner Williams, Jr.) and Jerry Goldsmith, in which pseudo-Wagnerian effects, including a large orchestra, fanfare choruses, and leitmotifs (and even, in the case of *E.T.*, direct quotations), have enjoyed an astonishing revival. Unmistakable traces of Wagner can be heard, for example, in the *Star Wars, Star Trek,* and *Superman* films, *E.T., Krull,* and *Conan the Barbarian,* as well as in *Jaws, Blue Lagoon,* and the *Raiders of the Lost Ark* series: George Lucas, Steven Spielberg, and John Milius have contracted a curious musical alliance here.[14]

---

12. Herzog wanted to use Wagner's music in his later film *Fitzcarraldo* (1982); according to the screenplay, he intended to use music from *Die Walküre* in the film's closing sequence, but in any event it is Italian opera and Caruso that dominate the film from beginning to end. Herzog produced *Lohengrin* in Bayreuth in 1987.

13. See also Rolf Thiele's witty and erotic film *Just Come Here, My Darling Birdie* (1968), the opening episode of which shows the old Germanic tribes setting out in search of women to the sounds of *The Ride of the Valkyries.*

14. In the context of the link between science fiction, fantasy, and Wagner (to which the theme of the Middle Ages ought also to be added) one should further mention the "space opera" briefly described earlier in this chapter and the comic strip version of the *Ring* published in the series *Histoires fantastiques.* It is symptomatic of this link that the artist Ul de Rico (Conte Ulderico Gropplero di Troppenburg, born 1944 in Udine) not only published a huge coffee table book with fantasy-style illustrations on the *Ring* (1980), but also designed the sets for the

An interesting case is that of Fritz Lang's famous two-part silent film *Die Nibelungen* of 1923–24. Although the film itself contains few reminiscences of the *Ring,* the distributors made both parts available abroad in shortened versions in 1925 and 1928 with music taken from Wagner's scores and arranged by Hugo Reisenfeld; and in 1933 a soundtrack was added to the film (once again cut and revised) with music made up exclusively of Wagner. Lang (who did not like Wagner) tried unsuccessfully to block the move. He emigrated to America in 1933 and divorced his wife, Thea von Harbou, who had written the screenplay for *Die Nibelungen* and who in the meantime had joined the National Socialist Workers' party. Wagner also figures in the remake of *Die Nibelungen* directed by Harald Reinl in 1966–67, not only in the music of Rolf Wilhelm but, to a far greater extent than in Lang's version, in the story too. And, as might be expected, he is also to be heard in Adrian Hoven's 1971 sex film *Siegfried and the Legendary Love Life of the Nibelungs.*

Film Versions of Wagner's Stage Works

Wagner was also one of the first composers whose works were made into films, initially in the form of short silent films (beginning with Thomas Edison's *Parsifal* of 1904 and 1910, and Franz Porten's *Lohengrin* of 1907, which starred his daughter Henny Porten as Elsa); later in "cinema operas" made by Delog (German Cinema Opera Company) and including *Lohengrin* (1915) and *The Flying Dutchman* (1919), both with a live orchestra and singers; and finally in a number of sound films (still heavily cut), of which the most notable are Max Calandri's 1948 *Lohengrin* and Daniel Mangrane's 1951 *Parsifal.* Both these last-named films were made in Italy, as were at least five earlier silent films. Time and again one finds excerpts from Wagner's music dramas in films about famous singers and impresarios, or which take place against an operatic background. Examples here include *Interrupted Melody* (USA, 1955), about the life of the soprano Marjorie Lawrence, and *The Big Broadcast of 1938* (USA, 1938) and *Two Sisters from Boston* (USA, 1946), with appearances by Kirsten Flagstad and Lauritz Melchior, respectively. The same is true of films based on books that are related to Wagner, such as Rolf Thiele's film of Thomas Mann's *Blood of the Wälsungs* (1964).

Holländer has always been a particularly profitable subject for feature films. The American director Albert Lewin was the first to transfer the opera to a modern setting in his film *Pandora and the Flying Dutchman* (1951), starring James Mason and Ava Gardner in the title roles;[15] but the first complete film of the opera (and, indeed, of any work by Wagner) was made by Joachim

---

ambitious, if not particularly successful, film *Unendliche Geschichte,* the most expensive science-fiction film made in Germany to date (Michael Ende, 1983).

15. This film is still worth seeing today. Although it contains no explicit reference to Wagner and does not include any of his music, this modern reworking of the Dutchman legend could scarcely have derived its inspiration from any other source. Transferred to a present-day setting, the film tells the story of a night club singer and a yacht owner, and in so doing quotes an astonishing number of elements from the plot of Wagner's opera.

Herz in the German Democratic Republic in 1964. Although little known in the West (in spite of a broadcast on Swiss television in 1983), Herz's *Dutchman,* expressly described as being "based on" Richard Wagner, remains the most impressive and convincing opera film to date.[16] By situating the work in the nineteenth century and by interpreting the action as Senta's vision (expressed by means of two different film formats), Herz can be seen, both here and in his other productions, at the very least to have exerted a fundamental influence on many later directors, including Harry Kupfer, who clearly took over a number of Herz's ideas in his 1978 Bayreuth production of the work. A second television version which also manages to break free from the theater, albeit with more conventional results, was made in Munich in 1975 by Václav Kašlík. Herbert von Karajan's 1981 television film of *Das Rheingold* (the first part of a planned but unrealized complete *Ring*) occupies a middle ground between a stage production (it started life at the Salzburg Easter Festival) and a studio version of the work.

The increasing popularity of televised opera broadcasts or television productions based on original stage performances has of course left its mark on Wagner. With the exception of *Die Feen,* all of Wagner's stage works, including even *Das Liebesverbot* and *Rienzi,* have been shown on television (often internationally) at least once, beginning in 1970 with *Die Meistersinger* from Hamburg. Other broadcasts have followed from Geneva, Graz, Munich, and Wiesbaden, and especially, of course, from Bayreuth. The undisputed high point so far has been the televised production of the complete *Ring* from Bayreuth, a documentary record of the stage productions seen there between 1976 and 1981, directed by Patrice Chéreau and conducted by Pierre Boulez. Reproduced for television, it enjoyed considerable success in many countries outside Germany, including France, Great Britain, and the United States. In stark and express contrast, finally, is Hans Jürgen Syberberg's film adaptation of *Parsifal* (1982), a special case in that Syberberg has consciously turned his back on the traditional opera film and created an autonomous work of cinematic art. The film overlays Wagner's *Parsifal* with a complex network of visual symbols and allusions, and in so doing both comments on and complicates Wagner's already complex work.[17] The soundtrack is provided by a high-quality recording of the work especially made for the purpose in France. Even those critics who dislike the film have been impressed by its technical sophistication and by the outstanding acting of its cast, especially Edith Clever as Kundry. Syberberg had already shown a highly unconventional approach to Wagner and his ideological implications in such earlier films as *Ludwig: Requiem for a Virgin King* (1972), *Confessions of Winifred Wagner* (1975, originally five hours in length), and *Hitler: A Film from Germany* (1977); the same

16. The 1983 Wagner Film Festival in Venice neither listed this film nor presented a showing of it. Herz's ideas on the subject were first published in 1962 and reprinted in Csampai-Holland 1982, pp. 223–233.

17. Syberberg's own commentary in Syberberg 1982 is indispensable for that very reason; see also his 1976 *Filmbuch.*

is true of Syberberg's later film *The Night* (1985), a six-hour recitation, also with Edith Clever. In the process he has certainly provided the most widely discussed (at least outside Germany) and, for many people, the most impressive contributions, aside from those of Joachim Herz, to the subject of Wagner and the cinema.

Translated by Stewart Spencer

Postscript (1991)

As I have already said in the introduction to this chapter, the influence of Wagner and his works on the various media is one which, in theory at least, will never cease expanding. Therefore it is not surprising that since 1986, when the original German text of this survey was published, there have been a number of events worth noting. I would also like to take this opportunity of drawing the attention of English-speaking readers to two publications not mentioned above which have made a contribution to the subject of Wagner's influence on English literature. They are Elliott Zuckerman's *First Hundred Years of Wagner's Tristan* (Zuckerman 1964) and Stoddard Martin's *Wagner to "The Waste Land"* (Martin 1982), both of which discuss the relationship of Wagner to English authors from Swinburne to Joyce and Eliot.

From the world of dance a noteworthy event was the ballet version of the *Ring* choreographed by Maurice Béjart for the Deutsche Oper in Berlin in 1990. And Reinhard Baumgart's *Wahnfried,* which appeared as a book in 1985, was turned into a television production.

Among the most interesting events in Germany have been the striking alternative versions of Wagner's music dramas which Uwe Hoppe has regularly mounted on the fringe of the Bayreuth festival since 1983 with his ensemble, Studiobühne Schützenhaus. The productions contain many parodistic elements, though they are not intended principally as parodies. Rather, their purpose is to make Wagner's works more relevant to modern concerns and to turn the deeper structures and layers of meaning which lie hidden beneath their surface into theatrical reality. Hoppe's productions so far include *Der Ring des Liebesjungen* (1983), *Paxiphall & Lohengrün* (1985), and *Thannreuther, Meistersinger* (1988). His ideas have even had an influence on the "normal" performances of the Bayreuth festival (they were observable, for instance, in Harry Kupfer's *Ring* production in 1988).

The *Ring* has proved to be a favorite not only with practically every major opera house of international repute but also with novelists in the English-speaking world, such as the South African author André Brink, who absorbs a number of Wagnerian topics into his highly critical confrontation with the present political situation in South Africa (*States of Emergency,* 1988). A utopian sequel to the *Ring* has been invented with a great deal of subversive irony by the Englishman Tom Holt (*Expecting Someone Taller,* 1987–88), and modern German history, Nazism, and Wagner are combined in the most grotesque way imaginable in the fictitious biography of an English brother and sister by the Canadian writer David Gurr (*The Ring Master,* 1987). In this context another book not mentioned in my earlier account should be noted: *Der Feuerkreis* (The Circle of Fire), written in 1971 by the Austrian novelist Hans Lebert.

The medieval tale of Parzival, including the way twentieth-century commentators have interpreted it with many allusions to Wagner, is the subject of *Parsifal: A Novel* (1988) by the Englishman Peter Vansittart. The life of the first conductor of Wagner's *Parsifal,* the Jewish conductor Hermann Levi, has also been turned by Rolf Schneider into a novel (*Die Reise zu Richard Wagner,* 1989).

Works: The Composer

CHAPTER 18

The Musical Works

WERNER BREIG

Early Instrumental Works

Wagner was not one of those composers who, like Schubert and Mendelssohn, manage to find their own "voice" while still in their youth. Rather, Wagner's early works display the sort of attachment to formative musical models that is decidedly epigonic. It was not until around 1840, during Wagner's sojourn in Paris, that he was able to eliminate these influences or, to put it more positively, to shape his own creative ideas in such a way that traditional elements were made to serve and not to dominate his intentions.

Wagner began his career as a composer of instrumental music. He wrote his earliest works while studying composition (1829–1831) with Christian Gottlieb Müller, a violinist in the Leipzig Gewandhaus orchestra, and subsequently (1831–32) with the cantor of St. Thomas's, Christian Theodor Weinlig.

Although Weinlig taught Wagner for only about half a year, his influence was lasting. In a letter written in 1834, Wagner described his lessons with Weinlig: "To give me a thorough grounding in harmony, he first took me through the strict, learned style [*gebundener Styl*] and he did not stop until he considered me thoroughly proficient in it. In his opinion, this learned style was the first and only foundation for the production of free and rich harmonies, as well as an essential tool for the learning of counterpoint. He then taught me counterpoint in the most secure form and according to the strictest principles" (SB I, 150; SL 18–19). Later Wagner gave a detailed description in his autobiography of the intensive tuition Weinlig gave him in the composition of fugue (ML 55). The influence of these studies is discernible in the fugal introduction to the finale of the Piano Sonata in A Major (WWV 26), although Wagner later recognized it as being stylistically out of place and deleted the passage (see SW 19, 115). Still more important than the content of Wagner's lessons was the fact that for the first time he was now devoting his attention to, and working intensively at, the craft of composition. If

Wagner's account of his teacher's assessment at the end of the course is accurate, Weinlig must have seen matters in a similar light: "Probably you will never write fugues or canons. What you have achieved, however, is self-sufficiency. You can now stand on your own two feet, and know that you can use the most refined techniques if you need to" (ML 56). (We should bear in mind that Wagner's recollection of this statement is probably colored by his main preoccupation when he dictated it. At the time—between November 1865 and March 1866—he was composing *Meistersinger*.)

The creative yield of these years is impressive in terms of quantity. We cannot, however, trace Wagner's musical works back to the very beginning because nearly all his instrumental works written before he began his studies with Weinlig fell victim to Wagner's self-criticism and were destroyed—a fact which in itself testifies to the fundamental importance of Weinlig's teaching. Among the works concerned were three piano sonatas, a string quartet, and at least four, or possibly five, overtures for orchestra (WWV, pp. 64–74). For the most part these works are mentioned only briefly in Wagner's autobiographical writings. He left a detailed account of just one of them—the Overture in B flat (WWV 10)—and of the one and only performance of the work, on Christmas Eve 1830 in Leipzig. The relevant passage in his autobiography (ML 53) includes a vivid description of a striking oddity devised by the seventeen-year-old composer—a drumbeat on the second quarter of every fifth bar—and its effect on the astonished audience. (Again, we have to remember that the passage not only documents this early composition, but is also a model example of Wagner's emphatic, and perhaps slightly exaggerated, way of telling a story.)

For the most part, Wagner's extant early works are either for piano or for orchestra. That the piano plays a significant part in these compositions is not to say that Wagner had a special affinity for the instrument and its expressive possibilities. In this respect the piano remained alien to him throughout his life; it was merely an easily accessible medium for musical thought that was universally in use. The significance Wagner attached to piano music is also shown in the musical forms he chose in his early works: he was not interested in composing character pieces like those written by "real" piano composers such as Chopin, Schumann, and Liszt; instead he wrote large-scale cyclical works in the classical mold. The B-flat Major Sonata op. 1 (WWV 21)—published in 1832 with a dedication to Weinlig—can be regarded as an example of Wagner's submission to the discipline demanded by his teacher. Wagner obeyed Weinlig's instructions and based the piece on "strict harmonic and thematic discipline"; the model recommended was "one of the most childlike sonatas of Pleyel" (ML 56). (For a more skeptical view of this passage in Wagner's autobiography, see WWV, p. 84.)

A formally and expressively expansive antithesis to this work of self-limitation is the F-sharp Minor Fantasia of November 1831 (WWV 22), a work consisting of 374 measures in the free-keyboard fantasia tradition of C. P. E. Bach. Beethoven's Fantasia op. 77 probably served as a model for

Wagner; the idea of basing a large section of the work on the principle of variation probably derives from the Beethoven work (mm. 261–304, for instance, are a variation of mm. 217–260). The F-sharp Minor Fantasia is the one early piano work in which Wagner in later years could still find something of himself. He played it for Cosima in November 1877, and she noted in her diary that it was "very touching! Inner absorption in the example of the great masters, dreamy simplicity—how different the juvenile works of today!" (CT, 17 November 1877).

The most ambitious of the piano works of these years, and indeed of all Wagner's piano works, is the *Große Sonate* in A Major op. 4 of 1832 (WWV 26). It not only imitates Beethoven's style throughout but shows its dependence on specific Beethoven works. The opening movement of the Third Symphony, for instance, obviously inspired the dactylic rhythm ♩♪♪ in the development section of the first movement of Wagner's sonata. Wagner's slow movement, headed "Adagio molto, e assai espressivo," is based on the slow movements of Beethoven's piano sonatas op. 106 and op. 110. And the Maestoso introduction of Beethoven's last sonata op. 111, with its double-dotted rhythms, clearly influenced the eighteen-year-old composer when he wrote the introduction (also headed "Maestoso") to the last movement of his own sonata.

Music for orchestra looms even larger than music for piano. Wagner's favorite genre was the overture, possibly because it was easier to organize performances of short works than of long works such as symphonies. One of Wagner's earliest extant compositions is an untitled orchestral work in E minor (WWV 13) that could well be identical with a lost overture written in 1830 for Schiller's play *Die Braut von Messina* (WWV 12). The overtures in D minor (two versions) and C major (WWV 20 and 27, respectively), as well as the overture in E minor to Ernst Raupach's tragedy *König Enzio* (WWV 24A), date from 1831 and 1832. (It is possible that two *Entr'actes tragiques* [WWV 25] were planned for the same drama; there are two extant sketches, the first of which is partially orchestrated.) The affinity of these works to Beethoven was stressed by Wagner himself in his autobiographical writings, and detailed analyses of the similarities can be found in Voss 1977 (pp. 48ff.).

Wagner wrote three more overtures during the years 1834–1837. The first, completed in January 1835, was for a tragedy titled *Columbus* by Wagner's friend Theodor Apel (WWV 37A). This was followed in 1836 by the overture *Polonia* (WWV 39), which reflected Wagner's sympathy for the unsuccessful Polish uprising against Russian rule in 1831. The third work in this group was the *Rule Britannia* overture of 1837 (WWV 42), which was not apparently prompted by any external cause. In all three works Wagner attempts to free himself to a certain extent from the hitherto overpowering influence of Beethoven. A new source of inspiration is Mendelssohn's *Meeresstille und glückliche Fahrt*. The *Columbus* overture is clearly modeled on it; indeed, in later years Wagner even went so far as to describe his overture to Cosima as a "plagiarism" (CT, 17 June 1879). The traditional folk melodies used in the two works that followed are another new source. We also know from Cosima's diaries that Wagner at this time was planning yet another overture, the subject of which was to be Napoleon: "He intended to depict his hero in all his glory up to the Russian campaign, from then on in his decadence. For the apex of the pyramid he needed a gong stroke, but began to doubt whether this was permissible in music, and asked somebody. Since he could not make up his mind to use the gong, he abandoned the whole thing" (CT, 12 July 1869).

Finally, the C Major Symphony (WWV 29), written in Prague in the early summer of 1832, has an important place among Wagner's early instrumental works. (A second symphony in E major [WWV 35], begun in 1834, was never finished.) According to Glasenapp, Wagner described the C Major Symphony in later years as a work that had been written "under the overwhelming influence of Beethoven's music, insofar as a man of twenty is capable of understanding and knowing it" (Glasenapp VI, 67, quoted in SW 18, I, p. xvii; for further details, see Kropfinger 1991 and Voss 1977). Nonetheless, the technical expertise of the young composer and the generous dimensions of the movements (475, 208, 447, and 442 measures, respectively) command respect. On Christmas Eve 1882, less than two months before his death, Wagner organized a revival of the symphony in Venice, which he conducted himself; he even made some revisions of the score for this occasion. A few days later he wrote an article about the performance, *Report on the Revival of an Early Work* (SSD X, 309–315), containing an appreciation of the symphony written some fifty years before that mixes affection with distance: "If there is something in this work that belongs unmistakably to Richard Wagner, it is at most boundless confidence; even at that time he was forging ahead regardless of, and staying immune to, the chicken-heartedness that was to become fashionable soon after and has since proved to be irresistible to the Germans" (p. 314). This view of the work is surprisingly close to Friedrich Wieck's impression of its first performance (on 15 December 1832 in Leipzig), at least according to a letter from his daughter Clara to Robert Schumann (SW 18, I, p. xiii).

Lieder to 1840

The lied was a peripheral genre for Wagner. If we disregard *Der Tannenbaum* (WWV 50) and *Gruß seiner Treuen* (WWV 71), which was originally written for a male choir, we can divide Wagner's extant lieder into three groups: the *Faust* compositions of 1831, the songs with French texts written between 1839 and 1840, and the Wesendonck lieder of 1857–58.

The lieder Wagner wrote between 1828 and 1830 survive as fragments and were probably never more than that (see WWV 7). The *Sieben Kompositionen zu Goethes Faust* (WWV 15), by contrast, have survived intact. They were written at the beginning of 1831 and—apart from possible revisions to the only complete source (a copy in another hand made in 1832)—are among Wagner's earliest extant compositions. In Paul Bekker's judgment they are better than one might expect because of the "unforced simplicity of the way the music illustrates pictorial images" (Bekker 1924, p. 80). For long stretches the seventeen-year-old composer tries to give some identity to the declamatory passages with a generous use of dotted rhythms, a style to which he later succumbed (though on a higher level) in *Holländer*. (In a letter to Theodor Uhlig of 25 March 1852, Wagner made some self-critical remarks about the declamation in *Holländer*.) The first signs of a personal voice in these settings are probably most discernible in the two Gretchen compositions in G minor (no. 6, *Gretchen am Spinnrade*, and no. 7, *Melodrama*, "Ach neige, du Schmerzenreiche"). An analysis of no. 6, however, shows the extent to which inexperience still impedes the development of Wagner's musical ideas. Certain technical weaknesses in this song indicate that it was not thoroughly revised in 1832. Awkward moments such as the consecutive fifths for the left hand in the sixth measure (and later passages parallel with it) and the botched voice-leading in the twenty-second would have been almost inconceivable after his studies with Weinlig.

Wagner wrote *Der Tannenbaum* in the autumn of 1838 around the time he began composing the first act of *Rienzi*. The text, by Georg Scheurlin (Wagner found it in the *Deutscher Musenalmanach für das Jahr 1838,* edited by Adalbert von Chamisso and G. Schwab), consists of a dialogue between a pine tree *(der Tannenbaum)* and a young boy. At the end the tree says: "Daß schon die Axt mich suchet / zu deinem Totenschrein, / das mach mich stets so trübe, / gedenk' ich, Knabe, dein." ("Whenever I think of you, boy / My heart with grief is seized / That the axe already seeks me / From whom your coffin will be made.") There are unmistakable parallels here to Eduard Mörike's poem *Denk es, o Seele,* which was written in 1856 (and set to music by Hugo Wolf in 1888). The setting identifies the two interlocutors by means of differing accompanying figures on the piano (eighth notes for the pine tree and sixteenth notes for the boy), a technique Wagner may have borrowed from the ballads of Karl Loewe—works which he held in high esteem throughout his life. As for the details, one is struck by Wagner's carelessness in tolerating an echo of Schubert's *Winterreise* (no. 11, "Da war es kalt und finster") in the two final lines of the vocal part. (Or is it possible that Wagner had not become acquainted with *Winterreise* since its publication in 1828?) The song nonetheless contains original elements that anticipate some of Wagner's later music. In particular the conversation about fate in *Der Tannenbaum* is reminiscent of the Norns scene in *Götterdämmerung,* including the first version of it in *Siegfrieds Tod* (as *Götterdämmerung* was originally called). The main thing that links them is the dark and remote key of E-flat minor, which Wagner, who was a kapellmeister in Riga when he composed *Der Tannenbaum,* jokingly referred to as the "Livonian key" (SB I, 357). (Livonia is now a region of the Baltic states and comprises southern Latvia and northern Estonia.) In addition, there are echoes of the early musical setting of the Norns scene in *Siegfrieds Tod* (sketched in 1850) in the instrumental figuration and in details of the vocal declamation.

At the start of Wagner's first stay in Paris he composed a number of songs with French texts in the hope that they would help him make a name for himself as a composer in the French capital. In his autobiography he wrote: "My friends now strongly advised me to write something on a smaller scale in the way of songs, which I could then offer to popular singers for performance at their frequent concerts" (ML 173). In the winter of 1839–40 Wagner produced six of these small-scale songs: *Dors mon enfant,* to a text by an unknown author (WWV 53); *Attente,* after Victor Hugo (WWV 55); *Mignonne,* after Pierre de Ronsard (WWV 57); *Tout n'est qu'images fugitives,* a setting of the poem *Soupir* by Jean Reboul (WWV 58); *Les deux grenadiers,* after a French translation by François Adolphe Loeve-Veimar of Heine's poem (WWV 60); and *Adieux de Marie Stuart,* after Pierre Jean de Béranger (WWV 61), a virtuoso coloratura piece intended for Julie Dorus-Gras, the celebrated soprano of the Paris Opera. (For a list of some of the singers Wagner had in mind for the other songs, see WWV 198.) Wagner also began two more songs but did not complete them: *Extase* (WWV 54) and *La tombe dit à la rose* (WWV 56), both to texts by Victor Hugo.

The French songs are technically competent; the melodies are well defined, and the piano accompaniments are richly executed and on occasion orchestrally colored. The form is also handled in an interesting way. Wagner later spoke, quite rightly, of "small pieces" of which he had "no reason to be ashamed" (ML 173). The songs did not meet with much success at the time, perhaps because they were too complicated for the function they were supposed to serve. Later, the setting of Heine's *Grenadieren* (replete with a retranslation of the text into German) became quite well known, perhaps because of the parallel with Robert Schumann's version (based on Heine's original text), which, like Wagner's, quotes the *Marseillaise* at the end.

The connection between Wagner's French songs and the popular Parisian romances of the time has not yet been explored. Stylistic traits that point in the direction of Wagner's later works, however, are easier to identify; they are evident in specific thematic characteristics that Wagner later took up in other contexts. Glasenapp was the first to point out that the principal theme of *Attente* (Example 1a) has an affinity with a moment in the third act of

Mon - te, é - cu - rueil, mon - te au grand chê - ne

Example 1a   *Attente,* mm. 5–6

Example 1b   *Tristan,* act 3, mm. 963–966 (bass clarinet and cello)

Tristan (Example 1b), which is reinforced by the fact that both passages illustrate an act of looking out from a high place (Glasenapp I, 348; in Ellis translation I, 283). Moreover, the melodic outline of the first vocal phrase of *Mignonne* (Example 2a) closely resembles the section in the same key in the Bridal Chamber scene in the third act of *Lohengrin* beginning with the phrase "Fühl' ich zu dir" (Example 2b). And the instrumental motif depicting the wavering of despair in *Les deux grenadiers* (Example 3a) is taken up again in a more strongly defined variant form in *Tannhäuser*'s Rome narration, again in the same key (Example 3b). (Glasenapp's view that the motif in *Les deux grenadiers* parallels a moment in the third act of *Parsifal*—from measure 373— is hardly convincing.)

Early Operas
Die Hochzeit

After completing the C Major Symphony, Wagner made his first serious attempt at writing the libretto and music of an opera. He probably did not realize the fundamental importance of this move at the time, but the composition of *Die Hochzeit* (WWV 31) in 1832 marks the de facto beginning of

Example 2a   *Mignonne*, mm. 2–3

Example 2b   *Lohengrin*, act 3, scene 2, mm. 29–30

Example 3a   *Les deux grenadiers*, mm. 30–31

Example 3b   *Tannhäuser*, act 3, scene 3 (Rome narration)

the dominance of music drama in Wagner's output, compared with which everything else was to seem peripheral. His decision to devote himself to the genre of opera is all the more remarkable when one considers that for a long time (that is, until the first performance of *Rienzi* in October 1842) none of his operas had successful performances, whereas at least some of his orchestral works did.

Wagner's first venture into the field of opera with *Die Hochzeit* foundered not on the problem of performance but even before the work was finished. The libretto was completed in November 1832, and the musical sketch of the beginning of the first act dates from 5 December. The music earned the nineteen-year-old composer "encouraging praise" from his teacher, Weinlig, "for its clarity and singability" (ML 68). In January 1833, as a result of criticism by his older sister, Rosalie, Wagner destroyed the libretto, so the musical sketch was all that remained. Although he had abandoned the opera as a whole, he orchestrated the fragment and wrote it out in full score (the date at the end is 1 March 1833) after his move to Würzburg, probably with a view to mounting a performance there. It is unlikely that such a performance ever took place. This fragment and Wagner's account of the text (ML 66–68) provide the only information about the work that remains.

It is difficult to determine whether this musical fragment displays any individual traits above and beyond sure technical mastery of the operatic tradition (the immediate model here was probably Marschner). Affinities can certainly be discerned between the characteristic instrumental bass motif, which recurs in the recitatives, and motifs in the *Ring*. Glasenapp even ventures to refer to this as the "earliest" leitmotif (Glasenapp I, 169; in Ellis translation I, 145; see also Cooke 1979a, pp. 249–252).

More significant, probably, than such questions of detail, which remain open to discussion, is a basic decision that Wagner made with *Die Hochzeit:* for here, in his first operatic work, Wagner is his own librettist, in complete contrast to his treatment of the song genre, in which all the texts he set to music were written by others. Long before any theorizing about the problem of the *Gesamtkunstwerk,* or synthesis of the arts, Wagner was obviously convinced that the nature of opera was such that text and music had to spring from a single source. Thus for Wagner, creative work in the field of music and drama could only mean the creation of both poetry and music.

Die Feen

Immediately after his destruction of the libretto for *Die Hochzeit,* Wagner undertook a project that was to become his first completed opera: *Die Feen* (WWV 32). The text was finished by January 1833, and on 20 February Wagner began the musical composition with a draft for act 1. (In the terminology used by the Bayreuth archive, a terminology that has become increasingly problematic, this is referred to as an "orchestral sketch" although WWV prefers "complete draft." See my excursus on the creative process in Wagner's music. later in this chapter.) The score was completed by 6 January 1834.

Wagner's hope that the Leipzig theater would accept the piece for performance was not realized. He never heard the work; its posthumous premiere did not take place until 1888 in Munich.

The genre of the three-act work is Romantic opera. With respect to the models for its text and music, Wagner gave the following account in *A Communication to My Friends:* "The 'Romantic opera' of Weber popular at the time, and the new appearance of Marschner in Leipzig, where I was living, inspired me to imitate it. I produced just what I wanted, an opera libretto: I set it to music according to my impressions of Beethoven, Weber and Marschner" (SSD IV, 252). The enumeration of Wagner's models establishes his basic indebtedness, but the list is incomplete. For example, the buffo duet between Drolla and Gernot in act 2 is suspiciously close to quotation from the Papagena-Papageno duet in the act 2 finale of *Die Zauberflöte,* and one of the most significant harmonic inventions is inconceivable without Mendelssohn's overture to *Midsummer Night's Dream* (see my discussion later in this chapter). In general it should be borne in mind that while Wagner was writing *Die Feen,* the repertoire with which he was intimately involved as choir director in Würzburg included works by Weber, Auber, Rossini, Cherubini, Beethoven, Paër, Hérold, and Meyerbeer. This served to keep Wagner in constant contact with the main currents of contemporary German, Italian, and French opera.

In a brief survey such as this, one is certainly entitled to pay special attention to characteristic and forward-looking elements as distinct from those that are merely epigonic or typical of contemporary styles, even if such elements are not central to the overall impression created by the work. From this perspective Wagner's power of expression and originality in scenes where the border states of consciousness are characterized in musical terms is particularly noteworthy: the falling asleep and awakening of Arindal in the finale of act 1, and above all the mad scene of act 3, of which Paul Bekker aptly said that here the youthful Wagner "stumbled on a fundamental aspect of his talent for the first time" (Bekker 1924, p. 89).

Seen from a different perspective, Wagner "stumbled on a fundamental aspect of his talent" with a harmonic invention connected with the heart of the *Feen* subject. This is the sequence of chords that can be considered a musical emblem signifying a spiritual change to the realm of the immortals. It appears throughout the work, first in the overture and then, with significant emphasis, in the final scene of act 3. There can be little doubt that Wagner was inspired by the sequence of chords at the start of Mendelssohn's *Midsummer Night's Dream* overture. (Like the overture to *Die Feen* and the final part of the opera, the Mendelssohn work is in the key of E major.) Mendelssohn uses two pairs of chords, the roots of which are descending fourths (E major to B major and A minor to E major); the first moves from the tonic of E major, and the second returns to it. The chordal movement of *Die Feen* is similarly based on descending fourths, which results in an unbroken sequence moving ever farther from the tonic (E, B, F sharp, C sharp, and G-sharp major). The composer does not bother for the most part to find a logical way to return from the distant chord of G-sharp major back to the tonic; instead he simply continues in E major.

This sequence is the first instance of those "magic" combinations of chords that play such a major role in the motivic arsenal of Wagner's mature works. The harmonic emblem, far-reaching as it is, still appears isolated in a context that is, in all other respects, harmonically quite conventional. In the final analysis, the problem of integrating such expressive details could be solved only by completely changing the way harmony was treated, a consequence Wagner probably did not envisage when he wrote this striking sequence in *Die Feen*.

Das Liebesverbot

Wagner had precise ideas about the ambience of his early operas. He envisaged *Die Feen* as set in the Nordic Middle Ages, a view he sought to realize against the wishes of the director when a performance in Leipzig was still under discussion. "Highly incensed, I fought against the insufferable turban and kaftan costumes and demanded energetically the knightly garb typifying the earliest period of the middle ages" (ML 79). He did, however, change the setting of *Das Liebesverbot* from the Vienna of its model, Shakespeare's *Measure for Measure,* to "the capital of fiery Sicily" (ML 83), and the German element is represented only negatively by the governor, Friedrich, who "attempts to introduce puritanical reforms and fails miserably in the process." (ML 83).

These settings are reflected by the musical idioms of contemporary opera from which the composer took his bearings. In the case of *Die Feen* this was German Romantic opera, and in *Das Liebesverbot* the models were French and Italian. The switch from one idiom to the other was as abrupt and immediate as Wagner's sudden adoption of the philosophy out of which the libretto of *Das Liebesverbot* grew. The essay *German Opera* (June 1834), which Wagner was writing when he started work on *Das Liebesverbot,* parallels the change; it contains an abusive attack on Weber's *Euryanthe* as the embodiment of "German profundity" in music. "Instead of quickly capturing a feeling with a single bold and telling stroke, he hacks to pieces the impression of the whole with petty details and detailed pettiness . . . Oh, this unhappy erudition—this source of all German ills!" (SSD XII, 2).

The music of *Das Liebesverbot* was written during 1834. On 23 January the composition draft was begun, and on 30 December it was completed; the score itself was probably finished in January 1835. The premiere (the only performance during Wagner's lifetime) took place on 29 March of the same year, at a time when the Magdeburg Opera company was on the brink of dissolution (ML 118ff.).

Wagner was engaged as a conductor at the Magdeburg theater while he was working out the composition of *Das Liebesverbot*. Aside from works by Weber and Marschner, the repertoire he conducted there consisted mainly of

Italian and French operas. The season included Rossini's *Otello* and *Il barbiere di Siviglia*, Bellini's *I Capuleti e i Montecchi*, Auber's *La muette de Portici* and *Fra Diavolo*, and Cherubini's *Le porteur d'eau*. This choice may provide certain clues to sources of influence, but no detailed study yet exists of Wagner's reception of these works.

Wagner's strenuous efforts in seeking to execute the work and its constituent parts on the largest scale are impressive, even if the result is not convincing. One often has the impression that his primary concern was to extend the length of the opera, and that filling it out with real musical substance was secondary. (The composer may have thought that the power and energy of a performance would compensate for the lack of substance in some sections.) Wagner was confronted here with a task that would play a significant role in his later works, namely, that of spanning long periods of time with musical means; the inexperienced composer of *Das Liebesverbot* did not solve the problem, although he attacked it with resolution.

As for particular features of the work that stand out as characteristic of Wagner's style, the most striking is the introduction of the duet between Isabella and Mariana (no. 3), which Wagner later included, almost as a direct quotation, as the Rome motif in act 3 of *Tannhäuser*.

A melodic shape that can be described as the Verdict motif (Example 4) is of more fundamental interest. The unison theme is meant to sound unwieldy, and what is impressive about it is, first and foremost, its characteristic, even graphic nature. Cosima Wagner, who heard the *Liebesverbot* overture in 1879 performed in a piano reduction within the family circle, praised the theme as "very good" because it was "soulless, legal, harsh, dramatic" (CT, 31 January 1879). Especially noteworthy, however, is the way this passage foreshadows Wagner as an innovator in the field of harmony. Here he creates an intervallic structure that is largely independent of its tonal context. Three of the seven pitches (apart from the final note they follow one another without repetition like the notes of a twelve-tone series) are alien to the key (ab', c#', a#), and neither the first nor the last note of the theme belongs to those scale degrees which identify C major, the main key of the overture. The uniformity of the intervals provides structural cohesion, for motion is only by major thirds (and the complementary interval of the minor sixth) and semitone steps. From the self-contained tranquillity of this motif Wagner creates some surprising harmonic effects in the overture by using the intervals as the basis of a succession of functionally unrelated harmonies (mm. 79ff.). The same motif also plays a significant part in Friedrich's extended solo in act 2 (no. 10: scene and aria),

Example 4   Overture to *Das Liebesverbot*, mm. 38–52

which, with the compactness of its orchestral setting and the eloquent melodic writing of the vocal part, is the most convincing single number in the work.

Rienzi

After trying his hand at the genres of German Romantic opera and grand comic opera in the French and Italian style, Wagner, now conductor at the theater in Riga, ventured to undertake a more ambitious work: *Rienzi* (WWV 49). As Wagner later wrote, it was an opera "suited only to the most brilliant forces for its performance; in the oppressive and straitened circumstances in which I found myself, I could never be tempted to present it to the public" (SSD IV, 258).

Wagner's description of *Rienzi* as a "grand tragic opera in five acts" refers to the genre of grand opera that had been dominant in Paris for a decade. Daniel-François-Esprit Auber's opera *La muette de Portici,* first performed in 1828 and accepted as the first grand opera, is based on a libretto by Eugène Scribe, who was to become the most influential librettist in the history of the genre. The sixteen-year-old Wagner became acquainted with *La muette* in Leipzig, in the year following its Parisian premiere, and later conducted it in Magdeburg. His enthusiastic description of this work in *Reminiscences of Auber* (SSD IX, 42–60), written in 1871, may also be regarded as an enumeration of those qualities of grand opera with which he sought to provide *Rienzi*. In *A Communication to My Friends* (1851), he describes his intentions: "'Grand opera,' with all its scenic and musical splendour, its richness of effects, its large-scale musical passion, stood before me, and my artistic ambition was not merely to imitate it, but with unbridled extravagance to surpass all its previous manifestations" (SSD IV, 258). (In the subsequent passage, however, Wagner stresses, no doubt rightly, that this did not mean subordination of plot to operatic convention.)

Wagner described a Berlin performance of Gaspare Spontini's *Fernand Cortez* in the summer of 1836 as a direct inspiration for the conception of *Rienzi*. The work belongs among the precursors of grand opera. Wagner writes in his autobiography that the style of performance, directed by the composer himself, gave him "a fresh insight into the inherent dignity of major theatrical undertakings, which in all their parts could be elevated by alert rhythmic control into a singular and incomparable form of art" (ML 124). The importance of Meyerbeer's opera *Les Huguenots* must not be overlooked as an influence on Wagner, although because of his hostility toward Meyerbeer at the time, he was unwilling to admit it.

Rienzi came into being in two phases, with a long interruption in between, a fact reflected by certain stylistic differences between the earlier and later parts. The first phase was from 7 August 1838 to 19 April 1839. During this period, in which Wagner was still in Riga, the score of the first act and the entire musical draft of the second were completed. Only in Paris on 15 February 1840 did he continue with the third act, and by 19 November 1840 the whole work was finished. Before resuming work on *Rienzi*, Wagner composed *Eine*

Faust-Ouvertüre (WWV 59) and most of the songs to French texts, discussed earlier. Work on the third and fourth acts of *Rienzi* overlapped with the beginnings of the textual and musical conception of *Holländer*.

The five-act structure of *Rienzi* is one of the external features that shows its adherence to the tradition of grand opera, as is the basic principle of the structure of each act, with crowd scenes (choral scenes in musical terms) forming the framework at the beginning and the end, and solo and ensemble numbers in the middle.

Yet the way in which Wagner as dramatist and musician exploited the remaining room for maneuver is quite original. With a symmetrical ordering of solo components over the whole work, Wagner invented a combination of numbers to illustrate parallels and opposites in the dramatic action. This is a principle of musical structuring to which Wagner adhered (albeit in radically altered forms) in his later works. A sketch of the overall structure (see Table 1) illustrates this. The greatest weight given to the role of the protagonist is in the crowd scenes (appropriately enough in terms of the content of the work). In each of the five acts Rienzi participates in the large concluding choral numbers, and in all acts other than the third he is also onstage during the introduction. In contrast to this Rienzi is involved in the solo middle sections of only the first and last acts—the parts in which Irene is also present.

Table 1   The structure of dramatic action in *Rienzi*

Rienzi's Rise		*Peripeteia*	*Rienzi's Fall*	
Act 1	2	3	4	5
Intro.	*Intro.*	*Intro.*	*Intro.*	*Intro.*
R. enters.	R. enters.	R. enters.		R. on stage.
	R. exits.	R. exits.		
Sc. a. Trio.	*Duet.*		*Duet.*	*Duet.*
R. exits.	Nobles		Citizens	R. exits.
	plot		plot	
	the	*Aria.*	the	
	assassination		downfall	
	of R.		of R.	
	Adriano		Adriano	
	resists		supports	
	the		the	
	plan.		plan.	
Duet.	*Trio.*		*Trio.*	*Sc. Duet.*
Adriano/Irene		Adriano		Irene/Adriano
Finale.	*Finale.*	*Finale.*	*Finale.*	*Finale.*
R. reenters.	R. reenters.	R. reenters.	R. reenters.	R. reenters.

Source: Deathridge 1977.

The dominant figure in the middle section of each act is Adriano, who sings the only large-scale aria in the entire work, which also happens to fill the center of the third—that is, the middle—act. The two conspiracy scenes in which Adriano participates (acts 2 and 4) and his duets with Irene in the first act (expressing agreement) and the fifth act (expressing discord) complete the symmetrical pattern.

This arrangement of plot and actors is underpinned by a musical development which for the most part adheres closely to the dramatic exposition and has only a few points of lyrical repose. In this respect Wagner came close in *Rienzi* to what he later praised as Auber's art in *La muette de Portici:* "Each of the five acts presented a graphic image of the most uncommon vividness, in which arias and duets in the conventional operatic sense could scarcely be perceived, . . . or at any rate did not function as such; it was always a whole act done like this with every bit of its ensemble that was fascinating and thrilling" (SSD IX, 45).

The close connection of expressive melody with dramatic movement is a forward-looking element in *Rienzi,* but the melodic structure is scarcely ever fused intimately with the form of the text. Rather, the shape of the vocal line is what Wagner later dismissively referred to as "absolute operatic melody." What he meant by this can be illustrated with one of the most effective melodic inventions of *Rienzi,* namely, the period "Doch hört ihr der Trompete Ruf," which constitutes the fundamental melodic idea of the final part of the introduction to act 1. This section consists of a tripartite ABA' scheme with a coda. Of the fourteen lines of text, lines 1–4 and 11–14 are the "framing" sections that shape the musical form of the eight-measure period. The first and last four lines read as follows in Wagner's original version of the libretto (that is, before he set them to music):

Rienzi

(1) Doch hört ihr der Trompete Ruf
     [*But when you hear the trumpet's call*]

(2) in lang gehalt'nem Tone schallen
     [*Resounding with a long-held note*]

(3) dann ziehet vor den Lateran
     [*Then march before the Lateran*]

(4) verkündigt sei Freiheit allen!
     [*Let freedom be declared for all!*]

Baroncelli, Cecco, the People

(11) Wir schwören dir Gehorsam treu
     [*To you we swear our loyalty*]

(12) und bald sei Roma wieder frei!
     [*And may Rome soon again be free*]

(13) Willkommen nennet so den Tag
     [*Greet with joy the day and hour*]

(14) er räche euch und eure Schmach!
     [*May it avenge your dishonor!*]

It is clear from the rhythm of the verse endings and the rhyme scheme that the final stanza was not originally intended to be sung to the same music as the opening stanza. Once the composer had decided on the ABA′ form, this created a textual problem of declamation; a further problem arose because Wagner's melodic idea for this part commences on the beat, whereas the beginning of all the verses of the text is unstressed. Example 5 shows the principal voice part of the first and last stanzas. A comparison of the final text with the original version reveals that Wagner tried to bring his drafted text more into line with his musical invention, although it was not possible to remove all the inconsistencies. The listener, however, is scarcely disturbed by the lack of unity between the declamation of words and music because his or her attention is held by the purely musical quality of the melody and by the extremely effective increase in intensity from the solo voice accompanied pianissimo by the repetition of the same music by the chorus and full orchestra.

The dramatic dialogues in the first two acts of *Rienzi* mainly employ the traditional technique of accompanied recitative—that is, vocal declamation partly accompanied by the orchestra and partly interrupted by it with interpolations that delineate mood and character. In acts 3 to 5, however—and this underlines the stylistic change from the Riga period to the Paris period—there predominates a tendency toward another kind of organization that is to a certain extent symphonic.

The dialogue between Adriano and Rienzi in the finale of act 3—"Zurück,

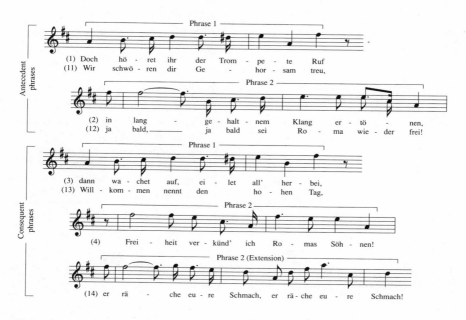

Example 5   *Rienzi,* act 1, no. 1: Introduction, mm. 359–366 and 392–400 (measure numbers follow SW)

zurück! Halt ein, Tribun!"—may serve as an example. The independence which Wagner's musical intentions have achieved can be observed in the fact that during the composition he felt it necessary to add four lines to the text (shown in brackets in Table 2). In terms of content this addition contains nothing that is new; its function is merely to provide sufficient text for the intended musical form. (See Deathridge 1977, pp. 91ff., for an account of the genesis of this recitative based on Wagner's sketches.) With this textual expansion the first phrases of the great dramatic dialogue could be given a musical form of conclusive single-mindedness and unity, as shown in Example 6. Table 2 illustrates this unity in the first section of the dialogue.

The homogeneity of this section is the result of a dense network of motivic relations: motif a in period I recurs in expanded form in period II and is also related diastematically to motif d; motif b is rhythmically related to motif c; and the chromatic bass motion of motif c is continued in period IV in connection with the upper voice of motif d. The formal progression appears to be both dynamic and closed; a determinant of this is that the "imploring"

Table 2   The organization of text and music in *Rienzi*, act 3, finale

Periods	Measures	Orchestral motifs	Text
I	231–237	a	*Adriano:* Go back, go back! Tribune! Stop fighting! Listen to me!
II	237–245	a (extended) b	*Rienzi:* Wretch, I pity you! You must curse your house!
III	245–252	c	*Adriano:* Stop! Once more I beg you. Try leniency, send me!
IV	253–263	d	[Without a word of your command I hasten to do what duty bids. But oh! all doors are closed. So I stand here and beg you to listen!]
V	263–271	c	Let me speak to my father, then no drop of blood shall flow!

Example 6

motif c (originally in period III) is taken up again after a development section (period IV, for which the additional text was used) in the manner of a recapitulation in period V. (Such an analysis could be applied equally well to the entire dialogue between Adriano and Rienzi.)

With the development of this symphonic technique for the dialogue, Wagner adopted a principle that could be developed even more expressively and with richer associations in his later works that relied on leitmotifs. The basic elements of the technique, however, remained essentially the same.

Eine Faust-Ouvertüre

Before resuming work on the interrupted composition of *Rienzi,* Wagner wrote *Eine Faust-Ouvertüre* (WWV 59), which, together with the *Siegfried-Idyll,* is the only one of his works to have entered the symphonic repertory. The composition draft was completed on 13 December 1839 and the score on 12 January 1840. Originally the piece was planned as the first movement of a Faust symphony (Wagner sketched a Gretchen theme for the slow movement), but he then abandoned this project and titled the work *Overture to Faust* (SB I, 378). According to a letter of 9 November 1852 to Franz Liszt, Wagner later thought of calling it "Faust in Solitude" or "The Solitary Faust: A Tone-Poem for Orchestra" (Wagner-Liszt, p. 248; SL 272), but in 1855 he decided to publish the work as *Eine Faust-Ouvertüre.* This published version (on which modern performances are based) reveals a number of changes from the original score. While still in Paris, Wagner replaced the abrupt fortissimo ending of the original with a gently fading pianissimo, a change that strikingly presages the concluding transfiguration Wagner added to the revision of *Holländer* in 1860. For the Dresden premiere in 1844 Wagner retouched the instrumentation, and in 1855 he made several substantial alterations, the most important of which was the expansion of the cantabile second subject, which had been recommended by Liszt.

Wagner later explained the creation of *Eine Faust-Ouvertüre* with reference to a new encounter with Beethoven's Ninth Symphony, which he heard, according to his autobiography, in a rehearsal of the Conservatoire Orchestra conducted by François-Antoine Habeneck, "a performance so perfect and so moving that the conception of this marvellous work which I had dimly formed in the enthusiastic days of my youth . . . suddenly stood before me bright as day and as palpable to my touch" (ML 174–175). As Egon Voss convincingly argues, however, Berlioz's *Romeo et Juliette* symphony was probably an even more significant source of inspiration (Voss 1982, pp. 9ff.).

Eine Faust-Ouvertüre is based on sonata form and can thus be represented schematically (the numbers indicate measures):

1–30   Slow introduction with preparation of the themes of the principal section

31–166	Exposition
	31–79 First subject
	80–117 Transition
	118–166 Second subject (mm. 144–166 added 1855)
167–324	Central section, beginning as last subject of exposition but soon merging into development
	276–308 Center of development
	309–324 Retransition
325–384	Recapitulation
	325–356 First subject (with development elements)
	357–384 Second subject
385–447	Coda: Transfiguration finale (probably revised 1841)

At first glance the most striking difference from regular sonata form is that the final theme of the exposition has been merged with the development to produce a coherent section (here referred to as the central section), so the usual division after the exposition does not occur. (This modification of sonata form is also found in Wagner's opera overtures.) But since the demarcation of formal elements from one another is not unambiguous, this scheme is not the only possible representation. Finally, Wagner is so free with the disposition of thematic figures and formal techniques that the sonata form appears to be no more than a vague point of orientation. Yet no clear logic peculiar to the form of the work and independent of sonata form is discernible.

Fascinating as *Eine Faust-Ouvertüre* is in the power of its thematic invention, its imaginative combination of themes, and the fluidity of its harmonies, it is hardly an instrumental work that is clearly articulated in form and meaning. Wagner later went so far as to describe it as more of a personal document than a communicative work of art: "It is difficult to perform it in a meaningful way," he wrote to Hans von Bülow in 1858. "I felt this myself when I had it performed a year ago. Therefore I should not have published it . . . Such things must remain private, be kept under lock and key" (Wagner-Bülow, p. 94). At any rate, *Eine Faust-Ouvertüre* brought home to Wagner that instrumental music was not his true forte, a realization which, in the Zurich essays, he had turned polemically into the general assertion that after Beethoven the age of instrumental music was at an end: "The art of music, now superseded by the arts of poetry and dance, is no longer an instinctively necessary art for mankind" (SSD III, 98).

Der fliegende Holländer

In retrospect, Wagner regarded *Holländer* as his first fully valid work. "The period during which I worked in obedience to the dictates of my inner intuitions began with the Flying Dutchman," he wrote to August Röckel on 23 August 1856. And in a letter to King Ludwig II of 2 September 1864 he described *Holländer* as "that earlier, less ambitious work that was nonetheless already typical of my true style." The breakthrough to his "true style," which Wagner achieved in *Holländer,* is intimately related to the genesis of the work, or more precisely to the original and unique way in which the central stylistic features of Wagner's music were grasped and set in place.

The earliest document is an outline, written in French (Wagner Lettres, pp. 31–35), which Wagner sent to Eugène Scribe on 6 May 1840 in the hope of enlisting his help in obtaining a commission to compose the work for the Paris Opéra. Three solo or choral numbers are built into the plot of this outline, all of them songs that reflect the reality of the stage action. Especially significant is a ballad which impresses the girl (she does not yet have a name), even more so than the portrait of the Dutchman. (Wagner took the idea of the portrait from Heine, whereas the ballad was his own invention.) "But above all she was moved by an ancient ballad that she had often heard her nurse sing, and that she herself repeated every day. This ballad told of the terrible fate of the pale, handsome man in the portrait. But nothing touched her more powerfully than the end of the ballad, containing the condition for the Dutchman's redemption, but at the same time indicating that he had not until then found a woman who had been faithful to him till death: at this she was inspired by an extreme exaltation and exclaimed: 'I, oh I would be capable of saving the wretched condemned man.'" Songs are also envisaged for the sailors celebrating their return home in the evening. The Scottish sailors (in the final version they became Norwegians) sing a "cheerful song," but the Dutchmen, angered by the Scotsmen's gibes, "reply that they will sing the kind of song one learns from sailing the seas for centuries. They sing a terrible, strange and frightening song."

In the summer of 1840, when Wagner was expecting to be asked to audition some of the music he had written for the opera, it was these three pieces for which he simultaneously dashed off both text and music (he had not even written a prose draft, let alone a libretto). The audition never took place. But these three numbers later proved to be the point of departure for a new way of writing music for opera.

Wagner started working systematically on the libretto and music in 1841. The libretto was completed on 28 May, and on 11 July he began the first complete draft of the music with the introduction to the first act. (In addition to the three numbers written for the abortive audition in 1840, he had also composed the Helmsman's Song and the Spinning Chorus in advance in 1841.) On 19 November 1841, with the completion of the score of the overture, the composition of the entire work was finished.

Wagner revised the work several times afterwards (Vetter 1982, and WWV pp. 239–241). Three of these later revisions stand out as particularly important. First, the opera originally consisted of one act divided into three scenes. For the Dresden premiere on 2 January 1843, Wagner divided it into three acts. The transitional music between the scenes in the original version was now adapted for the preludes and postludes to the acts. Second, in the first performance Senta's Ballad, together with the preceding twenty-eight measures, originally in A minor, was transposed to G minor because the original key was too high for Wilhelmine Schröder-Devrient, who was to sing the part. And third, for a concert in Paris at the beginning of 1860, Wagner composed a new ending to the overture. In place of the fortissimo finale of 1841 with the Dutchman motif, Wagner introduced a gentle, radiant ending in the style of *Tristan,* using the Redemption motif (from the refrain of Senta's Ballad). "Only now that I have written Isolde's final transfiguration," he wrote to Mathilde Wesendonck on 10 April 1860, "have I been able to find the right ending for the *Holländer* overture." Wagner also let the new ending of the overture stand as the definitive conclusion of the opera.

Wagner originally saw the work as belonging to the genre of Romantic opera; but he later came to regard it as breaking down opera's traditional limits. A few days after the Dresden premiere, Wagner wrote to his sister, Cäcilie Avenarius, that with *Holländer* he had "perhaps founded a new genre" (SB II, 204; Family Letters, p. 91). And in August 1843 he explained in a letter to Ferdinand Heine: "From the outset I had to abandon the modern arrangement of dividing the work into arias, duets, finales, etc., and instead relate the legend in a single breath." As a result, "in all its external details, it is so unlike anything we now understand by the term opera" (SB II, 314–315; SL 114–115). This remark takes up a passage from the novella *A Pilgrimage to Beethoven,* written in the autumn of 1840, in which Wagner makes Beethoven the mouthpiece of his criticism of the "patchwork" nature of opera, and of his vision of a future form of opera that would be "a true musical drama" (SSD I, 109; Wagner-Paris, p. 79).

Wagner's claim to have abandoned "the modern arrangement of dividing the work into arias, duets, finales, etc." appears to be disproved by the list of numbers in the opera, containing as it does all the traditional headings. Yet the relation of these titles to the corresponding music is extremely varied. If we were to try to describe Wagner's different approaches to them in *Holländer,* we could distinguish three categories:

1. Erik's arioso numbers in acts 2 and 3, as well as Daland's aria preceding the great duet in act 2, remain firmly within the conventions of opera. The form of these numbers and their tone (the sentimental nature of Erik's cantilenas and the buffo character of Daland's aria) corresponds to their role in the work as a whole. They characterize figures in the drama whose thinking remains bound by convention and who therefore face Senta's convention-shattering fate with inward estrangement.

2. In some numbers operatic convention is modified by differentiating and extending the form and intensifying its expression. The two large-scale solo numbers of the Dutchman and Senta, his entrance aria in act 1 and their duet in act 2, certainly fall into this category. These pieces are admirable in many musical details and in their psychological perceptiveness (one need only think of the double monologue at the beginning of the duet). Yet they are problem-

atic because they strain the underlying traditional forms to the breaking point. Indeed, Hanslick may have had this in mind when he wrote that he felt "disgruntled and disappointed" precisely where "the pathos of deep passion should come to the fore" and accused the composer of "overstraining purely external expression" (Hanslick 1860; Csampai-Holland 1982, p. 143). Symptomatic of this is the sheer hypertrophic length of these numbers, especially in relation to their position within a one-act work (which Wagner at one point intended to call a "dramatic ballad"); the aria (307 measures) and the duet (442) far outstrip anything comparable in the "grand opera" *Rienzi*.

3. A special position is occupied in *Holländer* by those five pieces that are actual songs in terms of the events played out onstage (see Deathridge 1982). Their function in the musical continuity consists of a complicated interplay of three separate elements. First, the songs create a caesura in the external musical progression; yet in a certain way they are not operatic numbers, since the singing of a song is an integral part of the dramatic action.

Second, the songs serve to establish wide-ranging connections. The first appearance and reprise of the Helmsman's Song in act 1 and the Sailors' Chorus in act 3 serve as a frame for large formal sections. The verses of the Spinning Chorus at the opening of act 2 fulfill a similar function.

And third, since a song is a sequence of symmetrically structured verses, it sets up strong expectations in the listener's mind. Thus, the technique of dislocating the anticipated sequence can be used to great effect. The second verse of the Helmsman's Song, for example, is not completed because the singer is overcome with fatigue. The third verse of the Spinning Song does not proceed beyond its introductory lines because Senta stops it in its tracks— "Oh! Macht dem dummen Lied ein Ende!" ("Oh! Stop that foolish song!")— and then sings the ballad herself. The ballad is in turn broken off before the regular ending of its third verse by Senta's decision: "Ich sei's, die dich durch ihre Treue erlöse!" ("It is I who will redeem you through my faithfulness!"). The second verse of the Norwegian Sailors' Chorus is disrupted by the increasing storminess of the sea, and the attempt to sing the third verse is completely distorted by the shouts of the Dutchman's crew, and has to be abandoned. The Phantoms' Chorus of the Dutchman's crew is the only one not to be cut off prematurely by some external force; it seems as indestructible as their accursed ship. With the interrupted song, Wagner forged a technique similar to the quotation of a motif that can be used to give the effect of variation and estrangement. It is a formal principle that he was later to use to great effect in *Die Meistersinger*.

As we have seen, Wagner composed three numbers in 1840, well before starting on the work as a whole. It was a crucial factor in another innovation that cannot be grasped in terms of a typology of opera: *Holländer* is permeated with a few musical themes that symbolize central dramatic and scenic elements. Examples 7a–7g show the most important of these, which Wagner later described as "thematic seeds" (SSD IV, 323). The arpeggio figure (Ex-

Example 7a   Dutchman motif (Ballad, Phantoms' Chorus)

Example 7b   Storm chords (Ballad, Phantoms' Chorus)

Example 7c   Wave figure (Ballad, Phantoms' Chorus, Sailors' Chorus)

Hoe!____ Hoe!____ Hoe!____ Hoe!____   Ho!__ He!__ Je!__ Ha!

Example 7d   Sailors' Call (Phantoms' Chorus, Sailors' Chorus)

Example 7e   Sailors' Dance (Sailors' Chorus)

Doch, daß der ar - me Mann noch Er - lö - sung fän - de auf Er - den,

Example 7f   Redemption Melody (Ballad): "Yes, that the poor man may still find re-demption on earth"

Example 7g   Arpeggio figure (composed later)

ample 7g) belongs only indirectly to this list, because it is not in one of the precomposed numbers. Wagner added it as a quotable motif, as it were, while working on the composition of the whole opera. It was originally written in connection with the Dutchman's aria—the section "Wie oft in Meeres tiefsten Schlund" ("How often in the sea's deepest abyss")—and subsequently included in the ballad (half-cadence at the end of the introduction of the verses and before the beginning of the refrain); it is also cited in the Senta-Dutchman duet, "Ach könntest das Geschick du ahnen" ("Oh, if you could know the fate"). The insertion of this motif is evidence that Wagner's way of manipulating motifs in *Holländer* was not as intuitive as he later claimed (SSD IV, 323).

Almost all of these basic thematic shapes relate to the sea, the natural element that is central to the action of *Holländer* (Wagner described the subject as a legend filled "with the pounding of the sea"; SB II, 314, and SL, 114). Limitless expanse and emptiness (a), storm (b), and waves (c) are the images associated with the main motifs of the ballad and the Phantoms' Chorus. They are supplemented by motifs from the Sailors' Songs (d, e), which, Wagner claimed, originated with his voyage on the *Thétis* (ML 162–164). The Redemption melody (f), the last of the basic themes to be composed in advance, is the musical antithesis of examples a–c in the minor key. The contrast is a musical analogy of the antithesis between eternal voyaging and redemption on which the dramatic action is based.

Wagner quotes these motifs mainly as follows:

Act I: the choral parts before Daland's entrance; the transitional passages before and after the Helmsman's Song; the Dutchman's aria; the choral section between the Dutchman-Daland duet and the repetition of the Helmsman's Song; the orchestral postlude.

Act II: the Spinning Chorus (motif d); Erik's Dream narration; various passages in the Senta-Dutchman duet.

Act III: the introductory choral scene and the finale, after the naming of the Dutchman.

The use Wagner makes of the basic themes ranges from isolated quotation (for instance, in the Dutchman's aria) to insertion within the structural process in the two sections of the work that are most advanced in terms of compositional technique. These are, first, the closing part of the Helmsman's Song, where the melody of the song is, to use Schoenberg's term, "liquidated" in the transition to the Dutchman's aria; and second, and most important, the double-chorus scene in the third act.

The idea in *Holländer* of themes that can encompass an entire work was not a system that Wagner could apply easily to other works. Yet he did remain committed to a more general principle: that quality of a work which he later described as "an uncommonly vivid colour of the greatest definition" (SB IV, 328). Achieving such a unified coloring, no matter how this was to be arrived at in musical and structural terms, became a requirement that henceforth determined Wagner's poetic and musical approach to any new work.

Das Liebesmahl der Apostel

At the beginning of 1843, shortly after the premiere of *Holländer* and before his appointment as kapellmeister at the court theater in Dresden, Wagner was offered the post of director of the local male choir, the Liedertafel. Wagner accepted but resigned in 1845, as he soon realized that the artistic and social style of the choir was alien to him. At first, however, he threw himself into his new duties with commitment and undertook to write a work for the big male choir festival at Dresden in the summer of 1843, in which all the Saxon singers converging on Dresden for the festival could be united. Wagner temporarily gave the work priority over the composition of *Tannhäuser* (WWV 70), for which he had completed the libretto at the beginning of April. The festival music for the choir occupied him from the middle of April until the end of June, so the planned performance on 6 July had to be rehearsed very hastily. Wagner describes his conception of the work in his autobiography:

> I decided that the monotony of such choral singing, which the orchestra would only enliven to a slight extent, could be made bearable solely through the introduction of some dramatic elements. I therefore conceived a quite large choral scene depicting the first feast of Pentecost and the outpouring of the Holy Ghost, and executed it in such a way that the whole thing would be sung by various choral groups in turn, completely avoiding any real solo parts in accordance with the dictates of the situation. What came out of this was my *Liebesmahl der Apostel* [Love-feast of the apostles], a work . . . which, given the specific circumstances in which I had to produce it, I am content to assign to the category of "occasional" works.   (ML 257–258)

The premiere was given by 1,200 singers and an orchestra of 100. In a letter to his sister Cäcilie of 13 July 1843, Wagner spoke of a spellbinding effect on the audience. Later he described his own impression of the performance as one of disappointment at the relation between the "colossal mass of human bodies" and the "disproportionately modest effect" that this mass produced. This experience, he concludes in his autobiography, "convinced me of the inherent foolishness of such gigantic choral undertakings, and produced in me a decided antipathy to concerning myself with them in any way in the future" (ML 258).

Das Liebesmahl der Apostel is difficult to assign to a genre; the original subtitle, *A Biblical Scene,* is hardly specific. Perhaps it would be best to call the work (it lasts about thirty minutes) a miniature oratorio. The choice of subject and the choral writing may well have been influenced by Karl Loewe's vocal oratorio for male voices titled *Die Apostel zu Philippi* (The apostles of Philippi) of 1835, which was given its first performance in Dresden in 1837, six years before Wagner's *Liebesmahl* (see Geck 1971, p. 21).

In a first sketch Wagner arranged the sequence of scenes as follows (SSD XI, 264):

1. Gathering: apostles in low spirits

2. Bad news: threats

3. Prayer

4. Enthusiasm: great unity of souls and property[1]

The completed work retains this structure, although it contains a significant moment not obvious from the sketch: namely, the words of the "Voices from on High" which follow the prayer: "Be of good cheer, for I am near you and my Spirit is with you. / Rouse yourselves! Joyfully speak the word / that will never pass away in eternity." This transitional section (it gives us pause to think of how important the notion of transition was for Wagner in later years; see Dahlhaus 1983, pp. 132ff.) is a moment worthy of Wagner the musical dramatist, despite the fact that he came to disparage the work, calling it, among other things, "a sort of Oberammergau play" (CT, 17 June 1879). At the Dresden premiere Wagner had this chorus sung from the dome of the Frauenkirche, an idea later taken up in *Parsifal*. The music from on high, sounding as if it had been transported into another world, leads directly to the orchestral entrance with the pianissimo drum roll. The music fills the whole vast space, conveying the experience expressed by the disciples with the words: "What mighty roar fills the air? What sounds, what ringing? / Is it not moving, the place where we are standing?"

Wagner did not in fact wait until *Parsifal* before continuing to develop the idea of the chorus of the Voices from on High. Already the Grail theme in *Lohengrin* can in a broad sense be regarded as a metamorphosis of the dome chorus from *Liebesmahl*. The idea of music as representing a "consoling sensory idea of the supernatural" (one of Wagner's comments on the *Lohengrin* prelude in SSD V, 179) from the heights, as if it were out of this world, is only hinted at by the spatial position of the voices in *Liebesmahl,* whereas in *Lohengrin* it is truly integrated into the composition by the violins playing in their highest register.

Two further important melodic ideas in the *Liebesmahl* are developed in *Parsifal*. The theme "Kommt her, die ihr hungert, die ihr dürstet" (Come unto me ye who hunger and ye who thirst) from the first chorus of the disciples reappears in a chromatic metamorphosis as the so-called Angel motif in *Parsifal* (it first occurs in Gurnemanz's narration in act I at m. 575); and the beginning of the phrase "Der uns das Wort, das herrliche, gelehret" ("He who taught us the glorious Word") from the final section of *Liebesmahl* is included in the chorus of the knights of the Holy Grail in act I of *Parsifal*. This further development shows that Wagner employed a wealth of invention in *Liebesmahl* that would only later bear fruit on a larger scale.

---

1. This would appear to be the first time that Wagner formulated a critique of property, which later became a central theme of the *Ring*. See also the passages in the scenario of *Jesus von Nazareth* (WWV 80) in which Wagner allows Jesus to speak out in favor of common property (SSD XI, 289ff.).

Tannhäuser

More than any other of Wagner's works, *Tannhäuser* (WWV 70) was for its creator what would nowadays be termed a work in progress, a piece whose shape was continually changing in the course of its performance history. Wagner always regarded the most recent version as the only valid one, superseding all the others. Today we are more inclined to regard at least the two main phases of the work as equally valid; in performance practice these are known as the Dresden and the Paris versions. The discussion in this section will concentrate initially on the version used for the Dresden premiere in October 1845 and will then give an overview of changes Wagner made in the shape of the work up to 1875.

Wagner worked on the libretto of *Tannhäuser* from June 1842 to April 1843 (at the time it was still called *Der Venusberg*). In the summer of 1843, while on holiday in Teplitz–Schönau, he devised the first part of the composition, the Venusberg music, which he had been "carrying around" in his head for some time (ML 260). In November of that year he resumed work on the composition, and on 17 January 1844 completed the draft of the first act. After a long interruption owing to unforeseen circumstances, he resumed work on the composition in September 1844, completing the draft of the second act by 15 October and that of the third act by 29 December. The score of the entire opera was finished on 13 April 1845.

The fact that the composition of *Tannhäuser* took one and a half years (by contrast, the composition of *Holländer* had taken a mere six weeks) brought the risk of impairing the unity and consistency of the work. (Wagner drew his conclusions from this experience and changed his working methods for the composition of his next opera.) He describes how he coped with this problem in *Tannhäuser* in a letter written in the summer of 1845 to the Berlin music critic Karl Gaillard: "In spite of the long interruptions that kept me away from the score for months on end, I was always able to reimmerse myself in an instant in the characteristic aura of the work, an aura which had so exhilarated me when I first conceived the piece" (SB II, 434; SL 122). By "aura" here he refers to the basic poetic and musical coloring permeating a work, giving it character and unity. Wagner had seen the unity of *Holländer* in similar terms, saying that he had succeeded in allowing "the whole aura of the legend to spread unchecked over the entire piece" (SB II, 314; SL 114).

Unlike the style of *Holländer,* that of *Tannhäuser* cannot be said to evolve from a uniform center. The aura of the work consists, musically speaking, of a constellation of different stylistic traits. Particularly prominent are the chromaticism of the Venusberg music, the ritual tone of the Pilgrims' Choruses and the Rome theme; the courtly music of homage for the entrance into the Wartburg, and the songs accompanied by the harp during the song contest. In contrast with *Holländer* and *Lohengrin,* the eponymous hero has no consistent musical signature. If one seeks to identify a musical figure with which he is especially associated, one would most likely choose the song the first three stanzas of which Tannhäuser sings to Venus, while the fourth in the song contest forms the peripeteia of the entire work. This song belongs in a general sense to the stylistic genre of the harp-accompanied singer's melody, although it does not fit this mode entirely. It would be more appropriate to define it musically in terms of the function it fulfills in its two contexts, the Venusberg scene and the song contest. In each of the two situations it brings about the abrupt transition into the respective countersphere, and in doing so precisely characterizes Tannhäuser in terms of Wagner's drama. With the musical invention of Tannhäuser's Song, Wagner ingeniously solved the problem which Reinhold Brinkmann formulated as "to write music which, in the Venusberg scene, has its feet on the earth close to the Wartburg, and yet, within the chivalric world, emphasises that element of unruliness which terrifies the old order" (Brinkmann 1970, p. 203).

The interlocking of various styles in the music of *Tannhäuser* was portrayable only in the context of a further relaxation of formal operatic conventions. Here for the first time Wagner abandoned the standard titles at the head of numbers and, adopting the practice of the spoken theater, simply divided the acts into scenes, although the new terminology sometimes only masks opera numbers in the old style (for example, Elisabeth's aria and the Elisabeth-Tannhäuser duet in act 2, and Wolfram's balladlike Song to the Evening Star in act 3). Nevertheless, sections which justify the use of the new terminology in terms of musical style predominate. Attention should be drawn to those parts which are most advanced in this respect: the introductory Venusberg scene; Tannhäuser's Rome narration, which Guido Adler regarded as an almost fully developed example of Wagner's "musico-dramatic style" (Adler 1904, p. 87); and finally the third scene of act 1 (Wartburg Valley), which is artistically one of the most successful parts of the entire work and can be regarded as a translation of Berlioz's *Marche de pélerins* (the second movement of *Harold en Italie*) into the realm of music drama.

The fact that music is a central component of the plot of *Tannhäuser und der Sängerkrieg auf der Wartburg* (Tannhäuser and the song contest at the Wartburg), to give the work its full title, means that the element of music on the level of reality in the stage action shapes the structure of the entire work to a far greater extent than was the case in *Holländer*. This again illustrates the ambivalence of the musical setting of stage action in terms of the opera's structure: on the one hand, a structure consisting of individual components is stressed; on the other hand, its conventional operatic pattern is nullified because the structure is determined by the stage action. The repetition or further development of stage music creates a network of relations spanning the entire opera, as shown in Table 3. (The instrumental introduction to act 3 has been included in the table because it quotes the first chorus of pilgrims; the two Pilgrims' Choruses are linked by a broken line because both of their central sections contain chromaticism as a symbol of contrition.)

Apart from the recapitulation of songs, only the large stretches of the Venusberg music in act 3, taken from the opening scene of act 1 (these passages

Table 3   Music on the level of reality in the stage action in *Tannhäuser*

Act 1
  Scene 1 — Sirens' Song
  Scene 2 — Tannhäuser's Song, Strophe 1 (D-flat major)
    Tannhäuser's Song, Strophe 2 (D major)
    Sirens' Song
    Tannhäuser's Song, Strophe 3 (E-flat major)
  Scene 3 — Shepherd's Song (shepherd playing on his pipe) heard together with Pilgrims' Chorus I (common time)
    Pilgrims' Chorus I
  Scene 4 — Hunting music
    Hunting music

Act 2
  Scene 4 — Processional music of allegiance
    Song contest with songs by
      Wolfram, Tannhäuser,
      Walther, Tannhäuser,
      Biterolf, Tannhäuser,
      Wolfram, then:
    Tannhäuser's Song, Strophe 4 (E major)
    Pilgrims' Chorus (finale)

Act 3
  Introduction — Tannhäuser's Pilgrimage, with quotations of lines from Pilgrims' Chorus I
  Scene 1 — Pilgrims' Chorus II (¾ time)
    Wolfram's Song to the Evening Star
  Scene 2 — Chorus of Younger Pilgrims
  Scene 3 — Pilgrims' Chorus II

were first introduced into the revised Dresden version, where they are associated with the reappearance of Venus), have a significant function in terms of the musical–dramatic structure. In contrast, the citation of individual motifs or phrases, the technique which in *Holländer* so powerfully prefigures Wagner's later use of leitmotifs, plays only a relatively minor role here.

From *Tannhäuser* onward it becomes increasingly clear that the new in Wagner's musical-dramatic oeuvre consists not only of the structure of relations between drama and music but also of the means of musical expression itself. The wealth and range of Wagner's new discoveries in the field of composition make him one of the great innovators—if not the greatest innovator—in the history of nineteenth-century music.

The main area of innovation is harmony. The most avant-garde music of the *Tannhäuser* score is the Venusberg scene at the beginning of the first act: here the harmonic activity, in keeping with the scenic turbulence of the bacchanal, is in a continual modulatory flux. (When Wagner revised this scene in the style of *Tristan* in 1860, he relied mainly on the set of motifs from 1843; this would not have been possible if the core of the *Tristan* harmony had not already existed in the first version.)

It is hardly surprising that Wagner's contemporaries did not know how to evaluate Wagner's harmony. For precisely his most characteristic harmonic creations, because of their chromatic and enharmonic qualities, do not allow any clear categorization in terms of the harmonic system as it was perceived at the time. Not only was an adequate analysis of certain Wagnerian harmonic turns impossible within the theoretical concepts of Wagner's age, but even today it can still be controversial.

The Venusberg scene contains a striking instance of Wagner's venturing beyond the accepted limits in harmonic terms, namely, the five-note chord (b-e′-g′-a♯′-d♯″) from the Sirens' Song (see Example 8). A harmonic analysis shows here a diminished seventh chord (e′-g′-a♯′-c♯″) that alternates between a dominant and subdominant function, whose treble entry is delayed by a suspension (d♯″-c♯″) and which is underlaid by a pedal point on b. The listener's attention is held (as later with the opening sounds of the *Tristan* prelude) more by the suspension than by the resolution. This is due in part to the greater length of the suspension, which is five times longer than the resolution. Yet the suspension has an intervallic structure that is so memorable that the listener's attention lingers on it, rather than relating it to its resolution. For if one here uses as a reference the twelve-tone chromatic scale, disregarding enharmonic differences, the sound of the Sirens' Song is revealed as a combination of a major and a minor triad with g′ as the common note: the three lower notes constitute an E minor triad in second inversion (b-e′-g′), and the three upper notes constitute an E-flat major triad in first inversion (g′-a♯′-d♯″ = g′-b♭′-e♭″).

The Sirens' Song is an early example of those Wagnerian harmonic advances which require a dual explanation, one that is inherent in the system and another that transcends it. The first shows the functional sense of the sound in its context, whereas the second explains why the listener's attention is held by a specific sound and does not perceive it merely as an accidental product of chord tones and melodic intentions. If one takes both explanations together

Naht euch dem Stran - - - de!

Example 8

and relates them to each other, one begins to understand the way in which the music achieves its effects. It is a simultaneous pulling away and an urge to rest, combined with a temporary loss of the harmonic sense of space (E minor–E-flat major). These effects are closely related to the dramatic situation and also have to do with how Wagner the poet-composer imagined the possibility of an adequate musical performance (see Wagner's letter of 30 January 1844 to Karl Gaillard, SB II, 358; SL 118).

This discussion has been based on the version of the score used for the first performance, with occasional reference to differences between the various other versions of *Tannhäuser*. I shall now summarize the history of the revisions, of which those for the Paris performance in 1861 are the most consequential but by no means the only ones.

Wagner began revising the night after the premiere (ML 312). Even at the end of his life, he did not regard his efforts to finalize the work as complete, as is shown by his oft-quoted remark to Cosima that he still "owed the world" his *Tannhäuser* (CT, 23 January 1883). The nature of the changes and the motivation behind them are so diverse that only the essentials can be outlined here. (A complete documentation of the different stages of the work's history will be given in volumes five and six of the *Sämtliche Werke;* overviews are provided in Steinbeck 1964, Strohm 1978, and WWV 287–295.)

The version generally known as the Dresden version today is not, in fact, that of the premiere; rather, it represents the result of Wagner's experiences with the Dresden performances from 1845 to 1848. This version was finalized in 1852 in connection with Wagner's article *On Performing "Tannhäuser"* (SSD V, 123–159) and the preparation of the new edition of the piano arrangement by Theodor Uhlig, published by C. F. Meser (for details, see WWV 70, pp. 282, 289).

The main changes to the original version are at the beginning and end of act 3. Wagner shortened the instrumental introduction (Tannhäuser's Pilgrimage) from 155 measures in the original to 92 (see SSD V, 137 for the reasons). The music and action of the act's ending were revised: Venus appears onstage and sings; Tannhäuser sinks down at Elisabeth's grave. The corresponding dramatic elements had originally been portrayed only by a glowing of the Hörselberg, specifically by torchlight from the Wartburg, and the tolling of the funeral bell. Wagner regarded the revised version "not as a change, but a correction," as "the previous ending contained, in scenic terms, only a *hint* of the *reality* that ought to be conveyed to the *senses*" (letter to Theodor Uhlig of 14 September 1851, emphasis in original; SB IV, 113). Some of the passages which Wagner had cut after the premiere were restored in the 1852 version. He provided detailed reasons for these "concessions made out of dire necessity" and their revocation in his article on the performance of *Tannhäuser* (SSD V, 130–141).

The main changes for the Paris production of 1861 were to scenes 1 and 2 of act 1. (In addition, he made numerous minor changes and—again—concessions which were later revoked.) The substantial expansion of the Venusberg scene was obviously a response to the Paris Opéra's insistence on a ballet. This external motivation, however, was coupled with Wagner's realization that only a revised version incorporating the advances of the musical technique of *Tristan* could fully exploit the musical potential of the themes in the Venusberg scene. The chromatic combinations of chords, the free modulations, and the subtly differentiated rhythms of the *Tristan* style inform the new Venusberg music, although the stock of basic themes from the Dresden version is hardly increased at all. The only thematic innovation is a motif which is barely hinted at in the original version but is of central importance here (see Example 9). It is a melodic figure which combines an echo of the Longing motif from *Tristan* (bracket a) with an anticipation of the Eva motif from the fourth scene of act 2 of *Die Meistersinger* (bracket b).

The following scene—between Tannhäuser and Venus—was also radically changed, especially the parts involving Venus. "I later came to the conclusion," Wagner wrote, "that the part had been treated all too sketchily in my work [in Dresden], and when I came to adapt it for Paris, I supplied everything I felt had been hitherto lacking by completely remodelling the part" (ML 304–305). The revisions to Tannhäuser's part are few; any alteration to the three-strophe song, which is the musical centerpiece of his part in the second scene and is quoted in the song contest of act 2, would have had consequences that were too far-reaching.

A third major change in act 1, namely the direct transition from the overture to the Venusberg scene, does not, strictly speaking, belong to the Paris version. Wagner intended this solution for the Paris production, but then agreed to the Paris Opéra management's wish and separated the two parts. The overture was not combined with the bacchanal until the Vienna production of 1875.

The Creative Process in Wagner's Music

Wagner's method of working out his opera texts remained virtually constant from his earliest works to *Parsifal*. Apart from brief preparatory outlines, it consisted of two phases, the prose draft and the final verse form. In contrast, his method of composing underwent certain changes in the course of his creative career. More precisely, one can say that basically his method remained constant until *Tannhäuser*. *Lohengrin* then marks the beginning of an intermediate, experimental stage, and his working method stabilizes again with the composition of *Tristan*. As his method of working first became a fundamental problem for Wagner between the writing of *Tannhäuser* and *Lohengrin*,

Example 9

this appears to be an appropriate point at which to include some discussion of the subject. It is—and this should be mentioned first—a subject which, quite apart from its purely technical aspects, opens up a perspective on questions of musical structure which must be addressed, at least in outline, if the dates of the genesis of each work are to mean anything.

Wagner discussed the problem of the musical elaboration of his works several times in his letters and his autobiography, but his remarks always referred to a specific situation, and he was never consistent in his use of terminology. When Otto Strobel started cataloguing the Bayreuth collection of Wagner's manuscripts in 1932, he found it necessary to devise a uniform nomenclature for the various types of musical sources. He distinguished three phases of a work's elaboration:

1. Single sketches (that is, preparatory records of themes, phrases, periods, movements, and so on).

2. The composition sketch (that is, a first written record of the entire course of a work, in which the vocal parts were complete but the instrumental parts were only scantily outlined, sometimes on only one staff). The composition sketch was not intended to be transferred directly to the score; instead, it was followed by step 3.

3. The orchestra sketch, which, in addition to the vocal parts, records the course of the orchestral part in greater detail, using at least two staves, although abbreviations are common. This orchestral sketch leads directly to step 4, the goal of the whole working process.

4. The score (that is, a version of the work in which all the details have been elaborated). In some cases Wagner also produced a version of the score in pencil before making a fair copy in ink.

This discussion will concentrate on the first three of these phases. They document that part of the creative process in which the problem is to develop a complex structure that goes toward making up an opera score out of both a global conception of the whole, such as is to be found at the beginning of all Wagner's works, and a series of isolated ideas. What is required is a purposefully organized working method which must be capable of accommodating both the spontaneous flow of musical ideas and the planning of the technical elaboration of all the details.

So far I have used Strobel's Bayreuth terminology not only because these are the official archival terms but also because they have been established in the literature on Wagner for decades. From a number of perspectives, however, it is doubtful whether this terminology is entirely satisfactory (see Deathridge 1974 / 5). Anyone seeking to understand the changes in Wagner's working methods from the names of the draft manuscripts will find Strobel's nomenclature too undifferentiated. Thus Robert Bailey, in his detailed study of Wagner's method of composition (Bailey 1979, a work to which this part of my essay is greatly indebted), has introduced more terms. He renames Strobel's "composition sketch" a "composition draft," and he replaces the term "orchestra sketch" with three terms whose purpose is to demonstrate the increasing degree of elaboration in this second draft: for works up to *Lohengrin* he uses the term "composition draft"; for works from act 1 of *Siegfried* to act 1 of *Meistersinger* he uses the term "developed draft"; and for act 2 of *Meistersinger* to *Parsifal* he uses the term "orchestral draft" (or "short score").

The catalogue of Wagner's musical works (WWV) does not provide a much greater degree of differentiation than the Bayreuth classification, but for the stages of elaboration between partial sketches and score it chooses the neutral term "complete draft" *(Gesamtentwurf)*, in the sense of the more familiar term "continuity draft" used in Beethoven studies, thus distinguishing quantitatively between "sketches" for parts and "draft" for the continuous whole. In this terminology the complete draft for works up to *Holländer* corresponds to the orchestra sketch. For *Tannhäuser* the composition sketch (which is still not a stage that is quite continuous for the whole, although it approaches the status of a draft) is given the rather contradictory name "fragmented complete draft," while the orchestra sketch becomes an "entire complete draft" *(vollständiger Gesamtentwurf)*. (From this point the catalogue includes Strobel's nomenclature in parentheses to avoid confusion.) For works from *Lohengrin* on, WWV simply distinguishes between a first and a second complete draft (respectively, Strobel's composition sketch and orchestra sketch). This essay follows the usage of WWV, unless a more detailed description proves necessary.

The procedure which Wagner followed up to *Tannhäuser* was to work out, on the basis of the completed libretto and of isolated musical ideas, several numbers or sections of the work as single sketches. This process used two staves, an upper one for the vocal part, and a lower one for an outline of the orchestral development (bass, harmony, important motifs). (In the case of *Tannhäuser,* these sketches, although individually elaborated, in fact contain a large part of the entire work.) Wagner then built on this basis by producing for each act a continuous complete draft, initially on no more than two staves. In appearance the whole thus resembles a piano arrangement, although no consideration is given to its playability on that instrument.

This method of sketching his works—which does not yet include a rough first complete draft in the sense of Strobel's composition sketch—allowed Wagner to note the overall course of his early works in a sufficiently rapid manner, without encumbering them with incidental details. His intentions were nonetheless recorded precisely enough so as to obviate difficulties with the elaboration of the score even if work was interrupted for a long period.

This method was seemingly inadequate for the composition of *Tannhäuser.* The reasons for this lie primarily in the increasing complexity of the music, for which traditional forms now provided scarcely any support. In addition, for the first time Wagner had to reconcile the composition of a major work with the demands of his duties as kapellmeister in Dresden. Under these circumstances the composition of *Tannhäuser* took a year and a half (not counting the working out of the score). This must have troubled Wagner, even though he insisted that his enthusiasm for the material always enabled him to immerse himself quickly into the aura of his original conception. In any event, his response was to produce a continuous rough musical draft for *Lohengrin* by means of a method of notation which until then he had used only for the preparatory sketches—that is, a sketch on two staves. This method proved its worth: *Lohengrin* was completely drafted in this highly abbreviated form in the summer of 1846. Afterwards, however, a second complete draft was still necessary as a transitional phase preceding the score. But this second version of the overall progression could now concentrate on the elaboration of details, although this did not exclude corrections to the first draft, which are particularly evident in *Lohengrin* (see Deathridge 1989).

The method of beginning with a first complete draft, which had proved its worth in *Lohengrin*, was retained in later works. Nevertheless, new problems with the further elaboration of this sketch arose with the very next work. When Wagner was about to transfer the first complete draft of *Das Rheingold* (written in eleven weeks) into a more elaborate notational form, he found that the part writing for the eight horns in the instrumental introduction (a musical idea that is not included in the composition sketch) could not be contained in a few staves. He therefore decided to proceed immediately from the first draft to the score. In the course of the first scene, however, he switched to an abbreviated short-score style of notation which he was never to use again. The third phase of composition was to make a fair copy of the score.

When composing *Die Walküre*, Wagner again began with a first complete draft, this time more detailed than those for *Lohengrin* and *Das Rheingold* (that is, it frequently used a number of staves for the orchestral part). He then immediately began work on the first version of the score, followed by a fair copy. But the greater length of *Die Walküre* in comparison to *Das Rheingold* led to a new problem. Since Wagner had written the first complete draft for all three acts before continuing to work them out, there was a time gap of up to a year in some instances between the draft and the first version of the score. In his autobiography (ML 526) Wagner relates that at times he had great difficulty in reconstructing his complex musical ideas from the bare outlines of the first draft.

To ensure that this difficulty did not recur, Wagner changed his method yet again from *Siegfried* onward. Now the second complete draft followed shortly after the first. Here the procedure varied: either both stages were worked out concurrently for one act, or the second complete draft was begun immediately after the first draft for the act had been completed. The adoption of this method meant that Wagner had to sacrifice the possibility of drafting an entire work in a short period, as he had done in the case of *Lohengrin, Das Rheingold,* and *Die Walküre*. Presumably this sacrifice seemed acceptable because the leitmotif technique which had become the basic compositional principle in *Der Ring* served to guarantee the music drama's homogeneity. The uniform musical coloring of a work—what Wagner in his *Tannhäuser* period had called its characteristic aura—had now found expression in the actual musical material, and Wagner could fall back on this as he continued composing.

The time intervals between his finishing the second complete draft and beginning work on the score varied. In the first two acts of *Siegfried,* Wagner inserted a first version of the score before the fair copy, so that here, exceptionally, the fair copy of the score is the fourth rather than the third stage of elaboration. From *Tristan* on, he abandoned this precautionary measure; instead, the first and second complete drafts became increasingly detailed. The genesis of the fair score of *Parsifal* illustrates how unambiguously the composition of the late works—with the exception of some instrumental details— is recorded in the second draft: Wagner was even able to draw the measure lines in the score before writing down the notes.

Lohengrin

After the end of the 1845–46 theater season, the highlights of which for Wagner had been the premiere of *Tannhäuser* and his conducting Beethoven's Ninth Symphony for the first time, he was granted three months' summer vacation by the theater management. He spent this time in the village of Großgraupa, near Pillnitz, where he hoped not only to have a rest but to "draw a deep breath before beginning a new work" (ML 336). He was referring to the musical elaboration of *Lohengrin* (WWV 75), the libretto of which had been completed in November 1845. Wagner "succeeded in sketching the music for all three acts of *Lohengrin,* if only in very hasty outline form" (ML 336) by 30 July 1846, during which process his new drafting procedure proved very useful.

In the second phase of elaboration Wagner began with the third act, which he refers to in his autobiography as an exceptional procedure. This was partly "for the sake of the musical material of the Grail narration"; but the main reason was the "criticism of the dramatic character of this act and its close" by the writer Hermann Franck (ML 337). Wagner had discussed the problem of the ending of the work with Franck, in terms of both the text and his intention "to use music . . . to complement [its] meaning" (SB II, 513; SL 131), wherever the text had left questions unresolved. In order to realize this intention, Wagner now sought from the beginning "to establish the act"— the problematic third act—"to my own complete satisfaction, as the core of the whole work" (ML 337). As it turned out, the second draft, particularly for the third act, required a number of significant changes from the first, with respect to both the music and the libretto. Later it became apparent that even in this stage of the working process not all of the problems of this act had been solved. Even in the score the Grail narrative had a continuation after the ending "Sein Ritter bin ich Lohengrin genannt" ("I am his knight called Lohengrin"), the ending we are familiar with today. It was only shortly before the Weimar premiere that Wagner undertook to cut the continuation, for he felt that it was "bound to create an impression of coldness" (letter to Franz Liszt of 2 July 1850; SB III, 345).

Wagner began work on the second complete draft of the third act on 9 September 1845, completing it on 5 March 1846. The elaboration of acts 1 and 2 was comparatively rapid (12 May to 2 August 1847), and on 28 August the draft of the prelude was also completed. The final stage of the process, the production of the score, took from 1 January to 28 April 1848. It was the last work Wagner composed in his Dresden period.

The transformation of the opera form into the "true musical drama," to quote the expression from his Beethoven novella of 1840 (SSD I, 109; Wagner-Paris, p. 79), entered a new phase with *Lohengrin*. The through-composed structure of major dramatic interrelations is already foreshadowed in the libretto. Robert Schumann, who was much preoccupied at this time with problems of opera composition, noticed this when Wagner first read the text of *Lohengrin* to an audience in November 1845. Wagner recounts in his autobiography: "Schumann also liked it, yet couldn't figure out the musical form I had in mind for it, as he couldn't find any passages suitable for traditional musical numbers. I then had some fun reading him different parts of my poem just as if they were in aria and cavatina form, so that in the end he smilingly conceded the point" (ML 326).

If Wagner dispensed with the formal means of shaping the material provided by the tradition of operatic composition, what alternative method did he discover? To begin with a negative observation, it is worth noting that the absence of traditional musical numbers includes the genre of song as stage music, which had played such an influential part in his previous operas, especially in *Tannhäuser*. This change was determined by the subject of the work itself. Kings, counts, and knights of the Holy Grail cannot as easily be brought onstage singing as can sailors, maidens, sirens, minnesingers, and pilgrims. Of the stage music in *Lohengrin,* only the Royal Fanfare achieves key importance, as we shall see later on. In contrast, the Bridal Chorus, the Herald's trumpeters, and the fanfares from the turret of the citadel remain episodic and can be regarded as relics of the opera tradition.

What is significant, however, for the development of music drama as Wagner understood it is a type of formal design whose structures cannot be described in terms of musical forms; rather, they constitute as it were translations of dramatic sequences into music and therefore can be illustrated only individually. Here are some examples:

1. The rondolike structure of the second scene of act 1, in which Elsa's related cantilenas in A-flat major and A-flat minor constitute the main section and the interspersed dialogue parts the episodes.

2. The combination of scenes 2 and 3 of act 1 as an intensified sequence of the three key areas of A-flat major, A major, and B-flat major: a succession of semitone rises which is prefigured, albeit on a smaller scale, in the three strophes of Tannhäuser's Venusberg Song.

3. The bridal scene in the third act, which begins very slowly ("sehr langsam") in ¾ time and ends in a very lively ("sehr lebhaft") manner in alla breve meter, combining this antithesis in a manner that foreshadows the art of transition ("Kunst des Übergangs") of the love scene in act 2 of *Tristan* (discussed later in this essay).

Particularly noteworthy is a technique of establishing musical connections that is based on a new relationship between vocal parts and orchestra. This is exemplified in part of the opening scene of act 2, the nocturnal dialogue of Ortrud and Friedrich. This is the scene to which Wagner refers in his autobiography in his account of a conversation with Ludwig Tieck in Potsdam in September 1847: "He assured me that he completely approved of my poem for *Lohengrin;* yet declared that he didn't understand how all this could be set to music without a fundamental change in the nature of opera, and was particularly concerned in this respect about such scenes as the one between Ortrud and Friedrich at the beginning of the second act" (ML 346–347). These are the same misgivings that Robert Schumann had expressed in 1845. By that time, however, Wagner had already finished the second complete draft of *Lohengrin*. So on this occasion, instead of resolving the matter with a joke, he was able to reply precisely: "I thought that I was arousing him to utmost enthusiasm when I began to elaborate to him in my own way on how I proposed to solve these apparent difficulties and set forth my ideas concerning the ideal of music drama" (ML 347).

Wagner may have explained to Tieck that musical connections in opera need not be based on closed vocal numbers, but that they can also be established by an interrelationship of orchestral motifs, as in Example 10. The example presents the sequence of motifs in the respective principal orchestral parts that are heard as a continuous chain. The transition from one form of motif to the next is achieved through an affinity of substance: a and b share an opening on the first beat of the bar and a falling fifth; b and c share

Example 10

diminished intervals and a wide ambitus. This succession of motifs, providing connections and expression, forms the background against which a dialogue such as the following can unfold in a free, recitativelike declamation (the correspondence of libretto and orchestral motifs is illustrated by bracketed motivic designations in the text):

Friedrich:	[a1] Ha! Now I understand his ban!
Ortrud:	Give heed! [a2] No one here has the power, [b]
	to draw the secret from him,
	but she, whom he has strictly warned
	to never seek to question [c1] him.
Friedrich:	Then Elsa must be goaded [c2]
	into asking him the question?
Ortrud:	Ha, you're quick to understand!
Friedrich:	But [c3] how can it be done?
Ortrud:	Listen!
	[c4] Above all, hither we must not
	flee; [c5] so sharpen your wits!
	In her to waken just suspicion.

[Friedrich:	[a1] Ha! Dann begriff ich sein Verbot!
Ortrud:	Nun [a2] hör! Niemand hier hat Ge- [b] walt,
	ihm das Geheimnis zu entreißen,
	als die, der er so streng verbot,
	die Frage je an [c1] ihn zu tun.
Friedrich:	So gält' es, Elsa zu verlei- [c2] ten,
	daß sie die Frag' ihm nicht erließ?
Ortrud:	Ha, wie begreifst du schnell und wohl!
Friedrich:	Doch [c3] wie soll das gelingen?
Ortrud:	Hör!
	[c4] Vor allem gilt's, von hinnen nicht
	zu fliehn; [c5] drum schärfe deinen Witz!
	Gerechten Argwohn ihr zu wecken.]

Such a correspondence between vocal parts and orchestra had already been present in Tannhäuser's Rome narration. The novelty in *Lohengrin* is that not only are the motifs worked out by the orchestra significant in this scene, but they form part of a group of principal themes throughout the whole opera. Thus the section just discussed is related to *Tannhäuser* in the way the music has been structured, but because themes are being used that span the entire work, it is more closely related to *Holländer*.

With this observation I begin to address the subject of how Wagner uses themes to unify an entire work, a procedure that later became known as the leitmotif technique. By merely alluding to *Holländer,* however, I certainly do not claim to do justice to the way the technique is used in *Lohengrin*. Whereas a basic stock of characteristic motifs for *Holländer,* deriving from vocal numbers Wagner had composed in advance, virtually fell into his lap, so to speak, bringing together the main themes for *Lohengrin* was clearly part of Wagner's strategy from the start. Only thus could a group of basic shapes be created that relate to one another, indeed that form a system. What Hanslick said of *Holländer* (basing his observation, of course, on Wagner's *Communication to My Friends*)—namely, that "this kind of concept is . . . not dramatic but symphonistic" (Csampai-Holland 1982, p. 140)—is not actually true until *Lohengrin*. In Hanslick's view the idea offended against the laws of the genre: "The opera composer must unravel the canvas of his drama as a succession of events, as something coming into being." Wagner certainly did not regard himself as about to destroy the musical-dramatic genre. On the contrary, he thought he was rescuing it as a fully valid aesthetic form. His conviction was that dramatic music "in order to constitute, as music, a work of art, must show the unity of a symphonic movement. It achieves this if, in closest affinity with the latter, it encompasses the whole drama, and not merely small individual parts of it that have been arbitrarily highlighted" (SSD X, 185).

The complex of themes spanning *Lohengrin* includes six separate themes, as shown in Examples 11a–11f. (The association with characters or moments in the drama is so clear-cut that there is no need to apologize for using descriptive labels. In this context I would also like to dispense with a discussion of the problematic use of the word *motif* to describe basic thematic shapes.)

The fact that this group of themes constitutes a system becomes even more apparent when one considers that all the themes—apart from the Forbidden Question melody—have a characteristic instrumentation and use a characteristic key. Other than the Royal Fanfare, however, they do not appear exclusively in this instrumentation and key, although the deviations may be understood as variants of the respective basic instrumentation or key. Thus in act 1, for instance, Lohengrin's theme is played by the woodwinds as long as he appears only vicariously in Elsa's reverie; as soon as he is actually present as the Grail Knight, his theme resounds with the "real" instrumentation, using three trumpets.

Dramatic theme	Characteristic instrumentation	Characteristic key
Grail	High strings	A major
King	Trumpets	C major
Elsa (Glance)	Oboe	A-flat major (modulating)
Lohengrin	Trumpets	A major
Ortrud	Low strings	F-sharp minor

C major, the center of the tonal system, is assigned to the king, the worldly central figure of the empire; the trumpet is the instrument traditionally associated with a ruler. Lohengrin's knightly theme also has the trumpet as its

Example 11a   Grail motif

Example 11b   Royal Fanfare

Example 11c   Elsa (Glance) motif

Example 11d   Lohengrin motif

Nie   sollst du mich be - fra - gen,   noch   Wis - sens   Sor - ge   tra - gen

Example 11e   Forbidden Question motif: "These questions ask me never, brood not upon them ever"

Example 11f   Ortrud motif

principal instrument. He, too, has the status of a ruler, but his kingdom is not worldly; rather it is the supernatural kingdom of the Grail, for which A major, which is a circle of three fifths higher than C major, is the appropriate key. The celestial kingdom of the Grail is characterized as unearthly and remote by the instrumentation of the prelude and the Grail narration (high notes or harmonics on the violins). Relative to the Grail sphere, the region of its adversaries (Ortrud) is defined as an opposing world through low strings and the key of F-sharp minor (the relative minor of A major). (The note of F sharp, the antithesis of C by the interval of a tritone, often represents evil in Wagner's works—for instance, in Alberich's curse on the ring in *Das Rheingold*.) Elsa's key is extremely close to Lohengrin's in terms of tonal space, but in terms of the system of key relationships it is extremely distant. Metaphorically speaking, the basic harmonic content of Elsa's key is the yearning of her key of A-flat major for Lohengrin's key of A major, which is striven for in a chromatic modulation. The gestural equivalent of this amounts to "the raising of her [Elsa's] eyes, which are transfigured with rapture" (SSD X, 191). Elsa's instrument is the oboe, which, according to Berlioz's treatise on instrumentation, is appropriate for expressing "naïve grace, pure innocence, silent joy and the sorrows of a sensitive nature" (Berlioz-Strauss 178).

Another important respect in which *Lohengrin* goes further than *Holländer* is that the principal themes are not merely quoted. To a certain extent Wagner's later description already applies here: "Basic themes, as in a symphonic movement, are opposed, supplement and re-shape one another, divide and combine: only that here the enfolding dramatic action establishes the laws of division and combination" (SSD X, 185; see also Siegele 1971). According to this, the relation between music and dramatic action is reciprocal. Although the passage just quoted, from Wagner's late essay *On the Application of Music to the Drama* (1879), stresses the justification of thematic processes through dramatic events, the converse also applies. Lohengrin's path from the world of the Grail to reality via Elsa's vision, Ortrud's ominous gesture at the end of act 2, Elsa's defeated look the morning after the fateful question has been asked: in all these events the thematic relationships in the music give the dramatist what he needs to illustrate and motivate the action, much as Wagner described in his letter to Franck (30 May 1846).

The tendency of the orchestral part at times toward structural autonomy through the relation of themes to one another finds a corollary in the vocal writing, which tends to fit the declamation of the words more exactly. Wagner had been coming to terms with the problem of the relation of his music to poetic language since *Holländer*. With *Lohengrin* this preoccupation entered a decisive stage.

In *A Communication to My Friends,* Wagner describes his predicament retrospectively from the position he had adopted with the text of *Siegfrieds Tod.* He refers to the "incompleteness of modern verse," attributing this deficiency to "its complete lack of true rhythm" (SSD IV, 326). Modern verse in this

Ein - sam in trü - ben Ta - gen / hab ich zu Gott ge - fleht, /

des Her - zens tief - stes Kla - gen / er - goß ich in Ge - bet; /

Example 12

context is verse with alternating end rhymes, which occupies a central place in Wagner's operatic writing from *Holländer* to *Lohengrin*. By "lack of true rhythm" Wagner means that verses with the same metrical structure can have different stress patterns (rhythm here refers to the regular recurrence of the same elements). This is not a specific property of Wagner's treatment of verse; it is one of the basic properties of alternating verse. If in such cases the composer opts for symmetrical, liedlike shaping of the melody, the musical garment will not fit all the verses of the text equally well. In the opening song of *Die Winterreise*, for instance, Schubert uses the same music for "Fremd bin ich eingezogen" and "Der Mai war mir gewogen"; its rhythm fits the stresses in the second instance, but not in the first. (The singer has to think how his performance can give a different value to "fremd" and "ein—".)

The priority of songlike symmetry over differentiated stresses dictated by the meaning of the text was something the musical dramatist in Wagner could not accept. What characters in opera say is not a *recital;* it is *speech.* Wagner describes his method in *Lohengrin* as follows: "Wherever . . . the expression of poetic speech was such a priority that I could only justify the melody in terms of it, then this melody, if it was not to do violence to the verse, had to lose almost all its rhythmic character" (SSD IV, 327). An example of this kind of composition of rhymed verses is the beginning of Elsa's Dream narration in scene 2 of act 1 (see Example 12). The musical setting of this four-line verse is unrhythmic in Wagner's sense; that is, there is no melodic-rhythmic correspondence between musical phrases (compare the method in *Rienzi* as illustrated in Example 5). This type of declamation, which Wagner also called "musical prose" (*Opera and Drama;* SSD IV, 114), is characteristic of long stretches in the music of *Lohengrin,* for instance in the Elsa-Lohengrin dialogue in act 3. It marks the most mature stage of Wagner's concern with the problem of words and music in his Romantic operas. In his subsequent works he was to find fundamentally new ways of handling the relationship between poetic and musical rhythm.

Der Ring des Nibelungen

The composition history of the *Ring*—the largest work in the history of music—is summarized in Table 4.

Table 4   Composition history of the *Ring* (synopsis)

Das Rheingold	Die Walküre	Siegfried (original title: Der junge Siegfried)	Götterdämmerung (original title: Siegfrieds Tod)
Text composed			
Oct. 1851–Nov. 1852 (Albisbrunn / Zurich)	Nov. 1851–July 1852 (Albisbrunn / Zurich)	May 1851–Nov. / Dec. 1852 (Zurich); modifications to Act I during composition of the music	Oct. 1848–Nov. / Dec. 1852 (Dresden / Zurich)
Music composed			
Nov. 1853–Sept. 1854 (Zurich); isolated sketches Feb.–Nov. 1853	June 1854–March 1856 (Zurich / London / Seelisberg / Zurich)	Sept. 1856–Aug. 1857 (Zurich) [to the end of the second complete draft of Act II]; Dec. 1864–Dec. 1865 (Munich) [orchestration of Act II]; March 1869–Feb. 1871 (Tribschen) [composition of Act III]; individual sketches from 1851 and (for Act III) from 1864	Oct. 1869–Nov. 1874 (Tribschen / Bayreuth); incomplete draft of *Siegfrieds Tod*: Summer 1850 (Zurich)
First performance			
22 Sept. 1869 (Munich)	26 June 1870 (Munich)		
First performance as part of the Ring *cycle*			
13 August 1876 (Bayreuth)	14 August 1876 (Bayreuth)	16 August 1876 (Bayreuth)	17 August 1876 (Bayreuth)

Source: Deathridge 1988.

Opera and Drama

When Wagner wrote the text of *Siegfrieds Tod* (later to become *Götterdämmerung*) in November 1848, he gave it the subtitle *Grand Heroic Opera in Three Acts*. The original text of *Der junge Siegfried* (later to become *Siegfried*), written in May 1851, however, he called a "drama." That this change of terminology refers to a fundamental distinction is made clear at the end of his essay *A Communication to My Friends* (here cited from the first version of August 1851): "[Whoever looks forward to the *Nibelungen* opus] with the expectation of experiencing something similar to opera, is completely mistaken. I no longer write operas: since I do not wish to invent an arbitrary term for this work, I am calling it a drama, because this describes most clearly the viewpoint from which my work must be received" (SW 29, I, 53).

Certainly the assertion with which the passage opens is an exaggeration and must be understood as an example of the futuristic emotiveness that dominates Wagner's remarks around 1850. Nevertheless, the change of terminology is undoubtedly a concrete indication that in the meantime Wagner had developed in his theoretical writings precise ideas about the structure of his envisioned "word-music drama." These are concepts which were first fully realized in *Der junge Siegfried* (and later in *Das Rheingold* and *Die Walküre*). (Incidentally, when revising the text for the conclusion of the tetralogy in 1852, Wagner did not bother to remove the operatic features which distinguish it from the other three parts. These relics of the opera tradition in *Götterdämmerung* are particularly evident in the choruses and the trio of vengeance in act 2.)

What happened between the "opera" *Siegfrieds Tod* and the "drama" *Der junge Siegfried*?

The libretto of *Siegfrieds Tod* is already a "drama" in the sense in which Tannhäuser and especially *Lohengrin* are. The acts are divided into scenes and are through-composed, and for the most part the text is in dialogue form. From *Lohengrin* Wagner had gathered experience in coping musically with such a text, and it led him to apply these insights even more emphatically in *Siegfrieds Tod*.

Some features of the text, however, are clearly conceived in terms of traditional opera. Several passages are predisposed to closed musical forms; this is particularly evident in the refrains of the Norns scene and the dialogue between Brünnhilde and the Valkyries. Furthermore, high points are marked by ensembles and choruses which, merely by virtue of the numbers involved, contribute to Wagner's formal strategy: the Blood Brotherhood duet and the ensemble of the Valkyries in act 1; the chorus of vassals, the trio of vengeance, and the oath in act 2; and the choral finale of act 3.

Of these potentially musical features of the text, only the first—that is, the stylizing of the dialogue—remained unproblematic for Wagner in terms of his more narrowly defined notion of music drama. He fell back on this technique in 1851–52, for example in the Riddle scene between Wotan and Mime in the first act of *Siegfried,* and in the new version of the Norns scene in the revised text of *Siegfrieds Tod*. But the use of ensemble and chorus is subjected to restrictions resulting from the theory he expounded in *Opera and Drama,* a theory oriented toward spoken drama.

In Wagner's view, Shakespeare's drama is superior to Greek drama because it has no chorus: "In Shakespeare the chorus is broken up into individuals taking part in the action, who act for themselves in accordance with their individual views and position, much as the principal hero; and even their apparent subordination within the artistic framework is a consequence only of their limited contact with the principal hero . . . wherever even the most subordinate character has to participate in the main action, he expresses himself entirely according to his own free discretion" (SSD III, 268–269). A music drama that does not want to relinquish what has been achieved with this "can only consider characters who by their necessary individual expression can exert at all times a decisive influence on the action"; such a character would be lost in an ensemble. For the same reason, "the *chorus* hitherto used in opera will have to be dispensed with in *our* drama" (SSD IV, 162).

Ensemble singing is not entirely eliminated from those parts of the *Ring* text elaborated in 1851–52. But wherever it does occur, it can be considered one of those "infrequent, completely justifiable cases necessary for the greatest comprehensibility" (SSD IV, 162) that Wagner allows. The Rhine Maidens and the eight Valkyries are groups of characters who are not given their full weight as individuals; the duets of Sieglinde and Siegmund in *Walküre,* and of Brünnhilde and Siegfried in *Siegfried,* particularly in the context of works in which dialogue is the norm, can be regarded as "speaking" in the sense Wagner undoubtedly intended here: the abandonment of individuality in the fulfillment of love.

Wagner did, however, strictly observe his own rule not to write choruses. It is clear from the first prose sketches for *Siegfried* that Wagner intended to bring the Nibelungen into the action as a chorus, but this plan was soon dropped; and in *Das Rheingold,* where the Nibelungen are essential in scenes 3 and 4, the only sounds they make are "cries and shrieks."

The possibilities of "operatic" musical richness that Wagner abandoned by adhering to this method are noted in a criticism of *Das Rheingold* by one contemporary listener: "No symmetrical form . . . no ensembles. We see the entire company of gods and giants, eight to ten characters, standing next to each other on the stage for half the evening, and none of them sing together at the same time. One after another they recite, slowly and with pathos, while the others look on, dumb and bored. Three solid hours in musical Indian file! . . . Would a chorus of Nibelungen dragging gold, or of gods finally entering Valhalla in triumph, have been undramatic?" (Hanslick 1875, pp. 310–311). Hanslick, who reviewed the premiere of *Das Rheingold* in 1869, is an authoritative witness to the correctness of Wagner's statement "I am going to write no more operas" (SW 29, I, 53). Hanslick saw very clearly that certain traditional operatic techniques were no longer being used. (He said that only during the offstage trio of the Rhine Maidens toward the end of the work did his "languishing ear positively revive.")

After the breaking of so many links—though not all—with the old operatic forms, the question arose, how can listeners come to terms with the musical course of a work such as the *Ring* through listening and analysis? Understandably, attention first focused on the leitmotif technique, which I discuss later in this essay. The literary concept of thematic connections, however, which sought to interpret the *Ring* on the basis of its use of leitmotif, was scarcely adequate to clarify the structure of the composition; rather, it seemed merely to confirm Hanslick's view that Wagner's work lacked musical form. Wagner himself expressed certain reservations about the idea of leading thematic threads proposed by his friend and acolyte Hans von Wolzogen. He pointed out that, because Wolzogen was not concerned with "the specific nature of music," he was more interested in "the dramatic significance and effect of what he called 'leitmotifs' than in their use in the musical construction" (SSD X, 185).

Given the length of the *Ring,* the task of describing its formal musical construction posed a challenge for musical analysis; within the traditional theory of musical forms, no conceptual apparatus was available to describe a musical structure that continues uninterrupted for up to two hours (*Götterdämmerung,* act 1, including the prologue). This challenge was not taken up by Wagner scholarship until the twentieth century, initially by Alfred Lorenz in the 1920s, and, after a lengthy pause, in the more recent work of Carl Dahlhaus. The discussion of problems of form in Wagner's works is still in a state of flux, so any attempt to outline definitive solutions is probably premature. It seems more appropriate to suggest some concepts which Wagner scholarship has developed in the twentieth century in order to answer the question of form. The three approaches I have selected are those of Alfred Lorenz, Carl Dahlhaus, and Patrick McCreless. (The criterion for this selection was that their work is not confined to isolated problems of musical analysis in the *Ring,* but takes into account the entire tetralogy.)

Between 1924 and 1933 four volumes of an analytical work by Alfred Lorenz, titled *Das Geheimnis der Form bei Richard Wagner* (The secret of form in the works of Richard Wagner), were published. The first volume is concerned with the *Ring.* (The later volumes deal with *Tristan, Meistersinger,* and *Parsifal.*) Lorenz's analyses were extremely influential for decades, if only because they were unrivaled in their thoroughness (all Wagner's works from the *Ring* onward are minutely analyzed).

The key concept of Lorenz's analysis was taken from Wagner's essay *Opera and Drama:* the notion of the poetic-musical period which "is determined by a principal key." "The work of art achieves the most complete expression," Wagner says in this context, "when many such periods are presented; to realise the highest poetic intent, each necessitates the next and they develop into a rich overall statement" (SSD IV, 154). On the basis of this passage and the preceding discussion about the coordination of meaning and harmony, Lorenz establishes a definition of the period based primarily on uniformity of key, but also including meter, tempo, thematic relations, and poetic content. According to Lorenz, the internal structure of the period can be strophic, archlike (ABA), a rondo or refrain, or in so-called bar form (AAB). He also distinguishes forms "raised to a higher power" (a whole bar, for example, can serve as a single A or B section of a superordinate bar), as well as interlocking and consecutive forms. By the same token, a number of periods can combine to make up larger complexes, which sometimes include entire scenes and acts; Lorenz analyzes *Rheingold* in its entirety in this way, describing it as a "consummate arch form."

Alfred Lorenz felt compelled to provide an answer to every question about form in Wagner's works. His voluminous analyses are undoubtedly a pioneering achievement, if only because they expose the limitations of the leitmotif theory (which really belongs to a literary genre) once and for all. In general terms, the limitation of Lorenz's approach, which went unnoticed for decades, is the assumption that there exists a secret of form in Wagner's works, which requires only that the curtain be drawn aside so that all can be revealed and presented in the form of schematic diagrams.

Carl Dahlhaus criticized the conception of form underlying Lorenz's analyses on the grounds that the "spatial, symmetrical and architectonic element of musical form" is dominant, and this, he says, "conflicts with Wagner's sense of form" (Dahlhaus 1969, p. 96). On the basis of his critique of Lorenz, Dahlhaus developed a "musico-dramatic conception of form," which he demonstrated in a series of publications from 1965 (some are reprinted in Dahlhaus 1983). Dahlhaus states four main objections to Lorenz's interpretation, in particular to the way he used Wagner's concept of the poetico-musical period for his own analytical ends:

1. Lorenz's periods are frequently far longer than anything that can be deduced from Wagner's discussions or from nineteenth-century conceptions of the musical period.

2. The length of these periods varies spectacularly in Lorenz's analyses, ranging from 14 to 840 measures.

3. The demand for tonal cohesion does not follow from Wagner's condition that each period should be "determined by a principal key."

4. The period cannot generally be defined in abstract musical terms; rather, it must be regarded as a rhetorical-musical form, taking into account the structure of the dialogue in the relevant section.

Dahlhaus describes Wagner's overall strategy in creating musical form, in which the period represents one phase:

> Musical form, in so far as it is intended, is realised as it were hierarchically; motives combine to form groups or complexes of motives, groups combine into "poetic-musical" periods, periods form scenes or parts of scenes . . . and scenes form the entire drama. However, form is . . . not equally distinctive at all levels of the hierarchy. A "closed" group of motives can coincide with "open" periodic structure—in relatively limitless combinations—and the manner in which the formal strength and clarity of individual periods and entire scenes relate to one another is not subject to any rule; rather, it constitutes one of the problems of an interpretative formal analysis that attempts to show why the forms exist rather than merely drafting alphabetical schemata. At any rate analogies between small and large forms cannot be assumed; rather the degree of agreement or divergence must be examined and understood as a characteristic feature. (Dahlhaus 1971, p. 84)

No less important than the principles cited here are Dahlhaus' exemplary analyses of numerous passages from the *Ring*. They are the practical background to the notion of an "interpretative analysis of form," which lend it persuasive force.

More recently Patrick McCreless has attempted to incorporate into his analysis of the formal principles of the *Ring* the changes in Wagner's conception of the work that took place over a period of decades. McCreless distinguishes three phases in the musical form-building process that superseded one another (McCreless 1982, esp. pp. 104ff. and 188ff.):

1. *Rheingold* is constructed from periods which are definable in terms of keys and are coordinated to one another.

2. In *Walküre* and in acts 1 and 2 of *Siegfried* the periods become longer and more digressive in their tonality; to a much greater extent they refer beyond themselves to the way a scene is unified.

3. In act 3 of *Siegfried* and in *Götterdämmerung* a more symphonic way of thinking gains in importance; the structure of the third act of *Siegfried,* for instance, is comparable with that of a symphony in five movements.

The work by McCreless is essentially a detailed analysis of *Siegfried:* the overall conception I have outlined is suggested rather than explained as such. I include it here because it is to be expected that the aspect of historical development which it emphasizes will play an even greater role in future analytical Wagner research. Indeed, the fact that nearly all Wagner's musical sketches and drafts are extant is a powerful incentive for further detailed study of this matter. (For an inventory of the sketches and drafts, see WWV. A brief summary of work done in this area is given in Chapter 7 of this volume.)

Alliterative Verse and Musical Declamation

Wagner used essentially two verse forms for the libretti of his operas up to and including *Lohengrin:* blank iambic verse with five stresses—the meter of classical drama—and rhyming iambic verse, usually four-line verse with an *abab* rhyme scheme. These two verse types tend to be associated with certain musical styles: the blank verse lends itself to recitative, and the rhyming stanza to more arialike passages. Up to *Lohengrin,* Wagner, in his role of composer, had to come to terms with this polarity of text, which retains an aspect of the traditional recitative-aria dualism, although his attitude toward it became increasingly distanced and problematic. (I have already offered examples of Wagner's musical treatment of blank and rhyming verse in *Lohengrin.*)

Given Wagner's new ideal of music and drama in the *Ring,* the polarity between blank and rhyming verse, and all that it implies from a musical point of view, was bound to be a fundamental problem. In any event, the stylistic difference between recitative and aria (or arioso) continues to play a role in the first two parts of the *Ring.* Wagner, however, was obviously seeking a form of text that did not commit him in advance to a particular kind of musical treatment and left him free for more variation of style. It had to be a form that contained certain principles of stylization to which musical symmetries could be related but, at the same time, was so close to prose that it conformed to the ideal of opera as dialogue.

It was an extremely significant coincidence that the Old Norse sources, which to a large extent provided the material for the *Ring,* stimulated Wagner into trying out a new kind of metrical treatment for the libretto. The source of this inspiration was Old Norse alliterative verse, key elements of which he incorporated into the text of the *Ring* (see Wiessner 1924 and Spencer 1985).

Wagner had already made up his mind to use alliterative verse when he started work on the text of the *Ring* in the autumn of 1848, and it is clear that he was aware of the significance of this innovation for the overall artistic shape of the work. It is true that Wagner did not formulate a detailed theory of alliterative verse until he wrote *Opera and Drama* in 1850–51, by which time the poem of *Siegfrieds Tod* was already two years old. Nevertheless, it can be said with certainty that even at the outset of his work with the new text form in the autumn of 1848, Wagner was aiming at a new relationship between language and music. For on 2 December 1848, when Wagner read the newly finished libretto of *Siegfrieds Tod* to Eduard Devrient, he evidently described the advantages of using alliterative verse as the basis of his opera so convincingly that Devrient later noted in his diary: "The man is a poet through and through . . . Alliteration as he uses it is a real discovery for the opera libretto; in fact, it ought to be made mandatory" (SW 29, I, 30).

The rules underlying Wagner's *Nibelungen* verse can be summarized as follows (certain peculiarities of the text for *Siegfrieds Tod,* which arise from the fact that it was the first libretto of the tetralogy to be written, have been omitted):

1. Each verse has one or two stressed syllables.

2. The number of unaccented syllables varies; in the upbeat and in the body of a verse it ranges from none to three, and at the conclusion of the verse from none to two.

3. Every verse forms an alliterative pattern either within itself (internal alliteration) or with a neighboring verse (connective alliteration); often both types of alliteration are combined.

4. Alliterative rhymes are formed when several stressed syllables begin with the same consonant or with different (rarely with the same) vowel.

5. Individual verses can be grouped into strophelike structures, but can also appear in irregular succession.

The most important metrical principle of Wagnerian alliterative verse (which is not identical in every respect with the Old Norse model) is not alliteration but rhythm. The variability in the number of unaccented syllables means that every verse stress can contain an accented syllable, that is, a focus of the language's meaning; indeed it must contain such a syllable, for only by this means is the verse accent apparent. Through this method Wagner gained what he found lacking in the alternating verse: "true" rhythm. Thus he could arrange the order of his verses in advance to accommodate, at least potentially, more flexible rhythm and melody in the music. It is significant that when he was trying to explain his musical intentions in a letter of 29 June 1851 to Franz Liszt, Wagner was keen to read part of the *Ring* libretto to him: "What I've written here [*Der junge Siegfried*] gives—I fear—such an inadequate impression of what I have in mind that if I could read it aloud to you—to at least indicate what I intend—this would certainly reassure me about the desired effect of my poem on you" (SB IV, 67).

A passage from the second scene of *Rheingold* illustrates the way in which the new verse scheme affects the melodic structure of the vocal parts. It consists of a text unit of nine lines from Wotan's dialogue with Fricka, presented first without music:

	Upbeat	1st foot		2d foot			3rd foot
1	Wo	frei-	er	Mut			frommt,
2	al-	lein		frag'	ich	nach	kei- nem.
3	Doch des	Fein-	des	Neid			
4	zum	Nutz	sich	fü-	gen,		
5		lehrt	nur	Schlau-heit	und		List,
6	wie	Lo-	ge ver-	schla-	gen	sie	übt.
7		Der	zum Ver-	tra-	ge	mir	riet,
8	ver-	sprach	mir,	Frei-	a	zu	lö- sen:
9	auf	ihn	ver-	lass'	ich	mich	nun.

The nine verses have nine different rhythmic structures, but there are only two basic metrical patterns: verses with two accented syllables (lines 3–4) and those with three accented syllables (lines 1–2 and 5–9). (The considerable preponderance of verses with three syllables over those with two in this example is not typical of the *Ring* as a whole.) The path along which the text can be articulated in musical form is therefore mapped out in advance. Any distance that remains constant is chosen for the stresses, and this establishes the rhythmic fixed points for the melody. The melody is then worked out, on the one hand, from the perspective of declamation and expression and, on the other hand, with meaningful formal organization of the section in mind. Finally, in some places orchestral motifs are also taken into account. (The setting of the vocal part in measures 950–953 of Example 13, for instance, is part and parcel of the chromatic sequence of chords associated with Loge which sound simultaneously in the orchestra.)

Here Wagner placed the accents on the first and third beats of a $\frac{4}{4}$ measure; a pause is inserted after verses with three accents so that the next verse begins at the beginning of a measure. (This arrangement of accents is so fundamental that Wagner described it as a prototype in *Opera and Drama*; see SSD IV, 125.) In verses 1–6 this ordering of accents is followed without exception (see Example 13). This melody is rhythmic in terms of Wagner's theory; that is, for particular verse lines it has corresponding melodic phrases. A glance at the continuation in Example 14 shows how the composer can progress from these simple declamatory shapes to more differentiated forms. Aside from the

Example 13

Example 14

minor displacement at the beginning, the metrical norm laid down by the vocal line in Example 13 (given in the notation above the upper system in Example 14) is broken in two places: at *a* the meter is halved; at *b* the values are twice as fast compared to what we expect. The declamatory purpose of these devices is clear: Loge's promise—to free Freia—is emphasized by lengthening (expansion of *b*). The effect of the deviation from the norm depends on the norm's being recognized as such. It is of course possible, in principle, to achieve such effects in composing music for alternating verse. But Wagner's principle of musical prose, as we have seen, meant that the technique of deviation had been exhausted for the purposes of achieving correct word and sentence stresses; that is, it was no longer fully available for rhetorical differentiation.

Leitmotif Technique

As early as December 1848 one of Wagner's basic ideas about the musical realization of his *Nibelungen* opera was that the orchestra should have "a significant role to play in its dramatic expression" (SW 29, I, 31). Looking back at the finished first draft of *Das Rheingold* in January 1854, he wrote to August Röckel that the work had "become a close-knit unity: There is scarcely a measure in the orchestra which does not develop out of preceding motifs" (Röckel-Briefe, p. 42; SL 310). One must not take this claim quite literally with respect to *Das Rheingold;* it is only true without qualification for *Siegfried* and *Götterdämmerung*. If we consider the qualitative change in the musical style of *Das Rheingold* compared with that of *Lohengrin,* however, the essential correctness of Wagner's claim is underlined.

What brought about this change? Three causes can be identified. First, the text had to be arranged in such a manner that it gave the necessary points of reference for a musical web of motifs. The genesis of the *Ring* libretto cannot be understood unless we assume that Wagner was intent on distributing the characters, the props, the inner motifs of the action, in short all the necessary ingredients for the development of the drama as if he were working with musical themes. This is the only way in which this extract from a letter of 11 February 1853 to Liszt after the completion of the *Ring* libretto can be understood: "The prospect of setting all this to music now attracts me greatly: as regards the form, it is already fully fashioned in my head" (Wagner-Liszt, p. 264; SL 280).

Second, for the most part the thematic system of the *Ring* music was based on such elementary motifs that the variation technique could be employed in a far more diverse manner than had been possible in *Lohengrin*. One of the most impressive examples of this variation technique is the first motif of *Das Rheingold* and its metamorphoses. The horn motif—the primal form of the so-called Nature motif—ascends upward in an E-flat major triad (Example 15a) and is compressed into a melodic form with the ambitus of a tenth in the passage that follows (Example 15b). On top of this comes a "swirling" figure (Example 15c); its rhythmic diminution (Example 15d) pervades long stretches of the scene at the bottom of the Rhine, where it represents the motion of the waves. The second of these forms is the starting point for a further process of variation. Its upward movement can be interpreted as a musical symbol of becoming; it is in these terms that the ascription to Erda of the motif variant (Example 16a) in scene 4 of *Rheingold* is to be understood: Erda, the goddess who depicts herself as knowing "how everything was, . . . how everything is, how everything will be." And the reversal of direction (Example 16b) stands for the opposite of becoming, for extinction, and particularly, as the context makes clear, for the perishing of the gods: "A sombre day dawns for the gods."

The metamorphosis of themes is often so radical that it seems to be—in fact is meant to be—a distortion of a theme's original character. Wagner himself interprets one such example in his essay *On the Application of Music to the Drama* (1879). The example is the combination of the Rheingold and Valhalla motifs accompanying Wotan's outburst in act 2, scene 3, of *Walküre:* "So take my blessing, / Nibelungen-son! / That which disgusts me deeply / I bequeath to you, / the empty glitter of the gods: / may your envy gnaw it greedily to pieces!" Wagner comments on the combination of themes, which is heard twice (Example 17a): "Once the simple nature motive [Example 17b] had been heard in the course of the drama at the first gleaming of the glittering Rhine gold, and another, hardly less simple motive [Example 17c] had also

Example 15a

Example 15b

Example 15c

Example 15d

Example 16a

Example 16b

been heard when Valhalla, the fortress of the gods, first loomed up in the redness of dawn, and each of these motives, in closely intertwined participation in the intensifying passion of the action, had undergone corresponding changes, I could, by means of a strange harmonisation present them together in such a way that this musical image, more than Wotan's words, gave an insight into the terribly darkened soul of the suffering god" (SSD X, 188).

The third reason for the change is that, in comparison to *Holländer, Tann-häuser,* and *Lohengrin,* the allocation of musical themes to characters, objects, and motifs for events in the action is now far more complex. This is shown

Example 17a

Example 17b

Example 17c

by the fact that it is difficult to find suitable descriptions even for motifs that play an important part in the *Ring*. Terms such as *escape* or *discontent* are at best aids to comprehension; they are certainly not adequate semantic definitions of the motifs concerned. But even where description is possible, the function of the motifs as a whole is not so much to characterize individual things as to differentiate among them by combining disparate elements. The mythical content allows plenty of scope for mingling characters, objects, and concepts. Thus there are motifs that designate both material things and abstractions (spear/contract), persons and material things (Loge/fire), or persons and abstractions (Freia/youth). Conversely, the minor characters (Erda, Gutrune) are characterized by only one motif, whereas the central characters are seen from several perspectives (Wotan: Valhalla/spear; Brünnhilde: Valkyrie/lover; Siegfried: the boy who blows his horn in the woods/the redeeming hero). And the revealing comments Wagner made when he had to compose for the second time the scene between Brünnhilde and Siegfried in *Götterdämmerung* shows how far from schematism and predictability Wagner's use of musical motifs can be: "In the scene between Brünnhilde and Siegfried in Götterdämmerung no theme from the love-scene [in *Siegfried*] recurs, for everything is determined by mood, not by thought, and the mood is a different one than the heroic idyll in *Siegfried*" (CT, 11 December 1869).

Wagner's leitmotif technique makes such a number of demands on the listener that a brief discussion of them seems appropriate here.

Wagner repeatedly stressed the symphonic ideal as the background to his method of composing with themes in his music dramas. The stock of basic themes which Wagner used in *Holländer* or in *Lohengrin* corresponds roughly to the number of themes used in a symphonic movement and is therefore similarly clear and memorable. This restriction meant, however, that in a musical-dramatic work only a small part of the work's whole course could be permeated by a group of basic themes. But if a music drama were to become "a close-knit unity" (see Wagner's letter to Röckel quoted at the beginning of this section), then this would be possible only by means of a set of themes more diverse than anything known in instrumental music. (Wagner's technique of combining groups of themes by variations on a basic shape common to them all makes the difference seem smaller; but it is there nonetheless.) The listener who wishes to follow the ramifications, variations, and combinations of themes throughout the work thus faces a task no less complicated than that of following the most ambitious symphonic works. Even the earliest well-meaning Wagnerians believed that this difficulty could be overcome merely by compiling lists of leitmotifs. Actually, there is probably nothing that has been as detrimental to an adequate appreciation of Wagner's music as the supposed shortcut of "thematic guides," a practice which Wagner did not initiate but tolerated. As a result, the misapprehension spread that the ability to identify motifs was identical with an understanding of the work. Commentaries based on this approach gave rise to a type of Wagner appreciation which George Bernard Shaw caricatured in *The Perfect Wagnerite:* "To be able to follow the music of *The Ring,* all that is necessary is to become familiar enough with the brief musical phrases out of which it is built, to recognize them and attach a certain definite significance to them, exactly as any ordinary Englishman recognizes and attaches a definite significance to the opening bars of *God Save the Queen*" (Shaw 1898, p. 103).

Wagner's remark that the "mood" of a scene is decisive for its composition should encourage the listener to put, albeit attentively, his or her trust in the flow of the music and to include the interplay of motifs in an appreciation of the work so that this interplay is accessible to the memory of what has already been heard. The main prerequisite for commentaries on Wagner's works is that they should enable listeners to follow musical processes rather than seduce them into merely labeling the motifs.

The Ring *Orchestra*

The range of orchestral sounds that Wagner requires for the *Ring* is just as extreme as the temporal dimensions of the work. The constitution and treatment of the orchestra in the *Ring,* however, is not the result of a sudden change but is rather a further development of tendencies which had already informed Wagner's previous works.

Because of the rich experience Wagner had gained at a young age in working with the orchestra, instrumentation was a craft whose techniques he had mastered thoroughly in his early works. In later years, when, referring to the music of *Das Liebesverbot,* Wagner self-critically described it as "dreadful," "appalling," and "disgusting," he did not include the orchestration in the damning criticism. In fact he told Cosima that the instrumentation was good: "That I could do in my mother's womb" (CT, 31 January 1879). This early technical assurance was the basis for the further development of Wagner's style of orchestration, in which the increased use of orchestral means became part of his musical invention, particularly in terms of "intensifying and interpreting the entire dramatic action of the opera through tone colours" (Voss 1970, p. 330).

Lohengrin is a milestone in the development of Wagner's orchestral technique. A notable innovative feature here is Wagner's use of the wind instruments, which Richard Strauss—himself one of the greatest virtuosi of orchestration in the history of music—graphically described in 1904:

> The treatment of the wind section in *Lohengrin* amounts—aesthetically—to an unprecedented peak of true perfection. The so-called third instruments (English horn, bass clarinet) incorporated for the first time into the woodwind section are already used in diverse combinations. The second, third and fourth horn parts, and the trumpets and trombones already attain polyphonic independence, and Wagner's characteristic doubling of melodic parts is executed with such sure awareness of tone and elaborated with such a sense of musical beauty that even today it commands our unqualified admiration. (Berlioz-Strauss, p. iii)

The first signs of the link between the use of instruments and musical–dramatic characterization can be seen in the way themes are associated with instrumental colors (see the chart in the section on *Lohengrin*).

All wind instruments are more strongly represented in the *Ring* orchestra than in *Lohengrin*. The flute, oboe, clarinet, trumpet, and trombone sections consist of four instead of three players, and there are eight horns. Occasionally the fifth through the eighth horn players are required to switch to tubas. Wagner also insisted on a number of new types of instrument for the *Ring*: the narrow-bore tuba with a French horn mouthpiece (the so-called Wagner tuba), bass trumpet, contrabass tuba, and contrabass trombone. Another novelty of the *Ring* orchestra is the precise number of strings required: sixteen first and sixteen second violins, twelve violas, twelve cellos, and eight double basses. The stringed instruments also include six harps.

The effect of this numerical reinforcement of the orchestra is not merely to increase the volume of the sound. Its primary function is to provide a rich palette of colors appropriate to the richness of the action. The eight horns in the instrumental introduction to *Das Rheingold* and in act 2, scene 2, of *Götterdämmerung* (Dawn); the chorus of tubas used for the Valhalla theme in *Das Rheingold* and at the beginning of the Announcement of Death scene in *Die Walküre;* the eight-part violin divisi at the sight of the gleaming gold in the second scene of *Das Rheingold:* all these are examples of Wagner's striking use of the *Ring* orchestra, and many similar instances could also be cited (see Berlioz-Strauss and Voss 1970).

The instrumental richness of the *Ring* score was to remain unique in Wagner's oeuvre. *Tristan* returns to the orchestra of *Lohengrin,* and the instrumental apparatus of *Die Meistersinger* even strongly resembles that of the classical symphony orchestra. The abandonment of extreme instrumental resources in these two scores does not merely amount to simplification but goes hand in hand with a refinement of the interaction between various families of instruments (see Voss 1970, pp. 334ff.). This development reveals a particularly interesting perspective on those parts of the tetralogy that were composed after *Meistersinger.* When Wagner returned to the *Ring* after writing *Tristan* and *Meistersinger,* the orchestra stayed the same. He had the benefit, however, of the additional refinements of instrumental technique that he had introduced in the two earlier operas. The nuances of the orchestral sound in the later parts of the *Ring* can be intuitively grasped as a new style, although so far there has been no detailed research on this subject.

Instrumental Works after 1850

Eine Faust-Ouvertüre, written during the period of *Rienzi,* was the last orchestral composition that Wagner intended to be a large-scale work, in the emphatic sense of the word. (It will be recalled that this one-movement piece was originally planned as the first movement of a symphony.) After *Holländer* Wagner became increasingly aware that his creative talents were destined for the theater; in his Zurich writings around 1850 he even proclaimed, generalizing, his conviction "that the last symphony [Beethoven's Ninth] has already been written" (SSD III, 97), and that the only valid artwork of the future could be the music drama. The fact that Wagner's contributions to instrumental music from 1850 on were only occasional and commissioned pieces is quite consistent with this philosophy.

With the exception of two unpretentious humorous compositions from the Zurich years, his piano pieces of this time are all "albumleaves," and not in the neutralized sense of the term (as, for example, in Schumann's op. 99 and 124) but in the functional sense of a musical dedication. The recipients were Mathilde Wesendonck (*Eine Sonate für das Album von Frau M. W.,* 1853; WWV 85), Princess Metternich (*In das Album der Fürstin M.,* 1861; WWV 94), Countess Pourtalès (*Ankunft bei den schwarzen Schwänen,* 1861; WWV 95), and Betty Schott, the wife of Wagner's publisher (*Albumblatt,* 1875; WWV 108).

Apart from these brief piano pieces of a private nature, which often seem like written-down improvisations (and as such are undoubtedly of interest), Wagner was specifically commissioned to write works for political personalities and causes. The first of these is the *Huldigungsmarsch* (WWV 97), a march of hommage for large military orchestra, composed in 1864 to mark the nineteenth birthday of Ludwig II (5 October 1864). The publisher C. F. Peters commissioned Wagner to produce a work to mark the founding of the German Empire in 1870, and after some hesitation Wagner accepted and wrote the *Kaisermarsch* (WWV 104) in 1871. In it the composer cites the melody of

Luther's chorale *Ein feste Burg ist unser Gott,* and concludes the piece with the choir singing ad libitum to the words "Heil! Heil dem Kaiser König Wilhelm." The last work in this category is the *Grand Festival March for the Opening of the Centennial, Commemorative of the Declaration of Independence of the United States of America* (WWV 110), to quote the title as it appeared on a piano score published in Cincinnati in 1876, the year in which it was written. As Cosima Wagner's diaries attest, Wagner's artistic misgivings about writing this work were at least as serious as those he had about the *Kaisermarsch,* but he received substantial remuneration for it ($5,000), and it satisfied his American patron.

Also an occasional work, although vastly superior in artistic value to the others, is the *Siegfried-Idyll* (WWV 103), which Wagner composed for Cosima's thirty-third birthday. The unofficial title in the dedicatory score reads: "Tribschen Idyll with Fidi-Birdsong and Orange Sunrise as Symphonic Birthday Greeting Offered to His Cosima by Her Richard, 1870." (The private allusions can be deciphered by consulting CT, 6 June and 14 June 1869.) In the first publication of 1878 the work was given the simpler title *Siegfried-Idyll,* which can be taken as referring either to Wagner's son Siegfried (born on 6 June 1869) or to *Siegfried* (the draft of which was finished in July 1869), from which the principal themes of the *Idyll* are taken.

In addition to the strings, the work uses five woodwinds (flute, oboe, two clarinets, and bassoon) and three brass instruments (two horns and trumpet). At the first performance on the staircase of the Tribschen villa on 25 December 1870, some string parts were played by one and some by two players, and today the *Idyll* is often performed purely as chamber music. The number of performers used at Tribschen was probably an impromptu solution dictated by the forces at hand; moreover, the title on the autograph score contains the term *symphony.* This, and the fact that on many occasions Wagner directed the work using a proper orchestra, is a sign that it was probably orchestrally conceived.

Almost the entire thematic substance of the *Idyll* predates the composition itself; only the second subject (mm. 50ff.) seems to have been written without recourse to preexisting themes. The main point of reference for the themes is act 3 of *Siegfried.* On occasion, however, the *Siegfried* themes themselves clearly date back to even earlier ideas. This inference is supported by an entry in CT, which was noted down during the time when act 3 of *Siegfried* was being composed (19 May 1869): "Before lunch R. plays for me what he has written and is delighted that several themes which date from the 'Starnberg days' and which we had jokingly earmarked for quartets and symphonies have now found their niche ['*Ewig war ich, ewig bin ich*']. Great surge of joy at this coming together of life and art."

The several themes from the Starnberg days (this was the decisive period in the relationship between Wagner and Cosima during the summer of 1864) can only refer to two themes: the theme referred to in the leitmotif guides as the Peace melody in E major (first encountered in m. 1478 of *Siegfried,* act 3; see Example 18a) and the World Treasure theme (first in m. 1497; see Example

Example 18a

Example 18b

18b). That the first of these themes is actually far older than act 3 of *Siegfried* is proved by a musical sketch of Wagner's from 14 November 1864 (reproduced in Westernhagen 1976, p. 175); no such evidence exists for the second theme. The use of both themes in *Siegfried* gives the impression—as Ernest Newman points out (Newman 1976, III, 271ff.)—of a mere quotation; to the further course of the tetralogy these themes are virtually irrelevant. It is just these two musical figures that are now used as the principal theme of the *Siegfried Idyll*. Originally conceived for instrumental works (quartets and symphonies), they found their real purpose in the *Idyll*, after a guest appearance of sorts in the music drama. (For a different view, see WWV 508–509 and Deathridge 1983.)

Three other themes or motifs from *Siegfried* were also incorporated into the *Idyll*: the horn theme first heard in measure 259 of the *Idyll*, which Wagner described as the "Theme of Joy" (CT, 13 June 1869; otherwise known as the Resolve to Love motif; see *Siegfried*, act 3, m. 1719); a triplet figure (mm. 275ff.) which first appears in *Siegfried*, act 3, measure 1581 ("Brach sie mein Bild, so brenn' ich nun selbst"); and the birdcalls, which first occur in the middle section (mm. 303ff.) and appear in this form in *Siegfried*, act 2 (mm. 1881ff.).

There are two further thematic elements which do not originate with *Siegfried* but also predate the composition of the *Idyll*. The lullaby that functions as the final subject in the exposition and recapitulation (first occurrence in mm. 91ff.) Wagner had written down as early as 31 December 1868 (facsimile and transcription in BB 170–171). And the birdcall which is introduced into the *Idyll* in conjunction with the Theme of Joy (mm. 262ff.) is prefigured in a single sketch, titled *Blackbird Singing* (published in Westernhagen 1976, p. 153, no. 25a), which presumably dates from 10 May 1870 (see CT).

The structure of the *Siegfried-Idyll* can be outlined as follows (the numbers represent measures):

1–28	Introduction: preparation of principal theme I
29–105	Exposition
	29–49 Principal subject, based on principal theme I (Peace melody), E major
	50–90 Transition and secondary subject, B major
	91–105 Final subject: Lullaby, B major
106–307	Central section
	106–133 Introduction (beginning as in mm. 1ff.), followed by developmentlike treatment of exposition elements
	134–147 Transition (trills and arpeggios)
	148–258 Central part of central section, based on principal theme II (¾ time version of World Treasure theme): (1) wind, A-flat major (mm. 148ff.); (2) strings, A-flat major–A major (mm. 181ff.); (3) wind and strings, contrapuntally combined with a ¾ variant of principal theme I, B major–A-flat major–F major (mm. 200ff.)
	259–285 Transitional section above pedal point G: (1) Theme of Joy with Blackbird Singing (mm. 259ff.); (2) triplet figure (mm. 275ff.)
	286–303 Apotheosis: combination of principal theme I with a diatonic variant in ¾ time of principal theme II, E major–C major
	303–307 Transition: birdcalls
308–387	Recapitulation
	308–350 Transition and secondary subject, E major
	351–365 Principal subject, based on principal theme I, E major
	366–372 Transition ("very calm"): Theme of Joy and Blackbird Singing
	373–387 Concluding subject: Lullaby, E major
388–405	Coda: combination of principal themes I and II

Sonata movement form is decisive for the opening and closing parts of the work. Between the exposition and the recapitulation, however, there is no development but rather an extensive central section in which the second principal theme is introduced, developed, and contrapuntally combined with the first. Moreover, the change of time and tempo introduce an element of several movements in one. As willing as Wagner was to fall back, at least partially, on the sonata form as a tried and tested means of coordination, it is clear that he did not have an overall form in mind when he composed the

Idyll but instead had a set of themes he wanted to include in the work. That the stock of themes is minted from programmatic ideas would have to be presumed, even if this were not supported by the private title and various comments to Cosima. It is interesting to speculate about details, although all such speculation must remain hypothetical. The allusions to private—even the most private—matters made the *Idyll* a highly personal shrine for Richard and Cosima Wagner ("Its fair tones our guardian angels," as Cosima once wrote; CT, 23 March 1882), and for this reason they were extremely reluctant to accede to Schott's wish to publish it, eventually agreeing only because of severe financial problems.

Wagner was aware of the special place of the *Siegfried-Idyll* among his occasional works. Cosima noted in her diary: "He plays me the sonata for Math. Wesendonck and laughs heartily at its 'triviality,' as he calls it. He says he has never been able to write an occasional piece—this sonata is shallow, nondescript, the *Albumblatt* for Betty Schott is artificial; only with the *Idyll* had he been successful, because in that everything came together" (CT, 30 August 1877). What came together was the private circumstances, with which Wagner identified; the succinctness of the themes, an effect that is due in part to the numerous associations with *Siegfried;* and finally the freedom to allow these themes to develop and to combine without the constraints imposed by a dramatic context.

This last point shows another connection in which the *Siegfried-Idyll* must be seen. A series of projects and individual thematic sketches by Wagner documents a longing for the symphonic idiom in his later years (see WWV, pp. 519–525). The symphonies which Wagner planned to write were not to conform to the dramatic ideal of the Beethoven type of symphony; Wagner's conception finds expression, for instance, in a conversation with Liszt on 17 December 1882: "If we write symphonies, Franz, then let us stop contrasting one theme with another, a method Beeth[oven] has exhausted. We should just spin a melodic line until it can be spun no farther; but on no account drama!" (CT, 17 December 1882). Only in the *Siegfried-Idyll* could such conceptions be translated into reality. It is therefore a forerunner to a number of instrumental works after *Parsifal* which Wagner considered but was not to realize.

The *Wesendonck-Lieder*

The *Wesendonck-Lieder* (WWV 91), Wagner's only songs of his mature period, are closely connected internally and externally with the development of *Tristan*. The texts by Mathilde Wesendonck were probably strongly influenced by Wagner's libretto for *Tristan* (see Voss 1983, p. 24). His decision to set to music "a number of pretty verses that were sent to me, something I have never done before" (Wagner-Liszt, p. 536) can be understood only in the light of his personal relationship with Mathilde Wesendonck, a relationship which was also a shaping force on the mood of *Tristan* (see Chapter 1 in this volume). And the music of the opera, which he was composing at the same time, had a marked influence on the style of the songs as a whole; the substantial affinities of *Träume* and *Im Treibhaus* with sections of acts 2 and 3 entitle us to describe these numbers as studies for *Tristan*.

The connection between the *Wesendonck-Lieder* and *Tristan* is illustrated in this chronological chart (the dates of the songs refer to the completion of the first written version):

1 October–31 December 1857	First complete musical draft of *Tristan*, act 1
30 November 1857	*Der Engel*
4 December 1857	*Träume*
17 December 1857	*Schmerzen*
22 February 1858	*Stehe still!*
3 April 1858	Completion of score of *Tristan*, act 1
1 May 1858	*Im Treibhaus*
4 May 1858	Continuation of work on *Tristan*, with complete musical draft of act 2

In 1862 the songs were published by Schott, with the title *Fünf Gedichte für eine Frauenstimme mit Pianoforte-Begleitung;* they were ordered as follows: *Der Engel, Stehe still!, Im Treibhaus, Schmerzen,* and *Träume.* In order to indicate that the poems were not by him without providing the name of the poet, Wagner first called the work *Five Dilettante Poems,* a title he later dropped, probably at the publisher's request.

Of the five songs, the most musically significant are *Träume* and *Im Treibhaus,* the studies for *Tristan.* The beginning and end of *Träume* run parallel to parts of the duet "O sink hernieder, Nacht der Liebe" in *Tristan,* act 2; and the major section of the piano part of *Im Treibhaus* recurs in act 3 (the instrumental introduction and beginning of Tristan's account of the "Weiten Reich der Weltennacht"). These two songs benefited from Wagner's musical invention in *Tristan.* Inevitably the remaining songs, in which Wagner referred more directly to the poems, fall short of the studies in thematic quality. Nevertheless, they retain something of the tone of *Tristan* and are sustained within the cycle by the two outstanding songs, which in the published version Wagner—no doubt intentionally—placed in the middle and at the end.

Tristan und Isolde

Nearly three years elapsed between the time when Wagner first became fascinated by the *Tristan* material during a period of intense involvement with Schopenhauer's writings in the autumn of 1854, and August 1857, when he began to elaborate the scenario. During this time, in which Wagner's idea of the work went in effect through a latent phase, the music of *Tristan* was also quietly maturing as Wagner worked on *Die Walküre* and the first two acts of *Siegfried*. Toward the end of 1856, elements began to enter Wagner's musical thinking that were not appropriate to *Siegfried,* a fact that must have played a significant part in his decision to stop work on *Siegfried* and to concentrate on the *Tristan* project. On 22 December 1856 Wagner wrote to Otto Wesendonck: "I am no longer attuned to *Siegfried,* and my musical sensibility already roams far beyond it, to where my mood belongs—into the realm of melancholy" (Wesendonck-Briefe, p. 44). The specific background to these remarks was that three days previously Wagner had written a melody in G major to the words "Sink hernieder, Nacht der Liebe," which (in modified form) was later taken up in act 2 of *Tristan* (see Bailey 1979, pp. 308ff.). An even more direct irruption of the *Tristan* sphere into the composition of *Siegfried* was a melodic idea Wagner had on 21 May 1856. He "at first did not know where to place it" (Wesendonck-Briefe, p. 70), but eventually thought of using it for part of the dialogue in the final scene of *Siegfried* (SSD VI, 171), as shown in Example 19. Wagner then realized that this phrase belonged to *Tristan* and used it in act 1 as the principal theme of Brangänge's song of appeasement, beginning with the words "So lebte der Mann" (ibid., pp. 318ff.). In spite of such confusions, Wagner still managed to finish the first complete draft of act 2 of *Siegfried* on 30 July 1857; but, as he had already noted as early as 18 June at the beginning of the second draft of act 2 (on which he was working concurrently with the first): "*Tristan* already decided on."

The operatic innovations which Wagner had developed up to and including the *Ring* and thought out theoretically in his writings around 1850 are three-fold: the conception of dialogue opera as a continuous whole, one act at a time; the emancipation of the libretto from traditional models; and the use of symphonic motifs. They were the obvious basis for the artistic shaping of *Tristan.* Nonetheless, Wagner's experiences in composing the first phase of the *Ring* and the requirements imposed by new material led to certain modifications in all three areas.

When Wagner proposed the idea of continuously composed dialogue opera in *Opera and Drama* (for which he refused to use the term *opera*), he insisted on a drastic reduction of ensemble singing and complete abandonment of the operatic chorus, requirements consistent with the parts of the *Ring* libretto written in 1851–52.

As far as ensemble singing is concerned, it is used even more sparingly in *Tristan* than in the *Ring*. Wagner confines it exclusively to the moments when two characters sing together and which, like the love duets in *Die Walküre*

Example 19

and *Siegfried,* count as one of the infrequent cases where it is necessary for the "greatest comprehensibility" of the action (see my discussion under "Opera and Drama").

In *Tristan,* however, Wagner revokes his demand for the abolition of the opera chorus, in that he assigns the ship's crew and Tristan's followers choral roles in the action. True, their involvement is limited to a few passages in the first act; nevertheless, the chorus has an important and striking role to play, reminding us that the background to the action is an affair of state, namely, Tristan's wooing of a bride on behalf of King Marke. The chorus is the backdrop for the shifting of the action to the inner, psychological plane in act 1; it is hard to think of any other device that would have allowed so vivid a contrast.

If one considers the metrical form of the text, which Wagner, with some justification, always regarded as anticipating the musical style of the composition, one first discovers that it retains that achievement of the *Ring* text which Wagner referred to as rhythmic verse: every verse stress corresponds to an emphasis in the meaning, so that the verse structure can be translated in a similar manner into musical declamation, as was shown earlier with an extract from the *Ring.* In addition, there are obviously some new features in the verses of *Tristan.* The most striking of these is the removal of alliteration from the central position it has enjoyed in *Opera and Drama* and the libretto of the *Ring.* Wagner continues to use it, but now in conjunction with end rhyme, which is again introduced on a large scale. In some cases a comprehensive linking of lines is established which uses neither alliteration nor end rhyme but depends on devices such as assonance, rhythm, and rhetorical figures. A brief example from act 1, scene 2, serves to illustrate the free alternation of different devices that can link the lines of the verse together:

> Mir erkoren,
> mir verloren,
> hehr und heil,
> kühn und feig—.
> Todgeweihtes Haupt!
> Todgeweihtes Herz!
>
> [Destined to be mine,
> lost to me,
> peerless and proud,
> brave and craven!
> Death-devoted head!
> Death-devoted heart!]

Lines 1 and 2 are linked by end rhyme, lines 5 and 6 by alliteration; line 3 is in itself an alliteration. Furthermore, the two lines in each of the three pairs are so closely parallel (in terms of rhythmic and syntactic analogy and word repetition) that the fact that lines 3 and 4 are linked only by assonance is scarcely noticeable.

The rhetorical device of parallelism plays a highly significant part in *Tristan* as a whole. To explain it, we must recall one of the most fundamental truths about the relationship between words and music in Wagner's works from the *Ring* onward, a truth taken so much for granted that it is easy to forget. Repetition of segments of the text, an extremely common means of fashioning musical form in the traditional aria (traces of it still remain in *Lohengrin*), no longer occurs. (The conspicuous absence of repetition has, of course, a great deal to do with Wagner's basic tenet that the text of an opera should be written so as to have the effect of dialogue.) This means that from the outset the text must be planned in such a way that it can accommodate the projected length of the music. This basic fact had already had a marked impact on the *Ring,* but it was only in *Tristan* that Wagner took this principle to its logical conclusion. The rhetorical figures of varying, intensifying, and antithetical repetition are present in the text in such profusion that they seem to anticipate the sequential style of the music. As an example of this, the lines at the start of the second scene of act 2 may be cited (the first part of the dialogue proper after the effusive introductory greeting). The key words, listed in the right-hand column of Table 5, are developed almost like musical motifs (shown by connecting lines). The entire section of text is permeated by antithesis (indicated in the diagram by facing arrows). This idea of opposites then serves as

Table 5   Parallelism in *Tristan*

Text (SSD VII, 37)		Key words
Isolde:	Wie lange fern!	lange ⟍ ⟋ fern
	Wie fern so lang!	fern ⟋ ⟍ lang
Tristan:	Wie weit so nah!	weit → ← nah
	So nah wie weit!	nah → ← weit
Isolde:	O Freundesfeindin,	Freundesfeindin
	böse Ferne!	→ ← Ferne
	O träger Zeiten	
	zögernde Länge!	Länge
Tristan:	O Weit' und Nähe,	Weit' → ← Nähe
	hart entzweite!	
	Holde Nähe,	Nähe ↓
	öde Weite!	Weite ↑
	. . . .	
Isolde:	Im Dunkel du,	Dunkel ↓
	im Lichte ich!	Licht ↑

a link between the opening twelve lines, which are homogeneous in content, and the continuation, which in turn introduces a new antithesis between darkness and light.

In these and similar parts of the text, where the question of end rhyme versus alliteration has become almost irrelevant, the art of transition stands out—that which Wagner, with reference to the music of *Tristan* in his famous letter to Mathilde Wesendonck of 29 October 1859, described as his "most delicate and profound art." That Wagner always wished to see this art appreciated fully "in the closest association with the poetic design" (ibid.) has its justification not only in the content of the text but also in its formal aspects.

When Wagner temporarily stopped work on the composition of the *Ring* in the summer of 1857 and started detailed work on *Tristan,* it was the second time that he had turned from an artistic enterprise of immense dimensions to one of more manageable proportions. A similar situation had occurred in 1840–41, when the extremely long "grand opera" *Rienzi* was followed by the "dramatic ballad" *Holländer.* Certainly such analogies must not be pushed too far; in this instance it should be noted that the absolute length of the works is not comparable, and that *Holländer* was not worked out in detail until after the completion of *Rienzi.* In contrast *Tristan* (like *Meistersinger* later) was interpolated into the tetralogy's process of development. Nevertheless, the parallels between the two situations are obvious and instructive. In both cases the change from the creation of wide-ranging connections to a more easily comprehensible conception was marked by a clear strengthening of internal musical cohesion.

In both cases, too, as one might expect, the text is the basis of this concentration of musical ideas. In *Holländer* Wagner could confine himself to the dramatization of an anecdotal story by Heinrich Heine, whereas the action of *Rienzi* had been spread over seven years. The process of concentration is hardly less in *Tristan.* If Wagner claimed to encompass nothing less than "the world's beginning and its end" (Wagner-Liszt, p. 267; SL 281) in the *Ring,* the essence of *Tristan* is that it is "the simplest, but most full-blooded musical conception" (Wagner-Liszt, p. 394; SL 324); the entire work is, "so to speak, just a love scene" (CT, 6 March 1870).

In *Holländer* the musical consequence of the concentration of the action was the emergence of the first signs of a unified set of themes permeating the entire work. In *Tristan* it was a way of composing which the composer himself described as symphonic. If one is to believe Wagner's later remarks, then the possibility of composing in a symphonic style was even a decisive factor in the conception of *Tristan.* In 1878 he explained to Cosima "his need at that time to push himself to the limit musically, since in the *Nibelungen* the requirements of the drama frequently forced him to restrict the musical expression" (CT, 1 October 1878). And later in that same year he said "he had felt the urge to express himself symphonically for once, and that led to *Tristan*" (CT, 11 December 1878).

For a musical-dramatic work to be described as symphonic, at least two conditions must be met. First, the orchestral part must have the decisive role in the musical continuation of long stretches of the work; and second, the thematic structure of the orchestral material must exhibit a considerable degree of stringency, which makes a restriction of thematic material necessary. For example, in the section "Nur einen sah ich, der sagte der Liebe ab" from Loge's narration in *Das Rheingold* (scene 2), the musical progress is entrusted to the orchestra, but, if one is to judge by the thematic structure, this section can scarcely be called symphonic; rather, it would be more appropriate to call it rhapsodic, for the rapidly changing orchestral motifs tell a story, the context of which can be understood only if we listen to what Loge is singing about. In contrast, it does not seem inappropriate to describe Isolde's Tantris narration (act 1, scene 3), which is based largely on a very limited number of motifs, as symphonic (for a detailed analysis, see Brown 1989).

   Another question must follow here: Does the symphonic aspect of *Tristan* consist only of a high degree of autonomy for the orchestral material, or is there in addition a special relationship to the forms of instrumental music, and especially to sonata form?

   If we consider act 1, scene 1 of *Tristan,* the following observations can be made. First, the thematic material of the orchestral part is dominated by two principal figures (Example 20 gives the "exposition" of theme a in 1 and its "development" in 2). Second, in terms of compositional technique a distinction can be made between tonally stable and modulatory sections as well as between passages that present themes and those that develop them. And third, the gravitational points of the harmonic structure of the scene are the principal tonic C minor and the relative major key of E flat.

   All three attributes are features of sonata form, although they are not used here in a way that would create such a form. For one thing, it is scarcely possible to decide which of the themes is to be regarded as the first subject. Also, one of the themes is presented for the first time in the scene itself (theme

Theme a

Example 20a

Theme b

Example 20b

a), whereas the other is taken from the instrumental introduction. And finally, after a short expositionlike passage, the remaining and considerably larger part of the scene is devoted to a process of development, so the recapitulation essential to the tripartite sonata form is missing.

In fact the sonata elements do two things: in general terms they give the musical continuity tautness, concentration, and consistency; and together with the dialogue and the action they help to shape the form. An interpretation of their function in this light leads to a correction of several of Lorenz's analyses. Lorenz says that the first scene of act 1 has the form of a "consummate arch" (Lorenz II, 30ff.). The sections of this arch are measures 33–55 ("Blaue Streifen") and 117–170 ("O weh! Ach! Ach! des Übels"). The two passages are meant to correspond as songs of Brangänge in E-flat major, whereas in actual fact their unrelatedness has to be masked by the rubric "symmetry of contrast." The course of the scene may be ordered more sensibly when one realizes that Brangänge's short introductory speech is part of the exposition, whereas the second speech, like Isolde's outburst which precedes it, is developmental in nature and thus becomes an almost equally important response. The sonata *elements,* dissociated from one another, do not constitute sonata *form;* but they have become the building blocks of a genuinely musical and dramatic formal process.

Of all the musical parameters of the *Tristan* style, its harmony has always been considered particularly advanced. If the characteristic elements of the *Tristan* harmonic idiom are considered on their own—the exploitation of sounds that are enharmonically ambiguous, the blurring of tonality by means of chromatic chord progressions, the use of modulating sequences—it can be clearly seen that none makes its first appearance in *Tristan.* Used in a cumulative and emphatic way, however, they add up to a harmonic style of striking novelty.

Nothing could demonstrate this more clearly than the beginning of the work, with its harmonic turns which have long puzzled analysts, who usually focus on the so-called Tristan chord (the name chord in this context is not quite correct). An exact citation of this beginning (see Example 21) is necessary for an analysis. Given the context and its cadencing effect, the first four-note (Tristan) chord must be regarded as a suspension. Its top note, g♯', resolves to a', so that at the end of the second measure a chord built of thirds and fourths results. Depending on the theorist's point of view, this chord can be regarded as an altered version of either a subdominant or a double dominant chord. Measure 3, after the resolution of a further suspension (a♯' to b'), brings a relatively stable dominant seventh chord in the tonic key A minor. Even at its initial appearance here, the first chord establishes an identity of its own in that it remains unresolved within one of the instrumental groups (upper two staves of Example 21). Thereby it is made clear that this sound must be heard as an entity in its own right. At the same time we are also being prepared for its use in other contexts (for example in the first scene of act 1; see Example 20b). Discussion about the chord's "real" significance is misleading, for its

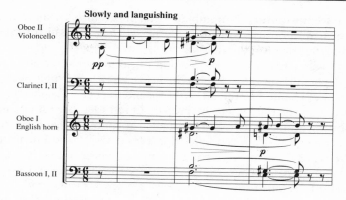

Example 21

expressive power lies precisely in the fact that it can take on many possible meanings.

Not only has the opening phrase of the *Tristan* prelude spawned countless analyses, but it has also played a prominent part (usually as a quotation) in the way composers have reacted to Wagner. (It is well known that Wagner himself was the first to quote *Tristan,* in the third act of *Meistersinger.*) Claude Debussy cites the melodic opening motif in *Golliwogg's Cakewalk,* the final piece in his piano suite *Children's Corner,* appending the sarcastic direction "avec une grande émotion." Conversely, Arnold Schoenberg's citation of the same motif in *Verklärte Nacht* is intended as an *hommage à Wagner.* The most profound citation, however, is in the final movement of Alban Berg's *Lyric Suite* for string quartet. Here the opening phrase, in a four-part version, is integrated within the musical context of the twelve-tone work in such a manner that it may be explained, as Berg said himself, in terms of a strict adherence to the twelve-tone row. The citation is not only an expression of admiration for Wagner's *Tristan* as a harbinger of the new music of the twentieth century, but also part of a secret program with references to Berg's love for Hanna Fuchs-Robettin, the sister of Franz Werfel (Perle 1977).

Die Meistersinger von Nürnberg

When Wagner decided, in the autumn of 1861, to write and compose *Die Meistersinger,* he was not turning to new material but reverting to a project dating from his Dresden period. That he should take up this plan again is surprising, however.

In the first place, Wagner had given his draft of 1845 to Mathilde Wesendonck in Zurich, from which one can conclude that he had jettisoned the subject from his future creative plans. This distancing from the *Meistersinger* material was logical at the time, for how could Wagner find a use for a piece in which sixteenth-century Nuremberg is far more than an incidental backdrop after he had rigorously argued in *Opera and Drama* that historical subjects are inappropriate for music drama?

Second, it was actually the continuation of the *Ring* composition that was on Wagner's agenda in 1861, from which his work on *Tristan* was to have been only a brief respite. In fact, after *Tristan* and the Paris *Tannhäuser,* Wagner again started work on the *Nibelungen* project. On 17 October 1861 he informed Franz Schott, whom Wagner had persuaded to publish the *Ring,* that "the entire project could easily be completed in two years" (Schott-Briefe, p. 20).

Soon afterward he must have had a change of mind, for in his next letter to Schott, dated 30 October 1861, Wagner wrote that he did not for the moment want to return to his great *Nibelungen* work but instead "to await a period of external successes" (Schott-Briefe, p. 23). Instead, his next plan would be "an easier, less demanding, and therefore more quickly completed work," namely *Meistersinger,* which he promised "to deliver finished and ready for performance by next winter" (ibid. pp. 23ff.). Luckily for Wagner (and probably also for his publishing house) Schott could not foresee that one year would turn into six; he accepted the offer.

As for the reasons behind this sudden change of heart, we must resort to speculation, for Wagner's autobiographical remarks are either vague or inscrutable. By way of comparison, one may look back to 1845, when, for the first time, Wagner's two "singer operas" stood side by side. Shortly after completing *Tannhäuser,* Wagner had written the first draft of the comic opera *Meistersinger,* a work that "could follow as a richly textured Satyr play" (SSD IV, 284). Similarly, in 1861, after writing the revised Paris version of *Tannhäuser,* Wagner drew up a plan for *Meistersinger* that was in keeping with his "present mood," which called for "cheering up and the occupation with something lighter" (Schott-Briefe, p. 23). In *My Life,* Wagner transfers the decision to write *Die Meistersinger* from 1845 to November 1861, a time he spent in Venice with Otto and Mathilde Wesendonck; the decisive impulse, according to this version, came from his contemplation of Titian's *Assunta* (Assumption of the Virgin), which "made a most exalting impression" on him. The composer felt within him his "old creative powers suddenly awakening . . . with almost their original primordial power" (ML 667). (The meaning of his attributing this composition to a specific event has been much discussed in German literary studies of Wagner; see Wapnewski 1978b, pp. 89ff.; Borchmeyer 1982, p. 282; Schubert 1983, pp. 212ff., especially pp. 235ff.)

Work on the libretto was soon under way, and by 19 November Wagner was able to send Schott the new prose draft, which had undergone considerable changes from the original draft of 1845; in January 1862 the libretto was complete. The musical composition, by contrast, initially took an unexpectedly long time: he began work with the prelude in the spring of 1862, but it was not until March 1866 that he was able to finish the score of act 1.

Work on the next two acts progressed more rapidly, and by 24 October 1867 the score of the entire work was finished.

The faltering progress of his work on act 1 can undoubtedly be ascribed largely to the circumstances of Wagner's life during those years, circumstances which often forced him to interrupt his work. But aside from this, one must not overlook the difficulties caused by the need to discover an appropriate musical style for a genre with which Wagner had no experience. Telling evidence of his initial uncertainty in this respect is provided by an early version of Walther's Prize Song (Example 22) that is sketched in a letter to Mathilde Wesendonck of 12 March 1862. Wagner's comment on this sketch was: "Listen to how simple it sounds." Later he obviously judged this kind of simplicity as lacking in distinctiveness and replaced this first attempt with a completely new version of text and music. Wagner had at first been inclined to equate lightness of musical tone with ease of creation (see the letter to Schott of 30 October 1861), but he soon realized that the appropriate tone for the musical comedy could be achieved only by careful reflection on how it was to be composed. This realization is echoed in the letter of 9 June 1862: "But it also torments me to be pressured in my work: the way I am working now, I cannot work quickly."

In the year after the completion of *Tristan*, Wagner wrote to Mathilde Wesendonck on 2 May 1860: "In a certain very deep sense which only the World Spirit can understand, I can now only repeat myself in new works: I can reveal no new essence of my nature." Even in view of his later works, Wagner never retracted these astonishing words; in fact he even repeated them in March 1879, when the draft of *Parsifal* was nearly complete: "In fact, he [Wagner] says, he has produced nothing new since *Tristan,* whereupon I observe that even from a technical point of view *Die Meistersinger, Siegfried,* and *Götterdämmerung* contain new ideas. But what he meant was that there had been no need for him to write a single note more; he could just have said, 'Do it as I do.' So he thinks!" (CT, 26 March 1879).

Cosima's tone of disapproval is understandable: she was reluctant to accept that the work of two decades, including the nearly completed Parsifal, should be degraded as mere recapitulation of earlier work. And that *Meistersinger,* act 3 of *Siegfried, Götterdämmerung,* and *Parsifal* are more than just stylistic recapitulation cannot seriously be disputed.

Fern—— mei-ner Ju-gend gold-nen To-ren zog—— ich einst aus—— in Be-
trach-tung ganz ver-lo-ren:

Example 22

But the concept of musical novelty is complex. Wagner's assertion was right insofar as he did not compose anything "new," in the sense of avant-garde, after *Tristan*. *Tristan* remained the spearhead of Wagner's work as a musical avant-gardist. After *Tristan,* the new was no longer achieved by compositional means but rather by the stylistic reorganization of what was already available.

In the Lilac monologue of act 2, Wagner provides a formulation of how this type of novelty in *Meistersinger* is to be understood: "It sounded so old but nevertheless was new." The "old sound" can in fact serve as a generic term for a series of stylizations, all of which are called forth by the subject of the work.

And here it must be considered not only that the subject matter is historical but especially that it is musical. Music is a sustaining element of the action, and within the very precise historical context of master song, which the *Riemann Musiklexikon* defines as "the art of singing ordered in guilds of bourgeois singing schools in German cities of the fifteenth and sixteenth centuries" (Sachteil 1967, p. 552).

For creating the historical and musical ambience of *Die Meistersinger* Wagner developed a musical style that is in no sense a copy of any earlier style. (That kind of approach would have been fundamentally alien to Wagner; the derivation of the guild motif from a historical Meistersinger melody is a stylistically insignificant triviality.) Historical music is present only insofar as certain elements of the old style are used in a manner of free association; the result is an idiom which had never before existed—no more than the supposed "Lydian mode" of Beethoven's "Hymn of Thanksgiving to the Divinity, from a Convalescent" in the op. 132 string quartet.

Three elements may be regarded as focal points of this historical stylization: diatonicism, the chorale, and counterpoint. Diatonic melody is highlighted in symbolic fashion right at the beginning of the prelude (Example 23). It has the effect of a motto, similar to the chromaticism at the beginning of the prelude to *Tristan*. This excerpt also illustrates the strange ambiguity of the diatonicism in *Meistersinger*. The upper voice begins with a leap of the fundamental fourth from c″ to g′ and then passes equally succinctly through the diatonic octave from e′ to e″. This is given a bass line which is also a simple diatonic structure: a descending scale interrupted by an octave leap in the second measure. But these simple outer parts clash with one another. From the second beat of the second measure to the first beat of the third measure

Example 23

the dissonant notes a and g sound against each other and require harmonic resolution. This is accomplished through the chromatic c♯′, which seems to justify the dissonant interval of a–g in that it integrates it within a dominant seventh chord on a. The anticipated resolution to D minor does not take place, however. Instead, the continuation reinforces the basic key of C major within the boundaries of its diatonic scale. Diatonicism appears—and this is characteristic of the *Meistersinger* style—as an artificially simple construct extracted from the possibilities of the chromatic *Tristan* style. Carl Dahlhaus has described it as a diatonicism that is somehow "dreamlike" (Dahlhaus 1979, p. 75).

It seems likely that Wagner received the stimulus for such a combination of chromaticism and diatonicism from Bach's four-voiced chorale movements, of which Wagner certainly knew at least those in the *St. Matthew Passion.*

The term *chorale* summarizes the second main element of the musical style of *Meistersinger*. In Wagner's earlier works chorales in the wider sense of the word were occasionally prominent: one need only think of the Pilgrims' Choruses in *Tannhäuser,* the choralelike tone of the *Lohengrin* prelude, and the prayers in the same work. In *Meistersinger* Wagner now writes movements whose direct relation to the historical model of choral harmonizations in the manner of Bach is unmistakable. The chorales in *Die Meistersinger* are not significant in number, but they appear in prominent places in the work. The first act opens with a chorale sung by the congregation of St. Catherine's church in Nuremberg, and no less effectively placed is the "Wach auf" Chorale in the Festival Meadow scene, which, in addition, is cited in advance in the instrumental prelude to act 3. (It is significant to the development of the musical idiom of *Meistersinger* that this chorale was one of its earliest ideas.) The choralelike passages in *Meistersinger* are not quotations; but they can be shown to be conscious and carefully considered backward glances similar to those in the diatonicism of the work.

Let us now consider the third focal point of historicizing stylization, that of counterpoint. We may recall that a highly developed contrapuntal technique is already to be found in *Tristan,* both in the independent leading of subsidiary voices and in the application of thematic combinations, whose high point is probably found in the development of the "mournful melody" (*traurige Weise*) in act 3. This technique in *Tristan* is a refinement of a technique which may be traced back to the first phase of Wagner's work on the music of the *Ring.* (Example 17 provides an illustration from act 2 of *Die Walküre.*) The difference between this technique and the contrapuntal technique of *Meistersinger* could be explained as follows: passages such as the example from *Walküre* or the combination in *Tristan* of the mournful melody with the motif of day allow counterpoint to be overlooked as a mere technical device to a large extent. Their purpose is to heighten the musical–dramatic meaning, and the means to this end is the combination of musical motifs as semantic elements. Of course, the use of counterpoint in *Meistersinger* is also justified in dramatic terms. But since art is a central element of the plot here, counterpoint—as art—has a dramatically legitimate place in the musical technique. The basic form of counterpoint in *Meistersinger* may be seen in the "craftsmanlike" technique, which, for instance, dominates the opening section of the prelude. This perspective on the one hand elucidates the sense of the parodistic counterpoint that typifies the pedantic, fossilized art epitomized in the drama by Beckmesser; on the other hand, craftsmanlike technique can undergo a sublimation and become meditative counterpoint, as in the prelude to act 3, where it symbolizes cerebral artistry. Ludwig Finscher, whose distinctions between craftsmanlike, parodistic, and meditative counterpoint I have noted (Finscher 1970), refers additionally to a category of affective counterpoint, which, however, is more a direct legacy of the *Tristan* style than a characteristic element of *Die Meistersinger*.

Another interesting link to the chorale may be seen in the final part of act 2, the so-called fight scene. According to Finscher's classification, this belongs to the parodistic sphere. Here the rhythmically augmented serenade by Beckmesser, "Den Tag seh' ich erscheinen," is implemented like a cantus firmus. It is not inconceivable that Bach's organ chorales, with their pedal cantus firmus, provided some inspiration here. If one sought a particular work, the most likely possibility might be the *Fantasia super "Komm heiliger Geist, Herre Gott"* (BWV 651), published in 1847 in volume 7 of the Peters edition of Bach's organ works. It is also possible, however, that Wagner became familiar with this genre much earlier, during his studies with Weinlig.

In addition to the elements of diatonicism, chorale, and counterpoint, there is one further stylization device: the reference to the Meistersingers' song, the rules of which are recited by Kothner in act 1 and interpreted by Sachs in act 3. The song is a central component of the plot; its success or failure is decisive for the outcome of the drama. That the invention and performance of songs should be part of the plot is itself enough to ensure that the song plays an important role in this composition. But in addition, the song as a principle of stylization embraces the musical form in various ways; one may go so far as to regard the entire three-act structure as being analogous to the bar form AA′B (Lorenz III, 8ff.).

The use of the "interrupted song," which had already been tested in *Holländer*, assumes tremendous significance here as an element for providing cohesion to large sections of the opera. The most wide-ranging example is Walther's Trial Song in the first act. The song itself stretches over 162 measures; but, together with the interpolated discussion by the masters about what they have just heard, it spans 376 measures. The principle of the interrupted song is used most artfully in the sixth and seventh scenes of act 2, as we can see in Table 6. (The numbers on the left refer to the measures at which each relevant section begins. Sections which contain neither songs nor material derived from them are enclosed in brackets.)

The symphonic structures which Wagner had developed in *Tristan* have a somewhat diminished importance in *Die Meistersinger,* but they have not by

Table 6   The interrupted song in *Die Meistersinger*, act 2

scene 6

850	[Conclusion of dialogue section from previous scene; orchestra: chordal accompaniment, tuning of Beckmesser's lute, Cobbler motif]
878	Cobbler's Song, verse 1, with comments by Eva and Walther
914	[Interruption of song by Sachs–Beckmesser dialogue]
923	Cobbler's Song, verse 2, with comments by Eva and Walther
959	[Renewed interruption of song by Beckmesser's objection to Sachs's singing]
976	Cobbler's Song, verse 3, with comments by Beckmesser; "Wahn" motif as contrapuntal contrasting voice (SSD XII, 348)
1012	Instrumental citation from Cobbler's Song together with "Wahn" motif, plus Eva–Walther dialogue and Beckmesser's remarks
1023	[Discussion between Sachs and Beckmesser leading to an agreement]
1202	[Night Watchman's Horn and Midsummer Night theme]
1217	Beckmesser attempts to begin his serenade, is disturbed by Sachs
1243	Beckmesser's Serenade, verse 1
1269	[Beckmesser's complaint]
1277	Beckmesser's Serenade, verse 2 (without fermata, and with richer orchestral accompaniment)
1303	[Sachs: "Seid ihr nun fertig?" (see act 1, m. 1795)]
1313	Beckmesser's Serenade, verse 3 (without pauses, breathless), plus Sachs's little "Merker" motto, David's entrance, neighbors' complaint about nocturnal disturbance

scene 7

1357	Fight scene; constructive elements: (1) fuguelike development of Fight motif; (2) cantus firmus–like quotations of parts of Beckmesser's Serenade in bass
1439	Night Watchman's Song with horn call, framed by Midsummer Night theme

any means been superseded. At times one can even speak of a permeation by osmosis of the song principle and the symphonic principle—a trait of the *Meistersinger* music which clearly exerted a powerful influence on Gustav Mahler's symphonic ideas.

Sachs's Lilac monologue in act 2, together with the motivic development which leads to it, provides an impressive example of the interweaving of songlike and symphonic elements. The text of the monologue is a reflection of Walther's Trial Song in act 1. If one is seeking an adequate musical technique for a reflective text, the technique of symphonic development seems to be a natural choice (although, as the "Wahn" monologue in act 3 demonstrates, it is not the only possibility). In any event, symphonic development technique characterizes the core of the Lilac monologue (mm. 315–349). Its thematic point of departure is a phrase that goes back to the opera's prelude. It is first encountered in the development in the E major section of the prelude (mm. 104ff.; see Example 24a) and then again in the melody of the Stollen (section a) of Walther's Trial Song (mm. 1718ff.; see Example 24b and, respectively, the second Stollen). After this the motif reappears in the Abgesang (section b) of the Trial Song (mm. 2042ff., "Es schwillt das Herz vor süßem Schmerz"). What is novel here is, first, the technique by which the motif is worked out over twelve measures, and second, the harmonization of the melody's leading tone with a five-note chord. As Sachs stands alone down-

Example 24a

Example 24b

Example 24c

stage at the end of act 1, it is in this harmonization that the motif imprints itself on his mind as the essence of Walther's song (Example 24c).

That a motif should be emphasized and, to a certain extent, worked out in Walther's Trial Song introduces an unsonglike element into the piece. In the Lilac monologue, by contrast, the reintroduction of this motif recalls the song as a whole. In the monologue the elaboration is lifted onto another plane, particularly through an expansive modulatory process, which—partly in dominant-to-tonic progressions, partly in sequences of thirds—leads through the keys of F–B flat–D flat–E–A–C–F major. The point of departure of the development process is the instrumental citation of the principal motif, asserted by Sachs's formulation of the problem: "And yet I can't be rid of it: I feel it—and can't understand it." At the end of the motivic-modulatory elaboration, the same motif is heard again in the opening tonality of F major, now no longer purely instrumental but described in Sachs's newly discovered formula for the source of Walther's artistry: "Spring's command, sweet need" (Sachs takes up this point in act 3 when he explains to Walther the difference between a "lovely song" and a "Meistersong.") The remainder of the text is a résumé, and the music flows into a simple period of eight measures with a folklike melody.

The song principle and the symphonic principle—which are demonstrated by the Lilac monologue, considered in the light of its previous history within the work—may be designated, and are distinguishable, as basic principles of compositional technique. Clear distinctions, however, cannot be made in sections where one or the other of these techniques is absolutely dominant. Their complex interaction has a lot to do with those same "laws of separation and combination laid down by the details and performance of the dramatic action" of which Wagner later wrote in *On the Application of Music to the Drama* (SSD X, 185) in a discussion of the role of fundamental themes in the music drama. In this sense the Lilac monologue is an object lesson in the subject of that essay.

Parsifal

When Wagner began working out the text and music of *Parsifal* in 1877, the year after the first Bayreuth Festival, he returned to his first prose draft of 1865. This in turn was the result of a preoccupation with the subject of Parsifal, which, in terms of his familiarity with the material, dates back to the 1840s and resulted in a first working plan in 1857.

There are considerable gaps in our knowledge of the work's prehistory. Thus, we can only speculate about the precise nature of the so-called Good Friday inspiration of 1857 (ML 547; see CT, 22 April 1879; and see also Chapter 1 of this volume), for Wagner's accounts all date from a later time. The music sheet with "Wo find ich dich, du heil'ger Gral" (SW 30, 13), which probably belongs in the context of an attempt to include Parsifal in act 3 of *Tristan* (ML 511), cannot be dated with any certainty. It is only from 1858 on that we have datable evidence of Wagner's intellectual efforts with his own conception of *Parsifal,* which then found a provisional result in the prose draft of 1865.

Neither is there any existing evidence of connections between preliminary work on the text and the musical ideas. The earliest extant musical sketch is for "Komm, holder Knabe" (SW 30, 21). This, however, is dated 9 February 1876, which places it shortly before the definitive elaboration of the work.

As for the elaboration itself, we have more precise information about *Parsifal* than about any of Wagner's other works. Both the writing of the libretto (March and April 1877) and the composition (September 1877 to January 1882) occurred in a period whose events and conversations Cosima Wagner recorded in meticulous detail in her diaries. These entries not only contain copious information on the chronology of *Parsifal,* but in addition report countless remarks by Wagner about his intentions and the attendant problems.

Frequently the diaries mention that the composer did not accomplish the entire work effortlessly. One morning Wagner was able to progress only some eight measures, but they "are exquisite, particularly the last two" (CT, 24 November 1878). Shortly afterward Wagner remarked to Cosima: "Sometimes it is just a few bars which hold one up terribly, till one can introduce the key one needs in such a way that it is not noticeable" (CT, 29 November 1878). Later she reports that "he has completed six measures, but they are very significant ones" (CT, 9 January 1879). Much conscious effort was devoted to working out the composition's technical details. One must be careful, Wagner remarks, "not to let oneself be led astray by the melodies" (CT, 14 December 1877). In another instance he struggled to find the appropriate tonality for a particular passage (CT, 9 June 1878). In many cases a passage already written would fall victim to Wagner's subsequent self-criticism. Cosima notes at one point that the revision of a passage required an entire morning (CT, 27 January 1879); on another occasion Wagner reports that "he has crossed out everything he did yesterday" (21 September 1878).

Many of the remarks noted by Cosima refer to passages which can be identified. As a whole, the diaries provide a documentation of the psychology of creation surrounding the conception of *Parsifal,* a topic that still awaits a comprehensive evaluation in connection with the written stages of the work's text.

The musical–dramatic structure of *Parsifal* does not contain any fundamentally new elements, but it does follow up the achievements of the *Ring* and *Tristan.* But *Parsifal* again demonstrates the flexibility of Wagner's conception. Important characteristics unique to the work can be understood in terms of fundamental musical–dramatic decisions. We should note three points in particular.

First, the only structural division of the work expressly indicated by Wagner is that of three acts. The subdivision into scenes that is found in earlier scores is dropped in the final version. A division into scenes could have been made without difficulty in at least two instances: in act 1 at Parsifal's intervention in the action (m. 742); and in act 2 at the rapid changeover to the Enchanted Garden (m. 427). What prompted Wagner in the first case to refrain from indicating any scene changes as such probably has to do with the transformations in acts 1 and 3 in which "time becomes space"; for transformation here is not merely a technical necessity but a dramatic event in its own right, with music of commensurate importance. As for act 2, it also contains a scene change which proceeds in stages, for it can scarcely be determined whether the great scene between Parsifal and Kundry begins with the shout "Parsifal!" (m. 739) or with the dialogue after the disappearance of the maidens (m. 781). Moreover, this scene only acquires a clear-cut musical profile in measure 827, with the *Herzeleide* (Heart-in-sorrow) narration. The establishment of scene divisions in act 3 would also have proved difficult. If the onstage presence of characters is taken as a criterion for defining a scene, it would seem natural to begin a second scene with Parsifal's entrance (m. 158); but in the musical development this break carries only a slight emphasis, in keeping with a dramatic structure in which the significance of Parsifal's entrance is only gradually revealed. The "art of transition," which Wagner described in 1859 with respect to a single scene (see my discussion of *Tristan*) is expanded in *Parsifal* into a means of shaping connections that range beyond the confines of a single scene.

A second point is that, according to Wagner's theory in *Opera and Drama,* music drama, like spoken drama, is based on dialogue; ensembles and choruses, with rare exceptions, have no place in it (see my discussion earlier in this essay). What Wagner meant by the "justified cases necessary for the highest understanding" (SSD IV, 162) may be gathered from those sections of the *Ring* written after 1851 and from *Tristan*. Insofar as ensembles occur, the characters therein are not individualized, or not fully individualized (that is, they are Rhine Maidens or Valkyries), or else they are pairs of lovers. The configuration of characters in *Parsifal* does not allow for ensemble singing. As a result, *Parsifal* is Wagner's sole music drama (if we discount the four-voice setting of the motif "Durch Mitleid wissend" for four squires in act 1) which is completely without ensemble singing.

The third point is that all three acts of *Parsifal* contain chorus scenes—in acts 1 and 2 quite extensive ones. In the Grail Hall sections of the first and third acts we hear the male chorus of the Grail Knights, supplemented on occasion by the higher voices of the boys. The chorus scene of the second act is entrusted to the Flower Maidens, comprising six soloists and two choir groups of soprano voices. The chorus scenes of acts 1 and 2 are at least decisive elements of the action; in musical terms they belong to the most impressive material of the entire work. Even in *Tristan* and *Meistersinger* Wagner broke his own rule from *Opera and Drama* banning the chorus; in *Parsifal* the chorus was decisively rehabilitated as a component of the music drama.

The text of *Parsifal* is, in its use of language, one of the most varied of

Wagner's libretti. His formal freedom is doubtless based on his previous experience of setting to music the most diversely structured texts *(Ring, Tristan, Meistersinger)*. To what extent the text of *Parsifal* was predetermined by musical conceptions is difficult to say. It is likely that Wagner the librettist worked to a large degree independently of Wagner the composer, justifiably convinced that the latter would be equal to any challenge.

In the libretto of *Parsifal,* Wagner avails himself of virtually every formal element used in the preceding works. But here the individual elements have become independent of the connection to a system which previously governed them (blank verse and five-stress iambics; alliteration and two- to three-stress verse with variable unaccented syllables).

Let us consider a few technical details of the verse form. The individual lines of the verses have between two and five accents. The rhythm of the verse usually alternates between iambic and trochaic; on occasion, however, the freely alternating unaccented syllables familiar from the *Ring* also occur. The lines are occasionally linked by end rhymes or alliteration, but for the most part they remain without any rhyme.

An example of the application of different metrical principles in a short space, and the translation of verse form into musical declamation, may be seen in Example 25, which contains a five-line excerpt from Gurnemanz's speech in the opening part of act 1. (Line endings in the text are indicated by a slash.) In line 1 we have a choice: either it can be regarded in isolation, or it can be linked to line 2 through the word *tragen,* which is common to both. Lines 2 and 3 are linked by end rhyme; and lines 4 and 5 are related to each other first by the alliteration between *siegreich* and *Siechtum,* and then by the rhetorical antithesis of *Herrn* and *Knecht.*

When setting this section (it is in $\frac{6}{4}$ time) Wagner used a recitativelike declamation in verse 1, which is animated at the end by the agonizing accented suspension. Lines 2 and 3 are in an expressive arioso style, in which the rhymes of the text also correspond musically. In the last two lines the vocal line and the simultaneously sounding orchestral motifs are in unison (this occurs more frequently in *Parsifal* than in the earlier works). In line 4 this is

Example 25

the "Titural variant of the Faith motif" (Lorenz IV, 26); and the last line is sung to the "Suffering motif of the Love Feast theme" (see mm. 2–3 of the prelude). The expression of this sequence of motifs is based not solely—or perhaps not even primarily—on the symbolic content of the motifs (which at this early stage of the work is only vaguely defined in the listener's mind); more fundamental is the harmonic turn from D-flat major in the first motif to E minor in the second.

Complementing the preceding example, whose expressivo is rich in nuances but on the whole somewhat restrained, is a passage in which the text declamation is heightened into a veritable psychological image of the character. It is a passage from the dialogue at the beginning of act 2, in which Klingsor exerts his magical power over a reluctant Kundry in order to make her into Parsifal's seductress. To Klingsor's speech (Example 26) Kundry replies (Example 27).

Example 26

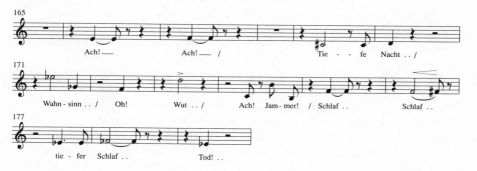

Example 27

The formal adjustment of these text parts is basically confined to limiting the length of the lines: Klingsor's speech comprises lines with three and four accents, whereas Kundry's speech consists of lines with two or three accents (in fact they disintegrate into single words). The lines are not linked either by end rhyme or by alliteration. The disposition of unaccented syllables is variable. Klingsor's speech tends toward a dactylic pattern, whereas, conversely, Kundry's speech is marked by the elision of unaccented syllables; the former gives the lines a powerful impetus, the latter paralyzes their movement.

What determines the initial musical impression evoked by this dialogue section is primarily the contrast between the two speeches, which are relatively homogeneous in themselves. Klingsor's biting and scornful speech is expressed musically in the rapid tempo of its delivery, the variety of tone length, the insertion of brief pauses, and the agility of intervallic usage. But Kundry's speech develops from an extremely realistic imitation of a way of speaking which is described in the stage directions as "uneven and disjointed, as if attempting to regain the power of speech."

Despite their relative uniformity, both speeches are differentiated in themselves. The wealth of nuances which the composer had in mind is suggested by informative evidence in Wagner's rehearsal instructions of 1882, which Heinrich Porges and Julius Kniese noted in their piano scores (see SW 30, 191). In measure 157 there must be "no accent" on "Vieh"; in measure 158 "the tone is to be accentuated with scorn, quite devilishly"; for measure 160 the note says, "Poco ritenuto, but should not become too slow"; the phrase "den reinen Hüter" in measure 161 is to be sung "more scornfully"; in the following phrase ("des Grales") the "seventh is to be sung especially scornfully"; and Wagner remarks of Klingsor's final phrase: "The triplets very even, one like the other; they represent the naturalness of the speech." Wagner gave particular instructions for the stammering speech of Kundry: the word "Wahnsinn" (m. 171) should be "somewhat more accented"; "Wut" (m. 173) enunciated "with an insistent accent"; "Schlaf" (m. 176) "still somewhat toneless"; and "Tod" (m. 179) "not short."

In his 1882 review of *Parsifal,* Eduard Hanslick wrote: "Those who have not been informed by Wagner's close friends would be bound to guess for themselves that generally he wrote the orchestral accompaniment first and then sketched the vocal parts above this. The symphonic, autonomous orchestral part is the coherent and unifying whole; whatever is sung to this are fragments, whose meaning lies in the words, not the music" (Csampai-Holland 1984, p. 149). This is correct insofar as the vocal melody did not obtain its concrete shape without the simultaneously sounding web of orchestral motifs (for this reason a complete analysis of the cited passage would have to include the instrumental components). As far as the genesis of Wagner's scores is concerned, today we know that Hanslick was misinformed. As the conclusion to his investigation of the sketches to *Tristan,* Robert Bailey could state: "The vocal part was in fact the generating element of the entire texture, no matter how elaborate or complicated it later became" (Bailey 1972, p. 241). This philological insight can certainly also be applied to *Parsifal*. If one combines this with Wagner's performance instructions, then there can be no doubt that the vocal parts of *Parsifal* are a relatively autonomous layer of the total artistic structure. It is not surprising that its astonishing novelty caused difficulties for performers and critics alike. If Adorno could say that the handling of dissonance in the passage "Amfortas! the wound!" in act 2 (mm. 994ff.) is poised on "the threshold of atonality" (Adorno 1981, p. 67), then it can be stated analogously of passages such as those cited here that in their declamatory style they belong to the early history of musical expressionism.

The motivic web which permeates the orchestral movement of *Parsifal* probably constitutes, with its wealth of nuances and variants, its ramifications and transitions, the pinnacle of artifice in Wagner's work. This can be demonstrated by the changes in one thematic figure. For this purpose a theme whose adaptability is not obvious at first sight is especially suitable: the prophecy given to Amfortas, "Durch Mitleid wissend, der reine Tor" ("Made wise through pity, the blameless fool"), abbreviated in the analytical literature as the theme of the Pure Fool. Example 28 states the theme at its first complete presentation (at the end of Gurnemanz's narration in act 1). It is a mantric formula, similar to the motif of the Forbidden Question in *Lohengrin,* with which the Pure Fool theme also shares the melodic element of the falling fifth. Another similarity with the motif of the Forbidden Question is that in general only the first half is cited. The Pure Fool theme is heard only once again in its complete form, namely in the hall of the Grail in act 1, as encouragement

Example 28

to Amfortas and as an exhortation to continue the liturgy of the Grail (mm. 1404ff.). The squires, to whom Gurnemanz communicates this promise at the conclusion of his narration, begin to repeat it (mm. 737ff.), but they are hindered by the increasingly perceptible cries of dismay at the killing of the swan (this is a device which did not occur to Wagner until he was working on the composition; see CT, 25 November 1877).

Before its actual exposition by Gurnemanz (see Example 28), the theme has been heard several times, but without its meanings being defined precisely; it is the kind of appearance of a leitmotif which Wagner described in *Opera and Drama* as a "presentiment" (SSD IV, 186). To Gurnemanz's words "Toren wir, auf Lind'rung da zu hoffen, / wo einzig Heilung lindert" ("Fools we are, to hope for balm / where only healing will cure him"; act 1, mm. 179ff.), the orchestra plays the first half-phrase of the theme (part a) as a hint of an intellectual association, which the speaker links with what has been said. The words "Ihm hilft nur eines, / nur der Eine!" ("Only one thing can help him, / only one man!"; mm. 189ff.) that follow soon after are accompanied by the orchestra only with the first phrase of the theme [a1]. The expected continuation is not heard, just as Gurnemanz is not prepared to answer the question of who the "one man" might be. It is then Amfortas himself who speaks the words (which are split up into phrases [a1] and [a2] with which his healer has been identified for him (mm. 319ff.). Thereby a mediating phase between "presentiment" and "presence" is reached. The Pure Fool theme makes its presence felt to the full more than four hundred measures later (mm. 728ff.), when Gurnemanz explains the meaning of the promise in detail.

Up to this point in its development the theme has gradually been constructed from its phrases into the basic form. With the partial repetition by the squires, a first subtle transformation of the theme begins to emerge. The E-flat major chord on the word "Tor" (fool) seen in the context of the entire theme, is a Neapolitan sixth, with reference to D minor or D major. If only the first part of the theme is cited, then the original Neapolitan chord is freed for a change of harmonic function. Thus the E-flat major chord as subdominant of B-flat major mediates the transition to Parsifal's entrance scene (mm. 742ff.). At the end of act 1, the Neapolitan chord to "Tor" (now C major, m. 1658) becomes—even more surprisingly—the tonic. Here the basic tonality of the Pure Fool theme is B minor, and its remoteness from the principal tonality of the context, C major, could be interpreted as an expression of the distance separating the promise of salvation from the actual situation.

Of the subsequent transformations of the Pure Fool theme, two variants that distinguish themselves by virtue of their originality and profundity, without appearing in the least spectacular, are worth emphasizing.

First, the great seduction scene in act 2 is introduced by Kundry's shout "Parsifal!" (m. 739), which is the first time the eponymous hero's name is uttered in the entire work. The name is sung to a broken triad. When Kundry repeats the name, this broken triad is set to an orchestral anticipation (Example

29a) of a phrase from the "Herzeleide" theme (mm. 831ff.), so the triadic motif does not seem to require further explanation. Somewhat later, however, Kundry explains the name Parsifal (following Josef von Görres, Wagner derived the name from Arabic), and this at the same time provides the etymology of the triad (Example 29b).

Second, at the end of act 3, before Parsifal, as the new king, celebrates the Grail service, a combination of motifs, to the words "Nicht soll der mehr verschlossen sein" ("No more shall the shrine be sealed") is to be heard in the orchestra (Example 30). Following phrase a1 of the Pure Fool theme (horns), the beginning of the Love Feast theme from the opening of the prelude is heard, but its continuation is now reshaped so that at the same time the Pure Fool theme is supplemented by its phrase a2; this is followed by a four-

Example 29a

Example 29b

Example 30

measure unfolding of the opening motif of the Love Feast theme on its own. The concluding aphorism, "Erlösung dem Erlöser" (Redemption to the Redeemer), has thus been fully expressed musically by this combination of motifs before it is ever spoken.

Translated by Paul Knight and Horst Loeschmann

Biography and Reception:
Bayreuth, Performance,
Musical Influence

CHAPTER 19

The Bayreuth Festival and the Wagner Family

MANFRED EGER

The Bayreuth Festival

Only by examining the events which led up to the foundation of the Bayreuth Festival is it possible to understand what it is that makes this festival so distinctive and unique, and to appreciate not only its importance in terms of cultural history, but also the utopian boldness of the idea behind it, the stages in its realization, including its initial failure, and its founder's larger-than-life achievement. The history of the Bayreuth Festival goes back to Wagner's childhood, when he attended the Dresden Kreuzschule and his teacher Professor Sillig inspired in him an "ardent desire" to study the language, mythology, and history of ancient Greece. This bent was further encouraged by his uncle Dr. Adolf Wagner. His choice of Bayreuth was also influenced by a youthful experience in the form of a journey in 1835 which brought the twenty-two-year-old music director his first encounter with Bayreuth, "pleasantly illuminated in the evening sun" (ML 104). As a twenty-six-year-old conductor in Riga, he was struck by the leisured society which attended the local theater and inspired by the steeply rising orchestra stalls, the half-dark auditorium, and the sunken orchestra pit to develop his own ideas for a future theater. And in 1840, at the Paris Conservatoire, he learned how effective a sound wall could be in producing a surprising concentration and transfigured unity of orchestral sound. At the same time his antipathy toward the visible orchestra increased.

In Dresden two decisive impulses followed in the form of Wagner's confrontation with Germanic mythology on the one hand and Greek mythology on the other. Jacob Grimm's *German Mythology* was an exciting revelation for him, and led to a "complete rebirth" (ML 260). Wagner's renewed interest in the Greek dramatists resulted from his reading of a translation of Aeschylus and the *Didascalia,* both by Johann Gustav Droysen. Before his eyes he could see and sense "the intoxicating vision" of a day-long festival of Attic tragedy, a dramatic performance which—accompanied and borne along by the suggestive force of *melos*—became a celebration at which the gods themselves were present and in which the whole of the populace shared as participants. "My ideas about the significance of drama, and especially of the theater itself, were decisively moulded by these impressions" (ML 342–343). The sense of national consciousness that was roused by the Wars of Liberation (1813–1815) found expression in widespread attempts to reform the theater, attempts which culminated in 1848 in the demand that the court theaters be abolished and replaced by a national state theater. As court kapellmeister in Dresden, Wagner modified these aims in his *Plan for the Organization of a German National Theater for the Kingdom of Saxony* (1848). Among the ideas that he proposed here was that of transforming the theater from a place of mere entertainment to an artistic institution in which art could maintain sufficient dignity to command respect and ennoble people's taste and manners. Only a state subsidy, Wagner concluded, could ensure that commercial considerations would not play a part, and that the repertory and performances could be planned according to purely artistic criteria. The rejection of his proposals made it clear to Wagner that ideas such as his could be realized only in the context of a political revolution.

In October 1848 Wagner completed *The Nibelung Legend (Myth),* the first prose draft of the poem of the *Ring,* a work which is inextricably linked with the conception and history of the Bayreuth Festival. Beginning with the end of the work, he wrote the earliest version of *Siegfrieds Tod* (later retitled *Götterdämmerung*). In his essay *Art and Revolution,* written after his flight to Switzerland, he intensified his attacks on the contemporary opera industry, its cheap showmanship, and its empty virtuosity. As a counterpoise to all this he proposed the art of the Greeks, an art in which the deepest and most noble aspects of the popular consciousness had found expression. He lamented the decline of tragedy in general, since he regarded the genre as the great and unified "expression of a free and beautiful commonalty," and became convinced that "only a great revolution involving the whole of mankind . . . can create this work of art for us." The ideas propounded in these essays are part of a process of fermentation and clarification that also encompasses the poem *Siegfrieds Tod,* as well as its musical realization and subsequent performance. Both the drama and its staging made demands that were far in excess of all usual notions. Wagner was not aiming at a mere renaissance or imitation of the Greek model. Admittedly he made important elements of that model his own, elements that include the idea of myth as the intrinsic subject for drama, the unity of drama and music, and the character of a national festival; but he gave these elements a different context, and one that was suited to another time and place. In his essay *The Art-Work of the Future* he made even further claims for such a work, insisting that it should unite the individually fragmented arts and artist together with the audience and allow them to share in a common experience, in other words, a work of art for the community. In formulating these ideas Wagner was also backing up the claims that would be made for his later festival. As for the theater building of the future, he demanded that it should not serve any architectural end in itself, nor should it fulfill a need for luxury; rather it should be intended solely and exclusively to serve the production.

Wagner began the music of *Siegfrieds Tod* in 1850 but soon abandoned it, his first concern being to create the conditions that were necessary for staging the work. In a letter written from Zurich to Ernst Benedikt Kietz and dated 14 September 1850, Wagner first announced his plans for a festival performance of the work. It was the "boldest of all plans," he told Kietz: he would "have a theatre erected here on the spot, made of planks, . . . and give three performances—free, of course—one after the other in the space of a week, after which the theatre would then be demolished and the whole affair would be over and done with." Less than a week later, on 20 September 1850, he wrote to tell Theodor Uhlig that, in allocating tickets, he would give preference to young people, universities, and choral societies. After the performances he would tear down the theater and burn the score. "Well," he asked Uhlig, "does that strike you as suitably insane?"

In *Opera and Drama* Wagner elaborated the theoretical and aesthetic bases for his continuing work on the drama by defining the new relationship between poetry and music in the music drama, in addition to discussing the importance of myth and leitmotif. Instead of returning to the musical setting of *Siegfrieds Tod,* however, he sketched out the poem *Der junge Siegfried* (later renamed *Siegfried*) in order, as he told Uhlig on 10 May 1851, to spare his audiences a long recital of past events, and to "impart the important myth by means of action on stage." In much the same spirit he then prefaced *Siegfried* with *Die Walküre,* before finally adding *Das Rheingold* as a prelude to the whole.

A Communication to My Friends contains the first public announcement of the *Ring:* "At a festival fixed for that express purpose I plan to perform those three dramas together with the prelude." The title of the tetralogy—*Der Ring des Nibelungen*—first appears in a letter to Uhlig of 12 November 1851, where it is described as a *Bühnenfestspiel,* literally a "Stage Festival Play." To this Wagner adds a remark of a politically explosive nature: "A *performance* is something I can conceive of only *after the Revolution;* only the Revolution can offer me the artists and listeners I need. The coming Revolution must necessarily put an end to this whole *theatrical business* of ours: they must all perish, and will certainly do so, it is inevitable. Out of the ruins I shall then summon together what I need: I shall *then* find what I require. I shall then run up a theatre on the Rhine and send out invitations to a great dramatic festival: after a year's preparations I shall then perform my entire work within the space of *four days: with it* I shall then make clear to the men of the Revolution the *meaning* of that Revolution, in its noblest sense." At the same time Wagner was thinking about his future artists: "I want decent actors who can sing," he told Franziska Wagner on 21 March 1852.

The poem of the entire *Ring* was published in a limited private edition in 1853. By the summer of 1857 Wagner had completed the musical composition of the tetralogy as far as the end of act 2 of *Siegfried*. He then broke off work on the *Ring* for seven years, although his plans for the work and for a festival performance of it were taken up again at the end of 1862, when he drafted a preface to the first public edition of the poem. In it he listed the conditions under which the *Ring* should be performed, including a festival production "free from the influences of the repertory routine that afflicts our existing theatres" (SSD VI, 273). The performances would be given "in one of Germany's less large cities," thus avoiding a big-city audience. There would be a "temporary theatre, as simple as possible, perhaps built solely of wood and taking account solely of the artistic suitability of its interior," with a steeply raked, amphitheaterlike auditorium and an invisible orchestra. Singers would be engaged from among the members of German opera companies. All lovers of art would be able to attend, and the audience would be clearly and specifically educated so that, away from their working environment and in a relaxed frame of mind, they would feel devotionally inclined from the very first mystic sound and thus be able to concentrate on the performance at hand. Wagner also hoped that such a festival would enable him to influence public and theatrical taste. At this stage he still allowed the possibility of performing new and original works by other composers in his planned festival theater. He saw two ways of financing the project: either by means of an association of wealthy men and women, or else through the establishment of a foundation by some German prince or other ("Will this prince be found?").

A year later Wagner did find himself in the presence of this very prince, Ludwig II of Bavaria, a man who was to play a decisive role in the history of the Bayreuth Festival (see Chapter 13). He gave Wagner an official commission to complete the *Ring*, a commission which provided the composer with the material conditions that would enable him to do so. The overall fee of 30,000 gulden, however, also gave Ludwig the copyright and performing rights to the work. The king's (abortive) plans to build a magnificent festival theater in Munich went far beyond anything Wagner had envisaged and in some respects actually ran counter to the composer's intentions. Nonetheless, the plans that were drawn up by Gottfried Semper contained a number of concrete ideas that would later be adopted at Bayreuth, including the amphitheaterlike auditorium (also intended as a democratic counterexample to the traditional horseshoe-shaped Court Theater with its tiers of boxes), the sunken and invisible orchestra, and the resultant "mystic abyss" between the reality of the auditorium and the mythic ideality on stage, and, finally, the double proscenium, which created an illusion of perspective by visually narrowing the inner frame surrounding the stage and thus making everything onstage seem larger.

The Establishment of the Festival at Bayreuth

A mere three months after his banishment from Munich, Wagner once again found thoughts of Bayreuth passing through his mind (see his letter to Hans von Bülow of 20 February 1866). In mid-May 1866 he dictated a further section of his autobiography to Cosima, recalling "pleasant memories" of his first journey through Bayreuth in 1835. On 24 July 1866 he suggested that Ludwig might choose Bayreuth as his "favourite residence." But the strongest impulse came, unwittingly and unintentionally, from Ludwig himself in the form of the first performance of *Das Rheingold* in Munich on 22 September 1869, a production which took place on Ludwig's orders but against Wagner's wishes. The experience shocked the composer deeply, but at the same time opened his eyes to the fact that a performance of the *Ring* as *he* intended it could only be staged away from Munich, in a place that was free from incomprehension and the intrigues of the Court Opera, and safe from intervention on the part of the king. But the place in question would have to be at the heart of Germany and be in Bavaria. His eyes once more turned toward Bayreuth. In the course of various conversations on the subject Hans Richter recalled the enormous stage of the Margraves' Opera House in the town. Alarmed by the news that the king was also intending to surrender *Die Walküre* to the Munich Court Opera, Wagner and Cosima got out their encyclopedia at the beginning of March 1870 and looked up the entry on "Baireuth": "R. had mentioned this place as one he would choose," Cosima noted in her diary on 5 March 1870. In other words, the choice had already been made by this date. Mention of the magnificent old opera house merely served to confirm that choice.

A whole series of astonishing circumstances and coincidences serves to place this choice in a remarkable light. One example among many is Jean Paul's remark, often described as a premonition, that "we are still awaiting the man who will both write and set a genuine opera." These words were written in Bayreuth in 1813, the year of Wagner's birth. Wagner knew nothing of these links when he wrote retrospectively to Friedrich Feustel on 1 November 1871, telling him that his "good daemon" had brought him to Bayreuth. Wagner arrived in town with Cosima on 17 April 1871 for his first unofficial visit. They visited the Margraves' Opera House, and although they found it unsuited to their purpose, they resolved to settle in the town and to build their own festival theater there. A week later Wagner began negotiations with Liszt's pupil Carl Tausig as provisional secretary of the festival enterprise, and on 12 May 1871, while in Leipzig, he announced that the first Bayreuth Festival would be held in the summer of 1873. Not until six months later, in the previously quoted letter of 1 November 1871, did he officially inform Friedrich Feustel, a local banker and the chairman of Bayreuth's municipal representatives, of his intention. For all their no-nonsense sobriety, the city fathers showed themselves to be open-minded and full of confidence, in addition to displaying far-sightedness and boldness of spirit. It was decided as early as 7 November 1871 to offer Wagner a building plot free of charge. He had originally selected a site at the end of the Hofgarten, but the land was not suitable for building, and so the authorities suggested an alternative site in the suburb of St. Georgen. When one of the landowners refused to sell, Wagner angrily threatened to abandon the whole project, but finally allowed himself to be persuaded by the advantages of a third plot of land on the present Festival Hill, a site which the town had acquired in the intervening period.

While these preparations were in progress, Wagner continued to work on the *Ring*. In his conversations with Nietzsche at Tribschen, the numerous conceptual and spiritual links between the *Ring* and his ideas for a festival on the one hand, and Greek tragedy and the festivals of classical antiquity on the other, had become clearer and more pronounced.

In order to finance the venture a patronage scheme was devised at the beginning of 1872 with the aim of selling one thousand patrons' certificates at 300 thalers each in return for the guarantee of a seat at all the performances. Emil Heckel offered the support of the first Richard Wagner Society, which he had founded in Mannheim. But the most active encouragement came from the Committee of Management, whose members included the mayor of Bayreuth, Theodor Muncker, Feustel, and the lawyer Dr. Käfferlein. They assumed responsibility for what was soon to become a gigantic business concern. In April 1872 Wagner and his family left Tribschen to settle permanently in Bayreuth. On 22 May 1872, his fifty-ninth birthday, he laid the foundation stone of his Festival Theater, enclosing with it the motto:

> Here may a secret be enshrined
> And rest for many a hundred year:
> For while this stone holds it confined
> The world will know what's hidden here.

Of their journey back from the ceremony Nietzsche wrote: "He fell silent and in doing so turned his gaze in upon himself . . . The whole of the past had been a preparation for this moment." That afternoon Wagner conducted a performance of Beethoven's Ninth Symphony in the Margraves' Opera House.

Whereas Wagner had earlier thought of Strasbourg as an alternative to Bayreuth, he now received offers—often highly attractive ones—from Darmstadt, Berlin, London, Chicago, and Baden-Baden; even Bad Reichenhall, with its twenty-five-piece band, attempted to lure him to the town, but of course in vain. Wagner continued to work on *Götterdämmerung* during this period while at the same time keeping up a tireless stream of correspondence and traveling around Europe in order to solicit benefactors, conduct concerts, settle questions of an administrative, technical, or artistic nature, and recruit singers—this alone a laborious and time-consuming task. He complained to Cosima on 6 November 1872, "What tremendous will power I need for my enterprise, yet inwardly how finished with life I am!"

The topping-out ceremony for the Festival Theater took place on 2 August 1873, but it was overshadowed by financial worries. Only a third of the patrons' certificates had been sold. Bills could not be paid. Bismarck, to whom Wagner had sent a copy of his essay *The Stage Festival Theater in Bayreuth* in order to "communicate this cultural concept to the great reviver of German hopes," did not even acknowledge the letter; and even King Ludwig, whom Wagner repeatedly begged to provide a "formal guarantee," remained deaf to his entreaties. At a meeting of delegates from the various Wagner societies, it was decided to send out an appeal to the whole of the German Reich; the net proceeds of the appeal were six thalers, sent in by a group of students from Göttingen. Building work had to be suspended. The undertaking was threatened with ruin. Wagner even addressed a petition to Kaiser Wilhelm I, asking him to declare the 1876 festival a quinquennial celebration of the peace treaty signed with France in 1871, and to set aside the sum of 100,000 thalers for that purpose; but this plan, too, came to nothing. Finally Wagner considered the idea of presenting the theater to the town of Bayreuth (CT, 18 January 1874). Not until the end of January 1874 did the king relent and agree to an advance of 100,000 thalers, a sum which he insisted must be repaid out of moneys received from the patrons. The construction of his villa, Wahnfried, caused Wagner further concern and increased the strain on his nerves. Only a few days before completing *Götterdämmerung* Wagner complained about the stress that was being placed on him by all these pressures: "It is madness—where am I supposed to get the strength?" (CT, 13 November 1874).

The preliminary rehearsals took place in 1875 in the still incomplete Festival Theater. It was an unforgettable experience for all who witnessed the moment when Wagner emerged from the orchestra pit to be greeted by the words, "Completed, the eternal work," sung by Franz Betz, Bayreuth's first Wotan. At the end of the year Bismarck prevented the kaiser from granting the loan of 30,000 thalers that the latter was considering making available to Wagner. The lack of money became so critical that Wagner spoke to Cosima of a "complete game of chance" (CT, 5 February 1876). Since the majority of the patrons' certificates had found no takers, there could no longer be any thought of free admission; instead, admission had to be charged on all the remaining seats, and the number of free seats, previously set at five hundred, had to be reduced to fifty.

The First Festival

The first Bayreuth Festival opened on 13 August 1876, an event which, in spite of all the concessions and shortcomings, marked the triumph of a utopian vision that had finally become a reality. Wagner himself described it as a "miracle" in a letter to Emil Heckel of 11 February 1877. Among the foreign and local visitors were two emperors, Wilhelm I of Germany and Dom Pedro II of Brazil. Writing retrospectively, Wagner claimed that "never before had an artist been so honoured" (SSD X, 105). King Ludwig stayed away; he had attended the rehearsals but did not come back to Bayreuth until the third cycle.

As far as the artistic aspect of the enterprise was concerned, Wagner's disappointment knew no bounds. "R. is very sad, says he wishes he could die," Cosima noted on 9 September 1876. Throughout the performances his principal feeling had been "never again, never again" (CT, 5 November 1876). Hostile critics had a field day: "The German nation has nothing in common with this appalling disgrace," Ludwig Speidel wrote. But even an adversary such as Paul Lindau was bound to concede that "Wagner has achieved what no artist before him had even presumed to attempt. Bayreuth . . . is without doubt the mightiest individual achievement that one could ever imagine."

The general public had left without giving the festival a second thought. "Not a single one of the princes . . . has asked R. what can be done for him," Cosima complained on 9 October 1876. "The whole thing had been a pleasure trip, something extraordinary, to be sure, but with no further significance or consequence" (SSD XII, 328). Wagner wrote to Heckel on 9 December 1876: "The enterprise that I have carried through so far was a question addressed to the German public: 'Is this what you want?'—I now assume that this is not what they want, and so I am finished." The deficit of 150,000 marks was Wagner's sole responsibility. In a letter to King Ludwig he suggested that either the German Reich or else Bavaria should take over the Festival Theater as its property and pay an annual subsidy of 100,000 marks, which would allow between five hundred and six hundred seats to be given away free to people who could not otherwise afford them (21 October 1876). The letter remained unanswered. A circular addressed to the patrons and appealing for help in settling the deficit met with a quite literally solitary response when a woman from Kolberg sent 100 marks. Wagner wondered whether to declare the enterprise bankrupt and to offer Wahnfried to the highest bidder in order to pay off his debts. He wished "to hear nothing more about the *Ring des Nibelungen*," and hoped "that the theater would go up in flames" (CT, 26 February 1877). Strenuous efforts to reduce the deficit by giving concerts in London brought in a pitiful £700 and made his heart condition worse. Cosima sacrificed the 40,000 marks she had inherited from her mother's estate. The couple considered emigrating to America, and even offered the Bayreuth staging of the *Ring* to the Court Theater intendancy in Munich. In September 1877 a new Society of Patrons was founded, and it was to them that Wagner elaborated his plan of staging all his works, from *Holländer* on, between 1878 and 1883 and, at the same time, training singers, musicians, and conductors. All these projects foundered. By the end of 1877 Wagner's mood was one of resignation: "I no longer place my hopes in the German spirit." Only after further futile negotiations did Ludwig finally relent on 31 March 1878 and offer an interest-bearing loan to cover what remained of the deficit of 100,000 marks; under the terms of the loan the sum was to be paid back (and was indeed paid back) out of the royalties on all performances of Wagner's operas in Munich.

In the meantime Wagner had begun work on the music of *Parsifal*. In the course of conversations on the future performance of the piece, he let slip the remark, "Oh, I hate the thought of all those costumes and greasepaint." He recalled "those dreadful artists' balls," adding: "Having created the invisible orchestra, I now feel like inventing the invisible theater!" (CT, 23 September

1878). He told the king that a drama in which the most sublime mysteries of the Christian faith were openly enacted onstage could not be presented to a frivolous audience alongside a traditional opera house repertory (see the letter of 28 September 1880). He called the work a *Bühnenweihfestspiel,* literally a Stage Dedication Festival Play, since he intended to dedicate a stage to it, and this stage, he argued, could only be the Festival Theater in Bayreuth. "There, and there alone, may 'Parsifal' be presented now and always." The king agreed, and undertook sponsorship of the next Bayreuth Festival. The full score of the work was finished on 13 January 1882. Preparations for the performances that summer went ahead under considerably more favorable conditions than in 1876. To Wagner's regret all the performances, with the exception of the first, which was reserved for the Society of Patrons, had to be opened up to the paying public. He tried to salvage at least a remnant of his fondest idea, and successfully appealed to Friedrich Schön to establish a foundation which would make it possible for people without means of their own to attend the festival free of charge. He called this Richard Wagner Bursary Foundation the "heart of the Bayreuth enterprise." It is still in operation today.

With his "farewell work to the world" Wagner came even closer to Greek tragedy, inasmuch as he turned here to the substance of a *living* religious faith. In his 1880 essay *Religion and Art* he had advanced the view that "where religion becomes artificial, it is reserved for art to salvage the nucleus of religion" by giving ideal form to the mythic symbols and thus allowing the profound truth concealed within them to be recognized. To Wagner's deep dismay the king stayed away not only from the world premiere on 26 July 1882 but also from the fifteen subsequent performances of the work, although a massive porch had been specially built for him at the entrance to the Festival Theater. On this occasion the composer was well satisfied with the overall artistic impression. A request which he addressed to the audience at one point to hold their applause was misunderstood, resulting in the tradition of banning all applause at performances of the work, a ban which he himself opposed in vain. When he shouted "Bravo!" at one performance of the Flower Maidens' scene, he was hissed by the rest of the audience (CT, 11 August 1882). At the final performance he himself took up the baton from the Transformation music on and conducted the work through to the end. It was a prescient gesture, but one which the audience failed to note.

The Wagner Family

Cosima Wagner

Soon after the 1882 festival was over, Wagner complained in a letter to Angelo Neumann of 29 September 1882: "My Bayreuth creation stands or falls with 'Parsifal.' Of course this creation will pass away with my death, for I know of no one, now or in the future, who could continue my work in the spirit of its creator." Indeed, the vacuum soon became evident following his death.

Attempts were made—unsuccessfully—to persuade Liszt or Bülow to assume control of the festival. The 1883 performances of *Parsifal* became a memorial to their creator. The singer Emil Scaria was placed in overall charge of the production, but he could not prevent the singers from falling back into their old exaggerated operatic gestures.

Cosima was kept closely informed of all deviations from the 1882 production, and she herself observed the two final performances in secret. What she saw appalled her. Her reaction was one which Wagner had never considered: she herself assumed control of the festival, with administrative support from Adolf von Gross, Feustel's successor and son-in-law. The very same year she drew up plans for festivals from 1884 to 1889, and when news reached her during the 1884 rehearsals that there was a lack of commitment on the part of the performers and that slovenliness was rife, she took direct and immediate action. Hidden behind a partition onstage, she followed the rehearsals and performances, passing notes to the conductor, Hermann Levi, and the director, Anton Fuchs, gently urging upon them her suggestions for correcting the production. "Her observations were so pertinent and so sensitive, and contained such important information concerning the art of performance that I learned more in these few days than in twenty years as a practising conductor," Hermann Levi wrote to his father on 7 August 1884. When the General Wagner Society, concerned for the future of the festival, decided to establish a Richard Wagner Foundation with the intention of introducing extensive artistic participation and including works by other composers in the festival repertory, Cosima refused categorically to countenance such a move. In doing so she also gave an effective demonstration of her standards and expectations. She assumed official responsibility for the festival in 1885, a year when no festival was held in Bayreuth. In keeping with Wagner's own intentions she gradually introduced all his works to the festival repertory, from *Holländer* on. The *Tristan* performances of 1886, under the baton of Felix Mottl, whom she herself had personally engaged, were presented to half-empty houses. For one of the performances only eleven tickets had been sold. By 1888, however, with her production of *Die Meistersinger,* she had managed to break down the barrier of skepticism on the part of potential audiences. Later performances were well attended and were received with tumultuous applause and cheering. Bayreuth's reputation as a model theater for the staging of Wagner's works was thus securely founded. The announcement that *Tannhäuser* was to join the repertory in 1891 elicited a storm of protest: the work was deemed unworthy of being staged at the Festival Theater, and a fiasco was widely predicted. In the end Cosima's production was widely hailed as the rebirth of an opera which had become debased by the repertory routine of ordinary opera houses.

The building of a Richard Wagner Festival Theater in Munich, based on Gottfried Semper's surviving plans and instigated by Ernst von Possart, was regarded by Cosima as a blow directed at Bayreuth. But the theater, later to be known as the Prinzregententheater and largely designed as a massive replica of the Bayreuth Festival Theater, never became a rival of Bayreuth. In 1901 Cosima petitioned the Reichstag in a vain attempt to extend copyright protection from thirty years to fifty. Equally unsuccessful was her request—this time supported by eighteen thousand signatures—that the performing rights to *Parsifal* be limited to Bayreuth. Still less was she able to prevent performances of the work from being given in New York in 1903 in a production that was denounced by the faithful as "the rape of the Grail" (the United States had not signed the Bern Convention and was therefore not subject to international copyright laws). In 1913 the term of copyright expired on all of Wagner's works, including *Parsifal,* and much to Cosima's dismay many theaters immediately took advantage of their new-found freedom. Indignation over the performances of *Parsifal* in America had found expression in anti-Semitic and nationalist pamphlets which helped to align Wahnfried with the *völkisch* mentality and cultural conservatism of Wilhelminian Germany. These trends were intensified in the Bayreuth circle which had formed around Houston Stewart Chamberlain, Cosima's son-in-law, and Hans von Wolzogen. Their mouthpiece, the *Bayreuther Blätter,* also encouraged the cult of genius with which Cosima surrounded the figure of her late husband.

The reproach that is often leveled against Cosima, namely that her productions were rigidly bound by tradition, is only partially justified. However insistently she appealed to "the master's will," she had nonetheless sufficient independence of mind to give free rein to her own personal taste. By discouraging exaggerated gestures and replacing them with a more intense and dignified language, she created a style of her own which was exemplary, at least by contemporary standards. Her attempt to establish the Festival Theater as a temple in no way lessens her achievement in having maintained and consolidated the Bayreuth Festival with astonishing energy and diplomatic skill. At the same time she influenced both stage design and style of acting in such a way that her productions were regarded as the yardstick against which to measure all other Wagner performances of the time.

Siegfried Wagner

Cosima had already reached her seventieth year when, in 1907, serious illness persuaded her to hand over the running of the festival to her thirty-eight-year-old son, Siegfried. As an only partially successful composer and librettist of operas on legendary and fairy-tale subjects, he was already acknowledged as a talented conductor. He had conducted the festival orchestra almost every year since 1896, and in 1901 and 1904 had also directed productions. In addition to his status as Wagner's son and his undoubted artistic authority, his affable and conciliatory nature was also a useful asset in discharging his functions as festival director. As early as 1900 he had installed a cyclorama and a new floodlighting system, and so created the necessary preconditions for lighting designs which he proceeded to exploit to considerable effect. In the face of strong objections he had the courage to make constant improvements to the staging of the various works, including his father's own production of *Parsifal*.

The years leading up to the First World War were marked by a series of family rows. In the so-called Beidler case, Isolde Beidler (née von Bülow) took her mother to court, demanding recognition as Richard Wagner's daughter and, out of consideration for her son, asked for the corresponding legal entitlements. At the same time Siegfried Wagner was the victim of a blackmail campaign which was waged against him for private reasons. Not only was the family's reputation threatened, but so too were the standing and very existence of the festival. It was presumably this circumstance which encouraged Siegfried to set up a Festival Foundation for the German Nation, which was intended to secure the Festival Theater, together with its assets and holdings. The outbreak of war prevented him from realizing the plan, and it was not until sixty years later that the scheme was put into effect by Siegfried's widow. (He married the eighteen-year-old English girl Winifred Williams in 1915, and their children, Wieland, Friedelind, Wolfgang, and Verena, were born between 1917 and 1920.)

Postwar inflation wiped out the festival's reserves. In 1921 the Wagner societies established a German Festival Foundation for Bayreuth. Calls for donations involved a national appeal, and these, together with a concert tour which Siegfried Wagner undertook in America, brought in sufficient funds to reopen the festival in 1924. The inaugural production of *Die Meistersinger* in the presence of General Ludendorff was turned into a demonstration of *völkisch* and nationalist sympathies, with the audience standing for Hans Sachs's final address and launching into the German national anthem at the end of the opera. Siegfried posted notices outside the auditorium asking the audience to refrain from political demonstrations within the Festival Theater, but unofficially he and his wife made no secret of their sympathy for right-wing opposition to the Weimar Republic, not least in recognition of that opposition's support for Bayreuth. In addition, the influence of the Bayreuth circle, which saw itself as a bulwark against cultural and racial decay, and in so doing invoked the name of Richard Wagner, made the family an easy target for the program and person of that passionate Wagner fanatic Adolf Hitler. He visited Wagner's house and grave in 1923, and also called on Houston Stewart Chamberlain, who responded with a fulsomely effusive letter (Field 1981, pp. 436–437). When Hitler was imprisoned following his abortive putsch in November 1923, Winifred Wagner's gifts to him in prison included the writing paper that he used for *Mein Kampf*. A close personal friendship developed between them during these years. The racist League of German Youth, founded in 1925, and the Battle League for German Culture, which was summoned into existence in 1928 by the Nazi ideologist Alfred Rosenberg gave the names of Bayreuth and Wagner a politically explosive force.

The family remained blind to this misuse of its name. Siegfried Wagner continued to engage Jewish artists and distanced himself, officially at least, from anti-Semitic propaganda. In the face of considerable opposition he engaged a foreign conductor, Arturo Toscanini, in 1930, and Toscanini responded by waiving his fee. Siegfried's productions were praised for the natural and compelling visual style of his handling of the individual singers and groups onstage. Together with the set designer Kurt Söhnlein, he developed an expressively stylized poetic realism which culminated in changes to individual sets in the *Ring* and *Parsifal* and, above all, in new productions of *Tristan* in 1927 and *Tannhäuser* in 1930. This last-named production was paid for by a grant of 100,000 marks from the various Wagner societies and from friends, and, thanks to Toscanini, it became Siegfried Wagner's greatest success. But he did not live to see it realized: he collapsed during the rehearsals and died on 4 August 1930, a mere four months after Cosima.

Winifred Wagner

As specified in his will, Siegfried's widow, Winifred, took over the running of the festival following his death. With a realistic sense of her limitations she entrusted the chief artistic responsibilities to three outstanding experts. The principal artistic director was Heinz Tietjen, who also collaborated as stage director and conductor. He was joined by the set designer Emil Preetorius and the conductor Wilhelm Furtwängler. The latter, however, resigned his post after only a year because of arguments over individual responsibilities. At the same time Bayreuth also lost Toscanini, who withdrew from the festival in 1931 when the audience at the rehearsal for Siegfried Wagner's memorial concert was charged admission: he felt that the Festival Theater had been profaned by a mercenary spirit. In later years he avoided the festival in protest at the anti-Semitic rabble-rousing propaganda which was now on the increase in Germany. Both incidents were extensively but unsuccessfully exploited by Winifred's opponents, but she refused to pay them any heed in her single-minded application to the strict running of the festival.

The Winifred Wagner era was more liberal than it appeared. The cultural propaganda which made emotional use of Wagner and the Bayreuth Festival, the annual visits of Adolf Hitler, who stayed with Winifred as her house guest every summer from 1936 to 1939, the mass turnout of prominent party members, and the forests of flags could not disguise the fact that the artistic heart of the festival remained largely untouched by events. Hitler, it must be said, made available on average 55,000 marks for each new production, but he respected the artistic competence of the festival administration. Winifred's personal relations with him enabled her to fend off unreasonable requests by a number of party members: she peremptorily rejected a plan to use the Festival Theater for a meeting of the German Youth Movement, and she calmly parried references to Tietjen's links with the Social Democratic party, insisting that what was important was not party membership but artistic achievement. When many of the festival's foreign visitors remained away in

1933 and—in spite of the cultural propaganda—a lack of demand for tickets gave rise to concern, the Nazi authorities and organizations bought up the remaining tickets in blocks. In 1934, for example, the Reich's Ministry of Propaganda bought tickets to the value of 327,000 marks, a third of the total proceeds for that year.

From an artistic point of view, this was undoubtedly a golden age in the history of the Bayreuth Festival. It brought together an elite band of singers and conductors. The impact of Preetorius' sets, with their heavily symbolic world of simplified and accentuated forms, was enhanced by the possibilities inherent in the new lighting system. The high point was the 1936 *Lohengrin*. The 1937 *Parsifal* marked Wieland Wagner's Bayreuth debut as a set designer. Criticism on the part of the building inspection authorities in 1936 persuaded Winifred Wagner to consider ways of renovating and improving the Festival Theater. The plans degenerated into a monstrous scheme which Hitler commissioned the architect Emil Rudolf Mewes to work out in detail. The intention was to erect a kind of Acropolis on Festival Hill, a vast horseshoe-shaped complex of classically inspired buildings, some of which were not unimpressive in design. The extensive rear portion of the central section was intended to include the original ("temporary") Festival Theater, leaving the auditorium unaltered but surrounding it on the outside with supports so that only the upper part of the fly tower would have remained visible. The outbreak of the Second World War prevented the scheme from being realized.

From the beginning Winifred, unlike Cosima, encouraged objective Wagnerian research. She wanted to call off the festival when war broke out, but Hitler insisted that it continue in the form of "wartime festivals." The audience, now admitted free of charge, was made up largely of wounded soldiers, munitions workers, and Red Cross nurses. As early as 1941 Winifred's sons Wieland and Wolfgang attempted to increase their artistic influence on the festival. The elder of the two brothers, supported and encouraged by Hitler, who exempted him from military service, came into serious conflict with Tietjen. He designed the sets for a new production of *Die Meistersinger* in 1943, a work which marked the end of Winifred Wagner's era in 1944.

After the war the Festival Theater was used for concerts and for performances of operas, operettas, musicals, and revues. Performances of Wagner were taboo for the next six years. Wahnfried had suffered serious bomb damage, and the adjacent building was requisitioned by the occupying authorities. Winifred had to move out, and the family's property was handed over to a trustee. A denazification court accused Winifred of having allowed the festival to be misused for propagandist ends by the Nazi dictators. Statements from witnesses made it clear that she had repeatedly and successfully interceded on behalf of persecuted individuals and that she had saved the lives of a number of Jews. The charge against her was upheld, nonetheless, and she was sentenced to 450 days' special labor and to confiscation of 60 percent of her private fortune. An appeals court decision in 1948, however, reclassified her as less incriminated.

Wieland and Wolfgang Wagner

Initially it seemed impossible that the Bayreuth Festival would ever reopen, a fear which led Wieland Wagner to consider establishing a festival in Switzerland. Bayreuth's mayor Dr. Oskar Meyer, attempting to salvage the Bayreuth tradition, appealed to Dr. Franz Beidler, the son of Isolde Beidler, who had been driven from Bayreuth following her court case in 1914. He drew up guidelines for reestablishing the Bayreuth Festival. No longer was the Wagner family to be responsible for its management but rather a Richard Wagner Festival Foundation. The council of trustees was to include Thomas Mann as its honorary president, an honor which Mann declined in amusement. The legality of Siegfried Wagner's will also began to be questioned, as did his widow's claims to a greater share in his estate than was given to her children. In 1949 she formally renounced all further involvement in the festival and entrusted its management to her sons. In this way she opened the door to a new beginning for the enterprise. Wieland made a decisive break with the past: "After Auschwitz there can be no more discussions about Hitler." In the period that followed the brothers justified the "political guarantee" that the town of Bayreuth had undertaken on their behalf. In order to finance the first postwar festival, Wagner's grandsons planned to sell original manuscripts from the family archives. The Society of Friends of Bayreuth, founded in 1949, intervened and blocked this move. As the years passed, the Society of Friends was to prove one of the festival's most energetic supports.

The first postwar festival opened with a performance of *Parsifal* in 1951. Thus began an era which, like none other before it, was to have a formative influence in matters of style on the whole of contemporary music theater. With the single exception of *Die Meistersinger* in 1951, Wieland and Wolfgang Wagner assumed responsibility for all productions during the next eighteen years, functioning as both directors and set designers. Throughout this period it was Wieland who carried the main burden of responsibility for the festival's administration and precarious finances. The productions that were staged during this era were marked by a particular style of acting—statuesque, economical, and expressive—by stylishly austere and symbolically suggestive sets, by a meaningful use of light and color, a Jungian interpretation of the works, and a permanent search for newer immanent aspects of their meaning. The Festival Theater became an artistic and intellectual workshop. The process of *Entrümpelung* (clearing away dead wood), as the Wagner brothers liked to refer to it, was not confined to the stage, but also found expression in articles by highly qualified contributors to the festival's program booklets, articles in which even provocatively critical voices were to be heard on occasion. The public image of Wagner and his works was freed of a distorting overlay, and the foundations were laid for a transformed and deeper understanding: new dimensions that had previously been hidden were now opened up. Right from the outset, Wieland's production of *Parsifal* revealed perhaps the closest approach to those elements of Greek tragedy which had helped to influence his grandfather's plans for a festival. This approach even went so far as to rein-troduce the classical *orchestra* as a disc-shaped acting area. The production remained in the repertory for twenty-three years, and became a symbol not only of New Bayreuth and the festival but also of Wagner's idea of a festival in general. Furious protests were leveled at Wieland's violation of his grand-father's stage directions, not least in his 1951 *Parsifal* and his 1956 production of *Die Meistersinger*. They led to the foundation of an Organization for the Faithful Presentation of Richard Wagner's Dramas, and even to a series of court cases. When Wieland died in 1966, the world of music theater mourned the passing of an artist of genius, while Bayreuth itself lost the most significant director in the festival's ninety-year history.

Since Wieland's death, Wolfgang Wagner has been the festival's sole direc-tor. In addition to his artistic contribution, he has made it his lasting concern to see to structural improvements made to the Festival Theater. By using identically shaped reinforced concrete beams to replace the wooden sections in the half-timbering on the outside of the building, he preserved the character of the original "temporary" structure, which by then had acquired the status of a historically registered building. And by undertaking constant technolog-ical innovations in the theater's stage fittings, and by erecting rehearsal stages and other ancillary buildings, he has ensured trouble-free working conditions and an improvement in gastronomical standards. Since 1969 he has sought to broaden the artistic spectrum by bringing in stage directors from outside Bayreuth. Throughout this period the festival has remained the goal of many an artist's ambitions and the springboard for countless international careers. Nationalist and national socialist tendencies in the productions or in audience attitudes are now no more than an embarrassing memory or a source of wry amusement. If ideological sensibilities continue to be stirred, it is for the most part by left-wing trends, and even then only rarely. When SS uniforms were seen in Götz Friedrich's production of *Tannhäuser,* there were protests not only against the dramaturgical quality of the allusion but also at what was assumed to be a Marxist provocation. The 1976 centenary *Ring* production by the young French team of Patrice Chéreau and Richard Peduzzi provoked the greatest scandal in the whole history of the festival. A number of gags travestying the work and reducing it to the level of an operetta opened up a new gulf between the idea and the reality of the festival, and at the same time blinded many in the audience to the very real qualities of, for example, the striking and often virtuosic handling of individual details. Audience reaction even took the form of threats, and many members of the orchestra rebelled. Opposition was fomented by an Action Committee for the Works of Richard Wagner. Wolfgang Wagner was himself caught in the cross-fire, but Bayreuth survived even this by no means minor crisis.

An important step in safeguarding the festival was taken in 1973 when, at the instigation of Winifred and with the support of Wolfgang Wagner, the Richard Wagner Foundation of Bayreuth was called into being. Apart from the Wagner family itself, the foundation's members include the Federal Republic of Germany and the Free State of Bavaria. The Festival Theater was transferred to the foundation, which in turn was to lease it back to the festival director of the day, guaranteeing him complete artistic freedom but also investing in him financial and administrative responsibility. The State of Bavaria is contractually obliged to make good any shortfall in the festival's subsidy. The transfer of Wahnfried to the town of Bayreuth allowed the house to be rebuilt and fitted out as a Wagner museum. The valuable family archives, acquired for 12.4 million marks, are now called the National Archives of the Richard Wagner Foundation of Bayreuth. At the same time, steps were taken to ensure the best possible successor as head of the festival, with members of the Wagner family enjoying preferential rights, together with the right of recommendation. In cases of dispute the decision is to be made by a commission composed of overseers from the leading opera houses in the German-speaking world, and, if necessary, the advisory board of the Richard Wagner Foundation itself. In this way the previously close and fruitful ties between the Bayreuth Festival and the descendants of its founder have been acknowledged as a tradition worthy of preservation.

Translated by Stewart Spencer

CHAPTER 20

Performance History: A Brief Survey

OSWALD BAUER

Performances during Wagner's Lifetime

Wagner's stage career began with a fiasco. The first performance of his second opera, *Das Liebesverbot,* took place in Magdeburg on 29 March 1836, with the composer himself conducting. The second performance had to be canceled: a mere six people had turned up to see it. No further performances of the work were given during Wagner's lifetime, and, indeed, *Das Liebesverbot* has never found a home for itself in the regular repertoire. New productions were staged in 1913, 1933, and 1983 to mark the centenary of Wagner's birth and the fiftieth anniversary and centenary of his death. Most of them were mounted by opera houses eager to include a complete cycle of Wagner's works in their season of performances. Berlin, for example, first heard the work in 1933, in a production directed by Franz Ludwig Hörth, conducted by Leo Blech, and with Marcel Wittrisch and Käthe Heidersbach in the leading roles. Munich followed fifty years later, when the work was directed by Jean-Pierre Ponnelle and conducted by Wolfgang Sawallisch; the principal singers were Hermann Prey and Sabine Hass.

Wagner's very first completed opera, *Die Feen,* fared even less well. It did not even reach the stage until after the composer's death, receiving its first performance at the Munich Court Theater on 29 June 1888. Like *Das Liebesverbot, Die Feen* has never been accepted into the standard repertoire, and if performed at all has tended to be presented within the framework of a cycle of all the composer's works.

Wagner's first genuine stage success was the first performance of *Rienzi* in Dresden on 20 October 1842. The part of Adriano was created by Wilhelmine Schröder-Devrient, who was to remain Wagner's ideal of a singing actress until the end of his life, and the title role was sung by Joseph Tichatschek. Wagner was unable to recreate the huge success of the Dresden production on the occasion of the Berlin premiere in 1847, in spite of the fact that he himself conducted the opening performances. Other theaters were initially hesitant to take up so vast a work, since it had acquired the reputation of being very expensive to stage.

On 2 January 1843, a mere two and a half months after the premiere of *Rienzi*, *Holländer* received its first performance. It, too, was given in the Dresden Court Theater, with Wagner himself conducting. The only vocal performance of any distinction was once again that of Schröder-Devrient as Senta. The new work soon disappeared from the repertoire, since Dresden audiences, expecting something spectacular to follow *Rienzi*, found the opera too slight and somber.

Productions of *Holländer* were mounted later the same year in Riga and Cassel. The composer Louis Spohr was responsible for preparing and conducting the Cassel performances, where the technical aspects of the production are said to have been especially impressive. The Berlin premiere followed in 1844 at the Schauspielhaus on the Gendarmenmarkt, the opera house having burned down. Wagner himself conducted the first two performances.

Dresden was again the scene of Wagner's next operatic venture, the first performance of *Tannhäuser*, given under the composer's baton on 19 October 1845. Expectations ran high, but the applause on opening night was no more than polite. Joseph Tichatschek, who again created the title role, had a magnificent tenor voice but came nowhere near meeting the histrionic demands of his exacting part. Wilhelmine Schröder-Devrient sang Venus, and Wagner's niece Johanna, then barely nineteen years old, created the part of Elisabeth. Wagner himself was impressed most of all by the performance of Anton Mitterwurzer as Wolfram. The magnificent sets were designed by Edouard-Désiré-Joseph Despléchin of the Paris Opéra, and the medieval costumes by Ferdinand Heine. There were seven additional performances of the work in 1845 and 1846 before its revival in 1847, when a new ending was added. The premiere of *Tannhäuser* was the first occasion on which the passionate partisanship of the innovative composer's supporters and critics made itself felt among the general public and in the press, a partisanship which was to mark all his premieres from that point on, so that the name of Richard Wagner was soon familiar even to those people who never set foot in an opera house.

Other opera companies were slow to include *Tannhäuser* in their repertoires, since it was regarded as a historical work requiring expensive sets and costumes; and the music, moreover, had little appeal among the broader public. Not until 1849, four years after the Dresden premiere, did Franz Liszt have the courage to stage the work, conducting it himself. In so doing he helped the opera achieve its decisive breakthrough. As early as 1852 productions began to follow in various theaters, including Schwerin, Breslau, and Wiesbaden. The larger court theaters of Vienna, Munich, and Berlin were less quick to reach a decision. Preparations for the Munich premiere were hampered by a campaign against Wagner the outlawed revolutionary, who, it was said, had no business appearing on the stage of a court theater. The first performance, on 12 August 1855, had all the signs of being a real sensation. Its success with local audiences rested first and foremost not with the music but with the sets and costumes, which evoked a resplendent picture of medieval pomp and ceremony. The Berlin premiere followed in 1856, and a year after that came the turn of Vienna, not at the Court Theater, however, but in the Thalia Theater in one of the city's suburbs. The opera was first heard in the Kärtnerthor Theater (then the home of the Court Opera) in 1859.

Completed in 1848, *Lohengrin* was initially intended to open in Dresden, but the plan came to nothing as a result of Wagner's involvement in the Dresden uprising of May 1849 and his subsequent flight to Switzerland. Once again it was Franz Liszt who had the courage to give the work its first performance. The premiere took place in Weimar on 28 August 1850 as part of the town's Goethe and Herder celebrations, with Liszt himself conducting. It was to be fifteen years before another of Wagner's works received its first performance.

Nonetheless, the 1850s finally saw an end to Wagner's limited status as merely a local celebrity. He became known throughout Europe not only as a composer but also as a writer—he was working at the time on his three great works on musical theory—and, last but not least, as a prominent political refugee. That he was known throughout the 1850s first and foremost as the author of *Tannhäuser* is also clear from Napoleon III's edict that the work be performed at the Paris Opéra in preference to *Tristan,* which had been completed in 1859 and which Wagner was energetically attempting to have staged in Paris. The Paris premiere of *Tannhäuser* on 13 March 1861 turned out to be the greatest theatrical scandal of the age. The reason lay primarily in Wagner's refusal to compose a ballet for the second act. As a result the Jockey Club—influential subscribers, many of whom were members of the aristocracy—disrupted the performance. In addition, the imperial decree was interpreted as a victory and as a sign of intrigue on the part of the German faction at court, since it had been enacted at the instigation of the Princess Metternich. Wagner was well satisfied with the progress of the rehearsals. The sets were designed by Despléchin, and as far as the cast was concerned, Wagner's wishes were met. Albert Niemann was engaged at vast expense to sing the title role, and the young Marie Sax sang the part of Elisabeth. Wagner was deeply impressed by her. After the third performance, however, which had again been accompanied by considerable uproar, Wagner withdrew his score, in spite of the fact that the subsequent performances were already sold out. He was unwilling to inflict such disruption on himself and his singers a moment longer.

Although the score of *Tristan* had been completed in 1859, another six years were to elapse before the work finally received its first performance at the Court Theater in Munich, and even then the premiere had to be postponed because of the soprano's indisposition. Karlsruhe had already rejected the work, and plans to open at the Vienna Court Opera were abandoned in 1863 after seventy-seven rehearsals. The piece was regarded as unperformable. Munich finally heard the work on 10 June 1865 in a performance Wagner described as perfect. The sets were designed by Angelo Quaglio (acts 1 and

3) and Heinrich Döll (act 2), and the costumes by Franz Seitz, all of whom followed Wagner's instructions to the letter. The conductor was Hans von Bülow. Isolde was sung by Malwina Schnorr von Carolsfeld, and Tristan by her husband, Ludwig. His performance left Wagner deeply stirred, and Schnorr became his ideal embodiment of a singing actor. Nine years were to pass before a second theater dared to attempt the work, once again in Weimar.

The greatest triumph of Wagner's career, however, was to be the first performance of *Meistersinger* at the Munich Court Theater on 21 June 1868. Again the sets were designed by Angelo Quaglio and Heinrich Döll, and Franz Seitz was responsible for the costumes. Both of the set designers went to Nuremberg expressly to study the local architecture. For the second act sets Wagner demanded working houses instead of the usual painted flats. The sets proved to be one of the main reasons for the opera's success. The conductor again was Hans von Bülow. As with *Tristan*, Wagner had engaged the most suitable singers from all over Germany, much to the displeasure of the local intendant and his ensemble. Franz Betz from Berlin was Sachs, Franz Nachbaur from Darmstadt sang Walther, and Max Schlosser from Augsburg played David, while Eva was performed by a young singer from the Munich ensemble by the name of Mathilde Mallinger. Only with the Beckmesser of Gustav Hölzel from Vienna was Wagner at all dissatisfied.

Once again it was the medium-sized theaters which were the first to take their courage in their hands and perform the new opera. It was heard in Dresden, Dessau, Karlsruhe, Mannheim, and Weimar in 1869. The court operas of Vienna and Berlin followed in 1870. Just as with *Tannhäuser,* it was the sets and costumes that were most admired, since the picture they gave of an idealized past coincided with the nostalgic nationalism of contemporary taste; but the music itself remained unintelligible. Critical debate among the general public and in the press was now conducted with greater intensity than for any other composer. The most widely held view was that Wagner's "music of the future" would never really catch on.

When plans to build a Festival Theater in Munich foundered, King Ludwig II ordered *Das Rheingold* and *Die Walküre* to be produced in Munich in 1869 and 1870, in spite of determined opposition on Wagner's part. There were serious disagreements between king and composer. Hans Richter resigned as conductor while the rehearsals were still in progress, and was relieved of his title of Director of Court Music. Franz Betz, who was to have sung Wotan, withdrew from the production. The complicated stage machinery was in the hands of Carl Brandt, who acquitted himself so admirably that he was later engaged for the first Bayreuth Festival. When *Die Walküre* premiered in 1870, it was again the technical side of the production and the sets which received the greatest praise. Wagner's experiences in Munich persuaded him to press on with plans for his own Festival Theater, in which he could work independently and perform the *Ring,* as he had planned it, as a self-contained cycle. The foundation stone of the Festival Theater was laid at Bayreuth on 22 May 1872. Preliminary rehearsals began in the summer of 1875, with the singers rehearsing their parts in Wahnfried and the orchestra in the still unfinished theater. Wagner himself assumed responsibility for both the musical rehearsals and the stage production. After all, roles such as those of Siegfried (Georg Unger) and Brünnhilde (Amalie Materna) had to be prepared from scratch. Franz Betz had taken on the part of Wotan, and Albert Niemann that of Siegmund. The task of designing the sets had been entrusted to no routine scene painter but to a landscape artist with limited theatrical experience, the Viennese Joseph Hoffmann. They were built in the Coburg studios of Max and Gotthold Brückner. Wagner was disappointed with the opulent historical costumes of Carl Emil Doepler. Carl Brandt had already collaborated with Wagner on equipping the new theater and installing the stage machinery, and he was now invited to assume overall technical control of the first festival. The Bayreuth Festival was inaugurated with a performance of *Das Rheingold* on 13 August 1876, and the event attracted international attention. The cycle was given three complete performances. Wagner was dissatisfied with the artistic results, and hoped to do everything better the following year. A repetition of the festival was out of the question, however, because of the deficit incurred in 1876. Other theaters, too, hesitated, with only *Die Walküre* being considered a potential box office draw.

The Leipzig opera director Angelo Neumann was courageous enough to present the entire *Ring* there in 1878, the same year in which a complete cycle was first heard in Munich; Vienna followed in 1879 and Hamburg in 1880. Since the Court Theater in Berlin had no plans to perform the *Ring*, Neumann's company brought their production to the city's Victoria Theater in 1881, where it met with enormous success. Wagner attended the performances, as did Kaiser Wilhelm and his family. In May and June 1882 Neumann gave guest performances of the *Ring* in London, and in September he and his company began their spectacular tour, taking the *Ring* to Germany, the Netherlands, Belgium, Switzerland, Austria, Hungary, and Italy. The tour was a huge success. In 1880 Wagner persuaded King Ludwig II to decree that, because of its unique character and content, his Sacred Stage Festival Play *Parsifal* should be performed solely and exclusively in his Festival Theater at Bayreuth. The first performance of the new work was given there on 26 July 1882. Hermann Levi conducted the Munich Court Opera orchestra. Paul von Joukowsky had followed Wagner's instructions to the letter in designing the sets and costumes, basing his designs for the Temple of the Grail on Siena Cathedral. As before, the sets were built by the Brückner brothers in their Coburg workshops. Since sixteen performances were planned, the principal roles had to be double- and triple-cast. The audience was profoundly impressed by the unusual work, and Wagner, too, was generally more satisfied with the artistic results than he had been in the case of the *Ring* six years previously. At the final performance he himself conducted the closing scene from the Transformation music on. It was his festival swan song: six months later he was dead.

From Wagner's Death to the First World War

Although Wagner was a European celebrity at the time of his death, his works had not yet managed to establish a place for themselves in international opera house repertoires. In particular the later music dramas from *Tristan* on were regarded as excessively modern and difficult, so during the 1870s it was only the earlier works—*Holländer, Tannhäuser,* and *Lohengrin*—which began to make any headway. The situation was to change after Wagner's death, however, and from the 1890s until around 1910 his works dominated the international opera scene as had those of no other composer before him. Their popularity was increased by the fact that, far from being abandoned on Wagner's death, as many people had assumed would happen, the Bayreuth Festival, after a shaky start, grew increasingly successful under Cosima Wagner. Every self-respecting opera house sought to adopt the Bayreuth trademark. Often this simply meant hiring individual Bayreuth singers or ordering copies of the Bayreuth sets from the Brückner brothers, who mass-produced them in their Coburg studios. The work of these theater studios (in addition to the Brückners and several smaller firms, the Viennese studio of Brioschi, Burghart, and Kautsky produced much-sought-after designs, providing the sets, for example, for the Metropolitan Opera in New York, while the Baruch studios did a flourishing trade in Berlin) resulted in a certain standardization and uniformity in set design. This uniformity was further encouraged by photographs and colored prints of the Bayreuth sets which were widely circulated and which created an iconographic model, especially for the smaller and medium-sized theaters. But even larger opera houses adopted this method; La Scala in Milan, for example, requested large colored photographs of the Bayreuth *Tannhäuser* for its first performances of the work in 1891, allowing the Milanese designer Giovanni Zuccarelli to reproduce the Bayreuth staging in every detail. An independent style, occasionally revealing a certain local color, emerged only at those opera houses which could afford to employ leading artists as scene painters and were not obliged to rely on mass products from the workshops. In their heavy and gorgeous colors, the sets which Carlo Brioschi designed for the Vienna Court Opera owe much to the style of Hans Makart, and the same is true of the work of Franz Angelo Rottonara. At the Paris Opéra Amable, Carpezat, Lavastre, and Jambon, often working together, produced designs that remained firmly within the Grand Opéra tradition. For La Scala, Carlo Ferrario designed richly colorful sets that were exceptionally lavishly ornamented and that were still very much indebted to the style of the great nineteenth-century Milanese set painters. A notable example of Ferrario's work was his 1898 *Meistersinger.* The general impression was that of the final colorful flowering of a great tradition, the virtuoso art of illusionistic scene painting.

In Paris Wagner's works were banned from the repertoire for two decades because of his partisan stance in the Franco-Prussian War of 1870–71 and, more especially, as a result of his unspeakable satire *Eine Kapitulation* (WWV 102). When Charles Lamoureux produced *Lohengrin* at the Eden-Théâtre in Paris in 1887, he was forced to abandon the production after only two performances, so violent were the protests that were staged outside the theater. The first performance of the same work at the Palais Garnier in 1891 led to the greatest protest demonstration in the history of Wagner productions. The square outside the Opéra had to be sealed off by mounted police to prevent the crowds of demonstrators from getting near the building, and several hundred people were arrested. These protests, however, took the sting out of any further opposition. The first performances of *Tannhäuser* at the Palais Garnier four years later were able to go on without being disrupted, and were a great success. The opera house in Brussels profited from Paris' abstinence, and throughout the 1880s and 1890s presented glittering premieres of several of Wagner's later works, sung in French, which many Wagnerians traveled from France to see.

But it was precisely during these years when Wagner was not performed onstage in France that *wagnérisme* developed as a uniquely French expression of enthusiasm for Wagner. People attended the Sunday concerts of Charles Lamoureux, Jules Pasdeloup, and Edouard Colonne. Wagner was discussed in the salons, which set the tone in matters of art and social mores. It became fashionable to travel to Bayreuth for the festival. Everyone who thought he was anyone not only took the waters at Marienbad, Karlsbad, and Baden-Baden during the summer months but also attended the Bayreuth Festival. "Bayreuth threatened to become a rendezvous for snobs," Siegfried Wagner wrote of this period. But the First World War put an end to all that.

During these decades it was customary to perform Wagner's works in the language of the country in which the production was taking place, be it Italian, English, or French. The trend toward singing a work in the original language did not develop until the twentieth century. But since even at this time globe-trotting opera stars were not unknown, performances were some-times given in a mixture of languages. It was traditional practice, too, to make extensive cuts in some of the works. *Die Meistersinger,* for example, was scarcely ever given in full; cuts were usually made in David's instructions to Walther in act 1 and in parts of the opening scene of act 3. Acts 2 and 3 of *Die Walküre* were rarely heard in their entirety. It was usually Wotan's mon-ologue in act 2 and the scene between Wotan and Brünnhilde in act 3 which suffered most. The same was true of *Tristan.*

In Bayreuth, meanwhile, Cosima worked single-mindedly and indefatiga-bly to combat the slovenliness in the way that most theaters ran their affairs. *Parsifal* was performed at Bayreuth in 1883 and 1884 as a requiem, so to speak, for the dead composer. In 1886 Cosima then began to build up the festival repertoire, beginning with *Tristan,* a work which brought no guar-antee of success with its audiences. But that was never Cosima's prime consideration, for what concerned her most was the realization of her self-appointed task. *Meistersinger* followed in 1888, and *Tannhäuser* in 1891, the latter to the accompaniment of violent protests on the part of diehard Wagnerians. *Lohengrin* entered the festival repertoire in 1894, and in 1896, twenty years after it had first been heard there, the *Ring* returned to Bayreuth. The 1901 production of *Holländer* completed the festival canon. No one will deny Cosima Wagner this achievement, her intensive musical and stage rehearsals, and her weeding out of careless routine. It is less easy to assess her attempts to establish her own theatrical style. In the case of works such as *Tristan* and *Meistersinger,* which had already been staged in model performances under Wagner's own supervision, she saw it as her task to recreate those earlier productions as faithfully as possible on the Bayreuth stage. With her new production of the *Ring* in 1896, everything was retained from 1876 that was felt to have been good, and the rest was changed. But here we come up against the problematic nature of a production style which legitimizes arbitrary choices by reference to the master's alleged intentions—intentions into which Cosima alone was initiated. Only with works such as *Tannhäuser,* for which there was no valid model that she could fall back on, did she reveal any greater artistic freedom.

The first generation of star Wagnerian singers to establish a reputation after Wagner's death was soon in demand all over Europe and abroad as well. One thinks, for example, of Lilli Lehmann, the first international Wagnerian prima donna. She had sung at the first Bayreuth Festival, and went on to introduce New York audiences (she was a member of the Metropolitan Opera company for many years) to all the leading Wagnerian roles. One thinks, too, of Anton van Rooy, the 1901 Bayreuth Dutchman; the Belgian tenor Ernest van Dyck, a famous Bayreuth Parsifal who sang Tannhäuser, Lohengrin, and Tristan in all the great opera houses; Milka Ternina of the Munich Opera, who sang Kundry in New York on the occasion of the "illegal" performances of *Parsifal* in 1903; Italo Campanini, the first Lohengrin in Bologna (1871), Milan (1873), and New York (1871), where he was famous for his costume of a helmet with a large blue plume and a magnificent cloak; Jean de Reszke, idolized from Paris to New York and famous as Lohengrin and Siegfried; the statuesque Felia Litvinne, who could sing Isolde in five different languages; Lilian Nordica; Olive Fremstad; Louise Grandjean, leading soprano at the Paris Opéra and a Bayreuth Venus; the boyish tenor Charles Dalmorès, who demanded exorbitant fees and received them; Leo Slezak, whose name is inextricably bound up with the part of Lohengrin; the legendary Emmy Destinn, the 1901 Bayreuth Senta; and Anna Bahr-Mildenburg, a famous Kundry and Isolde under Gustav Mahler. Even those star singers of the period who were not exclusively associated with Wagner were attracted by the success of his operas. Fyodor Chaliapin and Francesco d'Andrade, a famous Don Giovanni, both sang the Dutchman; Christine Nilsson, a true star singer, tried her hand at various soprano roles; and Nellie Melba, the prima donna assoluta of the turn of the century, sang Elisabeth and Elsa.

Among the notable conductors were Hans Richter, who conducted Wagner in London, Budapest, and Vienna; Anton Seidl, one of Wagner's assistants, who enjoyed great success in New York both as a conductor and as an orchestral and vocal teacher and whose labors were rewarded by an improvement of standards in Wagnerian performances there; Felix Mottl in Karlsruhe, Munich, and Bayreuth; Hermann Levi, the first conductor of *Parsifal,* who was general music director in Munich; the young Arturo Toscanini in Milan; the young Richard Strauss; and, in Vienna and New York, Gustav Mahler. In the days before film, television, and records, touring opera companies would travel to the remotest parts of the world, including Australia and South America, where they performed Wagner's works, often under the most difficult conditions and in an improvised fashion.

A special case in the performance history of the composer's works is his Sacred Stage Festival Play *Parsifal.* The very first person to break his stipulation that the work be performed only in the theater at Bayreuth was none other than King Ludwig II himself. Following Wagner's death he made special arrangements to have the entire production brought to Munich and presented there at private performances in the Court Theater in the spring and fall of 1884 and again in the spring of 1885. When Ludwig died in 1886, the Munich Court Theater demanded the rights to perform the work as it wished. When the Prinzregententheater was finally built as a special Wagner theater, Ernst von Possart renewed the same demand. In spite of these attacks, Bayreuth managed to retain the work for itself: performances of *Parsifal* were the festival's main attraction, and they were successful from a financial point of view, too. The piece was widely discussed, but it could be seen only in Bayreuth. Countless reports have survived, describing the performances and revealing a broad spectrum of emotions from the overwhelming sense of dislocation felt by Alban Berg to the total rejection expressed by Igor Stravinsky. In 1903 concert excerpts from *Parsifal* were performed in Paris under Alfred Cortot, and at La Scala under Toscanini. And on 24 December of the same year the work was performed at the New York Metropolitan Opera, a production which went ahead in the face of the most violent protests by Cosima Wagner and her Bayreuth circle, and which became famous as "the rape of the Grail." The production was a sensational success, and was sent on tour throughout the United States, where it ran for 130 performances.

The second such unauthorized production took place in Amsterdam on 20 June 1905, and was organized by the local Wagner Society. Neither country had signed the Bern Convention, which was intended to protect works of art. Protests on the part of composers, conductors, and Wagner societies were all in vain. The sets for both productions were built in the Vienna studios of Hermann Burghart. In spite of Cosima's petition to the Reichstag in 1901 and a renewed appeal in 1912, this time supported by eighteen thousand signatures, the government declined to extend the period of copyright beyond the statutory thirty years after the composer's death. From 1914 on, the Sacred Stage Festival Play was freely available for any theater to perform. The race was on. Monte Carlo and Zurich had already stolen a march with productions in 1913. In Barcelona the local premiere began on New Year's Eve 1913 and lasted until five o'clock in the morning on New Year's Day. Later that same day the piece was first heard at the Charlottenburg Opera in Berlin and at the German Theater in Prague. In the course of January alone some forty German theaters mounted productions of *Parsifal* including Halle, Wuppertal-Barmen, Kiel, Mainz, Königsberg, and Chemnitz. Elsewhere there were productions in Vienna, London, Brussels, St. Petersburg, Budapest, Madrid, Milan, Rome, and Paris, where the work was playing at three different theaters at once. Many theaters imitated Bayreuth by covering the orchestra pit, announcing the individual acts by means of fanfares, lowering the lights in the auditorium, and having hour-long intermissions.

Adolphe Appia and Stage Design

For one of the Bayreuth Festival visitors in 1886, a performance of *Tristan* was to trigger ideas that would have a profound effect on the future course of stage design. The visitor in question was Adolphe Appia. He was disappointed by the illusionistic painted flats, which seemed to him an inadequate substitute for the visions of space and light conjured up by the music. His idea was to interpret the music in optical terms rather than to design more or less precise historical settings. Stylization and abstraction, the most important innovations of twentieth-century production style, can be traced back to Appia. His basic demands were for a three-dimensional space with acting areas at various levels over which the performers could move freely, and for changes in lighting to interpret musical and psychological processes. His realization that "music, in and through itself, never expresses a phenomenon, but rather the inner essence of that phenomenon" shows how far he had moved from naturalism in the theater. He was no longer a classical scene painter but rather a designer of spatial compositions. In his seminal work *Music and Staging,* written in French between 1892 and 1897, and published in German in 1899, he expounded his basic ideas, adding his thoughts and concepts for various individual works. *Tristan* and the *Ring* in particular were the object of intensive study on his part at this time. But Appia was categorized as a theorist, and the *Journal de Genève* appealed in vain to the Geneva Theater management to engage him for their new production of *Tristan.* An additional problem was that, if his ideas were to be realized at all, the most up-to-date stage technology was indispensable, including a dimmer-controlled lighting board, special backdrops, and, at a later date, a cyclorama.

It was first and foremost those members of the audience who were not seeking a superficial spectacle in Wagner's works but who hoped that the performance might reveal the message of the piece who were no longer satisfied with a nineteenth-century production style. Significantly, perhaps, discussions centered on the *Ring*. When Romain Rolland saw the *Ring* in Bayreuth in 1896, he felt only an intellectual pleasure: the universal import of a work which he had compared to the *Iliad* had certainly not escaped him, but not because of anything he had witnessed on the Bayreuth stage. George

Bernard Shaw conceived of the *Ring* as a vast sociorevolutionary parable. And Konstantin Sergeyevich Stanislavsky wrote that even a Wagnerian god could be made to seem plausible by a psychological grasp of his innermost being. The ground was prepared for a new interpretation of Wagner. Nonetheless, the change in performance style did not proceed from any current production ideas or from a new type of acting but from modern set designers who were attempting to translate Wagner's theatrical visions into a visual language appropriate to the age.

A start was made with the new production of *Tristan* at the Vienna Court Opera in 1903 to coincide with the twentieth anniversary of Wagner's death. The conductor was Gustav Mahler and the designer Alfred Roller, a friend of Gustav Klimt and president of the Vienna Secession. Roller was a master of the subtle interplay of color and form that typified the work of the Vienna Secessionists, and he was able to bring that mastery to bear on his stage designs. His view was indisputably influenced by Appia, though by no means directly dependent on him. His lighting plot for act 2 has always been seen as an especially impressive example of his work: first of all the flaming red of the torch, followed, during the love duet, by a shimmering deep-blue night turning to purple, and then, at Melot's betrayal, by the pale and sulphurous yellow rays of dawn. He had also evolved an alternative way of using space in this act: instead of the traditional dense forest foliage with a castle tower, there was a vast starry vault with pale moonlight playing on the castle's marmoreal walls. For the opening act he was the first designer to use a two-level deck, dividing the chorus scenes from the more intimate scenes in Isolde's tent. He also showed the play of light on the surface of the sea. Mahler and Roller again collaborated in 1905 on *Das Rheingold,* the first installment of a new production of the *Ring* that was followed in 1907 by *Die Walküre,* given uncut for the first time in Vienna. The collaboration came to an end when Mahler left the Vienna Opera. Roller's production had been the first conscious attempt to break away from the overpoweringly dominant Bayreuth model of 1896. Grane the horse was relegated to the wings, as was Fricka's pair of rams, while the Ride of the Valkyries was merely indicated by projecting scudding clouds on the backdrop. The Viennese audience, brought up on the sumptuous scenery of Brioschi, Burghart, Rottonara, and others, was slow to accept the new style.

Typical of Appia's influence at this time are the observations which Vsevolod Meyerhold set down in writing on the occasion of his production of *Tristan* at the Maryinsky Theater in St. Petersburg. He interpreted *Tristan* as a myth, not as a historical piece, and therefore found the historicism of "metal helmets and shields that gleam like samovars" to be false. This of course was the very historicism that Bayreuth had authorized. For him and his designer Alexander Konstantinovich Shervachidze it was sufficient to show a sail in act 1, massive castle walls in act 2, and, in the final act, bare cliffs in front of an infinite, dreary horizon. Characteristically, Meyerhold also drew upon Noh drama and Japanese art in formulating his ideas, noting how the latter is capable of expressing the whole of spring in a single blossoming twig.

Attempts to come to terms with the *Ring* were especially fruitful in influencing set design. A new feeling for nature was a striking feature of the years immediately after the turn of the century, a feeling that was clearly indebted to the *plein-air* paintings of the Impressionists and therefore unlike the nature paintings produced by studio artists. The landscapes designed by Gustav Wunderwald for the Deutsche Oper in Berlin in 1914 are entirely in the style of Giovanni Segantini. All attempts at stylization failed, however, when it came to the forest scene in act 2 of *Siegfried,* which turned out to be somewhat conventional even in the work of the younger designers. Among names that deserve to be mentioned here are Hans Wildermann, who designed the sets and costumes for the Cologne Easter Festival's productions of *Tristan* in 1911 and the *Ring* in 1912, and especially the young Ludwig Sievert, who, together with the director Franz Ludwig Hörth, undertook a rigorous stylistic reinterpretation of the *Ring* in Freiburg in 1912–13. This was the first time that a continuous cyclorama and a revolving stage had been used. In *Das Rheingold* the gods stood on a segment of a globe in an open space no longer circumscribed by flats. Sievert later redesigned his sets for productions in Baden-Baden in 1917, Hanover in 1925, and Frankfurt in 1926–27, but much of the expressive power of the original was lost in the process.

That these new ideas initially came to fruition only in isolated instances is clear from the new production of the *Ring* that was staged at the Berlin Court Opera in 1913 to mark the centenary of Wagner's birth. Whereas the smaller theaters had already begun to reform their stage productions, grand opera continued to be presented in Berlin in an inferior nineteenth-century style. The sets on this occasion were designed by Hans Kautsky; the director was the theater's general intendant, Georg von Hülsen; and the conductor was Leo Blech.

Aside from the *Ring,* it was *Parsifal* above all which presented a challenge to new designers, not least because there were so many productions of the work being staged in 1913 and 1914. Here, too, the nature scenes show a clear rejection of the somber, ponderous, solemn style of nineteenth-century landscape painting. Bright spring landscapes with snow-covered mountains, fresh green birch trees, and sunny alpine pastures speckled with yellow flowers in the manner of art nouveau paintings were the dominant features here. By contrast, the sets for the temple scenes were often exaggeratedly lavish and closely based on historical models such as Montserrat, San Vitale in Ravenna, or Mainz Cathedral; sometimes gently colored contours in a bright art nouveau framework were preferred instead.

Parsifal also benefited in a particularly fruitful way from one of Appia's ideas. He had suggested making the smooth tree trunks in the forest scenes look like pillars, which would create a solemn atmosphere in the forest and, at the same time, could be transformed into the pillars of the Grail Temple.

Ludwig Sievert adopted this idea in Freiburg in 1914, as did Gustav Wunderwald in Berlin, Hans Wildermann in Breslau, Johannes Schröder in Bochum-Duisburg in 1921, Heinrich Wendel in Düsseldorf, and Rolf Christiansen in Antwerp in 1972. Günther Uecker's abstract metal rods in Götz Friedrich's 1976 Stuttgart production, and the forest of cypresses designed by Jürgen Rose for Vienna in 1979, are part of this same tradition.

Productions during the Weimar Republic and the Third Reich

With the outbreak of the First World War all attempts at theatrical reform and all questions of interpretation suddenly became unimportant. The Bayreuth Festival had to be suspended in 1914 and was not able to open its doors again until ten years later. In France, England, and the United States, performances of Wagner's works were banned for the duration of the war. Wagner, after all, was now the music of the enemy.

The music itself was less to blame for this state of affairs than the people who claimed it for themselves. For the nationalists of the Wilhelmine era, it was Wagner's subject matter—more than his music—that served to legitimize their own imperial ideology (this was especially true of *Lohengrin*), and to confirm their saber-rattling policies. Nothing was done in Bayreuth or Wahnfried to counter this view—far from it. It had always been demanded there that Wagner's cause should be made a national cause, and as early as 1896 the *Bayreuther Blätter* had described the Festival Theater as an "Aryan citadel." The names Bayreuth and Wahnfried no longer stood merely for the festival or for certain artistic goals, but for a limited, narrow-minded ideology that was nationalist in outlook. The warning voices of Maximilian Harden and Paul Bekker, for example, were simply ignored. Bekker had advised against claiming Wagner as an artist while at the same time turning Bayreuth from a place of art into a hotbed of aesthetic and political reaction under the leadership of Houston Stewart Chamberlain. Chamberlain, who had married Eva Wagner, Wagner's daughter by Cosima, in 1908, established in 1923 the first contacts between Wahnfried and Hitler, a move which marked the beginning of Bayreuth's descent into the camp of *völkisch* nationalist ideology. When the festival reopened in 1924 in the presence of Erich von Ludendorff, the audience sang the German national anthem at the end of *Die Meistersinger*. Siegfried Wagner was incensed, but he had already hoisted the black, white, and red flag on the theater roof, a gesture symbolizing resistance to the Weimar Republic.

Artistically, Bayreuth produced very few new ideas during the 1920s. Festival funds had been exhausted by the war and by the ensuing period of inflation, and no more income could be expected from royalties, the period of copyright having expired in 1913. In consequence there was little money available for sets and costumes. Bits of scenery from the prewar period were combined with new, three-dimensional sets, most notably in the *Ring*. Not until 1930 did Siegfried Wagner succeed in realizing his stage conception in a new production of *Tannhäuser*, in which Arturo Toscanini made his Bayreuth conducting debut. The Elisabeth of Maria Müller set new standards for this role.

For intellectuals, and indeed for anyone interested in the theater in the 1920s, Wagner's music was felt to belong to the past and to be out of fashion. After the excesses of the prewar years, there was now a feeling of satiety. This rejection of the composer's works was regarded as a challenge by theatrical designers and, more particularly, by a new generation of directors who sought to interpret them as topical, contemporary works of art. It is owing to such people that these works survived artistically at a time when they were being exploited by the forces of political reaction.

Above all it was *Lohengrin* that, as the favorite work of the German Nationalists, was now stripped of its Romantic vestment. Leo Pasetti's sets for the 1929 Munich production were austerely stylized and rhythmically structured, in the same tradition as Renato Mordo's 1928 production in Darmstadt, where the designer had been Lothar Schenck von Trapp. At the German Theater in Prague in 1933 Emil Pirchan designed solid structures in the Bauhaus style for the director Herbert Graf. In addition to *Lohengrin*, the *Ring* in particular was subjected to a thorough stylistic reappraisal. Leo Pasetti's designs for a production of the cycle first seen at the National Theater in Munich in 1921–22 were heavily influenced by Adolphe Appia, but without compromising any of Pasetti's own individual painterly style. The conductor on this occasion was Bruno Walter and the director Anna Bahr-Mildenburg, a former singer who had been schooled by Cosima to the extent that it is questionable whether her production could ever have matched the new style of staging the work. Both the scenery and the production itself of the 1924 *Ring* at the German Theater in Prague were graphically expressionist in style. The director was Franz Ludwig Hörth, the designer Emil Pirchan, and the conductor Alexander Zemlinsky. The same production was later seen, during the 1928–29 season, at the Prussian State Opera in Berlin. For the Entry of the Gods into Valhalla, a motion-picture projector was used. The overall impression was of a successful synthesis of production values and stage concepts; even the starkly symbolic colors of the costumes formed part of the basic stylistic conception.

The violent contrasts between light and shade that were popular with expressionist artists were also a characteristic feature of Oskar Strnad's designs for the Dresden Opera in 1930. In 1922–23 one of the leading directors of the time, Saladin Schmitt, collaborated with the designer Johannes Schröder on a new *Ring* in Duisburg which was brutally expressionist in style, with a visionary and monumental visual force.

The 1920s also witnessed the realization of the only designs of Appia's to reach the stage. In 1923 Toscanini gave him a chance to stage *Tristan* at La Scala. Appia took as his starting point the designs he had published in his book *Music and Staging*, but in an even more simplified version. Appia by this time had entered his abstract phase. The Milan audiences were deeply dismayed by the art of this inexorable Calvinist, as they called him. The orchard in act 2 was merely suggested by a couple of cypresses and lit by a cold white light. It was described as looking more like a prison courtyard. The production was conducted by Toscanini, and the cast included Nanny Larsen-Todsen as Isolde and Ezio Pinza as King Marke.

As a result of his work in Milan, Appia was invited by the producer Oskar Wälterlin to design a *Ring* for him in Basel. In this way Appia was finally given an opportunity to come to grips with a work that had been central to all his theorizing. But the production got no further than *Das Rheingold* and *Die Walküre* in 1925. The Basel stage equipment was inadequate: there was no cyclorama, although Appia's designs urgently needed one; the footlights which he had categorically refused to countenance had to be used after all; Valhalla could not be shown by means of projections; and so on. His expedient solution was a system of steps, platforms, and curtains. Perhaps the technical shortcomings of the Basel stage were not so decisive. But Appia's writings on the subject were by now thirty years out of date; he himself had developed in the meantime and had entered an abstract geometrical phase. In the intervening period he had worked with Jacques Dalcroze in Hellerau and Geneva, where audiences had again found his style to be excessively cold and lacking in atmosphere. In any event, his productions failed to leave a mark on the history of the theater. Appia's significance lay more in the influence he exerted as a theorist.

The new production of *Holländer* at the Kroll Opera in January 1929 proved a highly political affair. The director was Jürgen Fehling, the conductor Otto Klemperer, and the sets were designed by Ewald Dülberg. The original Dresden version of the score was used without the revised ending of the overture and the final scene, with its motif of redemption. Of Nordic folklore there was not a trace; the costumes were contemporary, with Senta looking for all the world as though she had just stepped out of a fashion illustration by Käthe Kollwitz. Dülberg's designs were in the Neue Sachlichkeit style and dispensed with any attempt to evoke an atmospheric magic. Up-to-date stylistic devices were used to realize Wagner's elemental drama, and to realize it, moreover, with such alarming immediacy that the audience was reduced to a profound and unprecedented state of shock. The *Dutchman* was no longer a charming fairy tale. Fehling also imposed a new expressionist style of acting on the performers. There was widespread protest against the production, with the state being called upon to intervene and restore order. A storm was clearly brewing.

Jürgen Fehling was also responsible for the new *Tannhäuser* at the Berlin State Opera in February 1933, staged to mark the fiftieth anniversary of Wagner's death. The sets were designed by Oskar Strnad, and the conductor was again Otto Klemperer. After four performances the production had to be canceled, following severe pressure from the Kampfbund, or Battle League. It was the last attempt to reinterpret Wagner in a modern idiom before the general *Gleichschaltung* (conformist streamlining) of the Third Reich. On this occasion, too, the original Dresden version was used. Fehling and Strnad departed from the visual model that had always been associated with *Tannhäuser* and, instead of depicting scenes of medieval beauty, presented a specific society with specific views on the role of the artist. Herein lay the topicality of their interpretation. Nonconformist types were not tolerated. Harshness, gloom, and tragedy were exposed as the real message and meaning of the work, not its beautiful surface. It was only natural that the production was banned.

For the propaganda machine of national socialism Richard Wagner was the representative German artist. Hitler's visits to the Bayreuth Festival were exploited for propagandist purposes by radio and newsreel. *Die Meistersinger* became the official opera of the Nuremberg party congresses. The Potsdam congress ended with a performance of *Die Meistersinger* on 22 March 1933. The international radio broadcast of the same work from the Bayreuth Festival later that summer was used by Goebbels to make a major propaganda speech. In 1939 an open-air production of *Rienzi* was staged as part of the summer festival in Berlin, the capital of the Reich, and turned into a mass spectacle with sets by the Reich's official designer, Benno von Arent. Performance figures for the 1930s, however, reveal that Wagner was no longer the most widely performed composer in Germany. He was falling off in popularity, having been surpassed by Verdi. Indeed, during the Second World War he even fell back to fifth place, behind Verdi, Puccini, Mozart, and Lortzing.

What the German theaters were now expected to present was not modern experimentation but performances that were true to the spirit of the work. Realistic sets were the order of the day. The country's cultural inheritance had to be cited in the scenery; autochthonous architecture was also practiced onstage. One example among many for the total conformity to propagandist aims is the work of Benno von Arent, whose sets and costumes for *Meistersinger* were personally authorized by Hitler. His designs for Sachs's workshop at the beginning of the third act were intended to express the message "Honor work, respect the workers." The Festival Meadow, with its row of flags receding into the distance and massed array of extras, resembled nothing so much as a Nuremberg rally, a Festival Meadow à la the Third Reich. Arent revived his official version of *Die Meistersinger* at Nuremberg and Berlin in 1935, at Munich in 1936, at Danzig in 1938, at Weimar in 1939, and at Linz in 1941.

If, in spite of pressure from above, Arent never worked in Bayreuth, it was because of the decision of Winifred Wagner, who was now in charge of the festival. By the end of the 1920s Siegfried Wagner had become conscious that sweeping reforms were now vitally necessary. The team he had in mind to institute these changes were the conductor and director Heinz Tietjen and the designer Emil Preetorius. When Siegfried died in 1930, Winifred began to work with them on a program of theater reform. In an age of state-decreed realism, Bayreuth was able to go its own artistically tenable way, having been granted free rein, to some extent, on the strength of its international importance. In the final analysis Bayreuth was needed as a cultural label. And the festival certainly used the freedom it had been given. Preetorius' sets for the *Ring*—and for *Lohengrin, Tristan,* and *Holländer*—were in muted colors, highly graphic in outline, with restful, arching contours and a sure sense of proportion. His Valkyrie rock in particular became a symbol of Bayreuth's stage reforms. In 1934 the old *Parsifal* production, which had survived almost unaltered since the work's first performances in 1882, was replaced by a newer one, a change which led to violent protests on the part of the older Wagnerians. The new sets were designed by Alfred Roller. These years also saw the first fruits of Wieland Wagner's work as a designer. He was responsible for the new *Parsifal* sets in 1937, and for the sets and costumes of the 1943 *Meistersinger*.

Mention should also be made of a curiosity which is, however, characteristic of the fascists' appreciation of Wagner. In 1938 a performance of act 2 of *Lohengrin* was given in Rome to mark Hitler's visit to the Eternal City. A real minster was created in the Foro Mussolini, with a tower some 130 feet high, facing a complete Norman castle several stories tall. The stage was 130 yards in width, and the chorus is said to have numbered some ten thousand. The soloists included Maria Caniglia and Ebe Stignani.

During these years, and even at the height of the Second World War, Wagner's works were not subjected to a boycott in countries at war with Germany, as they had been during the First World War. The old productions continued to be revived, with few innovations in terms of staging or design. For the many Wagnerian singers who were forced to emigrate from Germany at that time, it meant that there was at least the hope of finding work. And for audiences from Buenos Aires to New York and from London to Paris, this meant direct contact with many stars of what is fondly referred to as the golden age of Wagnerian singing.

Of the great names of the 1920s and 1930s, whose voices are almost all documented in the form of phonograph records, a mere list must suffice here: Lotte Lehmann, Maria Jeritza, Lauritz Melchior, Franz Völker, Set Svanholm, Kirsten Flagstad, Frida Leider, Martha Fuchs, Rudolf Bockelmann, Alexander Kipnis, Maria Müller, Max Lorenz, Josef von Manowarda, Jaro Prohaska, Gotthelf Pistor, Helen Traubel, Emmanuel List, and so on. Conductors who deserve to be named here include Wilhelm Furtwängler, Victor de Sabata, Hans Knappertsbusch, the young Herbert von Karajan, and Clemens Krauss.

As a political gesture toward the German Reich, which had concluded a border and friendship treaty with the Soviet Union in 1939, a production of *Die Walküre* was staged at Moscow's Bolshoi Theater in November 1940. The director was Sergei Eisenstein. Given the political situation, his production of *Die Walküre* was bound to remain an isolated phenomenon, although it anticipated much that was to come to fruition during the 1970s. Eisenstein wanted to achieve an "audio-visual unity" of stage picture and music: everything that was recounted in the music was to be visualized onstage. In order to realize this aim he invented the so-called mimic chorus, which accompanied

Sieglinde's narration in act 1, for example, performing a mime show. For the Ride of the Valkyries he demanded whole groups of flying Valkyries. His hope was to achieve a mobility of action and sets such as had been possible up to that point only in films. Eisenstein himself claimed that the performance was intended to be "realistic in its essential detail, mythological in its structure, epic in its generalized forms, and emotional in the changing variety of its musical and visual portrayal" (Burzawa 1989, p. 303).

When war broke out in 1939, Winifred Wagner wanted to close the Festival Theater, but Hitler ordered the so-called wartime festivals to proceed. The organization called Strength Through Joy was entrusted with the task of distributing tickets and entertaining festival visitors. Tickets were given by preference to soldiers and munitions workers. In 1943 and 1944 only *Die Meistersinger* was performed at the festival.

Postwar Productions

Whereas 1945 was of no great historical significance in the performing practices of most of the world's great opera houses, the situation in Germany was bound to be different. Many of the theaters had been destroyed, and an attempt was made to get by on what could be salvaged from the aftermath of war in order to meet the insatiable thirst for theater. New theaters began to rise from the rubble during the 1950s, and the opera most frequently chosen to open the first wave of newly constructed buildings was once again *Die Meistersinger,* just as it had been at the turn of the century. It was as though nothing had happened. A striking feature of these productions during the 1950s and early 1960s was the use of high and brightly lit church windows in act 1. In the rebuilding of the country's medieval churches, bright transparent glass had been installed in preference to opaque stained-glass windows. Was this symbolic of a new luminosity after an age of darkness and gloom?

Even if a lack of suitable materials forced many theaters to make an aesthetic virtue of necessity during the immediate postwar years, once supplies became more plentiful there still remained a reluctance to return to the realistic production style of the past. The early 1950s saw many ethereal, allusive, and stylized productions which nevertheless achieved a great deal of individuality within their self-imposed framework. The days of a unified style were over. The set designs of Emil Preetorius formed a bridge, as it were, between the 1940s and 1950s, representing continuity and standardization at one and the same time. Once he had developed his basic concept, Preetorius reproduced the same designs in a wide variety of opera houses with very few modifications. His 1938 Bayreuth *Tristan,* for example, reappeared in Amsterdam in 1948, in Munich in 1958, and in Vienna in 1959. The same was true of his sets for the *Ring,* which were still being used in Vienna in the 1970s. Plausible and tasteful, the Preetorius style was widely copied and gave rise to a sort of school.

The Bayreuth Festival finally reopened in the summer of 1951. Wagner's grandchildren Wieland and Wolfgang were now in charge, and the period of New Bayreuth, as it has been called, has without doubt been one of the most fruitful and influential in the whole performance history of Wagner's works. Even the opening production of *Parsifal* on 30 July 1951 had a programmatic message: it was no longer merely a question of stage reform but rather of coming to terms intellectually with the work. Wieland Wagner's *Parsifal* left a decisive mark on the New Bayreuth style, a style that is symbolized by his Grail Temple consisting of only four golden-red shimmering columns rising up out of the darkness. In his so-called *Parsifal* Cross Wieland gave visual expression to his understanding of the work. In the field of tension created by the polar opposites Mother-Savior, Klingsor-Titurel (or of the archetypes swan-dove, spear-chalice) Parsifal's spiritual and intellectual development is enacted in a perfectly symmetrical arch whose turning point is Kundry's kiss, representing the mystic center, climax, nadir, and circle of the path of salvation all in one. Wieland's production remained in the festival repertoire until 1973. In the mid-1960s he and Pierre Boulez began a comprehensive overhaul of the work both scenically and musically, but his death in 1966 left the plan incomplete.

Wieland's 1951 production of the *Ring* remained within the Bayreuth tradition of cautious stylization for the first two years of its existence, but 1953–54 saw a break with this tradition and a rigorous application of Adolphe Appia's ideas. A central disc as a raised acting area and a wide cyclorama created a symbolic space within which the intellectual drama of the *Ring* could unfold. Light was used for dramaturgical effect, with new color combinations and projections developed over long periods of intensive rehearsal. The costumes were no longer Germanic in style but were based instead on the costumes of classical Greek tragedy. Starting from the realization that the *Ring* is related to Greek mythology, Wieland was able to offer a new perspective on the work in which the nationalist element was rendered inconsequential in the face of an insight into the basic coherence of Western culture and the timelessness of myth. *Lohengrin* was staged by Wieland in 1958 as a highly stylized mystery play in blue and silver. His *Tannhäuser* in 1954 and again in 1961 was a drama of ideas in which the Middle Ages were merely a conceptual space symbolized by a golden background against which the action took place. His abstract production of *Meistersinger* in 1956 gave rise to a good deal of protest, and booing was heard for the first time within the precincts of the Festival Theater. The mastersingers without Nuremberg, it was called, and with some justification. The town no longer appeared as part of the background. The second-act set, with a stone surface and two huge umbels hovering above it in the infinite blue of a summer's night, was perhaps the most famous of Wieland's many designs.

The New Bayreuth style, with its tendency toward abstraction and stylization, was imitated everywhere, producing a kind of internationally valid performance style. As early as 1956, in his Hamburg *Ring,* Günther Rennert and his designer Helmut Jürgens had declared their support for a "concrete" presentation of the "emblems and symbols" contained in the *Ring*. In Rennert's opinion the *Ring* required the very objects that Bayreuth had dispensed with, since for him such objects as a tree or a hearth or a door were meaningful realities. Wieland, too, in his second *Ring* production in 1965 moved away from the timelessness of his first production and in the direction of concrete historical allusions: "Valhalla is Wall Street" became something of a catchphrase, in keeping with Hans Mayer's description of the *Ring* as a "bourgeois parable."

Even during the 1960s various attempts were made to break away from the existing scheme of *Ring* productions. In 1967 Gustav Rudolf Sellner collaborated with the sculptor Fritz Wotruba to produce a *Ring* in Berlin that was notable for its archaic blocklike structures. For their Metropolitan Opera production in the 1960s and for the Salzburg Easter Festival production of 1967–1970 Herbert von Karajan and Günther Schneider-Siemssen staged the *Ring* as a drama of vast cosmic spaces in which the elemental forces of nature—rain, storms, and scudding clouds—could be represented by means of a detailed lighting plot.

The New Bayreuth of the 1950s and 1960s not only saw the development of a new performing style, it also witnessed the emergence of a new generation of Wagnerian singers whose status is now legendary. Among those who deserve to be mentioned here are Astrid Varnay and Martha Mödl, Hans Hotter (the "regular Wotan"), Josef Greindl, Birgit Nilsson (*the* Brünnhilde and Isolde of her day), Jerome Hines, Theo Adam, Hans Beirer, Gottlob Frick, Wolfgang Windgassen (who sang all the great tenor roles), Elisabeth Grümmer (unforgettable as Elsa and Elisabeth), Leonie Rysanek and James King (for many years an ideal pair of Wälsung lovers), Marrti Talvela, Anja Silja (as Senta and Elisabeth), Ramon Vinay, Hans Hopf, and others. Among conductors, too, only a handful of names can be singled out: Eugen Jochum, Hans Knappertsbusch, Joseph Keilberth, the young Wolfgang Sawallisch, Rudolf Kempe, and Karl Böhm. Karajan has already been mentioned.

It was the school of Walter Felsenstein that provided the impetus necessary to supplant the New Bayreuth style as the dominant force in Wagner productions. Felsenstein believed in a realistic form of music theater with concrete historical allusions. In 1962 his pupil Joachim Herz produced *Holländer* at the Komische Oper in Berlin and, together with his designer Rudolf Heinrich, transferred the action to the bourgeois milieu of the 1840s, the date when the work was written. Daland's ship was a steamer, and the meeting between the Dutchman and Senta in Daland's parlor took place at a living room table. With its bourgeois realism, this was a *Holländer* set in the world of Ibsen.

The idea of locating Wagner's works at the time of their composition became thoroughly fashionable in the 1970s, as always happens when imitators take hold of an original idea. All of the composer's works, from *Meistersinger* to *Tristan* and *Lohengrin,* were now relocated in the nineteenth century. At the same time, particular weight was placed on authentic costumes. In the 1970s the *Ring* especially was subjected to the most exciting new interpretations. The centenary of the first Bayreuth Festival in 1976 provided many opera houses with an opportunity to mount new productions of the cycle. But there was also a deeper reason. The events of 1968 had made the *Ring* seem highly topical in the eyes of directors, designers, and conductors. Cassel was the first to make a start in 1970 (with the director Ulrich Melchinger and the designer Thomas Richter-Forgach); followed by Leipzig in 1973 (Joachim Herz directing and Rudolf Heinrich as designer); London in 1974 (with Götz Friedrich directing, Josef Svoboda as designer, and Colin Davis conducting); La Scala, also in 1974 (with director Luca Ronconi, designer Pier Luigi Pizzi, and conductor Wolfgang Sawallisch); and Geneva in 1975 (with director Jean-Claude Riber and designer Josef Svoboda). Whereas New Bayreuth had emphasized the *Ring*'s mythic timelessness, it was very much the work's historical specificity which was now being examined. The social questions of the nineteenth century and the history and criticism of ideology determined the way that the piece was interpreted. And the history of the cycle's reception and influence was now regarded as a part of the work itself, and it was staged accordingly. The main concern was to rescue the *Ring* from the vagueness of a classical setting and restore its topicality. One took the technique of alienation from the spoken theater. One no longer had to conform to a single binding style. Thus, depending on one's starting point, the *Ring* might be set in the 1870s, in the early years of the Industrial Revolution, in the era of Pop Art, or during the Third Reich; or German folklore or constructivism might be the dominant influence; and a collage technique might serve not only to point out the wealth of allusions that the *Ring* contains but also to draw attention to its inconsistencies.

The 1976 Bayreuth centenary *Ring,* directed by Patrice Chéreau, conducted by Pierre Boulez, and designed by Richard Peduzzi (sets) and Jacques Schmidt (costumes), became a milestone in the work's performance history. The starting point for Chéreau's interpretation was with the conditions of individual freedom that exist in a system of power such as that in which Wotan and Alberich operate. Individual human freedom is sanctioned by the gods only to the extent that it helps them maintain or regain their power. Even the freedom of Siegfried himself, ostensibly the freest of heroes, is programmed by Wotan. It was not only the political aspect of the cycle that Chéreau presented onstage, however, but also Wagner's human alternative as embodied by Siegmund's love for Sieglinde and Siegfried's love for Brünnhilde. And he also showed the bitterness and grief that is felt when that love is destroyed, betrayed, cheated, and sacrificed to the will to power. Chéreau saw in Wagner's return to Germanic myth an attempt to give a cultural foundation and a past to a certain period of history, and at the same time to depict the attitudes of his own generation. For him the *Ring* was "an allegory of the nineteenth century" which, "in the guise of myth," deals with us, too. His production style reflected this multilayered view of the work and used pictorial elements from various ages and stylistic movements, employing them both symbolically and referentially. One retains a memory above all of stunning stage pictures and of a handling of the individual singers that set new standards in operatic acting.

It is noteworthy that at the end of the 1970s a number of *Ring* productions came to grief and in some cases were never even completed. The reason did not always lie in technical difficulties; rather, the uses of this particular production style had already been exhausted. Making the work topical by locating it in an age of technology and thereby producing an alienation effect could illuminate individual aspects of the cycle at best, but the effectiveness of such a procedure was bound to be quickly depleted. In Nikolaus Lehnhoff's San Francisco *Ring* the nineteenth century was merely an excuse for evoking beautiful stage pictures in the style of Karl Friedrich Schinkel and Caspar David Friedrich.

A more independent line has been followed in Berlin with Götz Friedrich's production of the *Ring* (designed by Peter Sykora), and the same is true of Herbert Wernicke's Munich *Holländer* and Hamburg *Meistersinger* of 1984. New impulses in the 1980s were provided by Ruth Berghaus in Frankfurt and Harry Kupfer in Bayreuth.

Translated by Stewart Spencer

CHAPTER 21

Sprechgesang *or Bel Canto:*
Toward a History of Singing Wagner

JENS MALTE FISCHER

Fundamentals

As the turbulent Bayreuth Festival of 1983 came to an end, with controversies over the new *Ring* production and over strained vocal chords mainly because of the heavy demands placed on the Wagnerian tenors, the festival director Wolfgang Wagner gave vent to his despair and frustration and suggested that, given the excessive demands of today's audiences, the great Heldentenors of the 1920s and 1930s such as Lauritz Melchior and Max Lorenz would probably be booed. In view of the numerous recordings that exist of both these tenors, some of which were made from live recordings, anyone with an interest in historical opera and recordings knows that such a statement is untenable. But festival directors have always complained: "What good is it to me if I write such beautiful things and can't find a singer who understands how to perform them?" That was said by the grandfather of Wolfgang Wagner in 1875 to the singing teacher Julius Hey during preparations for the first festival. Difficulties with singers have always existed, and to answer the old, controversial question of whether singing today is much worse than it was sixty, eighty, or one hundred years ago is not the aim of this discussion. It is easy to deliver sweeping judgments on the "crisis in the art of singing," in the words of Wolf Rosenberg. To substantiate the indictment in individual cases is harder; and at any rate one must distinguish between types of voices and styles of opera, for although at present there are singers of the Italian and French tenor repertoire who are justly celebrated, the prognosis for Wagnerian tenors is an extremely gloomy one.

Much of what I am going to say will be dismissed by anyone who disagrees with it as mere subjective judgment. Nonetheless I believe that in the area of singing, objective judgments reach much farther than is generally supposed, and there is only one area in which taste is truly the decisive factor: namely the judgment of timbre, of the individual coloring of the voice and of vocal character. For all the other areas there are criteria which derive from several centuries of theoretical consideration of the problems of the art of singing, and according to which, for all the differences in detail, there is acknowledged to be a broad unanimity about basic issues. I cannot go into the fundamentals of singing here; I will just refer to the book by the singing teacher Franziska Martienssen-Lohmann, *Der wissende Sänger* (3rd ed., Zurich, 1981). Since I believe that the criteria for Wagnerian singing are fundamentally the same as those that are valid for singing in general (one of the main reasons for bad Wagnerian singing is that a basic difference is taken for granted), here are the ten commandments of Franziska Martienssen-Lohmann for faultless singing, which I place here as a signpost to my discussion:

1. Sovereign command of breath and body
2. Purity and certainty of intonation
3. Clarity and balance of vowels and their placement
4. Balanced timbre in all registers
5. Volume, carrying power, and resonance
6. Control of all degrees of volume
7. Calmness of floating notes
8. Naturalness of articulation and vividness of projection
9. Grasp of tempo, capacity to accentuate, rhythmic suspension
10. Legato and line—the heart of singing

Even a brief discussion of all these points would require a chapter of its own. Only a few need to be singled out as being of special significance for singing Wagner. One hears much lamentation these days about the shortage of the great voices which are supposedly required for Wagner. Yet in the wake of Karajan's *Ring* recordings and performances, the opportunity has also not been missed to interpret Wagner as a sort of chamber music for smaller voices. For what constitutes a big voice turns out, on closer inspection, to elicit little agreement. Some talk of volume, others of metal, intensity of sound, or carrying power. *Volume* is not something that a voice possesses by nature; it is the outcome of a maturing process for which spaciousness and expansiveness of the vocal apparatus are prerequisites. Volume is something that any voice can achieve in principle. Given two singers with equal potential for producing volume, in the end physical condition will be the deciding factor. This is the reason why large voices (which without question are necessary for Wagner) are seldom concealed in slim, slight figures, but are more readily found in singers with athletic builds (by which is not meant elephantine corpulence or striking obesity, as was characteristic of Ludwig Schnorr von Carolsfeld, the first Tristan, who was idolized by Wagner).

At a time when many singers who produce sounds of a certain loudness are considered Wagnerian singers, we must look briefly into the matter of loudness. In terms of acoustics, one must distinguish correctly between *loud-*

ness and *intensity of sound,* in addition to considering the loudness level as a concept in the psychology of perception. The relationship between two degrees of sound energy can be expressed as the differential in noise strength. The unit of measurement is the *phon.* The mean volume of singing voices lies between 65 and 85 phons; the fortissimo of a Heldentenor can reach 100 phons; the pain threshold is approximately 130 phons. It is important to point out that the subjective experience of loudness by no means corresponds exactly to the phon scale; thus a sound at double the number of phons is not experienced as being twice as loud. That is why in acoustics the concept of loudness is introduced (with its own measurement of *sone*), which does more justice to the subjective impression of hearing. Now, where the required volume of so-called dramatic voices is concerned, especially Wagnerian voices, it is necessary to ensure that the volume which is experienced as convincing loudness is based on the optimum development of the resonance cavities and on perfect breath technique; that is, the *carrying power* of the voice must also be correspondingly developed. It seems to me that one of the main problems of contemporary Wagnerian singing is that volume and carrying power are mistaken for each other. Carrying power, in which the so-called overtones play a large part (a topic on which I cannot expand further here), is wholly independent of loudness. But it plays a decisive role in creating the *impression* of loudness, and thus loudness is again decisive for giving the impression of a dramatic voice. Carrying power is also independent of the volume of a voice and can be at the disposal of small voices. So the tenor Tito Schipa was able, owing to perfectly developed carrying power, to fill the great houses, such as the Teatro Colón in Buenos Aires, tirelessly, although he perhaps possessed the smallest voice of all the great tenors of the past. What must be achieved equally by dramatic and by lyric tenors is *penetrating power,* which can rest on the one hand on physical requirements but, on the other hand, is also a matter of variable *dynamics.* Carrying power, volume, penetrating power, and dynamics decide, so to speak, the fate of a dramatic voice in general, and a Wagnerian voice in particular. When an originally lyric tenor gains the power of penetration, one calls him in Italy a *lirico spinto* tenor. It is a fatal mistake of many singers to think that volume and the effect of loudness can be supported by emphatic body work and increased air consumption. There were and are prominent Wagnerian singers with whom in fortissimo one can observe bulging neck veins and a wobbling head—an extremely bad sign. The problem is that many singers are absolutely convinced that they can increase the loudness of their notes by such means. For the listener (and this is the decisive factor) the carrying power of the voice actually diminishes through such tension, and the impression of loudness is decreased; thus the opposite effect from that striven for is attained. Anyone who wants to know how the impression of elemental vocal power and enormous volume can be achieved without resorting to tensed-up exertion should listen to the best records of the Italian baritone Titta Ruffo. Singers of Wagner can learn from him.

Wagner's Singers and the Bayreuth School

Wagner's reported complaints about his inability to find singers for his festivals are signs that he was defeated in a much more limited undertaking than the founding of the festival, namely the establishment of a music school dedicated to preparing singers to perform his works. In 1865 Wagner had submitted to his royal patron Ludwig II a proposal for a German music school to be established in Munich, but unfavorable circumstances prevented its realization. At the center of the curriculum for this school would have stood the development of singing. Even then Wagner located the difficulties of a German art of song in the peculiarities of the German language. Wagner saw the basic faults of the singers of his time, when they sang German opera, as being the thoughtless absorption of the prevailing Italian bel canto school into German operatic singing. In contrast to Italian vocalism, in German energetic speaking accents must take the foreground, being especially suitable for dramatic performance. But it must be emphasized that in his proposal to Ludwig, Wagner expressly says that the melodious sound of the Italian school should not thereby be sacrificed—a warning which would be painfully neglected in the Bayreuth school after Wagner's death.

Wagner always had conflicting feelings about Italian bel canto. It is probable that a traumatic childhood experience played an important part in this. In Wagner's mother's house the Italian castrato Sassaroli, a colleague of Wagner's sister Klara at the Dresden Opera, used to visit from time to time, and he alarmed the child, in spite of his good nature, with his shrieking laughter and his strange voice, arousing in Wagner, as he explains in *My Life,* a powerful hostility toward Italian singing and speech. The contrary influence to this came from Wilhelmine Schröder-Devrient, who was later to be his first Senta. The "demonic warmth of her human-ecstatic performance" was a model for him, and her occasional abandonment of singing tone for dramatic effect decisively shaped his idea of speech-song. An echo of how Schröder-Devrient must have affected him can be heard in the recordings of the great Lilli Lehmann (as a singer the younger woman was surely far more impeccable), who participated in the first Bayreuth Festival of 1876 and was Brünnhilde in the *Ring* in 1896. There is only one uncharacteristic Wagner excerpt on record, but perhaps the famous recording of Donna Anna's aria "Or sai chi l'onore" shows clearly what I mean.

After the failure of the Munich plans, Wagner had concerns other than the founding of a music school; but he never forgot those plans. When the first festivals in Bayreuth were over, they surfaced again, but now reduced to their core, namely as a sketch for a school specifically for training in the style of the master's works. But this idea also failed, among other reasons because there were not enough singers who were ready to, or in a position to, undertake a months'-long excursion to Bayreuth. In 1892 for the first time Cosima was able to open a school in style training, but of very reduced scope. The head was not Julius Hey, the experienced vocal adviser of the first festivals; instead Julius Kniese was appointed, and he also was in charge of training at the festivals. Kniese seems to have been the crucial figure in the negative development of the characteristic Bayreuth singing style of the turn of the century. Under Cosima's aegis and Kniese's direction, the Wagnerian idea of speech-song—or *Sprechgesang,* as it was later called—was wildly exaggerated. This was partly the result of a misunderstanding of Wagner's abiding doctrine, according to which he demanded a beautiful sound and insisted that there must be legato, something which he had declared indispensable in, for example, *Lohengrin,* and which was now wholly sacrificed. Leo Slezak, who once sang unsuccessfully in Bayreuth and then went on to become one of the leading Wagnerian singers outside of Bayreith, reported that with Cosima, and with Kniese as well, one had to sing in full voice at every rehearsal until one's voice was totally exhausted.

What has this to do with the idea of speech-song? Wagner thought that only a performer who understood how to recite his part in accordance with the intentions of the poet could sing in accord with the intentions of the composer. Work with his singers thus always began with detailed reading rehearsals. The dramatic effect of the sense should be intensified through "speech-sculpture." To rectify errors in intonation, Wagner made the singers first of all enunciate clearly during the singing; then he concentrated on correct breathing; and finally he formed the movement of the melodic line through swelling and accentuation. The models which Wagner always invoked for his speech-song were, on the one hand, Wilhelmine Schröder-Devrient as Leonore and, on the other hand, the scene between Tamino and the Speaker from Mozart's *Zauberflöte.* Mozart was on this point the founder of German declamation. In the Wagner recordings from the turn of the century a surprisingly clear division is noticeable. With singers who primarily sang Wagner in Bayreuth or underwent their training there (such as Pelagie Greef-Andriessen, Anton van Rooy, and Theodor Bertram, in individually varying degrees), the one-sidedness of this principle is painfully apparent: the legato principle is to a large extent abandoned; each syllable, each consonant, is gasped out with the greatest energy; breathing is often against the vocal line; and the most glorious vocal means (as, for instance, with Theodor Bertram, possibly the most powerful heroic baritone voice ever recorded) thereby achieve only an incomplete effect. Here begins what English critics have called the "Bayreuth bark," and what one wit has dubbed "can belto" instead of bel canto. If, by contrast, one listens to singers who came to fame and glory as Wagner interpreters outside Bayreuth, in Vienna perhaps or New York, one hears in many cases perfect Wagnerian singing which can still serve today as ideals. I mention here only the soprano Johanna Gadski, who sang primarily at the Metropolitan Opera, the tenors Leo Slezak and Jacques Urlus, and the contralto Ernestine Schumann-Heink. It was, paradoxically, precisely the Bayreuth doctrine of speech-song which gave support to the supposed unsingableness of the Wagnerian roles with the evidence of all too many ruined voices. It also made no difference that Wagner himself had already predicted to Julius Hey in 1875 that under the rubric of speech-song, unfortunately only a powerfully intensified speaking of the text would be understood, and that this would always be defeated in unequal combat with the orchestra. Under this absurd doctrine (as Wagner called it) many beautiful voices went to an early grave. But that was precisely the method that Bayreuth adopted after Wagner's death.

The master himself was not innocent, on account of many ambiguous utterances, of this development. Certainly he lacked ultimate insight into technical problems. In this respect one may note that during rehearsals for the first festival his Siegfried, Georg Unger, had to repeat the same phrase until he was exhausted, all because Wagner believed that Unger's basic problem, which was a strongly palatal approach to sound, could be corrected. But Wagner was sensible enough to seek as a balance the collaboration of the best singing teacher of his time, Julius Hey. Cosima, however, obviously did not understand much about singing, and Kniese was not a singing teacher but a choral director. Above all throughout his life Wagner retained a mental image of vocal beauty based on the recollection of the voice of his first Rienzi and Tannhäuser, Josef Tichatschek. Italian bel canto carried over into the Wagnerian parts as legato, the natural gift of a "lovely tremulous smile" in the voice, a tireless, virile, and radiant vocal organ: all that had indelibly imprinted on Wagner, according to his own testimony, the ideal of how a dramatic tenor must sound. Tichatschek had nonetheless in Wagner's view one decisive failing: he could not achieve access to the deeper dimensions of humanity, so he was not, above all, able to approach the accents of pain which Wagner demanded of Tannhäuser. This was in the right hands for the first time with Schnorr von Carolsfeld, the first Tristan, and a singer whom Wagner mourned long after his premature death (Hey nonetheless claimed that Schnorr had in no wise sung with impeccable technique). Albert Niemann, the Tannhäuser of the Paris scandal, was called upon by Wagner to be the first Siegmund in Bayreuth.

Wagner's ambivalent attitude toward the problems of singing is clear in his relationship to bel canto. His model of German opera singing he always described as German or "vaterländisch" bel canto. As I have mentioned, the castrato was for him the negative symbol of the Italian art of singing; yet he did not want to sacrifice the beauty of sound that resulted from the way voices were trained in Italy. On the one hand he mocked in the strongest terms "so-called Italian voice training," but on the other he praised Tichatschek's way of carrying over bel canto into the singing of his own music. The older Wagner, perhaps conditioned by his ever-longer sojourns in Italy, established a more positive attitude toward bel canto. Cosima noted in her diary for 3 August 1872: "Richard sings a cantilena from *I Puritani*, and remarks that Bellini wrote melodies lovelier than one's dreams. The melody recalls Rubini to him, how wonderfully he sang it" (Rubini was the most celebrated Italian tenor of the 1840s and 1850s). But Cosima seems to have suppressed such statements later; for example, in a letter of 1890 to Richard

Strauss, who had recommended a baritone to her, she writes: "I remember Herr von Milde. But I fear bel canto on his part, which will already be represented for us by Reichmann and Scheidemantel." One sees that bel canto has finally become a term of abuse. Additional evidence is provided by many leading Bayreuth singers of that time: a comparison between the interpretation of Wolfram by Anton van Rooy and by the great Italian baritone Mattia Battistini is very instructive in this connection.

One often encounters the view that the blame for this negative development is borne by Julius Hey's monumental *German Singing Primer* (Hey 1884), for Hey was the champion of the extreme speech-song ideology. That this view is false must be clear to everyone who looks carefully enough into Hey's work, which even today provides enthralling reading. Hey got to know Wagner in Munich in 1864 and was made technical singing adviser for the first festival. In Hey's memoirs we have a source of extraordinary richness for Wagner's demonstrations of the vocal interpretation of his works and for his rehearsal technique (Hey 1911). In Hey's primer on singing, which appeared a year after Wagner's death, we find the account of Hey's long experience as a successful teacher and as a collaborator with Wagner. As we have seen, Hey was not engaged for the festivals after Wagner's death. When he next visited Bayreuth, in 1902, he was horrified by Julius Kniese's technical preparation of most of the singers. Hey's primer on singing is interesting because it is in no way a bible of speech-song; instead its principles are much more along the lines of Wagnerian bel canto, to express it in simplified terms. Certainly Hey also saw in Wagner's thinking a difference between German and Italian styles of singing, but he never tired of asserting that for German dramatic singers the basic prerequisites of bel canto were of the greatest importance. One quotation from this work, whose aim is the training of the ideal Wagnerian singer, must suffice: "As we have seen, there is not a singing discipline of the Italian school, no region of vocal virtuosity, which the German singing-method could not develop just as exhaustively."

It is not difficult, in the light of turn-of-the-century recordings, among which recordings of Wagner had a place from the beginning, to test my theory that a gulf opened between Bayreuth on the one hand and Vienna and New York on the other, which became ever deeper through the ideological narrow-mindedness of the Bayreuth circle (one need only recall the battle over performing *Parsifal* outside Bayreuth). Julius Hey did not realize that his (and in many ways Wagner's) presentation of correct Wagnerian singing had caught on internationally. But in Bayreuth, too, the state of affairs I have described did not last. Under Kniese's successor at Bayreuth, Carl Kittel (who held this post from 1912 to 1939), relations improved markedly. Kittel often expressed his view about performance styles in the *Bayreuth Festival Guide (Festspielführer)* during the 1930s. As far as singing was concerned, he turned out to be wholly in Hey's camp, taking a careful middle course between speech-song and bel canto. The records that emerged from Bayreuth from the second half of the 1920s verify this with the greatest clarity. The broader tolerance of the festival director Siegfried Wagner and also of Winifred Wagner had beneficial results in this respect too. The engagement of Arturo Toscanini as a Bayreuth conductor would have been as unthinkable under Cosima and Kniese as that of a German bel canto singer such as Franz Völker, or of Gunnar Graarud, Maria Müller, or Alexander Kipnis, all singers who embodied the so-called bel canto style and therewith all those virtues which Wagner and Hey had had in mind.

Bass and Baritone

The fundamental power of the bass probably has to do with bigger vocal chords and with the particularly wide vocal tract which, according to its constitution, amplifies the basic tone and the deep overtones of the vocal chords. What a baritone is—statistically the most common male vocal range—receives only a fleeting word of explanation in the literature on vocal physiology. Art music for a long time was not even particularly interested in bass voices. Relatively early in the history of opera, with Monteverdi, the bass received its characteristic profile as basso profondo, with little higher vocal extension. Pluto, Neptune, and Charon are the typical Monteverdian bass figures, among whom Seneca in *L'incoronazione di Poppea* is certainly the richest; the essential features are the majestic, the solemn, and the manner of old age. In the nineteenth century, too, the authority of a bass voice is best revealed in the figures of priests, kings, and fathers. Among innumerable examples I will mention only the conversation between Philip and the Grand Inquisitor in Verdi's *Don Carlos,* where in two personages all three figures are, as it were, represented. After that there develops the aspect of the evil bass (Kaspar in *Der Freischütz,* Sparafucile in *Rigoletto,* Wagner's Hagen as a vast intensification of this tradition), which of course finds its ideal type in the evil principle itself, the devil, on the opera stage, an embodiment found in Berlioz as in Gounod and Boito. Busoni was the first to make a tenor out of him.

Let us leave to one side the question of the lyric baritone, which is represented in Wagner only by Wolfram. The appearance of the heroic baritone is of relatively late date. Wagner himself, so far as I can see, did not employ it but rather chose the description of bass. In the piano scores of Klindworth and Mottl one can read "high bass" for what we today would call a heroic baritone; Wotan is thus characterized, but also Alberich, Donner, Fafner, and Gunther, while the Wanderer in *Siegfried* is described as a bass whose tessitura indeed lies somewhat lower than that of Wotan in *Die Walküre.* The part of Hans Sachs is likewise known as a bass part, although it is mostly sung by heroic baritones and even by lyric baritones. As concerns the extension of the voice, there is virtually no distinction between Wagner's basses and heroic baritones; for both f′ is the upper limit, the difference lying only in that for the high bass or the heroic baritone the tessitura is higher; that is to say, the greater part of the role moves in the top third of the vocal register, which is not the case for pure bass parts. Such variation is to be found not only in Wagner but also in the Italian repertoire. Roles such as Simone Boccanegra, Iago, and also Scarpia lie deeper than Renato and di Luna and are cheerfully sung by heroic baritones who want to relax from the arduous business of the father of the gods.

In German opera the differences between bass and baritone developed in the first half of the nineteenth century. For a long time it was customary for actors to serve in the smaller, less important bass parts of fathers and intriguers. In a sketch which Carl Maria von Weber submitted in Dresden in 1817 he listed the opera personnel that in his opinion were indispensable. These deep male voices are included there: a first bass for character parts "in which acting is preeminent" and a bass for minor roles "of a comic or narrow range." The concept of the baritone is in general still not employed; likewise with Mozart there is no explicit distinction between bass and baritone. In Weber's *Der Freischütz* there are four bass roles: Kaspar, the Hermit, Kuno, and Ottokar, among whom Ottokar is today described and cast as a baritone. In Weber's *Euryanthe* we certainly have in Lysiart a foreshadowing of the Wagnerian heroic baritone, just as the title roles of Marschner's *Hans Heiling* and *Der Vampyr* not only prefigure the Dutchman in vocal characteristics, but also show that they are figures far removed from the cliché villain because they are men who have been hardened into gloom through horror and suffering; they are fallen angels, as Wagner said of the Dutchman. To put it in a nutshell, the heroic baritone emerged from the familiar distracted romantic heroes of literature.

In the present-day casting of Wagner's works the bass roles seem to present the fewest difficulties. There is a roster of basses, whether youthful or middle-aged, such as Kurt Moll, Matti Salminen, and Nikolaus Hillebrand, who give respectable, even expressive performances. Nonetheless, any reader who has the records to hand can test for himself whether in recent years he has heard a Hunding sung as Emanuel List sings him in the recording of act 1 of *Die Walküre* under Bruno Walter in 1935—a dangerous Hunding without exaggerations, whose tone in the bottom register is still resounding and neither hefty nor hollow. It is also worth asking whether there has been a Gurnemanz or a König Heinrich like Alexander Kipnis. This question is perhaps a bit unfair because superfluous in my eyes (and ears), for I take Kipnis to be the premier bass of our century, even above Chaliapin, whom he surpasses in versatility. Kipnis' repertoire embraced the whole Italian range, with Philip in the center; he sang Mozart, indeed Leporello as well as Sarastro and the Commendatore; he sang Wagner in Bayreuth until he emigrated; he sang Boris Godunov in the original tongue, for he came from Ukraine; he sang the Barber of Baghdad and Baculus in *Der Wildschütz;* and as if that were not enough, he was one of the finest lieder singers of his generation. One can scarcely find a richer and more cultivated bass voice on records, despite the fact that his timbre is not so exotic as Chaliapin's. In all the languages in which he sang, Kipnis was almost completely idiomatic (this too marks a difference from Chaliapin). That his fame in Europe was less than his due is the result of his having sung almost exclusively in New York after fleeing from the Nazis.

Wagner made greater demands on his heroic baritones than on his basses. For instance in *Höllander* he demanded from the singer of the title role an adequate range of color and above all the art of modulation, by which he meant the shading of sound. The dark, uneasy modulation of the vocal organ must be taken to its furthest limits. Julius Hey remarks in his singing primer that the Dutchman makes the heaviest dynamic demands, requiring powerful vocal expansion as well as broadly phrased cantilena. If one surveys the interpreters of the Dutchman on the complete modern recordings, one discovers deficiencies in all these respects, most evident in Norman Bailey, the Dutchman in Solti's recording of 1977. If one goes back to the beginning of recording, one finds that Anton van Rooy, the most celebrated Dutchman and Wotan of the turn of the century, is inadequate because he displays the negative characteristics of Bayreuth speech-song to a notable extent. Better are the records made about twenty years later featuring Friedrich Schorr, *the* Wotan and Sachs of the 1920s and 1930s, who in a recording from 1929 also sings a compelling Dutchman. Here we have the powerful vocal expansion next to which contemporary exponents strike one as small-scale, as well as the broadly phrased cantilena of which Schorr was capable, for he could manage his huge voice with astonishing flexibility. Many stiff notes of Schorr's are not to my taste, but nonetheless he is all in all the most convincing heroic baritone that the phonograph has vouchsafed us. For the generations after Friedrich Schorr and Rudolf Bockelmann, Hans Hotter has set the style for the Dutchman and Wotan. He remained active as a performer into his eighties and was already, as a very young singer, the Wotan of an incomplete *Walküre* which Bruno Seidler-Winkler conducted in 1938; then, having overcome a vocal crisis, he helped to mold postwar Bayreuth. Indeed it was astonishing how well the pathos of his performance and his tendency to grandiosity managed to fit in with the production concepts of the postwar period.

Only one singer seems to me to be equal to Schorr, if not superior to him, because he stands closer to our present-day idea of declamation, and that is George London, the sole baritone of the postwar period who in volume, metallic sound, and broad stream of tone embodies my idea of a heroic baritone. Serious illness prevented London from scaling the peak of the Wagnerian repertoire as Wotan. His *Rheingold* Wotan under Solti and his *Walküre* Wotan under Leinsdorf are indicative of what might have been possible, head and shoulders above everyone else by virtue of his incomparable timbre; nor should his darkly glowing Amfortas be forgotten.

We come now to Hans Sachs, a role that makes entirely different demands when compared with the Dutchman. While situations of the highest emotion and drama are concentrated in only three musical and dramatic high points, Sachs has to be onstage nearly continuously in a part which, to speak in the language of *Die Meistersinger* itself, also demands a large number of "tones and manners." He must range from the saucy to the tender, from broad muttering and grumbling to irony, from introspective moments to the artistic pathos of the final address. It is an old point of contention whether Sachs should be sung by a bass or by a heroic baritone. Wagner, as I have mentioned, indicated a bass, but he obviously intended a high bass, or heroic baritone, given the tessitura. Many renowned Wagnerian basses have given this role a wide berth (for instance Gottlob Frick, who on other than vocal grounds might have played the part); others, such as Josef Greindl, gave very convincing interpretations but had occasional difficulties with the higher reaches. The most significant Sachs interpreters were for this reason nearly always heroic baritones, but many singers of that type have had no (or only brief) access to Sachs, for instance Hans Hotter. At present it seems to be the custom to reserve the cobbler-poet for lyric baritones. Dietrich Fischer-Dieskau has sung it on records and also on the stage, and as of this writing Bernd Weikl is far and away the most-sought-after Sachs. These two voices are very different, and yet they remain, I think, lyrical in their basic character. This quality has nothing to do with volume or the art of declamation, but suggests only that a rather softer vocal character predominates, that the voice possesses less metallic ring, less fullness of resonance, less depth than is demanded of a heroic baritone—and also of the part of Hans Sachs, which one can regard as a bass, a high bass, or a heroic baritone, but which is certainly not one thing: a role for a lyric baritone. Of course such voices have no trouble with the top notes, do not have to make too much of an effort with the closing address at the end of an overlong evening, and can sing a beautifully tender "Johannisnacht." But the character of the role is altered fundamentally (and not as Wagner would have wished) when the top third of the part, in which a high bass or heroic baritone develops his greatest power of penetration and dynamics, becomes in effect the middle register for a lyric baritone, in which his dynamic possibilities are contracted. His own top register, which reaches up to a' and even beyond that, is in general not required; it is, so to speak, amputated. Such a Sachs, on dynamic grounds as well as by virtue of his register, quickly becomes monotonous and monochromatic. Moreover, he is not enough of a contrast with a perhaps dark-hued Stolzing tenor and hence does not embody sufficiently the distance in age and the experience of life, qualities which must be present if the relations among the characters of *Meistersinger* are to remain credible.

Sachs, as he should be, was and is for many cognoscenti Friedrich Schorr, who has left us many exemplary recordings. As a vocal ideal beyond Schorr, even if he is interpretively inferior to him, I would mention Hans Hermann Nissen, whose Sachs is best heard on a studio recording of the third act conducted by Karl Böhm in 1938 with the ensemble of the Dresden State Opera. Two years before, Nissen's career had crossed paths with that of the older Schorr. Schorr was booked for the production of *Meistersinger* which Toscanini conducted at the Salzburg Festival in 1936, but he fell out with the maestro during rehearsals and was replaced by Nissen. A technically inadequate recording from 1937 documents this noteworthy performance. Nissen possessed a most fitting voice for the role of Sachs, virile and flexible, technically superb, with a perfect mezza voce (which is not self-evident from the size of the voice) and a supported, resonant piano ("Johannisnacht" can never have been sung more beautifully). Nissen was a very straightforward Sachs, not too "sicklied o'er with the pale cast of thought"; today one would require more nuances, but as a singer he is hardly surpassable.

About the part of Wotan one does not need to say much because a lot of what applies to the Dutchman and Sachs is also valid for this character, who, as it were, unites in himself the demands of the other two roles. The touchstone for any Wagnerian singer is of course the end of *Walküre,* which shows Wotan as father and god, thereby taking up the old role clichés which were once allotted to the bass, but penetrating beyond them to the accents of suffering which were first expressed by the heroic baritone born of the Romantic spirit. The demands on the singer are correspondingly large: the greatest possible expansion of the voice has to triumph over the massive orchestra, but at the same time the legato line must remain firm and be available for inward piano tone. The Wotan type of singer has not been forthcoming in the recent past; but the situation has improved with Siegmund Nimsgern and James Morris. When we deal with the more distant past we are moving onto surer ground: Friedrich Schorr is here again a yardstick, with very minor reservations concerning intonation; Rudolf Bockelmann can be set next to him with his less personally colored but more supple voice; George London is almost at the same level; and finally there is Alexander Kipnis, who made a brilliant recording of Wotan's Farewell (originating from Berlin in 1926), showing that a bass too can conquer the part (which Kipnis sang not only in the studio).

Contralto and Mezzo-Soprano

In the summer of 1875, during the rehearsals for the first performance of the *Ring* as a cycle, which was to take place the following year, discussion in the inner circle (according to Julius Hey) came around to the work of Amalie Materna, the first Brünnhilde. The talk centered on the inadequate intellectual development of the admittedly gifted female singers with whom Wagner had had to deal in the course of his life. The master's statement on this was different from what one might expect:

> Should I only entrust my female roles to singers who are capable in each phrase that they sing of conducting profound reflections on the moral basis and permissibility of what I wanted? I want innate, natural singing talent combined with a musical disposition and adequate vocal organs, which achieve security and artistic completeness through reasonable training. Temperament is—according to my experience—the essence, because it provides the most valuable basis for everything, what the dramatic action demands vocally as well as in acting from the

stage-singer. A natural understanding of the word-content of a theatrical work belongs with that. The law for the artistic union of word and tone remains the province of appropriate instruction, which awakens the feeling for speech-rhythm and phrasing, and transmits it into song. Particular weight is to be put on this, because it has to serve as a guideline for effective speech-song. Led on the right way of vocal development and artistic understanding the female sex grasps everything else quickly and wins a secure overview. What need has a healthy instinct in general for long reflective fussing? Temperament takes to heart and grasps what is decisive. I hold that to be more worthwhile than when a hysterically inclined, highly intellectual woman with failing energies of will and without the necessary surplus of power comes to perform tasks which presuppose a healthy, robust physical constitution under all circumstances.   (Hey 1911, pp. 184–185)

Besides being remarks which are important for Wagner interpretation altogether, this quotation contains insights into Wagner's image of women which I cannot comment on here, and important remarks for the presentation of Wagner's female roles.

Pure contralto parts are not exactly common in Wagner and are really represented only by Erda in *Rheingold* and *Siegfried;* even one or another of the Valkyries and Norns does not have to be a contralto, even though they are designated as such in the score. In the eighteenth century the concept of the contralto voice was employed as much for castrati as for female singers. Later, as the castrati diminished in importance, it was reserved for women and developed as the third vocal designation after soprano and mezzo-soprano. If one listens to historical recordings of contralto voices and compares them with today's representatives of the genre, one is convinced that there are no more voices of a dark and equally voluminous type such as those of an Ernestine Schumann-Heink or a Clara Butt; all present-day Erdas give the impression that they would be happier singing Fricka. A phenomenon like Schumann-Heink, who besides being a primeval Erda could sing a contralto coloratura part in Donizetti's *Lucrezia Borgia,* has finally become a historical monument.

When we turn to mezzo-sopranos, we find ourselves on equally shaky ground as with the division between bass and heroic baritone. One hears, for example, frequent *Lohengrin* performances where the Ortrud and the Elsa can hardly be distinguished in terms of vocal color. On the one hand, one does not want to assign Ortrud to a contralto because the higher parts of the role, which must be sung with dramatic force, would present grave difficulties; yet on the other hand, there is no question that Wagner would have wanted a different singer for Ortrud than for Elsa, the former being distinguished by darker vocal coloring and other characteristics. The same goes for Kundry, of whom theater aficionados say that the first act of *Parsifal* needs a contralto, the second act a soprano. The distinction between soprano and mezzo-soprano is first notable in the middle of the eighteenth century. Then, for the first time in operatic history, parts were written for soprano which possessed a greater extension in the higher register and imposed virtuosic demands. But terminologically they were not always so distinguished: from contemporary reports of the most celebrated prima donnas of the late eighteenth century, Cuzzoni and Bordoni, with whom Handel worked in London, it emerges that Bordoni was first a mezzo, while Cuzzoni took charge of the highest soprano parts; but both singers described themselves as sopranos.

If one surveys complete post-war recordings of *Lohengrin,* one cannot really be satisfied with any of the Ortruds, if one is employing strict standards. What Wagner wanted from his Ortrud can be read in a letter which he wrote to Liszt in 1850, when Liszt was preparing the first performance of *Lohengrin.* It emerges that the most important features of the character are "frightful cunning" and "appalling madness," which must come out in the expression of the portrayal of this "gruesome political woman." There is for me only one singer who can convey all these qualities, and has brought them to real expression, and that is Margarete Klose, who not for nothing was *the* Ortrud of the 1930s and 1940s. Her Ortrud can best be heard in a live recording from the Berlin State Opera which Robert Heger conducted in 1943. This *Lohengrin* ensemble, with Klose, Jaro Prohaska as Telramund, Franz Völker as Lohengrin, and Maria Müller as Elsa, is not only historically remarkable but is an unsurpassable model. It has precisely the same cast as an even more famous *Lohengrin* performance of 1936 in Bayreuth, conducted by Wilhelm Furtwängler. From the 1936 performance there are unfortunately only some extracts which show that Völker and Maria Müller were fresher vocally, but even in the 1943 version they need fear no competition. Margaret Klose as Ortrud was unique because she was decidedly a contralto in vocal color but a soprano as far as volume, attack, and high notes were concerned—truly a rare combination. One can hear in the 1943 recording how at the beginning of the second act she realizes all of Wagner's instructions, such as "softly but grimly," "scornfully," "with terrifying mockery," how she gives the word "Gott" a demonic crescendo, and how she unleashes "Entweihte Götter" and hurls it out. One cannot doubt that this is a unique performance in Wagnerian singing, the recording of the century, if one chooses to call it that.

The Wagnerian Soprano

In the last sections we turn to the two vocal types which are regarded by many as the crown of Wagner's vocal creations, the soprano and the Heldentenor. The greatest popular interest is consequently brought to them, and a successful or even a declining Wagnerian tenor always causes more of a sensation than a heroic baritone. It must nonetheless be asked whether there really are soprano and tenor roles which surpass in interest those of Sachs or Wotan as far as vocal demands and dramatic depth are concerned; but the baritone has at all times received less attention and must live with this handicap.

The Wagnerian soprano roles are of three types: the lyric-dramatic soprano (this uncommon designation will be explained shortly), with varying degrees of emphasis on the first or second word (when one compares Elsa and Elisabeth, for instance); the youthful-dramatic soprano, as represented by Sieglinde; and the high-dramatic soprano, perfectly embodied in Isolde and the Brünnhilde of *Götterdämmerung* (but who in *Walküre* falls between the youthful-dramatic and high-dramatic soprano). The development which led to these vocal types took place during the nineteenth century. It was determined from two sides: from the cultural-sociological side of musical life, in which ever-larger concert halls and opera houses demanded ever-larger and more penetrating voices, and also from the side of the composers, who created ever more dramatic female figures—a development parallel to the birth of the heroic baritone from the pale romantic hero. Thus the heroine of the new type was born. With dramatic coloratura sopranos the coloratura element was more and more recessive. Suffering and despair expressed themselves no more in the head register, as in Bellini's Norma and Donizetti's Lucia, but in chest notes indicative of heroic-pathetic passion or revolt. Also, with reference to the diminishing virtuosity of German singers, composers such as Weber and Mendelssohn saw to it that virtuoso decoration was sacrificed and a virtue made out of a failing. It was one of the later Wagner's greatest deeds to correct the negative developments in Wagnerian singing, in particular the crude preference for loudness, through the ingenious idea of the sunken Bayreuth orchestra. According to Julius Hey, Wagner deplored the tendency toward raw shouting (citing Elsa as an example) and vocal power for its own sake. The arrangement of the Bayreuth orchestra was, and still is, a great advantage to the singers. Frida Leider has described how wonderfully lightly one can sing in Bayreuth, how no fortissimo from the orchestra can cover a well-trained voice.

I have already mentioned the lyric-dramatic soprano, a contradiction in terms, one might think. But let us consider Elisabeth in *Tannhäuser* and her entry aria, the so-called Hallenarie or Greeting to the Hall of Song. This is well known for its many changes, from the jubilant outburst of long-suppressed feeling to a lyrically sustained, bashful "Da er aus dir geschieden," and back again to the ringing triumph of "Wie jetzt mein Busen hoch sich hebet." Or let us recall the passionate moment when Elisabeth makes herself vulnerable and throws herself before Tannhäuser in the second act to shelter him from the swords of the Wartburg assembly. These contrasts are intended for the lyric-dramatic voice and are not available to Elsa. When we listen to famous interpreters of the role of Elisabeth from the past and present, we find only two completely satisfactory portrayals. That of Maria Müller is best heard in an abbreviated version of the work under Karl Elmendorff (Bayreuth, 1930) and embodies the ideal of a voice type which many maintain is only to be found in German singers. The most accomplished singer in this category was Müller's contemporary Margarete Teschemacher, and then later Elisabeth Grümmer. Where Maria Müller fell just short of perfection (she was better suited to Elsa) was in her range of feeling. In this respect we should consider a relatively little known singer, the Frenchwoman Germaine Lubin, who sang in notable performances of *Tristan* in 1939 under Victor de Sabata and was, as Isolde, the partner of Max Lorenz. A recording of the Hallenarie sung in French and recorded in 1929 I take to be the ideal rendition of this difficult piece.

Sieglinde in *Die Walküre* is an entirely different character, no mere enthusiastic virgin like Elsa and Elisabeth but a young woman hardened by suffering, and already somewhat mature. The tessitura of Sieglinde lies lower than that of the other two parts. It is a youthful-dramatic role with a tendency toward the high-dramatic; very often singers who later become Brünnhildes have begun as Sieglindes. A powerful voice with a good middle range and a developed chest register is thus required. Technically the part is not very difficult, and one therefore rarely hears a really bad Sieglinde. This also applies to successful contemporary performers, who even so must subject themselves to being compared with Lotte Lehmann in the recording of the first act under Bruno Walter. For those for whom the tone quality of Lehmann is already too mature on this recording, there is the much less well known recording of the last scene of the first act coupled with the whole of the third act which was made in New York in 1945 under the baton of Artur Rodzinski. Here one can listen to one of the most resplendent Wagnerian voices ever to undertake Sieglinde and Brünnhilde, that of the American Helen Traubel. She came to the Met in 1937, emerged as the equal of Flagstad and Melchior in 1939, and was, after Flagstad departed from New York in 1941, the leading Wagnerian soprano of that company. At the beginning of the 1950s her contract was not renewed, allegedly because she had worked as a nightclub and film singer, a combination which was intolerable at the time (today it would raise her status still higher). The absolute technical authority of her singing, the radiantly triumphant sound of her voice, the accent-free German: it is time that Helen Traubel was recognized as one of the truly great.

The high-dramatic soprano may seem to one person to be the crowning achievement of Wagner's female roles, to another a monumental misdevelopment straying far from the bel canto ideal. This voice type has undergone several transformations. Around the turn of the century, as the influential example of Johanna Gadski shows, a slenderer vocal character with greater penetrating power ruled. Frida Leider was still dedicated to this ideal, as was Helen Traubel. Then came the emphasis on bigness of voice with the incontestable high point of Kirsten Flagstad (naturally these developments, which can be only minimally controlled, depend on the emergence of the singers' personalities). Since then this trend has been reversed: Birgit Nilsson, the leading Brünnhilde and Isolde of the 1950s and 1960s, still largely corresponded to the older ideal, while the Isolde of Margaret Price (only on records) and the Brünnhilde of Hildegard Behrens are closer to a youthful-dramatic or even a lyrical type of voice. A previously much-debated question plays hardly any role at present: namely the matter of whether the high-dramatic soprano must or should be developed out of the soprano or mezzo or even the contralto voice. Hans Knappertsbusch once said that out of velvet (that is, mezzo and contralto) one cannot make satin (soprano), although it is said that he changed his mind when he heard Martha Mödl. There were always sopranos, like Mödl and Martha Fuchs, who came from "underneath" (in a sense Astrid Varnay, probably the greatest female Wagnerian singer of the postwar period, whose voice also possesses a marked mezzo quality, belongs in this group too). In many cases the cello sound of the mezzo made available to an Isolde or Brünnhilde nuances of much effectiveness, but it also often led prematurely to problems with the higher reaches of the parts.

As concerns Isolde, I am not happy with the tendency toward lightweight voices. When a lyric soprano with great power of penetration (a female lirico spinto in other words) sings Isolde, one is delighted with a radiant high register, which has a tremendous effect and is in no way unimportant. But it must also be recognized that if anything the middle register then sounds weak, and the low part of the voice often seems to be more of a speech than a chest register. An Isolde without middle or lower registers is no Isolde at all. The part can be managed only as Wagner intended and composed it, with the high peaks built on powerful foundations. We must remember that Wagner said unmistakably in a letter of 1859: "I need, especially for Isolde, voice, voice, voice!" It cannot be disputed that Isolde, even more than the Brünnhilde of *Götterdämmerung,* must possess an element of majesty and grandeur, like the unsurpassable Kirsten Flagstad, and which seems to have disappeared from *Tristan* since Birgit Nilsson (although it cannot be ruled out that a Jessye Norman or an Eva Marton may one day bring this element back again). Kirsten Flagstad possessed the most ample soprano voice of our time. Recordings give only an incomplete picture of its tonal character, as anyone agrees who was able to experience it in person. She was the only soprano who could match in vocal amplitude the overpowering Lauritz Melchior. The rightly famous *Tristan* recording of Furtwängler shows Flagstad at the advanced age of fifty-six, and it is undeniable, for all one's admiration, that her voice has taken on a maternal flavor, as Wagner first noticed once in the aging Wilhelmine Schröder-Devrient. Anyone not put off by technical shortcomings can hear Flagstad as Isolde with Melchior in a Covent Garden performance of 1936 (the conductor is Fritz Reiner) and will be addicted to these crowning, radiant sounds, but also spoiled for the leading Isoldes of our time.

As Brünnhilde, Flagstad was not so convincing; here she was surpassed by Frida Leider, who without doubt had the superior stage temperament. There may have been singers who surpassed Frida Leider in one or another respect, but none seems to me to have been so qualified all around. She was certainly the most complete female Wagnerian singer, a shining stage presence, a glorious voice which mastered perfectly the German style of bel canto required by Wagner; and we have it from her that she always tried to carry over the Italian vocal schooling into singing Wagner (one should listen to her Donna Anna). Not least her voice was supremely suitable for recording (more so than the essentially larger voice of Flagstad). It is not possible to sing Brünnhilde's Immolation better than she did.

The Heldentenor

The Heldentenor, as he is known to us, and who today causes heads of opera houses so many headaches, was not introduced into the history of music by Richard Wagner. Wagner's heroic tenor parts are only the peak (and, in retrospect, the end) of a development for whose origins one must look primarily toward the Italian opera composer Gaspare Spontini. Not by chance was Spontini named Napoleon's court composer. The heroic Napoleonic period, the Empire, was exactly the right time for him: it longed for heroic operas and it got them. Spontini's operas, and a bit later grand opera, required a new heroic type; no more the sentimental youngster like Edgardo in *Lucia di Lammermoor,* who knows only how to sing of death, the tomb, and renouncing love, but rather a young man who when necessary resists an enemy's superior force with his sword, like Masaniello in Auber's *La muette de Portici,* and Raoul in Meyerbeer's *Les Huguenots.* Such characters were no longer adequately portrayed with the head register or indeed in falsetto for their top notes, as was usual until then. What was now required was a superior force and sense of drama to project the voice across the footlights with convincing power (and therefore with corresponding loudness). This led to that oft-cited first high C sung in the chest register by the French tenor Gilbert Duprez as Arnold in Rossini's *Guillaume Tell* at the Paris Opéra in 1837; with this note he inaugurated the new epoch of the heroic tenor, from whom from now on fanfarelike high notes were demanded.

It is interesting to observe that uniquely in France a special kind of tenor has been preserved, whom the French call a *tenor de vaillance,* whose voice is often not very attractive, but who can serve up top C's and above through almost abnormal vocal trumpet thrusts. An amazing historical example is the French tenor Léon Escalaïs, who stands wholly in the tradition of Duprez, a tradition that produced, as one might expect (with one or two exceptions such as Paul Franz and Georges Thill) no tenor suitable for Wagner. Josef Tichatschek, Wagner's first Rienzi and Tannhäuser, was already one of the tenors belonging to the new type. By the middle of the nineteenth century the concept of the Heldentenor seems to have been generally accepted. For Julius Hey in his primer on singing (Hey 1884) the Heldentenor is not a vocal type in the sense of a basic nature or disposition but is rather the outcome of a long tradition. Hey sees the Heldentenor (and he means the Wagnerian Heldentenor) as developing out of the so-called deep tenor, whom on the basis of vocal quality one can often hardly distinguish from a baritone. Above all a powerful physical constitution is essential. Indeed, it is striking what value Wagner placed on the physical constitution of his heroes: the first Siegfried, Georg Unger, he obviously chose more on the grounds of his athletic physique than for his voice, and was mistaken in his assumption that the vocal problems would somehow look after themselves. This might seem to us today to be very naive, but surely the current lack of powerful voices (which, as I have said, Wagnerian singing cannot do without) is also a consequence of the changing ideals of physical beauty, to which the powerful physiques of Melchior and Slezak no longer correspond.

Naturally there are significant variations within the Heldentenor range in Wagner, from the almost lyrical extreme of Lohengrin to the heavyweight hero Siegfried or the heroic character-tenor, as one might call it, of Tannhäuser or Tristan. Only a few of these differences can be picked out by examples.

Of all Wagner's tenor parts Lohengrin is the one that has been calculated most clearly on a single level; it is dominated by distance and vulnerable rapture, which is shattered in the bridal chamber scene through very human emotions. It is important that the interpreter of Lohengrin should draw out a maximum of nuances within this small spectrum of emotion, so that one tone does not become monotonous. More important here than anywhere else in Wagner is the pure quality of the voice, and thus of timbre. Wagner himself wrote to Liszt as he prepared the first performance that the singer must possess one quality above all: luster in his appearance and in his voice. Beyond that a good Lohengrin must also sing a supported piano; he must command the art of mezza voce as well as that of messa di voce, of seamlessly swelling and then diminishing single tones; and he must have considerable legato technique. Only if these techniques are in place is that wonder of blue and silver that Thomas Mann associated with *Lohengrin* likely to materialize. These are no small demands, and it is not surprising that I find them met to an inadequate degree by prominent contemporary exponents of the part. Precisely on account of its legato demands the role of Lohengrin has often been taken on by singers of Italian training; indeed, in the nineteenth century *Lohengrin* was the most frequently performed of Wagner's operas in Italy.

In a newspaper report of a performance of *Lohengrin* in 1871 in Bologna Hans von Bülow wrote about the Italian tenor Cleofonte Campanini: "He sings the whole last act thrillingly. I have never heard the Grail Narration rendered by German singers in a way that approached his." Bülow was apparently not disturbed by the fact that this was a Lohengrin sung in Italian and that the swan was bidden farewell with the words "Addio mio cigno gentil." It is a little-known fact that in 1901 Enrico Caruso sang Lohengrin three times in Buenos Aires. He did not repeat it, however, and alas made no record of it. The most influential Italian Lohengrin remains Aureliano Pertile, Toscanini's favorite tenor, whose Lohengrin excerpts have textbook status as regards the art of phrasing, and who brought his mastery of messa di voce to the point of mannerism; what Pertile lacked was a beautiful voice. One can hear a Lohengrin à la Puccini in the Englishman Alfred Piccaver, the onetime idol of the Vienna State Opera. The velvet quality of the voice, with its perfect legato, gives Lohengrin surprising nuances, but the strong sensuality of his nasal tones completely loses the quality of distance. In the 1950s and 1960s the Hungarian Sandor Konya also sang a Pucciniesque Lohengrin with great success, which was very refreshing as a counterbalance to the all-too-German rendering of the role; the legato of Konya still lingers agreeably in many listeners' ears to this day. The American Jess Thomas too sang the role at that time impressively. That leaves the question whether Franz Völker in the 1930s perhaps set standards for Lohengrin which still have not been surpassed. The live recording from the Berlin State Opera of 1943, which I mentioned previously in connection with Margaret Klose, proves that he did; but because he is vocally fresher in the earlier studio recordings and live excerpts from Bayreuth in 1936, these performances are still more perfect. Before and since Völker no German Wagnerian tenor has possessed such legato culture without sacrificing vocal power (Völker was also a wonderful Siegmund). A particular artistic trick of Völker's was to make the consonants speak out softly. His notes come with astonishing delicacy, like balls of cotton wool; one must nonetheless grant that the clarity of diction which Wagner constantly demanded suffers somewhat. Völker is nonetheless far above the Wagnerian standard in his breath control (and there can be no legato without breath control). One need only compare the way Völker sings his greeting to the swan in act 3 with long breaths (a moment which, almost unsupported by the orchestra, counts among the trickiest in the part), whereas *all* the Lohengrins of later complete recordings break up the passage with frequent intakes of breath. About Franz Völker's Lohengrin there is little to cavil at or with which to find fault, and if I say that for me Völker's voice is still a shade too earthly, that is a comment apart from all issues of quality. At a time when I had given up the search for the ideal Lohengrin voice, that mixture of unearthly Grail radiance and suppressed sensuality, a recording of a concert came into my hands in which a few weeks before his death Jussi Bjoerling had sung the Grail narration for the first and last time in public. Even though the Swedish language is not unconditionally suitable for Lohengrin, and although this is only an interpretive beginning, is sung too boyishly, and also contains a musical error—here it is, the ideal Lohengrin voice!

The role of Tannhäuser, as is widely known, places the most taxing demands on a Wagnerian tenor, even though other parts may be far more difficult in terms of endurance. I recall a floundering Jess Thomas as Tannhäuser in Bayreuth, and the leading Wagnerian tenors of the present day have yet to show that they are up to this part. My recollection of Wolfgang Windgassen includes a distinguished portrayal in performance; Windgassen is not a singer for the recording studio because his voice lacks the required sensuous appeal. He stands as the exponent of an interpretation of a modern Tannhäuser, psychologically in extremis. One can hear what in my opinion is the best Tannhäuser, namely Max Lorenz, and note that Windgassen only takes Lorenz's example a stage further. Lorenz is a noteworthy case. Outside of Germany, in standard modern works on the history of the art of singing or of operatic interpretation on record he is a fringe figure, and for the most part not a very highly esteemed one. If I had to name the three greatest Wagnerian tenors of our century, however, they would be Lauritz Melchior, with Jacques Urlus close behind, and Max Lorenz, the character-tenor among Heldentenors, who achieved his best performances as Tannhäuser and Tristan, but who also had no need to fear any rivals as Siegfried.

Lorenz did not start out as a baritone but was from the beginning a genuine tenor, who as the Siegfried of *Götterdämmerung* was able to sing out the notorious high C in act 3 ("Hoi-ho, Hoi-he"—it is meant only as a kind of cry of delight by Wagner). Lorenz's timbre cannot be called outstandingly beautiful; his first recordings show from what recalcitrant material his performances were achieved. When fully developed his voice—which by no means possessed the volume of a Melchior—showed a remarkable power of penetration; like Damascus steel it flashed out over the strongest orchestral sound. Lorenz was the expressionist among the great Wagnerian tenors, as it were the German counterpart to the verismo of Aureliano Pertile, with whom he had in common a voice of little attractiveness. Expression was for him everything, and in his drive toward expression he often let note values go by the board. His singing always gave a suggestion of impetuous forward pressure. His Tannhäuser (in a Berlin radio performance of 1943 under Artur Rother) and his Siegfried (in a performance of *Götterdämmerung* at the Berlin State Opera in 1944 under Robert Heger, of which the final two scenes are preserved) are in any case Wagner recordings whose overpowering impact can hardly be denied.

The question can only be touched on here as to whether the genuine Heldentenor must be developed out of a baritone, as Lauritz Melchior deduced from his own development (he even established a foundation to support such schooling). This question is not new, and it is perhaps not one of general principle but rather one that must be decided for individual cases. Albert Niemann, the Tannhäuser of the first Paris performances and later the first Bayreuth Siegmund, seemed to be a disguised baritone; at any rate Hans von Bülow, who understood something about voices, characterized him as a toneless, pushed-up baritone. If anything the specialists are wary of this. We saw that Julius Hey derived the Heldentenor not from the baritone but from the deep tenor (which was for him a distinctly different thing), and he predicted vocal ruin for those tenors who could conquer the high notes which nature had denied them only by force. The great Italian tenor Giacomo Lauri-Volpi, who wrote many interesting books about singers and singing, expressed himself on the same problem, which is posed for Italian tenors by Otello, in a very similar way: "Baritones remain baritones and will never achieve a tessitura which needs clarity and squillo [by *squillo* the Italians mean the penetrating force of top notes] without endangering their vocal organs, and if a baritone wishes to transform himself into a tenor, he launches on a dangerous adventure, which may perhaps cost him his career, because he has overstepped the bounds of his natural endowment." In spite of these warnings, changes of type have always occurred (and with complete success): Jean de Reske, the most significant tenor of the era before Caruso and also a leading Wagnerian tenor, had been a baritone; the same was true of famous Otellos such as Giovanni Zenatello, Renato Zanelli, and Ramon Vinay.

Siegmund is the Wagnerian tenor role with the lowest tessitura, and technically at every point is attainable by a baritone. No wonder that many good interpreters of the part were previously baritones, for instance James King, the most convincing Siegmund of recent decades, and of course also Lauritz Melchior. Another tenor who is painfully neglected in Germany is Jacques Urlus. There are experts who claim that his voice is the most glorious in the Wagnerian tenor repertoire to have been preserved on records. His Sword monologue from *Die Walküre* offers at the cries of "Wälse!" a vocal expansion which can be compared with that of Melchior, if one allows for the primitive recording technique. Urlus, who was born in 1867 on the Belgian-German border, the son of Dutch parents, sang for only a short time in Bayreuth (1911–12) as Siegmund, and was then from 1912 on the leading Wagnerian tenor at the Met. There he took the place of de Reske in the German repertoire, and he was admired by Caruso. Urlus was (and in this he is comparable to Alexander Kipnis) a singer of astonishing versatility: he was at the climax of his career still a prized Tamino; he sang Otello and Samson; he was the tenor soloist in *Das Lied von der Erde* and a famed Evangelist in the *St. Matthew Passion*. Who among our present-day Wagnerian tenors is capable of that?

Not only was Urlus supreme as Siegmund, but we can also still hear his *Siegfried* recordings. This is precisely the role that today creates the most difficulty for casting offices. Urlus, Melchior, and Lorenz have all shown in different ways (and also, as is demonstrable, under performance conditions) that one can master the whole of this role brilliantly. Wagner himself claimed the title role in *Siegfried* to be his most difficult by far, and he laid the greatest stress on singing the high a's in the smelting and forging songs and also in the third act radiantly. Now this is precisely where the Heldentenors of the baritonal variety have their greatest trouble, while the "true" tenors find it easier to produce in a double sense the required cutting vocal quality in the first act. At the time of writing René Kollo seems to be the only one who can fulfill the demands of both Siegfrieds without resorting to excuses. Kollo prepared himself for a long time for Siegfried, a role for which he did not at first seem to be predestined; an attempt at it came too early in the Bayreuth Chéreau production and was abandoned. Kollo's tenor does not belong to the baritonal type, nor is it characterized by much metal. The directness of his singing and his superior stage presence have brought him to the summit of his repertoire. Many people claim that Peter Hofmann is the more impressive Siegfried, but Hofmann keeps well clear of such heavy Wagnerian roles, surely with good reason, and confines himself to Lohengrin, Siegmund, and Parsifal. Siegfried Jerusalem has not only the appearance but also a suitable Christian name and at present perhaps the most attractive voice in the Wagnerian tenor repertoire, although his lyrical basic material must be carefully tended and protected from excessive stress. Siegmund is for him a part that stretches him to his limits. It is therefore not a foolish idea to allow the young Siegfried to be sung by a "true" tenoral Heldentenor, and the Siegfried of *Götterdämmerung* by a baritonal tenor. Here the objection will readily be raised: But what about Lauritz Melchior! Still, I am not making a cheap escape when I call Melchior an absolute exception by virtue of his massive voice, which was in turn sustained by an equally massive physique and above all guided by his high level of artistic understanding. This claim is valid for the better part of his extraordinary career, although in later years even Melchior could, as live performances testify, deliver shockingly slack, undisciplined performances. No tenor, certainly, should be advised to follow Melchior's example unreflectingly, just as the majority who have sought to emulate Caruso's by no means conventional technique have failed. Melchior worked with an overly strong covering of the voice. This technique is recognizable in a darkening of the voice in the top register, deep placement of the larynx, and expansion of the passages above the glottis. In proper dosages the technique is necessary in order to make sure that the different registers are balanced out (as one can hear perfectly with Urlus). In the degree to which Melchior employed the technique, there is a danger that the positioning of the voice is pushed backwards, with the consequence that increased expenditure of power vainly seeks to compensate for the resulting reduction in sound. To put it as clearly as possible: Melchior's technique of covering the voice was in no way compatible with the golden rules of singing. It may have been a legacy from his years as a baritone, for baritones who are afraid of sounding too tenorish at the top apply it freely (more or less consciously). It remains Melchior's secret how he managed, apparently effortlessly, through this darkening of the voice to overcome the odds and achieve an effect with his top notes which one can compare with the sun breaking through the clouds. That his immense physical strength was a necessary ingredient is clear, but perhaps it is not enough to explain the phenomenon.

With this retrospective review of the great heavy Wagnerian tenors, a race of singers that is dying out, or perhaps already extinct (I confess that I hear in the Wagnerian tenors of our day none who can even approach performances of such quality, although there are certainly many with different views), I end this brief survey of the history and problems of singing Wagner. Much remains unsaid; many great voices of the past, as well as many respectable voices of the present, remain unnamed. It should be clear by now that it is in the spirit of Richard Wagner himself that one demands obedience to the commandments of the art of song, which Wagner's own term *German bel canto* first filled with meaning. It seems as though these commandments have altogether lost their status as obligations in today's Wagnerian singing, despite the persistence of impressive individual performances.

Translated by Michael Tanner

CHAPTER 22

Wagner's Musical Influence

CARL DAHLHAUS

Wagner's Successors and Imitators

Contrary to popular prejudice, stylistic imitation in opera is a complex phenomenon that is difficult to unravel. First, it generally consists not in the emulation of a single model but in the mingled influence of a number of models. Moreover, the significance we accord to a certain factor, such as the choice of subject matter, the dramaturgical structure, or the leitmotif technique, is dependent on the aesthetic position we adopt. (The idea that Wagner's own theory contains the only valid criteria with which to judge his successors is a dogma that probably has no followers among historians.) Second, in opera, in contrast to the symphony or chamber music, eclecticism within certain limits, which are not very closely defined, is aesthetically legitimate as long as it seems sufficiently justified in dramaturgical terms (for example, the stylistic breaks in *Holländer*). The commonplace which states that imitation leads to aesthetic failure, an idea which derives from the premise that art has to be new in order to be authentic, thus provokes the objection that, conversely, the charge of stylistic imitation is leveled only against works that are unsuccessful. In an opera such as Eugen d'Albert's *Tiefland* (1903), although its lack of originality is plain for all to see, it proves to be of no concern on account of the crude but nevertheless effective dramaturgy. Third, journalism, which historians despise in the present, but which is posthumously treated as an authentic source, tends, under the pressures of the trade, to regard conspicuous features as the essential ones; that is, critics are too quick to identify "Wagnerism" on the basis of chromatic harmony and rudimentary leitmotif technique, although the basic musical-dramaturgical pattern—with choral and ensemble scenes, inserted ballets, and lyrical episodes—betrays more of the influence of Meyerbeer (Edmund Kretschmer, *Die Folkunger*, 1874).

A fourth point is that stylistically imitative operas are as a rule only in part dependent on the idea of the *Gesamtkunstwerk:* the fact that subject matter, form of language, dramaturgy, and musical structure are interdependent in Wagner's works does not mean that it is necessarily wrong to focus on one or the other. Rather, adapting and transposing into another context new musical means of communication and musical-dramatic techniques is a wholly normal procedure that merely seemed unusual in Wagner's sphere of influence because everything connected with Wagner provokes emotions and imaginary plots, as if noticing or denying the influence of *Parsifal* on *Pelléas et Mélisande* (which to be sure was most clearly apparent in the orchestral interludes, and which Debussy cut for this reason) were a matter of faith. Fifth, a distinction must be made among Wagner's successors based on the works from which the influence emanated. Vincent d'Indy's *L'étranger* (1903) has recourse to motifs from *Holländer,* although in the context of a musical language that is in part derived from *Tristan*. Hans Pfitzner's *Der Arme Heinrich* (1895) is reminiscent of *Tannhäuser* in a way that might be fittingly described under the vague rubric of musical-scenic mood. Dietrich's narrative is virtually an exact replica of the Rome narrative, although stylistic imitation is difficult to pin down in detail. August Bungert's *Homerische Welt* (1896–1903), which was praised for two decades and then abruptly and irrevocably forgotten, was intended to be a counterpart to the *Ring* (whose Nordic mythological subject matter was in fact structurally derived from antiquity). *Guntram* (1894) by Richard Strauss, a "weltanschauung drama" (with a text by the composer), was influenced by *Parsifal* right down to certain small details. In other words, we must distinguish, as in the case of Beethoven's symphonies, between the overall reception of Wagner and the history of the influence of individual works. Sixth, Wagner's successors were able to take their bearings not only from the music dramas but also from aesthetic theory, be it the original Wagnerian one or the orthodox view propagated by Bayreuth. If we proceed from the idea that the musical drama as defined in the *Beethoven* festschrift of 1870 is a symphonic opera whose music expresses the "innermost essence of the world"—that is to say, which must be justified structurally without outside support—and additionally that the Bayreuth doctrine called for the cultivation of other genres in view of the fact that Wagner had perfected the mythological tragedy, then Friedrich Klose's *Ilsebill* (1903), a fairy-tale opera based musically on a dramatic symphony, would seem to be the purest example of a legitimate post-Wagnerian work.

Finally, the question of whether or not one could speak of Wagnerisms depended on the national operatic traditions which formed the critics' backgrounds and systems of reference, including non-German critics who toed their own national line. The claim that Verdi's late style, as manifested in *Don Carlos, Otello,* and even *Falstaff,* was less the result of an internal development than of external, Wagnerian influence has long since been discredited, yet it was still being pressed by a noted historian of opera, Hermann Kretzschmar, as late as 1919. It can be understood only if we take into account the tenacity of the genre tradition in Italian opera, which was the obverse of its popularity. In the case of late-nineteenth-century French composers, the pilgrimage to

Bayreuth was virtually obligatory. Saint-Saëns and d'Indy attended the Festspiele as early as 1876, to be followed in the 1880s by Duparc, Chabrier, Fauré, and Debussy. Yet what they appropriated musically, although the critics drew it to the fore, was restricted on the whole to the technique of orchestration and the tendency to develop chromatic harmony still further. Even operas whose subject matter reflects the example of music drama, such as Emmanuel Chabrier's *Gwendoline* (1886), Edouard Lalo's *Le Roi d'Ys* (1888), and Ernest Reyer's *Sigurd* (1884), remind one of the Wagnerian model less with regard to the basic traits of the musical and dramatic structure than in the use of advanced harmony—a common enough trait of the epoch, though it was forced to become a progressive feature, and a sign of the times, above all by Wagner, who insisted on it most. Sometimes it seems as if it was not the real influence of Meyerbeer but the inclination to call him by name that fell victim to the influence of Wagner.

Wagner and Operatic Realism

It would be both aesthetically and historically incorrect to associate closely the distinguishing features of the Wagnerian style with certain areas of dramatic subject matter: features such as chromatic harmony; the ability, if chromaticism is the norm, to hear diatonicism as an eloquent exception; musical prose and speech melody; the primacy of orchestral melody; the unending leitmotif web; and psychologically motivated polyphony. Rather, as Jules Massenet's *drame lyrique Werther* (1886) and Gustave Charpentier's naturalist opera *Louise* (1900) demonstrate, they can always be transferred to genres foreign to Wagner without a stylistic break over and above that which is permissible in opera. There can be no question of illegitimate appropriation, of the musical language of the Stage Festival Play being profaned in realistic opera, if on the one hand we proceed from compositional criteria and on the other realize that the symbolism that belongs to the implications of leitmotif technique was not foreign to the kind of naturalism espoused by Zola. The relationship of the music drama, a genre rooted in Romantic tradition, to the realistic tendencies that in the late nineteenth century began to gain currency even in opera, a seemingly antirealistic art form, is thus characterized by a peculiar paradox. Whereas on the one hand operatic realism, in the extremely diverse forms created by Bizet, Mussorgsky, and Janáček, represents the antithesis to music drama, it would on the other hand hardly have been possible without some of the musical techniques developed by Wagner. (*Carmen* is the exception which proves the rule.) That musical realism or naturalism would use Wagner's advanced harmony and instrumentation for descriptive purposes was predictable and self-evident (the word *naturalistic* as a term of abuse was already current among conservative critics). Of greater importance, however, is the musical-dramaturgical fact that realistic texts can hardly be set to music other than in the form of the musical prose to which Wagner progressed in the *Ring,* under the pressure of a kind of alliterative verse which is prose by musical standards. And musical prose in turn, in order not to fall apart into musically disparate declamatory phrases, needs the support of an unending orchestral melody, the structuring of which as a web or tissue of leitmotifs suggests itself inasmuch as it guarantees musical coherence and performs dramaturgical functions. In other words, the partial Wagnerism of a naturalistic opera such as Charpentier's *Louise* is not the result of a stylistic compromise, but rather the obvious (if not necessary) solution to a compositional problem that arose particularly in an operatic genre whose subject matter departed furthest from the mythical music drama.

Comedy and Fairy Tale

Hugo Wolf, Alexander Ritter, and Engelbert Humperdinck (Siegfried Wagner's composition teacher) were members of Wagnerian circles and even of the Bayreuth orthodoxy. The fact that Wolf wrote a musical comedy (*Der Corregidor*, 1896), and Ritter (*Der faule Hans*, 1885; and *Wem die Krone?*, 1890) and Humperdinck (*Hänsel und Gretel*, 1893) fairy-tale operas fit in with the Bayreuth doctrine that the history of musical tragedy based on mythological subject matter had been brought to an end by Wagner. The doctrine implied that it was impossible to add to the tradition, as August Bungert had dared to do with a gesture of defiance (*Homerische Welt*, 1896–1903), and suggested that musical comedy and fairy-tale opera were genres for which Wagner had merely paved the way (*Die Meistersinger,* and acts 1 and 2 of *Siegfried*) without pursuing them to their ultimate conclusion. The future was given something of a chance, but not much of one.

The problems that beset Wolf in *Der Corregidor*, however, were almost impossible to solve, in contrast to the difficulties (by no means small but nevertheless worth the effort of overcoming) which he encountered in his attempt to continue the Schumann tradition of lied composition in the spirit of Wagner's music. Wolf generally rejected the simple or apparent solution of commenting, as it were, by means of a declamatory vocal line on a piano piece consisting of a web of eloquent motifs; as a result he was forced to embark on precarious attempts to reconcile the strophic principle of the lied with a musical style that took its bearings from Wagner, whose motifs, harmony, and counterpoint tended in the direction of musical prose. But these very contradictions were among the preconditions and sources of inspiration of the complex textual interpretation, both prosodic and expressive, that has always been praised in Wolf's songs.

In the coarser genre of opera, by contrast, the dangers and disadvantages of a stylistically problematic situation are more apparent than the opportunities and advantages. The song scene at the beginning of *Der Corregidor*, a narrative painting lacking dramaturgical function, is untheatrical. The great Jealousy monologue, doubtless the central core of the opera, is dramatic to the extent that it transcends the limits of comedy: the specific drama of comedy, which is always convivial and social, unexpectedly turns to the tragic pathos of isolation. And Wolf, with a dramaturgical timidity that ruined the stage effect, evaded the crisis that ought to occur at the end, for he lacked the means to portray it musically.

Whereas *Der Corregidor* is a failure (though of the first order), whose short-comings can be gauged by comparing it with Verdi's *Falstaff,* Humperdinck's *Hänsel und Gretel* is depressingly provincial when we think of the great tra-dition of Russian fairy-tale opera extending from Glinka to Stravinsky and Prokofiev. It is easy to sympathize with Rudolf Louis, who in 1912 (*Deutsche Musik der Gegenwart*) claimed to be ashamed of his earlier enthusiasm. All in all, the kind of post-Wagnerian opera propagated or encouraged by Bayreuth, which consisted in eschewing tragedy in favor of fairy-tale opera or musical comedy, was a luckless undertaking. (*Der Rosenkavalier* became an outstanding "comedy for music" precisely because, after *Elektra,* Strauss renounced the idea of following in Wagner's footsteps, which at the same time had entailed trying to outdo him.) The authentic history of influence was the opposite of the orthodox one.

Wagner, Schopenhauer, and Instrumental Music

When he first elaborated it in *Opera and Drama* in 1851, Wagner's provocative assertion that the history of the symphony had come to an end was not as wrongheaded and egocentric as it was bound to seem retrospectively from the vantage point of the last quarter of the century, which was a second age of the symphony. In the 1850s and 1860s it was the symphonic poem that dominated the scene, not the symphony. Yet the symphonies of Bruckner and Brahms changed the situation in the 1870s; and Wagner responded as early as 1879, not without some spiteful polemics against Brahms but without a word about Bruckner, in the essay *On the Application of Music to the Drama,* the subject of which was the relationship between dramatic and symphonic music.

The postulate in *Opera and Drama* that music is or should be a means to the end of the drama was revised by Wagner, with some shifts in emphasis, from 1854 on under the influence of Arthur Schopenhauer's aesthetics of music (which is a metaphysics of absolute music inspired by Wackenroder and Tieck). The difference is most clearly apparent in *Beethoven* (1870). The idea that music expresses the innermost essence of the world, that, as Scho-penhauer claimed, it was not the music that illustrated or commented on a text or an action but rather the reverse, that the text or the action illustrated or commented on the music, made it necessary to require of music a wholly self-sufficient structure, for if it was to be considered essential form, it could not be dependent on the outside support of mere phenomenal form.

But in the 1879 essay Wagner, although adhering to the view of music drama as symphonic opera, seems to be evading the logical consequences of Schopenhauer's metaphysics. For one thing he warns against attempting har-monic-contrapuntal "audacities," which were justified by the action in dramatic music, in symphonic music, which lacked such justification. He then returns to the thesis of *Opera and Drama* that the formal law of dramatic music, despite its symphonic aspirations, is contained in the scenic action. "However, to be an artwork as music, the new form of dramatic music must have the unity of the symphonic movement; and this it attains by spreading itself over the whole drama, in the most intimate cohesion therewith, not merely over single smaller, arbitrarily selected parts. This unity consists in a tissue of basic themes pervading all the drama, themes which contrast, complete, re-shape, divorce and intertwine with one another as in a symphonic movement; only that here the needs of the dramatic action dictate the laws of parting and combining, which were there originally borrowed from the motions of the dance."

If we attempt to translate into compositional categories Wagner's theory that the classical symphony "originally" stems from the dance, this obviously means that a regular four-square syntax, in conjunction and interaction with comprehensible harmony based on the cadential model, constitutes the formal ground plan of instrumental music. The thematic and motivic development had its roots in the harmony and the syntax. In contrast to this, formal consistency had to be constituted and ensured primarily through thematic-motivic relationships the moment the regular periodic structure dissolved into musical prose and the harmony based on the cadential model disintegrated to become "wandering tonality" (Arnold Schoenberg). Wagner, it seems, could imagine a network of motivic relationships only without a clearly defined harmonic-syntactic basis as a dramaturgically motivated connection in which "the needs of the dramatic action dictate the laws of parting and combining."

Composers of symphonic music toward the end of the nineteenth and the beginning of the twentieth centuries, from Bruckner to Mahler, Strauss, and even Schoenberg, not only appropriated certain features extrapolated from the Wagnerian style, but (except for Bruckner, who was not given to reflecting about aesthetic matters) were also Wagnerians, disciples of the metaphysics of Schopenhauer, Wagner, and Nietzsche. This fact produced a complex configuration in the history of ideas on account of the conflicting nature of Wagnerian theory, which was a metaphysics of music and yet at the same time did not surrender the idea of the primacy of the drama. But it was precisely from the contradictory assumptions inherent in the intermingling of technical facts and aesthetic implications that certain specific conclusions were drawn. These, despite the extreme divergence between the composers of the fin de siècle, formed a complex of features that was characteristic for the epoch as a whole.

First, Strauss, Mahler, and Schoenberg were wholly convinced that music which expressed the innermost essence of the world had to be structurally self-sufficient, and that a support from without in the shape of a text, a program, or a scenic action could be nothing but a "pointer" (Mahler) whose task it was to lead to the interior of music conceived of as a metaphysically and thus formally self-contained "world unto itself" (Tieck). Second, the premise that music is the essence of form, and drama merely its appearance, led them to assume that instrumental music could also venture out to compositional extremes. The timidity with which Wagner in 1879 insisted on a dramaturgical justification of chromatic-motivic asymmetries and uncompromising motivic combinations could not be explained, strictly speaking, in terms of Wagnerian and Schopenhauerian metaphysics. The radical nature of Bruckner's compositional technique was, without his being aware of it, quite in keeping with the spirit, even if not with the letter, of the Wagnerian aesthetic. Third, Wagner's idea that musical form consists primarily in the relationship of themes and motifs implies nothing less than that, in contrast to the classical symphony, neither the four-square character of the writing, the regular periodic structure, nor the firmly established tonal ground plan is an absolutely essential precondition for musical consistency. Rather, musical prose (which Bruckner, however, eschewed) and wandering tonality are possible without the danger of formal disintegration if as a sort of counterbalance the network of thematic-motivic relationships is ever more tightly knit, something that is true for Brahms and Bruckner just as much as it is for Wagner.

The differences between absolute and program music and between the symphonic and the dramatic style, which were accentuated in the partisan musical squabbles of the day were actually of secondary importance in comparison with the tendency at the time, first, to understand music as the self-evident essence of form (aesthetically of primary importance); second, to take harmonic and syntactic irregularities to the extreme; and third, to seek stability of form in ever closer thematic-motivic links. In the history of composition the process whereby formal coherence (in contrast to the classical tradition) came to be ensured less by the harmonic-syntactic structure, which Eduard Hanslick called large-scale rhythm, than by a web of motivic relationships was precisely the reason why the way became open in harmony and syntax for experiments such as wandering tonality and musical prose. It was a path that finally led to the "emancipation of the dissonance" (Schoenberg) and to the abrogation of regular rhythm (Stravinsky); and, as a consequence of the emphasis placed on motivic relationships, it made twelve-tone technique possible. Progress from Romanticism to modernism was thus a process in which, in different ways, both Brahms and Wagner participated. Thus it is possible to understand why Schoenberg should have invoked both traditions and ignored the partisan polemics.

The Modernist Movement

Wagner's music is the embodiment of what those who were born after him characterize as the nineteenth century, no matter whether they long to return to the past or whether they affect an inner distance that does not become more credible for being exaggerated. Yet nothing could be further from the truth than to construct a mutually exclusive contrast between the fin de siècle, which stood compositionally in the shadow of Wagner, and the New Music of the twentieth century, whose epoch-making events were the abolition of tonality by Arnold Schoenberg (1908) and of regular rhythm by Igor Stravinsky (1913). Rather, the elucidation of the period between 1889, the year of Richard Strauss's *Don Juan* and Gustav Mahler's First Symphony, and the beginning of the 1920s—the collapse of expressionism, Schoenberg's discovery of twelve-tone technique, and Stravinsky's stylistic change to neoclassicism—is still an unsolved problem. The emphases we place determine the greater or lesser significance we accord to the subsequent history of Wagnerian compositional technique and aesthetics, a history that is easy to establish but difficult to evaluate historically.

Hermann Bahr termed the fin de siècle the modernist movement. Although at the time it was fashionable to compare the age with the decadence of late antiquity, it was in fact replete with a mood of awakening whose musical emblem seems to have been the beginning of Strauss's *Don Juan*. It is a mood that calls into question the expression "late Romanticism," a term that seems to allude to a final phase in a developmental process and derives from the polemics of the 1920s against the fin de siècle. Yet the enthusiasm for Wagner reached a stage in the 1890s which, without exaggerating, one might call frenzied delirium. That the modernist movement was influenced by Wagner in compositional and aesthetic terms would have been denied by no German composer of the era, despite striking stylistic differences—not by Strauss or Mahler, nor by Schoenberg or Pfitzner. Thus, inasmuch as we can speak at all of tangible features that were common to the composers of the modernist movement, in essence we are dealing with conclusions that were drawn from the Wagnerian tradition. It was a tradition that could be interpreted in many ways. The conviction that musical progress was primarily apparent in the extent to which one succeeded in constructing unusual chords and in relating them to one another in a compelling manner instead of letting them protrude from the context as isolated events stemmed from Wagner. So did the procedure of establishing an interaction between harmony and instrumentation, which makes it impossible to analyze one aspect of the writing without taking account of the other—and the principle of understanding musical form not as tonal architecture, the parts of which form a clear-cut whole by means of repetition and contrast, but as a web in which motifs that are to be understood as musical ideas are interwoven. Thus the Wagnerian tradition was not a late Romantic relic within the modernist movement but, precisely as in the case of the influence exerted by Liszt, a factor that encouraged compositional progress.

There are no doubt compelling reasons for the common habit of speaking of a musical revolution around 1910. Yet this turns the depiction of the subsequent effects of the Wagnerian style into a precarious undertaking, for it suggests an erroneous idea: the idea that a late Romanticism in the shadow of Wagner, or the nineteenth century, was at this time superseded by a New Music, with which the twentieth century openly confronted the past in the person of Wagner. In fact important and characteristic works of the time, such as Franz Schreker's *Die Gezeichneten* (1918) or Alexander Zemlinsky's *Lyric Symphony* (1923), are unmistakably part of the modernist movement which derived from Wagner, and yet they keep their distance from the New Music of Schoenberg and Stravinsky. But if the aesthetic stature of *Die Gezeichneten* and the *Lyric Symphony* convinces us that until about 1923 the initial phase of the New Music was paralleled by an equally authentic survival of the modernist movement (to speak of untimely works would be a violent distortion of the historical facts), this betokens the survival, until the beginning of the 1920s, of a legitimate (and not merely derivative) post-Wagnerian style. This state of affairs emerges with some clarity as soon as we relinquish the idée fixe that there is such a thing as "epochs proceeding in Indian file," in the words of Ernst Bloch.

Apart from this the concept of an epoch threshold, which, around 1910, was crossed independently by composers such as Schoenberg, Stravinsky, Alexander Scriabin, and Charles Ives, is not altogether unproblematic. It is precisely when we proceed from criteria whose origins lie in the reconstruction of a latent post-Wagnerian style that the concept of a New Music encompassing both Schoenberg's *Erwartung* and Stravinsky's *Sacre du printemps* seems to disintegrate or become strangely elusive. If Schoenberg's "emancipation of the dissonance," which meant that one was no longer compelled to resolve dissonances onto consonances, proved to be the extreme consequence of the chromaticism of *Tristan,* Stravinsky's harmony and rhythm, which were no less disconcerting, were the result of developments which in the nineteenth century ran parallel to the mainstream determined by Wagner, although their significance was at first not sufficiently realized. Stravinsky forces us to reconstruct the prior history of semitonal or atonal diatonicism in the nineteenth century. That is, he forces us to relinquish the common nineteenth-century prejudice that musical progress consists in the discovery of unusual and yet logically compelling chromatic chord progressions, on the grounds that it is altogether the wrong way of looking at it (as Nietzsche might have said). A history of diatonicism in the nineteenth century, corresponding to Ernst Kurth's *Romantic Harmony and Its Crisis in Wagner's "Tristan"* (Kurth 1920), still remains to be written.

The assertion that Schoenberg's atonality represents a consequence of the chromaticism of *Tristan* has long been a commonplace (and remains difficult to challenge). It is not, in fact, the result of historical research with which we could be wholly satisfied but rather a mere point of departure, and this because it has proved impossible to define which stage of the process is to pass as the qualitative leap by which a compositional state beyond Wagner was reached. (That Schoenberg's atonality was at first mocked by hostile critics as being the music of an imaginary future that would never come to pass and then, hardly two decades later, scorned as a survival of the "bad" nineteenth century, the dregs of the Wagnerian style, and hence consigned, so to speak, to the rubbish heap of the past, is typical of a situation in which the hostility to Wagner was the remnant of the post-Wagnerian style, which remained topical in the controversies about current aesthetic and compositional developments.)

We can make the problem comprehensible by examining complementary harmony, the procedure of relating chords to one another by the fact that the second consists entirely or almost entirely of notes not contained in the first. It is quite evident that the origins of the technique lay in the kind of chromatic alteration whose paradigm was Wagner's *Tristan,* namely in the contraction of a whole tone (g′-a′) to a semitone (g♯′-a′). This, being the "striving" of a leading note (g♯′) to its goal (a′), represents a dynamic factor. In Schoenberg's early atonal period semitone steps are the most common intervals between chords that complement one another to form a chromatic scale, which is not as self-evident as it might seem. Somewhere along the line, however (the vagueness of this statement is a sign of psychological uncertainty) the point is reached at which the chromatic striving suddenly changes to a kind of abstract complementarity—or, to put it more precisely, at which the dynamic element becomes a secondary, and finally an indifferent feature, or one that pales into insignificance. (When in dodecaphony, which in terms of harmonic technique is a generalization of complementary harmony, two chords are derived from the same twelve-tone row, the decisive and structural factor in compositional and aesthetic terms is the static complementary relationship and not the dynamic tendency of the one chord toward the other.) Thus it would be correct to regard the moment within the development of atonality when complementarity became detached from the sense of striving as the point where the influence of the Wagnerian style and the chromaticism of *Tristan* came to an end. (This moment cannot be precisely dated, though it had certainly occurred by the time dodecaphony came into being.)

Both the prolongation of modernism in the music of Schreker and Zemlinsky and the development of atonality between 1908 and 1923 are products of Wagner's influence that were deflected (respectively directly and indirectly) into areas of compositional method latent with ambiguity and gradual changes of meaning. By the early 1920s, with Schoenberg's transition to dodecaphony and Stravinsky's to neoclassicism (both a form of hostility toward Wagner raised to the status of a program), Wagner's influence as part of an "authentic" way of composing that was adequate to the historical situation had come to an end. All that remained was a negative influence in the shape of Stravinsky's and Brecht's polemics against Wagner's musical dramaturgy. Even if we resist the temptation of dogmatically equating anachronism with aesthetic failure in judging, say, Strauss's late work *Die Liebe der Danae* (1940), with its obvious indebtedness to Wagner, a distasteful feeling of embarrassment in such cases is unavoidable.

The History of Wagner's Technique of Composition

Whether an attempt to provide a rough sketch of the historical influence of Wagner's technique of composition manages to touch on essential or merely peripheral facts depends on the extent to which we succeed in understanding the links and interactions between harmony, instrumentation, motivic technique, counterpoint, and syntax. To isolate the parameters would be to distort precisely those features which are of crucial importance in the history of the reception of the Wagnerian style.

Whereas Wagner's chromatic harmony was emphatically praised as being the origin of the modernist movement, his counterpoint was treated with reserve insofar as it was not in fact described as being mere pseudopolyphony that exhausted itself in the paraphrasing of chords. Yet even the most cursory analysis of the emblem of the music of the future, the opening bars of the *Tristan* prelude, suffices to show how the compositional factors interlock in a manner from which criteria of a legitimate post-Wagnerian style may be deduced. The suspended g♯' before a', which leads to the genesis of the legendary *Tristan* chord, owes the fact that it can be drawn out to the length that is part of its expressive-symbolic character to a motivic-contrapuntal feature: the fact that it is an inversion of the suspended f' before e' in bar 1, and that between the motifs of the upper and lower voices, which together form the substance of the harmony, there exists the eminently contrapuntal relationship of strict contrary motion (f'-e'-d♯'-d' / g♯'-a'-a♯'-b'). Apart from this the impression that the progression is poised between being "open" and "closed," because the dominant-seventh chord is neither a conclusion in itself nor yet able to tolerate a trivial A-minor chord at the end, is the exact harmonic equivalent of the phenomenon typical of Wagner's melody: as a rule leitmotifs neither end in a cadence nor do they permit a cadence to be added to them. The feature peculiar to the motifs and the harmony, the evasion of the contrast between open and closed structures, is in turn a correlative of a syntax that tends in the direction of musical prose: the prolonging of the opening motif in *Tristan* is irregular (three bars) and in addition it is variable (extension in the second sequence). (It would be absurd to want to regulate the motivic complex by placing it in a four-square period with an antecedent and consequent that functions as large-scale rhythm. Rather, the motif is essentially prose, which is why it is necessary to continue with a sequence instead of a consequent.)

A measure of an authentic post-Wagnerian style may be the degree to which, in later works, the interaction of advanced harmony, eloquent counterpoint, irregular and variable phrasing, and a motivic structure that is harmonically and syntactically at one and the same time open and closed seems successful. If we admit this, then both Strauss's *Elektra* (1908) and Schoenberg's *Erwartung* (1909) can be reckoned to be among those works in which, precisely because there can be no talk of mere stylistic imitation, both the compellingly plausible and the precarious consequences became visible—consequences that were prefigured in a considered, intellectually evolutionary appropriation of basic traits of Wagnerian compositional technique.

Yet the most difficult problem at the time was not an issue as far as Strauss and Schoenberg were concerned. For composers with a less energetic cast of mind than was the case with the representatives of the modernist movement, this was syntax as a premise of formal organization. Since it seemed difficult to constitute palpable musical forms without the principle of large-scale rhythm, the correspondence between bars, groups of bars, half-periods, and periods, the temptation to return to the four-square pattern was not infrequently overwhelming. Operatic genres with an affinity for the song, such as the fairy tale *(Hänsel und Gretel)* and the comedy *(Der Corregidor)*—genres, that is, which were accepted in Bayreuth because they pursued paths other than the mythical tragedy perfected by Wagner—suggested a recourse to regular periodic structures in any case. But the relationship between four-square syntax on the one hand and leitmotif technique, expressive counterpoint, and chromatic harmony on the other became distorted. The compositional dubiety manifested itself aesthetically as stylistic disunity. The counterpoint, to put it in a nutshell, tended to become academic, the chromaticism forced, and the leitmotif technique didactic.

In contrast to this, the psychological counterpoint in *Elektra,* which the purists of the strict style suspected of being literary, proves to be legitimate in terms of the post-Wagnerian style in that in the first place it became possible only through musical prose, which permits an almost imperceptible appearance and disappearance of the vocal lines in interaction with the complex instrumentation; through leitmotifs, to which it owes its expressive-symbolic substance; and, above all, through a chromatic harmony rich in dissonance. This, supported by the instrumentation, conveys the feeling that music is, in the sense of Schopenhauer or even Freud, a language of the subconscious. (But the correlation of the parameters could be similarly reconstructed from every other starting point.)

It is nonetheless apparent in the case of composers of outstanding significance that it was precisely the incongruous nature of the compositional factors, whose inner coherence is one of the postulates of the Wagnerian style, that produced results which in one way or another promoted the process of historical change in a decisive fashion. In Schoenberg's orchestral works of the "critical years" *(Erwartung,* 1909; *Die glückliche Hand,* 1913), the harmony was a function of the counterpoint to an extent that threatened the balance of the compositional parameters. Yet in those works where the scoring did not permit a similarly rich or overrich polyphony *(Drei Klavierstücke* op. 11, 1909; *George-Lieder* op. 15, 1909), a new compositional situation was reached. As a result of the resolution with which the advanced harmonic level was nonetheless maintained, the emancipation of the dissonance, instead of remaining inconspicuous as a side product of excessive counterpoint, became the conspicuous event that made far-reaching technical and aesthetic consequences imperative, and in the final analysis led to dodecaphony.

In the case of Strauss the balance of the compositional parameters was endangered by the fact that in *Elektra* (1908) an at times rank growth of counterpoint embellishes a relatively simple harmony, whereas chords with an intricate structure and complex tone color not infrequently have to provide their own justification as isolated effects that are not justified in motivic and contrapuntal terms. The result was that a retraction of advanced harmony, which was accomplished in an almost programmatic manner in *Der Rosen-*

kavalier (1910), seemed possible without the composer's having to infringe on the fundamentals of the motivic-contrapuntal texture. In other words, both Schoenberg's transition from the modernist movement of the beginning of the century to the New Music and Strauss's simultaneous retreat from the modernist movement into a classicism far removed from the present were connected, by virtue of the fact that they were compositional decisions, with an exclusive emphasis on the complex of compositional parameters whose specific inner synthesis represented Wagner's essential compositional legacy. The compositional influence of Wagner was at an end the moment the modernist movement split into New Music on the one hand and classicism on the other—that is, when the simultaneous participation of Strauss and Schoenberg in the historical process reached a stage where they began to differ even though they were contemporaries.

Music Drama and New Music

If we consider Wagner's influence from a stylistic and a dramaturgical point of view, we may pursue the traces left by the music drama into the later decades of the New Music. It is not misguided to speak of an unbroken history of music drama in terms of a specific operatic genre invented by Wagner, a history that extends from Strauss's *Salome* (1905) and *Elektra* (1908), Schoenberg's *Erwartung* (1919) and *Moses und Aron* (1930–1932), and Berg's *Wozzeck* (1925) and *Lulu* (1937) to Bernd Alois Zimmermann's *Die Soldaten* (1965), despite the different musical languages of the various works.

Yet an important feature of the music drama tradition, precisely because it has achieved almost universal acceptance since the late nineteenth century, is now hardly ever seen as having come from Wagner. This is the assertion of a poetic claim comparable to that of the spoken drama, and the associated decline of libretto writing as a literary metier with fixed craft rules. (In the twentieth century there have really been only librettists of genius and bad librettists.) Arrigo Boito, to whom Verdi owed the texts of *Otello* and *Falstaff,* was a Wagnerian inasmuch as he wrote librettos that were no longer librettos as such but poetic works of the first rank. The origins of literary opera, in which the texts of plays are set to music literally, though of course in shortened form, can be understood, in the case of Debussy, Strauss, and Berg, as a consequence of the poetic ambition which, under the influence of Wagner, gained ground in the field of the libretto.

But the musical prose to which Wagner progressed in *Das Rheingold* first made it possible to base an opera on the unaltered text of a play. Yet musical prose, which was also tested independently of Wagner in Mussorgsky's unfinished opera *The Marriage* (1868), does not constitute a specifically Wagnerian tradition. Rather, in terms of the history of style, the decisive factor was initially the fact that it became a central problem of how to make possible a continual change in speech inflection in the vocal lines (the result of the influence of the dramaturgy of the spoken play) through orchestral writing that ensured musical consistency. The composition of a prose text, particularly in the case of a decidedly literary ambition that is aimed at interpreting the text, requires rapidly changing melodic inflections rich in nuances. In Berg's *Lulu,* the text of which omits hardly a single stylistic level of the language, from the hectic talk about stock prices to the hymnlike admission of love, the scale of melodic possibilities ranges in untold nuances from melodrama via recitative and arioso right up to emphatic cantabile writing. But the abrupt alternation of stylistic levels in the voice part makes it necessary to create musical coherence primarily by means of orchestral melody, as Wagner called it. The instrumental writing on which the dialogues are based can only consist of short repeated phrases, as in Italian opera, or of a symphonic web, as in music drama. In terms of music and dramaturgy, the decisive feature of the Wagnerian tradition in twentieth-century opera is thus the symphonic claim of the orchestral melody to be the basic foundation of a vocal dialogue which dominates literary opera as the historical consequence of the poetic pretensions of music drama.

That *Wozzeck* and *Lulu* belong to the tradition of Wagner is due not so much to the leitmotif technique, the significance of which remains secondary, as to a seemingly anti-Wagnerian feature: the self-contained forms on which Berg based individual scenes. They are almost exclusively instrumental forms (variation, sonata, invention), and the function they perform is the same as that of the Wagnerian tissue of leitmotifs. The symphonic orchestral writing forms the precondition and basis for a vocal dialogue which, as a form of interpersonal conflict, takes its dramaturgical bearings from the spoken play. Its model is the dialogue that by means of speech and counterspeech develops to a conclusion, and not the duet that presents a static emotional conflict. In terms of operatic history Berg's recourse to instrumental forms does not constitute a parallel to the restoration of classical vocal forms, for which Ferruccio Busoni made a plea at about the same time. Rather, it is its antithesis, if we proceed from the dramaturgical functions that are performed by the musical procedures. The complementarity of literary opera and instrumental forms is, in terms of genre history, a transformation of the Wagnerian idea of conjoining the development of the spoken play and that of the symphony, as represented by Shakespeare and Beethoven. And inasmuch as we see the principle of the *Gesamtkunstwerk* in the configuration of the dramaturgy of the spoken play and the symphonic style, and not in a vague idea of the interaction of the arts, the operatic practice of the Second Viennese School proves to be a legitimate post-Wagnerian style, although in an unorthodox sense.

Whereas the symphonic style in twentieth-century opera is generally seen as having been influenced, directly or indirectly, by Wagner, the tendency to favor epic theater, in the case of Igor Stravinsky (*L'histoire du soldat,* 1918) and Bertolt Brecht (*Aufstieg und Fall der Stadt Mahagonny,* 1930), seems to be the antithesis to music drama, although it is precisely in the *Ring,* Wagner's official magnum opus, that epic traits are unmistakable. The confusion, at least with regard to terminology, stems from the fact that the term *epic* functions as a collective name for tendencies opposed to the classical drama of closed forms, between which there is in part not the slightest connection. In the *Ring* the many-sided action, the aesthetic presence of the author in the work (in the shape of the leitmotif commentary), and the interpolation of narratives that move the action ahead only slightly appear to be epic features if we are thinking of the postulates of classical dramaturgy: the unity of the action, the absence of the author, and the consistent functionality of the narrative sections. Yet the epic quality of the *Ring* has nothing in common with the epic traits of the opera *Mahagonny:* the distance between actor and role, which is supposed to give the audience cause for reflection instead of empathy; the relative independence of individual situations; as well as the construction of a contrapuntal instead of a tautological relationship between music, language, and stage action. If we are not afraid of linguistic confusion, we can characterize music drama as epic theater. Yet the forms that are usually so termed represent the essence of a post-Wagnerian operatic dramaturgy.

Musical Criticism of Wagner

The musical criticism of Wagner in the late nineteenth and early twentieth centuries was in part mingled with reservations concerning dramaturgy, aesthetics, and cultural politics, although it nonetheless permits the isolation of certain technical features. It was directed primarily against the exaggerated lyrical pathos, the obtrusive and inflexible character of the leitmotif technique, the stereotypical nature of the sequential technique, and the lack of form given the appearance of metaphysical dignity by the term *unending melody*. Wagner's music was accused of forcibly taking possession of the emotions and chaining them up, thereby endangering the inner freedom of man, which is the basis of his humanity. In essence this is the same as Schiller's objection to the emotional effect of music as a whole. If, however, like Schiller, we understand form as the antithesis of emotion, then an evaluation of the real or possible ways of perceiving Wagner's music does not depend exclusively on aesthetic and anthropological assumptions. Above all it depends on the extent to which we are able to grasp and do justice to the formal precision of Wagner's music dramas.

Schoenberg's criticism of Wagner's sequence technique, the mania for saying the same thing twice (to put it mildly), represents the obverse of the compositional postulate of developing variation. Whereas the sequence technique that Wagner felt moved to use was the result of the fact that leitmotifs can rarely be complemented to form regular periods with antecedents and consequents, it remains open to doubt whether developing variation, which comes from the tradition of instrumental music leading from Beethoven to Brahms, is capable of performing a dramaturgical function. Wagner's sequences were a means of continuing leitmotifs, with their tendency toward isolation, in a meaningful way; and they served to intensify the lyrical emphasis. It is doubtful whether the principle of developing variation, with which Schoenberg compared the technique, can actually be used to criticize Wagner, for it is open to the charge of being unoperatic.

The fact that not even Debussy and Stravinsky shrank from mocking Wagner's stereotype leitmotifs in a stereotyped manner does not mean that they were right. First, the idea that leitmotifs are fixed little musical pictures is at least partially erroneous, or at least a coarse oversimplification in the face of the kind of variation technique that Wagner developed, especially in *Parsifal*. Second, in the *Ring* the relative constancy of the motivic manifestations is the obverse of dramaturgically indispensable submotivic relationships between the leitmotifs. And third, there can be no question of totally fixed meanings, as suggested by the guides. More to the point is Wagner's idea of placing leitmotifs in continually changing musical and symbolic contexts, so that gradually a host of associations that cannot be expressed by means of labels attaches to the identity of the motif.

In the final analysis the charge of formlessness rests on a concept of form based on the nexus of self-contained tonal coherence, periodic syntax, and the premise that musical form is tonal architecture. In contrast to this, the structure of the music dramas is characterized by wandering tonality, musical prose, and a kind of inner coherence that Wagner compared to a tissue. Thus the goal of an interpretation appropriate to Wagner is not the justification of the traditional theory of form by means of a forcible application of certain categories (as undertaken by Alfred Lorenz). Rather, it should be the explication of the specifically Wagnerian idea of form. It should try to make tangible how a nexus gradually results from open tonality, irregular syntax, and a motivic technique that does not, as in the case of Beethoven, form a goal-oriented developmental process, but an ever more densely knit network encompassing ever more of the past. And it should suggest that, just like the operatic numbers and symphonic movements of the classical traditions, this nexus may lay claim to being thought of as form.

Whereas the musical criticism of Wagner had its origins in the history of composition, the tendency to restore classical forms, the universal claim of the principle of developing variation in the Schoenberg school, or the sobering of the musical tone in the neoclassicism and the New Objectivity of the 1920s, it also constituted a challenge to Wagner exegesis in that it made plain that one could not counter the polemics with an apologia that attempted to suggest tonal coherence, regular syntax, and architectonic form by means of analytical contortions. In fact it was possible to counter the polemics only by understanding that what was new in Wagner was an antithesis to classical form. But it was form nonetheless.

Translated by Alfred Clayton

Works: The Writer

CHAPTER 23

The Prose Writings

JÜRGEN KÜHNEL

Richard Wagner heads a long line, which continues into the present day, of composers who are also active as authors, and whose writings are not restricted to questions of musical aesthetics but which also address political, contemporary, and philosophical issues. Wagner's writings are in addition a source, as yet far from exhausted, of insight into his musical and dramatic oeuvre. Moreover, the aesthetic writings of his Zurich years represent an important and thoroughly original contribution to discussions of the philosophy of art—particularly literary and musical theory—in the nineteenth century.

In this essay I have arranged Wagner's writings according to biographical periods. Within individual sections his work is grouped, where necessary, under thematic headings. I have also made a distinction between major, minor, and occasional writings. All the writings in SSD are included, as well as some that are not. [A checklist of the writings with the original German title, date of first publication, and location in SSD and the standard English translation of Wagner's prose works (Ellis) is provided as an appendix at the end of the chapter. Ed.]

Early Writings, 1834–1839

Wagner's early writings (indeed, his writings through 1848) are restricted to questions of musical aesthetics in the broadest sense. The July revolution of 1830, the decisive influence of which is brought out in the 1834 *Autobiographical Sketch* ("I only felt happy in the company of political writers"), did not find expression in his literary work. The writings from the years 1834–1839 are the direct result of Wagner's activities as *Opernkapellmeister* in Würzburg, Magdeburg, Königsberg, and Riga, but they also deal with the predominantly negative experiences with his first operas, *Die Feen* (1834) and *Das Liebesverbot* (1836). Consequently, they revolve around two topics—namely, the state of contemporary opera and German opera singing. Even though the emphases differ somewhat, the central aesthetic tenets of the Zurich writings (and also of the later theoretical work) nevertheless stand out clearly. An experience which left an indelible mark on Wagner's view of opera and opera singing during these years was a performance of Bellini's *I Capuleti e i Montecchi*, with Wilhelmine Schröder-Devrient in the role of Romeo, in Leipzig in March 1834.

Essays

German Opera (no. 1). This essay, written in Leipzig in 1834 and the first example of Wagner's literary work, is also the first in a series of writings by Wagner which deal critically with the state of contemporary opera. There are links to be found between this essay and the first part of *Opera and Drama*. Wagner here asserts the failings of German opera (and German drama) in the face of the "confusion of ideas" of "Germanomaniac music experts" and measured against dramatic truth (which is from the very beginning one of the major requirements of Wagnerian aesthetics for the musical theater). Contemporary German music is said to be exhausting itself in erudition with no meaning in life, in the sterile academic reproduction of handed-down musical genres and techniques such as the oratorio or "affected counterpoint." Judging on the basis of *Der Freischütz*, Wagner says that Weber had, at best, lyrical talent but "never knew how to handle singing" (that is, dramatic singing). Wagner compares this dismal situation with positive tendencies in Italian (Bellini in particular) and French opera (from Gluck through Grétry to Auber). Italian opera, he says, relies on "beautiful singing," which lends its protagonists (although individual characterization was admittedly weak) sensuousness and human warmth, and French opera since Gluck has developed a specifically dramatic music which (at the expense, in turn, of beautiful singing) stresses the "individual significance of the figures and characters." Wagner's ideal conception of opera, which he sees almost embodied in Mozart (it is noteworthy that Beethoven's Ninth Symphony is not yet referred to as the starting point of a new musical drama; see also SSD I, 10), and toward which he calls for the development of new musical-dramatic forms, turns out to be a "modern" synthesis of Italian and French opera.

Pasticcio (no. 2). Published under the eloquent pseudonym "Canto Spianato" (smooth singing), *Pasticcio* follows closely from the essay *German Opera*, which was only a few months old. Individual passages from the two pieces match verbatim. The call for an up-to-date synthesis of Italian and French opera leaning toward Mozart (and Gluck) is, however, stated more precisely here and is fully consistent with the principal aesthetic works of Wagner's Zurich years. What he postulates for the first time in *Pasticcio* is the concept of musical theater, which is esssentially poetry and as such captures the characters' inner being, their sensuousness and "passionateness"; similarly, words and notes are only an expression of this true essence of music drama. From this proposal, which represents nothing less than a "unity of poetry and song in the theater," Wagner derives further implications for opera singing in terms of both composition and actual singing. He firmly rejects an instrumental treatment of the human voice in the manner of J. S. Bach ("however much the uncritical admirers of this composer might protest") and declares himself in favor of a German version of "good Italian cantabile style," based on natural principles of breathing and articulation, in which he is fully prepared to include the bel canto art of ornamentation—not as an end in itself but as a means of expression dictated by "aesthetic-psychological necessity." Accordingly, he expects from the singer a combination of perfect technique and intensity of expression, of melody and declamation, combinations in which one component should never be neglected at the expense of the other, and which of necessity (in contrast, he says, to the practice on the German musical stage) should take account of the physical, technical, and psychological limitations to which the individual singer and his voice are subject. Here, too, numerous links can be found with later writings, in which Wagner states his position on questions of opera singing (*Report . . . concerning a German School of Music to Be Established in Munich,* no. 143; *On Actors and Singers,* no. 135; *The "Devotional Stage Festival" in Bayreuth,* no. 147).

Dramatic Singing (no. 3). This essay, which was written in Königsberg in 1837 but was not published until 1888 from the original manuscript, differs from the *Pasticcio* of 1834. The call comes again for the perfect singing technique found in the Italian school ("utmost purity of tone," "utmost precision and roundness," "utmost smoothness of the passages," "accurate delineation of the periods"; and, as a particular quality of the intended "German bel canto," the "utmost clarity of expression") as the indispensable principle of dramatic singing ("What can emotion achieve if it exceeds physical capacities?"). Wagner puts forward Wilhelmine Schröder-Devrient as the ideal example of a German dramatic singer, whose technical perfection (achieved after a second period of studying singing) makes the much-praised intensity and expressivity of her portrayals possible.

Bellini (no. 4). This essay, which was published in the Riga newspaper *Der Zuschauer* while Wagner was conducting his benefit performances of *Norma* 11–23 December 1837, also follows thematically from the *Pasticcio* of 1834. [See also Wagner's review of a performance of *Norma* in Königsberg on 8 March 1837, first published in Lippmann 1973.—Ed.] It is not so certain that he has a specific purpose here. Using Bellini and his *Norma* as a model (Bellini is one of the few composers about whom Wagner never made negative critical comments, even in later writings), Wagner again asserts the preeminence of Italian operatic singing over contemporary German opera. Bellini managed, albeit within a stereotypical framework, "to convey clearly pure passion on the stage" and to do that simply by means of "a clear, graspable melody": "Song, song and more song, Germans! For song is the language in which man communicates in music."

Shorter Occasional Pieces and Articles

Der Freischütz (no. 5) is a review of a production of Weber's opera in Magdeburg in which Wagner makes special mention of the singing ability of Karoline Pollert (a singer whom he encountered again in 1856) in the role of Agathe.

In *From Magdeburg* (no. 6) Wagner takes scornful pleasure in avenging himself on the "indifferentism" and lack of understanding of art shown by the public in the "commercial and military town" of Magdeburg, yet he also gives due credit to the qualities of Magdeburg's opera company ("opera in the process of dissolution") and their own achievements, including the first production ever of *Das Liebesverbot*. Nos. 7 and 8 are two newspaper advertisements from Riga, publicizing an opera (no. 7) and a concert (no. 8). The former publicizes a production of *Norma* in Wagner's honor, for which he had published the essay *Bellini* the day before. Here Wagner again characterizes Bellini's work as bringing together "the richest melodic fullness" with "an inner glow" and "the profoundest truth." In the latter Wagner announces his benefit concert of 14 March 1839, at which he would be bidding farewell to his Riga audiences and handing over the musical directorship to Heinrich Dorn. Other occasional articles from this period include the lost article (no. 9) written in Berlin in May 1836, which was intended for the *Neue Zeitschrift für Musik* but was not published by Schumann because of its polemics against the Berlin critic Ludwig Rellstab.

The Paris Years, 1839–1842

The writings from Wagner's years in Paris are the product of the journalistic work to which he turned out of financial necessity after his hoped-for success as an opera composer did not materialize and his occasional composition work for Maurice Schlesinger proved insufficient to keep him alive. The leading publications that printed Wagner's essays and reviews were the *Revue et gazette musicale* (published by Maurice Schlesinger, with Wagner's contributions appearing in French translation), the Stuttgart journal *Europa* (published by August Lewald), Schumann's *Neue Zeitschrift für Musik,* and the Dresden *Abendzeitung*. The contributions to the *Revue et gazette musicale* consist mainly of writings on issues of musical aesthetics, and in particular on opera, writings which occasionally take on a novelistic character in the tradition of the German musician novella, exemplified by E. T. A. Hoffman. Contributions to the German journals and newspapers are for the most part, by contrast, satirical feuilletons modeled on Heine's. In content these writings are increasingly concerned with Wagner's shifting assessment of French (and Italian) opera, a fact which can be attributed above all to his disappointment over the commercialization of art in Paris. These changes are reflected most clearly in Wagner's relationship with Meyerbeer. In the logical progression of his aesthetic views on musical drama, his turning (once again) to Beethoven acquires key significance in the Paris years.

Writings for the Revue et gazette musicale
On German Music (no. 10). In his first attempt for the *Revue et gazette musicale* Wagner presents for discussion to the French public his view of the development of German music, putting this development into a wide historico-

political and cultural-sociological context: that is, the history of German music, he says, was determined by the number and the small size of the German states, by German Protestantism, and by the tendency of German courts toward foreign models. It was inevitable under these circumstances that German music would become provincial and academic. The possibility of development existed particularly for instrumental music; vocal music continued to be limited to the field of Protestant church music but certainly achieved the greatest perfection within the structure of the great Passions and oratorios of Bach's age ("without question the most complete example we have of independent vocal music"). German opera is lacking, however (cf. no. 1, *German Opera*), because at the courts—where it could have developed—it was merely representational in form and "left to the Italians." Mozart's *Zauberflöte,* which Wagner judged an attempt to develop German opera on the basis of the popular Singspiel (which originated "far from the splendour of the court, among the people"), was certainly a masterpiece sui generis, but at the same time it had completely exhausted the finite limits of this folk genre. Wagner once again treats Weber's operatic oeuvre as a blind alley in musical history (cf. no. 1). Wagner records what he considers by contrast to be an enormous advance in French (and Italian) opera in the first third of the nineteenth century, an upsurge which he explains similarly in a historical and political context: "Is all this not a true reflection of the recent history of the French nation?" The essay ends with an enthusiastic tribute to Auber, whose opera *La Muette de Portici* has justifiably won for the "newer French school . . . hegemony over the civilized world." It is here alone that the future of German opera lies: "No two nations can be imagined whose brotherhood could produce greater and more perfect results for art than Germany and France." This tribute also comprises (cf. no. 11) a homage to Meyerbeer (not yet explicit here) and expresses Wagner's hope for his own success as a German composer of operas in Paris.

On Meyerbeer's "Les Huguenots" (no. 11). This essay, not published until 1911 (from a copy of Wagner's original manuscript), is a continuation—which for unknown reasons did not appear in his lifetime—of his first contribution to the *Revue et gazette musicale.* It is one of the most important sources on Wagner's relationship with Meyerbeer during his first years in Paris. The dating of 1837 suggested in SSD XII, 422, is undoubtedly incorrect and is clearly intended to play down this tribute to Meyerbeer in accordance with Wagner's later pronouncements on his former exemplar. Wagner repeatedly attributes the plight of German music, and particularly German opera, to the "non-existence of the Germans as a nation." Whenever German musicians did create works of world class, this usually happened on the other side of the German frontier: Handel, schooled in the Italian art of singing, brought about the culmination of English Protestant vocal music; Gluck carried through to fulfillment the "ancient, classical direction of French tragedy"; Mozart "raised the Italian school to perfection in a real sense." Meyerbeer is added to this list, just as, in the final section of the essay *On German*

Music, he, a German composer, is said to pick up from Auber in raising French opera to its zenith. A final point serves to limit slightly this hymn of praise to Meyerbeer: as the latter's achievements "cannot be surpassed"—like the work of Handel, Gluck, or Mozart, or even Beethoven, whose name appears for the first time at this point—completely new forms are required. The (unspoken) need is thus for a new hero in musical history, and there is no doubt that none other than Wagner himself is intended.

Pergolesi's "Stabat Mater" (arranged for full orchestra with choirs by Alexis Lvoff, member of the Academies of Bologna and St. Petersburg) (no. 12). In a careful review Wagner gives his full endorsement to the treatment of Giovanni Battista Pergolesi's *Stabat Mater* by the tsarist court composer Aleksej von Lwoff (1799–1871).

The Virtuoso and the Artist (no. 13; see also no. 22). In this first critical look at the cultural life of Paris, Wagner uses as his point of departure the story of the Mines of Falun told in allegorical form (see also SSD XI, 125–135 and Weiner 1982). He contrasts the figure of the self-satisfied virtuoso, who thinks only of his effect on the public, with the artist (meaning the performing artist), who, as "the person who conveys the artistic intention" and the "representative of the creative master," should ideally be only the "medium for the artistic idea, which achieves through him to a greater or lesser extent a real existence." The climax of the essay is his criticism of a performance in Paris of *Don Giovanni* in which he caricatures the celebrated tenor Giovanni Battista Rubini as the archetype of hollow virtuosity (see, for example, the passage: "On that evening Rubini took his famous trill from a′ to b♭′!").

A Pilgrimage to Beethoven (no. 14). In this, the first of Wagner's humorous musician novellas, the young German composer and Beethoven enthusiast "R . . . " from "L . . . " tells of his trip to Vienna, where, in the face of numerous obstacles caused in particular by a troublesome Englishman who dogs "R . . . ," he finally achieves his longed-for meeting with Beethoven. The novella makes use of the memoirs of Johann Friedrich Reichardt ("intimate letters, written on a trip to Vienna and the Austrian states in late 1808 and early 1809"), but "R . . . " from "L . . . " refers to Wagner himself. Wagner's (renewed) attention to Beethoven and his Ninth Symphony in 1840 was prompted by the orchestral concerts at the Conservatoire in Paris (SSD 1, 16). Wagner's theory of music drama here acquires a new quality compared with the writings from 1834 to 1839. In the closing part of the novella one of the axioms of this theory is spoken by Beethoven himself, to the effect that the last line of the Ninth Symphony is a connecting link leading to the development of "true music drama," with Wagner thus fulfilling what Beethoven had started. The combined effect of symphonic music and singing is seen by Beethoven, who is in the novella first and foremost Wagner's mouthpiece, as a synthesis bringing together on a higher plane supraindividual "elemental feelings" (represented by the instruments) and "individual emotion" (represented by song), the general and the particular, infinite nature and human individuality, with all its limitations.

On the Overture (no. 15). This essay is another important document in the development of Wagner's theories on music drama during his years in Paris. The function of the overture as an integral constituent of musical drama lies, according to Wagner, in the fact that the "characteristic idea of the drama would be reflected intrinsically by means of self-contained music and brought to a conclusion which anticipates, like a premonition, the task to be fulfilled by the scenic action." This function is fulfilled neither by the older "sinfonia" type of overture, which has the character simply of unconnected transitional and introductory music, nor by the modish potpourri overture, which Wagner deprecates as a "theatrical craving for admiration" and showmanship. In the main part of the essay he analyzes the overtures to Gluck's *Iphigénie en Aulide,* which was to occupy him again during his years as kapellmeister in Dresden, and to Mozart's *Don Giovanni* and Beethoven's *Leonore* Overture no. 3 as important steps toward the postulated ideal.

An End in Paris (no. 16). In his second musican novella Wagner deals freely with his worsening material crisis and his disappointment with cultural life in Paris, where talent means nothing and where patronage and money mean everything. "R . . . ," the hopeful young musician from *A Pilgrimage to Beethoven* (no. 14), is starving to death in Paris. On his deathbed he formulates a creed which points to some degree to Wagner's later ideas on the relationship between art and religion: "I believe in God, Mozart and Beethoven . . . ; I believe in the Holy Spirit and the truth of an indivisible Art; I believe that all shall be made Blessed by this art." The fragment *How a Young Musician Died in Paris* (no. 16a) is a draft which was produced as early as the late fall of 1840.

The Artist and His Public (no. 17) consists of fictional pages from the diary of the late "R . . . " (see nos. 14 and 16). The theme is the ambivalence of the artist who, on the one hand, has an "urge for publicity" without which he cannot fulfill himself but, on the other, is never understood by a public that wants only to be entertained.

Der Freischütz (no. 18) is an essay—containing a poetic retelling of the Weber opera—written with a view to the French premiere at the Grande Opéra in Paris (on 7 June 1841), and which attempts to explain the special features of this work to the Parisian public. Wagner refers once again to the problems of adapting works to French tastes (the German *Wald* is "quite different" from the French *bois*) and to performance conventions at the Opéra, which are not compatible with the absence of ballet, the spoken dialogue, and the songlike nature of the singing parts.

A Happy Evening (no. 19). The third of the Parisian musician novellas contains a fictional dialogue between "R . . . " and a friend on the relationship between absolute music and program music. "R . . . ," who is also Wagner's mouthpiece here, rejects tone painting and the programmatic interpretation of symphonic works such as Beethoven's Third and Sixth symphonies as incompatible with the nature of "true music." The composer welcomed ideas arising from external events ("for we are people and our fate is governed by external circumstances"), yet it is not these events that he treats musically but the sensations which are evoked by such events—"great, passionate and lasting sensations." They are raised to the level of the supraindividual and the universal through the language of symphonic music, because music "does not express the passion, love and longing of such or such an individual in such or such a situation, but passion, love and longing itself" (cf. his remarks on the relationship between instrumental music and singing in the final movement of Beethoven's Ninth Symphony in no. 14).

Halévy and "La Reine de Chypre" (no. 20). Wagner's last contribution to the *Revue et gazette musicale,* written on the occasion of the world premiere of Halévy's *Reine de Chypre* on 22 December 1841 at the Opéra, reveals the development of Wagner's theory of music drama during his years in Paris, particularly in the now clear distancing from French (and Italian) opera. It is true that he still praises Halévy as a "genuinely dramatic composer," but at the same time Wagner records the decline of French opera: it has been perverted into an "art industry," rendered superficial and "devoid of style" by "artistic corruption"; it has "descended into a system of clichés." Dramatic truth is "concealed by a smooth, conventional outer wall." The Wagner of the Zurich writings on art is already in evidence. Meyerbeer, once prized, is no longer mentioned (cf. no. 28, however). The introductory passages contain basic formulations of the relationship between verbal and tonal language and between verse and music in musical drama—formulations which offer variations on the pronouncements of "Beethoven" (that is, Wagner) in *A Pilgrimage to Beethoven* (no. 14) regarding the relationship between music and singing in Beethoven's Ninth Symphony (elemental feelings versus individual emotion) and on the functional purpose of symphonic music in the novella *A Happy Evening* (no. 19), which is the raising up of individual sensations into the supraindividual. While verbal language denotes and delineates "in clear, recognizable strokes" a limited reality, music has the capacity, through the "magic of the inexpressible," to blend this reality with "intimations of the Highest." The combined effect of poetry and music, poet and musician, is indispensable in musical drama, a decisive step toward the later idea of the synthesis of the arts.

Wagner or his publishers later put his individual contributions for the *Revue et gazette musicale* together in the series *Two Periods in the Life of a German Musician* (no. 21), the first publication of the German versions of nos. 14 and 16 under the individual titles *A Pilgrimage to Beethoven (from the papers of a musician who actually died)* and *An End in Paris (from the pen of a musician who is still alive); A German Musician in Paris: Novellas and Essays* (no. 22), a compilation of nos. 14, 16, 19, 10, 13, 17, and 27, in that order; *"Der Freischütz" in Paris* (no. 23), a compilation of no. 18 and the corresponding review for the Dresden *Abendzeitung* (no. 30); and *Two Essays for the "Gazette Musicale"* (no. 24), a compilation of no. 12 and the second part of no. 20 in the French versions.

Feuilletons for Europa

Parisian Amusements (no. 25) is a satirical critique of the *amusements* of the Parisian public in the theater, concerts, and salons, in particular of Rubini (see no. 13) and the dramatist and librettist Eugène Scribe ("Without Scribe no opera, no play—no real entertainment"). *Parisian Fatalities for the Germans* (no. 26) is an autobiographical tale, mixing truth and fiction, based on Wagner's experiences as a German artist in Paris: "All in all it is the most tiresome thing, being a German in Paris. Being German is splendid when one is at home, where there is warm-heartedness, Jean-Paul and Bavarian beer." The latter is a satirical companion piece to the novella *An End in Paris* (no. 16).

Contributions to Schumann's Neue Zeitschrift für Musik

Rossini's "Stabat Mater" (no. 27; cf. no. 22) is a satirical feuilleton which Wagner himself described as a humorous account occasioned by a performance of Rossini's *Stabat Mater,* with more digs at Rubini. "Valentino," the name Wagner uses as a pseudonym, is a conductor at the Salle St. Honoré, and Wagner blames his incompetence for the failure in Paris of his *Columbus Overture* (see Glasenapp, I, 395–396). *Special Edition from Paris* (no. 28) is similar in tone to the last contribution to the *Revue et gazette musicale* (no. 20). In this piece Wagner settles his account with French opera and Parisian cultural life. "Fashion" or "virtuosity" is all. Meyerbeer is described as a "deliberately sly fraud," the first of numerous defamatory statements against the Parisian who helped him and whom he once admired. The upshot: "We must abandon our belief in Paris."

Articles for the Dresden Abendzeitung

Reports from Paris for the Dresden *"Abendzeitung"* (no. 29) is a collective title for nine of Wagner's eleven articles for this newspaper in 1841–42, mainly satirical feuilletons dealing with various topics. The most prominent are the polemics against Liszt in the first and second articles and the predominantly positive assessment of Berlioz in the third article. Wagner considers Liszt a virtuoso interested solely in public acclaim and material success (their relationship was not to change until they met in Weimar in 1848). *Le Freischutz: A Report to Germany* (no. 30; cf. no. 23) is a satirical counterpart to no. 18. In the *Freischütz* essay for the *Revue et gazette musicale* Wagner tried to draw the attention of the Paris public to Weber's opera as a work of German Romanticism, but in this report for the *Dresdener Abendzeitung* he gives a satirical account of its adaptation for the Opéra, which he considered a failure (he cites the unfortunate translation of the libretto, the attempt to structure the plot more logically, the recitative which Berlioz composed subsequently, the ballet arrangement for the *Invitation to the Dance*). No. 31, *Report on a New Parisian Opera: Halévy's "La Reine de Chypre,"* is a counterpart to no. 20. The two essays cover largely the same ground. *A Paris Diary* (no. 32) should also be included among the Paris writings. It is an abandoned fragment of a planned diary, dated 23, 29, and 30 June 1840, which deals in particular with Wagner's poverty.

Writings from 1842 to 1848

In his years in Dresden up to 1848 Wagner's writing was limited to shorter occasional pieces of widely varying importance, such as the *Autobiographical Sketch* (no. 33) and the memoir (which was not in fact intended for publication) *Concerning the Royal Orchestra* (no. 42). Wagner was not stimulated into more extensive literary creativity again until the events of the Revolution of 1848. The survey that follows of the meager literary oeuvre of the Dresden period up to the revolution is presented chronologically.

Autobiographical Sketch (no. 33). After the overwhelming success of the premiere of *Rienzi* on 20 October 1842 in Dresden, Heinrich Laube gave Wagner the opportunity to reach a wider public in his *Zeitung für die elegante Welt*. This first autobiographical piece ends with Wagner's return from Paris to Germany: "I saw the Rhein for the first time, and with bright tears in my eyes I, a poor artist, vowed to be eternally faithful to my German fatherland." *Felix Mendelssohn-Bartholdy's "St. Paul" Oratorio* (no. 34), a review of the performance in Dresden of Mendelssohn's *St. Paul* Oratorio, conducted by the composer on Palm Sunday 1843, was possibly intended for a Dresden newspaper but never published. In an attempt to gain Mendelssohn's favor, as he had Meyerbeer's during his early years in Paris, Wagner praises the *St. Paul,* in contrast to his rejection elsewhere of the oratorio form, which he considered an anachronism (see no. 1), as a work "which is a testimony to the finest flowering of art and which fills us with justifiable pride at the age in which we live when we consider that it was created in our own times." Nos. 35 and 38 are *Two Letters to the Dresden Liedertafel*. The first is a call to the members of this choral society, which Wagner had just taken over as conductor, to participate in a music festival in the summer of 1843. Wagner's *Liebesmahl der Apostel* (WWV 69) was premiered in the course of this festival. In the second letter Wagner, who had given up conducting the Liedertafel owing to the pressures of work, recommends Ferdinand Hiller as his successor. Nos. 36 and 37 are two statements about the translation into German of the text for *Les deux grenadiers*. In Paris in 1840 Wagner had set Heine's *grenadiers* to music in a metrically free French version; he distanced himself in 1843 from a reprint published by Schott, in which the French text was subjected with Heine's original "to the most appalling stretches, contortions and perversions."

No. 39 is the *Oration on the Lying in Rest of Weber*. The transporting of Weber's mortal remains from London to Dresden and his burial in Dresden on 15 December 1844—against the declared wishes of the court—represented not only a posthumous honor to the former Dresden kapellmeister but also a political demonstration in which broad sections of the patriotically minded bourgeoisie took part. Wagner's funeral oration must be understood in this context. It celebrates Weber as a national composer, a composer "of the people." The critical tone which Wagner adopts elsewhere is missing. No. 40 is *On Beethoven's Ninth Symphony.* Wagner conducted this symphony on 5 April 1846 as part of the Palm Sunday concert in Dresden, a performance which represented a high point in the history of this work's reception in the nineteenth century. The three articles ("enthusiastic effusions"), which appeared anonymously in the *Dresdener Anzeiger,* were written to attune the Dresden public to the symphony, which Wagner calls a work of art "the like of which there has never been." In connection with this performance was the *Program to Beethoven's Ninth Symphony* (no. 41). Wagner expounds on the "higher human voices of the soul" which underlie the symphony's individual movements (see nos. 14, 19, and 20 with regard to this statement and comments on the function of symphonic music in other writings from the Paris period) with the help of passages from Goethe's *Faust. Concerning the Royal Orchestra* (no. 42) is a petition arising from the frequent clashes of interest between the Court Theater and the Royal Orchestra, in which Wagner makes detailed proposals (with estimates of cost) to the management responsible for both bodies on the reform and reorganization of the Royal Orchestra. Dated 1 March 1846, it was submitted on 2 March and turned down after a year's delay. *Artist and Critic, with Regard to a Specific Case* (no. 43) is Wagner's reply to a malicious review from the pen of the *Dresdener Tageblatt's* critic, Carl Banck, of a performance of *Figaro* he conducted on 6 August 1846. No. 44, *A Speech on Friedrich Schneider,* is a talk on the composer Schneider (1786–1853) given during a banquet for the Royal Orchestra on the occasion of the performance in Dresden of Schneider's oratorio *Das Weltgericht* (The Last Judgment) on 7 November 1846 (cf. no. 1, in which Wagner citicizes Schneider's "false stiffness" and "absurdity").

The Revolution Years, 1848–49

Wagner's literary activities resumed on a larger scale with the onset of the revolution in early 1848. The essays from the revolutionary years form two distinct groups. While in his early writings and in the writings from his years in Paris he had concerned himself mainly with questions of musical aesthetics, Wagner now turned to two new areas: politics and theater reform. The essays with a political content—revolutionary writings in the narrower sense—make it clear that Wagner was more than a revolutionary for art's sake. These pieces, which Wagner omitted almost without exception from the ten volumes of writings he edited himself (SSD I–X), show a further development in his political philosophy between the March disturbances in 1848 and the uprising in Dresden in May 1849, a development which can be seen as a radicalization and a growing tendency toward anarchism, probably under the influence of Bakunin. The writings on reforming the theater, which in certain respects prefigure Bayreuth—that is to say, an autonomous artistic organization free from all the usual (state) constraints—fit into the context of the revolution; their theme is to some extent the reform of the German theater in the spirit of the revolution. Both the genuine revolutionary writings and those on theater reform contain ideas that would recur in the writings on art from the Zurich period, which are a synthesis of the three thematic areas covered in the writings from 1834 to 1849: the aesthetics of musical drama, the overturning of established society, and the reform of cultural life.

Revolutionary Writings

Letter to Professor Franz Wigard, Member of the German National Assembly in Frankfurt (no. 45). The series of revolutionary writings opens, appropriately enough, with Wagner's letter of 19 May 1848 to the Saxon Paulskirche delegate Wigard, who belonged to the democratic left and was a member of the Rump Parliament after the dissolution of the Paulskirche. Wagner proposes to Wigard a thoroughly radical political program calling for: (1) the dissolving of the Bundestag of the German Federation ("The parliament therefore constitutes the only constructive authority" and has the right to appoint a provisional Reich government); (2) the arming of the people; (3) "an alliance of solidarity with France"; and (4) territorial reform "on the principle that states of less than 3 and more than 6 million should not be allowed." Wagner sees such territorial reform, which was designed to combat both particularism and the hegemony of one of the larger territories within Germany, as the central prerequisite for the realization of the new constitution: "How useless a constitution would be in the light of the present situation in Germany!" The rulers who would not accept this territorial reform, which cut deeply into their rights, should be "roundly placed in the dock; and the charge against them has a completely historical basis."

How Do Republican Aspirations Stand in Relation to the Monarchy? (no. 46). Wagner's famous address to the Dresden Vaterlandsverein on 15 June 1848, which had appeared anonymously the day before in the *Dresdener Anzeiger,* reveals in the first part exactly the same political attitude as in the letter to Wigard (no. 45). The viewpoint is a republican one: Wagner calls for the abolition of the two-chamber system in Saxony and for universal and equal suffrage—"the granting to every native adult of the unconditional right to vote"—a phrase which also presumably includes the right of women to vote. It is an antiaristocratic viewpoint, too, seeking the "end of the last glimmer of aristocratism" as an immediate political objective. This stance also has features of a Romantic, pre-Marxist anticapitalist stance, which in Wagner's case can be traced in large measure to his experiences in Paris (and to his reading of Proudhon). The ultimate aim of the revolution is the "complete emancipation of the human race" to achieve a society based on the "work of its members" rather than on the "workings of money" ("like a terrible nightmare, money, this demonic concept, will recede from us"), and which Wagner equates here with the "fulfilment purely of Christ's teaching" (see also the detailed draft which he produced later for *Jesus of Nazareth,* WWV 80).

Wagner nevertheless distances himself at the same time from communism in the sense of a mechanical and unthinking "mathematical distribution of wealth and income," presumably an allusion to the *Communist Manifesto,* which had appeared in February 1848.

The second part of the speech then takes an unusual turn: the emancipation of the human race must be followed by the "emancipation of the monarchy." For only the king—after, it should be said, the abolition of the aristocracy and therefore of all class differences—could become the head of the republic, as it is he who is "the first and most authentic republican" ("*Res publica* means 'public thing.' What individual could be more fitted than the ruler to be a part of this 'public thing,' with all his feelings, senses and endeavours"). The king is called upon at the end of the speech to declare Saxony a republic—a republic which would naturally be at the same time the hereditary Wettiner monarchy. This sentiment, which must be interpreted in the context of the idea of revolution from above, a familiar concept in the history of German political thought, also bears the distinct features of radical republicanism in the Rousseau mold: the king at the head of the republic represents the embodiment of a *volonté générale* as opposed to the *volonté de tous,* or of each of the many individual members of society.

To Intendant von Lüttichau on the Speech at the Assembly of the Vaterlandsverein (no. 47). Wagner's speech (no. 46) led to, among other things, the withdrawal of *Rienzi* from the repertory of the Court Theater. In his letter to Lüttichau on 18 June 1848 Wagner tries to justify himself to him by stressing the conciliatory nature of the speech, which, in spite of its republicanism, argued for the monarchy of the Wettiners. Wagner contends at the same time, however, that the progressive Republican party is the party "of the future" and that "by declaring that the republic [is] the best form of state" he had "committed no crime by contemporary standards." He also underlines once again his opposition to the aristocracy, "the continuing structure of the court with all its formality deriving from an earlier age," which he had been right to deem offensive.

The Wibelungs (no. 48). This historical-mythological treatment, which is directly connected with the draft for a drama, *Friedrich I,* and the first drafts for the *Ring,* can be counted among the revolutionary writings in only a very broad sense. In this essay, which may have been drafted in the late summer of 1848 (though certainly completed later; see WWV, pp. 328–329), and which contains a great deal of speculation, Wagner links the two subjects which he was then working on, and which had been ideologically charged in equal measure since the beginning of the nineteenth century. There was talk of India's being mankind's original home, a primordial kingdom in the mountains of Asia—to some extent mankind's Golden Age—and of the descent of the dynasties with claims on the world from the first Asiatic and Indian kings, through Troy and the "Trojan" Franks and Romans, to the Hohenstaufen rulers of the Middle Ages.

Wagner makes free use here of his knowledge of ancient and medieval mythology and literature (and their Romantic interpretations). There was a correspondence, in his view, between history and mythology: the Hohenstaufen ruler Frederick I (Barbarossa) and Siegfried, the hero of the Nibelungenlied, were the heirs and last representatives of the primordial kingdom—Barbarossa in history, Siegfried in mythology. Both the great German ruler of the Middle Ages and the great German hero are for Wagner "Nibelungs," so named after the hoard of the Nibelungs, symbol of the original dynasty and thus of the Golden Age, the "incarnation of all earthly power." "He who possesses it, who commands through it, is or becomes a 'Nibelung.'" Wagner thus reinterprets the name Ghibelline (or Waiblinger) for the Hohenstaufen imperial element as Wibelungen, a variation for alliterative purposes of Nibelungen (that is, *Wi*belungen as opposed to *We*lfen, or Guelphs). Barbarossa/ Siegfried's rule is endangered; just as the mythical hero falls to the dragon (Wagner is very free with his sources), so does Barbarossa's primevally inherited world dominion break up under pressure from the church's claims to power, German particularism as typified by the Guelphs, and the capitalism of the northern Italian city-states. The symbolic hoard is perverted, becoming real estate, or property. In place of the original kingdom, whose last representative in history was Barbarossa, comes the rule of the nobility and a class society in the widest sense. Yet the hoard lives on at the same time in the utopian idea of the Grail (which Wagner later identifies with the hoard of the Nibelungs).

This correspondence between history and mythology is structured in three dialectical stages. In 1848 Wagner had looked into Hegel's philosophy of history: a long process of historical decline follows the primitive age, the Golden Age of the hoard, an age based on property and rule by the aristocracy; the hope of a return to the Golden Age lives on, however, in the idea of the Grail. The contemporary relevance to the 1848 revolution is made clear: in the language of this essay on history and myth it signifies the return of Siegfried and Barbarossa, asleep in the Kyffhäuser. This piece therefore also bears witness to the political ideas which characterize Wagner's revolutionary writings proper—his opposition to the aristocracy and his (pre-Marxist) anticapitalism. The original conclusion to his treatise, with its exhortation for a return of Barbarossa/Siegfried ("When are you returning, Friedrich, magnificent Siegfried! to smite mankind's evil, gnawing worm?") is missing in the SSD version. As a sign, perhaps, of Wagner's resignation in his later years, this ends with the picture of an emperor still asleep in the Kyffhäuser ("There he now sits in the Kyffhäuser, Friedrich, old Redbeard; around him the Nibelungs' treasures, beside him the sharp sword which once struck down the furious dragon"). It is also noteworthy that in *The Wibelungs* Wagner does not yet interpret the hoard and the Nibelungs in terms of the *Ring* story.

Germany and Its Rulers (no. 49). In the first of the three essays which he published anonymously in Röckel's *Volksblätter,* Wagner again took up an anticapitalist (in the pre-Marxist sense) and antiaristocratic position, in a work which was more radical—and not only in tone—than the speech to the Vaterlandsverein ("Six months have gone by and what has happened?"). He inveighs against a society in which those who produce an abundance through their work have no interest in this very abundance. Indeed, they suffer deprivation because their work "does not receive its reward intact." This is true not only of farm workers and factory workers ("Look at the pale, grieving faces, the dull, lusterless eyes, the emaciated, naked, freezing bodies") but also of broad sections of the bourgeoisie. He also calls for the abolition of the nobility. Some of his maxims are: "A person can only have one income and that is his own"; the nobility's "privilege is an injustice . . . if justice is to be valid there must be no privilege"; "one person's idleness is the theft of another's work." Unlike in the speech to the Vaterlandsverein, his attacks are now also directed against the king, who still relies on his divine right and the accompanying princely rights and the duties of the people, "whereas there is only this: the rights of the people and princely duties."

Man and Existing Society (no. 50). The second essay for the *Volksblätter* similarly bears witness to the radicalization of Wagner's political opinions. Here, in fiery language Wagner describes the course of the revolution up to this point simply as the prelude and first stage of a far greater upheaval to come. He calls for the "struggle of men against the status quo," the most sacred and most sublime "which has ever been fought." He now puts forward a principle of utilitarianism, which states that everyone has the right to happiness: it is the purpose and the right of man "to achieve ever greater and purer happiness through the ever greater perfection of his spiritual, moral and physical capacities." Man can achieve this purpose and this right only by uniting with others in society; for it is the role of society to promote man's happiness. The status quo works against this purpose and this right; hence man has the right to overturn it.

The Revolution (no. 51). The third essay for the *Volksblätter,* which concluded the series of genuine revolutionary writings a few weeks before the May uprising in Dresden, is a melodramatic prose hymn to the "sublime goddess Revolution." Anarchistic views are represented here more sharply than in the previous essays, views which would be characteristic of Wagner's political thought from now on, through all the changes it would be subject to. The work of the revolution is above all that of destruction; it is the "productive destruction of things as they are," as Bakunin saw it. Only when the old world lay in ruins could the new world rise up, a world in which men not only lived together as brothers but above all were free—"free in their desires, free in their actions, free in their pleasures."

Writings on Theater Reform

Plan for the Organization of a German National Theater for the Kingdom of Saxony (no. 52). The second petition that Wagner submitted on 15 May 1848 to Minister of the Interior Martin Oberländer on questions of the reform of cultural life (cf. no. 42) attempts to put revolutionary ideas to work in the theater. Wagner proposes the reorganization of the Dresden Court Theater on democratic lines: the Royal Court Theater would be declared the National Theater, and the system of intendants answerable only to the king would be abolished. The theater's artistic (and technical) personnel would organize themselves into a collective, to be joined by a second collective formed by a regionally organized association of all "the Fatherland's" dramatists and composers. From the principle of collective self-management by the proposed National Theater, Wagner then adduces the nature of theatrical art, which he describes here for the first time—the idea of the *Gesamtkunstwerk*—as a synthesis of all the arts ("Its essence is socialization"), and the organizational structure of the theater must correspond to it. There are further proposals: the application of this organizational model to Saxony's other theaters; the founding of a theater school; the reorganization of the Royal Orchestra, which would become the National German Institute for Music in Dresden (and would be rid of royal intendants), consisting of the orchestra and the choral institute. He proposes in addition the introduction of self-management, with the musical director to be chosen by the orchestra and the regional organization of a "composers' association for the Fatherland," as well as the establishment of a choir school and an orchestra school (the institutes thereby generating their own new talent, as with the National Theater). Wagner calls for adequate pension arrangements for artists and, among other things, the abolition of music during plays to entertain the audience at intermission and during set changes, which he sees as a "demeaning duty for art." The petition was referred to the management by the minister.

On Eduard Devrient's "History of German Acting" (no. 53). Wagner uses an announcement intended for the Augsburg *Allgemeine Zeitung* for the third volume of Eduard Devrient's *Geschichte der deutschen Schauspielkunst* (1848) as an opportunity to develop further the principles underlying his petition of 1848 (no. 52). The most important demand is that the "free state" must guarantee the independence of the theater through subsidies. The announcement, which was not printed, dates from 8 January 1849.

Theater Reform (no. 54). In this essay Wagner intervenes in the discussions of Devrient's 1849 paper calling for reform, *Das National-Theater des neuen Deutschlands* (A National Theater for the New Germany). In this treatise Devrient put forward similar reforming ideas to those contained in Wagner's 1848 petition (no. 52), including the transformation of the Court Theater into a National Theater, its nationalization, and the founding of a theater school. Wagner defends Devrient against the Berlin critic "Scenophilus."

More on Theater Reform (no. 55) is a new statement in the public debate on Devrient's plans for reform (cf. no. 54). Wagner reinforces his position (cf. nos. 52, 53, 54). He calls for a law on the theater "which organizes freedom for the good of all, gives every part of the complex art system its rights and makes them all subordinate to one purpose, which they have to work towards through joyfully active cooperation, namely the purpose of the finest of all the arts: dramatic art." The call for self-administration of the theater by its artistic collectives is backed up historically by references to Shakespeare and Molière.

The only occasional piece from the years 1848–49 is *Toast on the Day Commemorating 300 Years of the Royal Orchestra in Dresden* (no. 56). The orchestra is described as the "worthy bearer of the spirit of German music, which has flourished and been enhanced in the present time by Beethoven's mighty aura." To this can be added two short articles (nos. 57 and 58), statements to the *Dresdener Anzeiger*. In the speech to the Vaterlandsverein on 15 June 1848 (cf. no. 46) Wagner had called for the general arming of the people rather than a standing army, and had referred to the shortcomings of the people's municipal guard, characterizing it as the "lying communal guard." Here he apologizes publicly for this derisive phrase and stresses the "great merit of such a traditional institution . . . which I myself have willingly supported."

Writings from the Years 1849 to 1864

This survey of Wagner's writings between 1849 and 1864—from his flight from Saxony after the unsuccessful May uprising in Dresden until he was called to Munich by King Ludwig II—starts with the major aesthetic works of the Zurich years, a period in which his literary activity undoubtedly reached its peak. In the three Zurich writings on art, Wagner brings together the theoretical initiatives and the areas of interest in his essays from the years between 1834 and 1849—the aesthetics of music drama, the reform of the theater, and political revolution—to form a comprehensive aesthetic theory in the tradition of German idealism and the Hegelian left (see Franke 1983). Particular mention should be made of Schiller's aesthetics *(On the Aesthetic Education of Man, in a Series of Letters)*, Hegel's philosophical history *(Lectures on the History of Philosophy)*, and above all Ludwig Feuerbach's critique of religion, and his concepts of anthropological materialism and utopian communism of love from *The Essence of Christianity: Principles for a Philosophy of the Future* (it was to this 1843 treatise by Feuerbach that Wagner was alluding in the title of his *Art-Work of the Future*).

The writings on aesthetics from Wagner's Zurich period required a thorough knowledge of Feuerbach's philosophy (this is particularly true of terms which appear constantly in Wagner's work: *nature, sensuousness, love, egoism/ communism*). Influences can also be seen of Ludwig Börne and Bruno Bauer, David Friedrich Strauss *(Life of Jesus)*, and Wilhelm Weitling *(The Gospel of the Poor Sinner)*, as well as the anarchism of Max Stirner *(The Individual and His Property)*, Pierre-Joseph Proudhon *(What Is Property?)*, and Mikhail Bakunin. It should be said, however, that Wagner probably knew some of these works only by hearsay. The three Zurich writings on art, moreover, form a coherent whole: *Art and Revolution* (no. 59) formulates the historico-philosophical principles of Wagnerian aesthetics; *The Art-Work of the Future* (no.

62) unfolds within this framework a general aesthetic theory which centers on what Wagner referred to only in passing as the Gesamtkunstwerk; and *Opera and Drama* (no. 63) finally gives concrete form to the aesthetics of the Gesamtkunstwerk as the aesthetics of music drama. The last, and most comprehensive, of these three works is dominated by discussions of literary and musical theory. Overall, the three Zurich essays on art probably represent the most important contribution to aesthetic questions of the Hegelian left.

The remaining writings between 1849 and 1864 are arranged by category: first, the short articles on aesthetics, which repeat for the most part the main ideas in the three larger essays, elaborating on and supplementing them and in some cases even moving in the direction of the late theoretical work; then the writings on theater reform and works which are autobiographical in character or deal with Wagner's own musical-dramatic work and its performance; and finally, the shorter occasional pieces and articles on various subjects.

Major Writings on Aesthetics from the Zurich Period

Art and Revolution (no. 59). The first of the Zurich treatises on art was written in a few days at the end of July 1849. It was initially intended for publication in the French periodical *National,* but was turned down for reasons of content and then published in Leipzig by Otto Wigand, "who correctly perceived that the author's notoriety might prove a commercial asset" (Gregor-Dellin 1983, p. 190). In the historical and defining philosophical framework of Wagnerian aesthetics during this period, the essay builds on the contrast between ancient Hellenism and modern civilization. Standing at this point in the full tradition of German idealism, Wagner sees the social and political ideal embodied in ancient Hellenism, particularly in the Athenian polis of the classical age. The individual and society, private and public interests, are here in constant harmony, whereas in modern, bourgeois civilization they are brought into direct opposition. The aim of the "great revolution of mankind," which Wagner expected (and hoped for) after the 1848–49 revolution failed, was to overcome this opposition.

This overcoming of the status quo did not, of course, mean a return to circumstances as they were in Greece, the ideal nature of the Athenian polis in Wagner's view being in the final analysis ideal only in appearance and already carrying within it the seeds of destruction ("We do not want to become Greeks, for we know what the Greeks did not know and why they were to perish"). The economic foundation of Greek society and culture was slavery. It was slavery—and here Wagner, committed to the Hegelian left, distances himself clearly from the mythological Greece beloved by German idealists— that led inevitably to the downfall of the Greek world. It was slavery, too, the "angel of doom of all earthly fate," which determined social and cultural progress from the collapse of the Athenian polis to the bourgeois civilization of the present.

In bourgeois society slavery simply manifests itself in a different form, namely in the legal position concerning property and the dominance of money (Wagner again adopts a pre-Marxist, anticapitalist standpoint). Modern civilization differs from the Athenian polis notably in that the polis included freemen and slaves, whereas under the banner of bourgeois emancipation not all men have become free by any means. In fact, everyone becomes a slave: all are slaves to capital, "taught today by bankers and factory owners to seek the purpose of existence in working for their daily bread." While Greek society and culture was, therefore, only an illusory ideal in which modern factors were already latent, the society of the future, which results from the great revolution of mankind, will be based on a genuine ideal. All the social conflicts of the bourgeois age will be removed, and in a radical overturning of the system of ownership (and the humiliating working conditions that go with it), mankind will be liberated from common slavery under its own terms. In this framework Wagner compares the "public art of the Greeks" with the "public art of modern Europe" and comes to the conclusion, consistent in his terms, that art is "quite simply not present . . . in modern public life": "With the Greeks it was present in the public consciousness, whereas today it is present only in the conciousness of individuals, as opposed to the unconsciousness of the public as a whole. When it was flourishing, Greek art was therefore conservative, because it existed in the public consciousness as a valid and relevant form of expression: for us, true art is revolutionary because it exists only in opposition to the public as it stands."

This is obvious to Wagner in the contrast between ancient and modern theater. According to Wagner, Attic tragedy is to the modern forms of drama—plays and opera—what the Athenian polis, as an (ostensibly) ideal political system, is to particularistic bourgeois society. In tragedy the spectator "found himself again," "indeed the noblest part of his being, combined with the noblest parts of the complete being of the whole nation." The Athenian people "streamed away from the state assemblies, from the forum, the country, ships, from military camps, from the most distant regions, thirty-thousand together filling the amphitheater in order to see the most profound of all tragedies, that of Prometheus, to gather together before the most powerful works of art, to understand themselves, grasp their own actions, to come together with their essence, their comradeship, their god, in the most intimate unity and to be together again in the finest, deepest tranquility, when a few hours before there had been restless excitement and distinct individuality." This public aspect does not apply to modern theater, both plays and operas, or it operates in a completely different form; for if it is the "expression of public life in the present time," so is it the "unnatural order of human things and circumstances" which characterizes these times. The loss of the public element, the privatization of art in bourgeois society, means at the same time its commercialization.

The basis of Wagner's criticism of bourgeois art is thus seen to be its status as a commodity in the bourgeois system of ownership and production, in the "emancipated slavery" of modern civilization: "Whereas the Greek artist was rewarded, apart from by his own pleasure in the work of art, by success and public approval, the modern artist is retained and—paid. So now we are starting to identify the essential difference clearly and distinctly, namely that public Greek art really was art, whereas ours is artistic trade." This last phrase should not be misunderstood. What Wagner means by "craft" (*Handwerk*) is industrial labor, with its concomitant alienation of the artist (who is no longer an artist under these conditions) from his product: "To the craftsman, what counts is only the end result of his efforts, the profit that his work brings him; the work that he does does not bring him pleasure, to him it is only hardship, unavoidable necessity which he would rather burden a machine with; his work is able to shackle him by force of circumstances." But "if he gives away the product of his work he has nothing left of it but its abstract monetary value—accordingly it is not possible that his work ever transcends the character of the activity of a machine."

The contrast between the public nature of Greek art and its privatization (also in economic terms) is reflected—and here Wagner is beginning to touch on the heart of his aesthetic theory—in the structure of dramatic art in the two periods. Greek tragedy, as the expression precisely of its public nature, was a Gesamtkunstwerk. But as art ceased "to be the expression of the public consciousness," so did "the common spirit fragment into a thousand egoistic directions and the great synthesis of the arts, tragedy, also broke up into the individual constituents of art contained within it." "Rhetoric, sculpture, painting, music, etc. left the round dance in which they had moved as one, in order now to go their own way, to develop independently, but alone and egoistically." The juxtaposition of opera, plays, ballet, and so on in the art of bourgeois society is the result of this fragmentation. Accordingly, Wagner expects from the great revolution of mankind not only the overturning of the contemporary social order, the restoration of the public nature of art, and an end to its character as a commodity, but also at the same time the rebirth of the "total work of art"—an aesthetic utopia which is the clear counterpart of the sociopolitical utopia. That is, the reuniting of the arts in the artwork of the future is the aesthetic expression of brotherly humanity united in love.

Particular attention should also be paid to the essay's religious and historical perspective, with its critique of Christianity. The Athenian polis and Greek tragedy operate under the banner of Apollo. This god was the idealized image of man from Greek antiquity, this "beautiful and strong, free people." Yet the cult of Apollo, which was alive in tragic art, was replaced by the Christian religion, which in its essence is the religion of slavery. (The central doctrine of Christianity, according to Wagner, is "patiently to sacrifice this miserable world for a better world in the next.") In the Christian religion not only is the loss of the public character of art visible; but for Wagner it is also one of the decisive ideological driving forces in the development of bourgeois society: "Whereas a Greek would meet for his moral edification in the amphitheater for a few hours of the most profound value, a Christian shuts himself in a monastery all his life; there the people's assembly passed judgement, here we have the inquisition; there the state adhered to an honest democracy, here to a hypocritical absolutism." The Christian Middle Ages gave way imperceptibly to bourgeois society, which stands under the banner of the god Mercury. "And so it is that we see with horror the spirit of Christianity embodied in all candour in a modern cotton factory; for the benefit of the rich, God has become industry, keeping the poor Christian worker alive only for such time until the heavenly commercial constellations bring about the merciful necessity of releasing him into a better world." Christianity is in this sense for Wagner distinct from the figure of Jesus of Nazareth, who (and this was also a central point in the draft for the drama *Jesus of Nazareth*) took up the basic contradiction of ancient society and showed through his life and endeavors "that we are all equal and brothers." In the society of the future, after the great revolution of mankind—and in contrast to the Athenian polis, in which the mass of slaves stood in opposition to the "beautiful and strong, free people"—all will thus be united in brotherly love, strong, beautiful, and free. This society, and with it the artwork of the future, will stand under the banner not only of the defeat of Mercury and the return of Apollo, but also of the brotherly union of Apollo and Jesus of Nazareth.

The first of the three major writings on aesthetics is supplemented by On *"Art and Revolution"* (no. 60). In SSD this heading covers: (1) two supplementary sections; (2) the epigraph on the title page of the book edition of 1849 ("Where once art was silent there began the wisdom of the state and philosophy; where now the wisdom of the state and philosophy is at an end, art begins again"); and (3) a paragraph deleted from the first ten volumes of SSD edited by Wagner, which contrasts the "feverish paroxysms" of Christian art with the deeply rooted "human art of the future . . . in the eternally fresh and vivid green of nature's earth." The first of the two supplementary sections contains a first overall plan of the Zurich writings, the three parts of which are *Art and Revolution* (no. 59), *The Artists of the Future* (no. 61, not completed), and *The Art-Work of the Future* (no. 62). To this Wagner added a number of quickly annotated thoughts on each of these three works. One of these thoughts ("Unartistic lovelessness against animals in which we see only goods for industry") is interesting in this context and prefigures a central idea in the later writings (see no. 125). The second supplementary section contains an evocation to German princes (cf. nos. 46 and 49) to help to free art "from the service of industry."

In the context of nos. 59 and 60 comes *The Artists of the Future* (no. 61). This heading in SSD combines sketches and ideas for a planned essay of that title which was to be the second of the Zurich writings on art, but which was never finished. This section also includes what is described in SSD as "Aphorisms on the Writings on Art from 1849–1851." The thoughts formulated in the first part of the section have almost all found their way into *The Art-Work of the Future* (no. 62). The fragments collected under the sub-heading "On the Principle of Communism" again make clear Wagner's radical political position, as shown in the Zurich writings on art: "real, simple historic life," he says, will begin only "with the downfall of the present system and with the start of the new communist world order."

The Art-Work of the Future (no. 62). The second of the writings on art from the Zurich period was finished as early as November 1849, and it, too, was published by Otto Wigand in Leipzig. It elaborates extensively on the aesthetic utopia of the Gesamtkunstwerk which Wagner sketched briefly in *Art and Revolution*. My description is limited to the main points.

The first of the five chapters, "Man and Art in General," again defines the framework within which Wagner develops his aesthetic theory. The three dialectical stages of historical development as defined in *Art and Revolution* (ancient Hellenism, modern civilization, and the society of the future) move toward Feuerbach's anthropological materialism. That is, a natural system is followed by a social system, a cultural system in which natural man is alienated; science and life, rationalism and sensuousness stand in direct opposition; and man, rather than participating in nature, has only his isolated existence and the abstract state. Natural needs have been replaced by luxury ("need where there is no need"), "which can only be produced and maintained by instead depriving the other side of necessities." At the same time, the soul of modern industrial society (Wagner's abstract thought process is here thoroughly political) "is killing man in order to use him as a machine." To overcome this social and cultural system is the purpose of the great revolution of mankind. This new and all-embracing revolution signifies specifically an end to man's "self-differentiation from nature" and the "break-up of science," in the sense of an "acceptance of life per se, immediate and self-determining—life as it actually is," and the "liberation of thought into sensuousness." It also means the nullification of the state, which "from a natural association of equally deserving cases" has become "an unnatural compression of undeserving cases, from a benevolent agreement to protect all, a malevolent means of protecting the privileged," and with it the removal of all isolationism and particularism, the "opening out of egoism into communism." The subject of this great revolution of mankind will accordingly be the people, as "the embodiment of all those who," forced by the luxury, which is the mark of the social system, "experience a common need."

Wagner also draws a parallel here between general social development and the development of art: the social and cultural system has no real awareness of art; fashion and affectation are more appropriate to luxury in society, having "no relationship of need with life"; the artist has been perverted into a human machine; and the dividing-up of the arts corresponds to social particularism and egoism. The overcoming of the social and cultural system through the great revolution of mankind also means as a consequence the overcoming of the opposition between art and life, and with it the realization of the artwork of the future, which in this formulation (which varies slightly from that in *Art and Revolution*) is a Gesamtkunstwerk in a double sense. On the one hand, it is "the great synthesis of the arts, which is to embrace all the branches of the arts in order to some extent to use and to destroy each of these branches as a means of achieving the common objective of them all, namely the unconditional, direct representation of perfect human nature." On the other hand, it is not "the arbitrary possible act of the individual" but "the necessarily conceivable common work of the people of the future." The artwork of the future—or, as Wagner now says, the "great universal art-work of the future"—thus means (and this is what makes it representative of an aesthetic utopia) the return to the "totality of nature" which the "spirit, unsatisfied in the modern present" in its particular existence longs for, but on a higher plane. The three-stage dialectic in which the history of man unfolds is therefore the consequence of nature, culture, and art.

Chapter 2, "The Artistic Person and the Art Derived Directly from Him," deals with the three "purely human kinds of art," namely the arts of dance, music, and poetry, which form an indivisible unit "in the original, primary art-works of lyric poetry, and in its later conscious, highest perfection, drama" (meaning Greek tragedy). Of the triumvirate, dance is the "most real of all the art types" because its artistic material is "the actual physical person and not just a part, but the whole." Its principle is rhythm. In it are set out the requirements of both music and poetry, since "a person who sings and speaks" must also "of necessity be a physical person." In drama, in which "man is both the material and the object of art in all his dignity," and in which the three arts "permeate, generate, and complement each other," the "principle of rhythm created" from art is (in that it coordinates movement) "the measure which governs the understanding of everything represented in it (i.e. in drama)"; in drama, furthermore, dance appears in refined form as mimic art. With the decline of Greek tragedy—Wagner compares it with the confusion of the tongues of Babel—there began the downfall not only of dance but also of the arts of music and poetry, which derive from it.

Wagner does not go into this decline in great depth. Instead he attempts to understand history, and in particular the history of music, as a movement which yearns for the original harmony of all the arts. Dance, music, and poetry are bound by the common principle of rhythm; music and poetry have melody in common; music's third property, harmony, is peculiar to it alone. In Wagner's opinion music had reached its most extreme alienation from the material substratum of sensory man in the age of counterpoint, the development of which he blames ultimately on Christianity's enmity to life and to the senses. Counterpoint is music which is detached from sensory man; it is "art playing with itself, the mathematics of feeling, the mechanical rhythm of egoistical harmony." By contrast the opera aria shows the binding of music, if not to the whole then at least to the "singing" person, while the classical symphony binds music again to the three-dimensional movement of the body; the symphony is "harmonized dance." Its development strives consistently for the Wagnerian idea of the music drama: Haydn's symphonies are characterized by the "rhythmic dance melody"; Mozart "breathed into his instruments the yearning breath of the human voice"; and finally Beethoven (whose Seventh Symphony is, according to Wagner's oft-quoted dictum, the "apotheosis of dance itself," "dance in accordance with its highest essence, the happiest act, as it were, of physical movement embodied in notes") returned music to the poetic word in his Ninth Symphony.

This last symphony by Beethoven is thus the "human gospel of the art of the future." Poetry has distanced itself from the original Gesamtkunstwerk, and tragedy most of all in contemporary closet drama ("outrageous: drama written for dumb reading!"). Yet the history of the play also repeatedly shows signs of overcoming its egoistical thinning out, for example in acting companies in Shakespeare's day. Of the attempts up until that time to reunite the three purely human types of art, Wagner rejects the oratorio as well as opera. The oratorio, he says, would certainly like "to be drama, but only as far as the music allows." And opera is no more than a common contract (Wagner borrows this term, not without irony, from the sphere of bourgeois society) "of the egoism of the three arts." Even Gluck and Mozart (Wagner here keeps essentially to his earlier view) "revealed only the capacity and the necessary will of music" to reunite with dance and poetry, "without being understood by its sister arts."

The third chapter, "Man as Artistic Creator from Natural Materials," compares the three purely human arts with the three visual arts of architecture, sculpture, and painting, in which "the artistic person yearning for artistic self-representation subordinates himself to nature in accordance with his artistic needs, so that it serves him in accordance with his highest purpose." Architecture in its essence provides a "condensed imitation of nature" (the Greek temple with its ambulatory is a "condensed representation of the grove of the gods"), sculpture the "condensed imitation of the human figure." Painting, as the last-born of the three "bildende Künste," already has its source in "the ardent need . . . to bring to mind once again the human, living art-work that has been lost." Its achievement lies in the "inner comprehension and presentation of nature." Wagner also describes the history of these three visual arts as the distancing process of art from life. Ancient architecture had a public function; it culminated in the building of the temple and the theater. Their decline started with their privatization in later antiquity. Wagner gives as an example the "disgusting appearance of the now monstrous pomp of the emperors' palace with the rich on one side, and the mere . . . utilitarianism of the public buildings." Greek sculpture thrived on the sensuous "beauty of the human body," which was the "foundation of all Hellenic art." (In this connection Wagner interprets the male Spartan state and its homoerotic basis as a "purely human, communal art-work," to some extent the natural state in which art and life were still undivided, and thus a counterpart to Attic tragedy.) Contemporary visual art lacks this connection with sensory man and therefore with life. It can relate only to the "mummy of Hellenism": "This newer art should learn to recognize man from this fine stone, not from the real life of the old world." Painting was from its very beginnings a product of the growing alienation of art from life. But at the same time, nineteenth-century landscape painting (recall Wagner's preference for stage sets in a historical style reminiscent of late Romantic landscape painting) is the augury of a new victory "of nature over a bad culture which demeans people."

Chapter 4, "Principles of the Art-Work of the Future," and Chapter 5, "The Artist of the Future," bring out the two aspects of the aesthetic utopia associated with the idea of the Gesamtkunstwerk: the artwork of the future as musical drama, in which the lost unity of the arts is restored, and the artist of the future as the free fellowship of all artists. The "people" are therefore seen as the embodiment of liberated humanity, just as art and life will no longer be able to be divided after the great revolution of mankind. Wagner believes that the artwork of the future will unite as musical drama not only the three purely human arts but also the three visual arts. Architecture will regain its public character in the building of theaters, and in the process will once again become both beautiful and useful. Painting, whose works had previously been seen only "on the secluded wall of an egoist's room" or "stacked on top of each other, unrelated, unconnected and disjointed in a picture store" (a museum), will "fill the broad framework of the tragic stage, making the whole area covered by the set testify to [the artist's] natural creative power." For sculpture, too, the artwork of the future means deliverance, the "freeing of stone from its thrall into human flesh and blood, from immobility into mobility, from the monumental [by which he means timeless and therefore alienated from life and nature] into the immediate"; that is, sculpture will be "liberated" into the performer, the "mimic dancer" who can both sing and speak. The development that distinguishes the artwork of the future from Greek tragedy is the symphonic orchestra, the "tonal language of Beethoven," the function of which is to raise the individuality of the portrayal into something superindividual, universal, "Allgemeinsame" (see his earlier comments on this subject in nos. 14, 19, and 20): "The orchestra is, as it were, the soil of infinite, universal feeling, out of which the individual feelings of each performer can grow to their greatest fullness." The loosely appended final sections give concrete form once again to a decisive element in the great revolution of mankind, namely the abolition of the bourgeois system of ownership and of the state, which serves perversely to preserve just this system of ownership. The treatise ends with a first sketch of the draft for a drama *Wieland der Schmied* (Wieland the smith), Wieland being the symbolic figure of the people, who, out of necessity, lead themselves to freedom.

Opera and Drama (no. 63). The third and most comprehensive of the Zurich writings on art was written in the winter of 1850–51 and was published by Johann Jakob Weber in Leipzig, after appearing in prepublication extracts in the *Deutsche Monatsschrift*. The immediate reason for its composition was the (anonymous) article *Die moderne Oper* in the encyclopedia published by Brock-haus, *Die Gegenwart: Eine enzyklopädische Darstellung der neuesten Zeitgeschichte für alle Stände* (The present: everyman's encyclopedic guide to recent contemporary history). For details of the history of its origin and publication of *Opera and Drama*, see Kropfinger 1984. The treatise, which can be conveyed here only in its broad outlines, is divided into three parts.

In part 1, "Opera and the Essence of Music," Wagner discusses the musical-dramatic form of opera and its history since the eighteenth century, returning to and elaborating on earlier statements on this subject. The introduction opens out into a terse verdict on opera. Wagner describes it as a mistake in music history, which could only lead to its destruction (*Vernichtung* is used here in the Hegelian sense, as it frequently is in the writings from the Zurich period): "The mistake in the opera genre was that a means of expression (the music) was made the purpose, while the purpose of the expression (the drama) was made the means." This is the heart of the matter, and in this context Wagner goes on in subsequent chapters to examine the opera form—that is, the relationship of music to drama, or, in other words, of musical composition to poetic composition. (*Drama*, or *poetry*, should not be misunderstood to mean "libretto.") It is not a question of "prima la musica, doppo le parole" or "prima le parole, doppo la musica."

Wagner's critical survey of the history of opera is ordered dialectically. The point of departure is a description of eighteenth-century opera before Gluck, when opera was a succession of arias, recitatives, and ballet numbers, with the main weight falling on the arias, which exist simply so that the singer can "display his artistic accomplishment": the "composer arranges the material for the singer, and the writer in turn for the composer, for [the singer's] virtuosity." The first factor to prompt a change in the history of opera, as Wagner describes it, was "Gluck's revolution," which consisted of a partial correction of this system. Here the composer "rebelled" against the "despotism of the singer." The expressive function of the music became the heart of opera: "Gluck tried consciously, in both declamatory recitatives and in sung arias, without departing in any way from these forms . . . , to reproduce feelings indicated in the text as truly as possible through musical expression." The singer thus became "an instrument of the composer's intention," a decisive step toward music drama in Wagner's sense, although the position of the writer in relation to the composer was untouched by this "revolution." Cherubini, Méhul, and Spontini carried on Gluck's work in this respect. The line from Gluck to Spontini is described by Wagner as the "intellectual"—that is, deliberately experimental—direction within the development of opera, and one that took place above all in French opera.

In the history of Italian opera, Wagner ascribes to Mozart alone a position equal to that of Gluck and his disciples; Mozart, however, is not an "intellectual" composer but—and this is the second step in the dialectic—the great "naive" who, like Gluck, leaving "the formal framework of opera actually completely untouched," found the "truth of dramatic expression" from the "simplicity of his purely musical instinct" alone. Both the intellectual and the naive directions taken by opera at the end of the eighteenth and the start of the nineteenth centuries represent, taken together, for all their shortcomings and the criticisms made against them, a serious development in the history of opera: namely, their movement toward music drama in the Wagnerian sense. With Rossini—the next dialectical step—this serious direction experiences a sudden change to frivolity. Rossini's work is dominated by "naked, ear-pleasing, totally melodic melody," cast off from the idea of drama and devoid of any expressive function.

The further history of the genre is thus marked out: "The history of opera since Rossini is basically nothing more than the history of operatic melody." Weber attempted the "restoration of the original tonal system of the folk song." Wagner again describes this approach as a blind alley in the history of opera. The influence of *Der Freischütz* was due in the last analysis solely to the fact that here drama was geared completely to traditional melody, whereas music must in reality be a function of the drama. Recent French opera—in dialectical opposition to Weber's "intimate" folk methods—began with opéra comique as "expanded vaudeville" but then progressed, in a further turning in the dialectic of its history, with Auber (and his librettist, Scribe) into great historical opera. This was no longer solely the work of the composer, who now strove for historical features of operatic melody which produced "curiosities," but also the work "of the set painter and theatrical costumier." At the end of the line of development stands Meyerbeer's grand opera. Its secret, which calls on all musical and theatrical means, is "effect," which Wagner describes as "effect without cause." With Meyerbeer the dramatic writer is deprived utterly of all function. Meyerbeer "created a situation whereby the most flattering thing you could say to him was that the texts of his operas were very poor and pitiful but look at what his music managed to make out of this miserable stuff! This was how he brought about the most complete triumph of the music: the composer had ruined the librettist utterly and the musician was crowned as the actual librettist on the debris of the opera librettist's art!" So it was that in the course of its history the mistake that the opera genre represents—in that "the means of expression [that is, the music] attempted to determine for itself the intention of the drama"—finally came into being. The musical drama envisioned by Wagner has no logical connection with opera. The historical point of reference for the drama of the future—set against the history of opera as a whole (and in complete accord with his earlier statements) in a further dialectical step—is Beethoven's symphonic work, particularly the Ninth Symphony.

Part 1 of *Opera and Drama* closes with an attempt to interpret the essence of music metaphorically. The most important elements of this wide-ranging metaphorical correlation can be quoted in summary as follows: "Music is a woman"; "the whole musical organism is by nature . . . a feminine one, it is the only one which gives birth but does not generate; generative power lies beyond it"; this generative power is the word of the poet. The "organism of music" is able "to give birth to true, living melody only if it is fertilized by the ideas of the poet, the music is the mother bearer, the poet the male begetter." The "secret of infertility" which the opera carries within it thus becomes apparent: opera reached the "height of madness" with Meyerbeer because here it "did not only want to give birth but also to beget." It was quite a different matter with the symphonies of Beethoven, who in his Ninth found himself "constrained to bring the life-giving seed to the . . . organism of music which was newly stimulated to life-bearing capacity, and removed from it the begetting capacity of the poet." Beethoven's work points to the essence of the music of the future: whereas Italian opera is a "floozy," French opera a "coquette," and German opera a "prude" ("We have seen the prude fall into all the vices of her Italian and French sisters, but sullied by the vice of hypocrisy and unfortunately devoid of all originality!"), the music of the future will be the "woman, who really loves."

Part 2, "The Play and the Essence of Dramatic Poetry," continues the dialectical sequence of ideas. After dealing with opera as a possible prefiguration of musical drama in part 1, Wagner now turns to the play as the most significant form of modern theater. While opera's mistake is that it tries to generate drama out of absolute melody, the play—another form of particularism in the arts in modern society—wants to be nothing other than a "branch of literature, a form of literary art like the novel or didactic poem, only with the difference that rather than merely being read it is intended to be learnt by heart by several people, declaimed, accompanied by gestures and lit by theater lighting." Wagner believes that the history of modern drama has dual origins: the novel on the one side and classicistic drama in a line from Aristotle on the other. In the dialectic of this analysis both stand in opposition as thesis and antithesis. The novel is for Wagner, who agrees with Hegel here, the real genre of the prosaic bourgeois age. Shakespeare's drama, which Wagner considers the start of the history of modern drama, is the adaptation of the novel for the stage. The structural relationship of the (Shakespearean) play to the novel manifests itself in two particular features: (1) in what Wagner describes as its multifariousness and enormous versatility (both terms refer to the Aristotelian polymyth), namely in its amorphous character (seen from the classical standpoint), the juxtaposition of several threads of plot, the constant scene changes, the large cast, and finally in what Volker Klotz has subsumed in the idea of the open-form drama; and (2) in the external resolution of the characters, that is, in their perseverance through historical and social circumstances. The novelist must, according to Wagner, "be circumstantial . . . in order to be understood"; he must make the plot "comprehensible from the external dictates of the circumstances," must establish it as the "social sediment" of "historical events." In both points—both in its versatility and in the external determination of the characters through history and social circumstances—the novel and its adaptation for the stage in the open-form drama correspond to the condition of bourgeois society; the amorphous nature of the novel and its adaptation is equivalent to particularism and the alienation of the individual, the external determination of the characters to the objectification of mankind in the bourgeois state. It is also within the internal logic of the bourgeois genre of the novel that it "increasingly stripped away its artistic guise . . . on its way to practical reality" and disintegrated "into the practical multiplicity of daily events." The novel "proceeded from the representation of reality, and the attempts were so genuine that it finally destroyed itself as an art form in the face of this reality." The history of the novel ends necessarily in practical politics.

The play is an adaptation of the novel for the stage and is thus ultimately—like opera—a historical error. Wagner sees the opposite pole to Shakespeare's "novelesque" play embodied in Racine's *haute tragedie,* the product of the highly confused assimilation of Aristotle, a simply external and therefore distorting "imitation and reproduction" of Greek tragedy, a closed-form drama—a historical dead end. "Between these two most extreme opposites, Shakespearean drama and Racinian drama," between the (English) open-form drama and classical (French) closed-form drama, "modern drama now developed . . . in its unnatural, hermaphroditic form" as it manifests itself, in Wagner's view, above all in classical (German) drama, and particularly Schiller's historical drama, which balances between Shakespeare and Racine and which Wagner (how could he do otherwise?) rejects: "The poet who tries to deal with historical subjects while circumventing chronological accuracy [and there is no other possible way of handling history in drama], and for this purpose makes use of the facts of history on the basis of arbitrary artistic and formal judgements, could create neither history nor even drama."

For Wagner the modern play, like opera, thus fails overall to provide the connecting link for the musical drama of the future as "real drama." And it is to this that Wagner turns after concluding the historical-critical outline, developing its structural characteristics—again completely according to the inner dialectic of his analysis—in terms of Greek tragedy and the antithesis of Greek tragedy to the bourgeois novel. Wagner contrasts the historical and social multifariousness and versatility of the novel with myth as the thematic kernel of the drama (which he now always means in the sense of his drama of the future), and not merely as the imitation and reproduction of ancient or archaic myths in the sense of Racinian high tragedy. Myth is for Wagner a "great story" "in a broad circle of relationships"—that is, not the "cropped" story, in the sense of the (pseudo-)Aristotelian unities. Instead it replaces "mirrored" reality (which the novel naturally strives for) with fiction, a conceived reality in which the great story in all its complexity appears to be brought together, compressed into a whole. The myth is thus an intensification and a heightening of reality; it does not suspend this reality but makes it accessible. There is also a second aspect: myth is a supraindividual expressive form of a new collectivity and as such presupposes the overthrowing of the prosaic and particular existence of mankind in bourgeois society. The external determination of the characters of the novel is superseded by the internal necessity of the plot. Whereas the novel "goes from out to in," drama goes "from in to out"; whereas in the novel the individuality of the character is determined by the "mechanism of the story" and therefore remains coincidental and particular, in the drama this individuality develops from the "organism of humanity" as the "essence of the form."

These statements might be summarized as follows: in its prosaic and externally determined plot, the novel "explains the bourgeois citizen to us" as one who is alienated from his essence in the bourgeois state and its system of ownership, while by contrast drama, in its mythic and internally determined plot, "gives us the person." The climax of these remarks is an analysis of the Oedipus myth, which Wagner uses not just as an example to explain his concept of myth but also, at the same time, to expound the historical requirements of drama: the destruction of the state and the bourgeois system of ownership. Wagner relates the tragedy of Oedipus to the conflict between the "free self-determination of the individual" and "arbitrariness" as the "essence of the political state," between the individual's "life and love urge" and his "negation" in the system of ownership. In Wagner's interpretation the Oedipus myth represents an intensified and heightened picture of the whole history of mankind from the beginnings of society to the necessary decline of the political state.

Opera and Drama is also a fundamentally political work. In the latter sections of part 2 Wagner develops still newer elements of the drama. The sequence of ideas develops in the three historical stages prefigured in *Art and Revolution* and in *The Art-Work of the Future:* the natural state (or Hellenism), the cultural state (or modern civilization), and the state of liberated mankind in the future. The natural state, or Hellenism, finds its adequate expression in the "Urpoesie" of lyric verse (and in Greek tragedy), modern civilization in the novel, and humanity united in brotherly love in the society of the future in the drama. Lyric poetry addresses itself to the emotions, the novel to the intellect (as the opposite pole to the emotions), and drama to the "emotionalization of the intellect": "In drama we must become aware through the emotions." Lyric poetry is borne along by the "original and creative bond" of the "language of gesture, music and words," from the *mousiké* in the Greek sense of the word; the novel, by contrast, from the language of words alone, the "organ . . . of the versifying intellect"; and the drama restores the original unity on a higher level: "The language of music is the beginning and end of the language of words, just as the emotions are the beginning and end of the intellect, myth the beginning and end of history, lyric poetry the beginning and end of creative writing." This sentence should not be misunderstood, for it is not intended cyclically (Wagner himself adds), signaling a "return" to the beginning, but is meant in the sense of a dialectical "progression towards the acquisition of maximum human capacity"—the drama as a return to lyric poetry on a higher level.

Wagner also develops his theory of alliteration here. Alliteration expresses the "sensuously versifying power of language"; it puts "related linguistic roots together in such a way that, just as they sound similar to the hearing organs, they also link together similar objects into an overall image, in which the emotions seek to reach a conclusion about them." Alliteration is an inherent part of the Urpoesie of lyric verse and carries within it a combination of the rhythmic bond, as it were, and the arts of dance, music, and poetry. "The extension of a section of melody" is determined by the "period of exhalation of one breath," this period being limited by the "number of particular stresses." These stresses coincide "with the gesture" and are then intensified "linguistically in the alliterative root words." End rhyme, by contrast, belongs to an age in which the "original unity" of the arts has already fallen away; it no longer has the function of marking out rhythm, but merely flutters "loosely on the end of ribbons of melody while the verse becomes increasingly arbitrary and intractable." The opposite extreme of alliterative verse is obviously the prose of the novel. The newly acquired unity of music, poetry, and theater in the drama of the future involves a revival of alliterative verse. The conclusion of part 2 goes back to the imagery of the last chapter of part 1: the "poetic purpose" is the "productive seed," which "induces the splendidly loving woman Music to bring forth matter."

Part 3, "Poetry and Music in the Drama of the Future," concludes the discussion in terms of the dialectical progression of ideas, describing the drama of the future as a synthesis of poetry and music. Wagner here takes up the objectives of the drama of the future as set out in the first two parts (and in the two earlier writings) and develops them in greater detail. Central to this part are observations on the connection between alliteration and (vocal) verse melody, on the poetic-musical period as the smallest formal unit of musical drama, "in which many such periods are presented with such richness that, in fulfillment of the highest poetic purpose, they are determined one by the other and develop into a powerful whole"; on the role of the orchestra, which has the ability, unavailable to vocal verse melody, "to express the inexpressible," and which in the drama of the future has the function of the chorus in tragedy; and on the technique of the interconnecting leitmotifs. "The life-giving center of dramatic expression is the performer's verse melody, to which the preparatory, absolute orchestral melody has an allusive relationship. The idea of the instrumental motif is gleaned through recollection of the orchestral melody." The orchestra makes a "continual contribution" to this network of motifs, "taking it in every direction and providing clarification: it is the moving maternal lap of music, from which the unifying bond of expression develops." In this sense its role corresponds to that of the chorus in the tragedy of antiquity. The leitmotifs become "through the orchestra emotional signposts, as it were, in the whole sinewy structure of the drama. Through them we become constant confidants to the most intimate secret of the poetic purpose." They correspond in terms of expression to the drama's leading motifs in terms of their content. The complex network of leitmotifs ensures "unity of expression, constantly recalling and summarizing the content according to its context"; at the same time this "solves uniquely and finally the problem hitherto of the unity of place and time." In the constant interchange of the idea, the present (the verse melody), and memory it also has the function of bringing the audience into the drama and making them "indispensable contributors to the work of art." (For details of these observations, which constitute overall a detailed commentary on Wagner's compositional technique from *Rheingold* to *Parsifal,* see the analysis in Kropfinger 1984, pp. 486–495.) In the concluding sections of this investigation Wagner stresses once again that his concept of drama represents an aesthetic utopia ("but this future existence will be what it can be only if it absorbs this art-work"). But at the same time all art is utopian in character: "The producer of the art-work of the future is none other than the artist of the present who divines future life and who yearns to be included in it. He who nourishes this longing in himself in his most intimate capacity, who already lives for a better life—only one person can do this: the artist."

Sketch for "Opera and Drama" (no. 64) supplements *Opera and Drama* and documents its origin. In this letter to Theodor Uhlig (12 December 1850) Wagner, who was then starting to plan *Opera and Drama,* records a scheme for a synthesis of the arts (part 1: "Description of Opera until the Present Day," with music as the "organism giving birth"; part 2: "Description of the Nature of Shakespearean Drama until the Present Day," with "poetic sense" as the "generative organism"; part 3: "Description of the Way the Poetic Intention Gives Birth through Perfected Musical Language"). Attached thereto is a graphic representation of the arts as they combine in the Gesamtkunstwerk of musical drama and their correspondence to the unity of the emotions, intellect, and reason in man; this diagram was not included in the published edition of *Opera and Drama.* The simplified version in SSD (XVI, 95) is taken from Wagner's letter (SB III, 478). A facsimile of the original version in Wagner's manuscript of *Opera and Drama* can be found in Kropfinger 1984, p. 464.

Minor Writings on Aesthetics, 1849–1864

Art and Climate (no. 65). In this essay, written in February 1850, Wagner tackles the accusation that in *Art and Revolution* and *The Art-Work of the Future* he "failed to take into account the influence of the climate on a person's aptitude to art," coming to the conclusion that "with respect to our art" we "are affected not by climatic nature but by far-distant history." The real effective power of the present is "civilization, which is totally indifferent to climate," and which bears the responsibility for "our hypochondriac, cowardly and grovelling citizens," the "toadies, privy councillors and the holier-than-thou" just as much as for "scrofulous linen weavers made of skin and bone." In connection with Feuerbach's anthropological materialism and "Liebescommunismus" Wagner then formulates his picture of a human future in which the present "sanctimonious, legalistic civilization" will be overcome.

Judaism in Music (no. 66). Wagner's essay, which was controversial even in his lifetime, can be read in a dual context. It stands first of all in the context of discussions among the Young Germans and the Hegelian left over the emancipation of the Jews. He comments on Ludwig Börne in the final section of the pamphlet: "From his special position as a Jew he came among us seeking liberation. He did not find it and had to realize that he would only find it when we too are liberated into truthful people. But for a Jew, becoming such a person together with us is as much as to say: Stop being a Jew." This is thoroughly in keeping with Wagner's sociopolitical ideas during the Zurich years, the same ideas that also feature in the three major writings on art from that period. He is waiting for the great revolution of mankind, which will end man's alienation from his nature. The emancipation of the Jews can be achieved only against this background, as part of the emancipation of the person from the citizen, which Wagner called for in *Opera and Drama*. This was exactly what he meant in his appeal to the Jews: "Join boldly in this work of liberation, which will bear fruit through self-destruction, then we [that is, humanity liberated into brotherly love] will be united and undivided!" Self-destruction is meant here in the Hegelian sense, while "united and undivided" is a reference to the "communism" of society to come; the Hegelian term *Vernichtung* resonates, too, in the final dictum on the "deliverance" of the Jews as the deliverance of the Wandering Jew at the end of the world (see no. 79 on the symbolism of the figure of the Wandering Jew in Wagner's writings during the Zurich period). All these observations have their direct parallel in Marx's essay *On the Jewish Question* (Marx 1975), where he writes: "The social emancipation of the Jews is the emancipation of society from Judaism."

Wagner's essay can equally well be read differently, however. The document does not cite any examples and deals with the history of modern anti-Semitism in a heavily anti-Jewish manner: Jews are "repugnant in appearance" ("We desire instinctively to have nothing to do with people that look like that"); their language is "gibberish" ("a hissing, shrill and botched form of expression," an "unsuitable use and willful distortion of words and phrase constructions"); they are responsible for capitalism and thus for all the misery of bourgeois society (these emphases are not found in the major writings on art). "The Jew is really already more than emancipated in the current state of things; he is in control and will be so for as long as power remains money, before which all our actions are unavailing." Jews are unsuited to art ("The Jew has never had his own art, so never a life of artistic substance"); he can at best reproduce art ("imitating human words and speech like parrots"), so there is also no genuine Jewish music. No more need be said.

The final section of the essay deals with Mendelssohn, who is portrayed as the "tragic" example of Jewish eclecticism in the history of music—tragic because he was aware of his "impotence"—and with "that famous opera composer" whom Wagner apotropaically leaves unnamed. He was referring, of course, to Meyerbeer, who is mocked once again: "We honestly believe that he would like to create works of art and yet knows at the same time that he will never manage to; in order to extricate himself from this painful conflict between desire and ability he is writing operas for Paris, which he then has no trouble having performed in the rest of the world—nowadays the safest way of acquiring fame as an artist without being an artist." Other passages are devoted to Heine, whom Wagner acknowledges as the first Jewish poet— something which could have been possible only at a time when "poetry became a lie with us." No comment is necessary here either.

On Musical Criticism (no. 67) is a letter to the editor of the *Neue Zeitschrift für Musik.* In it Wagner reacts to the question from Franz Brendel, the editor of *Neue Zeitschrift,* as to what part a journal of this kind "should have in the process which our music today has necessarily to go through." Wagner comments thoroughly on public discussions of musical and aesthetic issues and argues against "the utter waywardness of public taste," a "senseless and heartless mass," and the "rashness and lack of honour in criticism." He calls for a completely new type of audience and of criticism, something which in fact presupposes revolution in the cultural system (and society). This again gives him the opportunity to resume the ideas on the aesthetic utopia of the Gesamtkunstwerk in the double sense (see *The Art-Work of the Future*), which he developed in his major writings on art.

On 15 February 1852 Wagner sent a concert program (intended for 17 February) to Theodor Uhlig which contained an explanatory note on Beethoven's *Coriolan* Overture (cf. no. 109). Enclosed with it was a long letter justifying the musical and aesthetic arguments of the program note. The passages on Beethoven in the letter to Uhlig were included in SSD under the title *On Performing Beethoven* (no. 68). For Wagner, Beethoven's symphonies are at heart "poetry" which "attempts to portray" a "real object." To convey this object to the performers and the audience is the real duty of the conductor of Beethoven, who should therefore never be just a musician ("Mendelssohn's rendition of Beethoven's works was only ever interested in its purely musical essence, never its poetic content, . . . In spite of his great technical subtlety, Mendelssohn's conducting always left me unsatisfied in its essence." As poetry (not, it should be noted, in the sense of mere program music) Beethoven's symphonic work does, however, point toward Wagner's musical drama: "The purpose of these efforts?? *Drama!!*"

Wilhelm Baumgartner's Lieder (no. 69). As part of a review of the collection *Frühlingslieder* (Spring songs) op. 12, dedicated to Wagner, by the Zurich music teacher and composer Wilhelm Baumgartner, Wagner addresses himself in detail to the question of song composition: the art song as a kind of small-scale musical drama in which the "tonal structure" receives only the "necessary individual form" if the composer brings the "sensory phenomenon" of this tonal structure "into closest contact with another sensory phenomenon—poetry itself." Wagner recommends the poems of Gottfried Keller for setting to music.

Gluck's Overture to "Iphigénie en Aulide" (no. 70) is a report to the editor of the *Neue Zeitschrift für Musik.* In February 1854, in the course of his orchestral concerts in Zurich, Wagner conducted the overture to Gluck's *Iphigénie en Aulide* and composed a new ending to the overture for this purpose, as he was able to demonstrate—after a thorough study of the Paris version of a score which Gluck himself prepared—that the previous ending of the concert version, which went back to Mozart (the overture leads straight on to act 1 of the opera in Gluck's original), was the result of a misunderstanding of the tempi Gluck had intended. Wagner passes this musical discovery on to the musical public, together with a short analysis of the overture (see also no. 15).

Dante—Schopenhauer (no. 71). In his letter from London dated 7 July 1855 to Franz Liszt, who had told him of the plan for his *Dante* symphony, Wagner—who was himself occupied by the *Divine Comedy*—criticizes the project from the perspective of Schopenhauer's philosophy (or his understanding of it). The essay points in many places to the philosophical writings of the Bayreuth years. This is true not only of the evocation of Schopenhauer (man as "will for life"; the aesthetic experience as the unwilled experience of the outside world; the "act of the negation of the will" as the "real act of the saint") but also of the criticism of historical Christianity. (Christianity had been distorted throughout its history by "mixing with narrow-minded Judaism"; early Christianity, however, as—of all things—a "branch of venerable Buddhism," had shown "aspects of the perfect negation of the will.") Wagner admittedly sees the necessity of being able to speak through philosophical and religious insights in understandable images, but he points in so doing to the consequent danger of distortion. Nor did Dante avoid this danger, particularly in *Paradiso* ("When explaining divine nature he appears, at least on a number of occasions, like a childish Jesuit"). The emphasis that Liszt was planning admittedly minimized this danger, "for music is the very primeval image of real art in the world." The second early testimony of Wagner's understanding of Schopenhauer's writings appears in no. 72, *Metaphysics of Sexual Love*. In this unfinished letter from 1858 the composer of *Tristan* comments, in the context of a reference to Schopenhauer, on lovers' suicide pacts. He sees "even in the system of sexual love a healing path to self-knowledge and the self-negation of the will—and not just the individual will."

On Franz Liszt's Symphonic Poems (no. 73). Wagner's letter (dated 15 February 1857) to Marie von Wittgenstein contains a detailed appreciation of Liszt, first as a virtuoso who "showed the value and meaning of the works of his predecessors in their fullest light and thereby almost attained the same heights as the composer being performed" (cf. no. 29) and then as a composer. Wagner addresses himself to the criticism of formlessness made against Liszt's symphonic poems ("with the invention of this term more [was] won than one was to believe"), ascribing to these works a new form which he defines as "the form which was appropriate on each occasion to the object and its presentational development," the historical starting point of which he sees in Gluck's *Iphigénie en Aulide* and in Beethoven's *Leonore* Overture no. 3 (see nos. 15 and 70).

A Letter to Hector Berlioz (no. 74). Wagner had given three concerts in Paris, on 25 January and 1 and 8 February 1860; on 9 February 1860 Berlioz published a criticism in the *Journal des débats* entitled *Concerts de M. Richard Wagner—la musique de l'avenir*. In his reply Wagner argues against the description *musique de l'avenir,* the French equivalent of *Zukunftsmusik* (music of the future), which he considers to have a polemical quality, and he refers Berlioz to *The Art-*

Work of the Future. His claim that the term *Zukunftsmusik* was coined by the Cologne music professor and publisher of the *Niederrheinische Musikzeitung* Ludwig Bischoff (1794–1864), in reference to the title of the second Zurich treatise on art, is not, in fact, correct (see Gregor-Dellin 1980, pp. 873–874).

"Music of the Future": To a French Friend as a Preface to a Prose Translation of My Opera Poetry (no. 75). This preface to the French edition of the libretti of *Holländer, Tannhäuser, Lohengrin,* and *Tristan,* in the form of an open letter to the Louvre curator Frédéric Villot, intended for the French public, contains basically a short summary of the three major writings on art from Wagner's Zurich period. The letter is to a certain extent a French counterpart to no. 79. The definition of myth is interesting: "This primeval, nameless folk poem, which we find treated in new ways by the great poets in every age of artistic perfection. The conventional form of human relations which can only be explained by abstract reason disappears almost completely. Instead only what is eternally comprehensible and purely human appears in an inimitable concrete form, which lends each genuine myth an immediately recognizable identity of its own."

Writings on Theater Reform

On the "Goethe-Stiftung" (no. 76). In this open letter (dated 8 May 1851) to Franz Liszt, Wagner comments on Liszt's suggestion for a "Goethe endowment" in Weimar, the aims of which were to be to encourage German art by means of an annual competition in all the arts. Wagner rejects the suggestion on the grounds that a prize of this kind would only encourage the "egoism" of the individual arts ("With the complete fragmentation of our art into individual arts each of these arts would claim supremacy for itself") and the general commercialization of art (describing the Goethe-Stiftung as a "Goethe Art Corporation," he claims, "Members of this company will . . . find themselves at their most numerous and eager to pay if an art lottery is held on every Goethe Day"). Wagner's suggestion instead is a German *Originaltheater* in Weimar, "which would serve as a suitable vehicle most likely to realize the idea most characteristic of the German mind in the dramatic artwork"—meaning drama as the synthesis of the arts in the Wagnerian sense. Wagner refers in this context to the forthcoming appearance of *Opera and Drama.* (See no. 77 on the significance of the term *Originaltheater.*)

A Theater in Zurich (no. 77). In this essay Wagner recommends to the Zurich public a thorough reform of theater in that city in the light of the precarious financial position of the Zurich Theater. The troubles of German theater lie, in Wagner's opinion, in the infertile "imitation of the Paris stage," particularly (again) grand opera. What he calls for are "original German theaters." His plan for such a theater in Zurich touches to a certain extent on the artistic utopia of the artwork of the future, as outlined in particular in the second of the three major writings: the theater must once again "become a part of public life"; and artists must be recruited from the Zurich public, the point being "to draw their own unknown powers to the warming [light] of public love." That will "lead to a gradual fading of the status of actor" and thereby also to a reconciliation in this area between art and life: "We are nearer to this social humanization of art or the artistic development of society than we perhaps thought." In the end "theater in its present form," namely commercialized theater as an "industrial institution," will "completely disappear." For the success of the project Wagner proposes the appointment of a committee, and calls (in vain) on the Zurich public to support the project financially.

The Vienna Court Opera Theater (no. 78). Here Wagner makes (quite reasonable) suggestions on a reform of the Vienna Court Opera. The aim of a publicly funded theater should be (according to a maxim of Emperor Joseph II, which Wagner considered appropriate to quote in the context of Vienna) "to contribute to the refinement of the morals and taste of the nation." From this Wagner derives certain demands. The first is that, instead of presenting a "confused, colourful disarray" of "performances of all kinds, from areas of the most contrasting styles," the theater should concentrate on a few ambitious works (meaning above all his own, of course) which could not be adequately realized in a commercialized cultural system. This would lead in practical terms to a numerical reduction in productions by a half, and to more carefully prepared performances; the transfer of Italian and French operas to the commercial sphere (Wagner does, however, recommend that Italian operas be exclusively "performed by Italian singers and in the Italian language"); as well as the running of the opera by three coordinated directors (a director of singing, an orchestral director, and a stage director); and naturally the end of "prima donna tyranny" and the "demands of virtuosi." (See nos. 79 and 83, in which Wagner formulates his idea for a Festival Theater.)

Autobiographical Writings, Prefaces, and Remarks on
Wagner's Musical-Dramatic Works

The most significant piece of this nature from the years 1849 to 1864 is *A Communication to My Friends* (no. 79). The comprehensive preface to the book edition of the text of *Holländer, Tannhäuser,* and *Lohengrin* contains a literary self-portrait by Wagner. Included in the autobiographical sketch are not only brief summaries of the important theoretical writings, in particular the three Zurich treatises on art, but also short interpretations of his own musical-dramatic works. Wagner interprets the figure of the Flying Dutchman as a modern Odysseus and Wandering Jew, driven by "longing for peace away from the storms of life": "He longs for death, like the Wandering Jew, as the end of his suffering; but the Dutchman can only achieve this death, a deliverance which is still denied to the eternal Jew, through a woman who sacrifices herself to him out of love . . . Yet this woman is no longer the caring homely Penelope of Odysseus, liberated before her time, she is Woman herself, the unavailable, longed-for, divined endlessly womanly Woman—in a word: the woman of the future." Wagner makes the connection between the longing of the Dutchman for deliverance and his own exile in Paris (and in bourgeois society generally); here the yearned-for "woman of the future" is the "expression of the homeland, i.e. of the embrace of an intimately known universe, a universe which I did not yet know but which I now longed for even so": the homeland as a utopia. And he makes a further connection with the lack of fulfillment in his own creativity; in other words the woman of the future is the redeeming spirit of music (cf. *Opera and Drama:* "Music is a woman"). The figure of Tannhäuser is also marked by a desire "to fade away from the present, to die away in an element of endless ethereal love which only seemed attainable in death." This desire is founded on the "longing for love . . . which could not be satisfied on the repellent basis of modern sensuality." Here, too, Wagner draws parallels with his creativity, but for him the basis of modern sensuality "is achievable again only in the sense which I had already learnt to know as the exploitation of our miserable public culture." Wagner interprets *Lohengrin* as relating a modern version of the myth of Zeus and Semele. Lohengrin is the god who longs for the "absolute love" of a woman "to whom he has to explain or justify nothing": "With his keenest of senses, his most knowing awareness, he wanted to become and be nothing other than a whole, complete, warm-blooded person, an actual person rather than a god." The work of the religious critic Feuerbach lies behind this. Wagner makes the connection with art here, too: Lohengrin is the "absolute artist" who suffers from the alienation of art from life and, unredeemed, yearns for a full sensual life. Lohengrin's tragedy is the tragedy of the absolute artist in bourgeois society, and for Wagner this is the "very tragedy of the life principle in modern society." Wagner rejects a Christian interpretation of both *Tannhäuser* and *Lohengrin*. He interpreted the death of Jesus in the dramatic sketch for *Jesus of Nazareth* as a revolutionary act, namely as a "denial of a loveless world." The essay also contains a sketch for *Die Meistersinger*. It ends with a plan for a festival at which the *Ring* tetralogy would be performed over three days and a preliminary evening—a first indication in the theoretical writings of the actual realization, in the idea of the festival, of the aesthetic utopia of the artwork of the future.

Preface to an intended 1850 edition of *Siegfrieds Tod* (no. 80). Wagner justifies the (abortive) publication of a work actually intended for the musical stage in the form of a literary text (see Strobel 1930, pp. 59–60, on this project) in spite of the dual problem posed by the venture ("If the sight of his verse in print inspires melancholy in the artist, who only knows how to communicate blissful understanding to you, the public, in a living work of art, the fact that a musical work of his is being presented must cause utter horror in him"). He cites the state of musical theaters, which, "under the protection of the police," have become the forum of "false prophets" (presumably an allusion to Meyerbeer's opera *Le prophète,* which premiered in 1849) and "sumptuous charlatans' stalls."

Preface to the intended publication in 1850 of the plan for the 1848 *On the Organization of a German National Theater for the Kingdom of Saxony* (no. 81). Under the heading *To a Friend in the Homeland,* on 18 September 1850 Wagner sent to Theodor Uhlig a preface to his planned (but unrealized) publication of the 1848 petition on theater reform (no. 52). Wagner attributes the failure of his reform plans to his lack of radicalism. It is true, he says, that at that time he had turned against the system of court theaters and intendants, but he had never properly taken off his "court uniform": "I still had one arm in it . . . when I wrote that paper for reform and the biggest mistake in the work is that at that time I had still not extricated myself." Wagner now rejects the use of reforms for the purpose of changing the existing system and places his "only faith" in revolution.

Preface to the first (private) edition of the poem *Der Ring des Nibelungen* (no. 82). The *Ring* text is little more than a plan for "the work of art which is actually intended," namely the drama of the future, which can be achieved only in performance and therefore cannot yet be intended for the public. In his Preface to the second edition of the poem of the Stage Festival Drama *Der Ring des Nibelungen* (no. 83), Wagner outlines his idea for a festival drama. He foresees productions of the *Ring* which are "free of the effects of the repertory arrangement in our current theaters." The location: "one of Germany's smaller towns." "The most choice and excellent singers from German operatic theater would be called there, uninterrupted by any other kind of artistic activity, to practice the multi-part stage work written by me." The public, streaming in "from near and far," would be able to experience the performances "free of the worries of everyday existence." Wagner looks for a princely patron for this project: "Will this prince be found?"

Staging instructions for the 1850 production of *Lohengrin* in Weimar (no. 84). The instructions to Franz Liszt and the director Eduard Genast on the world premiere of *Lohengrin* in Weimar on 28 August 1850 show Wagner, as do the later writings on the staging of his works, to be an advocate of scenic historicism and musical-theatrical realism, but also an experienced stage practitioner, something he had developed into as a result particularly of his years as kapellmeister in Dresden. Each movement onstage must originate in the score: this is the director's guiding principle ("Strict attention must be paid above all to precise cohesion between the elements of the plot and the music"). Wagner calls for "as much individual life as possible" for the choruses. The set itself is described in detail (see, for example, the instructions about the scenery for act 2 and Wagner's appended notes: "The precise performance of this scene to the above specifications must be insisted upon, because without it the vividness of the plot will never come out clearly").

On Performing "Tannhäuser": A Communication to Conductors and Performers of this Opera (no. 85). This statement, dated 14–23 August 1852, first appeared as a small brochure sent to German theaters. It contains, in addition to detailed instructions on the production and performance of *Tannhäuser,* certain fundamental, practical comments by Wagner on performing musical-dramatic works. Wagner calls for a close link between staging and music. The production must be backed at all times by the score ("which the director must therefore get to know thoroughly with the help of the conductor"). The performers must, before studying their roles, come to terms with "the full range of the poetry itself." In Wagner's view they are "in the first place portrayers," or actors; the singing must be based on declamation appropriate to the sense ("My declamation is singing and my singing declamation"). The choruses must be divided up into individuals and varying groups and correspond in their "arrangement exactly to real life." Comprehensive instructions for the conductor, director, set designer, and performers of *Tannhäuser* are included.

On the "Tannhäuser" Overture (no. 86). On 18 March 1852 Wagner sent his concert program of 16 March (no. 110) to the Frankfurt conductor Gustav Schmidt on the occasion of a performance of the *Tannhäuser* overture for Good Friday 1852, giving him instructions on the interpretation of the individual parts, based on his experiences in rehearsing the work.

Remarks on Performing the Opera "Der fliegende Holländer" (no. 87). This document, dated 22 December 1852, also reveals Wagner to be an advocate of musical-dramatic realism, which requires the "precise correspondence of the events on stage with the orchestra" and the "most careful correspondence between the action and the music." According to Wagner, Senta should "be seen not in the sense of modern, morbid sentimentality" but as "a wholly robust Nordic girl," a "naive." Erik is a counterpart to the figure of the Dutchman: "stormy, fierce and gloomy, like the loner." And Daland should not slip over "into actual comedy."

Petition for amnesty to King Johann of Saxony (no. 88). In this (unsuccessful) petition (dated Zurich, 15 May 1856) Wagner admits his participation in the May 1849 uprising in Dresden but claims that he was a revolutionary "only for the sake of art": "Nor did I ever turn to a particular political party or share any of its specific theories or plans or hopes, but the belief in a complete transformation of the political and above all the social world gradually took hold of me so strongly that I began to flatter myself of a new order, one that I needed before I could conceive of achieving my ideal relationship of art to life." Wagner tries to play down the writings on art from his first years in Zurich as the product of a medicinal purging ("in the manner of a pathologically eliminated disease-producing agent"). Draft of a petition for amnesty to Saxony's Minister of Justice Behr (no. 89) is a plan for another (unsuccessful) plea for amnesty (dated Venice, December 1858). Wagner points out that he could not submit to the judicial examination necessary for amnesty because of his impaired health, and he also asks to be made an exception in view of the ten years which have elapsed since the events of 1848–49. In *Review of the Paris Production of "Tannhäuser"* (no. 90) Wagner gives a detailed report in letter form (dated 27 March 1861) on the events that occurred at the notorious production of *Tannhäuser* in Paris on 13, 18, and 24 March 1861.

Minor Occasional Pieces and Short Articles

Wagner wrote several obituaries and dedications during this period. In [*Obituary and*] *Recollections of Spontini* (no. 91), Wagner honors Gaspare Spontini,

who died in 1851, as "the last member of a series of composers whose first
member is to be found in Gluck; what Gluck wanted and first undertook so
thoroughly . . . was carried through—insofar as it could be achieved in the
musical opera form—by Spontini" (see also the relevant passages in part 1 of
Opera and Drama). Wagner combines the appreciation of Spontini with renewed attacks on Meyerbeer. In the SSD edition Wagner adds to the obituary
a report (extracted from his autobiography) of a meeting with Spontini in
Dresden when he conducted *Vestalin* there as a guest in the fall of 1844: "He
declared openly that he liked me and for that reason only now wanted to
persuade me to avoid the misfortune of continuing in my career as a dramatic
composer." In his dedication of the score of *Lohengrin* to Franz Liszt (no. 92)
Wagner dedicates the first edition (lithographed, not yet engraved) of the
score to Liszt in gratitude for the premiere in Weimar which Liszt conducted.
He again stresses that the musical drama becomes reality only with a "living
performance." The score is described as "the sketch of a work which only
acquires a real existence when . . . it appears in sensory form to the eyes and
ears." His *Obituary of Ludwig Spohr and Chorus-Master Wilhelm Fischer (By
letter to an old friend in Dresden)* (no. 93) honors Spohr and the Dresden chorus
master Wilhelm Fischer, a longtime companion of Wagner's, who died in
1859. The dating of the obituary in SSD as 1860 is incorrect. Wagner honors
Spohr as the last "in a series of noble, serious musicians . . . whose youth
was illuminated directly by Mozart's radiant sun, protecting the light received
with touching fidelity like Vestal virgins guarding the pure flame entrusted
to them and preserving it in the chaste home against all life's storms and
gales."

The writings of this period also include statements on various subjects to
the press. The first is *On the Musical Direction of Opera* (no. 94). In September
1850 Wagner had refused the position of musical director offered to him by
Philipp Walburg Kramer, director of the Zurich Aktientheater, and instead
recommended first the inexperienced Karl Ritter, and then, when this nomi-
nation failed, Hans von Bülow. In this newspaper announcement of 17 October 1850 Wagner asks the Zurich public to understand his decision and to
have confidence in his preferred candidate (see Gregor-Dellin 1980, pp. 318–
321). Wagner's *In Recommendation of Gottfried Semper* (no. 95) commends
Semper, whom he had already recommended to the Zurich official Karl
Ritteron on 22 February 1850 for a professorship at the Swiss Polytechnikum,
to the people of Zurich as an architect whose real achievement lay in having
overcome the conflict in modern architecture ("an arbitrary reproduction of
the ancients . . . in superfluous buildings") by developing new architectural
forms out of the needs of public and private life. In *On Musical Coverage in
the "Eidgenössische Zeitung"* (no. 96) Wagner justifies and underlines his caution
in the light of controversy in the press over his conducting of Beethoven's
Fifth Symphony on 28 January 1851: he did not want to influence "public
taste," except through his "artistic achievements" (cf. ML 470–471). In *Vieuxtemps* (no. 97) Wagner commends to the people of Zurich the violinist Henri
Vieuxtemps, then playing as a guest artist in Zurich, as the "greatest and most

masterful . . . of the violinists alive today." The two had met in Paris in 1841 (see, under no. 29, the first of the accounts from Paris to the Dresden *Abendzeitung*). *On Performing the "Tannhäuser" Overture* (no. 98) is a piece in which Wagner calls on conductors intending to perform the overture to refer to his comments in *On Performing "Tannhäuser"* (no. 85).

No. 99 is Wagner's invitation to a reading of the *Ring* poem on 17, 18, and 19 February 1853 in the Hotel Baur-au-Lac in Zurich (see Gregor-Dellin 1983, p. 244) and no. 100 announces concerts of extracts from Wagner's works, with Wagner conducting, on 18, 20, and 22 May 1853 in the same city. *In Support of the Founding of a String Quartet* (no. 101) commends a string quartet to the Zurich public composed of soloists from the Zurich orchestra—Heisterhagen, Honegger, Bauer, and Schleich—who were to perform Beethoven's C-Sharp Minor Quartet op. 131 in December 1854 (cf. no. 113). *On the Direction of a Mozart Festival* (no. 102) is Wagner's official declaration of his readiness, in spite of impaired health, to conduct a performance of Mozart's *Requiem* as part of the planned celebrations of the composer's one-hundredth birthday, but only on condition that enough patrons are found to ensure a "worthy performance." (The project failed to find support, and the concert did not take place.)

In *From the "Europe artiste"* (no. 103) Wagner presents himself to the Paris public on the occasion of the concerts held in January and February 1860 as a "foreign" and "exiled" artist asking for hospitality but also for a fair-minded reception of his works. He is not, he says, a "Marat of music": "My compositions do not have such revolutionary tendencies." No. 104, *From the Vienna Court Opera Theater,* is a review of the ballet *Gräfin Egmont* by de Rola at the Vienna Court opera which Peter Cornelius was commissioned to write but which, for tactical reasons, Wagner wrote instead (see WWV, p. 19). Here "P.C." flatters the management of the Court Opera for their intention "of producing Wagner's latest opera, *Tristan,* in spite of the strongest opposition from the German music critics." The planned production of *Tristan* at the Vienna Court Opera did not materialize, and in *From the "Ostdeutsche Post"* (no. 105) Wagner denies the claim in that journal that he received compensation for the cancellation.

There are also several letters of thanks from this period. Nos. 106 and 107, together with no. 206, appear in SSD as *Three Letters to the Management of the Philharmonic Society in St. Petersburg.* No. 106 is a letter accepting the invitation of the Philharmonic Society to conduct a concert in the spring of 1863; it is dated 12 December 1862. In no. 107, dated 30 March 1863, Wagner expresses his gratitude retrospectively for the successful concerts in St. Petersburg on 3, 10, and 18 March (Gregorian calendar): "You have done one artist, whose career has been thickly sown with thorns, a great service." (For details of Wagner's concerts in Russia, see Bartlett 1990, pp. 16–32 and appendix 1.)

The shorter writings on various subjects in this period also include a series of program notes. They are presented in detail in the checklist of writings at the end of this chapter (nos. 108–116). Only no. 108, *Beethoven's "Eroica" Symphony,* is of particular interest here. This program shows how Wagner sees the composer as a poet. Beethoven's Third Symphony is interpreted as a heroic human image in musical notes (the "hero as a complete, whole person"). The first movement ("Might") shows "all the sentiments of a rich, human nature in the most restless, youthfully vigorous emotion"; the second movement represents "profound and great suffering"; the third movement shows "the brightly and cheerfully active person"; the fourth movement is the "counterpart of the first movement" and, finally, "the complete whole person." In the "Preliminary Note" to the program for the Zurich festival concert in May 1853 (no. 112), Wagner justifies his selection of extracts from his own work "as pure pieces of music [which] express in precise tonal colors a major element of the poetic whole."

Writings from 1864 to 1883

We now turn to the writings from Wagner's Munich period (1864–65), his "second exile" in Triebschen (1865–1872), and the Bayreuth years (1872–1883). The themes change in ways which were foreshadowed to some extent in the writings from the 1850s and early 1860s. In addition to writings concerned with questions of musical history—the theme of Beethoven again—musical practice, and the drama, there are philosophical essays, comparable with the great writings of the Zurich period, in which political, theological, and aesthetic issues overlap. The first of these writings (*On State and Religion* and *German Art and German Politics*) were intended for the instruction of Ludwig II; the later pieces (*Religion and Art* and subsequent writings) represent something of a philosophical testament on Wagner's part. The influence of Schopenhauer increasingly makes itself felt. There is also a growing amount of aggressive anti-Semitism which bears the mark of utter paranoia and which in the late writings—in an intermittently abstruse-sounding conglomeration of Schopenhauer and Feuerbach, and ideas about socialism, vegetarianism, animal welfare, and so on, as well as racist arguments and anti-Semitic agitation—contains a "theoretical" foundation in an adaptation of Gobineau's racial doctrine. The writings on theater reform concentrate entirely—apart from the proposal for a school of music in Munich (1865)—on Bayreuth. The autobiography *My Life* has a special position. My discussion begins with this autobiographical work; the philosophical writings follow, then the writings on musical aesthetics and the drama, and on theater reform and Bayreuth. The last section covers in brief the shorter occasional pieces and documents relating to Bayreuth and the *Bayreuther Blätter*. The conclusion consists of additional occasional pieces and short articles, including obituaries and dedications, reviews, open letters and statements to the press on various subjects, and concert programs.

Autobiographical Works

My Life (no. 117). Wagner dictated his autobiography, in which he had been encouraged by Ludwig II, to Cosima between 17 July 1865 and March 1880 (the last section dates from 20 March 1880). A limited private edition of fifteen copies was intended for the king and Wagner's immediate circle of friends. These were reclaimed after Wagner's death and largely destroyed. A general edition did not appear until 1911. (See ML 741–756 for details on the background, development, and publication of the work.) In *My Life* Wagner tells his life story up until his decisive summons to Munich in May 1864. But this is not an authentic autobiography in every respect. The work is tendentious on many points, not least because of the fact that Wagner dictated the text to Cosima and his actual addressee was the king of Bavaria, a fact which affects the description of Richard's relationship with Minna Wagner as well as his account of the years of the revolution. To this should be added the subjectivity of the narrative, which makes itself felt particularly in descriptions of putative rivals among contemporary musicians and writers. Julius Kapp was one of the first to seize on some of Wagner's errors (Kapp 1913, pp. 215–216), and more recent biographers have followed suit (see Newman 1976 and Deathridge-Dahlhaus 1984). This does not affect in any way, however, the position which *My Life* holds in the history of autobiography or its significance as a cultural and historical document. The dictation of *My Life* was based on notes in a big red pocket book which Wagner began in 1835 in Frankfurt (see ML 107–108) and continued regularly into the 1860s. He dictated *My Life* from these notes up to Easter 1846 and then decided, in February 1868 and January 1869, to write them afresh. These new notes, which cover the years from 1846 to 1868, are known as the *Annals* (no. 118) and have survived intact. The original red pocket book, however, was destroyed except for the first four pages containing entries up to the point of Wagner's arrival in Paris in 1839. (These pages have been published with extensive editorial notes in SB I, 81–92.) The *Annals* were included in *The Diary of Richard Wagner 1865–1882: The Brown Book* (no. 119), which is not strictly speaking a diary but a collection of autobiographical notes, sketches, essays, poems, and other sundry items written down intermittently over a seventeen-year period. (The history of the document is described in BB 13–21.)

Philosophical Writings
On State and Religion (no. 120). This essay from July 1864 was not originally intended for publication. It is addressed directly to Ludwig II and replies to his question "whether and in what way [Wagner's] views on state and religion have changed since [his] writings on art in the years between 1849 and 1851." Wagner certainly tries to minimize the political and, specifically, the revolutionary and anarchic tendencies in the writings on revolution and art by claiming that "this or any other form of government, the dominance of this or any other party, this or any other change in the mechanism of our political system" has never been of real interest to him, and whoever wishes to attribute "the role of a political revolutionary" to him clearly knows nothing about him. At the same time, however, he does cling to the political core of his aesthetics: the great seriousness of his efforts on behalf of art has necessarily required that he "indeed seek and call for a legitimate foundation in the realm

of life, in the state and ultimately in religion." This essay features a number of ideas central to the writings of 1848–1851, including the independent monarchism shown in the speech to the Vaterlandsverein (no. 46) and elements of a utopian socialism in the call for "the equal distribution of labor" as a precondition for the "transformation of the corporate, bourgeois, one-sided bias in work into a universal activity which is natural to all," and "which should necessarily take on an intrinsically artistic character."

But there are different ways of looking at everything, and the essay *On State and Religion* can be seen, as a whole, as a conscious reinterpretation of a number of key aspects of the revolutionary and aesthetic writings in the spirit of Schopenhauerian philosophy. Wagner's point of departure is the "egoism of the individual," based on a "blindly clamouring will." He justifies the state on this basis as the "agreement whereby individuals, by dint of limitations on each side, sought to protect themselves against force from either side." The ideal of this state is embodied in the monarch, who represents to some degree the *volonté générale* (the key words "general will" stand in a comparable context in the essay *German Art and German Politics*, no. 121) as opposed to the *volonté de tous,* that is, of individuals. The individual is determined not only by the will, however, but also by illusion, which determines the "spirit of the genus" in opposition to the "egoism of the individual" alive in the will. This illusion expresses itself principally in the patriotism of the bourgeois individual, namely in the "illusion that a significant change to the state would have to hit and destroy him personally, so that he believes he cannot survive the change"; as a result the citizen "is set on averting the evil threatening the state as one he must suffer personally."

The king is also the symbol of this patriotism. The illusion of patriotism admittedly exceeds the will of the individual in only a limited sense, as it includes the possibility of "injustice and violence against other states and peoples." There is the danger, furthermore, of the "intentional exploitation and conscious deception" of patriotism through public opinion, whose organ is the press (all his life Wagner felt persecuted by the press). The press claims to be the "guarantee of humanity's continuous progress" but is in fact nothing more than "unsuccessful unadulterated commercialism": "Each acts according to his needs, and the press itself determines public opinion in practice through its attitude in that it can be had at any time for money and gain." Religion, by contrast, is a higher form of illusion, "the complete reversal of all the efforts . . . which the state has initiated and organized." This statement certainly does not refer to theology, which is the attempt "to explain religious dogma according to laws of cause and effect between the phenomena of natural and bourgeois life, and to reject as an illogical fantasy anything that goes against this form of explanation." Understood in this way, religion is will rather than illusion; it is the "voluntary suffering and self-denial" of saints and ascetics in whom egoism is "already nullified." The king is also a saint and martyr in these terms; his actions are the "denial" of any will, a "sacrifice" for the egoistic individuality of his people, and demonstrate an "unshakeable gentleness," manifested in "grace," which rises above the legislation of the state. The state is thus "destroyed," as it were, by the grace of the king and counterbalanced by religion. The king himself (Wagner accepts entirely that he is placing him in an "almost superhuman position") finds his salvation in art as the third and highest form of illusion, the "friendly life redeemer" who "in life, rises above life and makes it appear even to us as a game." Religion is also raised into art insofar as it alone can still be the "divine vision" that grasps the religious revelation which has become increasingly unrecognizable in the disputes among churches and sects. The crux of the essay is Wagner's promise to Ludwig II of salvation through his art, in which at the same time the truth of religion is dismissed (cf. no. 126, *Religion and Art*).

German Art and German Politics (no. 121). The essays collected under this title were also meant primarily for Ludwig II; their publication followed in the autumn of 1867 in the *Süddeutsche Presse,* a semiofficial organ partly financed by the king. Publication of the essays was stopped, however, on his orders after the twelfth issue, obviously on account of the content (see, for example, comments on the murder of the writer August von Kotzebue in issue no. 9). This then led to the publication in book form of all fifteen essays the following year.

The first essay has as its theme the "subjugation" of German culture by French civilization and the attendant gulf between the "spirit of the German people and the spirit of its princes"—French civilization being the counterpart of courtly absolutism, with Frederick the Great as the incarnation of this "influence as a destroyer of freedoms." The second essay contrasts this theme with that of "the rebirth of the German Spirit" in the eighteenth century (in the work of Winkelmann, Lessing, Schiller, Goethe, Mozart, Beethoven), which took place imperceptibly at first, independently of politics and the princes, then took definite political shape after 1813 in the person of "German youth." From here Wagner draws a connecting line to the immediate present in the form of the battle of Königgrätz, which he sees as a victory "of a German spirit which was otherwise eradicated" in spite of the considerable duration of the Restoration. Prussia's attitude is clearly the issue here. As early as 1867 Wagner's enthusiasm was thus marked by a not-insignificant element of skepticism, which later changed abruptly into an unequivocal rejection of the Prussian-German reich.

The third and fourth essays are variations on these themes. Wagner makes particular mention of the role of the theater in the national "renaissance." It is true that the forces of reaction dominated here: "The theater was taken from the heirs of Goethe and Schiller. Opera here, ballet there: Rossini, Spontini, the Dioscuri Vienna and Berlin which carried with them the Pleiades of the Restoration." The fourth essay ends with an appeal to the German princes: "The example of the appropriation of this rebirth for the purpose of enriching the spiritual life of the German people and for the purpose of founding a new, genuinely German civilization whose benefit would go even beyond our frontiers, must come from those in whose hands the political fate of the German people lies. Nothing more is needed for this purpose than for this proper example to be given to the German princes from among their number"—a reference to the hopes Wagner had of Ludwig II. The fifth essay follows logically. Wagner analyzes, in a thoroughly critical manner, the cultural policy of Ludwig II's predecessors Ludwig I and Maximilian II. The efforts of the former were stillborn, in spite of their exemplary effect on other princes, and the art encouraged by Maximilian II remained an inferior imitation, a verdict which applies in particular to the Munich circle of poets ("Even the series of gifted imitators, who bore powerful witness from Kleist to Platen of the inexhaustible gifts of the German spirit, had now come to an end"). Wagner's chief criticism of Maximilian II, as elsewhere, is that the king "ignored dramatic art out of suspicion and perhaps mistrust."

Essays six through eleven are devoted to the theater. Wagner sees in the theater the "seed and core of all the spiritual development of the nation's poetry and morality" in that "no other branch of the arts can ever truly flourish and educate the people which does not fully recognize and guarantee the all-powerful role of the theater." He weaves new meditations on the nature of theatrical art into a critical history of the theater from the ancient Greeks to the present, taking up the main ideas from part 2 of *Opera and Drama*. In theater the actor's "urge to imitate" and the poet's "urge to recreate" meet. It is up to the poet to "bring into being" an event from life, and to do that by "limiting" and "heightening" (cf. his comments on myth in *Opera and Drama*, myth now being defined more clearly as the "model of an event from life"; its achievement is to "idealize"). The poet's model, however, lives only through the actor and his work in the nation's theater. It is the actor who shows the poet "ever new and unprecedentedly rich possibilities in human existence"; he represents the "realistic" principle which must in turn be rendered "into a higher existence" by the poet alone. The nature of theatrical art therefore consists of a dialectical unity of realism (the actor) and idealism (the poet) (essays seven and eight). Wagner then describes the decline of German theater after the rise of German classicism as the result of reducing theatrical art to the art of the actor: "The actor is fed with delicacies and the poet is left to starve." This reduction manifested itself in virtuosity, the commercialization of the theater, and (indeed because of) empty official coffers ("that frightening ghost: Finance"), as well as the debasement of the public into a "Lower Chamber . . . of German theater-goers voting in taxes." Schiller's *Tell* and Goethe's *Faust* were replaced by the operas of Rossini and Gounod (Gounod's *Faust* being a "repellent, sweetly vulgar, affected concoction, with the music of an inferior talent who would like to achieve something and in his anguish grasps at any means"). For Wagner the prototype of this "new theatrical development in Germany" was Kotzebue, in whom literary and political reaction come together ("Kotzebue wrote his privy councillor's reports to Petersburg on the way things have changed nicely in Germany and was quite happy doing it"). Wagner celebrates his murder by the "German youth" Sand as "an unheard-of and ominously odd act." In the final section of essay eleven Wagner turns to education policy. In this context he formulates his famous maxim that "German" means "doing the thing one does for its own sake and for the joy of it; whereas utilitarianism, i.e. the principle whereby a thing is done because of an external personal objective, shows itself to be un-German." So Wagner identifies the "virtue of the Germans" with the "highest principle of aesthetics."

Using this definition, Wagner then goes on in essay twelve to criticize in particular attempts by the church and the state to misuse educational establishments for their own ends, referring to the "Pedagogical Province" in *Wilhelm Meisters Wanderjahren*. Essays thirteen through fifteen also use the definition of "German" as a starting point and end by defining a cultural and political utopia. The monarch is considered, on the basis of his right to bestow grace (see no. 120, *On State and Religion*), to be quintessentially exempt "from the principles of expedience binding upon the state" and the embodiment of the "condition of freedom which no other can attain, in which he is held by the general will." The monarch should gather about him an order in which "from every sphere of state and social organizations" those are called upon who in their activities and potential "exceed the generally legal standard of requirements set out of expedience"—a call for a new nobility, as it were, to take over from the old hereditary nobility. The theater, however—and here the circle closes—is to mediate between this aesthetic state, with its "exemption from the common utilitarian principle," and the sphere of the state and society, which is determined by utilitarian interests; the theater thus has an interest in both areas through the collaboration of the poet and the actor. The collection of essays thereby opens out into a new variation of the Wagnerian artistic utopia and his ideas on the social significance of theater reform. The concluding section links up with the first and second essays and reiterates, in the light of the Prussian victory at Königgrätz, that it was the German spirit which made the rebirth of the nation possible, and not the power politics of its princes (and Bismarck).

What Is German? (no. 122). This essay has the same origin as the collection *German Art and German Politics*, parts of it having been written as early as September 1865 for Ludwig II. It was finally published in 1878 with the addition of an introduction and a long epilogue. The central issue in the essay is again the famous pithy definition of "German" (see essay eleven in no. 121): "that everything beautiful and noble came into the world not for the sake of profit, not even for fame and recognition: . . . and only that which works in this way can lead Germany to greatness." The skepticism toward Prussia that marked the collection of essays from 1867–68 has changed by 1878 in the epilogue to this essay into an unambiguous rejection of the Prussian-German state. Here Wagner is countering a journalist who had reproached him, saying that after all it was not he alone who had taken a lease on the German spirit: "I noticed that and gave up the lease. On the other hand I was pleased when a common German imperial coin was brought out and in particular too when I learnt that it turned out to be so authentically

German that it did not fit in with any other coin from any of the other great nations of the world, remaining instead . . . out of circulation: I was told it was really dire for common usage but very profitable for bankers. My German heart also swelled when we voted liberally for 'free trade.' Of course there was and is much poverty in the country; the worker starves and trade is ailing. But 'business' is doing well."

The Prussian-German Empire of 1871 is here the embodiment of un-Germanness. Wagner cites Johann Sebastian Bach as a symbol of the German spirit: "His is the history of the innermost life of the German spirit during the terrible century of the utter extinction of the German people. Look at his head there, hidden under a ridiculous full-bottomed French wig, this Master—as a miserable choir-master and organist, trailing around among little Thuringian parishes, the names of which are hardly known, with meagre appointments, remaining so unnoticed that it required another whole century for his works to be pulled from oblivion. And now look what a world the immeasurably great Sebastian . . . built!"

The quotations are ample proof that the older Wagner was no partisan of Bismarck's empire—apart from a fleeting rapprochement—and show how little his nationalism had in common with the demonstrations of power and chauvinism of the national German state of 1871. Nevertheless, the essay's openly antidemocratic and anti-Semitic tendencies should not be overlooked. The Jews are portrayed as the representatives of the "un-German" utilitarian principle, as the profiteers of capitalism: "The Jew seized these advantages and the Jewish banker nourishes his enormous wealth on the crippled and declining national prosperity." Even the Junkers (young Prussian aristocracy) and law students are counted along with them: the Jews (*Juden*), Junkers, and jurists form, together with Jesuits and journalists, the five *J*'s, in which Wagner sees summed up all the negative features of his age, while astonishingly, "French-Jewish-German democracy" is seen as the real cause of the failure of the Revolution of 1848.

Modern (no. 123). In this inflammatory anti-Semitic pamphlet Wagner does not, it is true, actually accuse the Jews of being the authors of all the wrongs of "modernity," which he again deplores. Modernity here stems instead from France, and the first people to bring it into Germany were the Young Germans (near-contemporaries of Wagner himself, it should be noted, such as Gutzkow and Laube). They "started with the war against literary 'orthodoxy,' meaning belief in our great poets and sages of the previous century, fought against the so-called 'romantics' who succeeded them . . . , went to Paris, studied Scribe and E. Sue, translated them into masterfully sloppy German," and so on. He sees the Jews, however, as profiting from these conditions.

Shall We Hope? (no. 124). Just three years after the first Bayreuth festival (which in his view had failed ultimately as a concept), Wagner again turns to the question of the "relationship of art to our life," which he had examined in *The Art-Work of the Future*. He acknowledges that his idea of a festival could not be realized "until the ideas which I bring together in the 'art-work of the future' have been observed, understood and respected to their full extent," and he draws up an alarming balance sheet. The state is by nature "barbaric and thoroughly hostile to art"; his only concern is "to prevent it becoming something else." The Prussian-German empire alone set itself on expansion through force and in so doing endangered peace in Europe and failed "to associate us closely with our [political] neighbours"; but the Germans were destined to be "improvers of the world," not rulers, and the empire had offended against this principle (see the maxims in nos. 121 and 122). Science— meaning, as always, the natural sciences, "the false god of the modern world"—had failed; "a remedy against the starvation of unemployed fellow citizens" had not been found. Religion—meaning, as always, the official theology of the church—had become powerless. Public opinion was governed by a press which Wagner saw as "the worst poison for our spiritual and social system." This being the situation, Wagner poses the fateful question: "Shall we hope?" The answer he gives changes the nature of the question: "We must hope." Here lies the only hope—for Wagner's art, and also for the future of mankind.

Open Letter to Herr Ernst von Weber, Author of "The Torture Chambers of Science" (no. 125). The open letter, which Wagner wrote in October 1879 after a visit from Ernst von Weber to Bayreuth, supports Weber's antivivisection protest (*Die Folterkammern der Wissenschaft,* 1879). Wagner again turns on the "specter of science" (that is, the natural sciences), "which in our despiritualized age has risen from the dissecting table to the gun factory to become the demon of the cult of utilitarianism, which alone wins the favor of the state." He professes—and this idea appears here for the first time in his later writings—that sympathy, in the Schopenhauerian sense of enduring together, is the "only true basis of all morality." He sees in this "religion of sympathy"—this term also appears for the first time in Wagner's writings— the only possibility of overcoming the "dogma of utilitarianism" and the curse of modern civilization ("It seems that the march of civilization has transformed man into a rapacious wild animal"), in spite of (indeed because of) the opposite tendency in state and society, which "are so calculated, by the laws of mechanics, to operate without sympathy and charity," all the more so as it is "the military administration that is solely responsible, apart from the stock exchange, for ordering our national life." Wagner demands the unconditional abolition of vivisection and all animal experiments: "For our conclusion with regard to human dignity is that this dignity reveals itself at the very point where man is able to distinguish himself from animals by feeling pity for them."

Religion and Art (no. 126). In this essay and subsequent pieces (nos. 127– 130) Wagner summarizes the philosophy of his later years. In contrast to the major writings of the Zurich period this later oeuvre lacks a clear line of thought. The texts proceed largely by association of ideas and feature numerous repetitions and a verbosity which is tiresome in parts. The title *Religion and Art* strictly applies only to chapter 1 of the essay, which begins with the famous formulation: "It could be said that when religion becomes artificial it is the preserve of art to rescue its essence by apprehending the mythical symbols—which religion wishes to be believed true in a literal sense—according to their symbolic value, in order to reveal the profound truth hidden in them by representing them ideally." This sentence on the relationship between art and religion implies a whole philosophy of history drawing on Feuerbach and Hegel (albeit in strangely altered form). Religion must fade before the reality of utopia—which for Wagner is also an aesthetic utopia—can be achieved. The age of religion and its priestly agents is over; a binding interpretation of the world through the dogmas of the church, or, as the next sentence puts it, through a "growing accumulation of incredulities commended to faith," has become impossible. Religion has lost its function as an exciter of the senses. In this it has been replaced by art, or, better, it has been preserved and saved in art. Its salutary historical truths become mythical symbols, the medium of "ideal representation" (see no. 121, essays seven and eight, on this term) through the artist. It is the transformation of these salutary historical truths into symbols that reveals the "profound hidden truth" which lives in them under the dogmatic incrustation: religious utopia is liberated into the utopia of the work of art (Wagnerian, needless to say). Only when religion has become art completely will its fundamental essence be fully developed. These thoughts throw a clear light on the late musical-dramatic work *Parsifal,* which can in fact be seen in the spiritual context of the late writings. The "profound truth" of religion—"any true religion"—of Christianity as well as Buddhism (again pure Schopenhauer) is the "recognition of the frailty of the world" and the "teaching of liberation from it" through denial and sympathy (that is, suffering together), by "overturning the will." The religion of Jesus of Nazareth was a religion of compassion in this sense, with Jesus himself the Jesus of the poor "who called to him the weary and the oppressed, the suffering and the persecuted, the forbearing and the meek, the forgiving and the loving." His religion was thus "the most simple of religions." "But to the 'rich' it was too simple," and it therefore became alienated from its own essence through reworking and distortion, through the imposition of ideas by theologians. This alienation from its origins has determined the whole history of Christianity to the present day. The churches have become nothing more than the tool of power and property interests who have perverted Jesus' religion. This very alienation can be saved through art, for true Christianity is reborn in art, a work of redemption which achieves perfection in music, the "only art which corresponds fully to Christian faith."

Chapter 2 contrasts the reality of history with the truth of religion, the "overturning of the will." In his later years Wagner described history as the unimpeded progress of the will. Since its first dawning, history has shown man to be "a wild animal in a constant state of development. He conquers lands, subjugates the fruit-eating races, by subjugating other subjugators he founds great empires, forms states and establishes civilizations in order to enjoy his spoils in tranquility." This is also true of the ancient Greeks ("There is no blood-guilt that this beautifully creative people did not bring down upon their fellow beings in limb-tearing hate") and for the modern Prussian-German Empire, with its full armory, its "huge cannons and armour-plating which increases year by year." In reality, therefore, history knows no progress; instead it represents a single process of degeneration and irreversible decline. It was in this process of degeneration that the truth of Christianity (here the themes of chapter 1 are taken up again) was subverted and used as an instrument of power to back up the system of ownership and authority. In concrete terms this happened—and here Wagner's anti-Semitism emerges again—as a result of the assimilation of the Jesus of the poor and his religion of compassion into the "God of the Jews, Jehovah" and the religion of the Old Testament. Wagner consequently separates Christianity from Judaism on the basis of its origin and essence, interpreting its history instead as a progressive relapse into the Old Testament. In this situation, naturally, "it was not Jesus Christ, the Saviour, whom our military preachers recommend to the batallions gathered around them before the start of battle. Instead they name the one whom they have in mind: Jehovah, Yahweh, or an Elohim, who hated all gods apart from himself and therefore wished them to be subjugated by his true people." It was not only the church which had failed in the process of history, but also—and this too is not a new idea—the "so-called natural sciences," which have placed themselves fully in the service of the "agencies of war." In this context Wagner redefines the contrasting pair civilization and culture, setting history's civilization against a utopian culture: "power can civilize but culture must sprout from the soil of peace."

Chapter 3 raises the question of the possible reversal of this process of degeneration into a regeneration of humanity. The solution which Wagner intends might, in a time of alternative movements in many walks of life, appear less abstruse today than it was once seen to be. Wagner draws a connection between vegetarians, animal rights advocates, temperance societies (he mentions in this connection the "plague of drunkenness, which has emerged as the ultimate destroyer of all physical properties in our modern civilization" while providing the state with taxes), and socialism, on which Wagner continues to be quite open: "The resentment of the worker, who produces all that is beneficial in order to earn the least benefit proportionally for himself, points to the profoundest immorality of our civilization, which the latter's advocates can only counter with what in truth is malicious sophistry," a notable phrase in the years of the so-called socialist laws. Beyond this political solution, however, Wagner sees the real forum for regeneration— and the cycle of ideas in the essay now comes full circle—in art and in particular in "sacred music." Art and music lead to the "recognition of the need for redemption," the "profoundest principle of religion": "We have faith in such redemption in the sacred hour when all the outward images of the world dissolve from us as in ominous dreams, already experiencing foreboding: . . . then we hear only the sound, pure and yearning for peace, of the lament of nature, fearless, full of hope, all-soothing, redeeming the world."

This too provides an aid to the understanding of *Parsifal*. The final section of the essay again deals with the theme of degeneration and paints a thoroughly modern picture of the possible self-destruction of humanity as a consequence of permanently escalating armaments and preparations for war: "In the sea torpedoes and everywhere else shells of dynamite and so on. We should believe that all this, together with art, science, courage and honor, life and property, could one day go up in the air through an incalculable oversight."

"What Use Is This Knowledge?": An Epilogue to "Religion and Art" (no. 127). This first supplement to *Religion and Art* assesses the consequences of assertions made in that work: "We recognize the reason for the decline in historical man, and the need for regeneration; we believe in the possibility of such regeneration and devote ourself to its realization in every sense." Wagner again does not spare any criticism of the Prussian-German Empire: "German unity must be able to show its teeth everywhere, even when it has nothing more to chew with them." Bismarck is compared with "Robespierre in the Committee of Public Safety, as he tirelessly investigates how to increase his powers."

Remarks on "Religion and Art": "Know Thyself" (no. 128). This second coda to *Religion and Art* relentlessly pursues the criticism of civilization. As in the writings on the Revolution of 1848–49 and the years immediately afterwards, Wagner continues to see in property one of the roots of all the ills of modern civilization: "Property has been bestowed almost greater sanctity in our national and social conscience than religion." Capitalism also comes in for frank criticism: the invention of money signaled the fall of modern civilization, and "the faith that has disappeared has [been replaced] by 'credit,' this false assumption—that we are honest with each other—which has been maintained in ensuring artfully and rigorously against treachery and loss." Alberich's ring is apostrophized as a "stock exchange portfolio." Criticism of the system of property and capitalism is combined with renewed anti-Semitic attacks. Wagner admits that the Jews were not the inventors of capital ("It was our civilization which invented the art of making money out of nothing"), but he considers them its real exploiters (they are "virtuosi, where we are bunglers"). The idea emerges for the first time in this context that behind all the transient manifestations of civilization lies ultimately an "antagonism of the races," an idea which Wagner had adopted from Gobineau and which then becomes the theme of the third postscript to *Religion and Art* (no. 129). The idea of the global destruction of the Jews is at least alluded to (cf. SSD X, 274).

Remarks on "Religion and Art": Heroism and Christianity (no. 129). The central concern in the third epilogue to *Religion and Art* is the older Wagner's willful racial doctrine, a combination of Schopenhauer's and Gobineau's ideas. Wagner's starting point is the "unity of the human race"; this rests on the "capacity for conscious suffering," which in turn implies an "aptitude for the highest moral development." The antagonism of the races (see no. 128) stems from the variability of this very "capacity for conscious suffering," the "privilege of the white race," in whom this quality is heightened "to a particular degree."

Because of this privilege, the white race was chosen to be the prime mover in a historical process which will ultimately lead mankind from the depths of the will to a state of redemption in which—and this is to some extent an entelechial process—the inequality of the races will be removed. The race has not fulfilled its appointed function but—and this is the real cause of mankind's degeneration—has "founded a thoroughly immoral world order through domination over, and exploitation of the 'lower races.'" Wagner now links this racial doctrine—the height of abstruseness—with his idea of true Christianity: the blood of Christ, transcending all racial differences, is the quintessence of the "capacity for conscious suffering," the "incarnation of that very consciously willing suffering . . . which floods through the whole human race as the original source of divine compassion." Jesus died not "for the interest of a race so favored" but for the whole human race. True Christianity in Wagner's terms therefore offers the only possibility of destroying the antagonism of the races and thus also of the regeneration of mankind. For all its waywardness, this sequence of ideas does make clear how little Wagner's racial doctrine has in common with Gobineau's, and in particular with the ideas of racism and the German fascists, even if they always believed that they had to refer to Wagner.

On the Feminine in the Human (Conclusion to "Religion and Art") (no. 130). The planned fourth and last supplement to *Religion and Art* is given over to a further aspect of Wagner's critique of civilization: the relationship between the sexes and the need for the emancipation of women. The text remains a fragment; Wagner collapsed dying over the manuscript, which he had begun two days previously, at midday on 13 February 1883. The oppression of the woman, whose essence Wagner had defined to Cosima on 28 October 1881 as "sympathy with the male in his struggles against the outside world," is another symptom of the history of mankind's degeneration. Woman is the victim of power structures determined according to masculine principles and reproduction; she is a victim of the system of ownership, in whose interests marriages are arranged ("marriages of social convention based on ownership and property") and families founded. Female emancipation thus also forms part of the regeneration of mankind. The last sentences of the fragment deal with this theme. There are observations on Buddha, who at first wanted women to be "excluded from the possibility of sainthood" but then revised his attitude. "However," Wagner continues, "the process of the emancipation of women only proceeds in ecstatic convulsions." The words that follow are "Love—Tragedy," words whose meaning in this context may be illuminated by a conversation which Cosima records under the date 29 May 1882. The conversation related to Romeo and Juliet, Tristan and Isolde, and the tragic failure of their love: compelled by society—civilization—to marriages of social convention, backed ultimately only by property interests, Romeo and Juliet and Tristan and Isolde have to perish tragically.

Metaphysics. Art and Religion. Morality. Christianity (no. 131). A collection of aphorisms and supplementary remarks to the later writings, in particular to *Religion and Art* and its sequels.

Musical Aesthetics and Drama

On Conducting (no. 132). Wagner, who was himself one of the first star conductors in the history of modern music, draws on the sum of his conducting experience in this much-admired essay, to which Richard Strauss attributed canonical significance. Its maxims and analyses are embedded in his usual complaints about the parlous state of contemporary German music: poor training, insufficient financing, orchestras of inadequate size, promotion within the orchestra "according to the laws of seniority" ("In practice a German musician achieved his 'good position' . . . usually through simple application of the law of inertia: he moved upwards, by degrees"), arbitrary bowing technique, the additional composition of "spectacular endings," and so on. Even Meyerbeer and Mendelssohn had resigned themselves to this situation ("And this was Meyerbeer and Mendelssohn! So what will their dainty emulators be getting up to elsewhere?"). There is the usual polemic against a large number of contemporaries, including Brahms. Wagner gives a central position to the question of the correct tempo: "Its choice and determination immediately shows us whether the conductor has understood the piece of music or not." The correct time, however, is derived from a correct grasp of the *melos:* "Both are indivisible; one determines the other." The conductor's concern, however, should not be for a metronomically rigid reproduction but for the modifications to the main tempi prescribed; everything is subject to the "law of mutual relationships," and "these laws cannot be grasped too subtly or variously." Further key issues are the connection between the correct tempo and the "character of the particular performance of a piece of music," that is, "whether it inclines predominantly to the note that is held (the singing) or to the rhythmic movement (the figuration)"—it is on this contrast that the difference rests between "tempo andante" and "tempo allegro"—and the difference between "two forms of allegro," which Wagner (borrowing from Schiller) calls the naïve (as in Mozart) and the sentimental (as in Beethoven). The "sentimental form of more modern music" is characterized, in comparison to the naïve, as a mixed type: "The held and interrupted note, sustained singing and lively figuration are no longer opposites, kept formally apart—instead they are in direct contact, passing into each other imperceptibly."

Beethoven (no. 133). The publication in 1870—on the occasion of the centenary of Beethoven's birth—of a fictitious "speech at an ideal celebration of the great musician" is not only the most important document of Wagner's lifelong relationship with Beethoven, but also the major aesthetic work of Wagner's later years. The examination starts with a dilemma: Wagner intends in this anniversary year to establish "the relationship of the great artist to the German nation," but he realizes immediately that music, in contrast to poetry and the visual (plastic) arts, which are rooted in the nation and history linguistically and thematically, belong "in equal measure to all humanity" and possess in melody an "absolute language." This leads in the first part of the memorial tribute to a complete reappraisal of musical aesthetics based on the psychology (and metaphysics) of Schopenhauer, and in this framework to a new definition of the interrelationship of the individual arts. Wagner, following Schopenhauer, differentiates two sides of human consciousness, namely the will as "consciousness of oneself" and the "consciousness of other things"; whereas the latter is the "visual perception of the external world, the conception of objects," the will is "turned inwards." This introverted consciousness relates to visual perception as night does to day (it would be possible to develop an interpretation of *Tristan* on this basis); dream to reality (an "organ for dreaming" which achieves "real clarity of vision" while "our waking consciousness, turned in upon the day, feels only the powerful basis of our emotional will"); the sound wave to the light wave ("sound penetrates from this night into actual waking perception, as the direct expression of the will"); hearing to seeing. Whereas visual perception can never perceive more than the "appearance of things" and is based on a contrast between subject and object, the introverted consciousness is direct in character; it allows us "to understand the inner nature of things outside us." Subject and object coincide here: "Accordingly, seeing objects as such leaves us cold and disinterested, and only on becoming aware of the relationships between the objects seen and our will are our emotions stimulated."

In the field of aesthetics the visual arts are related to visual perception whereas music is linked to inner consciousness. The traditional aesthetic stems from visual art and transfers its laws to the other arts ("satisfaction through pure visual pleasure . . . as the criteria for all forms of aesthetic pleasure"), but music has its own rules. The concept of beauty in traditional aesthetics is based on the opposition between seeing (subject) and appearance (object); in music, by contrast, the "object, the perceived note, . . . coincides directly with the subject, the note produced." The visual artist makes the individual will "silent purely through seeing," whereas the musician arouses it to a universal will; he breaks through the "barriers of individuality" and "proclaims . . . himself as the conscious idea of the world." Although visual perception and visual art relate to categories of time and space, music touches "concepts of time" alone; its real element is the "harmony of sounds belonging neither to space nor time." By means of a "rhythmical arrangement" of sounds, however, the musician enters "into contact with the visual, plastic world"; without the "rhythmical sequence" music would "not be perceptible." Melody, the third element in music, is its form. The difference between these two art forms becomes clear in rhythm, however, which is the point of contact between visual art and music, for visual art (generally meaning the three-dimensional arts) "fixes gesture in space" and leaves "the reflecting idea to complement the movement"; music, by contrast, expresses "the inner essence of the gesture with such direct clarity that . . . we finally understand it without seeing it."

This sequence of ideas is supplemented toward the end of the second part of the analysis—after an appreciation of Beethoven's epoch-making significance—by reflections on the relationship of poetry and music, on drama in the Wagnerian sense. It becomes clear here that Wagner's new music aesthetic based on Schopenhauerian philosophy has led to a reevaluation of the views expressed in the Zurich treatises on art. In contrast to comments in *Opera and Drama*, particularly part 3, Wagner now judges "the relationship between music and poetry as a completely illusory one." Poetry can only represent "ideas contained in the phenomena of the world" and thus "make plain to the visual perception," whereas music is "itself an idea of the world," in fact "a comprehensive idea of the world." The poet can at best stimulate the musician; the "combining of music and poetry must therefore constantly lead to such a diminution of the latter, so it is all the more admirable how, in particular, our great German poets constantly reexamined the problem of unifying the two arts—or tried to." "We know," he goes on to state, "that the writer's verse—even if it is Goethe's or Schiller's—is not able to dictate the music." Every attempt to combine dramatic poetry and music must lead to opera, in which ultimately only seeing and hearing (the two sides of human consciousness) are alternately in play. Drama, in Wagner's terms, has nothing to do with poetry but—and here he arrives at a new definition of drama—"jumps . . . the barriers of poetry, just as music jumps all others." Its relationship with music is determined in that it is present a priori: because music "itself is an idea of the world," it "embraces drama in itself." It is to some extent an expression of this "agreed idea of the world which is equated to music." It is not the dramatic poem which is intended, however, but "drama which really moves before our eyes," a "counterpart of music given visible form, in which word and speech belong only to the plot and no longer to the poetic concept." This argument fits in with the definition of the drama in the essay *On the Term "Musikdrama"* (no. 185) as "acts of music made visible."

Within this aesthetic, for music just as for drama, Wagner now tries to establish Beethoven's epoch-making historical significance. He does this in three ways. Whereas music developed over the centuries exclusively "in the degrees in which the external side of music turned itself to the visual world"— that is, developed in particular—"a systematic edifice, its rhythmic period structure" and thus became part of an analogy with the pictorial arts, Beethoven penetrated through these "conventional forms" to the "innermost essence of music in the manner . . . in which he was again able to cast the inner light of the far-seeing, in order also to show these forms again in accordance with their inner meaning." In addition—and this is the second point—Beethoven raised the status of music, which in Germany (here Wagner makes his usual complaint about the cultural situation) had descended merely into a "pleasurable art . . . from its most special essence . . . to the pinnacle of its noble calling" and thus established a visible symbol. Wagner includes Beethoven in a series with Lessing, Goethe, and Schiller, seeing here the only possible answer to the question he first posed as to Beethoven's relationship with the German nation: for Wagner, Beethoven is an example of how "the German spirit redeems the spirit of mankind from deep disgrace." Beethoven is the consummate dramatist among musicians—not as an opera composer ("What is the dramatic plot of the text of the opera *Leonore* other than an almost hateful dilution of the drama experienced in the overture, a little like a boringly intoned commentary by Gervinus rather than a scene from Shakespeare") but, and here Wagner is fully consistent with his earlier writings, as a symphonist. The dramatist Beethoven is characterized by a kindredness of spirit with Shakespeare, for whom it is also "impossible to draw an analogy with any poet": "If we capture the complexity of Shakespeare's world, with the uncommon fullness of the characters contained in it and affecting each other, in an overall impression on our inner feelings, and compare it with the same complex in Beethoven's world of motifs with its irresistible insistence and certainty, then we cannot fail to notice that one of these worlds covers the other completely so that each is contained in the other." The third part of the tribute consists of Wagner's stereotypical complaint about contemporary (musical) culture, the "caprices of Parisian taste," all-powerful fashion, and so on. Wagner contrasts this civilization with its characteristics of degeneracy and decline, with the redeeming power of music: music, he says, "bursts . . . out of the chaos of modern civilization" and "neutralizes it, as daylight does to lamplight."

On the Destiny of Opera (no. 134). This paper, which was completed in March 1871, was presented on 28 April of the same year before members of the Royal Academy of Arts in Berlin. Wagner again summarizes his idea of "musically conceived drama," as he now calls it (cf. no. 185), and he does this (while recalling to some extent *Opera and Drama,* particularly parts 1 and 2) with reference to the new conception of drama contained in the *Beethoven* festschrift. His description certainly does point out several new aspects of this idea. Initially it involves a reassessment of the two forms of the modern play, which Wagner differentiates in part 2 of *Opera and Drama,* as the classical "literature drama" (the closed form) and Shakespearean drama (the open form). In examining classical literature drama Wagner takes as his point of departure the terms *emotionalism* and *purpose.* He distinguishes between the "naive poet of the old world" and the "modern cultural poet," who "uses the forms of naive poetry only to make philosophical theses understood in a popular, abstract sense." In this way literature drama replaces the "effect of the directly observed living picture" (as in ancient tragedy, for example) with "purpose." Its means of expression is a "poetical-rhetorical style" and its effect "poetic emotionalism." Wagner sees this reduction of drama to rhetoric and emotionalism as the real historical error of literature drama—even of the great classics of Lessing, Goethe, and Schiller. In the "dramatic conceptions of our lesser theater writers" this poetic emotionalism changes abruptly into bathos, the secret of which lies in effect (see the definition of *effect* in *Opera and Drama*). He contrasts "emotional literature drama" of recent times (Wagner calls a "complete history of theatrical 'emotionalism'" essential) with Shakespeare's theater. For him Shakespeare (as he maintained in the *Beethoven* festschrift) was not a poet but, like Lope de Vega, Molière, and Aeschylus, an "actor and impresario." He defines Shakespeare's drama, in contrast to modern literature drama, as "fixed mimic improvisation of the very highest poetic worth." Shakespeare is the dramatist par excellence and as such stands "apart from the real poet, and the actor himself, from whose real nature he must step forth if he wishes to "hold his mirror up to life" like a poet.

Wagner had already commented similarly in 1867 in *German Art and German Politics* (no. 121) on the nature of theatrical art and its character, which is realistic (by way of the actor) and idealistic (by way of the writer) at the same time. Whereas in *Opera and Drama* open-form Shakespearean drama is classified as close to the bourgeois novel in the same way as closed-form, classical literature drama was classified as a historical error, it now becomes an important basis for Wagner's idea of musically conceived drama. The other point of departure is in his thoughts on opera. Opera too now appears in a gentler light. This much-abused genre (see part 1 of *Opera and Drama,* as well as the *Beethoven* essay) has, we now read, "shown up the decline of the theater," but it did not cause this decline. In fact, it "can be seen very clearly from its present dominant influence that opera alone can be called upon to restore our theater." That, precisely, is the "destiny of opera" referred to in the title—but not, of course, in its historical (and obsolete) repertoire form. It is because of the "power of music" that opera carries this destiny within it. This became clear in the music of Beethoven, which is marked by the same "immediacy of presentation" as Shakespeare's drama and which has to some extent an improvisational character. Wagner thus carries on where he left off in the *Beethoven* festschrift. His idea of musically conceived drama (the description stresses the dominant, active role of music) therefore—and this is the new definition—proves to be the "heightening" of theatrical mime (conceived in a similar way to Shakespeare's drama) through the medium of Beethoven's symphonies. Wagner defines this idea as "mimic-theatrical improvisation of accomplished poetic value brought about through the highest artistic thoughtfulness."

On Actors and Singers (no. 135). In this piece Wagner continues the reflections contained in his lecture to the Berlin Academy of Arts (no. 134) on the nature of acting. The desired reform of the drama as well as the theater system requires new principles for the actor's and the opera singer's art, based on the "mimic" as it is understood (as the art of improvisation) not only in Shakespearean drama, which goes beyond the literary, but also in the subliterary "Punch and Judy shows in our fairs": "The most lowly genre is the only place left in Germany where good theater is played." Wagner's report of a Punch and Judy production in Heidelberg (see Cosima's note dated 14 May 1871) is one of the highlights of the treatise, which is rich in anecdotes: "In the player of this puppet theater and his quite incomparable performances—with which he held me breathless, while the public from the street seemed to forget their daily routine in their passionate interest in him—the spirit of the theater came alive for me once again for the first time for ages. Here the improvisor was writer, director and actor at the same time, and his magic brought the poor puppets to life before me with the truthfulness of inexhaustibly eternal folk characters."

On the Performance of Beethoven's Ninth Symphony (no. 136). Wagner gives an account of his experiences at a performance on 22 May 1872 in the margravial opera house in Bayreuth on the laying of the foundation stone of the Festival Theater. His premise is that Beethoven, unlike Haydn and Mozart, who conceived their works on the basis of the abilities of their orchestra, orchestrated his works not only within a historically given framework, but also went "immeasurably far" beyond this limitation "in the nature of his musical conceptions." On this basis Wagner justifies a series of interventions in the score he has made, using as his prime criteria clarity and the "safeguarding of melody."

Public and Popularity (no. 137). In this tract from August 1878 Wagner makes a generalized attack on the German public, "brought up among the mediocre and the bad." He goes so far as to claim that the "workshops of what is good in art" lie "far from the actual public," and that "nothing good would ever come about . . . if from now on it was taken into account when performing to an audience." His polemic is aimed in particular at the "popular" academic types of the Prussian-German Empire, both the students ("with their children's caps on one side of their head, in jackboots, carrying before them their swelling beer-bellies") and the teachers (with a dig in passing at Nietzsche, whose *Human, all too Human* had appeared in May 1878).

The Public in Time and Space (no. 138). In this essay Wagner uses the "fate of Liszt's music" as the basis of an examination of the importance of space and time (the environment in terms of the age and the world) in how literary and musical works are received. He approaches this question by citing the examples of Plato, Dante, and Calderón, as well as Attic tragedy and Mozart's operas. He reaches two conclusions. First, factors of time and space dictate "the fate of great geniuses to the extent . . . that their influence—if it is understood at all in their lifetime—has no effect on higher intellectual life, and it is left to a posterity which has gained in true knowledge as a result of their guidance (which remained incomprehensible to contemporaries) to grasp the true sense of their revelations." According to Wagner, for example, in the history of his reception Dante was recognized as being exceptionally great only after the "reality of the medieval spectre of faith" that bound his contemporary public had lost its power and the "elevated mind of the poet" could be seen as a "world judge of ideal purity." But second, "attempts to revive . . . Attic tragedy in our theaters" show how great works of art which were once the perfect expression of their time and were received as such can become over the centuries "completely alien" until they are accessible only through the mediation of scholars, "who actually do not understand anything about" them. The fact that Liszt's symphonic poems found only hesitant acceptance was a consequence of the "laziness" of the German public: "Anyone who is familiar with German concertgoers and their heroes, from the general to the corporal, knows the kind of mutual society for talentlessness he is dealing with here."

On Poetry and Composition (no. 139). The three writings from 1879 on this theme (nos. 139–141) are variations, maintaining in part an informal tone reminiscent of the Paris feuilletons, of individual sections of *Opera and Drama,* especially parts 1 and 2. The first of these three is really nothing more than a collection of witty aperçus. The second essay, *On Opera Poetry and Composition in Particular* (no. 140), contains for the most part detailed investigations of the relationship between the text and the music in the German operas of Marschner and Weber, as well as in Beethoven and Rossini ("Rossini received a lot of abuse: but it was only his originality that annoyed us"). The third piece, *On the Application of Music to the Drama* (no. 141), deals again with symphonic composition (instrumental music) as the starting point for Wagnerian drama. The central element—which Wagner explains with examples from the *Ring*—is the technique of motifs; Wagner is less interested in Hans von Wolzogen's leitmotifs and "their dramatic significance and effect" than in their "use in building musical composition," the multiple linking of themes, their variations, and their interrelationships.

Letter to H. von Stein (no. 142). Wagner's last completed written work (dating from 31 January 1883), a letter to the philosopher Heinrich von Stein which was intended as an introduction to his book *Heroes and the World: Dramatic Sketches,* contains reflections on seeing and being silent and a final definition of drama. Being silent is the "only possible reconciliation of the seeing person" with a world in which "there is not a decade which is not filled almost totally with the shame of the human race": "It seems very easy to talk about the things of this world because everybody talks about them. But to portray them in such a way that they speak for themselves is only given to the few." What is needed is silence: only out of "seeing silence" does "the power to portray what is seen develop." It was from silent seeing that Shakespeare created his world, namely drama, which "is not a form of poetry but the mirror of the world reflected from our silent soul."

Theater Reform and Bayreuth
Report to His Majesty the King Ludwig II of Bavaria Concerning a German School of Music to Be Established in Munich (no. 143). The last of Wagner's great petitions on the reform of art and music was finished on 23 March 1865 and appeared in print in the same year. Ludwig II had asked Wagner for his suggestions on reforming the Munich Royal Conservatoire of Music. Wagner starts by seeing a problem in the term *Conservatoire*: it is the function of such an institution to "conserve" a classic style of performance; but as there is no German performing style, an institution of this kind (unlike in France or Italy,

with the style-forming conservatoires in Paris, Milan, and Naples) is condemned to redundancy and failure. He then quickly turns to the issue that concerns him, namely the realization of the festival idea which he first formulated in 1863 (see no. 83). He calls on the king to construct an ideal theater for the performance of the *Ring* cycle (it is here that the idea of an unseen orchestra appears for the first time), from which "a genuinely valid style for the performance of works of decidedly German originality can be founded." As this particularly gifted and well-educated performer stipulates, however, what is first needed is the "founding of a suitably organized singing school."

In a digression Wagner again presents his ideas on the art of German singing (see nos. 2 and 3). What he has in mind, as before, is a careful adaptation of the "Italian school" to the peculiarities of the German language. He is looking for a "proper development of singing on the basis of the German language," a language "with generally short and mute vowels which can only be extended at the expense of clarity of meaning, hampered by admittedly highly expressive consonants which are, however, piled up utterly regardless of all harmony," and to which the "model of Italian singing" cannot be applied directly. The risk of "stunting harmonious singing" is to be counteracted by a "thoughtful study of Italian singing." In addition to singing instruction in the narrow sense, Wagner calls for comprehensive teaching in music, speaking technique, voice development, gymnastics, and the "development of a vivid technique and acting ability." He suggests as a second stage the expansion of the singing school into a "general music school"; the third stage would then be its further development into a "theater school." The decision on the order could be taken by the festival theater itself, an institution to which "the German nation can return at a particular time every year and the best and finest works of its masters are produced in an exemplary fashion, which from then on—if the manner of the production sufficiently justifies it—could be passed on to other theater institutions in Germany for more frequent repeat performances using the same model." This kind of festival theater would thus be a "monument to the German artistic spirit."

Report to the German Wagner Society on the Circumstances and Fate Which Accompanied the Composition of the Stage Festival Play "The Ring of the Nibelung" (no. 144). In his 1871 report Wagner first gives an overview of the creative history of the *Ring* tetralogy. His indication of a structural connection between the Siegfried and Tristan myths is interesting here: "Their consistent similarity lies, however, in the fact that Tristan, like Siegfried, marries a woman intended for another in ancient law through deception, making this act an unfree one, and finds his downfall as a consequence of the resulting mismatch." The second part is devoted to the idea of a festival.

The Stage Festival Theater in Bayreuth (no. 145). A letter to Marie von Schleinitz (dated 1 May 1873) is followed by Wagner's account of the laying of the foundation stone for the Festival Theater, for which, in his festival address, he expressly rejects the name National Theater in Bayreuth ("Where might this nation be that built itself this theater?" he asked in 1872, one year after the founding of the Prussian–German Empire). Wagner then goes into the qualities of his theater house: the unseen orchestra, the amphitheater style, the lack of boxes, the "mystical abyss" which "is there to divide the real from the ideal." Between the spectator "and the scene which is to appear there is nothing clearly noticeable, merely a distance between the two prosceniums which is held 'in suspension,' as it were, through the architecture. The scene, which is thus at one remove from the spectator, has the inaccessibility of a dream, while the ghostly sounding music from the 'mystical abyss' . . . puts him into an enraptured state of clear-sightedness in which the scene watched now becomes for him the most faithful reproduction of life itself." The account is accompanied by six architectural plans.

A Look Back at the 1876 Stage Festivals (no. 146). Wagner makes a careful assessment of the first festivals ("Was I expected to repeat them?"). The main point of the report is to thank his collaborators, particularly Otto Brückwald (the architect of the Festival Theater), Karl Brandt and Joseph Hoffmann (stage manager and designer respectively), Albert Niemann (Siegmund), Karl Hill (Alberich), Gustav Siehr (Hagen), Franz Betz (Wotan), and Hans Richter (the conductor of the performances): "There was a fine, deeply enthusiastic will about everything here."

The "Devotional Stage Festival" in Bayreuth in 1882 (no. 147). Wagner comments in retrospect on the production criteria which governed the premiere of *Parsifal* under his overall guidance at the second festival in 1882. He is again speaking as an opera director here (see also nos. 84, 85, and 87). He starts by discussing singing, and in doing so rejects all forms of expressive singing ("The impassioned style which has become a characteristic of opera singers in contemporary theater, where every line of melody is usually run through without variation, should never be heard here"). Clarity and melody are for him the supreme and equal principles of the art of singing (see no. 136 on these principles). It is precisely at dramatic points that he expects his singers to show appropriate reticence—both "in the use of the breath and in life-like movement." The highest law with regard to the actor's gestures and movements is economy: "In those places where we had become accustomed in opera to acting the passions with outstretched arms as though calling for help, we were to find that a half lift of an arm, even a characteristic movement of the hand, the head, is quite enough." Movements should ultimately be dependent on the "liveliness of the dialogue." The principle of "solemn simplicity" applies for costumes and decor.

A series of shorter occasional writings and documents on Bayreuth and the *Bayreuther Blätter* follows. No. 148, *To the Presidents of Wagner Societies,* dated 1 January 1877, is a call for the formation of a "Patrons' Association for the fostering and maintenance of the Stage Festivals at Bayreuth," to which Wagner attributes the function of a "university for dramatic and musical interpretation" with a role in developing a style (see no. 143). *Prospectus Published with the Statutes of the Patronatverein* (no. 149) is a program (dated 15 September 1877) for the Bayreuth "School of Style" (see no. 148) for the years 1878–1883. *Introduction to the First Number of the "Bayreuther Blätter"* (no. 150) is Wagner's foreword to the first issue of the *Bayreuther Blätter,* which, after the failure of the School of Style, was intended to serve as "communications within the Association" (meaning the Patronatverein) with no further pretensions. In number 151, *A Word of Introduction to Hans von Wolzogen's "On the Decline and Restoration of the German Language,"* Wagner complains about the lack of willingness of "serious-minded musicians" to collaborate on the *Bayreuther Blätter* so that "for the time being those of my friends who splendidly feel called to address their full attention only to the further cultural objective behind my efforts are taking care of . . . the bulletin side." Number 152 is the *Announcement to the Members of the Patronatverein,* dated 15 July 1879. The festival performances which had originally been planned for 1880 had to be postponed, as did the "establishing of the anticipated practice of periodically repeating the stage festival plays." *Introduction to the Year 1880* (no. 153) is Wagner's merciless reckoning with the culture and cultural policy of the Prussian-German Empire (dated Christmas 1879). According to no. 154, *To the Honored Patrons of the Stage Festivals at Bayreuth,* dated 1 December 1880, *Parsifal* was to be premiered in 1882 in a production reserved for Bayreuth (see no. 209). No. 155 is *Introduction to Count Gobineau's "Ethnological Résumé of the Present Aspect of the World."* As in the writings on *Religion and Art,* here Wagner also links a racial doctrine, inspired perhaps by Gobineau (Gobineau "tested the blood in the blood of mankind and must have found it irreparably corrupt"), with his interpretations of "true Christianity" as the religion of compassion, from whose redemption alone regeneration could come. No. 156, the *Letter to H. von Wolzogen,* dated 13 March 1882, concerns the dissolution of the Patronatverein, which had fulfilled its purpose with the forthcoming 1882 festival. The stage festivals were to take place annually henceforth and thereby take over the function of the "school for the style founded by me." The *Bayreuther Blätter* is to continue as an independent publication. No. 157, *Open Letter to Herr Friedrich Schön in Worms,* dated 16 June 1882, is a call to found a new Patronatverein, which would enable needy people to attend festival performances. After the "patron of the work of art" we now had the "patron of the public."

Several documents were gathered together in SSD XII and XVI under the heading "On the History of the Work of Bayreuth." They include *To the Patrons of the Stage Festivals in Bayreuth* (no. 158), dated 30 August 1873. Financial difficulties at the outset of the first festival (planned for 1875) prompted Wagner to invite the patrons to Bayreuth on 1 October 1873. In no. 159, *Essential Announcement,* dated 16 February 1874, Wagner vetoes concert performances of extracts from *Die Walküre* in light of the festival. In *The Press on Rehearsals,* (no. 160), dated 1875, Wagner dismisses negative reports in the press of the rehearsals which took place in 1875. *To the Honored Patrons of the 1876 Stage Festivals* (no. 161), dated 11 October 1876, is an appeal to the patrons to make good the deficit following the "successful" conclusion of the festival. No. 162 is Wagner's *Speech to the Delegates of the Bayreuth Patronat* (taken down in shorthand by Franz Munckler), during discussions in Bayreuth on 15 September 1877 on the continuation of the festivals. *Announcement of the Production of "Parsifal"* (no. 163), dated 8 December 1877, announces, among other things, the *Bayreuther Blätter* and the world premiere of *Parsifal* (set for 1880). *Founding of the Festival, the Patronat, and the Wagner Societies* (no. 164), *On the Laying of the Foundation Stone* (no. 165), *On the First Festival in 1876* (no. 166), and *On the Second Festival in 1882* (no. 167) are documents on various aspects of the festivals from Wagner's pen.

Short Occasional Pieces and Articles

Among Wagner's obituaries and dedications of this period is no. 168, *My Recollections of Ludwig Schnorr von Carolsfeld,* in which he pays tribute to the first singer to portray Tristan (on 10, 13, and 19 June and 1 July 1865 in Munich) and who died unexpectedly shortly afterward in Dresden on 21 July 1865. Wagner refers to Ludwig Schnorr von Carolsfeld as an exceptional singer and actor who set new standards with his portrayals of Tannhäuser and Tristan.

No. 169, *Fragment of an Essay on Berlioz,* is an introduction to an abandoned obituary of the composer, who died on 8 March 1869: "It is easy to give a fair assessment if artistic merit alone is not hard to judge. This becomes a most difficult task, however, if the impact of this artist appears equally unclear both to his contemporaries and to posterity, yet the excellent qualities of the artist himself have to be recognized as beyond question." No. 170 is *On the Dedication of the Second Edition of "Opera and Drama" to Constantin Frantz,* the "conservative federalist" (*Quid faciamus nos?* 1856; *Studies of the Balance in Europe,* 1859). Wagner attempts to rework his anarchistic views on the "destruction of the state" as the indispensable precondition for the artwork of the future (see part 2 of *Opera and Drama*) by linking them with Frantz's idea of a central European federal system, which, in the tradition of the medieval empire, would be an open and flexible political grouping—not a state but an "institution of public peace." Frantz, who rejected a national German state, called this federation the German Empire. Wagner takes up this concept in these terms. His subsequent rejection of Bismarck's empire (nos. 122 and 127) is prefigured here.

Reminiscences of Auber (no. 171). In this obituary Wagner refers to his encounters with Auber, who died in Paris on 12 May 1871 at the age of eighty-nine, praising in particular his opera *La muette de Portici* (premiered in 1828) as a musical drama of the highest order: "a 'great opera,' a full five-act tragedy, entirely in music." "Each of the five acts shows a graphic picture of the most uncommon vividness, in which arias and duets in the usual operatic sense are hardly to be seen and, with the exception of a prima donna's aria in the first act, hardly worked as such." He mentions in particular the "unusual conciseness and vivid compression of form": "The recitatives thundered down on us like thunderbolts; it moved from them to the choral ensembles like in a storm and amid the raging chaos suddenly the energetic exhortations to calm, or renewed appeals; then again frantic jubilation, murderous turmoil and in between once more a moving, fearful supplication, or a whole people whispering its prayers." Wagner sees the French people's spirit as alive in this work: Auber's music has raised this spirit "to the highest glory possible for it, like the revolution persuading the can-can dancing guttersnipe onto the barricade in order to have him boldly challenge the murderous bullet there, draped in the tricolore." He also defines the role of *La muette de Portici* in the July revolution of 1830.

Wagner's reviews include in particular the collection of *Notices* in the SSD. In *Notices I: W. H. Riehl* (no. 172) Wagner interprets the novellas of Wilhelm Heinrich Riehl (1823–1897), cultural historian and father of German folklore (*Cultural-Historical Novellas,* 1856; *New Book of Novellas: Stories from Olden Times,* 1862–1865), as typical products of the German idyll in the period of the Restoration: "The German, decaying in lowly circumstances and prevented from any kind of power at every step," was able, "pushed by unhelpfulness into helplessness, pressurized into a sphere of narrow bourgeois influence," only "to shape the world entrusted to him into an idyll, and to declare in frequently moving variations that he is happy and requires nothing of his idyll." Wagner accuses Riehl of playing down social pressure ("Real, genuine innocence—oh! what a source of all that is sublime!"). A supplement from 1872 relates to Riehl's *Music's Expressive Features* (written after 1853, not concluded until 1877). Wagner argues against Riehl's call for German composers to return to the naiveté of older music and to write in a less reflective manner.

No. 173, *Notices II: Ferdinand Hiller,* is a confused polemic against Hiller, whose two-volume work *From the Musical Life of Our Time* (1867) Wagner denigrates as "feuilleton nonsense." In *Notices III: Recollections of Rossini* (no. 174) Wagner gives an account of his encounters in Paris in 1860 and 1861 with Rossini, who died on 18 November 1868. Obviously greatly impressed by Rossini's nobility and internationalism, Wagner objects that his relationship with the master of Italian opera is being used in polemics, and particularly as the subject of jokes. Wagner praises Rossini as the representative of a certain cultural-historical era: "In the same way as Palestrina, Bach and Mozart belonged to their own time, so does Rossini belong to his." Where criticisms are to be made of Rossini (see, for example, part 1 of *Opera and Drama*), they should be leveled "not at his talent nor his artistic conscience, but simply at his audience and his environment, which made it more difficult for him to rise above his age and thereby to share in the greatness of true artistic heroes."

Notices IV: Eduard Devrient (no. 175). Wagner argues against Devrient's book *My Recollections of Felix Mendelssohn-Bartholdy,* which appeared in 1868, the publication of which, twenty-one years after Mendelssohn's death, he considers superfluous. He criticizes especially the use of numerous supporting quotations and the book's "quite unbelievably clumsy style." Wagner rejects the "Hamlet-like tragedy in Mendelssohn's operatic destiny" which Devrient regrets ("We, for our part," Wagner writes, "regret that we are seldom able to cite three words by the author without coming up with something non-sensical").

Notices V: Elucidation of "Judaism in Music" (no. 176). In the letter to Marie Muchanoff of 1 January 1869, presented as a preface to the second edition in book form of the essay *Judaism in Music* (no. 66), Wagner tries to justify this new edition. He sees himself as the helpless victim of a growing conspiracy of international Jewry (supposedly the cause of the failure of *Tannhäuser* in Paris in 1861) and worldwide "Jewish agitation." After Meyerbeer and Mendelssohn it is now the turn of Jacques Offenbach and Eduard Hanslick to come in for vilification. Hanslick's epochal work *On Musical Beauty* (1854) is denounced as mere propaganda in the interest of "musical Judaism." In this work Hanslick has "raised the beauty of Jewish music into a complete dogma . . . and achieved the tacit acceptance of this dogma completely imperceptibly, adding Mendelssohn to the line of Haydn, Mozart and Beethoven as if it was quite natural." Wagner retracts the closing passage of the 1850 essay, which forms part of the historical context of arguments involving Young Germany, on the emancipation of the Jews (see no. 66). He now contemplates "the forcible ejection of the corrupting foreign element." The second edition of the notorious pamphlet thus manifests a clarity which—unlike the 1850 version—leaves no doubt as to the malice in Wagner's anti-Semitism (cf. the quite different tone in no. 178, however). Wagner added a preface to the collection of *Notices* in SSD VIII, in which he prepares his reader for the polemical tone of the texts.

Several other brief writings belong in the context of the *Notices* by virtue of their content (see nos. 173 and 176). In *Observations on an Alleged Comment by Rossini* (no. 177) Wagner applies a dictum by Rossini, reported by Hiller, to Hiller's opera *Der Advokat* (1855): "If the magic of the notes has really enchanted the listener, the word will certainly always come off second best. But if the music fails to hit home then what use is it? It is then unnecessary, or becomes superfluous or even intrusive." No. 178 is *On "Judaism in Music."* After a successful production of *Lohengrin* in Berlin, Karl Tausig, Wagner's young Jewish friend, had telegraphed Wagner that *Lohengrin* had made the Jews forgive him again (the second edition of the defamatory *Judaism in Music* had appeared shortly before; see no. 176). In his letter of reply, dated April 1869, Wagner claims that he had been misunderstood ("It really would be no bad thing if my pamphlet was only read really by clever and sophisticated Jews, but it seems now that nobody can read any more"), and he calls the piece "the corpus delicti, which for me comes under the statute of limitations," two statements which are at best incomprehensible in view of the *Elucidation of "Judaism in Music"* (no. 176). Furthermore, he does not expect "forgiveness" from the Jews ("I have already experienced an uncommon amount of good naturedness from Jews"—and so he had). Instead, he expects a "really sophisticated Jew" to give "to this whole question a great and positive new turn, but who will himself give an extremely important position to our most important cultural affairs"—whatever that might mean. No. 179, *Open Letter to Dr. Friedrich Stade,* dated 31 December 1870, is Wagner's letter of thanks to the Leipzig musicologist for sending a polemical piece against Hanslick's work on musical aesthetics, *Beauty in Music.*

Among the shorter writings on various subjects are the collected "Open Letters and Shorter Essays" in SSD. The *Letter on Acting to an Actor* (no. 180), dated 9 November 1872, to Ernst Gettke, an actor from Kassel, is connected with the essay *On Actors and Singers* (no. 135), written shortly before. Wagner explains the essence of the art of acting in terms of (Dionysian) ecstasy. Unlike Greek tragedy, in which "in the few ceremonial cases" any educated person could be an actor, Wagner sees the danger in more recent professional acting of the "degradation of artistic performances which are required every day, through the dulling and weakening of the power of the state of ecstasy in which each should proceed." This danger can be combatted only by "doing justice to the . . . task to be resolved in the dramatic work," through an "ideal truthfulness" which shows up the "vanity" of daily routine in the theater. Wagner is skeptical of the possibility of teaching acting at appropriate schools ("I believe rather that real actors would only be able to learn among themselves"). He also recommends "improvisations of scenes and whole plays," because "the basis and crux of all acting talent lies without doubt in improvising" (see also nos. 134 and 135).

A Look at German Opera Today (no. 181). This is Wagner's detailed report of his visit with Cosima to theaters in the provinces from 10 November to 15 December 1872 to acquire artistic personnel for the planned first festival. It contains a merciless judgment on the routine operation of German opera houses. In witnessing productions in, for example, Würzburg (*Don Giovanni*), Frankfurt (*Le prophète*), Mannheim (*Tannhäuser*), Mainz (*Fidelio*), Cologne (*Die Zauberflöte*), Bremen (*Die Meistersinger*), and Dessau (*Orfeo ed Euridice*), he established that it was not just his works which suffered from inadequate performance conditions. In fact "the same inability to achieve what is right in performance" was to be found "in every type of opera music, in Mozart's just as in Meyerbeer's." Among other things Wagner criticizes the lack of production; arbitrary bowing technique; the singers' lack of training; and especially the inadequacy of the conducting ("this utterly worthless German conducting, which remains inviolate moreover because of life-long appointments and carefully maintained coteries of city families, often holding on to incompetent people for some fifty years") and the conductors' inability to direct the singers correctly and to inspire them to perform to the extent of their talents and range; the use of the wrong tempi; insufficient familiarity generally with the work to be performed ("our practitioners of opera no longer know anything of the actual text, i.e. the actual, real content of a work"); a lack of vision as to the all-important "effect of the whole"; and finally, the "dull insensibility" of the audience, who get themselves up "in amazing luxury" ("Everything was magnificent in velvet and gold") and simply expect "the singer to sing something nice." Wagner's maxim for conductors is "in opera heed, if you are otherwise good musicians, only what happens on the stage . . .; your principal endeavor should be that this series of events, heightened and spiritualized through involvement with the music, achieves the 'fullest clarity.' If you achieve this clarity you can be assured that you have instinctively produced both the right tempo and the right performance from the orchestra." Wagner praises only a production of Gluck's *Orfeo* in Dessau: "I declare out loud that I have never experienced a more refined or perfect overall performance in a theater."

Letter to a Friend on the Production of "Lohengrin" in Bologna (no. 182). In a letter to Arrigo Boito (not named in SSD) on 7 November 1871 Wagner reacts to the success of the production of *Lohengrin* in Bologna on 1 November, the first performance of a Wagnerian work in Italy. In addition to the typical complaint about the inadequacy of productions on the German stage, the letter also contains hints of Wagner's cautious rapprochement with Italian opera, particularly Bellini (see the earlier writings, above all nos. 4, 7, and 8). Bellini, whom he had spared his polemics even during his bitterest quarrel with Italian opera (see, for example, *Opera and Drama*), now appears to Wagner the incarnation of "frankly revelatory, sensitive artistic receptivity in every way" and the representative "through the strange century of Italian decadence with its castrato-type singing and pirouetting" of that "productive spirit of the people . . . to which the new world owes all its art since the Renaissance." Wagner doubts the possibility—a surprising statement to be making in 1871—of a rebirth of art on national lines alone ("although we still have a longing, reminding us of the fact that we do not embrace the whole essence of art") and hopes for a "new congress" of the "genius of peoples." He evaluates the success of his *Lohengrin* in Bologna in these terms, as a symbolic "love match" "which would marry the genius of Italy with that of Germany."

Letter to the Burgomaster of Bologna (no. 183). This is Wagner's letter of thanks of 1 October 1872 for the conferment of honorary citizenship following the spectacular success in Bologna of *Lohengrin* (see no. 182). In this letter he again expounds on his relationship with Italian opera. He links—and this is not in itself a new idea—the criticized virtuosity and the cult of the prima donna with courtly absolutism, which has kept "Italy no less than Germany in a state of impotence and fragmentation." He sees at the same time, however, in the shared historical past and in the shared battle against historical circumstances the preconditions for a future "marriage of Italian with German genius" (see also the very similar statement in no. 182) under the banner of freedom, or "Libertas" (an allusion to the city of Bologna's coat of arms).

To Friedrich Nietzsche, Professor of Classical Philology at Basel University (no. 184). In this letter to Nietzsche, dated 12 June 1872, Wagner attacks the philological criticism of Nietzsche's *Birth of Tragedy,* and in particular Ulrich von Wilamowitz-Möllendorf's reply, *Philology of the Future* (1872). He combines the polemic against Wilamowitz with a fundamental attack on philology, which he criticizes—comparing it with French academicism—as sterile and abstract: "As a consequence it is only philologists themselves who instruct each other and presumably for the sole purpose of teaching other philologists, that is to say only high school teachers and university professors, who then can do no more than train other high school teachers and university professors. I can understand that; the point here is to uphold the purity of science and to keep the state in such awe of this science that it feels honor bound constantly to grant large salaries for philology professors etc." Wagner exhorts Nietzsche to use his professorship to revive German education.

On the Term "Musikdrama" (no. 185). Wagner rejects the term *Musikdrama* for his work (it was coined by Theodor Mundt in his essay *On Opera, Drama, and Melodrama in Their Relationship to Each Other and to the Theater*, which appeared in the periodical *Blätter für Literarische Unterhaltung* in 1831): *Musikdrama* means "drama in the service of the music," exactly the opposite of what he, Wagner, intends (see part 1 of *Opera and Drama*; Wagner's linguistic analysis is not convincing, incidentally). For similar reasons Wagner rejects the term *musical drama*, which he himself used at first. He describes his dramas as "acts of music made visible"—a phrase which suggests the new concept of the synthesis of the arts defined in the tribute *Beethoven* in 1870 (no. 133)—and finally he gives up suggesting a term of his own, adding sardonically that the description *opera* was not judged suitable by his critics. He commends his works as "nameless artistic acts." In *Prologue to a Reading of "Götterdämmerung" before a Select Audience in Berlin* (no. 186), the introductory remarks to the reading of *Götterdämmerung* in Berlin on 17 January 1873, Wagner again summarizes in a few paragraphs his idea of a musical drama as set out in *Opera and Drama*.

In terms of subject matter the open letters and shorter essays lead us to *On an Opera Production in Leipzig* (no. 187). This letter to the editor of the *Musikalishes Wochenblatt*, Ernst Wilhelm Fritzsch, begins with a detailed examination of the function of musical publications: "Who reads such music papers? Who is influenced and governed by even the best of the opinions expressed in them?" The professional musician is concerned only as to whether he is praised or not, while the public are not interested in "thoroughly complex and philosophically elucidatory" dissertations. This is followed by a detailed review of a production of Spohr's *Jessonda* in Leipzig (on 20 December 1874). Wagner once again expresses his views—completely within the spirit of the earliest writings (see nos. 1 and 10)—on the problem of German opera. For Wagner, the inadequacies of the production being criticized are accordingly "the inevitable result of the peculiarly immature operatic genre which 'opera' has developed into here in Germany." No. 188, *Report on the Revival of an Early Work,* is a review, dated 31 December 1882, submitted to Fritzsch, of a performance at the Teatro Fenice on 24 December 1882 (the evening before Cosima's birthday) of the Symphony in C Major (WWV 29), which had originated exactly half a century before. The review contains affable reminiscences of Mendelssohn (Wagner reports being "surprised at the excellence of the achievements of this master, who was so young at that time").

Wagner's statements to the press of this period include *A Reply to the Essay*

"*Richard Wagner and Public Opinion*" (no. 189), his circumspect reply to an article in the Augsburg *Allgemeine Zeitung* on 19 February 1865, written by Oskar Freiherr von Redwitz-Schmölz, the author of the Catholic-conservative verse novel *Amaranth* (1849) and a Bavarian senator. He had criticized Wagner as an "occasional man of the barricades" who misuses his position as the king's favorite and "puts himself between the people of Bavaria and its king." Wagner ripostes—incorrectly, without a doubt—that he was working in Munich "under the terms of a contract" on the completion of the *Ring* tetralogy, for which he had received privileges which "had not exceeded what Bavarian kings had already granted in respect of similar commissions for works of art and science." "Entitled, therefore, to regard myself not as a favorite but as an artist who is well-paid entirely in keeping with his work, I believe first of all that I do not have to give an account to anyone of the employment I put my earnings to, as though I had to excuse myself for having found the same appropriate reward for my work that painters, sculptors, architects, scholars etc. have found on many occasions."

In *The Munich Court Theater* (no. 190) Wagner responds to an article in the Augsburg *Allgemeine Zeitung* of 6 September 1869 in which he was criticized by an anonymous writer—clearly, however, someone close to the manager of the Munich Hoftheater, Karl von Perfall—for his refusal to collaborate on the planned world premiere of *Das Rheingold* (the dress rehearsal was held on 25 August and the premiere on 22 September), which was "a scheme arranged well in advance against the management." Wagner justifies his noninvolvement by arguing the impossibility of performing the work adequately in the routine framework of the Court Theater, referring to his *Report . . . Concerning a German School of Music to Be Established in Munich* (no. 143) and the plans for reform it contains. Nos. 189 and 190 are brought together in SSD under the heading "Two Statements in the Augsburg *Allgemeine Zeitung*." No. 191, *Invitation to the First Performance of "Tristan und Isolde,"* is a letter dated 18 April 1865 to the editor of the Viennese journal *Der Botschafter*, Friedrich Uhl, whom Wagner asks to publish a mention of the planned premiere of *Tristan* (on 10 June 1865). Uhl printed the full letter, which gives a detailed background of this noteworthy production and the difficulties associated with it. Nos. 192 and 193 also form part of this group. In *Speech to the Court Orchestra in Munich before the Dress Rehearsal for "Tristan und Isolde" on the Morning of 11 May 1865* (no. 192) Wagner justifies his decision not to take on himself the musical direction of the performance, the first ever of the opera, on account of his poor health as well as the high standard achieved by the orchestra: "They do not need me. They have absorbed my work and presented it back to me: I can enjoy it calmly . . . Difficulties, the like of which have not arisen before, have been overcome. The task has been accomplished, and the artist's salvation has been achieved—Oblivion! He is forgotten!" In the *Letter of Thanks to the Munich Court Orchestra* (no. 193), dated 19 July 1865, Wagner thanks the orchestra for its "important" and "incomparable" performance at the premiere of *Tristan*. No. 194 is *An Article from the Munich "Neueste*

Nachrichten" of 29 November 1865. This fateful article, in which Ludwig II is advised "to remove two or three persons who do not enjoy the slightest respect among the people of Bavaria" (meaning the government officers Pfistermeister and von der Pfordten), led to Wagner's expulsion from Bavaria. Nos. 190–193 are grouped together in SSD under the heading "From the Munich Period."

In his *Statement in the "Berner Bund" of 10 June 1866* (no. 195) Wagner protests—following the visit of Ludwig II to Tribschen on 22 May 1866—against renewed and now voluble public criticism, including articles in the Munich *Volksbote* and *Punsch,* that he "had literally stormed the king's treasury in an indefensible manner" and set up a "desperate race to the cabinet treasury." In a second *Statement in the "Berner Bund" of 16 September 1869* (no. 196) Wagner firmly rejects criticisms of his noninvolvement in the world premiere of *Rheingold* in Munich (although he gives no arguments). No. 197 is *Four Statements in the "Signale für die musikalische Welt."* The first, dated 23 January 1869, contains a correction to the article on Hans von Bülow which had appeared in the journal. In the second statement, dated 19 March 1869, Wagner rejects an article from the Parisian *Chronique illustré,* which was reproduced in *Signale,* on his failure to participate in the Paris premiere of *Rienzi* on 6 March 1869 as "fabricated by German Jews in Paris." In the third statement, dated 20 June 1870, Wagner attacks a report in *Illustrierte Zeitung* on 18 June 1870 that he had turned down an invitation to conduct Beethoven's Ninth Symphony on the centenary of his birth "gratefully acknowledging the commission, which was an honor for me." He calls this "quote" a "euphemism"; in fact he had not replied to the letter of invitation because it was signed by, among others, Hanslick. In the fourth statement, dated 12 November 1871, Wagner confirms the publicized gossip about his letters to Napoleon III and his private secretary Mocquard in connection with the production in Paris of *Tannhäuser.*

No. 198 is *Two Statements in the Augsburg "Allgemeine Zeitung" on the Opera "Theodor Körner" by Wendelin Weißheimer.* The Augsburg *Allgemeine Zeitung* had claimed on 3 May 1872 that the world premiere of Wendelin Weißheimer's *Theodor Körner* arose as a result of his influence. Wagner attacks the claim in both statements and asserts again that this opera "was refused by me on account of its extremely dubious quality." No. 199 is *Two Corrections in the "Musikalische Wochenblatt": I, Correction; II, Objection.* In the first statement, dated 29 June 1872, Wagner corrects a number of points in a report by the Berlin Akademischer Wagner-Verein on his biography and "development" (the financial support supposedly provided by Meyerbeer during the Paris years, for example). In the second statement, dated 25 March 1873, Wagner rejects the claim in the Wagner entry in the 1873 supplement to the Brockhaus encyclopedia that "influential friends at the Prussian Court" had in 1871 tried to install Wagner "in Berlin in the position of general musical director, which had been vacant since Meyerbeer's death."

Five letters on the circumstances of Wagner's art abroad form a further group of shorter pieces and articles. No. 200 is *To Frau Judith Gautier on the Forthcoming Production of "Rienzi" in Paris*. In this letter, dated March 1869, Wagner justifies not having involved himself in the Paris premiere of *Rienzi* on 6 March 1869: "It would look as though I was putting myself at the head of a theatrical enterprise with the aim of winning back through *Rienzi* what I lost through *Tannhäuser*. The press, at least, would interpret my coming as such." He did not "in any way" scorn success in Paris, particularly for *Rienzi*, which was "utterly made for Paris" and "never shown there" but which for him still possessed "all its youthful freshness." In no. 201, *To Champfleury*, dated 16 March 1870, Wagner welcomes an initiative from Jules Champfleury, director of the Sèvres porcelain factory, to found a magazine with the aim of "uniting the French and German spirit" (it was to be called *L'imagérie nouvelle*). He himself speaks of the idea, which goes back to Napoleon III (see no. 205), of founding an "International Theater" in Paris with comparable aims. Wagner again praises Méhul, who was to take up "a foremost place" in this theater. No. 202, *To the Editor of the "American Review,"* is a letter to Dexter Smitte, dated June 1874. Wagner explains his 1876 plans for Bayreuth and asks for support from the American public.

In no. 203, *To Professor Gabriel Monod in Paris*, dated 25 October 1876, Wagner tries to justify himself to the French historian for his "comedy" *Eine Kapitulation* (WWV 102): "Everything that I have ever written on the subject of the French mind was composed in German and solely for Germans, which shows that I could not have had it in mind to offend nor indeed to provoke the French, but simply meant it for my own countrymen." All the "Germans' culture which is publicly discernible" (an old theme) is nothing more than "clumsy" Gallicism—where, that is, it is anything more than "symptoms of barbaric crudeness." He goes on, "How ridiculous a Frenchman must find this broken version of his cultural observations to a foreigner." No. 204 is *To the Duke of Bagnara, President of the Music Conservatoire in Naples*. On 21 April 1880 Wagner had gone to a concert in the Naples Conservatoire. In his letter of thanks, dated 22 April 1880, he comments on the training of musicians at the Conservatoire. He recommends a thorough study of Mozart's *Figaro*, Gluck's two *Iphigénie* operas, and *Vestalin*. Young musicians would learn from such works to offer the public "not what it is used to finding in the theater but exactly what is not found there: style!" This group of letters is joined by no. 205, *Thoughts on the Significance of German Art for Foreigners*. The text probably originated in 1869. Wagner returns once again to the failure in Paris of *Tannhäuser* and points to the "weaknesses in our one-sided national development, which in many cases we are more sensitive about exposing than in touching upon personal failings," and he bemoans the idea of an international theater expressed by Napoleon III on the occasion of the World Exhibition in Paris (see no. 201).

Other letters in SSD include no. 206, the third letter (see nos. 106/107) to the management of the Philharmonic Society in St. Petersburg, in which Wagner offers his thanks, on 8 November 1866, for a further invitation to

St. Petersburg but refuses on account of commitments in Munich. In no. 207, *On Performing Music: On the Andante in Mozart's Symphony in E-Flat Major,* a letter to Bülow dated 13 March 1868, Wagner's remarks include the fundamental advice that everything depends "in Mozart almost exclusively on the song in his motifs." No. 208 is *To the Managing Committee of the Wagner-Verein in Berlin.* The managing committee of the Berlin Wagner-Verein, Ernst Dohm and Georg Davidsohn, were negotiating in 1873 with the General Intendant in Berlin, von Hülsen, about a benefit performance of *Lohengrin* for the planned festival in Bayreuth. The plan failed as a result of Wagner's insistence, made clear and justified in the letter of 18 March 1873, on an unabridged performance. In *To King Ludwig II on the Production of "Parsifal"* (no. 209), dated 28 September 1880, a letter that had many consequences, Wagner insists that *Parsifal* remain the preserve of Bayreuth alone. He justifies this by virtue of the discrepancy between his "so ideally conceived work" and "theatrical and public practices, which are acknowledged to be profoundly immoral." The final piece to be included among the miscellaneous writings is no. 210, *Personal: Why I Do Not Reply to the Numerous Attacks on Me and My Views on Art,* a collection of nine aphorisms on the relationship between the artist and criticism.

The list of prose works concludes with the series of concert programs *"Die Meistersinger von Nürnberg": Prelude to the Third Act* (no. 211); *On "Die Walküre"* (no. 212); *On "Götterdämmerung"* (no. 213); and *"Parsifal": Prelude* (no. 214).

The "autobiographical" account in English, *The Work and Mission of My Life,* which is occasionally quoted, was the work not of Wagner himself but of Hans von Wolzogen. It is true that Wagner did sign the original English manuscript, but he immediately distanced himself from the text (see CT, 1 May 1879) and refused to allow a reprint after the unauthorized retranslation into German appeared in September 1879.

Translated by Simon Nye

Appendix: Checklist of Writings

[Dates refer to first publication unless otherwise stated. The list does not claim to be complete or to have settled some complex questions of chronology and authenticity. A detailed catalogue and a modern scholarly edition must await further research.—Ed.]

Early Writings, 1834–1839

ESSAYS AND AUTOBIOGRAPHICAL NOTES

1. *Die deutsche Oper* (German Opera), 10 June 1834, *Zeitung für die elegante Welt* (anonymous), SSD XII, 1–4 (Ellis VIII, 55–58).

2. *Pasticcio,* 6 and 10 November 1834, *Neue Zeitschrift für Musik* (signed "Ng."; authenticity doubtful, see Konrad 1987, pp. 218–223), SSD XII, 5–11 (Ellis VIII, 59–66).

3. *Der dramatische Gesang* (Dramatic Singing), written 1837, SSD XII, 15–18.

4. *Bellini,* 7–19 December 1837, *Der Zuschauer* (Riga; signed "O"), SSD XII, 19–21 (Ellis VII, 67–69).

SHORTER OCCASIONAL PIECES AND ARTICLES

5. *Der Freischütz,* 7 November 1835, *Magdeburgische Zeitung* (signed "r"), SSD XVI, 57–58.

6. *Aus Magdeburg* (From Magdeburg), 3 May 1836, *Neue Zeitschrift für Musik* (anonymous), SSD XII, 12–14.

7/8. Two newspaper advertisements from Riga, 8 December 1837, 8 March 1839, SSD XVI, 3–4.

9. Article by Wilhelm Drach [pseudonym], lost, written in Berlin in May 1836 (see SB I, 274–275, 319).

The Paris Years, 1839–1842

WRITINGS FOR THE *REVUE ET GAZETTE MUSICALE*

10. *Über deutsches Musikwesen* (On German music), 12 July 1840, SSD I, 149–166 (Ellis VII, 83–101).

11. *Über Meyerbeers "Hugenotten"* (On Meyerbeer's *Les Huguenots*), probably written 1840 (not published in the *Revue*), SSD XII, 22–30.

12. *"Stabat Mater" de Pergolèse* (Pergolesi's "Stabat Mater"), 11 October 1840, SSD XII, 401–405 (Ellis VII, 102–107).

13. *Der Virtuos und der Künstler* (The virtuoso and the artist), 18 October 1840. The original French version differs considerably from the German version in SSD I, 167–179 (Ellis VII, 108–122 = trans. of German version).

14. *Eine Pilgerfahrt zu Beethoven* (A pilgrimage to Beethoven), 19, 22, 29 November and 3 December 1840, SSD I, 90–114 (Ellis VII, 21–45).

15. *Über die Ouvertüre* (On the overture), 10, 14, 17 January 1841, SSD I, 194–206 (Ellis VII, 151–166).

16. *Ein Ende in Paris* (An end in Paris), 31 January, 7 and 11 February 1841, SSD I, 194–206 (Ellis VII, 46–68).

16a. *Wie ein armer Musiker in Paris starb* (How a young musician died in Paris), sketch for no. 16, written late autumn 1840, SSD XVI, 235.

17. *Der Künstler und die Öffentlichkeit* (The artist and his public), 1 April 1841 (signed in error "Werner"), SSD I, 180–186 (Ellis VII, 134–141).

18. *"Der Freischütz": An das Pariser Publikum* (*Der Freischütz:* to the Paris public), 23 and 30 May 1841, SSD I, 207–219 [= retranslation into German from the French text] (Ellis VII, 169–182). Original German text in Voss 1976, pp. 117–137.

19. *Ein glücklicher Abend* (A happy evening), 24 October, 7 November 1841 (written 12 May 1841 in Meudon; original title, *Über Instrumentalmusik*), with revisions in SSD I, 136–149 (Ellis VII, 69–82).

20. *Halévy und die "Königin von Zypern"* (Halévy and *La reine de Chypre*), 27 February, 13 March, 24 April, 1 May 1842, SSD XII, 131–148, 406–413 (Ellis VIII, 175–200).

21. *Zwei Epochen aus dem Leben eines deutschen Musikers* (Two periods in the life of a

German musician) = nos. 14 and 16 in German translation published in the Dresden *Abendzeitung* from 30 July–10 August 1841.

22. *Ein deutscher Musiker in Paris* (A German musician in Paris) = nos. 14, 16, 19, 10, 13, 17, and 27 collected as a group in SSD I, 90–193.

23. *"Der Freischütz" in Paris* = nos. 18 and 30 collected as a group in SSD I, 207–240.

24. *Zwei Aufsätze für die "Gazette Musicale"* (Two essays for the *Gazette musicale*) = nos. 12 and 20 (second part) collected as a group in SSD XII, 401–413.

FEUILLETONS FOR *EUROPA* (STUTTGART)

25. *Pariser Amüsements* (Parisian amusements), spring issue, April 1841 (under the pseudonym W. Freudenfeuer), SSD XII, 31–45 (Ellis VIII, 70–86).

26. *Pariser Fatalitäten für Deutsche* (Parisian fatalities for the Germans), summer issue 1841 under the pseudonym V. [sic] Freudenfeuer, SSD XII, 46–64 (Ellis VIII, 87–107).

CONTRIBUTIONS TO SCHUMANN'S *NEUE ZEITSCHRIFT FÜR MUSIK*

27. *Rossini's "Stabat Mater,"* 28 December 1841 (under the pseudonym H. Valentino), SSD I, 186–193 (Ellis VII, 142–150). See also no. 22.

28. *Extrablatt aus Paris* (Special edition from Paris), 5 February 1842, under the pseudonym H. V[alentino], SSD XVI, 58–60.

ARTICLES FOR THE DRESDEN *ABENDZEITUNG*

29. *Pariser Berichte für die Dresdener Abendzeitung* (Reports from Paris for the *Dresdener Abendzeitung*), in 1841 on 19–22 March (I), 24–28 May (II), 14–16 June (III), 2–4 August (IV), 23 August (V), 1–2 October (VI), 4–8 December (VII), 25 December (VIII), and in 1842 on 10–11 January (IX), SSD XII, 65–130 (Ellis VIII, 108–171).

30. *Le Freischutz: Bericht nach Deutschland* (*Le Freischutz*: Report to Germany), 20 July 1841, SSD I, 220–240 (Ellis VII, 183–204).

31. *Pariser Bericht über eine neue Oper "La Reine de Chypre"* (Report on a new Parisian opera: Halévy's *Reine de Chypre*), 26–29 January 1842, SSD I, 241–257 (Ellis VII, 205–222).

OTHER PARIS WRITINGS

32. *Ein Tagebuch aus Paris* (A Paris diary), written June 1840, SSD XVI, 4–6.

Writings from 1842 to 1848

33. *Autobiographische Skizze* (Autobiographical sketch), 1 and 8 February 1843, *Zeitung für die elegante Welt,* revised SSD I, 4–19 (Ellis I, 1–19). Original text SB I, 95–114.

34. *Das Oratorium "Paulus" von Mendelssohn-Bartholdy* (Felix Mendelssohn-Bartholdy's St. Paul Oratorio), written Easter 1843, SSD XII, 149–150.

35. *An die Dresdener Liedertafel: Aufruf* (First letter to the *Dresden Liedertafel*), written April 1843, SSD XVI, 6–7.

36/37. *Zwei Erklärungen über die Verdeutschung des Textes "Les deux grenadiers"* (Two statements about the translation into German of the text for *Les deux grena-*

diers), 15–19 May and 19 June 1843 *Neue Zeitschrift für Musik,* SSD XVI, 10–11.

38. *An die Dresdener Liedertafel: Niederlegung der Leitung* (Second letter to the Dresden Liedertafel), written 14 November 1845, SSD XVI, 8–10.

39. *Rede an Webers letzter Ruhestätte* (Oration on the lying in rest of Weber), delivered 15 December 1844, SSD II, 46–48 (Ellis VII, 235–237).

40. *Zu Beethovens Neunter Symphonie* (On Beethoven's Ninth Symphony), 24 and 31 March, 2 April 1846 *Dresdener Anzeiger,* SSD XII, 205–207 (Ellis VIII, 201–203).

41. *Programm zur 9. Symphonie von Beethoven* (Program to Beethoven's Ninth Symphony), 5 April 1846, SSD II, 56–64 (Ellis VII, 247–255).

42. *Die Königliche Kapelle betreffend* (Concerning the Royal Orchestra), dated 1 March 1846, SSD XII, 151–204.

43. *Künstler und Kritiker, mit Bezug auf einen besonderen Fall* (Artist and critic, with regard to a specific case), 14 August 1846 *Dresdener Anzeiger* (dated 11 August), SSD XII, 208–219 (Ellis VIII, 204–214).

44. *Eine Rede auf Friedrich Schneider* (A speech on Friedrich Schneider), delivered 7 November 1846, SSD XVI, 61–62.

The Revolution Years, 1848–49

REVOLUTIONARY WRITINGS

45. *Ein Brief an Professor Franz Wigard* (Letter to Professor Franz Wigard), written 19 May 1848, SSD XVI, 11–12.

46. *Wie verhalten sich republikanische Bestrebungen dem Königtum gegenüber?* (How do republican aspirations stand in relation to the monarchy?), 14 June 1848 *Dresdener Anzeiger* (anonymous), SSD XII, 220–229 (Ellis IV, 136–144).

47. *An den Intendanten v. Lüttichau über die Rede in der Versammlung des Vaterlandsvereins* (To Intendant von Lüttichau on the speech at the assembly of the Vaterlandsverein), written 18 June 1848, SSD XII, 12–16 (Ellis IV, 145–148).

48. *Die Wibelungen* (The Wibelungs), Leipzig 1850 (written 1848–early 1849; see WWV, p. 329), SSD II, 115–155 (Ellis VII, 257–298), conclusion of 1850 edition reprinted in SSD XII, 229.

49. *Deutschland und seine Fürsten* (Germany and its rulers), 15 October 1848, *Volksblätter* (anonymous), SSD XII, 414–419.

50. *Der Mensch und die bestehende Gesellschaft* (Man and existing society), 10 February 1849, *Volksblätter* (anonymous), SSD XII, 240–244 (Ellis VIII, 227–231).

51. *Die Revolution* (The revolution), 8 April 1849, *Volksblätter* (anonymous), SSD XII, 245–251 (Ellis VIII, 232–238).

WRITINGS ON THEATER REFORM

52. *Entwurf zur Organisation eines deutschen National-Theaters für das Königreich Sachsen* (Plan for the organization of a German national theater for the Kingdom of Saxony), completed 11 May 1848, SSD II, 233–273 (Ellis VII, 319–360).

53. *Über Eduard Devrients "Geschichte der deutschen Schauspielkunst"* (On Eduard Devrient's *History of German Acting*), written January 1849, SSD XII, 230–232 (Ellis VIII, 218–221).

54. *Theater-Reform* (Theater reform), 16 January 1849 *Dresdener Anzeiger* (signed J.P.–F.R.), SSD XII, 233–236 (Ellis VIII, 222–225).

55. *Nochmals Theater-Reform* (More on theater reform), 18 January 1849, *Dresdener Anzeiger* (signed J.P.–F.R.), SSD XII, 237–239.

OCCASIONAL WRITINGS

56. *Trinkspruch am Gedenktage des 300 jährigen Bestehens der königlichen musikalischen Kapelle in Dresden* (Toast on the day commemorating 300 years of the Royal Orchestra in Dresden), delivered 22 September 1848, SSD II, 229–232 (Ellis VII, 313–318).
57/58. *Zeitungs-Erklärungen* (Two statements to the *Dresdener Anzeiger*), 20 and 22 June 1848, SSD XVI, 27.

Writings from the Years 1849 to 1864

MAJOR WRITINGS ON AESTHETICS FROM THE ZURICH PERIOD

59. *Die Kunst und die Revolution* (Art and revolution), Leipzig 1849, SSD III, 8–41 (Ellis I, 21–65).
60. *Zu "Die Kunst und die Revolution"* (On *Art and Revolution*), written 1849, SSD XII, 252–253 (Ellis VIII, 362–363, incomplete).
61. *Das Künstlertum der Zukunft* (The artists of the future), written 1849–1850, SSD XII, 254–282 (Ellis VIII, 343–361).
62. *Das Kunstwerk der Zukunft* (The art-work of the future), Leipzig 1850 (completed 4 November 1849), SSD III, 42–177 (Ellis I, 69–213).
63. *Oper und Drama* (Opera and drama), Leipzig 1852 (extracts published in 1851), SSD III, 222–320, IV, 1–229 (Ellis II), Kropfinger 1984.
64. *Eine Skizze zu "Oper und Drama"* (Sketch for *Opera and Drama*), written 12 December 1850, SSD XVI, 93–95, SB III, 476–478.

MINOR WRITINGS ON AESTHETICS

65. *Kunst und Klima* (Art and climate), April 1850 *Deutsche Monatsschrift für Politik, Wissenschaft, Kunst und Leben*, SSD III, 207–221 (Ellis I, 249–265).
66. *Das Judentum in der Musik* (Judaism in music), 3 and 6 September 1850, *Neue Zeitschrift für Musik* (under the pseudonym K. Freigedank), Kneif 1975, pp. 51–77 (WNS, 9/i [January 1988], pp. 20–33), rev. ed. January 1869, SSD V, 66–85 (Ellis III, 79–100 with notes of differences between the two versions). See no. 176.
67. *Über musikalische Kritik* (On musical criticism), 25 January 1852, *Neue Zeitschrift für Musik*, SSD V, 53–65 (Ellis III, 59–74).
68. *Zum Vortrag Beethovens* (On performing Beethoven), extracted from a letter to T. Uhlig written between 13 and 15 February 1852 (SB IV, 285–290), SSD XVI, 77–83.
69. *Wilhelm Baumgartners Lieder,* 7 February 1852, *Eidgenössische Zeitung,* SSD XII, 286–288.
70. *Glucks Ouvertüre zu "Iphigenia in Aulis"* (Gluck's overture to *Iphigénie en Aulide*), 1 July 1854, *Neue Zeitschrift für Musik,* SSD V, 111–122 (Ellis III, 153–166).
71. *Dante–Schopenhauer,* from a letter to F. Liszt of 7 July 1855, SSD XVI, 95–101.
72. *Metaphysik der Geschlechtsliebe: Bruchstück eines Briefes an Arthur Schopenhauer* (Metaphysics of sexual love: fragment of a letter to Arthur Schopenhauer), written during 1858, SSD XII, 291.
73. *Über Franz Liszts symphonische Dichtungen* (On Franz Liszt's symphonic poems),

10 April 1857, *Neue Zeitschrift für Musik,* SSD V, 182–198 (Ellis III, 235–254).

74. *Ein Brief an Hector Berlioz* (A letter to Hector Berlioz), 22 February 1860, *Journal des débats,* SSD VII, 82–86 (Ellis III, 285–291).

75. "*Music of the Future,*" Paris and Leipzig 1861 (written September 1860), SSD VII, 87–137 (Ellis III, 293–345).

WRITINGS ON THEATER REFORM

76. *Über die "Goethestiftung"* (On the *Goethe-Stiftung*), 5 March 1852, *Neue Zeitschrift für Musik* (completed 8 May 1851), SSD V, 5–19 (Ellis III, 5–22).

77. *Ein Theater in Zürich* (A theater in Zurich), 27 June, 4 and 11 July 1851, *Neue Zeitschrift für Musik* (also separately printed in Zurich in 1851 by the Schulthess Press), SSD V, 20–52 (Ellis III, 23–57).

78. *Das Wiener Hof-Operntheater* (The Vienna Court Opera Theater), October 1863, *Der Wiener Botschafter,* SSD VII, 272–295 (Ellis III, 361–386).

AUTOBIOGRAPHICAL WRITINGS, PREFACES, AND REMARKS ON WAGNER'S MUSICAL-DRAMATIC WORKS

79. *Eine Mitteilung an meine Freunde* (A communication to my friends), Leipzig 1851, SSD IV, 230–344 (Ellis I, 267–392). Original ending SW 29/I, 52–54.

80. Preface to an intended 1850 edition of *Siegfrieds Tod,* written May 1850, SSD XVI, 84–85, SW 29/I, 34.

81. Preface to an intended publication in 1850 of the 1848 *Plan for the Organization of a German National Theater for the Kingdom of Saxony* (see no. 52), written 18 September 1850, SSD XVI, 86–92.

82. Preface to the first (private) edition of the poem *Der Ring des Nibelungen,* Zurich 1853 (see WWV, pp. 352–353), SSD XII, 289–290.

83. Preface to the second edition of the poem of the Stage Festival Drama *Der Ring des Nibelungen,* Leipzig 1863, SSD VI, 272–281 (Ellis III, 274–283).

84. Staging instructions for the 1850 production of *Lohengrin* in Weimar, SSD XVI, 63–73.

85. *Über die Aufführung des "Tannhäuser": eine Mitteilung an die Dirigenten und Darsteller dieser Oper* (On performing *Tannhäuser:* a communication to conductors and performers of this opera), 14–23 August 1852, then in extracts in *Neue Zeitschrift für Musik* on 3 and 24 December 1852, 1, 7, and 14 January 1853, SSD V, 123–159 (Ellis III, 167–205).

86. *Über die "Tannhäuser"-Ouvertüre* (On the *Tannhäuser* Overture), written 18 March 1852, SSD XVI, 74–77.

87. *Bemerkungen zur Aufführung der Oper "Der fliegende Holländer"* (Remarks on performing the opera *Der fliegende Holländer*), dated 22 December 1852, SSD V, 160–168 (Ellis III, 207–217).

88. Petition for amnesty to King Johann of Saxony, dated 15 May 1856, Gregor-Dellin 1983, pp. 542–545.

89. Draft of a petition for amnesty to Saxony's Minister of Justice Behr, written December 1858, SSD XVI, 24–27.

90. *Bericht über die Aufführung des "Tannhäuser" in Paris* (Review of the Paris production of *Tannhäuser*), 7 April 1861, *Deutsche Allgemeine Zeitung,* SSD VII, 138–149 (Ellis III, 347–360).

MINOR OCCASIONAL PIECES AND SHORT ARTICLES: OBITUARIES AND
DEDICATIONS

91. [*Nachruf und*] *Erinnerungen an Spontini* (Recollections of Spontini), 11 February
    1851, SSD V, 86–88 (Ellis III, 123–127).

92. Dedication of the Score of *Lohengrin* to Franz Liszt, beginning of August 1852
    (written May 1852), SSD XVI, 73–74.

93. *Nachruf an Ludwig Spohr und Chordirektor Wilhelm Fischer* (Obituary of Ludwig
    Spohr and chorus master Wilhelm Fischer), 2 December 1859, *Neue Zeitschrift
    für Musik,* SSD V, 105–110 (Ellis III, 145–152).

PRESS STATEMENTS

94. *Über die musikalische Direktion der [Züricher] Oper* (On the musical direction of
    [the Zurich] Opera), 17 October 1850, *Eidgenössische Zeitung,* SSD XVI, 16–18.

95. *Zum Empfehlung Gottfried Sempers* (In recommendation of Gottfried Semper), 6
    February 1851, *Eidgenössische Zeitung,* SSD XVI, 18–19.

96. *Über die musikalische Berichterstattung in der Eidgenössischen Zeitung* (On musical
    coverage in the *Eidgenössische Zeitung*), 7 February 1851, SSD XVI, 19–20.

97. *Vieuxtemps,* 20 September 1852, *Eidgenössische Zeitung,* SSD XVI, 20.

98. *Über die Aufführung der "Tannhäuser" Ouvertüre* (On performing the *Tannhäuser*
    Overture), 30 October 1852 *Neue Zeitschrift für Musik,* SSD XVI, 20.

99. Invitation to a reading of the poem of *Der Ring des Nibelungen,* 12 February 1853,
    SSD XVI, 21.

100. Announcement of concerts arranged for May 1853, 2 April 1853, SSD XVI, 21–
    22.

101. *Empfehlung einer Streichquartett-Vereinigung* (In support of the founding of a new
    string quartet), October 1854, *Eidgenössische Zeitung,* SSD XVI, 23.

102. *Über die Leitung einer Mozart-Feier* (On the direction of a Mozart festival), 15
    February 1856, *Eidgenössische Zeitung,* SSD XVI, 23–24.

103. *Aus der "Europe artiste"* (From the *Europe artiste*), November 1859, SSD XVI, 28.

104. *Vom Wiener Hofoperntheater* (From the Vienna Court Opera Theater), 8 October
    1861, *Österreichische Zeitung* (signed "P. C."), SSD XII, 292–296.

105. *Aus der "Ostdeutschen Post"* (From the *Ostdeutsche Post*), November 1861, SSD
    XVI, 28.

LETTERS OF THANKS

106/107. *Drei Schreiben an die Direktion der Philharmonischen Gesellschaft in St. Petersburg*
    (Three letters to the management of the Philharmonic Society in St. Petersburg)
    I, II, 12 December 1862, 30 March 1863, SSD XVI, 29–31 (III, see no. 206).

PROGRAM NOTES

108. *Beethovens "Heroische Symphonie"* (Beethoven's "Eroica" Symphony), for a con-
    cert in Zurich on 26 February 1851, SSD V, 169–172 (Ellis III, 221–224).

109. *Beethovens Ouvertüre zu "Coriolan"* (Beethoven's "Coriolan" Overture), for a
    concert in Zurich, 17 February 1852, SSD V, 173–176 (Ellis III, 225–228).

110. *Ouvertüre zu "Tannhäuser"* (*Tannhäuser* Overture), for a concert in Zurich on 16
    March 1852 (title *Der Venusberg*), SSD V, 177–179 (Ellis III, 229–231).

111. *Ouvertüre zum "fliegenden Holländer"* (*Der fliegende Holländer* Overture), for a concert in Zurich, 25 April 1853, SSD V, 176–177 (Ellis III, 228–229).

112. *Zu Tannhäuser* . . . (From *Tannhäuser:* I. Entry of the Guests at the Wartburg; II. Tannhäuser's Journey to Rome. Prelude to *Lohengrin* [titled "The Holy Grail"]; from *Lohengrin:* I. The Men's Scene and Bridal Procession [from act 2]; II. Wedding Music and Bridal Chorus), for the festival concerts in Zurich, 18, 20, and 22 May 1853, SSD XVI, 167–170; V, 179–181 (Ellis III, 231–233); preface to the program notes for the Zurich May concerts 1853, SSD XVI, 22–23.

113. *Beethovens cis-moll-Quartett (op. 131)* (Beethoven's C-Sharp Minor Quartet op. 131), dated 12 December 1854, SSD XII, 350 (Ellis VIII, 386).

114. *Tristan und Isolde: Vorspiel* (Prelude to *Tristan und Isolde*), for a concert in Paris on 25 January 1860, SSD XII, 346–347 (Ellis VIII, 388–387; repr. in Bailey 1985, pp. 47–48).

115. *Die Meistersinger von Nürnberg: Vorspiel* (Overture to *Die Meistersinger von Nürnberg*), for a concert in Löwenberg, Silesia, 2 December 1863, SSD XII, 347–348.

116. *Tristan und Isolde: Vorspiel (Liebestod) und Schlußsatz (Verklärung)* (*Tristan und Isolde*: Prelude [Liebestod] and Conclusion [Transfiguration]), for a concert in Vienna, 27 December 1863, SSD XII, 347.

Writings from 1864 to 1883

AUTOBIOGRAPHICAL WORKS

117. *Mein Leben* (My life), written between 17 July 1865 and 25 July 1880, first (private) edition, Basel 1870–1875 (vols. 1–3), Bayreuth 1880 (vol. 4); SSD XIII–XV, ML.

118. *Annalen* (Annals), written in February 1868 (covering the years 1846–January 1868) and January 1869 (covering the year 1868), BB 93–124, 166–169.

119. *Das braune Buch: Tagebuchaufzeichnungen 1865 bis 1882* (The diary of Richard Wagner, 1865–1882: The Brown Book), first entry 10 August 1865, last entry between 21 March and 9 April 1882, BB.

PHILOSOPHICAL WRITINGS

120. *Über Staat und Religion* (On state and religion), completed 16 July 1864, SSD VIII, 3–29 (Ellis IV, 3–34).

121. *Deutsche Kunst und deutsche Politik* (German art and German politics), 24 September–19 December 1867, *Süddeutsche Presse* (partial publication), Brussels and Leipzig 1868 (full publication in French and German respectively), SSD VIII, 30–124 (Ellis IV, 35–135). Foreword to 1868 ed. in SSD XVI, 92–93 (BB 127).

122. *Was ist deutsch?* (What is German?), first published with added introduction and epilogue *Bayreuther Blätter*, February 1878 (written September–October 1865; introduction and epilogue added for first publication), SSD X, 36–53 (Ellis IV, 149–169). First published complete in König-Briefe, IV, 5–34.

123. *Modern*, March 1878, *Bayreuther Blätter*, SSD X, 54–60 (Ellis VI, 41–49).

124. *Wollen wir hoffen?* (Shall we hope?), May 1879 *Bayreuther Blätter*, SSD X, 118–136 (Ellis VI, 111–130).

125. *Offenes Schreiben an Herrn Ernst von Weber, Verfasser der Schrift "Die Folterkammern der Wissenschaft"* (Open letter to Herr Ernst von Weber, author of *The Torture Chambers of Science*), October 1879, *Bayreuther Blätter*, SSD X, 194–210 (Ellis VI, 193–210).

126. *Religion und Kunst* (Religion and art), October 1880, *Bayreuther Blätter,* SSD X, 211–252 (Ellis VI, 211–252).

127. *"Was nützt diese Erkenntnis?":* Ein Nachtrag zu "Religion und Kunst" ("What use is this knowledge?": an epilogue to *Religion and Art*), December 1880, *Bayreuther Blätter,* SSD X, 253–263 (Ellis VI, 253–263).

128. *Ausführungen zu "Religion und Kunst": "Erkenne dich selbst"* (Remarks on *Religion and Art:* "know thyself"), February–March 1881, *Bayreuther Blätter,* SSD X, 263–274 (Ellis VI, 264–274).

129. *Ausführungen zu "Religion und Kunst": Heldentum und Christentum* (Remarks on *Religion and Art:* heroism and Christianity), September 1881, *Bayreuther Blätter,* SSD X, 275–285 (Ellis VI, 275–284).

130. *Über das Weibliche im Menschlichen: Als Abschluß von "Religion und Kunst"* (On the feminine in the human: as a conclusion to *Religion and Art*), fragment, written 11–13 February 1883, SSD XII, 343–345 (Ellis VI, 333–337 and VIII, 396–398).

131. *Metaphysik. Kunst und Religion. Moral. Christentum* (Metaphysics. Art and religion. Morality. Christianity), written between 1870 and 1882, SSD XII, 337–342 (Ellis VIII, 390–395).

MUSICAL AESTHETICS AND DRAMA

132. *Über das Dirigieren* (On conducting), Leipzig 1869, SSD VIII, 261–337 (Ellis IV, 289–364).

133. *Beethoven,* Leipzig 1870 (written 20 July–11 September 1870), SSD IX, 61–126 (Ellis V, 57–126).

134. *Über die Bestimmung der Oper* (On the destiny of opera), Leipzig 1871, SSD IX, 127–156 (Ellis V, 127–155).

135. *Über Schauspieler und Sänger* (On actors and singers), Leipzig 1872, SSD IX, 157–230 (Ellis V, 157–228).

136. *Zum Vortrag der neunten Symphonie Beethovens* (On the performance of Beethoven's Ninth Symphony), 4 and 11 April 1873, *Musikalisches Wochenblatt,* SSD IX, 231–257 (Ellis V, 229–253).

137. *Publikum und Popularität* (Public and popularity), April, June, August 1878, *Bayreuther Blätter,* SSD X, 61–90 (Ellis VI, 51–81).

138. *Das Publikum in Zeit und Raum* (The public in time and space), October 1878, *Bayreuther Blätter,* SSD X, 91–102 (Ellis VI, 83–94).

139. *Über das Dichten und Komponieren* (On poetry and composition), July 1879, *Bayreuther Blätter,* SSD X, 137–151 (Ellis VI, 131–147).

140. *Über das Opern-Dichten und Komponieren im Besonderen* (On opera poetry and composition in particular), September 1879, *Bayreuther Blätter,* SSD X, 152–175 (Ellis VI, 149–172).

141. *Über die Anwendung der Musik auf das Drama* (On the application of music to the drama), November 1879, *Bayreuther Blätter,* SSD X, 176–193 (Ellis VI, 173–191).

142. *Brief an H. v. Stein* (Letter to H. von Stein), January–March 1883, *Bayreuther Blätter,* SSD X, 316–323 (Ellis VI, 323–332).

THEATER REFORM AND BAYREUTH

143. *Bericht an seine Majestät den König Ludwig II. von Bayern über eine in München zu errichtende deutsche Musikschule* (Report to His Majesty King Ludwig II of Bavaria

concerning a German school of music to be established in Munich), spring 1865, SSD VIII, 125–176 (Ellis IV, 171–224).

144. *Bericht an den Deutschen Wagner-Verein über die Umstände und Schicksale, welche die Ausführung des Bühnenfestspiels "Der Ring des Nibelungen" begleiteten* (Report to the German Wagner Society on the circumstances and fate which accompanied the composition of the Stage Festival Play *The Ring of the Nibelung*), Leipzig 1872, SSD, in two parts with further additions, VI, 257–281 (Ellis III, 255–273) and IX, 311–322 (Ellis V, 309–319). Conclusion of 1872 edition, SSD XVI, 110–111.

145. *Das Bühnenfestspielhaus zu Bayreuth* (The Stage Festival Theater in Bayreuth), Leipzig 1873, SSD IX 322–344 (Ellis V, 320–340).

146. *Ein Rückblick auf die Bühnenfestspiele des Jahres 1876* (A look back at the 1876 stage festivals), December 1878, *Bayreuther Blätter*, SSD X, 103–117 (Ellis VI, 95–109).

147. *Das Bühnenweihfestspiel in Bayreuth 1882* (The "Devotional Stage Festival" in Bayreuth in 1882), November–December 1882, *Bayreuther Blätter*, SSD X, 297–308 (Ellis VI, 301–312).

148. *An die geehrten Vorstände der Richard Wagner-Vereine* (To the esteemed presidents of the Wagner societies), dated 1 January 1877, SSD X, 11–15 (Ellis VI, 15–18).

149. *Entwurf veröffentlicht mit den Statuten des Patronatvereins* (Prospectus published with the statutes of the Patronatverein), dated 15 September 1877, SSD X, 16–18 (Ellis VI, 19–21).

150. *Zur Einführung (Bayreuther Blätter, Erstes Stück)* (Introduction to the first number of the *Bayreuther Blätter*), January 1878, SSD X, 19–24 (Ellis VI, 22–27).

151. *Ein Wort zur Einführung der Arbeit Hans von Wolzogen "Über Verrottung und Errettung der deutschen Sprache"* (A word of introduction to Hans von Wolzogen's *On the Decline and Restoration of the German Language*), February 1879, *Bayreuther Blätter*, SSD X, 24–26 (Ellis VI, 28–29).

152. *Erklärung an die Mitglieder des Patronatvereines* (Announcement to the members of the Patronatverein), dated 15 July 1879, SSD X, 26 (Ellis VI, 30).

153. *Zur Einführung in das Jahr 1880* (Introduction to the year 1880), January 1880, *Bayreuther Blätter*, SSD X, 27–32 (Ellis VI, 31–35).

154. *Zur Mitteilung an die geehrten Patrone der Bühnenfestspiele in Bayreuth* (To the honored patrons of the stage festivals at Bayreuth), dated 1 December 1880, SSD X, 32–33 (Ellis VI, 36–37).

155. *Zur Einführung der Arbeit des Grafen Gobineau "Ein Urteil über die jetzige Weltlage"* (Introduction to Count Gobineau's *Ethnological Résumé of the Present Aspect of the World*), May–June 1881 *Bayreuther Blätter*, SSD X, 33–35 (Ellis VI, 38–40).

156. *Brief an H. von Wolzogen* (Letter to H. von Wolzogen), April 1882 *Bayreuther Blätter*, SSD X, 286–290 (Ellis VI, 285–291).

157. *Offenes Schreiben an Herrn Friedrich Schön in Worms* (Open letter to Herr Friedrich Schön in Worms), July 1882, *Bayreuther Blätter*, SSD X, 291–296 (Ellis VI, 293–300).

158. *An die Patrone der Bühnenfestspiele in Bayreuth* (To the patrons of the stage festivals in Bayreuth), dated 30 August 1873, SSD XII, 317–323. (For a second message to the patrons, dated 15 September 1873, see SSD XVI, 146–147.)

159. *Notgedrungene Erklärung* (Essential announcement), dated 16 February 1874, SSD XII, 323–324.

160. *Die "Presse" zu den "Proben"* (The "press" on "rehearsals"), dated 1875, SSD XII, 324.

161. *An die geehrten Patrone der Bühnenfestspiele von 1876* (To the honored patrons of the 1876 stage festivals), dated 11 October 1876, SSD XII, 324–325.

162. *Ansprache an die Abgesandten des Bayreuther Patronats* (Speech to the delegates of the Bayreuth Patronat), delivered 15 September 1877, SSD XII, 326–334.

163. *Ankündigung der Aufführung des "Parsifal"* (Announcement of the performance of *Parsifal*), dated 8 December 1877, SSD XII, 334–336 (Ellis VI, 36–37).

164. *Begründung des Festspiels, des Patronats und der Wagner-Vereine* (Founding of the Festival, the Patronat, and the Wagner societies), dated 12 May, 18 May, and 25 December 1871, SSD XVI, 131–140.

165. *Zur Grundsteinlegung* (On the laying of the foundation stone), various announcements and speeches dated 1 February, 16 March, 24 May and June 1872, SSD XVI, 141–146.

166. *Zum ersten Festspiel von 1876* (On the first festival in 1876), fourteen announcements about administration and related matters written between September 1873 and August 1876, SSD XVI, 146–164.

167. *Zum zweiten Festspiel von 1882* (On the second festival in 1882), announcement to the local presidents of the Wagner societies and a vote of thanks to the citizens of Bayreuth, dated 15 January 1878 and 3 September 1882 respectively, SSD XVI, 162–164.

SHORT AND OCCASIONAL PIECES AND ARTICLES: OBITUARIES AND DEDICATIONS

168. *Meine Erinnerungen an Ludwig Schnorr von Carolsfeld* (My recollections of Ludwig Schnorr von Carolsfeld), 5 and 12 June 1868, *Neue Zeitschrift für Musik,* SSD VIII, 177–194 (Ellis IV, 225–243; BB 134–145).

169. *Fragment eines Aufsatzes über Hector Berlioz* (Fragment of an essay on Hector Berlioz), written 8 March 1869, SSD XII, 312 (Ellis VIII, 376).

170. *Zur Widmung der zweiten Auflage von "Oper und Drama": An Constantin Frantz* (On the dedication of the second edition of *Opera and Drama* to Constantin Frantz), dated 26 April 1868, Leipzig 1869 (= 2nd edition of *Opera and Drama*), SSD VIII, 195–199 (Ellis II, 3–7; BB 128–131).

171. *Erinnerungen an Auber* (Reminiscences of Auber), 10 November 1871, *Musikalisches Wochenblatt,* SSD IX, 42–60 (Ellis V, 35–55).

REVIEWS AND STATEMENTS

172. *Zensuren I: W. H. Riehl ("Neues Novellenbuch")* (Notices I: W. H. Riehl), November 1867, *Süddeutsche Presse* (anonymous), reprinted with new supplement on 22 March 1872, *Musikalisches Wochenblatt,* SSD VIII, 205–213 (Ellis IV, 253–260).

173. *Zensuren II: Ferdinand Hiller ("Aus dem Tonleben unserer Zeit")* (Notices II: Ferdinand Hiller), November 1867, *Süddeutsche Presse* (anonymous), SSD VIII, 213–220 (Ellis IV, 261–268).

174. *Zensuren III: Eine Erinnerung an Rossini* (Notices III: Recollections of Rossini), 17 December 1868, Augsburg *Allgemeine Zeitung,* SSD VIII, 220–225 (Ellis IV, 269–274).

175. *Zensuren IV: Eduard Devrient ("Meine Erinnerungen an Felix Mendelssohn-Bartholdy")* (Notices IV: Eduard Devrient), Leipzig 1869 (under the pseudonym Wilhelm Drach), SSD VIII, 226–238 (Ellis IV, 275–288).

176. *Zensuren V: Aufklärungen über "Das Judentum in der Musik"* (Notices V: Elucidation of *Judaism in Music*), Leipzig 1869, SSD VIII, 238–260 (Ellis III, 101–122). See also no. 66.

177. *Bemerkungen zu einer angeblichen Äußerung Rossinis* (Observations on an alleged comment by Rossini), date uncertain (according to SSD 1855), SSD XII, 313 (Ellis VIII, 376–377).

178. *Zum "Judentum in der Musik"* (On *Judaism in Music*), dated April 1869, SSD XVI, 102–103.

179. *Offener Brief an Dr. phil. Friedrich Stade* (Open letter to Dr. Friedrich Stade), January 1871, *Musikalisches Wochenblatt*, SSD XVI, 103–108.

SHORTER WRITINGS ON VARIOUS SUBJECTS

180. *Brief über das Schauspielerwesen an einen Schauspieler* (Letter on acting to an Actor), 1873, *Almanach der Bühnengenossenschaft*, dated 9 November 1872, SSD IX, 258–264 (Ellis V, 257–262).

181. *Ein Einblick in das heutige deutsche Opernwesen* (A look at German opera today), January 1873, *Musikalisches Wochenblatt*, SSD IX, 264–287 (Ellis V, 263–284).

182. *Brief an einen italienischen Freund über die Aufführung des "Lohengrin" in Bologna* (Letter to an Italian friend on the production of *Lohengrin* in Bologna), end 1871, *Norddeutsche Allgemeine Zeitung*, dated 7 November 1871, SSD IX, 287–291.

183. *Schreiben an den Bürgermeister von Bologna* (Letter to the Burgomaster of Bologna), 11 October 1872 (dated 1 October) *Musikalisches Wochenblatt*, SSD IX, 291–294 (Ellis V, 289–291).

184. *An Friedrich Nietzsche, ordentlich Professor der klassischen Philologie an der Universität Basel* (To Friedrich Nietzsche, professor of classical philology at Basel University), 23 June 1872, *Norddeutsche Allgemeine Zeitung*, SSD IX, 295–302 (Ellis V, 292–298).

185. *Über die Benennung "Musikdrama"* (On the term *Musikdrama*), 8 November 1872, *Musikalisches Wochenblatt*, SSD IX, 302–308 (Ellis V, 299–304).

186. *Einleitung zu einer Vorlesung der "Götterdämmerung" vor einem ausgewählten Zuhörerkreise in Berlin* (Prologue to a reading of *Götterdämmerung* before a select audience in Berlin), 7 March 1873, *Musikalisches Wochenblatt*, SSD IX, 308–310 (Ellis V, 305–306).

187. *Über eine Opernaufführung in Leipzig* (On an opera production in Leipzig), 8 January 1875, *Musikalisches Wochenblatt*, SSD X, 1–10 (Ellis VI, 1–11).

188. *Bericht über die Wiederaufführung eines Jugendwerkes* (Report on the revival of an early work), 11 January 1883, *Musikalisches Wochenblatt*, SSD X, 309–315 (Ellis VI, 313–321).

STATEMENTS TO THE PRESS

189. *Zur Erwiderung des Aufsatzes "Richard Wagner und die öffentliche Meinung* (A reply to the essay *Richard Wagner and Public Opinion*), 22 February 1865, Augsburg *Allgemeine Zeitung*, SSD XII, 297–303.

190. *Das Münchener Hoftheater: zur Berichtigung* (The Munich Court Theater: a correction), 16 September 1869, Augsburg *Allgemeine Zeitung*, SSD XII, 304–308.

191. *Einladung zur ersten Aufführung von "Tristan und Isolde"* (Invitation to the first performance of *Tristan und Isolde*), 21 April 1865, *Der Wiener Botschafter*, SSD XVI, 32–41 (Ellis VIII, 239–248).

192. *Ansprache an das Hoforchester in München vor der Hauptprobe zu "Tristan"* (Speech to the Court Orchestra in Munich before the dress rehearsal for *Tristan und Isolde*), 15 May 1865, *Bayerische Zeitung,* SSD XVI, 42–43.

193. *Dankschreiben an das Münchener Hoforchester* (Letter of thanks to the Munich Court Orchestra), dated 19 July 1865, SSD XVI, 43–44.

194. *Ein Artikel der Münchener "Neuesten Nachrichten" vom 29 November 1865* (An article from the Munich *Neueste Nachrichten* of 29 November 1865), signed "fr," SSD XVI, 44–47.

195. *Erklärung im "Berner Bund" 10 Juni 1866* (Statement in the *Berner Bund* of 10 June 1866), SSD XVI, 47–48.

196. *Erklärung im "Berner Bund" 16 September 1869* (Statement in the *Berner Bund* of 16 September 1869), SSD XVI, 48 (date wrongly given as 1866).

197. *Vier Erklärungen in den "Signalen für die musikalische Welt"* (Four statements in the *Signale für die musikalische Welt*), 23 January and 19 March 1869, 20 June 1870, 12 November 1871, SSD XVI, 49–51.

198. *Zwei Erklärungen in der Augsburg Allgemeinen Zeitung über die Oper "Theodor Körner" von Wendelin Weißheimer* (Two statements in the Augsburg *Allgemeine Zeitung* on the opera *Theodor Körner* by Wendelin Weißheimer), 1 and 10 June 1872, SSD XVI, 51–52.

199. *Zwei Berichtigungen im "Musikalischen Wochenblatt"* (Two corrections in the *Musikalisches Wochenblatt*), 29 July 1872, 25 March 1873, SSD XVI, 53–54.

OPEN LETTERS, MISCELLANEOUS FRAGMENTS AND CONCERT PROGRAMS, 1864–1883

200. *An Frau Judith Gautier über die bevorstehende Aufführung des "Rienzi" in Paris* (To Frau Judith Gautier on the forthcoming production of *Rienzi* in Paris), 10 March 1869, *La liberté,* SSD XVI, 114–117. Drafted by Cosima Wagner (CT, 21 February 1869).

201. *An Champfleury* (To Champfleury), dated 16 March 1870 (in French), SSD XVI, 117–118 (in German).

202. *An den Herausgeber der "Amerikanischen Revue"* (To the editor of the *American Review*), dated June 1874 (in English), SSD XVI, 118–120 (in German).

203. *An Professor Gabriel Monod in Paris* (To Professor Gabriel Monod in Paris), dated 25 October 1876, SSD XVI, 120–124.

204. *An den Herzog von Bagnara, Präsidenten des Konservatorium der Musik in Neapel* (To the Duke of Bagnara, president of the Music Conservatoire in Naples), dated 22 April 1880, SSD XVI, 125–127. Drafted by Cosima Wagner (CT, 23 April 1880).

205. *Gedanken über die Bedeutung der deutschen Kunst für das Ausland* (Thoughts on the significance of German art for foreigners), written probably 1869, SSD XII 314–316.

206. *Drei Schreiben an die Direktion der Philharmonischen Gesellschaft in St. Petersburg* (Three letters to the management of the Philharmonic Society in St. Petersburg) III, 8 November 1866, SSD XVI, 31–32 (see nos. 106/107).

207. *Zum musikalischen Vortrag: Zum Andante der Es-dur Symphonie von Mozart* (On performing music: on the Andante in Mozart's Symphony in E-Flat Major), letter written 13 March 1868, SSD XVI, 102–103.

208. *An den Vorstand des Wagner-Vereins zu Berlin* (To the managing committee of the Wagner-Verein in Berlin), written 18 March 1873, SSD XVI, 111–114.

209. *An König Ludwig über die Aufführung des "Parsifal"* (To King Ludwig II on the production of *Parsifal*), written 28 September 1880, SSD XVI, 128.

210. *Persönliches: Warum ich den zahllosen Angriffen auf mich und meine Kunstanschauungen nichts erwidere* (Personal: why I do not reply to the numerous attacks on me and my views on art), dates uncertain, probably written between 1855 and 1882, SSD XII, 309–311 (Ellis VIII, 381–384).

211. *Die Meistersinger von Nürnberg: Vorspiel zum III. Akt* (*Die Meistersinger von Nürnberg:* prelude to the third act), probably 1869, SSD XII, 348–349 (Ellis VIII, 388).

212. *Zur Walküre . . .* (On *Die Walküre*), program notes for a concert in Munich on 11 December 1869, SSD XVI, 171–172.

213. *Zur Götterdämmerung . . .* (On *Götterdämmerung*), program notes for a concert in Vienna on 1 March 1875, SSD XVI, 173–175 (see also WWV, pp. 416–417).

214. *Parsifal: Vorspiel* (*Parsifal:* prelude), program note for the private performance given for Ludwig II in Munich, 12 November 1880, SSD XII, 349 (Ellis VIII, 388–389).

Bibliographical Abbreviations
Acknowledgments · Contributors · Indexes

Bibliographical Abbreviations

Abbate 1985   Carolyn Abbate. "The 'Parisian' Tannhäuser." Ph.D. diss., Princeton University, 1985.

Abbate 1985a   ——— "Der junge Wagner malgré lui: Die frühen *Tannhäuser*-Entwürfe und Wagners 'übliche Nummern . . . '" In WlWf, pp. 59–68.

Abbate 1989   ——— "Symphonic Opera, a Wagnerian Myth." In Abbate-Parker, pp. 92–123.

Abbate 1991   ——— *Unsung Voices: Opera and Musical Narrative in the Nineteenth Century.* Princeton, 1991.

Abbate-Parker   Carolyn Abbate and Roger Parker, eds. *Analyzing Opera: Verdi and Wagner.* Berkeley, 1989.

Adler 1904   Guido Adler. *Richard Wagner: Vorlesungen gehalten an der Universität zu Wien.* Leipzig, 1904; 2nd ed. 1923.

Adorno 1947   Theodor W. Adorno, "Wagner, Nietzsche, and Hitler." *Kenyon Review,* 9 (1947): 155–162. Reprinted in Theodor W. Adorno, *Gesammelte Schriften,* vol. 19, pp. 404–412. Frankfurt a.M., 1984.

Adorno 1952   ——— "Selbstanzeige des Essaybuches 'Versuch über Wagner.'" *Morgenblatt für Freunde der Literatur,* no. 3 (25 Sept.), p. 5. Frankfurt a.M., 1952. Reprinted in Theodor W. Adorno, *Gesammelte Schriften,* vol. 13, pp. 504–508. Frankfurt a.M., 1971.

Adorno 1981   ——— *In Search of Wagner.* Trans. R. Livingstone. London, 1981. [All citations are to this edition.] Original German ed. *Versuch über Wagner.* Berlin, 1952; reprint ed. 1964.

Altmann 1905   Wilhelm Altmann. *Richard Wagners Briefe nach Zeitfolge und Inhalt: Ein Beitrag zur Lebensgeschichte des Meisters.* Leipzig, 1905; reprint ed. 1971.

Angelucci 1928   Arnaldo Angelucci. "Il fenomeno della sublimazione nell'arte studiato nelle opere di Michelangelo—Wagner—Berlioz." *Archivio di ottalmologia,* 35 (1928): 385–428, 433–475, 481–528, 529–557.

Anonymous 1901   "[11] Briefe Ludwigs II. an Richard Wagner." In *Jahrbuch für sexuelle Zwischenstufen mit besonderer Berücksichtigung der Homosexualität,* ed. M. Hirschfeld, vol. 3 (1901), pp. 588ff. Reprint (selections in 2 vols.), ed. W. J. Schmidt, vol. 1, pp. 166–175. Frankfurt a.M., 1983–84.

Arro 1965   Elmar Arro. "Richard Wagners Rigaer Wanderjahre: Über einige baltische Züge im Schaffen Wagners." *Musik des Ostens,* 3 (1965): 123–168.

Bailey 1968   Robert Bailey. "Wagner's Musical Sketches for 'Siegfrieds Tod.'" In *Studies in Music History: Essays for Oliver Strunk,* pp. 459–494. Princeton, 1968.

Bailey 1969   —— "The Genesis of 'Tristan and Isolde,' and a Study of Wagner's Sketches and Drafts for the First Act." Ph.D. diss., Princeton University, 1969.

Bailey 1972   —— "The Evolution of Wagner's Compositional Procedure after Lohengrin." In *International Musicological Society: Report of the Eleventh Congress Copenhagen 1972,* vol. 1, pp. 240–246. Copenhagen, 1974.

Bailey 1977/8   —— "The Structure of the 'Ring' and Its Evolution." *Nineteenth-Century Music,* 1 (1977/8): 48–61.

Bailey 1979   —— "The Method of Composition." In *Wagner Companion,* pp. 269–338.

Bailey 1985   ——, ed. *Richard Wagner: Prelude and Transfiguration from Tristan and Isolde* (Norton Critical Score). New York, 1985.

Barth-Mack-Voss   Herbert Barth, Dietrich Mack, and Egon Voss, eds. *Wagner: Sein Leben, sein Werk und seine Welt in zeitgenössischen Bildern und Texten.* Vienna, 1975; reprint ed. 1982. Trans. London, 1975; rev. and enlarged Egon Voss, Munich, 1982.

Bartlett 1990   Rosamund Bartlett. "Wagner and Russia: A Study of the Influence of the Music and Ideas of Richard Wagner on the Artistic and Cultural Life of Russia and the Soviet Union, 1841–1941." Ph.D. diss., Oxford University, 1990.

Baudelaire 1861   Charles Baudelaire, "Richard Wagner et Tannhaeuser à Paris." *Revue européenne,* Paris (1 April 1861). Also *Oeuvres complètes,* ed. C. Pinchois, vol. 2, pp. 794ff. Trans. P. E. Charvet, in *Baudelaire: Selected Writings on Art and Artists,* pp. 325–357. Cambridge, 1972.

Bauer 1983   Oswald Georg Bauer. *Richard Wagner: The Stage Designs and the Productions from the Premières to the Present.* Foreword Wolfgang Wagner. New York, 1983.

Baur-Fischer-   Erwin Baur, Eugen Fischer, and Fritz Lenz. *Menschliche Erb-*
Lenz 1936   *lehre.* Munich, 4th ed. 1936.

Bayreuther Blätter   *Bayreuther Blätter,* ed. Hans von Wolzogen. Chemnitz, 1878–1938.

BB   Richard Wagner. *The Diary of Richard Wagner 1865–1882: The Brown Book.* Presented and annotated Joachim Bergfeld; trans. George Bird. London, 1980. [All citations are to this edition.] Original German ed. *Das braune Buch: Tagebuchaufzeichnungen, 1865 bis 1882,* Zurich, 1975.

Becker 1978   George Becker. *The Mad Genius Controversy: A Study in the Sociology of Deviance.* Beverly Hills, Calif., 1978.

Bekker 1924   Paul Bekker. *Richard Wagner: Das Leben im Werke.* Stuttgart, 1924. Trans. M. M. Bozman. London, 1931; reprint ed. 1970.

Berlioz-Strauss   Hector Berlioz. *Instrumentationslehre.* Rev. and enlarged Richard Strauss. 2 vols. Leipzig, [1905]. Trans. Theodore Font, *Treatise on Instrumentation.* New York, 1948.

Bertau 1982   Karl Bertau. "Tristan und Narziss." In *Programmhefte der Bayreuther Festspiele: "Tristan und Isolde."* Bayreuth, 1982.

Birnbaum 1920   Karl Birnbaum. *Psychopathologische Dokumente: Selbstbekenntnisse und Fremdzeugnisse aus dem seelischen Grenzlande.* Berlin, 1920.

BKB   *Bericht über den internationalen musikwissenschaftlichen Kongress Bayreuth 1981.* Ed. Christoph Mahling and Sigrid Wiesmann. Kassel, 1984.

Bloch 1985   Ernst Bloch. "Paradoxes and the pastorale in Wagner's music." In *Essays on the Philosophy of Music,* pp. 84–105. Trans. Peter Palmer. Cambridge, 1985. Original German text "Paradoxa und Pastorale in Wagners Musik." *Merkur,* 13 (1959): 405–435.

Bonaparte 1933   Marie Bonaparte. *Edgar Poe: Sa vie—son oeuvre. Etude psychoanalytique.* Foreword Sigmund Freud. Paris, 1933; reprint ed. 1958. Trans. John Rodker, *The Life and Works of Edgar Allan Poe: A Psycho-Analytic Interpretation.* London, 1949.

Borchmeyer 1982   Dieter Borchmeyer. *Das Theater Richard Wagners: Idee—Dichtung—Wirkung.* Stuttgart, 1982. [All citations are to this edition.] Trans. Stewart Spencer. Oxford, 1991.

Borchmeyer 1983   ———, ed. and afterword. *Friedrich Nietzsche. Der Fall Wagner. Schriften—Aufzeichnungen—Briefe.* Frankfurt a.M., 1983.

Botstein 1987   Leon Botstein. "Wagner and Our Century" (review of Mann 1985 and Katz 1986). *Nineteenth-Century Music,* 11 (1987/8): 92–104.

Boucher 1948   Maurice Boucher. *Les idées politiques de Richard Wagner: Exemple de nationalisme mythique.* Paris, 1948. Trans. Marcel Honoré. *The Political Concepts of Richard Wagner.* New York, 1950.

Bowen 1897   Anna Maude Bowen. *The Sources and Text of Richard Wagner's Opera "Die Meistersinger von Nürnberg."* Munich, 1897; facsimile reprint New York, 1977.

Brandl 1985   Rudolf Maria Brandl. "Musik und veränderte Bewußtseinszustände." In Bruhn-Oerter-Rösing 1985, pp. 423–432.

Breig 1973   Werner Breig. "Studien zur Entstehungsgeschichte von Wagners 'Ring des Nibelungen.'" Habilitation diss., University of Freiburg i. Br., 1973.

Breig 1980   ——— "Der 'Rheintöchtergesang' in Wagners 'Rheingold.'" *Archiv für Musikwissenschaft,* 37 (1980): 241–263.

Brink 1924   Louise Brink. *Women Characters in Richard Wagner: A Study in "The Ring of the Nibelung."* Nervous and Mental Disease Monograph Series, no. 37. New York, 1924.

Brinkmann 1970   Reinhold Brinkmann. "Tannhäusers Lied." In Dahlhaus 1970, pp. 199–207.

Brinkmann 1971   —— "Szenische Epik—Marginalien zu Wagners Dramenkonzeption im 'Ring des Nibelungen.'" In Dahlhaus 1971a, pp. 85–96

Brinkmann 1972   —— "'Drei der Fragen stell' ich mir frei': Zur Wanderer-Szene im I. Akt von Wagners 'Siegfried.'" In *Jahrbuch des Staatlichen Instituts für Musikforschung*, pp. 120–162. Berlin, 1972.

Brinkmann 1978   —— "Mythos—Geschichte—Natur: Zeitkonstellationen im 'Ring.'" In Kunze 1978, pp. 61–77.

Brinkmann 1979   —— "Wonder, Reality, and the Borderline Between." In *Programmhefte der Bayreuther Festspiele: "Lohengrin,"* pp. 23–43. Bayreuth, 1979.

Brinkmann 1982   —— "Richard Wagner der Erzähler." *Österreichische Musikzeitschrift,* 37 (1982): 297–306.

Brown 1989   Matthew Brown. "Isolde's Narrative: From Hauptmotiv to Tonal Model." In Abbate-Parker, pp. 180–201.

Bruhn-Oerter-   Herbert Bruhn, Rolf Oerter, and Helmut Rösing, eds. *Mu-*
Rösing 1985   *sikpsychologie: Ein Handbuch in Schlüsselbegriffen*. Munich, 1985.

Brussel 1963   James A. Brussel. "The Brobdingnag of Bayreuth." *Psychiatric Quarterly Supplement,* 37 (1963): 212–229.

Bugard 1932   Pierre Bugard. *Musique et symbolisme en psychologie normale et pathologique*. Bordeaux, 1932.

Burke 1963   Kenneth Burke. "The Thinking of the Body: Comments on the Imagery of Catharsis in Literature." *Psychoanalytic Review,* 50 (Fall 1963): 25–68.

Burrell 1898   Mary Burrell. *Richard Wagner: His Life and Works from 1813 to 1834*. London 1898.

Burrell 1929   *Catalogue of the Burrell Collection*. Compiled anonymously. London, 1929.

Burzawa 1989   Ewa Burzawa. "'Die Walküre' von Sergei Eisenstein: Versuch der Rekonstruktion." In Müller 1989, pp. 299–311.

Buschinger 1984   Danielle Buschinger. "Die Wagner-Rezeption in der französischen Literatur des 20. Jahrhunderts." In Salzburg Symposium, pp. 351–410.

Busoni 1911   Ferruccio Busoni. *Sketch of a New Esthetic of Music*. Trans. Theodore Baker. New York, 1911. In *Three Classics in the Aesthetics of Music*, pp. 73–102. New York, 1962.

Cabanès 1920[?]   [Augustin] Cabanès. *Grands névropathes: Malades immortels*. 2 vols. Paris, 1920[?]; reprint ed. 1953.

Caftale 1933   R. Caftale. "Psicoanalisi e grafologia: Osservazioni sulla scriptura di Riccardo Wagner." *Rivista italiana di psicoanalisi,* 2 (1933): 372–384.

Caïn 1982   Jacques and Anne Caïn. "Freud, 'absolument pas musicien . . .' (18. 1. 28)." In J. and A. Caïn, G. Rosolato, J. Rousseau-Dujardin, P. Schaeffer, J. G. Trilling, and A. de Mijollaet. *Psychanalyse et Musique,* pp. 91–137. Paris, 1982.

Canzler 1987   Peter Canzler. "Parsifal und das Mitleiden des Psychoanalyti-
                    kers." In *Jahrbuch der Psychoanalyse,* ed. H. Beland, F.-W.
                    Eickhoff, W. Loch, et al., vol. 21, pp. 33–57. Stuttgart,
                    1987.

Carassus 1966   E. Carassus. *Le snobisme et les lettres françaises de P. Bourget à
                    M. Proust, 1884–1914.* Paris, 1966.

Chamberlain 1900   Houston Stewart Chamberlain. *Richard Wagner.* Trans. G. Ain-
                    slie Hight, rev. by au. London, 1900. [All citations are to
                    this edition.] Original German ed. Munich, 1896.

Chamberlain 1923   ———— *The Wagnerian Drama.* London, 1923. Original German
                    ed. *Das Drama Richard Wagners: Eine Anregung,* Leipzig,
                    1892; reprint ed. 1973.

Chessick 1983   Richard D. Chessick. "'The Ring': Richard Wagner's Dream
                    of Pre-Oedipal Destruction." *American Journal of Psychoanal-
                    ysis,* 43 (1983): 361–374.

Cody 1975   John Cody. "Richard Wagner and the Ur Maternal Sea." *Bul-
                    letin of the Menninger Clinic,* 39 (1975): 556–577.

Coeuroy 1965   André Coeuroy. *Wagner et l'esprit romantique.* Paris, 1965.

Comuzio-Ghigi 1983 Ermano Comuzio and Giuseppe Ghigi, eds. *L'immagine in me
                    nascota. R. W. . . . Un itinerario cinematografico.* Venice, 1983.

Cooke 1979   Deryck Cooke. *I Saw the World End: A Study of Wagner's
                    "Ring."* Oxford, 1979.

Cooke 1979a   ———— "Wagner's Musical Language." In *Wagner Companion,*
                    pp. 225–268.

Cosima 1980   *Cosima Wagner: Das zweite Leben. Briefe und Aufzeichnungen,
                    1883–1930.* Ed. Dietrich Mack. Munich, 1980.

Cox 1926   Catherine Morris Cox. *The Early Mental Traits of Three
                    Hundred Geniuses.* Stanford, 1926.

C. P. 1873   [Carl Pringsheim?]. *Richard Wagner und der "Specialist der Psy-
                    chiatrie": Eine Beleuchtung der Puschmann'schen Studie.* Berlin,
                    1873.

Cremerius 1971   Johannes Cremerius, ed. and intro. *Psychoanalytische Biogra-
                    phien.* Frankfurt a.M., 1971.

Csampai-   Attila Csampai and Dietmar Holland, eds. *Richard Wagner, Die
  Holland 1981   Meistersinger von Nürnberg: Texte, Materialien, Kommentare
                    (rororo opernbuch 7419).* Reinbek, 1981.

Csampai-   ———— *Richard Wagner: Der fliegende Holländer. Texte, Materi-
  Holland 1982   alien, Kommentare (rororo opernbuch 7346).* Reinbek, 1982.

Csampai-   ———— *Richard Wagner, Tristan und Isolde. Texte, Materialien,
  Holland 1983   Kommentare (rororo opernbuch 7770).* Reinbek, 1983.

Csampai-   ———— *Richard Wagner, Parsifal. Texte, Materialien, Kommentare
  Holland 1984   (rororo opernbuch 7809).* Reinbek, 1984.

CT   *Cosima Wagner: Die Tagebücher, 1869–1883.* Ed. and annotated
                    Martin Gregor-Dellin and Dietrich Mack. 2 vols. Munich,
                    1976/7. Trans. and intro. Geoffrey Skelton. 2 vols. London,
                    1978/80.

d'Annunzio 1893   Gabriele d'Annunzio. "Il caso Wagner." *La tribuna* (Rome): 23
                    July, 7 and 9 August 1893.

Dahlhaus 1965   Carl Dahlhaus. "Wagners Begriff der 'dichterisch-musikalischen Periode.'" In *Beiträge zur Geschichte der Musikanschauung im 19. Jahrhundert,* ed. Walter Salmen, pp. 179–187. Regensburg, 1965.

Dahlhaus 1969   —— "Formprinzipien in Wagners 'Ring des Nibelungen.'" In *Beiträge zur Geschichte der Oper,* ed. Heinz Becker, pp. 95–129. Regensburg, 1969.

Dahlhaus 1970   ——, ed. *Das Drama Richard Wagners als musikalisches Kunstwerk.* Regensburg, 1970.

Dahlhaus 1970a   —— "Zur Geschichte der Leitmotivtechnik bei Wagner." In Dahlhaus 1970, pp. 17–40; reprinted in Dahlhaus 1983, pp. 86–104.

Dahlhaus 1970b   —— "Soziologische Dechiffrierung von Musik: zu Theodor W. Adornos Wagnerkritik." *International Review of Music Aesthetics and Sociology,* 1 (1970): 137–147.

Dahlhaus 1971   —— *Wagners Konzeption des musikalischen Dramas.* Regensburg, 1971.

Dahlhaus 1971a   ——, ed. *Richard Wagner—Werk und Wirkung.* Regensburg, 1971.

Dahlhaus 1974   ——"Wagners 'Kunst des Übergangs.' Der Zwiegesang in 'Tristan und Isolde.'" In *Zur musikalischen Analyse,* ed. Gerhard Schuhmacher, pp. 475–486. *Wege der Forschung,* vol. 257. Darmstadt, 1974. Reprinted in Dahlhaus 1983, pp. 132–138.

Dahlhaus 1979   —— *Richard Wagner's Music Dramas.* Trans. Mary Whittall. Cambridge, 1979. [All citations are to this edition.] Original German ed. *Die Musikdramen Richard Wagners.* Velber, 1971.

Dahlhaus 1983   —— *Vom Musikdrama zur Literaturoper. Aufsätze zur neueren Operngeschichte.* Munich, 1983.

Dahlhaus 1985   —— "Chronologie oder Systematik? Probleme einer Edition von Wagners Schriften." In WlWf, pp. 127–130.

Darcy 1989   Warren Darcy. "Creatio ex nihilo: The Genesis, Structure and Meaning of the 'Rheingold' Prelude." *Nineteenth-Century Music,* 13 (1989/90): 79–100.

Deathridge 1974/5   John Deathridge. "The Nomenclature of Wagner's Sketches." *Proceedings of the Royal Musical Association,* 101 (1974/5): 75–83.

Deathridge 1977   —— *Wagner's 'Rienzi': A Reappraisal Based on a Study of the Sketches and Drafts.* Oxford, 1977.

Deathridge 1977a   —— "Wagner's Sketches for the 'Ring.'" *Musical Times,* 118 (1977): 383–389.

Deathridge 1979   —— "Wagner und Spontini. Mit einem unveröffentlichten Brief Richard Wagners." In *Jahrbuch der Bayerischen Staatsoper 1979,* pp. 68–76. Munich, 1979.

Deathridge 1981   —— Review of Westernhagen 1978. *Nineteenth-Century Music,* 5 (1981): 81–89.

Deathridge 1982   —— "Introduction to the Flying Dutchman." In ENO, *Der fliegende Holländer* (1982), pp. 13–26.

Deathridge 1983 ——— "Cataloguing Wagner." *Musical Times*, 124 (1983): 92–96. Enlarged version in *The Richard Wagner Centenary in Australia*, ed. Peter Dennison. *Adelaide Studies in Musicology*, vol. 14, pp. 193–197. Adelaide, 1985. See also Deathridge-Voss 1985 and WWV.

Deathridge 1988 ——— "The Ring: An Introduction." In *DGG* booklet with recording of *Die Walküre*, cond. James Levine, pp. 41–58. Hamburg, 1988.

Deathridge 1989 ——— "Through the Looking Glass: Some Remarks on the First Complete Draft of 'Lohengrin.'" In Abbate-Parker, pp. 56–91.

Deathridge-Dahlhaus 1984 John Deathridge and Carl Dahlhaus. *The New Grove Wagner*. London, 1984.

Deathridge-Voss 1985 John Deathridge and Egon Voss. "Wagnerforschung—*Und weiter nichts?? Weiter nichts?? Zur Einführung in das Wagner-Werk-Verzeichnis.*" In WlWf, pp. 181–194.

Dettmering 1969 Peter Dettmering. *Dichtung und Psychoanalyse: Thomas Mann—Rainer Maria Rilke—Richard Wagner*. Munich, 1969.

DiGaetani 1978 John DiGaetani. *Richard Wagner and the Modern British Novel*. Cranbury, N.Y., 1978.

Dinger 1892 Hugo Dinger. *Richard Wagners geistige Entwicklung*. Leipzig, 1892.

Donington 1963 Robert Donington. *Wagner's 'Ring' and Its Symbols: The Music and the Myth*. London, 1963.

Donington 1965 ——— "Wagner and Beethoven." Response to Jacobs 1965. *Music Review*, 26 (1965): 363ff.

Dorn 1879 Heinrich Dorn. *Gesetzgebung und Operntext. (Eine Schrift für Männer.) Zeitgemässe Betrachtungen*. Berlin, 1879.

Drews 1931 Arthur Drews. *Der Ideengehalt von Richard Wagners dramatischen Dichtungen im Zusammenhange mit seinem Leben und seiner Weltanschauung, nebst einem Anhang: Nietzsche und Wagner*. Leipzig, 1931.

DS Richard Wagner. *Dichtungen und Schriften,* ed. Dieter Borchmeyer. 10 vols. (annotated selection from SSD). Frankfurt a.M., 1983.

Dujardin 1931 Edouard Dujardin. *Le monologue intérieur*. Paris, 1931.

Eck 1979 Claus D. Eck. "Psychoanalytiker deuten Gestalten und Werke der Literatur." In *Die Psychologie des 20. Jahrhunderts,* ed. Gion Condrau, vol. 15, pp. 851–67. Zurich, 1979. Reprinted in *Kindlers "Psychologie des 20. Jahrhunderts." Psychologie der Kultur*, vol. 2, pp. 377–393. Weinheim, 1983.

Eckart 1929 Richard Graf Du Moulin Eckart. *Cosima Wagner: Ein Lebens- und Charakterbild*. Munich, 1929. Trans. C. A. Phillips and intro. E. Newman. 2 vols. London, 1929.

Eckstein 1936 Friedrich Eckstein. *"Alte unnennbare Tage!" Erinnerungen aus siebzig Lehr- und Wanderjahren*. Vienna, 1936.

Eger 1979 Manfred Eger. "The Letters of Richard and Cosima Wagner: The History and Relics of a Destroyed Correspondence."

Programmhefte der Bayreuther Festspiele: "Das Rheingold," pp. 25–47; "Die Walküre," pp. 25–55. Bayreuth, 1979.

Ehrenfels 1896 — Christian von Ehrenfels. "Die musikalische Architektonik." Bayreuther Blätter, 19 (1896): 257–263.

Ehrenfels 1913 — ———— Richard Wagner und seine Apostaten. Vienna, 1913.

Ehrenfels 1931 — ———— "Wagner und seine neuen Apostaten." Der Auftakt: Moderne Musikblätter, 11 (1931): 5–12.

Ehrenzweig 1949 — Anton Ehrenzweig. "The Origin of the Scientific and Heroic Urge (The Guilt of Prometheus)." International Journal of Psycho-Analysis, 30 (1949): 108–123.

Eilert 1978 — Heide Eilert. "Im Treibhaus: Motive der europäischen Décadence in Theodor Fontanes Roman 'L'adultera,'" Jahrbuch der deutschen Schillergesellschaft, 22 (1978): 496–517.

Ellis — William Ashton Ellis, ed. and trans. Richard Wagner's Prose Works. 8 vols. London, 1892–1899; reprint ed. 1972.

Engels 1985 — Friedrich Engels. The Origin of the Family, Private Property, and the State. Trans. Alick West, intro. Michèle Barrett. New York, 1985.

ENO — English National Opera and the Royal Opera. Opera Guides. London. Tristan und Isolde, 1981; Der fliegende Holländer, 1982; Die Meistersinger, 1983; Die Walküre, 1983; Siegfried, 1984; Götterdämmerung, 1985; Das Rheingold, 1985; Tannhäuser, 1988.

Ewans 1982 — Michael Ewans. Wagner and Aeschylus: The Ring and the Oresteia. London, 1982.

Family Letters — Family Letters of Richard Wagner. Trans. W. A. Ellis, enlarged ed., notes and intro. John Deathridge. London, 1991.

Fehr — Max Fehr. Richard Wagners Schweizer Zeit. Vol. 1 (1849–1855), Aarau, 1934; vol. 2 (1855–1872), Aarau, 1954.

Feis 1910 — Oswald Feis. Studien über die Genealogie und Psychologie der Musiker. Vol. 71 of Grenzfragen des Nerven- und Seelenlebens, ed. L. Loewenfeld and H. Kurella. Wiesbaden, 1910.

Field 1981 — Geoffrey G. Field. Evangelist of Race: The Germanic Vision of Houston Stewart Chamberlain. New York, 1981.

Finscher 1970 — Ludwig Finscher. "Über den Kontrapunkt der Meistersinger." In Dahlhaus 1970, pp. 303–312.

Fischer 1977 — Jens Malte Fischer. "Dekadenz und Entartung. Max Nordau als Kritiker des Fin de siècle." In Fin de siècle: Zur Literatur und Kunst der Jahrhundertwende, ed. R. Bauer, E. Heftrich, et al., pp. 93–111. Vol. 35 of Studien zur Philosophie und Literatur des neunzehnten Jahrhunderts. Frankfurt a.M., 1977.

Fischer 1980 — ————, ed. and intro. Psychoanalytische Literaturinterpretation: Aufsätze aus "Imago: Zeitschrift für Anwendung der Psychoanalyse auf die Geisteswissenschaften" (1912–1937). Munich, 1980.

Floros 1982 — Constantin Floros. "Studien zur Parsifal-Rezeption." In Richard Wagner: Parsifal, ed. Heinz-Klaus Metzger and Rainer Riehn, pp. 14–57. Munich, 1982.

Flugel 1936   J. F. Flugel. "The Tannhäuser Motif." *British Journal of Medical Psychology,* 15 (1936): 279–295.

Foster 1954   Milton Painter Foster. "The Reception of Max Nordau's 'Degeneration' in England and America." Ph.D. diss., University of Michigan, 1954.

Franke 1983   Rainer Franke. *Richard Wagners Zürcher Kunstschriften.* Hamburg, 1983.

Freud 1907   Sigmund Freud. "Delusions and Dreams in Jensen's *Gradiva.*" In SE, vol. 9, pp. 1–95.

Freud 1908   ———— "Creative Writers and Day-Dreaming." In SE, vol. 9, pp. 141–153.

Freud 1910   ———— "A Special Type of Choice of Object Made by Men." In SE, vol. 11, pp. 163–175.

Freud 1912   ————"On the Universal Tendency to Debasement in the Sphere of Love." In SE, vol. 11, pp. 177–190.

Freud 1914   ————"The Moses of Michelangelo." In SE, vol. 13, pp. 209–236.

Freud 1925   ————"An Autobiographical Study." In SE, vol. 20, pp. 7–70.

Freud 1928   ————"Dostoevsky and Parricide." In SE, vol. 21, pp. 173–194.

Freud 1933   ————Foreword to Bonaparte 1933. In SE, vol. 22, p. 254.

Frommel 1933   Gerhard Frommel. *Der Geist der Antike bei Richard Wagner.* Berlin, 1933.

Fuchs, E. 1923   Eduard Fuchs. *Das individuelle Problem.* Vol. 2 of *Geschichte der erotischen Kunst.* Munich, 1923.

Fuchs, H. 1903   Hanns Fuchs. *Richard Wagner und die Homosexualität.* Vol. 7 of *Studien zur Geschichte des menschlichen Geschlechtslebens.* Berlin, 1903.

Fuchs-Kind 1913   Eduard Fuchs and Alfred Kind. *Die Weiberherrschaft in der Geschichte der Menschheit.* 2 vols. with suppl. Munich, 1913; new ed. Vienna, 1930.

Furness 1982   Raymond Furness. *Wagner and Literature.* Manchester, 1982.

Gay 1986/87   Peter Gay. *The Tender Passion.* Vol. 2 of *The Bourgeois Experience: Victoria to Freud.* New York, 1986/87.

Geck 1970   Martin Geck. *Die Bildnisse Richard Wagners.* Munich, 1970.

Geck 1971   ————*Deutsche Oratorien 1800 bis 1840: Verzeichnis der Quellen und Aufführungen,* Quellen-Kataloge zur Musikgeschichte 4. Wilhelmshaven, 1971.

Geck 1988   ————"Parsifal: A Betrayed Childhood. Variations on a Leitmotif by Alice Miller." WNS, 9/2 (April 1988): 75–88.

Glasenapp   Carl Friedrich Glasenapp. *Das Leben Richard Wagners in sechs Büchern dargestellt.* Leipzig. Vol. 1, 5th ed. 1923; vol. 2, 5th ed. 1910; vol. 3, 5th ed. 1921; vol. 4, 4th ed. 1908; vol. 5, 5th ed. 1912; vol. 6, 3rd ed. 1911. Trans. vols. 1–2, 3rd ed. W. A. Ellis. In vols. 1–3 of *Life of Richard Wagner.* London, 1900–3; reprint ed. 1977.

Glass 1982   Frank W. Glass. *The Fertilizing Seed: Wagner's Concept of Poetic Intent.* Ann Arbor, Mich., 1982.

Glatzel 1986   Johann Glatzel. "Literatur und Schriftsteller in psychiatrischer Betrachtung." In Langner 1986a, pp. 18–45.

Gold 1960   Milton Gold. "The Early Psychiatrists on Degeneracy and Genius." *Psychoanalysis and the Psychoanalytic Review*, 47/4 (Winter 1960); 37–55.

Golther 1902   Wolfgang Golther. *Die sagengeschichtlichen Grundlagen der Ring-dichtung Richard Wagners.* Berlin, 1902.

Golther 1907   ——— *Tristan und Isolde in den Dichtungen des Mittelalters und der neuen Zeit.* Leipzig, 1907.

Graf 1911   Max Graf. *Richard Wagner im "fliegenden Holländer": Ein Beitrag zur Psychologie künstlerischen Schaffens.* Vol. 9 of *Schriften zur angewandten Seelenkunde,* ed. Sigmund Freud. Leipzig, 1911.

Graham 1978   Lindsay A. Graham. "Wagner and *Lohengrin,* a Psychoanalytic Study." *Psychiatric Journal of the University of Ottawa,* vol. 3/1 (March 1978): 39–49.

Greenblatt 1983   Robert Greenblatt. "Richard Wagner (1813–1883): The Voluptuary Genius." *British Journal of Sexual Medicine,* 10:93 (March 1983): 17–18.

Gregor-Dellin 1973   Martin Gregor-Dellin. *Richard Wagner: Die Revolution als Oper.* Munich, 1973.

Gregor-Dellin 1980   ——— *Richard Wagner: Sein Leben—Sein Werk—Sein Jahrhundert.* Munich, 1980.

Gregor-Dellin 1983   ——— *Richard Wagner: His Life, His Work, His Century.* Trans. J. Maxwell Brownjohn. London, 1983. Abridged version of Gregor-Dellin 1980.

Gregor-Dellin 1985   ———"Recent Researches on Wagner (His Mother's Secret)." *Programmhefte der Bayreuther Festspiele: Parsifal,* pp. 50–58. Bayreuth, 1985.

Gregor-Dellin/ Soden 1983   Martin Gregor-Dellin and Michael von Soden, eds. *Richard Wagner: Leben, Werk, Wirkung.* Düsseldorf, 1983.

Grey 1987   Thomas Grey. "Wagner and the Aesthetics of Musical Form." Ph.D. diss., University of California, 1987.

Groddeck 1927   Georg Groddeck. "Der Ring." *Die Arche* 3/11 (November 1927): 11–31. Trans. M. Collins. "The Ring, A Text-Book of Psycho-Analysis." In *Exploring the Unconscious,* pp. 132–153. London, 1933.

Groeben 1972   Norbert Groeben. *Literaturpsychologie: Literaturwissenschaft zwischen Hermeneutik und Empirie.* Stuttgart, 1972.

Groeben/ Vorderer 1986   Norbert Groeben and Peter Vorderer. "Empirische Literaturpsychologie." In Langner 1986a, pp. 105–143.

Großmann- Vendrey 1976   Susanna Großmann-Vendrey. "'Wagner in Italien': Bemerkungen zur Rezeptionsforschung." *Die Musikforschung* 29 (1976): 195–199.

Großmann- Vendrey 1977/83   ——— *Bayreuth in der deutschen Presse: Beiträge zur Rezeptionsgeschichte Richard Wagners und seiner Festspiele.* 3 vols. Regensburg, 1977/83.

Grunsky 1906   Karl Grunsky. "Wagner als Sinfoniker." In *Richard Wagner-Jahrbuch,* ed. Ludwig Frankenstein, vol. 1, pp. 227–244. Leipzig, 1906.

Grunsky 1907 ——— "Das Vospiel und der erste Akt von 'Tristan und Isolde.'" In *Richard Wagner-Jahrbuch,* ed. Ludwig Frankenstein, vol. 2, pp. 207–284. Berlin, 1907.

Grunsky 1935 Hans Alfred Grunsky. *Seele und Staat: Die psychologischen Grundlagen des nationalsozialistischen Siegs über den bürgerlichen und bolschewistischen Menschen.* Berlin, 1935.

Grunsky 1943 ——— "Einer der uns fehlt: Dem Gedenken von Alfred Lorenz." In NWF, pp. 35–42.

Grunsky 1951 ——— "'Parsifal' im Lichte der Tiefenpsychologie." *Programmhefte der Bayreuther Festspiele: Parsifal,* pp. 6–28. Bayreuth, 1951.

Guichard 1963 Léon Guichard. *La musique et les lettres en France au temps du Wagnérisme.* Paris, 1963.

Guichard 1964 ———, ed. *Richard et Cosima Wagner: Lettres à Judith Gautier.* Paris, 1964.

Gutman 1968 Robert Gutman. *Richard Wagner: The Man, His Mind, and His Music.* New York, 1968.

Haesler 1985 Ludwig Haesler. "Musik und Psychoanalyse." In Bruhn-Oerter-Rösing 1985, pp. 259–265.

Haisch 1953 Erich Haisch. "Über die psychoanalytische Deutung der Musik." *Psyche,* 7 (November 1953): 81–88.

Halász 1987 László Halász, ed. *Literary Discourse: Aspects of Cognitive and Social Psychological Approaches.* New York, 1987.

Hall 1951 Calvin S. Hall. "What People Dream About." *Scientific American,* 184 (May 1951): 60–63.

Hall 1983 ———"Wagnerian Dreams: One Hundred Years after Richard Wagner's Death, a Study of the Composer's Dreams Offers Clues to His Odious Behavior." *Psychology Today,* 17 (January 1983): pp. 34–39.

Hall/Van de Castle 1966 Calvin S. Hall and Robert L. Van de Castle. *The Content Analysis of Dreams.* In Century Psychology Series, ed. Richard M. Elliott, Gardner Lindzey, and Kenneth MacCorquodale. New York, 1966.

Halm 1916 August Halm. *Von Grenzen und Ländern der Musik.* Munich, 1916.

Hanslick 1860 Eduard Hanslick. "'Der fliegende Holländer' von Richard Wagner." *Die Presse,* 13/284 (Vienna, 1860); reprinted in Csampai-Holland 1982, pp. 140–144.

Hanslick 1875 ——— *Die moderne Oper: Kritiken und Studien.* Berlin, 1875.

Hanslick 1894 ——— *Aus meinem Leben.* Berlin, 1894; reprint ed. 1971.

Hermand 1962 Jost Hermand. "Gralsmotive um die Jahrhundertwende." *Deutsche Vierteljahrsschrift für Literaturwissenschaft und Geistesgeschichte,* 36 (1962): 521–543.

Herrmann 1873 Franz Herrmann. *Richard Wagner: Streiflichter auf Dr. Puschmann's psychiatrische Studie.* Munich, 1873.

Hey 1884 Julius Hey. *Deutscher Gesangs-Unterricht.* 3 vols. Mainz, 1884.

Hey 1911 ——— *Richard Wagner als Vortragsmeister, 1864–1876: Erinnerungen.* Leipzig, 1911.

Hight 1925   George Ainslie Hight. *Richard Wagner: A Critical Biography*. 2 vols. London, 1925.

Hirsch 1894   William Hirsch. *Genius and Degeneration: A Psychological Study*. New York, 1896; London, 1897. Original German ed., *Genie und Entartung: Eine psychologische Studie*. Berlin, 1894.

Hodges 1980   Donald A. Hodges, ed. *Handbook of Music Psychology*. Lawrence, Kans., 1980.

Holland 1975   Norman Holland. *Five Readers Reading*. New Haven, 1975.

Hollinrake 1970   Roger Hollinrake. "The Title-Page of Wagner's 'Mein Leben.'" *Music and Letters*, 51 (1979): 415–422.

Hopkinson 1973   Cecil Hopkinson. *Tannhäuser: An Examination of Thirty-six Editions*. Tutzing, 1973.

Hostinsky 1877   Otakar Hostinsky. *Das Musikalisch-Schöne und das Gesamtkunstwerk vom Standpunkte der formalen Aesthetik*. Leipzig, 1877.

HSA   Adolf Hitler. *Sämtliche Aufzeichnungen, 1904–1924*. Ed. E. Jäckel. Stuttgart, 1980.

HSC   *Hitler's Secret Conversations, 1941–1944*. Trans. N. Cameron and R. H. Stevens. New York, 1953.

Hugbald 1910   Hugbald. "Verwandtschaften im Nibelungenring." In *Schaubühne*, 6 (21 April 1910): 436.

Ingenschay-   Dagmar Ingenschay-Goch. *Richard Wagners neu erfundener My
Goch 1982   thos: Zur Rezeption und Reproduktion des germanischen Mythos in seinen Operntexten*. Bonn, 1982.

Jachino 1894   Carlo Jachino. "Wagner è un degenerato?" *Rivista musicale italiana*, 1 (1894): 130–137.

Jäckel 1931   Curt Jäckel. *Richard Wagner in der französischen Literatur*. Breslau, 1931/2.

Jacobi 1958   Jolande Jacobi. "Archetypisches im Ring des Nibelungen." In *Programmhefte der Bayreuther Festspiele: Das Rheingold*, pp. 1–8, 18–22. Bayreuth, 1958. Reprinted in *Richard Wagner und das neue Bayreuth*, ed. Wieland Wagner, pp. 136–149. Munich, 1962.

Jacobs 1965   Robert L. Jacobs. "A Freudian View of *The Ring*." *Music Review*, 26 (1965): 201–219.

Jacobs-Skelton 1973 Robert L. Jacobs and G. Skelton, eds. and trans. *Wagner Writes from Paris . . .* London, 1973.

Jacobson 1932   Anna Jacobson. *Nachklänge Richard Wagners im Roman*. Vol. 20 of *Beiträge zur neueren Literaturgeschichte*, Neue Folge. Heidelberg, 1932.

Jones 1925   Katherine Jones. Review of Brink 1924. *International Journal of Psycho-Analysis*, 6 (1925): 229ff.

Jones 1959   ——— "King Mark Disguised as Himself." *Imago*, 16 (Summer 1959): 115–125.

Josephson 1979   Nors S. Josephson. "Tonale Strukturen im musikdramatischen Schaffen Richard Wagners." *Die Musikforschung*, 32 (1979): 141–149.

Jung 1911/12   Carl Gustav Jung. *Symbols of Transformation* (Collected Works 5). Trans. R. F. C. Hull. London, 1956.

Jung 1930   —— "Psychology and Literature." In *The Spirit in Man, Art, and Literature* (Collected Works 15), pp. 84–105. Trans. R. F. C. Hull. London, 1956.

Jung 1932   —— "On the Relation of Analytical Psychology to Poetry." In *The Spirit in Man, Art, and Literature* (Collected Works 15), pp. 65–83. Trans. R. F. C. Hull. London, 1956.

Jung 1974   Ute Jung. *Die Rezeption der Kunst Richard Wagners in Italien.* Regensburg, 1974.

Just 1978   Klaus Günther Just. "Richard Wagner—ein Dichter? Marginalien zum Opernlibretto des 19. Jahrhunderts." In Kunze 1978, pp. 79–84.

Kalfus 1984   Melvin Kalfus. "Richard Wagner as Cult Hero: The Tannhäuser Who Would Be Siegfried." *Journal of Psychohistory,* 11 (Winter 1984): 315–382.

Kandinsky   [*Wassily*] *Kandinsky: Complete Writings on Art,* ed. Kenneth C. Lindsay and Peter Vergo. 2 vols. London, 1982.

Kaplan 1912   Leo Kaplan. "Zur Psychologie des Tragischen." *Imago* 5 (May 1912): 132–157; reprinted in Fischer 1980, pp. 33–63.

Kapp 1913   Julius Kapp. *Wagner: Eine Biographie. Neunte und Zehnte durchgesehene und erweiterte Auflage.* Berlin, 1913.

Karbaum 1976   Michael Karbaum. *Studien zur Geschichte der Bayreuther Festspiele.* Regensburg, 1976.

Karpath 1906   Ludwig Karpath. *Zu den Briefen Richard Wagners an eine Putzmacherin. Unterredungen mit der Putzmacherin Bertha: Ein Beitrag zur Lebensgeschichte Richard Wagners.* Berlin, 1906.

Kastner 1878   Emerich Kastner. *Wagner-Catalog: Chronologisches Verzeichnis der von und über Richard Wagner erschienenen Schriften, Musikwerke, etc., etc., nebst biographischen Notizen.* Offenbach, 1878; reprinted 1966.

Katz 1986   Jakob Katz. *The Darker Side of Genius: Richard Wagner's Anti-Semitism.* London 1986. [All citations are to this edition.] Original German ed. *Richard Wagner: Vorbote des Antisemitismus.* Königstein, 1985.

Kerman 1961   Joseph Kerman. "Wagner: Thoughts in Season." *Score,* 28 (1961): 9–24.

Kerman 1983   —— "Wagner and Wagnerism." *New York Review of Books,* 22 (December 1983): 27–37.

Kerman 1989   —— *Opera as Drama.* Rev. ed. Boston, 1989.

Kester 1984   Sally Kester. "An Examination of the Themes of Love, Power, and Salvation in Richard Wagner's 'The Ring of the Nibelungen': The Study of a Failed Individuation Process." Ph.D. diss., University of Western Australia, 1984.

Kinderman 1980   William Kinderman. "Dramatic Recapitulation in Wagner's *Götterdämmerung.*" *Nineteenth-Century Music,* 4 (1980/1): 101–112.

Kinderman 1983   —— "Das Geheimnis der Form in Wagners 'Tristan und Isolde.'" *Archiv für Musikwissenschaft,* 40 (1983): 174–188.

Klein 1979   H. F. G. Klein. *Erst- und Frühdrucke der Textbücher von Richard Wagner: Bibliographie.* Tutzing, 1979.

Klein 1983   —— *Erstdrucke der musikalischen Werke von Richard Wagner: Bibliographie.* Tutzing, 1983.

Kneif 1975   Tibor Kneif, ed. *Richard Wagner: "Die Kunst und die Revolution," "Das Judentum in der Musik," "Was ist deutsch?"* Munich, 1975.

Koch 1875   Ernst Koch. *Richard Wagners Bühnenfestspiel im Verhältnis zur alten Sage und zur modernen Nibelungendichtung.* Leipzig, 1875.

König-Briefe   *König Ludwig II. und Richard Wagner. Briefwechsel.* Ed. O. Strobel. 5 vols. Vols. 1–4, 1936; vol. 5, 1939.

Konrad 1987   Ulrich Konrad. "Robert Schumann und Richard Wagner: Studien und Dokumente." In *Augsburger Jahrbuch für Musikwissenschaft,* vol. 4. 1987.

Koppen 1973   Erwin Koppen. *Dekadenter Wagnerismus: Studien zur europäischen Literatur des Fin de siècle.* Berlin, 1973.

Kropfinger 1984   Klaus Kropfinger, ed. *Richard Wagner, Oper und Drama.* Stuttgart, 1984.

Kropfinger 1991   —— *Wagner and Beethoven: Richard Wagner's Reception of Beethoven.* Rev. ed. Trans. Peter Palmer. Cambridge, 1991. Original German ed. *Wagner und Beethoven: Untersuchungen zur Beethoven-Rezeption Richard Wagners.* Regensburg, 1975.

Kubizek 1954   August Kubizek. *Young Hitler: The Story of Our Friendship.* Trans. E. V. Anderson. London, 1954; reprint ed. 1973. Original German ed. *Adolf Hitler: Mein Jugendfreund.* Graz, 1953.

Kudszus 1980   Winfrid G. Kudszus. "Literaturwissenschaft und Psychiatrie." In *Die Psychologie des 20. Jahrhunderts,* ed. U. H. Peters, pp. 1121–30. Zurich, 1980.

Kunze 1978   Stefan Kunze, ed. *Richard Wagner: Von der Oper zum Musikdrama.* Bern, 1978.

Kurth 1920   Ernst Kurth. *Romantische Harmonik und ihre Krise in Wagners "Tristan."* Bern, 1920; reprint ed. 1975.

Kusche 1967   Ludwig Kusche. *Wagner und die Putzmacherin, oder Die Macht der Verleumdung.* Wilhelmshaven, 1967.

Laing 1973   Alan Laing. "Tonality in Wagner's 'Der Ring des Nibelungen.'" Ph.D. diss., University of Edinburgh, 1973.

Lange-Eichbaum 1967   Wilhelm Lange-Eichbaum and Wolfram Kurth. *Genie Irrsinn und Ruhm: Genie-Mythus und Pathographie des Genies.* 6th ed. Munich, 1967; reprint ed. 1979.

Langner 1986a   Ralph Langner, ed. and intro. *Psychologie der Literatur: Theorien, Methoden, Ergebnisse.* Weinheim, 1986.

Langner 1986b   —— "Literatur in der Sicht der Komplexen Psychologie [C. G. Jungs]." In Langner 1986a, pp. 46–77.

Large-Weber 1985   David Large and William Weber, eds. *Wagnerism in European Culture and Politics.* Ithaca, N.Y., 1985.

Lee 1932   Vernon Lee (= Violet Paget). *Music and Its Lovers: An Empirical Study of Emotion and Imaginative Responses to Music.* London, 1932.

Lehmann 1986 — Herbert Lehmann. "Jung contra Freud/Nietzsche contra Wagner." *International Review of Psychoanalysis*, 13 (1986): 201–209.

Levin 1959 — Irving Levin. "Some Psychoanalytic Concepts in Richard Wagner's 'The Ring of the Niblung [sic].'" *Archives of Criminal Psychodynamics*, 3 (Spring 1959): 260–316.

Lewin 1984 — David Lewin. "Amfortas's Prayer to Titurel and the Role of D in *Parsifal:* The Tonal Spaces of the Drama and the Enharmonic C♭/B." *Nineteenth-Century Music*, 7/3 (1984): 336–349.

Lippert 1927 — Woldemar Lippert. *Richard Wagners Verbannung und Rückkehr, 1849–1862.* Dresden, 1927. Trans. Paul England, *Wagner in Exile, 1849–1862.* London, 1930.

Lippmann 1973 — Friedrich Lippmann. "Ein neu entdecktes Autograph Richard Wagners." In *Musicae scientiae collectanea: Festschrift Karl Gustav Fellerer,* pp. 373–379. Cologne, 1973.

Lloyd-Jones 1982 — Hugh Lloyd-Jones. "Wagner." In *Blood for the Ghosts: Classical Influences in the Nineteenth and Twentieth Centuries,* pp. 126–142. London, 1982.

Lombroso 1891 — Cesare Lombroso. *The Man of Genius.* New York, 1891; rev. ed. 1914.

Lombroso 1897 — ——— *Genio e degenerazione 1: Nuovi studi e nuove battaglie.* Palermo, 1897; enlarged ed., 1907.

Lorenz — Alfred Lorenz. *Das Geheimnis der Form bei Richard Wagner.* 4 vols. Vol. 1, *Der musikalische Aufbau des Bühnenfestspieles Der Ring des Nibelungen.* Berlin, 1924; reprint ed. 1966. Vol. 2, *Der musikalische Aufbau von Richard Wagners "Tristan und Isolde."* Berlin, 1926; reprint ed. 1966. Vol. 3, *Der musikalische Aufbau von Richard Wagners "Die Meistersinger von Nürnberg."* Berlin, 1930; reprint ed. 1966. Vol. 4, *Der musikalische Aufbau von Richard Wagners "Parsifal."* Berlin, 1933; reprint ed. 1966.

Lorenz 1914 — Emil Franz Lorenz. "Die Geschichte des Bergmanns von Falun, vornehmlich bei E. T. A. Hoffmann, Richard Wagner, und Hugo von Hofmannsthal." *Imago* 3 (1914): 250–301.

Lunacharsky 1965 — Anatoly Lunacharsky. "Richard Wagner: On the Fiftieth Anniversary of His Death." In *On Literature and Art,* pp. 340–354. Moscow, 1965. See also Bernice Glatzer Rosenthal's articles in Large-Weber 1985 and *Wagner in Retrospect.*

M. 1870 — M. "Richard Wagner's Musikdramen und die Sittlichkeit." *Neue Zeitschrift für Musik,* 36 (25 November 1870): 433–434.

Maas 1932 — Paul Maas. Review of Drews 1931. *Gnomon,* 8 (1932): 174–176.

Mack 1978 — Dietrich Mack, ed. *Theaterarbeit an Wagners Ring.* Munich, 1978.

Magee 1990 — Elizabeth Magee. *Richard Wagner and the Nibelungs.* Oxford, 1990.

Mann 1933	Thomas Mann. "Leiden und Grösse Richard Wagners." *Neue Rundschau* (Berlin), April 1933. Trans. Allan Blunden, "The Sorrows and Grandeur of Richard Wagner." In Mann 1985, pp. 91–148.
Mann 1985	—— *Pro and Contra Wagner* [collected writings on Wagner]. Trans. Allan Blunden; intro. Erich Heller. London, 1985.
Marcuse 1963	Ludwig Marcuse. *Das denkwürdige Leben des Richard Wagner.* Munich, 1963.
Martin 1982	Stoddard Martin. *Wagner to "The Waste Land": A Study of the Relationship of Wagner to English Literature.* London, 1982.
Marx 1975	Karl Marx. "On the Jewish Question." In Karl Marx and Friedrich Engels, *Collected Works,* vol. 3, pp. 146–174. London, 1975.
Marx-Letters	*The Letters of Karl Marx.* Selected, trans., and intro. S. K. Padover. Englewood Cliffs, N.J., 1979.
Mayer 1966	Hans Mayer. *Anmerkungen zu Wagner.* Frankfurt a.M., 1966.
Mayer 1976	—— *Richard Wagner in Bayreuth, 1876–1976.* Stuttgart, 1976; trans. London, 1976.
Mayer 1978	—— *Richard Wagner: Mitwelt und Nachwelt.* Stuttgart, 1978.
Mayreder 1936	Rosa Mayreder. "Von Wagner zu Nietzsche: Ein Jugenderlebnis." *Die Glocke: Wiener Blätter für Kunst und geistiges Leben,* 2 (1 February 1936): 8–15.
McCreless 1982	Patrick McCreless. *Wagner's "Siegfried": Its Drama, History, and Music.* Ann Arbor, Mich., 1982.
McCreless 1989	—— "Schenker and the Norns." In Abbate-Parker, pp. 276–297.
McGrath 1965	William McGrath. "Wagnerism in Austria." Ph.D. diss., University of California, 1965.
McGrath 1974	—— *Dionysian Art and Populist Politics in Austria.* New Haven, 1974.
Meinck 1892	Ernst Meinck. *Die sagenwissenschaftlichen Grundlagen der Nibelungendichtung Richard Wagners.* Berlin, 1892.
Meyer 1978	Michael Meyer. "Musicology in the Third Reich: A Gap in Historical Studies." *European Studies Review,* 8 (1978): 349–364.
Michel 1948	André Michel. "Les guerres péniques chez Wagner." In *Psychanalyse de la musique,* pp. 66–86. Paris, 1951. Original pub. *Psyché,* 25 (November 1948).
Michel 1965	—— *L'école freudienne devant la musique.* Paris, 1965.
Miller 1988	Alice Miller. *Der gemiedene Schlüssel.* Frankfurt a.M., 1988.
Millington 1984	Barry Millington. *Wagner.* London, 1984.
Mitchell 1967	William J. Mitchell. "The *Tristan* Prelude: Techniques and Structure." *Music Forum,* 1 (1967): 162–203.
Mittelalter-Rezeption	Jürgen Kühnel, Hans-Dieter Mück, et al., eds. *Die Rezeption des Mittelalters in Literatur, Bildende Kunst und Musik des 19. und 20. Jahrhunderts.* Göppingen, 1982.

ML

Richard Wagner, *My Life,* trans. Andrew Gray, ed. Mary Whittall. Cambridge, 1983. [All citations are to this edition.] Originally published in 4 vols.: 1–3 privately in Basel, 1870–75; 4 privately in Bayreuth, 1881. Abridged ed. vols. 1–4, Munich, 1911. [Suppressed passages first published in *Die Musik,* 22 (1929/30): 725–731; trans. Ernest Newman, *Fact and Fiction about Wagner,* pp. 199–202. London, 1931.] Unabridged ed. M. Gregor-Dellin, Munich, 1963, 1976, 1983.

Moll 1910

Albert Moll. *Berühmte Homosexuelle.* Vol. 71 of *Grenzfragen des Nerven- und Seelenlebens,* ed. L. Loewenfeld and H. Kurella. Wiesbaden, 1910.

Moloney/ Rockelein 1948

James Clark Moloney and Laurence A. Rockelein. "An Insight into Richard Wagner and His Works (A Psychoanalytical Fragment)." *American Imago,* 5 (November 1948): 202–212.

Montinari 1985

Mazzino Montinari. "Nietzsche-Wagner im Sommer 1878." In *Nietzsche-Studien: Internationales Jahrbuch für die Nietzsche-Forschung,* ed. E. Behler et al., vol. 14 (1985), pp. 13–21.

Mora 1964

George Mora. "One Hundred Years from Lombroso's First Essay 'Genius and Insanity.'" *American Journal of Psychiatry,* 121 (1964/5): 562–571.

Moreau 1859

Jacques-Joseph Moreau de Tours. *La psychologie morbide dans ses rapports avec la philosophie de l'histoire ou de l'influence des névropathies sur le dynamisme intellectuel.* Paris, 1859.

Morel 1857

Bénédict Auguste Morel. *Traité des dégénérescences physiques, intellectuelles et morales de l'espèce humaine et de ses causes qui produisent ces variétés maladives.* Paris, 1857.

Mork 1990

Andrea Mork. *Richard Wagner als politischer Schriftsteller.* Frankfurt, 1990.

Moser 1938

Max Moser. *Richard Wagner in der englischen Literatur des 19ten Jahrhunderts.* Schweizer anglistische Arbeiten, no. 7. Bern, 1938.

Motte-Haber 1979

Helga de la Motte-Haber. "Musikpsychologie." In *Brockhaus Riemann Lexikon,* vol. 2, ed. Carl Dahlhaus and Hans Heinrich Eggebrecht. Wiesbaden, 1979.

Mühlen 1977

Patrik von zur Mühlen. *Rassenideologien: Geschichte und Hintergründe.* Berlin, 1977.

Müller 1862

Franz Müller. *Der Ring des Nibelungen: Eine Studie zur Einführung in die gleichnamige Dichtung Richard Wagners.* Leipzig, 1862.

Muller 1981

Philippe Muller. *Wagner par ses rêves.* Brussels, 1981.

Müller 1982

Ulrich Müller. "Parzifal 1980—Auf der Bühne, im Fernsehen und im Film." In Mittelalter-Rezeption, pp. 623–640.

Müller 1985

———— "Richard Wagners ungeschriebene Oper von 'Erec und Enide.'" *Zeitschrift für Germanistik,* 6 (1985): 180–188.

Müller 1986

———— "From 'Parsifal' to the Ban on Love: Wagner and the Middle Ages." WNS, 7 (1986): 110–125.

Müller 1989

Ursula and Ulrich Müller, eds. *Richard Wagner und sein Mittelalter.* Anif/Salzburg, 1989.

Müller- Freienfels 1919	Richard Müller-Freienfels. *Persönlichkeit und Weltanschauung: Psychologische Untersuchungen zu Religion, Kunst, und Philosophie.* Leipzig, 1919.
Musique en jeu 1972	Bibliography (Music and Psychoanalysis). *Musique en jeu,* 9 (November 1972): 119–122.
Natoli 1984	Joseph Natoli, ed. *Psychological Perspectives on Literature: "Freudian Dissidents and Non-Freudians," a Casebook.* Hamden, Conn., 1984.
Natoli/Rusch 1984	Joseph Natoli and Frederic L. Rusch. "A Survey of Psychocriticism." In *Psychocriticism: An Annotated Bibliography,* pp. xi–xxiii. London, 1984.
Nattiez 1980	Jean-Jacques Nattiez. "Chéreau's Treachery." *October,* 14 (Fall 1980): 71–100.
Nattiez 1983	——— *Tétralogies—Wagner, Boulez, Chéreau: Essai sur l'infidélité.* Paris, 1983.
Nattiez 1990	——— *Wagner androgyne: Essai sur l'interprétation.* Paris, 1990.
Newcomb 1981/2	Anthony Newcomb. "The Birth of Music out of the Spirit of Drama." *Nineteenth-Century Music,* 5 (1981/2): 38–66.
Newman 1949	Ernest Newman. *The Wagner Operas.* New York, 1949; reprint ed. 1961, 1977, 1988.
Newman 1976	——— *The Life of Richard Wagner.* 4 vols. Cambridge, 1976. Original ed. New York, 1937–46.
Nietzsche 1910	Friedrich Nietzsche. *The Case of Wagner/Nietzsche contra Wagner.* Trans. Anthony Ludovici. London, 1910.
Nietzsche 1967	——— *The Birth of Tragedy and The Case of Wagner.* Trans. Walter Kaufmann. New York, 1967.
Nietzsche 1976	——— *Nietzsche contra Wagner: Out of the Files of a Psychologist* (1888). In *The Portable Nietzsche,* ed. W. Kaufmann, pp. 661–683. New York, 1976.
Nietzsche 1978	——— *Briefwechsel.* Ed. Giorgio Colli and Mazzino Montinari. Vol. 3, May 1872–December 1874. Berlin, 1978.
Nietzsche 1979	——— *Ecce Homo.* Trans. R. J. Hollingdale. New York, 1979.
Nietzsche 1983	——— *Untimely Meditations.* Trans. R. J. Hollingdale. Cambridge, 1983.
Nietzsche Werke	*Nietzsche Werke.* Ed. Giorgio Colli and Mazzino Montinari. New York, 1967–.
Noll 1983	Justus Noll. "'*Es* wollte ihn wecken'—oder: Bach auf gehacktem Fleisch spielen. Ein Versuch über die Träume Richard Wagners." *Neue Zeitschrift für Musik,* 144/2 (1983): 4–8; 144/3 (1983): 12–15.
Nordau 1895	Max Nordau. *Degeneration.* New York, 1895. Original German ed. *Entartung.* 2 vols. Berlin, 1892.
NWF	*Neue Wagner-Forschungen.* Ed. Otto Strobel. Karlsruhe, 1943.
O. Wesendonck- Briefe	*Briefe Richard Wagners an Otto Wesendonck, 1852–1870: Neue vollständige Ausgabe.* Ed. W. Golther. Berlin, 1905.
Pahlen 1981	Kurt Pahlen, ed. *Richard Wagner: "Tannhäuser und der Sängerkrieg auf Wartburg."* Munich, 1981.

Panizza 1895 Oskar Panizza. "Bayreuth und die Homosexualität: Eine Erwägung." *Die Gesellschaft: Monatsschrift für Literatur, Kunst und Socialpolitik,* 11 (1895): 88–92. Trans. and intro. Isolde Vetter. WNS, 9 (1988): 69–75.

Panizza 1899 Hans Dettmar [= Oskar Panizza]. "Tristan und Isolde in Paris" [poem]. *Zürcher Diskußionen* [sic], 2 (1899), no. 20–1: 13ff.

Panizza 1900 ——— "Tristan und Isolde in Paris" [prose]. *Zürcher Diskußionen* [sic], 3 (1900), no. 25–6: 1–12.

Park 1935 Rosemary Park. *Das Bild von Richard Wagners Tristan und Isolde in der deutschen Literatur.* Vol. 9 of *Deutsche Arbeiten der Universität Köln.* Jena, 1935.

Perle 1977 George Perle. "The Secret Programme of the Lyric Suite." *Musical Times,* 118 (1977): 629ff., 709ff., 809ff.

Petsch 1907 Robert Petsch. "Der Ring des Nibelungen in seinen Beziehungen zur griechischen Tragödie und zur zeitgenössischen Philosophie." In *Richard Wagner-Jahrbuch,* ed. Ludwig Frankenstein, vol. 2, pp. 284–330. Berlin, 1907.

P.H. 1907/8 P. H. "Pathologie Wagnérienne: Tannhäuser." *Revue de l'Université de Bruxelles,* 13 (1907/8): 398–402.

Plesske 1971 Hans Martin Plesske. *Richard Wagner in der Dichtung: Bibliographie deutschsprachiger Veröffentlichungen zusammengestellt von Hans Martin Plesske.* Bayreuth, 1971.

Porges 1983 Heinrich Porges. *Wagner Rehearsing the "Ring": An Eye-Witness Account of the Stage Rehearsals of the First Bayreuth Festival.* Trans. Robert L. Jacobs. Cambridge, 1983. Original German ed. *Die Bühnenproben zu den Bayreuther Festspielen des Jahres 1876.* Leipzig, 1877.

Prox 1986 Lothar Prox. *Strukturale Komposition und Strukturanalyse: Ein Beitrag zur Wagner-Forschung.* Regensburg, 1986.

Pudor 1891 Heinrich Pudor. *Sittlichkeit und Gesundheit in der Musik.* Dresden, 1891.

Pudor 1907 ——— "Richard Wagners Bisexualität." *Geschlecht und Gesellschaft* (Munich), 2/3 (1907): 140–144. Supplement 2/10 (1907): 475ff.

Pudor 1934 ——— *Dr. Heinrich Pudor, ein Vorkämpfer des Deutschtums und des Antisemitismus.* [Bibliography of Pudor's writings, 1890–1934.] Leipzig, 1934.

Puschmann 1873 Theodor Puschmann. *Richard Wagner: Eine psychiatrische Studie.* Berlin, 1873.

Racker 1948 Enrique Racker. "Ensayo psicoanalitico sobre la personalidad e la obra dramatica di Ricardo Wagner." *Revista de Psicoanálisis* (Buenos Aires), 6 (1948): 32–81 [with abstract in English, French, and German].

Rank 1911 Otto Rank. *Die Lohengrinsage: Ein Beitrag zu ihrer Motivgestaltung und Deutung.* Vol. 13 of *Schriften zur angewandten Seelenkunde,* ed. Sigmund Freud. Leipzig, 1911.

Rank 1912 ——— *Das Inzest-Motiv in Dichtung und Sage: Grundzüge einer Psychologie des dichterischen Schafferns.* Leipzig, 1912; 2nd ed. 1926; reprint 2nd ed. Darmstadt, 1974.

Rather 1979   L. J. Rather. *The Dream of Self-Destruction: Wagner's "Ring" and the Modern World.* Baton Rouge, La., 1979.

Rauschenberger 1937   Walther Rauschenberger. "Richard Wagners Abstammung und Rassenmerkmale." *Die Sonne: Monatsschrift für Rasse, Glauben, und Volkstum im Sinne Nordischer Weltanschauung und Lebensgestaltung,* 14 (1937): 161–71; reprinted in Walther Rauschenberger, *Erb- und Rassenpsychologie schöpferischer Persönlichkeiten,* pp. 140–152. Jena, 1942.

Rauschning 1940   Hermann Rauschning. *The Voice of Destruction.* New York, 1940.

Renk 1978   Herta E. Renk. "Anmerkungen zur Beziehung zwischen Musiktheater und Semiotik." In Mack 1978, pp. 275–288.

Ritter 1936   Gerhard Ritter. *Die geschlechtliche Frage in der deutschen Volkserziehung.* Foreword H. Schwarz. Berlin, 1936.

Röckel-Briefe   *Briefe an August Röckel von Richard Wagner.* Ed. La Mara [M. Lipsius]. Leipzig, 1894. Trans. E. C. Sellar; intro. H. S. Chamberlain. Bristol, 1897.

Roncoroni 1899a   L. Roncoroni. "Il carattere di Riccardo Wagner." *Annali di Freniatria,* 9 (1899): 1–36, 101–121.

Roncoroni 1899b   —— "L'emotività in Wagner." *Archivio di psichiatria: Science penali en antropologia criminale per servire allo studio dell'uomo alienato e delinquente,* 20 (1899): 92–134.

Rose 1982   Paul Lawrence Rose. Review of Westernhagen 1978. *Historical Journal,* 25 (1982): 751–763.

Sadger 1912   Isidor Sadger. "Von der Pathographie zur Psychographie." *Imago,* 1/2 (May 1912): 158–175. Reprinted in Fischer 1980, pp. 64–85.

Salzburg Symposium   *Richard Wagner 1883–1983: Die Rezeption im 19. und 20. Jahrhundert.* Ed. Franz Hundsnurscher, Ulrich Müller, and Cornelius Sommer. Stuttgart, 1984.

Sartre 1948   Jean-Paul Sartre. *Portrait of the Anti-Semite.* London, 1948.

SB   Richard Wagner. *Sämtliche Briefe.* Ed. Gertrud Strobel, Werner Wolf, Hans-Joachim Bauer, and Johannes Forner. Leipzig, 1967–.

Sch   Arthur Schopenhauer. *Sämtliche Werke.* Ed. W. Freiherr von Löhneysen. 5 vols. Stuttgart, 1961–1965. [All citations are to this edition.] Single works relevant to Wagner: trans. E. F. J. Payne, *The World as Will and Representation.* 2 vols. New York (Dover Publications), 1966; *Parerga and Paralipomena.* 2 vols. Oxford, 1974.

Schachter/   S. Schachter and J. E. Singer. "Cognitive, social, and physiological determinants of emotional state." *Psychological Review,* 69 (1962): 379–399.
  Singer 1962

Schadewaldt 1970   Wolfgang Schadewaldt. "Richard Wagner und die Griechen: Drei Bayreuther Vorträge." In *Hellas und Hesperien,* vol. 2, pp. 341–405; 2nd ed. Zurich, 1970.

Schemann 1925   Ludwig Schemann. *Lebensgefährten eines Deutschen.* Leipzig, 1925.

Schickling 1983   Dieter Schickling. *Abschied von Walhall: Richard Wagners erotische Gesellschaft.* Stuttgart, 1983.

Schickling 1989 ——— "Richard Wagners Männer und Frauen: Zur emanzipatorischen Psychologie des 'Ring.'" In *In den Trümmern der Eignen Welt: Richard Wagners "Der Ring des Nibelungen,"* ed. Udo Bermbach, pp. 163–180. Berlin, 1989.

Schmid 1988 Manfred Hermann Schmid. "Metamorphose der Themen: Beobachtungen an den Skizzen zum 'Lohengrin'—Vorspiel." *Musikforschung,* 41/2 (1988): 105–126.

Schorske 1980 Carl E. Schorske. *Fin-de-Siècle Vienna: Politics and Culture.* New York, 1980.

Schott-Briefe *Richard Wagners Briefwechsel mit B. Schott's Söhne.* Ed. W. Altmann. Mainz, 1911.

Schubert 1983 Bernhard Schubert. "Wagners 'Sachs' und die Tradition des romantischen Künstlerselbstverständnisses." *Archiv für Musikwissenschaft,* 40 (1983): 212–253.

Schuh 1936 Willi Schuh, ed. *Die Briefe Richard Wagners an Judith Gautier.* Zurich, 1936.

Schüler 1971 Winfried Schüler. *Der Bayreuther Kreis von seiner Entstehung bis zum Ausgang der wilhelminischen Ära.* Münster, 1971.

Schuré 1875 Edouard Schuré. *Richard Wagner: Son oeuvre et son idée.* Paris, 1875; rev. 4th ed. 1895.

SE *The Standard Edition of the Complete Psychological Works of Sigmund Freud.* Trans. James Strachey, with Anna Freud, Alix Strachey, and Alan Tyson. London, 1953–74.

Sehulster 1979/80 Jerome R. Sehulster. "The Role of Altered States of Consciousness in the Life, Theater, and Theories of Richard Wagner." *Journal of Altered States of Consciousness,* 5 (1979/80): 235–258.

Seidl 1895 Anton Seidl. "Nordau's Theory of Degeneration. II. A Musician's Retort." *North American Review,* 160/463 (June 1895): 740–743.

Sessa 1979 Anna Dzamba Sessa. *Richard Wagner and the English.* London, 1979.

Sexau 1963 Richard Sexau. *Fürst und Arzt: Dr. med. Herzog Carl Theodor in Bayern [1839–1909].* Graz, 1963.

Shaw 1895 George Bernard Shaw. "A Degenerate's View of Nordau." *Liberty* (New York), 9/6 (27 July 1895): 2–10. Rev. ed. with intro. *The Sanity of Art: An Exposure of the Current Nonsense about Artists Being Degenerate.* New York, 1908; 2nd rev. ed. In *Major Critical Essays,* ed. Michael Holroyd, pp. 309–360. New York, 1986.

Shaw 1898 ——— *The Perfect Wagnerite: A Commentary on the Nibelung's Ring.* London, 1898; 4th ed. 1923; reprint ed. 1972.

Siegele 1971 Ulrich Siegele. "Das Drama der Themen am Beispiel des 'Lohengrin.'" In Dahlhaus 1971a, pp. 41–51.

Sigismund 1984/85 Volker L. Sigismund. "Ein unbehauster Prinz: Constantin von Sachsen-Weimar (1758–1793). Der Bruder des Herzogs Carl August—Eine biographische Skizze." In *Jahresgabe 1984/85 der Ortsvereinigung Hamburg der Goethe-Gesellschaft in Weimar.*

Silbermann 1981   Alphons Silbermann. *Der ungeliebte Jude: Zur Soziologie des Antisemitismus.* Zurich, 1981.

SL   *Selected Letters of Richard Wagner.* Trans. and ed. Stewart Spencer and Barry Millington. London, 1987.

Soden-Loesch 1983   Michael von Soden and Andreas Loesch, eds. *Richard Wagner: Die Feen.* Frankfurt a.M., 1983.

Sontag 1980   Susan Sontag. "The Eye of the Storm." *New York Review of Books,* 21 February 1980.

Sontag 1987   ———— "Wagner's Fluids." *London Review of Books,* 9/22 (10 December 1987): 8–9.

Spencer 1985   Stewart Spencer. "The Language and Sources of 'The Ring.'" In ENO, *Das Rheingold,* 1985, pp. 31–38.

Spielrein 1912   Sabina Spielrein. "Die Destruktion als Ursache des Werdens." In *Jahrbuch für psychoanalytische und psychopathologische Forschungen,* ed. E. Bleuler, S. Freud, C. G. Jung, vol. 3 (1912), pp. 465–503; reprinted in Spielrein, *Sämtliche Schriften,* vol. 2, pp. 98–143. Freiburg i. Br., 1987.

Spitzer 1877   Daniel Spitzer. "Briefe Richard Wagners an eine Putzmacherin." *Neue Freie Presse,* Vienna, 17 June and 1 July 1877; reprinted Vienna, 1906. Trans. Sophie Prombaum, *Richard Wagner and the Seamstress.* Intro. and epilogue Leonard Liebling. New York, 1941.

Spitzer 1881   ———— *Wiener Spaziergänge,* vol. 3. Vienna, 1881.

SSD   Richard Wagner. *Sämtliche Schriften und Dichtungen.* 16 vols. Leipzig, n.d. [1911–16]. [All citations are to this edition.] Vols. 1–10 originally published under Wagner's supervision as *Gesammelte Schriften und Dichtungen.* 10 vols. Leipzig, 1871–83. For Eng. trans., see Ellis.

Stein 1950   Leon Stein. *The Racial Thinking of Richard Wagner.* New York, 1950.

Stein 1960   Jack M. Stein. *Richard Wagner and the Synthesis of the Arts.* Detroit, 1960; reprint ed. 1973.

Steinbeck 1964   Dietrich Steinbeck. *Inszenierungsformen des "Tannhäuser" (1845–1904): Untersuchungen zur Systematik der Opernregie.* Regensburg, 1964.

Steinbeck 1984   Wolfram Steinbeck. "Die Idee des Symphonischen bei Richard Wagner: Zur Leitmotivtechnik in 'Tristan und Isolde.'" In BKB, pp. 424–436.

Stekel 1909   Wilhelm Stekel. *Dichtung und Neurose: Bausteine zur Psychologie des Künstlers und des Kunstwerkes.* Wiesbaden, 1909. Trans. "Poetry and Neurosis." *Psychoanalytic Review,* 10 and 11 (1923–4); reprinted New York, 1963.

Stekel 1917   ———— "Nietzsche und Wagner: Eine sexualpsychologische Studie zur Psychogenese des Freundschaftsgefühls und des Freundschaftsverrats." *Zeitschrift für Sexualwissenschaft und Sexualpolitik,* 4 (1917): 22–28, 58–65.

Stephan 1970   Rudolph Stephan. "Gibt es ein Geheimnis der Form bei Richard Wagner?" In Dahlhaus 1970, pp. 9–16.

Sternagel 1989   Sigrid Sternagel. "Psychophysiologische Reaktionen während der Rezeption der 'Meistersinger von Nürnberg' von Richard Wagner: Eine Feldstudie." Master's thesis, Justus-Liebig University, Gießen, 1989.

Stone 1966   Alan A. Stone and Sue Smart Stone. *The Abnormal Personality through Literature*. Englewood Cliffs, N.J., 1966.

Strobel 1930   Otto Strobel, ed. *Richard Wagner: Skizzen und Entwürfe zur Ring-Dichtung: Mit der Dichtung "Der junge Siegfried."* Munich, 1930.

Strobel 1943   ———— "Ziele und Wege der Wagnerforschung." In NWF, pp. 15–32.

Strohm 1978   Reinhard Strohm. "Zur Werkgeschichte des 'Tannhäuser.'" In *Programmhefte der Bayreuther Festspiele: Tannhäuser*, pp. 64–76. Bayreuth, 1978.

Strunz 1986   Franz Strunz. "Der Erlösungstraum Richard Wagners." *Psyche*, 40 (June 1986): 557–562.

Sutor 1893   Sutor. "Un capitolo di Max Nordau sopra Wagner." In *Cronaca wagneriana*, vol. 1, pp. 10ff. Bologna, 1893.

SW   Richard Wagner. *Sämtliche Werke*, ed. Carl Dahlhaus, Egon Voss, et al. 31 vols. Mainz, 1970–.

Swisher 1923   Walter Samuel Swisher. "The Symbolism of Wagner's 'Rheingold.'" *Psychoanalytic Review*, 10 (October 1923): 447–452; reprinted New York, 1963.

Syberberg 1982   Hans Jürgen Syberberg. *Parsifal: Ein Filmessay*. Munich, 1982.

Symons 1909   Arthur Symons. "Notes on Wagner at Bayreuth." In *Plays, Acting, and Music: A Book of Theory*. London, 1909.

Tanner 1979   Michael Tanner. "The Total Work of Art." In *Wagner Companion*, pp. 140–224.

Tappert 1903   Wilhelm Tappert, ed. *Richard Wagner im Spiegel der Kritik: Wörterbuch der Unhöflichkeit*. 2nd ed., rev. and enlarged, Leipzig, 1903 [first published 1877]; reprint ed. Munich, 1967 and 1984.

Teillard 1948   Ania Teillard. "Anima—Animus (L'amour selon Jung)." *Psyche*, 3 (February 1948): 191–202.

Vaget 1984   Hans Rudolf Vaget. "Die Auferstehung Richard Wagners: Wagnerismus und Verfremdung in Syberbergs Hitlerfilm." In *Film und Literatur*, ed. S. Bauschinger, S. L. Cocalis, and H. A. Lea. Bern, 1984.

Vaget 1987   ———— "Strategies for Redemption: *Der Ring des Nibelungen* and *Faust*." In *Wagner in Retrospect*, pp. 91–104.

Vauzanges 1913   Louis M. Vauzanges. *L'écriture des musiciens célèbres: Essai de graphologie musicale. Avec quarante-huit réproductions d'autographes*. Paris, 1913.

Vehrs 1987   Wolfang Vehrs et al. "Zur Reliabilität und Validität der kontinuierlichen Skalierung mit dem Vehrs-Hebel." Paper presented at the Twenty-Ninth Conference of Experimental Psychologists, Aachen, 12–16 April 1987.

Vergo 1981   Peter Vergo. *Art in Vienna, 1898–1918*. 2nd ed. Oxford, 1981.

Vetter 1953   Walther Vetter. "Richard Wagner und die Griechen." *Musik-forschung*, 6 (1953): 111–126.

Vetter 1979   Isolde Vetter. "Der 'Ahasverus des Ozeans'—musikalisch unerlöst? Der Fliegende Holländer und seine Revisionen." In *Programmhefte der Bayreuther Festspiele: Der fliegende Holländer*, pp. 70–79. Rev. and enlarged in Csampai-Holland 1982, pp. 116–129.

Vetter 1980   —— Review of Groβmann-Vendrey 1977[/83]. *Musikforschung*, 31 (1980): 66–67.

Vetter 1982   —— "Senta und der Holländer—eine narziβtische Kollusion mit tödlichem Ausgang." In Csampai-Holland 1982, pp. 9–19.

Vetter 1982a   —— "'*Der fliegende Holländer*' von Richard Wagner: Entstehung, Bearbeitung, Überlieferung." Ph.D. diss., Technical University of Berlin, 1982 (microfiche).

Vetter 1988a   —— "Das Kunstwerk der Zukunft aus der Perspektive psychiatrischer Vergangenheit: Richard Wagner und Theodor Puschmann." In *Das musikalische Kunstwerk: Geschichte, Ästhetik, Theorie. Festschrift Carl Dahlhaus zum 60. Geburtstag*, ed. Danuser, de la Motte, Leopold, et al., pp. 269–284. Laaber, 1988. Trans. WNS, 10 (1989): 96–110.

Vetter 1988b   —— "'Leubald: Ein Trauerspiel,' Richard Wagners erstes (erhaltenes) Werk." In *Programmhefte der Bayreuther Festspiele: Die Meistersinger*, pp. 1–19. Bayreuth, 1988. Trans. pp. 53–68.

Vetter-Voss 1988   Isolde Vetter and Egon Voss. "Richard Wagner: Leubald. Ein Trauerspiel (Erstveröffentlichung)." In *Programmhefte der Bayreuther Festspiele: Die Meistersinger*, pp. 95–208 (with three facsimiles). Bayreuth, 1988.

Vogt 1986   Matthias Theodor Vogt. Index of Essays in the Bayreuth Festival Programs, 1951–1986 (alphabetical by author). In *Programmhefte der Bayreuther Festspiele: Das Rheingold* (A–F). *Die Walküre* (G–O), *Siegfried* (P–T), *Götterdämmerung* (V–Z). Bayreuth, 1986.

Vordtriede 1958   Werner Vordtriede. "Richard Wagners 'Tod in Venedig.'" *Euphorion*, 52 (1958/9): 378–396.

Voss 1970   Egon Voss. *Studien zur Instrumentation Richard Wagners*. Regensburg, 1970.

Voss 1976   ——, ed. *Richard Wagner: Schriften eines revolutionären Genies*. Munich, 1976.

Voss 1976/7   —— "Die Richard Wagner-Gesamtausgabe: Ein Projekt der Bayerischen Akademie der Schönen Künste." In *Jahrbuch der historischen Forschung*, pp. 53–56. Stuttgart, 1976/7.

Voss 1977   —— *Richard Wagner und die Instrumentalmusik: Wagners symphonischer Ehrgeiz*. Wilhelmshaven, 1977.

Voss 1978   —— "Wagners 'Sämtliche Briefe'?" *Melos/Neue Zeitschrift für Musik*, 4 (1978): 219–223.

Voss 1981   —— "Wagner's 'Meistersinger' als Oper des deutschen Bürgertums." In Csampai-Holland 1981, pp. 9–31.

Voss 1982	———— "Wagnerliteratur und Wagnerforschung." In *Quellenforschung in der Musikwissenschaft: Wolfenbütteler Forschungen*, vol. 15, pp. 75–79. Wolfenbüttel, 1982.
Voss 1983	———— "Richard Wagner: Fünf Lieder nach Gedichten von Mathilde Wesendonck . . . " *Neue Zeitschrift für Musik*, 144/1 (1983): 22–26.
Voss 1983a	———— "Once Again: The Secret of Form in Wagner's Works." WNS, 4 (1983): 66–79. Original German text in Mack 1978, pp. 251–267.
Voss 1984	———— "Wagners 'Parsifal'—das Spiel von der Macht der Schuldgefühle." In Csampai-Holland 1984, pp. 9–18.
Wagner Companion	*The Wagner Companion*. Ed. Peter Burbidge and Richard Sutton. Boston, 1979.
Wagner et la France	*Wagner et la France*. Ed. M. Kahane and Nicole Wild. Paris, 1983 [exhibition catalogue].
Wagner in Retrospect	*Wagner in Retrospect: A Centennial Reappraisal*. Ed. and intro. Leroy R. Shaw, Nancy R. Cirillo, and Marion S. Miller. Amsterdam, 1987.
Wagner Lettres	*Lettres françaises de Richard Wagner*. Ed. J. Tiersot. Paris, 1935.
Wagner-Bülow	*Richard Wagner, Briefe an Hans von Bülow*. Jena, 1916.
Wagner-Liszt	*Franz Liszt-Richard Wagner Briefwechsel*. Ed. and intro. Hanjo Kesting, Frankfurt a.M., 1988. Original German ed. (1887) trans. F. Hueffer, London 1888; rev. ed. 1897.
Walter 1956	Richard D. Walter. "What Became of the Degenerate? A Brief History of a Concept." *Journal of the History of Medicine*, 11 (1956): 422–429.
Wapnewski 1978a	Peter Wapnewski. *Richard Wagner—Die Szene und ihr Meister*. Munich, 1978; 2nd ed. 1983.
Wapnewski 1978b	———— *Der traurige Gott: Richard Wagner in seinen Helden*. Munich, 1978; 2nd ed. 1980.
Wapnewski 1981	———— *Tristan der Held Richard Wagners*. Berlin, 1981.
Wapnewski 1984	———— "Rivale Faust: Beobachtungen zu Wagners Goethe-Verständnis." In *Jahrbuch des Freien Deutschen Hochstifts, 1984*, ed. Christoph Perels, pp. 128–156. Tübingen, 1984.
Wapnewski 1985	———— "Überlegungen zu einer Inszenierung des *Tannhäuser* (insbesondere des Ersten Aufzugs)." In WlWf, pp. 223–232.
Weiner 1982	Marc A. Weiner. "Richard Wagner's Use of E. T. A. Hoffmann's 'The Mines of Falun.'" *Nineteenth-Century Music*, 5 (1981/2): 201–214.
Weingart/Kroll/ Bayertz 1988	Peter Weingart, Jürgen Kroll, and Kurt Bayertz. *Rasse, Blut, und Gene: Geschichte der Eugenik und Rassenhygiene in Deutschland*. Frankfurt a.M., 1988.
Wesendonck-Briefe	*Richard Wagner an Mathilde Wesendonck: Tagebuchblätter und Briefe, 1853–1871*. [Ed. Wolfgang Golther.] Berlin, 1904. Trans. William Ashton Ellis. London, 1905.
Wessling 1983	B. W. Wessling, ed. *Bayreuth im Dritten Reich*. Weinheim, 1983.
Westernhagen 1956	Curt von Westernhagen. *Richard Wagner: Sein Werk, sein Wesen, seine Welt*. Zurich, 1956.

Westernhagen 1963   ———— "Die Kompositions-Skizze zu 'Siegfrieds Tod' aus dem Jahre 1850." *Neue Zeitschrift für Musik,* 124 (1963): 178–182.

Westernhagen 1966   ———— *Richard Wagners Dresdener Bibliothek, 1842–1849.* Wiesbaden, 1966.

Westernhagen 1976   ———— *The Forging of the Ring.* Trans. Mary Whittall. Cambridge, 1976. Original German ed. *Die Entstehung des "Ring."* Zurich, 1973.

Westernhagen 1978   ———— *Wagner: A Biography.* Trans. Mary Whittall. 2 vols. Cambridge, 1978. [All citations are to this edition.] Original German ed. *Wagner.* Zurich, 1968; rev. and enlarged, 1978 [Eng. translations based on this edition].

Weston 1896   Jessie Laidlay Weston. *The Legends of the Wagner Dramas: Studies in Mythology and Romance.* London, 1896.

Wiessner 1924   Hermann Wiessner. *Der Stabreimvers in Richard Wagners "Ring des Nibelungen."* Berlin, 1924; reprint ed. 1967.

WlWf   *Wagnerliteratur-Wagnerforschung: Bericht über das Wagner-Symposium München 1983.* Ed. Carl Dahlhaus and Egon Voss. Mainz, 1985.

WNS   *Wagner* [Journal of the London Wagner Society], New Series. Ed. Stewart Spencer. 1980–.

Wolzogen 1878   Hans von Wolzogen. *Die Sprache in Wagners Dichtungen.* Leipzig, 1878.

Woolley 1931   Lawrence Grange Woolley. *Richard Wagner et le symbolisme français.* Paris, 1931.

Wulffen 1928   Erich Wulffen. *Sexualspiegel: Von Kunst und Verbrechen.* Dresden, n.d. [1928].

WWV   *Wagner Werk-Verzeichnis: Verzeichnis der musikalischen Werke Richard Wagners und ihrer Quellen,* ed. John Deathridge, Martin Geck, and Egon Voss. Mainz, 1986.

Wyzewska 1934   Isabelle Wyzewska. *La revue wagnérienne: Essai sur l'interpretation esthetique de Wagner en France.* Paris, 1934.

Zademack 1921   Franz Zademack. *Die Meistersinger von Nürnberg: Richard Wagners Dichtung und ihre Quellen.* Berlin, 1921.

Zelinsky 1976   Hartmut Zelinsky. *Richard Wagner: Ein deutsches Thema—Eine Dokumentation zur Wirkungsgeschichte Richard Wagners, 1876–1976.* Frankfurt a.M., 1976; rev. ed. Berlin, 1983.

Zelinsky 1978   ———— "Die 'feuerkur' des Richard Wagner oder die 'neue religion' der 'Erlösung' durch 'Vernichtung.'" In *Wie antisemitisch darf ein Künstler sein?,* ed. Heinz-Klaus Metzger and Rainer Riehn, pp. 79–112. Munich, 1978.

Zelinsky 1982   ———— "Rettung ins Ungenaue: Zu Martin Gregor-Dellins Wagner-Biographie." In *Richard Wagner: Parsifal,* ed. Heinz-Klaus Metzger and Rainer Riehn, pp. 74–115. Munich, 1982.

Ziehen 1895   Ludwig Ziehen. "Entartung." *Bayreuther Blätter,* 18 (1895): 358–366.

Zimmermann 1978   Michael Zimmermann. "Gegenwärtige Tendenzen der Musikästhetik." In *Funkkolleg Musik,* ed. Carl Dahlhaus et al., pp. 44–83. Mainz, 1978.

Zuckerman 1964   Elliott Zuckerman. *The First Hundred Years of Wagner's Tristan.* New York, 1964.

Acknowledgments

The editor of the English-language edition would like to thank all the translators most warmly, especially for their unfailing courtesy in answering his queries. Special thanks go to Alfred Clayton, Peter Palmer, and Stewart Spencer, who also kindly assisted with a number of editorial problems. Jean-Jacques Nattiez provided valuable information for the checklist of writings at the end of the final chapter, and Horst Loeschmann and Isolde Vetter offered valuable assistance on many bibliographical details and points of translation. Patricia Williams made the bold decision to transform this book into English; many thanks are due her for consistent help and encouragement. Amanda Heller undertook the mammoth task of copyediting the final manuscript with great acumen. Last and by no means least, Margaretta Fulton waited patiently in the "other" Cambridge for each section to cross the Atlantic, often after considerable delay caused by the sheer amount of detail involved and the pressure of other commitments.

Grateful acknowledgment is made to the following for permission to quote from the publications indicated: to Cambridge University Press for quotations from the translation of Wagner's biography, *My Life*, translated by Andrew Gray and edited by Mary Whittall (1983); to Dent for quotations from *Selected Letters of Richard Wagner*, translated and edited by Stewart Spencer and Barry Millington (1987); and to Harcourt Brace Jovanovich and William Collins for quotations from *Cosima Wagner's Diary*, translated by Geoffrey Skelton (1978).

J. D.

Contributors

OSWALD BAUER
General Secretary, Bavarian Academy of Fine Arts, Munich

DIETER BORCHMEYER
Professor of Modern German Literature and Theatre Studies, University of Heidelberg

PETER BRANSCOMBE
Professor of Austrian Studies, University of St. Andrews

WERNER BREIG
Professor of Musicology, University of Wuppertal

CARL DAHLHAUS
Ordinarius and Professor of Musicology, Technical University of Berlin, at the time of his death

JOHN DEATHRIDGE
Fellow and Director of Studies in Music, King's College, University of Cambridge

MANFRED EGER
Director of the Richard Wagner Museum and the National Archive of the Richard Wagner Foundation, Bayreuth

JENS MALTE FISCHER
Professor of Theatre Studies, University of Munich

ERNST HANISCH
Professor of Modern Austrian History, University of Salzburg

ERWIN KOPPEN
Professor of Comparative Literature, University of Bonn, at the time of his death

RÜDIGER KROHN
Professor of German Philology, Universities of Karlsruhe and Stuttgart

JÜRGEN KÜHNEL
Teacher of German Medieval Literature, University of Siegen; founder of the Studio Theatre (1979)

VOLKER MERTENS
Professor of Old German Literature, Free University of Berlin

GÜNTER METKEN
Critic and art historian, Paris

ULRICH MÜLLER
Professor of Medieval German Literature, University of Salzburg

HARTMUT REINHARDT
Professor of Modern German Literature, University of Trier

ISOLDE VETTER
Professor of Aesthetics and Educational Psychology, *Musikhochschule*, Karlsruhe

PETER WAPNEWSKI
Professor of German Philology, Technical University of Berlin; founding Rector (1981–1986) and permanent Fellow, *Wissenschaftskolleg*, Berlin

Index of Wagner's Musical Works

Index of Wagner's Writings

General Index